Short Story Criticism

Guide to Gale Literary Criticism Series

For criticism on	Consult these Gale series
Authors now living or who died after December 31, 1999	*CONTEMPORARY LITERARY CRITICISM (CLC)*
Authors who died between 1900 and 1999	*TWENTIETH-CENTURY LITERARY CRITICISM (TCLC)*
Authors who died between 1800 and 1899	*NINETEENTH-CENTURY LITERATURE CRITICISM (NCLC)*
Authors who died between 1400 and 1799	*LITERATURE CRITICISM FROM 1400 TO 1800 (LC)* *SHAKESPEAREAN CRITICISM (SC)*
Authors who died before 1400	*CLASSICAL AND MEDIEVAL LITERATURE CRITICISM (CMLC)*
Authors of books for children and young adults	*CHILDREN'S LITERATURE REVIEW (CLR)*
Dramatists	*DRAMA CRITICISM (DC)*
Poets	*POETRY CRITICISM (PC)*
Short story writers	*SHORT STORY CRITICISM (SSC)*
Literary topics and movements	*HARLEM RENAISSANCE: A GALE CRITICAL COMPANION (HR)* *THE BEAT GENERATION: A GALE CRITICAL COMPANION (BG)*
Asian American writers of the last two hundred years	*ASIAN AMERICAN LITERATURE (AAL)*
Black writers of the past two hundred years	*BLACK LITERATURE CRITICISM (BLC)* *BLACK LITERATURE CRITICISM SUPPLEMENT (BLCS)*
Hispanic writers of the late nineteenth and twentieth centuries	*HISPANIC LITERATURE CRITICISM (HLC)* *HISPANIC LITERATURE CRITICISM SUPPLEMENT (HLCS)*
Native North American writers and orators of the eighteenth, nineteenth, and twentieth centuries	*NATIVE NORTH AMERICAN LITERATURE (NNAL)*
Major authors from the Renaissance to the present	*WORLD LITERATURE CRITICISM, 1500 TO THE PRESENT (WLC)* *WORLD LITERATURE CRITICISM SUPPLEMENT (WLCS)*

ISSN 0895-9439

Volume 89

Short Story Criticism

Criticism of the Works of Short Fiction Writers

Rachelle Mucha
Thomas J. Schoenberg
Lawrence J. Trudeau
Project Editors

THOMSON

GALE

Detroit • New York • San Francisco • San Diego • New Haven, Conn. • Waterville, Maine • London • Munich

Short Story Criticism, Vol. 89

Project Editors
Thomas J. Schoenberg, Lawrence J. Trudeau, and Rachelle Mucha

Editorial
Jessica Bomarito, Kathy D. Darrow, Jeffrey W. Hunter, Jelena O. Krstović, Michelle Lee, Russel Whitaker

Data Capture
Frances Monroe, Gwen Tucker

Indexing Services
Factiva®, a Dow Jones and Reuters Company

Rights and Acquisitions
Margaret Abendroth, Lori Hines, Timothy Sisler

Imaging and Multimedia
Dean Dauphinais, Leitha Etheridge-Sims, Lezlie Light, Mike Logusz, Dan Newell, Christine O'Bryan, Kelly A. Quin, Denay Wilding, Robyn Young

Composition and Electronic Capture
Amy Darga

Manufacturing
Rhonda Dover

Associate Product Manager
Marc Cormier

© 2006 Thomson Gale, a part of The Thomson Corporation. Thomson and Star Logo are trademarks and Gale is a registered trademark used herein under license.

For more information, contact
Thomson Gale
27500 Drake Rd.
Farmington Hills, MI 48331-3535
Or you can visit our internet site at
http://www.gale.com

ALL RIGHTS RESERVED
No part of this work covered by the copyright herein may be reproduced or used in any form or by any means—graphic, electronic, or mechanical, including photocopying, recording, taping, Web distribution, or information storage retrieval systems—without the written permission of the publisher.

This publication is a creative work fully protected by all applicable copyright laws, as well as by misappropriation, trade secret, unfair competition, and other applicable laws. The authors and editors of this work have added value to the underlying factual material herein through one or more of the following: unique and original selection, coordination, expression, arrangement, and classification of the information.

For permission to use material from the product, submit your request via the Web at http://www.gale-edit.com/permissions, or you may download our Permissions Request form and submit your request by fax or mail to:

Permissions Department
Thomson Gale
27500 Drake Rd.
Farmington Hills, MI 48331-3535
Permissions Hotline:
248-699-8006 or 800-877-4253, ext. 8006
Fax 248-699-8074 or 800-762-4058

Since this page cannot legibly accommodate all copyright notices, the acknowledgments constitute an extension of the copyright notice.

While every effort has been made to secure permission to reprint material and to ensure the reliability of the information presented in this publication, Thomson Gale neither guarantees the accuracy of the data contained herein nor assumes any responsibility for errors, omissions or discrepancies. Thomson Gale accepts no payment for listing; and inclusion in the publication of any organization, agency, institution, publication, service, or individual does not imply endorsement of the editors or publisher. Errors brought to the attention of the publisher and verified to the satisfaction of the publisher will be corrected in future editions.

LIBRARY OF CONGRESS CATALOG CARD NUMBER 88-641014

ISBN 0-7876-8886-X
ISSN 0895-9439

Printed in the United States of America
10 9 8 7 6 5 4 3 2 1

Contents

Preface

Short Story Criticism (*SSC*) presents significant criticism of the world's greatest short-story writers and provides supplementary biographical and bibliographical materials to guide the interested reader to a greater understanding of the authors of short fiction. This series was developed in response to suggestions from librarians serving high school, college, and public library patrons, who had noted a considerable number of requests for critical material on short-story writers. Although major short-story writers are covered in such Thomson Gale series as *Contemporary Literary Criticism* (*CLC*), *Twentieth-Century Literary Criticism* (*TCLC*), *Nineteenth-Century Literature Criticism* (*NCLC*), and *Literature Criticism from 1400 to 1800* (*LC*), librarians perceived the need for a series devoted solely to writers of the short-story genre.

Scope of the Series

SSC is designed to serve as an introduction to major short-story writers of all eras and nationalities. Since these authors have inspired a great deal of relevant critical material, *SSC* is necessarily selective, and the editors have chosen the most important published criticism to aid readers and students in their research.

Approximately eight to ten authors are included in each volume, and each entry presents a historical survey of the critical response to that author's work. The length of an entry is intended to reflect the amount of critical attention the author has received from critics writing in English and from foreign critics in translation. Every attempt has been made to identify and include the most significant essays on each author's work. In order to provide these important critical pieces, the editors sometimes reprint essays that have appeared elsewhere in Thomson Gale's Literary Criticism Series. Such duplication, however, never exceeds twenty percent of an *SSC* volume.

Organization of the Book

An *SSC* entry consists of the following elements:

- The **Author Heading** cites the name under which the author most commonly wrote, followed by birth and death dates. Also located here are any name variations under which an author wrote, including transliterated forms for authors whose native languages use nonroman alphabets. If the author wrote consistently under a pseudonym, the pseudonym will be listed in the author heading and the author's actual name given in parentheses on the first line of the biographical and critical introduction. Uncertain birth or death dates are indicated by question marks. Single-work entries are preceded by the title of the work and its date of publication.

- The **Introduction** contains background information that introduces the reader to the author and the critical debates surrounding his or her work.

- A **Portrait of the Author** is included when available.

- The list of **Principal Works** is ordered chronologically by date of first publication and lists the most important works by the author. The first section comprises short-story collections, novellas, and novella collections. The second section gives information on other major works by the author. For foreign authors, the editors have provided original foreign-language publication information and have selected what are considered the best and most complete English-language editions of their works.

- Reprinted **Criticism** is arranged chronologically in each entry to provide a useful perspective on changes in critical evaluation over time. All short-story, novella, and collection titles by the author featured in the entry are printed in boldface type. The critic's name and the date of composition or publication of the critical work are given at the beginning of each piece of criticism. Unsigned criticism is preceded by the title of the source in which it appeared. Footnotes are reprinted at the end of each essay or excerpt. In the case of excerpted criticism, only those footnotes that pertain to the excerpted texts are included.

- Critical essays are prefaced by brief **Annotations** explicating each piece.

- A complete **Bibliographical Citation** of the original essay or book precedes each piece of criticism. Source citations in the Literary Criticism Series follow University of Chicago Press style, as outlined in *The Chicago Manual of Style,* 14th ed. (Chicago: The University of Chicago Press, 1993).

- An annotated bibliography of **Further Reading** appears at the end of each entry and suggests resources for additional study. In some cases, significant essays for which the editors could not obtain reprint rights are included here. Boxed material following the further reading list provides references to other biographical and critical sources on the author in series published by Thomson Gale.

Indexes

A **Cumulative Author Index** lists all of the authors that appear in a wide variety of reference sources published by Thomson Gale, including *SSC*. A complete list of these sources is found facing the first page of the Author Index. The index also includes birth and death dates and cross references between pseudonyms and actual names.

A **Cumulative Nationality Index** lists all authors featured in *SSC* by nationality, followed by the number of the *SSC* volume in which their entry appears.

An alphabetical **Title Index** lists all short-story, novella, and collection titles contained in the *SSC* series. Titles of short-story collections, separately published novellas, and novella collections are printed in italics, while titles of individual short stories are printed in roman type with quotation marks. Each title is followed by the author's last name and corresponding volume and page numbers where commentary on the work is located. English-language translations of original foreign-language titles are cross-referenced to the foreign titles so that all references to discussion of a work are combined in one listing.

In response to numerous suggestions from librarians, Thomson Gale also produces an annual paperbound edition of the SSC cumulative title index. This annual cumulation, which alphabetically lists all titles reviewed in the series, is available to all customers. Additional copies of this index are available upon request. Librarians and patrons will welcome this separate index; it saves shelf space, is easy to use, and is recyclable upon receipt of the next edition.

Citing *Short Story Criticism*

When citing criticism reprinted in the Literary Criticism Series, students should provide complete bibliographic information so that the cited essay can be located in the original print or electronic source. Students who quote directly from reprinted criticism may use any accepted bibliographic format, such as University of Chicago Press style or Modern Language Association (MLA) style. Both the MLA and the University of Chicago formats are acceptable and recognized as being the current standards for citations. It is important, however, to choose one format for all citations; do not mix the two formats within a list of citations.

The examples below follow recommendations for preparing a bibliography set forth in *The Chicago Manual of Style,* 14th ed. (Chicago: The University of Chicago Press, 1993); the first example pertains to material drawn from periodicals, the second to material reprinted from books:

Morrison, Jago. "Narration and Unease in Ian McEwan's Later Fiction." *Critique* 42, no. 3 (spring 2001): 253-68. Reprinted in *Short Story Criticism.* Vol. 57, edited by Janet Witalec, 212-20. Detroit: Gale, 2003.

Brossard, Nicole. "Poetic Politics." In *The Politics of Poetic Form: Poetry and Public Policy,* edited by Charles Bernstein, 73-82. New York: Roof Books, 1990. Reprinted in *Short Story Criticism.* Vol. 57, edited by Janet Witalec, 3-8. Detroit: Gale, 2003.

The examples below follow recommendations for preparing a works cited list set forth in the *MLA Handbook for Writers of Research Papers,* 5th ed. (New York: The Modern Language Association of America, 1999); the first example pertains to material drawn from periodicals, the second to material reprinted from books:

Morrison, Jago. "Narration and Unease in Ian McEwan's Later Fiction." *Critique* 42.3 (spring 2001): 253-68. Reprinted in *Short Story Criticism.* Ed. Janet Witalec. Vol. 57. Detroit: Gale, 2003. 212-20.

Brossard, Nicole. "Poetic Politics." *The Politics of Poetic Form: Poetry and Public Policy.* Ed. Charles Bernstein. New York: Roof Books, 1990. 73-82. Reprinted in *Short Story Criticism.* Ed. Janet Witalec. Vol. 57. Detroit: Gale, 2003. 3-8.

Suggestions are Welcome

Readers who wish to suggest new features, topics, or authors to appear in future volumes, or who have other suggestions or comments are cordially invited to call, write, or fax the Associate Product Manager:

Associate Product Manager, Literary Criticism Series
Thomson Gale
27500 Drake Road
Farmington Hills, MI 48331-3535
1-800-347-4253 (GALE)
Fax: 248-699-8054

Acknowledgments

The editors wish to thank the copyright holders of the excerpted criticism included in this volume and the permissions managers of many book and magazine publishing companies for assisting us in securing reproduction rights. Following is a list of the copyright holders who have granted us permission to reproduce material in this volume of *SSC*. Every effort has been made to trace copyright, but if omissions have been made, please let us know.

PHOTOGRAPHS APPEARING IN *SSC*, VOLUME 89, WERE RECEIVED FROM THE FOLLOWING SOURCES:

Thomson Gale Literature Product Advisory Board

The members of the Thomson Gale Literature Product Advisory Board—reference librarians from public and academic library systems—represent a cross-section of our customer base and offer a variety of informed perspectives on both the presentation and content of our literature products. Advisory board members assess and define such quality issues as the relevance, currency, and usefulness of the author coverage, critical content, and literary topics included in our series; evaluate the layout, presentation, and general quality of our printed volumes; provide feedback on the criteria used for selecting authors and topics covered in our series; provide suggestions for potential enhancements to our series; identify any gaps in our coverage of authors or literary topics, recommending authors or topics for inclusion; analyze the appropriateness of our content and presentation for various user audiences, such as high school students, undergraduates, graduate students, librarians, and educators; and offer feedback on any proposed changes/enhancements to our series. We wish to thank the following advisors for their advice throughout the year.

John Barth
1930-

(Full name John Simmons Barth) American short story and novella writer, novelist, essayist, and nonfiction writer.

The following entry presents criticism from 1971 to 2005 on Barth's works of short fiction. For further information on Barth's short fiction, see *SSC*, Volume 10.

INTRODUCTION

Barth is regarded as one of the most important contributors to literary postmodernism, a contemporary movement that comprises works characterized by structural experimentalism, an eclectic mixture of cultural references, incorporation of word games, and a self-conscious examination of fiction writing and the interaction between reader and text. Concerned with transcending the strictures of literary realism, Barth constructs labyrinthine plots and parodies mythical and historical tales. In "The Literature of Exhaustion," the first essay to advance an aesthetics of postmodern fiction, Barth describes the contemporary experimental writer as one who "confronts an intellectual dead end and employs it against itself to accomplish new human work." This essay has been construed as a vital manifesto proposing various keys to fiction's survival in the face of seemingly exhausted possibilities. Barth's volume of short stories *Lost in the Funhouse* (1968) and collection of novellas *Chimera* (1972) present fictional treatments of his literary theories and are considered among his most experimental and distinguished works.

BIOGRAPHICAL INFORMATION

Barth was born May 27, 1930 in Cambridge, Maryland to John Jacob Barth and Georginia Simmons. His childhood and adolescence were largely quiet and uneventful. He attended Cambridge High School, and, after graduating, attended Juilliard School of Music in New York City. After a few months in New York, Barth was forced to return home because he lacked the funds necessary to meet the expenses of tuition and living in the city. He later attended Johns Hopkins University in Baltimore, receiving his B.A. in 1951 and his M.A. in creative writing in the spring of 1952. Barth received the National Book Award in 1973 for *Chimera*. He also received the F. Scott Fitzgerald Award for outstanding

achievement in American literature in 1997, and in 1998 Barth received the PEN/Malamud Award and the Lannan Literary Awards lifetime achievement award.

MAJOR WORKS OF SHORT FICTION

A series of fourteen pieces, *Lost in the Funhouse* evinces Barth's search for alternatives to conventional writing through his use of diverse styles and his exploration of the creative process. As suggested by the collection's subtitle, "Fiction for Print, Tape, Live Voice," stories in this volume draw on a variety of media sources, with some requiring the reader to listen to tape recordings. Barth also experiments with visual dimensions, as in the first story, "Frame-Tale," which contains only the words "Once upon a time there / was a story that began" printed along the edge of the page with instructions to cut out the words and construct a Möbius strip out of them. Commentators have noted that the resultant structure in which the words twist and loop back upon themselves to repeat the same message is emblematic of ways in which characters and themes are repeated throughout *Lost in the Funhouse.* Stories in the volume may generally be divided into three categories: narratives that focus on the maturation of the protagonist, Ambrose Mensch, from conception through adolescence; metafictional pieces that trace the development of storytelling; and stories based on classical mythology. Stories in the first category depart from traditional narrative techniques, often parodying literary convention. "Night-Sea Journey," for example, is a mock heroic epic told from the perspective of a sperm on its voyage to a mysterious "Shore," or egg, which upon fertilization will eventually develop into Ambrose. The elevated tone that the sperm-narrator adopts heightens the artifice and humor of the story. "Lost in the Funhouse," which is frequently interpreted as a parody of James Joyce's *A Portrait of the Artist as a Young Man,* features a third-person omniscient narrator who comments on various literary techniques throughout the exposition of the story. Thirteen-year-old Ambrose goes on a seaside outing with his parents, uncle, older brother, and a teenage girl named Magda to whom both Ambrose and his brother are attracted. Ambrose's attempts to engage in a relationship with Magda are frustrated by self-reflexive thoughts that inhibit his ability to enjoy a sexual encounter. Structured to resemble the disorientation that characterizes a trip through a fun house, the story includes repeated and distorted images that continually draw attention to the self-conscious and, at times, inhibitive nature of storytelling. Several tales in *Lost in the Funhouse* focus on the process of fiction writing. In "Life-Story" the narrator reflects on the seeming impossibility of writing new, inventive fiction in the late twentieth century and laments that he can only offer "another story about a writer writing a story! Another regressus in infinitum!" Barth urges the reader to assume an active role in his stories, as in "Title," in which the narrator rejects several false starts and ultimately encourages the reader to engage in the narrative. Barth's method of retelling classical myths is perhaps best displayed in "Menelaiad," which is frequently compared in structure to a set of Chinese nesting boxes—each of which, when opened, reveals another of similar yet smaller appearance. In this story, the Greek hero Menelaus recounts his life story, recalling past events and conversations, which he distinguishes from present circumstances by adding a separate set of quotation marks to the story. In "Anonymiad," a story also based on Greek mythology, Barth relates the tale of a minstrel who has been marooned on an island. In his isolation the minstrel writes stories and casts them out to sea, inventing and revising narrative forms until he believes he has exhausted all possibilities. His commitment to writing, however, is renewed when a jar containing a message washes ashore and he realizes that others also need to communicate.

Barth also uses ancient tales in *Chimera,* a collection of three interlinked novellas. Written during Barth's middle years when he experienced difficulty writing, the novellas metaphorically represent ways of surpassing the exhausted possibilities of writing. The first novella, *Dunyazadiad,* is based on the story of Scheherazade, the heroine of the classical Arabian frame-tale *The Thousand and One Nights.* In the original, Scheherazade is held captive by King Shahryar, who intends to make love to her and then kill her; however, Scheherazade escapes death each night by telling such a compelling story that the king spares her life in order to hear more. Barth combines modern and anachronistic diction in his retelling of the story and also shifts the main point of view away from Scheherazade. *Dunyazadiad* is narrated by Scheherazade's sister, Dunyazade, who witnesses her sister's predicament and is similarly threatened by the king's brother, Shah Zaman. Furthering the story-within-a-story motif, Barth introduces the character of the Genie, a mask for the contemporary figure of Barth himself, who is able to read stories from *The Thousand and One Nights* to Scheherazade and Dunyazade that will provide them with their life-saving narratives. In the next novella, *Perseid,* Barth creates a colloquial version of the story of the Greek hero Perseus. At the midpoint of his life, Perseus wishes he could repeat the heroic deeds of his past but eventually realizes that to move forward he cannot simply repeat his former actions but must change their pattern to succeed. In the last novella, *Bellerophoniad,* the Greek figure Bellerophon confronts middle age and harbors doubts about the significance of his life. Throughout the narrative, he attempts to imitate the actions of previous heroes to secure his own heroic status; yet, unlike Perseus, he never succeeds because he merely repeats the examples of former heroes and, according to at least one critic, lacks individuality. *Bellerophoniad* both exemplifies and parodies the dead end that writers face when they conform to a historic past and fail to assert originality in their retelling of stories.

Barth's *On with the Story* (1996) is a collection of short stories—many involving middle-aged academics and writers—that are ostensibly being told by a husband and wife to one another while they are vacationing. His *The Book of Ten Nights and a Night* (2004) is comprised of eleven stories that are told—but not set—during the eleven days between September 11, 2001 and September 21, 2001, and has been regarded as evocative of Bocaccio's *Decameron* and as a parody of *A Thousand and One Nights.* The stories in *The Book of Ten Nights and a Night* are related on the night of and for ten nights following the terrorist attacks on the World Trade Center and Pentagon on September 11, 2001, and treat such themes as sexuality, human relationships, social structure, aging, and the role of fantasy and fiction in everyday life. Three novellas—*Tell Me, I've Been Told,* and *As I Was Saying*—comprise *Where*

Three Roads Meet (2005), in which Barth presents the characters from his novel *The End of the Road* (1958) in narratives that examine sexuality, heroism, and the creative process.

CRITICAL RECEPTION

The extremely complex and metafictional nature of Barth's short fiction has inspired countless exegeses on the direction of contemporary literature. During the late 1960s and early 1970s, many critics condemned Barth's focus on the writing process as self-indulgent and charged that his works produced a sense of elitism by appealing only to an academic audience. Numerous other commentators faulted Barth's emphasis on the depleted potentialities of narrative forms and his rejection of realism in *Lost in the Funhouse* and *Chimera* as nihilistic. Later critics, however, have interpreted Barth's exploration of the possibilities of literature as an affirmative message that equally challenges writer and reader. Barth has been hailed as a uniquely insightful commentator on religion and mythology, and his works have been likened to those of such authors as W. B. Yeats and James Joyce. Reviews of Barth's most recent works of short fiction have been mixed. Critics have faulted *On with the Story, The Book of Ten Nights and a Night,* and *Where Three Roads Meet* for containing less effective versions of the type of narratives offered in his earlier short works, but some commentators have praised these recent collections as well-written, imaginative, and as socially and culturally relevant to the twenty-first century world. Robert L. McLaughlin declared that *The Book of Ten Nights and a Night* is "a beautiful and most worthy addition to the oeuvre of one of our greatest writers."

PRINCIPAL WORKS

Short Fiction

Lost in the Funhouse 1968
Chimera 1972
On with the Story 1996
The Book of Ten Nights and a Night 2004
Where Three Roads Meet 2005

Other Major Works

The Floating Opera (novel) 1956; revised edition, 1967
The End of the Road (novel) 1958; revised edition, 1967

The Sot-Weed Factor (novel) 1960; revised edition, 1967
Giles Goat-Boy; or, The Revised New Syllabus (novel) 1966
LETTERS (novel) 1979
*The Literature of Exhaustion, and The Literature of Replenishment (essays) 1982
Sabbatical: A Romance (novel) 1982
The Friday Book (essays and nonfiction) 1984
The Tidewater Tales (novel) 1987
The Last Voyage of Somebody the Sailor (novel) 1991
Once upon a Time: A Floating Opera (novel) 1994
Further Fridays: Essays, Lectures, and Other Nonfiction, 1984-1994 (essays, lectures, and nonfiction) 1995
Coming Soon!!!: A Narrative (novel) 2001

*These two essays were originally published in the journal *The Atlantic Monthly* in 1967 and 1980, respectively.

CRITICISM

Richard Boyd Hauck (essay date 1971)

SOURCE: Hauck, Richard Boyd. "The Fruitful Fruitless Odysseys: John Barth." In *A Cheerful Nihilism: Confidence and "The Absurd" in American Humorous Fiction,* pp. 201-36. Bloomington: Indiana University Press, 1971.

[*In the following excerpt, Hauck traces Barth's transcendence of the limitations of reality, fiction, meaning, and absurdity in the stories in* Lost in the Funhouse.]

"One must needs make and seize his soul . . ."

Burlingame

1 · ODYSSEY IN THE FUNHOUSE

When asked if the discussion of suicide in *The Myth of Sisyphus* had colored his characterization of Todd Andrews in *The Floating Opera,* John Barth replied, "There certainly may be similarities between them, but it didn't color my work because I haven't read *The Myth of Sisyphus.* I believe Camus says the first question that a thoughtful man has to ask himself is why he is going to go on, then make up his mind whether to blow his brains out or not; at the end of *The Floating Opera* my man decides he won't commit suicide because there's no more reason to stop living than to persist in it."[1] Thus Barth showed that thoughtful men ask similar questions and arrive at similar answers without having to read each other's books. Barth's character formulates one simple and direct response to the absurd dilemma: "there's no more reason to stop living than to persist in it." Having arbitrarily decided to live, Andrews simply continues to live and to invent action. One of his actions is the writing of *The Floating Opera,* his own history. John Barth himself seems to have transcended the dilemma by writing stories. "There is a Hindu thing that I've always wanted to go clear through," he said. "It's called *The Ocean of Story . . .* Four feet long. Wouldn't it be wonderful to have written that?"² The basic motivation for writing stories is the "impulse to imagine alternatives to the world. . . ." What the writer really wants to do, Barth said, is to "reinvent philosophy and the rest—make up your own whole history of the world." The motivation for absurd creation is, then, the recognition that the universe has meaning only when a man assigns it meaning. The man who controls the meaning best is the highly inventive man—the artist.

The motivation for comic absurd creation is the recognition of the fun to be had revealing the inseparability of the real and the fictional world. The comic novelist is not a serious historian because he believes that it is impossible to record a truth without changing it into a new truth. The question of being a "realist" in fiction is a question that can be made to look silly because reality and fiction are already indistinguishable. A book, whether its technique is "realistic," "surrealistic," "romantic," or whatever, always has life as its subject and is itself one of the facts of life, with its own reality. Furthermore, life outside books can be just as fabulous as fables. A work of history is a selection and interpretation of events and is, therefore, a story. Even what men take to be reality is a story: "God wasn't too bad a novelist, except he was a Realist. Some of the things he did are right nice: the idea that ontogeny recapitulates phylogeny is a master stroke; if you thought that up you'd be proud of yourself." Any model of reality is a story about reality's story, just as a mathematical model of a phenomenon represents the plot of that phenomenon. What is hilarious is the way men accept models of reality as reality and forget that the model has a story reality of its own. Immediately observable information, in fact, becomes a story the moment it is perceived and can then be seen as simultaneously real and unreal: "Robert Louis Stevenson could never get used to the fact that people had two ears, funny-looking things, and eye-balls in their heads; he said it's enough to make you scream. I agree."³ Barth is not too interested in trying to write "realistic" fiction: "One ought to know a lot about Reality before one writes realistic novels. Since I don't know much about Reality, it will have to be abolished. What the hell, reality is a nice place to visit but you wouldn't want to live there, and literature never did, very long. . . . Reality is a drag."⁴

The storyteller who transfers the simultaneous reality and unreality of the world to his own cosmos does not

decide which is which; he re-creates the phenomenon as a dilemma or joke. The title of Barth's *Lost in the Funhouse* is a metaphor for the artist's ambiguous position. This book is a "sequence" of related short stories, some previously published, but the whole arranged loosely as an exercise in the problems the absurd creator as storyteller faces. Appropriately, some of the stories are quasi-autobiographical. A few are designed for conventional printing, with a narrator speaking in the third person or with a first-person narrator telling his own story. Other pieces are composed for oral recitation by the author or live voices other than the author's. One piece, titled **"Autobiography,"** is from a tape designed to be played while the author sits quietly in view of an audience. Several of the stories are told in such a way that the difference between author and narrator is deliberately reduced until the two are indistinguishable.

These devices create frames in which the processes of storytelling in the world of the book and the processes of John Barth's telling of the story before the reader's eyes are constantly being examined at the same time. Thus there are stories within stories within stories and narrators quoting narrators quoting narrators. In **"Menelaiad,"** for example, Barth (or the implied author—Barth writing in his persona as writer) retells the story in the words of a modernized Menelaus who in turn quotes others and recalls his own earlier tellings:

" ' "Nothing for it but to do as Eidothea'd bid me," ' "
I say to myself I told Telemachus I sighed to Helen.⁵

The narrative levels continue to accumulate. There is even a storytelling Menelaus whom Menelaus imagines:

" ' " ' " 'By Zeus out of Leda,' I commenced, as though
I weren't Menelaus, Helen Helen, 'egg-born Helen was
a beauty desired by all men on earth. . . .' " ' " ' "⁶

The storytellers involved in these passages are John Barth, professor at Buffalo and writer at large; John Barth, implied author of the story; Menelaus, the "I" of the story but also Barth's re-creation of an ancient literary figure; the Menelaus of the past who told his story before; and a storytelling Menelaus who is a figment of Menelaus's imagination. Little wonder this story begins "Menelaus here, more or less."⁷

The stories in *Lost in the Funhouse* are arranged to encompass various stages in the life of the artist from his conception through his late years of deepening involvement with unanswerable questions. The first piece in the book is a preface to this arrangement and is a metaphor for the endless activity to which the author in and of the book commits himself: the infinite creation of story. It is printed on a vertical strip running from bottom to top on both sides of a single sheet. Instructions are included for cutting out the strip, twisting it once, and joining the ends together. The result is a Möbius strip, a continuous one-sided surface upon which one can now read the words, for as long as he lives if he so desires, "ONCE UPON A TIME THERE WAS A STORY THAT BEGAN ONCE UPON A TIME THERE WAS A STORY THAT BEGAN ONCE UPON A TIME THERE WAS A STORY THAT BEGAN. . . ."

The next story, the first portrait of the artist, is called **"Night-Sea Journey"** and is a satirical allegory of man's absurd quest for the meaning of his existence. The satire begins as the story opens:

> "One way or another, no matter which theory of our journey is correct, it's myself I address; to whom I rehearse as to a stranger our history and condition, and will disclose my secret hope though I sink for it."

> "Is the journey my invention? Do the night, the sea, exist at all, I ask myself, apart from my experience of them? Do I myself exist, or is this a dream? Sometimes I wonder. And if I am, who am I? The Heritage I supposedly transport? But how can I be both vessel and contents? Such are the questions that beset my intervals of rest."

The tone of the passage and the clichés the narrator uses suggest that Barth is making the questions into a joke. The disturbing factor in the joke is that these questions are, in spite of their absolute familiarity, man's most basic ones—and they are unanswerable. Therefore, the joke is not only on the narrator but on everybody, author and reader included. The serious joke grows as the reader learns that the narrator's familiar questions have to do with the purpose of mankind's commonest experience, the journey of life. The narrator swims with millions of his companions through dark seas towards an unknown destination. The goal of the journey is a personified female entity whose warmth can be sensed by some of the travelers. The existence of the quest's objective cannot be proved by anyone, and many fear that the joy of union with "Her" spells oblivion as well as ecstasy. These doubts and uncertainties are the conflicts embodied in all theologies. The ultimate joke of the story hinges on the reader's discovery that the narrator and his companions are spermatozoa.

To the reader's delight, the sperm-narrator talks about his dilemma in the terminology of the absurd:

> "If at times, in certain humors—stroking in unison, say, with my neighbors and chanting with them 'Onward! Upward!'—I have supposed that we have after all a common Maker, Whose nature and motives we may not know, but Who engendered us in some mysterious wise and launched us forth toward some end known but to Him—if (for a moodslength only) I have been able to entertain such notions, very popular in certain quarters, it is because our night-sea journey partakes of their absurdity. One might even say: I can believe them *because* they are absurd.

> "Has that been said before?"

The spermatozoa swim bravely upstream for two measures, flailing their tails, then must rest, sliding backwards one measure. During these periods of inactivity, the narrator ponders and soliloquizes. Thousands of his companions drown every instant, while the survivors sustain one another by singing "Love! Love!" The narrator recalls that some, including himself in his nihilistic moments, have speculated that the journey is without meaning. He answers the question of suicide in a way that echoes Todd Andrews's arbitrary logic: " 'Indeed, if I have yet to join the hosts of the suicides, it is because (fatigue apart) I find it no meaningfuller to drown myself than to go on swimming.' " He has heard some say, " ' "The night-sea journey may be absurd, but here we swim, will-we nill-we, against the flood, onward and upward, toward a Shore that may not exist and couldn't be reached if it did." ' " The choice for the thoughtful swimmer is, then, "give over thrashing and go under for good, or embrace the absurdity; affirm in and for itself the night-sea journey; swim on with neither motive nor destination, for the sake of swimming, and compassionate moreover with your fellow swimmer, we being all at sea and equally in the dark."

The narrator tries to insist that he does not find the embracing of absurdity acceptable: "If not even the hypothetical Shore can justify a sea-full of drownèd comrades, to speak of the swim-in-itself as somehow doing so strikes me as obscene. I continue to swim—but only because blind habit, blind instinct, blind fear of drowning are still more strong than the horror of our journey." With this, the joke seems genuinely nihilistic: if the swimmers cannot elect to like their condition, then nothing moves them but meaningless chemical processes. The narrator admires swimmers who strike off in their own directions, asserting their independence even though it costs them their lives, and he envies the hedonists. But he rejects both blatant nonconformity and egoism as being "more dramatically absurd, in our senseless circumstances, than tailing along in conventional fashion. Suicides, rebels, affirmers of the paradox—nay-sayers and yea-sayers alike to our fatal journey—I finally shake my head at them." But even as he rejects these alternatives, he is dedicating himself to the more intrinsically absurd, if not the more dramatically absurd, solution: swimming on in full awareness of the absurdity of swimming on. He does not reject the absurd mode after all; where others say *nay* or *yea,* he says both at once.

Being perfectly lucid, the narrator acknowledges the absurdity of his choice to remain in the intrinsically absurd situation: " 'A poor irony: that I, who find abhorrent and tautological the doctrine of survival of the fittest . . . may be the sole remaining swimmer! . . . Chance drowns the worthy with the unworthy . . . and makes the night-sea journey essentially *haphazard* as well as murderous and unjustified.'"[8] Ironically, his guess is correct. His attempts to reject an absurd solution and his philosophical discourse itself are terminated by his being the spermatozoon who unites with "Her." The union is an ambiguous event, just as traditional mystical union with the godhead is ambiguous: it is ecstasy but it is also intellectual annihilation. The hero protests his flood of joy: " 'I am not deceived. This new emotion is Her doing; the desire that possesses me is Her bewitchment. Lucidity passes from me; in a moment I'll cry "Love!" bury myself in Her side, and be "transfigured." Which is to say, I die already; this fellow transported by passion is not I; *I am he who abjures and rejects the night-sea journey! . . .* I am all love. "Come!" She whispers, and I have no will.' "[9] His last effort to defy love fades as he broadcasts a warning to the fluid, a message to those who may come behind him: " 'Stop Your hearing against Her song!' " He disappears into the warm globule shouting, " 'Love! Love! Love!' " The final twist of the joke is that the ecstatic union produces a new life but the consciousness that went into the union is gone and will never know that new consciousness is born. The conception is both rebirth and death, and this ambivalence is the basic truth of cyclical life.

Three of the stories in the collection are about a boy named Ambrose, who may or may not be the issue of the union depicted at the end of the **"Night-Sea Journey"** (by inference, of course, he is). The stories are deliberately Joycean portraits of the artist as a young man, and Barth may have intended Ambrose to resemble Barth. The reader is invited to make these comparisons because Barth has deliberately built the parallels between himself, Ambrose, and Joyce into the stories. To compound the joke, he has drawn Ambrose as a budding author who is deliberately imitating Joyce's conscious literary apprenticeship.

Ambrose is thirteen, and he thinks of himself as being at the awkward age. In the first of his stories, **"Ambrose His Mark,"** Ambrose does the telling—in the first person. In the second two stories, the author uses third person, but we have the impression—probably because the first story was told by an "I"—that Ambrose is still telling his own story. Thus in **"Lost in the Funhouse"** it is impossible not to equate the author's speculations with Ambrose's. "Is it likely," says the storyteller, whoever he is, "does it violate the principle of verisimilitude, that a thirteen-year-old boy could make such a sophisticated observation?"[10] A third possibility is that Barth lets Ambrose tell his own story in retrospect. This blending of narrator identities makes **"Lost in the Funhouse"** structurally tight in spite of constant interjections about the difficulties of writing a story. "There is no *texture of rendered sensory detail*," the teller complains about his story, and he feels that it lacks the conventional diagrammatic rise and fall described by Freitag's Triangle.[11] He constantly worries about using clichés and italicizes them to show that he is conscious of them. The subject of the story is story-writing, and its satire centers on the conventional things people talk about when they talk about story-writing.

The interjections complement the story's plot. Ambrose, trying to impress a girl friend, hopes to act sophisticated and nonchalant when he accompanies her through the funhouse at a carnival. He actually fears that he will get lost in there and imagines what might happen if he does. His imaginings are directly related to the subject of storywriting. As the teller (Barth or the older Ambrose) talks about writing the story, young Ambrose of the plot is imagining how the story of being lost in the funhouse would be written. In turn, being lost in the funhouse itself is a storytelling situation, because, when lost, one has nothing left to do but sit down in some corner to await rescue or death, telling stories to oneself to avoid going insane. One ending Ambrose imagines for the story is "He died telling stories to himself in the dark; years later, when that vast unsuspected area of the funhouse came to light, the first expedition found his skeleton in one of its labyrinthine corridors and mistook it for part of the entertainment."[12] This sentence is a condensation of Barth's and Ambrose's idea of the curious status of the storyteller.

At points in this book, Barth appears to be more than cynical about the process of absurd creation, even as he accepts it as inevitable. In a piece called **"Title,"** he rambles across various stock problems of composition, having begun with an axiom: "Everything leads to nothing: future tense; past tense; present tense. Perfect. The final question is, Can nothing be made meaningful? . . . If not, the end is at hand. Literally, as it were."[13] Later, he seems bitter but resigned: "There's only one direction to go in. Ugh. We must make something out of nothing. Impossible. Mystics do. Not only turn contradiction into paradox, but *employ* it, to go on living and working. Don't bet on it. I'm betting my cliché on it, yours too. What is that supposed to mean? On with the refutation; every denial is another breath, every word brings us closer to the end." Following this, he recognizes that the alternative to having no hope is to supply some alternative, making something out of nothing after all. Still, "That's no alternative. Unless I make it one. Just try; quit talking about it, quit talking, quit!" And finally, he plunges into the ludicrous, noting that writing is a matter of filling sentence-structure boxes: adjective into adjective slot, noun into noun, verb into verb. What the writer and his story are doing is creating each other—an absurd notion complicated by the possibility that in **"Title"** the story itself may be telling its own story: "that's what I'm leading up to, me and my bloody anticlimactic noun, we're pushing each other to fill in the blank."[14]

The author's condition may thus be wretched; John Barth—whoever he is—says in this book that he believes it is. The teller's proper point of view is "first person anonymous," and we must accept this as a description of whoever it is that speaks here.[15] The problem and its solution are inseparable, completely reversible, one and the same: "To be moved to art instead of to action by one's wretchedness may preserve one's life and sanity; at the same time, it may leave one wretcheder yet."[16] The writer finally can do nothing but stay on his Möbius strip, telling stories ever onward and upward and downward and backward. **"Lost in the Funhouse"** ends with the simultaneous problem and solution neatly stated: "He wishes he had never entered the funhouse. But he has. Then he wishes he were dead. But he's not. Therefore he will construct funhouses for others and be their secret operator—though he would rather be among the lovers for whom funhouses are designed."[17]

As readers, we are constrained to doubt the story's last claim. As we look into Barth's funhouses, we must declare that we who are outside looking in cannot help but envy the builder just as he envies lovers and readers. Is there really, after all, a difference between doers in the world, lovers in the funhouse, readers in their chairs, and authors in their books? And whether we are lost or found, we are still in the house of fun. In Barth's own terms, the only way to transcend the absurd is to put our sense of it to work, realizing that creating absurd alternatives is a high and difficult variety of fun. It is fun to write stories. It is fun to read stories. It is even fun to read and write about reading and writing stories.

Notes

1. John Enck, "John Barth: An Interview," *Wisconsin Studies in Contemporary Literature,* VI (Winter-Spring, 1965), 12.

2. Ibid., p. 4.

3. Ibid., p. 8.

4. Ibid., p. 11.

5. John Barth, *Lost in the Funhouse* (Garden City, 1968), p. 140.

6. Ibid., p. 153.

7. Ibid., p. 130.

8. Ibid., pp. 3-6.

9. Ibid., p. 12. This story shows some startling resemblances to Twain's "The Great Dark" and "Three Thousand Years Among the Microbes." The night-sea journey was discussed extensively by Jung, who saw it as part of a cycle of quest myths, all of which reflect the longing to attain rebirth through a return to the womb.

10. Ibid., p. 73.

11. Ibid., p. 89.

12. Ibid., p. 95. One of the writers Barth admires most is Jorge Luis Borges, one of whose works is titled *Labyrinths.* Speaking of this book, Barth said, "That brings us to his favorite image of all, the labyrinth. . . . A labyrinth, after all, is a place in which, ideally, all the possibilities of choice (of direction, in this case) are embodied, and . . . must be exhausted before one reaches the heart. Where, mind, the Minotaur waits with two final possibilities: defeat and death, or victory and freedom." See "The Literature of Exhaustion," *The Atlantic,* CCXX (August, 1967), 29-34.

13. *Lost in the Funhouse,* p. 105.

14. Ibid., pp. 111-13.

15. John Barth, "Anonymiad," *Lost in the Funhouse,* p. 199.

16. Ibid., p. 183.

17. *Lost in the Funhouse,* p. 97.

Michael Hinden (essay date April 1973)

SOURCE: Hinden, Michael. "*Lost in the Funhouse*: Barth's Use of the Recent Past." *Twentieth Century Literature* 19, no. 2 (April 1973): 107-18.

[*In the following essay, Hinden remarks on Barth's treatment of the dilemma of "exhausted" possibilities faced by contemporary writers, and by modern culture in general, in* Lost in the Funhouse.]

"Historicity and self-awareness, he asseverated, while ineluctable and even greatly to be prized, are always fatal to innocence and spontaneity. Perhaps adjective period Whether in a people, an art, a love affair, on a fourth term added not impossibly to make the third less than ultimate."[1] Arriving at this judgment, the narrator of **"Title"** in Barth's **Lost in the Funhouse** concludes that today's writers, schooled in criticism, burdened with self-consciousness, laboring in vineyards harvested by their recent predecessors, have been reduced to pushing each other literally "to fill in the blank," (p. 109). The "blank," he suggests, is what remains (or what does not remain) of our recent literary past. "Love affairs, literary genres, third item in exemplary series, fourth—everything blossoms and decays, does it not, from the primitive and classical through the mannered and baroque to the abstract, stylized, dehumanized, unintelligible blank." (p. 105). Discounting irony, the mood recalls that darkest of all passages in *Ecclesiastes.* Vanity of vanity, says the Preacher: "For in much wisdom is much vexation, / and he who increases knowledge increases sorrow."

The plight of Barth's monologist reflects not merely a crisis in *belles lettres* but the predicament of the age itself which, like its counterpart, prose fiction, appears to be "about played out" (p. 105). Too much is known, too much has been tried, too much is now over with, yet nothing has been settled, Barth intimates, striking a tone peculiarly appropriate for the seventies. Certainly it seems painfully clear that for all our striving after systematic truth (especially in moral philosophy and aesthetics) we do seem to have lost our capacity for zest to the extent that our thought processes have become self-conscious and historical. Familiarity denatures insight; what can be analyzed in terms of origin or motive soon loses its power to enthrall us.

These observations are neither startling nor new, yet in one sense the dilemma of the contemporary writer is unique. In the compressed space of several generations a dozen literary movements have flourished and been catalogued, manifestos studied, techniques codified and perfected, ranks assigned, order imposed. Sheer volume is reason in itself to explain Barth's observation that literature by now has exhausted the vast seed bag of potentialities that were brought to flower in the recent past. In his essay, **"The Literature of Exhaustion,"** Barth specifies: "By 'exhaustion' I don't mean anything so tired as the subject of physical, moral, or intellectual decadence, only the used-upness of certain forms or exhaustion of certain possibilities—by no means necessarily a cause for despair."[2] The "real technical question," he elaborates, "seems to me how to succeed not even Joyce and Kafka, but those who've *succeeded* Joyce and Kafka," namely, Beckett and Borges.[3] In Barth's evaluation of Borges's work there can be found a suggestion of the direction he himself has embarked upon as a means of transforming art's paralysis. Borges's "artistic victory, if you like, is that he confronts an intellectual dead end and employs it against itself to accomplish new human work."[4] As the narrator of **"Anonymiad"** remarks in *Lost in the Funhouse,* the point is that "one can't pretend to an innocence outgrown or in other wise retrace one's steps, unless by coming full circle." (p. 174). Borges is willing to make this voyage, employing as method a unique conception of the Baroque, which he defines as "that style which deliberately exhausts (or tries to exhaust) its possibilities and borders upon its own caricature."[5] Moreover, in fiction the possibilities opened by such procedure suggest "how an artist may paradoxically turn the felt ultimacies of our time into material and means for his work—*paradoxically* because by doing so he transcends what had appeared to be his refutation. . . ."[6] The final possibility (adds the narrator of **"Title"**) might then be for the artist to "turn ultimacy against itself to make something new and valid, the essence whereof would be the impossibility of making something new." (p. 106).

In *Lost in the Funhouse* Barth brings these conceptions to realization. Based on his notion of ultimacy turned against itself by means of a style that is self-exhausting and yet comically triumphant, the book reveals a dazzling display of modernist techniques even while it examines the depletion of certain forms of modernist expression and the unbearable self-consciousness of intellectual life. Myths, symbolism, interior monolog, time shifts, varieties of point of view, mixed media, esoteric word play—all are employed, parodied, and refreshened as Barth's vision of the funhouse is defined.

Like Borges, Barth is convinced that his artistic victory can be gained only by confronting the recent past and "employ[ing] it against itself to accomplish new human work." Therefore, in an attempt to exhaust the possibilities of its own tradition, *Lost in the Funhouse* begins as an elaborate parody, revival, and refutation of Joyce's masterpiece, *A Portrait of the Artist as a Young Man.* That Barth consciously is engaged in this endeavor there can be no doubt. Joyce himself is mentioned twice in the title story as an originator and authority on techniques of modern fiction (p. 71, p. 85), and the recycling of Joycean/Homeric materials, especially the Daedalus-labyrinth motif (**"Night-Sea Journey," "Lost in the Funhouse," "Echo," "Menelaid"**) is intentional. In the true spirit of caricature, Barth's attitude toward his model is both respectful and subversive. This, unlike Joyce's Stephen who at the conclusion of *A Portrait of the Artist* escapes (at least temporarily) the nets of his imprisonment, young Ambrose in Barth's story wanders deeper into the funhouse labyrinth "wherein he lingers yet." (p. 91). While Stephen's soul prepares to soar in the final passage of *A Portrait of the Artist*— "Old father, old artificer, stand me now and ever in good stead"[7]—the narrator of **"Autobiography"** mocks: "Father, have mercy, I dare you! Wretched old fabricator, where's your shame? Put an end to this, for pity's sake! Now! Now!" (p. 36). And the speaker in **"Night-Sea Journey,"** a sperm caught up in the surge of life against his will, undoes Stephen's affirming cry—"Welcome, O life! I go to encounter for the millionth time the reality of experience and to forge in the smithy of my soul the uncreated conscience of my race"[8]—with a life-negating moan: "Whoever echoes these reflections: be more courageous than their author! An end to night-sea journeys! Make no more!" (p. 12).

Joycean patterns dominate *Lost in the Funhouse* and may be found in the determinative structural elements of the work as well as in minute intricacies of style. For instance, Stephen's advocacy of an Olympian artist who "like the God of creation, remains within or behind or beyond or above his handiwork, invisible, refined out of existence, indifferent, paring his fingernails,"[9] is adopted as a basis for Barth's narrative point of view, but is driven beyond logical limits in **"Echo," "Autobiography," "Life Story," "Title,"** and **"Anonymiad."**

Echo says Tiresias is not to be trusted in this matter
. . . none can tell teller from told. Narcissus would appear to be the opposite from Echo: he perished by denying all except himself; she persists by effacing herself absolutely. Yet they come to the same . . . the
voice persists, persists.

(**"Echo,"** p. 99)

Repetitions of various special phrases and psychological perceptions from *A Portrait of the Artist* also are
conspicuous in Barth's stories, additionally strengthen-
ing the connection between the works. Two examples
may suffice. Both Stephen and Ambrose are fascinated
by the sounds of words and the denotative meaning of
colloquial phrases. Thus, Stephen:

> Suck was a queer word. . . . Once he had washed his
> hands in the lavatory of the Wicklow Hotel and his fa-
> ther pulled the stopper up by the chain after and the
> dirty water went down through the hole in the basin.
> And when it had all gone down slowly the hole in the
> basin had made a sound like that: suck. Only louder.[10]

Ambrose in **"Lost in the Funhouse"**:

> Funhouses need men's and ladies' rooms at intervals.
> Others perhaps have also vomited in corners and corri-
> dors; may even have had bowel movements liable to be
> stepped in in the dark. The word *fuck* suggests suction
> and/or flatulence. Mother and Father; grandmothers and
> grandfathers on both sides. . . .

(p. 76)

Stephen:

> And when Dante made that noise after dinner and then
> put up her hand to her mouth: that was heartburn.[11]

Ambrose:

> By looking at his arm a certain way he could see drop-
> lets standing in the pores. It was what they meant when
> they spoke of *breaking out in a cold sweat*: very like
> what one felt in school assemblies, when one was wait-
> ing in the wings for the signal to step out onto the
> stage.

(**"Water Message,"** p. 49)

But Barth's most significant use of Joycean materials
concerns the collapse of credibility of the artist-as-hero
theme in modern literature and the question raised as to
whether there is "anything more tiresome, in fiction,
than the problems of sensitive adolescents" (**"Lost in
the Funhouse,"** p. 89). In this regard the key story is
"Ambrose His Mark," a mock-heroic portrait of the
artist's birth and infancy with an account of the derivation of his name. In memory of the baby's painful encounter with a hive of swarming bees, his uncle suggests that he be named after St. Ambrose, who "had the
same thing happen when he was a baby. All these bees
swarmed on his mouth while he was asleep in his fa-

ther's yard, and everybody said he'd grow up to be a
great speaker" (p. 31). Grandfather counters that, "the
bees was more on this baby's eyes and ears than on his
mouth," whereupon Uncle Konrad adds, "So he'll grow
up to see things clear" (p. 31). But the fact of the matter is that Ambrose grows up to lose himself in his own
reflection. Perhaps, then, the ultimate significance of the
story lies in the outrageous pun implicit in its action—a
portrait of the artist as a "stung" man. (The pun, I venture to submit, is Barth's, not mine.)

Yet Barth's resources in *Lost in the Funhouse* extend
far beyond the limited form of parody. According to
Barth's conception of the Baroque, a work eventually
must serve as model to *itself*, defining and exhausting
its own possibilities of invention and procedure as if to
caricature its own emerging form. *Lost in the Funhouse* clearly attains this end. Barth announces in the
"Author's Note" that the stories here should be approached as "neither a collection nor a selection, but a
series" (p. ix), and viewed in this light, they do reveal a
pattern of progressive unity. The particular sequence of
the stories itself suggests an aesthetic circularity which
is of major thematic significance, beginning with
"Frame Tale," a Moebius strip (to be cut out and
fastened) on which is printed: "Once upon a time there
/ Was a story that began" (repeating itself in perpetuity
band to band), and ending with **"Anonymiad,"** a fanciful slice from Homer's banquet that pretends to be the
world's first instance of autobiographical prose fiction.
The interim tales are connected in various ways, the
most important being the treatment of the growth of
consciousness in a given mind (the artist) and the confusion resulting from hyper-consciousness transmuted
into art. Four of the stories, appropriately, are specifically about the difficulties of writing stories.

"Night-Sea Journey," following **"Frame Tale,"** is a
delightful *tour de force* which at a blow appears to exhaust the possibilities of first person point of view and
autobiographical fiction as a whole, while simultaneously opening up new areas for narrative experiment.
The artist carries us back to a journey prior to his own
conception, speaking as a cell endowed (to his chagrin)
with the collective wisdom of the human race. From
this perspective Barth scrupulously examines the major
details of the ancient archetypal pattern of the **"Night
Journey"** as described by Arthur Koestler (even to the
point of suggesting a direct borrowing from Koestler's
model):

> Under the effect of some overwhelming experience, the
> hero is made to realize the shallowness of his life, the
> futility and frivolity of the daily pursuits of man in the
> trivial routines of existence. This realization may come
> to him as a sudden shock caused by some catastrophic
> event, or as the cumulative effect of a slow inner devel-
> opment, or through the trigger action of some appar-
> ently banal experience which assumes an unexpected

significance. The hero then suffers a crisis which involves the very foundations of his being; he embarks on the Night Journey, is suddenly transferred to the Tragic Plane—from which he emerges purified, enriched by new insight, regenerated on a higher level of integration.[12]

Barth's narrator concludes that the night-sea journey he has undertaken (the cause of life itself) appears to have no meaning, that the struggle "onward and upward" is absurd. His last moments of awareness are addressed to "You who I may be about to become"; his advice is to "terminate this aimless, brutal business! Stop your hearing against Her song! Hate Love!" (pp. 11-12). Yet even at this instant of refusal the speaker is propelled toward an unwilling union and reintegration with the "She," a transfiguration and renewal of the endless cycle.

Since it occurs to the narrator that "Makers and swimmers *each generate the other*" (p. 8), the story suggests a biological parallel to the fictional circularity of **"Frame Tale."** The similarity is intentional, for in this early story Barth establishes a complicated pattern of allusions to be developed later stressing the interrelatedness of bungled life and art. Thus, **"Ambrose His Mark,"** which follows **"Night-Sea Journey,"** takes as its subject the artist's birth, weaning, and belated christening. **"Autobiography,"** the fourth story in sequence, is **"Night-Sea Journey"**'s companion piece, exploring the self-recorded birth pangs of a piece of fiction "still in utero, hung up in my delivery" (p. 36). Here too the argument is posed for an "interrupted pregnancy," but with as little success as the plea for contraception in **"Night-Sea Journey."** Two other Ambrose stories follow, concerning identity crises and the growing sensitivity of the artist and his problems. These are separated by a tale intended to shed light on both, **"Petition,"** Barth's central parable of the incompatibility of instinct and self-scrutiny. This witty fable takes the form of a plea for severance by the self-loathing partner in a Siamese twin relationship, a literal over-the-shoulder observer whose entire life has been "a painful schooling in detachment" (p. 61). "To be one: paradise! To be two: bliss! But to be both and neither, unspeakable." (p. 68).

In **"Water Message"** (which obviously is indebted to Joyce's "Araby") Ambrose, fascinated by words and already isolated from his playmates, experiences the preadolescent confusion of lost innocence centered around the mysteries of a secret boys' club and the seduction of an idolized older girl by her "moustachioed boyfriend." The story is one of both initiation and exclusion, and the "sea-wreathed" bottle which washes ashore at the conclusion with its effaced message and blank signature is a perfect emblem of the boy's wonder at his own blurred image of identity. Indeed, the boy's

discovery harks back to the ending of **"Ambrose His Mark"**: "Yet years were to pass before anyone troubled to have me christened or to correct my birth certificate, whereon my surname was preceded by a blank" (p. 32). But it also anticipates the driving theme of **"Title"**: "The story of our life. This is the final test. Try to fill the blank. Only hope is to fill the blank. Efface what can't be faced or else fill the blank" (p. 102).

It is the function of the artist to find means of filling in the blank: thus, in order to create a self, to discover meaning and identity, Ambrose determines in the pivotal seventh story, **"Lost in the Funhouse,"** to become an artist. Yet the central image of the book reveals our hero in the funhouse maze frustratingly thrown back upon "the endless repetition of his image in the mirrors . . . as he *lost himself in the reflection* [Barth's italics] that the necessity for an observer makes perfect observation impossible" (p. 90). In **"The Literature of Exhaustion"** Barth has written that, "a labyrinth, after all, is a place in which, ideally, all the possibilities of choice . . . are embodied, and—barring special dispensation like Theseus'—must be exhausted before one reaches the heart."[13] At length, then, Ambrose contemplates exhaustion.

> How long will it last? He envisions a truly astonishing funhouse, incredibly complex yet utterly controlled from a great central switchboard like the console of a pipe organ. Nobody had enough imagination. He could design such a place himself, wiring and all, and he's only thirteen years old. He would be its operator: panel lights would show what was up in every cranny of its cunning of its multifarious vastness; a switchflick would ease this fellow's way, complicate that's, to balance things out; if anyone seemed lost or frightened, all the operator had to do was.
>
> He wishes he had never entered the funhouse. But he has. Then he wishes he were dead. But he's not. Therefore he will construct funhouses for others and be their secret operator—though he would rather be among the lovers for whom funhouses are designed.
>
> (pp. 93-94)

It is particularly ironic that Ambrose loses himself in the funhouse after pursuing big-busted Magda, whose sex appeal entices him, ignoring the warning of the narrator of **"Night-Sea Journey"** to hate love, but also failing to duplicate his self-transforming discovery of union. "Can spermatozoa properly be thought of as male animalcules when there are no female spermatozoa? They grope through hot, dark windings, past Love's Tunnel's fearsome obstacles. Some perhaps lose their way" (p. 77). At this point the first sequence in the book's cycle of stories is complete.

The next seven stories turn increasingly from a perspective on the problems of the artist as an individual to a perspective on the problems of his art, though both themes, of course, are closely intertwined. In **"Echo"** a mythic frame enlarges Ambrose's dilemma through the inverted image of Narcissus, prisoner of his own reflection, lost in a cavern where *he* has fled to avoid his female (and male) admirers. In the cave he finds Tiresias, who with foresight prophesied to Narcissus' mother that her son would lead a long and happy life only if "he never came to know himself" (p. 90). Like Ambrose, Narcissus is destroyed by self-observation, and linked to hapless Echo and Tiresias, he symbolizes passion turned to impotence, the exhaustion of the artist's voice and prophet's vision. This theme is taken up again briefly in **"Two Meditations"** and again in **"Glossolalia,"** which features six speakers who prophesy and who share the common experience of being misunderstood by their respective audiences.

"Title," spaced between **"Two Meditations"** and **"Glossolalia,"** is the most forthright of the stories in its analysis of the bankruptcy of modern fiction. "The narrator has written himself into a corner" (p. 108), and his most plausible alternative (a forecast of literature's future?) is: "General anesthesia. Self-extinction. Silence" (p. 106). Here Barth acknowledges the view of Beckett, who, "weary of [art's] puny exploits, weary of pretending to be able, of being able, of doing a little better the same old thing, of going a little further along a dreary road," prefers "the expression that there is nothing to express, nothing with which to express, no desire to express"—and yet who still admits some "obligation to express."[14] **"Life Story"** continues this mood. The "writer of these lines" (as the narrator identifies himself) toys with the idea that his own life might be a fictional account and begins work on a tale in which an author "comes to suspect that the world is a novel, himself a fictional personage" (p. 113). The story frames soon multiply out of hand until the author silences himself, complaining that "in his heart of hearts he disliked literature of an experimental, self-despising, or overtly metaphysical character, like Samuel Beckett's Marian Cutler's, Jorge Borges's" (p. 114). The enterprise of fiction now is on the brink of suicide.

> To what conclusion will he come? He'd been about to append to his own tale inasmuch as the old analogy between Author and God, novel and world, can no longer be employed unless deliberately as a false analogy, certain things follow: 1) fiction must acknowledge its fictitiousness and metaphoric invalidity or 2) choose to ignore the question and deny its relevance or 3) establish some other, acceptable relation between itself, its author, its reader.
>
> (p. 125)

One course lies open. The words of **"Frame Tale"** curl round again with their infinite repetition, and literature begins anew. Barth returns to Homer.

"Menelaid" and **"Anonymiad"** are the true masterpieces of *Lost in the Funhouse,* each tale obviously deserving more detailed analysis than would be practi-

cable here. Suffice it to say that **"Anonymiad"** brilliantly recapitulates the thematic materials of the previous stories. Its premise of the stranded minstrel who single-handedly invents and exhausts the major categories of literature, then sets his works adrift in the wine jugs which inspired them, is a perfect symbol of modern art's dilemma of narcissism and estrangement.

> *Amphora*'s my muse:
> When I finish off the booze,
> I hump the jug and fill her up with fiction.
>
> (p. 164)

(The story also brings full circle the thematic strands begun in **"Night-Sea Journey"** and **"Water Message."**) But perhaps the achievement of greatest significance in *Lost in the Funhouse* is **"Menelaid,"** as remarkable in its structure as in its vision of the Trojan War.[15] (The title pun, of course, suggests both Helen's promiscuity and the varied layers of the story.) Constructed as a labyrinth to disguise yet at the same time enhance the simple proclamation at its heart, **"Menelaid"** is the complicated rhetorical mechanism foreshadowed by the narrator of **"Life Story,"** an interminable narrative "whose drama lies always in the next frame out" (p. 117). The truth at the heart of things which it asserts is "the absurd, unending possibility of love" (p. 162); its premise is that it was Menelaus' mistrust of instinct, his self-scrutiny and hyper-consciousness, that drove Helen into the arms of Paris and issued in the Trojan War; its mechanism is the tale within a tale extended to infinity as Proteus threatens to dissolve all frames through his capacity to change his shape and voice at will.[16] The chief significance to Barth of the story's final image is suggested by his comments on the subject in **"The Literature of Exhaustion."** Menelaus on the beach at Pharos, he declares,

> is genuinely Baroque in the Borgesian spirit, and illustrates a positive artistic morality in the literature of exhaustion. He is not there, after all, for kicks (any more than Borges and Beckett are in the fiction racket for their health): Menelaus is *lost,* in the larger labyrinth of the world, and has got to hold fast while the Old Man of the Sea exhausts reality's frightening guises so that he may extort direction from him when Proteus returns to his 'true' self. It's a heroic enterprise, with salvation as its object—one recalls that the aim of the Histriones is to get history done with so that Jesus may come again the sooner, and that Shakespeare's heroic metamorphoses culminate not merely in a theophany but in an apotheosis.[17]

Like Camus's redoubtable hero of the absurd (though rather more comic than Promethean in guise), Menelaus discovers that he may *multiply* what he cannot unify and that (in Camus's words again) his "nostalgia for unity, this fragmented universe and the contradiction that binds them together,"[18] in other words, his experience of the absurd, is the only bond uniting him to reality. The image further suggests Barth's own conception of his relation to past literary tradition which, despite his grasp (or because of it), continues to deny him substance yet remains for him an indissoluble bond. As Camus asserts: "The first and, after all, the only condition of my inquiry is to preserve the very thing that crushes me, consequently to respect what I consider essential in it. I have just defined it as a confrontation and an unceasing struggle."[19] Tension, the vitality of combat, is for Camus that sole element which ennobles man and fortifies him to repudiate suicide which itself is a negation. In contrast, the absurd man "can only drain everything to the bitter end, and deplete himself. The absurd is his extreme tension, which he maintains constantly by solitary effort, for he knows that in that consciousness and in that day-to-day revolt he gives proof of his only truth, which is defiance."[20]

However, Barth's characters in *Lost in the Funhouse* are neither capable nor desirous of maintaining a posture of heroic defiance; for them suicide proffers a continual seduction. As noted earlier, the sperm cell in **"Night-Sea Journey"** abjures and rejects his swift-running course toward life. Similarly, the story telling itself in **"Autobiography"** begs, "if anyone hears me . . . and has the means to my end, I pray him do us both a kindness" (p. 37). The narrator of **"Petition"** discloses that his soul "lusts only for disjunction" (p. 62), and in **"Lost in the Funhouse"** Ambrose remarks that if there were "a button you could push to end your life absolutely without pain . . . he would push it instantly" (p. 86). Narcissus, too, we are told, "desired himself defunct before his own conception" (**"Echo,"** p. 100). Menelaus alone, through his "peculiar immortality" (p. 124), knows he cannot die and refuses the false solace of the death wish. Yet impulse, not conviction, drives him on, habit, not determination. And, indeed, impulse, not determination, drives the sperm toward union with the egg; only against his better judgment does Narcissus finally grow fond. Impulse and habit, too, are the forces which continue to animate art, but no rational justification for prolonging it seems possible. The writer finds his sentences stringing themselves out as though he were a "recidivist" engaging in a nasty habit he cannot manage to suppress. "Or a chronic forger, let's say; committed to the pen for life. Which is to say, death. The point, for pity's sake. Not yet. Forge on" (**"Title,"** p. 103). One recalls Vladimir's observation in *Waiting For Godot* that "habit is a great deadener." When Estragon complains, "I can't go on like this," the answer he receives is: "That's what you think."[21]

Against unreasonable demands, through impulse, habit, dread of stopping, sheer perversity, perhaps, and no doubt, also, through the joy of making labyrinths, Barth does go on—or has gone on, at least until now. What more remains for him to do? Put another way, what edi-

fice will Barth attempt (with Theseus' dispensation) to raise atop this labyrinthine cavern? He has prepared us for the dazzling and the bizarre, yet it would not be surprising if in the future Barth's literary design began to take a more traditional, familiar form—for only to a limited extent does Camus's evaluation of Nietzsche's position in modern philosophy seem applicable to Barth's relationship to contemporary fiction and aesthetics. Of Nietzsche Camus writes that, "with a kind of frightful joy [he] rushes toward the impasse into which he methodically drives his nihilism. His avowed aim is to render the situation untenable to his contemporaries. His only hope seems to be to arrive at the extremity of contradiction. Then if man does not wish to perish in the coils that strangle him, he will have to cut them at a single blow and create his own values."[22] In like manner Barth challenges the writers and critics of contemporary fiction to cut the coils that bind them to the recent past. But that same past, as *Lost in the Funhouse* paradoxically demonstrates, already has furnished Barth with new materials for art, providing thereby for a Prodigal Son's circuitous return.

Notes

1. John Barth, *Lost in the Funhouse* (New York: Bantam, 1969), p. 106. Future page references to *Lost in the Funhouse* are drawn from this edition and will be cited parenthetically in the text along with individual story titles when the text reference is not otherwise clear.

2. John Barth, "The Literature of Exhaustion," reprinted in *On Contemporary Literature,* ed. Richard Kostelanetz (New York: Avon Books, 1969), pp. 662-675. The article originally was published in *The Atlantic Monthly,* Vol. 220, No. 2 (August, 1967), pp. 29-34.

3. *Ibid.,* pp. 664-665.

4. *Ibid.,* p. 668.

5. Barth quoting Borges, "The Literature of Exhaustion," p. 672.

6. *Ibid.,* p. 669.

7. James Joyce, *A Portrait of the Artist as a Young Man,* ed. Chester G. Anderson (New York: The Viking Critical Library, 1968), p. 253.

8. Joyce, pp. 252-253.

9. Joyce, p. 215.

10. Joyce, p. 11.

11. Joyce, p. 11.

12. Arthur Koestler, *The Act of Creation* (New York: Dell, 1964), p. 358. The hero as embryo motif, of course, is derived from *The Oxen of the Sun* epi-

sode in *Ulysses.* Joyce discussed his intention in that section in a letter to Frank Budgen dated March, 1920: "Am working hard at *Oxen of the Sun,* the idea being the crime committed against fecundity by sterilizing the act of coition. . . . Bloom is the spermatozoon, the hospital the womb, the nurse the ovium, Stephen the embryo." Stuart Gilbert, ed., *James Joyce: Letters, Vol. I* (New York: The Viking Press, 1966), pp. 139-140.

13. "The Literature of Exhaustion," p. 674.

14. From "Three Dialogues by Samuel Beckett and Georges Duthuit," *Samuel Beckett: A Collection of Critical Essays,* ed. Martin Esslin (Englewood Cliffs, N.J.: Prentice Hall, 1965), pp. 16-22, p. 17.

15. Throughout *Lost in the Funhouse* Barth's use of Greek materials is discerning. In "Menelaid" he draws upon the tradition which holds that Aeschylus wrote a satyr play called *Proteus* (now lost) in comic counterpoint to Agamemnon's tragedy. In the words of the Greek scholar, George Thomson, "the *Proteus,* which followed the trilogy of the *Oresteia,* dealt with the adventures of Menelaos after the Trojan War as a *scherzo* to his brother's tragic homecoming; and it is not difficult to imagine a *Proteus* charged with the romantic atmosphere of the *Odyssey* which would round off in a whirl of irresponsible gaiety the liturgical grandeur of th*e Oresteia.*" *Aeschylus and Athens* (New York: Grosset and Dunlop, 1968), p. 228. Barth also draws on Euripides' *Helen,* which follows the legend that a phantom was sent to Troy in Helen's place while the real Helen spent the war years in Egypt under the protection of Proteus. The circumstances in "Anonymiad" also seem based upon a little known Greek tradition, again recounted by Thomson, "of a minstrel at Mycenae, to whom Agamemnon had entrusted the guardianship of his Queen—evidently a vassal of high standing." *Aeschylus and Athens,* p. 60.

16. The narrative frames in "Menelaid" are inspired by Menelaus' digressions in Book IV of the *Odyssey* describing his encounter with Proteus on the beach at Pharos. In Barth's version Telemachus and Peisistratus arrive at Menelaus' palace (as in the *Odyssey*) to obtain information about Odysseus. Their arrival is recounted in frame II. (In frame I Menelaus addresses the reader.) Menelaus begins by telling them the tale of his reunion with Helen (frame III), who postponed their coupling by demanding the story (frame IV) of how Menelaus managed to capture Proteus. In that tale Proteus in turn demands to know Menelaus' reasons for capturing him—which entails (frame V) the story of Menelaus' encounter with Proteus' daughter, Eidothea, and the story she elicited from him concerning the ending of the Trojan War (frame VI). At this stage Barth's Menelaus simultaneously is telling the story of his repossession of Helen to Eidothea, the Eidothea story to Proteus, the Proteus story to Helen, the Helen story to Telemachus and Peisistratus, the story of that story to the reader. One further coil: the subject matter of frame VI (the ending of the Trojan War) necessitates frame VII, the reasons for the Trojan War: but Menelaus demands *that* story of himself. Just as the centerpiece of *Lost in the Funhouse* is the title story placed seventh in a sequence of fourteen, so the seventh frame here is the centerpiece of "Menelaid," the heart of the labyrinth, and the remaining frames in sequence work their way back out again from VII to I.

17. "The Literature of Exhaustion," p. 674.

18. Albert Camus, *The Myth of Sisyphus and Other Essays,* trans. Justin O'Brien (New York: Vintage Books, 1961), p. 37.

19. Camus, p. 23.

20. Camus, p. 41.

21. Samuel Beckett, *Waiting for Godot* (New York: Grove Press, 1954), p. 60.

22. Albert Camus, *The Rebel,* trans. Anthony Bower (New York: Vintage Books, 1956), p. 71.

Clayton Koelb (essay date fall 1974)

SOURCE: Koelb, Clayton. "John Barth's 'Glossolalia.'" *Comparative Literature* 26, no. 4 (fall 1974): 334-45.

[*In the following essay, Koelb highlights the metrical qualities of "Glossolalia" compared to poems such as the odes of Pindar as a means of facilitating "a new understanding of the relationships that obtain in practice among the notions of meter, verse, and prose."*]

One of the most fundamental distinctions in literary criticism is the one between verse and prose. Every literary text, it is assumed, is either one or the other, or occasionally some mixture of the two. The possibility of a third category is rarely entertained. The chief difference between verse and prose, it is also assumed, is meter. The *Oxford English Dictionary* says that the principal signification of *prose* is "the ordinary form of written or spoken language, without metrical structure; esp. as a species or division of literature." *Verse* is defined in an analogous but opposite fashion: "Metrical composition, form, or structure; language or literary work written or spoken in metre; poetry, esp. with reference to metrical form."

Such a simple set of definitions for prose and verse has been weakened, or at least made far more complicated, by the general acceptance of "free" (that is, nonmetrical) verse. Though there are still many dissenters, a large number of critics are willing to admit that there are non-metrical texts which nevertheless ought to be called verse. In this essay I propose to complicate matters further by examining a text which is metrical in a perfectly unambiguous way but which remains in spite of its meter a piece of prose. To make the issues as clear as possible, I shall establish the metrical structure of this text by comparing it to another one which, though metrical in exactly the same way as the first, happens to be verse. It is hoped that out of this dramatic confrontation will come a new understanding of the relationships that obtain in practice among the notions of *meter, verse,* and *prose.*

John Barth's collection **Lost in the Funhouse** contains a group of six short paragraphs collectively entitled **"Glossolalia."** It is, in spite of its brevity, a formidably complex fiction, one that requires an especially imaginative and attentive reader. Each paragraph is composed in a different narrative voice. And each paragraph, one notices, is metrically equivalent to the others. For the reader's convenience, I quote **"Glossolalia"**[1] in its entirety:

> Still breathless from fending Phoebus, suddenly I see all—and all in vain. A horse excreting Greeks will devour my city; none will heed her Apollo loved, and endowed with clear sight, and cursed when she gainsaid him. My honor thus costlily [sic] purchased will be snatched from me by soldiers. I see Agamemnon, my enslaver, meeting death in Mycenae. No more.

> Dear Procne: your wretched sister—she it is weaves this robe. Regard it well: it hides her painful tale in its pointless patterns. Tereus came and fetched her off; he conveyed her to Thrace . . . but not to see her sister. He dragged her deep into the forest, where he shackled her and raped her. Her tongue he then severed, and concealed her, and she warbles for vengeance, and death.

> I Crispus, a man of Corinth, yesterday looked on God. Today I rave. What things my eyes have seen can't be scribed or spoken. All think I praise His sacred name, take my horror for hymns, my blasphemies for raptures. The holy writ's wrongly deciphered, as beatitudes and blessings; in truth those are curses, maledictions, and obscenest commandments. So be it.

> Sweet Sheba, beloved highness: Solomon craves your throne! Beware his craft; he mistranslates my pain into cunning counsel. Hear what he claims your hoopoe sang: that its mistress the Queen no longer worships Allah! He bids you come now to his palace, to be punished for your error . . . But mine was a love song: how I'd hymn you, if his tongue weren't beyond me—and yours.

> Ed' pélut, kondó nedóde, ímba imbá imbá. Singé eru. Orúmo ímbu ímpe ruté sceléte. Ímpe re scéle lee lutó. Ombo té scele té, beré te kúre kúre. Sinté te lúté sinte kúru, te ruméte tau ruméte. Onkó keere scéte, tere lúte, ilee léte leel' lúto. Scélé.

> Ill fortune, constraint and terror, generate guileful art; despair inspires. The laureled clairvoyants tell our doom in riddles. Sewn in our robes are horrid tales, and the speakers-in-tongues enounce atrocious tidings. The prophet-birds seem to speak sagely, but are shrieking their frustration. The senselessest babble, could we ken it, might disclose a dark message, or prayer.

Apparently Barth did not find the attentive and imaginative readers he needed. Many readers (or at least some reviewers) failed to realize who each of the six glossolalists are, and they also missed the responsion. In the second (paperback) edition, Barth felt compelled to add an elaborate note of explanation:

> The six glossolalists of **"Glossolalia"** are, in order, Cassandra, Philomela, the fellow mentioned by Paul in the fourteenth verse of his first epistle to the Corinthians, the Queen of Sheba's talking bird, an unidentified psalmist employing what happens to be the tongue of a historical glossolalist (Mme Alice LeBaron, who acquired some fame in 1879 from her exolalic inspirations in the "Martian" language), and the author. Among their common attributes are 1) that their audiences don't understand what they're talking about, and 2) that their several speeches are metrically identical, each corresponding to what in fact may be the only verbal sound pattern identifiable by anyone who attended American public schools prior to the decision of the U.S. Supreme Court in the case of *Murray v. Baltimore School Board* in 1963.

Actually, there are several versions of the Lord's Prayer in common use, and the verbal sound pattern most identifiable by public school pupils begins "I pledge allegiance to the flag . . ." But, working back from the rhythms of **"Glossolalia,"** I venture to guess that the sound pattern in Barth's mind is that of Matthew vi. 9-13:

> Our Father which art in heaven, hallowed be thy name. Thy kingdom come. Thy will be done in earth as it is in heaven. Give us this day our daily bread. And forgive us our debts, as we forgive our debtors. And lead us not into temptation, but deliver us from evil: For thine is the kingdom, and the power, and the glory, forever. Amen.

This version seems "wrong" to me, as it doubtless would to others who are accustomed to the phrase, "forgive us our *trespasses,* as we forgive *those who trespass against us."* I mention this only because Barth's assumption that anyone familiar with the Lord's Prayer would recognize the sound pattern of his six paragraphs is not entirely justified. Nevertheless, the version from Matthew vi is very likely the most popular, particularly since it is the version used in the frequently performed musical setting. Indeed, one can practically sing **"Glossolalia"** to this music, though the effect is more than a little grotesque, and I do not recommend it.

This points up the truth of Barth's assertion that **"'Glossolalia'** will make no sense unless heard in live or recorded voices, male and female, or read as if so heard."[2] Barth was annoyed that some reviewers apparently found this and similar pronouncements about other pieces in **Lost in the Funhouse** "pretentious." In the case of **"Glossolalia"** at least, the author's annoyance makes more sense than the reviewers' criticism. Until the reader recognizes that there is a *seventh,* unspoken paragraph belonging to the series, a paragraph that is a prayer, the point of the whole piece will be lost. This "babble" does, when we ken it, disclose both a dark message and a prayer.

It is not my purpose here to delve into the considerable subtleties of Barth's piece, though that would be an interesting and profitable enterprise. Rather, I am interested in exploring the questions raised about the nature of "meter" and of "verse" by the existence of this piece of very metrical prose.

But is it really prose? To be sure, Barth prints it as prose, but perhaps this is part of the plan of the fiction. Maybe this is "verse in disguise," just awaiting the clever critic to strip away the false beard of prose-style printing. In a sense, one could claim that such is in fact the case; for it is easy enough to practice upon **"Glossolalia"** the mystical art of colometry and to arrive at a consistent policy for line division. For example, it would be perfectly legitimate (in a sense) to print the first paragraph in the following form:

(1) Still breathless
(2) From fending Phoebus,
(3) Suddenly I see all—
(4) And all in vain.
(5) A horse excreting Greeks will devour my city;
(6) None will heed her Apollo loved,
(7) And endowed with clear sight,
(8) And cursed when she gainsaid him.
(9) My honor thus costlily purchased
(10) Will be snatched from me by soldiers.
(11) I see Agamemnon,
(12) My enslaver,
(13) Meeting death in Mycenae.
(14) No more.

This division is based on the simple procedure of determining where Barth consistently makes a pause marked by the end of a word (exclusive of proclitics like "the"). This slight pause, often called "hiatus" or "diaeresis," is more accurately termed *obligatory juncture.* Its symbol is +. Following this procedure and an analogous one for determining where more prominent (ó) and less prominent (o) syllables occur, one can schematize the metric pattern of the piece (poem?) in this way:

(1) o ó o +
(2) o ó o ó o +
(3) ó o o ó o ó +
(4) o ó o ó +
(5) o ó o ó o ó o o ó o ó o +
(6) ó o o ó o ó o ó +
(7) o o ó o o ó +

(8) o ó o ó o ó o +
(9) o ó o ó o ó o o ó o +
(10) o o ó o ó o ó o +
(11) o ó o o ó o +
(12) o o ó o +
(13) o o ó o o ó o +
(14) o ó (o) + +

If we follow the example of many classical scholars, we could claim that the division offered above gives not just fancy printing but represents "true lines." "Quae lineae sinistra a paginae margine proficiscuntur, sunt veri ϛτίχοι, in quorum finibus . . . hiatum . . . exstare licet."

The Latin quotation is from C. M. Bowra's preface to the Oxford edition of the odes of Pindar.[3] It may seem outrageous to thus imply a comparison between the epinician, that ancient Greek song of victory, and Barth's modern American parable of defeat and despair. But, from the metrical point of view at least, the comparison appears to me inevitable. Of course, there is very little likelihood that Barth was consciously or unconsciously influenced by Pindar, although the use of classical characters and the very *un*victorious theme make one wish a case for such influence might be made. The metrical comparison, though, remains valid even if Barth does not know an epinician from an alcaic.

Granted the basic differences between Greek and English meter, cannot a case be made that, in spite of those differences, **"Glossolalia"** is remarkably like (to take only one possible example) the sixth Pythian ode? If one is allowed to say that the meter of "Evangeline" is "the same" as that of the *Aeneid* (and critics do so regularly), one ought to be allowed to say that the metrical systems followed by Barth and Pindar are virtually equivalent.

Let us examine the scheme of *Pyth.* VI. I will give only the pattern, to save the printing of quantities of Greek. As it happens, this ode has six strophes, and it is *monostrophic*; that is, all six strophes follow precisely the same metrical pattern. The analysis given here follows that of Turyn:[4]

(1) ŏ ō ŏ ō ŏ ŏ ŏ ō ŏ ō ŏ ō ō +
(2) ŏ ō ŏ ō ŏ ŏ ō +
(3) ŏ ŏ ŏ ō ŏ ŏ ō ŏ ō̃ ō ŏ ŏ +
(4) ŏ ŏ ō ō ŏ ŏ ō ō ŏ ō ŏ +
(5) ō ō ŏ ō ŏ ŏ ō ŏ ō ō ŏ ō ō +
(6) ŏ ŏ ō ŏ ŏ ō ŏ ō ō ō ŏ ŏ ō +
(7) ŏ ō ŏ ō ō +
(8) ō ō ŏ ō ŏ ŏ ŏ ō +
(9) ŏ ō ō ŏ ō ŏ ŏ ō ŏ̃ ō ŏ ŏ + +

Now, no claim is made that there is any relationship between Pindar's arrangement of long and short syllables and Barth's arrangement of stressed and unstressed syllables. There is no need to, since Pindar's arrangement presents no pattern of recurrent elements. The lines are completely heterogeneous, just as they are in **"Glosso-lalia."** If one examines a single strophe without relation to the others in the same poem, such an isolated strophe exhibits no metrical properties whatsoever. This is true both in Pindar's and in Barth's pieces, provided one realizes that there are really seven strophes in **"Glosso-lalia,"** one of which is not expressed. In Pindar as in Barth, the meter can only be perceived by comparing one strophe with another. Both are constructed, in the terminology of classical scholarship, κατὰ ϛτποφήν.

In poems constructed κατὰ ϛτποφήν, there is no requirement that any pattern of recurrence be present within the individual strophe. But from strophe to strophe, the recurrence is exact. "Strophic response is usually very close, and often undeviatingly precise, syllable by syllable, for long stretches."[5] This is as one would expect when the responding units are so large. Extensive liberties would tend to destroy utterly the metrical quality. The degree to which groups of syllables—usually asserted to be various kinds of "cola"—differ from one another within Pindar's strophes varies. The so-called "aeolic meters" (*Pyth.* VI is an example) are heterogeneous to a frustratingly high degree. The only thing that can be said for certain about such aeolic strophes is that there is a strict response, long with long and short with short, between the strophes.

There are of course no "longs" and "shorts" in English prosody, but rather more and less prominent syllables. There is a long tradition in English verse of imitating classical meters by substituting more prominent (stressed) syllables for longs, less prominent (unstressed) syllables for shorts. The criticism has been made that such imitations by no means reproduce the character of the originals, and this is on the whole true. But, while the character of the classical models may indeed be falsified, the *system* is reproduced accurately. English imitations of the dactylic hexameter, for instance, are poor imitations in that the English dactyl (ó o o) is a three-beat rhythm, whereas the classical dactyl (ō ŏ ŏ) has four beats. But they are on the whole good imitations in that they follow accurately the metrical *principles* (though not the phonological realities) of their models.

Barth's **"Glossolalia"** is comparable to *Pyth.* VI in a similar sense. The principles of response in Pindar are, of course, based on the natural durational prosody of Greek, whereas Barth uses the ordinary English system of more and less prominent syllables. Such fundamental differences in the phonological bases must be acknowledged. But, having acknowledged them, we are quite at liberty to forget them in observing the principles of response that are at work. We can do the following: Let us call Greek long syllables "A syllables" and Greek short syllables "B syllables"; let us also call English stressed syllables A and English unstressed syllables B. We can write a rule for the meter of *Pyth.* VI:

A strophe is composed or found, and is taken as the "model" strophe. The pattern and number of A and B syllables in the model strophe is not fixed. One or more strophes are then composed according to this model, wherein the pattern of A and B syllables must correspond virtually exactly with that of the model.

This rule applies equally well to *Pyth.* VI and to **"Glossolalia."** It could be applied to any system in any language in which a contrasting base pair can be found. Thus, one could compose κατὰ ϛτροφήν in Chinese, using as A and B syllables those with "level" and "deflected" tones. One could *not* compose in this manner in French, at least not using the usual French system of versification, and an adequate literary translation of **"Glossolalia"** into French would appear extraordinarily difficult. In principle, though, the rule could be applied with equal success with any set of A and B syllables. And so, in principle, *Pyth.* VI and **"Glossolalia"** are metrically identical.

The fact that classical scholars are able to take almost any series of syllables in Greek verse and divide them into strings of "cola," each of which bears an impressive appellation, changes nothing. These cola are, in A. M. Dale's phrase, merely "pieces of rhythm," entities that sometimes enter into systematic relationships with each other, but often do not. Even if we assume that Pindar composed the sixth Pythian by putting together various cola—an assumption difficult to support—nothing is changed. There is no pattern at the level of the colon in *Pyth.* VI, and that is that. I can assert that I am composing this page by assembling various iambs, trochees, spondees, dactyls, anapests, and so forth. And you cannot absolutely disprove it. But you can say that there is no structure of such entities visible, and that is all that matters. Colometry has no *metrically significant* information to give about *Pyth.* VI.

For the sake of completing the comparison, though, let me say that one can, as I suggested above, practice "colometry" upon **"Glossolalia."** I propose the following rhythmic analysis which divides the strophe into "pieces of rhythm" (syllable groups one could call "cola" if one wished) in this way:

    (1) amphibrach +
    (2) iamb amphibrach +
    (3) dactyl cretic +
    (4) iamb iamb +
    (5) iamb iamb iamb anapest amphibrach +
    (6) choriamb iamb iamb +
    (7) anapest anapest +
    (8) iamb iamb amphibrach +
    (9) iamb iamb dactyl trochee +
    (10) anapest iamb amphibrach +
    (11) iamb 3rd-paeon +
    (12) 3rd-paeon +
    (13) 3rd-paeon amphibrach +
    (14) iamb ++

One might then point out that the rhythm of the whole is mainly iambic, with amphibrachs forming a strong secondary figure. The principal rhythms are announced clearly in the first two lines, and they return in the last two. The cadence of lines 11-14 is made more powerful by the series of third paeons preceding the return to the "dominant-tonic" sequence of amphibrach-iamb.

The preceding is done somewhat tongue-in-cheek, but this kind of analysis is by no means worthless in the context of the single strophe, where rhythms of a sort, but not meter, can be perceived. It is the kind of analysis that will work perfectly well on prose. The Lord's Prayer, a piece of prose, can be so analyzed in isolation (though it should be mentioned that a "colometry" based on such an analysis in isolation would probably differ from the one given here for **"Glossolalia"** as a whole), but since there is no "periodicity," no regular recurrence of cola or other elements, it is neither metrical in the usual sense nor rhythmic in the strict sense.

The piece as a whole *is* metrical, not because of the alleged presence of cola and of "rhythm" in the looser, nonperiodic sense, but because there is a precise recurrence of elements at the strophic level. It is metrical in exactly the same way that Pindar's sixth Pythian ode is metrical. The structure of the two pieces is so similar that what is claimed or denied about the one (regarding metrical structure) must also be claimed or denied for the other.

The logical conclusion is that, if the sixth Pythian is verse, **"Glossolalia"** must be verse also.

Having reached this logical conclusion, have we not now explained the "real" nature of Barth's fiction? Sad to say, I do not think so, for the logic here is deceptive. It appears that we have an unambiguous syllogism of the following form:

Major Premise: What is true of *Pyth.* VI regarding metrical
                structure is true of "Glossolalia" as well.
Minor Premise: *Pyth.* VI is verse.
Conclusion: "Glossolalia" is verse, but disguised as prose.

That seems straightforward enough, but serious difficulties exist. The major premise is sound: that is what has just been shown in some detail. The minor premise and conclusion, though, deserve some scrutiny.

One of the main problems centers upon the notion of "verse." While I do not think anyone would disagree with the opinion that *Pyth.* VI is verse, I think there are some uncertainties about just why there is no disagreement. The most logical explanation (once again we try to be logical) would follow from the definition of verse offered by the *OED* (quoted earlier) and, more scientifically, by John Lotz: "In most languages there are texts in which the phonetic material within certain syntactic frames, such as sentence, phrase, and word, is numerically regulated. Such a text is called verse, and its distinctive characteristic is meter."[6] If we accept this, it is clear that *Pyth.* VI is verse by definition. The phonetic material within the framework of the strophe is very strictly regulated in both *Pyth.* VI and in **"Glossolalia."**[7] That the strophes individually show no metric structure is no obstacle, for these are examples of "astichic" verse. Lotz's definition is reasonably precise and quite adequate to the material. And yet, though I think Lotz's definition is an excellent one, I do not think it tells us why we all accept *Pyth.* VI as verse. It explains why *he* would take it to be so, but that is a different matter. Everyone who knows German literature accepts Goethe's "Prometheus" as verse, though it is not metrical. Lotz says, "A non-metric text is called prose."[8] So much for "Prometheus," which according to Lotz, should be called prose. I point this out, not to criticize Lotz's very successful definition, but merely to demonstrate that it neither reflects nor explains commonly held views on these matters. It was not meant to.

The lack of correspondence between Lotz's definition and the ordinary usage of criticism, between his rigor and the usual laxity, tells us something about the content of the term "verse" as it is commonly employed. Verse is, in a very real and very legitimate sense, literature presented in short units each printed on a single line. It is, in effect, a kind of presentational mode, a conventional signal used by authors to condition the responses of their readers. I do not claim that this is what "verse" ought to mean, or what it always used to mean, or what everyone thinks it means now, but only what its most common function is today.

Although Northrop Frye tends to support the view which I here oppose, that the difference between verse and prose is defined chiefly by meter, his description of the chief points of opposition between the two lends evidence supporting the view I advocate.[9] "When the sentence structure takes the lead, and all patterns of repetition are subordinated to it, we have prose." While the difference between prose and verse is alleged to find its *expression,* and its *differentia specifica,* in a difference in rhythmic organization, he evidently sees the ultimate origin in a difference in intention: "The aim [of prose] is to present a certain content or meaning in as unobtrusive and transparent a way as possible," or to give the reader the *impression* that such an unobtrusive and transparent medium is being employed. "Verse is able to absorb a much higher concentration of metaphorical and figurative speech than prose . . ." Though Frye sees this ability to "absorb" figurative speech as a result of metrical organization, one might equally well ascribe it to the intention of the versifier, whose aim is not to render language transparent, but in fact to draw attention to language.

Prose, then, in this revision of Frye's position, is the presentational mode that tries to render language transparent (or pretends to do so); and verse is the mode that draws attention to language (or pretends to do so). **"Glossolalia,"** it seems to me, is an example of the former, of a "prose intention"; and *Pyth*. VI (at least as its modern editors understand it) is an example of the latter, of "verse intention."

I believe it is instructive, therefore, to observe that Pindar's epinician odes are today always printed divided into lines, though this is not necessary and was not done in early manuscripts. That is how editors feel Pindar *ought* to be presented, because they evidently feel that his intention was similar to that of writers known to use the presentational mode of verse. Even more instructive, I think, is that John Barth chose not to so divide his paragraphs in **"Glossolalia."** I do not mean that he "chose" in the sense that he considered the two alternatives and selected one—though it is possible he did this. I mean only that *he* considered his piece to be prose, that he included it in a collection of prose works, and that he intended his readers to accept it as prose. He knew very well that **"Glossolalia"** is metrical. Indeed, he had to point out that fact to most of us. But the meter did not make him wish to present it as verse.

My conclusion, perhaps paradoxical, is that even though Pindar and Barth use identical metrical principles, Pindar's work "is" verse and Barth's work "is" prose. I use the quotation marks to emphasize that "to be verse (or prose)" frequently means, in the speech of today's scholars and poets, "to be intended as or presented as verse (or prose)."

I cannot convince myself that saying Barth's piece is "verse disguised as prose," as I suggested above, does justice to the facts. We would be obliged to accept this view if we apply Lotz's definition of verse to **"Glossolalia."** One must ask, what has Barth disguised? Certainly not that the piece is metrical: he has gone out of his way to make sure we understand that it is. Has he "disguised" the fact that there is in **"Glossolalia"** a higher degree of linguistic organization and complexity than in his other works? I am certain he would deny that such a difference exists, and I would be inclined to agree with him. No, there is no falsification in presenting the piece as prose, because it "is" prose—metrical prose. And Barth has made it so largely by the very act of so presenting it.

I believe it is useful for critics to be able to distinguish between pieces like Goethe's "Prometheus" and Barth's **"Glossolalia"** by calling the former verse and the latter prose. This we could not do if we were to accept Lotz's view that all metrical texts are verse, all nonmetrical texts prose. The distinction frequently made between "prose" and "poetry" seems to me to be something else,

an opposition rather different from that between prose and verse. While **"Glossolalia"** reflects what I have called a "prose intention," one would be hard put to argue (as I once tried to do) that it is "prosaic." While the language is not as allusive, ambiguous, or "dense" as much poetic speech—as Goethe's "Prometheus," for example—it is far more so than much very prosaic material composed in meter. Frye would argue that the "poetic" language of **"Glossolalia"** is made possible to some degree by the presence of meter. It is my contention that meter has in fact no connection whatever with either "verse" or "poetry."

While this is not a position that is frequently taken today, it is by no means a new one. "People link up poetic composition with meter and speak of 'elegaic poets,' 'epic poets,' not treating them as poets by virtue of their imitation, but employing the term as a common appellation going along with the use of meter. And in fact the name is also applied to anyone who treats a medical or scientific topic in meter, yet Homer and Empedocles actually have nothing in common except their meter; hence the proper term for the one is 'poet,' for the other, 'science writer' rather than 'poet.'" This, of course, is from Aristotle's *Poetics*.[10] Though the distinction he is trying to maintain is not precisely the same one for which I argue, his point is relevant. The presence or absence of meter is not invariably connected with the presence or absence of other characteristics of the text. Thus a piece that is metrical may be verse (*Pyth*. VI) or may not (**"Glossolalia"**), may be poetic (**"Glossolalia"**) or may not ("There once was a hermit named Dave . . . ," etc.). Non-metrical texts may also be verse ("Prometheus") or may not (Baudelaire's "L'Étranger"), may also be poetic ("L'Étranger") or may not (*The Congressional Record*). The use of meter may be a considerable ally in creating language that is poetic (as Frye rightly suggests), but works such as Goethe's "Prometheus" and Baudelaire's "L'Étranger" show clearly that its assistance is by no means always necessary.

It is really not strange, then, that two works so different as **"Glossolalia"** and *Pyth*. VI turn out upon analysis to be formally almost identical. That one is presented as prose and the other as verse means neither that the formal identity is an error of analysis nor that the distinction proposed by the presentation is unreal. It means only that meter is a matter of form and that the distinction between prose and verse is a matter of presentation. The same form does not entail the same presentation, and while we have come to expect that works composed in meter will be presented as verse, as is the case with *Pyth*. VI, it need not always be so. There can be metrical compositions that are not verse. **"Glossolalia"** is not verse. It is a complex and highly structured piece of prose, an elegant tale of catastrophe composed κατὰ στροφήν.[11]

Notes

1. From the book *Lost in the Funhouse.* Copyright © 1968 by John Barth. Published by Doubleday & Co., Inc. Barth's comments, and the text itself, I quote from the Bantam paperback edition of 1969. The comments appear on page xi, the text on pp. 111-12.

2. From the "Author's Note" that did not appear in the first edition, taken here from p. ix of the Bantam edition.

3. *Pindari Carmina,* 2nd ed. (1947), pp. viii-ix.

4. *Pindari Carmina cum Fragmentis* (Cambridge, Mass., 1952), p. 116.

5. *Oxford Classical Dictionary,* 2nd ed., p. 684.

6. "Elements of Versification" in *Versification, Major Language Types,* ed. W. K. Wimsatt (New York, 1972), pp. 4-5.

7. It is evident that Lotz considers the strophe (at least as it appears in Greek lyric verse) to fit the definition of a "syntactic frame." He cites the late Sapphic strophe as an example of metrical utterance (i.e., verse), and even acknowledges that "occasionally strophic enjambement does occur" (p. 7). Since Pindar's strophes are no different in this regard, I think there is little question that Lotz would accept *Pyth.* VI as verse.

8. Wimsatt, p. 5.

9. This discussion of Frye's position is based on his article on "Verse and Prose" in *Encyclopedia of Poetry and Poetics,* ed. Preminger, Warnke, and Hardison (Princeton, 1965), from which quotations are taken.

10. The translation is my adaptation of Else, *Aristotle: Poetics* (Ann Arbor, 1967), pp. 16-17. Else translates μέτρα as "verse," a procedure that could only create confusion in the present context.

11. I should like to acknowledge the helpful suggestions of Craig La Drière and W. K. Wimsatt, both of whose criticisms saved me from a number of errors and resulted in substantial improvements in the essay. The errors that remain are, of course, mine alone.

Gerald Gillespie (essay date summer 1975)

SOURCE: Gillespie, Gerald. "Barth's *Lost in the Funhouse*: Short Story Text in its Cyclic Context." *Studies in Short Fiction* 12, no. 3 (summer 1975): 223-30.

[*In the following essay, Gillespie views the stories in* Lost in the Funhouse *within the context of "Forrest L. Ingram's category of the 'completed' cycle."*]

While the short story **"Lost in the Funhouse"** can stand as an independent work, it also is the pivotal story in the book of stories bearing its name. Thus an adequate appreciation of its qualities must take into account the special dimensions that it acquires, and helps create, in the book. I find it difficult to explicate John Barth's fiction more clearly than he himself does in interviews and essays or internally in his works. But since critical attention has focused mainly on his novels, it is useful to consider in detail the sense of his fourteen short stories grouped under the name of *Lost in the Funhouse,* which as a story was first published separately just a few months after his manifesto, **"The Literature of Exhaustion"** (August 1967), in *The Atlantic Monthly.* This essay, to which I shall turn, deals with the same questions as his experimental cycle then well underway. The opening paragraph of the "Author's Note" to the first edition of the book *Lost in the Funhouse: Fiction for Print, Tape, Live Voice* (New York: Doubleday, 1968) makes it plain:

> This book differs in two ways from most volumes of short fiction. First, it's neither a collection nor a selection, but a series; though several of its items have appeared separately in periodicals, the series will be seen to have been meant to be received "all at once" and as here arranged. Most of its members, consequently, are "new"—written for this book, in which they appear for the first time.
>
> (*B* ix)[1]

Besides corroborating that the set in its entirety constitutes a genre, Barth's definition independently parallels Forrest L. Ingram's category of the "completed" cycle.[2] To seven stories separately published from 1963 to 1968, Barth added seven more and rearranged the order of occurrence within a larger scheme with its own logic and rhythms; but that scheme had evolved from the initial subject of 1963.

In the following outline, the left-hand column shows the titles of stories one through seven of the cycle, and the right-hand column stories eight through fourteen. Those in italics appeared in advance of the cycle, as well as in it. Figures preceding a title indicate its rough number of pages; figures in parentheses, the year of original publication.

2	"Frame-Tale" (68)	3	"Echo" (68)
9	*"Night-Sea Journey"* (68)	1	"Two Meditations" (68)
19	*"Ambrose His Mark"* (63)	8	*"Title"* (67)
4	*"Autobiography"* (68)	1	"Glossolalia" (68)
16	*"Water-Message"* (63)	13	"Life-Story" (68)
13	*"Petition"* (68)	35	"Menelaiad" (68)
25	*"Lost in the Funhouse"* (67)	31	"Anonymiad" (68)

"Completion" of the cycle was accomplished—in Ingram's terms—by "rounding off" its themes, symbolism, and total pattern in the longer, sub-divided story

"Anonymiad," and by capturing the whole work in a terse "frame," aptly called **"Frame-Tale."** With its brevity and abstraction **"Frame-Tale"** stands in relation to the length and specificity of **"Anonymiad"** within the compass of all fourteen stories as **"Frame-Tale"** stands to the first preponderantly contemporary, biographical sequence culminating in **"Lost in the Funhouse,"** and as **"Echo"** stands to the second preponderantly historical and mythic sequence culminating in **"Anonymiad."** By counterbalancing and juxtaposing forms, Barth preserves the tension between the individuality of each of the stories and the necessities of the larger unit; not surprisingly, his book discusses such formal relationships. Thus the earliest published **"Ambrose His Mark"** still exudes the independence of being which its storytelling conventions imply and, in itself, gives the appearance of being a segment of "real" time, involving named "persons," a slice of life in an American community. But, in its position as third story, its motifs and themes—wine, roses, honey, birth, sex, poetic election—intermesh with those of the cycle. In the way **"Frame-Tale"** and **"Anonymiad"** bracket the other stories, they reinforce the impression of disproportionate size and type. This relationship, paradoxically, both relativizes the apparent uniqueness of any single tale, such as the "life" of Ambrose depicted at some intersection or the recognized "pattern" underlying disparate utterances in **"Glossolalia,"** and also affirms the validity of each story through its archetype.

Neither our getting lost in the mythic and universal, nor our emerging from the simultaneity of things and thoughts into the clear light of a distinct moment, but rather our movement between planes of consciousness is the key experience. In the beginning, the outer mask of the book is the fragmentarily developed *persona* of an artist, a well established "modern" *topos* (therefore, implicitly "exhausted" and ripe for post-modern interpretation in Barth's view). This protagonist appears in traditional guises as the special child in **"Ambrose His Mark,"** as the adolescent undergoing the inner puberty rite of election in **"Water-Message,"** and finally as the ineluctably committed artificer "who will construct funhouses for others and be their secret operator" (*B* 94) in **"Lost in the Funhouse,"** the story that as conclusion of the first half and mid-point of the entire cycle fittingly bears the name of the cycle. The interlaced experimental stories of the first half of the cycle, **"Autobiography: A Self-Recorded Fiction"** (IV) and **"Petition"** (VI), more decisively shift toward the philosophic treatment of the nature of memory, story, and identity that already has been probed, with delayed impact, in the grimly humorous **"Night-Sea Journey"** (II). The more "advanced" stories of the first half of the cycle keep apart and envelope the more "traditional" core (III, V) so that the final meaning of the Ambrose strand transcends the standard implications of the model of the sentimental education of an individual human be-

ing. The "depersonalized" analysis of the relationship between consciousness and story-telling comes emphatically to the fore in the second half of the cycle, which, because it consists almost wholly of added stories, exhibits—in Ingram's terms—the consistency of a "composed" subcycle. The involved bracketing of internal narrations in the story **"Menelaiad"** (XIII) fully confirms the reader's assumption of deliberateness on Barth's part, but **"Night-Sea Journey"** has already provided sufficient initial evidence that the incapsulation of a superindividual "message," "heritage," or "code" will be a structural principle, as well as theme, throughout the book.

Each half of the cycle *Lost in the Funhouse* moves through seven stories; each half is parallel in the way it unfolds from a nucleus story containing the generative cosmic propositions. This implicit reference to a seven-step dialectic, which operates, metaphorically and literally, in an organic continuum often mentioned in the book, is not just a far-fetched esoteric whim of Barth's. He uses cabbalistic and theosophic patterns because they express the hidden, labyrinthine "code" that supposedly underlies both life and art. The two halves of the story cycle mirror each other, symbolizing the primal moment out of which spring all the manifold relationships of "reflection." Beyond the discovery of perspectivism, the Renaissance had discovered man's bondage to transience, the possible multiplicity of worlds, and the haunting concept of infinity. When Il Parmigiano painted his self-portrait before a convex mirror (1523) and hit upon the play of perspectivistic distortions, the new mode was called mannerism. In the actual labyrinth of the title story, **"Lost in the Funhouse,"** a chamber of mirrors compound to infinity the grotesque and beautiful, eternal and fleeting vision. Artifice is an ambiguous mystery created in response to life, its ultimate foil. The opening **"Frame-Tale"** of the cycle illustrates how radical is Barth's impulse to reduce phenomena to pattern. Because it involves a trick, some critics will redundantly dismiss it as a lamentable instance of "mannerism"—an issue I defer for now, but one Barth constantly addresses. **"Frame-Tale"** consists of instructions and pre-printed words for making a Möbius band and that, once followed, reads forever: ONCE UPON A TIME THERE WAS A STORY THAT BEGAN . . . Or, depending on where we intersect the syntax, A STORY THAT BEGAN ONCE UPON A TIME THERE WAS . . . , and so forth, variously. This series is infinite since it flows on a time belt that is a single plane, even though its motion creates the illusion of other dimensions. It therefore fulfills the motto spoken by the voice of the Posttape of *Giles Goat-Boy* (1966): "Unwind, rewind, replay." Except that the simpler model of the Möbius band and clarifies not only the awesome complexity of a computerized world running on, and the principle of the cycle, but also dialectic process *per se*.[3]

But recognition of our role seems close to impossible, once we have eaten of the candied apple on the boardwalk of the Maryland ocean front and, with artist-elect Ambrose, become among those "lost in the funhouse." In the "Seven Additional Authors Notes," Barth carefully dissociates himself from the "triply schizoid" authorial voice of an interior monologue (for stereophonic performance), entitled **"Title,"** which relates "the Author's difficulties with his companion, his analogous difficulties with the story he's in process of composing, and the not dissimilar straits in which, I think mistakenly, he imagines his culture and literature to be [thus Barth as outsider to his own book]" (*B* x-xi). That voice bemoans, nonetheless, that "Love affairs, literary genres, third item in exemplary series, fourth—everything blossoms and decays, does it not, from the primitive and classical through the mannered and baroque to the abstract, stylized, dehumanized, unintelligible, blank" (*B* 105). With all due caution in distinguishing aspects of voice, one can scarcely miss the relevance of such statements to Barth's own similar public pronouncements regarding *ultimacy* as a governing principle of our times or to the developmental logic flowing from his own achievements in *The Sot-Weed Factor* and *Giles Goat-Boy*. In the second half of the cycle *Lost in the Funhouse,* we wander in the maze of reflection, and even the *persona* of the artist, no longer spellbinding as a mask, evolves into sheer "voice," as act and content.[4]

In the *Sot-Weed Factor,* Barth converts "actual" history into humoristic "fiction" by having its protagonist test out a set of his own age's concepts of itself; the internal model of this revision by Barth is the satirical Marylandiad which results from Ebenezer's hard encounters and awakening (for double irony, a Marylandiad founded on the obscure, but actual work of a late seventeenth-century colonial namesake). The "redone" story is thus "living" myth, since the approach of the novel embodies the Western heritage of irony. We do not read the "Revised New Syllabus" in *Giles Goat-Boy* merely as a retrospective allegory of the immediate past, but as a composite, experimental "myth" which widens the scope of the American story in accordance with its newly perceived "anthropological" dimensions. And similarly, the title story of the cycle *Lost in the Funhouse* advances Barth's basic conviction that what we like to term "real" history (e. g., the Second World War glimpsed offshore from the amusement park at Ocean City) is just a specific intersection in a composite myth, but all mythic communities, such as those of ancient Greece and Maryland, are linked as manifestations of a code in a mysterious continuum.

The many internal hints within single stories therefore justify viewing the title story of the book, **"Lost in the Funhouse,"** in several already-mentioned cyclical relationships. By its position and development of themes, it represents structurally within the whole book the simultaneous "middle," "beginning," and "end" of which Barth often speaks. It ties together the apparently ordinary and recently experienced present of Maryland and seemingly remote but imaginatively re-experienced past of Greece. It completes the series of probes into the figure of Ambrose and successfully links him to a universal pattern. Hence, once the ontology and biology of the perceiving mind has been fully suggested, the second half of the cycle can recapitulate these rhythms, dispensing with the fiction of the ego or personality called Ambrose. The story **"Anonymiad"** eventually fulfills the propositions that attain their first complex exposition when, in **"Lost in the Funhouse,"** Barth pierces the web of a twentieth-century identity and escapes through it as through a net.

The title story of the book skillfully evokes the realm of appearances as the funhouse, the maze of mirrors, the mental and temporal labyrinth whose titular divinity is the laughing fat lady, named Fat May. Her raucous, infectious laugh reveals for some, disguises for others, the ridiculousness of existence and unifies the aspects of Venus Urania and Maya. In Ambrose's fantasy, which answers his desire for initiation by his father into the secret of getting through the funhouse, the father confirms the distinction between appearance and reality. In a probable allusion to the Dedalus line of artificers in Joyce's *Portrait of the Artist,* Ambrose's surrealistic nightmare of failure to negotiate the funhouse properly with Magda and his loss of her to his shadow-brother Peter ("Penis") pose an anguish analogous to that of the later written Chang-Eng-Thalia triangle of **"Petition."**[5] As Ambrose suffers in the "mirror-maze" and "[loses] *himself in reflection,*" he "[sees] once again, more clearly than ever, how readily he deceived himself into supposing he was a person" (*B* 90) and even anticipates that he will relapse constantly into that illusion. His compensatory fantasies include the key one of himself in the artist-hero role as "one of Western Cultures truly great imaginations" (*B* 92)—a stab by Barth, not so much at himself, as at our collective myth of the West, centered on the heroic ego.[6]

Obviously, Barth is not original in his attack on the concept of identity. In *Steppenwolf* (1927), Hermann Hesse had already derided even the commonplace definition of schizophrenia as one of many efforts by Western civilization to patch the holes in its threatened system of illusion. In Hesse's and other related writing, the romantic exploration of Oriental religious insights recur with a vengeance. Hesse had also seen the logic of expressing the break-up of Western ideology by using its own already highly developed mode of irony, the humoristic tradition. But, as Baudelaire realized, laughter had become ambiguous, a potentially reintegrative or disintegrative self-critique. We may then legitimately view the cycle *Lost in the Funhouse* (1968) and the novel *Giles Goat-Boy* (1966) as manifesting the tension between a negative assessment and positive aspiration with regard to "our" civilization. Within the title story **"Lost in the Funhouse,"** Ambrose vacillates between the polarities of confidence and disillusionment. We note that after his oblique vision of the hidden mechanisms and operator of the funhouse, nonetheless "he couldn't be sure he hadn't dreamed part or all of the sight" (*B* 84); and, adding further complication, now reality surges as superreality through consciousness: "The town, the river, himself, were not imaginary; time roared in his ears like wind; the world was *going on!* This part ought to be dramatized. The Irish author James Joyce once wrote. Ambrose M——— is going to scream" (*B* 85).

This passage, and the opening sentence of the following paragraph,—"There is no *texture of rendered sensory detail,* for one thing"—illustrates Barth's method and message. The focus switches suddenly; the fiction is both a story and an essay. Tenses constantly switch; and as Lowry Nelson has shown with respect to the rise of this technique in baroque literature, the movement among various planes of time or points of view constitutes a dramatic perspectivism.[7] From the start, the commentary on conventions and devices of fiction parallels each phase of the story in an involved way. Page one bores directly through the armor of nineteenth-century practice which gives "the illusion of reality," but "it is an *illusion* that is being enhanced, by purely artificial means" (*B* pp. 69 ff.). The general consideration of art gradually evolves into a particular reflection on details of the story of Ambrose in progress; ironically, an authorial voice that usually seems to be congruent with various time layers of Ambrose's mentality criticizes the story from the vantage of conventional realism; and the story, in self-contradiction to its own internal critique that there is "nothing in the way of a *theme*" (*B* 74), actually elaborates the theme explicitly through its tightly woven symbolism. The authorial problem expounded in the Sternean editorial first-person ("We haven't even reached Ocean City yet: we will never get out of the funhouse" [ibid.]) undergoes permutation into Cervantine third-person ironic narration ("At this rate our hero, at this rate our protagonist will remain in the funhouse forever" [ibid.]). When it moves into the implicitly limited intersection in the cosmic process, the voice gives temporal, spatial, and cultural co-ordinates, which it even compares to the scientific methodology of fixing a reference point (*B* 70). Some details are covered by supercompressed historical notes, e.g., "as mentioned in the novel *The 42nd Parallel* by John Dos Passos" (ibid.). Despite internal denials about *texture,* details possess a remarkable lucidity and vibrance, and the probes into the passing scene, coeval with World War II, are nothing less than clairvoyant.

In the story **"Ambrose His Mark,"** the protagonist has been associated with service to and descent from Venus, whose incarnation is the mother, and with the mellifluous and melic through his baptismal name Ambrose and nickname Der Honig (the honey). That story and **"Water-Message"** have established his acute sensitivity about the organic chain of being both as a familial and as a personal trait. Projected, or projecting himself, as the narrator of the story **"Lost in the Funhouse,"** and becoming the essayistic voice, the Ambrosian mind contemplates the story of its native region as a long skein of sexual acts. *The Sot-Weed Factor* is tacitly cited in this very literally described procreative start and continuity of Maryland (*B* 76). Many motifs—groping in the Love Tunnel, submarines off shore which must launch torpedoes, etc.—reiterate the seeking of the sperm. But also the manneristic trap of endlessness—a variation upon the Möbius band motif of **"Frame-Tale"**—opens when Ambrose wanders the two-and-one way of consciousness into "this other part [of the funhouse], that winds around on itself like a welk shell . . . around the right part like the snakes on Mercury's caduceus" (*B* 80). He perceives corruptibility and transcience in the minutest details, for the texture of the surface of life confronts him in the debris of the boardwalk of Ocean City. The organically limited perceiver is detached from, yet chained to, self: "In the funhouse mirror room you can't see yourself go on forever, because no matter where you stand, your head gets in the way." This statement is equally applicable to the sperm, which thrusts its "message" forward in the darkness toward a possible continuance through merger with the egg; or to the mind that, for all its infinite posturings, gets in the way by analyzing to pieces its own fiction and interferes with the organic process it fears as a captivity and delusion.

As Leslie A. Fiedler wrote just over a decade ago, Barth has gone his own way, heedless of fashion, quite aware of the canons of realism but resolutely suspicious of them. It is still true, as in 1961, that Barth "is, on one level, a historical scholar; and his books, even when they deal with contemporary or nearly contemporary events . . . give the odd effect of being worked up from documents, carefully considered and irreverently interpreted. He finds in history not merely the truth, not really the truth at all—for each of his novels exploits the ambiguities of facts and motives—but absurdity."[8] The cycle *Lost in the Funhouse* still considers one hard reality in this day of vanishing certainties: mankind is an organic continuum whose events betray an underlying cyclic pattern. But in interpreting the positivistic data of an excerpted life in an "historical" locale and moment as a mere convention of fiction, and relativizing the story of the protagonist psyche as an interesting variation upon an abstract, finally irreducible, pattern that pervades all fiction of all time, Barth departs—perhaps decisively—from history into myth.[9] The structure of the story cycle so exactly corresponds to his sense of a multifarious, fragmented human identity which our age of accelerated accumulation of information has hastened that, in purely formal terms, it is an extraordinary success. The cycle permits control over its implied infinity by a finite agent, the artist, who grasps for one last access to unending significance.

Notes

1. Since Barth added notes in 1969, I shall cite the convenient Bantam paperback (second) edition as *B,* followed by page number. The position of stories within the cycle will be indicated in Roman numerals. Barth's other works will be cited by page number in their respective original editions.

2. Forrest L. Ingram, "The Dynamics of Short Story Cycles," *The New Orleans Review,* 2 (1970), 7-12.

3. In the novels, Barth uses a series of containing frames that he inherits from Cervantes to comment on and distance himself from the narrative process, while at the same time underscoring the nature of his authorial perception. *Giles Goat-Boy* inherits the two-and-one androgyne and trinitarian configurations from *The Sot-Weed Factor*; and in turn, *Giles Goat-Boy*'s various polarities and mirrorings, and its repeated triple series of seven, foreshadow the symbolism of *Lost in the Funhouse.*

4. It bears repetition that Barth was contemplating the nature of "voice" and much specific story matter that turns up in the 1968 cycle at least as early as his essay "The Literature of Exhaustion." For example (p. 34):

   > But Menelaus on the beach at Pharos, for example, is genuinely Baroque in the Borgesian spirit, and illustrates a positive artistic morality in the literature of exhaustion. He is not there, after all, for kicks (any more than Borges and Beckett are in the fiction racket for their health): Menelaus is lost, in the larger labyrinth of the world, and has got to hold fast while the Old Man of the Sea exhausts reality's frightening guises so that he may extort direction from him when Proteus returns to his "true" self. It's a heroic enterprise, with salvation as its object—one recalls that the aim of the Histriones is to get history done with so that Jesus may come again the sooner, and that Shakespeare's heroic metamorphoses culminate not merely in a theophany but in an apotheosis.

5. That Barth was probably thinking of Joyce intently as he worked on the title story is revealed in "The Literature of Exhaustion" (p. 32):

   > This "contamination of reality by dream," as Borges calls it, is one of his pet themes, and commenting upon such contaminations is one of his favorite fictional devices. Like many of the best such devices, it turns the artist's mode or form

into a metaphor for his concerns, as does the diary ending of *Portrait of the Artist as a Young Man* or the cyclical construction of *Finnegans Wake.*

6. Beagle traces the "cosmopsis" crisis back to Jacob Horner in *End of the Road* for whom the Doctor prescribes a Hesse-like mythotherapy, in Barth's text:

   > ". . . a man's integrity consists in being faithful to the script he's written for himself . . . It's extremely important that you learn to assume these masks wholeheartedly. Don't think there's anything behind them: there isn't. *Ego* means *I,* and *I* means *ego,* and the ego by definition is a mask. Where there's no ego—this is you on the bench—there's no *I.* If you sometimes have the feeling your mask is *insincere*—impossible word!—it's only because one of your masks is incompatible with another. You musn't put on two at a time. . . ."

7. Lowry Nelson, *Baroque Lyric Poetry* (New Haven: Yale University Press, 1961).

8. Fiedler, "John Barth: An Eccentric Genius," *New Leader,* February 13, 1961, p. 22.

9. Barth's experimentation with cyclic structure exhibits a richness and maturity that most recent brief articles, such as in *Critique,* 13 (1972), fail to address. The connection of the cyclic principle with Barth's "rediscovery" of myth as pure story is also evident in the cyclic stories of *Chimera* (1972).

Thom Seymour (essay date summer 1979)

SOURCE: Seymour, Thom. "One Small Joke and a Packed Paragraph in John Barth's 'Lost in the Funhouse.'" *Studies in Short Fiction* 16, no. 3 (summer 1979): 189-94.

[In the following essay, Seymour examines Barth's expression of reader and author awareness of text and plot devices in "Lost in the Funhouse."]

One of the most puzzling things about the John Barth short story **"Lost in the Funhouse"** is its apparent neglect. It has not been neglected by the reading public, presumably; after all, the story first appeared in a mass-market magazine and has since been included in a volume of Barth's short fiction (available in a paperback edition from a mass-market publisher), not to mention the current edition of *The American Tradition in Literature.* I mean, rather, the neglect, in recent years, of commentators. When it first appeared, in 1968, the volume that contains **"Lost in the Funhouse,"** *Lost in the*

Funhouse, received generally unfavorable reviews. Though perforce hastily conceived, these reviews were not entirely wrong, for there are a number of pieces in the book that strike us today, as they did then, as mere baubles, toys for and of an exhausted imagination. Indeed, this is the line of attack most reviewers took toward the work: you have circled back so fully on your own self-awareness, Mr. Barth, where can you go from here?[1] But what the reviewers failed to see is that this question is largely answered by the book itself. For the two stories that were most frequently praised were **"Menelaid"** and **"Anonymiad,"** Barth's retelling of Greek myths, in which the telling not the tale is updated. Thus, these stories anticipate the brilliant novellas of *Chimera,* which in turn anticipate God-knows-what. It seems that Barth, if he wanted to, could go on in this vein forever.

Still, as good as **"Menelaid"** and **"Anonymiad"** are, the finest piece in *Lost in the Funhouse* must be the title story. Even admitting, as Gerhard Joseph does of *Giles Goatboy,* that "one reader's imaginative profundity [may be] another's puerile shallowness and irresponsible navel-gazing,"[2] **"Lost in the Funhouse"** is still extraordinary, if only because of its perfect technical integration. From the baldest "reality" to the sublest distortion to the most labored pedantry—the cutbacks, false turns, dead ends, and mirror images all reenforce each other on every level of the narrative. The story is extraordinary as well because it is what it says it is, a *fun*house. What sets this story apart from the sterility of so much "experimental" fiction, what makes it (and, indeed, most of Barth's writing) such a delight, is the sense of play, of pure fun-ness, that pervades it. For something which in outline is so serious, even sentimental, the tale is riddled with howlers, puns, silliness, and simple small jokes, in all of which we too become lost, and like Fat May, the mechanical laugher on the boardwalk, are left wheezing and clutching our sides.

THE JOKE

One of the smallest jokes in **"Lost in the Funhouse"** is an even smaller mystery. The joke is a throwaway, really, but one that involves both craftiness and craft. In the mode of phony *roman à clef* of preceeding centuries, Barth refuses to give us either the last names of his characters or the year (even decade) of the story's events. Hard on the heels of this refusal, however, comes Barth's pedantic explanation that this is nothing more than a gimmick of fiction used to heighten the illusion of fact. Of course, by making such an admission, Barth obviously destroys any illusion of factuality in his own piece of fiction.

Yet the joke is just beginning. For imbedded in the matrix of the narrative are all the clues we need to come up with the exact date (more accurately, the exact day

in one of two possible years) on which the events of the story take place. Early on, we are told that it is *"Independence Day, the most important secular holiday of the United States of America,"* in the year 19__.[3] July fourth it is, but what of the decade? The principals travel to Ocean City in a "black 1936 LaSalle sedan" (p. 74), so it is at least the late thirties. But we know further, from numerous small references, that it is wartime. There are references to matchbook covers advertising "U.S. War Bonds and Stamps" (p. 74) or "warning that A Slip of the Lip Can Sink a Ship" (p. 80); there is a scarcity of tobacco (p. 76); there is talk of "tankers torpedoed offshore" (p. 79); there are the prizes in the digger machines in the penny arcade, prizes "made now in USA" (p. 84); there is mention of a "brown-out": "on account of German U-boats, . . . streetlights were shaded on the seaward side" (p. 85). The examples go on and on. So we know that it is World War II—July 4th, 1942, at the earliest; the U.S. was not in the war on any Independence Day before that. On the other hand, because of the fear of German U-boats, it cannot be as late as 1945; the war in Europe was over before July of that year. The story must take place on July 4th, 1942, 43, or 44. Yet even one of these years can be eliminated. Nineteen forty-two is out once we are told that "some of the [digger] machines wouldn't work on white pennies" (p. 84). During the war, to save precious copper, the U.S. government minted a penny with a greatly reduced copper content. This coin, with its zinc and steel coating, was called a gray or white penny. However, this penny was minted only in 1943. So, granting even that white pennies were in wide circulation in Maryland by July of that year, the events of the story could have happened only on July 4th of 1943 or (more likely) 1944.

But what is the point of all this? There isn't any. That's the point. Needless to say, the exact date of the story's events matters not at all. And that, of course, is part of the joke; that Barth would go to such trouble to conceal from us, yet provide all the clues to the discovery of, an essentially meaningless fact. After all our careful groping down this one dark passage in the funhouse of this fiction, we come upon just one more dead end, and must turn around and stumble back and start over again.

THE PARAGRAPH

Gerhard Joseph has said that "*Lost in the Funhouse* provides ample evidence that, aside from all questions of aesthetic success, [Barth] is one of the two or three most aware, most technically experimental writers of acknowledged power at work in America today."[4] As goes the book, so goes the story. **"Lost in the Funhouse"** is a technical *tour de force.* Barth molds together in this tale so many aspects of the technique of fiction, and yet does it so brilliantly and with such seeming ease, that all questions of aesthetic success are definitely not aside. Barth can crack jokes, offer asides, re-write, question the validity of his characters, question the worth of his story, question the worth of himself as a storyteller, while at the same time he can keep what narrative line there is going, and keep the reader interested in it and in the jokes, asides, etc. And this is to say nothing of Barth's dazzling manipulation of language itself.

"Trust the tale not the teller" is, with **"Lost in the Funhouse,"** a foolish admonition, for the tale amounts to little more than this: a pubescent boy, his family and would-be girlfriend, take the family's usual Independence Day outing to Ocean City, Maryland's answer to Atlantic City. After one or two minor adventures on and under the boardwalk, the boy gets lost in the funhouse, from which he presumably escapes or gets rescued, though we never find out (another of the story's small jokes). All the while, he attempts to come to terms with his budding, befuddling sexual cravings and his increasing sense of alienation from those around him and from the world in general. It is, in short, one version of the classic modern tale of the outsider, the sensitive, grown-up child with powerful gifts of observation and rumination who must inevitably settle for the oyster of art since the pearl of love apparently will forever elude him. The character is, of course, cliché and sentimental, as is the whole story. But this is hardly a concern. There is so much else going on here that the shabbiness of the story's impetus is neither readily apparent, nor, once discerned, of any import. As with much contemporary fiction, we are not really expected to learn of "life" from the story, to be instructed by the author in the ways of the world. The "message," we know now, is not the enduring quality of any piece of fiction. More important, many contemporary writers know it as well. Therefore, they (and Barth is a good example) have become increasingly uninterested in preaching at the reader or in convincing him that that which he is reading is "real." They have become, in other words, story-*tellers* instead of *story*teller. **"Lost in the Funhouse"** is a product of this shift in emphasis; the tale itself counts for very little, so the telling—if not the teller—is all.

It is not possible to get at, briefly, all or even most of the ways in which **"Lost in the Funhouse"** works. Nor does such an analysis seem quite appropriate. A close textual analysis of the entire story would prove most boring, and for that reason, if for no other, would violate both the "beingness" of the story and its appeal. But **"Lost in the Funhouse"** clearly merits careful consideration, and to that end the synecdochic approach should suffice, with one paragraph selected to stand for the whole.

> But though he had breathed heavily, groaned as if ecstatic, what he'd really felt throughout was an odd detachment, as though someone else were Master. Strive

as he might to be transported, he heard his mind take notes upon the scene: *This is what they call* passion. *I am experiencing it.* Many of the digger machines were out of order in the penny arcades and could not be repaired or replaced for the duration. Moreover the prizes, made now in USA, were less interesting than formerly, pasteboard items for the most part, and some of the machines wouldn't work on white pennies. The gypsy fortuneteller machine might have provided a foreshadowing of the climax of this story if Ambrose had operated it. It was even dilapidateder than most: the silver coating was worn off the brown metal handles, the glass windows around the dummy were cracked and taped, her kerchiefs and silks long-faded. If a man lived by himself, he could take a department-store mannequin with flexible joints and modify her in certain ways. *However*: by the time he was that old he'd have a real woman. There was a machine that stamped your name around a white-metal coin with a star in the middle: A_____. His son would be the second, and when the lad reached thirteen or so he would put a strong arm around his shoulder and tell him calmly: "It is perfectly normal. We have all been through it. It will not last forever." Nobody knew how to be what they were right. He'd smoke a pipe, teach his son how to fish and soft-crab, assure him he needn't worry about himself. Magda would certainly give, Magda would certainly yield a great deal of milk, although guilty of occasional solecisms. It don't taste so bad. What if the lights came on now.

(pp. 84-85)

Apart from the simple story line, there are at least four major aspects to the narrative of **"Lost in the Funhouse,"** all of which, in varying degrees, are evidenced in this paragraph. One of the most obvious aspects involves comments by the author on the story in progress, comments directed sometimes to the reader, sometimes to himself, frequently to both. The sixth sentence, the one that begins, "The gypsy fortuneteller machine, . . ." is obviously an example of this. These comments are inserted not just for humor, but also to push the reader back from the story. They keep him reminded of the fact that the story is indeed a fiction, an artifact, a creation from experience, not experience itself.

Aligned with this is the second major aspect, the sense of the story as unfinished, a rough draft, perhaps, full of uncompleted thoughts, false starts, and options expressed but not exercised. This has much the same effect as the author's running commentary, for it too forces the reader to remember that a fiction is a made object, that regardless of how inevitable a story seems when finished, it is shaped and directed from the outset. The third from last sentence is a perfect example of the literal "rough draftness" of the story: whether Magda "gives" or "yields" her milk will have to be decided during a later revision.

Related to this, but somewhat more subtle, is the third major aspect, the illogicality of the narration. Throughout the story, and clearly in this paragraph, sentence frequently follows sentence as a total *non sequitur.* How exactly, for example, we get from the experiencing of sexual passion to a discussion of the condition of the digger machines in the penny arcades is not at all clear. What we have here is a form of stream-of-consciousness. However, it is not a character's stream flowing by, but the author's. In other words, we are taken back to an earlier stage in the manufacture of a story, back to the point before the story itself and the author's fabrication of it have been separated.

Finally, one of the most intriguing of these narrative aspects is Barth's handling of the distinction between author/narrator and protagonist. Barth cunningly refuses either to maintain the distinction steadfastly or to collapse it entirely. At one point he even asks (who? the reader? himself?), "Is there really such a person as Ambrose, or is he a figment of the author's imagination?" And in the paragraph quoted above, for example, we begin inside the protagonist's thoughts: "he heard his mind take notes upon the scene. *This is what they call* passion. *I am experiencing it.*" The comments that follow on digger machines and their worsening prizes are clearly those of the narrator. So far so good. But what of this: "If a man lived by himself, he could take a department-store mannequin with flexible joints and modify her in certain ways"? Or this: "Suppose the lights came on now"? Whose notions are these, and how can we tell? The point is, of course, that not only can we not tell, but that it does not matter. More properly, it matters that we *not* be able to distinguish here between the narrator and the protagonist. For by blurring the distinction between the two, Barth is able, subtly, to raise questions about the relationship between biography and fiction, reality and imagination—questions important not only to this particular story, but to much contemporary fiction, if not, indeed, to all fiction of all times everywhere.

In sum, the whole of **"Lost in the Funhouse,"** on every level, from title to tag, is very, very artfully managed. The apparent off-handed handling of the story's immense technical problems is in itself simply stunning. But to approach the story on that level alone—technical problems invented, technical problems solved—is surely a mistake, for that takes much of the fun out of the funhouse. Barth himself insists that technique is the means not the ends. On the dust jacket of *Lost in the Funhouse,* he is quoted as saying, "My feeling about technique in art is that it has about the same value as technique in love-making. That is to say, heartfelt ineptitude has its appeal and so does heartless skill; but what you want is passionate virtuosity." Still, the story's concerns with technical questions cannot and should not be avoided. **"Lost in the Funhouse"** does seem to be more of an artifact than, say, something by I. B. Singer. And the major thrust of its technical investigation comes in the area of authorial self-

awareness. One hates to use the inverted logic of some modern criticism (more in the plastic arts than in literature) which suggests that a difficult and obscure work is in fact a simplification, a return to basics. But that is really what we have here: a case of new being old, complication simplicity, and obfuscation ingenuousness. For the question of the writer's self-awareness—and the reader's consequent awareness of him as well—so integral a part of **"Lost in the Funhouse,"** emphasizes the (generally unacknowledged) *sine qua non* of any piece of fiction: the author and the words. We have always discussed plot and theme, mood and character as if they existed on their own, as if their creation existed independent of their creator. If Barth does nothing else in **"Lost in the Funhouse,"** at least he moves us a step closer to a realization of this error in our ways. And if we can thank Barth for nothing else, we can thank him for having the honesty to report, on his return from the literary wars, that he has met the enemy and found, as did Pogo, that it is he.

Notes

1. Of this sort of review, Tony Tanner's, in *Partisan Review,* 2-1969, is the most telling.

2. Gerhard Joseph, *John Barth* (Minneapolis: University of Minnesota Press, 1970), pp. 37-38.

3. John Barth, "Lost in the Funhouse." *Lost in the Funhouse* (New York: Doubleday and Company, 1968), p. 72. All subsequent quotations from this work will be indicated by page number in the body of the essay.

4. *John Barth,* p. 38.

Jeff Rackham (essay date autumn 1980)

SOURCE: Rackham, Jeff. "John Barth's Four-and-Twenty Golden Umbrellas." *The Midwest Quarterly* 22, no. 2 (autumn 1980): 163-75.

[*In the following essay, Rackham asserts that Barth offers important textual clues to readers toward the proper mode for approaching his works in* Lost in the Funhouse.]

For the last decade or so the fictions of John Barth—and others such as Coover, Gass, Barthleme and Pynchon—have clashed with most assumptions and expectations we bring to the act of reading. Critics like Robert Scholes have moved deftly through various rationales—fabulism, metafiction, structuralism—and the brilliance of explanation has almost lulled us into saying, well yes, now we understand, and we do in part. We know a great deal about the new fiction. But when we come back to the works themselves, trying to reconcile those complex verbal constructs, the quality of the reading experience and much of the truth of the experience still seems inarticulated. A number of readers have ploughed ahead with conventional exegesis, finding in a work like Barth's *Lost in the Funhouse,* for example, a traditional organic unity in verbal patterns, or various themes arising out of an even more traditional character development, or mythic strategies similar to or in parody of James Joyce. Some thirty or forty of these essays have been published in the last ten years. And again we say, well yes, if we chalk up the rest to mere style, perhaps *Lost in the Funhouse* is after all only another bildungsroman, a portrait of the artist as young spermatazoon. But when, as readers again, we mole our way through the text, many of these analyses seem reductive of the total experience. Where is the bewildering frustration, the outright laughter, the sense of mystery, the intellectual pleasure of literary gamesmanship, the tedium punctuated with sudden insight that Barth evokes in most readers?

Perhaps what we need now is not another reading of the work, but a new reader. Like the art of writing, reading is bound up in generic traditions, and when genres change or forms blur and merge, as they seem to be doing in contemporary fiction, the reader must renegotiate his role. In a 1975 *PMLA* essay, Father Walter J. Ong describes the historical role of readers as one enforced upon them by writers in every age. Writers, Ong reminds us, must fictionalize their readers as much as they fictionalize their stories. A writer cannot write without an audience and by the nature of his medium, cannot know who that audience is, cannot know his reader's individual characteristics. He must fictionalize the qualities of his readers, must make certain assumptions about them (consciously or unconsciously), must allow them certain educational and cultural parameters, and certain goals in reading—entertainment, adventure, insight into human affairs. In turn, the audience, if it is to share the experience of the writer, must accept the role the author has devised. The process was clearly expressed by Wayne Booth in *The Rhetoric of Fiction.* "The author creates . . . an image of himself and another image of his reader; he makes his reader, as he makes his second self, and the most successful reading is one in which the created selves, author and reader, can find complete agreement" (p. 161).

The importance of this fact to the new fiction is clear. We have become habituated to the realistic novel, and especially as academics, we have been conditioned to expect—even in older "experimental" writers like Joyce and Beckett—to find relationships between technique and some element of our reality. Faced now with writers like John Barth who, if not denying reality, have gone beyond believing that any substantial truth can be found in it for fiction, we have trouble trying to read the simple words on the page.

The novel, a form which had become through endearing familiarity a comfortable mode of communication, has now forced us into negotiation, something that always happens when writers of any era begin to negate the former norms. Negotiation compels the reader to reconsider not only the genre but the dailiness of his life that the older norms supported. To continue to look for "epiphanies" or "solidity of specification," let alone "character development," or "social issues," is essentially to impose the standards of one genre onto another. The new fiction is clearly not realism, and Jerome Klinkowitz, Raymond Federman, Philip Stevick and others have begun the task of defining a new aesthetic for it. But it is one thing to identify basic characteristics of a form, another thing entirely to read a story in the proper role. What we need is another author like Henry Fielding, willing to step in and instruct us in that role, and to a limited extent, we find him in John Barth's *Lost in the Funhouse*—if, that is, we look to clues Barth provides us at the beginning.

The initial difficulty most readers encounter with *Lost in the Funhouse* is the disorder of beginning without clear referents, *in medias res.* **"Night-Sea Journey,"** the first fiction in the work, usually evokes confusion, groping, perhaps even a sense of being offended by what seems deliberate and unnecessary abstraction. For many readers it is not until the center of the story, at the point where the narrator's voice speculates that in "possibly a single night-sea per thousand, say, one of its quarter-billion swimmers . . . achieve[s] a qualified immortality," that the narrator's identity as a sperm can be confirmed. For some, like several early reviewers and most of my students, this identity is never successfully comprehended. They finish the work believing the narrator is a fish, or that the whole of it is a prose essay composed of philosophical meanderings. The problem of narrator identity is central to the type of reader Barth is here fictionalizing. If we approach the work as we would approach conventional forms—and all our training enforces this approach—we anticipate that the narrator will be either a "character" in the work or will soon point out to us a main "character" for us to identify with or follow adventurously or psychologically. At the very least, we expect the narrator to be a central intelligence, who, puzzled as he may be, will at least through sensitive observation help us to know something, to find meanings. None of this occurs. We may feel baffled, even angry. But earlier textual clues have been passed over.

In *Lost in the Funhouse* a two-page **"Frame Tale"** precedes **"Night-Sea Journey"** and performs several important readerly functions. Barth provides us with instructions on how to cut and paste the tale into a Mobius strip: "Once Upon A Time There Was A Story That Began Once Upon A Time There Was A Story That Began . . ." etc. Several critics have dealt sufficiently with the various formal relationships of the frame tale to the book as a whole. But as readers we need to take seriously the words on the page. When a writer clearly frames the whole of his fiction with "Once Upon A Time," we had better review our assumptions. Fairy tales and folk tales do not deal in "character development" (except perhaps implicitly through morals learned). If to read such tales with full enjoyment we must adopt an attitude of child-like immediacy, then Barth must be signalling for what might be called a temporary suspension of literary sophistication—at least in part. Apparently we must be prepared to accept the philosophical conflicts of a sperm attempting to find reason in blind chaos on its literal level, not as symbol or metaphor of a more daily reality. We will have to accept the literalness of the sperm's quest as we would accept the literalness of a young princess searching for magic words to free her from Rumplestiltskin. Since neither folk nor fairy tale are ultimately profound forms—their primary function seeming to provide joyful sublimation—Barth seems to suggest that our first need as new readers is to rid ourselves of the high seriousness that realist fiction has led us to expect.

Our habitual conditioning toward realism makes us skeptical that a fairy tale opening should be taken at its worth, but the element of play in Barth (and in Coover, Barthleme, certainly in Borges) is perhaps the "most equal" of several major elements. Barth has even been criticized for not dealing with social values or major cultural issues. To allow the validity of such criticism means we must equally chastise the Brothers Grimm. Simply because there are serious elements in Barth, elements that function as cognition rather than as sublimation, we cannot ignore the relationship of the fairy tale opening to the remainder of the text. Nor can we impose upon Barth a judgment applicable to writers of an historically different form. Such criticism occurs not because the new fictionists have abandoned social responsibility, but because the reader's role is confused. The words on the page say, "Once Upon A Time." To ignore them, or to assume they don't relate to **"Night-Sea Journey"** and the other fictions included in *Lost in the Funhouse* is to do violence to the art of reading.

But of course Barth's frame tale is not composed solely of "Once Upon A Time." Barth gives ironic twist to the conventional fairy tale opening by shaping it as Mobius strip: a multi-dimensional/single-dimensional tale that goes on repeating itself forever, something folk and fairy tales do not do, but which mythic cycles, in their promise of eternal rebirth, do endlessly. Two more clues then. We are not after all to be wholly naive, child-like readers of fantasy—no hobbits here. We are also to see this tale in ironic dimension, and we must prepare ourselves for reading it on the deeper imaginative level of mythic cycle.

But how can the nature of reader of fairy tale be fused with the nature of reader of irony? And how can the committed seriousness of myth be fused with the escapist entertainment of fantasy? Barth's famous essay on **"The Literature of Exhaustion"** offers the thesis that contemporary writers have found it necessary to employ older forms against themselves, ironically, to "accomplish new human work." I believe too much has been made of the negative in this essay. To read Barth solely as writer of ironic fairy tale or ironic myth, pitting one form against the other, or against the ultimacies of themselves, is to take the ironic aspect as metaphor of exhaustion, as metaphor of contemporary loss, rather than as a strategy that functions to accomplish new human work. Such a reading is a return to Modern realism with its heavy emphasis on irony and all its serious reflections on the contemporary nature of world disorder. The exhaustion of older forms, and the ironic use of them, does not represent a death of fiction or whatever. Barth insists that the greatest writers always work with ultimacies of form, forcing form to the extremes of possibility. Jorge Luis Borges, whom Barth offers as example, has employed form against itself "precisely to make new and original literature." Thus we cannot limit our vision of mobius strip irony to one of irony impressed on fairy tale. The reverse relationship also exists and moderates the implications.

The fairy tale aspect of the mobius strip suggests that "irony" in *Lost in the Funhouse* does not necessarily partake of high seriousness, and that it is not necessarily metaphoric. In turn, the relationship of irony to "Once Upon A Time" reveals a highly sophisticated literary pleasure in discovering how a conventional form can indeed be forced to its ultimacy. It reveals also a rather simple aesthetic pleasure in what might be called imaginative play. Perhaps there is an aspect of Barth's irony here which suggests that its role is closer to that of "wit" in eighteenth century literature than to the use of irony in Modern realism.

Appreciation of **"Night-Sea Journey,"** then, begins in the need for believing in the immediacy of fantasy, for accepting innocently the once-upon-a-time adventures of a sperm, while at the same time allowing one's self the luxury of recognizing the ingenious and highly literate irony of spermatic tale and all its historical and formal referents. By luxury, I mean the luxury of reading for wit rather than for high (academic) seriousness. The temptation to take it all as symbolic or metaphoric needs to be resisted because it inevitably sends one off on a chase for antecedents and allusions, or forces a rationalized reconciliation with reality.

Neither is John Barth employing myth (or mythic cycles) as did earlier Modern writers. T. S. Eliot has said that Joyce used myth as a "way of controlling, or ordering, of giving shape and significance to the immense panorama of futility and anarchy which is contemporary history." Eliot himself used it as a mode of perception or vision in *The Waste Land*. The temptation is to assume that all myth in an age of irony must function in a similar way. Barth has said in an interview, however, that much as one might admire such writers, their use of myth is one-dimensional. They used classical myth to make an ironic contrast with contemporary reality. "I think it's more interesting," Barth observes, "if you find yourself preoccupied with mythic archetypes or what have you, to address them directly" (Bellamy, pp. 8, 9). Which is what he attempts in *Lost in the Funhouse*. There, the author-hero discovers that he must work through layerings of myth, ultimately to become a part of myth. Thus in **"Night-Sea Journey"** the sperm finds himself *in medias res* because all myth, as part of a larger cycle, begins in the middle (and no doubt because all human experience as we know it begins that way). The sperm attempts to find sense in the confusion of conflicting claims as to the meaning of it all, and he perceives that in some way he is to be the tale bearer of his generation. Later, as Ambrose, he is marked by the gods to have a honey'd tongue, and in the title fiction (**"Lost in the Funhouse"**), he attempts to tell his first tale about himself. Having become a nameless writer he struggles at writing any fiction—first in the voice of others (**"Echo"**), later in debate with his own inner voice (**"Title"**) and finally as a teller of fictions about a writer of fiction who discovers he is fictionalized (**"Life Story"**). The series of tales progresses humorously and absurdly, from that of a specific sperm and named child, to an unnamed author and finally to an abstract voice (in **"Menelaid"**) telling tales within tales. In the final selection (**"Anonymiad"**) the hero learns his ultimate lesson. As all great writers must, he moves beyond the struggle with voice, beyond the difficulty of the story and its unfolding: he becomes the thing itself—in this case, an anonymous bard in ancient mythic times casting seminal fictions into the salt sea to be reborn again in another form. He has discovered that an authentic identity is both unique and at the same time an anonymous element of a larger whole. The movement is from the "created" (a sperm shot off on a quest against odds as great as any faced by a prince off to find a magical princess) to the "creator" (the bard, drawing forth from his imagination a world of heroes, villains, and destinies). In Mobius-strip fashion we move from the lowest level of prose tale ("Once Upon A Time") to the highest level ("In the beginning God created . . ."), and in the passage we discover these are not mutually exclusive genres; they are continuous ("Continued, continued," Barth repeats parenthetically at the bottom of the frame tale page).

What it demonstrates of course is that all myth is a fictive way of organizing experience, that to "address myth directly" is to deal directly with human intelligence, with the unstable subjective self struggling to make sense of the multiple systems of order imposed on us all; to find, if you will, a way to transcend historical mode (i.e., taking form to its ultimacies), and to transcend individuality.

The frame tale now takes on its fullest meaning. If Barth is addressing myth directly, even though ironically, then the new reader must confront *Lost in the Funhouse* in a similar fictive role, not as a seeker after the nature of reality—a Mobius strip is only illusion—and especially not as realistic interpreter—for those who live and experience myth, even ironic myth, are not necessarily the same as those who later interpret it—but as full and wondrous participant in the ritual of telling. In the same way that we as readers must in part accept the givens of primal fantasy as truth (talking frog, philosophizing sperm), we are led to acknowledge by the multiple dimensions of a Mobius strip, by the eternally recurring story that begins "Once Upon a Time," that we must assume the historically earlier role of partaker of myth, looking not to myth to explain or contrast with contemporary reality, but to create the experience of confronting internal truth directly. The mythic element in Barth, and other contemporary writers like Robert Coover, is not to give shape and significance to the futility and anarchy of our lives, but to express it in all its confusions, idiocies, and discontinuous realities. We are not being asked to believe in the truth of chairs or electricity, nothing here to be measured and weighed, but to believe in the fable of order itself, in the wonderful myth that order establishes value and meaning in human activity.

Barth's hero, like ourselves, must work through the myths of life, rejecting old forms which nevertheless impose themselves on us. And hence the irony: this is not formlessness, not absurdity as so many realist readers have charged; this is the opposite—this is excess of form, excess of meaning, as in our daily lives. I believe that in this paradox lies the truth of the reading experience. In the act of reading the text we replicate the meaning of the text. The reader is thrust into a confused sea of forms, mythic forms, realistic forms, fantastical forms—competing forms—none of which in itself provides total coherency, each of which claims its own truth.

Walter J. Ong asserts that the writer enforces a role on the reader, and that is what Barth does here. The reader is forced to go on a quest, like a sperm, like Ambrose, and especially like the nameless writer searching for a voice. All the confusion, the frustration, the unexplained mysteries, the tedium punctuated with insight and disgust must be struggled through and overcome, is overcome in the triumph of the voice that becomes the tale, is overcome in the reader who receives the whole of it "all at once" as Barth suggests we should in an author's note.

If we approach *Lost in the Funhouse* as realist readers prepared to explicate only selected elements, we negate the fullness the work attempts to express. Among other things, it is the reductive aspect of realism and realistic techniques that contemporary writers have had to abandon as unreal, and nore importantly, untrue. The realists made us feel stable, secure. We have character, plot, linear time, and insights into common feelings. All of which now seem like an idealized vision of life, certainly a reductive vision that refines the chaos of existence and makes it manageable. Realism perpetuates the illusion that life can be explained. The new fiction, by immersing itself in illusion, forces the reader to recognize that the relationship to life exists in the experience of the reading, in the interaction between text and reader, much as might be said of music. We can now say we have moved from Henry James' illusion of reality to John Barth's reality of illusion. What we can no longer ignore is that the quality of the reading experience is, in the new fictionists, the meaning itself. Illusion, fantasy, myth are the only truths they offer.

How then is the new reader to read? A demand for a highly literate and cultivated background combines with an equal demand for accepting fiction as pure play; that in turn is confounded with the need to believe that magic is real, that fairy tale and dream are true to the inner self, as of course they are. Our job with the new fiction is not to analyze—as it seemed to be in realism—but to synthesize. We must draw together the paradoxes instead of attempting to cut through them. The story, **"Petition,"** one of the least discussed works in *Lost in the Funhouse,* might illustrate. An oddity among oddities, the tale purports to be a letter to

> His most Gracious Majesty Prajadhipok, Descendent of Buddha, King of North and South, Supreme Arbiter of the Ebb and Flow of the Tide, Brother of the Moon, Half-Brother of the Sun, Possessor of the Four-and-Twenty Golden Umbrellas.

The letter asks for relief for siamese twins of opposing natures, joined belly to back, and forced through their freakishness to perform in a lewd travesty of sexuality with a contortionist named Thalia, a woman who at times also seems to have two realities. The elements of fantasy and bawdiness are joined with comic pathos as the forward twin narrates his humiliations and degradations. It is important for the reader to have enough literary background to recognize the letter-device as an important early form in fiction, especially one used often by Richardson and others to reveal right moral action, something which this letter parodies. It can also help if the reader is familiar with the dual natures of Thalia,

the muse of comedy in Greek myth. And it is fun to know that His Majesty Prajadhipok was a real king of Siam, that Barth lifted verbatim much of the actual language concerning the King from a *Time* magazine report of the King's visit to America, April 20, 1931. An interpreter might analyze each of these elements and many more, demonstrating that all are intricately unified in the tale. But how the story as a whole fits into the narrative of *Lost in the Funhouse* has presented problems. The tale seems to have no apparent relationship to accounts of Ambrose which precede it and follow it, except as one or two critics have suggested, as "representation" of conflict between Ambrose and his brother Peter.

If we recall, however, that we are dealing with a mythic cycle, we will remember that a conventional element of most mythologies is the concern for the duality of human nature. **"Petition"** strikes on one level at the heart of conflict between all brothers, as an allegorical parody of Cain and Able. But on a more prophetic level, the story presents an ironic inversion of the metaphysic of yin and yang, a bawdy dream, if you will, of the mirrored dichotomies of male and female. This is yin and yang as mythic illusion, as unreal as the King of Siam and all his four-and-twenty umbrellas, and paradoxically as true as the mythic order of world vision he symbolizes. The Mobius strip suggests our reading pattern then: **"Petition"** must be seen as a single-dimensional tale of conflict between brothers ("representative" of the conflict between Ambrose and Peter, Cain and Able, etc.) and as an illusory, multiple-dimensioned tale of the conflict in human nature itself between male and female, light and dark, good and evil. Barth has brilliantly synthesized two major elements of mythology, and he has done so with hilarious irony. If we, as readers, are to see the whole of it, we must accept the truth of the illusion.

Barth and other contemporary writers, especially Gass, Coover and Pynchon, are exploring man's relationship to himself, to his paltry means for making intelligence of his life and the universe. Not the real universe, whatever that is, but the universe of the imagination where myth can still express cosmogony, where the struggle of telling the tale itself makes manifest the radial complexity of human nature. The new reader of the new fiction must be open to the ambiguity of experience in which the writer, confronting the formal finalities of his time, turns back to the sources of creation, to fantasy, dream, and myth, like Homer, like Borges, telling tales in the dark, beyond the reach of science and reality— making art. Sociology, psychology, anthropology, history and other social sciences have taken over realism. The artist has had to go elsewhere to find his truths about the human condition, and the reader must follow. Does it leave something out? Of course. This is not real wholeness, only the fable that it can be found. But as

John Gardner has said, "You redeem the world by acts of the imagination" (Bellamy, p. 178).

Bibliography

Barth, John. "The Literature of Exhaustion." *Atlantic,* August, 1976.

Bellamy, Joe David. *The New Fiction: Interviews with Innovative American Writers.* Urbana, 1974.

Booth, Wayne C. *The Rhetoric of Fiction.* Chicago, 1961.

Ong, Walter J., S. J. "The Writer's Audience Is Always a Fiction." *PMLA.* January, 1975.

Carol Schloss and Khachig Tololyan (essay date winter 1981)

SOURCE: Schloss, Carol, and Khachig Tololyan. "The Siren in the Funhouse: Barth's Courting of the Reader." *The Journal of Narrative Technique* 11, no. 1 (winter 1981): 64-74.

[*In the following essay, Schloss and Tololyan interpret Barth's complex narratives in* Lost in the Funhouse *as direct invitations to readers to read actively and maintain individual perspective, and as illustrations of the inherent challenge of writing for an unknown audience or of determining an author's intent.*]

"You dogged, uninsultable print-oriented bastard," says one of John Barth's narrators to the reader, "it's you I'm addressing, who else, from inside this monstrous fiction."[1] Barth profanes his readers with almost ritual insistence and objects to them as an audience, even as he insists that he needs their presence; *Lost in the Funhouse* develops the insult as a form of invitation. The paradoxical attitude which motivates such development may be interpreted as disdain for the performance that is underway, or it may be said to show Barth so much in control of the interaction between writer and reader that he can toy with it at will. By speaking in contradictions, by spinning out some mimetic fictions, as well as grotesqueries and revamped mythologies, Barth plays aggressively with his craft. In his hands, the hidden costs of writing assume the status of a plot. Intent on making the invisible visible, Barth ensures that those who are usually absent from a text—writer and reader—are dramatized, and that the process by which they communicate are exposed. His book lacks (because it avoids) the coherence of a traditional novel, with its singleness of perspective and unified progression of a ground situation; instead, a kind of self-dramatization becomes central to Barth's enterprise. The relation of a writer to his materials, and the changing, sometimes hostile relation of a writer to his readers become his

dogged, recurrent preoccupations. He begins by arousing in his reader an expectation which he repeatedly frustrates, an expectation that a number of possible scenarios for the relation between writer, reader and tale will be enacted and tested in order to discover a more valid and privileged community of reading.

This recurring masquerade of "teller. tale. told," is ingenious and intriguing. It begins by generating its own set of problems, for Barth chooses to reveal a displeasure that is one result of his own decision to communicate through novel-writing. His readers are captive and necessary witnesses to the author's dramatization of the dilemma inherent in literary transactions. In part, Barth's hostility can be dismissed: much of the book is a verbal jest and a virtuoso performance. To the extent that it can be seen as an exercise undertaken for the pleasures of technical mastery, its motives are questionable. But its manipulations of convention and self, however playful and self-mocking, have a basis in real dissatisfaction and from **"Night Sea Journey,"** through the assortment of fragments and stories which constitute this book, we can watch Barth restlessly testing and rejecting ideas and formulas for reconstructing the literary relationships which hound him by their seeming immutability: one can play with convention, but one needs play-goers. The dramatization of an authorial self through the act of writing demands an audience which, in turn, extracts its price.

What can be said of a text which questions the value of the very communication it is designed to provide? Richard Poirier would see in Barth's self-parody, in his proclivity to speak and simultaneously to discredit what is spoken, a scepticism about the whole endeavor of literature.[2] While he rightly observes internal contradictions in the text, his assessment of their consequences seems too extreme. For if Barth questioned this enterprise as wholeheartedly as Poirier suggests, he would not write, not even to parody the activity of writing—such a parody is to some extent a confirmation of the importance of what it parodies. Thus, the existence of any text implies that its author seeks something in a literary transaction beyond jovial insult, perhaps even beyond a repetitive exposure of the fictitiousness of mimetic representation.

A partial answer may lie in the author's attempt to move readers away from their traditionally flaccid reading postures. What Barth looks for in us is difficult to assess, but it seems to involve a willingness to play with deceptions and the ability to learn, ultimately, what to do with them. The book is a finished product which pretends to record its own composition. It parades the choices and frustrations of writing as if they were generated haphazardly in the reading present. If these moves are made in the interests of increased candor, they fail. In narrative, every gesture of spontaneity inevitably involves a conscious decision. Barth is always in control of his medium, working in the manner of the funhouse operator of his title story, inviting participants to enter into a game whose counters are "units of information." The book's cycles of concealment, exposure, false revelation, and discovery are set up to challenge readers who, Barth feels, are pathetically eager to accept the illusions of traditional narrative as the recompense of a communicated vision. We are asked not to receive information passively; on the other hand, it would be too optimistic to assert that we are invited to participate in a genuinely cooperative, meaning-bestowing activity, as those who stress the role of the reader in fiction would have it. Quite simply, Barth *challenges us not to be taken in, to survive the surface permutations of the text with our own perspectives intact.*

This invitation promotes, and is designed to promote, analytic postures in reading that are useful beyond our encounter with this single, self-announced fiction. In this respect, *Lost in the Funhouse* belongs to the narrative category which advocates "reading" all the world (whether encountered on TV, in political statements, or in print) as fiction, as a system of duplicitous signs. We are to meet these cultural givens with an active, countering intelligence; we are not to be taken in. Like some of the lovers in his text, Barth wants a partner of equal agility. However, what he creates as a funhouse-labyrinth, as a place for a rewarding kind of intellectual hide-and-seek become, instead, a "chronicle of minstrel misery" (193). The creation of infinitely regressing verbal corridors, however excellent the motive, proves to be self-defeating: communication, when it is so displaced, prohibits the very confirmation of self that Barth seeks.

These generalizations have as their basis the observation that the stories in *Lost in the Funhouse* are not simply about what they purport to discuss. As Donald Barthelme once observed, in an essay on advertising,[3] the youthful figures frolicking in a pastoral setting often serve the purpose of selling the cigarettes discreetly tucked away underneath the glossy images; commercial pseudo-art often uses pure forms in the service of a "content" or message shunted into the background. Similarly, in the chapters or "stories" of *Lost in the Funhouse,* Barth inevitably has two subjects. Regardless of the ostensible subject of the stories, *he makes them function ultimately as extended metaphors-of-self, as a means for the author to image forth the difficulty of his and his readers' position.* Being lost, being lost in a funhouse, being twins, being neither one nor quite two, sending anonymous messages to unknown receivers—all are used in the service of this central preoccupation. They are the mediating structures between the details of the stories on the one hand, and the inferrable, transcending concerns of the author.

These strange metaphors assume special importance in the text because they serve to qualify what is an apparent authorial ideology. The narrator, in whom are subsumed all the lesser narrative voices of "I" and "he," seems unable to repress comments about his own boredom and his sickening self-consciousness: "God, but I am surfeited with clever irony," "History and self-awareness . . . are always fatal to innocence and spontaneity," "The fact is, the narrator has narrated himself into a corner." These and similar comments so frequently interlace the other ground situations of the fiction that they assume an independent dramatic status: by depending too exclusively on these, and by reading Barth's essay on the subject, commentators have classified *Lost in the Funhouse* as a pure example "the literature of exhaustion" and Barth as a writer detached and amused by his own solipsism.

While it is doubtless valuable to observe Barth's explicit, self-mocking despair, it is of equal importance to find the *common metaphoric antecedent* to the various fictional situations in the text, to understand the principle which unifies what first appear to be grotesquely disparate items. Sperm swimming, twinning, funhouse mazes, ancient lyricists all assume coherence, albeit a jarring one, as aspects of the writer's autobiography. More clearly than the petulant, cranky narrative voice, these metaphoric renderings define the kinds of transaction Barth considers possible between himself and his readers.

"Let us leave, if possible, *myself,*" Laurence Sterne suggested to himself, as *Tristram Shandy*'s narrator, but then he thought better of it. ". . . 'tis impossible,—I must go along with you to the end of the work." His jest works because it is grounded on the certainty that a narrator is indispensable to a narrative. That the opposite might also hold true, that a reader might be equally necessary to the transaction, is not discussed as directly—a remarkable circumstance in a book that questions almost every other convention of writing.

Sterne's apparent unconcern, his self-confident address to the audience, stands in marked contrast to Barth's stridency: "Why has he as it were ruthlessly set about not to win you over but to turn you away? Because your own author bless and damn you, his life is in your hands!" (124). The issue for Barth is one of power, or conversely, one of frustration at the inability of the writer to exist in his role as the creator of a text without the consent of his readers; their refusal to read would signal the non-existence, or at any rate the inefficacy of the efforts of his imagination. In one sense, Barth articulates a real and widespread fear first discussed by the philosopher, Hume—that one's performance, not observed, can be said to have no real existence. But in another way, the issue raised is bogus. Anybody who receives Barth's message concerning his fears has already guaranteed the closure of a transaction. Barth knows he has readers; he apparently wishes he could redefine their relation to him.

Barth's uncertainty has at its root a more far-reaching disturbance—the breakdown of a communal metaphor for understanding the world, and thus the created worlds of fiction. No longer standing in relation to his book as God once supposedly stood in relation to the universe, as a dispenser of orderly, authoritative, and interpretable meanings. Barth posits that all literary relationships must be realigned: his own to his materials, and his readers' to him. The problem of a bankrupt author: God analogy is posed explicitly in **"Life Story,"** where an unnamed voice observes that "certain things follow" from this realignment:

> 1. fiction must acknowledge its fictitiousness and metaphoric invalidity, or
>
> 2. choose to ignore the question and deny its relevance, or
>
> 3. establish some other, acceptable relation between itself, its author its reader.

The problem is also explored metaphorically in **"Night Sea Journey,"** where a sole, surviving sperm acts as the "tale bearer of a generation" (9). This vignette is, of course, the record of a swimmer's attempt to understand the predicament of "swimming." In that no sperm can tell his own tale, the story is literally impossible; but in another sense, because all sperms bear tails, the pun is almost too ingeniously literal. Both of these dimensions contribute to the narrative's effect, for they allow the author to pass playfully from the apparent situation of swimming spermatozoa to a discussion of his own position. The pun establishes the analogy: the story launches a book about the development of a writer and his art, the articulate sperm swims in a sea of literary traditions and because of it, the concerns of the small, bewildered voyager assume wider implications. His struggle to understand the phenomenal world, to ascribe meaning to his experience, results significantly in indeterminacy. Various models of the structure of the sperm-world are posited as possible—that "makers and swimmers each generate each other" (8) that there are cycles within cycles in the universe, that swimmers unwittingly gravitate toward and eventually penetrate "Her," a shore of some kind, and that union of shore and swimmer results in a loss of self. It is here that Barth first raises the issue of merged identities, of becoming, "something both and neither" that continues to preoccupy him throughout, but especially in **"Petition,"** where the Siamese twins are "both and neither," while remaining individuals in some other, more mundane sense.

All models for the possible structure of the sperm-world remain partial; they are carefully left at the conjectural level, as hypotheses which the speaker-swimmer cannot verify. In fact, at any point where the speaker seems to endorse one theory, he is careful to undercut that support: "Naturally I hooted with the others at this nonsense." Similarly, efforts to assign a purpose to the journey are undermined, and indeed, are never set forth as more than speculation: "Very likely, I have lost my sense" (9), "Perhaps . . . I am drowned" (9), "Alternately he liked to imagine . . ." (8). The "author's" refusal to elevate any one preferred construct of reality to an authoritative position tells us pointedly that he considers all categories and structures to be equally good and consequently any choice among them impossible, if not meaningless. This refusal to choose inevitably results in contradictions, and the sperm-swimmer, approaching the shore and his impending merger with "Her," finds solace in resistance—"Hate love!"—at almost the same time that he succumbs, crying, "Love! Love! Love!" (12). After a fashion, this is a very American, very Whitmanesque posture: "Do I contradict myself? / Very well then I contradict myself; / I am large, I contain multitudes." (*Song of Myself,* section 51, 1324-6). But unlike his expansive predecessor, Barth appears not to enjoy this multiplicity, not to find in it a possible or satisfactory solution to epistemological uncertainty.

These are the same kinds of uncertainties that shape **"Life Story"** and **"Menelaid,"** with the extended circumstance that in the later vignettes the activity of "telling" usurps the status usually accorded the substance of the tale. The existence of the speaking voice, as it "composes itself," is primarily important; the metaphors of a pained, divided self retreat further into the background. With the distinctions between "fiction" and "life" or "illusion" and "reality" blurred, the old king in the **"Menelaid"** is able to give only a halting account of the siege of Troy and Helen's subsequent evasion of him. It is a story peppered with unorthodox typography, and critics have labored over it, trying to identify speakers and times, and to disentangle the narrative layers supposedly implied by these typographic oddities and also by Barth's regression of dramatized listeners: " " ' "Nothing for it but to do as Eidothea'd bid be," ' " I say to myself I told Telemachus I sighed to Helen" (136). And indeed, this the problem dramatized in the text. As Menelaus observes; " ' "Hard tale to hold onto, this" ' " (139). He then endeavors to "hold fast to layered sense by listening as it were to Helen hearing Proteus hearing Eidothea hearing me; critic within critic, nestled in my slipping grip . . .' " (145). As suggested previously, this organizing exercise is futile. Had Barth intended for these frames to be deciphered, he might have used a ridiculous number of quotation marks, but he would have closed the quotes according to the opening orders established; the grammatical code would have been consistent. That the punctuation is erratic ("Why?" ' " ' ") (e.g. 148, 150) identifies the playfulness of the artifice: if textual reality is a frame-up, then any frame is appropriate.

As in *Tristram Shandy,* these forms are intended to obfuscate. Thus, when Menelaus asks in the text, " " ' "What's going on?" " Proteus's response is uninterpretable: " " ' " 'Son of Atreus!' . . . Don't imagine I didn't hear what your wife will demand of you some weeks hence, when you will have returned from Egypt . . . Don't misbehave yesterday, I warn you . . . (145). Such apparently organized comments, which are actually internally contradictory, do not always constitute an invitation to critics to discover a significant order concealed behind the verbal surface. A warning, even one from Proteus, cannot be applied to past actions any more than a future utterance can be heard in the present unless one posits that the categories of past, present, future, and uniform duration are inoperable. This is probably exactly what readers should suppose—that the fiction of the text abolishes the convention of progressively organized time.

A similar challenge to critics seems implicit in Menelaus's inability to recount what did happen at Troy, an inability, incidentally, which the narrator of the **"Lost in the Funhouse"** story shares, since he refuses to sort out Ambrose's fate—did the boy escape the funhouse or die wandering in its mazes? In one version of Menelaus's tale, Helen was a traitor and willing adulteress. In another, she was never in Troy; Paris had made love to "cloud-Helen" while Helen herself languished chastely in Pharos. The permutations continue, including the possibility that the Trojan fiasco was a dream of Zeus's and that Menelaus is himself a cloud. As Proteus and Menelaus tell it, the past becomes another story, or a series of stories, invented in retrospect, and hence not subject to verification. "Place and time, doer, done-to have lost their sense" (p. 160). Barth, as protean narrator, refuses the clarities of singular voice and identifiable narrative progression, even as he had declined to select a meaning for the **"Night Sea Journey."**

There are moral implications in this studied indecision. Insofar as Barth pictures himself in his sperm "tale bearer" or Menelaus's struggle with a proliferation of possible but inconclusive meanings, he offers us an explanation of his inability to advocate any subject as a fit topic for fiction. Since even fictional truth has become an irrelevant standard, his mind is free to play over myriad possibilities. With the fond indifference of a funhouse operator, aware of the absurdity of choice, he will pick his distortions at will.

"Petition" works in a similar way, although its implications are of a different order. By spinning out a grotesque image of self-conscious dependence. Barth again directs our attention away from the problems of "teller and tale" toward his grudging relations with those who are "told," his audience. The literal parameters of the piece are highly comic, and equally improbable; the petition is a plea for royalty to separate embarrassingly

joined Siamese twins. Coupled front to back, one twin acts while the other observes from behind. One wants to absorb, literally, the observer on his back; the other wants to control, and failing this, ("My attempt to direct our partnership ended in my brother's denying . . . my reality," (61) to become separate and independent. Impotent to affect his own destiny, he writes to call attention to the humiliating genetic fate: "To be one: paradise! To be two: bliss! But to be both and neither is unspeakable. Your Highness may imagine with what eagerness his reply to this petition is awaited . . ." (68). The situation is jarring and unseemly on the literal level—it takes us through intricacies of bodily maneuvers that are exhilarating feats of imagination, if nothing else. Nonetheless, it allows Barth to explore, in a bemused and exotic way, the issues of self-consciousness, observation and dependence. He has, as in **"Night Sea Journey,"** extended the second term of a metaphor-of-self and treated it as the literal predicament of a hapless being. To some extent, the translation of any text from the literal to a secondary, implied level of meaning is inevitably conjectural. In the case at hand, Barth has provided insufficient "cues" to unequivocally distinguish the second term of the implied analogy. The twins collectively serve as a model for the writer. They are a faustian creature, divided against itself, unable to act without self-scrutiny, and thus unable to act effectively, even in love. Thalia, their acrobatic lover, will not marry either twin in their dual condition. Looked at in this light, Barth has provided a pathetic image of the divided consciousness similar to Kenneth Fields' "other walker," or J. V. Cunningham's "Identity, that spectator / Of What he calls himself."

There is room here to see the problem as one of relationship, where being "both and neither" describes a literal duality. Whether we think of twin and twin or author and reader, there is a curious recurrence of simultaneous resentment and dependency. The twins are bound, their fates so inextricably woven that life for either one of them depends upon the union. In positing this bizarre situation, the narrator realizes in frustration that symbiosis maintains vitality, yet the observer's yearning for independence, for self control and self-definition is unmistakable. In short, the cooperative system does not work, especially for the desperately observant twin, and one who can imagine the control and the cooperation he is unable to achieve.

For a writer to compare himself to a grotesquely misshapen creature, even with this indirection, involves almost comic self-pity. Barth risks the pity because, with the virtue of exaggeration, the analogy emphasizes the ambiguous position of a man whose identity is dependent upon another for confirmation. The desperation he exhibits resembles that expressed in the narrator's later, grudging reflection about writers and readers: ". . . don't you think he knows who gives his creatures their lives and deaths? Do they exist except as he or others read their words? Age except we turn their pages? And can he die until you have no more of him?" (124). To be "both and neither" is apparently Barth's way of discussing an uncomfortable dependence: being locked into a system where one's only identity is established in participation when one would prefer self-sufficiency.

The point is clear: Barth wants to annoy his readers rather than engage them. It is just their annoyance which links them to him, through his text. If he is impotent to change the structural basis of narrative transaction, to obliterate the need for teller, tale, told, he can at least heckle his literary conspirators: "You've read me this far, then? Even this far? For what discreditable motive?" (123). The insult is explicit, yet this is a point in the text when an explicitly articulated ideology seems to be counter-balanced by more implicit authorial postures. Barth's disdainful voice obfuscates by its own garrulousness, for the problem the author dramatizes is not just the one he articulates. It is not entirely caused by the presence or the absence of readers, nor by problems of consent or dependency alone. There is also a problem emanating from the tension between writing and loving, a contrast/parallel which runs through much of the text.

Throughout the book, Barth plays on an analogy between writers and lovers. It is implicit in **"Petition,"** where the writer-twin is also a marriageable twin engaging the attentions of a young contortionist. It runs beneath **"Night Sea Journey,"** where the speaker is not simply a man-on-the-street or someone who could raise existential questions with equal plausibility, but a sperm, the literal bearer of love's genetic code. The most accessible image of this preoccupation is placed strategically at the end of the book, in the **"Anonymiad."**

In the manner of Beckett, who pictured the writer as a lone entrepreneur in a room, in a bottle, in a trash can, writing out, Barth presents his minstrel-turned-prose-artist as a solitary, abandoned islander. The fiction of the story is that it records the writing of itself, as an unnamed contemporary of Menelaus uses squid ink to cover a hide of a goat with his history-to-date. Unlike Beckett, who manipulates in a closed self-referential system of language, Barth metaphorically remains in a communicative posture: his island writer humps the jug that will bear his message out to sea, and in this curious, highly "conceited" way, Barth exposes and joins his preoccupations with writing and love. The story provides the least devious self-image of a painfully contorted book, but it holds the key to Barth's dilemma.

This analogy is accomplished through an energetic, but by now familiar word play: Barth uses a figure of speech as the basis for a supposedly literal predicament. Thus, our convention of referring to artistic creation as

the offspring of an artist's intimacy with his muse becomes, here more than anywhere else in the text (though it is implied throughout), a literal copulation. Abandoned on an island with nine amphorae of wine, the minstrel names them after the nine muses, and one by one, drinks the spirits, uses each jug first as a sexual partner and then as a vessel for his sea-bound message. As he indicates in his own song:

> Amphora's my muse:
> When I finish off the booze,
> I hump the jug and fill her up with fiction.
>
> (164)

The "Minstrel's Last Lay" is both a song and a coupling, and the less genteel metaphors of sexual encounter describe his use of the wine bottles: he breaks their seals, corks them, and makes each "the temporary mistress of my sole passion" (164). In short, by creating a purposeful semantic confusion, the writer can manipulate the metaphors of sex to identify the literal acts of writing. The implications of this correlation then become obvious: the solitary minstrel, who has left his honeyheaded beauty in the arms of another, more virile man, suggest the cuckoldry and its resultant solitude are inevitably the fate of artists. Commenting on the writing of his own history, he observes: "His corresponding professional sophistication, at the expense of his former naive energy, was to be rendered as a dramatical correlative to the attrition of his potency with Merope . . ." (191). The message seems to be that expertise at writing is achieved at the expense of human involvement. Thus the solipsism of the minstrel's position is not begun, but merely extended by his removal to an island.

Yet even this is a position Barth is careful to undercut. We are clearly given to understand that the minstrel-narrator considers his imagination to provide recompense for the more tangible pleasures of the flesh. The muses become his initial lovers and his writing a form of intercourse with a larger world. Unable to love the available woman, he turns to unknown others, the recipients of his "water messages," for the kinds of self-validation that supposedly characterize the transactions of lovers. By extension of the analogy, any reader or recipient of an author's communication becomes a lover of sorts. Indeed, the anonymous minstrel confirms this conjecture when he seals his final message in its sea-going bottle. He remarks, "I could do well by you now, my sweet, to whom this and all its predecessors are a continuing, strange love letter." (193).

The problem is that this is a false analogy, incapable of closure and bound inevitably to disappoint. A reader is not a surrogate lover. Nameless, faceless, uncommitted to the literary transaction except as it pleases or annoys him, he cannot validate a writer's self in the same way that men and women confirm each other's worth. This is especially true when an author has nothing in particular to say. TO WHOM IT MAY CONCERN / YOURS TRULY (53) is a statement which may delight Ambrose when he finds this anti-message in a bottle, but as a model for literature, it is bleak. It is here that we detect the results of a growing impersonality of the text, the eclipse of the author and his narrators in favor of the creation of a disembodied, performing voice. Leaving in the "blanks" of a text because alternatives are unlocatable, or unchooseable, as the case may be, leaves precisely that: a series of blanks. To substitute for "vision" a cheerful but tiresome commentary on the impossibility of writing is hardly a fecund alternative. Even Barth intimates that he knows this when he has a confused Menelaus ask: "When will I reach my goal through its cloaks of story? How many veils to naked Helen?" (140).

It is thus that this playful verbiage turns sour, and the repeated admonitions of the text assume an awkward sincerity: "Love! Love! Love!" Barth has reduced a clever verbal labyrinth to a tale of "minstrel misery," to the articulated frustrations of a man imprisoned by his obsession with language, and pained by the poverty of his broken efforts to reach out.

Ambrose is not, but wishes he were, among "the lovers for whom funhouses are designed" (94). If this, too, is a metaphor-of-self, it is naive and painfully revealing. Though Barth may have taught us to read in such a way as to survive his protean text with our wits intact and bristling with an annoyed caution, he has done so at great price. To control, to parade with feckless, changing voice through a brilliantly patterned but hollow text, may be masterul, but it is also solipsistic; it promotes an independent and wary intelligence in readers at the expense of a more satisfying confirmation of the specific narrator or artist. If we are lovers, we are not so in relation to Barth, even in the oblique fashion required by his nostalgia. In this respect, despite his trickster's aplomb, it is Barth who has lost.

This is not to deny Barth's achievement in *Lost in the Funhouse,* but rather to claim that it does not consist of achieving a new and better communication between writer (whether the narrator, or John Barth) and reader, or of a better balance between loving and writing. Instead, Barth begins by giving voice (the word) to a sperm engaged in the process of making a body of flesh, and ends with the successful creation of a disembodied voice, a voice which is reminiscent of, and mutilated like those of Beckett's novels (*L'Innommable* especially). To dwell on those paradoxes and to attempt to construct a community of reader and writer mediated by the text is what we as critics almost instinctively do. It is also what we are finally asked, by Barth to resist.

Notes

1. John Barth, *Lost In The Funhouse,* (New York: Bantam, 1969) Further references to this volume will be given in the text.

2. Richard Poirier, *The Performing Self* (New York: Oxford University Press, 1971), p. 21

3. Donald Barthelme, "(Review of) the 40th Annual Editorial and Art Design Awards," *Harper's* (October 1967), pp. 30-32

Jan Marta (essay date June 1982)

SOURCE: Marta, Jan. "John Barth's Portrait of the Artist as a Fiction: Modernism through the Looking-glass." *Canadian Review of Comparative Literature* (June 1982): 208-22.

[*In the following essay, Marta surveys Barth's commentary on Modernist techniques and theories in* Lost in the Funhouse.]

Introversion is a dominant trend of Modernist literature, but what happens when introversion turns back on itself; when Modernism looks at itself as a movement characterized by self-reference; looks at itself looking at itself?

John Barth's *Lost in the Funhouse,* whose subject matter is literature and whose predominant technical device is *mise en abyme*[1] or self-reference, lies beyond the Modernist period in a position to reflect on the movement from which it has evolved. It exposes Modernist commonplaces and truisms, and parodies the attempts of earlier Modernists, like Joyce in *Ulysses,* to treat the whole tradition of literature. Using the very techniques of Modernism to destroy that movement, *Lost in the Funhouse* attempts to regenerate literature, to provide an antidote to the post-Modernist blank of silence to which writers like Beckett lead. Barth revitalizes 'exhausted literature' through innovation in structure, theme, mode, genre, language and style, and through his self-conscious exploration of the relationships between reader, writer and text, and reader, writer, text and critic.

Although Barth's novels *The Sot-Weed Factor* and *Giles Goat-Boy* have positive elements, *Lost in the Funhouse* is perhaps the most positive of his works and a most positive view of the fate of post-Modernist literature. We would therefore like to highlight the ways in which *Lost in the Funhouse* regenerates literature while casting a parodic look at Modernism. In so doing we will also show how *Lost in the Funhouse* adheres to many Modernist trends. As we have stated, introversion is a dominant trend of Modernist literature and a predominant technical device of *Lost in the Funhouse.* Our study concludes then with a look at how this work makes particular use of introversion to regenerate literature. Throughout, we have placed considerable emphasis on the (implied) reader's reaction to the work since *Lost in the Funhouse,* like other Modernist texts, invites reader participation in the creation of the work.

According to traditional genre definitions, *Lost in the Funhouse* would be considered a collection of short stories. Yet *Lost in the Funhouse,* a 'series . . . meant to be received "all at once" and as here arranged' (p. ix), can be read as a single text.[2] Not only the Author's Note quoted above, but also the work of critics such as Michael Hinden, Gerald Gillespie, and Beverly Gray Bienstock, attest to the unity of the text.[3] Most important, *Lost in the Funhouse* proclaims itself a single tale. The Author's Note and Seven Additional Author's Notes by the omission of the customary signature or initials of the author become a part of the fiction as well as a commentary on it. Their injunction, 'On with the story. On with the story' (p. ix), repeated on page 170, asserts the singleness of the tale to follow. Also, the '(continued)' which brackets **'Frame-Tale'** reinforces its theme of literature's infinite repetition of a single tale, making the story a fragment of that one repeated tale, and a fragment of *Lost in the Funhouse*'s one story.

Two sub-texts, consisting of the first seven stories and the second seven respectively, divide the macro-text. Each story, in itself a complete text composed of smaller units, participates in these two larger wholes—the subtext and the macro-text. Cross reflections confirm the interrelationship of the stories. The stinging of Ambrose, the central event in **'Ambrose His Mark'** reappears as analepsis in **'Water-Message'** and **'Lost in the Funhouse.'** 'Ambrosia' figures in Eidothea's advice in **'Menelaiad,'** and in **'Anonymiad'** in the forms of 'honeyed diction,' and 'bee-sweet form,' 'clover voice' and 'honey tongues.' The tongues of **'Glossolalia'** recur in **'Life-Story'** and **'Anonymiad'**; the latter's amphorae and writings echo **'Night-Sea Journey'**'s 'vessel and contents'; **'Echo'** mythologizes Ambrose's mirror-house experience; and so on. Thus, although *Lost in the Funhouse* moves from voice to voice and perspective to perspective, changing character and situation, the stories are linked by metaphoric association, a principle of concatenation in Modernist literature where the imposition of equivalence over contiguity, or following Jakobson, of metaphor over metonymy, blurs the distinction between poetry and prose. Proteus, the 'old fabricator' (p. 36), symbolizes the tale's chameleon nature. There is innovation here regarding the standard division of narrative into genres based on length and scope—short story as opposed to short novel as opposed to novel—and variation on the use of metaphor to blur genre distinctions. *Lost in the Funhouse* is a novel composed of short stories.

On the diegetic level, the major tale of *Lost in the Funhouse* is a portrait of the artist as a fiction—a self-referential subject in the Modernist tradition of James Joyce's *Portrait of the Artist as a Young Man.* The chronological development of the artist from conception through birth, childhood, adolescence and manhood to death parallels the inception, genesis, death and regeneration of fiction. **'Night-Sea Journey'** describes the immanent conception of a human being; **'Ambrose His Mark,'** the birth and naming of a baby. In **'Water-Message'** Ambrose receives a sign of his call to writing, a vocation he accepts in **'Lost in the Funhouse.'** At this point the first section of *Lost in the Funhouse,* the *Künstlerroman,* and the second section, the *Bildungsroman,* merge. The writer works unsuccessfully at his craft, and at his personal relationships in **'Title.'** **'Life-Story'** continues the development of his art, this time inspired by the writer's suspicion that he is a fiction. In **'Menelaiad'** all that remains of the writer is his printed voice, his narration; in **'Anonymiad'** the writer has no existence except for his work. In the same way that 'this isn't the voice of Menelaus; this voice *is* Menelaus, all there is of him' (p. 125), this tale is not the tale of Anonymous, this tale *is* Anonymous; Proteus' prophecy that 'when the voice goes he'll turn tale, story of his life, to which he clings yet, whenever, how-, by whom- recounted' (pp. 161-2) comes true—the artist is a fiction. The tale's end rejoins its beginning, **'Frame-tale,'** the first story of *Lost in the Funhouse* and the one which opens the series of stories more exclusively dealing with fiction as their subject. This series comprises **'Autobiography,'** the short story's self-examination; **'Echo,'** its discussion of voice and perspective; and **'Glossolalia,'** its exercise in stylistic experimentation; as well as **'Title,'** **'Life-Story'** and **'Anonymiad'** where living and writing become almost the same act.

The diegesis or strictly 'fictional' aspect of the work engenders myriad subthemes, some of which we will elaborate upon in the course of this paper. First briefly, as a literary portrait, the subject spawns meta-textual themes: the history of literature, a theory of genre, the evolution of literary criticism, a credo regarding realism, and an esthetics involving the dichotomy between print and oral narration, between the medium and the message. Since the primary figure in the portrait is the artist, a group of themes cluster around the creative process or enunciative structure of literary communication: the genesis of a work, sources of material and inspiration, the work as autonomous structure, the author as hero, *poeta,* priest, as man, failed lover and neurotic, and the reader necessary to the writer's creation. Textual themes—technical questions of voice, perspective, style, structure, plot progression, and characterization—also derive from the portrait of the artist as fiction. Fictionality gives rise to transcendental themes of the relationship of fiction to reality, of art to life.

Two themes, the dialectic between fiction and reality and that between art and love, deserve close attention. They are key to the work's philosophy of literary regeneration and exemplary of its fourfold frame structure, a pattern integral to that philosophy. Structurally *Lost in the Funhouse* comprises many 'frames' each of which is a reflector and creator of theme. The 'Frame-Tale' establishes this structure and itself provides one of the frames. The message of 'Frame-Tale''s Moebius strip, 'Once upon a time there was a story that began Once upon a time there was a story that began Once . . .' (pp. [1-2]) *ad infinitum,* asserts the autogenous nature of fiction, yet the frame, or instructions, imply a creator of the Moebius medium and its message, as well as a re-creator to follow his direction. Thus the cyclical structure of *Lost in the Funhouse,* beginning and ending with fiction and imitated within 'Frame-Tale,' operates along with a frame structure homologous to that of the 'realistic' author-reader frame bracketing any fictive work.

In this fictive work, the realistic frame dissolves into its fictive centre, first in 'Frame-Tale' where the creator and re-creator are merely structures implied by the fiction, then in the whole tale. Anonymous, the narrator-protagonist of the tale's concluding segment, 'Anonymiad,' constitutes both a reader and writer figure. The ex-minstrel writes artistic messages sealed in amphorae, but also receives and reads one:

> I never ceased to allow the likelihood that the indecipherable ciphers were my own; that the sea had fertilized me as it were with my own seed. No matter, the principle was the same: that I could be thus messaged, even by that stranger my former self, whether or not the fact tied me to the world, inspired me to address it once again.
>
> (pp. 189-90)

Both identities, writer and reader, derive from the fictional message. Shortly, the dead, nameless, Anonymous will be known only as the character in his writings.

The tale's end thwarts reader expectation since customarily the character gains in realism through his association with the author. *Lost in the Funhouse* fictionalizes reality instead of 'realizing' fiction as nineteenth-century literature and Modernism both aimed to do, though in different ways.[4] Furthermore, since certain indicators imply that the text is autobiographical—the Maryland setting, the birthdate of 'Life-Story''s author figure, the meta-textual *mise en abyme* of Barth's own literary career in 'Anonymiad'[5]—John Barth the man, or at least the writer, dissolves into fiction, as does his corollary, the 'real' reader.

The dissolving frames bring reality and fiction on to the same plane, just as the twist of a circle creates the single plane of a Moebius strip. Distinguishable dimensions

are mere illusion. The two opposites resolve into a cycle which at once returns to the point of origin and generates literature anew. The unending 'closed' circle is paradoxically open-ended. Linear progression occurs, although as part of a dialectical advance. The dialectic, a Modernist view of history, contradicts those critics like Gillespie, Slethaug and Morris who see mainly stasis, nihilism, and absurdity in Barth's works.[6]

The same fourfold pattern—circle, dissolving frames, joined poles and open-ending—occurs with other pairs of thematic opposites which underpin the stories. For example, the tales of *Lost in the Funhouse* return perpetually to the polarization of art and love, introduced as antithetical and mutually destructive in 'Night-Sea Journey,' Here siren love menaces the narrator-sperm, 'author' of 'these reflections,' who enjoins 'whoever echoes these reflections' to 'hate love!' (p. 12). The adolescent Ambrose of 'Lost in the Funhouse' does not hate love but leaves it aside in his decision to be an artist. He will be a creator of funhouses in their literary context, rather than a lover-appreciator of them in their sexual aspect:

> He wishes he had never entered the funhouse. But he has. Then he wishes he were dead. But he's not. Therefore he will construct funhouses for others and be their secret operator—though he would rather be among the lovers for whom funhouses are designed.
>
> (p. 94)

In 'Life-Story' the author's wife puts an end to his writing activity, 'kissing him et cetera to obstruct his view of the end of the sentence he was nearing the end of . . .' (p. 126).

Yet there is progression in this perpetual return, since 'Menelaiad' transcends the art-love schism. The centre holding its many narrative frames is the 'absurd, unending possibility of love' (p. 162). With the 'real' narrator, Menelaus, corporally dead, his voice—into which Proteus has changed himself—growing 'scratchy, incoherent, blank' and his tale doomed to expiration in ten or ten thousand years, Menelaus will still survive 'in Proteus's terrifying last disguise, Beauty's spouse's odd Elysium: the absurd, unending possibility of love' (p. 162). Although the final section of the tale describes the dissolution of narrator, narration, and narrated into love, this very love, anthropomorphized by Helen, 'cause of every mask and change of state,' 'first cause and final magician' (p. 127), generates both the diegesis and the *récit* of the tale. She is responsible for all the events, she 'turned the Argives into a horse, loyal Sinon into a traitor, yours truly [Menelaus] from a mooncalf into a sea-calf, Proteus into everything that is'(p. 127). She lies at the vortex of tales spiralling out in time and space:

> " ' " ' " ' " ' "Speak!" Menelaus cried to Helen on the bridal bed,' I reminded Helen in her Trojan bedroom," I confessed to Eidothea on the beach,' I declared to

Proteus in the cavemouth," I vouchsafed to Helen on the ship,' I told Peisistratus at least in my Spartan hall," I say to whoever and where- I am. And Helen answered:

" ' " ' " ' "Love!" ' " ' " ' "

(p. 150)

Love as the prime generator of art, discovered through the dissolution of frames, represents a progression in *Lost in the Funhouse*'s circular return to the two poles of art and love. Their conjunction leaves literature's possibilities open-ended.

As a theme repeated with variation throughout the work, the theme of art and love is reflected syntagmatically and at the same time forms a paradigm for the whole. Its two poles develop paradigmatically into a discussion of traditional literary critical views of the telos of a text. The concern with art in itself asserts the autonomy of literature, while love constitutes an object of literature's mimetic function. Barth implicitly assigns historical co-ordinates to the two attitudes, writing a literary critical history in addition to an aesthetics. Both teloi have been exhausted, one through nineteenth-century Realism: 'On, God damn it; take linear plot, take resolution of conflict, take third direct object, all that business, they may very well be obsolete notions, indeed they are, no doubt untenable at this late date, no doubt at all . . .' (p. 109); the other through Modernist solipsism: '. . . the so-called "vehicle" itself is at least questionable: self-conscious, vertiginously arch, fashionably solipsistic, unoriginal—in fact a convention of twentieth-century literature' (p. 114). Obsolete as nineteenth-century Realist techniques may be, reality exists, 'people still fall in love, and out . . . and what goes on between them is still not only the most interesting but the most important thing in the bloody murderous world, pardon the adjectives' (p. 109). The danger in not finding an alternative means of expression other than self-consciousness is the post-Modernist blank of silence.

In preventing this silence, the union of art and love in 'Menelaiad' regenerates literature, at once returning it to a mythic point before the telic split into autonomy and mimesis and advancing it with knowledge of that split. 'Menelaiad' employs modernist self-referential techniques, feigns perdition into abstraction, yet tells a love story and conveys a strong message on the life and death cycle of literature. *Lost in the Funhouse*'s reworking of Homeric material, the Proteus-Menelaus-Helen myth, makes former literature an object of imitation—self-referentiality is mimetic. Similarly, parody, an eighteenth-century precursor of Modernist introversion and a Barthian device, must imitate literature to create literature. This regeneration of literature through the union of two literary opposites, introversion

and mimesis, is the telos of *Lost in the Funhouse,* the *raison d'être* of its subject, themes and patterning, the ultimate paradigm of the work.

Lost in the Funhouse, then, regenerates literature through genre modification, structural innovation, and at the thematic level, through the union of fiction and reality, of art and love, of autonomy (Modernist) and mimesis (nineteenth-century Realist). Moreover, it gives literature new life by revitalizing the literary medium. Print and oral communication vie with each other throughout the collection, the one dominant in **'Petition,'** the other in **'Night-Sea Journey,'** but coalesce in narrator-author figures such as Anonymous, and in Menelaus' 'printed voice' (p. ix). In **'Anonymiad,'** *Lost in the Funhouse* returns to a mythic point before the invention of writing and progresses through the genesis of the medium—goatskin (paper), squid (ink), and characters (letters). It emphasizes the materiality, immortality and flexibility of written works. The history and nature of the medium become the message; the medium determines the message in a concrete way: Anonymous divides 'Helen's hide in half to insure the right narrative proportions' (p. 172), then for lack of goatskin intends to present Part Three, his 'crux' and 'core,' as 'a mere lacuna.'

The overt declaration of this intention exposes the hermeneutics of any literary text, all of which require reader co-operation whether obedient or active. Here the reader expects to postulate actively the 'blank chapter,' but Anonymous replaces this participation with obedience when he fills in the chapter himself. The play with reader expectation asserts the narrator's authority and reflects the reading process. We have already referred to this process and will return to it. The relationship between author and reader provides one frame or context for the text and following the Modernist tradition engages the reader in the creation of the work more actively than does classically Realist literature. Still Barth maintains a tension between the author-narrator as authority on the work and the reader as participant in its creation. On the other hand, at times both dissolve into the fiction as in the example from **'Anonymiad'** cited above.

Lost in the Funhouse fits yet another frame. Anonymous' genre experimentation with mytho-historical fiction, 'religious narrative, ribald tale-cycles, verse-dramas, comedies of manners' (p. 187), constitutes a literary history which implies actual period coordinates as does the aesthetic debate on autonomy and mimesis. Anonymous' desire to create a work uniting tragedy and satire, verse and prose, 'whimsic fantasy, grub fact, pure senseless music,' in a word 'adventuresome, passionately humored, merry with the pain of insight, wise and smiling in the terror of our life' (p. 191), recounts his invention of the novel genre, more explicitly identified through Barth's puns: 'But the whole conception of a literature faithful to daily reality is among the innovations of this novel opus!' (p. 176). Like the other narrator-authors of *Lost in the Funhouse,* Anonymous struggles with the codes of fictionality and of narrativity. These struggles are inherent in the novel, 'an unstable compound inclining always to break into its constituent elements,'[7] and in narrative in general:

> Poised between the direct speaker or singer of lyric and the direct presentation of action in drama; between allegiance to reality and to the ideal; it is capable of greater extremes than other forms of literary art, but pays the price for this capability in its capacity for imperfection.[8]

While *Lost in the Funhouse* reflects the evolution of fiction and adds a step in its development—that of a novel comprised of short stories—it also reflects the evolution of literary criticism, thereby giving new positive direction to literature in all its facets. In particular, *Lost in the Funhouse* is a retrospective fictional reflection of Barth's own critical views in **'The Literature of Exhaustion.'**[9] The same operative principles, historical view and aesthetics found in *Lost in the Funhouse* form the thesis of Barth's 1967 article on Borges. Barth admires Borges who not only exemplifies but makes artistic use of aesthetic ultimacies: '[Borges'] artistic victory, if you like, is that he confronts an intellectual dead end and employs it against itself to accomplish new human work.'[10] One way of so doing is to reproduce a work of art with ironic comment on the genre and history of the art (rather than on the state of the culture). Barth's portrait of the artist as a fiction, as a parody of Joyce's *Portrait of the Artist as a Young Man,* does just that.

Lost in the Funhouse, through the explicit difficulties of its author figures, reflects a second Borgesian device described by Barth in the article and exemplified in 'Pierre Menard, Author of the *Quixote,*' where Borges 'writes a remarkable and original work of literature, the implicit theme of which is the difficulty, perhaps the unnecessity, of writing original works of literature.'[11] Most importantly, *Lost in the Funhouse*'s fourfold structure in its cyclical return which destroys opposites to regenerate them, brings to fruition Barth's belief in **'The Literature of Exhaustion'** that 'an artist may paradoxically turn the felt ultimacies of our time into material and means for his work—*paradoxically* because by doing so he transcends what had appeared to be his refutation.'[12]

As a corollary, Barth believes that 'the artifices of languages and literature—such far-out notions as grammar, punctuation . . . even characterization! Even *plot*!' can be 'rediscover[ed] validly' with awareness of immediate precedent in literary history.[13] The use of quotation marks in **'Menelaiad'** reflects this credo. They reverse

the tendency away from punctuation and grammar in Modernist stream-of-consciousness towards an extreme reliance on punctuation in order to signify speaker, listener and tale. Their multiplication has both comic and serious effects drawing attention to the medium of the message, to its limitations and to the interchange between 'reality' and 'fiction' in the tale. The frames isolating particular tales, tellers and listeners interfuse; punctuation marks play with time, space and verisimilitude. They form one tale of a Modernist here-and-now fictional reality; they reflect the effects Barth ascribes in **'The Literature of Exhaustion'** to the story-within-the-story turned back on itself—metaphysical perturbance of the reader, literary illustration of the *regressus in infinitum,* an image of the exhaustion or attempted exhaustion of literary possibilities.

The implied frame, **'The Literature of Exhaustion,'** can be found embedded in its reflector, *Lost in the Funhouse,* through echoed phrases: '. . . it's [Borges' artistic victory is] a matter of every moment throwing out the bathwater without for a moment losing the baby.'[14] Compare:

> Why could he not begin his story afresh x wondered, for example with the words why could he not begin his story afresh et cetera? y's wife came into the study as he was about to throw out the baby with the bathwater. "Not for an instant to throw out the baby while every instant discarding the bathwater is perhaps a chief task of civilized people at this hour of the world."
>
> (p. 116)

More significantly these phrases illustrate Barth's regeneration of language through his literary style. A cliché of the idiom, a tired signifier, gains new meaning by its union with an irregular, ideological signified. The resulting sign, at once exoteric and esoteric, has both a humorous and a sober impact. Socio-linguistic extremes dissolve into one recycled expression.

Although a refreshing device, this method of composition plays on the standard literary use of metaphoric association. Barth himself exposes the commonplace, and his version, by openly challenging the reader's expectation of symbolic import:

> Fat May's laugh came suddenly from the funhouse, as if she'd just got the joke; the family laughed too at the coincidence. Ambrose went under the boardwalk. . . . If the joke had been beyond his understanding, he could have said: *"The laughter was over his head."* And let the reader see the serious wordplay on second reading.
>
> (pp. 82-3)

The mocking exhortation to a second reading creates another form of stylistic cyclical patterning. A third derives from verbal repetition, for example, 'I would advise in addition the eschewal of overt and self-conscious discussion of the narrative process. I would advise in addition the eschewal of overt and self-conscious discussion of the narrative process' (p. 116). Repetition becomes so ubiquitous that 'ditto' provides a convenient replacement as does 'et cetera.' The latter indicates repetition but also open-endedness.

The same recycling with open end occurs at the syntactical level. The segment: 'A single straight underline is the manuscript mark for italic type, *which in turn* is the printed equivalent of oral emphasis of words and phrases as well as the customary type for titles of complete works, not to mention' (p. 69), begs re-reading since the grammatical structure and the syntactic norms of the text lead to the expectation of a grammatical completion. Alternatively, the segment begs re-writing because 'not to mention' can be made to fit if it replaces 'as well as.'

The diegetic level also engages the reader in the artistic task of 'filling the Blank,' asking 'How in the world will it ever   ' (p. 110). In a story where the 'real' author becomes narrator-writer-reader, becomes protagonist-character, becomes fiction, the 'real' reader also becomes writer, and thus allied with all the writer-protagonists and their metamorphosis into fiction, not only because of *Lost in the Funhouse*'s plot and Anonymous' end, but also as a result of its style. Barth achieves his 'regnant idea' of 'turning as many aspects of the fiction as possible—the structure, the narrative viewpoint, the means of presentation, in some instances the process of composition and/or recitation as well as reading or listening—into dramatically relevant emblems of the theme' (p. x).

The aim and its realization are Modernist, even though the *tour de force* may be borrowed from the post-Modernist Borges. While proclaiming the impossibility of literary creation, *Lost in the Funhouse*'s portrait of the artist as a fiction generates literature anew and illustrates literature's self-regeneration. It is modernist in its self-reference and beyond Modernism in that self-referentiality has become a stale convention which it must renew to keep alive. Indeed, the primary device for regeneration in *Lost in the Funhouse* is *mise en abyme* or self-reflection, as we have suggested earlier. Accordingly, we will now turn to the fourteen short stories which compose *Lost in the Funhouse* and for which the macro-text is an object of reflection, that is, of contemplation and of mirroring.

'Life-Story,' for example, is a meta-textual *mise en abyme* which conducts a critical commentary on the state of twentieth-century literature. It echoes *Lost in the Funhouse* and its critical frame **'The Literature of Exhaustion.'** The conventionality of narrative introversion, the dullness of *tranche-de-vie* realism, the self-despising, overtly metaphysical experimentation of the

avant-garde are lacking humour, adventure, and romance. Gone are the attractive heros, values, and deeds. The print medium and narrative genre seem 'moribund if not already dead' (p. 118). While age, occupation, and marital status identify the protagonist, an author figure, with John Barth, the 'real' reader is 'deuteragonist' (p. xi) addressed directly 'from inside this monstrous fiction' (p. 123). In other words, the reader is he who agonizes through the reading of Modernist literature. As in the single tale of *Lost in the Funhouse,* in **'Life-Story'** producer and receiver of the work unite in the fictional 'hero' of the story who concludes:

> . . . one or more of three things must be true: 1) his author was his sole and indefatigable reader; 2) he was in a sense his own author, telling his story to himself, in which case in which case; and/or 3) his reader was not only tireless and shameless but sadistic masochistic if he was himself.
>
> (p. 124)

The final pages of **'Life-Story'** recount the reader's role in giving life to the work and to its implied author's act of creation. Both reader and writer read and compose the work; their activities are analogous and mutually essential.

'Lost in the Funhouse' reflects in greater detail the processes of creation and reception as well as their context. Ambrose's imagination translates external stimuli and autobiography into stories. His union with the narrator-writer who has theoretical, if not practical, knowledge of literary techniques adds craftsmanship to the creative act. However, the story also supports parodically the view of the author as elect. Although Ambrose in his adolescent awkwardness is more anti-hero than hero, his sensitivity, introversion, vocation, and celestial name set him apart from other men.

This dual perception of the writer as *poeta* and priest mirrors the parody of the classical views of the writer conducted throughout the book. The writer whom Ambrose becomes inherits his imagination as well as the narrator's concern for, and difficulty with, technical devices; **'Glossolalia'** plays 'divine inspiration' against medium and message; Anonymous has his Muses. Unsuccessful relationships with the opposite sex, jealousy of a successful member of the same sex, creative difficulties and suicidal despair plague every author figure of the work. In the end the artist, *poeta* and priest, a solitary solipsist, creates his world and himself.

As auto-critic the narrator-writer of **'Lost in the Funhouse'** becomes receiver of his own text and illustrates the reading process, while satirizing the excesses of Modernist literature. His criticism of the lack of direction, prolixity, futility or implausibility of his narration reflects the teleological orientation of reading as well as reader expectations of coherence, logic, intelligibility, and verisimilitude. His discussion of technical devices, including those derived from the print medium, period convention, and genre norms, is meta-exegetical, revealing textual signposts for the reader. Like the old man who betrays Ambrose, these *points de repère* may be deceptive and often are in Modernist literature. Just as Ambrose realizes too late the importance of the process of going through the funhouse rather than the getting through, Modernist literature deflects reader attention from the end of the work to its operation.

The story 'Title' mirrors the prototype for the critical side of *Lost in the Funhouse* as well as the origin of its patterning, Barth's 'The Literature of Exhaustion.' The fiction of 'Title' imitates its own genesis and that of *Lost in the Funhouse*: the idea of progressive regeneration as applied to literature; its development to this point and its projected end; its *raison d'être,* the exhaustion of literature; and its purpose, to find new ways of treating old themes.

This emphasis on literary means echoes a Modernist concern with structures of composition and results in a variety of textual *mises en abyme*. A *mise en abyme* of the print-oral dichotomy, such as 'Autobiography' where the tape-recorded fiction supposedly narrates itself though the author is its father and the machine its mother, draws attention to the linguistic nature of fiction. Here the medium is secondary to the verbal code. 'Autobiography' mirrors Barth's contemporary technological resolution of the print-oral dichotomy, the creation of prose fiction for 'Print, Tape, Live Voice.' Barth retains the prose narrative format but writes works to be read, listened to, or performed.

In whatever format, Barth writes works to be understood. The importance of the text as a coded message which can be deciphered is emphasized by the linguistic theme explored in 'Ambrose His Mark' and in 'Glossolalia.' The illusion of senselessness in *Lost in the Funhouse* is only an illusion—Ambrose may get lost in his own reflection but he eventually sees his vocation clearly through a Modernist existential *prise de conscience*. The six passages of 'Glossolalia' have greater meaning when one recognizes the speakers thanks to Barth's Seven Additional Author's Notes. Only the fifth message remains unintelligible. Thus 'Glossolalia' ultimately reflects Roman Jakobson's theory of the necessity of a common code between enunciator and receiver for there to be linguistic, literary or narrative communication. The author's concluding statement, 'The senselessest babble, could we ken it, might disclose a dark message, or prayer' (p. 112), a parody of Modernist literature and the attitude into which it has trained reader and critic, paradoxically proves true.

Barth here also challenges the conventional operation of the *mise en abyme,* at least Dällenbach's explanation thereof, since to understand the first meaning of the reflection in 'Glossolalia,' one must grasp its second-order significance. His modernist irreverence for tradition inverts the common Modernist device employed conventionally in Henry James' 'Real Thing,' for example.

Reflection as a device forms the object of textual *mises en abyme* in Barth's work—introversion turns back on itself to discuss its own operation. This occurs most specifically in the title story, 'Lost in the Funhouse,' when Ambrose looks into the funhouse mirror:

> In the funhouse mirror-room you can't see yourself go on forever, because no matter how you stand, your head gets in the way. Even if you had a glass periscope, the image of your eye would cover up the thing you really wanted to see.
>
> (pp. 81-2)

The inevitable imposition of the real reflecting object makes pure reflection impossible, reinforcing the union of self-reflection and mimesis, as we have seen at the macro-textual level. Similarly, literary reflection remains linked to mimesis by the posited reality of the reflecting object or at least by the perceiver of the reflection.

As the 'story' points out in 'Autobiography,' time lapse and the properties of memory also prevent perfect reflection: 'I'm his [the author's] bloody mirror! Which is to say, upon reflection I reverse and distort him' (p. 34). 'Echo' specifies the distortion since the nymph 'edits, heightens, mutes, turns others' words to her end' (p. 97). More important, self-reflection leads away from self-knowledge to self-destruction whether as victim of parody, misrepresentation, or the union of reflected, perceiver and reflection as in Narcissus' case. Neither omniscience, perspective, nor voice can provide reliable knowledge of fiction. Reflection needs mimesis. Barth concretizes here the third possibility for regenerating the novel as he describes it in 'Title.' He turns 'ultimacy against itself to make something new and valid, the essence whereof would be the impossibility of making something new' (p. 106). He regenerates the device of reflection through the same dialectical pattern which informs the work, and in so doing does make something new.

Self-reference in *Lost in the Funhouse* exhibits the characteristics of Modernist narrative introversion—it includes self-conscious narration, it presents the work as a structured whole, it emphasizes form and it approaches symbolism through the Proteus figure. However, when *Lost in the Funhouse* holds a mirror to introversion, it unites with the other, mimetic, tendency of Modernism. *Lost in the Funhouse* makes explicit and urgent in practice what Modernist theory already knew but neglected—that literature cannot entirely destroy or divorce itself from an alternate reality.[15] In turning inward to regenerate itself, *Lost in the Funhouse*'s auto-representation proves that 'structural introversion is more than the narcissistic contemplation of art.'[16] It shows how narrative introversion surpasses the 'danger of decadence from inbreeding' and the 'danger of avoiding the force and pressure of history' to regenerate Modernism through its own regeneration.[17]

Our initial question then was not mere rhetoric. When Modernism reflects on itself, it allows introversion to revitalize literature and through union with its mimetic counterpart, to avoid the blank of silence. An entertaining text in its own right, *Lost in the Funhouse* mirrors the literary past and prefigures new directions for the literary future.[18]

Notes

1. Our concept of *mise en abyme* follows Lucien Dällenbach's theory in *Le Récit spéculaire: essai sur la mise en abyme* (Paris: Seuil 1977).

2. John Barth, *Lost in the Funhouse: Fiction for Print, Tape, Live Voice* (New York: Bantam Books 1969). References to this work are given in the text in brackets.

3. Beverly Gray Bienstock, 'Lingering on the Autognostic Verge: John Barth's *Lost in the Funhouse*,' *Modern Fiction Studies,* 19 (Spring 1973) 69-78; Gerald Gillespie, 'Barth's *Lost in the Funhouse*: Short Story Text in its Cyclic Context,' *Studies in Short Fiction,* 12 (1975) 223-30; Michael Hinden, '*Lost in the Funhouse*: Barth's Use of the Recent Past,' *Twentieth Century Literature,* 19 (1973) 107-18.

4. See Damian Grant, *Realism* (London: Methuen 1970), on conscientious and conscious realism.

5. David Morrell, *John Barth: An Introduction* (University Park: Pennsylvania State University Press 1976) 95

6. Gillespie, op. cit.; Christopher D. Morris, 'Barth and Lacan: The World of the Moebius Strip,' *Critique,* 17 (1975) 69-77; Gordon E. Slethaug, 'Barth's Refutation of the Idea of Progress,' *Critique,* 13, No. 3 (1972), 11-29

7. Robert Scholes and Robert Kellogg, *The Nature of Narrative* (London: Oxford University Press 1966) 15

8. Ibid., 16

9. John Barth, 'The Literature of Exhaustion,' *The Atlantic Monthly,* 220 (August 1967) 29-34

10. Ibid., 31

11. Ibid., 31

12. Ibid., 32

13. Ibid., 31

14. Ibid., 32

15. José Ortega y Gasset, 'The Dehumanization of Art,' in *The Idea of the Modern in Literature and the Arts,* ed. Irving Howe (New York: Horizon Press 1967)

16. J. Fletcher and Malcolm Bradbury, 'The Introverted Novel,' in *Modernism: 1890-1930,* ed. Malcolm Bradbury and James McFarlane (Middlesex: Penguin Books 1976) 414

17. Ibid., 414

18. Linda Hucheon draws similar conclusions in her recent monograph *Narcissistic Narrative: The Metafictional Paradox* (Waterloo: Wilfrid Laurier University Press 1980). This work takes a broader look at contemporary auto-referential fiction including analyses of *Lost in the Funhouse* and others of Barth's publications.

Marilyn Edelstein (essay date spring 1984)

SOURCE: Edelstein, Marilyn. "The Function of Self-Consciousness in John Barth's *Chimera*." *Studies in American Fiction* 12, no. 1 (spring 1984): 99-108.

[*In the following essay, Edelstein argues that Barth addresses "linguistic and artistic self-consciousness" as well as "human self-consciousness" in* Chimera.]

Much recent American fiction has become increasingly self-conscious, displaying an awareness of itself as fiction, as artifice that diminishes the role of a central human consciousness or self in the fiction. The fictional *process* is in the foreground of much contemporary fiction where the narrative human *presence* once was. Yet, both fictional process and human presence serve similar structural functions within the text, which suggests that the creation of a fiction resembles the creation of a human self, real or imaginary. The provisional reality of self-conscious fiction is like the provisional reality of the "post-modern" self, prone to self-questioning, constituted by process rather than substance, multiple, changeable, perhaps even illusory.

John Barth's novel *Chimera* is a supremely self-conscious fiction. Barth's use of the three central narrators in the three sections of the novel—the *Dunyazadiad,* the *Perseid,* and the *Bellerophoniad*—foregrounds the relationship between diffusion of identity and artistic self-consciousness within the novel. Although an individual, by definition, should not be susceptible to division or separation into parts without losing its identity, the narrators in *Chimera,* like the novel's sections, are all divisible, incomplete, or inter-changeable. Definitions of identity often include elements such as continuity, functional unity, consciousness, recognitive memory, personality, or awareness. Yet, there is still a question about the relation of a self so constituted to *self*-conscious fiction.

Both "self" and "identity" are dual terms, used both to indicate a presumed psychological center or unity and as reflexive, even mathematical terms. "Self-consciousness" can mean consciousness of a Self, of an "I," of a core unity, or it can refer to the consciousness of itself by an entity (a person, a novel). In the case of a person, both meanings can come together, since consciousness can only presume a self by knowing itself. In the case of a text, reconciling both meanings becomes more problematic. If a text flaunts its own artificiality, if its even provisional reality is constantly being undercut, if its author's presence *in* and not just *behind* the text is constantly being emphasized, it is commonly called a "self-conscious" text. The cohesive function, the underlying, organizing intelligence, whether of the author or of the narrator, inscribed within the text can be considered the "self" of the text. If this textually created self is in some ways analogous to a human self, perhaps the human self is only a "linguistic configuration rather than an ontological entity."[1]

Prior to the advent of modernism, neither the existence of a substantial human self nor the value of the literary project itself was generally questioned explicitly within a work of fiction (except in precociously self-conscious novels such as *Don Quixote* or *Tristram Shandy*). The twentieth-century suspicion of the concept of stable identity was bound to have profound effects on the shape of fiction. While many modernist works explored the human self and human consciousness in bold new ways, in many "post-modernist" works an intensified linguistic and artistic self-consciousness seems to have supplanted concern with human self-consciousness. Yet, in the work of a writer like John Barth, the two concerns frequently intersect.

The issue of representation itself is raised when one tries to understand the relationship of a human self (or even a human being) to its seeming counterpart in the fictional character. Obviously, a three-dimensional physical organism bears little overt relation to a series of written signs. In fact, one of the reservations a writer like Barth has about the usual depiction of human beings as characters in fiction derives from his awareness of the reductionism implicit in linguistic formulations of experience. As Albert Cook has written, "language, for the knower of the self, serves as a kind of trap, and

also as a kind of instrument, the only one at his disposal. As soon as a self-awareness objectifies itself into words, the words stand with their own syntactic order, their own associations, out and away from the self and its awareness."[2]

The novel as a genre assumed some of the characteristics of the autobiography, with its insistence on, and assertion of, the "self" of the autobiographer. Because the novel developed from a story-telling, narrative tradition, it has always consisted essentially of the telling of a story by one "person" to another, who may exist within the fiction as another character or outside the fiction as the reader. The use of a first-person narrator as the central percipient was one means of obviating certain epistemological problems because, as Barth noted in an interview, "[we] still imagine ourselves to be characters, and our lives are influenced by other people around us whom we see as characters and our relations to whom we perceive in a dramatic, in a dramatical, way."[3] Since most people feel their own consciousness at the center of their perceptions, the use of a first-person narrator within the novel can create at least a fictional self within the work. People can go on believing in a concept of subjectivity, seemingly discredited by philosophers and theoreticians, just as they live their own lives in "calendar and clock time" and believe in cause and effect, even if physicists or philosophers have discredited both concepts.[4]

It may be impossible to get rid of the last remnant of the subject, as the selecting, shaping, interpreting consciousness behind the work, without creating pure chaos (unorganized phonemes, complete nonsense), although a conscious, language-using creature might not be able to create pure randomness anyway. Recent writers like Robbe-Grillet or Barthelme may attempt to reduce this human presence to a minimum, rejecting the anthrocentrism of earlier fiction in a struggle for linguistic or phenomenological purity (although, as Barth has very astutely pointed out, Robbe-Grillet and others may merely be replacing earlier versions of realism with a far "hipper" "epistemological realism").[5] Barth, however, wants the novel to be technically innovative but also, as the Genie puts it in *Chimera,* "'seriously, even passionately, *about* some things as well.'"[6] Barth considers Beckett and Borges as among those few current writers "whose artistic thinking is as hip as any French new-novelist's, but who manage nonetheless to speak eloquently and memorably to our still-human hearts and conditions, as the great artists have always done."[7] Barth considers Marquez's novel *One Hundred Years of Solitude* a postmodernist masterpiece precisely because it is "not only artistically admirable but humanly wise, lovable, literally marvelous."[8] Barth himself, at his best, manages to be eloquent, wise, and artistically sophisticated.

Self-consciousness thus becomes both a philosophical and a technical concern in *Chimera.* Barth uses named, finally recognizable, if not always stable or unified, first-person central narrators in the novel. First-person narration, in addition to solving epistemological problems, generally gives the reader a sense of familiarity, an expectation that a story is being told by a person with whose experience the reader can perhaps identify, in whose reality the reader can believe, at least for the duration of the fiction. Yet, Barth uses Protean characters (like the shape-shifter Polyeidus), multiple layers of narrative structure, differing perspectives on the same events (as in Durrell's *Alexandria Quartet*), shifting narrators, and changing names for the same characters (as in many of Beckett's works) to inhibit this complacent process of identification, to force the reader to grapple with the complexities of life and language as Barth himself has. The reader's role is complicated when the writer's role is complicated, as it is in *Chimera,* in which the narrators are painfully aware of themselves as the "writers" of the books that are being read. Yet, each tale within the work has more than one writer (and speaker) in it; the authorship of the Text must finally be attributed to the ultimate puppeteer, Barth. Fictional "reality" thus becomes as problematic as "reality" itself (if, in fact, the two are different, which Barth has contested).

The tales in *Chimera* are being told in retrospect, to the reader and to another character within each tale. The stories are told as if they are taking place in the present tense, although the central events in the story have already taken place (all except the outermost frame, which occurs in the "present"). Memory thus plays a primary role in the narrative structure of the novel, and it is also an integral aspect of most definitions of the self. As Louis Dupré has noted, "the self can only be remembered. It is present merely as the *re-* of representation."[9] Thus the self assumes the status of any signified, fated always to be re-presented, never simply present.

The transcendence of time through art becomes an especially poignant problem in a novel two-thirds of which (the *Perseid* and the *Bellerophoniad*) concern the heroes' attempts in mid-life to recover, renew, and write about their pasts. The first section (the *Dunyazadiad*) makes the connection between story-telling and mortality even more explicit, for the archetypal story-teller Scheherezade can only live as long as she can tell new tales (and within the *Dunyazadiad,* she can only "live" as long as her new master Barth deigns to continue his story of her). The characters themselves try to negate time, aging, and the imminence of death through love (and through story-telling). The analogy Barth draws in the novel between the narrative process and a love relation reveals once again how he explores "human" concerns through narrative technique.

Chimera, though ostensibly a set of tales, is really a novel "whose 'plot' is not the continuity of what happens to a sustained character, but what happens to the story-teller himself as he moves through the series."[10] Like the mythical chimera, part lion, goat, and serpent, the novel is composed of three vitally connected, if at first seemingly disparate, parts. Each of the three tales is self-referential and mutually referential; each has one or more frame tales and one or more tales-within-tales; each tale reflects on artifice, on mortality, on the nature of fiction, on the nature of love, and on the nature of "reality" (a term Barth almost always uses with quotation marks). Both Bellerophon and Perseus are supposed to be extra-fictionally immortal, Perseus as a constellation and Bellerophon as the text of the *Bellerophoniad*; Dunyazade and her sister Scheherezade are immortal story-tellers. Of course, all of the characters are immortal because they are transfigured into art (and inscribed in language) by Barth. Perseus and Bellerophon, especially, seem to have more linguistic reality than "human" reality, even within the world of the novel. The characters themselves call their own "reality" into question, wondering if they do exist only in words. Scheherezade says,

> "Little Doony . . . pretend this whole situation is the plot of a story we're reading, and you and I and Daddy and the King are all fictional characters. In this story, Scheherezade finds a way to change the King's mind about women and turn him into a gentle, loving husband. It's not hard to imagine such a story, is it? Now, no matter what way she finds—whether it's a magic spell or a magic story with the answer in it or a magic anything—it comes down to particular words in the story we're reading, right? And those words are made from the letters of our alphabet: a couple-dozen squiggles we can draw with this pen. This is the key, Doony! And the treasure, too, if we can only get our hands on it! It's as if—as if the key to the treasure *is* the treasure!"

(p. 8)

At these properly enigmatic words, the Genie (Barth) appears, for he has had the same revelation at the same moment, while trying to find his way out of a writer's block. This is how all magic formulae (if not all words) operate, the magic syllables make the absent thing present. This magic operation may, in fact, be the key (to the treasure) that is itself the treasure. The words make Barth and Scheherezade one, for they are both conscious of exactly the same thought at exactly the same moment. The words produce action, however, as well as thought; thus, the magical potency of words is implicitly affirmed, even though elsewhere in the book it may be explicitly denied. The tale of Bellerophon tells "how he rode the heroic cycle and was recycled. Loosed at last from mortal speech, he turned into written words: Bellerophonic letters afloat between two worlds, forever betraying, in combinations and recombinations, the man they forever represent" (p. 138). The power of letters both to betray and to re-present, make present once again, is here asserted.

Christopher Morris delineates two important motifs in Barth's work: first, "the wholly contingent nature of naming (a condition into which, as Barth reiterates, one is born without choice); second, the rupture between the visual and perceptible world, centered in the self, and the world of language, which exists without a center."[11] The power of language to reveal and to conceal, to trap and to re-present, to make illusions and to shatter them gives it its dual character as presence and absence. Perseus and Medusa, at the end of the *Perseid,* now both constellations, are at ease with the condition of their representation. Perseus says, "I'm content. So with this issue, our net estate: to have become, like the noted music of our tongue, these silent, visible signs; to *be* the tale I tell to those with eyes to see and understanding to interpret; to raise you up forever and know that our story will never be cut off, but nightly rehearsed as long as men and women read the stars" (pp. 133-34). Perseus is preserved, conserved in signs; he can be "read" by stargazers; he is satisfied. Yet, Bellerophon also kills the Chimera with a pencil; words can be weapons and destroyers, too. Words can also bring self-knowledge (even knowledge that one's self consists of words).

In *Chimera,* as in much contemporary fiction, "the self is not to be found in the personality of the author or narrator or reader but rather . . . in the interrelationship of the three a new collective identity is created."[12] Using mythic characters in two of the three tales, and legendary characters (and legendary story-tellers) in the first, is a means of reinforcing this transpersonal vision of the self. As Hans Meyerhoff notes, "the quest for mythical roots may not be a quest for personal identity but for an identification with mankind in general. Myths may convey a sense of temporal continuity and structural unity for the 'self' of man."[13]

Chimera is truly a meta-novel, a novel about its own creation, a parable and parody of its own coming into being. The characters are supremely, almost paralyzingly self-conscious, as is the fiction as a whole. The narrators are aware of themselves as telling stories within stories within stories. It is difficult to tell which are the largest frame layers and which merely subtexts. Barth himself makes repeated appearances (as the Genie, as Jerome B. Bray). The *Bellerophoniad* begins with the reading of the *Perseid.* Parts of the stories repeat motifs and even whole sentences from Barth's earlier works. The Text and the subtexts all discourse on themselves. Bellerophon even becomes the pages of his own story floating down onto Barth's Maryland marshes. Barth's Genie in the *Dunyazadiad* speculates on whether a clever writer might "'conceive a series of, say, *seven* concentric stories-within-stories, so arranged

that the climax of the innermost would precipitate that of the next tale out, and that of the next, et cetera'" (p. 24). Barth himself writes this imagined text in *Chimera.* The novel truly is a chimera, a grotesque and incongruous artistic work, an absurd creation of the imagination. All its narrative tricks serve to emphasize the artifice of the work, the hand of the author wielding his pencil over the blank pages. Barth tries to decipher the essence of story-telling *through* the act of story-telling. The repetition and patterning essential in myth, and necessary for any systematic construction, dominate in this novel.

Perseus is a true mythic hero, even though he and his story are self-centered and involuted. He renews his life by re-living it ironically (and by re-telling it ironically). His heroic immortality is assured, first by his having been made a constellation, then by having the story of his story become part of a story by Barth. Bellerophon is a failed hero; in fact, his heroic identity is found to be a lie when he discovers that he is not the demigod Bellerus but his human brother Deliades; the *Bellerophoniad* is about a phony Bellerophon. Mirroring his failed heroic career, his stories fail, his lovemaking generally fails, and, finally, Barth's own *Bellerophoniad* seems to fail (perhaps intentionally, to extend the reflected Bellerophonic failure as far as possible). Dunyazade is aware of herself as a runner-up to her sister's title as story-teller extraordinaire. Barth is interested in the struggle of a person, or a fictional character, to become what he or she is by recognizing what he or she has (or has not) been, and where he or she is going (or failing to go). Perseus says to Calyxa, "'thus this endless repetition of my story: as both protagonist and author, so to speak, I thought to overtake with understanding my present paragraph as it were by examining my paged past, and thus pointed, proceed serene to the future's sentence'" (pp. 80-81). Barth seems to have viewed his *Chimera*-writing as a similar process for himself at mid-life.

Perseus' story is a spiral because he does transcend his past and realize his immortal aesthetic identity; Bellerophon's story is a circle because he "never does transcend himself, merely repeats himself rather than recycles."[14] Just as Todd and Jacob, in Barth's first two novels, are disabled by excessive habits of self-reflection, so Bellerophon's phonic involution disables him.

The one hope for escape from disabling self-consciousness in *Chimera* seems to be in the relational world of love. The first story involves Dunyazade and her spouse Shah Zaman, and Scheherezade and her spouse, King Shahryar. The penultimate frame of the story involves Dunyazade telling the other stories to the man she loves. The tale of Perseus involves his love for Calyxa and Andromeda and, finally, Medusa (who can turn men to stone but with whom Perseus is turned into stars and words). Bellerophon is involved, rather unsuccessfully, in various love affairs (with Melanippe and Philonoë, primarily) but seems incapable of transcending his self-absorption in order to love genuinely. With the increase in self-consciousness (of both characters and text) from the first tale to the last comes a decrease in the characters' capacity for monogamy, an increase in the number of lovers, a decrease in the number of genuinely loved. The ***Dunyazadiad*** consists almost exclusively of dialogue, of conversations between lovers; there seems to be almost no frame until the very end of the tale, when a writer (most likely Barth himself) appears. Perseus addresses Medusa, his beloved, from their stars at the end of the tale, while Bellerophon addresses the reader (in fact, becoming the text in midsentence).

Scheherezade and Barth seem to be having a love affair, too. He gives her the stories that save her life for 1,001 nights; actually, her stories allow him to write *this* text, thus enabling him to "live" in words. He collapses time by re-presenting himself as the master of an ancient well-beloved predecessor. The text itself collapses the distance between it and the reader, by involving the reader in the love-relation of interpretation. As the Genie says to Scheherezade,

> "narrative, in short—and here they were again in full agreement—was a love-relation, not a rape: its success depended upon the reader's consent and cooperation, which she could withhold or at any moment withdraw; also upon her own combination of experience and talent for the enterprise, and the author's ability to arouse, sustain, and satisfy her interest—an ability on which his figurative life hung as surely as Scheherezade's literal"

>   (p. 26)

Perhaps because Perseus *can* love, can enter into true relation to another, he becomes both words and star, forever able to live with his beloved Medusa. Bellerophon becomes a text, a fiction, because he is so aware of his own self-creation, so perpetually concerned with his own metaphorical existence, that he is incapable of relating to an Other. He says, at the end of the novel, "I hate this, World! It's not at all what I had in mind for Bellerophon. It's a beastly fiction, ill-proportioned, full of longueurs, lumps, lacunae, a kind of monstrous mixed metaphor—" (p. 308). Bellerophon often speaks of himself in the third person; he objectifies his own existence in his obsessive search for its meaning. He makes his own consciousness a text for consciousness to read, but he cannot avoid the trap of solipsism.

Yet, the self-consciousness of the novel itself, apart from contributing to an extremely funny and brilliant book, serves a purpose and does not finally disable the fiction. Barth believes one should "acknowledge and embrace the artificial aspect of art, which you can't get rid of anyway."[15] He also refers to a well-known statement by Borges that "those moments in literature when the characters within a work begin to comment on, or be aware of, the fiction that they're in disturb us because such moments remind us of the fiction that *we're* in."[16] As Tony Tanner has said of Barth's novels, "if there is no one fixed 'reality' then the self can improvise a theoretically endless succession of roles to play *in* the world, just as the author can invent an 'endless succession of names' *for* the world."[17] The endless spirallings of a reflexive fictional creation produce the sense of a world with infinite possibilities, both within and without the fiction. As John Stark notes, "the main kind of process in Barth's work is artistic. Because of their meandering plots and talkative narrators his books seem to be open-ended almost as if they were being created right before the reader."[18] They *are* being created in front of the reader; the process of fictional creation is made as transparent as possible (given the great number of tricks the Genie Barth has up his sleeve) in order to reveal a mind at work, shaping language, creating fictional equivalents of human selves, mimicking gods making worlds and peopling them.

As Robert Alter has pointed out, the creation of art, even self-conscious art, is still a gesture demonstrating "human order against a background of chaos and darkness, and it is the tension between artifice and that which annihilates artifice that gives the finest self-conscious novels their urgency in the midst of play."[19] In recent fiction, self-consciousness within the text engages issues outside the text. As Frederick J. Hoffman notes, "the modern philosophical hero is almost invariably a split self: the self who exists and the self who reflects upon his role as an existing being."[20] Similarly, the work of fiction both exists as an aesthetically enjoyable object to be read and experienced, and also comments upon its existence as such an object; by so doing, perhaps it can encourage its readers to reflect on their own existence, to explore the relations between self-creation and aesthetic creation. As Barth himself has written, art "may both inspire and reflect" cultural changes.[21] Barth manages to explore larger personal, philosophical, psychological, and cultural concerns (love, sexual roles, aging, youthful ideals, mortality) through literary innovation.

By creating works wherein the very identities of the characters are in constant doubt or flux or self-questioning, books whose sequences of events yield and require multiple interpretations, whose multiple layers of narrative both hide and manifest multiple layers of reality, writers like Barth explore the need for self-definition, for creation of individually meaningful existence, for individually defined reality. Readers must create unity, sense, and structure from the text, just as they must from their own experience. As participants in the hermeneutical act required by a work such as *Chimera,* which manifests its own processes of creation, readers are assisted in their own processes of self-creation.

Notes

1. Robert Detweiler, "Theological Trends of Postmodern Fiction," *Journal of the American Academy of Religion,* 44 (1976), 229.

2. Albert Cook, *Prisms: Studies in Modern Literature* (Bloomington: Indiana Univ. Press, 1967), p. 152.

3. Joe David Bellamy, "Having It Both Ways," *The New Fiction: Interviews with Innovative American Writers,* ed. Joe David Bellamy (Urbana: Univ. of Illinois Press, 1974), pp. 15-16.

4. Bellamy, p. 16.

5. Bellamy, p. 15.

6. John Barth, *Chimera* (New York: Random House, 1972), p. 28. All further references to this work appear in the text.

7. John Barth, "The Literature of Exhaustion," *The American Novel Since World War II,* ed. Marcus Klein (Greenwich: Fawcett, 1969), p. 270.

8. John Barth, "The Literature of Replenishment," *Atlantic Monthly* (Jan., 1980), p. 71.

9. Louis Dupré, "Alienation and Redemption Through Time and Memory: An Essay on Religious Time Consciousness," *Journal of the American Academy of Religion,* 43 (1975), 675.

10. Frank D. McConnell, *Four Postwar American Novelists: Bellow, Mailer, Barth, and Pynchon* (Chicago: Univ. of Chicago Press, 1977), pp. 118-19.

11. Christopher Morris, "Barth and Lacan: The World of the Moebius Strip," *Critique,* 17 (1975), 71.

12. Detweiler, p. 230.

13. Hans Meyerhoff, *Time in Literature* (Berkeley: Univ. of California Press, 1960), p. 82.

14. David Morrell, *John Barth: An Introduction* (University Park: Pennsylvania State Univ. Press, 1976), p. 151.

15. Bellamy, p. 15.

16. Bellamy, p. 10. The reference is to Jorge Luis Borges, "Magies partielles due *Quichotte,*" *Les temps modernes,* 10 (1955), 2130; the passage Barth cites has been translated in numerous works.

17. Tony Tanner, *City of Words: American Fiction 1950-1970* (New York: Harper and Row, 1971), p. 230.

18. John O. Stark, *The Literature of Exhaustion: Borges, Nabokov, and Barth* (Durham: Duke Univ. Press, 1974), p. 148.

19. Robert Alter, *Partial Magic: The Novel as a Self-Conscious Genre* (Berkeley: Univ. of California Press, 1975), p. 235.

20. Frederick J. Hoffman, *The Mortal No: Death and the Modern Imagination* (Princeton: Princeton Univ. Press, 1964), p. 319.

21. "Literature of Replenishment," p. 69.

E. P. Walkiewicz (essay date 1986)

SOURCE: Walkiewicz, E. P. "'Water-Message.'" In *John Barth,* pp. 84-109. Boston, Mass.: Twayne Publishers, 1986.

[*In the following essay, Walkiewicz maintains that the Möbius strip "Frame-Tale" that opens* Lost in the Funhouse *serves as an analogy for the entire collection, which cycles back to its beginning in the final story, "Anonymiad."*]

If a significant segment of the reading public has come to associate Barth's name with innovation, experimentation, and exhaustion, his fiction with self-reference and self-indulgence, this reputation is based to a large extent on the two books that appeared in the decade following the publication of *Giles Goat-Boy.* Timing seems to have had a great deal to do with this, for *Lost in the Funhouse* and *Chimera* were issued in a period during which a number of factors conjoined to insure that the works would become both highly visible and susceptible to a certain kind of interpretation. *The Sot-Weed Factor* had earned Barth a fair amount of critical attention and something akin to a cult following, *Giles Goat-Boy* had won him a much wider audience, and revised editions of his first three books had been published by Doubleday in 1967, generating a new wave of reviews. Moreover, by the late 1960s and early 1970s, developments in literary criticism had begun to catch up with developments in contemporary fiction, the rapid proliferation of critical studies on earlier authors had encouraged growing numbers of scholars to focus on the work of contemporary writers, and the popularization of the ideas of Marshall McLuhan had created an atmosphere conducive to an acceptance of the "intermedia" experimentation of *Lost in the Funhouse.* Finally, even if many of them, as Barth claims, widely misinterpreted it, a good number of readers took his essay on Borges as a prologemena to any future fiction, linked **"The Literature of Exhaustion"** with the stories and novellas Barth produced in the same period, and came to view the latter, therefore, as representing the clearest and most definitive embodiments of his aesthetic and metaphysics.

While the validity and usefulness of such valuations are debatable, what is more certain is that *Lost in the Funhouse* and *Chimera* are integral parts of the continuum that is Barth's oeuvre. The former, for instance, continues, and perhaps in a way completes and reverses ("Unwind, rewind, replay"), the retrograde recapitulation of the evolution of the species Homo poeticus that characterizes the development of Barth's earlier fiction. Having previously parodied realism, reorchestrated some of the conventions of the eighteenth-century novel, and created a comic Old Testament, in *Lost in the Funhouse* he seemingly brings not only the novel but literature itself full circle by taking us back "to the oral tradition out of which literature comes."[1] Whether it is interpreted as an authorial pretense or a statement of authorial intention, the "Author's Note" to the volume indicates that many of its "members" are meant for "recorded authorial voice," or "live authorial voice," "live or recorded voices," or to be "read as if heard so."[2] *Dunyazadiad* in *Chimera,* of course, reaches back through the tradition in a different way, playing upon one of the most famous oral storytelling situations recorded in literature.

Barth's "Fiction for Print, Tape, Live Voice" (the subtitle of *Lost in the Funhouse*), moreover, is just as progressive as regressive, for in "exploring the possibilities" opened up by the use of tapes he is suggesting that one may escape literary exhaustion not only by "investigating roots" but also by employing the fruits of modern technology. Exploiting the potential of the electronic medium, he has indicated, is "a way of having it both ways." On the one hand, you "have the authorial voice, after all, telling the stories when you work on tape. On the other hand, unlike purely oral literature, a tape has some of the virtues of print: it's interruptable and referable. You can stop a tape, as you can't stop a live storyteller, and you can go back to a particular point—two things that you *can* do on the page that you can't do in the movie theatre, for example, and that you couldn't do with the live oral tradition very easily." Like this experimentation with the means of presentation, the use of myth in both *Lost in the Funhouse* and *Chimera* also represents a kind of progressive regression. Whereas *The Sot-Weed Factor* and *Giles Goat-Boy* are informed by the pattern of the "monomyth" and replete with allusions to mythological figures and situations, in composing many of the pieces in the two later volumes Barth decided to reject the "mythopoeically retrograde" approach of writing "about our daily experiences in order to point up to the myths," choosing instead "to address" the "mythic archetypes" more "directly."[3]

Although the two books are linked to and advance Barth's earlier work in numerous other ways, such as the facts that both play a great number of new variations on the triangle and on the principle that ontogeny

recapitulates phylogeny, what is perhaps most apparent to the reader is the seemingly more blatant emphasis on resonance and increased preoccupation with "the secret adventures of order." One of the "Seven Additional Author's Notes" that appear in the Bantam edition of *Lost in the Funhouse,* for instance, states that the "regnant idea" behind the author's indicating "ideal media" of "presentation" is "the unpretentious one of turning as many aspects of the fiction as possible—the structure, the narrative viewpoint, the means of presentation, in some instances the process of composition and/or recitation as well as of reading or listening—into dramatically relevant emblems of the theme" (x). Its fourteen pieces, the author tells us, "are meant to be received 'all at once'" and to be perceived as constituting "neither a collection nor a selection, but a series" (ix). The first of them is an emblematic **"Frame-Tale,"** and many play with such patterns as the "regressus in infinitum" (114). The title of *Chimera* emblemizes its nature as "a kind of monstrous mixed metaphor."[4] Here Chinese boxes again abound, and the fictional universe appears to be governed by the principles of numerology. One of its constituent parts, *Perseid,* exhibits a "complicated structure" that is based upon "the Fibonacci series of numbers as it manifests itself in the logarithmic spiral" and that Barth himself once termed "almost, but not quite, completely arbitrary."[5]

A MOEBIUS STRIP

Whereas the geometry of *Perseid* is spiral, the structure of *Lost in the Funhouse,* we are led to believe, is a closed loop. Its **"Frame-Tale"** is a kit for constructing a Moebius strip which the reader is free to regard as "one-, two-, or three-dimensional" (ix). Once it is completed mentally or physically, the loop becomes an emblem of the "Law of Cyclology" and all its corollaries, including the propositions that make up the "monomyth." As a continuous tape, it not only reminds us of the Grand Tutor's "endless tapes" but also suggests the means of presentation of many of the pieces in the book, and it is thus emblematic of Barth's recycling of elements of his own fictions and of the oral-literary tradition. This connection with the tradition is further reinforced by the nature of the message that is both conveyed by and inscribed on the **"Frame-Tale."** For in joining headpiece to tailpiece, the reader helps to bring into being a story that reads "ONCE UPON A TIME THERE WAS A STORY THAT BEGAN ONCE UPON A TIME . . ." (ad infinitum), serves as midwife at the birth of a headless, tailless, and at least theoretically endless tale that may have been conceived as a result of Barth's love affair with Scheherazade.

As a participant in a panel discussion that took place in March of 1975, Barth talked about the ramifications of a typographical error in *Perseid,* stated that he does not know what he has "written when" he has "written a book," and went on to add the following remarks:

My hair was raised (that's a metaphor) when I was doing some homework in *The Thousand and One Nights* for a piece I was writing, and I realized the formula in the Arabic . . . for beginning a story like *The Thousand and One Nights,* after the invocation to Allah, is the following: "There is a book called *The Thousand and One Nights* in which it is written that there was this king Shahryar, this vizier, and his daughter Scheherazade," and the rest. Now we're reading it, and on the page it says: "There is a book called *The Thousand and One Nights* in which it is said. . . ." Where is that book? At that moment I realized that while I thought I was an Aristotelian, I am in fact a Platonist, and that all novelists are practicing Platonists. Because if that book exists anywhere, it is in the heaven of ideas.[6]

If such comments lead us to interpret **"Frame-Tale"** as indicating that the book is but a copy of the Book, what Barth says elsewhere may lead us to interpret it as suggesting that the book is also one that copies itself. In **"The Literature of Exhaustion"** he points out that one of Borges's "frequenter literary allusions is to the 602nd night of *The 1001 Nights,* when, owing to a copyist's error, Scheherazade begins to tell the story of the 1001 nights, from the beginning. Happily, the King interrupts; if he didn't there'd be no 603rd night ever, and while this would solve Scheherazade's problem—which is every story-teller's problem: to publish or perish—it would put the 'outside' author in a bind." The Argentine artificer who, as Barth suspects, "dreamed this whole thing up," himself states the "now infinite and circular" story embraces itself "monstrously," its reiteration representing a "curious danger" to the "transfixed" auditor.[7] What both Barth and Borges find "hairraising" are the ontological questions raised. "Why does it make us uneasy," Borges asks, to know that "the thousand and one nights are within the book of *A Thousand and One Nights*?" The answer, he proposes, is that such "inversions suggest that if the characters in a story can be readers or spectators, then we, their readers or spectators, can be fictitious. In 1833 Carlyle observed that universal history is an infinite sacred book that all men write and read and try to understand, and in which they too are written."[8]

It is these troubling ontological implications that add the twist to Barth's **"Frame-Tale,"** alerting us to the presence in *Lost in the Funhouse* of the phenomenon Douglas R. Hofstadter has labeled "Strange Loopiness." In his fascinating, Pulitzer Prize-winning work *Gödel, Escher, Bach: An Eternal Golden Braid,* Hofstadter indicates that the "'Strange Loop' phenomenon occurs whenever, by moving upwards (or downwards) through the levels of some hierarchical system, we can unexpectedly find ourselves right back where we started." Although Hofstadter examines many "Tangled Hierarchies," or systems "in which a Strange Loop occurs," the one most nearly analogous to *Lost in the Funhouse* is the world of M. C. Escher, the Dutch graphic artist who was himself enamored of the Moebius strip:

In some of his drawings, one single theme can appear on different levels of reality. For instance, one level in a drawing might clearly be recognizable as representing fantasy or imagination; another level would be recognizable as reality. These two levels might be the only explicitly portrayed levels. But the mere presence of these two levels invites the viewer to look upon himself as part of yet another level; and by taking that step, the viewer cannot help getting caught up in Escher's implied chain of levels, in which, for any one level, there is always another level above it of greater "reality," and likewise, there is always a level below "more imaginary" than it is. This can be mind-boggling in itself. However, what happens if the chain of levels is not linear, but forms a loop? What is real, then, and what is fantasy?[9]

Implicit in the "Tangled Hierarchies" of Escher's drawings or Borges' "story-within-the-story turned back upon itself" or Barth's **"Frame-Tale"** is a basic conflict between the finite and the infinite that gives rise to "a strong sense of paradox,"[10] and this is something else that links *Lost in the Funhouse* to Barth's earlier fiction, for, as we have seen, the exposure of the inherent paradoxes in hierarchical systems has always been a useful strategem for him to employ, serving both as a means of creating aesthetic resolution and as an expression of his satiric attitude.

Constituting a "Strange Loop" that bears an affinity to Scheherazade's six hundred and second tale, **"Frame-Tale"** serves, then, as an invitation to lose ourselves in an ontologically perplexing funhouse where distortions of distortions generate finite representations of the infinite and the first and last members of Barth's "series" appear to link up, turning the terminal into the perpetual, the linear into the cyclical. The existence of the "Funhouse," of course, requires the interaction "of three terms—teller, tale, told—each dependent on the other two but not in the same ways" (**"Life-Story,"** 118), and while it offers the possibility of substituting "almost death" for death, its closed loops and infinite regressions threaten, like Scheherazade's ploy, to put not only the "outside" author but the reader/auditor "in a bind." For if Scheherazade is permitted to persist, if **"Frame-Tale"** is permitted to continue along its recursive course, there can be no six hundred and third night ever, Barth's story can never really begin, and to be put in the position of Shahryar, to have one's desire for completeness and consummation perpetually frustrated, may be a less than satisfying experience. By placing his Moebius strip in our hands, where we may turn it until our own exhaustion takes over, Barth may be acknowledging both the necessity of our participation and the limits to our sufferance. Moreover, just as one must ignore the trompe l'oeil in an Escher drawing in order to get caught up in a chain of levels, so too must we avoid noticing that Barth's closed loop is a feat of legerdemain if we are to remain "fixed" and continue repeating the refrain. Handling it according to his instructions, we may find that the illusion has been quickly dispelled, that our attention has almost inevitably been drawn to the Real, to pulp and ink. Discovering that the strip is not multi- but merely three-dimensional, we may also be led to discover the inviolate level that exists below every tangled hierarchy.[11]

LOST IN THE FUNHOUSE

To become convinced that **"Frame-Tale"** is indeed emblematic of the "Funhouse" as a whole, one need only move on to the first piece in the series proper, for **"Night-Sea Journey"** is marked by recycling, depends on a bit of gimmickry, and invites the reader to become enmeshed in a tangle of physical and metaphysical hierarchies. The narrator who both swims in and generates this ocean of story is a spermatozoon, "tale-bearer of a generation" (9). Ontogeny here is the recapitulation of ontology, and "the Heritage" (4) transported is not only genetic but literary and mythic. Barth's choice of narrator is yet another thing that links his work with Sterne's, for in recounting the circumstances of his conception, Tristram Shandy refers to the general sixteenth- and seventeenth-century belief that each spermatozoon contains a homunculus, a little man "as much and as truly our fellow-creature as my Lord Chancellor of England." Speaking of the dangers his "little gentleman" must have faced in his solitary travels, Tristram wonders what might have happened had he "got to his journey's end miserably spent" and "in this sad disorder'd state of nerves . . . laid down a prey to sudden starts, or a series of melancholy dreams and fancies. . . ."[12] Similarly, Barth's own homunculus is "exhausted and dispirited," wonders whether he has lost his senses, and indicates that he too is "vulnerable to dreams" (3, 9). Unlike Sterne's minute voyager, however, Barth's swimmer raves to himself (10); believing that he is "the sole survivor" of a "fell journey" (9), that, like Melville's Ishmael, he "Only" has "escaped alone to tell" (Job 1:14-19), he howls of the loss of "the best swimmers of" his "generation" (4) and questions Job-like the nature and design of his "Maker," the purpose of his trial.

In considering the possibility that he may be a "Hero" and in referring to his trial as a "night-sea journey," the "tale-bearer" engages in a bit of mythopoetizing, defines his absurd swim as the archetypal voyage of the sun, the passage through the earth womb or in the belly of the whale, the descent into the underworld that begins with an entry into a labyrinth or spiral.[13] The maze he has entered is both anatomical and speculative, for as he is drawn inexorably "Herward" (9), he engages in a series of "eschatological" musings that in jest "perhaps illumine certain speculations of Lord Raglan, Carl Jung, and Joseph Campbell" (x), while seeming to illustrate in utero the truth of one of Borges's favorite Platonic utterances: "It is an arduous task to discover the

maker and father of this universe, and, after discovering him, it is impossible to declare him to all men."[14] Just as Plato offers us in dialogue the words of Socrates and Timaeus, Barth's brooder conveys the conjectures of one of his "late companions," including such tangled hierarchies as a universe in which "Makers and swimmers *each generate the other*," or one consisting of "cycles within cycles, either finite or infinite" where "the 'night-sea,' as it were, in which Makers 'swam' and created nightseas and swimmers like ourselves, might be the creation of a larger Maker, Himself one of many, Who in turn et cetera" (8). Like his biblical forebear, however, this garrulous gamete "multiplieth words without knowledge" (Job 35:16). Talking to himself, "to keep" his "reason in" the "awful darkness" (10), he finds that such "recesses from swimming" are what "sustain" him "in the swim" but must acknowledge that the purpose of his journey is ultimately unspeakable; even when mythologized it can be described only in the same abstractions that fail to define the goal of the Goat-Boy's quest: *"consummation, transfiguration, union of contraries, transcension of categories"* (3, 10).

Reciting his companion's hypotheses, he temporarily loses and finds himself in eddies of reflection, his words drowning out for a time the call of selfless "Love," the name we give to "our ignorance of what whips us," what draws us toward a paradoxical consummation that is "the death of us, yet our salvation and resurrection; simultaneously our journey's end, mid-point, and commencement" (4, 10). "Rehearsing" (3; pun surely intended) many of the stances assumed by Barth's earlier imaginative progeny, he attempts to identify himself as an "utterest nay-sayer," as *"he who abjures and rejects the night-sea journey"* (12, 11). Yet, even though he tries to resist, though he hopes to convince his unseen auditor, the being he will become, to stop his hearing against the siren's song and "Make no more," he is compelled to join in repeating the refrain: "Love! Love! Love!" (12). In true Menippean fashion, his speculations buy him time but account for nothing, and if we are cognizant of his "actual nature" and realize that his words are "merely correct" (x), the labyrinth of abstraction becomes transparent, revealing the machinery of natural law, and the tide of the speaker's vagrant prose becomes synonymous with the tragicomic ebb and flow of the Real.

Mythic pretensions, water symbolism, and the extended use of the phylogenetic conceit link **"Night-Sea Journey"** with **"Ambrose His Mark,"** the first of three stories in the series explicitly about the would-be "Maker" Ambrose M _____ (Mensch). While it may be true that it was a colleague who suggested he use "Ambrose," Barth could hardly have settled on a more resonant Christian name for his nascent artist-hero.[15] Not only is it associated with lucidity and illumination (the Ambrose Lightship), hallucination and immortality (ambrosia), but also, via St. Ambrose, with the Word and the Book. A fourth-century bishop of Milan, Ambrose is known for having possessed great oratorical power, composed magnificent hymns, and introduced antiphonal singing and the use of neumes to represent musical notes. Perhaps most significant, he was, Augustine tells us, the first person to read silently, beginning what Borges refers to as "the mental process" that "would culminate, after many centuries, in the predominance of the written word over the spoken one, of the pen over the voice," initiating the "strange art" that "would lead, many years later, to the concept of the book as an end in itself, not as a means to an end."[16]

As mock myth, **"Ambrose His Mark"** begins anew the night-sea journey, revealing the unusual aspects of the archetypal hero's birth and the sign of his vocation, recording the seemingly portentous circumstances surrounding his naming. The spermatozoon may have called for an end to making, to the "'immortality-chain,'" the "cyclic process of incarnation" (8), but if he has generated Ambrose and the tale he bears, flesh and word have been made again. Furthermore, since the "Law of Cyclology" seems to be operant, the apparently synchronous patterns of bildungsroman, *Künstler-roman,* and romance begin to reemerge, if only through parody, as both hero and text develop along generic lines and struggle to make "Sense" (12).

In recalling the eighteenth chapter of *Moby-Dick* ("His Mark"), the title of this first chapter of Ambrose's history suggests that *his* mark, like Queequeg's, is not only a significant sign expressing his secret name, nature, and destiny but also a signature left by his Maker, a key to the mysterious plan that makes sense of both ontogeny and cosmology. When Melville's heathen enrolls among the Pequod's company, he signs his name by making "an exact counterpart of a queer round figure" that is "tattooed upon his arm," one of the many "hieroglyphic marks" written on his body by "a departed prophet and seer" and constituting "a complete theory of the heavens and the earth, and a mystical treatise on the art of attaining truth." Thus, Ishmael tells us, "Queequeg in his own proper person was a riddle to unfold; a wondrous work in one volume" revealing the mysteries not of any particular sect, but the universal truths disclosed to those cosmophilists who have been initiated into "the great and everlasting First Congregation of this whole worshipping world."[17]

Just as Queequeg must bear the misnomers "Quohog" and "Hedgehog," so too must Ambrose respond to "*Honig*" and even "Christine" until a "naming-sign" (30), an extraordinary swarming of bees about the birthmark on his face, leads his relations to name him after the saint who as a child allegedly shared a similar experience. The occurrence seems auspicious since, as Uncle Konrad notes, the swarm of bees that settled on the mouth of Ambrose's namesake was interpreted as an omen indicating that "he'd grow up to be a great speaker" (31). Moreover, the descriptions of a baptismal service being enacted nearby, the etymology of his name itself, and the mythic association of bees and honey with "Her" milk, with the maternal water of life, all appear to mark Ambrose as not only a potential master of words but as a bringer of the Word, an artist-hero capable of completing the night-sea journey to gain immortality by discovering and transmitting the secrets of the Great Mother.

The narrative mode of the story, however, is first-person usual; the tone Ambrose employs in telling his tale is, if anything, *mock*-heroic; and the points of congruence between his account of his birth and naming and Tristram Shandy's own recollection of those significant events may cause one to wonder whether all this "ado" (25) is about nothing, whether Uncle Konrad's notions about the importance of portents have as much relevance as Walter Shandy's theories about names and noses. Both Queequeg's hieroglyphic tattoos and Ambrose's mark may connote gnosis, but the harpooneer cannot "read" the "mysteries" inscribed on his "living parchment"[18] and Ambrose's birthmark is "ambiguous" (32). To "Aunt Rosa" "its three lobes" resemble "the wings and abdomen of a bee in flight," yet she may be misconstrued as calling it a *B* ("'Oh boy,' Konrad sighed. 'Nah, it is a bee! A regular bee! I declare'"), and if it looks like a "purple bee" flying "upside down without benefit of head," it also looks like those anatomical features that make "the *Honig*" an Ambrose and not a Christine (29-30). (*B*, of course, is indeed the signature of his Maker, the jester who has a good deal of fun in the story with double entendres involving drones and stingers.)

Our hero himself notes that it "was to be" his "fate to wonder at that moniker, relish and revile it, ignore it, stare it out of countenance into hieroglyph and gibber," knowing full well that he and his "sign are neither one nor quite two" (32). His use of "moniker" is apt, for it is a term in which the single sign has doubled (monogram and marker), emblemizing his remarks about the duplicity of language, remarks reminiscent of Jacob Horner's own comments about the inaccuracy of words, the necessary distortion involved in assigning names to things. If all the signposts lend themselves to misinterpretation, if the hieroglyphs are ambiguous, then the way through the labyrinth is not clearly marked and Ambrose cannot accurately translate the book of himself. Even if the swarming of bees on his eyes and ears may be taken as a sign that "he'll grow up to see things clear" and not as an indication that he will be blinded by Oedipal innocence, will be stung by or stop his "hearing against Her song" (**"Night-Sea Journey,"** 12), the bees do not light on his mouth as they did on the saint's, and there is nothing to foretoken that his vision will be anything but "unspeakable." Rather than returning him to the font, the womb of guiding "Grace" (25), Ambrose's unorthodox baptism results in his being "weaned not only from" his mother's "milk but from her care" (29). His birthmark, thus, becomes also the mark of his solitude and exile, the mark of Cain. It would be years, he tells us, "before anyone troubled" to complete his "birth certificate, whereon" his "surname was preceded by a blank" (32), a blank he must in a sense fill in himself, perhaps like that other *B*, Henry Burlingame, by asserting, choosing "his gods and devils on the run," and quilling "his own name upon the universe."

The concept that, as Borges puts it, "universal history" is a "Sacred Scripture" we "decipher and write uncertainly," or that "we are the versicles or words or letters of a magic book,"[19] is one of the basic conceits Barth toys with in *Lost in the Funhouse,* and it is again predominant in the second Ambrose story in the series. Corresponding to the stage in the hero's journey known as "the call to adventure," **"Water-Message"** once more confronts the would-be reader of signs with a blankness. Here and in the title story, water imagery carries us not only to the womb-font and Clio's spring, but also to Actaeon's stream, Narcissus's pool, and the Abyss.

Remaining close to Ambrose's point of view and employing a tone that tempers mild mockery with indulgence, a narrator takes us through his subject's preadolescent awakening to *Nature's Secrets* (43). Comic allusions indicate that, in this context at least, the "monomyth" is to be interpreted as an elaborate metaphor for the innocent's initiation into the mundane secrets of Mars and Venus. "Scylla and Charybdis," for example, is the name Ambrose gives to a particularly dangerous part of his route home from school, a place where he must navigate between a vicious "Spitz dog" and "Crazy Alice" (39), and where he one day encounters the belligerent Wimpy James. Escaping this ogre by "playing the clown," and feeling that he is therefore "No man at all," he recoups by imagining himself as "Odysseus steering under anvil clouds" or a Herculean hero borne "aloft to the stars" (41-44).

Ignorant of and insecure about the "facts of life" (40), Ambrose creates fictions in which he performs heroically in worlds that are not the case. Too young to be initiated into "the Occult Order of the Sphinx" and share the sexual knowledge of older boys such as his appropriately named sibling, Peter, he hopes that mastery of the word will be the key to the mysteries of the flesh, pores over *The Book of Knowledge,* turns over names and phrases as if they were magical, transformative. When he discovers a note in a bottle, therefore, he believes that "the word" has "wandered willy-nilly to his threshold," illuminating not only the rites conducted

in the older boys' "Den" at the heart of the "voluptuous" and mysterious "labyrinth" called "the Jungle," but also a "greater vision, vague and splendrous, whereof the sea-wreathed bottle" is "an emblem" (46, 52). If we forge a connection between this "water message" and Barth's spermatozoon, who is also both "vessel and contents" (3), then we may share in Ambrose's anticipation, expect him to receive phylogenetic knowledge and the Great Mother's guidance. Indeed, the narrator leads us on, describing the paper the message is written on in language ("tablet," "thrice," 53), subtly suggestive of hermetic wisdom.

Like those other "Saints," Eben and George, however, Ambrose finds that the world refuses to meet his expectations, for this MS. found in a bottle consists only of a general salutation—"To Whom it may Concern"—and a complimentary close—"Yours Truly" (53). The rest is a blank, and, noticing that "those shiny bits in the paper's texture" are "splinters of wood pulp" (54), he has his attention drawn to the Real, just as ours is if we look closely at the book's **"Frame-Tale."** The demystifying message the sea sends is that it may be taken as a void, an emblem of the world's arbitrariness and finality, of the cruel and seductive call of Love, or a surface in which one may see his reflection, stare at his moniker, and fill in the blank with and by himself. The only apparent alternative to joining in singing "Her" senseless song is to answer "Ambrose, Ambrose, Ambrose, Ambrose!" (**"Ambrose His Mark,"** 32).

These alternatives are more elaborately emblemized in the title story of the series, one of the most widely known and frequently critiqued of Barth's works, and the last of the three pieces focusing on Ambrose per se (three for the trinity, Hermes Trismegistus, the lobes of his mark, etc.). By the time we reach this spot on the loop, ontogeny has progressed to the point of pubescence, the mythic quest to the stage of the hero's trials in the bowels of the labyrinth. The figure who presides over adolescent Ambrose's adventures in the Ocean City funhouse is "Fat May the Laughing Lady," a steatopygous Venus, mechanical Great Mother, whose amplified chuckles, groans, and tears may be a response to the comic absurdity of the night-sea journey or to his efforts to escape it by playing the clown. Having become painfully aware of the enticements of Magda, a well-developed companion, whose name designates her as an avatar of the archetypal Virgin-Whore, Ambrose enters "Her" domain. Unable to find his bearings in this frowzy and fantastic kingdom by the sea, he, like the "tale-bearer," is at best ambivalent about the groping passage through "Love's Tunnel's fearsome obstacles" (77). The funhouse may be fun for lovers or cosmophilists, but for "Ambrose it is *a place of fear and confusion*" (69) where something inexplicable whips us, generation after generation, to engage in mechanical multiplication, where "Her" song is the "shluppish whisper, continuous as seawash round the globe," that "tide-like falls and rises with the circuit of dawn and dusk" (76-77). Confronting the facts of life in the funhouse-world, he finds that any view of it is a distortion, "that *nothing*" is "what it" looks "like," each person a fabricator who practices "mythotherapy" and views "himself as the hero of the story" (87).

He realizes, moreover, that in "the funhouse mirror-room you can't see yourself go on forever, because no matter how you stand, your head gets in the way" (81-82)—self-consciousness makes one aware of the inviolate level that enables the illusion of a tangled hierarchy to come into existence; self-awareness makes one conscious that what the mirror sees is funny and that "She" offers but a "poor sort of immortality" (**"Night-Sea Journey,"** 10). In contrast to the presumably less (self)-conscious Peter and Magda, who find "the right exit" and go "all the way, through," (82, 77), Ambrose falls prey to Barth's "metaphysical emotion," is led by ontological speculation into a "Strange Loop," a spiral part of the funhouse "that winds around on itself like a whelk shell" (80). The "simple, radical difference about him," either "genius" or "madness," makes it impossible for him simply to "*be*" (85, 79), to accept unconsciously and satyrically the arbitrariness and finality of a natural order in which "millions of living animals devoured one another" (87), even though he knows that "the world" is "*going on,*" that the "town, the river, himself," are "not imaginary" and time is real (85). He wishes he could end his "life absolutely without pain" (86), but he cannot. He finds a "name-coin" that may be "suggestive" of lucidity and immortality as well as "the famous lightship" and "his late grandfather's favorite dessert" (90), but, like George's assignment, it belongs or belonged to someone else, and he encounters no signs that can be simply translated to reveal the maze's "secret" (85). He and we may imagine alternative "possible endings" characterized by heroic struggles, miraculous rescues and escapes, or the revelation of the "funhouse operator" (83-84), but such "stories" told oneself "in the dark" (92) have a tendency to degenerate from romance to cliché. Having "strayed into" this "pass *wherein he lingers yet,*" Ambrose cannot pass and may even "have ceased to search" for the "way" (91-92). And so, though it will not alter his loneliness or the likelihood that he will die talking to himself to keep his reason, "though he would rather be among the lovers," he decides as consolation to "construct funhouses for others and be their secret operator" (94). If it is difficult for him to be one kind of Maker he will try his hand at becoming another; if he is unable to interpret and voice the book that is world or self, he will try to design one that is an end in itself.

In the reading, of course, **"Lost in the Funhouse"** is a good deal less solemn and straightforward than the preceding summary would indicate. The narrator himself plays the clown, lacing his language with puns, pointing to pregnant passages, and burlesquing his role and ours through the use of "heavy-footed" symbolism (90), particularly of the Freudian and Jungian sorts. His labored and labyrinthine narrative gets sidetracked, backtracks, and diverges, explores numerous culs-de-sac. When we are told that Ambrose "fell into" the "habit of rehearsing to himself the unadventurous story of his life, narrated from the third-person point of view" (92), we are threatened with Scheherazade's monstrous tale. When we learn of his decision to become an artificer, we are being invited to help create and lose ourselves in an infinite regression, a hall of mirrors in which *A,* a constructor of funhouses, exists in a funhouse constructed by *B,* who exists. . . .

Much of the narrative ado in the story consists of the exposure of the limits and artifices of literary realism, and of the narrator's infertility, aesthetic and technical faux pas, and false starts, his inability to complete his inquiry. Like dilapidated Ocean City, the house that James built would appear to be decrepit, "worn out" (85), and the uninspired narrator seems incapable of completing the passage, laments the fact that he may be repeating a tired and tiresome refrain. There have been readers who, interpreting such devices and comments as authorial statements, have concluded that Barth believes that the possibilities of fiction have been exhausted and that he has been reduced to making the most of what some of them find to be an annoyingly self-indulgent brand of self-consciousness. Not only is it true that the same things could conceivably be said of Sterne, but also that this kind of response fails to do justice to Barth's use of "the narrative viewpoint" and "the process of composition" as "dramatically relevant emblems" (x).

For one thing, the way in which Barth plays the role of author in the tale helps to create the aforementioned chain of levels of reality, fostering the illusion that in this fiction it may be possible to "go on forever," suggesting the type of *regressus in infinitum* that, according to Borges, may be used to convince oneself that "what all idealists admit" is correct—"the world is hallucinatory."[20] At the same time, however, by showing his hand, "the author . . . of this story" almost inevitably reminds us of the existence of a very mortal Maker who has constructed a funhouse out of perishable ink and paper and who owes that existence to the fact that "in approximately the year when Lord Baltimore was granted charter to the province of Maryland by Charles I, five hundred twelve women . . . received into themselves the intromittent organs of five hundred twelve men" (76). The effect is much the same as that produced by the Escher lithograph "Drawing Hands" in which a pair of hands appear to arise out of a picture within the picture and draw each other as well as the picture of which they are, and are not, a part. Just as

"Lost in the Funhouse" puts a tangle in the hierarchy consisting of teller and tale, Escher's piece twists together the hierarchical levels of drawer and drawn while also calling attention to the process of composition and, therefore, to the undrawn hands of the artist and the invisible inviolate level where, from one point of view, the "immortality chain" can "terminate" (**"Night-Sea Journey,"** 8).[21] Both works of art interweave the mundane and the mad dream and display an apparent conflict between the finite and the infinite, but Barth's "Funhouse" evokes an especially strong sense of paradox arising out of a conflict between the Real and the Ideal. The very ordinariness of Ambrose's "difference," the at times banal universality of his attempts to escape the reality of natural law by inventing adolescent fantasies, makes the story, moreover, a dramatization not only of an aesthetic dilemma (or of the satyric satirist's paradoxical position), but of the fix Ambrose, the author-narrator, the invisible author, indeed all of us may be in.

By the time we have made our way through **"Lost in the Funhouse,"** then, "teller, tale," and "told" have come together to emblemize the paradoxes contributing to and implicit in the artist-hero's decision to construct funhouses. Since the book is a "series," **"Autobiography,"** and **"Petition,"** the two pieces that fit between the three Ambrose stories, also contribute to this evolutionary process. Both "vessel and contents," teller and the tale he bears, the speaker of **"Night-Sea Journey"** seemingly evolves into more than one "unimaginable embodiment" of himself (12), generates not only Ambrose, and consequently the pseudo-autobiographical **"Ambrose His Mark,"** but also **"Autobiography: A Self-Recorded Fiction."** The first-person narrator of this "garbled or radical" "translation," this "reflection" of the tale-bearer's "reflections" (**"Night-Sea Journey,"** 12), is the story itself, speaking of itself and existing only "in a manner of speaking" (33). A disembodied voice, "contentless form," it is a "monstrosity" sired upon a recording machine, "a mere novel device," by an author who "found himself by himself with pointless pen" (33, 35, 34). As the "bloody mirror" of its father, "upon reflection" it reverses and distorts him; as "a figure of speech" (34) it is part thing, part grammar book, and completely neither. "Being an ideal's warpèd image," its "fancy's own twist figure," it consists of words that cannot be made flesh. Still "in utero, hung up in" its "delivery," it parodies the ironic prayer of Joyce's artist-hero, Stephen Dedalus, begging its Maker to turn it off: "*Wretched old fabricator, where's your shame? Put an end to this, for pity's sake!*" (36).[22] Its plea to have its plight terminated is echoed by the monstrous correspondent of **"Petition,"** a suicidal supplicant who signs himself "Yours truly" (68), claims to be a Siamese twin, and writes the King of Siam to ask him to become concerned with their "case" (67). Whereas Ambrose expects the sea to send him the word, the peti-

tioner transmits a message to the "Supreme Arbiter of the Ebb and Flow of the Tide," begging him to help terminate his "freakish" (55) existence as a creature of "introspection," "revery," and "fancy" (60) attached to a lustful, beastly brother. In contrast to the speaker of **"Autobiography,"** the petition writer wishes he had never been made flesh and ponders the paradoxes of incarnation, yet he too finds it "unspeakable" "to be both and neither" (68).

Pretending to be pure voice and found document respectively, **"Autobiography"** and **"Petition"** are signs pointing to the twin traditions Barth attempts to pull into the "Funhouse" in order that he may "have it both ways." In each case, moreover, it would appear (or sound), initially, as if the author-Maker has escaped the bind he has been put in, for he seems to have disappeared like the author of "The Revised New Syllabus" or to have traded the role of creator or narcissist for that of oracle or historian. In performance, or imagined performance, however, the father of **"Autobiography"** is visibly present if silent (ix) while the story refers to its mode of presentation as "a mere passing fancy who didn't pass quickly enough," a "mere" gimmick, "just in style, soon to be commonplace" (34). And if the author fails to disappear when creating an illusion of absence, so too does he foil himself when trying to hide behind a seemingly independent presence, for the fictive petitioner is revealed to be a blank, his condition may be but a monstrous metaphor, and his definition of what is the case is a blatant parody of that literary commonplace, the doppelgänger motif, that calls into question the integrity of the document by signaling the existence of a maze of intertextual relationships not only with the fiction of Makers such as Poe, Stevenson, and Nabokov, but with Barth's own. "No matter how you stand" in the mirror-room of the funhouse, "your head gets in the way."

In terms of ostensible point of view, **"Autobiography"** and **"Petition"** are the products of a process of narrative differentiation that recapitulates the evolution of narrative stances in Barth's earlier books while taking us in this one from first-person accounts, through the multiple points of view of **"Lost in the Funhouse,"** to the indeterminate perspective of **"Echo."**

If **"Frame-Tale"** is indeed a frame-tale, then **"Echo"** is located in the middle of *Lost in the Funhouse,* and whereas, as critics have noted, at the center of Joyce's "Portrait of the Artist" we discover silence, at the center of Barth's, at the heart of the night-sea journeyer's Dedalian labyrinth, we encounter a completely reflective surface that confounds us with reverberations and mirror images. "Afflicted with immortality," the title character has turned "from life" and learned "to tell stories with such art that the Olympians implore her to repeat them," a decision she pays for when Hera discovers she has been deceived and punishes Echo by rendering her incapable of speaking for herself (97). As a result, in "her ultimate condition," an author's note tells us, the nymph "repeats the words of others in their own voices," and "the words of 'Echo' on the tape or the page may be regarded validly as hers," those of the other characters (Narcissus and Tiresias), the author's, "or any combination or series of the four." "Inasmuch as the three mythical principals are all more or less immortal," moreover, and Tiresias "can see both backward and forward in time, the events recounted may be already past, foreseen for the future, or in process of occurring as narrated" (x). The presence of Narcissus, the indication that Echo's transformation is a kind of punishment, and the reminder that "saturation," "telling the story over as though it were another's until . . . it loses sense," is one "cure for self-absorption" (95), all suggest that the author has not completely escaped the paradoxes of self-consciousness. Nonetheless, **"Echo"** is a technical tour de force in which the unseen author comes as close as he does anywhere in the book to achieving the illusion of godlike detachment espoused by Joyce's Dedalus, and which demonstrates, following Ambrose's decision to construct funhouses for others, that Barth himself possesses the ability to create for us a fictive universe where the laws of time and space need not apply.

On the other side of this looking glass, in the second half of the series, we discover a continued proliferation of perspectives and an ostensibly greater preoccupation with "the secret adventures of order." **"Echo,"** with its numerous possible permutations of point of view, is immediately succeeded, for instance, by a pair of meditations, the "triply schizoid monologue entitled **'Title'**" (x), and the six visions of **"Glossolalia."** Similarly, the complexity of the central tale's multiple simultaneous narratives is reflected in the Chinese boxes of **"Life-Story"** and the tales within tales that constitute **"Menelaiad."** While we may be led by this to infer that, having traced the twist in the strip, we arrive at a surface that reflects everywhere the concept that the book is an end in itself, this is not precisely the case, for in the pieces in this section of the work we still feel the tug of the tide and find signs that may be read as directing us to the visionary or the Real. To ignore rather than try to work through paradox is to accept the blindness of innocence. The Moebius strip is itself both "both and neither"; the third segment of the hero's cyclical journey concerns itself with the possibility of a return to the world.

"There's no future for prophets" (100) someone punningly says in **"Echo,"** and the three pieces that follow it all involve soothsayings of sorts. **"Two Meditations,"** for example, presents from a mock-omniscient point of view the propositions that the patterns that govern the universe are unpredictable and that knowledge, as Oedi-

pus learned, always comes too late. ("To know is to recognize," Borges reminds us, "but it is necessary to have known in order to recognize, but to know is to recognize.")[23] The six "speakers in tongues" of **"Glossolalia"** share in common the facts "that their audiences don't understand what they're talking about" and "that their several speeches are metrically identical" (xi). Their seemingly senseless "babble, could we ken it, might disclose a dark message, or prayer" (112), or merely a pattern of hieroglyphs cut in time. And the fictional "author" of **"Title"** predicts that the "worst is to come" (102).

His schizoid "*monologue interieur*" (xi) is one of the most relentlessly self-indulgent expressions of paralyzing self-consciousness in the series, and it is obviously informed by two of the book's regnant conceits: corpus = corpus; fiction making = love making. Experiencing sexual "difficulties with his companion," "analogous difficulties with the story he's in the process of composing," and believing his "culture and its literature to be" in similar "straits" (x-xi), he has become a naysayer fixed "in the middle, past the middle, nearer three-quarters done, waiting for the end" (102) of his affair, his life, his story, his culture, and the book itself. Thinking he must "Efface what can't be faced or else fill the blank" (102), he enumerates several possibilities, echoing some of Barth's own statements in **"The Literature of Exhaustion"**: the "rejuvenation" of exhausted forms from their "own ashes"; the supplanting of the "moribund" by the "vigorous new"; the strategy of turning "ultimacy against itself to make something new and valid, the essence whereof would be the impossibility of making something new" (105-106). These alternatives, reflections of "historicity and self-awareness" (106), are voiced in counterpoint to the utterances of another voice which we may, if we like, associate with "Her," and which points out that the fact "that some writers lack lead in their pencils does not make writing obsolete" (108) and that "people still fall in love, and out . . . and what goes on between them is still not only the most interesting but the most important thing in the bloody murderous world" (109). To go all the way with "Her," however, is to end up "Blank," and, since the other options are "tiresome," "unlikely," and "nauseating," the "author" continues to narrate "himself into a corner" (108), embracing a last possibility— "Self-extinction. Silence" (106)—to indefinitely suspend his final sentence: "How in the world will it ever   " (110). A parody of the strategy Barth predicted Samuel Beckett would employ, this ultimate attempt to make nothing meaningful ironically makes the "author"'s self-defeating prophecy self-fulfilling if the reader/auditor decides mercifully to complete the sentence and fill in the blank with the "end."

In spite of the fact that it has been occasionally quoted out of context as if it did, **"Title,"** rather obviously, does not contain Barth's last words on the topic, nor, for that matter, "Hers." Indeed, in the remaining stories in the volume Barth increases the volume of "Her" self-less song, permitting "Her" in **"Life-Story,"** for example, to interrupt the naysaying, obstruct the narrator's view of his "private legacy of awful recollection and negative resolve" (**"Night-Sea Journey,"** 11). The hyphenated title of this piece is at least triply emblematic, suggesting not only a disjunction or a forged connection, but the linking of hierarchical levels that creates a twisted chain, in this case a potentially infinitely complex variation on what Hofstadter calls the "author-ship triangle," a "Strange Loop" in which author *Z* exists only in a novel by author *T,* who exists only in a novel by *E,* who exists only in a novel by *Z.*[24] Barth's version is more baroque since the "author," a writer of novels, stories, and this life-story, both suspects that his own life is a fiction and conceives of a story containing a character who not only has the same suspicion but is writing a similar account, the situation replicating itself "in both ontological directions" potentially ad infinitum (113-14). One option he might pursue is to continue stringing out himself and his story, exhausting the possibilities one by one, but to take this route would be to sentence himself to the tedium of an endless tale "whose drama always lies in the next frame out" (117). At any point he might take a different tack and tie the tail ends of his life-story together, but because he may be "in a sense his own author, telling his story to himself" (124), this would put him in a triple bind, to say nothing of the "outside" author and reader. Taking neither to the end of the road, he instead employs a syllogism (a form of logic that may be refuted by use of a *regressus ad infinitum*)[25] to demonstrate that "the story of his life" is "a work of fact." Permitting "his real wife and imaginary mistresses" to enter "his study," he cedes control, allowing "Her" to wish him a "Happy birthday" and kiss him "to obstruct his view of the end of the sentence he" is "nearing the end of" (125-26). Illustrating that one "way to get out of a mirror-maze is to close your eyes and hold out your hands" (**"Title,"** 108), he presumably accepts the ambiguous embrace "She" offers and "caps his pen," thereby to "end his ending story endless by interruption" (126).

When he speculates that "'his' story" may have begun "at his birth or even generations earlier," that it may be "a *Bildungs-roman,* an *Erziehungsroman, a roman fleuve*" (122), the "author" of **"Life-Story,"** is of course correct, for his tale is indeed part of a larger saga of formation and education, of a "stream novel" in which the tide of prose first takes us up to, and then carries us away along the course that proceeds from, Ambrose's conscious choice of vocation. Discovering that his mark is ambiguous, the message he has received a blank, resisting the sirens' instinctual refrain while doubting, perhaps, that the mermaids will sing to him, Ambrose finds himself lost in the protean labyrinth of the world

and resolves regretfully but also pridefully to design funhouses "vaster by far than any yet constructed," "incredibly complex yet utterly controlled" (**"Lost in the Funhouse,"** 93). The danger is that in attempting to escape in fear and confusion from the song of Love that may only be the summons of Death (**"Night-Sea Journey,"** 10), he will lead himself from the heart of one mirror-maze to the center of another.

As the "self-styled narrator" (106) of **"Title"** and the "author" of **"Life-Story"** discover, it is just as possible to lament losing yourself in self-reflection or in infinite mirror rooms of your own creation, just as distressing to see yourself going on forever, as to despair at being possessed by "Her bewitchment" (**"Night-Sea Journey,"** 11), at realizing you are at sea in creation, or that "what is 'immortal'" is "only the cyclic process of incarnation, which itself might have a beginning and an end" (**"Night-Sea Journey,"** 8). The petitioner's fear of "coupling" and absorption (62), Ambrose's self-consciousness about sexual potency, his confusion at losing control and being unable to interpret conclusively the shifting design of the cheap tablet that is the book of the world, become on the other side of the mirror the self-absorbed artist's fear of schizophrenia, his self-consciousness about creative impotence, his distaste for the unimpassioned tedium and frustration of becoming obsessed "with pattern and design for their own sakes," (**"Life-Story,"** 115), of possessing total control over a book that is an end in itself yet only a "warped" image of the Book itself. The tale-bearer's speculations about phylogeny and his resistance against the drive that compels him to repeat the refrain echo as the tale-teller's reflections on "historicity" and his reaction to the exhaustion that he believes condemns him to do likewise. The quest for the meaning of Making translates into the struggle to make meaning, the "horned" dilemma of being made to end into the difficulty of making an end. As the Grand Tutor in all his wisdom tells us, "our books stay reconciled, but who in modern terms can tell heads from tales?"

Caught in mid-passage through the dark tunnels of life-story, one may "abjure"—court suicide, "make no more," cap one's pen—or find a comfortable corner in which to "rehearse" "a series of last words, like an aging actress making one farewell appearance after another" (**"Title,"** 108), stringing out an ultimate performance that terminates in a dumb show. Or else one may teach oneself to swim, to strike out or inscribe as if one could follow a line to that destination that is "the death of us, yet our salvation and resurrection; simultaneously our journey's end, mid-point, and commencement." The message of Fat May's laughter, "could we ken it," may be that the best laid strategies of silence, exile, and cunning do not alter the accuracy of the "actuarial tables" (**"Life-Story,"** 118), that, however, much ado we may make about nothing, when all is said and done the only viable course is accepting the value, and seeking to overcome the difficulties, of achieving consummation with another, forging a bond, if only through a kenning, with lover, audience, world.

While all the tales in the series address this course and its perils in manners straightforward or circuitous, self- or subconscious, the two at the tail-end, **"Menelaiad"** and **"Anonymiad,"** offer, if not a solution, at least a resolution, one that carries over from this saga-cycle to the next, from *Lost in the Funhouse* to *Chimera.* The self-mocking hero of **"Menelaiad"** reveals himself in many guises, both those others have made for him— "The fair-haired boy? Of the loud war cry! Leader of the people. Zeus's fosterling"—and that which he has made himself: "this isn't the voice of Menelaus; this voice *is* Menelaus, all there is of him" (127). In a vital, though sometimes overlooked, passage of **"The Literature of Exhaustion,"** Barth, drawing on Borges, notes that a "labyrinth, after all, is a place in which, ideally, all the possibilities of choice (of direction, in this case) are embodied, and—barring special dispensation like Theseus'—must be exhausted before one reaches the heart. Where, mind, the Minotaur waits with two final possibilities: defeat and death, or victory and freedom." Unlike the favored Theseus, "Menelaus on the beach at Pharos" is "genuinely Baroque in the Borgesian spirit," for he "is *lost,* in the larger labyrinth of the world, and has got to hold fast while the Old Man of the Sea exhausts reality's frightening guises so that he may extort direction from him when Proteus returns to his 'true' self. It's a heroic enterprise, with salvation as its object—one recalls that the aim of the Histriones is to get history done with so that Jesus may come again the sooner, and that Shakespeare's heroic metamorphoses culminate not merely in a theophany but in an apotheosis."[26] In the case of Barth's version of the Homeric episode, Menelaus's struggle takes the twisted form of seven tales nesting within tales, seven frames or Chinese boxes, the outermost of which consists of Proteus, become the voice of Menelaus, telling the story of how that came to be, the story of Menelaus's tale; the rest, the tale of Menelaus's life as told by him to various auditors.

In order to explain himself and complete his life-story, Menelaus is compelled to suspend frame-tale after frame-tale and to move to the next frame in where the drama may lie, make his way toward the center of the labyrinth where the Minotaur's twin possibilities await. Although he suggests that his purpose is "Truth to tell" (130), to peel off the "cloaks of story," remove "Her" "veils" to reach "naked Helen" (140), the overwhelming question that wraps him in this argument of insidious intent is "Why me?" (150), why did Helen choose

him, less than others, above all others. Telling his way away from and toward "the seed and omphalos of all" (148), he rephrases the question, asking "Who am I?" and:

each time drawing a blank (153, 148).

The maze of story and typography through which he and we proceed is in a sense an elaborate (self)-deception or ruse, for all the voices that are so meticulously distinguished may be seen as Menelaus's or Proteus's or Barth's, or no one's, ink on pulp. At its heart lies a simple, if deceptive and ambiguous, answer:

" ' " ' " ' " Love! " ' " ' " ' "

(150)

But, while this is the word that can trigger the implosion of the entire edifice, Menelaus cannot take it to heart. Proteus tells him "Helen chose" him "without reason because she loves" him "without cause," advising him to "embrace her without question and watch" his "weather change" (156); Helen enjoins him to "woo" the "senseless answer to our riddle" and "espouse" her "without more carp" (159). Menelaus, however, in fear of being fooled, rejects their comebacks, holds on to himself, fills the blank by himself, and thereby loses himself, makes himself not a hero but "a fool," "chimaera, a hornèd gull" (139). Choosing to remain "undeceivèd Menelaus, solely, imperfectly" (161), he becomes not the "eternal husband" (127), but the eternal cuckold. Since he has "lost course" (128), his "voice yarns on," and "when the voice goes he'll turn tale, story of his life, to which he clings yet, whenever, how-, by whom-recounted" (161-62).

Unlike Homer's hero Menelaus (*Odyssey,* 4) and Vergil's bee-keeper, Aristaeus (*Georgics,* 4), who, assisted by nymphs and fortified by ambrosia and nectar, wrest direction from Proteus the ever-truthful, perform the proper acts of faith, and succeed, respectively, in bringing forth buzzing bees from rotting carcasses and reaching the Elysian Fields, Barth's Menelaus, his "carcass" "long wormed" (161), resides somewhere in "Hades" (128). Unwilling to trust, to let go of self-knowledge, he, or rather all that remains of him, is woven into the tangled hierarchies of a life-story that resembles in form the structure of *Lost in the Funhouse* itself. The "Old Man of the Sea," however, has the last word: "Then when as must at last every tale, all tellers, all told, Menelaus's story itself in ten or ten thousand years expires, yet I'll survive it, I, in Proteus's terrifying last disguise, Beauty's spouse's odd Elysium:

the absurd, unending possibility of love" (162). His "dark message, or prayer" metamorphoses into the book's consummating tale and points, if we trust it, to the possibility of another kind of heroism, that of "the Thesean *hero,* who, confronted with Baroque reality, Baroque history, the Baroque state of his art, need *not* rehearse its possibilities to exhaustion," need "only be aware of their existence or possibility, acknowledge them, and with the aid of *very special* gifts . . . go straight through the maze to the accomplishment of his work."[27]

"Anonymiad," the last item, if we wish, in the series, is a marooned minstrel's "Last Lay," the history of a life-story that recapitulates the development of *Lost in the Funhouse,* Barth's corpus, and all of literature; the evolution of "the author," Barth's career, and homo poeticus. The "tale-bearer," at once a singular Homeric bard and all Makers, has been seduced by love and world, deceived into exile, has fallen into fits of self-consciousness, feared exhaustion, and, like many of his predecessors/descendants in the book, has faced a blank. Halfway through his story he finds "there, at the heart, never to be filled, a mere lacuna" (177). But having acknowledged the possible existence of this lake, this pit, the bottomless well of self-reflection, the gap between word and world, shifting appearance and ideal form, he avoids drowning in Narcissus's pool, losing his way in Echo's or Proteus's caves. Leaving "unsaid" what "must be blank" (193), he goes on through this gesture of cynicism to recount how, inspired by his own water, he "developed a kind of coded markings to record the utterance of mind and heart," and, inspired by the gods, came to launch "his productions worldward" (186). Although distressed as he became older by the possibilities that there might be nothing new to say, no "new way to say the old," that "the 'immortality' of even the noblest works" he knew might be but "a paltry thing" (188), he was saved from the despair of Barth's **"Title"** character, the fate of his Menelaus, by a water-message and a change in point of view.

Discovering a largely blank and wholly indecipherable parchment washed up in an amphora, he was roused to "imagine that the world contained another like" himself, "might be," indeed, "astrew with islèd souls, become minstrels perforce, and the sea a-clink with literature" (189). Though the amphora and its ciphers may have been his own, this mattered not, for "the principle" he decided, "was the same: that" he "could be thus messaged, even by that stranger" his "former self, whether or not the fact tied" him "to the world, inspired" him "to address it once again" (190). Yearning "to be relieved of" himself, he shifted to his "only valid point of view, first person anonymous" (192), to become, perhaps, like Borges's Shakespeare "nothing" and "everything that all others are," no one and god-like.[28]

Buoyed up by these gestures of faith, having "taught" himself "to swim," he was enabled, despite the void in the center, to put "Headpiece" and "Tailpiece" of his **"Anonymiad"** together in their container and set "afloat" a work that may be both and neither an end in itself and a means to an end. Praising Apollo and committing himself to "Her" call, he calls his tale "a continuing, strange love letter" and says he has "ceased to care whether" it "is found and read or lost in the belly of a whale" (193). "Will anyone have learnt its name?" he asks. "Will everyone?" "No matter," he tells us, for:

> Upon this noontime of his wasting day, between the night past and the long night to come, a noon beautiful enough to break the heart, on a lorn fair shore a nameless minstrel
>
> Wrote it.
>
> (194)

The minstrel's epitaph, his testament, is both a death sentence and a prayer that holds open the possibilities of theophany and apotheosis, in Todd's terms, both "a gesture of temporality" and "a gesture of eternity" (*Floating Opera,* 50).

Contained within **"Frame-Tale"** and linked in numerous ways to the first story in the series, his last lay may be interpreted as beginning the cycle again, leading us back to retrace our way through a labyrinth we may never leave. His final words, set adrift by themselves, suggest, however, a different course. Kenned in another way, they translate into a signaling device in the hand of the "outside author" pointing to the inviolate level outside the closed and twisted loop, into signs directing us to follow the thread that spirals out of the Funhouse and through *Chimera.*

Notes

1. Bellamy, *New Fiction,* 8.

2. *Lost in the Funhouse: Fiction for Print, Tape, Live Voice* (New York, 1969), ix; hereafter cited in the text; this edition contains all of the author's notes Barth has written.

3. Bellamy, *New Fiction,* 8-9.

4. *Chimera* (New York, 1973), 320; hereafter cited in the text.

5. McKenzie, "Pole-Vaulting," 137. For a discussion of Barth's use of "Chinese boxes" see Stark, *Literature of Exhaustion,* 124-25.

6. McKenzie, "Pole-Vaulting," 141. Charles Caramello has also linked "Frame-Tale," Scheherazade, and death. See the section on Barth in his *Silverless Mirrors: Book, Self & Postmodern American Fiction* (Tallahassee, 1983), 112-21.

7. "The Literature of Exhaustion," 33; Jorge Luis Borges, "Partial Enchantments of the *Quixote*," in [his *Other Inquisitions 1937-1952*, trans. Ruth L. C. Simms (New York: Simon & Schuster, 1965)], 45.

8. Borges, "Partial Enchantments," 46.

9. Douglas R. Hofstadter, *Gödel, Escher, Bach: An Eternal Golden Braid* (New York: Vintage, 1980), 10, 15. One reviewer has compared Hofstadter's book to Barth's *LETTERS*; see Gary Thompson, "Barth's Letters and Hawkes' Passion," *Michigan Quarterly Review* 19, no. 2 (1980):270.

10. "The Literature of Exhaustion," 33; Hofstadter, *Gödel*, 15. For an extensive examination of the role of paradox in Barth's fiction, see Tharpe, *John Barth*.

11. See Hofstadter, *Gödel*, 686-92, for an explanation of how every system contains a "protected" or "inviolate" level, "unassailable by the rules on other levels, no matter how tangled their interaction may be among themselves."

12. [Laurence Sterne, The Life and Opinions of Tristram Shandy, Gentleman (Boston: Houghton Mifflin, 1965)], 4-5.

13. For a description of some of the forms of the mythic "night-sea journey," see, for example, Erich Neumann, *The Great Mother: An Analysis of the Archetype* (Princeton: Princeton University Press, 1972), 157-58, 177.

14. See Borges, "On the Cult of Books," in *Other Inquisitions*, 117. Borges, of course, quotes the *Timaeus*.

15. See Morrell, *John Barth*, 88-89.

16. Borges, "On the Cult of Books," 117-18.

17. Herman Melville, *Moby-Dick; or, The Whale* (New York: W. W. Norton, 1967), 84, 399, 83.

18. Ibid., 399.

19. Borges, "On the Cult of Books," 120.

20. Borges, "Avatars of the Tortoise," in *Other Inquisitions*, 114.

21. My discussion of the Escher lithograph draws upon the analysis by Hofstadter, *Gödel*, 689-90.

22. For further speculation on Barth's response to Joyce's work, see Michael Hinden, "*Lost in the Funhouse*: Barth's Use of the Recent Past," *Twentieth Century Literature* 19, no. 2 (1973): 107-18; reprinted in *Critical Essays on John Barth*, ed. Joseph W. Waldmeir (Boston, 1980), 190-200.

23. Borges, "Avatars of the Tortoise," 114.

24. Hofstadter, *Gödel*, 688-89.

25. See "The Literature of Exhaustion," 34.

26. Ibid.; Borges's "Histriones," he notes, are a heretical sect "who believe that repetition is impossible in history and therefore live viciously in order to purge the future of the vices they commit." Shakespeare's "heroic metamorphoses," according to Borges, won him a conversation with God. See Jorge Luis Borges, "Everything and Nothing," in *A Personal Anthology*, ed. Anthony Kerrigan (New York: Grove Press, 1967), 115-17.

27. "The Literature of Exhaustion," 34.

28. Borges, "From Someone to No One," in *A Personal Anthology*, 120-21.

Selected Bibliography

PRIMARY SOURCES

BOOKS

Chimera. New York: Random House, 1972; paperback edition, New York: Fawcett Crest, 1973.

The End of the Road. Garden City, N.Y.: Doubleday & Co., 1958; rev. ed., Garden City, N.Y.: Doubleday & Co., 1967; paperback edition, New York: Bantam Books, 1981.

The Floating Opera. New York: Appleton-Century-Crofts, 1956; rev. ed., Garden City, N.Y.: Doubleday & Co., 1967; paperback edition, New York: Bantam Books, 1981.

Giles Goat-Boy; or, The Revised New Syllabus. Garden City, N.Y.: Doubleday & Co., 1966; paperback edition, New York: Bantam Books, 1981.

LETTERS: A Novel. New York: Putnam, 1979; paperback edition, New York: Fawcett Columbine, 1982.

Lost in the Funhouse: Fiction for Print, Tape, Live Voice. Garden City, N.Y.: Doubleday & Co., 1968; paperback edition, New York: Bantam Books, 1969.

Sabbatical: A Romance. New York: Putnam, 1982; paperback edition, New York: Putnam, 1982.

The Sot-Weed Factor. Garden City, N.Y.: Doubleday & Co., 1960; rev. ed., Garden City, N.Y.: Doubleday & Co., 1967; paperback edition, New York: Bantam Books, 1969.

NONFICTION

"The Literature of Exhaustion." *Atlantic Monthly,* August 1967, 29-34.

INTERVIEWS AND STATEMENTS

Bellamy, Joe David. "Having It Both Ways: A Conversation Between John Barth and Joe David Bellamy." *New American Review* 15 (1972): 134-50.

————. "John Barth." In *The New Fiction: Interviews with Innovative American Writers,* 1-18. Urbana: University of Illinois Press, 1974. Reprint of the previous entry.

McKenzie, James. "Pole-Vaulting in Top Hats: A Public Conversation with John Barth, William Gass, and Ishmael Reed." *Modern Fiction Studies* 22, no. 2 (1976): 131-51.

SECONDARY SOURCES

BOOKS

Morrell, David. *John Barth: An Introduction.* University Park: Pennsylvania State University Press, 1976. Provides extremely useful background information about all the works through *Chimera.* Particularly helpful for those interested in biography, sources, and the process of composition.

Tharpe, Jac. *John Barth: The Comic Sublimity of Paradox.* Carbondale: Southern Illinois University Press, 1974. An excellent study covering the major works through *Chimera.* Tharpe's main focus is on the philosophical content of Barth's books, and he deals extensively with the author's interest in ethics, ontology, cosmology, epistemology, aesthetics, and logic.

Waldmeir, Joseph, ed. *Critical Essays on John Barth.* Boston: G. K. Hall, 1980. A fine collection of essays surveying Barth's work and the state of Barth criticism, and of reviews of and articles about each of his first six books. Contains a number of the best short critical studies produced so far.

PARTS OF BOOKS

Caramello, Charles. *Silverless Mirrors: Book, Self & Postmodern American Fiction.* Tallahassee: University Presses of Florida, 1983. The chapter on Barth and Eugene Wildman represents one of the most convincing attempts to read Barth's work in the context of contemporary critical theory. The book as a whole is one of the best studies of postmodern fiction available.

Stark, Jack O. *The Literature of Exhaustion: Borges, Nabokov, and Barth.* Durham, N.C.: Duke University Press, 1974. The long section on Barth includes a useful analysis of language and technique, but Stark occasionally goes overboard in attempting to link the fiction to "The Literature of Exhaustion."

Julius Rowan Raper (essay date fall 1989)

SOURCE: Raper, Julius Rowan. "John Barth's *Chimera*: Men and Women under the Myth." *The Southern Literary Journal* 22, no. 1 (fall 1989): 17-31.

[*In the following essay, Raper studies the contrast between fixed, archetypal characters and those who exhibit variable traits in* Chimera *to examine how Barth* "exhausted the familiar heroic myth in order to release the energies of other myths waiting at the periphery of Western consciousness."]

Surely John Barth is our most inventive contemporary novelist. He may also be our most creative and, considering his contributions to postmodernism, our most influential. Among the themes developed in his complex trilogy of tales, *Chimera* (1972), the opposition between Protean characters and those with a fixed destiny may not, at first, appear as important as other subjects treated, including competition between the sexes and the nature of storytelling. Yet Barth's contrast of character types serves a central purpose, for it helps bring together the other, more obvious topics. At the same time, because the contrast is not the foreground of the book, taking it for focus gives a reader a place to stand in responding to *Chimera,* a perspective a degree freer of Barth's own metafictional commentary that, by pre-empting discussion of the overt themes, tends to dominate readings of the book.

A position outside Barth's commentary may prove helpful. For Barth's meanings often lie hidden beneath his brilliant surfaces. The great modernist texts of Eliot, Joyce, Pound, and Faulkner employed the tortured beauty of fragments, ellipses, and associative syntax to bypass the censors, both personal and social, while exploring otherwise unthinkable sexual and social issues important to the early century. In the same way, Barth employs convoluted phantasies and metafictions in the style of postmodernism to open the mind to problems of the late twentieth century that readers might otherwise prefer to deny. To put the censors at ease, he removes his tales from the moralized, canonical myths of our era and focuses on non-canonical myths of the ancient Middle East. His ploy sets him free to play, to explore, to revise our mythology as his inward urges insist—a process that leads to healing discoveries about the roles men and women play in an age when the feminist revolution has put the underlying myth of our culture in question.

The contrast between Protean and fixed characters in *Chimera* is what the reader should expect from the novelist who, when he created Henry Burlingame as a central figure in *The Sot-Weed Factor* (1960), pioneered the exploration in contemporary American literature of Protean freedom.[1] In *Factor,* Burlingame tells his opposite number, Ebenezer Cook, whose *fixed* identity is that of virgin and poet (204-05), that "your true and constant Burlingame lives only in your fancy. . . . In fact you see a Heraclitean flux: whether 'tis we who shift and alter and dissolve; or you whose lens changes color, field, and focus; or both together" (349). Barth had moved steadily toward this clear opposition of character types in his two earlier novels, when he played absurdist Todd Andrews against chameleon-like Harrison

Mack (28-29, 49-50) in *The Floating Opera* (1956), and self-canceling Jacob Horner (67) against dangerously consistent Joe Morgan (68, 152-55) in *The End of the Road* (1958). After Burlingame, the clear contrast appeared a second time in *Giles Goat-Boy or, The Revised New Syllabus* (1966), where George Giles, destined to be the Grand Tutor, struggles against shape-shifting Harold Bray. This opposition of types, therefore, may be the central conflict of Barth's books, certainly of his early ones.

After *Giles Goat-Boy,* the opposition reemerged in several short pieces in **Lost in the Funhouse** (1968). In "**Echo**" Barth contrasts the beautiful youth Narcissus, who obsessively denies "all except himself," with sad Echo, who effaces "herself absolutely" (102-03). Narcissus's dogged pursuit of self causes him to languish away by the mirroring pool. Echo's self-effacing allows her to survive, but only as the Protean repetition of others' voices. In Barth's interpretation, the opposite types "come to the same" end, for "it was never himself Narcissus craved, but his reflection" (103), his visual echo. Consequently, as late as "**Echo,**" no exit from the dilemma represented by narcissism and Proteanism seemed available for Barth's characters (cf. Bienstock 77-78).

In the same book, Barth carried the freedom afforded by Protean variability to its alphabetical extreme in the obsessive "**Life-Story.**" There, an author who one afternoon considers "that his own life might be a fiction, in which he [is] the leading or an accessory character" (116), goes on for a dozen pages to become one letter (C?) in a literal alphabet of narrators, A to Z, all of them writing stories about other authors while trying to escape an (alphabetically) earlier narrator's fiction. Presumably, if the process continued, narrator Z would be, in Barth's recurring Moebius fashion, the author of A's story, so that the cycle could twist upon itself and continue. Even though none of the authors seems to care for such artifice-acknowledging fictions, none can go back to writing straightforward mimetic tales.

Barth's infinite regress of narrators appears to be an inevitability not only of twentieth-century literature's commitment to self-consciousness, but also of twentieth-century philosophy. Here Edmund Husserl's phenomenological ideal of the transcendental ego—a mainstay of twentieth-century culture especially after purification into Sartre's existential consciousness called "being-for-itself"—finds its literary incarnation in the device of framing stories. Authors who transcend the swamp of their earlier life by making that past a fiction of which they are the author have discovered a convenient device for liberating "being-for-itself." They seek the anguish of existential freedom to escape the nausea of a defined identity, of being bogged down in the story of one's past. At the same time, they remain true to Alain Robbe-Grillet's proposition that the purpose of contemporary fiction is to lead the way to imaginative freedom by showing how one invents the work and, thereby, the world and one's own life (Robbe-Grillet 156).

But in avoiding the nausea of fixed identity, "**Life-Story**" dramatized the malaise of phenomenology. Although the situation, an alphabet soup of narrators, is absurd and suitable for satire or parody, the tone nonetheless has the feel of heartfelt parody. The shape-shifting of the narrator from identity to alphabetical identity becomes frenzied. His need never to be controlled by an externally determined or authored self leads to a flood of fears—of abstract formalism, of fantasy, distortion, fragmentation, obsession—eventually of schizophrenia and suicide (**Lost** 118, 124). Protean freedom is one thing, Protean fragmentation another altogether. And here the line between the two is easily blurred. Indeed, the distance between high-spirited Henry Burlingame and the troubled narrator of "**Life-Story**" is much less than the 280 years that separate them would imply. The act of connecting the two in the reader's imagination draws a reasonably straight line through Barth's Moebius-turned universe.

The distance between the "**Life-Story**" narrator and the pre-historic Greek Polyeidus in **Chimera** is even shorter—and yet not less than that between Bellerophon, intent on becoming a mythical Greek hero, and Ebenezer Cook or George Giles, each with his sense of destiny. Bellerophon and Polyeidus represent the most obvious developments in **Chimera** of Barth's pattern of playing fixed characters against Protean figures. But other characters, male and female, in the three novellas provide clarifying variations of the contrast. In **Perseid,** for example, Barth opposes the rigidity of Andromeda to the flexible constancy of Medusa, and plays petrifying, middle-aged Perseus off against his younger heroic self. In **Bellerophoniad,** the varied contrasts include the imitative Anteia and one-dimensional Philonoe opposed to the multi-dimensional Melanippe, as well as role-dominated Deliades/Bellerophon set against shape-shifting Polyeidus. In **Dunyazadiad,** the culminating tale though placed first for the publisher's misguided commercial reasons (Morrell 162), Barth plays off a Faustian Scheherazade against her sister Dunyazade who remains her own woman; the tale also frames the one-role Shahryar with the more complex Shah Zaman. In addition, **Dunyazadiad** offers the passionate Genie to contrast as author to the mutable and self-effacing Polyeidus and the imitative Jerome B. Bray of **Bellerophoniad.**

For all these characters except Polyeidus and Bray, gender roles present major problems. And central to gender role is the myth of the hero so brilliantly stated and developed in **Perseid,** the first of the tales Barth wrote (Morrell 140-43). Perseus's problem sounds the obvious theme of the three-part novel: how are men and women ever to transcend the myth of heroic maleness that, *Bellerophoniad* reminds us, has dominated Western culture since the overthrow of the matriarchy some 3500 years ago (*Chimera* 277).[2] As the son of Zeus and the princess Danae, Perseus may originally have taken to the heroic part naturally enough. Morrell is correct, therefore, in saying that Perseus is "his own man finally" (152). But, from the start, Perseus seems benighted; his heroic behavior arises from a great reservoir of unconsciousness. His eagerness in middle life to feel heroic again suggests that the heroic pattern is the only masculine role he knows or feels comfortable playing (91).

Whatever its source in Perseus's life, the myth serves useful purposes. The way Perseus ponders the murals in Calyxa's temple indicates that the pattern lends meaning, an external one, to a demigod's life (80-81). His anxiety that his cousin Bellerophon may challenge his greatness in Athene's eyes implies that the heroic role helps satisfy his masculine need to feel special (93). This specialness, as his relationships with Athene, Calyxa, Andromeda, and especially Medusa (who loved her beheader) demonstrate, is a feeling that not only Perseus but perhaps all heroes acquire from the way women respond to their heroic feats (87-88, 90, 93).

Dependency of heroes on the impressionability of women combines with Perseus's recurring anxieties about his sexual potency and the size of his organ (66, 68-70) to suggest a very modern explanation for an ancient pattern of behavior: that heroic role-playing compensates for deepseated sexual anxieties by enabling heroes to deny their anxieties. Barth draws some of his best comedy from such anachronistic connections that would have been as unthinkable in a heroic shame culture, as in a modern locker room or barracks. When Calyxa asks Perseus if he is "really so naive as to equate love-making, like a callow lad, with mere prolonged penetration," his twice-told reply is: "Yes, 'I'm *a hero!*' I indicated with a sweep of my relieved glories [the murals]. . . . 'Virtuoso performance is my line of work!'" (70). Perseus's anxiety here cannot be altogether a product of his mid-life crisis, for even if potency was not a problem of his youthful heroic cycle, it is still unlikely that his member has shrunk during the intervening years. In short, like Napoleon, he has had something to compensate for, for a long time.

In this playful manner, even in the most heroic and most sympathetic to males of the three novellas, Barth has begun his exploration of weaknesses that hide behind the myth of maleness. Because Perseus's heroic behavior is in part compensatory, a way to deny anxieties, it belongs to a dimension of the demigod's self that is largely a pretense and therefore false. As a result, even when the hero succeeds in fooling women with his heroism, he feels the pretense in himself. In this manner, the heroic pattern generates its own form of anxiety (80). Perseus may have succeeded in selling his heroic role to the Calyxas and the Medusas of the pre-historic Middle East, but in moments of self-doubt he is the first to admit that "No man's a mythic hero to his wife" (87). For long years Andromeda has been house-training and henpecking her rescuer and onetime hero (76), and may have henpecked him into his present psychosexual weakness (76, 87). Yet the anxiety about size must surely antedate both Andromeda and the heroic feats.

Some of Perseus's psychosexual difficulty, however, appears to be situational, the product of a mixed marriage—Argive and Ethiopian (77)—man and woman. Andromeda's ceaseless struggle for parity has taken the starch out of Perseus's stiff image of himself as hero, and, in the process, has wrecked the marriage (77). As Perseus sees their relationship, "the more she became her own woman, the less" she is his (85). In their second-cycle's final encounter, all she wants, she claims, is "to build as best she [can] a life of her own"—alone (125). Unfortunately for Perseus, even Calyxa enjoys her "free, independent life" (109) and cannot offer him heaven on earth. The situation between men and women appears to be all oil and vinegar—especially when, as Andromeda points out, the male is a mythic hero with an "insufferable ego" that proposes "three parts Perseus to one Andromeda" (77).

If in his first cycle Perseus passionately pursued the fixed destiny of the heroic myth, he learns here in his second cycle the necessity of incorporating an opposite sort of behavior: "[B]eyond a certain point [he] must permit things to come to [him] instead of adventuring to them" (94). Such behavior, of course, has little place in the heroic pattern.

Nor is Perseus's new behavior, "beyond a certain point," part of the usual male pattern. The man's traditional part, according to Jungian analyst Robert Johnson, was to go on a quest, to initiate action. The woman's role, in contrast, was to wait for extraordinary events to come to her (41). From Johnson's perspective, Perseus, in the second half of his life, has to develop the other half of his personality—the so-called feminine traits—so that he can become something more than the marble facade he became as a Greek hero. In his second cycle, he is required to become less heroic and more perfectly human.

This mandate comes from the hooded woman who visits him in *Nao Athinis,* the Temple of Athene (94), bearing the wisdom of his half-sister Athene (94). His instructress is Medusa herself, and her goal is to steer him toward his deeper humanity so that finally, through mutual commitment, they may become immortal stars together.

If Medusa is Athene's surrogate, she is also Andromeda's antithesis. For although Andromeda later claims
she loved "Perseus the man" (124), she has dealt with
Perseus chiefly in his heroic roles, as both golden rescuer and has been, each of which she obviously resents
(77-78). In contrast, Medusa seeks a Perseus with an
expanded repertoire of behavior.

But Medusa too has known the hero, and, in an ambivalent manner, has, like Andromeda, been rescued by
him. As she tells her story, the chance she might "be as
Gorgon as her sisters," those "snakehaired frights,"
made her welcome decapitation by Perseus as deliver-
ance from the coldness to which ravishment by Poseidon had doomed her (89-90). In emotional terms, Perseus's arrival unwittingly freed her from the cold, man-
petrifying rage that followed her rape. Medusa strangely
awaited the coming of Perseus as "a golden dream"
(90).

The myth of Medusa, told from her point of view, thus
lends a far different meaning to Perseus's bloody deed—
and Medusa's life. It shows that beneath the role Medusa played as Perseus's monster/victim lived a complex woman. As Perseus claims, she was both his "true
adversary and chief ally"—not because beheading her
made him famous, as he once thought (78), but because
their stories are linked in ways he originally did not
recognize. And because her true identity is veiled from
Perseus, the narrator, the coherence of her personality
easily escapes the reader.

As Perseus was Medusa's unwitting rescuer, she is his
unrecognized guide through the second cycle of his life.
Her face hidden by the hood, she advises him (84, 86),
instructs Calyxa on mural scenes from his life (86),
submits to his anxiety-ridden embraces (94-95), saves
him from drowning (97-98), and repeatedly informs
him that he must relinquish his heroic cunning and act
forthrightly (93-94, 99). She poses questions about his
quest for rejuvenation that Calyxa reinterprets as the
riddle crucial to his later life: "How can Being Perseus
Again be your goal, when you have to be Perseus to
reach it?" (100). It is a mystery that goes beyond the
goal-directed behavior of heroes, a paradox no hero
without instruction can be expected to understand or
answer. For it distinguishes being from doing, and a
hero comprehends one thing, the willful action that a
quest brings into being. For a hero, that action is the
single mode of being that has value. Everything else
belongs to a malaise, the boredom of waiting for the
quest.

Medusa underscores Perseus's heroic blindness when
she lets him make love to her again (100-01). Because
he does not comprehend that Medusa, the goal of his
quest, is already at hand, his pursuit of Perseus-like
heroism has once more blinded him to the human Per-

seus whom Medusa sees, loves (106-07), and patiently
assists into being. He has confused a role, a means to
an end, heroism, with a state of being, loving Medusa,
an end in itself.

Perseus spends the remainder of his tale not only coming to terms with his ambivalence about Andromeda
(110-11, 120, 125) but realizing that estellation, endless
stardom, requires not heroic action but restraint and
committed loving. The extent of his eventual growth
becomes clear when, having figuratively slain the
"young Perseus," his double, by clobbering Andromeda's new lover, Danaus (122-23), he sufficiently masters his heroic vanity to forego murdering the raging
Andromeda and, in the same heartbeat, embraces "the
paradoxic precious" Medusa (125). As from the first
words ("Good evening") Medusa has been a constant
but invisible audience, so through the second cycle of
his life she has been both an invisible guiding presence
and waiting goal, his future already present—because
she has loved him constantly since his heroic past (105).

Medusa, or her spirit, is also felt as an invisible presence in the other two novellas. Clearly, Bellerophon
seeks his own Medusa in Melanippe, and, even though
Dunyazade is the primary narrator of her own tale rather
than primary audience as were Medusa and Melanippe,
she is the spiritual heir (or progenitor, depending on
which direction one moves along the Moebius-strip
chronology) of Medusa. In each tale, the Medusa figure
offers the chief positive alternative to the dominate
myth of masculine heroism. Medusa-like qualities that
recur in the other figures include an inner vision that
leads to constant goals, a measure of flexibility, and remarkable powers of empathy, even extending to monsters and adversaries (127).

Medusa and Perseus have one distinct advantage over
their parallels in ***Bellerophoniad.*** As Perseus tells her
in their eternal epilogue: "at the time we were archetypes, not stereo types; reality, not myth" (129). Only in
his second cycle did Perseus "wish his time turned
back" (133) so that he could relive his heroic youth,
and the second cycle eventually brings him the wisdom
to put that "unpleasant middle Perseus . . . to death
. . . forever" (124). Even when he tried to imitate his
youthful self, the attempt itself sprang from a spontaneous need within the aging man.

Not so Bellerophon. His effort to recycle his earlier life
is part of a conscious, life-long imitation of the heroic
pattern, especially as he, on his fortieth birthday, finds
it set forth in the story of Perseus, his model hero (137-
38). When we discover that Bellerophon is, in fact, Deliades (306), we see that, as with Perseus, the need to
behave in a heroic manner is at base a grandiose compensation for underlying inferiority. In the case of
Bellerophon/Deliades, inferiority comes not from

Perseus-like anxiety about penis size, but from playing second fiddle to Bellerus, who their mother Eurymede claimed was Poseidon's son, a "demigod destined for the stars" (151). Having begun life "circumspect, prudential," moderate, and wise (151), Deliades became his brother's "mortal killer" and buried himself under the name "Bellerophon" (the voice, or murderer, of Bellerus) "to live out in selfless counterfeit, from that hour to this, [his] brother's demigoddish life" (306)—thus creating a myth not of heroism, but of role-playing, the counterfeit life, inauthenticity. The significance of Bellerophon's myth—and of *Chimera* itself—is clearly that "by imitating perfectly the Pattern of Mythic Heroism, [one becomes], not a mythic hero, but a perfect Reset [ie. a perfect imitation of the Pattern of Mythic Heroism]" (303). That is the fate of Bellerophon, would have been the fate of Perseus had Medusa not been his constant guide, and would have been the fate of Shah Zaman had he not had Dunyazade as audience and possessed inner resources not visible in his public role of heroic (that is, compensatory) manhood.

But Deliades/Bellerophon shares his fate with his father, Polyeidus. As Bellerophon finally recognizes, "only Polyeidus's son could have mimed a life so well, so long" (306). Inasmuch as Polyeidus is not a demigod or a hero—at most the mere verbal/pictorial pattern of the hero's life (260-61)—Barth through Polyeidus indicates that imitation of the received role of male heroism is only part, a significant part, of a larger problem—the counterfeit life that one takes from the external world rather than spins from the central self. For Polyeidus, whose name means "Many-shapes," is Barth's most Protean character, excepting Proteus himself in **"Menelaiad"** from *Lost in the Funhouse.* But, whereas Proteus turned, in his daughter's words, "first into animals, then into plants and wine-dark sea, then into no saying what" (*Lost* 160), Polyeidus, as though captured by Professor Henry Higgins or a contemporary French critic, turns, as he becomes increasingly self-conscious, into mere words, documents epistolary, literary, or historical (152-53). In his final identity, the intentionally botched mock epic *Bellerophoniad,* he becomes, much like Barth's Echo, an anonymous grouping of "false letters" that spell out his imitative son's tale.

The fate of father and son here is a far cry from that of Perseus and Medusa who became "these silent, visible signs [stars and words]; to *be* the tale I [Perseus] tell to those with eyes to see and understanding to interpret; to raise you up forever and know that our story will never be cut off, but nightly rehearsed as long as men and women read the stars . . ." (133-34). In contrast to the exhilaration the reader feels with *Perseid,* the reader of *Bellerophoniad* can scarcely wait to finish and move on to the next story, or, if he/she has read them in the unfortunate order imposed by the publisher, recycle the novellas by turning back to *Dunyazadiad.*

Impatience with *Bellerophoniad* does not mean that the tale fails to do what Barth asks of it, only that it functions far less effectively as an ending than as the middle of a fiction. For it introduces new characters who help fill the wide gap between extremes found throughout Barth's works that play off Protean characters against those with a fixed destiny. At the same time it develops themes stated in *Perseid,* by introducing figures who clarify the opposition between role-players like middle Perseus, on the one hand, and characters, on the other, who, like Medusa and the final Perseus, remain their own man or woman.

Such integrity of character is a difficult concept to treat in postmodern fiction, for the age is largely phenomenological and post-moralistic. The heritage of phenomenology, especially through Sartrean existentialism, has stressed Being as discontinuous moments of consciousness of objects. A consistent self is more and more viewed as a construct (a fiction) of reflexive consciousness. One's essence is said to be what one has been, one's past. Each man, like Proteus, "makes his essence as he lives" (Sartre 630). At the same time, in the anti-moralizing literary culture inherited from modernism, especially from New Criticism, an author who stresses integrity of character is likely to sound didactic.

Barth avoids both problems. No contemporary author, with the possible exception of Thomas Pynchon, has created characters more Protean than Barth's Henry Burlingame, Harold Bray, Proteus, and Polyeidus. And yet Barth does not embrace such figures enthusiastically, the way a committed phenomenologist would. His shape-shifters may not seem simpletons like his characters who pursue a fixed destiny—Ebenezer Cooke, George Giles, and Bellerophon. But comparison of Polyeidus and Bellerophon, variable father and simple son, reveals that the two sets of characters are alike in one fatal way. All are role-players. Whether they pursue an abstract role, like those who set out toward a certain destiny, or whether, Proteus-like, they play a seemingly boundless series of parts, all conform to externals. Like phenomenological man, each Barthian shape-shifter or destined hero lives a decentered existence. Indeed, in Sartre's persuasive ontology, the concept of a center makes no sense, except as bad faith—self-deception. But, despite Sartre's brilliant exposition, Barth, in *Chimera,* quietly, with no didactic flourishes, in an understated fashion, presents a contrasting group of characters—Medusa, Melanippe, Dunyazade, even the men Shah Zaman and the Genie/author—who appear to act from a constant center without assuming grandiose roles.

Melanippe, for example, stands in stark contrast to Anteia and, less starkly, to Philonoe. In a sense, both Melanippe and Anteia are seduced by the male heroic myth, but their reasons are very different, Melanippe's largely cultural, Anteia's narrowly personal. Melanippe recounts her culture's myth of the Amazons and their opposition to "the forcible suppression of their sex" (218). But the source of Anteia's seduction by the hero myth is the ludicrous penis envy produced by a culture in which it is not men and women, but only heroes, who behave in ways the culture is conditioned to value. Her longing to be a hero turns her into a grotesque parody of male heroism when she becomes Queen (sic) of the new absolute matriarchy of Tiryns. Her subsequent revision of western mythology will obviously serve the vanity of female supremists as effectively as old myths served male supremists (277-78). Anteia may thus be an Aristotelean pendulum swing away from Bellerophon—but she is, like Bellerophon, a role-playing imitation of the pattern of the mythic hero.

Anteia's sister Philonoe, though perceptive and articulate (208-09), is one of those women, so pitied in our age, who appear to "love" directing all their time and energy toward an external object, a husband or child or both. Self-neglect and sacrifice for her husband have caused Philonoe, as she admits, to grow "dull and uninteresting . . . just at the time when [her husband and marriage] most need a spot of perking up" (236). Although dutiful wifeliness may arise from deep-seated inner needs, it remains a role taken from the external world, not from within.

In contrast to Philonoe, Melanippe maintains her center no matter what role or roles she plays. Like Anteia, she is an Amazon (146), but a lifelong Amazon, not a mid-life convert. Like Polyeidus, she is a shape-shifter with "a kind of limited Protean capacity," but only "when sexually in extremis" (215). Despite this Protean quality and the Amazon behavior that comes to her like her name ("one of a dozen-odd given names" the Amazons use) as a cultural role, Melanippe lives from a center:

> For distinct from her "Melanippe-self" [her cultural role], . . . Melanippe knows a private, un-categorizable self impossible for her ever to confuse with the name *Melanippe*—as Perseus, she believes, confused himself with the mythical*persona* *Perseus*, Bellerophon *Bellerophon*. . . .
>
> (238)

Even as "the only true Amazon in a courtful of falsies," "she feels herself to be by no means comprehended by that epithet" (237). For she is *herself*, a category of one that fits her better, she feels, than even the two categories, "human being, female" (237).

This private self gives her the energy to reject Bellerophon's effort to impose a Medusa-like role on her as the audience of his tale. She interrupts his pseudo-*Perseid* daydream: "I can't believe you wrote this mess. . . . It's a lie! It's false! It's full of holes!" (291).

The protest that follows seems to come from her heart: "I'm tired of Amazoning; I'm tired of being a demigod's girlfriend. . . . [W]hat I want is a plain ordinary groovy husband and ten children, nine of them boys" (293). The myth of matriarchy satisfies the inward Melanippe as little as did the myth of patriarchy.

Whatever the name Melanippe ("dark mare") may have meant to Amazons, as a dark "horse" she *is* a Medusa figure, for her function and value, like those of Medusa, are carefully understated. Yet both women emerge as the character in their tales best exemplifying a self that is centered, constant, and capable of initiating concerted action. Understatement with Melanippe again permits Barth, without becoming didactic, to represent integrity to an age intrigued by Protean variability.

The title character of **Dunyazadiad** serves a similar purpose. Dunyazade, who for much of the story seems a mere passive reporter of events, ultimately stands in bold contrast to Shahryar and her sister Scheherazade and in shaded contrast to Shahryar's brother Shah Zaman, while receiving surprising thematic reinforcement from the Genie/author.

The overt power of **Chimera**'s true conclusion comes from Scheherazade, who, Faust-like, puts on in turn the disciplines of knowledge her age provides—politics, psychology, mythology, and folklore—in an impassioned effort "to stop Shahryar from killing [a virgin every night] and wrecking the country" (5-7). Swallowed by hatred of Shahryar (21), Sherry at the climax of the tale, instructs her sister to act, after their double weddings, as she will act: geld her husband, choke him with his own genitals, then slit her own throat (38). The grandiosity of Scheherazade's righteous white rage, justified though it may be, very nearly consumes them all.

But Dunyazade has from the early days of their scheme sensed the one-dimensional quality of the hatred her sister expresses, chiefly because she intuits the ambivalence of Scheherazade's relationship to Shahryar. She suspects that Sherry takes "a kind of pleasure despite herself" (21) in her sexual confrontations with Shahryar. The tale's ending, in which the two royal couples relinquish their rigid social roles—tyrants and victim/rebels—to become joint authors of the book in which they appear (55), signifies that Sherry's behavior to this point, like that of the two kings, has been an assumed part, not the complete expression of needs at her core. She has been under the spell of a social and sexual role.

Sherry's spell is the obverse mirror of that which, the Genie/author says, has deranged the brother kings (22) and that, by implication, consumed middle Perseus and Bellerophon: the spell of the male myth. For Perseus, the myth of the hero compensated for his imagined organ inferiority. For Bellerophon/Deliades, it covered an imagined inferiority to his brother Bellerus. For the two kings in this climactic tale of *Chimera,* the myth of male heroic superiority is the way men save face, the way Shah Zaman, for example, keeps from seeming "chicken-hearted and a fool" (55)—or, worst yet, from seeming a cuckold. But this tale penetrates farthest into causes of the grandiose myth of male heroic power. It indicates that men set themselves up as patriarchs with life-and-death control over women to compensate for an ultimate powerlessness (43-44)—shared by the deluded ifrit of Sherry's favorite story (5)—to control the sexual activity of women, an anxiety that may have loomed larger than ever in the 1970s after Masters and Johnson demonstrated how much more sexual women, in fact, may be than men.

Because the two shahs are men with social power, the evil of their reactions to female sexual power is magnified: their "private apocalypse" infects the state. As one observer of culture has remarked: "wars, dynasties, social upheavals, conquests, and religions are but the superficial symptoms of a secret psychic attitude unknown, even to the individual himself, and transmitted by no historian"; "the whole history of the world" ultimately springs "as a gigantic summation from . . . hidden sources in individuals" (Jung 148-49). Consequently, the psychosexual anxieties of men like the two Shahs, who fall back on traditional models or myths of male behavior, are, as the tale suggests and the novel underscores, of paramount social significance.

Barth, like many contemporary writers (in contrast to Eliot, Pound, and the modernists), recognizes that imitation of past models cannot create a way of life free of the mistakes of masculine heroism (199). For 3500 years, as Barth's tale illustrates, men (and women) have died for the story of the hero—that is, to save face. Only embracing the great *as if,* which allows Shah Zaman to free himself from the myth of male behavior and to express elements truer to his own nature (47, 52), can lead to a culture that differs in the way his (or our) survival requires. *Chimera* reminds us that we must regularly go back into the treasure-house of our culture. But we must use its resources up as quickly as possible—exhaust them—in order to free the imagination from the past, at best only prologue to free invention, on the chance that we will discover the something new the situation requires.

Because the imagination works from the self's center, it can effectively use the past as a resource. But the past, *Bellerophoniad* shows, must not be looked to for models. Instead, it is a treasure-house of mirrors, a literal funhouse. A modern writer, exhausted and blocked like the Genie/author of *Dunyazadiad* or the author with Barth's resume whose lecture is interjected into *Bellerophoniad* (198-203), can employ non-canonical figures like Perseus and Bellerophon as mirrors for projections

to use up the emotional possibilities of the past. In honoring the past thus, the author avoids repressing its mistakes, an error that would lead to archaic behaviors returning when least desired. Taking on the past in Barth's manner, an author may clean out the inner storage (earth?) closet (254) and so work through to other, less explored mirrors like Medusa, Melanippe, Shah Zaman, Dunyazade. This process of exhaustion and discovery thaws possibilities otherwise frozen at the core. It reverses the energy exchange that modernism fostered through symbolic mimesis (199). Rather than have modern characters—Wastelanders, Leopold Blooms, Joe Christmases—unwittingly imitate patterns passed down, Barth's approach addresses the archetypes directly, frames them, uses them up, and moves to less explored mythic and psychological territory.

Clearly Barth is warning that the archetypal life lived slavishly becomes a stereotypic evasion of life, an abstract ideal held in the mind. In his resistance to abstraction Barth stands solidly in the mainstream of southern literary culture. At the same time, however, by pointing toward the original energies of Perseus and the less familiar energies of Medusa, Melanippe, Dunyazade, and his Genie-self, he is reminding us that the archetypes, even for Jung, are *not* the seemingly universal figures and images of myths, legends, religions, and folklore—not the symbols—but the human *energies*—the elemental instincts and behaviors—those images express.[3] Only the less familiar, noncanonical myths of our civilization, or newly invented ones, can set the central energies of the human spirit, the psyche, free from the patterns into which the canonical myths we take for reality have channeled the inward resources. Read in proper order, the tales of *Chimera* record the process whereby their author exhausted the familiar heroic myth in order to release the energies of other myths waiting at the periphery of Western consciousness.

Notes

1. After Ralph Ellison's Rinehart and Saul Bellow's Augie March, with Herman Melville's Confidence Man and James Weldon Johnson's Ex-Colored Man as distant predecessors. See Lifton's forceful defense of Protean man (37-63).

2. Although asserted by Anteia, a flawed, generally satirized character, the existence of a matriarchy prior to the emergence of Homer's Mycenaean heroes accords with modern historical reconstructions of the eastern Mediterranean (McNeill 109-28), especially following Spyridon Marinatos's excavations of Akrotiri on the Greek island of Thera that show the role the Thera eruptions played in destroying the Minoan civilization and opening the way for the Mycenaeans (Vermeule 155 n). Artifacts in the National Archeological Museum in Iraklion, Crete, reveal the overthrow

of the older earth goddesses of the matriarchy by the younger sky gods of the patriarchy led by Zeus and closely tied to the western heroic myth. But Anteia's claim that the matriarchy was "the original and natural" order of things makes no allowance for the hunting culture of the much older cave dwellers around the great central sea.

3. Harris effectively describes the Jungian and Campbellian implications of the struggle that goes on in the novel between masculine and feminine energies (130-55, esp. 143). The pattern, however, according to which characters compensate for inferiority with the myth of the male hero echoes Adler (*Science* 1-2), as perhaps does the reliance on *as-if* solutions to problems (*Individual* 360). But Barth's attitude toward the great *as-if* is far more positive than Adler's. My interpretation of masculine compensation as defensive grandiosity draws on the Self Psychology of revisionist psychoanalyst Heinz Kohut (*Self Psychology* 135-36, 141-60, 193, 245; "Disorders" 416-17, 419, 421).

Works Cited

Adler, Alfred. *The Individual Psychology of Alfred Adler.* Eds. Heinz L. Ansbacher and Rowena R. Ansbacher. New York: Harper and Row, 1956.

———. *The Science of Living.* Ed. Heinz L. Ansbacher. Garden City, NY: Doubleday, 1969.

Barth, John. *Chimera.* New York: Random House, 1972.

———. *The End of the Road.* New York: Bantam, 1969.

———. *The Floating Opera.* New York: Avon, 1956.

———. *Lost in the Funhouse.* Garden City, NY: Doubleday, 1968.

———. *The Sot-Weed Factor.* New York: Grosset & Dunlap, 1964.

Bienstock, Beverly Gray. "Lingering on the Autognostic Verge: John Barth's *Lost in the Funhouse.*" *Modern Fiction Studies* 19 (Spring 1973): 69-78.

Campbell, Joseph. *The Hero with a Thousand Faces.* Princeton: Princeton UP, 1972.

Harris, Charles B. *Passionate Virtuosity: The Fiction of John Barth.* Urbana: U of Illinois P, 1983

Johnson, Robert A. *She: Understanding Feminine Psychology.* New York: Harper & Row, 1977.

Jung, C. G. "The Meaning of Psychology for Modern Man." *Civilization in Transition.* New York: Bollingen, 1964.

Kohut, Heinz, and Ernest S. Wolf. "The Disorders of the Self and their Treatment: An Outline." *International Journal of Psycho-Analysis* 59 (1978): 413-25.

Kohut, Heinz. *Self Psychology and the Humanities.* Ed. Charles B. Strozier. New York: Norton, 1985.

Lifton, Robert Jay. *Boundaries: Psychological Man in Revolution.* New York: Vintage, 1970.

McNeill, William H. *The Rise of the West: A History of the Human Community.* New York: Mentor, 1963.

Morrell, David. *John Barth: An Introduction.* University Park, PA: Pennsylvania State UP, 1976.

Robbe-Grillet, Alain. *For a New Novel: Essays on Fiction.* Trans. Richard Howard. New York: Grove, 1965.

Sartre, Jean-Paul. *Being and Nothingness: An Essay on Phenomenological Ontology.* Trans. Hazel E. Barnes. New York: Philosophical Library, 1956.

Vermeule, Emily. *Greece in the Bronze Age.* Chicago: U of Chicago P, 1972.

Beth A. Boehm (essay date 1989)

SOURCE: Boehm, Beth A. "Educating Readers: Creating New Expectations in *Lost in the Funhouse.*" In *Reading Narrative: Form, Ethics, Ideology,* edited by James Phelan, pp. 102-19. Columbus: Ohio State University Press, 1989.

[*In the following essay, Boehm analyzes Barth's attempt to "educate" his readers—who must be, Boehm argues, "steeped in the high modern aesthetic"—about their traditional expectations of literature and about his nontraditional approach, so that readers can ultimately "appreciate his virtuosity" in* Lost in the Funhouse.]

In **"The Literature of Exhaustion,"** which appeared in 1967, the year before *Lost in the Funhouse,* John Barth makes the distinction between ideas worth discussing and things worth doing and suggests that because anyone can talk about ideas, he prefers the type of art that not many people can *do.* Comparing the pop artists of the Sixties with the acrobats who delighted him as a child, Barth claims that he is "on the whole more impressed by the jugglers and acrobats at Baltimore's old Hippodrome . . . : genuine *virtuosi* doing things that anyone can dream up and discuss but almost no one can do" (30).

This preference for doing over talking, for the performance over the idea, for the process over the substance, is at the very heart of *Lost in the Funhouse,* but the consequences of Barth's preference have been denounced more than they have been applauded. Alter, for instance, objects to Barth's emphasis on the writer's virtuosity, calling it "a peculiarly elitist and miraculist notion of literary continuity and renewal" (227). Claiming that the metafictional techniques employed in *Lost in the Funhouse* and *Chimera* are gratuitous and indulgent, Klinkowitz further suggests that Barth's performance results in very unsatisfying art: in these works, he claims, Barth "confuses the product of art with the conditions of its inception, a process which obviously fascinates Barth . . . but which often results in simple bad writing" (7). Shloss and Tololyan, on the other hand, applaud Barth's virtuosity, but they raise a serious question about the effect of performance literature on the relationship between the author and his reader: "To control, to parade with feckless, changing voice through a brilliantly patterned but hollow text, may be masterful, but it is also solipsistic; it promotes an independent and wary intelligence in readers at the expense of a more satisfying confirmation of the specific narrator or artist" (73). The objection that Barth's performance alters the nature of the literary transaction so that it is less satisfying than that of more traditional narratives has ominous implications. Cynthia Ozick, for example, claims that experimental fiction which seeks to create "wholly different" expectations subverts "not only literature but *the desire to have a literature*" (243). These objections deserve serious consideration, for like the charges of elitism and gratuitousness, they extend beyond *Lost in the Funhouse* to metafictional strategies in general. But in order to evaluate the consequences of Barth's preference for the performance over the idea, it is first necessary to look more closely at the nature of *Lost in the Funhouse.*

The author's note to this collection is the first indication of his preference for doing over saying. Indicating the ideal methods of presentation for each of his fictions, he claims that the story called **"Title,"** "makes somewhat separate but equally valid senses in several media; print, monophonic recorded authorial voice, stereophonic ditto in dialogue with itself, live authorial voice, live ditto in dialogue with monophonic ditto aforementioned, and live ditto interlocutory with stereophonic et cetera, my own preference; it's been 'done' in all six" (ix). Despite the obvious facetiousness of this note, many readers have taken his suggestions at face value, either claiming as one critic has, that many of the pieces in *Lost in the Funhouse* do indeed "lose much meaning in print and have to be imagined spoken" (Hutcheon 99) or suggesting, as another has, that Barth has capitulated to "the forces of an imperfectly understood Marshall MacLuhan" (Helgeson). While Barth's note does not offer any helpful suggestions for ways of *reading* his collection (and after all, the printed version is in fact the only way it's been 'done'), it does indicate that he is an author intensely aware of his medium. But that awareness shines through his choices within his medium for talking about media: his use of words like "aforementioned" and "et cetera," and his repetition of "ditto" (which, of course, indicates repetition itself) work to undercut the literal content of his statement and to satirize—rather than capitulate to—the intermedia artist. The quotation above, for example, is difficult to process when heard, but when the referents

to all those dittoes and aforementions are stabilized on the printed page, it is simply a matter of backtracking according to grammatical conventions to discover meaning. Barth's note on possible and preferred medium, then, leads back to an implicit claim for the distinctiveness of—and his virtuosity with—written language.

This preference for doing over saying creates an interesting rhetorical problem for the author of *Lost in the Funhouse.* Like all virtuosos, Barth needs an audience who can appreciate his considerable skills. Yet as Peter Rabinowitz suggests, Barth seems to belong to a group of writers who "have intentions which are so subtle and complex that they can only write for an authorial audience which they know to be, at best, but a tiny portion of their actual audience" (126).[1] Others have likewise suggested that "Barth wants to annoy his readers rather than engage them" (Shloss 71). The rhetorical strategies of *Lost in the Funhouse,* however, suggest a different intention and a different attitude toward the authorial audience. Barth seems to have believed, in 1968 anyway, that this audience was unprepared to participate fully in the process of making meaning from the type of art he could do best. These readers know the conventions of realistic literature, and they generally expect fiction to reveal some truth about the world outside of the text; in other words, Barth writes for an audience steeped in the high modern aesthetic. His rhetorical difficulty, then, is that he must on the one hand make his readers self-conscious about their expectations of what literature should be and thus teach them the falseness of those expectations; and on the other hand, he must perform in ways that teach the reader to appreciate his virtuosity. He must be both pedant and acrobat, talker and doer.

In handbook fashion, the narrator of **"Lost in the Funhouse"** explains the traditional functions of the parts of a narrative: the beginning should "introduce the principal characters" and "establish their initial relationships," while the middle has the "double and contradictory function of delaying the climax while at the same time preparing the reader for it and fetching him to it" (73-74). Although Barth is hardly conventional, he nevertheless loosely follows this strategy in order to instruct and woo his reader. Thus the collection is roughly divided into three parts, with the first part introducing his fictional concerns through narratives that his audience will be able to enter with the conventions they already understand. The metafictional middle of the book has the double function of making explicit statements about the nature of conventional narratives and of preparing the reader for his unconventional ones. The stories of the third part, then, reward Barth's steady pupils and provide a type of climax—the author is finally allowed to escape his self-consciousness and to perform his type of art.

Let me begin by examining two stories from the first part of the collection, **"Night-Sea Journey"** and **"Peti-**

tion." On the narrative level, the first is about the journey of a sole surviving sperm, blindly pursuing the egg, and the second is the letter of an embittered Siamese twin petitioning for independence from his crude brother; but these stories actually introduce Barth's theme of the writer's solitary endeavor and begin to establish his notion of the uneasy relationship between writers and readers. Barth's swimming "tale-bearer" (Shloss and Tololyan have already pointed out the pun—sperm bear tails while authors bear tales) posits many possible purposes for the journey, but he is unable to choose one that best explains his situation. The contemporary author faces a similar difficulty: though capable of creating many patterns that might explain or structure his experience, he ultimately cannot impose any single *one* on the world because "Truth" is not only relative but ultimately indeterminate. Barth furthers the analogy between swimmer and writer by suggesting that the sperm cannot determine the meaning of the journey any more than "he could say what would happen after She and Hero, Shore and Swimmer, 'merged identities' to become something both and neither" (10). The writer's endeavor, like the sperm's, becomes meaningful only when received by another; but as Iser suggests, "reading removes the subject-object division that constitutes all perception" (293), and though the text can be given life only by a reader, it becomes something that partakes of both reader and writer—and yet is neither. The petitioner's dependence upon his brother likewise mirrors the writer's upon the reader. The brother who writes the letter says he is solitary, articulate but mute, "an observer of life, a meditator, a taker of notes, a dreamer" (59); his twin, on the other hand, is "incoherent but vocal," ignorant, uncompromising, and uncooperative. They depend on each other for existence, yet fight each other for supremacy. The petitioning brother craves his independence—an identity not merged with another's: "Death itself I would embrace like a lover, if I might share the grave with no other company. To be one: paradise! to be two: bliss! But to be both and neither is unspeakable" (68). In "Petition," the fact of dependence is threatening, particularly to the writer, who can assert power only by pulling against his brother (reader), spoiling his pleasure, and halving his force (61). But the Siamese twin, like Barth, realizes that he will always be dependent on another and imagines a new type of relationship, "something more congenial and sympathetic" (67).

While these stories from the beginning of Barth's collection introduce his fictional concerns, they are not metafictional. That these stories are implausible does not make them necessarily unconventional; they do, in a manner, offer "truths" about the conditions of their narrators. No intrusive narrator reminds us of the fictionality of these fictions, of the fact that a sperm could not tell his story, and it is possible to enter the narrative audience in the same way we make the leap of faith

when Kafka's narrator tells us that Gregor Samsa awoke one morning to discover he had been metamorphized into a cockroach. Similarly, the analogy between sperm and writer is not explicit in the text; we discover it, from implicit clues in the text, using the same process we use to find analogies in traditional fiction. What is perhaps also implicit in Barth's bizarre choice of narrators is the belief of many postmodern writers that it is almost impossible to write anything new.

This postmodern concern forms the conflict at the heart of the collection's title story, which has two separate narratives competing for its audience's attention: the first, a seemingly typical story of an adolescent's growing self-consciousness as he makes his way through a funhouse in Ocean City, is continually interrupted—and finally overtaken—by the story of the narrator's growing self-consciousness as a writer. This narrator knows that his authorial audience does not come fresh-eyed to his text, that his readers have a great deal of experience reading fiction, and that this experience has created expectations that the narrator simply cannot fulfill. The narrator similarly believes that his readers will measure his story, not against their experience in the everyday world, but against their experience as participants in fictional worlds. By writing, for example, "When Ambrose and Peter's father was their age, the excursion was made by train, as mentioned in the novel *The 42nd Parallel* by John Dos Passos" (70), the narrator relies for support not upon the historical correctness of his observation, but upon the reader's recognition of a fictional precedent. Similarly, when he worries that a remark attributed to Ambrose might seem too sophisticated for a thirteen-year-old boy, he wonders not if some real teenager could think like that, but if he is violating the fictional principle of verisimilitude. And after writing that Ambrose and his brother were "stimulated by the briny spume," he recalls that "The Irish author James Joyce . . . uses the adjectives *snot-green* and *scrotum-tightening* to describe the sea. Visual, auditory, tactile, olfactory, gustatory" (71). The narrator recognizes that in comparison his own adjectives are trite and will fail to engage the reader's imagination.

Failure of imagination occurs at every level of "**Lost in the Funhouse.**" On the narrative level, both Ambrose and the narrator are imaginatively paralyzed by their self-consciousness. The lonely adolescent, who feels "different" from everyone around him, recognizes that funhouses appeal to lovers and attempts to imagine one where it would be impossible to get lost: "He would be its operator: panel lights would show what was up in every cranny of its cunning of its multifarious vastness; a switch-flick would ease this fellow's way, complicate that's, to balance things out; if anyone seemed lost or frightened, all the operator had to do was" (93). Lost in the conventional form, Ambrose is unable to approach the problem freshly, so he is unable to imagine a better funhouse. Similarly, the narrator's awareness of his literary predecessors renders him incapable of completing even a simple metaphor, and the story is thus full of open-ended statements such as this: The brown hair on Ambrose's mother's forearms gleamed in the sun like" (70). Unwilling to simply complete the fictional formulas he knows readers expect and unable to imagine new formulas, he leaves them blank.

But Ambrose and the narrator are not the only ones lacking imagination. Implicit in this story is a condemnation of the authorial audience's dependence upon pat fictional formulas. Barth's accomplishment in this story is that by beginning to make readers conscious of the falseness of their aesthetic expectations—by revealing the artifice of those techniques that make literature seem "real," he also makes them complicit in the writer's failure to fulfill their expectations to tell the Truth with artifice.

Barth moves from implicit suggestion in **"Lost in the Funhouse"** to explicit statement in **"Title"** and **"Life-Story,"** narratives which seem to support Klinkowitz's contention that the author's obsession with the processes of composition results in "simple bad writing." These stories are not only uninteresting apart from what they have to tell us about fictionality, but they are *purposely* tedious—they are perfect illustrations of Barth's belief that it is far easier to talk technique than it is to make art. But each of these stories works in two ways to instruct the reader and alter his or her expectations of what literature should be. On the first level, the narrators clearly articulate problems all contemporary authors must face: the used upness of old forms, the difficulty of impressing readers who are all too familiar with conventional techniques, and perhaps most important, the fact that "the old analogy between Author and God, novel and world, can no longer be employed unless as a false analogy" (125). Barth's narrators, then, not only desire to abandon old forms, but to abandon likewise the mimetic notion that fiction can really tell us anything about how real people behave; in other words, Barth wants us to acknowledge "the fictitiousness and metaphoric invalidity" (125) of even purportedly realistic fiction.

But in addition to articulating these concerns, Barth instructs his reader through the manipulation of technique. In **"Title,"** for instance, the narrator is so overwhelmed by ennui at the prospect of writing another predictable story that he frequently writes like this: "In this dehuman, exhausted, ultimate adjective hour, when every humane value has become untenable, and not only love, decency, and beauty but even compassion and intelligibility are no more than one or two subjective complements to complete the sentence" (103-4). Unlike the narrator of **"Lost in the Funhouse"** who is unable to fill in the blanks because of his consciousness

of the reader, this narrator substitutes grammatical terms for what should be content words in order to frustrate the reader's expectations that the author should fill in the blanks for her. In addition to making her aware of the writer's role as performer, this substitution of form for substance makes her more conscious of her activity as a reader. That is, even a "passive" reader of traditional narratives anticipates certain means by which the author will complete things, even sentences. When, for example, a reader meets with this beginning, "The house on the hill was," she might anticipate some physical description, such as "white" or "sprawling," and if the author fulfills that expectation, she processes the information without taking much notice of it. If, on the other hand, the author completes the sentence with a less familiar description—with "haunted" or "in flames" for instance—the reader automatically recognizes that this minor departure from the anticipated is significant and forms new narrative expectations based on it; the reader, however, is surprised only by the content, not by the form, and she is able to process the information without consciously contemplating her activity. But when the author simply completes the sentence with "adjective," the reader is unable to process it passively, for instead of meeting the anticipated content word, she meets a term describing the function of the word she expected. Her reading thus disrupted, she is forced both to contemplate her own expectations and to attend more closely to the words that actually appear on the page.

And Barth rewards his authorial audience for this heightened self-consciousness through verbal play. The narrator of **"Title,"** for instance, comments upon his metafictional techniques and suggests that "it's self-defeating to talk about it instead of up and doing it; but to acknowledge what I'm doing while I'm doing it is exactly the point. Self-defeat implies a victor, and who do you suppose it is, if not blank?" (107). The reader is invited to fill in that blank in two ways: the writer, of course, is victorious in that, having talked about technique, he will now be able to perform; but the reader is likewise a winner, for having acknowledged the fictitiousness of conventional structures, she is able to participate in a different type of process.

At this point, Barth acknowledges the necessity of an audience to appreciate his virtuosity and makes explicit the dependent relationship developed in **"Night-Sea Journey"** and **"Petition"**:

> . . . your own author bless and damn you his life is in your hands! He writes and reads himself; don't you think he knows who gives his creatures their lives and deaths? Do they exist except as he or others read their words? Age except we turn their pages? And can he die until you have no more of him?
>
> (124)

Despite the necessity of readers, the narrator of **"Life-Story"** risks alienating them, or as one critic has put it,

"John Barth heckles his literary coconspirators" (Shloss 71) with explicit insults:

> The reader! You, dogged, uninsultable, print-oriented bastard, it's you I'm addressing, who else from inside this monstrous fiction. You've read me this far, then? Even this far? For what discreditable motive? How is it you don't go to a movie, watch TV, stare at a wall, play tennis with a friend, make amorous advances to the person who comes to your mind when I speak of amorous advances? Can nothing surfeit, saturate you, turn you off? Where's your shame?
>
> (123)

Where indeed? The story itself has no plot, and the narrator's self-conscious sophistry is tedious and unaffecting. The reader who forbears and continues reading, despite the narrator's pleading that he put an end to the miserable story by closing the book, must be different from the narrative audience.

Linda Westervelt suggests that John Barth "gives the readers signals that his narrators are not to be identified with him in any simple fashion" (48). Similarly, the authorial audience is not to be identified with the narrative audience that the writer in **"Life-Story"** addresses. Barth is, in part, distinguished from his cranky, bored narrator by his verbal virtuosity, his playfulness, and by his ability to imagine a more congenial relationship between author and reader. The reader who can survive the surface of the printed page is likewise distinguished from the reader who desires more traditional narratives by his willingness to delight in play. The insult is aimed at readers who must have their expectations for action and mimesis fulfilled; as the narrator of **"Anonymiad"** says, "if you must have dialogue and dashing about, better go to the theater" (172). (And the implication here is that other mediums—film, television, theater—fulfill certain narrative functions, while the printed word offers different types of narrative and verbal satisfactions.) The insult hurled at these "incompetent" readers, then, becomes a compliment to Barth's authorial audience, which is made up of a select community of print-oriented people who are willing to engage a difficult written text.

The more congenial relationship between author and reader, or teller and told, is the one implicit in **"Menelaid"** and **"Anonymiad,"** the last stories in the collection. Although both are clearly meant for print, as Barth's experimenting with punctuation marks unique to written language indicates, the underlying relationship between writer and reader is that of the teller and auditor of the oral tale. As Ong suggests, the oral narrator's audience already knows the tale; the pleasure comes from the surprising manner in which it is told. The teller's performance likewise depends upon his audience; according to Ong, the more active and delighted the audience, the more involved the tale (9-21). In the oral narrative, then, both auditor and teller are more concerned with the performance than with the substance of the tale; the purpose of the narrative occasion is not only to instruct the audience by providing insights into the human condition (although these well-told tales do that as well), but also to engage and entertain the audience. Thus for the final stories in the collection, Barth chooses classic tales he expects his authorial audience to have read, and he playfully retells them. Fiction becomes the source of more, original fiction, with the emphasis shifting from the substance to the performance, a shift for which the previous stories in the collection have prepared his audience.

While the reader's awareness of literary precedents paralyzes the narrators of the metafictions in the middle of *Lost in the Funhouse,* Barth turns his audience's literariness to his advantage in **"Menelaid."** Here, the audience's familiarity with the characters and events of the *Odyssey* is a prerequisite for understanding and appreciating Barth's imaginative revision of a small part of Homer's epic. **"Menelaid"** has more substance—more "story"—than **"Title"** or **"Life-Story,"** but the effects of Barth's fiction depend upon its departures from, and additions to, the classic tale. By employing the mythic tale, Barth thus controls the conventions to which his readers must appeal and leads them to those of the epic and the oral tale.

Like Barth's postmodern narrators, Menelaus is worried about his role as "story-teller." The "voice" of **"Menelaid"** recounts the story told to Telemachus (Odysseus's son) and Peisistratus (Nestor's son) when they came to Sparta for news of Odysseus. Within this recounting, however, are other "tellings" of the events leading to his marriage to Helen, the Trojan War, his ambush of Proteus, and his "reconquering" of Helen to several different audiences: Helen, Porteus, his daughter Eidothea, Telemachus and Peisistratus, and finally, the auditor of his current telling, the reader of Barth's book. Each telling envelops the previous telling, resulting in a convoluted attempt to distinguish between discourses: " ' " ' " 'Why?' I repeated," I repeated,' I repeated," I repeated,' I repeated," I repeat" (148). The action of telling takes on greater significance (and takes up more space) than the tale itself, and each occasion for the recounting alters and becomes part of the tale.

And like the previous narrators of *Lost in the Funhouse,* Menelaus is uncertain about his own existence; he is only a "voice," and his story—and his existence as a character in it—can only unfold through a narrative situation. The presence of auditors, then, is necessary for Menelaus to affirm his existence, but by participating in the narrative event, each auditor alters the tale, for every question, utterance, response is incorporated in the next telling. Menelaus, momentarily confused about the occasion of a particular telling, wonders to whom he's speaking: "Got your ear, have I? Like to know how it was, I suppose? Where in Hades are we? Where'd I go? Whom've I got hold of? Proteus? Helen?" (128). His auditor's response indicates both the mythic nature of Menelaus's narrative and that the events of the tale are already well-known:

> " 'Telemachus Odysseus'-son,' the lad replied, 'come from goat-girl Ithaca for news of my father, but willing to have his cloak clutched and listen all night to the tale How You Lost Your Navigator, Wandered Seven Years, Came Ashore at Pharos, Waylaid Eidothea, Tackled Proteus, Learned to Reach Greece by Sailng up the Nile, and Made Love to Your Wife, the most beautiful woman I've ever seen, After an Abstinence of Eighteen Years.' "

(129)

The capitalized phrases act as chapter headings for the events in Menelaus's life and emphasize the story-like quality of that life. But Telemachus's interpolation regarding Helen's beauty arouses the teller's suspicions about his auditor's real reasons for coming to Sparta and gives him another reason to hold tight to Telemachus's cloak and entertain him all evening with his well-told tale. What is a minor event in Homer's *Odyssey,* the purpose of which is very specific—Menelaus must tell about Proteus's news of Odysseus—assumes major importance in Barth's **"Menelaid,"** for the auditor's participation in the tale gives the teller another purpose: to figuratively hold Telemachus captive with his tale in order to keep him out of Helen's bed. And by creating these suspicions, Telemachus ensures that this narrative occasion will become the next episode in Menelaus's life-story, as well as the frame for the current telling.

Unlike the modern writer who cannot wrestle his readers to the ground, Menelaus physically compels his auditors to authenticate his existence. He holds tight to Proteus's tail as he exhausts his animal guises, just as he hangs on to Telemachus's shirt tail; even Helen, confronted in her Trojan bedroom, must hear their history rehearsed by a sword-wielding Menelaus. But eventually it is the version of reality that the tale provides that wins over Telemachus. Smitten by Helen (who is herself a clever fiction-maker), Odysseus's son is a gullible member of the narrative audience and anxious to believe her story—that Proteus "made a Helen out of clouds" to take her place in Troy, while she languished, "chaste and comfy," in Pharos, waiting for her true husband to return. Menelaus, despite his doubts about the truthfulness of her tale, chooses to incorporate his wife's fiction into his own, not because he wants to believe her faithful, but because her fiction proves that he is "loved"; for in his version of the Cartesian dictum, to be loved is to be.

Wise Nestor's son is more like the "modern" reader who must be held only by the tale and is concerned with consistency of both fact and technique, but be-

cause he is an auditor of an oral tale, Peisistratus is able to interrupt Menelaus's narrative and ask questions of the principal characters. He skeptically asks, for instance, why it is that Proteus, who can see both past and future, must depend upon Menelaus's tale in order to discover Eidothea's treachery. Peisistratus's rational questions thus cast doubt upon the "realism" of Menelaus's tale and increase the narrator's doubts about his own reality, despite his attempts to ignore his auditor. When, for example, Menelaus reaches the very center of his narrative, which unfolds the story of why Helen chose him to be her husband over her more heroic suitors, he switches to third-person, as if he cannot quite believe he is the hero of his life-story and as if the story, so often repeated to so many different auditors, no longer belongs exclusively to him. Just as Menelaus is about to repeat his climactic "why," Peisistratus begs leave to ask two questions, but Menelaus, responding as though his auditor is referring to the question so important to the narrative, impatiently corrects him:

> " 'One! One! " ' " 'There the bedstead stood; as he swooning tipped her to it his throat croaked "Why?" ' ' "
>
> " ' " ' "Why?" asked Eidothea.'
>
> " ' " 'Why why?' Proteus echoed." '
>
> " 'My own questions,' Peisistratus insisted, 'had to do with mannered rhetoric and your shift of narrative viewpoint.'
>
> " ' " 'Ignore that fool!' Proteus ordered from the beach." '
>
> " 'How can Proteus—' 'Seer,' 'So.' 'The opinions echoed in these speeches aren't necessarily the speaker's.' "

(149-50)

Like Barth, who distances the insults aimed at incompetent readers through a series of narrators, Menelaus refrains from insulting Peisistratus directly and from thus risking the loss of his most attentive, if least gullible, auditor by attributing his impatience to Proteus, whose ability to see future events clearly includes future narrations.

Although Peisistratus is a comic characterization of the modern reader who lacks imagination, he also possesses many traits of the authorial audience Barth attempts to create throughout *Lost in the Funhouse*: while he wants playfulness, Peisistratus is engaged, actively involved, and willing to work as hard as his narrator. His pragmatic questions frustrate and annoy Menelaus, but Peisistratus's attention to details would surely earn Barth's admiration (after all, it is through Peisistratus's observations that Barth exhibits his own ability to "read" closely). And while other auditors seek in the narrative support for their own versions of truth, Peisistratus approaches the narrative disinterestedly, as simply a story, though a story whose characters' actions and motives should be psychologically realistic.

It is likewise important to remember that while Menelaus suffers from the same insecurities as the narrators of **"Lost in the Funhouse," "Life-Story,"** and **"Title,"** Barth himself is liberated from the solipsism of those stories through his use of Menelaus's tale. Instead of worrying about writing for an audience incapable of appreciating his abilities, Barth writes for the reader who, having made his way through the funhouse, has, at least temporarily, consented to Barth's type of fiction. While Menelaus must coerce and force his auditors to attend to his tale, Barth knows that his audience can be held only by the force of his words, and he writes with a confidence missing from the earlier stories in the collection. Unlike the narrator of **"Title"** who feels he must explain the paradox inherent in the term "self-defeat," the author of **"Menelaid"** writes for a reader whose consciousness of linguistic play has been raised by the previous stories in *Lost in the Funhouse.* Having replaced the reader's expectation for plot and mimesis with an expectation for verbal virtuosity, Barth grants the reader his or her freedom to discover and appreciate that play. Menelaus, for example, relates Helen's response to his story about the capture of Proteus, which he tells while holding her on the deck of his ship off Pharos: " " ' "Hard tale to hold onto, this," declared my pooped spouse' " (139). The author does not explain that tale is a homonym for tail and thus refers not only to the convoluted story, but also to the literal tail by which Menelaus holds Proteus and to the figurative one by which he holds Helen, nor does he explain that Helen is not only pooped by the attempt to follow the tale, but also literally "decked." He allows the reader to discover the reverberations and double-entendres, and his clever use of sexual euphemisms, anachronisms, and American idioms reveals not a weariness with writing, but rather a love affair with the printed word, a love he seeks to share with his reader.

Love is the overriding theme of this collection, from its inception and night-sea journeying sperm through its final anonymous narrator, who suggests that "The trouble with us minstrels is, when all's said and done we love our work more than our women. More, indeed, than we love ourselves" (177). Throughout *Lost in the Funhouse* it seems, as Linda Westervelt has suggested, that "lover and designer are mutually exclusive roles. . . . On the one hand, the narrator-agents of **"Lost in the Funhouse"** and **"Life-Story"** are envious of the 'lovers for whom funhouses are designed' and characters in 'rousing good yarns,' and they hope to interest those kinds of readers in their fiction; on the other hand, they realize the futility of that hope" (51). But, as I suggested earlier, through the use of Menelaus and the anonymous minstrel, Barth distances himself from these narrative complaints and from this type of futile relationship with his readers. Through the medium of his fiction, he engages in a type of mutually satisfying love-making with his readers. The Genie who appears to Scheherazade in Barth's next work, *Chimera,* is a char-

acter not so distant from his author: "a light-skinned fellow of forty or so, smooth-shaven and bald as a rock's egg," with "queer lenses that he wore in frame over his eyes" (16). A writer from the twentieth century, he laments that "the only readers of artful fiction were critics, other writers, and unwilling students who, left to themselves, preferred music and pictures to words" (17). And it is the Genie who most clearly articulates the relationship Barth seeks with his authorial audience: narrative, says the writer, is "a love-relation, not a rape: its success depended upon the reader's consent and co-operation, which she could withhold or at any moment withdraw; also upon her own combination of experience and talent for enterprise, and the author's ability to arouse, sustain, and satisfy her interest" (34). Instead of antagonizing his reader as does the narrator of **"Life-Story"** or resenting his dependency and his role as a solitary observer, a dreamer, a taker of notes as does the petitioning Siamese twin, Barth—in **"Menelaid"** and **"Anonymiad,"** as in *Chimera*—grants his reader her independence and power at the same time that he seeks to share with her his love of language and his artistry.

If Barth's preference for doing over saying gives his book this type of rhetorical construction, a construction that necessitates his persuading the reader to consent to his performance, then how troubling are the various objections cited at the outset? Critics like Shloss and Tololyan find the analogy between reader and lover to be false, "incapable of closure and bound inevitably to disappoint. A reader is not a surrogate lover. Nameless, faceless, uncommitted to the literary transaction except as it pleases or annoys him, he cannot validate a writer's self in the same way that men and women confirm each other's worth" (Shloss 73). On a certain level this complaint is valid, as Barth himself seems to suggest in **"Menelaid,"** for Menelaus is clearly pitiable for his inability to accept Helen's love, for his need to find authenticity through narration, and for his need to force his auditors to comply—to "rape" his narratees. But what happens to the characters in the literary work (whether that work is *Lost in the Funhouse* or something more traditional, like *Middlemarch*) is not what happens to the flesh and blood reader or writer of that work; the transaction between reader and writer exists not in the text, but through the text, through the medium of the printed page. Throughout *Lost in the Funhouse,* Barth seeks to educate his readers in order that they can appreciate not the man John Barth, but his verbal performance; similarly, Barth writes not for an audience that seeks verification of its own truths in his work, but for one that consents to participate in that virtuoso performance. In other words, Barth uses the analogy between reader and lover not in the romantic sense that Shloss and Tololyan do—that lovers share a heartfelt emotional and moral bond—but in a sexual sense—that reader and writer luxuriate in each other's skillful performances.

For what Shloss and Tololyan simply ignore—or refuse to grant—is the metafictionist's basic assumption that the false analogy is the romantic one that equates author and god and replaces religion with literature, and it is ultimately Barth's refusal to communicate a "vision" that frustrates and disappoints readers like them. By making the reader aware of the text as art, metafictional strategies take away the emotional satisfaction of losing the self to the author's vision. A heightened consciousness of the artifice in a literary work brings about more than just a "wary intelligence" and a freedom to discover and delight in the text's offerings; it also relinquishes to the reader a disconcerting responsibility for his or her own moral life. For Barth, literature is not sacred (as his willingness to "rewrite" Homer indicates), and to those of us who are critics, writers, and teachers of those "unwilling students," this is his biggest affront. By turning literature into a sexual experience—a fondly remembered one-night stand—Barth denies the possibility of true transcendence through art. As *Chimera*'s Genie suggests, "the treasure of art . . . could not redeem the barbarities of history or spare us the horrors of living and dying" (25).

It is no wonder, then, that Robert Scholes suggests that Barth is a chronicler of our "despair over the exhausted forms of our thought and our existence" (123). For if the desire to have a literature is connected to man's desire to bring order to the chaotic facts of the world, the metafictionist's exposing the artificiality of that order would indeed seem to undermine that desire. Eagleton's objection to Roland Barthes's "hedonistic" critical approach likewise applies to performance literature:

> Caught up in this exuberent dance of language, delighting in the textures of words themselves, the reader knows less the purposive pleasures of building a coherent system, binding textual elements masterfully together to shore up a unitary self, than the masochistic thrills of feeling that self shattered and dispersed through the tangled webs of the work itself. . . . Far from returning the reader to himself, in some final recuperation of the selfhood which the act of reading has thrown into question, the modernist text explores his or her secure cultural identity, in a *jouissance* which for Barthes is both readerly bliss and sexual orgasm.
>
> (82-83)

Metafiction is not an inherently asocial form (one need only look at Borges or Coover to discover strong political and cultural concerns), but like most writers of this genre, Barth does despair over literature's failure—and ultimately its inability—to redeem mankind through the construction of ordered systems representative of "reality." Yet Barth's metafictional strategies suggest that reading can offer sustenance of another kind: an intellectual and aesthetic repast, a pleasant, joyful exercise of mind that differs from, but nevertheless coexists with, other happy diversions like playing tennis, watching acrobats or movies, and wandering through funhouses.

Performance literature is thus a retreat from the prosaic and chaotic facts of everyday existence—the stuff of which realistic literature is constructed—and its linguistic play is a source of readerly bliss. And play for play's sake may indeed by a worthwhile cultural value, for the writer of metafiction, like this character in Tom Robbins's *Jitterbug Perfume,* seems to be "convinced that play—more than piety, more than charity or vigilance—was what allowed human beings to transcend evil" (197).

In addition to the pleasure of play, however, performance literature offers a more enduring satisfaction. While it may not return the reader to a secure cultural identity, its self-referential language does return to the reader a certain power over linguistic structures by emphasizing the "man-madeness" of those structures. Language may not be able to corral the random facts of the world into a coherent order, but readers can actively create order from the words that appear on the page. The fact that language is contextual and meaning is slippery may be a source of anxiety for semanticists and truth-seekers, but for writers and readers of metafiction, it is a source of intellectual stimulation. Rather than despairing at the multiple meanings of words and the structures made from them, readers are encouraged to celebrate their ability to decipher and find meaning in these man-made structures.

The metafictional performance does, however, make the literary work only an "artful trinket" which, while having no redemptive power, "at least sustained, refreshed, expanded, ennobled, and enriched our spirits along the painful way" (*Chimera* 25). The emphasis on the pleasure offered by the author's performance, then, is paramount and perhaps lends credence to Alter's and Klinkowitz's charges of elitism and gratuitousness. Barth draws our attention to the suppleness of language and to its complete tractability in his hands, and some critics find the metafictionist's flaunting of his virtuosity gratuitous because his "artificial" structures never seem to point to anything outside of themselves. As many readers have suggested, Barth, like Ambrose, seems lost in a structure with no way out; but unlike Ambrose, Barth is lost in structures of his own making. By employing what he sees as worn out conventions and themes against themselves, by making them the subject of his writing, Barth attempts to educate his readers to the pleasures of performance literature, and far from being gratuitous, Barth's "performance" is thus integral to his work. In fact, the performance is ultimately all there is, and this does put a particularly elitist, and perhaps egotistical, emphasis on Barth's own ability as a performer. Alter, for instance, suggests that "Barth seems to be saying, we have come to such a pass that it is virtually impossible to write anything at all. Nevertheless, a few geniuses, having recognized that difficult task, will somehow manage to create" (227). If the reader of Barth's fiction is made to feel elite, a member of a select community of print-oriented people, how much more elite is the author who is able to entertain this select group.

What distinguishes Barth from many other experimental writers is his attempt to initiate a broader audience to the pleasures of performance literature. Rather than writing for a tiny portion of his actual audience, as Rabinowitz has suggested that he does, in *Lost in the Funhouse,* Barth instructs his actual audience in order that he may include them in this authorial audience. Indeed, in "The Literature of Replenishment," Barth wrote that the postmodern writer should aspire to make his work more democratic:

> He may not hope to reach and move the devotees of James Michener and Irving Wallace—not to mention the lobotomized mass-media illiterates. But he should hope to reach and delight, at least part of the time, beyond the circle of what Mann used to call the early Christians: professional devotees of high art.
>
> (70)

Barth attempts to reach an audience that extends beyond other writers, critics, and unwilling students, for his simple explanations of critical issues like structuralism and reception theory, and his deconstructionist musings about the disparity between sign and meaning are not directed toward already knowledgeable critics, nor are they an attempt to flaunt his own knowledge. Rather, Barth's instructional comments are directed toward the reader steeped in the high modern aesthetic who may find questions raised by current literary theory terribly esoteric, and by educating this reader with his handbook, Barth seeks to count him or her among the "elite."

This didactic quality may make *Lost in the Funhouse* a work whose rhetorical strategies create their own obsolescence. Wayne Booth, for instance, asks "Why do some works of intricate narrative obliquity, like John Barth's **'Lost in the Funhouse,'** seem thinner and thinner the longer one studies them?" (446). I have already suggested that stories like **"Life-Story"** and **"Title"** are tedious apart from what they can teach us about fiction, and the failure of these stories to sustain our interest during subsequent readings has to do, in part, with their textbook quality: once a reader grasps the issues raised in these fictions and becomes skillful at deciphering the puzzles offered, these didactic stories, like an old McGuffey reader, are no longer necessary or satisfying. Although the second, third, and fourth readings of any work differ from each other, sometimes revealing new depths, sometimes answering old questions, and sometimes betraying serious flaws, subsequent readings of a metafictional text that seeks to teach its reader to read itself, offer little remuneration for the effort.

But also responsible for the apparent "thinness" of these stories is the ephemeral nature of the transcendence offered by Barth's literary performance. By focusing on

the activity of reading rather than the content offered by the text. Barth dissolves meaning into a free play of language—play which lasts only as long as the activity itself continues. Although he accepts the importance of the reader in the literary transaction and acknowledges her independence, the more congenial relationship Barth establishes is not that of the Iserian "co-creator." "The teller's role," *Chimera*'s Genie suggests, "regardless of his actual gender, was essentially masculine, the listener's or reader's feminine, and the tale was the medium of their intercourse" (34). Although the Genie goes on to suggest that the "femininity" of readers was not a "a docile or inferior condition" (34), the fact remains that it is the "masculine" author's role to arouse the feminine reader's interest by leaving blanks for her to fill and by creating puzzles for her to solve. This sexually defined relationship ultimately stresses the potency of the author, upon which the reader's bliss depends (and interestingly enough, the mythic heroes of the last two stories in *Chimera* are worried about impotency). But as she becomes increasingly conscious of her activity as a reader and increasingly familiar with the text's intricacies, the rarer are the delights offered by the text—and the thinner that text seems. Because the pleasures offered by Barth's text are primarily intellectual (the satisfaction of deciphering and uncovering meanings which the author has made for the reader) and esoteric (the satisfaction of suddenly finding oneself a member of the select group of readers who are print-oriented rather than of the disdained group which needs dialogue and dashing about), they are not as intensely felt during the second or third reading; it is not that the structures—the puns and double-entendres—are no longer clever or amusing, but rather, that the novelty of discovering them for oneself wears off when the text has seemingly exhausted itself.

These failures, however, testify to the overall success of Barth's rhetorical strategies in *Lost in the Funhouse.* The text itself may fail to bring enduring delights to the individual reader; but by initiating readers to the almost hedonistic delights offered by performance literature, Barth creates an audience of active, self-conscious readers capable of re-experiencing the pleasures of discovery whenever they are confronted with a new puzzle. While he may not share a vision, he does share his wonder at the joyful power of man-made structures to sustain and refresh us, and in the process, he creates an authorial audience that can appreciate his verbal acrobatics. Writers of metafiction may indeed attempt to create "wholly different expectations" and to alter the relationship between the reader and the writer, but inherent in their strategies is the realization that the reader must consent to their performance and must willingly enter the authorial audience. Rather than attempting to destroy our desire to have a literature, writers of metafiction seek to make us more self-conscious readers of literature. Those who make it through the Barthian funhouse emerge, perhaps not as better people or better lovers in the "real" world, but as better readers and better lovers of the printed word.

Note

1. He uses the term "authorial audience" to describe the hypothetical audience for whom the author fashions rhetorical effects, and I have adopted his term and definition for the purposes of this article.

Works Cited

Alter, Robert. *Partial Magic: The Novel as Self-Conscious Genre.* Berkeley: University of California Press, 1975.

Barth, John. *Chimera.* Greenwich, CT: Fawcett, 1972.

———. "The Literature of Exhaustion." *Atlantic Monthly* 220 (August 1967): 29-35.

———. "The Literature of Replenishment." *Atlantic Monthly* 245 (Jan. 1980): 65-71.

———. *Lost in the Funhouse.* New York: Bantam Books, 1969.

Booth, Wayne. *The Rhetoric of Fiction.* 2d ed. Chicago: University of Chicago Press, 1983.

Eagleton, Terry. *Literary Theory: An Introduction.* Minneapolis: University of Minnesota Press, 1983.

Helgeson, Susan. "Fictions that Teach Readers How to Read—And Writers How to Write." Unpublished essay.

Hutcheon, Linda. *Narcissistic Narrative: The Metafictional Paradox.* Waterloo, Ontario: Wilfrid Laurier University Press, 1980.

Iser, Wolfgang. "The Reading Process: A Phenomenological Approach." *The Implied Reader: Patterns of Communication in Prose Fiction from Bunyan to Beckett.* Baltimore: Johns Hopkins University Press, 1974.

Klinkowitz, Jerome. *Literary Disruptions: The Making of Post-Contemporary American Fiction.* Urbana: University of Illinois Press, 1975.

Ong, Walter J., S. J. "The Writer's Audience is Always a Fiction." *PMLA* 90 (1975): 9-21.

Ozick, Cynthia. "Innovation and Redemption: What Literature Means." *Art and Ardor: Essays.* New York: Dutton, 1984.

Rabinowitz, Peter J. "Truth in Fiction: A Reexamination of Audiences." *Critical Inquiry* 4 (1977): 121-141.

Robbins, Tom. *Jitterbug Perfume.* New York: Bantam Books, 1984.

Scholes, Robert. *Fabulation and Metafiction.* Urbana: University of Illinois Press, 1979.

Shloss, Carol, and Khachig Tololyan. "The Siren in the Funhouse: Barth's Courting of the Reader." *Journal of Narrative Technique* 11 (Winter 1981): 64-74.

Westervelt, Linda. "Teller, Tale, Told: Relationships in John Barth's Latest Fiction." *Journal of Narrative Technique* 8 (Winter 1978): 42-55.

Carol Booth Olson (essay date summer 1990)

SOURCE: Olson, Carol Booth. "Lost in the Madhouse." *The Review of Contemporary Fiction* 10, no. 2 (summer 1990): 56-63.

[*In the following essay, Olson contends that* Lost in the Funhouse *depicts the postmodern artist as "an incoherent voice muttering in a void."*]

In John Barth's ***Lost in the Funhouse,*** the artist, confronted by the bankruptcy of existing forms of fiction, searches for a way to salvage the literature of exhaustion. This quest is a futile one, however, because the protean persona loses his way and his mind in the "labyrinthine corridors" of language. The further he ventures into the "mirror-maze" of art, the more entrapped he becomes in the distorting reflections of his own psyche. Midas-like, everything he touches turns into fiction while reality recedes from his grasp. Ultimately, he is reduced to an incoherent voice muttering in a void.

Although the speaker of **"Life-Story"** protests that he is not "unmanageably schizophrenic," indications that the narrator of the sequence suffers from irremediable fragmentation appear throughout. In the opening monologue, **"Night-Sea Journey,"** for example, the existential voyager (a spermatozoon) admits,

> "Very likely I have lost my senses. The carnage at our setting out; our decimation by whirlpool, poisoned cataract, sea-convulsion; the panic stampedes, mutinies, slaughters, mass suicides; the mounting evidence that none will survive the journey—add to these anguish and fatigue; it were a miracle if sanity stayed afloat."[1]

He feels that the night-sea journey toward conception is "without meaning" and, therefore, yearns for some "unimaginable embodiment" of himself to "terminate this aimless, brutal business." Born out of this despair, Ambrose comes to fear "schizophrenia, impotence creative and sexual—in short living and dying."[2]

Again, in **"Life-Story,"** the narrator simultaneously acknowledges and mocks the fact that he is psychologically disturbed:

> One manifestation of schizophrenia as everyone knows is the movement from reality toward fantasy, a progress which not infrequently takes the form of distorted and

fragmented representation, abstract formalism, an increasing preoccupation, even obsession, with pattern and design for their own sakes . . . to the (virtual) exclusion of representative "content."

(115)

At least one critic has also noticed that "the narrator-speaker, in fact, sounds a bit mad himself as he raves on at a maniacal, yet halted pace, urging himself to stop and then in desperation pleading to his father to do it for him: 'Put an end to this, for pity's sake!'"[3]

At first glance, *Funhouse* appears to be a collection of arbitrarily ordered short stories. However, upon closer inspection, one discovers a certain cohesiveness in the tales. In the preface to the book, the author maintains that the volume is "neither a collection or a selection, but a series" of reflections meant to be received "all at once." The central symbol for the structure of the work is the Möbius strip "which begins and ends only to begin again," as Kyle notes, continually turning in upon itself. Likewise, the "plot doesn't rise by meaningful steps but winds upon itself, digresses, retreats, hesitates, sighs, collapses, expires."[4]

Several well-planned "coincidences" in the series reinforce the connection between the individual narratives. The spermatozoon in **"Night-Sea Journey,"** for instance, emerges in the following story (or chapter) as the neglected and long nameless Ambrose. When Ambrose reaches that "awkward age," he, in turn, wonders whether some spermatozoa "perhaps lose their way" in the "hot, dark windings, past Love's Tunnel's fearsome obstacles." The "talebearer of a generation" recurs once again in **"Autobiography"** as the voice of fiction who vows to continue the "tale" of his "forebears." It is also significant that at the end of the book the minstrel in **"Anonymiad"** launches his chronicle of "misery" in an amphora; for a similar water-message floated in on the tide earlier in the sequence, filling Ambrose's spirit with "new and subtle burdens."[5]

Characterization plays an important role in Barth's creation of interwoven tales. Echo is the key figure here. On one level, she is the author who "edits, heightens, mutes, turns others' words to her ends." But on another level, she symbolizes the fact that the various personae are "all of a piece," as William Carlos Williams would say; that is, they recall and reflect one another. This is implicit in the image of the funhouse in which the individual is replicated in an endless succession of mirrors. For example, the triad of Ambrose, Magda, and Peter in **"Lost in the Funhouse"** is repeated in **"Petition"** with the competition between two Siamese twins for Thalia; in **"Echo"** with the first, second, and third person relationship of Narcissus, Echo, and Tiresias; in **"Menelaiad"** with the cuckolding of Menelaus by Helen and Paris; and in **"Anonymiad"** with the betrayal of the

minstrel by Merope and Aegisthus. But the protagonists in the sequence have more in common than a compromising relationship in a ménage à trois. The narrator of **"Menelaiad"** sums up their mutual predicaments: "One thing's certain: somewhere Menelaus lost course and steersman, went off track, never got back on, lost hold of himself, became a record merely, the record of his loosening grasp" (128).

Midway through **"Lost in the Funhouse"** the speaker asks, "What is the story's theme?" and then answers his own question: "Ambrose is ill." In a sense, the entire book depicts the process of psychic breakdown, of the "loosening grasp" of a consciousness. In the same way that Eliot explores the symptoms of spiritual bankruptcy in the wastelanders through various voices (Marie, Ferdinand, Tiresias, et al.), Barth chronicles the fragmentation of a composite persona (Ambrose, Menelaus, the minstrel, et al.). The symbol of their collective state of mind is the labyrinth.

In *The Garden and the Map,* John Vernon identifies both the map and its counterpart, the labyrinth, as schizophrenic images because they imply an area that is "fragmented in all ways, spatially, physically, temporally." Everything exists in "discrete, mutually exclusive units; hence there is no process; the world is immobile."[6] As Barth writes in **"The Literature of Exhaustion,"** the labyrinth "is a place in which, ideally, all the possibilities of choice (of direction, in this case) are embodied, and—barring special dispensation like Theseus's—must be exhausted before one reaches the heart."[7] However, his characters become paralyzed when confronted by limitless alternatives and, ultimately, "lose their way and their souls" in the funhouse. Kierkegaard discusses this dilemma in *The Sickness unto Death*:

> Now if possibility outruns necessity, the self runs away from itself, so that it has no necessity whereto it is bound to return—then this is the despair of possibility. The self becomes an abstract possibility which tires itself out with floundering in the possible, but does not budge from the spot. . . .[8]

The personae in *Funhouse* all exhibit certain destructive patterns of behavior and undergo similar crises as they "flounder" through their lives that indicate the gradual disintegration of their psyches. At the heart of these problems is a decided lack of a sense of self. Ambrose is continually plagued by feelings of unreality, feelings that surface whenever he is in the presence of other people. For instance, when Ambrose becomes separated from Peter and Magda in the funhouse, the narrator comments: "Ambrose understood not only that they were all so relieved to be rid of his burdensome company that they didn't even notice his absence, but that he himself shared their relief. Stepping from the treacherous passage at last into the mirror-maze, he saw once again, more clearly than ever, how readily he deceived himself into supposing he was a person" (89-90). The minstrel in **"Anonymiad"** also admits "uneasiness in the world" and in his "own skin," describing himself as a "lad the contrary of solipsistic, who felt the world and all its contents real except himself." Beverly Bienstock's assessment of Menelaus is appropriate for all the speakers: "And so Menelaus comes in his own mind to be a mere shadow, a zero, an Echo."[9] In essence, their collective point of view is, as the minstrel says, "first person anonymous."

In *The Divided Self,* R. D. Laing writes that "if the individual cannot take the realness, aliveness, autonomy, and identity of himself and others for granted, then he has to become absorbed in contriving ways of trying to be real, of keeping himself or others alive, of preserving his identity, in efforts, as he will often put it, to prevent him from losing his self."[10] For the speakers in *Funhouse,* the act of writing is the one thing that gives them any sense of self. In the world of fiction, they can assume any "identity" they choose and create and destroy people and places with the stroke of a pen. Unfortunately, they cannot seem to integrate thought and action, words and things, mental and physical. Their commitment to the imagination is at the expense of (and obviously a replacement for) a meaningful existence in everyday life.

Ambrose, for example, is a spectator rather than a participant; he can only watch himself watch other people relate to one another. When he is alone with Magda, Ambrose has to tell himself, "This is what they call passion. I am experiencing it." But his mind is too busy "taking notes on the scene" to enable him to feel anything but an "odd detachment." Ambrose does not feel that he belongs in the funhouse of love, but he likes to think that he will build a funhouse of words "vaster by far than any yet constructed." The speaker in **"Petition"** is even more divorced from other human beings and the physical world. He draws his sustenance solely from "introspection," "revery," and "fancy," and would like nothing better than to be severed from the sexual drives and bodily needs represented by his "gross," inarticulate twin brother. In essence, the mind has completely dissociated itself from the body.

Although the narrator-speakers in the book value the written word above all else, each, ironically, suffers from an inability to verbalize his thoughts and feelings. Afflicted with self-consciousness, an existential despair about the lack of meaning in his life and his craft, and a severe case of indecision, the artist (or rather artist manqué) balks at every turn in the mirror-maze of fiction. Puzzled by the problem of narrative progression, the author of **"Lost in the Funhouse"** muses: "We should be much farther along than we are; something has gone wrong; not much of this preliminary rambling

seems relevant. Yet everyone begins in the same place; how is it that most go along without difficulty but a few lose their way?" (75). In **"Life-Story,"** the character in the fiction-within-a-fiction voices his creator's concern that he must "retain his self possession to the end" of the sentence or he may "go mad" and perhaps "destroy himself and/or others." Try as they might, no one seems to be able to reach to the heart of the labyrinth, to complete a story.

One of the factors which encumbers the progress of these would-be writers is their own self-absorption. They question every thought, carefully structure and critique each statement before conversing and, in short, analyze the spontaneity out of their lives. Like Narcissus, they have become prisoners of their own reflection. The dilemma of the speaker in **"Title"** is typical of most of the personae. He feels that fiction is in an irrevocable process of attrition and that its demise mirrors the decline in "humane" values like love, decency and compassion. Confronted by a world without meaning, he cannot find any justification for perpetuating the "passionless" art of writing, an art which has become "an exhausted parody of itself." But he is so obsessed with his plight that he spends every available hour bemoaning the fact that he cannot think of anything to say: "And I think. What now. Everything's been said already, over and over; I'm as sick of this as you are; there's nothing to say. Say nothing. / What's new? Nothing" (102). The speaker's effort to "fill in the blank" becomes increasingly laborious with each sentence. There is no possibility of a dialogue with his wife because he has to concentrate on choosing the appropriate preposition or noun to sustain the endless chain of fragments which are designed to ward off "General anesthesia. Self-extinction. Silence." Aware of the debilitating effects of his "obscene verbal problem," the narrator pleads, "Somebody please stop me"; but he continues to ramble on compulsively:

> Oh God comma I abhor self-consciousness. I despise what we have come to; I loathe our loathesome loathing, our place our time our situation, our loathsome art, this ditto necessary story. The blank of our lives. It's about over. Let the *dénouement* be soon and unexpected, painless if possible, quick at least, above all soon. Now now! How in the world will it ever
>
> (110)

Even if he had the strength of purpose and the confidence in the validity of his craft to resume the "Progress of Literature," the writer would still encounter obstacles in his path. For he must *choose* which direction to take in the labyrinth—arrive at a decision and act on it. Suffering from Kierkegaard's "despair of possibility," he cannot bring himself to make this kind of commitment. Laing explains that "there is something final and definitive about an act, which this type of person regards with suspicion. Action is the dead end of possibility. It scleroses freedom. If it cannot be utterly eschewed, then every act must be of such an equivocal nature that the 'self' can never be trapped in it" (87). So, like Eliot's Prufrock, the speakers pretend that there will be time "for a hundred indecisions / And for a hundred visions and revisions," but, somehow, they sense that their procrastination and vacillation is not liberating but stagnating.

The protagonist's own psychological handicaps and his "negative resolve" about the future of art and society combine to make his existence an impoverished one. In order to cope with his sense of unreality, fear of impotence, mental paralysis, and feelings of estrangement, he elects to "efface what can't be faced or else fill in the blank" with fantasy. Perhaps because from the moment of his birth there is doubt as to both his legitimacy and his name, Ambrose never develops ontological security. He is so uncomfortable in his own body and in the company of others that he often longs to push a button and "disappear" himself. Other protagonists in the sequence exhibit a similar inclination to self-destruct. "Narcissus desired himself defunct before his conception" (as did the spermatozoon); the minstrel admits, "I yearned to be relieved of myself: by heart failure, bolt from Zeus, voice from heaven"; and Echo persists "in effacing herself absolutely," living only by giving back "other's delight regardless of hers." Suicide would seem to be the logical resolution to the problem, but it involves both choice and action—commitment and conduct that the schizoid speaker fears worse than death. The spermatozoon's position on this matter is characteristic of them all: "'Indeed, if I have yet to join the hosts of suicides, it is because (fatigue apart) I find it no meaningfuller to drown myself than to go on swimming'" (4).

John Vernon points out that "one of the primary devices the schizophrenic uses to cover himself is to retreat into fantasy."[11] While the personae in *Funhouse* frequently ponder self-extinction, they usually opt for withdrawal from reality. Ambrose is constantly conjuring up stories, rewrites of the scripts of everyday life in which he is courageous, decisive, and beloved rather than timid, vacillating, and ignored. For instance, in **"Water-Message,"** after the boys discover Peggy Robbins and her lover in the Sphinx's Den, Ambrose concocts a fiction in which she returns to the "Jungle" and begs his forgiveness for being unfaithful. His vision is clearly romantic (although Barth's is obviously mock-romantic) and hackneyed: "then he bore her from the Jungle, lovingly to the beach, into the water. They swam until her tears were made a part of Earth's waters; then hand in hand they waded shoreward on the track of the moon" (50). A certain amount of daydreaming is healthy and normal for a young boy; but almost all of Ambrose's adventures take place in the realm of fantasy rather than

in the real world. Indeed, the brother in **"Petition,"** Echo, Menelaus, the minstrel—all of these characters may be figments of Ambrose's imagination.[12] The entire sequence may be the result of his effort to work out his own problems in fiction. But then, perhaps Ambrose is the creation of an anonymous narrator who, in turn, feels that he is the product of some elusive master novelist.

Regardless of who the source of this composite consciousness is, all of the personae in *Funhouse* suffer from "too much imagination." The process of fiction-making begins to snowball and it is impossible to reach through the levels of the tale to any concrete reality. Hence Menelaus pleads with Proteus, "When will I reach my goal through its cloaks of story? How many veils to naked Helen?" As the speaker becomes lost in the funhouse of fiction, he becomes imprisoned in his own solipsistic universe. The minstrel of the **"Anonymiad"** is actually relieved when Aegisthus abandons him on the island because he can embrace the world of art exclusively and leave the "real" world to "clip and tumble, burn and bleed": "I had imagination for realm and mistress, and her dower language! Isolated from one world by Agamemnon, from another by my own failings, I'd make Mycenaes of which I was the sole inhabitant, and sing to myself from their golden towers the one tale I knew" (185).

Eventually, the speakers in the sequence cut themselves off from everything that is essential to any kind of creative interchange—including their own bodies. The brother in **"Petition"** who most explicitly identifies with ratiocination, articulation, and the spirit vehemently repudiates the flesh:

> I am slight, my brother is gross. . . . He's ignorant but full of guile; I think I may call myself reasonably educated, and if ingenuous, no more so I hope than the run of scholars. My brother is gregarious. . . . For my part, I am by nature withdrawn; an observer of life, a meditator, a taker of notes, a dreamer if you will. . . . We have nothing in common but the womb that bore, the flesh that shackles, the grave that must soon receive us. If my situation has any advantage it's only that I can see him without his seeing me; can therefore study and examine our bond, how ever to dissolve it . . .
>
> (59-60)

As a result of this irremediable fragmentation, Prufrock gradually becomes Gerontion—a disembodied voice reiterating "thoughts of a dry brain in a dry season." And while Echo, the author of **"Title,"** the speaker in **"Life-Story,"** and Menelaus reflect, ponder and rehearse, this voice "becomes hoarser, loses its magnetism, grows scratchy, incoherent, blank." For the divorce of imagination and reality depletes the vitality of both. By the end of the sequence, the persona is merely "a survival expert with no will to live," recording chronicles of his own misery. One has to wonder if there ever was any "water-message"—if these narrators were ever capable of creating works of fiction or if they could and still can only reproduce the nothingness they perceive in themselves and in the world around them. For these personae, language and literature seem to have outlived their usefulness; both the characters and their art appear to have reached "the end of the road."

Although the speaker in **"Title"** identifies the situation he finds himself in as more "tsk tsk than boo hoo," the future is bleak for all of the protagonists. "Where there's life there's hope," the speaker bravely asserts but, shortly thereafter, he concedes that "there's no hope." In *Howards End,* E. M. Forster writes of Margaret Schlegel: "Only connect! That was the whole of her sermon. Only connect the prose and the passion, and both will be exalted, and human love will be seen at its height. Live in fragments no longer." The schizophrenic personality in **Funhouse** cannot connect the fragments of his existence. Art and life, self and other, even mind and body are irreparably severed. He is lost in the madhouse, imprisoned in the "labyrinthine corridors" of his own mind. There will be no breakthrough from breakdown.

Many critics have discussed **Funhouse** as an amusing series of stories that "turn daily life into mythology while turning mythology into domestic comedy," as *Time*'s reviewer put it. But the plight of the speakers is hardly a comic one and, more often than not, the laughter is tinged with hysteria. In **"Life-Story,"** the narrator wonders if he is a character in another man's fiction and if "his author might as probably resemble himself and the protagonist of his own story-in-progress." This statement may be Barth's way of indicating how closely he identifies with his characters. As a contemporary writer, he shares their concern over the apparent depletion of literary forms and possibilities. Moreover, their obsessions and neuroses may be a reflection of his own doubts and fears. Tony Tanner felt at the time that "this account of seemingly futile writing in endless solitude" was an "analogue" for Barth's own situation and that he had "temporarily trapped" himself "inside that verbal circle, which moves, but never progresses."[13] The difference between Barth and his personae, of course, is that he was capable of creating and completing this work and several others out of his own struggle with the written word.

Notes

1. John Barth, *Lost in the Funhouse* (1968; New York: Bantam, 1969), 9. Hereafter cited parenthetically.

2. The narrator of "Life-Story" makes this comment about himself (121) but it characterizes Ambrose perfectly: see note 12 below.

3. Carolyn A. Kyle, "The Unity of Anatomy: The Structure of Barth's *Lost in the Funhouse,*" *Critique* 13 (1972): 36.

4. Kyle, 32.

5. Barth also notes that the "sea journey launched by the minstrel at the end" echoes "the book's first piece," "Night-Sea Journey": see Douglas Davis, "The End Is the Beginning for Barth's 'Funhouse,'" *National Observer,* 16 September 1968, 19.

6. John Vernon, *The Garden and the Map: Schizophrenia in Twentieth Century Literature and Culture* (Chicago: Univ. of Illinois Press, 1973), 26.

7. In John Barth, *The Friday Book* (New York: Putnam's, 1984), 75.

8. Quoted in Tony Tanner, *City of Words: American Fiction 1950-1970* (New York: Harper & Row, 1971), 259.

9. Beverly Bienstock, "Lingering on the Autognostic Verge: John Barth's *Lost in the Funhouse,*" *Modern Fiction Studies* 19 (1973): 73.

10. R. D. Laing, *The Divided Self: An Existential Study in Sanity and Madness* (Baltimore: Penguin, 1965), 42-43.

11. Vernon, 23.

12. Robert Kiernan also suggests that Ambrose may be trying to escape from himself by creating the other fictions in the sequence: see "John Barth's Artist in the Funhouse," *Studies in Short Fiction* 10 (1973): 373. The narrator notes that "now and then" Ambrose "fell into his habit of rehearsing to himself the unadventurous story of his life, narrated from the third-person point of view" (92).

13. Tanner, 258.

Stan Fogel and Gordon Slethaug (essay date 1990)

SOURCE: Fogel, Stan, and Gordon Slethaug. "*Lost in the Funhouse.*" In *Understanding John Barth,* pp. 107-30. Columbia: University of South Carolina Press, 1990.

[In the following essay, Fogel and Slethaug provide an in-depth critical analysis of the stories in Lost in the Funhouse.*]*

The Floating Opera and *The End of the Road* attracted a broad base of readers, including those who enjoyed familiar, realistic conventions governing setting, plot, and characterization as well as those who preferred novels of ideas—philosophical inquiries into existentialism and nihilism. Although *The Sot-Weed Factor* and *Giles Goat-Boy* were Barth's first books to depart from this predominantly realistic format, *Lost in the Funhouse* and *Chimera* did so in an even more distinctly experimental way. Those who had found Barth's first two books easy to read and master, to be "readerly" texts in Roland Barthes's words, discovered new and often discomfiting qualities in *Lost in the Funhouse* and *Chimera.* His texts had become "writerly," not easily assimilated, mastered, and consumed; they played language games in ways that kept the text fresh but always difficult.

Probably the most relentlessly experimental of his works, *Lost in the Funhouse* and *Chimera* are, paradoxically, often Barth's most popular. Possibly because of their relative brevity, but most likely because of the raptly suspenseful nature of the accounts, they ensnare readers who like both taut thrillers and self-scrutinizing methods. The books are also engaging because the short pieces are collected into an integrated series. Whether a spermatozoon fulfills its quest, or Bellerophon achieves his self-definition, or Dunyazade triumphs in her storytelling—these may not sound like the makings of absorbing fiction (especially since they are told with many sets of quotation marks to indicate multiple tellers in a confined space)—nonetheless, these accounts succeed, no doubt because of the way they offer, and yet qualify, tried and true tales.

Lost in the Funhouse: Fiction for Print, Tape, Live Voice, a series of fourteen stories, is fundamentally about telling and listening to stories. As Alfred Appel, Jr., observes, "it is a cerebral, hard-surfaced, often fantastic fiction, whose forms evolve constantly in unexpected, quantum-quick ways."[1] However delightful this experiment, Barth showed some uneasiness about his new style when the book appeared in 1968. Though he had previously published several of these stories in journals, as early as 1963, the collection showed a much different side to Barth's work than the previous novels and might, therefore, have seemed to warrant some defense. The dust jacket of the first edition warns the readers about the experimentation and provides an apologia. In this apologia, taken from an interview at McGill University, Barth says:

> I've been trying to compose pieces which will be quite short, which will have to be published finally in a volume because they'll take some of their resonance from each other—but of which most won't really be designed for the printed page at all. These are experimental pieces . . . [but are not] cold exercises in technique. My feeling about technique in art is that it has about the same value as technique in love-making. That is to say, heartfelt ineptitude has its appeal and so does heartless skill; but what you want is passionate virtuosity.

Although many of these stories have similar modes of presentation and characters, their relation to one another is more difficult to establish, because they do not follow a linear development, and because Barth tries to frustrate the tendency to put ideas and methods into neatly unified patterns. Some deal with the growth of heroes, and some explore the development of techniques and processes of fiction. Although all of Barth's books deal with the way people perceive and articulate experience, *Lost in the Funhouse* is the first that self-consciously treats the communication act so explicitly. Stories that deal with questions of love, heroism, identity, maturation, and war and peace are also self-consciously about narration, structural forms, and audience reception.

Those critics who explore content include Beverly Gray Bienstock, Harold Farwell, Charles B. Harris, and Edgar H. Knapp. Bienstock writes about the book as a search for "one's identity amidst the tangled skeins of past, present, and future."[2] Farwell discusses Barth's vision of absurd love: "Love is not," he says, "something we can create or preserve in opposition to a world gone mad, but . . . the image of that world and its absurdity."[3] Harris explores the relationship between sexuality and language.[4] Knapp takes a more comprehensive view, using the title story to illustrate that Barth plays with nineteenth-century conceptions of mankind, myth, and artistry.[5]

Michael Hinden, Heide Ziegler, and E. P. Walkiewicz are among those who focus on structure and technique. Hinden argues that the book "examines the depletion of certain forms of modernist expression [especially Joyce] and the unbearable self-consciousness of intellectual life."[6] Ziegler thinks that the book is about the writer and the act of writing. To her the volume's primary purpose is structural: "to dissolve genre, narrative mode, authorial voice, and consecutive time sequence."[7] Walkiewicz sees the book as about literary cycles, and he buttresses his view by reference to Douglas R. Hofstadter's study, *Gödel, Escher, Bach: An Eternal Golden Band.*[8] This connection is fascinating, for Hofstadter says of loops: "Implicit in the concept of Strange Loops is the concept of infinity, since what else is a loop but a way of representing an endless process in a finite way."[9] The infinite within the finite is an idea that Barth has explored since *Giles Goat-Boy.*

In the infinite, looping universe of this text, four of the initial stories, set in tidewater Maryland in 1943 and the years following, are conventional treatments of the growth of Ambrose Mensch, the protagonist, from sperm to budding author. These include **"Night-Sea Journey," "Ambrose His Mark," "Water-Message,"** and **"Lost in the Funhouse"**; but **"Frame-Tale"** and **"Petition"** are also relevant. Several of the middle stories, which deal with the middle period of life, treat the development of fiction; fiction, itself, is the hero of these tales. These stories include **"Echo," "Glossolalia," "Two Meditations," "Autobiography: A Self-Recorded Fiction," "Title,"** and **"Life-Story."** The terminal stories, paradoxically dealing with the later middle stages of the heroes' lives and the beginning stages of their fiction, return to more realistically drawn characters and situations, drawn from Greek myth, *The Iliad,* and *The Odyssey.* These stories explore the origins of heroic models and storytelling, and include **"Menelaiad,"** and **"Anonymiad."** In acknowledging the roots of literature Barth also refers to Joyce's *Ulysses,* which has stamped the modern use of classical tradition with its imprint. Together, the stories in this series explore the ways in which fiction and heroes are at once fresh and new as well as traditional and old. They are primarily about the ways in which human experience and literary technique are both like and unlike those preceding them. Nothing is ever wholly the same; nothing is completely different. Life *almost* repeats life; art *almost* repeats art; and life and art *almost* repeat each other.

One of the ways art and life almost repeat one another is through their structural sequences. In the Aristotelian literary scheme, fiction has beginnings, middles, and ends, and for Freitag, following this model, the introduction, rising action, and resolution take the shape of a triangle. Ambrose's discussion of these concepts in **"Lost in the Funhouse"** reminds the readers of the importance of such views on plot development and structure and helps to situate the rest of the stories, for this book is, like **Chimera,** a more-or-less three-sectioned creature, an image reinforced by the central birthmark of the headless, upside-down bee in **"Ambrose His Mark."** But, just as Ambrose's bee is truncated, so this book tends to dwell on beginnings and middles; the endings are either beginnings (the optimistic view) or total collapses (the pessimistic view).

Beginnings are central to the first stories of *Lost in the Funhouse.* Taken together, these stories constitute a kind of novella in the classic tradition of the *bildungsroman,* or initiation and growth of the hero. And, since Ambrose is, *LETTERS* confirms, the author of the entire book, each tale can also be understood as fiction about the development of an artist.

In the first of these tales, **"Night-Sea Journey,"** the fundamental human dilemma is laid bare through the dramatic monologue of a sperm, vigorously swimming toward an unknown goal. The arrival, in the story's conclusion, of the sperm at its goal presumably accounts for the conceiving of Ambrose. As the swimming sperm strokes along, he wonders why he is adrift in a sea of other swimmers who seem better equipped than he to deal with the rigors of the night-sea journey. Philosophical in nature, he asks himself the hard questions of life, those that Ambrose later asks: Is there a Maker? Who is he, and what are his nature and motives? Are his intentions benevolent or malevolent? What is the final goal, and how is it attained? Why does

one creature succeed and the rest expire? These questions, which are germane to the existence of every thinking being, are given a distinctly humorous cast as they relate to the act of procreation. When readers recognize that the story is about the act of conception, the sperm's other questions become especially meaningful: Did the Maker release the sperm intentionally or inadvertently? Did he want to prevent the sperm from reaching the shore or assist it? Was the Maker "stupid, malicious, insensible, perverse, or asleep and dreaming?"[10] Was the act moral or obscene? Are the swimmers important in themselves or only as they assure the Maker's immortality? The sperm's philosophical sense of the absurd is accentuated by his literary imagination. When he laments, "I have seen the best swimmers of my generation go under. Numberless the number of the dead!" (4) or "Ours not to stop and think; ours but to swim and sink" (5), he invokes Ginsberg, Conrad, and Tennyson. Barth's word play on "Maker" as God, sexual adventurer, and author is beautifully executed and helps the readers to see the various overlapping patterns in the book; it also helps the readers to understand that all such patterns are the product of the human ability to create fictions.

"Ambrose His Mark" extends this discussion of the origins and purposes of life, especially with regard to Ambrose and his family—his bawdy and flirtatious mother Andrea; his conniving, unscrupulous Grandfather Mensch who uses Andrea's fecundity to attract a swarm of bees; the pedantic Uncle Konrad and simple Aunt Rosa who register embarrassment over Andrea's sensuality; and his brother Peter, for whom he feels affection and competition. This story deals with Ambrose's birth and naming as well as his familial and social infrastructure. Konrad's "discourse upon the prophetic aspect of swarming among various peoples" (22) is a key to the story and the collection overall, for it presents the many ways that this infrastructure can be interpreted. His comment illustrates the view that everything is open to acts of interpretation. Few things, if any, can be regarded as neutral. Certainly, Ambrose's "mark" is not one that escapes such cultural scrutiny. The mark is, first of all, his birthmark, and the family members attempt to read it the way others might a Rorschach test. The mark is more a blob than an explicit picture, but Andrea finally declares it to be a three-sectioned, upside-down, headless bee in flight. She draws this conclusion because of the bees swarming when she is breastfeeding Ambrose. The "mark" is also Ambrose's name or signature; but since he is called many names, including Christine, Honey, and Ambrose, since he is not baptized or given his Christian name until the age of thirteen, and since the identity of his father is not certain his name and identity are decidedly questionable. Then, too, the "mark" can be linguistically considered. A mark within structuralist linguistic theory indicates the significant difference between any two meaningful sounds or signs in a given language system. Ambrose is marked or different from other members of his family, though he shares certain characteristics with them.

His marking will continue to change: When Ambrose is weaned, when he begins to make decisions for himself, when in **"Water-Message"** he finds the message in the bottle on the beach, or when in **"Lost in the Funhouse"** he gets lost and decides to be an operator of funhouses rather than a player or lover, his identity shifts and changes. These alterations indicate the fluid and indeterminate nature of meaning: Identity is not static, and nothing can ever be interpreted precisely the same from person to person or time to time.

Something that is open to interpretation is language, and young Ambrose is fascinated with words and perplexed about their various meanings. **"Water Message"** and **"Lost in the Funhouse"** are primarily about this developing interest. Words represent knowledge for Ambrose; to understand words is to comprehend life. He is drawn to words that seem unusual or elicit unusual responses, words like "facts" and "facts of life," which may be used to indicate factual knowledge or sexual mysteries, or metaphorical phrases like "lump in the throat" or "breaking out in a cold sweat" that describe his adolescent feelings. The very sound of words attracts him, but more than that, he is interested in words in relation to the values of his changing milieu and the way in which literature affects attitudes. When he finds the "water-message" in the bottle, it represents a special act of communication and knowledge to which only he is privy.

As a child in the fourth grade (**"Water-Message"**), he is undersized and studious, the target of the bullies in the school, but he has a vivid sense of language and a rich literary imagination. He thinks of the twin terrors of his neighborhood, the Spitz dog and Crazy Alice, as Scylla and Charybdis, names that he chose from *The Book of Knowledge*. He names the boys' club the Occult Order of the Sphinx, though he is considered too young to join it. He wants to be initiated into the whispered mysteries that the older boys seem to understand, the reason for their laughing about what Peggy Robbins did with Tommy James at the clubhouse. Chagrined to be cowardly, young, and excluded from the discourse of the older boys, he dreams a literary dream of heroism, rescuing Peggy Robbins from distress, loving and forgiving her for her indiscretion and unfaithfulness, and, putting aside his personal dislike of Wimpy Jones, saving him too. He thinks of Peggy as his courtly love, and he describes her in the most conventional romantic language.

Ambrose's choice of vocabulary, and hence perception, is influenced by what he reads. When he describes his encounters with childhood rivals and potential sweet-

hearts as "Odysseus steering under anvil clouds" (45) or thinks of himself as slashing his "way under portcullis and over moat, it was lay about with mace and halberd" (46), when he wants access to the boys' club, the Occult Order of the Sphinx—he has brought Odysseus, King Arthur, and Huck Finn into a working relationship with his contemporary existence. These fictions influence the way Ambrose thinks about himself and reality; they inform his vision, mold his thoughts, and direct his emotions. In Barth's terms life does imitate art, not just in the sense that certain events resemble those described in art, but also in the sense that the concepts of fiction really do influence or "contaminate" our view of events.

Because perceptions are governed by words and cultural constructions, descriptions tend to be recycled endlessly, but always with some differences. The title story, **"Lost in the Funhouse,"** especially stresses the function of repetition and distortion, sameness and difference. The story concerns the thirteen-year-old Ambrose, taken on an Independence Day holiday to Ocean City. With him are his mother, father, and Uncle Karl, as well as his fifteen-year-old brother Peter and fourteen-year-old Magda G———, whom both brothers fancy. The story details the ride to the beach, Ambrose's discovery of raw sexuality under the boardwalk, the teenagers' foray into the funhouse with its peculiar distorting mirrors, and Ambrose's getting lost. The story, written in strained, self-conscious, third-person prose, conveys Ambrose's increasing awareness that all expression is learned and hence sufficiently alien. He is also aware that his developing sexuality is estranging—part of him, but not one with him. He recognizes that he is like other youths in his developing sexual awareness and desires, but he thinks of himself as a less confident and able lover than his brother Peter or the anonymous sailor in the funhouse. At the same time, he realizes that, while all his family and acquaintances speak the English language, he has more facility with it and more interest in the conventions of literature. Both sex and language are, consequently, "natural" and estranging. This same-different, conformity-alienation pattern is visually presented in the image of the funhouse mirrors. These mirrors give back a reflection to the viewer, but that reflection is a one-dimensional imitation and not the original. Moreover, in a funhouse the glass itself is distorting—shortening, broadening, or elongating the viewer, so that repetition differs more than usual. Life and art, Ambrose and the funhouse of fiction, do repeat socially and literarily established images and patterns, but they also change and distort them.

Appropriately, the more style-oriented stories reflect similar concerns. The first story, **"Frame-Tale,"** is also about repetition, but primarily the codified or repetitive introductions to tales. "Once Upon a Time" and "There Was a Story That Began" are two such formulaic beginnings, which, when combined, suggest the unending "beginningness" of stories. This device not only suggests that literature depends upon patterns of repetition but, in inviting the reader to cut, twist, and link the ends, emphasizes that no form perfectly reduplicates its predecessor. As the lead story in the collection, **"Frame-Tale"** establishes the book's commitment, not to content or realism and all its conventional accoutrements, but to form itself.

In its distinctly gothic, nonrealistic presentation, **"Petition"** also establishes the importance of repetition and emphasizes the notion of "sameness" and "difference." The story deals with the written petition to a visiting dignitary, Prajadhipok, that he assist in separating the narrator, an unnamed Siamese twin, from his brother. The narrator has become increasingly burdened with the behavior of his brother to the point that he wants a radical solution. "Fastened front to rear," the Siamese twins are the same: sharing the same life blood and muscle tissue, they are unenduringly part-and-parcel of each other. But they are also different. One is earthy, sensual, bawdy, gregarious, realistic, and vocal; the other (the narrator-writer) is cerebral, solitary, romantic, and unable to speak. Although the narrator is aware of their differences, he seems unable to cope with his dilemma: "I affirm our difference—all the difference in the world!—but have endeavored in vain to work out with him a reasonable cohabitation" (62). The narrator cannot abide being both identical and different: "To be one: paradise! To be two: bliss! But to be both and neither is unspeakable" (71). In terms of form, to follow in the tradition of renowned masterpieces is preferable; to be completely new and original is acceptable; but to be both new and repetitive, to be the twist in a loop, is intolerable. Presented within the imagery of twinship and doubleness, the story is, in certain respects, about the artist's difficulty in trying to adhere to tradition and break from it. These tales all stress the beginnings of life and fiction. No beginning or birth can be seen as a wholly unique event, for each duplicates existing patterns and species. Yet, each beginning, however repetitive, is also in some significant way unique. To recognize this combination allows one (self or story) to get on with the plot.

The stories that constitute the second section of the book, the middle period of life and "rising action" literature, are those beginning with **"Echo."** These are the most difficult tales exploring lives and styles of writing which, like a needle caught in the groove of a record, seem trapped in predictable responses and patterns or doomed to failure. As the title suggests, **"Echo"** is a variant of the Narcissus legend, told here not only from the female perspective but one that centers on Echo's storytelling abilities. Beginning with the gift of divine narrative, telling lively stories of her own fabricating, Echo is condemned by "the Queen of heaven" to repeat the voices of others. Her repetition is echoed by others

within the tale—Narcissus who falls in love with his reflection in the spring of Donacon and Tiresias who has lived so long, heard so many stories, and given so much advice that he can no longer keep one separate from another. Such apparently mechanical repetitions do not, however, lead to identical meanings or conclusions, for as the narration affirms, "A cure for self-absorption is saturation: telling the story over as though it were another's until like a much-repeated word it loses sense" (98). Repetitive excess can lead to a different message from the original; excessive repetition undermines origins. But not all repetition leads to excess. Echo, for instance, "never, as popularly held, repeats all, like gossip or mirror. She edits, heightens, mutes, turns others' words to her end" (100). She is a writer, echoing previously written works, but always choosing words offered by her culture to create new fiction. Her echo is both a tribute to and a distortion of the originals. Her response prolongs her life and storytelling, whereas Narcissus dies in his attempts to embrace his reflection and to perpetuate what is intimately known and familiar.

Although the first stories raise questions about the individual speaker/writer in relation to communication codes, certain middle stories (**"Title"** and **"Life-Story"**) decry the apparent falseness and staleness of overused patterns: "Beginning: in the middle, past the middle, nearer three-quarters done, waiting for the end. Consider how dreadful so far: passionlessness, abstraction, pro, dis. And it will get worse. Can we possibly continue?" (105). In **"Title"** the narrative becomes its own narrator, lamenting its literary conventions, hating the medium in which it is told. It recognizes its similarity to other stories and feels crippled by its lack of individuality and spontaneity. By having the stories describe their own frustration and weaknesses, Barth emphasizes his central working premise: Words and literary patterns are so common that the idea of going beyond them to new beginnings often seems impossible. Since speakers can only use language generally available and commonly understood, and since previous literary works provide the basis of all further writing, an author/narrator/story may quite legitimately feel that everything has been said before, an attitude that can preclude further writing: "What now. Everything's been said already, over and over; I'm as sick of this as you are; there's nothing to say. Say nothing" (105). Notions of growth and progress, both on human and literary levels, give way to exhaustion, resignation, and ultimately, despair. Instead of prolonging life or the text, repetition may lead to blankness of vision and a lack of stirring vitality, and for the writer this awareness leads to another blankness: a failure to put anything at all on the page. Self-consciousness about the failure of vision and writing as a result of disillusionment following youthful romanticism can lead to emotional and textual breakdown. The distressed narrator of **"Title"** says it well: "We're more than halfway through, as I remarked at the outset: youthful vigor, innocent exposition, positive rising action—all that is behind us. . . . In this dehuman, exhausted, ultimate adjective hour, . . . every humane value has become untenable, and not only love, decency, and beauty but even compassion and intelligibility are no more than one or two subjective complements to complete the sentence . . ." (107). Unable to finish his penultimate sentence, the narrator still hopes that self-consciousness can be used against itself in order "to turn ultimacy against itself to make something new and valid, the essence whereof would be the impossibility of making something new" (109).

"Life-Story" is also about the seeming impossibility of individuality, but this latter tale is not self-engendered, as **"Title"** claims to be; it has an author, whose life the reader learns about. This author laments his own self-consciousness and bemoans his birth in the age of modernism rather than in a period that valued heroism and heroic rhetoric, that is, a "conservative, 'realistic,' unself-conscious" style with "arresting circumstance, bold character, trenchant action" (116, 118). Because he is a product of his age, his style slips into the "self-conscious, vertiginously arch, fashionably solipsistic, [and] unoriginal" (117). He begins to wonder if the world is not itself a novel and he a character, or he himself a fiction with thoughts that are also fictions. In that event, his story becomes a frame-tale of a story within a story. Ultimately, this narrator cannot discover what is real and what is fabricated or what he wills and what is willed for him. Unable to control his style and content he is lost in the funhouse of fiction as much as Ambrose, but, in the middle period of his life, with fewer resources. Instead of believing he is in control, he has to accept the likelihood that he is controlled, that he is someone else's fiction, and that he has no other identity. Ironically, in talking about his problems in writing, the author-narrator fashions a story about the impossibility of fashioning a story.

The last two stories in the series concern the late middle years of the characters' lives, but not old age. There is no final or grand conclusion to these stories, for as in **"Lost in the Funhouse"** and **"Life-Story,"** a crisis or end also marks a beginning. These last two stories are set in the ancient Greece of Odysseus and Penelope, Menelaus and Helen, and Agamemnon and Clytemnestra. These tales do not concern the glories of the battles, but rather the origins of storytelling. Menelaus, the narrator of the **"Menelaiad,"** has come back from the Trojan Wars and is living his later years at home with Helen, visited on this particular evening by Telemachus, the disguised son of Odysseus. As a means of keeping Telemachus from sleeping with the still beautiful Helen, Menelaus keeps him by the fire with his stories. He begins his storytelling by describing their present circumstances but then tells of past conversations, which are placed in separate quotation

marks, each set moving the reader ever further from the verifiable present. As he describes past events and conversations, Menelaus fears that he is only a narrating voice without any substantial identity: "One thing's certain: somewhere Menelaus lost course and steersman, went off track, never got back on, lost hold of himself, became a record merely, the record of his loosening grasp. He's the story of his life, with which he ambushes the unwary unawares" (131). What Menelaus grapples with is that the essence of each person is only his or her story. Telemachus is not a real visitor, trying to bed Helen, but only a voice, responding to Menelaus's and Helen's. Despite her great sexual appeal, the allure of Helen is mainly her words. Her perplexing statement that she loves Menelaus undoes him for years until Proteus advises him to "beg Love's pardon for your want of faith. Helen chose you without reason because she loves you without cause; embrace her without question and watch your weather change" (161). Each person has a narrative that intersects with other narratives, but the reality, the truth, at the bottom of these narratives is impossible to locate. The quotations within quotations stress that there is no guarantee of meaning from the act of speech; there is no center or locus of meaning, and life has to be lived in spite of that knowledge.

The narrator of the penultimate story is also left only with words. Paid to be a minstrel in Agamemnon's court, he stays there while the warriors go off to the Trojan Wars. While the others are absent, he is charged by Agamemnon with observing Clytemnestra to make certain that she remains faithful. Clytemnestra and her lover Aegisthus, however, arrange to dispose of the poet, and he is tricked into going aboard a ship and abandoned on an uninhabited island. There he writes his works, sending them to sea in empty amphorae.

An innocent minstrel, he was not prepared for the fruits of his introduction to court life, and too late he discovered that his minstrelsy inflamed the passions of Clytemnestra and Aegisthus. His political responsibility of spying on Clytemnestra in order to prevent her infidelity and his artistic mission of telling interesting stories that calm the passions are completely undermined, and he is exiled. In exile, he finds his art growing, though he has few resources—nine amphorae of wine, squid ink, and his pen, and no papyrus except for the skin of the goats he butchers.

Since he has not been allowed to live out the rest of his life in society, he begins his writing "in the middle—where too I'll end, there being alas to my arrested history as yet no denouement" (169). He later concludes, "there's no denouement, only a termination or ironical coda" (200). He has only memories of a once-active court life: "Merope's love, Helen's whoring, Menelaus's noise, Agamemnon's slicing up his daughter for the weatherman—all the large and deadly passions of men and women, wolves, frogs, nightingales; all this business of seizing life, grabbing hold with both hands . . ." (171). In isolation, he plans great works of art— his own life story, the Trojan wars, Agamemnon's court, and Clytemnestra's infidelity. He writes these in many genres, but his last, the one before the goatskin runs out, is to be his life story in nine parts. These intentions are never quite realized. The nine parts are not perfectly executed. He has a part called "1 1/2," and "3" does not exist, for he says, "Three, my crux, my core, I'm cutting you out;———; there, at the heart, never to be filled, a mere lacuna" (183).

Despite Anonymous's discouragement that he cannot fulfill his intentions and that the manuscript has not gone as he hoped, despite his feelings of defeat and exhaustion, and despite his view that no one will probably ever read his manuscripts, he does accomplish something. His writing saves him from suicide. Had he not been able to "tell" (though to no certain audience), he would have been bereft of hope. No matter how amateurish, decayed, or incomplete the work of art, it functions to save the author and, potentially, the reader. By a remote chance his works may communicate something to someone. Dubious whether his amphorae stuffed with manuscripts will ever reach an audience, he himself finds a jar washed up on his own beach. Whether his own or another's he does not know, but he does not care: "Now I began to imagine that the world contained another like myself. Indeed, it might be astrew with isled souls, become minstrels perforce, and the sea a-clink with literature! Alternatively, one or several of my messages may have got through." He then adds, "I never ceased to allow the likelihood that the indecipherable ciphers were my own; that the sea had fertilized me as it were with my own seed. No matter, the principle was the same: that I could be thus messaged, even by that stranger my former self" (196). An artist can be "messaged" by his or her own work; communication between past and present or between persons can exist. Literature does have a function, and the communication act does not have to be aborted, though the message may be somewhat misunderstood. These concluding stories do not affirm heroic endings and structured documents, but they affirm the possibility of new beginnings and new cycles. They suggest that living and writing, while repetitive and without individuality, may still have purpose, however apparently undiscoverable.

These new cycles and patterns of repetition depend fully upon the relationship between author, text, and reader or what Barth calls teller, tale, and told. *Lost in the Funhouse* rejects a belief in the author as a genius, one who with divine intuition creates a work beyond the abilities of more common human beings. Rather, Barth advances the view that writing is hard work, with

the artists never fully in control and with no divine reassurance or insight behind them. The unpredictability of writing is further complicated by the role of the reader, who the narrator of **"Life-Story"** calls "you, dogged, uninsultable, print-oriented bastard" (127). If potential readers refuse to read the work, then it dies, regardless of the intrinsic merit of the text itself. The narrator of **"Life Story"** argues that a story cannot even commit suicide without the reader's decision to close the book. "You who listen give me life in a manner of speaking" (35). Although a story may be conceived by the author, if it remains unread, its life is aborted. Readers have considerable independence and bring certain attitudes and understandings to bear on the text, so that the author's intentions, if ever known, are never wholly fulfilled. Meaning and immortality of the text are generated by both author and reader, text and interpreter. The message the author intends may be perceived quite differently by readers who have their own concerns and structures. Acts of reading, however repetitive, are always different, as are acts of writing. The writer and reader together create the text. Like an infinite loop, the interaction of text and reader seems always open to new possibilities, but insofar as the text itself is finite, the possibilities are not truly infinite.

Notes

1. Alfred Appel, Jr., "The Art of Artifice," *The Nation* 207 (28 Oct. 1968): 441.

2. Beverly Gray Bienstock, "Lingering on the Autognostic Verge: John Barth's *Lost in the Funhouse*," *Modern Fiction Studies* 19 (Spring 1973): 70.

3. Harold Farwell, "John Barth's Tenuous Affirmation: 'The Absurd, Unending Possibility of Love,'" *Georgia Review* 28 (Summer 1974): 290-306.

4. Charles B. Harris, *Passionate Virtuosity: The Fiction of John Barth* (Urbana: University of Illinois Press, 1983) 106.

5. Edgar H. Knapp, "Found in the Barthhouse: Novelist as Savior," *Modern Fiction Studies* 14 (Winter 1968-69): 446-53.

6. Michael Hinden, "*Lost in the Funhouse*: Barth's Use of the Recent Past," *Twentieth Century Literature* 19 (Jan.-Oct. 1973): 108.

7. Heide Ziegler, *John Barth* (London: Methuen, 1987) 50.

8. E. P. Walkiewicz, *John Barth* (Boston: Twayne, 1986) 84-109.

9. Douglas R. Hofstadter, *Gödel, Escher, Bach: An Eternal Golden Band* (New York: Vintage Books, 1980) 15.

10. John Barth, *Lost in the Funhouse: Fiction for Print, Tape, Live Voice* (Garden City, N.Y.: Doubleday, 1968) 7. Further references will be noted parenthetically in the text.

Benzi Zhang (essay date spring 1995)

SOURCE: Zhang, Benzi. "Paradox of Origin(ality): John Barth's 'Menelaiad.'" *Studies in Short Fiction* 32, no. 2 (spring 1995): 199-208.

[*In the following essay, Zhang traces how Barth re-works Greek myth in "Menelaiad" to create a new story and addresses the issue of establishing identity by tell-ing the story from a variety of viewpoints.*]

> It is not difficult to imagine why Homer has fascinated men's minds to this day: the enigma has its attraction and the blatant commonplace its unknown side.
>
> —Kirsti Simonsuuri
>
> *Homer's Original Genius* (3)

For the late twentieth-century writers, the myth of origin(ality) is at once a source of excitement and a cause of anxiety. The miraculous spring that nourished Homer's afflatus seems out of reach of today's writers, whose desperate yearning for inspiration only indicates the coming of an age of "exhaustion." The pervasive feeling that exists amongst these writers is the sense of "used-upness" concerning the sort of story they write and its possible repetition of the past. As John Barth observes in **"The Literature of Exhaustion,"** discuss-ing Jorge Luis Borges:

> for one to attempt to add overtly to the sum of "origi-nal" literature by even so much as a conventional short story, not to mention a novel, would be too presumptu-ous, too naive; literature has been done long since. . . . His *ficciones* are not only footnotes to imaginary texts, but postscripts to the real corpus of literature.
>
> (*Friday* 73)

The problem Barth perceives is a state of "depletion"—a fearsome loss of the "prestige of origins" in contempo-rary literature. "What does one do when all the stories are told?" "How can one be original when origin(ality) is exhausted?" One possibility, as Barth's **"Menelaiad"** demonstrates, is to turn "exhaustion" of old stories into "replenishment" of new ones, and to acknowledge old stories by "iterating" them in new and creative ways, thereby affirming one's own "re-origination." Re-origination is to parody, to play with the inevitable complicity with a tradition, and to recontextualize ironi-cally the echoing of the past. In Barth's story, tradition is as important as innovation, since for Barth writing is always an "inter-art" that involves the consciousness of literary history. As John Barth himself points out, the effort to assimilate the past and the future can be called a *modus operandi* of "trans-telling"—"go back to the beginning of things, narrative things, to see to what contemporary uses they might be put" (Glaser-Wöhrer 229). As C. B. Harris observes, quoting Mircea Eliade, "The *return to origins* gives the hope of a rebirth" (116). Trans-telling, however, does not mean to follow, but to enter into a dialogue with the past.

John Barth's **"Menelaiad"** contains an ancient story from the *Iliad* and the *Odyssey,* which has been told and retold throughout the centuries. In defiance of the fact that he is taking the risk of repetition, however, Barth translates the mythological story into a postmod-ern "trans-tale," a tale that plays with the tension be-tween the past and the present and indicates a paradoxi-cal trans-relation between originality and repetition. The aim of Barth's trans(re)lation of mythology is to show how literature can renew itself by "remarking" its origin(ality) and by trans-relating the ancient to the present. "This re-mark," according to Jacques Derrida, "can take on a great number of forms and can itself pertain to highly diverse types" (229). Barth's remark-ing takes the form of re-mythologizing that serves as a means for him to re-work and re-originate the "iterable" contents and forms of myth. In a sense, Barth's re-mythologizing in his postmodern-ancient story suggests what Derrida calls the "paradoxical historicity in the experience of writing." "The writer," Derrida observes, "can be ignorant or naive in relation to the historical tradition which bears him or her, or which s/he trans-forms, invents, displaces" (54), but the writer must al-ways write against a prior "non-saturable context" of old stories (63). What **"Menelaiad"** illustrates is the possibility that a storyteller can, instead of keeping si-lence in the age of exhaustion, turn origin(ality) into a paradox and employ it to re-create new stories.

In re-creating his tale of Menelaus, Barth weaves into the narrative network different versions of the same story in order to re-mark its origin, or rather de-originate it. These versions are layered as different narrative lev-els within the story, and each level indicates a step fur-ther away from the origin. All these levels construct a radically regressive Chinese box, which "dehistoricizes" the narrative voice of Menelaus who trans-tells the iter-able tale(s) of his history to himself and to various au-diences on different levels. To use Derrida's words, Me-nelaus's "text is thereby dehistoricized, but historicity is made of iterability." For Derrida, the paradox is that "there is no history without iterability, and this iterabil-ity is also what lets the traces continue to function in the absence of the general context or some elements of the context" (64). Apparently, the "iterability" of his-story makes Menelaus not only eternally "dehistori-cized" but also recontextualized and developed, since his trans-tale is not the same at each (re)telling. The historical levels in the story confuse themselves, as Me-nelaus attempts to trans-relate and transcend all the pe-riods of time in his re-telling(s) of the tale(s) of his life (lives).

The multi-layered trans-tale that Menelaus tells is a story of origin/truth vs. masks/disguises. At the center of the story is the enigmatic Helen, the origin(ality) of his love and puzzlement. Menelaus says:

She's the death of me and my peculiar immortality, cause of every mask and change of state. On whose account did Odysseus become a madman, Achilles woman? Who turned the Argives into a horse, loyal Sinon into a traitor, yours truly from a mooncalf into a seacalf, Proteus into everything that is? first cause, and final magician: Mrs. M.

(130-31)

Searching for decipherment of the magic beauty, Menelaus traverses between and beyond narrative levels and constantly asks himself, "When will I reach my goal through its cloaks of story? How many veils to naked Helen?" (144). Before Helen chooses him as her husband, Menelaus knows that he is the least hopeful of her admirers, of whom "Menelaus alone paid the maid no court" (153). But as the chosen "fit mate" for the fairest Helen, Menelaus is bedeviled with self-doubt. "Why me?" he asks (155). Despite her tender words, he cannot believe in her love for him—"To love is easy; to be loved, as if one were real, on the order of others: fearsome mystery! Unbearable responsibility" (156). Even after begetting their daughter, Menelaus still questions the originality of Helen's love:

It wasn't Zeus disguised as Menelaus who begot her, any more than Menelaus disguised as Zeus; it was Menelaus disguised as Menelaus, a mask masking less and less. Husband, father, lord, and host he played, grip slipping; he could imagine anyone loved, no accounting for tastes, but his cipher self. In his cups he asked on the sly their house guests: "Why'd she wed me, less horsed than Diomedes, et cetera?" None said.

(151)

Menelaus thinks of himself as a non-original re-mark of love or a shadow of someone else. In this self-doubt condition he invites Paris into his home, and that invitation eventually results in the Trojan War. After the war, Menelaus continues to search for answers to his inexplicable relationship to Helen: Why does the magic beauty choose to wed Menelaus who is "less crafty than Diomedes, artful than Teucer, et cetera?" (154) Menelaus "doggedly" looks for a cause-and-effect logic of truth, for a logical origin of reality. His puzzlement is ultimately boiled down, in the center of his story, to an ontological question: "Who am I"? He goes off to consult an oracle at Delphi with his question. The oracle's answer is several sets of blank quotation marks: " ' " ' " ' " " ' " ' " ' " ' " (158). The mystic effect is like breaking boxes on all layers only to find that there is nothing at the center.

The prospect of finding nothing in the central box suggests the effect of a paradox—"the effect of the same a-logical 'logic' of the singular and iterable mark" in literary language (Derrida 66). The blank at the center of oracle's answer implies that language is a paradox that denies the certainty of any original "truth." Ora-

cle's puzzling answer is like a Zen master's enlightenment, which is paradoxically above human language yet must be communicated in it. "When Buddha speaks of his enlightenment," D. T. Suzuki writes,

he describes his experience as something which cannot be comprehended by any of his followers because their understanding can never rise up to the level of Buddha's. It is another Buddha who understands a Buddha, Buddhas have their own world into which no beings of ordinary calibre of mentality can have a glimpse. Language belongs to this world of relativity, and when Buddha tries to express himself by this means his hearers are naturally barred from entering his inner life.

(52)

What results from this contradiction between the non-communicable Buddha's "inner life" and the need to express it within the limits of language is the paradoxical nature or "a-logical logic" of all language products, particularly literature. It is for this reason that Zen masters try to avoid the use of language, since the meaning that can be put into words is not the original meaning, and the name that can be named is not the original name. "One of the statements Zen is always ready to make is: 'No depending on words'" (57).

Suzuki and Zen masters never offer adequate explanations in words of the very paradox inherent in the statement "No depending on words." This paradox, in effect, is an original truth about all fiction and literature. If a writer should be like a Zen master, as Barth claims in "How to Make a Universe" (*Friday* 22), he should accept this paradox, which may present itself as an *au courant* alternative to modernist tendency to silence—to abandon language as an "exhausted" tool. If Modernism stressed "kaputness" of language and inadequacy of individual's struggle with language, Barth's **"Menelaiad"** re-marks a return to language, and to the paradoxical, a-logical dimensions of language. Menelaus does not abandon insistence on origin(ality) that may be translated as "truth," "reality," or "ultimacy," but he accepts its paradox and bewilderment. In his quest for true and original answers to the question of "whether I was the world's chief fool and cuckold or its luckiest mortal" (133), Menelaus is trapped in a bottomless Chinese box of language with compounded ironies, evasions, and disguises. As narrative boxes build layer upon layer around a center that is empty, it is the productiveness of uncertainty that stands out most. The narrative artifice, featured as much in the narrative language as in the ingenious structure of the Chinese box, simultaneously affirms both the power of language and its inadequacy to an ultimate origin(ality). As uncertainty accumulates within the layers of the story, the paradox of "no depending upon words" contributes to both the construction and deconstruction of an origin. When the story exuberantly raises epistemological and ontological questions such as "had he [Menelaus] ever been in Troy?"

(166), and "Who am I [Menelaus]?" it radically challenges our common sense of history and reality—the conventional, habitual origin(ality) for truth. Within the paradox of language, as Barth's story suggests, "meaning," "reality" and "truth" must be tentative and relative, since there are too many versions for reality, too many repetitions for an origin, and too many trans(re)lations for history. Literature is a type of iterable discourse that may produce various utterances independent of their origin(ality), yet they are inevitably situated in a "non-saturable context" in which a new text constantly interacts with older co-texts. Within such a world of interactive and co-optative simultaneity, legendary Menelaus and Helen retain their original mystery in Barth's artful "re-cycling" of classical mythology in a postmodern trans-tale that unfolds betwixt and between origin(ality) and repetition.

Barth's trans-telling of ancient myth seems to mark, in a sense, a reiteration of Northrop Frye's claim of the interrelatedness of all literature. But Barth's return to ancient myth is not merely confined to the sense of interrelatedness. Frye is certainly right in stressing the mythic aspect of modernism and insisting that the twentieth century is "once again a great mythopoeic age" (423). But he never explores the difference between modernism and postmodernism. Although Barth and other "postmodernists" have inherited the mythic impulse from modernism, their attitude to myth seems different from those of earlier writers. In Kirsti Simonsuuri's words, the modernist "looked at the culture of antiquity . . . from the standpoint of a stranger," and mythology is, as a result, "alienated" as a distant, historical marvel (26). If modernists such as T. S. Eliot, Thomas Mann, and Marcel Proust were attracted to the life and glory in the mythic past, Barth seems to be drawn to myth more by a sense of simultaneity, co-existence as well as trans-relating iteration. In "Literature of Replenishment," Barth quotes the seventeenth-century mystic Thomas Browne as saying, "Every man is not only himself . . . men are lived over again" (*Friday* 74). This implies a "sense of the merging of times" or what Mikhail Bakhtin calls "an authentic fullness of time" that opposes historical priority and indicates co-existence of the past and the present (36). This trans-relating co-existence, as Beinstock observes, does not involve simply "consecutive progression but simultaneity." So Barth does not use myth as T. S. Eliot, for instance, used it to contrast past glory with present mundaneness; rather, for Barth the ancient myth is a (re)current matter because the past is always the present on time's ever-turning wheel of regression, repetition and eternal return (see Beinstock 203-04). The image of the Möbius strip, which contests the genealogy of "origin," is surely a good analogue to this sort of regressive progression.

Barth's paradoxical concept of perpetual return in progression informs his attitude toward myth and time. The success of **"Menelaiad"** depends, by Barth's own account, on his ability to trans-relate the mythic past to the literal present. In Barth's opinion, the mythos of realism is in essence deeply mythic. Barth's idea that realism relies on myth as the origin for truth leads him to the paradoxical rethinking of the traditional assumptions underlying literary representation. The importance of "insisting on paradox" has been observed by Derrida:

> To insist on this paradox is not an antiscientific gesture—quite the contrary. To resist this paradox in the name of so-called reason or of a logic of common sense is the very figure of a supposed enlightenment as the form of modern obscurantism.
>
> (43)

In **"Menelaiad,"** Barth de-originates myth by relocating the mythic archetypes outside the "logic of common sense." While he employs the dismantled pieces of myth—what Claude Lévi-Strauss calls the "mythemes" (211), Barth challenges the idea of assuming myth as the origin(ality) for literary representation. In this paradoxical posture he is simultaneously a re-mythologizer who reworks on old material, and a playful, anti-mythologizing fabricator who, like Lévi-Strauss's *bricoleur,* breaks traditional assumptions in order to experiment with possibilities of new freedom from a denominating myth. In this way, Barth does not rewrite old myth but re-trans(re)lates it into a new tale. As one of Barth's best short stories, **"Menelaiad"** is intended to reconsider the prestigious origin(ality) of Western myth, to reconfigure the old mythic pattern, to recondition the Western literary tradition, and finally, to reconstruct a larger room of narrative maneuvers for new fiction. Therefore, Barth's **"Menelaiad"** dislodges, to a degree, the mythos, or the origin(ality), of traditional realism which, as Barth would believe, is not adequate for "reality" of life.

In Barth's opinion, traditional realism relies on underlying myths for production of meaning, and as a result, constitutes an epistemic hegemony through which literary production is seen and judged according to myth's ideal form. Therefore, traditional literature, controlled by myth-determined discourses, always depends on "mythic archetypes." Barth's intention in using mythic material, however, is to re-address the relation between literature and myth. In a sense, Barth's re-mythologizing story is a trans-myth tale that links the past to the future. To use Bakhtin's terminology, trans-myth suggests "the necessity of the past and necessity of its place in a line of continuous development . . . and finally, the aspect of the past and present being linked to a *necessary future*" (36). In **"Menelaiad"** Barth connects the two ends—the past and the future with a twist to make a vicious circle in which the old myth is de-stereotyped, de-originated and dehistoricized. The past is the future in Barth's story. Menelaus, therefore, does not echo our ideal heroic archetype; instead, we find Menelaus to be a comical anti-hero, a bewildered "postmodern" story-teller: "My problem was, I'd too much imagination to be a hero" (142). As he (re)tells his story, Menelaus sinks into a maze of Chinese box in which he tells a story in which he retells the story in which he trans-tells that story. By using the Chinese box strategy, Barth skillfully positions his "anti-hero" within settings as well as in tellings, keeping the two convoluted together. Barth simultaneously places his narrator in the para-doxical telling, retelling and trans-telling processes to re-mark an extreme version of the complex and ironic de-origination that dismantles myth-supported realism and heroism.

As our expectation of heroic development is frustrated, our sense of origin(ality)—reality and history that are rooted deeply in myth—is challenged. Barth's **"Mene-laiad,"** which is based on the Trojan War, actually runs against the grain of our historical, or rather, common knowledge of the Trojan War. For instance, Helen's story of the origin(ality) of Trojan War, which mediates between history and imagination, would surely re-set the values of our rational knowledge of historical origin into the dark:

> your wife was never in Troy. Out of love for you I left you when you left, but before Paris could up-end me, Hermes whisked me on Father's orders to Egyptian Proteus and made a Helen out of clouds to take my place. . . . All these years I've languished in Pharos, chaste and comfy, waiting for you, while Paris, nothing wiser, fetched Cloud-Helen off to Troy, made her his mistress.
>
> (164)

According to Helen herself, the Trojan War was fought over a spurious Helen "made of clouds," while the "original" Helen remained chastely at home. While numerous soldiers fought, bled and died in vain, and while Penelope, Odysseus's "faithless" wife, gave "herself to all one hundred eight of her suitors, plus nine house-servants" (161), Helen waited continently for the return of Menelaus—"Husband, I have never been in Troy," and "I've never made love with any man but you" (163). Menelaus comes to believe in Helen's account that renders more than 10 years of his own experience into fic-tion. Following Helen, he denies history as the origin(ality) of truth and translates reality into fiction for the sake of love. Menelaus accepts his wife's ad-visement—"Espouse me without more carp! The sense-less answer to our riddle woo, mad history's secret, base-fact and footer to the fiction crazy-house our life: imp-slayer love, terrific as the sun! Love! Love!" (165) and loses himself in the "a-logical" discourse of the it-erable love and fiction. This may remind the reader of

what Joseph Frank calls the "transformation of the his-torical imagination into myth." "Modern literature has been engaged in transmuting the time world of history into the timeless world of myth" (64). Frank's explana-tion for this is that "time is the very condition of that flux and change from which . . . man wishes to escape when he is in a relation of disequilibrium with the cos-mos" (60). In a sense, Menelaus as a story-teller trans-gresses the boundary of reality, time, and origin(ality) into the domain of art, timelessness and non-origin(ality)—and in so doing he cuts himself off from the ontological "cosmos." In other words, Menelaus in Barth's story finally escapes from time-determined origin(ality) or truth. He closes his eyes to Helen's infi-delity as Barth to his infidelity to original myth. Mene-laus embraces Helen and stops bothering himself with the question about the origin(ality) of her love.

For Menelaus, telling the story and loving Helen are in-tertwined together. Actually, love, or rather, the ques-tion of love, is the main concern of the story. The Chi-nese box strategy, however, treats the question of love in a strikingly new way. The question at the center of the concentric circles of Menelaus's story—" ' " ' " 'Why?' I repeated," I repeat' I repeated," I repeated,' I repeated," I repeated' " (152) is answered by Helen: " ' " ' " 'Love!' " ' " ' " (155). In spite of the numerous hints that suggest Helen's unfaithfulness, Menelaus de-cides to believe her "non-original" love and to accept Proteus's "a-logical" explanation: "Helen chose you without reason because she loves you without cause; embrace her without question" (161). Similarly, Mene-laus comes to accept the limitation of words in spite of the possible untruthfulness of them. If acceptance of the "a-logical logic" is necessary for both love and fiction, he will take it or be taken in by it without question: "'Yes, well, so,' is what I'd say. I don't ask what's changed the wind, your opinion, me, why I hang here like, onto, and by my narrative" (162). In fact, Helen's "love" is analogous to the nature of postmodern narra-tive which, without a sense of temporal superiority, in-dicates an unending process of iterable re-origination. Menelaus eventually gives up his "sense-making" ques-tion to accept Helen's "non-sense" answer. He declares that he has suspended his search for "originality" sim-ply because he loves her: "I believe all. I understand nothing. I love you" (162). In other words, Menelaus is not deluded by Helen, but he is willing to be sur-mounted by Helen's love: "I was taken in, it's a gift, a gift-horse, I shut my eyes" (167). Both in love and in fiction, "we can no longer even talk here of an *event,* of the event of such a text," as Derrida observes; "we can no longer question its *meaning* except by falling short of it, within the network of values which it has *in prac-tice* put into question" (112). Because of "the dogged-ness with which he clung to the dream of embracing despite all Helen" (153), Menelaus successfully works his way out of the Chinese box of love and fiction without questioning the origin(ality) of meaning and love. Menelaus adheres to his originless love and story as he hangs on to the never-original Proteus; he does not divorce love from his art, or repetition from re-creation: each enhances the other. For Menelaus, story (re)telling and love (re)making are the same—both are the gracious and a-logical acts of the desire to repeat and re-create.

Barth's remarkable achievement in **"Menelaiad,"** then, is his "original" trans-telling of old myth, which gives rebirth to an ancient story, and consequently suggests a new alternative for postmodern fiction. This new alternative is more than the technique that Jorge L. Borges describes in his story "Pierre Menard, Author of Don Quixote": "the technique is one of deliberate anachronism and erroneous attributions. This technique with its infinite applications, urges us to run through the *Odyssey* as if it were written after the *Aeneid*" (51). Since the ancient mythology with its variant versions comes to be ironically bound within the a-temporal perspective of Barth's **"Menelaiad,"** the ostensible "origin" of Barth's story becomes a product within that story through the contextualizing mobility of the Chinese box strategy; in other words, the mythic outer box of Barth's story—the Menelaus-Helen myth is *mise-en-abym*ed into an inner box in Barth's **"Menelaiad."** In this reversal lie the con-textual perspectives offered by the Chinese box strategy: Barth's postmodern trans-telling seems to make of all texts the pretexts of other texts. In **"Menelaiad,"** an ever-receding horizon of narrative brings about an endless proliferation of old myth, in which Menelaus appears as a diminishing point on the hallucinated horizon of his own story. In this sense, Barth's re-mythologizing challenges what Derrida calls "logocentrism," a Western predisposition to connect the meaning of a story/text to a point of origin—myth, history or "reality." Mining the distance of time and space, **"Menelaiad"** iterates the mythic story of Menelaus through an ever-evolving ontology of narration: in a paradoxical regressive progression, origin(ality) can only be seen as *trompe l'oeil*.

Works Cited

Bakhtin, Mikhail. *Speech Genres and Other Late Essays*. Ed. C. Emerson and M. Holquist. Trans. V. W. McGee. Austin: U of Texas P, 1986.

Barth, John. *Lost in the Funhouse*. Garden City: Doubleday, 1968.

———. *The Friday Book*. New York: Putnam's, 1984.

Beinstock, B. G. "Lingering on the Autognostic Verge: John Barth's *Lost in the Funhouse*." *Critical Essays on John Barth*. Ed. J. J. Waldmeir. Boston: Hall, 1980. 201-09.

Borges, Jorge Luis. *Fictions*. Ed. Anthony Kerrigan. London: Calder & Boyars, 1974.

Derrida, Jacques. *Acts of Literature*. Ed. Derek Attridge. New York: Routledge, 1992.

Eliade, Mircea. *Myth and Reality*. Trans. Willard R. Trask. New York: Harper, 1968.

Frank, Joseph. *The Idea of Spatial Form*. New Brunswick: Rutgers UP, 1991.

Frye, Northrop. *Fearful Symmetry*. Princeton: Princeton UP, 1969.

Glaser-Wöhrer, Evelyn. "First Conversation with John Barth, Baltimore, Nov. 5, 1975." *An Analysis of John Barth's Weltanschauung: His View of Life and Literature*. Salzburger Studien zur Anglistik und Amerikanistik, 5. Salzburg: U of Salzburg, 1977.

Harris, C. B. *Passionate Virtuosity*. Urbana: U of Illinois P, 1983.

Lévi-Strauss, Claude. *Structural Anthropology, Volume I*. Trans. C. Jacobson and B. G. Schoepf. New York: Basic Books, 1963.

Simonsuuri, Kirsti. *Homer's Original Genius*. Cambridge: Cambridge UP, 1979.

Suzuki, D. T. *Mysticism: Christian and Buddhist*. London: Allen, 1970.

D. Quentin Miller (review date spring 1997)

SOURCE: Review of *On with the Story*, by John Barth. *The Review of Contemporary Fiction* 17, no. 1 (spring 1997): 172.

[*In the following positive review of* On with the Story, *Miller contends that Barth "is still a master of the short story."*]

Although **On with the Story** is John Barth's first collection of short stories since **Lost in the Funhouse** (1968), readers of his recent novels will find themselves in familiar territory. Barth once again puts fiction under a microscope to show us how it works, to remind us of its fundamental elements, and to push these elements as far as they will go. He insists that stories are not absolute in any sense, underscoring his point by beginning the book with a story entitled **"The End: An Introduction"** and concluding the book with continuations of the eleven stories that precede the conclusion, in reverse order.

This inconclusive conclusion is just one of the many dazzling ways in which Barth knits together this collection of stories. Another is the series of interchapters depicting a vacationing husband and wife who exchange stories in bed. In this aspect, the book resembles a Barth novel like *The Tidewater Tales* or *The Last Voyage of*

Somebody the Sailor in which storytelling becomes a kind of serious game, as it once was for Barth's favorite literary predecessor, Scheherazade in *The Thousand and One Nights.*

This is not to say that there is nothing new in this collection. Barth has in fact discovered any number of new ways to illustrate his ideas about the nature of fiction. In the manner of Italo Calvino, he relies on physics to explain the motivations or actions of characters. (Laws of physics run rampant throughout the book; the first epigraph is a Heisenberg equation, and the book's final chapter has one character inscribing Schrödinger's wave-function equation across the buttocks of his naked lover). At one point, Barth cleverly puts *On with the Story* into the hands of his characters, one of whom has torn out a page from it to use as a bookmark in another book. Perspectives shift, worlds are brought into a new focus, objects or characters resurface, and the reader can only shake his head in admiration.

This *is* to say that even though the novel has been Barth's genre of preference, this collection proves that he is still a master of the short story. Not only does he issue graceful pronouncements about the state of fiction, he also manages to tell good stories. Especially admirable in this respect are **"On with the Story," "'Waves,' by Amien Richard,"** and **"Ever After."** The characters are thoroughly developed and easily recognizable, the plots are engaging, and one can almost feel the warm sand under one's feet or taste the dry Chablis that the author describes so lovingly. There is a cheerful, honest texture to these stories for all of their intellectual play that makes them enjoyable while still stimulating. *On with the Story* could just as easily be a beach book as a classroom text. Barth wouldn't have it any other way.

W. Todd Martin (essay date spring 1997)

SOURCE: Martin, W. Todd. "Self-Knowledge and Self-Conception: The Therapy of Autobiography in John Barth's *Lost in the Funhouse.*" *Studies in Short Fiction* 34, no. 2 (spring 1997): 151-57.

[*In the following essay, Martin concentrates on the self-identity and sexuality of the protagonists in* Lost in the Funhouse.]

Many of John Barth's works are marked by an attempt to sort out the maze of self-conception and to determine the effects that too much self-knowledge has on the individual. Barth's protagonists flounder to establish their place in the world, questioning whether they are living out the lives of their true selves or those of selves that they project upon themselves. Delving to the core of

such themes, Harold Farwell observes that "as a rejoinder to the notion that the unexamined life is not worth living, Barth once quipped, 'King Oedipus and I aren't so sure'" (Farwell 58). The implication is, of course, that while a degree of self-knowledge may be important for a life to be full, an excessive amount could be detrimental to the mental and spiritual being of the individual. Nevertheless, Barth continually forces the protagonists in his fiction—along with the readers thereof—to confront themselves with intense scrutiny.

It is in the experimental *Lost in the Funhouse* that one can best begin to draw conclusions about the world in which Barth's protagonists dwell, the discrepancies that they find within their selves, and possible ways of dealing with hyper-self-consciousness. The novel[1] is, on its most basic level, the autobiography of Ambrose Mensche, a highly perceptive and self-conscious young man. Told from the depths of the funhouse, Ambrose's narrative looks both to his past and to his future, hoping to create a sense of order in his life.

Following the broken but deliberate narrative from Ambrose's conception[2] through his pre-teen years,[3] Ambrose's entrance into the funhouse in the title story signals the beginning of his adolescence. Ambrose realizes his inexperience with sexuality and is aware of—but does not necessarily understand—the changes that his body undergoes as he develops sexually. Like most teenagers, despite acute self-consciousness, he has sexual drives that force him to focus his attentions on something other than himself; they coerce him outward toward the opposite sex, to such characters as Magda, an adolescent girl whose "figure [is] exceedingly well developed for her age" (78). Ambrose is obliged to become much more conscious of the world and the people surrounding him.

Unfortunately, the insecurity and uncertainty of what, exactly, is happening within his body cause him to shrink from any direct contact with the outside world and especially with the opposite sex. He fears that such contact would reveal his faults and weaknesses. On a family holiday, for example, Ambrose decides not to swim with the other youth, thinking, ". . . the cold water shrank you up so" (79). Rather than join the crazy diving-board antics of the others in the pool, Ambrose chooses to sit and observe. Doing so, he guards against possible embarrassment and emasculation; however, he forgoes the opportunity to have fun, to live. Even in a premeditated moment—staged to look like an accident—Ambrose recoils. He places his hand on the seat directly behind Magda as she leans forward, but he draws it out of the way an instant before she slides back onto the seat (74-75). In order to experience the outside world, one must take certain risks; Ambrose, however, must overcome his self-consciousness before he can venture from his self-isolation.

But Ambrose does not suffer only from sexual desire and the insecurities of puberty. As the author of his autobiography, he must also deal with his role as an artist. He is new and inexperienced with this endeavor; yet, he is eager to be understood and well received. Like the adolescent Ambrose, the artistic Ambrose faces many difficulties that result from an oversensitive awareness of oneself and the surrounding world. The artist, like the pubescent youth, is haunted by the assumption that others are aware of one's every thought, idea, emotion, and intention. Telling the story of *Lost in the Funhouse*, for example, Ambrose is acutely conscious of the devices that he uses throughout the story's text, especially in the title story. Fictional devices have always been used to "enhance the illusion of reality" (69). But the narrator explains: "Interestingly, as with other aspects of realism, it is an *illusion* that is being enhanced, by purely artificial means" (69-70). In order to portray reality, the author must employ artificial techniques. Doing so, the author is anxious that the reader may be all too aware of his faltering attempts.

Reciting the account of his life, imagining that there is an unseen admirer who transcribes the story as he tells it, Ambrose employs and deliberately reviews various devices that might be used in a written version of his story. He contemplates the purpose of underlining and italics; he discusses the use of description, metaphor and plot structure; he even questions the realism of his character. In the middle of the narrative, the narrator stops short and asks: "Is it likely, does it violate the principles of verisimilitude, that a thirteen-year-old boy could make such a sophisticated observation?" (70). Later, in mid-sentence, the narrator further intrudes and contemplates whether he should change the age of his protagonist: "better make him eighteen at least, yet that would render other things unlikely . . ." (90). In sum, Ambrose's account of his life must be filtered through language and numerous fictional devices, despite his desire to achieve realism. What Ambrose is doing, in essence, is adapting the story of his life to fit the structures of a conventional story. In the same way, he must adjust his self to accommodate more readily the structures and expectations that exist outside of him as he enters puberty.

The funhouse, then, metaphorically represents both the confusion and self-consciousness of the adolescent who must deal internally and externally with a maturing body and the self-consciousness of the artist who must create a maze of fictional devices in the struggle to portray reality. According to Jac Tharpe, "'**Lost in the Funhouse**' is a record of awareness. It has two main, disparate connected themes, art and love." It is an "awareness of awareness, self-consciousness about roles" (96). Thus, at the same time that Ambrose worries about others discovering his thoughts and intentions as both adolescent and author, he ". . . can ob-serve himself lost, aware of being lost, and aware of the deliberate attempt to discover himself" (Tharpe 96). In the end, however, while procreation and artistic creation continue to be juxtaposed, Ambrose decides to concentrate on the creation of art rather than seeking sexual satisfaction.[4] This is attributed largely to the circumstance that, having entered the funhouse with Magda, he loses her to his brother, Peter.

Upon entering the funhouse, Magda and Peter blindly follow the path laid before them as it winds its way to the exit; they remain unaware of the construct of the funhouse. Ambrose, on the other hand, is immediately aware of its construct and its purpose—"to watch the girls get their dresses blown up" (85). Ironically, despite Ambrose's keen awareness—or because of his distracting preoccupation with it—Ambrose strays from the regular path and wanders into "some new or old part of the place that's not supposed to be used . . ." (80). He becomes lost. Laura Rice-Sayre explains in "The Lost Construction of Barth's Funhouse" that the artist

> who names the world in which others simply exist bears the knowledge of the artificial and arbitrary nature of what the rest of us call reality; this knowledge is both his burden and his freedom.
>
> (471)

The burden is that the artist is liable to become trapped within the labyrinth of self-awareness.

Ambrose realizes the artificial and arbitrary nature of both the literal funhouse and the funhouse of life, and, after wandering aimlessly through the numerous passages of the funhouse, he slumps in the dark corner of an abandoned corridor, mentally paralyzed. This state of mind, which Barth elsewhere terms "cosmopsis,"[5] occurs when an individual becomes overwhelmed with the macrocosm of the world and thus realizes the insignificance and futility of one's own life. Mesmerized by this realization, one has difficulty making a decision, knowing that any choice is arbitrary. Entering the funhouse, Ambrose becomes aware of the construct of the funhouse and of all of the options open to him as he gropes through the passageways. Likewise, within the funhouse of adolescence, he discovers that there are many roles that he may play, depending upon whom he encounters.

Similarly, as an artist, Ambrose discovers all of the options that are open to him. He realizes that the things that he can create are infinite and the methods whereby he can create them are numerous. Ambrose is overwhelmed by the overall complexity of the decisions that he must make and, more importantly, by the knowledge that any action he takes is finally arbitrary. Thus, Ambrose's inability to find his way about, just like his becoming lost in the funhouse, does not necessarily stem from the fact that he can never somehow find his way back to the exit; rather, confronted with the labyrinth of possibilities, he finds himself paralyzed, unable to make the first step in an attempt to find his way out.

Trapped, with nothing else to do, Ambrose begins to retrace his steps from the very beginning, wondering where he could have gone wrong. The result is his autobiography. According to a doctor who appears in Barth's *The End of the Road* to treat a similar case, telling one's own story is precisely the prescription needed for an individual who suffers from such a predicament as cosmopsis. The reason is quite simple. As the doctor declares: "everyone is necessarily the hero of his own life story. . . . Not only are we the heroes of our own life stories," he continues:

> we're the ones who conceive the story, and give other people the essence of minor characters. But since no man's life story as a rule is ever one story with a coherent plot, we're always reconceiving just the sort of hero we are, and consequently just the sort of minor roles that other people are supposed to play.

(End of the Road 88-89)

By retelling his story, Ambrose has stumbled upon the cure for his paralysis without even knowing it. He reconceives the events of his past and, in his own mind, recreates his self.[6]

The idea of creating one's self anew by mentally rearranging the past is what Barth's fictional doctor calls "Mythotherapy":

> This kind of role-assigning is myth-making, and when it's done consciously or unconsciously for the purpose of aggrandizing or protecting your ego—and it's probably done for this purpose all the time—it becomes Mythotherapy. . . .
>
> Now many crises in people's lives occur because the hero role that they've assumed for one situation or set of situations no longer applies to some new situation that comes up, or—the same thing in effect—because they haven't the imagination to distort the new situation to fit their old role.

(End of the Road 89)

In order to protect the ego, the individual must conceive of himself or herself as the main character, the hero or heroine, of one's own story. This is usually accomplished subconsciously and without difficulty. However, because he is intensely self-aware, Ambrose must deliberately and consciously readjust his role to fit his circumstances. He can no longer deal with the world in which he exists; so he must imagine himself changed. Ambrose accomplishes this by writing his autobiography, adjusting and readjusting himself and the events of his life to create a new self.

In *The Story-Shaped World,* Brian Wicker demonstrates the parallels between the need for stories and for the self to be re-created. Wicker maintains—especially in his book's first part—that stories are an integral part of any society. Stories, he claims, aid in helping to explain both the outer world and the inner self. He feels that it is possible to know at least some of the characteristics of the whole (the world or the self) through a brief glimpse of its parts. A story provides such a glimpse of life; it portrays a much more organized and constructed view of life. Despite fictional constructs, any story reveals various characteristics of reality. Among the types of stories to which he gives careful attention is the autobiography. This is particularly relevant to **Lost in the Funhouse.** Echoing points addressed earlier, Wicker says:

> It is worth noting finally, in this discussion of the explanatory powers of stories that narrative is not only a unique instrument for describing certain kinds of truths about the external world, it is also, for similar reasons, uniquely important in explaining what happens inside oneself. Thus, the autobiographer is one who is trying to make sense of himself in relation to the world by recollecting his past in a narrative. For he knows that it is only in the retelling of his own story that he can put his life in order and shore up the fragments of his past against his ruin.

(Wicker 46)

Just as Wicker suggests, to deal with his situation in the funhouse, Ambrose attempts to reconceive his self. He has lost control over what he is, so he decides to reinstate his control by reciting his story, incorporating any needed changes. He writes his autobiography, creating and re-creating his former self. He creates a new identity by rearranging and changing his memory, telling his story the way that he wishes it had been. In doing so, he simultaneously hopes to recreate his present self. He is attempting to create a self who is capable of escaping the funhouse.

Too much self-knowledge led Ambrose into the depths of the funhouse, where he continues the struggle to release himself—just as it led Oedipus to his downfall and destruction. On the other hand, the construction of **Lost in the Funhouse,** Ambrose's autobiography, acts as a therapeutic endeavor. It is Ambrose's attempt to readapt himself to a world that has become alien to his former role. Like the schizophrenic narrator of **"Title,"** he ponders, "Can't we start over? What's past is past. On the contrary, what's forever past is eternally present. The future? Blank. All this is just fill in" (102). Ambrose's autobiography is an attempt, in essence, to erase and fill in the blank that makes up his life. It is an attempt to fill in the blank that precedes his surname on his birth certificate (32); it is an attempt to fill in the blank message that he finds in a bottle on the shore (53); it is an attempt to fill the void of his life that could not be filled by his baptism and first communion or his initiation into the Boy Scouts (85, 93); it is an attempt to redefine his identity. Art provides possible healing effects, allowing one to put one's life in order and even to create oneself anew.

Notes

1. Despite the unconventional form and methods of the book, I view *Lost in the Funhouse* as a novel. In the author's note at the beginning of the work, Barth says that it is "neither a collection nor a selection, but a series; though several of its items have appeared separately in periodicals, the series will be seen to have been meant to be received 'all at once' and here arranged" (vii). Barth qualifies this author's note further in an interview:

> No doubt it depends on how far you want to stretch the term "novel" or "series." . . . It's meant to be a series in that there is an exfoliation and a development, one with a double motion. As the apparent narrator in most of the stories in the series goes through his biographical development, the time of the stories tends to move back from the present into the mythic past, and then at the end, of course, there's a circling back.

(Lampkin 489)

2. One realizes Ambrose's potential for hyper-awareness in "Night-Sea Journey" as the spermatozoon that consummates Ambrose's conception contemplates its existence. It realizes the absurdity and futility of the life it leads, believing its existence is a mere formality with little purpose.

3. Reaching pre-adolescence in "Water-Message," Ambrose can no longer merely accept things as they are; rather, he must define everything in relation to himself. In order to assure his centrality in the universe in which he lives, Ambrose creates a fantasy world in which he resides as the hero who always gets the girl and who unselfishly saves those who have recently thwarted him. It is a defense mechanism, and at this point in his life, such a fictive portrayal of his self is acceptable. However, finding the bottled message on the shore later in the story, he is reminded of the outer world. It is this encounter, a blank message, that makes him utterly aware that he is not the individual around whom the world revolves. The fantasy world of his childhood begins to falter.

4. The stories that follow "Lost in the Funhouse" continue to focus on the plight of the artist facing the postmodern dilemma, particularly the search for or retention of one's identity. In "Life-Story," Barth creates a situation in which the narrator, an author, is faced with the possibility that he is a fiction created by yet another author; likewise, the narrators of "Echo" and "Menelaiad" have difficulty divorcing themselves from their stories and their voices from those of others, a theme further developed in Barth's collection of novellas, *Chimera*; "Anonymiad" depicts a sexually impotent narrator who ejaculates into jars that contain the manuscript of his life story, which has been meticulously structured, drawing the sexual and artistic notions of creation found in "Lost in the Funhouse" together.

5. Cosmopsis has become one of Barth's trademarks. Many of the main characters of his novels suffer minor cases of this variety of paralysis, which results from an inability to impose some sort of order upon their lives.

6. Two characters from Barth's *The Sot-Weed Factor,* Ebenezer Cooke and Henry Burlingame, raise certain ideas that are helpful in looking at the healing effects of Ambrose's autobiography. Ebenezer, the primary protagonist of the novel, for instance, believes that memory is "the house of Identity, the Soul's dwelling place! Thy memory, my memory, the memory of the race: 'tis the constant from which we measure change . . ." (141). Henry Burlingame, Ebenezer's tutor, however, rebuts by claiming that, in the first place, no one's memory is complete; there are breaks in memory. There is also no means through which to solve a dispute about memory. Burlingame goes on to explain that in remembering things, one has the tendency to remember only those incidents one wants to remember, forgetting the rest, and even the things that are remembered are usually colored and remembered as one wishes them to have been. The last item on Burlingame's list of the weaknesses of memory is exposed when he asks, "suppose the thread [of memory] gets lost completely, as't sometimes doth. Suppose I'd had no recollection of my past at all?" (142).

Works Cited

Barth, John. *The End of the Road.* New York: Doubleday, 1967.

———. *Lost in the Funhouse.* New York: Bantam, 1981.

———. *The Sot-Weed Factor.* New York: Doubleday, 1960.

Farwell, Harold. "John Barth's Tenuous Affirmation: 'The Absurd, Unending Possibility of Love.'" *Critical Essays on John Barth.* Ed. Joseph J. Waldmeir. Boston: Hall, 1980. 55-67.

Lampkin, Loretta M. "An Interview with John Barth." *Contemporary Literature* 29 (1988): 485-97.

Rice-Sayre, Laura. "The Lost Construction of Barth's Funhouse." *Studies in Short Fiction* 27 (1980): 463-73.

Tharpe, Jac. *John Barth: The Comic Sublimity of Paradox*: Carbondale: Southern Illinois UP, 1974.

Wicker, Brian. *Story-Shaped World: Fiction and Metaphysics: Some Variations on a Theme.* Notre Dame, Indiana: U of Notre Dame P, 1975.

Salvatore Marano (essay date 1999)

SOURCE: Marano, Salvatore. "Dedalus through the Looking-Glass: John Barth's *Lost in the Funhouse*." In *America Today: Highways and Labyrinths,* edited by Gigliola Nocera, pp. 107-15. Siracusa, Italy: Grafia' Editrice, 2003.

[*In the following essay, first presented at the 15th Biennial Conference of the Associazione Italiana di Studi Nord Americani in 1999, Marano outlines Barth's use of* mise en abysme—*a type of labyrinthine "frame story" in which the central narrative summarizes some aspect of the "framing story"—in* Lost in the Funhouse.]

> Étant sans cesse à court de temps (ou vous imaginant l'être), pris sous les échéances, les retards, vous vous entêtez à croire que vous allez vous en sortir en mettant de l'ordre dans ce que vous avez à faire. Vous faites des programmes, des plans, des calendriers, des échéanciers. Sur votre table et dans vos fichiers, combien de listes d'articles, de livres, de séminaires, de courses à faire, de téléphones à donner. Ces paperolles, en fait, vous ne le consultez jamais, étant donné qu'une coscience angoissée vous a pourvu d'une excellente mémoire de vos obligations. Mais c'est irrépressible: vous allongez le temps qui vous manque, de l'inscription même de ce manque. Appelons ceci la compulsion de programme (on en devine le caractère hypomaniaque); les États, les collectivités, apparemment, n'en sont pas exempts: combien de temps perdu a faire des programmes? Et comme je prévois de faire un article là-dessus, l'idée de programme devient elle-même une compulsion de programme.
>
> Roland Barthes, *Roland Barthes par Roland Barthes*

0.

As the title suggests, this [essay] is focused on the labyrinths of perception at the core of John Barth's ***Lost in the Funhouse.***[1] Since the book is a sustained example of the literary device known as *mise en abyme,* I thought it appropriate to read John Barth in the mirror of Roland Barthes. Since it plays with the autobiographical genre, I chose *Roland Barthes par Roland Barthes,* the epigraph of which reads:

> Tout ceci doit être considéré comme dit par un personnage de roman.

1.

A convincing example of the mirror labyrinth is to be found in *Minotaurus,* Dürrenmatt's variation on Borges's "La casa de Asterión," a story where the Theseus myth is told from the Minotaurus's point of view.[2] In **"The Literature of Exhaustion,"**[3] the essay that in 1967 opened the discussion on postmodern literature, Barth never mentions Dürrenmatt, but points out the influence exerted by Borges on the writers of his generation. According to the lesson of the Argentinean, Barth conceives his mytopoietic universe as a self-mirroring circuit of permutational narrative units providing the reader with an endless fugue of "Tales Within Tales Within Tales."[4] An intertextual step further, then, *Lost in the Funhouse* intertwines mythological themes and motifs with an underground discourse on literary conventions that adds to narration the distinctive touch of creative theory. As a result, when the opening **"Frame-Tale"** starts with the fairy-tale formula "Once upon a time", the reader is equally driven to the incipit of *The 1001 Nights* as well as to Propp's *Morphology of the Fable.*

2.

Barth's work has been read as a deviant example of American humor. In his dialogue with the Borgesian abyme of labyrinths and mirrors, just to make one example, his personal *regressus in infinitum* is accomplished through the parodic reflection in one of Borges's twentieth century avatars. As part of a tetralogy comprising **"Night-Sea Journey," "Ambrose His Mark,"** and **"Water-Message,"** the title story is a take on Joyce's *Portrait of the Artist as a Young Man,*[5] with Ambrose playing the role of an awkward Stephen Daedalus whose perceptual shift from the chaos of the explorer to the order of the architect—i.e. from the Thesean to the Daedalian experience of the labyrinth—is paired with the dangling *dénouement* of taking "a wrong turn, strayed into the pass *wherein he lingers yet*" (*LF,* 91).

Parody, irony and humor are in themselves strategies of mirroring. Whereas Joyce opens his book with the awakening of the five senses of his hero, Barth delays a complete sensorial description of the protagonist until the opening paragraph of **"Ambrose His Mark."** To refine the specularity of his approach, in the story that follows the narrative loop of **"Frame-Tale," "Night-Sea Journey,"** he uses a sustained wordplay to magnify the senseless situation of the narrator, a sperm about to reach the ovule:

> in our *senseless* circumstances . . . Very likely I have lost my *senses* . . . But even that were *Sense,* and there is no *sense,* only *senseless* love, *senseless* death.
>
> (*LF,* 6, 9, 12; italics added)

With the inside story of the conception of his hero, a second Tristram Shandy embedded in a pattern that echoes Joyce's motif of the embryo-artist, Barth pays homage to the modern tradition at the roots of post-modernist poetics. A cinematic parallel involving a tragic detective story and its comic pendant is in Orson Welles's *The Lady from Shangai* (1946) and Woody Allen's *The Manhattan Murder Mystery* (1993).[6] Where the former plays with the idea of the classical Cretan labyrinth—the one at the center, for instance, of Lawrence Durrell's *Dark Labyrinth*—and uses it as an emblem of his noir, the latter creates a layer of additional meaning by means of parody.[7]

3.

In the "Author's Note," itself a frame to the **"Frame-Tale"** that in a hall of mirrors displaces the actual reader somewhere between the autobiographical author and its narratological shadow, one is informed that the book "differs in two ways from most volumes of short fiction" (*LF,* vii). In reverse order, the first of these differences is that many stories were conceived for either live or recorded voice. The opposition between orality and the literacy expressed in the subtitle suggests that the dominant senses of the collection are sight and hearing. Consistently, the punning reference to Echo and Narcissus in the penultimate paragraph of **"Night-Sea Journey"** prepares the reader for the aural and visual labyrinths to come with the statement: "Whoever *echoes* these *reflections*: be more corageous than their author!" (*LF,* 12; italics added).

The second difference pointed out in "The Author's Note" is that the book is "neither a collection nor a selection, but a series" (*LF,* vii). Commentators have invariably failed to appreciate the mathematical implications of such statement. For if *Lost in the Funhouse* is neither an author's selection nor a collection, why should the word *series* describe it more accurately—in fact, so accurately that Barth's description of his next book, *Chimera,* reads: "a *series* of three novellas"?[8] The doubt is cleared as soon as we think of the mathematical meaning of the term. That mathematics preside over the structure of the book is unmistakable, according to the formula "borrowed from the Argentine writer Jorge Luis Borges" that "good literature [. . .] involves and requires both the algebra and the fire; in short, passionate virtuosity."[9] Hence, in terms of numerical symbolism, the insistent recurrence of numbers two and seven throughout the text.

Like Queneau in *Le Chendant,*[10] Barth is obsessed by seven. In a 1981 interview he points out that *LETTERS,* a seven-letter titled novel where the character of Ambrose reappears as Ambrose Mensch to meet all the protagonists of Barth's previous novels, "abounds in sevens: seven chapters, seven narrators, etc."[11] Origi-

nally published in 1968, *Lost in the Funhouse* was reissued the following year with "Seven Additional Author's Notes," two pages that have become a permanent part of it ever since. In seven sections is the story entitled **"Glossolalia,"** provided that the title is one of them. Seven are the chapters of the closing stories, **"Menelaiad"** and **"Anonymiad,"** with the former conceived as a typographic labyrinth of inverted commas and parenthesis, a visual-and-aural maze in the tradition of concrete writing turned into an emblem of the *mise en abyme* after one of the fathers of the Ouvroir de Littérature Potentielle, Raymond Roussel:

" ' (") ('(("What?"))') (")'

" ' " ' " 'Why?' I repeated," I repeated,' I repeated," I repeated,' I repeated," I repeat." ' " ' "

And the woman, with a bride-shy smile and hushèd voice, replied: 'Why what?'

Doux salons où sitôt qu'ont tourné deux talons
((En se divertissant soit de sa couardise
(((Force particuliers quoi qu'on leus fasse ou dise
Jugeant le talion d'un emploi peu prudent
Rendient salut pour oeil et sourire pour dent))[12]

If seven shows itself in disguise, two is well in sight throughout the text. Duplications prompted by the Echo and Narcissus motif at all the levels of reflection "de l'*énoncé* . . . de l'*énonciation* et . . . du *code*"[13] abound: the siamese twins of "*Pet*ition" and Ambrose's brother/antagonist, aptly named *Pet*er; the two sections of **"Two Meditations"**; the mirroring format of such titles as **"Frame-Tale," "Night-Sea Journey," "Water-Message," "Life-Story,"** all fastened with the hyphen, *et cetera.*

At least two combinations of seven and two are relevant to the structure of the book. First of all, *Lost in the Funhouse* consists of fourteen (i. e. twice seven) stories. Secondly, the sum of seven and two gives nine, a number suggestive of creation in two ways. Literally, since the time-span elapsed between **"Night-Sea Journey"** and **"Ambrose His Mark"** covers the nine months needed by the embryo to become a human being; and metaphorically, since in the fourteenth story, **"Anonymiad,"** its association with the Muses draws a parallel between onto- and/or philogenetic creation on the one hand, and artistic creativity on the other. Barth's numerology, then, is self-explicatory: two, the token of doubling, is what the reader finds in a labyrinth of sight and hearing like the funhouse; seven, the Biblical number of creation, points to an ironic author/God who brings to life his fictional universe in digits.

4.

If the book is a series, i. e. the sum of a finite or infinite number of terms which keep a constant relationship to each other, the reader has to search for its *k*-factor; otherwise it will be impossible to decide, metaphorically speaking, what kind of series it is. For the paradox implied by the *mise en abyme,* of which the facing mirrors imagery of the funhouse is a clear analogue, consists in the power to suggest the infinite by means of a finite number of elements. In **"The Literature of Exhaustion"** Barth describes this kind of *regressus in infinitum* that he admires in Borges—the latter after the anonymous author of *The 1001 Nights*—as "an instance of the story-within-the-story turned back upon itself."[14] The expression used bears more than a trace of the infinite. The uncertainty about the status of **"Night-Sea Journey"** as either the first or the second story of Barth's series depends on the fact that **"Frame-Tale"** is conceived in such a way as to form a Möbius strip reading "Once upon a time there was a story that began . . . (to be continued)." Like Georg Cantor's aleph zero, a notion used to describe the infinite set of the natural numbers, it is an autotelic marker of all the other mirroring plots; or, like its geometrical match, it is a part containing the whole which in turn contains it.

A weird Borromeian ring or rather a knot that cannot be fastened, reverse image of the Freitag triangle—the diagram open at one side discussed in the title story—, the one-dimensional surface with two sides known as the Möbius strip is a queer topological item. Topology, the branch of mathematics that studies this blueprint of postmodern literature, deals with the invariant properties maintained by geometrical figures after certain types of transformation have taken place.[15] From the zero *degré* of isometry to the border limit of affinity—the realm of the shadows—, through all sorts of omotetic and isomorphic changes in the progressive modification of shape, orientation, length, width or height, topology provides Barth with a structural pattern where the literary text comes to be seen as a process of endless repetition of the same old story.

Last threshold before the self-effacing narrative to follow and self-effacing narrative itself, the Möbius strip tale is an icon of the labyrinth, the powerful "archetype of space"[16] controlling the word-system, because *the solution of a labyrinth is a topological problem.* The way out of a labyrinth with one entrance and one exit is found by going ahead and touching the wall always on the same side, say the right. After a long *détour* you will either reach the center, if the labyrinth has one, or the exit. But if a cycle surrounds the center, you will be sent back to the entrance from the other side, *because you have walked on a planar Möbius strip.*[17]

The Thesean vision of the labyrinth, then, is a matter of perception; at this point, the shift from topology to Kurt Lewin's notion of the topological field of experience, where the real meets the imaginary and space its psychological cognition[18] is only a matter of perspective. As a matter of fact, the second labyrinth of the book is

the underground tunnel of the Falloppian tubes in **"Night-Sea Journey"** *as it is perceived* first by the spermatozoa, then by the reader in his/her response to the text. The tactile experience of the character is conveyed through visual and aural metaphors because the reader must be aware that Barth's literary construct is but an audiovisual labyrinth of words. If we take as the starting point **"Frame-Tale,"** the double center of the book consists of **"Lost in the Funhouse"** and **"Echo."** Otherwise, while the former reflects *ad libitum* the title, the latter appears in the magnificent isolation of a new *abyme,* the hearing labyrinth mirrored in the ear's labyrinth of its virtual listener.

5.

But what kind of mirrors are those at the center of the funhouse? As a threshold phenomenon between the semiotic and the symbolic,[19] the mirror belongs to the phenomenological dialectics of the inner and outer space of identity. In the title story, Ambrose disappears in the funhouse as a writer-to-be at the age of thirteen. This is to say that the mathematical limit to the series of his fictional years tends to the unattainable threshold of the magic number fourteen, the numerological emblem of his peculiar *rite de passage.* Since the character is already grown up, to invoke Lacan's notion of the mirror stage is pointless. However, inside the funhouse Ambrose faces a set of distorting mirrors, a "point of catastrophe"[20] for the catoptric and the semiosic because even if we accept distortion "as if we were in a fairytale,"[21] we cannot escape the impression that the distorted mirror reflection somehow retains the semiotic faithfulness—the *eikon,* as opposed to the *eidôlon*[22]—of the looking-glass image. Not surprisingly, psychologists Pierre Mounoud and Annie Vinter have noted that even children between 12 and 15 years of age have experienced problems in front of the threshold of a threshold.[23] Like the character of Proteus in **"Menelaiad,"** suggesting the topological sameness of isomorphic shapes, the funhouse labyrinth is located in the hyperbolic space of anamorphosis.[24]

6.

Yet from the Falloppian tubes to the map of the funhouse, Barth's labyrinths are all variations on the unicursal model of the classical one rather than rhyzomatic molds. It is for this reason that the controlling numbers of the series are two and seven. Leaving aside the endless numerological implications of these sacred ciphers, they refer respectively to "the maze's inherent duality as the embodiment of simultaneous artistry and confusion, order and chaos, product and process, depending on the observer's (or the writer's) point of view"[25] and also to the seven volutes of the Cretan labyrinth.[26] The decisive difference is in the twist of his Möbius strip version, which suggests the infinite variations of storytelling despite—or rather because of—the finiteness of its constituents.

Thresholds, entrances, passages; self-effacing images, *mise en abyme*, echoes: we can speculate if ***Lost in the Funhouse*** is a *series* of narratives between two genres, the novel and the short story, that belongs neither to the former nor to the latter. *Amb*rose, whose *amb*iguity is already nominalistic, was christened after the saint who set the model for the Medieval genre of the *speculum*; and **"Night-Sea Journey,"** the narrative of his conception, is a condensed story of the western thought, a black humor speculation on the meaning of life. Is it a coincidence that in 1943 Ambrose was 13 years old, like the real author of **"Lost in the Funhouse"**?

7.

On the route from philogenesis to ontogenesis we find again the Roland Barthes displaced at the beginning of this paper. If in planning his book Barth shares the Daedalus vision and sees the labyrinth of his fiction "above its space,"[27] in front of the mirror he cannot but shift to the inside vision of Theseus. An in the endless oscillation between the two he produces the most extraordinary of the anamorphoses, the inscribed shadow self, a "hierogliphic double"[28] trapped in the funhouse that reflects neither the former nor the latter but both: Asterión, the Minotaurus.[29]

In an autobiographical piece collected in *The Friday Book* entitled—and the title is indeed a-mazing—"Some Reasons Why I Tell the Stories I Tell the Way I Tell Them Rather Than Some Other Sort of Stories Some Other Way," having introduced his twin-sister, at a certain point Barth writes: "My books tend to come in pairs, my sentences in twin members"[30] At the end of his search, at the very center of the labyrinth, Theseus finds a mirror. Borges has written more variations on this theme than anybody else; once he used these words:

> A man sets himself the task of portraying the world. Through the years he peoples a space with images of provinces, kingdoms, mountains, bays, ships, islands, fishes, rooms, instruments, stars, horses and people. Shortly before his death, he discovers that that patient labyrinth of lines traces the image of his face.[31]

Notes

1. The first edition of the book was published by Doubleday in 1968. My reference throughout the text will be to the 1969 Bantam Books edition—hereafter referred to as *LF*—which adds to the original the "Seven Additional Author's Notes". In both editions the sequence of the stories is: "Frame-Tale," "Night-Sea Journey," "Ambrose His Mark," "Autobiography," "Water-Message," "Petition," "Lost in the Funhouse," "Echo," "Two Meditations," "Title," "Glossolalia," "Life-Story," "Menelaiad," "Anonymiad."

2. Friederich Dürrenmatt, *Minotaurus*, Zürich: Diogenes Verlag AG, 1985; Jorge Luis Borges, "La

casa de Asterión" (1949), in *Obras completas*, Buenos Aires: Emecé Editores, 1974.

3. John Barth, "The Literature of Exhaustion", in *The Friday Book. Essays and Other Nonfiction*, New York: Perigee Books, 1984.

4. John Barth, "Tales Within Tales Within Tales", in *The Friday Book*, cit.

5. James Joyce, *A Portrait of the Artist as a Young Man* (1916), New York: Viking Press, 1964.

6. Orson Welles, *The Lady from Shangai*, USA 1946; Woody Allen, *The Manhattan Murder Mystery*, USA 1993.

7. Lawrence Durrell, *The Dark Labyrinth* (1947), New York: Pocket Book, 1963. The setting of the final scene of Welles's movie is in the Crazy House, a funhouse with tunnels, a set of distorting mirrors, and other paraphernalia. Note also that Woody Allen has some funny sperm characters in his *Everything You Always Wanted to Know about Sex (but were afraid to ask)* (USA 1972).

8. John Barth, "Algebra and Fire", in *The Friday Book*, cit., p. 169; author's italics.

9. Ibid., p. 167.

10. Raymond Queneau, *Le Chendant* (1933), Paris: Gallimard, 1974.

11. Charlie Reilly, "An Interview with John Barth", *Contemporary Literature*, 22, 1 (1981), p. 15.

12. The quotations are respectively from *LF*, 148; Michel Foucault, *Raymond Roussel*, Bologna: Cappelli, 1978, p. 136. As for Barth's relationship with the Oulipo, note that in "The Literature of Replenishment," his 1980 follow-up to "The Literary of Exhaustion," the author includes both Queneau and Calvino in his tentative map of postmodernism (*The Friday Book*, cit., pp. 193-206).

13. Lucien Dällenbach, *Le récit speculaire. Essay sur la mise en abyme*, Paris: Éditions du Seuil, 1977, p. 61.

14. John Barth, "The Literature of Exhaustion", cit., p. 73.

15. On the topological nature of *LF* see Victor J. Vintanza, "The Novelist as Topologist: John Barth's *Lost in the Funhouse*", *Texas Studies in Language and Literature*, 19, 1 (1977), pp. 83-97.

16. Abraham Moles and Elisabeth Rohmer, *Labirinti del vissuto. Tipologia dello spazio e immagini della comunicazione* (1982), Venezia: Marsilio, 1985, p. 58.

17. The system does not work in 3-D labyrinths with tunnels and bridges, and in arborescent labyrinths with cycles on the "touch" side; in this case an

explorer trapped in the close circuit would not even reach the entrance if the starting point were an inside cross! The algorithm that solves all sorts of connected labyrinths is: from the starting point go straight on and take an unexplored path at each cross; if all the crosses have already been explored, take one that has been explored only once; if you walk all the paths twice in both directions, and never take a path that has been explored twice, you will be certain to (1) reach the exit and (2) explore the whole of the labyrinth. It must be noted that, because of its peculiar configuration, also the surface of a Möbius strip needs to be walked twice in order to be fully experienced: always in the same direction, but each time on a different side.

18. Abraham Moles and Elisabeth Rohmer, op. cit., p. 20.

19. Umberto Eco, "Sugli specchi" (1985), in *Sugli specchi e altri saggi*, Milano: Bompiani, 1987, p. 11.

20. Ibid., p. 37.

21. Ibid.

22. Andrea Tagliapietra, *La metafora dello specchio. Lineamenti per una storia simbolica*, Milano: Feltrinelli, 1991, p. 94.

23. *Il bambino, il riflesso, l'identità*, ed. by Angela Molina, Firenze: La Nuova Italia, 1995, p. 237.

24. See Jurgis Baltrusaitis, *Anamorphoses ou Thaumaturgus opticus*. Paris: Flammarion, 1984.

25. Penelope Reed Doob, *The Idea of the Labyrinth from Classical Antiquity through the Middle Ages*, Ithaca: Cornell University Press, 1990, p. 39.

26. Hermann Kern, *Labirinti* (1981), Milano: Feltrinelli, 1981, p. 13.

27. Wendy B. Faris, *Labyrinths of Language*. Symbolic Landscape and Narrative Design in Modern Fiction, Baltimore: The John Hopkins University Press, 1988, p. 4.

28. John T. Irwin, *American Hieroglyphics*. The Symbol of the Egyptian Hieroglyphics in the American Renaissance, New Haven: Yale University Press, 1980, p. xi.

29. Very interestingly, Lacan points out that the Möbius strip challenges the binary opposition of Aristotelic logic, as it provides "an image which is simultaneously one and two" (Christopher D. Morris, "Barth and Lacan: The World of the Möbius Strip," *Critique*, 17.1, 1975, p. 70), that is, another.

30. John Barth, "Some Reasons Why I Tell the Stories I Tell the Way I Tell Them Rather Than Some Other Sort of Stories Some Other Way" (*The Friday Book*, cit., p. 3).

31. Quoted in Wendy B. Faris, op. cit., p. 95.

Marjorie Worthington (essay date spring 2001)

SOURCE: Worthington, Marjorie. "Done with Mirrors: Restoring the Authority Lost in John Barth's Funhouse." *Twentieth-Century Literature* 47, no. 1 (spring 2001): 114-36.

[*In the following essay, Worthington views the metafictional properties of* Lost in the Funhouse *and explores Barth's treatment of the thematic and structural significance of the self, the author, and authority.*]

Although narrative self-consciousness is by no means specific to the contemporary period, the particularly rampant metafictional self-reflexivity demonstrated in **Lost in the Funhouse** has often been touted as one of the principal traits of postmodern fiction. As Linda Hutcheon says, "What we tend to call postmodernism in literature today is usually characterized by intense self-reflexivity and overtly parodic intertextuality" ("Historiographic" 3). Postmodern fiction, then, often exhibits a metafictional quality. Metafiction is typically defined as "fiction about fiction—that is, fiction that includes within itself a commentary on its own narrative and/or linguistic identity" (Hutcheon, *Narcissistic* 11). In other words, metafiction focuses as much if not more on its own processes of creation as on a "story" in the usual sense. John Barth, widely considered to be the preeminent American metafictionist, directly confronts issues of selfhood and authorship in his **Lost in the Funhouse** series.[1]

However, instead of challenging the primacy of authorship, Barth's metafictional experiments serve to cement the author into a position of authority over the text. Linda A. Westervelt writes: "John Barth . . . takes the inner division that results from self-consciousness and, by metaphoric extension, makes it a resource—namely, the subject of his fiction" (42). Many of Barth's works not only employ but also thematize the complications arising from an increasingly intrusive narrative self-consciousness that arises, according to Jerome Klinkowitz, from Barth's sense that his era

> had rejected the Cartesian definition of ego so central to traditional novelistic design. A hero could no longer speak with confidence and coherence and so define himself, since under contemporary philosophical pressure the old *cogito, ergo sum* had become a farcically painful lie.
>
> (408)

Although Barth's heroes are unable to define themselves through their narratives, they experience an almost desperate need to continue the attempt. The result is that most of the stories in the series depict narrators as authors so aware of themselves and so concerned with the effect of this awareness on their waning creative powers that they cannot avoid continually inserting their presence into the stories they narrate. Their overt authorial presence threatens to derail the narratives, making them unable to come to a fruitful end. Instead, they twist and turn on themselves, leaving the reader with the difficult and perhaps impossible task of sorting out product from process, story from narration.

Because of the intricacy of these stories, much of the critical discussion surrounding *Lost in the Funhouse* has focused on the increased burden of interpretation that metafiction forces on the reader. The argument has often been made that the intricacy of the text, coupled with the apparent failure of the narrator to control and shape the story, forces the reader to construct a meaning for the text and thereby to participate in the construction of the work itself. In the face of postmodern indeterminacy, interpretive authority no longer resides with authors, and singularity of meaning no longer exists. As Deborah A. Woolley puts it, criticism about metafiction

> substitutes a heroics of text and language for the older heroics of creative genius and imagination. The text . . . accepts the existentialist challenge to confront the lack of a center at the heart of language and to dwell in that void.

(460)

Many critics have pointed out that *Lost in the Funhouse* invites such an interpretation by repeatedly suggesting that traditional narrative forms and the authors who construct them have lost their power to find or depict a coherent meaning.

However, what is often overlooked is metafiction's inherent and inevitable preoccupation with the creative power of the author. At the same time that they lament the diminished capacity of the narrator to construct a proper story, the self-conscious moments in *Lost in the Funhouse* point necessarily to the existence of a creator, of an author. When I use the term *author,* I am not referring to the actual figure of John Barth but to what Inger Christensen calls the "fictional author," the narrator who is ostensibly also the author of the text he narrates. As Christensen says,

> The historical author will of course always exist outside and apart from the work itself, so that metafiction only operates with an additional factor: the fictional author [who] places himself inside the fictional world and figures as a structural element in the novel.

(13)

What I will focus on is not the historical or actual figure of John Barth, but rather the extent to which authorship and authority are thematic and structural concerns

in his series. *Lost in the Funhouse* is not merely a *Künstlerroman*-esque chronicle of the life and development of an author; the structural strategies it employs serve also as an attempt to recenter—to reauthorize—the author in twentieth-century fiction.

There are several avenues through which critics have approached the idea that metafiction in general and *Lost in the Funhouse* in particular allow more freedom or demand more responsibility for interpretation from the reader.[2] Beverly Gray Bienstock anticipates this critical focus on Barth's readers by arguing that *Lost in the Funhouse* addresses the issue of "the capricious immortality of the work of art" by asking, "how does the reader fit into this masquerade of immortal possibilities?" (72). To answer this question, some critics have employed elements of reader response theory in order to argue that the self-conscious intricacies of Barth's text demand that readers become skillful enough to follow this difficult text to its end. While mastery of the text may still elude them, these readers will have been initiated into the select group qualified to read metafiction. Beth A. Boehm points out this connection between Barth's work and reader response theory when she says: "Barth creates an audience of active, self-conscious readers capable of re-experiencing the pleasures of discovery whenever they are confronted with a new puzzle" (118).[3] Linda Hutcheon makes this same argument about metafiction in general when she posits that self-consciousness forces the reader to acknowledge a text's fictionality and to participate, to "engage himself intellectually, imaginatively, and affectively in its co-creation" (*Narcissistic* 7). Although reader response critics maintain that all texts demand such interpretive participation from readers, Hutcheon argues that the role of the reader is of even more crucial importance in metafiction. Because the text is so self-consciously fictional, she argues, the reader's interpretation is particularly necessary to imbue the text with meaning.

Deconstructionists have made a similar case for the importance of the role of the reader—in all texts, not just metafictional ones—by means of the Derridian concept of decentering, which results in the free play of linguistic signifiers and posits that meaning is not fixed but contextual, fleeting, nonexistent. Such a theory, Brian Edwards argues, "insists (minimally stated) upon reader participation in creating meaning and texts within the freeplay of language" (266).[4] The reader is charged with the responsibility for making meaning and interpreting the text because, the deconstructionist argument goes, the text no longer provides a singular, authoritative meaning—if indeed it ever did.

This "reduction of traditional forms of authority" clears the way for reader participation in the construction of textual meaning (Edwards 265). Many critics have pointed out the extent to which *Lost in the Funhouse* invites such an interpretation by asserting, as the selection called **"Life Story"** does, that "the old analogy between Author and God . . . can no longer be employed" (*Lost* 125). The text further lends itself to a deconstructive reading in that many of the stories are about the inability to tell a proper story or the inability of traditional narrative forms to hold up to contemporary narrative needs, as if "the medium and genre in which he worked . . . were moribund if not already dead" (*Lost* 118). Thus, the text almost asks to be deconstructed, as it claims that authority once did but no longer does rest with either the author or the text. In fact, the narrator of **"Life Story"** emphasizes the immense responsibility of the reader when he says: "your own author bless and damn you his life is in your hands. . . . Don't you think he knows who gives his creatures their lives and deaths? Do they exist except as he or others read their words?" (124). The implication here is that it is the reader, not the author, who holds the ultimate power over a narrative.

It is, however, not that simple. What the text suggests on one hand, it denies on the other. At the same time that *Lost in the Funhouse* proclaims the supremacy of the reader and reduces the author from the status of godlike creator to struggling fictional character, it nevertheless makes that author-character the thematic and structural crux of many of the stories it contains. Even as the metafictional elements of *Lost in the Funhouse* project a new direction for late twentieth-century fiction, closer examination reveals that they also serve to revalidate the very tenets of traditional narrative that they ostensibly repudiate: the centrality of authorial authority and the creative power of the individual. Similarly, while metafiction in general allows, even demands, a new and more powerful role for the reader, it simultaneously demonstrates the continuing need for a consciously constructing authorial figure. What I mean is: a text that thematizes a self-conscious awareness of the processes of its own construction unavoidably thematizes the importance of its *constructor*. Works that constantly point to themselves as texts or fictions, that refer continually to their fictionality, simultaneously point to the necessity of the existence of the artist or author who created them. By claiming to be unable to control the story he is crafting, the author-narrator demonstrates his continued presence in and creative influence over the text. By asserting his failure, he simultaneously asserts his (albeit waning) power, illustrating that the self-consciousness, the self-reflexivity of metafiction is simultaneously and necessarily a recognition of authorial presence.

The argument that metafiction is inherently author-focused is particularly relevant to a discussion about *Lost in the Funhouse* because both its structure and its content focus on issues of narrative and authorship. Although deconstructionists have rightly pointed to this text as a demonstration of how meaning and authority are decentered, *Lost in the Funhouse* represents at the same time an attempt to maintain a firm grasp on the power of author-ity. Despite the critical celebration of the "birth of the reader" that surrounds metafiction (Barthes 148),[5] a close textual reading of *Lost in the Funhouse* reveals one of its primary projects to be the resuscitation of a supposedly dead author who struggles to retain the ability to construct a narrative. *Lost in the Funhouse* juxtaposes elements of the self-reflexive narrative with the self-conscious creator in order to posit an intricate, inextricable relationship between them, thereby reaffirming the notion that at the helm of every narrative there must exist an agenic creator, or author. What has often been touted, then, as the preeminent postmodern urtext actually represents a simultaneous attempt to reestablish the authority of the author, the center of the subject, and the literary traditions of an earlier period.[6]

Many of the stories in this series feature a self-reflexive narrator who, we are led to understand, is the actual creator, the "fictional author" of the narrative. This fictional author bewails the fact that he cannot seem to construct a story in which his own presence does not overwhelm the action, a plight that, according to Heide Ziegler, illustrates that the "Romantic author who consciously begins to intrude into his own fiction must eventually become the postmodern author who is no longer able to withdraw from it" (91). Simultaneously, the protagonist that this too-present narrator describes is struggling with the different but related problem of an overdeveloped self-consciousness which keeps him from directly experiencing his own life.

This pairing of the stultifying self-consciousness of the main character and the crippling self-reflexivity of the narrative is evident, for example, in **"Life Story,"** which is about an author struggling to write an entertaining and meaningful story at the exact midpoint of his life, which is exactly two-thirds of the way through the twentieth century. It seems to him that the literary vehicle available to him at this time (Monday, June 20, 1966) is too "self-conscious, vertiginously arch, fashionably solipsistic, unoriginal—in fact a convention of twentieth-century literature" (114). Thus the narrator recognizes that the problems he is facing are problems facing literature in general at this point in the century. He describes his literary efforts this way:

> Another story about a writer writing a story! Another regressus in infinitum! Who doesn't prefer art that at least overtly imitates something other than its own processes? That doesn't continually proclaim "Don't forget I'm an artifice!"? That takes for granted its mimetic nature instead of asserting it in order (not so slyly after all) to deny it, or vice-versa?
>
> (114)

However, the apparent response to this claim that contemporary literature is too self-involved is *Lost in the Funhouse*—a series of stories that repeatedly depict that very self-consciousness. Similarly, the narrator in the story called **"Title"** laments, "Oh God comma I abhor self-consciousness. I despise what we have come to" (110), but then embarks on that very self-consciousness as a "temporary expedient" in order "to turn ultimacy, exhaustion, paralyzing self-consciousness and the adjective weight of accumulated history . . . against itself to make something new and valid, the essence whereof would be the impossibility of making something new. What a nauseating notion" (106). This is one of the basic contradictions or paradoxes of this text: although the narrators deplore the seeming ubiquity of contemporary narrative self-consciousness, no other means of construction is available to them. They hate being "meta" but cannot seem to avoid it.

At work here is Barth's oft-cited notion that his writing represents what he called "the literature of exhaustion." In his 1967 essay by that title, Barth describes the literature of exhaustion as representing "the used-upness of certain forms or exhaustion of certain possibilities" in literature (70). Novelistic fiction, Barth argues, has already said, done, and imagined everything that can be said, done, or imagined; it is no longer possible for fiction to follow the modernist imperative to "make it new."[7] For example, the narrator of **"Life Story"** gets most of the way through his narration and is still unable to establish what he calls a "ground-situation," or a basis for a good or meaningful story in this medium which is "moribund if not already dead" (*Lost* 118). In **"The Literature of Exhaustion,"** however, Barth says that the fact that the genre is moribund is "by no means necessarily a cause for despair" (70).[8] Instead, this lack of meaningful story can *become* the meaningful story, which thereby "turns the artist's mode or form into a metaphor for his concerns" (78). In other words, Barth argues that fiction should both portray and become—or be performative of—the postmodern exhaustion he discusses. Similarly, the **"Life Story"** narrator eventually realizes that he should regard "the absence of a ground-situation, more accurately the protagonist's anguish at that absence and his vain endeavors to supply the defect, as itself a sort of ground-situation" (*Lost* 123). Neither the article nor the story is saying, then, that art is no longer possible or that art can no longer have meaning (as Barth is often misunderstood as having said). Rather, the argument is that because traditional narrative forms have been "exhausted," a good artist must respond by depicting that very exhaustion.

And that is ostensibly what the narrator of **"Life Story"** attempts to do. After spending two-thirds of his lifetime writing novels, "it was perhaps inevitable that one afternoon the possibility would occur to the writer of these lines that his own life might be a fiction, in which he

was the leading or an accessory character" (113). He decides to write a story about a character who believes he is a character in someone's fiction, which would of course be a story about himself. This character suddenly and self-consciously recognizes his creator's, his *author's,* existence, and **"Life Story"** starts out to be about the *writing* of that story. However, in the process of writing the story, the narrator recognizes that he cannot be a fictional character because

> he could demonstrate by syllogism that the story of his life was a work of fact: though assaults upon the boundary between life and art, reality and dream, were undeniably a staple of his own and his century's literature as they'd been of Shakespeare's and Cervantes's, yet it was a fact that in the corpus of fiction as far as he knew no fictional character had become convinced as he had that he was a character in a work of fiction. This being the case and he having in fact become thus convinced it followed that his conviction was false.
>
> (125-26)

Whereas critics like Patricia Waugh argue that it is this metafictional self-consciousness that helps to blur the line between art and reality, and to "explore the possible fictionality of the world outside the literary fictional text" (2), it is this very self-consciousness that assures the narrator of **"Life Story"** that he is indeed real, that his life is factual. In the case of **"Life Story,"** narrative self-consciousness does not lead to the recognition of the fictionality of life; instead, the narrator's awareness of himself as a self-conscious being allows him to conclude that he is not, after all, a character in someone else's fiction. However, while the narrator's self-consciousness serves to reestablish his personhood or reality by convincing him that he could not possibly be fictional, that same self-consciousness stands in the way of his successfully completing the story he set out to write. Once he recognizes that he is *not* a fictional character in someone else's fiction, it suddenly becomes impossible for him to write the story about a character who is.

"Life Story" is indicative of many of the stories in *Lost in the Funhouse* in that, perhaps in response to **"The Literature of Exhaustion,"** it acts as an attempt to demonstrate the "used-upness" of modern literary traditions. In this series, seemingly pointless and meandering stories chronicle the ostensible inability of contemporary narrative forms to tell a proper or interesting story or to provide any manner of or route to "truth."

For example, the story titled **"Echo"** depicts the character of Narcissus looking into the pool and desiring immediate and direct access to the image he sees there, not knowing that that image is of himself—and not even of himself undistorted, but an image of himself inaccurately reflected by the pool. Narcissus tries but cannot truly find, see, or know himself without the interference of a screen of reflection. Heide Ziegler calls attention to "the double meaning of the word 'self-reflection'" as Narcissus moons over the reflection of himself that he sees in the pool, and becomes lost thereby in self-reflection—in reflecting on that self—until the gods pity him and turn him into the eponymous flower (91).

Narcissus spends eternity loving, longing for, and being denied unmediated access to himself. Instead, he can only see his image, or the narrativized reflection of reality his image in the pool represents. He is so taken with his own reflection that he can do nothing but stare at it and sigh. Both the narrative of his life and the narrativized image created by his reflection in the pool end here in the cave, mired in Narcissus's fascination with himself, stuck in his self-reflection. "Echo," then, makes a clear connection between the character of Narcissus and the author of the self-reflexive narrative (yet a third meaning for the term *self-reflection*)[9] in order to demonstrate the unfortunate result when an author (Narcissus) can do nothing but refer endlessly to his own narrative reflection. The story of Narcissus represents the self-reflexive narrative so in love with itself that it cannot do other than refer to itself and cannot, therefore, achieve self-knowledge or a properly fruitful narrative end[10] but can only "linger forever on the autognostic verge" (*Lost* 100). "Echo," then, serves as a warning that the self-reflexive fiction so popular at the time of its publication can act as a trap, alluring yet ultimately unproductive and stifling.

But Narcissus is not alone in the cave. When he attempts to speak, his words are reflected back to him by Echo, the nymph whose wonderful storytelling kept Hera distracted while Zeus frolicked with mountain nymphs, and who was subsequently cursed forever merely to repeat what is said in her presence. Echo is no longer able to make up her own stories; she can only reproduce those told her by others. The narrator of the story warns, however, that although her words are not her own, Echo still manages to be a storyteller through the manner in which she repeats what is told: "She edits, heightens, mutes, turns others' words to her end" (*Lost* 97). When Narcissus enters the cave with the pool, Echo instantly falls in love with him and repeats, alters, and shapes his words into a love narrative of her own:

> I can't go on.
>
> Go on.
>
> Is there anyone to hear here?
>
> Who are you?
>
> You.
>
> I?

> Aye.
>
> Then let me see me!
>
> See?
>
> A lass! Alas.
>
>   (98)[11]

In thus speaking to Echo, Narcissus believes he is speaking to himself, or at least a strange and oddly reflected version of himself, and he cannot resist that reflection: "No use, no use: Narcissus grows fond; she speaks his language" (99-100). What Narcissus really loves is not himself but the narrativized version of himself that he gets from Echo and from his reflection in the pool: "it was never himself Narcissus craved, but his reflection, the Echo of his fancy" (99). Echo fools Narcissus into loving her story when he thinks he loves only himself, illustrating that she is still able to construct a convincing narrative despite the fact that the words she must use are not original and not even her own.

Furthermore, Echo's attempts at narrative construction are more successful than Narcissus's; while Narcissus "perishes by denying all except himself," Echo "persists by effacing herself absolutely" (99). While Ziegler refers to Echo's love for Narcissus as "the story [being] in love with its author" (93), my argument establishes Echo as the author in love with the figure she attempts to narrativize: Narcissus. As author, Echo effaces herself absolutely in order to reflect and depict the story of Narcissus, and is thus able to persist by creating a more traditional, un-self-reflexive narrative. However, although she has withdrawn as much as possible from the narrative she constructs, she cannot withdraw completely; her authorial authority remains present and intact. In this way, Echo represents the successful author as a realist, constructing mimetic narratives by repeating what she has witnessed, yet exerting constant creative influence over those narratives as she "edits, heightens, mutes, turns others' words to her end." It is Echo who is ultimately able to survive long after the demise of poor self-reflexive Narcissus. The implication in "Echo," then, is that traditional mimetic fiction will outlast current metafictional narrative trends and that the individual creative genius of the author necessarily lurks behind every successful narrative construction no matter how mimetic that narrative may seem.

It is somewhat surprising perhaps to encounter this notion of the actively constructing author embedded in what is usually considered to be the quintessential postmodern or "experimental" work of fiction. The ostensible purpose of these experiments was to sound the death knell of traditional narrative enterprises, which had lost their power to create meaningful fiction. Both critics and Barth himself have usually agreed that the project of *Lost in the Funhouse* was to comment on the failure and exhaustion of traditional narrative forms and strategies and to create art from the self-conscious assertion that new art is no longer possible. Clearly, I am making an altogether different claim, in concert with Max F. Schultz's assertion that Barth "is not an errant realist guilty of formalist perversions so much as a radical preservationist looking for ways to conserve old and new storytelling" (408). Rather than being an argument for new fictional forms, the reclamation of the authorial authority demonstrated in **"Echo"** acts as the revalidation of traditional narrative techniques.

The concentration on authorial authority in this story is striking, especially since the time of its publication roughly coincides with the first literary theoretical rumblings about the death of the author and the rise of the importance of reader involvement in the text. My point is that at the same time that *Lost in the Funhouse* seems to invite increased reader participation in the construction of textual meaning, it also engages in an attempt to revalidate the figure of the author as a powerful and conscious constructor of narrative. This move appears in opposition to the idea that traditional novelistic forms are no longer powerful enough to result in great fiction, or that the authority for meaning-making no longer resides with an author. Rather, reestablishing the importance of the author serves simultaneously to reestablish those traditional forms as the very ones that can save postmodern fiction from the self-centered slump of metafictional reflexivity.

This endeavor to reinstate the author as the center of textual importance is evident in many of the stories in *Lost in the Funhouse,* including the story that is arguably the most notable (and noted) example of self-reflexive narrative: **"Lost in the Funhouse."** This story depicts a young boy named Ambrose getting lost in a funhouse on a beach boardwalk and vacillates between telling that story and discussing the telling of that story:

> He has come to the seashore with his family for the holiday, *the occasion of their visit is Independence Day, the most important secular holiday of the United States of America.* A single straight underline is the manuscript mark for italic type, *which in turn* is the printed equivalent to oral emphasis of words and phrases as well as the customary type for titles of complete works, not to mention.
>
> (69)

This digression from the story to a discussion of the use and meaning of italics calls attention simultaneously to the fact that the book is a piece of printed material and to the fact that the narrative itself is also a construction where certain words are emphasized, certain parts considered more noteworthy than others.

Interestingly, however, this construction—this narrative—is apparently moving increasingly beyond the constructor's control. Several pages into this rambling, digressive story, we are informed that

> We should be much farther along than we are; something has gone wrong; not much of this preliminary rambling seems relevant. Yet everyone begins in the same place; how is it that most go along without difficulty but a few lose their way?
>
> (75)

The narrative is stalled somehow, snagged on its self-conscious deviations, and we are left to wonder why it is that, while "most go along without difficulty," this narrative seems to have lost its way. Not only is it not progressing fast enough, but the narrator worries at regular intervals that "we will never get out of the funhouse" and "At this rate our hero, at this rate our protagonist will remain in the funhouse forever" (74, 75). The failure of the narrative to progress in a timely fashion will trap little Ambrose forever in the funhouse, making him similarly unable to progress. Just as Ambrose is lost in the funhouse, then, so are the narrator and reader lost in the funhouse of this narrative construction.

In fact, the connections are many between Ambrose's plight and the plight of this narrative. Just as the narrative is focused more on its own processes than the telling of a realistic story, the character of Ambrose is consistently too conscious of himself to engage directly with his surroundings. Ambrose narrates his existence to himself, and instead of simply having an experience, he feels the constant need to distance himself from that experience through a veil of mental description. For example, during a sexual encounter he had once had with Magda:

> though he had breathed heavily, groaned as if ecstatic, what he'd really felt throughout was an odd detachment, as though some one else were Master. Strive as he might to be transported, he heard his mind take notes upon the scene: *This is what they call* passion. *I am experiencing it.*
>
> (81)

Like so much in this story, what happens in and to the narrative is mirrored by what happens to Ambrose. The fear expressed by the narrator that the story is stuck and will never be able to progress to a proper ending mirrors Ambrose's similar fear that he will be trapped in the funhouse forever. And just as Ambrose masks or copes with his fears by consciously constructing a veil of story between himself and the events around him, the narrator constructs a similar veil of self-reflexive musings about the nature of narrative around the story of Ambrose in the funhouse. The self-reflexivity of the narrative serves to exteriorize Ambrose's self-conscious self-narration.

It is while he is at his most self-absorbed that Ambrose takes the wrong turn that gets him lost in the funhouse. In a truly Narcissistic move, Ambrose gets lost in self-reflection while viewing his altered image in the fun-house mirrors. Unlike Narcissus, however, Ambrose realizes that the mirrors do not provide a truly accurate reflection and do not allow him direct access to himself: "In the funhouse mirror room you can't see yourself go on forever, because no matter how you stand, your head gets in the way" (81-82).[12] Nevertheless, Ambrose gets so involved in his own reflections on his own reflection that it is here in this room that both he and the story go astray. He takes a wrong turn and suddenly, now "Ambrose is off the track, in some new or old part of the place that's not supposed to be used" (80). The narrator informs us that it is here, in the mirror room, that the misstep occurs: "That's just where it happened, in that last lighted room: Peter and Magda found the right exit; he found one that you weren't supposed to find and strayed off into the works somewhere" (82). Just as the narrative has become preoccupied with its own workings, Ambrose has become lost in the inner workings of the funhouse; just as the narrative has gone off its track toward the proper conclusion, Ambrose has gone off the track toward the end of the funhouse. It is important to note that the moment Ambrose goes astray into the inner workings of the funhouse is the moment when he is at his most self-reflexive.

Furthermore, Ambrose's experiences in the funhouse can be directly correlated to the trajectory of the narrative entire. In the same way that his self-awareness prevents Ambrose from forgetting himself long enough to have an experience unalloyed by self-narration, the self-conscious preciousness of the narrative prohibits it from progressing with the story. While Ambrose worries that he will never become a "regular person," the narrator evinces a certain amount of anxiety over whether this story will follow the traditional narrative structure described (and illustrated) as a variant of Freitag's Triangle (93, 91)—in other words, whether this will become a "regular narrative."

But it won't. At the same time that Ambrose gets lost by going "off the track, in some new or old part of the [funhouse] that's not supposed to be used," the narrative has similar problems: "the plot doesn't rise by meaningful steps but winds upon itself, digresses, retreats, hesitates, sighs, collapses, expires" (92). Clearly, the narrative itself has taken on the attributes of a funhouse—a funhouse in which we and it have become trapped and lost, with little hope of getting to the proper end. The narrator knows what that end should be, but is unable for some reason to bring it about: "The climax of the story must be its protagonist's discovery of a way to get through the funhouse. But he has found none, may have ceased to search" (92). This story, then, is performative in that it simultaneously depicts the failure of the protagonist and the narrative itself to reach the expected resolution. Just as Ambrose's self-reflections caused him to get lost and now he cannot

find his way out of the funhouse, the story is too focused on its own construction to make sufficient progress toward a conclusion and cannot, therefore, find its proper ending.

However, his self-consciousness serves an important purpose for Ambrose, who is often upset by the suspicion that he is not a real human being but rather a character in the story of his or someone else's life and that this story is a kind of "portrait of the artist as a fiction" (Marta 210). Ambrose realizes that if he is a fictional character, he is a character doomed to a heightened self-awareness that others do not possess—doomed therefore to the recognition that he *is* merely a fictional character. This realization saddens him, as he thinks

> how readily he deceived himself into supposing he was a person. He even foresaw, wincing at his dreadful self-knowledge, that he would repeat the deception, at ever-rarer intervals, all his wretched life, so fearful were the alternatives.
>
> (90)

Paradoxically, however, it this very sense of being too self-conscious to be a real person that simultaneously provides Ambrose with the means to construct a narrative subjectivity for himself. His constant self-conscious narration of events allows him to construct a selfhood where he worries there may be none. If he cannot be a person, he can at least construct himself a persona and thereby become, in a sense, the author of himself. So even if he feels, like Narcissus, that he does not have direct access to real experience (access not mediated by a film of self-constructed narrative), these narrative constructions represent his attempts to convince himself that he actually does exist. Through his constant narrativizing, Ambrose constructs a portrait of himself as a fiction and his narratives constitute his selfhood. Ambrose is the artist and his selfhood is his art.

Instead of continuing to search for the way out of this funhouse once he gets lost in the mirror room, Ambrose begins constructing narratives, "rehearsing to himself the unadventurous story of his life, narrated from the third-person point of view" (92). He fantasizes about meeting someone in the dark of the funhouse, of opening his soul to that person and helping her escape; he fantasizes about returning one day to the funhouse with his wife and child, of hugging his child to him when he wants to know what a funhouse is. "He dreams of a funhouse vaster by far than any yet constructed; but by then they may be out of fashion, like steamboats and excursion trains" (93). While lost in this funhouse, stuck in this narrative, Ambrose decides, "He could design such a place himself" (93). The story ends as Ambrose, still lost in the funhouse, realizes somewhat unhappily that he is destined to be a person who will "construct funhouses for others and be their secret operator—

though he would rather be among the lovers for whom funhouses are designed" (94). In other words, he decides reluctantly to be an author, a creator of narrative funhouses, despite the dreary recognition that they may be going out of style.

Thus, not only is **"Lost in the Funhouse"** a narrative about the failure of self-reflexive narrative, as I have shown and as many others have argued,[13] but it is also about the creation of an author. As the narrative fails, trapping its protagonist in the funhouse forever, that protagonist determines simultaneously to become an author. The failure of this narrative seemingly necessitates the emergence of a writer, of a creator—someone to witness and document that failure. In fact, **"Lost in the Funhouse"** is the story of the creator of this particular story as well as the story of its own creation. I would argue that Ambrose himself actually is the narrator (and therefore the ostensible constructor) of the story.

As noted earlier, Ambrose told to himself the events of his life from the third-person point of view; this story is also narrated in the third-person point of view, so it is not unreasonable to suspect that the narrator actually is Ambrose. Furthermore, earlier in the story that third-person point of view is interrupted by one of the instances where the narrator bemoans the slow progress of the story—the only instance, however, that is in the first person: "I'll never be an author" (83). It is instructive to examine the entire paragraph in which that statement occurs:

> "Let's ride the old flying horses!" Magda cried. I'll never be an author. It's been forever already, everybody's gone home, Ocean City's deserted, the ghost-crabs are tickling across the beach and down the littered cold streets. And the empty halls of clapboard hotels and abandoned funhouses. A tidal wave; an enemy air raid; a monster-crab swelling like an island from the sea. *The inhabitants fled in terror.* Magda clung to his trouser leg; he alone knew the maze's secret. "He gave his life that we might live," said Uncle Karl with a scowl of pain, as he. The fellow's hands had been tattooed; the woman's legs, the woman's fat white legs had. *An astonishing coincidence.* He yearned to tell Peter. He wanted to throw up for excitement. They hadn't even chased him. He wished he were dead.
>
> (83)

The paragraph begins in the present of the story, with Magda's suggestion. Then the narrator's show of discouragement leads into a description of the deserted Ocean City boardwalk. From that description emerge several of Ambrose's frequent fantasies about becoming a hero as the narrative once again resumes the third person, and the paragraph ends with an internal description of Ambrose's thoughts. The brief emergence of first-person narration is quickly glossed over and compensated for, but the connection is nonetheless made between the self-conscious narrator and the similarly self-conscious Ambrose; as Ambrose the child loses himself in the reflection of the funhouse mirrors, Ambrose the narrator reveals himself through his constant self-conscious reflections.

Thus, at the heart of this failed or failing narrative, there is the consciously constructing figure of the narrator, who, while he may not always be able to control the progress of the narrative, nevertheless acts as guide through and constant commentator on the action. Furthermore, this constructing presence is simultaneously narrator and author of the story he is narrating. The figure of Ambrose as author is constructed through and by the telling of this story, an argument that becomes more convincing in light of the myriad connections between the narrative and the character. In addition to its being a story about an author telling a story about the creation of an author, the story, through its telling, performatively transforms the main character Ambrose into an author ultimately able to narrate the story of his own creation as author. Here we have the connection between the self and the ostensible author made overt. The author, Ambrose, needs the narrative in order to narrate himself a "self." In turn, this need causes him to become an author. He determines to create funhouses for others because the curse of his self-consciousness denies him the ability simply to enjoy them. Ambrose needs the narrative—he needs to narrate—in order to be a person, in order to have a self.

However, in the case of the *Lost in the Funhouse* series as a whole, that need is reciprocated: as much as the author needs the narrative, the narrative simultaneously needs the author. For example, the story **"Lost in the Funhouse"** is in constant threat of breaking down, of not finding the appropriate end, of not getting through, or even into, the funhouse. Things are not progressing as they should: "we will never get out of the funhouse" (74) at this rate, "I'll never be an author" (83). The story threatens permanently to detour into one of its narrative perversions when it should merely suggest—but not pursue—the possibility of a perverse ending.[14] In fact, it has been argued that **"Lost in the Funhouse"** does end without the proper resolution, in that it ends without Ambrose's triumphant emergence from the funhouse.[15] And actually, Ambrose never does find his way out of the funhouse; he does not gain the knowledge we expect him to gain—knowledge of "the way out." So at first glance, this story does not seem to have the proper ending, because it does not end the way one would expect.

On closer examination, however, it becomes clear that Ambrose *does* gain a kind of knowledge—the sad knowledge that he is destined never to leave the funhouse. His calling is not only to remain in the funhouse forever, but to construct funhouses for others' enjoyment—to become an author. Ambrose does not "linger on the autognostic verge" but instead is imbued with an Oedipal self-knowledge of his true identity as an author. Thus this narrative *does* end productively: it creates an author out of Ambrose. Furthermore, for Ambrose, the autognostic moment—the moment in which this becomes a productive narrative—is the same moment in which Ambrose is confirmed in his authorship of this story about how he became an author. That moment of recognition is the moment in which Ambrose the author brings this, the story of his rise to authorship, to a productive close. Furthermore, as I argued earlier, this narrative creates its own author, as it is Ambrose himself who constructs the story **"Lost in the Funhouse."**

Subsequently, the ultimate savior of this highly successful depiction of narrative exhaustion must necessarily be a powerfully constructing author. To some extent, Barth himself recognizes this necessity in **"The Literature of Exhaustion"** when he concludes that contemporary fiction must wend its way through the labyrinth of all that has already been said and done and all that it is possible to say or do. He compares the author to Menelaus, who "has got to hold fast while the Old Man of the Sea exhausts reality's frightening guises so that he may extort direction from him when Proteus returns to his 'true' self" (82). Menelaus, then, becomes the strong author figure who holds out and holds on until truth is revealed.

In fact, in the *Lost in the Funhouse* story **"Menelaiad,"** Menelaus wants both to win back the love of his wife Helen and to be able to tell the story of that winning; he grasps the sea god for help. As in the essay, the Menelaus of the story wants desperately to get through the lies and illusions to the real story, to get through the layers of clothing to his wife. While holding on to Proteus, he cries, "When will I reach my goal through its cloaks of story? How many veils to naked Helen?" (140). Interestingly, however, the self that Proteus turns into is Menelaus himself, and Menelaus notices that the instructions he receives from Proteus are spoken from his own mouth. By holding on, Menelaus has become empowered to tell the story, and Menelaus the storyteller emerges as the "true self," making clear the connection between Barth's essay and his series of stories.

Lost in the Funhouse represents a fictional enactment of the essay's rebellion against the death of the author, or what Barth calls the tendency of the "intermedia arts" to eliminate "the most traditional notion of the artist: the Aristotelian conscious agent who achieves with technique and cunning the artistic effect" (**"Exhaustion"** 71). In the essay, Barth scoffs at the notion that a text is less the result of one person's artistic effort than an amalgam of different voices and forces. He argues to the contrary that "not just any old body is equipped for this labor": an author is "the virtuoso, the Thesean *hero*" who must "with the aid of *very special* gifts . . . go straight through the maze to the accomplishment of his work" (83, emphasis Barth's). Thus the author is necessary if we are going to navigate through the exhausted forms of modern literature toward newer and truer possibilities (which, as I have already argued, requires a simultaneous return to older traditions). Furthermore, Barth argues that the author is the true hero of contemporary literature and must therefore be strong, capable, centered, and fully developed. So for Barth, there truly is no need for despair, because the disintegrating narrative forms will be either salvaged or recast by the heroic virtuosity of the author.

In addition, this authorial virtuosity obviates the necessity for the interpretive participation of the reader, as is demonstrated by the last story in *Lost in the Funhouse*. The series ends with the image of the anonymous author of the **"Anonymiad,"** having just launched his final missive into the sea, convinced that no one will ever decipher, read, or even find it. What is the writer's response to the idea that his work will encounter no readers? "No matter," he sighs, it is enough for him to know that on "this noontime of his wasting day . . . on a lorn fair shore a nameless minstrel / Wrote it" (194). As this passage demonstrates, the interpretive involvement of the reader is not necessary for the success of a text; the virtuosity of the author is sufficient.

Clearly, this viewpoint does not so much signal an embrace of a reader-centered literary aesthetic as a reaction against it. It is certainly possible from my analysis to draw the conclusion that Barth is not the harbinger of postmodern indeterminacy and malaise that he is so often deemed to be. More likely, what it means to be "postmodern," in Barth's case at least, is quite different from what we usually imagine. I have argued that the project of *Lost in the Funhouse* is not simply to demonstrate the exhaustion of modernist narrative forms but to reinvigorate them by combining them with contemporary narrative strategies such as self-conscious self-reflexivity. This rejuvenation, however, requires a return to traditional principles of narrative, particularly that of the powerfully creative virtuosity of the author. As much as the ever-present metafictional self-consciousness illustrates the failure of language to construct a fixed and coherent meaning and asks or even demands a greater interpretive investment from the reader, it also requires a recognition of the creative enterprise of the fictional author. The true paradox of metafiction is that at the same time that it suggests an increased responsibility of the reader, it also represents an attempt to restore and recentralize the authority of the author.

Furthermore, this recentering of the author could be viewed as a recentering of an essentialized, coherently depicted subject. It seems to me that Barth's argument that a talented author figure is necessary to lead literature through the maze of exhausted forms is also a recognition of the necessity of a coherent, if constructed, subjectivity at the heart of the narrative. If the narrative threatens to fail, it can and must be rescued by the centralized figure of a coherent constructing subject as author. Whereas Barth argues for the necessity in contemporary literature for the heroic author who tries to control the narrative proceedings and who, in **"Lost in the Funhouse,"** takes the form of the narrator, I would suggest that equally necessary in Barth's work is the coherent yet self-constructing subject of Ambrose, narrating his life to himself in the third person. In *Lost in the Funhouse* (and possibly other metafiction) the *self* in self-consciousness and self-reflexivity refers not only to the narrative but also to an actual self constructed within that narrative—a self that is essential for the narrative's purposes.

Notes

1. In the author's note, Barth writes that the book is "neither a collection nor a selection, but a series; though several of its items have appeared separately in periodicals, the series will be seen to have been meant to be received 'all at once' and as here arranged" (*Lost* ix). Most critics, myself included, take this to mean that the stories in the book can and should be taken as able both to stand independently and to be read together.

2. My analysis could productively be broadened to include some of Barth's other texts such as *Chimera* or *Letters,* which also focus on innovations in narrative structure and on authorial agency. However, because it is widely considered to be one of the preeminent metafictional texts, *Lost in the Funhouse* often serves as the springboard for critical discussion of metafiction in general. I have chosen to focus solely on this series in an effort not only to reevaluate major critical readings of the text but also to reframe our understanding of the genre of metafiction as a whole.

3. See also both Westervelt and Marta.

4. See also Bell.

5. See also Foucault.

6. Others have also identified elements in *Lost in the Funhouse* that recuperate particular narrative forms. Heide Ziegler discusses what she calls the "neo-Romanticism of the postmodern author" (90). Max F. Schulz, through a reading of *Lost in the Funhouse* as a unified novel instead of a collection of short stories, argues that Barth attempts "to fuse into one viable contemporary form the different novelistic modes . . . of the nineteenth and twentieth centuries, and thereby to rejuvenate the storytelling conventions of Western culture" (397).

7. In a later essay, "The Literature of Replenishment," Barth further outlines his definition of postmodernism and comments on his 1967 essay by saying:

> What my essay "The Literature of Exhaustion" was really about, so it seems to me now, was the effective "exhaustion" not of language or of literature but of the aesthetic of high modernism: that admirable, not-to-be-repudiated, but essentially completed "program" of what Hugh Kenner has dubbed "the Pound era."

> (66)

8. Or, as the narrator in "Title" states, this is "a state of affairs more tsk-tsk than boo-hoo" (108). I mention this passage in order to illustrate the connection between "The Literature of Exhaustion" and *Lost in the Funhouse*; the latter is clearly a fictional embodiment of the ideas espoused in the former.

9. In fact, Hutcheon uses the term *narcissistic narrative* to refer to the kind of textual self-awareness typified by metafiction.

10. Judith Roof writes:

> As ideology, this pattern of [narrative's] joinder to product also accounts for the countless analogies to child/product—knowledge, mastery, victory, another narrative, identity, and even death— that occupy the satisfying end of the story.

> (xvii)

11. The fact that this exchange dimly echoes the ending of Beckett's *The Unnameable* ("I can't go on, I'll go on" [414]) is probably not coincidental, as this and many of the other stories in *Lost in the Funhouse* are preoccupied with reaching a satisfactory narrative ending.

12. Jan Marta discusses this part of the story in an effort to make more explicit the connection between the issues of this story and those of the series as a whole, saying: "The inevitable imposition of the real reflecting object makes pure reflection impossible, reinforcing the union of self-reflection and mimesis, as we have seen at the macro-textual level" (221).

13. See in particular both Olson and Slaughter.

14. Peter Brooks has argued that narrative must tend toward "the correct end," and that this end is threatened by "the danger of short-circuit: the danger of reaching the end too quickly" (103-04). Brooks argues that these possible short circuits or "perversions" are part of the pleasure of narrative in that we enjoy the threat that the story *might* go awry only because we *know* that eventually it will not.

15. See both Westervelt and Schulz.

Works Cited

Barth, John. "The Literature of Exhaustion." *Atlantic Monthly* 220 (Aug. 1967): 29-34. Rpt. in *The Novel Today: Contemporary Writers on Modern Fiction.* Ed. Malcolm Bradbury. Manchester: Manchester UP, 1977. 70-83.

———. "The Literature of Replenishment." *Atlantic Monthly* 245 (Jan. 1980): 65-71.

———. *Lost in the Funhouse.* New York: Bantam, 1969.

Barthes, Roland. "The Death of the Author." *Image Music Text.* Ed. and trans. Stephen Heath. London: Fontana, 1984. 142-48.

Beckett, Samuel. *The Unnameable. Three Novels by Samuel Beckett.* New York: Grove, 1991.

Bell, Steven M. "Literature, Self-Consciousness, and Writing: The Example of Barth's *Lost in the Funhouse.*" *International Fiction Review* 11.2 (Summer 1984): 84-89.

Bienstock, Beverly Gray. "Lingering on the Autognostic Verge: John Barth's *Lost in the Funhouse.*" *Modern Fiction Studies* 19.1 (Spring 1973): 69-78.

Boehm, Beth A. "Educating Readers: Creating New Expectations in *Lost in the Funhouse.*" *Reading Narrative: Form, Ethics, Ideology.* Ed. James Phelan. Columbus: Ohio State UP, 1989. 102-19.

Brooks, Peter. "Freud's Masterplot" *Reading for the Plot: Design and Intention in Narrative.* Ed. Peter Brooks. Cambridge: Harvard UP, 1984. 90-112.

Christensen, Inger. *The Meaning of Metafiction.* New York: Columbia UP, 1981.

Edwards, Brian. "Deconstructing the Artist and the Art: Barth and Calvino at Play in the Funhouse of Language." *Canadian Review of Contemporary Literature* 12.2 (June 1985): 264-86.

Foucault, Michel. "What Is an Author?" *Textual Strategies: Perspectives in Post-Structuralist Criticism.* Ed. Josue V. Harari. Ithaca: Cornell UP, 1979. 141-60.

Hutcheon, Linda. "Historiographic Metafiction." *Passionate Doubts: Designs of Interpretation in Contemporary American Fiction.* Ed. Patrick O'Donnell. Iowa City: U of Iowa P, 1986. 3-32.

———. *Narcissistic Narrative: The Metafictional Paradox.* New York: Methuen, 1980.

Klinkowitz, Jerome. "John Barth Reconsidered." *Partisan Review* 49 (1982): 407-11.

Marta, Jan. "John Barth's Portrait of the Artist as a Fiction: Modernism through the Looking-Glass." *Canadian Review of Comparative Literature* 9.2 (June 1982): 208-22.

Olson, Carol Booth. "Lost in the Madhouse." *Review of Contemporary Fiction* 10.2 (Summer 1990): 56-63.

Roof, Judith. *Come As You Are: Sexuality and Narrative.* New York: Columbia UP, 1996.

Schulz, Max F. "The Thalian Design of Barth's *Lost in the Funhouse.*" *Contemporary Literature* 25.4 (1984): 397-410.

Slaughter, Carolyn Norman. "Who Gets Lost in the Funhouse." *Arizona Quarterly* 44.4 (Winter 1989): 80-97.

Waugh, Patricia. *Metafiction.* New York: Methuen, 1984.

Westervelt, Linda A. "Teller, Tale, Told: Relationships in John Barth's Latest Fiction." *Journal of Narrative Technique* 8 (1978): 42-55.

Woolley, Deborah A. "Empty 'Text,' Fecund Voice: Self-Reflexivity in Barth's *Lost in the Funhouse.*" *Contemporary Literature* 26.4 (1985): 460-81.

Ziegler, Heide. "John Barth's 'Echo': The Story in Love with Its Author." *International Fiction Review* 7 (1980): 90-93.

Judith Fletcher (essay date spring 2003)

SOURCE: Fletcher, Judith. "Lost in the Underworld: John Barth Reads the *Odyssey.*" *Classical and Modern Literature* 23, no. 1 (spring 2003): 65-76.

[*In the following essay, Fletcher highlights the ways in which Homer's* Odyssey *informs* Lost in the Funhouse, *particularly in terms of how "Homer and Barth share a special relationship to storytelling technology which bears on the form of their own narratives and which creates meaning beyond the irretrievable construction of authorial intent."*]

Traditions of the Underworld, which course through a stream of literature from the earliest Mesopotamian epics to Homer, Vergil, Dante, and beyond, have a special significance for the postmodern author whose project, as identified by Jean-François Lyotard, is "to share collectively the nostalgia for the unattainable."[1] Salman Rushdie's *The Ground Beneath Her Feet* reworks Vergil's version of the Orpheus and Eurydice myth to serve as a postcolonial metaphor for the Indian diaspora; in *Angels and Insects,* A. S. Byatt reconfigures the Odyssean Nekyia as a woman's psychic journey.[2] One of the earliest exponents of postmodern fiction, John Barth's ***Lost in the Funhouse,*** is characteristic of this backward-looking gaze.[3] For Barth, the process of becoming a writer involves a symbolic catabasis which causes an apparent fragmentation of the traditional story line, yet simultaneously aligns his tale with a narrative pattern of deep antiquity—the mythical hero's quest so often associated with coming of age rituals.[4] In this article, I undertake an examination of the Odyssean allusions in *Lost in the Funhouse,* not simply to catalogue their correspondences and conclude that the ancient and postmodern texts share an initiatory theme but also to suggest that these rites of passage and their implications of death and regeneration are significant in terms of the history of the mechanical production of the text itself. Homer and Barth share a special relationship to storytelling technology which bears on the form of their own narratives and which creates meaning beyond the irretrievable construction of authorial intent. The poet we know as Homer practiced his craft at the juncture of an oral tradition and the invention of writing. Perhaps he dictated his epic poems to a scribe, perhaps they were preserved orally for generations until the introduction of writing, but the Greek alphabet was, if not already born, at least about to be. Comparative philology reveals that Homer composed the *Odyssey* from a large corpus of traditional tales and narrative building blocks preserved only by their telling. The *Odyssey* is oral poetry made permanent by writing. Homer came at the end of a tradition in existence for centuries, but the oral tradition was permanently altered and ultimately rendered obsolete by the creation of an alphabetic writing system around 750 BCE. So in this respect, Homer comes at the beginning of literary history. Now the epic tradition could be fixed, concretized and preserved. This permanence altered the nature of storytelling, for although the oral tradition existed alongside the written, with rhapsodes and Homeric guilds still reciting the epics well into the fifth century, the fixity of the written text took precedence.[5]

Barth is also a story maker on the threshold of a new technology: a communications revolution as profound as the invention of the alphabet. Although the electronic highway was not up and running when Barth wrote this collection in the late 1960s, just as writing may not have existed when Homer composed his epics, *Lost in the Funhouse* seems to anticipate the new electronic medium, to herald its incipient arrival, even perhaps to postulate the need for its existence. In 1967, Barth forecast a nonlinear form of narrative not transmitted by physical paper texts or "hardcopy."[6] With *Lost in the Funhouse,* which claims to be "fiction for print, tape, live voice," Barth seems to fulfill his own prophecy, although in reality the work continues to be "read" in a traditional format.[7] Yet Barth was prescient in ways that he could not have imagined: technology has created new opportunities for fiction, while simultaneously provoking a new theoretical approach to literature. The postmodern movement has intersected with information technology at a critical point. While hypertext novels such as *Uncle Buddy's Phantom Funhouse,* an electronic derivative of *Lost in the Funhouse,* have not re-

placed print-based novels, word processing techniques and an awareness of the internet contribute to the paratactic structure and open-endedness of postmodern narrative. The more dynamic and process centered conception of electronic discourse that uses the computer as a medium in its own right contributes to the idea that a text need not be authoritative or immutably fixed.[8] Postmodernism's playful borrowing from the ancient canon, and its tendency to rearrange narrative building blocks and juxtapose them in provocative new ways, has its analogue in word processing. We can cut and paste sections of our text in the same way that the postmodern author creates a story.

By reworking and adapting his ancient predecessor, Barth is replicating the very process that Homer used to create the *Odyssey.* Homer and Barth are bookends of an interlude in textual transmission that privileges the physical permanence of literature; both face toward another world of storytelling. Homer is poised on the doorstep of the written text; Barth is approaching cyberspace. Accordingly, late twentieth-century storytelling shares some similarities with oral techniques. Reassembling bits and pieces of preexisting stories, Homer was a *bricoleur* who used traditional material and tools not specifically designed for the task at hand.[9] In his appropriation of the *Odyssey,* Barth uses the same technique: for example, he borrows the first-person narrative of Menelaus to Telemachus, told in *Odyssey* 4, but he plays with the convention of embedded narrative so that Menelaus' account of his capture of Proteus is surrounded by nine sets of quotation marks at one point. The tale of Proteus becomes a metonym for the protean narrative and a vehicle for a meditation on the nature of the authorial voice.[10] Barth's expropriation of this Homeric sequence is yet another filament in an intertextual tissue that includes the Aristaeus episode in Vergil's *Fourth Georgic,* which recasts the encounter with Proteus as a bucolic amoebaean featuring a watery catabasis to the depths of the ocean. The story itself is a shapeshifting enterprise which mutates from generation (and genre) to generation.

As Barth tells us in his "Author's Note" (speaking as an extradiegetic voice from beyond the completed text), his compilation of stories is derived from the idea of a story cycle, such as the epic cycle. The *Odyssey* (1.1) begins when the narrator asks the Muse to sing of the man of many twists and turns. Barth commences his cycle of stories in another way: the opening "story" entitled **"Frame-tale"** consists of a band of paper which reads "Once upon a time there was a story which began"; beside this are instructions to twist the paper and join the ends to form the Möbius strip. The gimmick is a simple one, suggesting that storytelling is a cyclic activity, full of twists and turns from which we may pause as audience or teller, but which exists in an infinite capacity. Furthermore, the narrative structure of Barth's book of tales is as convoluted as a Möbius strip, always, it seems, turning in on itself; in this respect, too, it alludes to the complex structure of the *Odyssey*. Although a Muse is not mentioned explicitly in **"Frame-tale,"** they turn up in the other stories; for example, as Thalia (the Muse of Comedy), who is the lover of a set of Siamese twins, one of whom pens a querulous letter in the 6th story, **"Petition."** Thalia is a contortionist in a circus, a fitting Muse for Barth, and the personification of his Möbius-like story.

The second story, **"Night-sea Journey,"** evokes Odysseus swimming to shore at the end of Book 5, ultimately the single survivor of many:

> Two measures onward and upward, flailing with the rest, then I float exhausted and dispirited, brood upon the night, the sea, the journey, while the flood bears me a measure back and down.
>
> (4)

The narrator, a sperm, is aware that he is "transmitting the heritage" (3, 4) but unaware of the nature of his journey and identity.[11] He tries to resist the siren call of the large looming egg and exhorts his audience to ignore her song:

> I am all love. "Come!" she whispers, and I have no will. . . . You to whom, through whom I speak, do what I cannot: terminate this aimless, brutal business! Stop Your hearing against Her song!
>
> (12)

The rebellious sperm muses on the possibility of a Father god who is responsible for his existence; he wonders why he is swimming, where he is swimming; he scoffs at the possibility of a not-He, a Her towards whom he and all his brethren are swimming. Yet he is drawn inexorably towards the egg; his final thoughts are recorded as he plunges "into Her who summons, singing . . . 'Love, Love, Love'" (13).

The story suggests a number of Odyssean themes, including the reunion of Odysseus and Penelope whose eventual embrace is the purpose of the story. The *Odyssey* is propelled by Odysseus' desire to sleep with his wife again, which mirrors the desire of the reader to complete the tale. Their eventual embrace is described in the famous simile of a swimmer reaching shore, a simile which melds husband and wife in its imagery (*Od.* 23. 233-240). As he journeys home, Odysseus is offered different endings to his tale, a life of immortality with the nymph Calypso, for instance, or the lure of the Sirens. Any man who succumbs to the Sirens loses his identity through death, as the sperm lost his identity through absorption by the egg, but sexuality and narrativity are linked in other ways in the Siren episode. The implications of the *textual* allure of the Sirens goes back to Homer. The Sirens, as Pietro Pucci has noticed,

address Odysseus by his Iliadic epithet and refer to him in terms of the Trojan war; they invite him back into a tale where he enjoyed military renown.[12] But Odysseus is casting off the persona of the Iliadic hero and moving towards life and a different story.

The seminal narrator of **"Night-sea Journey,"** burdened with the weight of an unperceived narrative tradition, becomes (or at least we assume) Ambrose, whose story is told in three other sections of the collection. The sperm, his existence about to be subsumed by the egg, seems to speak to us from a position just outside the story itself, that is just prior to the conception of Ambrose and his narrative, and the loss of the sperm's individuality. A physical metamorphosis, or creative annihilation, occurs which gives rise to another state of being. In what follows I look at the Ambrose stories and their relationship to certain themes and questions in the *Odyssey* to offer a comparative reading of the two texts which reflects their liminal position in the history of communication technology. As I have already suggested, both the *Odyssey* and ***Lost in the Funhouse*** bear the marks of a literature on the threshold of a communications revolution. I have looked at this transitional status from outside the text by considering the external conditions of its production. Now I would like to investigate how this sense of moving from one state to another is produced within the text. My general idea here is that the texts' position on the brink of new ways of preserving a story has its analogy in the themes of a rite of passage. Certainly the motifs of conception and birth are suggestive in this regard.

The third story in the collection, **"Ambrose His Mark,"** deals with the naming of Ambrose, whose recollections include life within his mother's womb, and at her breast. Apiculture, a prevalent and significant motif, redolent of the Aristaeus episode in the *Fourth Georgic* (and its allusions to *Odyssey* 4), establishes a contiguity with the **"Menelaiad"** in which Menelaus recounts his hallucinatory experience with *ambrosia*. The narrator's grandfather is a bee keeper, who like Aristaeus needs to replenish his hive. Although he is affectionately called *Honig,* or Honey, by his extended family, the infant Ambrose remains unnamed for months after his birth. Around noon one Sunday, as a christening is in progress at a nearby church, he is visited by a swarm of bees who light on the bee-shaped birthmark on his head and are then herded into his grandfather's hive. Thenceforth he is Ambrose, after Saint Ambrose, who had a similar visitation. His family believe that this "naming sign" indicates that "he will see things clear." And since Ambrose is an author in the making, his name is prophetically significant.

The bees themselves have a swarm of literary antecedents. Bees and honey symbolize poets, literature, rhetoric, and philosophy for Classical writers: Homer praises the speech of Nestor, which flowed like honey from his tongue (τοῦ χαὶ ἀπὸ γλώσσης μέλιτος γλυχίων ῥέεν αὐδή, *Il.* 1.249). Horace called himself *apis Matinae,* "the bee of Matina" (*C.* 4.2.27) and describes his work as *poetica mella* (*Epp.* 1.19.44). According to Artemidorus, a dream about honey signified τὴν εὐέπειαν τῆς ϛοφίας, "the eloquence of wisdom" (*Oneir.* 5.83), or "seeing things clear."[13] The ancients also believed bees to be asexual (which stands in ironic contrast to the implied wantonness of Ambrose's mother); they were symbols of chastity and hence spontaneous regeneration.[14] Vergil's *Fourth Georgic* describes the bizarre rite of the *bugonia* as a way of recreating a lost hive; pummeled bull-flesh is transmuted into a swarm of bees. Rebirth and regeneration, a movement from one state to another, are running themes in the Ambrose stories. After his naming, and due to an untimely bee sting on her nipple, Ambrose's mother stops nursing him. Since a significant movement in initiatory stories is the separation of mother and son, Ambrose's naming and weaning coincide in a meaningful way.

Ambrose's history also alludes to important motifs of birth and naming in the *Odyssey*. Before he can return home, the Trojan hero, Odysseus, needs to be reinvented, domesticated, and thus reborn. He discards his identity when he escapes from the Cyclops by naming himself "Nobody." In essence he becomes a nobody, stripped of his ships, his companions, status, and even his clothing. His visit to the Underworld is a kind of spiritual death and rebirth. Odysseus' catabasis figures into a universal signifying scene; myths of death and rebirth are powerful and ubiquitous symbols of transition from one social state to another. Rick Newton has noted a birth metaphor in the hero's penultimate journey from Ogygia, the island of Calypso, to the shores of Phaeacia where he is met by Nausicaa.[15] Newton likens this to the birth process: a journey through water (another night-sea voyage, if you will), in which Odysseus casts off even the clothing he is wearing and, naked as a newborn, is greeted by a nubile young woman to whom he later says "You gave me life." (8.466) When Odysseus finally returns to Ithaka, he is still nobody at home: in disguise as a beggar and abused by his wife's suitors. He is recognized by his old Nurse, Eurykleia: as she is washing his feet, she sees the scar which sets off her reverie and the poet's digression on how Odysseus took his name.[16] Like Ambrose, he was nameless for a prolonged period, and like Ambrose, he took his name from his mark in the company of his male relatives. The motif of naming and scarification hint at an initiatory theme; young men achieving their name and identity through a mark, a rite of passage, a transition from one social state to another.

This initiatory theme recurs in the fifth story. In **"Water-message,"** Ambrose is a young lad whose daily trip home from school is fraught with challenges including dogs and social misfits whom he nicknames Scylla and Charybdis. His older brother is a member of a secret society, the Occult Order of the Sphinx, with mysterious initiation rites, which Ambrose is too young to undergo. On one particular occasion, the boys learn that their clubhouse is being used for a sexual rendezvous. Ambrose inadvertently reveals his innocence about such matters and is sent away by the older boys. As he waits for his brother on the ocean shore, Ambrose discovers a message in a bottle, a letter, but all that remains is the salutation, "To Whom It May Concern," and the close, "Yours Truly." The text has been washed away, but the tablet seems to summon Ambrose to his position in an authorial lineage. In the final story of the collection, **"Anonymiad,"** we learn who has been casting messages into the sea: the bard, left behind by Agamemnon to watch over Clytemnestra and sent to a desert isle by Aegisthus (*Od.* 3. 267-71). Barth fleshes out this marginal character and gives him a story and a voice, although not a name. He is on intimate terms with the Muses, nine amphoras of wine which the poet fills with semen and texts, another linkage of sexuality and storytelling. The island is a *locus amoenus* where he spends his days watching the flocks like one of the singing herdsmen of Theocritus or Vergil, for whom portentous events occur at noon. One noon, an amphora containing a parchment and watery script is washed up ashore. Unsure if he was the author of this text, the bard speculates:

> I had thought myself the only stranded spirit, and had survived by sending messages to whom they might concern: now I began to imagine that the world contained another like myself. Indeed, it might be astrew with islèd souls, become minstrels perforce, and the sea a-clink with literature!
>
> (196)

This prospect, or the possibility that "the sea had fertilized me as it were with my own seed," so excites the bard that he slaughters his last goat to use as parchment, breaks the seal of his one remaining amphora, Calliope, for his "last lay," and on the noon that the story ends casts his story into the sea.[17]

It seems that there is a connection between this ancient nameless bard and young Ambrose. Ambrose's creativity has been suggested throughout **"Water-message."** He is prone to imagining dramatic scenarios in which for instance he dies a tragic death, lamented by the sexy school Nurse. In another flight of fancy, he is "Odysseus steering under anvil clouds" (45) and committing feats of daring. Like Odysseus, Ambrose is a storyteller; for all his feats of cunning and strength, Odysseus' greatest talent lies in spinning a tale. So we learn that there is something special about Ambrose, that he sails the ocean of literature, that he will be initiated into a different order, the ranks of authors.[18]

These themes are picked up in the title story: **"Lost in the Funhouse."** The thirteen-year-old Ambrose, his family, and a pretty girl named Magda visit Ocean City. Throughout, Barth insistently refers to the authorial process by interjecting technical commentaries on literary devices and plot structure.[19] The story presents a mazelike and meandering challenge to traditional linear narrative. Among the seemingly random details offered is the fact that Ambrose has only recently been baptized and, although "intimidated by the ancient mysteries," (88) did not feel changed; even at the Boy Scout initiation campfire "he only pretended to be deeply moved." Ambrose's rite of passage includes a solitary perusal of the detritus under the boardwalk of Ocean City, but his real initiation will be completed in the Funhouse, a labyrinth, a test which Ambrose must pass before he becomes the secret operator of "a truly astonishing funhouse . . . although he would rather be among the lovers for whom funhouses are designed." (97) While lost in the funhouse, Ambrose imagines different versions of his story. One has him finding another lost person in the dark: "They'd match their wits together against the funhouse, struggle like Ulysses past obstacle after obstacle." (84)

In another version, he died of starvation telling stories to himself. Unbeknownst to him, a pretty young girl transcribed his every word. Although deeply in love with Ambrose, she realized that here "was one of Western Culture's truly great imaginations, the eloquence of whose suffering would be an inspiration to unnumbered." (96) So she let him die. These multiple versions of the story, with their labyrinthine points of entry and exit, are a type of narrative funhouse whose ludic quality is sustained by a playful evocation and transformation of ancient literary tropes. Ambrose's initiation into the role of the author, the operator of the funhouse, has a parallel in classical poetry. Hesiod, Theocritus, Callimachus, Vergil, and Propertius all create scenes in which they are inducted into the halls of poetry. Hesiod is visited by the Muses while pasturing sheep on a mountain (*Theogony* 1-34); Theocritus' 7th idyll features a visitation from an Apollo-like figure at noon.[20] Water is a prevalent motif in the "consecration of the poet": Callimachus drinks from a fountain of poetry; he delicately avoids attempts at epic, which he admires but likens to an Ocean (*Hymn to Apollo,* 107).[21]

So Ambrose is inaugurated into the elite order of authors at Ocean City. His experience in the Labyrinth of Stories, the hall of mirrors of the funhouse, may recall the labours of Theseus, whose trials in the Minoan Labyrinth most certainly correspond to male initiation rituals. Yet the most common metaphor for initiation is a visit to the Underworld, since initiates must experience a symbolic death as they exchange one social identity for another. An allusion to Hermes, who leads souls to the underworld, suggests the catabatic function of the funhouse, which "winds around the right part like the snakes on Mercury's caduceus." (83) Ambrose's visit to the funhouse can be read as a visit to the Underworld: its entrance is a Devil's mouth (89). Like many visitants to the Underworld, he must pay a special price: as Aeneas gives the golden bough to the Cumean Sybil, Ambrose accidentally gives the witchlike ticket taker a disc with his name stamped on it instead of a coin. Like Odysseus, he then loses his identity. If we consider Odysseus' catabasis as the forerunner of Ambrose's visit to the funhouse, we realize that Hades is a place crowded with stories of Queens, Homeric heroes, and spectacular sinners. The Underworld functions as a place where all stories are eventually completed. Indeed, *Lost in the Funhouse,* the book, ends when the nameless minstrel dies. In one version of his story, Ambrose does actually die; but in a sense, the unformed, childlike Ambrose undergoes a symbolic death and is reborn as a mature creator himself. "He wishes he had never entered the funhouse. But he has. Then he wishes he were dead. But he's not. Therefore he will construct funhouses for others and be their secret operator" (97).

The funhouse is ostensibly a tunnel of love, designed specifically for couples; Ambrose is unique in his solitary journey through it. His brother accompanies Magda, and as the couple wait for Ambrose to find his way out, they name their imaginary children. Here the narrator asks, "Can spermatozoa properly be thought of as male animalcules when there are no female spermatozoa? They grope through hot, dark windings, past Love's Tunnel's fearsome obstacles. Some perhaps lose their way" (80). Ambrose thus replicates the voyage and transformation of his spermatozoan predecessor and Odysseus, literature's first lost hero.

This is the final transformation for Ambrose, whose stories end here. But the stages of Ambrose's investiture as an author are part of a larger programme of self-reflexivity. Shloss and Tololyan describe *Lost in the Funhouse* as "a finished product which pretends to record its own composition."[22] We are reminded again and again of the processes of both composition and reading. The technological aspects of writing fiction include **"Autobiography: A Self-recorded Fiction,"** which according to Barth's postscript is the voice of an author's tape recorder.

"Anonymiad" supposedly survives because it has been written on a goat skin with squid ink. This is the final challenge for the nameless bard who records the process of trapping and skinning materials required for his composition, which, we are asked to believe, is a written composition. When Barth asks his reader to cut and twist a paper band representing the never ending cycle of stories, he highlights the physicality of his text in a different way; yet the gesture is coincident with a semiotic sleight of hand that reminds us that the paper band only signifies a tale, just as the words on the succeeding pages are signs of a story. The *Odyssey* is similarly self-reflexive. Its hero is a master storyteller, but more to the point, Homer gives us a plausible reconstruction of preliterate narrative performance and composition in the persons of Phemius and Demodocus. Homer admits no writing into his narrative world, but the *Odyssey* recreates a performance environment that includes the audience and their response.[23]

Both Homer and Barth represent the mode of storytelling with which they are both most familiar, reciting and writing, and which are both about to be replaced by a more technically sophisticated storytelling method. It is unlikely that either author had any idea of the magnitude of the changes that were about to occur in information technology, yet readers' awareness of the texts' transitional status in this respect lends a resonance to the initiatory motif. Readers on the doorstep of a new millennium can look back to the *Odyssey* and ***Lost in the Funhouse,*** cultural products of the past. Our backward-looking gaze—which is transformative, for reading a text is always a transformative process— lends new life and meaning to those stories. It is possible for us to historicize those texts, to read them both in the context of the technologies which produced them and the technologies which would follow them. Reading thus becomes a rite of passage itself, and while this is true for any reader of any text, it is a phenomenon which mirrors the initiation themes employed by Homer and Barth. But I have made claims beyond this: the written texts of the *Odyssey,* the record of an accumulation of oral performances, and ***Lost in the Funhouse,*** which is full of an awareness of the potential of other physical means of recording a story, are each situated in a transitional moment in the history of the mechanical transmission of narrative. The postmodern readers of these narratives have not only a privileged awareness of all these technologies and their capacity for shaping the way a story is told but also an opportunity to speculate on how changes in the mechanical means of preserving a tale resonate with one of the most basic narrative patterns of storytelling.[24]

Notes

1. Jean-François Lyotard, *The Postmodern Condition: the Report on Knowledge* trans. G. Bennington and B. Masumi (Manchester: Manchester U Pr, 1986), 35. Studies of the Underworld theme in literature include: Raymond Clark, *Catabasis: Virgil and the Wisdom Tradition* (Amsterdam: B. R. Gruner, 1979).

2. See Judith Fletcher, "An Odyssey Rewoven: A. S. Byatt's *Angels and Insects,*" *Classical and Modern Literature* 19.3 (1999): 217-231.

3. John Barth, *Lost in the Funhouse* (New York: Anchor Books, 1968, 1988)

4. The initiatory theme in *Lost in the Funhouse* has also been observed by Brian Edwards in "Deconstructing the Artist and the Art: Barth and Calvino at Play in the Funhouse of Language," *Canadian Review of Comparative Literature* 12.2 (1985): 264-286, at 282-283. Also see Laura Rice-Sayre, "The Lost Construction of Barth's Funhouse," *Studies in Short Fiction* 17 (1980): 463- 473.

5. The bibliography on this controversial issue is extensive and on-going. Milman Parry was the pioneer of the widely accepted theory of Homeric oral composition, based on the use of traditional formulae: *The Making of Homeric Verse: The Collected Papers of Milman Parry,* ed. Adam Parry (Oxford: Clarendon Pr, 1971). Norman Austin has argued against the narrowness of the oralist theory *Archery at the Dark of the Moon* (Berkeley: University of California Pr, 1975); see also David M. Shive, *Naming Achilles* (Oxford: Oxford U Pr, 1987). Using cognitive psychology, Elizabeth Minchin argues that Homer composed and performed the *Odyssey* and *Iliad* without the aid of writing. The texts that we possess were only written down later as records of oral performances: *Homer and the Resources of Memory: Some Applications of Cognitive Theory to the Iliad and the Odyssey* (Oxford: Oxford U Pr, 2001). In general, I concur with Joseph Russo: "But whatever we think about the genesis of the texts before us, there can be no doubt that their style has some resemblance to an oral style and some indebtedness to a long oral tradition. . . . My personal view is that the Homeric epics were composed without the aid of writing, but with a high degree of deliberate artistry," *Commentary on Homer's Odyssey* v. 3 (Oxford: Oxford U Pr, 1992): 15-16.

6. J. Barth, "The Literature of Exhaustion," *Atlantic* 220: 2 (1967): 29-34.

7. Barth himself, although he expresses a fascination with hypertextuality, has not in fact experimented with the new technologies of storytelling. He has, however, incorporated the concept of hypertext in a recent short story "Click," *Atlantic* (August 1997).

8. Ilana Snyder, *Hypertext: The Electronic Labyrinth* (New York: New York U Pr, 1996).

9. John Peradotto, "*Odyssey* 8.564-571: Verisimilitude, Narrative Analysis, and Bricolage," *Texas Studies in Literature and Language* 15.5 (1974): 803-832.

10. Cf. Edwards (above, note 4), 282-283.

11. "In that no sperm can tell his own tale, the story is literally impossible: but in another sense, because all sperms bear tails, the pun is almost too

12. Pietro Pucci, "The Song of the Sirens" in *Reading the Odyssey: Selected Interpretive Essays,* ed. Seth L. Schein (Princeton: Princeton U Pr, 1996): 190-199: 196.

13. Lucretius wrote of *Musaeo melle* "honey of the Muses" (4.22); See Jasper Griffin, "The Fourth Georgic, Virgil and Rome," *Greece and Rome* 26 (1979): 61-80: 78.

14. Examples of the bee as a symbol of chastity include Semonides' Bee Woman (7.83-93).

15. R. M. Newton, "The Rebirth of Odysseus," *GRBS* 25 (1984): 5-20. Newton detects birth imagery in Odysseus' voyage from Calypso to Scheria where he is reborn, naked with ears and eyes swollen from the salt water.

16. "Bending closer / she started to bathe her master . . . then, / in a flash, she knew the scar, that old wound / made years ago by a boar's white tusk / . . . give the boy the name I tell you now . . . so let his name be Odysseus . . . the son of Pain;" *Od.* 19. 445-460. Irene de Jong has effectively argued that Eurykleia is the focalizer of this reverie. I. J. F. de Jong, "Eurykleia and Odysseus' scar. *Odyssey* 19.393-466," *CQ* 35 (1985): 517-518.

17. Noon is the conventional time for bucolic poetry contests: Theocritus *Id.* 1 and 7 feature high-noon literary showdowns; Virgil has Aristaeus confront Proteus at noon (*G.* 4.401).

18. "The older Ambrose . . . may be read as the latent artist-hero at the threshold of discovery: the figure of the threshold may represent, indeed, the perpetual condition of the postmodernist hero whose task is to discover not answers but uncertainty itself." Edwards (above, note 4), 272.

19. "In his hands, the hidden costs of writing assume the status of a plot. Intent on making the invisible visible, Barth ensures that those who are usually absent from a text—writer and reader—are dramatized, and that the process by which they communicate are exposed." Shloss and Tololyan (above, note 11), 64.

20. Theocritus is very playful in his depiction of the investiture of the goatherd Simichidas by Lycidas (i.e., Apollo). For a more detailed discussion and bibliography see F. Williams, "A Theophany in Theocritus," *CQ* 21 (1971): 137-45. A similar investiture takes place in Vergil's Sixth Eclogue where Linus, son of Apollo, hands the pipes of poetry to Gallus. See D. Ross, *Backgrounds to Augustan Poetry,* (Cambridge: Cambridge U Pr, 1975), 18-39.

21. Propertius tastes of the "water of Philetas" (i.e., elegiac poetry), 3.3.51. See G. Luck, *The Latin Love Elegy* (Methuen: London, 1959), 140-141.

22. Shloss and Tololyan (above, note 11), 65.

23. It has never been conclusively established what the single reference to ϛήματα λυγρά in the tale of Bellerophon refers to (*Iliad* 6.168-170).

24. Versions of this paper were read at the meetings of the Modern Language Association in Washington, D.C., December 2000 and the Classical Association of Canada, May 2001.

Abbreviations

C: Horace's *Carmen Saeculare* (*Secular Hymns*)

CQ: *Classical Quarterly*

Epp: Horace's *Epodes*

G: Virgil's *Georgica* (*Georgics*)

GRBS: *Greek, Roman, and Byzantine Studies*

Id: Theocritus' *Idylls*

Il: Homer's *Iliad*

Od: Homer's *Odyssey*

Oneir: Artemidorus' *Oneirocritica*

Theogony: Hesiod's *Theogony*

Publishers Weekly (review date 15 March 2004)

SOURCE: Review of *The Book of Ten Nights and a Night: Eleven Stories,* by John Barth. *Publishers Weekly* 251, no. 11 (15 March 2004): 53-4.

[*In the following review, the critic offers a largely negative assessment of* The Book of Ten Nights and a Night, *maintaining that it contains "a few bright spots in an otherwise dismal bunch."*]

In Barth's latest collection, [**The Book of Ten Nights and a Night**] one of his stand-ins, C. P. Mason, a writer/teacher who is trying to fit a whole short story around a sentence he remembers from a dream, remarks: "Has any storyteller, from Homer to Hemingway, Poe to Pasternak, attempted to fabricate a narrative something out of so nearly nothing?" Such minimalist flourishes are not what one would expect from the former creator of gargantuan metafictions. Barth calls this collection a Hendecameron, and refers to both *The Arabian Nights* (which he pillaged to better effect in **Chimera**) and the *Decameron*. Instead of the plague from which Boccaccio's narrators have fled, Barth's stories are told over 11 days that include and succeed 9/11. The intervals between stories are filled with a lot of cutesy converse- and asterisk-laden copulation between a Barth stand-in—Graybard—and his muse, Wysiwyg (Barth, one of nature's true acronym maniacs, got the name Wysiwyg from computer slang—it stands for "What you see is what you get"). The stories themselves proliferate with other Barth stand-ins—retired professors who are writers or retired writers who are professors—and smart, sexy, Wysiwygish women. The few bright spots in an otherwise dismal bunch include the first night, a strongly written fragmentary description of the retirement of a Chesapeake Bay boatman, Capt. Claude Morgan, the oldest story here; the 11th night, which is Wysiwyg's story; and an interesting theme story on the universe as a shrinking mass, paralleling the human aging process, **"The Big Shrink."** The rest are filled with the gaseous, colorless chitchat characteristic of Barth's late style. Distressingly, Barth's inversion of the old writer's adage, "show, don't tell," has led him to a garrulous abyss: he tells and tells, but has nothing to show, leaving the reader with no reason to read him.

Robert L. McLaughlin (review date summer 2004)

SOURCE: McLaughlin, Robert L. Review of *The Book of Ten Nights and a Night: Eleven Stories,* by John Barth. *The Review of Contemporary Fiction* 24, no. 2 (summer 2004): 128-29.

[*In the following laudatory review of* The Book of Ten Nights and a Night, *McLaughlin declares that in this collection Barth "makes a valuable case for the importance of self-conscious fiction as a bridge between us and our world."*]

This book [*The Book of Ten Nights and a Night*] brings together several uncollected stories, a couple from the 1960s, most from the 1990s. At this presumably late stage in his career, John Barth is quietly confident in his ability to entertain us, making even the most mundane incidents—finding a lost wedding ring, a spat between lovers—funny and moving. Although the recurring theme here is aging, the focus is on the everyday and the delight to be found in life and love. Of course, this being a Barth book, these tales all tackle the knotty problem of how language and narrative seek to represent experience: the stories lie in the tension between the desire for transparent representation (the what-you-see-is-what-you-get theme) and the playful recognition of slippery language as a necessary medium of representation. This tension is at the heart of the book's framing device, in which Barth's imagination, here called Graybard, comports with his muse, WYSIWYG (What You See, etc.), over eleven nights—specifically, the nights between September 11 and 21, 2001. While the author shares the rest of the country's horror, Gray-

bard and WYSIWYG debate the value of mere storytelling at such a time, tentatively concluding, "to tell *irrelevant* stories in grim circumstances is not only permissible, but sometimes therapeutic." But the irrelevance of storytelling is exactly what the book refutes: with continual reminders of 9/11 seeping in, the stories explore the ways language and narrative try (and sometimes fail) to make the world, experience, and even the self knowable. One narrator asks, "what is *the self itself,* if not what has been aptly called a 'posited center of narrative gravity' that . . . continuously spins trial scenarios, telling itself stories about who it is and what it's up to, who others are and what they're up to; that finally *is,* if it is anything, those continuously revised, continuously edited stories." This book is too self-effacing to be a manifesto, but it makes a valuable case for the importance of self-conscious fiction as a bridge between us and our world. This is a beautiful and most worthy addition to the oeuvre of one of our greatest writers.

Charles A. S. Ernst (essay date November 2004)

SOURCE: Ernst, Charles A. S. "Night-Sea Journeying: The Text-World and Life-Text of John Barth." *Cithara* 44, no. 1 (November 2004): 45-66.

[*In the following expanded version of an essay that was first published in* Cithara, *Ernst discusses Barth's oeuvre as "a grand, extended text of numerous published installments, a megatext, the master narrative of the Barthian text-world," supporting his conclusions with an analysis of "Night-Sea Journey."*]

> It is not, however, principally to warn, correct, lament, or save the world that I make up and set down stories, but rather to add to the human inventory of its artful artifacts; not to preach, teach, engage, escape, celebrate, or bear witness (although I may by the way do any and all), but chiefly to discover what my muse has up her sleeve, let's say, by way of encore. If (to change the metaphor) having delivered, she declares a postpartum respite before reimpregnation, I'm patient, as a rule.
>
> John Barth, COMING SOON!!! (60)

For the reader who has journeyed through each of John Barth's published novels, novellas, short story collections, non-fiction publications, and autofiction (*Once upon a Time: A Floating Opera,* 1994), each text in sequence may be viewed as the expansion of an ever-increasing text-field, of a single Barthian discourse. While the experience of any writer's published corpus, whether or not read in sequence, may provide a sense of that writer's fictive world, not all writers complicate reader response as relentlessly and resiliently as Barth has done by using readings in later works to condition or dramatically transform the response to his earlier text.

The reading experience so described is not quite the same as that achieved, for example, by reading William Faulkner's fiction, which additively enlarges the reader's sense of that writer's Yoknapatawpha territory to make of his short stories and novels a species of extended narrative within a carefully delineated fictive surround. The effect in reading Barth may not be as immediately felt when reading his earliest texts sequentially, but in reading them all in the order published, the result is ultimately more extreme. To move from early texts (fifties/sixties) to writings in mid career (seventies/eighties), to later-period texts (nineties/present) is finally to reconsider Barth's project, from the viewpoint of a reading strategy, not as a series of separate texts, but as a grand, extended text of numerous published installments, a megatext, the master narrative of the Barthian text-world, in which points of reference between various Barthian texts come to seem so thickly strewn and repeatedly appropriated, with modifications in amplitude of meaning, that the connections seem less *inter*textual than *intra*textual.

While **"Night-Sea Journey"**—a particular story from Barth's *Lost in the Funhouse* collection (1968)—will provide, in the latter part of the study, a means of supporting this contention, it must be acknowledged that it is not simply the wandering hero connections between Barth's third and fourth novels, *The Sot-Weed Factor* (1960) and *Giles Goatboy* (1966), that have given rise to the notion of a Barthian megatext as a reading strategy; or the artist as hero in *Sot-Weed* and the "Ambrose" stories in *Lost in the Funhouse* (1968), or the emergent mythmaking found in all three of the foregoing publications, and further extended in the collection of novellas entitled **Chimera** (1972).

Nor is it the ambitious achievement of Barth's fifth novel, the intermittently readable, though heroically conceived, *LETTERS* (1979), although this is admittedly the first of his texts to link unequivocally all prior published work by recuperating selected characters from previous texts through a novel-length series of epistolary exchanges between them, regardless of differences in historical setting—or, as Susan Poznar puts it, "Barth's own seduction of his past fiction into a replenishing cooperation" (67). In this novel Barth's anagrammatic antics identify it as *"an old time epistolary novel by seven fictitious drolls & dreamers* [including the **Funhouse** Ambrose], *each of which imagines himself actual"* (49), of whom the seventh dreamer, as the back flap of the book jacket notes, is "the Author himself, none other." In extending to *LETTERS* the reproductive conceit of this study's epigraph ("a postpartum respite before reimpregnation"), a Barthian narrator in COMING SOON!!! (2001) observes that *LETTERS* was "an enormous, intricate fiction meant to be my U.S. Bicentennial novel, but so long in the muse's womb that it bade to become my personal semicentennial novel instead"

(82). When published, *LETTERS* had indeed invited consideration as a prism for viewing Barth's earlier texts by establishing itself as a central text coordinating intertextual connections between the others. In *American Fictions, 1940-1980* Frederick Karl called it a "landmark fiction" (486) and deliberately made it a recurring centerpiece in his treatment of Barth's earlier writings (457). However, it would take more experimental work within the developing Barthian canon, regarding the middle and (especially) later periods, to enable a persevering reader exposed to Barth's publications in chronological order, including **"Night-Sea Journey,"** to begin to conceive of Barth's writings in *toto* as forming a single Barthian discourse, or at least to be willing to view them in that way as an experimental reading strategy.

A step in this direction from Barth's middle period, though limited to two texts, involves the reader's eventual discovery that the whole of *Sabbatical,* Barth's sixth novel, turns out to be a fiction generated by Franklin Talbott (413-14), a character in Barth's seventh novel, *The Tidewater Tales.* This phenomenon is perhaps the first indicator that two separately published novels by Barth might function *intra*textually, rather than *inter*textually. Actually, Barth also manages to link *The Tidewater Tales* to his eighth novel, *The Last Voyage of Somebody the Sailor* (1991). Whereas Barth inserts or transports into *The Tidewater Tales* the putative or actual characters and storied backgrounds of Odysseus, Don Quixote, and Scheherazade, the process is reversed in *The Last Voyage of Somebody the Sailor:* A present-day protagonist, Simon Behler, is transported to the time and place of Sindbad the Sailor, where both, by turns, tell stories, the earliest of Simon's sounding much like fictionalized excerpts from Barth's own life, in his growing up along the Chesapeake in Dorchester, Maryland.

One determinant supporting the notion of reading Barth's collected publications as if they were a single massive discourse is the playful assimilation of autobiographical elements (as in the novel just referred to) that accumulate trace associations from text to text. Even Barth's self-references in his nonfiction (*The Friday Book,* 1984; *Further Fridays,* 1995) begin to seem capable of absorption into a text-world ever expanding to accommodate autobiography as well as fiction with significant modifications in meaning. Indeed, by the time one has read two of Barth's four most recent publications, *Once Upon a Time* and COMING SOON!!!, it is as if Barth's text-world—the fictive world of his collected texts viewed as a single discourse—has been absorbed into what may be called Barth's developing "life-text."

In this study, "life-text" refers not only to autobiographical elements in various publications by Barth, but includes the subjective formation of himself in a number of his texts as a fictive Barthian character in various guises, sometimes more "Barth" (the narrative voice and Barth-identified character in *Once Upon a Time*), or less "Barth" (a caricatured Barth figure as sensitive sperm in *The Tidewater Tales*), and sometimes assuming more than one prospective role in a single text (the aforementioned Barthified sperm and in a sense, without straining credulity, its authorial progenitors Franklin Talbott and, later, Peter Sagamore in *Tidewater Tales*).

For an earlier example, one might consider the text following *Lost in the Funhouse*; i.e., *Chimera*. Here Barth had pursued his interest in mythical heroes—to replenish canonical literature without exhausting it—in two of the publication's three novellas, *Perseid* and *Bellerophoniad* as well as his interest in frame-tales, particularly the Arabian Nights stories of Scheherazade in *Dunyazadiad,* the first novella in the group, but last written. In *Dunyazadiad* the boundary between art and life begins to blur with the introduction of a tall Barth-like genie, "bald as a roc's egg" (8) and bespectacled, a persona isomorphic to the "author," in what becomes increasingly a narrative exploration involving, as in Barth's *Funhouse* stories, a "recentering of the author" to provide "a coherent, if constructed, subjectivity" (Worthington 133)[1]. Barth's subsequent project, *LETTERS,* was also distinguished by the inclusion, already noted, of a virtual Barth character, a life-text construct, as one of the letter-writing "*drolls & dreamers*" (49) in that novel[2].

The notion of reading Barth's corpus as one huge, expansive discourse in which life-text is folded into text-world is given particular support by the appearance of two of Barth's later-period publications previously acknowledged, *Once Upon a Time* and his latest novel, *COMING SOON!!!* (2001). In these publications the life-text seems to swamp Barth's text-world, until they appear as one and the same—the life in the story, the story in the life—as part of an extended discourse comprised of all Barth's texts, and perhaps at a further extreme, *all* the fiction that Barth has read and has referred to in published work as well, to the extent that characters in the likeness, e.g., of Sindbad and Don Quixote make appearances in his fiction, too, as in *The Last Voyage of Somebody the Sailor* (1991).

In particular, Barth's *Once Upon a Time* is a mapping of autobiography onto fiction, or the reverse, for which the term autofiction may be a useful shorthand. In his "next" last novel, *COMING SOON!!!* one of Barth's narrators—the Barthian character whose pedigree includes all of the real Barth's novels—refers to *Once Upon a Time* as "a novel/memoir," and "a little life-tale written under the aspect of Vocation" (83)[3] *Once Upon a Time* is thus comprised of real and "virtual" characters and episodes, with the journey motif invoked to thematize the Barthian character's vocation as a writer, as Barth

puts into practice the narrative claims of the voice of Menelaus in Barth's *Funhouse* story **"Menelaid"**: "He's the story of his life, with which he ambushes the wary unawares" (128). As Zack Bowen observes,

> All autobiography contains elements of personalized self-fiction. The difference with *Once Upon a Time* is that few writers since Dante have embarked on a semi-fictionalized biography, making themselves relatively unexceptional subjects, warts and all, at the same time allowing the present fiction and creativity to speak for itself, even while the writer's past fictional work is intertwined and explicated as a part of the writer's own "Heart-mysteries."
>
> (199)

As an erstwhile musician, Barth himself acknowledges in *Once Upon a Time* that this "quasi-novel or quasi-memoir" (*Further Fridays* 191) is "meant to wrap up riffs that I've been noodling for forty years. Like . . . floating operas, water-messages and night-sea journeys, lost paths and last voyages . . ." (*Once* 382). Because the text intercuts, and undercuts, fact with fiction, blurring the boundary in a seamless story-telling, it enables Barth to recontextualize readings of his past fictions with autobiographical references, building on meanings already established, yet extending them and possibly modifying one's view of them. In consequence, to hold in mind what a single referent might mean, given its occurrence in one of Barth's texts, is to try to consider simultaneously its various usages throughout the entire corpus, because Barth never seems finally to be done with anything of consequence that he has used in his fiction, but accumulates references and adds new ones, maintaining and extending meanings simultaneously in an ever expanding Barthian text-world comprehending what is arguably a single massive discourse (the cumulation of Barth's published texts), with many points of access.

The tendency to view Barth's corpus as a single expanding discourse is further reinforced by a reading of Barth's latest novel, *COMING SOON!!!* (2001), which—like *Once Upon a Time*—willfully continues to blur fiction/nonfiction boundaries with a virtual Barth-type character and spousal counterpart. The myriad references to elements in earlier work by Barth make *COMING SOON!!!* challenging to read, but encourage one to try to map the whole of Barth's corpus upon this single text to tease out its allusions, while recognizing that the range of meanings threading through this novel are virtually dependent upon all of Barth's texts taken together, of which *COMING SOON!!!*—to be considered in more detail later in the study—is another demonstration of Barth's expanding narrative universe.

To recapitulate, while it is certainly possible to continue to read Barth's several texts independently of each other (even *LETTERS*), it may be argued that the effect of reading all of Barth's publications sequentially, especially after reading *Once Upon a Time* and *Coming Soon!!!*, is to find oneself viewing them, as previously asserted, as components of a single expanding discourse in which the ever increasing presence of autobiographical elements threatens to turn Barth's text-world inside out, as a function of his life-text, until one appears indistinguishable from the other in the cumulative Barthian corpus, or "Barthiad." From another perspective, in acknowledgment of *The Arabian Nights* and other favored Barthian sources, Barth's collective texts may be viewed as one writer's equivalent of the ocean of story that has become one of Barth's recurring metaphors for the endless process of story-telling and the seemingly endless stories so engendered, including his own.

The notion of Barth's collected works as a single discourse, from the perspective of a particular reading strategy, began to take shape for this reader while tracking the frequency of allusion in his writings to the wandering hero, and particularly in a specific form encountered in one of Barth's short stories, referred to before, from the *Lost in the Funhouse* collection: **"Night-Sea Journey,"** featuring a solipsistic sperm as a kind of epic hero. One might have supposed that an entire story devoted to this cast of one (although multitudinous others of its kind are mentioned) would have exhausted this material. However, there would seem to be little of consequence, as previously noted, that Barth introduces and develops that does not eventually, through imaginative extension, get recycled in his texts, chronologically considered, including Barth's sperm-and-egg, or wandering hero, motif, which recurs at various points in later work. For example, the remarkable reformulation, with autobiographical coloring, of the so-called "night-sea journey" itself in *Once Upon a Time* encourages especially a transformative rereading of the short story with that title in light of its new accommodation in this later text, as subsequent discussion will show.

In short, what has been claimed in general for Barth's work applies to **"Night-Sea Journey"** as well. Although one can arbitrarily limit one's response to **"Night-Sea Journey"** as a separate short story or, more appropriately, as a story situated in relation to the other stories of Ambrose in *Lost in the Funhouse,* it becomes difficult, after exposure to other Barth texts, and especially to *Once Upon a Time,* to read **"Night-Sea Journey"** without taking Barth's other work into account, without rereading **"Night-Sea Journey"** as a functioning narrative within a single, larger Barthian discourse, combining text-world with life-text. This reading perspective, when privileged, may provide arguably the best lens for viewing Barth's writings generally, fiction and nonfiction. While one can only suggest, in the space permitted, that particular themes and motifs in other Barth texts could similarly be tracked to make the same point, one contention of this study is that a critical scrutiny of **"Night-Sea Journey,"** including its subsequent recycling in later publications by Barth, makes a compelling case in support of the reading strategy of viewing the Barthian corpus as a single expanding discourse, fusing text-world with life-text, while simultaneously enriching the sperm-and egg or wandering hero symbology so examined.

The remaining intent of this study, then, is twofold: (1) To track the sperm-and-egg motif from **"Night-Sea Journey"** in its various manifestations to show its remarkable recycling in later texts, after first providing a detailed contextualization and analysis of the story itself, but without immediate reference to later texts by Barth, in order to provide a baseline reading; and, from that platform, (2) to use it as a test case in supporting the notion of reading Barth's publications (in chronological order) as an ever expanding, single discourse, in which Barth's text-world and life-text are (eventually) seen as one. At various turns in the discussion it may be necessary to set aside for a time the sperm-and-egg conceit to acknowledge the cumulation of life-text elements in his writings, with special emphasis on the fusion of fiction and autofiction in *Once Upon a Time* and *Coming Soon!!!* and their effect on readers and styles of reading. However, the figure of the wayward spermatozoon in its night-sea journey as a wandering hero within the Barthian discourse, along with related references, will remain a recurring focal point in this study.

To contextualize **"Night-Sea Journey"** from the twentieth-century perspective from which Barth was writing, it is instructive to observe by direct quotation how a few selected precursors over centuries, or millennia, chose to treat the imagined exploration of origins from their own respective vantage points in time. For example, in A.D. 397, St. Augustine acknowledged in his *Confessions* (I.vi) "that I do not know whence I came to be in this mortal life or, as I may call it, this living death. I do not know where I came from. . . . I have heard from the parents of my flesh, him from whom and her in whom you [the Maker] formed me in time. For I do not remember" (6). Thirteen hundred and sixty-three years later Laurence Sterne—in his novel *Tristram Shandy* (1760)—was confident of offering greater detail by positing in Chapter II, according to the science of his day, the "HOMUNCULUS," a minute flesh-and-blood version of humankind, "in how-ever low and ludicrous a light he may appear, in this age of levity" (6), but whose initial and future existence is made to depend on the parental perturbations of its begetting. What, then,

> if any accident had befallen him in his way alone?—or that, thro' terror of it, natural to so young a traveller, my little gentleman had got to his journey's end miserably spent;—his muscular strength and virility worn down to a thread;—his own animal spirits ruffled beyond description,—and that in this sad disorder'd state

of nerves, he had laid down a prey to sudden starts, or a series of melancholy dreams and fancies for nine long, long months together—I tremble to think what a foundation had been laid for a thousand weaknesses both of body and mind, which no skill of the physician or the philosopher could ever afterwards have set thoroughly to rights.

(6)

Two hundred and six years later, the supposed difficulties of this microscopic middle passage, with the homunculus supplanted by human sex cells, would be transformed by Barth into an existential journey of the wandering hero, recast as a deeply introspective spermatozoon. This unlikely protagonist is a seeker of Goethe's *ewige Weibliche* (the Eternal Feminine) in its most pristine form, the ovum, a Barthian version of the Great Attractor reduced to a microscopic universe in this Theater, or Natatorium, of the Absurd.

Having moved from nihilistic comedy in his first novel, *The Floating Opera* (1956), to nihilistic tragedy (Morrell 13) in his second novel, *The End of the Road* (1958), to nihilistic extravaganza in *The Sot-Weed Factor*, that parodic, mock-heroic, eighteenth-century pastiche of history and pseudo-history, Barth afterward deepened his knowledge of the putative hero in that novel, the radically innocent self-proclaimed poet laureate of Maryland, Ebenezer Cooke, by an examination of several texts. These texts are (1) Otto Rank's *The Myth of the Birth of the Hero*; (2) Lord Raglan's *The Hero: A Study in Tradition, Myth, and Drama,* with its "linear catalog" (Barth, *Once* 314) of twenty-two characteristics of herohood; and especially (3) Joseph Campbell's *The Hero With a Thousand Faces,* which "turns Raglan's linear catalogue into a [diagrammatic] counterclockwise circle, or cycle" (Barth, *Once* 314), presenting the life stations of the mythic hero's mysterious and then tragic experience.[4] Applying that knowledge to the eponymous hero of his fourth novel, *Giles Goat-Boy*, with its messianic allegory of the campus as world in a "revised new syllabus," Barth then sought, given his developing interest in the Bildungs- or Künstlerroman, to apply the mythic pattern of the wandering hero to his own portrait of the artist as a young man—with numerous fictional asides and divertissements on the nature of story-telling itself—in something other than a novel; i.e., the series of short stories collectively entitled *Lost in the Funhouse*[5].

Having published in 1963 (*Lost* vi) two short stories (**"Ambrose His Mark," "Water-Message"**) about a prospective artist-hero, the youthful Ambrose, and eventually including in 1967 a third story of Ambrose (entitled **"Lost in the Funhouse"**) who, apparently like Barth at age twelve or thirteen, is momentarily lost in a funhouse (Barth, *Once* 341), Barth began to conceive of a series of stories—independent yet capable of interre-

lation and presentable by mixed media—that would link thematically the more realistic Ambrose pieces with stories more redolent of fantasy and myth (*Once* 340). During the winter of 1965-66, his first in Buffalo, NY, the Barthian persona in *Once Upon a Time* says Barth wrote **"Night-Sea Journey"** as "the first story expressly meant for the new book: The monologue of an exhausted and disillusioned spermatozoon in unwitting mid-reenactment of the cycle of ritual mythic heroism" (340), a story first appearing in the June '66 issue of *Esquire* (*Lost* vi; *Once* 340-41) and then in 1968 as the first piece of some length for the *Lost in the Funhouse* publication.

The title **"Night-Sea Journey"** is specifically drawn from one of the named stages or stations of the Urmyth of the wandering hero in Campbell's circular diagram, as further annotated by Barth, and represents one of the mysterious "initiatory trials and ordeals" to be faced after the hero emerges from an "obscure childhood across the threshold of adventure" (*Once* 121), leading eventually to a transcendent experience and a return to the other side of the circle, as Barth says, to "translate enabling revelation into worldly work . . ." (*Once* 121). In Barth's story the spermatozoon's swim, "in the dark" and "at sea" (**"Night-Sea Journey"** 5) like that of the protagonist's companions, "a quarter-billion strong" (4), is the initiatory and mysterious ordeal. The imagined merger with the mysterious Other as ovum, expressed as a *"consummation, transfiguration, union of contraries, transcension of categories"* (11), is the transcendent experience. The tragic consequences of a return to the world for meaningful work, in the context of heroic endeavor, presumably encompass the fertilized egg, the developing embryo, subsequent delivery of the fetus nine months later, and in particular the lived experience of the individual human being, all latter components taking the reader beyond the confines of Barth's story.

The passage of thirty-eight years after the original publication of **"Night-Sea Journey"** may cause one to forget that the mysterious circumstances facing its flailing protagonist—or "existential voyager" (Olson 56) or "muse-sperm" (Mistri 151)—were challenging also to first-time readers, at least initially, who might be forgiven for likening the sex cell's thrashing ordeal to a salmon run. A subsequent reading makes one appreciate Barth's difficulty, not so much in gradually establishing the ground-situation (if it can indeed be called that) of this fiction, as in establishing the conditions for voicing it. Certainly a striking feature of the story is Barth's endowment of the sperm with consciousness, intelligence, memory, language, reasoning ability, and emotion—attributes to be lost in merger with the egg, though eventually regained in the guise of the human without the benefit of subsequent remembrance of sex cell experience. But since this sperm, alone of all its com-

rades, has survived the arduous swim by simply floating when it is not flailing, Barth's first-person narrative
has to frame itself in the opening paragraph as the
sperm's self-told story[6]. The microscopic narrator begins, then, with a Whitmanesque "it's myself I address"
(**"Night-Sea Journey"** 3)[7] and proceeds to rehearse its
"history and condition," as if rendered "to a stranger"
(3). In providing an account more or less complete and
coherent on its own treacherously uncertain terms, the
narrator tries to accommodate the critical discrimina-
tions of an imagined audience, that suppositional
"stranger" or addressee to whom it refers (Barth's implied reader, as it happens).

Crammed with queries about the nature of its being and
the limits of its knowing, including a nod to set theory—
"how can I be both vessel and contents?" (3)[8]—the second paragraph signposts the story title's three words by
the narrative voice's allusion, for the second time, to a
posited journey, as well as to the night, the sea, and
also the "Heritage" (3) the protagonist bears. These
worrisome interrogative reflections serve mainly to en-
large the meager narrative space with which the text
has just begun, in acknowledgment of the narrator's apparent situation as "a voice addressing itself and pon-
dering what self-consciousness implies about language's
power of reference" (Woolley 468).

By the third paragraph the mythos of the swim is introduced and insistently interrogated for much of the rest
of the story. The protagonist's conceptual leap in that
paragraph to a supposed first cause, "a common Maker"[9]
(**"Night-Sea Journey"** 3), has apparently been stimulated, as one later discerns, by the inspired lucubrations
of a "cynical companion" (5). This other sperm, long
since drowned, functions variously as a proto-
theologian, "a seer of sorts or a good guesser" (Slaughter
83), or even "a nihilistic sperm!" (Mistri 152), because
it has apparently speculated about multiple Makers
(Biblical) or Fathers (Freudian) who may have created
without purpose the conditions of the swim as Holocaust.

These grim surmisings are relieved by the reader's eventual recognition of Barth's absurdly comic transference
of what, on other terms, are serious human concerns
(philosophical, theological, and cosmological) to the
imagined consciousness of a gallivanting gamete. Also,
the stupendous loss of so many living organisms is
counterbalanced by the intrinsically euphoric nature of
the swim. Driven by "Love" toward an imagined distant "Shore" (**"Night-Sea Journey"** 4), the swimmers
become the victims, as Barth writes, "of their unremit-
ting *joie de nager*" (4), a *jouissance* matching, perhaps,
the pleasures of the text[10] for readers captivated, in spite
of themselves, by the cleverness of Barth's reproductive
conceit. Nevertheless, this conceit is always perilously
courting, by turns, the sophomoric and the serious, the

former tempered by the weight of storied reflection, the
latter relieved by Barth's ironizing wit.

For those returning to **"Night-Sea Journey"** after long
absence, a pleasure well remembered is the comic appropriation of other literary texts to reinforce the mock-
heroic tone of Barth's microscopic Ishmael, the long-
tailed "tale-bearer of a generation" (9). If the best "lack
all conviction," courtesy of Yeats, so does Barth's protagonist (3). The doughty cries of "Onward! Upward!"
(3), as these sex cells surge forward on the amniotic
sea, may call to mind Tennyson's *Charge of the Light
Brigade*, rerouted to a uterine journey. Several pages
later the battle cry becomes, "Ours not to stop and think;
ours but to swim and sink" (5). The protagonist does a
linguistic turn on the Erasmian fool (in the latter's
Praise of Folly) when Barth's (anti-)hero considers the
genealogical and teleological notions of his skeptical
quondam comrade, who had said, "I can believe them
because they are absurd" (3). Allen Ginsberg's "Howl"
is alluded to when the protagonist bemoans lost comrades: "I have seen the best swimmers of my generation
go under" (4). Yet the main character echoes the reasoning of Todd Andrews, the suicidal protagonist of
Barth's first novel, *The Floating Opera*, to justify the
decision to endure: ". . . it is because . . . I find it no
meaningfuller to drown myself than to go on swimming" (4). After a possible corruption of Ian Fleming's
You Only Live Twice to "you only swim once" (6), the
protagonist tries momentarily to dismiss the chapter-
and-verse rubric that sustains the swim in a loose parody
of Matthew 18:3, "Except ye drown, ye shall not reach
the Shore of Life" (6). At one point the treacherous nature of the swim is regarded in Darwinian terms as "the
survival of the fittest" (6) and somewhat earlier is implicitly equated with "Being," in language distinctively
Heidiggerian: the so-called "swim-in-itself" (6). Such
tidy philosophical formulations are filled to bursting
when the protagonist, echoing that drowned friend,
imagines

> two sorts of creators, contrary yet complementary, one
> of which gives rise to seas and swimmers, the other to
> the Night-which-contains-the-sea and to What-waits-at-
> the-journey's-end: the former, in short, to destiny, the
> latter to destination. . . .
>
> (11)

The first creator is imagined, from a Freudian perspective, as being possibly malevolent—"Our Father" as
"adversary and would-be killer!" (7)—desiring in various instances to prevent the protagonist's companions
from "fulfilling their destiny" (7)—and so "thrash,
splash, and be merry, we were soon enough drowned"
(11). The reader is presented with a list of Homeric terrors that have annihilated the ranks of fellow swimmers
"by whirlpool, poisoned cataract, sea-convulsion; the
panic stampedes, mutinies, slaughters, mass suicides"

(10). In spite of "the mounting evidence that none will survive the journey" (10) the protagonist continues to endure, a swimmer spent, "no longer young," and "disabused of every illusion" (10), yet apparently having inherited the hero's mantle by default, if the narrator is not in fact already drowned or dreaming.

With a sudden and surprising "calming of the sea" (10), followed by a warm and gentle turning of the tide to produce a veritable "flood of joy" (11), more and more attention is focused on the destination itself, no longer conceptualized as a "hypothetical Shore" (5), "a happy place" (6). Instead, it is now referred to as "a mysterious being" (10), suggestive of "a kind of vasty presence, song, or summons" (10). Because spermatozoa are figured as male and can scarcely imagine what a gendered counterpart would be like, this being is mysteriously referred to, nevertheless, as a "She" (9), a "Ulyssean siren" (Mistri 152) or, with Barth again invoking the hypothetical Heidiggerian patois, "Other-than-a-he" (**"Night-Sea Journey"** 10).

Awareness of this "sea-change" (9) is followed, with about two-thirds to three-quarters of the story completed, by the sperm's admission of "a certain desperate resolve, the point of my chronicling" (9). Having surmised that merger with the Other may obliterate present consciousness yet produce another Maker, with another Holocaust of swimmers in the making, the protagonist's resolve is this: Not to resist the Other's siren song, an impossible feat, but to encourage resistance in "You who I may be about to become, whatever You are . . ." (12)—to "terminate this aimless, brutal business!" (12). This second-person addressee had been introduced several paragraphs earlier when the protagonist momentarily denied, in a fit of self-raving, the reality of the Other, "There is no She!" (10), and seemingly his own reality as well. But rather than saying, "There is no me," the protagonist cries instead, "There is no You!" (10), encompassing not only the self as sperm and the *other* "self" the protagonist will instantly become after merging with the egg, but also the reader, a later version of that self. By the last two paragraphs this burdened referent has become "You to whom, through whom I speak" (12) and "Whoever echoes these reflections" (13), as someone who might break the circuit of desire,[11] even as the protagonist instead completes the circuit by plunging "into Her who summons" (13), singing the last words of the story as if in a Motown frenzy, "Love! Love! Love!" (13).[12]

If the completed **"Night-Sea Journey"** frames the Ambrose stories to follow, with sperm and egg the zygotic precursors of Ambrose, it also provides, in spite of its swimmer's ironic call to resistance, for the perpetuation of the reproductive cycle within its own text (gamete, human, gamete, human, *ad infinitum*) and of storytelling itself—the sperm as "fact" searching for its fiction, an Idea in quest of its Muse[13]. **"Night-Sea Journey"** also gestures toward the same cyclical activity of sexual conception and imaginative reception in its human readers. Hence it is a frame-tale with an ironic twist, reminiscent of the literal twist in Barth's introductory two-page Möbius-strip frame-tale ("ONCE UPON A TIME THERE WAS A STORY THAT BEGAN")[14], a text that never ends its beginning (1-2), but nonetheless precedes and frames all *Funhouse* stories, Barth's world of fiction, and the world's corpus of fiction generally.

Similarly, Barth's **"Anonymiad,"** the last story in the *Funhouse* series, is somewhat reminiscent, with its "Headpiece" (168) and "Tailpiece" (199), of the spermatozoon's swim in **"Night-Sea Journey."** The anonymous island-stranded minstrel and former goat-herder, coeval with Agamemnon and Menelaus, sets adrift his storied messages in bottles or amphorae named after the nine muses. He hopes that each floating opus, collectively a floating *opera,* will make contact with his beloved Merope. Longingly, he says of her, "I've taught myself to swim, and if some night your voice recalls me, by a new name, I'll commit myself to it, paddling and resting, drifting like my amphorae, to attain you or to drown" (200), like the sole surviving sperm in **"Night-Sea Journey,"** who proceeds by alternately swimming and floating—its message a genetic text, the "Heritage" (3) of which it speaks—to gain a new identity by inscribing itself, through merger, with the Other-as-She.

Through such associations, the last story in Barth's *Funhouse* is linked to **"Night-Sea Journey,"** the series' first story of some length, to create a labyrinth of language, or Möbius strip of funhouse stories, with no definitive way out, recapitulating by example the narrative mantra of the initial two-page frame-tale: "ONCE UPON A TIME THERE WAS A STORY THAT BEGAN" (1-2). Yet by fictively creating his tiny, self-aware, and skeptical protagonist in **"Night-Sea Journey,"** Barth admits, as a later Barthian narrator in *Once Upon a Time* (1994), that he sought thereby to "purge" his imagination of the wandering hero to which he had been so deeply committed in *Sot-Weed Factor* and *Giles Goat-Boy,* to "extricate" himself "from the maze, by a reduction to absurdity [in **"Night-Sea Journey"**] of the [mythic] model (though indeed the 'life history' of a spermatozoon hauntingly replicates the Ur-myth)" (Barth, *Once* 119). Instead, as Barth says, "I succeeded only in reimpregnating myself with it: self-insemination where I had intended abortion" (*Once* 119). Thus Barth not only continued to compose fiction with wandering-hero-and-journey motifs and allusions, but would eventually, and then more or less continually, include his sperm-and-egg conceit as a recurring *topos.*

In consequence, the reproductive conceit finds expression in altered form through much of Barth's increasingly postmodernist experimentation in the post-*Funhouse* seventies, eighties, nineties, and beyond. Such wandering-hero and other texts, whether momentarily sex-cell-centered or not, further particularize Barth's enlarging text-world. For example, in *LETTERS* one notes the character Ambrose's repeated attempts, "Mensch" that he is, to impregnate Germaine Pitt, Lady Amherst, who acknowledges his unfortunately "low-motile swimmers" (380) and says that Ambrose "examines bemused beneath a microscope his swarmy semen, giving names to (and odds on) individual spermatozoa in their blind and general race" (61).

In *Sabbatical* the converging of the York River Entrance Channel and the York Spit Channel into the Chesapeake Channel, with its tidal ebb and flow ("the one inbound, the other outbound; or, in tidewater, the one on floods, the other on ebbs"), is made analogous to the convergence of fallopian tubes into the vaginal canal: "Sperm swim up; ova float down" (137). This particular "Night-Sea Journeying" conceit is echoed in Barth's most recent novelistic excursion, *COMING SOON!!!* Serving as the unlikely narrator for what may be considered the novel's prologue and epilogue, the "odd-looking grizzled entity" (294) identified as "Ditsy-Belle, Ditsy-Boy" (1)—the "gender free or ambigendered 'Ditsy' from [his show-boating vessel's] Maintenance" (294)—recycles *Sabbatical*'s reproductive ebb-and-flow conceit in describing the Chesapeake Bay:

> . . . she's as tall and slim and shallow as the female lead in a dumb-blonde joke, is Ms. CB. And she *is* a she, make no mistake as you could with me: Your Old Man River might just keep rolling with his one-track male nomind, but our vagrant Chess not only ebbs and flows like the moonstruck mother she is—any old off-the-shelf ocean does *that*—but mixes salt and fresh till her average salinity just about matches that of the sack we all first swam in, or for that matter human tears.
>
> (3)

To return to *Sabbatical,* the notion of swimmers and floaters is later developed as a dream the couple Fenwick Turner and Susan Seckler simultaneously experience. In the dream Fenwick and his swimming CIA colleagues appear as male sex cells, while Susan and her sister Mims appear as "big, elastic, floating eggs," i.e., "white-water canoers" (205) without the canoe. Somewhat later Susan's mother Carmen explains her "alternate generations" theory (240), that humans are parents of sex cells only, and therefore grandparents of their human children (240-42). Captivated by this "child-grandchild conceit" (330), Fenwick imagines, regarding spermatozoa, what he calls the "water marathon" of "hordes of urgent swimmers" (331) and, without having read Barth's **"Night-Sea Journey,"** recontextualizes—as one piece of fiction retailing another—its tacit premise as one of "the sundry isomorphies of the cycle of mythic-heroic adventure" (331), centering on

the career of the rare successful spermatozoon, from its virgin birth, . . . through its threshold-crossing; its dark sea journey; the loss of its companions (and ultimately its own identity and tail); its election . . . to an extraordinary, transcendent union; its—rather, henceforward, *their*—subsequent serial metamorphoses, as ontogeny recaps phylogeny in the gestatory flight; its recrossing of the threshold and rebirth into the light. . . .

(331)

In *The Tidewater Tales*—which, with *Sabbatical,* gives the reader "two novels, but one postmodernist narrative, a single self-reflexive tale in two parts" (Schulz 149)[15]— the recycled premise of **"Night-Sea Journey"** is grandly expanded as the "abortive seminal television script" (618) of amateur writer Franklin Talbott who, with his wife Leah (413-14), are the actual script-inspired dreamers of such a sperm-and-egg drama, "the ovum as a sort of Penelope, beset by spermatozoic suitors" (167). As noted earlier, however, the entire *Sabbatical* novel is revealed to be Talbott's re-creation (413-14) of himself and his wife Leah as Fenwick and Sue respectively. Sue's mother Carmen, with her child-grandchild conceit, is really Leah's mother Carla, who shares the same view. Disenchanted with his "night-sea journey" script, Talbott jettisons Act I and later Act II by means of empty "Alert-and-Locate" flare cannisters (403) into the bay waters, where both, in sequence, are separately discovered by established writer Peter Sagamore of less-is-more fame, who partly overcomes writer's block by composing in novelistic prose an Act III for Talbott possibly to rework in script form.

Talbott's play is entitled *SEX EDUCATION* and appears in stages, as it is discovered and completed, in *The Tidewater Tales*. Through *SEX EDUCATION,* Barth—in his self-styled "Theater of the Womb" (419)—re-envisions the existential Angst of **"Night-Sea Journey,"** with its "sperm-and-egg conceit" (*Tidewater Tales* 419) as farcical romance comedy, featuring millions of spermatozoa testing themselves "against the Night, the Sea, the Journey itself" (386). One of its readers, Katherine Sherritt, associates it with "Woody Allen comedies" (161), presumably the last sequence in particular, of Allen's 1972 *Everything You Always Wanted to Know About Sex (But Were Afraid to Ask)*. By contrast, the material is presented from the ovum's point of view, this time producing two eggs, self-styled floaters May and June, the former surviving by learning to swim back upstream and, after teaching June to do likewise, begrudgingly allowing herself to be ravished by swarms of swimmers in snug-fitting wet suits. This selfless act permits June's temporary escape (*Tidewater Tales* 392-93) with a bespectacled ("Barthian") gentleman swimmer (374), previously met and to some extent patronized, but willing to exchange reproductive knowledge. Like the protagonist in **"Night-Sea Journey,"** this swimmer has endured by floating as well as swimming and, having gained June's trust in eluding throngs of his fellow swimmers, to whom, as noted, May eventually sacrifices herself as a distraction, June and her bespectacled swimmer friend paddle, neither up nor down, but crosswise, to temporary refuge from his companions. Floater and swimmer now renamed and further humanized as Mimi and Fred (628), they inevitably end their floating (soap) opera by imagining what their progeny would be like (629-31) from a transcendent union that begins to occur, while they repeat again and again, till their voices are one, the first four timeless words of Barth's Möbius strip, "Once upon a time" (632).

The celebration of sexual vitality through the mythic-heroic quest of the tale-bearing sperm is extended in *The Tidewater Tales* to include a form of consciousness in Katherine Sherritt (Sagamore)'s developing twin embryos, then fetuses, who serve periodically as a uterine chorus, affirming or gainsaying the scattered observations of their parents, as if in earshot, through what the twins claim is their "umbilical connection with transcendency" (235). Such "transcendency" is in force until the moment of their Jack-and-Jill delivery, like the actual dizygotic twins Jack and Jill Barth in 1930 (Reilly 602). Barth will refer to the latter in *Once Upon a Time* while reviewing there, in simulated **"Night-Sea Journey"** reverie, the confluences of river channels, forking paths (like Borges), and fallopian tubes: ". . . father-sperm and mother-egg conjoin[ing] to make an entity that's both and neither—and Jack and Jill are prenatally twinned into JackandJill" (*Once* 228). In *The Tidewater Tales,* the Sagamore couple's twins before delivery, having previously been referred to by probably fourscore names and more, in binary combinations like Pride and Prejudice, Yin and Yang, are then called, not Jack and Jill, but Adam and Eve—"Welcome to your garden!" (638). Then, in novel-concluding verses, they are referred to, while suckling their mother, as Kith and Kin, and finally as "Exhaustion and Replenishment" (654), after Barth's twin essays of 1967 and 1979 respectively.[16]

In *The Last Voyage of Somebody the Sailor,* the protagonist Simon Behler, who later survives in an Arabian sea, like a good night-sea journeyer, by floating as well as swimming (512), sings earlier in the novel to his beggerly comrades a song beginning,

> *We all commence our journey as a little sperm and egg;*
> *Yet some wind up as millionaires, while others have to beg.*

(15)

By novel's end, in perhaps a round-about tribute to Barth's twin sister Jill, the entire story of Simon and Sindbad (pronounced Simon in Arabic) turns out to have been the narrator's gift to Bijou, his twin sister in the story, while both are still babes in the maternity ward. This sister is described as "stethoscoped, green-tunicked, multifunction-digitaled—his audience he now recognizes to have been all along his oldest friend" (573), who in turn calls him "fellow ovum, comrade, pal" (573) and recalls their former "weightless" ride in the uterine "spaceship," "making ready to go Outside" (573).

The bespectacled (Barthian) spermatozoon in *The Tidewater Tales* and the reference (given the dizygotic twinning of the actual Barth and his sister Jill) to dizygotic twins in that novel and to twins in *The Last Voyage of Somebody the Sailor,* as quoted above, show that the gradual accretion of autobiographical references, generally, within the text-world of Barth's extended discourse is also to be found in the recycled use of his sperm-and-egg motif. However, the weight of such life-text references in critical discussion is increased considerably with the publication of *Once Upon a Time.* When Zack Bowen refers to Barth's text as "the latest [at the time] and most obviously personal version of his ur-story" (200), it is in acknowledgment of Barth's self-referentiality in previous texts. These writings not only have their own intertextual connections, but more and more appear to encourage if not require, as a condition of their several meanings, the life-text readings available through the cumulative publications forming Barth's text-world, considered not just as separate texts, but from the viewpoint of a single, expanding discourse susceptible to *intra*textual readings. *Once Upon a Time*—a self-reflexive fictional memoir or, as Bowen puts it, "a fiction or near-fiction within a fiction" (201)—is a fulfillment of that perception. Barth's greatly expanded textual life in *Once Upon a Time* becomes the dominant feature of his developing text-world. He reorients or reconditions past readings of his work by the large-scale assimilation in *Once Upon a Time* of his relentlessly textualized life in that publication.

In particular, even after this study has considered the extended usage of the sperm-and-egg motif in subsequent texts by Barth, the dialogic use in *Once Upon a Time* of **"Night-Sea Journey"** itself—as one (of several) fictional glosses upon Barth's newly textualized life—causes one to reimagine this short story, within Barth's text-world, as a function of Barth's expanding life-text as well. This assertion is supported by the emergent *intra*textual relations, increasingly evident, between his fictions and what is inevitably to be seen in *Once Upon a Time* as the autofictional journey of Barth's personal veerings and moorings in the context of his literary and academic career.

Thus, the floating/flailing sperm as wandering hero in **"Night-Sea Journey"** is given a remarkably personal sounding in the intermittent allusions of *Once Upon a*

Time to Barth's "marital night-sea journey" (336) in the 1960s, "a tempestuous night-sea that scuttled my domestic vessel" (120). As Barth observes, "On tranquil Langford Creek, I review my writings from that troubled time and shake my head at their . . . desperate attempts at affirmation. 'Love! Love! Love!' cries the disenchanted spermatozoon of **'Night-Sea Journey,'** just before he takes the final plunge" (*Once* 352). Thus, having mapped Campbell's heroic cycle of emplotment on the putative life of a sex cell in **"Night-Sea Journey"**—a microscopic Odysseus beset with ontological doubts—Barth's application of Campbell's initiatory (or night-sea journeying) phase to his own life-text in *Once Upon a Time* recalibrates the sex cell's story-ending love-cry, before union with the Other, as a wistful affirmation sensitive to the terminal condition in the sixties of Barth's first marriage, ending in 1969 (Fogel and Slethaug 2). More appropriate to Barth's fluctuating mood at the time is the resigned conclusion of Ambrose in the short story **"Lost in the Funhouse"** to "construct funhouses for others and be their secret operator—though he would rather be among the lovers for whom funhouses are designed" (95).

However, in Barth's *Funhouse* story **"Menelaid,"** the oft-quoted last words—"the absurd, unending possibility of love" (167), which Barth says in *Once Upon a Time* "had carried both him [Menelaus] and me through its sore and growing complications" (365)—are reenacted as an affirmation fulfilled, with creative implications for his post-*Funhouse* writings, in Barth's second marriage on December 28, 1970, to former Penn State student and subsequent high school teacher Shelly Rosenberg.[17] Their initial re-meeting and eventual wedding are recounted in *Once Upon a Time* (366-79) and earlier in his 1986 "birthday tribute to her" (*Further Fridays* 3), eventually published as "Teacher: The Making of a Good One," in *Harper's* (November, 1986) and reprinted in Barth's second Friday book (1995), *Further Fridays* (4-21) as "Teacher" (Barth's preferred title), including photos.[18]

Nicholas Birns has observed that "Barth's postmodernism is not a tyranny of textuality but a reconciliation between fiction and reality" (114), or as Richard Bradbury says, "a kind of postmodernism which is fundamentally synthetic in its approach" (60).[19] Barth himself has observed in a subsequent text (**"Ad Infinitum: A Short Story"**), "The story of our life is not our life; it is our story" (*On With the Story* 14). Nevertheless, like Elvis sightings, identifications of one or both Barths (husband and wife) in some loosely textualized form in most of Barth's fictions written during or after 1970 are difficult to resist as incremental life-text additions to Barth's developing text-world, in spite of caveats against biographical poaching: The genie in *Dunyazadiad* as noted before, but also accompanied by reference to his "young lady" (16); Barth as the virtual (and

actual) "Author," and self-identified letter-writer, in *LETTERS*; the Chesapeake-boating couple Fenwick (Scott Key) Turner and Susan (Rachel Allan) Seckler in *Sabbatical*; the several Chesapeake-boating couples like Peter Sagamore and Katherine Sherritt, and Franklin and Leah Talbott, in *Tidewater Tales* (including an unplanned visit by Scheherazade to a Chesapeake-boating genie and his Jewish wife); the Chesapeake-boating Simon Behler in *The Last Voyage of Somebody the Sailor*; the textualized version of the Chesapeake-boating Barth and his wife, as well as his twin sister Jill, in *Once Upon a Time*—that "story-that-is-not-a-story, autobiography-that-is-neither-auto-nor-biography" (Bowen 202); perhaps the husband and wife who provide dialogic interludes in Barth's most recent collection, or collocation, of short fiction **On With the Story** (1996); and more surely Barth's autofictional "Barth" character, an elder eminence in postmodern letters, and his spouse ("the wife") in his latest novelistic conception (or contrivance), COMING SOON!!!

In this novel, Barth's ninth, the intertextual allusions and fiction-blurring life-text elements are so deliberately composed and so thickly strewn that COMING SOON!!! readily reinforces the gradually developing impression, strongly supported by *Once Upon a Time* and more diffusely by the cumulative reading of his other writings in sequence, that the Barthian corpus is best read as a single discourse or megatext, a cornucopian encyclopedia of "fact-fictional" Barthiana, studded with intertextual—or is it *intra*textual?—cross-references, as this study reconceives them. As in *Once Upon a Time*, and intermittently in other earlier work, life-text elements so overwhelm Barth's burgeoning text-world that each begins to seem, depending on one's vantage point, a palimpsest of the other, with no sure way of determining whether life-text authorizes text-world or the opposite. Yet each new contribution to the Barthian corpus prompts a rereading of earlier texts in light of the most recent, as is true also of the sperm-and-egg motif which this study has traced.

If *Once Upon a Time* encourages readers (without abandoning responses previously rehearsed) to reinterpret **"Night-Sea Journey"** as being also the hopeful product of Barth's negotiation with contemporary life-text issues, COMING SOON!!! mainly refocuses attention, through its own title, on the completed work itself, whether **"Night-Sea Journey"** or some other, as the gestational result of artful imagining. At its simplest, COMING SOON!!! represents the prediction of its own arrival, but justifies that transparent interpretation through a plot-complicating nexus of life-text and text-world associations, as a brief account will show.

Although a few examples of sperm-and-egg allusions of varying kinds from COMING SOON!!! (3, 60) have already been adduced, the recycling of the reproductive conceit in this novel is given nominal expression, early on, when the ambisexual character Ditsy, in same-sex reverie mode, is put in mind—by the title COMING SOON!!!—of "a hopeful ejaculation" (5). The title, however, belongs to "a Ziploc™'d computer disk" (4), fished out of the marshes by Ditsy while engaged in "progging"; e.g., "to pick and poke about, to scavenge and scrounge"; "to beachcomb where no beach is" (31). When screened, the disk's contents turn out to be authored ostensibly by a "Novelist Aspirant" (70) or "N.A." (98), the "young J. 'Hop' Johnson" (87). Spelled out, Johnson's first two names, "Johns" and "Hopkins," refer to the educational association of his parents, but also to Barth's alma mater and final institutional affiliation. Hop's "half-hatched hybrid COMING SOON!!!" (87), a "proposed M.A.-thesis-novel" (90), is "a work whose ontological status—fact or fiction?" (87)—appears to have correspondences in its use of shared and recycled life-stories with the simultaneously gestating narrative of his "Great-Uncle Ennie" (70). As the latest version of a virtual Barth or Barth-like persona, Great-Uncle Ennie is an N.E.—a "Novelist (semi-retired . . .) Emeritus" (70). He is also variously referred to as "Coach Emeritus" (98), the "aging Possibly-Last Novelist" (279), "GreatUnc" (79), "Great Unc Ennie" (372), the "Elder Talester" (81), and even, when referring to the elderly gentleman's wife, as "her semi-retired-novelist-quote-emeritus husband" (79. Both wife and husband are also referred to as "Miz and aging Mister So-and-So" (62).

Each writer, "unofficial mentor and mentee" (279)—and at times, seemingly "comrades-in-arms" (279), at other times "rivals" (279)—is working on a narrative (to be identified as COMING SOON!!!), involving a planned show boat production and illustrating, the reader is told, the "Young-Fart/Old-Fart Novelist theme" (283), "the N.A./N.E. Rivalry theme" (282), or the "Youth and Strength" versus "Age and Cunning" theme (279). Both writers hope that each one's own text, with Hop's COMING SOON!!! version "a venerable cliché [in its title] of showbiz hype" (88), may reach completion sooner than the other. Great-Uncle Ennie, the Novelist Emeritus, is uneasy with the way that Hop accretes and then subsumes in his work everyone else's facts, fictions, lives-as-stories/stories-as-lives. Nor is the Novelist Emeritus comfortable with Hop's suggestion at a so-called "ontological Drydock lunchbreak" (151) that by year's end "they combine their separate versions-thus-far of the Ur-novel COMING SOON!!!" (151).

Criticizing Hop (the Novelist Aspirant), the Novelist Emeritus ironically opines that "*at least some of us elder specimens still honor the useful distinction between fact and fiction, art and life*" (232). Nevertheless, while aping the e(lectronic)-fiction that the novel parodies in print, Barth continues to revel in metafictional layers of fact/fiction, of textual worlds and worlds within texts,

of outer/inner frames that blur their boundaries, of multiple narrators/authors and of authors authoring themselves, as when both Hop (in e-fiction) and the Novelist Emeritus (in p-fiction) lay claim to "The Novelist Emeritus Character" (312) in their writing. The Novelist Emeritus speaks of himself as "The original of the [novelized] N.E. Character" (312), but eventually relents and permits the Novelist Aspirant's showbiz appropriation of "The N.E. Character—*my* N.E. Character, in *my* p[rint]-fictive COMING SOON!!!" (313).

The title COMING SOON!!! comes to stand, then, for a revived set of show boat visitations along the Chesapeake on a refurbished show barge (yet another Barthian floating opera, or metaphorical ark, Noah's, of course) and also the name for the show barge's "play-in-progress" (279); that is, the show itself, "so fluid and morph-prone a production!" (278). COMING SOON!!! also alludes to the prospect of an apocalyptic end-time written into the production, as originally mooted by millennialist sensibilities regarding the impending year 2,000 (in addition to Y2K concerns, also mentioned) and the direction-shifting narrative threat of "Tropical Storm Zulu" (316). Finally, the title identifies the intended millennial, but actually post-millennial, novel of 2001, the virtual COMING SOON!!! as awaited text (N.A.'s and/or N.E.'s) and, initially and ultimately, as the actual book-of-the-text held in the putative reader's hands—the titular interpretation with which this scrutiny of Barth's "next" last novel began.

Even this necessarily incomplete synopsis makes clear Barth's knowing complicity (1) in appropriating prior texts, his and others'; (2) in accreting life-text elements, which themselves become recurring features of an expanding text-world; and (3) in recycling particular motifs in refigured form—sperm-and-egg allusions and much else—that require new or altered readings to accommodate the latest reconfiguration in what may be read with profit as a single discourse with many entry points.

In genetics, as in writing, "the key to the treasure *is* the treasure," as not only Scheherazade exclaims in the story of her sister Doony (***Dunyazadiad*** 8), but also the Barth-like genie who, having simultaneously inscribed it within his own time and place, now appears in theirs to reaffirm it (11). In applying this well-worn phrase to Barth's second novel, *The End of the Road*, it may be observed that the "weatherless" protagonist Jacob Horner's adoption of a so-called Mythotherapy regimen—"the systematic assumption of borrowed or improvised personae to ward off paralysis in cases of ontological vacuity" (*LETTERS* 581)[20]—may be seen, in an ultimate sense, as having been reinscribed by Barth, *for* Barth as writer, in the form of an imaginative exploration of wandering heroes, in myths made and myths received, including the elevation to mythic status of human sex cells, beginning with Barth's **"Night-Sea Journey."** More generally, in the omnibus novel *LETTERS,* the same Jacob Horner's reliance on what is now called a *Scripto*therapy regimen to avoid paralysis may indeed be every fictionist's writing cure to tell the story of one's life without mistaking one's life for one's story. This observation may be affirmed even when, in Barth's case, text-world and life-text become deliberately intertwined in his *Once Upon a Time* to create—as expressed in Barth's **"Hold On, There"** coda to **"Stories of Our Lives"**—". . . life-stories. Life-or-death stories. Stories-within-stories stories, tails in their own mouths like the snake Ouroboros. Bent back on themselves like time-warps" (*On With the Story* 180).[21]

The reading commitment required to engage Barth's texts, whether as separate publications or as a single grand discourse combining text-world with life-text, may be increasingly elusive, as new readers find themselves awed by the expanding network of associations, confused by the range of protean meanings so generated, or indifferent to the interpretive needs of such a fiction. Contributing to such responses is the cultural phenomenon of reading habits altered and attention spans shrunk with the decade-old arrival of the Internet. A similar concern is actually sounded in Barth's Coming Soon!!!, which deliberately plays off a younger generation's e-text against an older generation's p-text. In *The Gutenberg Elegies,* Sven Birkerts laments the "displacement of the page by the screen" (3), or in other terms, the seemingly gradual attenuation, in generation after generation, of a "participatory" reading experience (32) in the "duration[al] state" (32) that it requires, involving the millennia-old hand-held book, as "an agency of self-making" (87), in contrast to the competing claims of high-definition screens, including the electronic print medium of hypertextual options, which is the challenging prospect explored at length in Barth's Coming Soon!!!, given the alternating currents of e-fiction and p-fiction (88) repeatedly discussed.

Barth's representation of Hop, the story's much younger alter ego narrator (and hypertextual enthusiast), shows recognition of the changing reading environment in the late twentieth and early twenty-first century. Hop readily embraces the new electronic medium, offering a satirical welcome to prospective readers of his own text: "As Robert Frost invites, You come, too, Comrade Reader . . . here in Virtualville . . ." (76). However, as if in agreement with Birkerts, the surrogate Barthian narrator or "real" Barth in Coming Soon!!!—having previously referred to his prospective new-millennial reader as "Mouseclicker, Option-opter, whatever" (86)—ruefully interjects at a later point, "Maybe we'll all rediscover *reading*? Don't hold Your breath, dear disappearing Reader" (151), while in the same breath coaxing the reader to read on anyway.[22]

Nevertheless, one cannot forget in an earlier fiction Barth's invoking—in the guise of a more hopeful authorial presence imagining a more congenially receptive reader—his now-familiar reproductive conceit, but used on the occasion to valorize the intersubjectivity of a writer whose text inscribes its reader, and a participatory reader self-inscribed by that text in the implicit context of a family romance, perpetually recycled. Thus in *The Tidewater Tales,* the writer Peter Sagamore muses that "if stories *were* children, their readers wouldn't be *their* children; they'd be one of their parents, and the author the other. The Mother and Father of Invention" (410). Given that conceptive role for readers, Barth invites all who would pore over novelistic messages in bottles, lose themselves in funhouses and mazes, finesse the function of authorial personae, and re-enter the ever lengthening Möbius strip of inter- and intratextual wandering heroes and night-sea journeys that have made the expanding discourse of Barth's burgeoning text-world and developing life-text a stimulating, if demanding, postmodern adventure.

Notes

1. Cynthia Davis declares unequivocally that "the Genii is clearly Barth himself" and shortly refers to "Barth as Genii" and "Genii-Barth" (217). Max F. Schulz also refers to the genii character in *Dunyazadiad* from Barth's *Chimera* as "the Genii Barth" (137).

2. Molly Hite, remarking on Barth's *LETTERS,* reminds readers that *LETTERS* includes "the author 'John Barth,' already an ontologically unsettling character [the genii] in *Chimera*" (712). Considering Barth's corpus up to *The Last Voyage of Somebody the Sailor,* and in consideration especially of the texts from *Lost in the Funhouse* onward, Alan Lindsay says, "Barth presents us with the author as Proteus" (78).

3. The Barthian narrator in Coming Soon!!! provides his own discourse on the problematic reception of life-stories as fiction, given the example of *Once Upon a Time*:

   Having delivered that novel/memoir (a problematic genre, inasmuch as one's interest in the two categories proceeds from antithetical presumptions: If you retail to me over lunch the "story" of your love affair in Lisbon, my interest in it presumes your account to be factual, even though in fact you may be exaggerating, omitting relevant details, even flat-out lying. If on the other hand you write a novel about its narrator's love affair in Lisbon, your story must interest me despite my presumption that it's a total fabrication—even though I may happen to know that in fact it's not.

   (Coming Soon!!! 84)

4. The Ur-myth template of the wandering hero originally appeared in Joseph Campbell's *The Hero*

With a Thousand Faces (1949) and is given on page 245 in the second edition (Princeton, NJ: Princeton UP, 1968). John Barth reproduced Campbell's diagram, preceded by material from Lord Raglan's *The Hero: A Study in Tradition, Myth, and Drama,* in "Mystery and Tragedy: The Twin Motions of Ritual Heroism," originally composed as a lecture presented on December 10, 1964, at SUNY at Geneseo ("Mystery" 41) and included in an essay in *The Friday Book* (New York: Putnam's, 1984) 44. Into this lecture Barth assembled "a little Raglan, a little Jung, and a few odds and ends I had up my own sleeve," which "came out a fascinating pattern indeed" (44). The Ur-myth diagram as it originally appeared in Campbell's text is reproduced with acknowledgment by one of Barth's *"seven fictitious drolls & dreamers"* (49), Ambrose Mensch (of *Lost in the House* fame) in Barth's "writerly," if not always "readerly," encyclopedic novel *LETTERS* (New York: Putnam's, 1979) 647. Barth's *own* annotated version of Campbell's diagram, first appearing in *The Friday Book* essay, is reproduced, along with several pages of commentary, in his fictional memoir *Once Upon a Time: A Floating Opera* (Boston: Little, Brown, 1994) 314-16. In a further postmodern gesture of self-reflexive recycling, Campbell's Ur-myth template is also explicitly discussed or referred to in Barth's *The Tidewater Tales* (New York: Putnam's, 1987) 312-13; and, yet again, in *Once Upon a Time,* pp. 115-16, 119-21, 302, and 309-11, with further use of the term "Ur-myth" in *Once Upon a Time* on pp. 323-24, 340-41, and 355-56.

5. Treating the series of stories in *Lost in the Funhouse* as a novel, W. Todd Martin cites "the author's note at the beginning of the work" (identifying the 1981 edition, p. vii), where "Barth says that it is 'neither a collection nor a selection, but a series, [and] though several of its items have appeared separately in periodicals, the series will be seen to have been meant to be received "all at once" and here arranged'" (151n1). Carolyn Norman Slaughter's study concurs with this minority view (81). Evelyn Glaser-Wöhrer argues that when the stories are "read *like* [italics mine] a novel," *Lost in the Funhouse* "turns out to be a Künstlerroman (with autobiographical traits)" (147-48). Finally, Alan Lindsay also numbers *Lost in the Funhouse* among Barth's novels, "though it is on one level a collection of short stories" (3), which brings the discussion full circle.

6. Reminding readers that "both the 'Authors Notes' and 'Seven Additional Notes' appear in the 1969 [second] edition of *Lost in the Funhouse*" (4n5), George Kurman and Roger W. Rouland point to Barth's complication of the sperm as narrator in

that Barth calls to the attention of "critics and readers that the narrator of 'Journey' is 'quoted from beginning to end by the authorial voice'" (Kurman and Rouland 4), which authorizes while ventriloquizing its tale-telling persona, although the Barthian persona in *Once Upon a Time* simply says that "Night-Sea Journey" is "narrated in the first person by a spermatozoan afflicted with self-awareness and skepticism" (119).

7. Zenobia Mistri relates the first line of Barth's story to "the opening line of Dante's *Divine Comedy,*" one of several "Dantean allusions" (151).

8. Deborah A. Woolley observes that the phrase "both vessel and contents" implies that "narrative voice [as in "Night-Sea Journey"] has a double nature: it is both personality and the vehicle by which personality is conveyed—both signified and signifier" (470).

9. Stan Fogel and Gordon Slethaug emphasize in this story "Barth's word play on 'Maker' as God, sexual adventurer, and author" (113), which accretes further meaning in Barth's narrative COMING SOON!!! as the putative head of the Tidewater Foundation (33), variously abbreviated as the (transcendental-hyphenated-signified) "GEE DASH DEE" or "G-D" or "Her-Slash-Him" (29), in the chapter titled "Is There a Gee Dash Dee?"

10. For an extended discussion linking Barth and Roland Barthes, see Lindsay, *Death in the FUNhouse,* particularly pages 1-2, 5-8, 13, 21, 34-38, 43-46, 51-69, 73-74, 103-13, 130-31, 133-35, 139, 154, 166.

11. As Harold Farwell notes, "The ultimate irony, of course, is that all these cries against 'senseless love, senseless death' are voiced just before the narrator gives himself completely to the singing . . ." (61) and subsequent merger with the Other-as-She.

12. Mistri suggests instead a storied conclusion, more appropriate in allusion, to Donne (152).

13. Apropos of Barth's "muse," the increasing life/fiction entanglements of Barth's later fiction—what are referred to as the "tangled tango" of "Fact and Fiction" (70), "our factfictional tango" (70), in Barth's most recent novel, COMING SOON!!!—are evident in this Barthian aside from that same publication: "Muse or Mrs . . . (they are not the same female entity, although their Venn Diagrams, so to speak, most certainly and fortuitously overlap)" (84-85).

14. In this vein, Michael Hinden observes that "since it occurs to the narrator" of "Night-Sea Journey" that "'Makers and swimmers *each generate the*

other' (p. 8), the story suggests a biological parallel to the fictional circularity of 'Frame Tale'" (194).

15. In addition, Schulz also speaks of "the complex fictive-'factual' intertextual symbiosis of *Sabbatical* and *The Tidewater Tales,*" regarding "the mechanics of crossbreeding and fecundating his [Barth's] fiction with his past fiction . . ." (150). In particular, Fogel and Slethaug note that "*Sabbatical* is, then, the nucleus of a clever and innovative frame tale, which is revealed and supplemented by numerous other small framing devices in *The Tidewater Tales*" (199).

16. For further discussion of *SEX EDUCATION* and the reproductive connections between *Sabbatical* and *The Tidewater Tales,* see Schulz 149-54 and Fogel and Slethaug 190-202.

17. Addressing directly the question of authorial privacy when the writer himself deliberately engages in an autobiographical "fiction," Zack Bowen says, "After all these years of dismay with what he considered a violation of his privacy by biographical critics, John Barth has published his own semifictionalized autobiography, or at least as much as his wife, Shelly, would permit—if we are to believe Barth's latest narrator [in *Once Upon a Time*]" (195). On the "'reality' intertext" (Lindsay 142) or "intertext of Barth's life" (Lindsay 143) in relation to his fiction, nonfiction, and autofiction, see Lindsay 142-49. For Barth's acknowledgment of particular autobiographical elements in *Once Upon a Time,* see Reilly 608-09.

18. As Barth notes in the introduction to this essay (*Further Fridays* 3-4), "*This Friday-piece was [originally] written in 1986 for a little anthology [edited by Louis D. Rubin, Jr.] called* An Apple for My Teacher . . . , *subtitled* Twelve Authors Tell About Teachers Who Made the Difference" (3).

19. Continuing, Bradbury relates this observation to the author function as increasingly played out in Barth's texts: "Within the narrative structures this [commitment to synthesis] creates a tension between the desire to eliminate the omniscient narrator as a symptom of a unitary voice and the reinstatement of that omniscient narrator as the only presence capable of achieving the synthesis towards which the text is geared" (61), another motive in recentering the narrator while straddling the margins of fiction and fact.

20. Hite provides this definition: ". . . Mythotherapy, an existential version of psychoanalysis that aims to compensate for the fundamental nonexistence of the subject by helping the analysand invent the self as an arbitrary but consistent character" (711).

21. Given this confluence of self-reflexive life-stories in Barthian tale-telling, Woolley would repudiate the notion that Barth's stories are a retreat from the world into text merely, primarily because of Barth's privileged voicing of the text: "But self-reflexive narrative is still narrative; as such, it is pervaded by voice. Any tendency of postmodern fiction to collapse into linguistic freeplay or mere 'text' is counterbalanced by narrative's irrepressible evocation, through voice, of a narrative presence characterized by certain acts, qualities, and intentions . . ." (481).

22. The anxiety of print-culture in the lengthening shadow of e-text alternatives is a theme explored at length by Fitzpatrick 518-59, especially through the interrogation of two kindred self-reflexive texts, Barth's *LETTERS* and Richard Powers' *Galatea 2.2* (1995).

Works Cited

Augustine, Saint, Bishop of Hippo. *Confessions.* Trans. and introd. Henry Chadwick. New York: Oxford UP, 1991.

Barth, John. "Ambrose His Mark." Barth, *Lost in the Funhouse* 14-34.

———. "Anonymiad." Barth, *Lost in the Funhouse* 168-201.

———. *Bellerophoniad. Chimera* 137-308.

———. *Chimera.* New York: Random House, 1972.

———. *COMING SOON!!! A Narrative.* Boston and New York: Houghton Mifflin, 2001.

———. *Dunyazadiad. Chimera* 3-56.

———. *The End of the Road.* Garden City, NY: Doubleday, 1967.

———. *The Floating Opera.* Garden City, NY: Doubleday, 1967.

———. "Frame-Tale." Barth, *Lost in the Funhouse* 1-2.

———. *The Friday Book: Essays and Other Nonfiction.* New York: Putnam's, 1984.

———. *Further Fridays: Essays, Lectures, and Other Nonfiction, 1984-1994.* Boston: Little, Brown, 1995.

———. *Giles Goat-boy; or, The Revised New Syllabus.* Garden City, NY: Doubleday, 1966.

———. *The Last Voyage of Somebody the Sailor.* Boston: Little, Brown, 1991.

———. *LETTERS: A Novel.* New York: Putnam's, 1979.

———. "The Literature of Exhaustion." Barth, *The Friday Book* 62-76.

———. "The Literature of Replenishment: Postmodernist Fiction." Barth, *The Friday Book* 193-206.

———. *Lost in the Funhouse: Fiction for Print, Tape, Live Voice.* Garden City, NY: Doubleday, 1968.

———. "Lost in the Funhouse." Barth, *Lost in the Funhouse* 72-97.

———. "Menelaid." Barth, *Lost in the Funhouse* 130-67.

———. "Mystery and Tragedy: The Twin Motions of Ritual Heroism." Barth, *The Friday Book* 41-54.

———. "Night-Sea Journey." Barth, *Lost in the Funhouse* 3-13.

———. *Once Upon a Time: A Floating Opera.* Boston: Little, Brown, 1994.

———. "Once Upon a Time: Storytelling Explained." Barth, *Further Fridays* 183-96.

———. *On With the Story: Stories.* Boston: Little, Brown, 1996.

———. *Perseid. Chimera* 59-134.

———. *Sabbatical: A Romance.* New York: Putnam's, 1982.

———. *The Sot-Weed Factor.* Garden City, NY: Doubleday, 1960.

———. "Teacher." Barth, *Further Fridays* 3-21.

———. *The Tidewater Tales, A Novel.* New York: Putnam's, 1987.

———. "Water-Message." Barth, *Lost in the Funhouse* 40-57.

Birkerts, Sven. *The Gutenberg Elegies: The Fate of Reading in an Electronic Age.* New York: Fawcett Columbine, 1994.

Birns, Nicholas. "Beyond Metafiction: Placing John Barth." *Arizona Quarterly* 49.2 (Summer, 1993): 113-36.

Bowen, Zack. "Setting the Möbius Strip Straight: John Barth's *Once Upon a Time: A Floating Opera.*" *Critique: Studies in Contemporary Fiction* 40.3 (Spring, 1999): 195-202.

Bradbury, Richard. "Postmodernism and Barth and the Present State of Fiction." *Critical Quarterly* 32.1 (Spring, 1990): 60-72.

Campbell, Joseph. *The Hero With a Thousand Faces.* New York: Pantheon Books, 1949.

Davis, Cynthia. "'The Key to the Treasure': Narrative Movements and Effects in *Chimera.*" Waldmeir 217-27.

Farwell, Harold. "John Barth's Tenuous Affirmation: 'The Absurd, Unending Possibility of Love.'" Waldmeir 55-67.

Fitzpatrick, Kathleen. "The Exhaustion of Literature: Novels, Computers, and the Threat of Obsolescence." *Contemporary Literature* 43.3 (Fall, 2002): 518-59.

Fogel, Stan, and Gordon Slethaug. *Understanding John Barth.* Understanding Contemporary American Literature. Ed. Matthew J. Bruccoli. Columbia, SC: U of South Carolina P, 1990.

Glaser-Wöhrer, Evelyn. *An Analysis of John Barth's Weltanschauung: His View of Life and Literature.* Salzburger Studien zur Anglistik und Amerikanistik 5. Ed. Erwin Stürzl. Salzburg, Austria: Institut für Englische Sprache und Literatur Universität Salzburg, 1977.

Hinden, Michael. "*Lost in the Funhouse*: Barth's Use of the Recent Past." Waldmeir 190-200.

Hite, Molly. "Postmodern Fiction." In *The Columbia History of the American Novel.* Ed. Emory Elliott. New York: Columbia UP, 1991. 697-725.

Karl, Frederick. *American Fictions, 1940-1980: A Comprehensive History and Critical Evaluation.* New York: Harper and Row, 1983.

Kurman, George, and Roger W. Rouland. "Conrad's *Heart of Darkness* as Pretext for Barth's 'Night-Sea Journey': The Colonist's Passage Upstream." *International Fiction Review* 20.1 (1993): 3-13.

Lindsay, Alan. *Death in the FUNhouse: John Barth and Poststructuralist Aesthetics.* Studies in Literary Criticism and Theory 2. Ed. Hans Rudnick. New York: Peter Lang, 1995.

Martin, W. Todd. "Self-Knowledge and Self-Conception: The Therapy of Autobiography in John Barth's *Lost in the Funhouse.*" *Studies in Short Fiction* 34.2 (Spring, 1997): 151-57.

Mistri, Zenobia. "Absurdist Contemplations of a Sperm in John Barth's 'Night-Sea Journey.'" *Studies in Short Fiction* 25.2 (Spring, 1988): 151-52.

Morrell, David. *John Barth: An Introduction.* University Park, PA, and London: Pennsylvania State UP, 1976.

Olson, Carol Booth. "Lost in the Madhouse." *Review of Contemporary Fiction* 10.2 (Summer, 1990): 56-63.

Poznar, Susan. "Barth's 'Compulsion to Repeat: Its Hazards and Possibilities.'" *Review of Contemporary Fiction* 10.2 (Summer, 1990): 64-75.

Raglan, Fitzroy Richard Somerset, Baron. *The Hero: A Study in Tradition, Myth, and Drama.* London: Methuen, 1936.

Rank, Otto. *The Myth of the Birth of the Hero, and Other Writings.* Ed. Philip Freund. New York: Vintage Books, 1964.

Reilly, Charlie. "An Interview With John Barth." *Contemporary Literature* 41.4 (Winter, 2000): 589-617.

Schulz, Max F. *The Muses of John Barth: Tradition and Metafiction From* Lost in the Funhouse *to* The Tidewater Tales. Baltimore and London: Johns Hopkins UP, 1990.

Slaughter, Carolyn Norman. "Who Gets Lost in the Funhouse." *Arizona Quarterly* 44.4 (Winter, 1989): 80-97.

Sterne, Lawrence. *The Life and Opinions of Tristram Shandy, Gentleman.* Ed. and introd. Ian Campbell Ross. Oxford: Clarendon P, 1983.

Waldmeir, Joseph J., ed. *Critical Essays on John Barth.* Critical Essays on American Literature. Ed. James Nagel. Boston: G. K. Hall, 1980.

Woolley, Deborah A. "Empty 'Text,' Fecund Voice: Self-Reflexivity in Barth's *Lost in the Funhouse.*" *Contemporary Literature* 26.4 (Winter, 1985): 460-81.

Worthington, Marjorie. "Done With Mirrors: Restoring the Authority Lost in John Barth's Funhouse." *Twentieth-Century Literature* 47.1 (Spring, 2001): 114-36.

Publishers Weekly **(review date 22 August 2005)**

SOURCE: Review of *Where Three Roads Meet,* by John Barth. *Publishers Weekly* 252, no. 33 (22 August 2005): 34.

[*In the following review, the critic responds favorably to* Where Three Roads Meet.]

Teller, tale, torrid (and torpid) inspiration: Barth's 17th book [***Where Three Roads Meet***] brings these three narrative "roads" together inimitably, and thrice. It employs all of his familiar devices—alliteration, shifts in diction and time, puns ("Leda lays egg, Egg hatches Helen, Helen lays Paris, Paris lays waste to Troy")—to tease and titillate, while at the same time articulate—obliquely, sadly, angrily, gloriously—a farewell to language and its objects: us. The first of three lightly linked novellas, ***Tell Me,*** introduces the three Freds: Alfred, Winifred and Wilfred, post-WWII collegemates who play jazz together, talk frankly and joustingly into the night, and form two alternating pas de deux. One particular set of exchanges sets the course of Wilfred's career; the whole story is a look back by him, a near lifetime later, at the before and after of that moment. The second piece, ***I've Been Told,*** presents a hero's tale that speaks in the first person (the story itself is the narrator)—"that story *c'est moi* guys, and here's how I go, now that I've got myself cranked up and more or less under way"—and puns endlessly. (It also has Freds). The third, ***As I Was Saying,*** uses the title's participle to riff on writing's eroticism: its three sisters, unreliable narrators all, use a *Krapp's Last Tape*-type conceit to tell of the sexual maelstrom of their adult lives, within which an infamous, Barthian novelist (Manfred F. Dickson Sr.) wrote. Wrote? The story ends in a mix of the past, present and future progressive: "As I was saying . . ."

FURTHER READING

Bibliographies

Vine, Richard Allan. *John Barth: An Annotated Bibliography.* Metuchen, N.J.: The Scarecrow Press, 1977, 106 p.

  Concise bibliography of Barth's works and secondary criticism.

Weixlmann, Joseph. *John Barth: A Descriptive Primary and Annotated Secondary Bibliography, Including a Descriptive Catalog of Manuscript Holdings in United States Libraries.* New York: Garland Publishing, Inc., 1976, 219 p.

  Thorough primary and secondary bibliography.

Criticism

Bell, Steven M. "Literature, Self-Consciousness, and Writing: The Example of Barth's *Lost in the Funhouse.*" *The International Fiction Review* 11, no. 2 (summer 1984): 84-9.

  Examines literary self-consciousness in *Lost in the Funhouse.*

Blake, Nancy. "Fiction as Screen Memory." *Delta* 21 (October 1985): 95-104.

  Focuses on the representation of point of view in Barth's short stories.

Brown, Robert E. Review of *The Book of Ten Nights and a Night,* by John Barth. *Library Journal* 129, no. 7 (15 April 2004): 127-28.

  Mixed review of *The Book of Ten Nights and a Night.*

Curran, Ronald T. Review of *On with the Story,* by John Barth. *World Literature Today* 72, no. 1 (winter 1998): 131-32.

  Favorable review of *On with the Story.*

Davis, Cynthia. "'The Key to the Treasure': Narrative Movements and Effects in *Chimera.*" *The Journal of Narrative Technique* 5, no. 2 (May 1975): 105-15.

  Studies the "tale-within-a-tale" narrative format of *Dunyazadiad,* and asserts that the novella contains "seven concentric stories that climax in a series 'like a string of firecrackers.'"

Harris, Charles B. "'A Continuing, Strange Love Letter': Sex and Language in *Lost in the Funhouse.*" In *Passionate Virtuosity: The Fiction of John Barth,* pp. 106-26. Urbana: University of Illinois Press, 1983.
Examines Barth's frequent habit of equating sex with other forms of human endeavor, such as art.

Kiernan, Robert F. "John Barth's Artist in the Funhouse." *Studies in Short Fiction* 10, no. 4 (fall 1973): 373-80.
Attempts to evaluate the unity of the different stories in *Lost in the Funhouse.*

Review of *The Book of Ten Nights and a Night,* by John Barth. *Kirkus Reviews* 72, no. 5 (1 March 2004): 191.
Negative review of *The Book of Ten Nights and a Night* that assesses the collection as "initially stimulating, increasingly puzzling, ultimately dissatisfying."

Review of *Where Three Roads Meet,* by John Barth. *Kirkus Reviews* 73, no. 15 (1 August 2005): 801-02.
Mixed review, asserting that *Where Three Roads Meet* "will appeal mostly to Barthophiles who want still more after 16 volumes."

Krier, William J. "*Lost in the Funhouse*: 'A Continuing, Strange Love Letter.'" *Boundary 2* 5, no. 1 (fall 1976): 103-16.
Discusses the composition of *Lost in the Funhouse* and notes that is not as free of structure as some critics have claimed.

Kurman, George, and Roger W. Rouland. "Conrad's *Heart of Darkness* as Pretext for Barth's 'Night Sea Journey': The Colonist's Passage Upstream." *The International Fiction Review* 20, no. 1 (1993): 3-13.
Asserts that reading Barth's "Night Sea Journey" with its literary inspiration—Joseph Conrad's *Heart of Darkness*—in mind "illuminates and expands" both the meaning of Barth's story and offers insight into the imagery used in Conrad's novel.

Mistri, Zenobia. "Absurdist Contemplations of a Sperm in John Barth's 'Night-Sea Journey.'" *Studies in Short Fiction* 25, no. 2 (spring 1988): 151-52.
Argues that "Night-Sea Journey" simultaneously embodies "nonsense and sense."

Rice-Sayre, Laura. "The Lost Construction of Barth's Funhouse." *Studies in Short Fiction* 17, no. 4 (fall 1980): 463.
Examines the alterations Barth made to several of the stories in *Lost in the Funhouse* before publication.

Shulz, Max F. "The Thalian Design of *Lost in the Funhouse.*" In *The Muses of John Barth: Tradition and Metafiction from* Lost in the Funhouse *to* The Tidewater Tales, pp. 1-15. Baltimore, Md.: The Johns Hopkins University Press, 1990.
Asserts that Barth successfully "rejuvenate[s] the storytelling conventions of Western culture."

Tobin, Patricia. "*Lost in the Funhouse* (1968) and *Chimera* (1972): The Hero Minors in Metaphor." In *John Barth and the Anxiety of Continuance,* pp. 84-102. Philadelphia: The University of Pennsylvania Press, 1992.
Examines the "literary experimentation" of *Lost in the Funhouse* and *Chimera.*

Wooley, Deborah A. "Empty 'Text,' Fecund Voice: Self-Reflexivity in Barth's *Lost in the Funhouse.*" *Contemporary Literature* 26, no. 4 (winter 1985): 460-81.
Observes the reader's text as distinct from the author's text in *Lost in the Funhouse.*

Ziegler, Heidi. "The supra-*Kunstlerroman*: *Lost in the Funhouse* and *Chimera.*" In *John Barth,* pp. 49-63. London: Methuen, 1987.
Applies the notion of the self-reflexive hero to *Lost in the Funhouse* and *Chimera,* and contrasts it with the notion of the *bildungsroman.*

"The Birthmark"

Nathaniel Hawthorne

The following entry presents criticism of Hawthorne's short story "The Birthmark" (1843). For further information on Hawthorne's short fiction, see *SSC*, Volume 3; for discussion of the short story "Young Goodman Brown," see *SSC*, Volume 29; for discussion of the short story "The Minister's Black Veil," see *SSC*, Volume 39.

INTRODUCTION

Hawthorne's "The Birthmark" (1843) was first published in the journal *The Pioneer* and later collected in *Mosses from an Old Manse* (1846). Critics regard this story as one of Hawthorne's most complex short works, often maintaining that it offers at once a cautionary tale of scientific responsibility, an astute examination of human psychology, an exploration of humankind's struggle to cope with mortality and ambiguity, a nuanced portrayal of the nature of romantic love, and an analysis of the limits of philosophical and spiritual thought. The broad range of critical discussion of "The Birthmark" is illustrative of the story's depth and complexity, and a testament to Hawthorne's status as one of America's most prominent and influential short fiction writers.

PLOT AND MAJOR CHARACTERS

In "The Birthmark," Aylmer, a highly skilled scientist, falls deeply in love with and marries Georgiana, a woman who is flawlessly beautiful except for a reddish, hand-shaped birthmark on her cheek. While he is initially not bothered by the birthmark, Aylmer soon becomes obsessed with it and dreams that he and his laboratory assistant, Aminadab, perform surgery to remove it. When Aylmer relates his feelings of disgust and the events in his dream to Georgiana, she becomes profoundly distressed and encourages her husband to try everything within his power to remove the birthmark from her face, so that she can again be viewed by him as the "ideal" beauty she once was. Aylmer's vast library of scientific tomes includes several works by famous alchemists, and he engages in various alchemical experiments, ultimately concocting a liquid that suc-

cessfully removes yellow spots from the leaves of a geranium. When Georgiana drinks the liquid, she falls into a deep sleep and Aylmer sits by her bedside and carefully records the gradual fading of the birthmark, failing to note his wife's death in his excitement over his "successful" experiment.

MAJOR THEMES

Scholars generally agree that Hawthorne wrote "The Birthmark" shortly after his marriage to Sophia Peabody. Because "The Birthmark" centers around a newlywed couple, numerous critics have speculated on the autobiographical sources for the story, concluding that the subject matter of the story may stem, at least in part, from Hawthorne's own anxiety about marriage and the power of love. A more prominently studied theme of "The Birthmark" is the role and social responsibility of the scientist. Sharing the European Romantics' mistrust of science, Hawthorne perceived great danger in attempts to manipulate nature, particularly if the aim of the endeavor is to somehow improve upon natural creation. Imperfection, Hawthorne asserts, is an integral part of humanity; to remove it is to remove life. Aylmer represents the Romantic archetype of the scientist: like Mary Shelley's Victor Frankenstein, Aylmer attempts to usurp divine powers, and like Johann Wolfgang von Goethe's Faust, he allows his intellectual curiosity to overcome his morality and spirituality, ignoring the redemptive power of love. While Aylmer is presumed at the outset of the story to represent humankind's possibilities and achievements, and his assistant, Aminadab, humankind's baser nature, in light of Aylmer's actions, the characters prove to be less clearly defined. This juxtaposition of character types engaging in morally ambiguous behavior is thought to be one of the ways in which Hawthorne depicts the dangers and failures of various schools of scientific, philosophical, and religious thought. When Georgiana represents the idealized "object" of romantic love she is content, but her willingness to risk her life to regain this status in her husband's eyes demonstrates the extent to which her existence is dependent upon her appearance, as well as the potential dangers and cruelties inherent in romantic love.

CRITICAL RECEPTION

Critics have consistently offered praise for "The Birthmark," but the focus of their commentary has varied widely. In addition to studies tracing possible autobiographical elements in "The Birthmark," critics have highlighted literary precedents for the story in works by such authors as William Shakespeare, Goethe, and in Ovid's treatment of the legend of Pygmalion. Critics have remarked on "The Birthmark"'s complex symbolism and a narrative style that has been viewed as alternately conveying lightness and darkness through Hawthorne's skillful manipulation of language and tone. Some commentators have emphasized Hawthorne's use of specific symbols, such as the hand, the heart, alchemy, and the birthmark itself, to elucidate his moral, philosophical, and spiritual themes, and others—like Charles L. Proudfit—have observed how, particularly through his careful characterization of Aylmer, Hawthorne anticipates such works as *The Ego and the Mechanisms of Defence*, published by esteemed psychologist Anna Freud in 1936. Such scholars as Judith Fetterley have interpreted "The Birthmark" as a distinctly feminist work, revealing what Fetterley calls the "sickness of men," rather than "the flawed and imperfect nature of women."

PRINCIPAL WORKS

Short Fiction

Twice-Told Tales 1837
Twice-Told Tales [second series] 1842
Mosses from an Old Manse 1846
The Snow-Image, and Other Twice-Told Tales 1851
A Wonder-Book for Girls and Boys 1852
Tanglewood Tales for Girls and Boys; Being a Second Wonder-Book 1853

Other Major Works

Fanshawe: A Tale (novel) 1828
The Scarlet Letter: A Romance (novel) 1850
The House of the Seven Gables, A Romance (novel) 1851
The Blithedale Romance (novel) 1852
The Marble Faun; or, The Romance of Monte Beni (novel) 1860; published in England as *Transformation; or, The Romance of Monte Beni,* 1860
Our Old Home (essays) 1863
Passages from the American Notebooks of Nathaniel Hawthorne (journal) 1868
Passages from the English Notebooks of Nathaniel Hawthorne (journal) 1870
Passages from the French and Italian Notebooks of Nathaniel Hawthorne (journal) 1872
Septimius Felton; or, The Elixir of Life (unfinished novel) 1872
Doctor Grimshawe's Secret: A Romance (unfinished novel) 1883

CRITICISM

Karl P. Wentersdorf (essay date 1963)

SOURCE: Wentersdorf, Karl P. "The Genesis of Hawthorne's 'The Birthmark.'" *Jahrbuch für Amerikastudien* 8 (1963): 171-86.

[*In the following essay, Wentersdorf investigates possible sources—including scientific writings, works by William Shakespeare, and events in Hawthorne's life—on which Hawthorne may have drawn to write "The Birthmark."*]

In the spring of 1838, Hawthorne met and fell in love with Sophia Peabody. Though she refused to consider marriage for the time being in view of her indifferent state of health, they were secretly engaged by the beginning of 1839, and Hawthorne began making plans for the future. He obtained political employment for a while, and then the Brook Farm episode intervened; neither experience was congenial to his personality or conducive to literary work, much less to good work. In the meantime, Sophia had recovered completely and there was no reason for further delay; they were married in July 1842 and went to live at the Old Manse in Concord. Hawthorne's life there during the next three years seemed like an extended honeymoon: as he confided to his journal on August 5, 1842, "Happiness has no succession of events, because it is a part of eternity; and we have been living in eternity, ever since we came to live at this old Manse."[1] Eight months later, he was still writing in the same vein: "The longer we live together—the deeper we penetrate into one another, and become mutually intertwined—the happier we are."[2]

It is hardly surprising that he produced some of his best work during that period. "As to the daily course of our life," he recorded on March 31, 1843, "I have written with pretty commendable diligence, averaging from two to four hours a day; and the result is seen in various magazines."[3] The work of these idyllic months clearly bears the stamp of his new-found happiness, and on few tales is it more deeply impressed than on **"The Birthmark,"** the story of a scientist who endeavors to remove the one physical imperfection in the beautiful young wife he dearly loves and in doing so destroys her. It was written in the winter of 1842-43, first published in *The Pioneer* in March 1843, and reprinted in *Mosses from an Old Manse* (1846).[4]

II

Source-hunting is not always a satisfying tool of literary criticism, inasmuch as the determination of an author's sources may raise more questions than it answers. Frequently, however, it does explain his intentions, clarifying points that might otherwise remain obscure; and where it is a question of his better work, it almost always throws valuable light on the working of his mind and the nature of his art. It is from these standpoints that it is instructive to consider the origin and development of **"The Birthmark."**

The idea for the story is found embryonically in an entry which Hawthorne made in his notebook in 1837: "A person to be possessed of something as perfect as mortal man has a right to demand; he tries to make it better and ruins it entirely."[5] This laconic note was written before he had become acquainted with Sophia. When the idea again occurred to him as a suitable theme for fictional treatment, in 1840, it had already undergone transformation through the experience of love: "A person to be the death of his beloved in trying to raise her

to more than mortal perfection, yet this should be a comfort to him for having aimed so highly and so holily."[6]

Hawthorne still needed ideas for a setting, and these were not forthcoming until 1842. In the summer of that year, following his withdrawal from Brook Farm and subsequent marriage, he resumed his interrupted reading and notemaking. Among the books to which his catholic tastes led him was a scientific work by the physiologist Combe, and one passage was of sufficient interest to warrant summarizing in the notebook: "The case quoted in Combe's *Physiology,* from Pinel, of a young man of great talents and profound knowledge of chemistry, who had in view some new discovery of importance. In order to put his mind into the highest possible activity, he shut himself up, for several successive days, and used various methods of excitement; he had a singing girl with him; he drank spirits; smelled penetrating odors, sprinkled cologne-water round the room, & c. & c. Eight days thus passed, when he was seized with a fit of frenzy, which terminated in mania."[7] This story of a young chemist whose experiments with a new and important discovery ended in disaster evidently recalled to Hawthorne's mind the idea about a person trying to raise his beloved "to more than mortal perfection" and killing her in the process. He realized the possibilities inherent in a combination of the two themes: the scientist to be a person of great knowledge and ability; the "new discovery" to be the means by which he hoped to rid his beloved of an imperfection; the experiment to be conducted in seclusion "for several successive days" and with the use of "various methods of excitement"; the proceedings to move the scientist to a state of frenzied exaltation and to terminate not (as in Combe's case) in mania but in a profound and sadder wisdom.

Yet the conception of a theme was still only the beginning of the creative act: it had to undergo a period of gestation before Hawthorne was ready to deliver it to the world.[8] And so he dropped it into what Henry James succinctly describes as "the deep well of unconscious cerebration,"[9] waiting patiently for the flash of inspiration which, in view of the congeniality of the theme to his mind, could hardly be long in coming.

III

During the process of maturing, the theme did not remain unchanged. "Put an idea into your intelligence," wrote Oliver Wendell Holmes, "and leave it there an hour, a day, a year, without ever having occasion to refer to it. When, at last, you return to it, you do not find it as it was when acquired. It has domiciliated itself, so to speak,—become at home,—entered into relations with your other thoughts, and integrated itself with the whole fabric of the mind."[10] In the case of **"The Birthmark,"** the theme remained in the matrix of Hawthorne's imagination for a period of several months, and the shape in which it finally emerged illustrates the validity of the Autocrat's observation.

The nature of the transformation is exemplified, in the first place, by the use which Hawthorne was ultimately to make of the stimuli mentioned by Combe. In the apartment where Hawthorne's hero conducted the experiment, there were "perfumed lamps" to provide "an atmosphere of penetrating fragrance"; and perfume from a "small vial," thrown into the air, "filled the room with piercing and invigorating delight."[11] The singing girl was not a necessary element because of the participation of the experimenter's beloved wife; furthermore, Hawthorne must have felt that the "drinking of spirits" as a means of stimulation would be unsuitable in a tale about a man who was to be shown as having "aimed so highly and so holily." But the two ideas nevertheless remained dormant in the recesses of his mind; and when he finally came to write the story, they rose to the surface of his consciousness in an artistically fused and sublimated form at the point where the scientist asks his wife to sing: "So she poured out the liquid music of her voice to quench the thirst of his spirit. He then took his leave with a boyish exuberance of gayety. . . ."

Even more typical of Hawthorne's methods is his use of a mysteriously concocted potion as the means of removing the wife's imperfection. The 'magic potion' theme is as old as literature itself, and it would be idle to speculate on the immediate source of the motif as it appears in **"The Birthmark."** Yet the choice of a nostrum as the "new discovery" is by no means accidental. Hawthorne was fascinated throughout his life by the idea of decoctions with supernatural properties: the motif occurs again and again in his works, centrally and incidentally, from the early tales right up to the fragmentary romances on which he was working just before his death, until at last—as one of Hawthorne's biographers remarks—the elixir theme "becomes an allegory in which he himself has a role."[12]

It is in certain facets of the character of the scientist in **"The Birthmark"** that one finds perhaps the most telling evidence of the imprint made by Hawthorne's personality on the chosen theme. Superficially, at least, Aylmer represents the type of investigator who was attempting to discover "the secret of creative force," and for whom the field of science was the only religion. There can be no doubt that Hawthorne strongly deprecated the tendency to deify the scientist striving for "ultimate control over nature."[13] Paradoxically enough, however, his portrait of Aylmer—a man who makes such an attempt and fails—contains some reflections of his own character. As Hawthorne was well aware, the fruits of his penetrating self-knowledge went into the

making of many of his fictional characters, both good and evil.[14] He created a whole series of characters—Coverdale, Holgrave, and Kenyon are the prime examples of the group—who manifest a "combination of coldness and aloofness with much outward charm, brilliancy, sensitiveness to impressions, and intellectual curiosity or eagerness to discover the secret of life."[15] Now this coldness and curiosity, of which Hawthorne was fully and somewhat unhappily aware in himself,[16] are paramount among the qualities of the hero in **"The Birthmark"**: Aylmer is a sensitive and brilliant man of irreproachable moral character and lofty aims; but in his coldly scientific quest for perfection, he overlooks the claims of humanity and so destroys the very being whom he had hoped to perfect.[17] "Perhaps every man of genius in whatever sphere," wrote Hawthorne in the story, "might recognize the image of his own experience in Aylmer's journal." There is certainly a partial image of Hawthorne in the scientist—not by any means a portrait, but a reflection of some of his essential traits.

IV

While in the deep well of Hawthorne's subconscious mind, the outline for his tale underwent changes that were conditioned not merely by his own temperament and predilections but also by contact with ideas gleaned from the writings of others. The mind of the literary artist is crammed with words, images, and scraps of dialogue retained in the subconscious; there, original ideas coalesce with unwittingly memorized fragments and enter, transmuted, into the flow of conscious thought at the moment of composition. The wider a writer's reading has been, the more the well of memory is likely to hold; and the extant list of books Hawthorne borrowed from the Salem Athenaeum alone is very suggestive as to the extent of his reading.[18] His work might therefore be expected to reveal evidence of a great variety of sources.

To state that Hawthorne did unconsciously assimilate and even at times consciously exploit fragments memorized or copied from the many books he had read is not to detract either from the quality of his art or from the honesty of his literary methods; in this respect, his creative process was no different from that of other great imaginative writers. Some scholars, it is true, believe that Hawthorne's mind did not work in this manner, and that he derived little from the books of others "apart from his beloved Bunyan, from Milton, or from Spenser."[19] Even Austin Warren, who draws attention to the extent of his reading "in both older literatures and contemporary publications," nevertheless asserts that "when he sat down to write, he was—literally and metaphorically—in a bare room populated only by the creatures of his imagination."[20] It is difficult to agree with this view: it may still be, as Arlin Turner once stated, that "we have as yet learned little about his literary borrowings,"[21] but this statement is less an acknowledgment that there is little or nothing to be learned than a tribute to the subtlety of Hawthorne's art and to the thoroughness with which ideas from sources were assimilated to the cast of his own mind. The point is underlined by Randall Stewart in an examination of Hawthorne's debt to *The Faerie Queene*: "Since he was no learned plagiary of other writers, the student of Hawthorne must not expect, in any obvious way, to track him in their snow. Shadowy traces of Hawthorne's reading, however, may be found in his works," and these traces "may serve to emphasize and illuminate some of his characteristic interests and methods."[22]

Modern research has drawn attention to many of Hawthorne's sources.[23] His earliest and most enduring allegiance was to the literature of the sixteenth and seventeenth centuries; and the strongest influence, except perhaps that of the two great allegorists, Spenser and Bunyan, came from Shakespeare. "As soon as he could read with ease," wrote his sister Elizabeth, "we began to read Shakespeare, which perhaps we should not have done if books of more entertainment had been as plentiful as they are now."[24] Hawthorne apparently found the plays somewhat more entertaining than his sister did, since he returned to them repeatedly in later years. Interestingly enough, the period of greatest concentration on Shakespeare seems to have been the three happy years at the Old Manse. "No one hunts us out in the evening," wrote Sophia Hawthorne to a friend on December 30, 1842. "Then Mr. Hawthorne reads to me. At present, we can only get along with the old English writers, and we find that they are the hive from which all modern honey is stolen. They are thick-set with thought, instead of one thought serving for a whole book. Shakespeare is preëminent. . . ."[25] During the following winter, 1843-44, Hawthorne was again reading Shakespeare aloud to his wife; in a letter of December 1843 to her mother, Sophia specifically mentions *The Tempest, The Two Gentlemen of Verona*, and *Love's Labour's Lost*.[26] And to another correspondent, Sophia wrote: "We have passed the happiest winter, the long evenings lifted out of the common sphere by the magic of Shakespeare. Mr. Hawthorne read aloud to me all the plays. And you must know how he reads, before you can have any idea what it is. I can truly say that I never comprehended Shakespeare before; and my husband was pleased to declare that he never himself understood him so well, though he has pored over the plays all his life."[27]

Hawthorne, then, had not only studied Shakespeare all his life but had developed an enthusiasm which made it a delight to read the plays aloud. Through Sophia's eyes, one catches glimpses of another Hawthorne, different from the reticent, unemotional man known to the world as a listener rather than a talker. During those long winter evenings in the lamp-lit study, while Sophia sat near him and sewed, he shed the shyness which sometimes made him almost tongue-tied in the presence of others, entering through the Shakespearean cosmos into that communion with humanity which the sensitiveness and aloofness of his nature prevented him from achieving with his own outer world, and enjoying the catharsis which only one who was himself a poet at heart could fully experience.

Critics have not always done justice to the fundamentally poetic aspect of Hawthorne's character,[28] yet it was this that made him so receptive artistically to the work of Shakespeare. The influence exerted by the great Elizabethan on the nineteenth-century American can be traced in his diction, in his descriptive passages, and occasionally in his characterization. But it was primarily Shakespeare's attitude toward the problem of good and evil that impressed itself on Hawthorne's receptive mind: the same all-embracing sympathy with humanity which finds its noblest expression in the inner conflicts of the tragedies manifests itself in Hawthorne's writings in his preoccupation with the duality of human nature. Moreover, even the allegorical element in his work, at its subtlest, is less in the manner of his obvious models than in that of Shakespeare.[29] It is hardly surprising to find one critic arguing that "Hawthorne can have gone to school with no one but Shakespeare for his inspiration and model."[30] The rebellious Puritan was in fact something of a link between the past and the future: he was the last of the allegorists in the Puritan tradition and the father of the psychological novel; and in his attempt to create an idiom "at once poetic and psychological," a modern but poetically inspired medium for the truth of the human heart, "who besides Shakespeare could have helped him?"[31]

V

There can be little doubt as to the aspects of Shakespeare's work that fascinated Hawthorne most. "Shakespeare," he wrote, "has surface beneath surface, to an immeasurable depth, adapted to the plummet-line of every reader; his works present many phases of truth, each with scope large enough to fill a contemplative mind. Whatever you seek in him you will surely discover, provided you seek truth. There is no exhausting the various interpretation of his symbols."[32] This interest in Shakespeare's style is reflected, as might have been expected, in the work done at the Old Manse. In **"The New Adam and Eve,"** which Hawthorne wrote in the fall of 1842, there are palpable echoes of King Lear's denunciation of hypocrisy; **"Earth's Holocaust,"** written in November or December 1843, contains parallels of thought and theme to *Measure for Measure*.[33] But the influence of Shakespeare is most obvious in **"The Birthmark,"** which falls chronologically between the two tales just mentioned.

There is nothing in Hawthorne's notebooks to indicate when or how he arrived at the idea of endowing the heroine of his tale with a birthmark as the physical imperfection which her scientist-husband was to attempt to remove, but there are grounds for thinking that the motif came from one of Shakespeare's plays. As a means of recognizing long-lost children, the birthmark is, of course, a common element in the older literatures; one finds it, for example, in *The Faerie Queene,* where a "rosie marke" facilitates the recognition of Pastorall (VI. xii. 7 [8-9] and 15 [6]), and in *Cymbeline,* where a blood-colored mole establishes the identity of Prince Guiderius (V. v. 364-69). In both of these instances, with which Hawthorne must have been acquainted, the marks serve a utilitarian purpose and have no symbolic meaning, whereas in Hawthorne's tale the birthmark was to have a double significance: it was to be the cause of the heroine's death and at the same time to symbolize imperfection in human nature. In both of these aspects, it reflects another birthmark theme in Shakespeare, again in *Cymbeline.* It will be recalled that the lovely Imogen, "whiter than the sheets," whose lips are "rubies unparagon'd," has

> on her left breast
> A mole cinque-spotted, like the crimson drops
> I' the bottom of a cowslip.
>
> (II. ii. 15-18 and 37-39)[34]

The blemish proves almost as fatal to her as it does to Hawthorne's Georgiana, although for different reasons; and when Iachimo refers to "this stain upon her" (II. iv. 139), in adducing false evidence that she had been unfaithful to her husband, the mark becomes at that moment an unmistakable though deceptive symbol of moral imperfection.[35]

Hawthorne's elaboration of the idea illuminates the way in which his imagination functioned. In his tale the defect took the form of a reddish mark, shaped like a miniature hand: its presence symbolized "the fatal flaw of humanity"; by its shape, "the crimson hand expressed the ineludible gripe in which mortality clutches the highest and purest of earthly mould, degrading them into kindred with the lowest"; and its habit of varying distinctness, "now lost, now stealing forth again and glimmering to and fro with every pulse of emotion," typified the tendency of human failings to fluctuate in intensity.[36] Moreover, the "stain on the poor wife's cheek," standing out under the stress of emotion "like a bas-relief of ruby on the whitest marble," is interpreted by Aylmer as "the symbol of his wife's liability to sin, sorrow, decay, and death."

The parallels to *Cymbeline* are of various kinds. Imogen's crimson mole and Georgiana's crimson mark are both described as a stain, and both marks are explicitly referred to as symbols of sin; but in view of Georgi-

ana's purity, Aylmer's feeling of "trouble and horror" at the sight of the "frightful object" seems inadequately motivated and probably should be regarded as an echo of the horror which Posthumus experiences at the thought of his wife's alleged sin.[37] The occurrence of the color contrast *white-ruby* in the description of both heroines could be coincidental; but the Shakespearean expression "cinque-spotted" (II. ii. 38) may well have given Hawthorne a hint for the five-fingered shape of his birthmark, and the reference to Guiderius's mole as "the natural stamp" that was "wise nature's end" (V. v. 367-68) is reflected in Hawthorne's description of Georgiana's mark as "the fatal flaw of humanity which Nature, in one shape or another, stamps ineffaceably on all her productions."[38]

Furthermore, though the presence of the potion element in **"The Birthmark"** cannot be attributed to the potion incident in *Cymbeline,* Hawthorne's treatment of the element reveals some similarities to that of Shakespeare. In *Cymbeline,* the Queen commands a physician to bring her some "poisonous compounds" that will cause "a languishing death"; when he questions her intentions, she explains that after having learned to make perfumes, she now wishes to experiment with poisons in order to test their "several virtues and effects." (I. v. 7-23) The drug which the doctor supplies is not, however, one of the desired "strange lingering poisons" but merely a cordial that will "stupify and dull the sense awhile" (I. v. 33-43); and when Imogen takes it (IV. i. 38), she sinks into a deathlike trance from which she later awakens unharmed. In **"The Birthmark,"** Aylmer first shows his wife a vial containing a powerful perfume and then produces a flask of "precious poison": "by its aid," he explains, "I could apportion the lifetime of any mortal. . . . The strength of the dose would determine whether he were to linger out years, or drop dead in the midst of a breath." While he is concocting the draught that is to remove the blemish, Georgiana assures him that she would take even "a dose of poison" if he offered it to her; and when she drinks the elixir, she falls into a deep slumber from which she awakens only to die.

From these minor links between *Cymbeline* and **"The Birthmark,"** it is possible to sense something of the spell which Shakespeare's colorful romance cast over Hawthorne's mind, particularly the scene in Imogen's beautifully decorated bedchamber in the royal palace. It is in this room, "*hanged* with *tapestry* of silk and silver," that the innocently slumbering woman—whose very breathing "*perfumes* the chamber" while "the *flame* of the taper bows toward her"—is spied upon by the lustful Iachimo. (II. ii. 18-20; II. iv. 68-69)[39] Fragmentary memories of this scene provided Hawthorne with some of the details for his description of the sumptuous apartments where Aylmer installed his wife for the purpose of the experiment: the walls were "*hung* with gorgeous *curtains* . . . from the ceiling to the floor" and light was provided by "*perfumed* lamps emitting *flames* of various hue." Iachimo's desire to touch and kiss the sleeping Imogen (II. ii. 16-17) suggested to Hawthorne the idea that many an admirer of his heroine "would have risked life for the privilege of pressing his lips to the mysterious hand." And it was undoubtedly Shakespeare's reiteration of this theme, in Iachimo's false report that he had kissed Imogen's mole as being "worthy the pressing" (II. iv. 134-37), which prompted Hawthorne to write the incident in which Aylmer, likewise watching the sleeping Georgiana, suddenly yielded to a "strange and unaccountable impulse" and "pressed" the birthmark with his lips.[40]

VI

Fascinated though he was by the birthmark theme in *Cymbeline*, Hawthorne did not find there the inspiration he needed to transform the already conceived outline into a tale; that inspiration was to come from another Shakespearean play. If Combe's *Physiology* had yielded an appropriate setting for **"The Birthmark,"** and Shakespeare's *Cymbeline* the basic symbol together with some descriptive details, it was *The Tempest* which provided Hawthorne with an allegorical foundation and with valuable material for the main characters.

It is no wonder that he was attracted to and influenced by *The Tempest*: of all Shakespeare's works, this is the most clearly allegorical and therefore the one most nearly in tune with Hawthorne's way of thinking and literary method. In his writings, Hawthorne alludes more frequently to *The Tempest* than to any other Shakespearean work, and one passage in particular strongly affected his imagination. There are good reasons why he should have been inspired by the play at precisely this time: it contains one of the most idealistic romances in the Shakespearean canon, that of Ferdinand and Miranda. No misunderstandings or partings mar the flowering of their love for each other; not a discordant note spoils the harmony of their idyllic engagement. Hawthorne must have felt unusually responsive during the late fall of 1842 to the romantic story of Ferdinand's courtship, and there can be no doubt that this was one of his favorites among the plays that he read aloud to Sophia. Did he not look upon the Old Manse as a modern Paradise, and on himself and his bride as a new Adam and Eve?[41] And did he not feel the "lonely island" with its "pretty Miranda" to be likewise, as the notebooks show, a symbol of Paradise?[42] In the treatment of the deep love between Aylmer and Georgiana, therefore, he draws both on his own experiences[43] and on *The Tempest*: just as Ferdinand tells Miranda, the "top of admiration," that she is "perfect and . . . peerless" (III. i. 38, 47), so Aylmer, gazing with "fervid admiration" on his beloved, assures Georgiana that she will "soon be all perfect"; and when she dies, she is indeed the "perfect woman".

There is, however, more to Shakespeare's romance than the love story. *The Tempest* is also an allegory on the eternal conflict between the spiritual and the sensual in humanity. Prospero, a man of science and reason, personifies intellectuality; his servant Caliban, a creature of brute ignorance and rank desire, typifies animality. They are paralleled in **"The Birthmark"** by Aylmer and Aminadab. Basically, Aylmer is the traditional scientific figure of romantic fiction, with his books, experiments, and ambitions. But he is much more than a New England version of the Gothic scientist (as was Hawthorne's Doctor Heidegger): Aylmer and, above all, his laboratory assistant are endowed with traits that link them unmistakably with Prospero and Caliban. Aminadab, Hawthorne states, "seemed to represent man's physical nature," whereas Aylmer with his intellectuality was "no less apt a type of the spiritual element." Some critics have commented briefly on this contrast in the characterization of the two men as reminiscent of *The Tempest*[44]; but the Shakespearean echoes in **"The Birthmark"** are more than just vaguely suggestive of one pair of characters in Shakespeare's play. The pervasive influence of *The Tempest* in the tale shows that Hawthorne had assimilated many ideas from his favorite drama and was exploiting them to an unusual degree.

Prospero, Duke of Milan, a man "reputed / In dignity, and for the liberal arts / Without a parallel," neglects worldly ends in order to concentrate on his "secret studies." (I. ii. 72-77) Exiled by his evil brother, he is compelled to spend many years on a lonely island, where he continues his occult studies and activities. With the aid of his book of magic, he is able to put his daughter to sleep (I. ii. 186),[45] to immobilize his enemies by drawing them into a charmed circle (V. i. 58, S. D. [stage direction]; see also I. ii. 463, S. D.), and to conjure up a masque of spirits for the entertainment of Ferdinand and Miranda (IV. i. 59, 148-50). Nor is Prospero's ability restricted to such elementary manifestations of the magician's art: he has at his command the forces of nature, from the winds, thunder, and lightning of the skies to the underground causes of earthquakes; and his power extends even into the world of the hereafter, for at the command of his potent art graves have opened, and their occupants have risen from the dead. (V. i. 41-50)

Aylmer is likewise devoted to the scientific study of nature's secrets, "an eminent proficient in every branch of natural philosophy" and famous for "discoveries in the elemental powers of Nature that had roused the admiration of all the learned societies in Europe." Whether or not he possesses "faith in man's ultimate control over Nature" is a question that Hawthorne leaves unanswered.[46] Certainly he has not only investigated the arcana of nature, from the highest clouds to the deepest mines, but also "studied the wonders of the human frame, and attempted to fathom the very process by which nature assimilates all her precious influences from earth and air, and from the spiritual world, to create and foster man, her masterpiece." His laboratory is full of old tomes, the most engrossing being a folio in which he has "recorded every experiment of his scientific career," a book which is "rich with achievements that had won renown for its author" and which constitutes both a history and an emblem of his ambitious and imaginative life. In order to distract Georgiana's mind "from the burden of things," he demonstrates optical phenomena which create the illusion that he "possessed sway over the spiritual world." But for all his modern science, there is something of the medieval magician about Aylmer: confident in his insight into the supernatural, he feels that "he could draw a magic circle round Georgiana within which no evil might intrude." He tells her that "it was altogether within the limits of possibility" to discover the philosopher's stone, and he more than intimates his ability to concoct the elixir vitae.

The protagonists of the play and the tale have much in common. Both are eminent scientists of integrity, international repute, and deep knowledge. Both have investigated the mysteries of the elements, and both lay claim to powers over life and death. In each case, the intensive studies are connected with a vital book: Prospero's volume, the source of his magic powers, develops—in typical example of Hawthornesque elaboration—into the ponderous folio which is at once the record and the symbol of Aylmer's scientific powers. Even Prospero's ability to place friend or foe within a charmed circle is reflected in Aylmer's somewhat unexpected belief that he could shield his wife from harm in the same manner.

The resemblance between Caliban and Aminadab is equally striking. Caliban the "man-monster" is a "freckled whelp, hag-born, not honour'd with / A human shape." (I. ii. 283-84, III. i. 14) Fathered by the Devil himself, the deformed creature could only "gabble like / A thing most brutish," until Prospero taught him human speech and trained him to perform such menial duties as carrying logs. (I. ii. 311-13, 319-20, 355-58) Though possessing intelligence, he has no understanding of virtue (I. ii. 351-53), and not all the careful instruction he has received has availed to reform his evil nature.[47] "Earth" and "filth" are appropriate epithets for "the beast Caliban" (I. ii. 314, 346; IV. i. 140), because he responds to humane treatment with an attempt to violate Miranda's honor; and when Prospero reminds him of the attempted crime and its punishment, he merely chuckles and wishes that he had succeeded. (I. ii. 344-51) This "born devil" with ugly body and cankered mind, a "mis-shapen knave" and "thing of darkness" (IV. i. 188-92; V. i. 268, 275), thus personifies the Aristotelian concept of bestiality in human nature and symbolizes gross sensuality.

The very appearance of Aminadab recalls the grotesque figure of Caliban, since he is described by Hawthorne as "a man of low stature but bulky frame, with shaggy hair hanging about his visage." He is Aylmer's underworker and tends the scientist's hot and sooty furnace, being "admirably fitted for that office by his great mechanical readiness." With his vast strength, smoky aspect, and "indescribable earthiness," he is the veritable embodiment of "man's physical nature." His "harsh, uncouth, misshapen tones" are "more like the grunt or growl of a brute than human speech." Though he is not called upon for advice, he expresses the muttered opinion that he would not part with the birthmark if Georgiana were his wife. At the climax of the experiment, when Aylmer draws back the curtain, permitting daylight to fall on Georgiana's face, Aminadab emits a "gross, hoarse chuckle," his customary expression of delight. And when the experiment terminates in disaster, the "clod" or "earthly mass" (as his master calls him) is perversely pleased, and his "hoarse, chuckling laugh" is heard again. He is the scientist's "base, demonic alter ego,"[48] not merely in the sense of a confidential assistant, but also as the symbolic projection of the sensual self that rejoices when the spiritual faculties fail to achieve perfection.

The servants in both works, then, are ugly, stunted in growth, and of great strength; both are well-suited to the offices they have to perform, both spring to carry out the master's commands, and both are the objects of angry and contemptuous outbursts. Both are described as "earth," in order to emphasize the predominance of the physical in their nature. Caliban is capable only of gabbling "like / A thing most brutish" before he is taught to speak, and Aminadab's talk is "more like the grunt or growl of a brute than human speech." The description of the laboratory assistant's tones as "misshapen" might seem surprising, were the epithet not recognizable as a fragment from one of Prospero's comments on his servant. Of course, the element of unrestrained animality in Caliban's make-up inevitably underwent a transformation in Hawthorne's mind, in the same way that certain details in Combe's account of the experimenting chemist were sublimated; the offense of which Caliban was guilty was completely suppressed, but there may be muted hints of his sensuality in Aminadab's muttered wish that Georgiana were his wife, in Aylmer's desire to protect her from possible harm, and in the gross chuckle with which Aminadab reacts when the daylight falls on Georgiana's face.[49]

Finally, Hawthorne's debt to *The Tempest* is such that even the milieu of his tale reflects sundry details of Shakespeare's setting. The description of Aylmer's rooms as a scene that "looked like enchantment" recalls the enchanted island of Prospero: the apartment with its "gorgeous" furnishings and its air of "grandeur and grace" moves Georgiana to think that "it might be a pavilion among the clouds," in an evident reflection of Prospero's vision of "cloud-capp'd towers" and "gorgeous palaces" (IV. i. 152). The echo was not fortuitous: the famous speech with which Prospero concludes the revels was one of the Shakespearean passages that had deeply impressed Hawthorne, and more than once in his writings he uses phrases culled from it.[50] In view of the intimate way in which the development of **"The Birthmark"** was bound up with Hawthorne's memories of *The Tempest*, it was almost inevitable that other fragments from the "revels" speech would crop up among the descriptive passages of the tale. Only a few lines after the already mentioned echo in Georgiana's first reaction to her surroundings ("*gorgeous . . . pavilion . . . clouds*"), Hawthorne describes an experiment performed by the scientist with the object of relaxing her: "Aylmer now put into practice some of the light and *playful* secrets which science had taught him among its profounder lore. *Airy figures,* absolutely *bodiless* ideas, and *forms* of *unsubstantial beauty* came and *danced* before her, *imprinting* their momentary *footsteps* on beams of light. Though she had some indistinct idea of the method of these optical phenomena, still the *illusion* was almost perfect enough to warrant the belief that her husband possessed *sway* over the *spiritual world.*"[51] There are obvious reflections here of the scene in which Prospero entertains the lovers with a show of spirits performing a "*graceful dance*" (IV. i. 138 S. D.), urges Ferdinand to "be cheerful," and then adds:

> Our *revels* now are ended. These our actors,
> As I foretold you, were all *spirits* and
> Are melted into *air,* into thin *air:*
> And, like the baseless fabric of this *vision,*
> The *cloud*-capp'd towers, the *gorgeous palaces,*
> The solemn temples, the great *globe* itself,
> Yea, all which it inherit, shall dissolve
> And, like this *insubstantial pageant* faded,
> Leave not a rack behind. We are such stuff
> As dreams are made on, and our little life
> Is rounded with a sleep.
>
>   (IV. i. 148-58)

Some of the vocabular and conceptual elements in the account of Aylmer's experiment that are not found in the above lines derive from other Shakespearean passages—for example, from the lines in which Prospero renounces his powers of "command" (V. i. 48) over the spiritual world:

> Ye elves of hills, brooks, standing lakes, and groves;
> And ye that on the sands with *printless foot*
> Do *chase* the ebbing Neptune . . .
>
>   (V. i. 33-35)

The account of the experiment also echoes the memorable comment on the poetic process which Shakespeare wove into one of his early romantic plays:

> And as imagination *bodies* forth
> The *forms* of things unknown, the poet's pen

Turns them to *shapes,* and gives to *airy* nothing
A local habitation and a name.

>   (*A Mids. Night's Dream,* V. i. 14-17)

VII

In theme and diction, therefore, **"The Birthmark"** received its distinctive color through the merging of Hawthorne's original ideas with fragments from Shakespeare, primarily from *The Tempest.* Even the allegorical significance of Hawthorne's characters is partially Shakespearean, but there the resemblance between the two works ends. In Shakespeare's play, the conflict between spirituality and sensuality ends with the triumph of good over evil: Prospero vanquishes his foes and abandons his studies (V. i. 7-12, 56-57); Caliban vows to reform and "seek for grace" (V. i. 294-95). Not so in **"The Birthmark"**: there the studies culminate in the defeat of the man who typifies the "spiritual element."

The failure of Aylmer's attempts to raise his wife to a state of physical perfection symbolizes, at one level of meaning, the frequent defeat of the spirit in its eternal struggle with the sensual. At the moment when the scientist's triumph turns into tragedy, the hoarse laughter of his other self resounds through the laboratory, and Hawthorne comments sadly: "Thus ever does the gross fatality of earth exult in its invariable triumph over the immortal essence." At another level of meaning, the attitudes and experiments of Aylmer reflect the conflict between materialism and dualism, the tendency of many of Hawthorne's contemporaries to regard science as a substitute for religion[52] and to believe that the achievement of mortal perfection was merely a matter of time. But the vital meaning of the tale, the moral which impressed Melville as being "wonderfully fine,"[53] is expressed in the concluding words: "Yet, had Aylmer reached a profounder wisdom, he need not have flung away the happiness which would have woven his mortal life of the selfsame texture with the celestial. The momentary circumstance was too strong for him. He failed to look beyond the shadowy scope of time, and, living once for all in eternity, to find the perfect future in the present." Even while striving after perfection in the moral and physical spheres, man must accept imperfection as one of the fundamental aspects of life, beyond the power even of the scientist to remove completely. Aylmer's tragedy is that he lacks the wisdom and humility to admit and accept this limitation.

The moral is doubly interesting because it reveals yet another way in which Hawthorne's personal situation at the time of writing **"The Birthmark"** is reflected, though inversely, in the tragic love of Aylmer and Georgiana. Their story ends in disaster because the scientist "failed to look beyond the shadowy scope of time, and, *living once for all in eternity,* to find the perfect future in the present." Hawthorne, as an already quoted journal entry shows, felt that he himself had found that perfect future: "We have been *living in eternity,* ever since we came to live at this old Manse." This feeling gives **"The Birthmark,"** in spite of its tragic ending, an undertone of sustained if subdued exaltation that is rare in Hawthorne's tales and novels, and that helps to endow the story with its unique appeal.

Notes

1. *The American Notebooks by Nathaniel Hawthorne,* ed. Randall Stewart (New Haven, 1932), p. 145. This work is hereafter cited as *Notebooks.*

2. *Notebooks,* p. 173.

3. *Ibid.,* p. 173.

4. On its place in the chronology of Hawthorne's works, see Elizabeth L. Chandler, "A Study of the Sources of the Tales and Romances Written by Nathaniel Hawthorne Before 1853," *Smith College Studies in Modern Languages,* VII, no. 4 (1926), 55-63.

5. *Notebooks,* p. xxv.

6. *Ibid.,* p. xxv.

7. *Ibid.,* p. 97. Hawthorne's source was Andrew Combe's *Principles of Physiology* (New York, 1836), pp. 233-34.

8. As Randall Stewart has calculated, the period that elapsed between the recording of a basic idea in Hawthorne's notebooks and the publication of a tale based on it averages almost six years. See *Notebooks,* p. xci.

9. Preface to *The American,* first published in vol. II of the New York Edition (1907), reprinted in *The Art of the Novel: Critical Prefaces by Henry James* (New York, 1934), p. 23.

10. *The Autocrat of the Breakfast Table* (1858) in *The Complete Works of Oliver Wendell Holmes* (Riverside Edition: Boston, 1891), I, 134.

11. Citations from Hawthorne's "The Birthmark" in this article are from the Standard Library Edition of *The Works of Nathaniel Hawthorne* (Riverside Press: Boston, 1882), II, 47-69. This edition is hereafter cited as *Works.*

12. Mark Van Doren, *Nathaniel Hawthorne* (New York, 1949), p. 260. On the 'elixir of life' theme in Hawthorne's works, see Richard H. Fogle, *Hawthorne's Fiction* (Norman, 1952), pp. 198-206.

13. It has been argued plausibly by Robert B. Heilman, "Hawthorne's 'The Birthmark': Science as Religion," *South Atlantic Quarterly,* XLVIII (1949), pp. 575-583, that the process of deification is underscored by the all-pervasive use of religious imagery. "The language pattern of the story indicates," he points out (p. 577), "that in the religion of science Aylmer is less priest than god." Roy R. Male, *Hawthorne's Tragic Vision* (Austin, 1957), pp. 81-82, agrees with Heilman: "Aylmer becomes virtually the god of the new religion of science. He has subverted the old creed; Aminadab, a High Priest in the Bible, has been transformed into his laboratory assistant."

14. Hawthorne did not believe in direct self-expression; indeed, in the Custom House essay, he deplored the practice of authors who "indulge themselves in such confidential depths of revelation as could fittingly be addressed, only and exclusively, to the one heart and mind of perfect sympathy" (*Works,* V, 17-18). In a letter to Horatio Bridge (*Works,* III, 385-86), he asserted that even in his prefaces, he had been "especially careful to make no disclosures respecting [himself] which the most indifferent observer might not have been acquainted with"; but while insisting that he had discussed "his external habits, his abode, his casual associates, and other matters entirely upon the surface," and that "these things hide the man instead of displaying him," he also added: "You must make quite another kind of inquest, and look through the whole range of his fictitious characters, good and evil, in order to detect any of his essential traits."

15. Amy L. Reed, "Self-Portraiture in the Work of Nathaniel Hawthorne," *Studies in Philology,* XXIII (1926), 48. Randall Stewart, *Notebooks,* pp. lxii-lxiii, disagrees with Miss Reed's view that "Hawthorne's young heroes and his mature villains are compounded of the same materials and that both are varieties of self-portraiture," but he nevertheless singles out three of Hawthorne's characters as being noteworthy for "their powers of penetrating observation and their aloofness" and adds that "these three characters—the artist in 'The Prophetic Pictures,' Coverdale, and Kenyon—are the closest approaches to self-portraiture in Hawthorne's fiction."

16. For an interesting account of Hawthorne's self-knowledge, his fear of coldness, and his "hatred" of his own intellectual curiosity, see Mark Van Doren, pp. 56-58.

17. William B. Stein, *Hawthorne's Faust: A Study of the Devil Archetype* (Gainesville, 1953), pp. 91-92, regards Aylmer as a Faustian character with two conflicting loves—one for his scientific studies, the other for his wife. As Stein demonstrates (*ibid.,* pp. 23-34), Hawthorne was undoubtedly acquainted with the Faust myth in its Goethean form, and several of his characters are torn by the same

kind of inner conflict that troubles Goethe's hero. There is, however, little in "The Birthmark" to justify the view that such a struggle was going on in Aylmer's breast: from the very beginning, he seems to experience merely abhorrence at the thought of his wife's blemish rather than any doubt as to the desirability or rectitude of his desire to remove it.

18. See "Books Read by Nathaniel Hawthorne, 1828-1850. From the 'Charge Books' of the Salem Athenaeum," *The Essex Institute Historical Collections*, LXVIII (1932), 65-87. An excellent summary of Hawthorne's reading is given by Mark Van Doren, pp. 31-35.

19. Stanley T. Williams, "Nathaniel Hawthorne," chapter 27 in *Literary History of the United States*, ed. Robert E. Spiller *et al.* (New York, 1946; revised one-volume edition, 1953), p. 420.

20. Austin Warren, "Hawthorne's Reading," *New England Quarterly*, VIII (1935), 482.

21. Arlin Turner, "Hawthorne's Literary Borrowings," *PMLA*, LI (1936), 543.

22. Randall Stewart, "Hawthorne and *The Faerie Queene*," *Philological Quarterly*, XII (1933), 196-206.

23. Many of Hawthorne's sources are referred to in the notes to *Notebooks*. See also Chandler (footnote 4), pp. 1-64; Arlin Turner (footnote 21), pp. 543-562; Arlin Turner, "Hawthorne's Methods of Using His Source Materials," *Studies for William A. Read* (Baton Rouge, 1940), pp. 303-304; and Frank Davidson, "Hawthorne's Hive of Honey," *Modern Language Notes*, LXI (1946), 14-21.

24. Randall Stewart, "Recollections of Hawthorne by His Sister Elizabeth," *American Literature*, XVI (1944), 319.

25. Rose Hawthorne Lathrop, *Memories of Hawthorne* (Boston, 1897), p. 54.

26. *Ibid.*, pp. 66-67.

27. *Ibid.*, p. 75. This undated letter is printed between others dated August 20 and August 15, 1844.

28. A notable exception is Q. D. Leavis in her study of "Hawthorne as Poet," *Sewanee Review*, LIX (1951), 179-205 (Part I) and 426-458 (Part II).

29. See Leavis, *loc. cit.*, p. 181. The work of "the essential Hawthorne," says Leavis, "is not comparable with the productions of the eighteenth-century 'allegorical essayists' nor is it in the manner of Spenser, Milton, or Bunyan—whom of course it can be seen that he has not merely studied but assimilated."

30. *Ibid.*, p. 182.

31. *Ibid.*, p. 439.

32. "Recollections of a Gifted Woman," in *Our Old Home* (*Works*, VII, 131-32).

33. The relevant passages are quoted by Davidson (footnote 23), pp. 16-17.

34. Citations from Shakespeare's plays in this article are from *The Complete Works of Shakespeare*, ed. W. J. Craig (Oxford, 1930).

35. Heilman (footnote 13) comments (p. 579) that "Hawthorne could hardly have found a better symbol than the birthmark, which speaks of the imperfection born with man, with man as a race. Here is original sin in fine imaginative form."

36. The coming and going of color in the face of an agitated person is a common image-object in Shakespeare, as is pointed out by Dr. Caroline Spurgeon, *Shakespeare's Imagery* (Cambridge, 1935), pp. 58-63; and it may be that there are traces of this image in the fluctuating color of the birthmark. Hawthorne's notebooks contain, however, an entry about a gambler with a scar on his forehead which, at moments of excitement, would flush a deep red. (*Notebooks*, p. 102) What relation this passage bears to Georgiana's blemish is difficult to say, as the entry is undated; it was apparently made some time after the extract from Combe's *Physiology* in 1842 and shortly before another entry dated July 27, 1844. Presumably the anecdote of the gambler postdates "The Birthmark."

37. It would certainly be wrong to regard Aylmer's horror as anything more than a pale reflection of Posthumus's disgust; but it is noteworthy that in Shakespeare, the image of a mark stamped on the face or body frequently implies immorality. (See also footnote 39.)

38. Hawthorne may also have had in mind the well-known passage in *Hamlet*:

> So, oft it chances in particular men,
> That for some vicious mole of nature in them,
> As, in their birth . . . ,
> Carrying, I say, the stamp of one defect,
> Being nature's livery or fortune's star,
> Their virtues else, be they as pure as grace,
> As infinite as man may undergo,
> Shall in the general censure take corruption
> From that particular fault.

(I. iv. 23-36)

39. It is interesting to note that the same scene (*Cymbeline*, II. ii) called forth similar echoes in T. S. Eliot's *The Waste Land*, lines 77-106. Maynard Mack *et al.*, editors of *Modern Poetry*, vol. VII in

the "English Masterpieces" series (New York, 1950), p. 127, comment as follows in a footnote to lines 77f.: "The many reminiscences in Eliot's lines of Shakespeare's description of Imogen's room in *Cymbeline* suggests [sic] that to the atmosphere of love and lust invoked here the pretended 'rape' of Imogen is also relevant."

40. The symbol was destined to have another literary echo. Just as Imogen's almost fatal blemish was recalled during the writing of "The Birthmark," so Hawthorne's treatment of the motif came back to Melville's mind while he was writing the tragic story of the handsome sailor with the fatal stammer. In chapter 2 of *Billy Budd,* Melville alludes to "the beautiful woman in one of Hawthorne's minor tales," and in both works the flaw plays a vital role. The interest taken by Melville in "The Birthmark" and the reflection of Hawthorne's story in *Billy Budd* (written more than forty years after the publication of the tale) are discussed by F. Barron Freeman, *Melville's Billy Budd* (Cambridge, 1948), pp. 117-20.

41. Mark Van Doren, p. 118.

42. *Notebooks,* pp. 271-272.

43. See, for example, F. O. Matthiessen, *American Renaissance* (New York, 1941), p. 254: "it is hardly accidental that 'The Birthmark' . . . was one of the first tales composed by Hawthorne after his own marriage."

44. For instance, Randall Stewart, *Notebooks,* p. xlv: "In order to emphasize the purely ideal qualities in this character [Aylmer], Hawthorne, in a contrast reminiscent of *The Tempest,* has introduced the very mundane figure, Aminadab." See also Austin Warren, *Nathaniel Hawthorne: Representative Selections* (New York, 1934), p. 367: "Aminadab is a reminiscence of Caliban, and plays the same role relative to Aylmer that the brute bears as servant to Prospero in *The Tempest.*"

45. The Cambridge Edition of *The Tempest,* ed. Arthur Quiller-Couch and J. Dover Wilson (1921), adds at this point a specific stage direction: "He traces a magic circle on the grass."

46. According to Randall Stewart, *Nathaniel Hawthorne: A Biography* (New Haven, 1948), p. 249, "Aylmer confidently believed that the scientist 'would ascend from one step of powerful intelligence to another, until he should lay his hand on the secret of creative force and perhaps make new worlds for himself.'" What Hawthorne says, however, is that some of the "ardent votaries" of science believed this, and he then adds: "We know not whether Aylmer possessed this degree of faith in man's ultimate control over nature."

47. See John E. Hankins, "Caliban the Bestial Man," *PMLA,* LXII (1947), 793-801. As Hankins stresses (p. 798), Caliban is "the embodiment of Aristotle's bestial man. The dramatist has sought to realize in the flesh the philosopher's concept of a primitive savage who has not attained the level of humanity."

48. The phrase is used by Daniel G. Hoffman, *Form and Fable in American Fiction* (New York, 1961), p. 184: the scientific interests of Chillingworth link him "with the base, demonic alter ego of the alchemist Aylmer in 'The Birthmark'—a monster stained with soot."

49. Hawthorne's choice of the name *Aminadab* is puzzling. The fact that it was "often used by the English dramatists of the 18th century to designate a Quaker" (Clarence L. Barnhart, *The New Century Handbook of English Literature* [New York, 1956], p. 35) is hardly pertinent here. It is the name of more than one high priest mentioned in the Old Testament; and William R. Thompson, "Aminadab in Hawthorne's 'The Birthmark,'" *Modern Language Notes,* LXX (1955), 413-15, suggests that at the figurative level, Aminadab "typifies religion subverted to the ends of science," that he is "a symbol of early authority which is now discredited," and that he represents the type of the "contemptuously regarded" priest who no longer has any votaries; he is not by any means without compassion, but he must answer "to the beck and call of the imperious *new* man as personified by Aylmer." If Aylmer is indeed a god of science, then Aminadab might well be a subordinated high priest. But why did Hawthorne select this particular high-priestly name? Neither the meaning ('my people is princely') nor the little that is known about the Biblical Aminadabs (one was Aaron's father-in-law, another the head of a Levitical family) suggests that Hawthorne chose it for considerations such as may have led Melville to name the demonic captain in *Moby Dick* after King Ahab.—There is, incidentally, no clearly demonstrable source for the appellation *Caliban.* Shakespeare was reading a translation of Montaigne's essay *Of the Caniballes* at the time of writing *The Tempest* (see E. K. Chambers, *William Shakespeare* [Oxford, 1930], I, 494) and was much influenced by it in the creation of his "man-monster." It has therefore been argued that *Caliban* is an anagram of *canibal* (see, for instance, F. S. Boas' Introduction to the Arden Edition of *The Tempest* [1897], p. xxiv; and Hankins [footnote 47], p. 796). Did Hawthorne use *Aminadab* because it is an anagram of "bad *anima*" and could therefore suggest the evil spirit in man? There is ample testimony in the stories and the notebooks that Hawthorne was greatly interested in suggestive names,

and it may be significant that Miranda uses the expression "ill-spirit" in the sense of *bad soul* (*The Tempest*, I. ii. 454-56).

50. Randall Stewart draws attention (*Notebooks*, p. 325) to two such echoes: in the American notebooks, "the *great globe itself*"; in the English notebooks, *"leave not a wrack* [sic] *behind."*; A third occurs in a letter of 1837 to H. W. Longfellow: "I have seen so *little* of the *world*, that I have nothing but *thin air* to concoct my stories of, and it is not easy to give a *life*-like semblance to such shadowy *stuff*" (cited by Mark Van Doren, p. 62). All three echoes are, of course, from Prospero's vision speech (*The Tempest*, IV. i. 148-58).

51. The italics in this and the following quotations are the present writer's.

52. Heilman (footnote 13), p. 578, makes the point that Aylmer is confused and that "the language of the story defines his confusion very precisely—defines it as the mistaking of science for religion." Heilman adds (p. 582): "In the marriage of science and humanity we see the inevitably catastrophic interaction of a mechanical perfectionism . . ."

53. Matthiessen (footnote 43), pp. 253-54.

Richard Harter Fogle (essay date 1964)

SOURCE: Fogle, Richard Harter. "'The Birthmark.'" In *Hawthorne's Fiction: The Light and the Dark*, 1952. Revised and expanded edition, pp. 117-31. Norman: University of Oklahoma Press, 1964.

[*In the following essay, Fogle assesses Hawthorne's use of "light and dark"—his clarity of design and lucid language versus tragic complexity and black tonality of narrative—in "The Birthmark."*]

It is strange but natural that **"The Birthmark"** should combine an explicit moral with some of Hawthorne's densest ambiguities. If this sounds strange but unnatural, one may reflect that, in Coleridge's words, "Extremes meet"; that is, a strong impulse in one direction evokes an equally strong opposite impulse in reaction to it. Or it may be a question of Hawthorne's artistic judgment, which perceives a need for enriching bareness and abstraction with the compensations of complexity.

The moral is adumbrated at the beginning of the story and stated at the end. Aylmer, a dedicated scientist, marries the beautiful Georgiana, with consequent complications. "Such a union took place, and was attended with truly remarkable consequences and a deeply im-

pressive moral." Georgiana is physically perfect except for a birthmark on her cheek. Aylmer, a passionate perfectionist, tries to eradicate it; he succeeds, but as with Beatrice Rappaccini it is at the cost of Georgiana's life. The story concludes, "Yet, had Aylmer reached a profounder wisdom, he need not thus have flung away the happiness which would have woven his mortal life of the selfsame texture with the celestial. The momentary circumstance was too strong for him; he failed to look beyond the shadowy scope of time, and, living once for all in eternity, to find the perfect future in the past." The proposition is quite clear: Aylmer, to state the case moderately, has made a serious mistake.

Yet Hawthorne's attitude is so removed and imperturbable that nothing in the story can be taken simply; in **"The Birthmark"** he reaches his furthest range of disengagement. The point of view is so detached that his irony is frequently universalized and objectified into humor, and as in **"My Kinsman, Major Molineux"** the action is a consummate joke upon the principal actors. There is an airy levity, for instance, in the observation that Aylmer "had left his laboratory to the care of an assistant, cleared his fine countenance from the furnace smoke, washed the stain of acids from his fingers, and persuaded a beautiful woman to become his wife." Hawthorne's humor has been little investigated, it may be from its delicacy, and Anthony Trollope's penetrating comment on the humor of *The Scarlet Letter* has never been adequately pursued:

> But through all this intensity of suffering, through this blackness of narrative, there is ever running a vein of drollery. As Hawthorne himself says, "a lively sense of the humorous again stole in among the solemn phantoms of her thought." He is always laughing at something with his weird, mocking spirit. The very children when they see Hester in the streets are supposed to speak of her in this wise: "Behold, verily, there is the woman of the scarlet letter. Come, therefore, and let us fling mud at her." Of some religious book he says, "It must have been a work of vast ability in the somniferous school of literature." "We must not always talk in the market-place of what happens to us in the forest," says even the sad mother to her child. Through it all there is a touch of burlesque,—not as to the suffering of the sufferers, but as to the great question whether it signifies much in what way we suffer, whether by crushing sorrows or little stings. Who would not sooner be Prometheus than a yesterday's tipsy man with this morning's sick-headache? In this way Hawthorne seems to ridicule the very woes which he expends himself in depicting.

Trollope, in true nineteenth-century fashion, is puzzled and amused by Hawthorne's gloom, for which he sees little occasion in reality. Hawthorne's humor is therefore all the more piquant to him from the shock of finding it; and it is, one may add, omnipresent in his fiction. *The Scarlet Letter*, as Trollope sees, is the most interesting instance of his humor because of the intensity and lack of relief of the book in its total effect.

We have spoken of the detachment of Hawthorne's attitude. Humor, however, traditionally involves sympathy, and Hawthorne shows a great deal of sympathy for his hero Aylmer. As Cleanth Brooks and Robert Penn Warren have remarked in *Understanding Fiction,* "The author is sympathetic to him, and obviously sees in his ruinous experiment a certain nobility." Again it is a case of Coleridge's meeting of extremes. As I have used these terms, irony in Hawthorne is lifted and objectified into humor, since irony contains a certain animus that interferes with objectivity, while humor sees the whole steadily and to a degree affectionately. Hawthorne's attitude and "tone" are then subtly varied and complex, and nowhere are more so than in **"The Birthmark."**

Aylmer is shown to be wrong, no doubt of it; but Aylmer is given a remarkably good run for his money. If he hangs himself, Hawthorne gives him a very long rope. The author is more engaged in his Faustian quest for knowledge and his Romantic pursuit of infinite development than most critics have seen, since the keenest critics of the story have usually been anti-Romantic. That at the last he can disengage himself is the more notable because of his sympathy with Aylmer.

This stress between detachment and sympathy renders **"The Birthmark"** one of Hawthorne's most intellectually lively tales, and with its richness of texture one of his best. It comes close to Poe in searching out abnormal experience and phenomena for their own sakes, for the wonders of Aylmer's laboratory resemble the perverse music and art with which Roderick Usher surrounds himself. This element of wondrous perversity is worth examining at some length. Its presence in the story is supported by one of Hawthorne's sources for it, as recorded in his *American Notebooks* in 1842, the approximate date of the story (1843). He cites

> the case quoted in Combe's *Physiology* from Pinel, of a young man of great talents and profound knowledge of chemistry, who had in view some new discovery of importance. In order to put his mind into the highest possible activity, he shut himself up, for several successive days, and used various methods of excitement; he had a singing girl with him; he drank spirits; smelled penetrating odors, sprinkled cologne-water around the room & c & c. Eight days thus passed, when he was seized with a fit of frenzy, which terminated in a mania.

In **"The Birthmark"** the various stimuli act upon Georgiana, not Aylmer, who is in fact their source. They are a means both of amusing her and of preparing her mentally and physically for the change she must undergo. "Georgiana . . . found herself breathing an atmosphere of penetrating fragrance, the gentle potency of which had recalled her from her deathlike faintness. The scene around her looked like enchantment." Aylmer has converted the "smoky, dingy, sombre rooms" of his customary laboratory into chambers of fantasy, in which gorgeous curtains, "concealing all angles and straight lines, appeared to shut in the scene from infinite space. For aught Georgiana knew, it might be a pavilion among the clouds." Significantly Aylmer, excluding the natural sunlight "which would have interfered with his chemical processes," had supplied its place with perfumed lamps, emitting flames of various hue, but all uniting in a soft, impurpled radiance."

To sooth and distract Georgiana's mind, Aylmer calls upon his scientific skill to surround her with wonders. "Airy figures, absolutely bodiless ideas, and forms of unsubstantial beauty came and danced before her, imprinting their momentary footsteps on beams of light." The illusion of these "was almost perfect enough to warrant the belief that her husband possessed sway over the spiritual world." When she wishes to look out, "immediately, as if her thoughts were answered, the procession of external existence flitted across a screen." (Here one is inclined to suspect that Aylmer has invented television, and to wish him damned accordingly and forthwith. But there is an escape for him; his scenes are painted rather than photographed, imitations rather than copies of reality. "The scenery and the figures of actual life were perfectly represented, but with that bewitching, yet indescribable difference which always makes a picture, an image, or a shadow so much more attractive than the original.") Next Aylmer produces a flower of miraculously swift growth, and bids his wife pluck it. "But Georgiana had no sooner touched the flower than the whole plant suffered a blight, its leaves turning coalblack as if by the agency of fire. 'There was too powerful a stimulus,' said Aylmer thoughtfully."

Later he tries to take Georgiana's portrait "by a scientific process of his own invention," which involves "rays of light striking upon a polished plate of metal." The result is "blurred and indefinable; while the minute figure of a hand appeared where the cheek should have been." As the experiment goes on, he speaks to her of the elixir of life, which is within his option to perfect; shows her a small vial containing a perfume "capable of impregnating all the breezes that blow across a kingdom"; and finally exhibits to her "a gold-colored liquor" that is "the most precious poison that ever was concocted in this world," in a small crystal globe. During this time Georgiana begins "to conjecture that she was already subjected to certain physical influences, either breathed in with the fragrant air or taken with her food. She fancied likewise, but it might be altogether fancy, that there was a stirring up of her system—a strange, indefinite sensation creeping through her veins, and tingling, half painfully, half pleasurably, at her heart." Failing to eradicate the birthmark by all lesser methods, Aylmer finally concocts "a liquor colorless as water, but bright enough to be the draught of immortality." It turns out to be so indeed, since it eliminates first "the birthmark of mortality" and shortly afterward Georgiana herself—presumably to Aylmer's consternation, though this too remains ambiguous.

This account is perverse insofar as it explores extreme and unnatural experience for its own sake, as Poe explores the abnormal sensations of the hypersensitive Roderick Usher. The perversity of it shades off into the pleasure of aesthetic contemplation: the chambers, golden liquids, crystal globes, and the like, are presented to us as beautiful. Thus far Hawthorne indulges in a kind of Romanticism that should not be ignored in him. One must add, of course, a meaning and morality quite different from Poe's. Most obvious is the suggestion of illusion: everything that Aylmer has created is false and unnatural, like the gorgeous flowers of Rappaccini's garden. The light is artificial, the figures are shadows, the plant dies at the touch of reality, and the draught of immortality is the draught of death. The images all reflect Aylmer's spirituality, emphasized throughout the story; and this spirituality of his is spurious.

Under the beautiful illusion he has evoked is the grim bareness of his reality, which Georgiana at length penetrates in his laboratory.

> The first thing that struck her eye was the furnace, that hot and feverish worker, with the intense glow of its fire, which by the quantities of soot clustered above it seemed to have been burning for ages. There was a distilling apparatus in full operation. Around the room were retorts, tubes, cylinders, crucibles, and other apparatus of chemical research. An electrical machine stood ready for immediate use. The atmosphere felt oppressively close, and was tainted with gaseous odors which had been tormented forth by the processes of science. The severe and homely simplicity of the apartment, with its naked walls and brick pavement, looked strange, accustomed as Georgiana had become to the fantastic elegance of her boudoir.

This scene evokes, like Melville's chapter on "The Whiteness of the Whale," John Locke's famous doctrine of secondary attributes in the perception, in which we ourselves attribute color, form, and life itself to a world intrinsically blank and unknowable. The doctrine underlies Addison's *Spectator* essays on "The Pleasures of Imagination," and the fact is relevant, for Locke's theory makes Addison's "imagination" a lovely and charming illusion, and the world a painted charnel house. Now, Aylmer is figuratively an artist and a practitioner of the imagination, who has created an artistic world for his beloved to dwell in; but it is false.

Something remains to be said of the reality, as also of what has so far been treated as illusion. Our first impression of the laboratory is simply its matter-of-fact bareness. Yet the furnace has a diabolic air, like the lime-kiln of **"Ethan Brand,"** and the circumstance that

its sootiness makes it seem "to have been burning for ages" reminds us of the blackened prison of *The Scarlet Letter,* the emblem of time, sin, and death. More favorably, too, it is the furnace of the human heart, like Robert Danforth's smithy, or the huge central chimney that is the heart of the house of the seven gables. Its reality is more than a bare negation.

There is also another side to be presented of Aylmer's creativity. The chambers and the laboratory are the image of his mind and moral being, and here lies a deep ambiguity. What if artistic illusion be awarded a reality of its own? Aylmer is an idealist in pursuit of the infinite, and the scene he has created appears to be shut in "from infinite space." "For aught Georgiana knew, it might be a pavilion among the clouds." To say too suddenly that his illusion is delusion is to ignore an important and an evident portion of Hawthorne's sensibility, which delights like Shelley's in paradoxes of airy form and insubstantial solidity. "Its wheels are solid clouds," says Shelley (*Prometheus Unbound*) of his Earth-Child's chariot, and Hawthorne would have approved the figure. Georgiana's chambers suggest his **"Hall of Fantasy,"** which admits "the light of heaven only through stained and pictured glass, thus filling the hall with many-colored radiance . . . so that its inmates breathe, as it were, a visionary atmosphere. . . ." This hall substitutes like the chambers of Georgiana, a "purple atmosphere for unsophisticated sunshine." It is not to be lived in always or by everyone, but it is the appropriate residence of the artist. Of it is remarked on the one hand that "the fantasies of one day are the deepest realities of a future one," and on the other that "The white sunshine of actual life is necessary in order to test them."

One repeats that Hawthorne's sensibility has its Shelleyan side, and that the affinity is more than superficial. In **"Earth's Holocaust"** he singles him out: "methought Shelley's poetry emitted a purer light than almost any other productions of his day." To document more generally the light of imagination, one might also adduce the north light of the artist, as Miriam explains its necessity to Donatello in *The Marble Faun* when he visits her studio. One cannot, in fact, deny to the imagination a provisional reality and value, a place (to speak advisedly) in the sun; and Aylmer is imaginative artist as well as scientist.

From still another angle the situation is less favorable to him. Georgiana's regimen, with its gradually increasing steps of unseen and dimly felt influence, represents one of Hawthorne's portrayals of an entrapment. It is most like the insidious process by which Dr. Rappaccini entangles Giovanni Guasconti, although less elaborate; it resembles the subtle temptation of Goodman Brown by the Devil; and Georgiana's sensations are similar to the Reverend Mr. Dimmesdale's while he is being mentally tortured by the unsuspected Chilling-worth. Aylmer's purposes are less insane than Rappaccini's, and unlike the Devil and Chillingworth he seeks his patient's or victim's good. His policy is no worse than a well-meaning physician's, who confides to his patient only a part of his method of treatment. Nevertheless there is an ugly element of concealment and perfidy in it, and we feel that Aylmer tries to play God and succeeds in playing the devil instead. Thus there are continual ironies from his misconceptions, as when, after talking of his powers, he bids Georgiana "consider how trifling, in comparison, is the skill requisite to remove this little hand [the birthmark]." He does not, as Robert Heilman says confusing the symbol with the reality, comprehend that in trying to change her he is undertaking incomparably the most difficult as well as the most impious task of all.

Aylmer is artist, idealist, God, and unwitting devil; and as Heilman maintains in his classic essay "Hawthorne's **'The Birthmark'**: Science as Religion," he is scientist-priest as well. Heilman notes that science and religion are interchangeable in the story, both in Aylmer's terms and the terms that are used to describe him. One might comment, too, that as scientist (and of course as artist) Aylmer plays the role of wizard.

Both Aylmer's gifts and his aspirations approach to wizardry. The story is set at a time when "the comparatively recent discovery of electricity and other kindred mysteries of Nature seemed to open paths into the region of miracle," although it is also, we must note, specified that "We know not whether Aylmer possessed this degree of faith in man's ultimate control over Nature." Watching over his wife, he is confident "that he could draw a magic circle round her within which no evil might intrude." Of his swift-growing plant Georgiana explains, "It is magical!" In his aspirations he cites the alchemists; and his wife says fearfully that "It is terrible to possess such power, or even to dream of possessing it." In his library are "the works of the philosophers of the middle ages, such as Albertus Magnus, Cornelius Agrippa, Paracelsus, and the famous friar who created the prophetic Brazen Head."

Hawthorne's conception of science has generally been considered rather comically old-fashioned, but with the growth of the twentieth century the joke would seem to have turned against his critics. For most of us the chemist, the nuclear physicist, and the biologist are indeed wizards, and the disproportion between scientific and humanist advances in knowledge has become a commonplace, as has the power of scientism. Aylmer's claims seem less striking when one considers current progress in creating life, in indefinitely prolonging it, and of course in exploring and mastering space, motion, and matter itself. With this power, too, inevitably comes the claim, not necessarily from the scientist, that it is all-sufficient. Thus Heilman says of Aylmer that "His tragedy is that he lacks the tragic sense; he is, we may say, a characteristic modern, the exponent of an age which has deified science and regards it as an irresistibly utopianizing force. His tragic flaw is to fail to see the tragic flaw in humanity." **"The Birthmark,"** in short, raises vital and explosively timely issues, and Aylmer represents the claims of modern scientism.

He is not, however, only a scientist, as has already been shown at length. He is also a Romantic and transcendental artist, holding like Owen Warland, the artist of the beautiful, Platonic conceptions of reality in form and idea. Aylmer does not, like Warland, catch "a better butterfly than this," or if he does it is with a supreme and Aristotelian irony of reversal; and Warland does not, like Aylmer, trifle with a human being. Nor so far as we can tell does Aylmer achieve self-knowledge as does the Artist; instead, as with Giovanni Guasconti the conclusion leaves him high and dry. Still, as I have said, Hawthorne gives him a very long rope, as artist, as thinker, and as man.

Among the several notebook memoranda for the story is "A person to be the death of his beloved in trying to raise her to more than mortal perfection; yet this should be a comfort to him for having aimed so highly and holily" (1839). Here the balance is remarkably even, and *holily* cannot be passed over. Aylmer is, as Heilman brands him, "a romantic perfectibilitarian, who suffers from a dangerous fastidiousness in the presence of complex actuality," but perhaps Heilman feels a little worse about this than Hawthorne did. Aylmer's distaste for the birthmark arises from an aesthetic and moral sense of disharmony in it. "Had she been less beautiful,—if Envy's self could have found aught else to sneer at,—he might have felt his affection heightened by the prettiness of this mimic hand . . . but seeing her otherwise so perfect, he found this one defect grow more and more intolerable with every moment of their united lives." He sets out to remove the flaw in the spirit of Pygmalion.

Aylmer's purposes are controlled by morality. Whereas Rappaccini "would sacrifice human life, his own among the rest, or whatever else was dearest to him, for the sake of adding so much as a grain of mustard seed to the great heap of his accumulated knowledge," there are some experiments that Aylmer will not undertake. He believes, for example, that the *elixir vitae* lies within his grasp, but does not attempt it, since he also believes "that it would produce a discord in Nature which all the world, and chiefly the quaffer of the immortal nostrum, would find cause to curse." Again, he possesses "the most precious poison that ever was concocted in this world. By its aid I could apportion the lifetime of any mortal at whom you might point your finger." He does not intend to use it thus, however: "its virtuous potency is yet greater than its harmful one."

Aylmer's notebook, which Georgiana comes upon, expounds his case most sympathetically and fully. In it he has recorded every experiment of his scientific career. "The book, in truth, was both the history and emblem of his ardent, ambitious, imaginative, yet practical and laborious life. He handled physical details as if there were nothing beyond them; yet spiritualized them all, and redeemed himself from materialism by his strong and eager aspiration towards the infinite. In his grasp the veriest clod of earth assumed a soul." Georgiana concludes her reading with a love and reverence more profound than ever for her husband, but a lesser confidence in his judgment. "Much as he had accomplished, she could not but observe that his most splendid successes were almost invariably failures, if compared with the ideal at which he aimed." One might appeal to *The Marble Faun* to denominate this praise, recalling how the novel prefers the rough sketch of the artist to the finished picture. Aylmer's volume is "the sad confession and continued exemplification of the shortcomings of the composite man, the spirit burdened with clay and working in matter, and of the despair that assails the higher nature at finding itself so miserably thwarted by the earthly part. Perhaps every man of genius in whatever sphere might recognize the image of his own experience in Aylmer's journal." If this is so, this is the human condition itself, not likely to be cured by adjurations to accept it.

Reflecting further, Georgiana reconsiders the character of Aylmer

> and did it completer justice than at any previous moment. Her heart exulted, while it trembled, at his honorable love—so pure and lofty that it would accept nothing less than perfection nor miserably make itself contented with an earthlier nature than he had dreamed of. She felt how much more precious was such a sentiment than that meaner kind which would have borne with the imperfection for her sake, and have been guilty of treason to holy love by degrading its perfect idea to the level of the actual; and with her whole spirit she prayed that, for a single moment, she might satisfy his highest and deepest conception. Longer than one moment she well knew it could not be; for his spirit was ever on the march, ever ascending, and each instant required something that was beyond the scope of the instant before.

This is an expression of purest Romantic dynamism, Whitman's "O farther, farther, farther sail!" or more appropriately still Emerson's

> *Have I a lover noble and free?*
> *I would he were nobler than to love me.*

Unquestionably the passage contains a profound irony, in such phrases as "his honorable love—so pure and lofty," "nor miserably make itself contented with an earthlier nature," "that meaner kind which would have

borne with the imperfection for her sake," "been guilty of treason to holy love by degrading its perfect idea," and "with her whole spirit she prayed." But the irony is indeed so deep that it is almost unfathomable; it questions without implying an answer. Aylmer is entangled in great complications, and his problem is treated with great and imaginative sympathy. Hawthorne himself is taken up with the desire of the moth for the star, in despite of the fall.

Lewis B. Horne (essay date 1969)

SOURCE: Horne, Lewis B. "The Heart, the Hand and 'The Birthmark.'" *American Transcendental Quarterly*, no. 1 (1969): 38-41.

[*In the following essay, Horne traces Hawthorne's use of the hand and the heart as symbols of mortality and spirituality in "The Birthmark."*]

Certainly one of Hawthorne's most pervasive assumptions is that man is imperfect. Frequently in his work he correlates spiritual and physical imperfection so that a diabolic character displays some kind of physical deformity; for the physical frame, he writes, is but a shadow of the moral system.[1] In **"The Birthmark,"** however, one finds an exception. The blemish of the tiny hand on Georgiana's left cheek indicates a physical imperfection only; it expresses "the ineludible gripe in which mortality clutches the highest and purest of earthly mould" (p. 205). Spiritually, she is perfect. From the "gripe" of her own mortality, Georgiana has little to suffer. But from the "gripe" of her husband, she is in much more danger, for Aylmer, when he makes Georgiana the subject of his experiment, makes her victim to his own mortal imperfection.

The adjective "mortal" is advisable because Aylmer, despite the ruin he brings to his wife, is no demon. Most critics of the story point this out. Brooks and Warren find more of aspiration than the monstrous in him; Robert B. Heilman describes him as a confused man, "a romantic perfectibilitarian"; and Hyatt H. Waggoner finds him acting from "a motive not itself wrong."[2] All see the nature of his imperfection in basically the same way, a way perhaps best described by Heilman: Aylmer, confusing science and religion, mixes spiritual yearning with a deadly exercise of power.[3] What has not been pointed out, however, is the way in which the image of the hand registers this imperfection of Aylmer's, indicating at the same time the scientist's effect upon his wife.

More often remarked upon is the image of the heart, an image integrally related in the story to that of the hand. For just as, in Aylmer's dream, Georgiana's birthmark is rooted in her heart, so in the daytime world of **"The Birthmark,"** Aylmer's flaw, indicated by the hand, is rooted in his. Indeed, it is more deeply rooted; for while Georgiana's flaw is physical, Aylmer's is spiritual. And the seat of the spiritual in Hawthorne's work is the heart, that repository of good and evil. Hawthorne at the end of **"Earth's Holocaust"** indicates this best when his narrator reflects:

> How sad a truth, if true it were, that man's agelong endeavor for perfection had served only to render him the mockery of the evil principle, from the fatal circumstance of an error at the very root of the matter! The heart, the heart,—there was the little yet boundless sphere wherein existed the original wrong of which the crime and misery of this outward world were merely types.

> (p. 372)

This thought has been prompted by the provocative comment of the stranger:

> unless they [reformers] hit upon some method of purifying that foul cavern [the heart], forth from it will reissue all the shapes of wrong and misery . . . which they have taken such a vast deal of trouble to consume to ashes.

> (p. 371)

Of importance in this second passage is Hawthorne's reference to the heart as a cavern, for this image is not restricted to **"Earth's Holocaust."** In fact, one of his most detailed allegorical descriptions in *The American Notebooks* implies that through the cavern of the heart one can make a figurative journey of discovery:

> The human Heart to be allegorized as a cavern; at the entrance there is sunshine, and flowers growing about it. You step within, but a short distance, and begin to find yourself surrounded with a terrible gloom, and monsters of divers kinds; it seems like Hell itself. You are bewildered, and wander long without hope. At last a light strikes upon you. You peep towards it, and find yourself in a region that seems, in some sort, to produce the flowers and sunny beauty of the entrance, but all perfect. These are the depths of the heart, or of human nature, bright and peaceful; the gloom and terror may lie deep; but deeper still is the eternal beauty.[4]

This entry was made sometime in 1842, **"The Birthmark"** written in the fall of that year, and **"Earth's Holocaust"** in the year following.[5] To see Aylmer's laboratory in these same terms as a kind of giant heart is not difficult: it has an entryway and its own deepening recesses; it has its "monsters"; it is, indeed, cavern-like. Finally, John W. Schroeder has demonstrated how Hawthorne makes "outward objects function . . . as projected symbols of the heart."[6] The journey into Aylmer's heart, is, in effect, what the reader makes with the unwitting and loving Georgiana when she moves into her husband's laboratory; and the clues to her danger appear in the references to Aylmer's hand.

An examination of the story shows that it falls readily into four sections with a prologue and an epilogue:

> (Prologue)
> The discussion about the birthmark
> The decision to remove the birthmark
> The sojourn in the laboratory
> —the threshold of the laboratory
> —the apartment of the laboratory
> —the laboratory itself
> The experiment
> (Epilogue)

The third section, the sojourn in the laboratory, is the longest in the story and the most important for my purpose. To move from the threshold into the apartment is to move nearer the *heart* of the laboratory—and deeper into the heart of Aylmer himself. "Georgiana," he has told his wife shortly before, "you have led me deeper than ever into the heart of science" (p. 207). But the distance Aylmer's obsession will drive him is indicated earlier in the reflection after his dream: "Until now he had not been aware of the tyrannizing influence acquired by one idea over his mind, and of the *lengths* which he might find in his heart to go for the sake of giving himself peace" (p. 207). (My emphasis here and in the following quotations.) A man obsessed, he has united his love of science with his love of woman, and done it unevenly. "What will be my triumph," he exclaims, revealing a greater love of science than love of wife, "when I shall have corrected what Nature left imperfect in her fairest work" (p. 208). The strength of his passion for science, as he expresses it here, the passion that virtually fills his heart, finds embodiment in the image of the laboratory as the man's heart.

Of the three stages of the journey through the heart described in the *Notebooks* entry—the entrance, the hellish inner regions, and the heavenly depths of the heart—Aylmer's laboratory corresponds to the second. Georgiana, apparently never frightened by the outside of the area, faints "but a short distance" over the threshold. The "penetrating fragrance," "gorgeous curtains," and "perfumed lamps" that she finds when she revives are deceptive: "the scene around her," Hawthorne writes, "looked like enchantment"; but he adds that the magnificent surroundings had been converted from "smoky, dingy, sombre rooms" (p. 209). The achievements Aylmer shows Georgiana for her entertainment do not please her. She responds sometimes as though the quickly growing flower or the elixir of immortality and death are too like those "monsters of divers kinds" to be found in the heart's cavern. Most interesting to her are not the proofs of Aylmer's success, but the evidence of his failures. In these failures the hand of mortality lies like unwilling sleep upon the man.

While Aylmer continues his work, Georgiana examines his library and finds there in a volume "from her husband's own *hand*" this evidence of failure:

. . . he had recorded every experiment of his scientific career, its original aim, the methods adopted for its development, and its final success or failure, with the circumstances to which either event was attributable. The book, in truth, was both the history and emblem of his ardent, ambitious, imaginative, yet practical and laborious life. He *handled* physical details as if there were nothing beyond them; yet spiritualized them all, and redeemed himself from materialism by his strong and eager aspiration towards the infinite. In his *grasp* the veriest clod of earth assumed a soul.

(p. 214)

Yet much as Georgiana admired these achievements,

she could not but observe that his most splendid successes were almost invariably failures, if compared with the ideal at which he aimed. His brightest diamonds were the merest pebbles, and felt to be so by himself, in comparison with the inestimable gems which lay hidden beyond his reach [his mortal "gripe"?]. The volume, rich with achievements that had won renown for its author, was yet as melancholy a record as ever *mortal hand* had penned.

(p. 214)

As Georgiana's nearly perfect beauty is flawed by the hand on her cheek, so Aylmer's ideal achievements are flawed by the comparative failures Georgiana finds described here in his own hand. Such another relative achievement is Georgiana to become.

And she becomes this willingly. As an enduring human relationship depends upon compromise, so must one effect a balance between what one has and what one expects: the fact of human imperfection hangs on one side of the scales; the dream of the ideal on the other. Confronting the reality of a flawed wife with a shudder and demanding the ideal in this temporal world, Aylmer upsets the balance of their relationship. He rejects compromise. He does not recognize his own flaw. Nor does he see that Georgiana, in accepting him, has compromised. To take from Aylmer his mortal weakness is to find a different man. We say sometimes of a person, changed after a long period of time or calamity: "He was hardly the same person." So Aylmer without his aspiration would not be Aylmer. That Georgiana accepts Aylmer with his flaw, that this mortal Aylmer and no ideal one is her husband, is apparent when she takes the fatal potion from his hand, taking it because it comes from his hand and not because of what it is.

Her husband, of course, is not of the same make. His unrelenting obsession with scientific achievement coupled with his aspiration for the perfect places a seal upon Georgiana's fate. Nor does Georgiana try to avoid that fate. When Aylmer leaves her in the vast luxuriant chamber after she sings to him, Georgiana, wanting "to inform Aylmer of a symptom which for two or three hours past had begun to excite her attention," follows

him into the laboratory for the first time (p. 215). The scene of Aylmer's labors, the place of his triumphs and failures, the laboratory as it is described reverberates with echoes of the description of the hidden cavern of the heart—the air "close" and full of "gaseous odors"; Aylmer himself "pale as death"; the monster Aminadab slaving there (pp. 215-216).

When Aylmer sees Georgiana he rushes to her, seizing "her arm with a *gripe* that left the print of his fingers upon it" (p. 216). These fingerprints come from the same hand that has already penned such melancholy mortal failures. Though Aylmer warns Georgiana of danger, she is still ready to continue with the experiment. For she accepts the fact of her husband's mortality:

I shall quaff whatever draught you bring me; but it will be on the same principle that would induce me to take a dose of poison if offered by your *hand*.

(p. 216)

Like Beatrice Rappaccini she drinks a fatal potion, but only at her lover's request.

The use of the word "hand" in the passage above is not accidental. For Hawthorne made the earlier reflection about Aylmer's notebooks (see above) Georgiana's own and not the author's. When she offers to drink whatever potion comes from Aylmer's hand, the earlier reflection may already have left her mind. But it should not have left the reader's. For consider the last paragraph of the story in which Hawthorne writes: "The fatal hand had grappled with the mystery of life, and was the bond by which an angelic spirit kept itself in union with a mortal frame" (p. 220). The complete sentence refers to Georgiana's hand. But the first half of the sentence— "The fatal hand had grappled with the mystery of life"—has a suggestive ambiguity that echoes the earlier reflection. Following directly as it does Georgiana's death speech, "the fatal hand" is most certainly Aylmer's also. Its fatefulness is scarcely disputable.

By taking the reader with Georgiana into Aylmer's laboratory, Hawthorne has taken the reader into the heart of the man, into those regions "with a terrible gloom, and monsters of divers kinds." Whether or not Aylmer moves onward in his journey to the sunnier meadows where all is "perfect," the reader does not know. For Hawthorne never tells us whether or not Aylmer felt any remorse or guilt for Georgiana's death. In one sense, he has triumphed, for the birthmark is gone; but he has triumphed at the cost of his wife's death. Was the price too dear? Georgiana tells Aylmer it was not. But Hawthorne the author avoids comment: instead, he leaves the reader in the laboratory, in the darkest recesses of Aylmer's heart, with the scientist viewing what his hand has wrought.

Notes

1. "Egotism, or the Bosom Serpent," in *Hawthorne: Selected Tales and Sketches* (New York: Rinehart Editions, 1964), p. 190. All other references within the text are to this paperback edition, selected because it is more readily available than the standard Riverside Edition.

2. Cleanth Brooks and Robert Penn Warren, *Understanding Fiction* (New York: Appleton-Century-Crofts, Inc., 1943), p. 104. Robert B. Heilman, "Hawthorne's 'The Birthmark': Science as Religion," *The South Atlantic Quarterly,* XLVII (October, 1949), p. 578. Hyatt H. Waggoner, *Hawthorne: A Critical Study,* Rev. Ed. (Cambridge, Mass., The Belknap Press, 1963), p. 108.

3. Heilman, p. 581.

4. Randall Stewart (ed.), *The American Notebooks* (New Haven: Yale University Press, 1932), p. 98.

5. For dating of the stories I depend upon Elizabeth L. Chandler, *A Study of the Sources of the Tales and Romances Written by Nathaniel Hawthorne before 1853,* Smith College Studies in Modern Languages, Vol. VII, No. 4 (Northampton, Mass., 1926), pp. 55-63.

6. "'That Inward Sphere': Notes on Hawthorne's Heart Imagery and Symbolism," *PMLA,* LXV (March, 1950), p. 107.

Robert D. Arner (essay date spring 1972)

SOURCE: Arner, Robert D. "The Legend of Pygmalion in 'The Birthmark.'" *American Transcendental Quarterly,* no. 14 (spring 1972): 168-71.

[*In the following essay, Arner examines parallels between "The Birthmark" and Ovid's retelling of the legend of Pygmalion.*]

Optimistically anticipating that his attempt to remove the hand-shaped stigma from the left cheek of his otherwise perfect wife, Georgiana, will end in success, the scientist Aylmer, central figure in Hawthorne's **"The Birthmark,"** boasts: "'I feel myself fully competent to render this dear cheek as faultless as its fellow; and then, most beloved, what will be my triumph when I shall have corrected what Nature left imperfect in her fairest work! Even Pygmalion, when his sculptured woman assumed life, felt not greater ecstasy than mine will be'."[1] Elsewhere in the story, Hawthorne insists upon the significance of the allusion by comparing Georgiana to a statue, the "Eve of [Hiram] Powers," and her complexion to "the purest statuary marble" (p. 51). He describes the birthmark as "a bas-relief of ruby

on the whitest marble" (p. 53), and, still later, speaks of Georgiana's "marble paleness" (p. 74) after she has drunk of the goblet prepared for her by her husband. So persistent a pattern of imagery and allusion, then, seems to call for some examination of Aylmer's concept of himself as a modern descendant of Pygmalion.

Only a few of Hawthorne's many critics have addressed themselves to this problem, and then only in passing. Robert B. Heilman views Aylmer's boastful comparison as evidence of the scientist's dream of infinite creative power,[2] and Roy R. Male, relating Aylmer to Shem Drowne of **"Drowne's Wooden Image"** and Owen Warland of **"The Artist of the Beautiful,"** finds in the allusion a statement of Hawthorne's organic theory of art. According to Male, these three artist figures share with Pygmalion an overmastering wish to liberate the perfect forms inherent in their materials and to create an art product which is both of and superior to nature "in that it embodies Nature's essence, and thus magically combines the ideal with the particular."[3] Finally, Daniel Hoffman, writing specifically of **"Drowne's Wooden Image,"** follows Male's lead in pronouncing the Pygmalion myth a fundamental one to Hawthorne's conception of the artist.[4]

As explanations of the Pygmalion allusion in **"The Birthmark,"** these interpretations seem to me incorrect for several reasons. In the first place, both Male and Hoffman, by placing this one reference to the famous Greek sculptor in the context of Hawthorne's other "Pygmalion" stories, tend to overlook the differences among Drowne, Warland, and Aylmer and to ignore the vastly different results of each man's endeavor. Only Aylmer's experiment ends in the death of his subject rather than in the creation of beauty out of inanimate materials, so that, if he is to be viewed as Pygmalion, we must acknowledge some ironic qualifications of the legend before the parallels make sense. A second problem, this one apparent in Heilman's approach, is the assumption that Pygmalion shared Aylmer's obsessive desire to create a perfect being. This is not the case, however, either in the original legend or in Ovid's retelling of it, where Hawthorne is most likely to have encountered it; indeed, there is some doubt as to who created the statue Pygmalion adored,[5] and although this does not enter into Ovid's version of the myth, neither do the themes of artistic striving, alienation, or pride in achievement. The sculptor seems to fashion a perfect woman almost accidentally. The artist's lonely struggle to create beauty, a romantic vision which plays a role in **"Drowne's Wooden Image"** and **"The Artist of the Beautiful,"** does not appear to underlie Hawthorne's intentions in this story. In order to understand those intentions, I believe, we must move beyond romantic tradition and consult the classical version of the story.[6]

In Ovid's retelling of Pygmalion's tale, the Greek sculptor is portrayed as one who, "loathing their lascivious life [sic], / Abhorr'd all womankind, but most a wife."[7] Determined to live by himself and yet not fall a prey to idleness, the "nurse of ill," he

> carv'd in iv'ry a maid, so fair,
> As nature could not with his art compare,
> Were she to work; but in her own defence,
> Must take her pattern here, and copy hence.
>
> Pleas'd with his idol, he commends, admires,
> Adores; and last, the thing ador'd, desires.
> A very virgin in her face was seen
>
> . . . . .
>
> He knows 'tis madness, yet he must adore,
> And still the more he knows it, love the more.
>
> (p. 440)

In testimony of his great love for the statue, Pygmalion presents it with rich and exotic gifts and lavishly furnishes a bridal chamber for his idol. At last, unable to bear the pain of his hopeless love any longer, he attends the feast of Venus and prays to her, "Give me the likeness of my iv'ry maid" (p. 441). Venus, well knowing that he means the statue itself, does better than he asks; she animates the cold marble and blesses the marriage bed of the two lovers. A son, Paphos, is later born of this union, a living creation which stands in contrast to the cold, lifeless statue that Pygmalion carved as the result of his denial of the power of passionate love.

Thus synopsized, the sculptor's story contains several key parallels to Hawthorne's tale. In the two protagonists, first of all, we have men whose work suggests the triumph of man's creative intellect over nature. Pygmalion's statue is more beautiful than any merely natural beauty, and Aylmer's researches aim at a similar superiority to the limitations imposed by nature. Further, both men give evidence of a certain sexual squeamishness when confronted by real, flesh-and-blood women instead of ideal types. Pygmalion retreats from feminine sexuality and finds an outlet for his creative energies in his art. Once he becomes obsessed with his wife's imperfection, which speaks of her "liability to sin, sorrow, decay, and death" (p. 52), Aylmer attempts a similar kind of retreat by using his science to break Georgiana's bond with the natural world. He attempts to create a perfect woman, a being above mortality and the laws of nature. In a sense he may be said to have succeeded, for in death Georgiana's perfect "angelic spirit" is liberated from its "normal frame" (p. 76) and ascends heavenward. Surely, however, in human terms at least, this liberation of his wife's immortal part must be viewed as an ironic contrast, rather than as a direct parallel, to Pygmalion's emancipation of a beautiful form from cold marble or to Shem Drowne's release of a figure of ideal beauty from a block of solid oak.

Once we become aware of this fundamental difference between Aylmer and Pygmalion, others come readily to

mind. For one thing, Pygmalion's art improves upon nature, whereas Aylmer's journals speak only of his unsuccessful attempts to rise above the power of natural forces. A natural law, death, triumphs over him even in his most ambitious and carefully planned experiment. He has, therefore, yet to reach Pygmalion's level of achievement, and, consequently, he lacks the sculptor's broader perspective. For Pygmalion, having attended perfection in art, finds that he prefers the imperfections of a mortal woman after all; only a living being can satisfy his love by responding to it and returning it. He prays to Venus to permit his artistic creation to enter into the realm of nature, subject to all the frailties and imperfections flesh is heir to, without daring to hope that his prayer will be granted. In contrast, Aylmer strives to remove Georgiana beyond nature's dominion. Presumably, if some of his earlier endeavors to master nature had succeeded, he would have known, as Pygmalion came to acknowledge, that the accomplishment was not worth the effort and was certainly not worth his wife's life. Nor does Aylmer invoke a deity beyond himself and his own knowledge, whereas Pygmalion bows to the power of Venus, and it is she, not the sculptor, who animates the statue. Aylmer, possibly misled by the romantic image of Pygmalion as a life-creating god in his own right, fails to remember this crucial fact when he compares himself to the sculptor. He does not follow Pygmalion's path from art to love and faith. There is no development of his self-knowledge but rather a willful self-deception, and so there can be no miracle of new life at the end of his quest.[8]

In this context, Hawthorne's references to the "marble paleness" of Georgiana assume an ironic significance. They not only describe the purity of her complexion, but they also foreshadow the denouement of the tale and her eventual metamorphosis from a warm, living woman into a cold, rigid "statue," marble in the doman of death. Thus Aylmer's story exactly reverses Pygmalion's, for it ends where the legend began, with a perfect but lifeless idol. In its broadest sense, then, the Pygmalion myth provides Hawthorne with a basic narrative structure as well as with certain ironic dimensions of meaning and allusion.

Pygmalion's story, moreover, may have given Hawthorne a clue for his central symbol, the hand-shaped birthmark. Certainly hints of perfection marred by passion appear in Ovid's account of Pygmalion's mad embracing of his marble maiden:

> And straining hard the statue, [he] was afraid
> His hands had made a dint, and hurt his maid:
> Explor'd her, limb by limb, and fear'd to find
> So rude a gripe had left a livid mark behind.
>
> (pp. 440-441)

That "livid mark" which Pygmalion fears to find on the marble would, of course, be hand-shaped. The sculptor here performs the same action that Aylmer also performs while exploring Georgiana's perfection in search of a blemish, which he finds too easily. Pygmalion observes no evidence of imperfection so long as his statue remains marble. But when it comes to life, the same handprint image is employed to emphasize her mortality and Pygmalion's joyous recognition of her earthly imperfections:

> But next his hand on her hard bosom lays:
> Hard as it was, beginning to relent,
> It seem'd, the breast beneath his fingers bent;
> He felt again, his fingers made a print,
> 'Twas flesh, but flesh so firm, it rose against
>   the dint.

(p. 442)

Hawthorne seems to have been struck by the hand-print as an image of passion, for in **"The Birthmark"** he uses the device to indicate that Aylmer's devotion to science surpasses his love for Georgiana. When she enters the laboratory to watch the proceedings, Aylmer, fearful that she will not go through with the experiment if she learns of the danger to her life and angry at this invasion of his privacy, rushes towards her and seizes her arm "with a gripe that left the print of his fingers upon it" (p. 69). The episode occurs precisely at the moment when, in the original Pygmalion story, the amazed sculptor is watching the life enter his beloved, so that Hawthorne's intention would once again seem to be ironic.[9] For the red mark of Aylmer's hand, a second birthmark, associates the scientist with imperfection by revealing his liability to passion, if only to the passion of his quest for knowledge.[10]

Whether or not Hawthorne derived the symbol of the birthmark from the legend of Pygmalion, however, he appears to have possessed much more than a superficial knowledge of it and to have constructed his tale on a plan that incorporated the myth into the basic narrative pattern. The irony of the allusion most interested him, for the legend recounts the growth of one who went from art to faith and love. For various reasons, but most importantly because of his total devotion to science rather than to another human being, Aylmer was unable to follow that path and left, as the end product of his researches, only a beautiful statue from which the life had departed.

Notes

1. "The Birthmark," in *Mosses from an Old Manse, The Writings of Nathaniel Hawthorne* (Boston and N. Y.: Houghton Mifflin, 1900), IV, 55-56. Further references to Hawthorne's story are to this edition and volume; page numbers will be indicated in parentheses.

2. "Hawthorne's 'The Birthmark': Science as Religion," *SAQ*, 48 (1949), 577.

3. "'From the Innermost Grain': The Organic Principle in Hawthorne's Fiction," *ELH*, 20 (1953), 219-220. The passage quoted in this paper is itself quoted by Male from Richard Harter Fogle, "The World and the Artist: A Study of Hawthorne's 'The Artist of the Beautiful'," *TSE*, 1 (1949), 39.

4. "Myth, Romance, and the Childhood of Man," *Hawthorne Centenary Essays,* ed. Roy Harvey Pearce (Columbus, O.: Ohio State Univ. Press, 1964), p. 198.

5. H. J. Rose, *A Handbook of Greek Mythology* (N. Y.: E. P. Dutton, 1959), p. 340A.

6. Perhaps the best example of the romantic Pygmalion is Thomas Lovell Beddoes' "Pygmalion, or The Cyprian Statuary," *The Works of Thomas Lovell Beddoes,* ed. Edmund Gosse (London: Fanfrolico Press, 1928), II, 346-352. Although Beddoes' "Pygmalion" was written in 1825, it was not published until 1851 and thus would not have been available to Hawthorne as a source.

7. "Pygmalion," fr. Ovid's *Metamorphoses,* Book X, trans. John Dryden; in *The Latin Poets,* ed. Francis R. B. Godolphin (N. Y.: Modern Library, 1949), p. 440. Further references to the text of Ovid's poem are to this edition of Dryden's translation and will be indicated by page number only.

8. Hawthorne was not, of course, suggesting that Aylmer acknowledge the power of a pagan goddess, but rather of the human (and Christian) love she represents. Hoffman, p. 209, notes Hawthorne's tendency to combine classical myths with Christian messages.

9. See Hoffman, p. 198.

10. Note Hawthorne's use of a similar image, again in connection with the idea of earthiness in a woman, in "Rappaccini's Daughter." The morning after Beatrice has seized Giovanni's arm in an effort to prevent his touching the poisonous purple shrub, the young man finds on the back of his hand "a purple print like that of four small fingers, and the likeness of a slender thumb upon his wrist." *Mosses,* in *Writings,* IV, 159.

Roberto di Pietro (essay date 1972)

SOURCE: di Pietro, Roberto. "Hawthorne's 'The Birthmark': Puritan Inhibitions and Romantic Appeal in the Context of the Faustian Quest." *Studi e Ricerche di Letteratura Inglese e Americana* 2 (1972): 239-57.

[*In the following essay, di Pietro asserts that in "The Birthmark" Hawthorne explores the metaphysical limitations of both Puritanism and Romanticism.*]

«Or, figliuol mio, non il gustar del legno
fu di per se' la cagion di tanto esilio,
ma solamente il trapassar del segno».

Dante—*Paradiso*—Canto XXVI

The acceptance of human imperfection was the central pivot in Hawthorne's religious beliefs. By contrast, this was connected in his speculations with the capital sin of pride—the Sin par excellence—which, as he felt, originated a syndrome of negative manifestations, especially on an existential level.

While Hawthorne deprecated the unreality of the Romantic[1] deification of man because it was ingenuously blind to man's intrinsic limitations, he also lamented the Puritans' exacerbated sense of perfectionism which somehow entailed the incapability on their part of recalling Jesus' rebuke: «Thou hypocrite,.cast out first the beam of thine own eye, and then shalt thou see clearly to pull out the mote that is in thy brother's eye».

On the one hand he thought that the orthodox Christian premise of imperfection from original sin was good because it was realistic; on the other he frowned upon the inability—both Puritan and Romantic through opposite faults—to achieve a «profounder wisdom» which he associated with the acceptance of man's liability to sin and of the Bunianesque conception of a common lot of toil and sorrow, as well as with his peculiar idea of a democracy founded on a resigned Christian sense of brotherhood in guilt, involving mutual forgiveness and charity. **«The Birthmark»**, a tale which dramatizes the leitmotiv of the search for perfection, draws all these background considerations into an elaborate counterpoint.

In its bare outline, this is the story of a scientist, Aylmer, who discovers soon after his marriage that a diminutive birthmark vaguely shaped like a «pygmy hand» on his wife's cheek overshadows the woman's otherwise perfect beauty. He begins to grow fretful and gradually becomes obsessed with the dream of removing the mark with a knife, following it down to his wife's very heart. Georgiana who is made very unhappy by her husband's affliction and withering stare not only consents to, but wishes for, an operation. She is less sanguine than Aylmer as to its upshot—and indeed she dies: the stigma is at last completely effaced by alchemical fluids—Georgiana is now perfect but dead.

The primary starting point in the story is religiously orthodox and distinctly anti-Emersonian. Aylmer, by Hawthorne's standards of judgement, is anything but wrong in his awareness of a «fatal flaw of humanity which Nature, in one shape or another, stamps ineffaceably on all her productions, either to imply that they are temporary and finite, or that their perfection must be wrought by toil and pain.» That this «fatal flaw» has been exter-

nalized and has become physical («the visible mark of earthly imperfection») is relevant in so far as its tangibility may prove to the doubting Emersonian liberal that its existence is incontrovertibly *real*. Yet how disabling should this blemish be considered and how far does it actually affect the fundamentals of human existence? As Hawthorne tells us, in itself the birthmark is nothing, only «a singular mark» on Georgiana's left cheek, which «in the usual state of her complexion—a healthy though delicate bloom—. . . wore a tint of deeper crimson, which imperfectly defined its shape amid the surrounding rosiness. When she blushed it gradually became more indistinct, and finally vanished amid the triumphant rush of blood that bathed the whole cheek with its brilliant glow.» Except for that slightly detracting imperfection, the woman's beauty is glorious—so much so that it prompts the author's comment: «Masculine observers, if the birthmark did not heighten their admiration, contented themselves with wishing it away, that the world might possess *one living specimen of ideal loveliness* [my italics] without the semblance of a flaw.» But it is the very excellence of his wife's physical appearance which somehow whets Aylmer's passionate perfectionism: «Had she been less beautiful,—if Envy's self could have found aught else to sneer at,—he might have felt his affection heightened by the prettiness of this mimic hand . . . ; but seeing her otherwise perfect, he found this one defect grow more and more intolerable with every moment of their united lives.»

The spiritual and moral correlatives of the strictly physical considerations may, of course, be taken for granted in the description of Georgiana's looks. Hawthorne's familiarity with Spenserian theories perhaps unconsciously drove him into the Neoplatonic habit of equating the somatic qualities and defects with their spiritual and moral counterparts. This becomes apparent in the author's statement that Aylmer, obsessed with the presence of the mark, had selected it «as the symbol of his wife's liability to sin, sorrow, decay and death» and that his «sombre imagination was not long in rendering the birthmark a frightful object, causing him more trouble and horror than even Georgiana's beauty, whether of soul or sense, had given him delight.»

In this tendency to exaggerate and make too much of a *real* but none the less *acceptable* flaw, Hawthorne takes the measure of Aylmer's Puritanism. That this particular aspect of the scientist's attitude reflects Hawthorne's idea of the Puritans' error of judgement one can hardly deny: like them, Aylmer shows a commendable amount of realism in detecting the basic «flaw»—but, like them also, he is incapable of ascribing to it the proper degree of importance. This, it will be found, is related to the author's argument in **«The Maypole of Merry Mount»**. The part of wisdom which the young protagonists of that story finally learn lies in their realistic, orthodox acceptance of a fallen state which, in Hawthorne's opinion, is not so unfortunate after all if one knows how to make the best of a bad job. The appreciable value of «troubled joy»—almost a philosophical meditation on the quality of «light» which Keats poetically described as «. . . what from heaven is with the breezes blown / through verdurous glooms and winding mossy ways»— should never be underestimated. Hence how much happier those «desperate» swains who «would have risked life for the privilege of pressing» their «lips to the mysterious hand!» How much more sensible those who had often called Georgiana's imperfection «a charm!».

Aylmer is first cousin to Giovanni Guasconti, in **«Rappaccini's Daughter»**, who stands hopelessly nonplussed before the combination of good and evil which he finds in the uncanny garden. Vis-à-vis the elusive, mystifying quality of Beatrice's composite personality, Giovanni can only think of the woman either as an angel or as a demon: he blunders in his failure to accept her simply as a human being. Not unlike Digby, the stern Puritan in **«The Man of Adamant»**, or any of the innumerable Puritan introverts in Hawthorne's fiction, Aylmer broodingly concentrates on the darkness, the «frightful» part, and thereby forgets the share of lingering Edenic afterglow with which human nature has been mercifully endowed since the Fall. Here Goodman Brown's desperate conclusion that «there is no good on earth . . . devil . . . to thee the world is given» is clearly called in question. As an operative force in life, evil is perhaps neither to be condoned nor condemned: it is to be *understood* as an unavoidable portion of human destiny. Aylmer's noxious monomania leads from the initial failure to appreciate the good all the way to its final, complete destruction.

We dare say that Mr. Heilman[2] makes a partly deficient statement when he asserts that Aylmer's «tragedy is that he lacks the tragic sense; he is, we may say a characteristic modern, the exponent of an age which has deified science and regards it as an irresistibly utopianizing force. His tragic flaw is to fail to see the tragic flaw in humanity . . . He is a Romantic perfectibilitarian, who suffers from a dangerous fastidiousness in the presence of complex actuality.» Aylmer, it is our opinion, does *see* the flaw only too well: Hawthorne has even made it concrete enough for him to feel with his hand and be haunted by. He is no Transcendental optimist who misses the «wrong», the essential patch of darkness on the light background which is at the core of true human tragedy. Of course, if one considers Aylmer's action per se, one is anything but unjustified in romanticizing the protagonist into «the exponent of an age which has deified science,» a utopistic Emersonian attempting to erase the term and meaning of evil. In Aylmer's belief that it was possible to discover «the secret of creative force» or perfection itself, there is indeed the equivalent presumption that marked scientific thought in Hawthorne's day. I am afraid however that, by supporting this view

alone, one tends to slur too casually over the workings of the scientist's «sombre imagination» and the author's delineation of Aylmer's frame of mind in the process of pursuing his goal. While the Transcendentalists would not so much as acknowledge the existence of any «birthmark» Aylmer recognizes—and is tantalized by—its dark «horror.» Of course, on the face of it, the shade of meaning between perfectionism and belief in perfectibility is perhaps too slight for one to cavil about. But the former, we believe, engages the mind in a much more strenuous activity. Aylmer's perfectionism is too intensely obsessive to be mistaken for the Transcendentalists' lighthearted way of bypassing the darker issues by simply ignoring them altogether.

At any rate, whether one prefers to stress Aylmer's 'Puritanism' in his inability to *rest content with* human imperfection, or his 'Romanticism' in that his action ultimately *misses* the essence of human tragedy, the fact remains that Hawthorne basically considers him blameworthy for this attitude: «Had Aylmer reached a profounder wisdom, he need not thus have woven his mortal life of the self-same texture of the celestial.» Hawthorne invariably deplores this human lack of discrimination between Time as the criterion of the limits and moral burdens of earthly existence, and Timelessness, which man should properly regard as belonging exclusively to a celestial hereafter[3].

The «ambiguity» which critics have almost unanimously proclaimed begins to be noted when we stop to consider how far Hawthorne condemns, and is inclined to condone, Aylmer in his strictly 'Romantic' Faustian quest as a dedicated scientist.

H. J. Lang[4], on the basis of two somewhat conflicting notebook entries of Hawthorne's has thought himself entitled to state that «the story itself has a birthmark» and in dismissing it, therefore, as a failure for ethical ambiguity. The first entry, dating from 1837, reads: «A person to be in the possession of something as perfect as mortal man has a right to demand; he tries to make it better, and ruins it entirely.» The second entry of 1839 reads: «A person to be the death of his beloved in trying to raise her to more than mortal perfection; yet this should be a comfort to him for having aimed so highly and loftily».

While the earlier entry entirely confirms the orthodox argument that we have seen, the later one has a somewhat contradictory 'Romantic' connotation which seems to have bothered Mr. Lang so much as to have made him throw up the sponge in despair of a consistent interpretation. Is Aylmer, one may wonder, to be considered an idealist aiming as «highly and loftily» as Owen Warland in **«The Artist of the Beautiful»**? Does his Transcendental imagination, which is not dissimilar from the Artist's, ultimately provide «a comfort» not unlike the lasting sense of spiritual conquest which attended the destruction of Warland's perfect butterfly? Mr. Lang cuts the Gordian knot by making the tongue-in-cheek remark that if praise of this «comfort» were the last word, «it might induce people to improve their wives by surgery, at whatever risk.»

The obvious difference in the moral issue is enough to dispel all such doubts: to improve *a human being* is a very strange, presumptious aspiration and, in so far as he uses his wife as a means rather than as an end, Aylmer deserves to be judged as rigorously as Rappaccini, Chillingworth, Westervelt, or Ethan Brand. To objectify the human, to make it a guineapig for detached studies is always a negative enterprise, in Hawthorne's opinion. Even artists, such as the author himself in **«The Old Apple Dealer»**, or the consummate painter in **«The Prophetic Pictures»**, or the poet Coverdale in *The Blithedale Romance,* no less than scientists and mesmerists, have been portrayed by Hawthorne as prone to, and guilty of this conceit. Aylmer thereby makes Georgiana, in the words that describe the death of Beatrice Rappaccini, «the poor victim of man's ingenuity and of thwarted nature, and of the fatality that attends all such efforts of perverted wisdom.» This «perverted wisdom» belongs to the proud mortal who aspires to superior knowledge, who attempts to modify the order of natural things and to usurp Faust-like the role of God. The «mimic hand» on Georgiana's cheek was the inescapable token of mortal frailty, a mysterious bond «by which an angelic spirit kept itself in union with a mortal frame.»[5] When the mark disappears, death must ensue because it is not for man to shuffle off the yoke of finiteness during his earthly existence.

Whether with regard to Aylmer's urge to perfection, or Rappaccini's to invulnerability, or the unnatural yearning of the four old people in **«Dr. Heidegger's Experiment»** for perennial youth, or the desire of **«The Ambitious Guest»** for immortal glory on earth, Hawthorne's message is invariably the same: heaven exists and earth exists, accept your earthly imperfections and bide your time. Life is «troubled joy» which partakes of both heaven and earth. Hawthorne suggests the realistic acceptance of man's dual nature: the earthly and the celestial, which should never be confused. What Mr. Lang[6] slightly dismisses as a platitude—«. . . man's radically mixed, his good and evil being (one of the great metaphysical discoveries of the New Critics) . . .» actually plays a prominent part in Hawthorne's views.

The difficulty is, however, that man wants heaven immediately. This irrational desire he cannot master, but can only hold in check at best[7]. Few are those who, like Matthew and Hannah in **«The Great Carbuncle»**, are able to reach healthy conclusion that «. . . the blessed sunshine and the quiet moonlight shall come through our window. We will kindle the cheerful glow of our hearth, at eventide, and be happy in its light. But *never again will we desire more light than all the world may share with us . . .»* [my italics] Our Progenitors' sin was that the Garden, with its bounty of trees and fruits did not gratify them, they wanted then and there the perfection of Heaven which must include also that one *forbidden* tree. That tree was «the birthmark» of their Eden, a restriction which they, like all their mortal progeny since, could not learn to abide. For Aylmer, too, «the momentary circumstance was too strong . . . ; he failed to look beyond the shadowy scope of time and, living once for all in eternity, to find the perfect future in the present.»

Hawthorne's treatment of his Faustian heroes is Marlowian in that they always meet with final doom. And yet it must be emphasized that the lesson which Dr. Faustus' «aspiring mind» ultimately learned—or Marlowe's own, for that matter, after the phase of Tamburlaine's titanism—falls far short of Hawthorne's principles. At the outcome of his adventure, Faustus reaches the conclusion that science can at most teach him 'quod est'; provide, that is, a vision of the wondrous laws of universal order without disclosing 'quid est', the reason for the existence of the created universe. The effect of this realization, however, has no moral consequence with him: Faustus does not finally acknowledge the excess of his superhuman aspirations, but rather laments the deficiency of human possibilities. He commits a serious error of judgement in so far as his pride remains uncurbed. The tragedy, in its terms, is exclusively existential, it catches no glimpse of anything beyond this world, it is hopeless in its suggestion of Luciferian despair[8]. While, in large measure, Hawthorne's preoccupation was also existential in this respect—one need hardly stress the author's view of guilt as a responsible agent in disrupting the harmony of the individual's «intercourse with the world»—it was not dissevered from a basic eschatological concern which Marlowe lacked altogether.

Of course the Renaissance—Hawthorne must have thought—anthropocentric though it was in its philosophy, had at least one commendable advantage in this particular Marlowian aspect over the kindred attitude of modern Transcendentalism, in so far as it was willing to acknowledge *the reality* of human imperfection. But the Christian in Hawthorne, as opposed to the Renaissance man in Marlowe, firmly believed in the admonishment of Revelation—that «Pride goeth before destruction, and an haughty spirit before a fall.» (Proverbs XVI, 18). Through a wide range of fictional characters and circumstances, Hawthorne voiced his fundamental execration of scientific humanism. The butt of his invectives is often symbolized by a deceitful plant which is invariably a poisonous growth—such as the crimson flower coruscating with haunting luridness in *Septimius*

Felton, or the hybrid blossoms in Dr. Rappaccini's garden, which have «an appearance of artificialness indicating that there had been such commixture and, as it were, adultery, of various vegetable species, that the production was no longer God's making, but the monstrous offspring of man's depraved fancy, glowing with only an evil mockery of beauty.»

Towards the close of his career, in a series of inchoately amorphous attempts at a comprehensive romance, including *Doctor Grimshawe's Secret, Septimius Felton,* **«The Ancestral Footstep»**, and *The Dolliver Romance,* Hawthorne returned to the theme of Faustus' damnation, concocting with the renewed passion of his Puritan forefathers ever fresh illustrations of the sin of 'libido sciendi' and the fall of the proud sinner in the hands of and Angry God[9].

At the beginning of *Septimius Felton,* in the conversation between the minister and the young protagonist who is uncertain whether he should proceed in his study of theology, Hawthorne evaluates the pros and cons of the Faustian quest. The priest advises Septimius to let himself be guided by the tranquil faith of his happier days, without racking his brains unduly over the lures and snares of scepticism which, though ineluctable, are unessential. The better course, as it is upheld by the priest, lies in peaceful acquiescence in one's earthly lot.

In his reply, Septimius clearly expounds the opposite theory: peaceful acquiescence, should it become an accepted belief and practice, would be a delusion. In his opinion, the reality of human life is to be found only in our moments of restless doubt, of uplifting spiritual yearning, when the veil of customary devotion has been boldly rent to reveal gaping chasms beyond. At such times only is the Goethian 'Schaudern' experienced, the thrill of horror intermingled with exultation. Boundless desires, dreams of absolute power, of glory, and of reform, all originate from it—and this hectic experience can best promote progress by goading man on to a hazardous and hence maturing challenge of the destructive forces. This problematic option between resigned acquiescence and a restless quest is constantly open to man: whether to gratify the heart's longing for peace or the mind's striving after the fulfilment of all conceivable cravings.

Hawthorne's intention in *Septimius Felton* was to illustrate once more the negative upshot of the later alternative and, therefore, to show how much preferable the former.

And yet, was there not a touch of nobility in this striving, in this Goethian 'Streben'[10] which is ardently championed by Septimius? Dante's exemplar Christianity did not prevent him from harbouring some ill-concealed admiration for the 'humanity' of his Ulysses whom he as-

signed to the depths of his «Inferno» (and with this Dantesque episode Hawthorne is likely to have been familiar). Even Milton's more or less unexceptional religious orthodoxy did not after all keep him from bestowing upon his Eve, in the ninth book of «Paradise Lost,»[11] a heroic dimension in her courage to challenge death and unavoidable chastisement rather than give up Knowledge.

True enough, Hawthorne is incapable of going to the same Romantic lengths as Melville in exploring the human compulsion to achieve superior knowledge. Ethan Brand, the Hawthornesque creation which bears perhaps the closest resemblance to Ahab, is condemned without any apparent trace of sympathy. Brand has committed «the one only crime for which Heaven could afford no mercy»—which is the philosophical equivalent of supreme knowledge. Hawthorne does not possess Melville's insight into the drama of the soul engaged in the quest of a truth which it perceives to be forbidden and is yet unable to renounce since renunciation would be death in life[12]. Nevertheless, we must give him his due by admitting that—if only this once, in his 'ambiguous' portrayal of Aylmer—he nearly approaches the same discernment.

As Mr. Fogle, who takes up the pro-Romantic suggestions of Cleanth Brooks and Robert Penn Warren, has aptly noted[13]: «Aylmer is shown to be wrong, no doubt of it; but Aylmer is given a remarkably good run for his money. If he hangs himself, Hawthorne gives him a very long rope. The author is more engaged in his Faustian quest for knowledge than most critics have seen, since the keenest critics have been anti-Romantic.»

By introducing us to the secrecy of Aylmer's notebook, which Georgiana is conveniently made to come across, Hawthorne obliquely advocates the Romantic cause of his protagonist. «The book, in truth,» as we are told, «was both the history and emblem of his ardent, ambitious, imaginative, yet practical and laborious life. He handled physical details as if there were nothing beyond them; yet spiritualized them all, and redeemed himself from materialism by his strong and eager aspiration towards the infinite. In his grasp the veriest cold of earth assumed a soul.»

Georgiana concludes her reading with a love and reverence more profound than ever for her husband, but a lesser confidence in his judgment. «Much as he had accomplished, she could not but observe that his most splendid successes were almost invariably failures, if compared with the ideal at which he aimed.» That failure is a foregone conclusion Hawthorne cannot deny. However, it seems apparent that the ideal quest which in **«The Artist of the Beautiful»** he had ventured to praise because, while it did involve considerable moral problems, these were not half so committing as the ones that arise here, begins to fascinate him even in these perilous circumstances.

«Considerate la vostra semenza: / Fatti non foste a viver come bruti»—that, in Dante's words, is the essence of the human condition, and Hawthorne seems to catch a fortune glimpse of it.

One of Goethe's most famous conceptions (with which Hawthorne may very well have been acquainted) referred to the existence of two souls in man's breast, the one clinging to the things of the earth, the other striving to attain its supersensual origins. Great talent in particular, as Goethe maintained—Imagination[14] in the ascendant—was compulsively inclined to challenge the accepted standards of perfection. It must seek its origins in the spiritual realms where values are eternal. Such was the critical alternative; and Hawthorne seems to be paraphrasing Goethe in describing Aylmer's diary as «the sad confession and continued exemplification of the shortcomings of the composite man, the spirit burdened with clay and working in matter, and of the despair that assails the higher nature at finding itself so miserably thwarted by the earthly part. Perhaps every man of genius, in whatever sphere, might recognize the image of his own experience in Aylmer's journal.»

But Hawthorne lacked Melville's 'negative capability'[15] of being awed by Ahab's titanic feats in the stormy seas without bothering to rationalize his admiration for the captain. Hawthorne felt that if his hero was to be even slightly approved of, he must be made worthy of as much respect as possible. As far as Rappaccini «was not restrained by natural affection from offering his child in this horrible manner as the victim of his insane zeal for science,» he and Aylmer are guilty of the same hideous sin—and Rappaccini's monstrosity is indeed condemned by the author without qualifications. Hawthorne sees to it, therefore, that, unlike Rappaccini's, Aylmer's purposes are shown to be controlled by at least a semblance of morality.

Mr. Fogle[16] has not lost sight of these moral justifications. Whereas reprobate Rappaccini «would sacrifice human life, his own among the rest, or whatever else was dearest to him, for the sake of adding so much as a grain of mustard seed to the great heap of his accumulated knowledge,» there are some experiments which, as Hawthorne tells us, Aylmer will not undertake. The scientist, for example, believes that the elixir vitae lies within his grasp but does not attempt it since he also believes (and his belief is dictated by the author's own orthodoxy) «that it would produce a discord in Nature which all the world, and chiefly the quaffer of the immortal nostrum, would find cause to curse.» Again, he possesses «the most precious poison that ever was concocted in this world. By its aid I could apportion the

lifetime of any mortal at whom you might point your finger.» And yet Hawthorne makes sure that his protagonist repudiates its use, and makes him wisely assert that «its virtuous potency is yet greater than its harmful one.»

If the suggested identification of the character of Rappacini with Shakespeare's Prospero[17] is completely ironical, the situation here would seem to warrant a more valid parallel between the «virtues» of Aylmer and those of the Shakespearian wizard. In so far as both Rappaccini's and Aylmer's «art» may be considered a type of 'applied science', this is not wholly unsanctioned by the standards of American Puritanism. But Rappaccini's «art» is comparable rather to the «natural» magic of goetist Sycorax, whereas Aylmer's may be more appropriately likened to Prospero's theurgy[18].

Of course Aylmer is not, any more than Rappaccini, quite a Promethean figure in the sense that Prospero may be called one: neither of Hawthorne's scientists steals the 'fire' of wisdom for the use of mankind, since their motivation is instinct with selfish pride. The sense of humility, resignation and acceptance which is detectable in Prospero's so-called valedictory speech of renunciation («Ye elves of hills, brooks, standing lakes and groves . . .») lies mostly beyond their Faustian experience. In the light of the sheer facts in the narrative, both of them appear to be guilty of the Marlowian error of judgement. Hawthorne does not reveal, and leaves it entirely up to us to decide, whether at the outcome of their adventure their character is spiritually matured through self-knowledge. Even if this possibility is taken into account, a vague feeling remains, however, that their comparative realization of «the horror» does not ultimately rescue them—as it did not Konrad's Kurtz—from the «heart of darkness». Still, Aylmer's sensible restraint, his more responsible attitude as compared with that of other Hawthornesque scientists, does partake in some degree of Prospero's «nobler reason»—which is not pure scientific rationalism, but a long search for patience and self-control.

Through the revelations contained in Aylmer's journal, and by vesting his hero with some qualities of moderation and discipline, Hawthorne perhaps tried to acquit himself partly of the responsibility of putting words of praise for Aylmer in the mouth of the latter's dying wife: «. . . you have aimed loftily; you have done nobly. Do not repent that with so high and pure a feeling, you have rejected the best the earth could offer».

Mr. Fogle[19] has even suspected some elements of irony in the description of Georgiana in the act of reconsidering the character of her husband—which, if they really exist, would confirm Hawthorne's inveterate reluctance to deviate from the Puritan path in the face of a Romantic flash of intuition.

The passage in question reads:

> Her heart exulted, while it trembled, at his [Aylmer's] honorable love—so pure and lofty that it would accept nothing less than perfection nor miserably make itself contented with an earthlier nature than he had dreamed of. She felt how much more precious was such a sentiment than that meaner kind which would have borne with the imperfection for her sake, and have been guilty of treason to holy love by degrading its perfect idea to the level of the actual; and with her whole spirit she prayed that, for a single moment, she might satisfy his highest and deepest conception. Longer than one moment she well knew it could not be; for his spirit was ever on the march, ever ascending, and each instant required something that was beyond the scope of the instant before.

In Mr. Fogle's opinion, «this is an expression of purest Romantic dynamism, Whitman's 'O farther, farther, farther, farther sail!' or more appropriately still Emerson's 'Have I a lover noble and free? I would he were nobler than to love me». «Unquestionably», Mr. Fogle goes on to comment, «the passage contains a profound irony, in such phrases as 'his honorable love—so pure and lofty', 'nor miserably make itself contented with an earthlier nature', 'that meaner kind which would have borne with the imperfection for her sake,' 'been guilty of treason to holy love by degrading its perfect idea', and 'with her whole spirit she prayed'».

Incidentally, it may also be noted that irony from an equal motivation appears in the close of **«The Great Carbuncle»**. The themes are indeed very similar in both tales—the «party of adventurers» are Aylmer's counterparts in so far as they are bound on a forbidden quest; as they smugly begin to rejoyce in the discovery of the precious stone, they are punished either by death or by moral and physical torment. Woe to those who reach for the forbidden fruit, says Hawthorne, and of course, on this basis, the closing paragraph of **«The Great Carbuncle»** must clearly be intended as ironic:

> Some few believe that this inestimable stone is blazing as of old, and say that they have caught its radiance, like a flash of summer lightning, far down the valley of the Saco. And be it owned that, many a mile from the Crystal Hills, *I saw a wondrous light around their summits, and was lured, by the faith of poesy, to be the latest pilgrim of the Great Carbuncle.*
>
> [my italics]

However, just because the irony is so apparent that it refuses a literal interpretation, one is tempted to consider the possibility of its being a 'cover'—and probably not so unconscious a cover—for a contrary intimation. But then here the noncommittal attitude is stressed, the author's disavowal of Romanticism more outspoken.

In **«The Birthmark»**, on the other hand, «the irony», to quote Mr. Fogle again, «is indeed so deep that it is almost unfathomable; it questions without implying an answer. Aylmer is entangled in great complications, and his problem is treated with great and imaginative sympathy. Hawthorne himself is taken up with the desire of the moth for the star, in despite of the fall».

There is an entry (1835) in Hawthorne's *American Notebooks* which, we feel, is much more than just 'a note' for the subject of a possible story: «A person to be writing a tale, and to find that it shapes itself against his intentions; that the characters are otherwise than he thought; that unforeseen events occur; and a catastrophe comes which he strives in vain to avert. It might shadow forth his own fate—he having made himself one of the personages». This is indeed a situation with which Hawthorne must have frequently been faced in his profession as allegorist-symbolist, every time that his reasoned allegories got out of hand under the stress of ill-smothered irrational claims and he himself, as a symbolist *malgré soi* got as helplessly involved as his fictional characters[20].

It has been cleverly suggested[21] that Hawthorne's own singled-minded effort to explore—in and through his various symbols—the mystery of life, the «quid est» which is beyond human ken, is in itself a type of Faustian quest, and from a religious point of view a re-enactment of Adam's Fall. Even as he describes and rationally condemns the error of his personages, Hawthorne the symbolist, it is maintained, instinctively reaching for Melville's «image of the ungraspable phantom of life» whether in Ethan Brand's fire, or in the birthmark, or in the great carbuncle, perpetrates—and feels guilty of—the self-same sin that he outlaws in his fiction. This, all things considered, will be seen to labour upon and to particularize the argument of many an authoritative critic regarding Hawthorne's suspicion of his «haunted mind»[22]; so that, if it holds true, the horns of the author's dilemma as a symbolist appear even more fiendishly pointed than one might estimate: «Would that Faustus could be romantically absolved—and I with him!» Aylmer alone of all Hawthorne's Faustian characters, as it seems, is treated with the half-insight, half-wishful-thinking that there may exist a satisfactory solution to the problem after all.

Far from being marred by ethical ambiguity—as Mr. Lang would have it—**«The Birthmark»** remains one of Hawthorne's intellectually most lively tales. Both in the «multiple-choice» obscurity of its central symbol and in its subtle ambivalence between orthodox detachment and Romantic sympathy, it possibly argues that the narrator's moralism was surreptitiously sapped by one of the most urgent philosophical theses of his day—the critique of human reason and of its cognitions, which tended to question the absolute value of our insights into Nature, human and otherwise, on the score of their subjectivity.

The sharp-witted, we concede, may object that it is at best arbitrary to interchange metaphysical with ethical conclusions; to infer, that is, that scepticism in metaphysics may actually extend to and confuse the moral issues—all the more since Emmanuel Kant himself made a point of showing that the moral dictates of the «practical reason» were strong enough to overcome all doubts concerning the validity of metaphysical knowledge. In deference to the hypercritical, let us then remain strictly within the sphere of metaphysics. What we find is that one of the premises of Kant's transcendental dialectic regards the inability of the «Vernunft» (Imagination, or Emerson's Reason) to rest content with the workaday perceptions of the «Verstandt» (Understanding), its strong urge to conquer the absolute essence of reality, to transcend the phenomenical experience and reach for the ungraspable noumenon. That failure in this enterprise cannot be averted is immaterial: the Imagination has peremptory claims of its own which are inherent in human nature and human destiny. This suggestion alone, if none other of all Kant's theories which had been more or less correctly assimilated into Transcendentalist doctrine, must have proved in itself disquieting enough to the intellect of Nathaniel Hawthorne—regrettably so to him, though luckily for posterity. It must have lurked in the darkest repository of his mind and waged secret war against the stringent orthodoxy of his Puritan extraction.

If Kant's shadow, as well as Goethe's, may here be suspected to loom tentatively alongside that of Jonathan Edwards across the path of the author's pilgrim's progress (a fact which Mr. Lang does somehow acknowledge but uses disappointingly in support of his argument for unresolved ambiguity), the result, we believe, is hardly failure from ethical inconsistence but rather a stimulating undercurrent of meaning, a viable inner tension encouraging an intellectual venture which, by Hawthorne's standards, is exceptionally audacious.

Notes

1. The terms 'Romantic' and 'Romanticism', while retaining for the most part their specific, traditional acceptation, have been deliberately stretched in this essay to cover—and to some extent to become synonymous with—the 'liberal' trend of mid-nineteenth-century American philosophic and religious thought as is perhaps best epitomized in R. W. Emerson's, *Divinity School* Address. «T. E. Hulme, in his 'Speculations', defined as 'Romantics' all those who reject the doctrine of Original Sin, and this is perhaps of all definitions the most useful and the best. For the Romantics saw Man as a sinless being surrounded by a sinless Nature. The fall of Man, they thought, had been greatly exaggerated. In fact, there had been no Fall at all». (Quoted from Randall Stewart,

American Literature and Christian Doctrine, Baton Rouge, 1958, p. 46).

The felicitous use of the word with respect to American liberalism has been too cogently justified by Mr. Stewart in the above-mentioned publication for us to dwell on it any further here. It may be noted, however, that the choice is all the more warranted since, as far as we are aware, F. O. Matthiessen alone of all Hawthorne's most prominent critics appears to have cautiously refrained from adopting the term in his «American Renaissance», as has been pointedly remarked by Renato Poggioli, in a review first presenting the Italian translation of Matthiessen's masterpiece to the Italian public in 1954 (the review was published in «Prospetti 10», Florence, Copyright 1955 by International Publications Inc., New York, N.Y., p. 108 ff.).

2. Quoted by Richard H. Fogle, *Hawthorne's Fiction: The Light and the Dark,* Norman, University of Oklahoma Press, 1952-1964, p. 127.

3. R. W. B. Lewis (*The American Adam: Innocence, Tragedy, and Tradition in the Nineteenth Century,* 1955, Chicago, p. 119) has extensively shown how this view, as it is set forth in most of Hawthorne's fiction, may be contrasted with the opposite Transcendental belief that «the Now was the only portion of time important to the writer, because if the immediate could be jostled long enough, beams of the Eternal would begin to show in it». Mr. Lewis states that the «angelic imagination» of the Romantic Transcendentalists (as Allen Tate chose to call it) «was prompted by the assumption that humans, like angels, can have direct perception of timeless essences.» «Now», he goes on to comment, «if anyone was certain that men were not in any respect like angels, it was Nathaniel Hawthorne; though he was restless enough and heretical enough to wish sometimes that they were and to tell, as in the tale of Owen Warland or of Aylmer in «The Birthmark», the sad story of someone who thought so».

4. H. J. Lang, *How ambiguous is Hawthorne?* contained in *Hawthorne, A Collection of Critical Essays,* edited by A. N. Kaul, New Jersey, 1966, p. 95.

5. On the splendid artistic achievement of Hawthorne in the selection of this 'multiple-choice' symbol, see A. Lombardo, *I Racconti di Hawthorne,* contained in *Il Simbolismo nella letteratura Nord-Americana,* La Nuova Italia, Firenze, 1965, p. 136. The birthmark as a mysterious symbol—very much like Hooper's black veil, or the great carbuncle, or the fire in «Ethan Brand»—eludes precise definition. It transcends the purely allegorical

because it cannot be explained in rational terms. It is as impenetrable as the mystery of life: and just because the author himself refrains from stating exactly what it stands for, it becomes a tentative instrument of knowledge; it poses a question which neither the author nor the reader can answer.

6. *Ibid.,* p. 86.

7. As Richard H. Fogle aptly observes (*ibid.,* p. 213), Hawthorne's «positive sinners are too much set on heaven, an ideal, or simply an occupation». Mr. Fogle devotes a full chapter of his book, under the heading «Hawthorne's Heaven and Earth», (p. 212 ff.) to this specific aspect of the writer's philosophy.

8. For an interesting discussion of this aspect of Marlowe's tragedy, see Salvatore Rosati, *Christopher Marlowe, Due Drammi, Edward II e Doctor Faustus,* Edizioni Scientifiche Italiane, Napoli, 1962.

9. See Elemire Zolla, Introduction to *Septimius Felton,* Vicenza, 1966.

10. There are some significant lines in W. Goethe's, *Faust* (Part II, Act II) which we wish to quote in full (the translation is ours):

    FAUST:

    «I do not seek my salvation in imperturbable quietude. In man's thrill, I know, is the best of humanity. And try though the world will to dampen the ecstasy of such moments, Man, when he is thus moved, will capture a profound sense of prodigy».

    MEPHISTOPHELES:

    «May thou sink, then! Or I might say rise! It is all one . . .».

11.

    «Great are thy Vertues, doubtless, best of Fruits,
    Though kept from Man, and worthy to be admired,
    Whose taste, too long forborn, at first assay
    Gave elocution to the mute, and taught
    The Tongue not made for Speech to speak thy praise:
    Thy praise hee also who forbids thy use,
    Conceales not from us, naming thee the Tree
    of Knowledge, knowledge both of good and evil;
    Forbids us then to taste, but his forbidding
    Commends thee more, while it infers the good
    By thee communicated, and our want:
    For good unknown, sure is not had, or had
    And yet unknown, is as not had at all».

12. See Agostino Lombardo, *La Ricerca del Vero,* Rome, 1961, pp. 171-212 (Chapter entitled 'La Ricerca di Melville').

13. *Ibid.,* pp. 119-20.

14. The antithesis Understanding-Imagination is pervasively present in English Romanticism and is most fully and philosophically developed in S. T. Coleridge, to whom Emerson is largely indebted.

Understanding is the lower faculty by which man perceives the world as material. It is concerned with mundane affairs, the data of the senses, the appearances, the temporal. Imagination, on the other hand—a faculty which Emerson peculiarly and misleadingly called Reason—apprehends the innate spiritual reality and truth of things. The Understanding functions by logic, demonstration, proof; the Imagination by intuitive perception and it endows the world with life, unity and meaning.

It is noteworthy that Emerson's idea of «Reason» bears directly on his conception of «self-reliance». As an antirationalist, by proclaiming that the ultimate reliance of a human being must be on his own mind, he of course could only mean «mind» as synonymous with «soul», the intuitive faculty as opposed to the rational one.

15. John Keats, in his famous letter of November 22, 1817, to his friend Bailey, refers to his valuable discovery of the «negative capability»—«. . . that is when man is capable of being in uncertainties, mysteries, doubts, without any irritable reaching after fact and reason». «Coleridge, for instance», says Keats—and, for that matter he could just as appropriately be talking of Hawthorne—«would let go by a fine isolated verisimilitude caught from the penetralium of mystery, from being incapable of remaining content with half knowledge».

16. *Ibid.,* p. 129.

17. See A. Lombardo, *I Racconti di Hawthorne,* ibid., p. 156.

18. Frank Kermode's introduction to Shakespeare's *The Tempest,* Arden Shakespeare Paperbacks, 1964, provides an interesting explanation of the basic difference between Prospero's magic and that of Sycorax.

19. *Ibid.,* pp. 130-31.

20. Charles Feidelson Jr., (*Symbolism and American Literature,* Chicago and London, 1953, pp. 6-15 ff.) has expertly studied the different psychology underlying Hawthorne's resource now to traditional Spenserian and Bunianesque allegorism, now to a more complex, subtle, ambiguous form of symbolism. The author's firm beliefs, it is observed, tended to get expressed within the solid framework of allegory; the deep-set intimations stirring within his sensibility and eluding definition—of which he was aware, but felt that he could neither fully discover nor convey them as clearcut theory—he entrusted to a form of mythopoetic symbolism as the most suitable means of combining expression and a personal speculative quest in the process. However, relinquishing the strictly allegorical mode of expression for the

other involved a choice which was practically on a moral level with him and, as such, it created considerable misgivings. While for Emerson and Whitman faith in symbolic or otherwise imaginative reality became an explicit metaphysical principle, the symbolism for Hawthorne was no more than a sporadic intuition which flickered unsteadily in a perpetually scrutinized opposition between «fiction» and «reality», «imagination» and «actuality», the teachings of Romanticism and those of down-to-earth eighteenth-century Puritanism. Hawthorne's love of the well-defined, logical proposition thus drove him generally to the sterility of reasoned allegorism. With this his Puritan morality was quite content, but the man-of-his-century in him was imaginatively dissatisfied. When his imagination hovered in the proximity of intuitive, «half-waking» truths, his Puritan sensibility smarted and made him morally suspicious of the absolute irreproachableness of such indefinite revelations coming from a mind which he regarded as discreditably «haunted».

21. See A. Lombardo, *I Racconti di Hawthorne,* ibid., pp. 145-46.

22. See note No. 20 to this essay. For an interesting illustration of the workings of Hawthorne's «haunted mind», see also F. O. Matthiessen, *ibid.,* pp. 229-241, and Hyatt H. Waggoner, *Hawthorne: A Critical Study,* Cambridge, Mass., 1955-63-67, pp. 8-11 et alibi.

Theodore Colson (essay date autumn 1976)

SOURCE: Colson, Theodore. "Analogues of Faulkner's *The Wild Palms* and Hawthorne's 'The Birthmark.'" *Dalhousie Review* 56, no. 3 (autumn 1976): 510-18.

[*In the following essay, Colson illuminates various similarities in symbolism, theme, and characterizations between "The Birthmark" and William Faulkner's* The Wild Palms.]

In the summers of 1925 and 1926 when Faulkner vacationed in Pascagoula he fell in love with a girl named Helen Baird. She only tolerated him, and married another man, but characters in two of Faulkner's novels were drawn from her—Patricia Robyn in *Mosquitoes* and Charlotte Rittenmeyer in *The Wild Palms*. Both represent a type of beauty Faulkner was drawn to. But Helen Baird had some bad scars, and Faulkner did not hesitate to transfer them to Charlotte. Why? Joseph Blotner, Faulkner's biographer, suggests that the suffering indicated by the scars was partly what drew Faulkner to Helen Baird.[1] Charlotte's scars suggest her vulnerability; she is associated with Aphrodite, but she is all too mortal.

There are some remarkable parallels between *The Wild Palms* and Hawthorne's **"The Birthmark"**, beginning with the marks on the heroines' faces.[2] Hawthorne's story is romantic and Faulkner's is naturalistic, but both stories have the force of parable, and the parables are similar: in each the lovers are totally committed to love, and that love is symbolized by the physical perfection of the woman; in each they try to make that perfection total through an operation, and the operation is fatal. In *The Wild Palms* Charlotte deserts her husband for Harry, an intern. Their total commitment to sexual love is uninterrupted until she becomes pregnant. She finally persuades him to perform an abortion, and it kills her. In **"The Birthmark"** the scientist Aylmer marries Georgiana, who is an utterly perfect woman except for the birthmark on her cheek, in the shape of a tiny hand. He becomes obsessed with removing it, and he finally does, but it kills her.

Georgiana's mark is a sign to Aylmer of humanity's fallen state: "It was the fatal flaw of humanity which Nature, in one shape or another, stamps ineffaceably on all her productions, either to imply that they are temporary and finite, or that their perfection must be wrought by toil and pain." It is the "symbol of his wife's liability to sin, sorrow, decay, and death." Charlotte has "a faint inch-long scar on one cheek which he recognized as an old burn, doubtless from childhood." And when she first meets Harry, Charlotte tells him that it is also on her shoulder and side and hip, and she got it while fighting her brother. Her scars are not given any weight of meaning, like Georgiana's. Yet, as R. V. Cassil points out in the introduction to the Signet edition, the story is of course not realistic. Georgiana's birthmark is like the scar of Melville's Ahab or Milton's Satan, and though Charlotte acquires hers naturalistically rather than supernaturally, her scars have the same significance. They are similar to the symbol of Caddy's muddy drawers in *The Sound and the Fury* (also acquired after fighting with her brother) which we associate with knowledge of good and evil and of death as we see Caddy peering in at Damuddy's funeral from the Compson tree of knowledge. But once Faulkner establishes the fact of Charlotte's scars he does not elaborate on it; it is her pregnancy that becomes the 'birthmark'.

Both couples fit very nicely in the whole Edenic tradition of American fiction.[3] They hope that by removing the symbol they can remove the condition of original sin and return to Edenic innocence and timelessness. Temporality is inextricably part of the fallen impure state they abhor. Aylmer specifically hates the birthmark as a sign that nature's work are "temporary and finite". The theme of return to Eden is clear enough in Harry and Charlotte's idyllic retreat to the lake. "Well, Adam," she says as soon as they are alone. Charlotte displays an Eve-like unconsciousness of temporality, but Harry is tormented by the diminishing row of cans of food, and when he is driven to make a calendar, he reconstructs the count of days by using Charlotte's menstrual periods.

The stories are one more demonstration of Hawthorne's and Faulkner's somewhat similar concerns for and their different approaches to the theological problem of the imputation of Adam's sin to the rest of mankind. The clearest statement in Faulkner's work is Quentin Compson's saying, "theres a curse on us its not our fault is it our fault." Hawthorne's characters are simply and orthodoxly born with original sin—the birthmark comes at birth. He plays with this idea most intricately in *The Scarlet Letter*: Pearl asks if she will get a scarlet letter when she grows up, but of course she is already herself the embodiment of *the* scarlet letter. Caddy and Charlotte are not born with the symbols of sin, the muddy drawers, the pregnancy, but come by them in a natural fashion. But the parallels are clear: Caddy and Pearl, Hester and Charlotte have the same problem. There are other symbols of the Adamic curse in Faulkner: the commissary ledgers in "The Bear", or Joe Christmas' ambiguous color, but I think his general approach is best represented by Caddy and Charlotte.

Both Faulkner's and Hawthorne's worlds are filled with men who are outraged and tormented by the thought of impurity. The convict in the "Old Man" story, whose chapters are interleaved with *The Wild Palms,* is one of these men. And of course both Georgiana's birthmark and Charlotte's pregnancy are symbols of impurity— the kind that is often symbolized by loss of virginity (Quentin Compson's attitude is an example). But virginity is valued in neither story; both are in a sense about the chastity of wedded love that Milton hymns, with the very great exception that Harry and Charlotte explicitly, and Aylmer and Georgiana in their fashion, scorn ordinary husband and wife relationships. Both stories are about absolute purity of love—of sexual love. The sexuality is, characteristically, only hinted at in Hawthorne's story, and the lovers try to make it totally spiritual in spite of its physicality. In Faulkner's story the flesh is insisted upon. This is not a minor difference, since it nicely represents the distance of the century from 1843 to 1939. But the similarity, the concern with total commitment to love, is greater than the difference.

Georgiana's love is so great that when she knows intuitively that Aylmer's experiment will kill her she still encourages him: "Her heart exulted while it trembled at this honorable love—so pure and lofty that it would accept nothing less than perfection nor miserly make itself contented with an earthier nature than he had dreamed of. She felt how much more precious was such a sentiment than that meaner kind which would have borne with imperfection for her sake, and have been guilty of treason to holy love by degrading its perfect

idea to the level of the actual." And Charlotte's commitment to "holy love" is equally obsessed: "It's got to be all honeymoon, always. Forever and ever, until one of us dies. It can't be anything else. Either heaven or hell! no comfortable safe peaceful purgatory between for you and me to wait in until good behavior or forbearance or shame or repentance overtakes us." Both couples set up "holy love" as their ultimate value, and to give in and accept their respective birthmarks would be treason to it.

Allen Tate's criticism of Poe's "Ligeia" could apply almost exactly to **"The Birthmark"**: "The hero professes an impossibly high love of the heroine that circumvents the body and moves in on her spiritual essence. All this sounds high and noble, until we begin to look at it more narrowly, when we perceive that the ordinary carnal relationship between a man and a woman, however sinful, would be preferable to the mutual destruction of soul to which Poe's characters are committed."[4] For Georgiana death is preferable to treason to holy love. And with some curious inversions Tate's observation is apropos to *The Wild Palms.* Harry and Charlotte's relationship is carnal all right, but it is carnality of a peculiar kind, elevated as a supreme value; "the ordinary carnal relationship" may want to prevent having a baby, but it will permit other human activities to exist along with the sexual. Not Charlotte and Harry.

Both Hawthorne and Faulkner eschew respectability because it is the appearance of goodness which can cloak the worst evil. But Harry and Charlotte hate and fear respectability because only in an aura of obvious adultery can they preserve the intensity of their wholly sexual relationship. As soon as Harry finds himself with a job and a home, settling down, becoming a *husband,* they must flee. And the pregnancy is the ultimate threat. A child is a bond between husband and wife, but the child asserts its own claims. Charlotte says she doesn't want a child because "they hurt too damn much." At first Harry thinks she is talking about childbirth, but then he realizes she is talking about the emotional pain of the relationship; she has left two children with her husband, and try as she might she cannot forget or stop loving them. She wants nothing between herself and Harry; she does not want a developing of love, but a stasis of love. In pleading for an abortion she says, "It's not us now . . . I want it to be us again, quick, quick, quick. We have so little time. In twenty years I can't any more and in fifty years we'll both be dead."

Charlotte has made sexuality their god, and confronted it with a titanic hubris: They will rule it. But, as Edwin Arlington Robinson says in "Eros Turannos," they

> That with a god have striven
> Not hearing much of what we say
> Take what the god has given.

Charlotte has some Aphrodite-like features herself, for to Harry she embodies the godly power of sexuality. And here is another parallel with **"The Birthmark"**: the hubris of trying to act godlike is doomed. This theme is explicit in Hawthorne's story; like Rappaccini, Aylmer develops an ambition to usurp God's unique power: he says he has had "thought which might have enlightened me to create." He forgets that nature "permits us indeed to mar but seldom to mend, and, like a jealous patentee, on no account to make."

This hubris is what Allen Tate (again writing of Poe) calls the "angelic imagination"—that kind of mind in which "neither intellect nor will is bound to the human scale, their projection becomes god-like, and man becomes an angel."[5] In the "angelic" apiration, writes Tate, the three classical faculties are hypertrophied. In hypertrophy of feeling "a nightmare of paranoia, schizophrenia, necrophilism, and vampirism supervenes, in which the natural affections are perverted by the will to destroy."[6] Such perversion of feeling is apparent enough in Faulkner's world (we have only to think of "A Rose for Emily"), and certainly though less obviously present in Hawthorne's. "The second hypertrophy is the thrust of the human will beyond the human scale of action," and the third is "the intellect moving in isolation from both love and the moral will." Clearly in characters like Ethan Brand, Hollingsworth, and Sutpen the imagination is "angelic". Aylmer's and Charlotte's imaginations are "angelic", and Georgiana and Harry in admiration acquiesce. The hypertrophy of feeling and will is apparent enough in both couples' exaltation of love. The hypertrophy of interest is obvious in Aylmer's confidence in his science, and in Charlotte's demands on Harry's science. Georgiana's situation is clear cut; she is the passive female victim of the experiment; she goes into it with masochistic knowledge that she is victim. Harry's situation is much more complicated: he is male, and has to wield the knife, but he is also the passive member of this couple, and seems the more victimized of the two. But clearly enough the partners in both couples mutually victimize each other.

Both stories use the knife image. The knife as a sexual image could never be more explicit than in Faulkner's story: when Harry attempts the abortion Charlotte says, "We've done this in lots of ways but not with knives, have we?" and the policeman who arrests him says, "Using a knife. I'm oldfashioned' the old way still suits me. I dont want variety." In Hawthorne's story Aylmer has a dream in which he operates on the birthmark: "but the deeper went the knife, the deeper sank the hand, until at length its tiny grasp appeared to have caught hold of Georgiana's heart; whence, however, her husband was inexorably resolved to cut or wrench it away."

Each of these stories gains in stature by their juxtaposition. Hawthorne's is clearly one of his romances; it is

far-fetched and obviously allegorical. *The Wild Palms* on the other hand is so grossly—apparently—committed to the physical that its main intention might be seen as pornographic (well, that is to the hypothetically stupidest of all possible readers). But the stories are transformations of the same thematic structure. *The Wild Palms* is the naturalistic fulfilment of the idea of **"The Birthmark"**: outside of romance women do not have hand-shaped birthmarks that represent original sin, but lots of women get pregnant. On the other hand **"The Birthmark"** is the allegorical statement of the situation of *The Wild Palms,* and the pregnancy is seen to be the birthmark of original sin—not in that the adultery is sinful, though having like Dimmesdale's and Hester's "a consecration of its own", but the pregnancy is for them a symbol of temporality, "liability to sin, sorrow, decay, and death."

Both couples see time as the great enemy—a theme of both stories is one theme of Shakespeare's sonnets, love's war upon time. All four lovers' ambition is to defeat time and mortality symbolically, since it finally cannot be done any other way, cannot be done in the flesh. Aylmer would achieve this by 'creating' an utterly perfect, flawless Georgiana. Charlotte's method is simply to ignore time and in the experience of love escape, transcend time (just as Ike McCaslin and Hightower do in their mystical visions). Harry tries to articulate this (in very Faulknerian rhetoric): "you are one single abnegant affirmation, one single fluxive Yes out of the terror in which you surrender volition, hope, all—the darkness, the falling, the thunder of solitude, the shock, the death—. . . but forever afterward you will know that . . . for one second or two seconds you were present in space but not in time . . ." (His friend McCord reacts to this somewhat as Allen Tate does to the love of Poe's Ligeia: "Sweet Jesus . . . If I am ever unlucky enough to have a son, I'm going to take him to a nice clean whorehouse myself on his tenth birthday.")

Georgiana, predictably, has the most spiritual vision: "I might wish to put off this birthmark of mortality by relinquishing mortality itself in preference to any other mode. Life is but a sad possession to those who have attained precisely the degree of moral advancement at which I stand." This "degree of moral advancement" is the kind of love that D. H. Lawrence finds so abominable: "The lust of hate is the inordinate desire to consume and unspeakably possess the soul of the hated one, just as the lust of love is the desire to possess, or to be possessed by the beloved, utterly. But in either case the result if the dissolution of both souls, each losing itself in transgressing its own bounds."[7] She worships Aylmer to the point where she is willing, indeed eager, to die for him and his obsession. "Do not repent" she says, "that with so high and pure a feeling, you have rejected the best the earth could offer. Aylmer, dearest Aylmer, I am dying!" In justice to Georgiana, she does not at all think her degree of moral advancement is the highest: "Were I weaker and blinder it might be happiness. Were I stronger it might be endured hopefully. But being what I find myself, methinks I am of all mortals the most fit to die."

Charlotte certainly does not think she is at the best moral point for death, but she is willing to risk death, and in her pain wishes for it: "Then take the knife and cut it out of me. All of it. Deep. So there won't be anything left but just a shell to hold the cold air . . ." Charlotte would scorn the sublimating away of physical sex in Hawthorne's story, but could readily understand the passion which makes both Aylmer and Georgiana willing to risk Georgiana's body for "holy love". Her idea of love is as wholly sexual as she can make it, but it is a deity. When she begs Harry to do his first (and successful) abortion for their friends she says, "This is for love too. Not ours maybe. But love."

Each author ends his story by drawing a moral, each in his characteristic rhetoric. There are two steps in Hawthorne's moral. First, "the parting breath of the now perfect woman passed into the atmosphere, and her soul, lingering a moment near her husband, took its heavenward flight." And of the cloddish servant Aminidab's laughter, Hawthorne comments: "Thus ever does fatality of earth exult in its invariable triumph over the immortal essence which, in this dim sphere of half development, demands the completeness of a higher state." So there is a higher, a "celestial" state where Georgiana's and Aylmer's perfect love could exist. But Hawthorne must add: "Yet had Aylmer reached a profounder wisdom, he need not thus have flung away the happiness which would have woven his moral life of the selfsame texture with the celestial. The momentary circumstance was too strong for him; he failed to look beyond the shadowy scope of time, and living once for all in eternity, to find the perfect future in the present." I suppose similar advice might have been given to Charlotte and Harry—that they could have woven mortal lives of jobs and respectability with their celestial sexual love. That is what their friend McCord thinks.

That the moral of Faulkner's story must be from Harry's point of view is in one sense ironic, because of these four characters Harry is the least idealistic, the most practical, and therefore the most anguished by the whole business. Like Georgiana he must try to understand and to articulate what is happening. He chooses not to try to escape from the police, and not to use the cyanide pill that Charlotte's husband offers him, but to live out his life imprisonment. He seems to have reached a "degree of moral advancement" stronger than that of Georgiana, who welcomed death. And in this story there is no higher, celestial state. Faulkner's Harry is rigorously naturalistic: the physical is *all* there is; when he is gone nothing will be left of what he and

Charlotte had, and so, to honor that—religiously—he will stay alive. The concluding lines of *The Wild Palms* approach Faulkner's best work:

> Now he could see the light on the concrete hulk, in the poop porthole which he had called the kitchen for weeks now, as if he lived there, and now with a preliminary murmur in the palm the light offshore breeze began, bringing with it the smell of swamps and wild jasmine, blowing on under the dying west and the bright star; it was the night. So it wasn't just memory. Memory was just half of it, it wasn't enough. *But it must be somewhere,* he thought. *There's the waste. Not just me. At least I think I dont mean just me.* Hope I dont mean just me . . . But after all memory could live in the old wheezing entrails; and now it did stand to his hand, incontrovertible and plain, serene, the palm clashing and murmuring dry and wild and faint and in the night but he could face it, thinking, *Not could. Will. I want to. So it is the old meat after all, no matter how old. Because if memory exists outside of the flesh it wont be memory because it wont know what it remembers so when she became not then half of memory became not and if I become not then all of remembering will cease to be.—Yes,* he thought, *between grief and nothing I will take grief.*

Faulkner did not, like Hawthorne, collect morals in notebooks and then make stories to fit them; but that this moral is important to Faulkner is made clear by his asserting it in a wholly different context in one of the sessions that went into *Faulkner in the University*: "between grief and nothing man will take grief always."[8]

Hawthorne's conclusion is that human imperfection "demands the completeness of a higher state," yet at the same time people would be better off putting up with 'birthmarks', somehow accommodating them with a sense of eternal life. In his fiction he frequently appeals to heaven; in Hawthorne's personal theology skepticism and faith were generally able to coexist; his view of the world is stylistically perfectly represented in his much commented on device of multiple possibilities. But, when his back was to the wall, he hesitatingly pinned his hopes on heaven. And so that is what he does with Georgiana.

Faulkner is quite different, the naturalistic humanist; he must pin his hopes on man. Of course his other works frequently end in hopelessness, as in *Sanctuary*—or with hope for the simple and good like Lena Grove or Dilsey, but none for the complex and tormented, like Quentin Compson. But in the conclusion of *The Wild Palms* he puts some affirmation, what must be about the most minimal affirmation there is, in Harry, who would be one of the simple, yet has been forced by Charlotte into this much complexity. It is a minimal affirmation and yet it is great. Harry is, in the sense of Faulkner's Nobel Prize speech, "prevailing".

But of course the great interest of both stories is not in their conclusions but in the psychological and spiritual development of these couples, and especially of Georgiana and Harry. That development is sick, by standards of normal mental health, and yet it is heroic.

Notes

1. *Faulkner: A Biography* (New York: Random, 1974), p. 512, and passim.

2. Though several critics have written about parallels of Hawthorne and Faulkner, no one has convincingly demonstrated that there was any direct influence. The only Hawthorne book in Faulkner's library in 1939 when he published *The Wild Palms* was the *Blithedale Romance* (*William Faulkner's Library—A Catalogue,* compiled by Joseph Blotner. Charlottesville: University Press of Virginia, 1964). The texts I have used are *Mosses from an Old Manse, The Complete Works of Nathaniel Hawthorne,* ed. George P. Lathrop (Boston: Houghton Mifflin, 1886), II, and *The Wild Palms* (New York: Random House, 1939).

3. For example, consider R. W. B. Lewis, *The American Adam* (University of Chicago Press, 1955), Charles L. Sanford, *The Quest for Paradise* (Urbana: University of Illinois Press, 1961), Leo Marx, *The Machine in the Garden* (New York: Oxford University Press, 1961).

4. Allen Tate, "The Angelic Imagination," *Collected Essays* (Denver: Swallow, 1959), p. 435.

5. *Ibid.,* p. 443.

6. *Ibid.,* p. 434.

7. D. H. Lawrence, writing of Poe's "Fall of the House of Usher" in *Studies in Classic American Literature* (1922), in *The Shock of Recognition,* ed. Edward Wilson (New York: Modern Library, 1952), p. 982.

8. *Faulkner in the University: Class Conferences of the University of Virginia 1957-1958,* eds. Frederick L. Gwynn and Joseph Blotner (Charlottesville: University Press of Virginia, 1959), p. 25.

Elizabeth R. Napier (essay date November 1976)

SOURCE: Napier, Elizabeth R. "Aylmer as 'Scheidekunstler': The Pattern of Union and Separation in Hawthorne's 'The Birthmark.'" *South Atlantic Bulletin* 41, no. 4 (November 1976): 32-5.

[*In the following essay, Napier maintains that Hawthorne uses the "pattern of union and separation" in "The Birthmark" to depict and investigate aspects of human psychology.*]

The psychological complexity of Hawthorne's **"The Birthmark"**—often overshadowed by an Aylmer-like attraction to the tale's central symbol—derives from patterns of imagery that unify the narrative and point deliberately to its "deeply impressive moral" (p. 48).[1] One pattern of images in **"The Birthmark"** deserves particular attention. It cautions against a reading of the tale as simple parable, directing consideration instead to the polarity that recurs on the level of the story's form and theme. The pattern is one of union and separation.

In the early German alchemical tradition, a man like Aylmer would have been called a *Scheidekünstler* (literally, an "artist of separation"). The term is in origin a technical one, referring to the chemical process of distillation, but Goethe in his *Wahlverwandtschaften* (*Elective Affinities*)—a tale employing motifs surprisingly similar to those of Hawthorne's **"Birthmark"**[2]—suggested that the word could be used to draw an analogy between the world of chemistry and that of human personality. In Goethe's usage, the term came to express a preoccupation with phenomena of attraction and repulsion not in the chemical but in the psychological domain.[3] Broadly speaking, Goethe (as well as many of the German philosophers of Goethe's time) stressed the desirability of a coexistence of opposite psychological principles and warned against the dangers of attempting to "separate out" any single aspect of the psyche.

From the beginning of **"The Birthmark"** the problem of unity and separation occupies a central position in the narrative. Hawthorne speaks of "affinities" (p. 47), "unions" (p. 48, 69), "marriages" (p. 48). Images of weaving and intertwining frame the tale; there is a strange nuptial ceremony. The chief representative of these images of union is Georgiana. Georgiana, mortal and magic, hideous and beautiful, stained and pure, "mediates between extremes. She is the best that earth and heaven can offer here and now."[4] Symbolic of Georgiana's unity is the mysterious birthmark upon her cheek. It is the birthmark that is the center of her reconciliatory nature, which joins her simultaneously to the world of men and the realm of the fairies. Even Georgiana's name exemplifies the harmony of her inner self: the stem carrying with it connotations of the earth, and the suffix (*iana*) implications of upward movement toward heaven.[5] In addition, her name combines masculine and feminine: George and Anna.

Counterpointing Georgiana's images of mystic union are Aylmer's images of removal and separation. Aylmer repeatedly speaks of "removing" (p. 48, 51, 52, 56, 58), of "cutting" and "wrenching away" (p. 52); he dreams of surgical operations; the distilling apparatus that dominates his laboratory is a fitting emblem of his obsession to disjoin. Aylmer's predilection for settings of seclusion, his insistence upon the theoretical separation of spirit and intellect, and the immiscibility of his idealism and his human affection evidence an unconditional rebellion against Georgiana's principles of union and harmony. The hint of debility in the scientist's name serves as a repeated reminder of the spiritual malaise that underlies his philosophy of disintegration.

Throughout **"The Birthmark,"** a controlled transference of images deepens the implications of Hawthorne's psychological theme. By shifting images of union to Aylmer and images of separation to Georgiana, Hawthorne maintains a significant tension between the two polar images of the tale. The result is that in Aylmer's hands images of union become grotesquely distorted—his passion for Georgiana increases in disturbing proportion as the possibilities for fulfillment wane. Aylmer's systematic employment of the language of sensual pleasure in the context of his scientific inquiries heightens the acuteness of his emotional inversion. He repeatedly refers to the "ecstasy" (p. 53, 68) of his investigations; in the intervals between his studies and experiments he appears to Georgiana "invigorated," "flushed and exhausted" (p. 58). Similarly, the mock marriage and consummation which are enacted within his laboratory "boudoir" are a hideous parody of what should be. Aylmer, simply enough, is unable to check his compulsion to separate and distill. Georgiana, in a like manner, cannot check her tendency toward union: she is able to justify her own death and her husband's failure through an unhesitating redefinition of her marital role.

Aylmer's compulsion toward separation is intensified by the realization that he himself is unmistakably a "split" personality. The "pale, intellectual" (p. 55) Aylmer is an almost allegorical representative of man's spiritual nature, while his shaggy assistant, Aminadab, is "no less apt a type" (p. 55) of the physical. Clearly, Aminadab is Aylmer's "other half," his *Doppelgänger,* the physical, earthly side of his personality which the scientist has, for some reason, "distilled out."

Aylmer's resentment of the birthmark stems in part from an inability, inherent in his very nature, to tolerate the union of physical and spiritual principles which he encounters in his wife. On a deeper level, his experiment upon the birthmark is an attempt to "reorganize"[6] Georgiana's psyche, to elicit, from the synthesis of opposites which maddens him, that single "golden principle" (p. 58) of his wife's nature. But in point of fact the tiny birthmark is not (like Aylmer's Aminadab) a detachable aspect of Georgiana's being. It is "deeply interwoven . . . with the texture and substance of her face" (p. 48). The final eradication of the birthmark dissolves the organizing principle of Georgiana's psyche—and what appears at first to be Aylmer's scientific failure becomes, in an ironic twist, the ultimate figuring forth of his philosophy.

By the end of **"The Birthmark,"** Aylmer has attained the status of a literal *Scheidekünstler.* He is guilty not only of Georgiana's death but—like Miles Coverdale and the Puritan society that condemned Hester Prynne—of a more abstract, spiritual crime: the violation of psychological integrity. Aylmer's attempt to "separate out" the single, unknown part of Georgiana's psyche indicates an ominous and tragic inability to deal with the complexity of being human.

If **"The Birthmark"** concludes (as R. B. Heilman has remarked)[7] with no startling self-insight and no renunciation, perhaps it is because the nature of Aylmer's psychological motivations (and Hawthorne's attitude toward them) is never satisfactorily resolved. Possibly, in a private campaign for self-betterment, Aylmer wishes to render Georgiana physically perfect—a purer partner to his own dominating spiritual sense; possibly his desire to remove the birthmark manifests a need to eliminate the last trace of the psychic opposite he abhors. But even as Hawthorne maintains sympathy toward his scientist, it is indisputably true that Aylmer does, in Fogle's words, "hang himself."[8] It is, therefore, at least equally possible that his efforts transcend any desire for psychological unity and represent instead the impulses of an unnatural and negative faith.

Notes

1. All references to "The Birthmark" are to *The Works of Nathaniel Hawthorne,* ed. George P. Lathrop (Boston: Houghton, Mifflin & Co., 1882), vol. 2.

2. "That is true!" the Captain exclaims to Eduard and Charlotte in the midst of a scientific explanation that foreshadows the tragic destiny of the novel's characters. "And those cases are indeed the most important and remarkable, wherein this attraction, this affinity, this separating and combining, can be demonstrated, the two pairs, as it were, crossing over; where four elements, until then joined in two's, are brought into contact and give up their former combination to enter a new one" (J. W. von Goethe, *Elective Affinities,* trans. Elizabeth Mayer and Louise Bogan [Chicago: Henry Regnery Co., 1963], p. 42). "Affinities," observes Eduard, "really become interesting only when they bring about separations" (p. 40). The impact of events in Goethe's novel, as in "The Birthmark," depends upon a precise control of the patterns of union and separation that impel the action of the plot and form the basis for its psychological theme. Here, as to a lesser extent in Hawthorne's tale, the psychological effects of "dissociation and taking possession" (p. 42) and the questions of fate and free will are examined in detail.

3. One hundred years later, Jung's studies of ancient alchemical texts were to lend interesting corroboration to Goethe's theories on the correlations be-

tween chemical and psychic structure. Here, as in other respects, the investigations of Goethe and Hawthorne anticipated, with curious exactitude, the psychological studies of Freud and Jung. On Hawthorne's interests, see Roy R. Male, Jr., "Hawthorne and the Concept of Sympathy," *PMLA,* 68 (1953), 138-149.

4. Alfred S. Reid, "Hawthorne's Humanism: 'The Birthmark' and Sir Kenelm Digby," *American Literature,* 38 (1966), 337-351. The reference here is to p. 351.

5. Reid draws similar conclusions, p. 351.

6. The term is R. B. Heilman's. See his "Hawthorne's 'The Birthmark': Science as Religion," *South Atlantic Quarterly,* 48 (1949), 575-583.

7. Heilman, p. 583.

8. Richard Harter Fogle, *Hawthorne's Fiction: The Light and the Dark* (Norman: Univ. of Oklahoma Press, 1964), p. 119.

David M. Van Leer (essay date 1976)

SOURCE: Van Leer, David M. "Aylmer's Library: Transcendental Alchemy in Hawthorne's 'The Birthmark.'" *ESQ: A Journal of the American Renaissance* 22, no. 4 (1976): 211-20.

[*In the following essay, Van Leer details the resonance of "pre-Newtonian science" and alchemy in "The Birthmark," tracing Hawthorne's treatment of the biography of Neoplatonist scientist Sir Kenelm Digby and the works of other scientists in the story.*]

When in 1842, after an unproductive term at the Boston Custom House and an even less congenial stay at Brook Farm, Hawthorne, newly married and comfortably settled at Emerson's Old Manse, begins again to write tales, there is a subtle difference in the kind of story he tells.[1] Whereas the earlier works are located in a recognizably Puritan setting, these new tales seem more unreservedly allegorical, less specifically historical. Yet Alfred Reid's demonstration[2] that in **"The Birthmark,"** the earliest of the new tales, the career of the idealist-perfectionist Aylmer has its prototype in the history of Sir Kenelm Digby, Neoplatonist scientist, suggests that we might want to revise that judgment. The later works may indeed be even more carefully wrought "histories" than were the earlier tales; if the atmosphere of old Boston and of the Salem witch trials might perhaps be the natural inheritance of a New England writer, surely the more foreign matter of Renaissance Neoplatonism must have been deliberately "got up."[3] **"The Birthmark"** thus poses two problems to those who would

view Hawthorne's historical settings as more than the backdrop for stiff allegories of the head and the heart: first, whether or not sense can be made of the scattered references to a tradition of pre-Newtonian science; and second, if the story is in some significant way *about* the alchemists, what motivated such an interest in mid-nineteenth-century America?

I

The place to start, obviously, is with Reid's illuminating discovery of the relevance of Sir Kenelm Digby to the tale. Although Reid's demonstration of a point by point correspondence between the science of Aylmer and Digby may be overstated, his more general outlines of influence are undeniable. Digby's interest in the resuscitation of plants through the application of a nitrous salt solution to the soil surely lies behind Aylmer's experiments with his liquid which similarly cleanses a blighted geranium. Even more clearly does the invigorating perfume with which Aylmer refreshes the air of his wife's room recall the vial of "fresh spirits" Digby claims that Cornelius Drebel kept to animate the exhausted air of his guest chamber. And most certainly Hawthorne found the original of his birthmark in Digby's entertaining pages on the treatment of sympathetic moles. In particular, Digby's story of the strawberry mark which grew inflamed in the berry season until it was finally cauterized by an obliging surgeon simply presents an earlier, happier version of Georgiana's hand and the operation on whose "perfect practicability" her husband is so misguidedly insistent.[4]

Yet, as Reid shows, the most tantalizing similarities between the two scientists relate not to the Platonist's science but to his romance. Acting on his principle that "a handsome lusty man that was discreet might make a vertuose wife out of a brothell-house," Digby marries, against the wishes of his friends, the bewitching Venetia Stanley, in the courteous phrase of one biographer, "a driver in pleasure's chariot with a very light touch on the reins of virtue." Sharing with Aylmer an unwillingness to admit the earthly limitations of his flawed wife, he proceeds to defend Venetia through three hundred pages of "Loose Fantasies."[5] In the curiously mixed style of autobiography as allegorical romance, our scientist, renamed "Theagenes," retells the story of his pursuit of Venetia, rather disconcertingly idealized into a celestial "Stelliana." The defense, though not without charm, is hardly convincing, as Venetia's claim to a virtue of Richardsonian dimensions is decidedly undercut by Digby's arguments throughout the narrative that her experience and few trivial failings enhance rather than lessen her suitability as a mate. Nor are Theagenes' own attempts to seduce the girl entirely consistent with his assertions of her inviolability.

But the inadequacies of Digby's literary picture of the true nature of Venetia's fragile humanity pose a more immediate problem when they reappear in the real-life history of her death; and it is this finale to the idealized love affair that lies most directly behind Hawthorne's tale. Upon Venetia's death, rumors circulate that her husband has killed her by making her drink as a beauty aid viper wine, a drink "vitalized" with a snake extract believed to have restorative powers. Although Digby does not, as one vicious gossip claimed, attribute the putrefaction of Venetia's brain to the restorative, he does, in trying to answer the rumors, admit that he frequently offered the wine to her as physic. "My wife attributed her vigorous health to it; for these ten yeares her head never aked and of late she looked better and fresher than she had done in seven yeares before."[6] Whether true or not, the rumors do at least point to the virtuoso's very real willingness to treat his wife with drugs too dangerous to be prescribed by an amateur. As Hawthorne sees, the step is not far from the Neoplatonist's blindly confident recommendation of the venom as a beauty aid for his "Stelliana" to Aylmer's fatal attempt to conform his earthly Georgiana to his ideal image of her.

To recognize that the story is in important ways about Sir Kenelm Digby, Renaissance Neoplatonist and virtuoso, however, is not to resolve all problems, but merely to exchange one set for another. To be sure, Aylmer's perfectionist monomania appears less hyperbolic when we understand that his notions simply develop the potential tragedy of a real man's career, that the melodrama almost occurred. But while the story seems less distant, less mechanical as history than as allegory, the new problem arises of the peculiar significance of Digby for Hawthorne. The immediate impulse is to platonize Digby into a representative figure of some sort. The interest in Puritan history that informs Hawthorne's early tales is understandable; we can recognize why an American author might consider Ann Hutchinson or John Endicott properly native material.[7] But a story about Kenelm Digby introduces history too obscure to be taken straight, as antiquarian biography.

This desire to broaden the scope of the story is not, however, merely a function of our modern discomfort with what we fear to be Hawthorne's taste for the arcane and remote. Hawthorne himself encourages this breadth as he places in Aylmer's library "the early volumes of the Transactions of the Royal Society" (p. 48). The reference might at first seem another innocent biographical note. Digby was, of course, a charter member of the Society; he sat on its first council, and the observations about plants which so interested Hawthorne were presented at one of the Gresham College convocations. Yet, in fact, the association of Digby and the Royal Society is an allusion very different in kind from those clues used to identify Digby in the first place. The scientist's brief connection with the Society at the end of his career had no great influence on his biography; indeed, he died before the group even began to publish

the *Transactions* that Aylmer reads. The reference to this somewhat later community of scientists, then, serves not to recall one more detail about Digby, but rather to evoke a broader context. The allusion raises the questions of why Hawthorne brings together Digby, Aylmer, and the Royal Society, how Aylmer's perfectionist goals reflect those of the new science, and, in the most interesting inversion of all, why it is Digby, not Newton, who most clearly embodies for Hawthorne the essence of the Society and its method.

Hawthorne's claim that "the members, knowing little of the limits of natural possibility, were continually recording wonders, or proposing methods whereby wonders might be wrought" (p. 48) suggests that Digby stands as representative scientist primarily in his gullibility. The Society itself, though hardly acknowledging Digby as their epitome, sadly remarks his credulity. One enemy of the new method, the hostile Henry Stubbe, called Digby "the Pliny of our age for lying" because he championed the magic powder of sympathy and believed in the petrified city of Ongila. Much to the chagrin of the more discerning scientists, Stubbe then proceeded to read Digby's failing as symptomatic of the problems of the Society as a whole. Recalling this attack, the Society could not, in their otherwise favorable obituary notice of Digby, help but regret the "credulity or want of veracity" which had by association so hurt their own credibility. Yet Hawthorne is right to sense with Stubbe the degree to which this gullibility is shared by most of the virtuosi. The early *Transactions* do seem naïve, mixing precise accounts of mining and tides with fanciful tales of monstrous births, stone-eating worms, and the "marvellous" power of pennyroyal to kill rattlesnakes. Even more fantastic are the records of the Society's first five years, where the fellows note the ability of spiders to escape from the center of a circle of powdered unicorn horn; and the minutes record with pathetic regularity the suggestion that someone remember to bring the miraculous sympathy powder to the next meeting.[8]

Yet were Digby's presence in the story only to remind us of the credulity of the early virtuosi, Hawthorne's critique might seem too easy, rather a cheap shot. The real significance of the coupling is not so much to emphasize the degree to which Digby's gullibility characterized the entire Royal Society as, conversely, to allow the Society's program to place Digby's experiments within a specific context of religious overbelief. As in *The Scarlet Letter* where Digby, mentioned by name, is said to have made scientific discoveries "hardly less than supernatural," so here the attempt is to depict an age "when the comparatively recent discovery of electricity and other kindred mysteries of nature, seemed to open paths into the region of miracle" (p. 36).[9] The seventeenth century itself recognized the miraculous potential of science as forecast by the Gresham College meetings. One thinks of Dryden's praise in his "Essay of Dramatic Poesy" for the virtuosi's revelation of a "new Nature"; or of Thomas Sprat's claim in his history of the Society that "we may well ghess that the absolute perfection of the *True Philosophy,* is not now far off."[10] Robert Heilman has already noted how **"The Birthmark"** plays on a general confusion of science and religion, whereby Aylmer is transformed into a priest-like figure offering communion from a deadly cup. With the reference to the Royal Society, we are meant to localize this confusion historically as part of that tense transition from medieval to modern science, and to draw on our own familiarity with the hopefully expectant tone of the age to fill in a background within which Aylmer can operate. Thus **"The Birthmark,"** rather than remaining a biographical account of a single virtuoso, expands to become Hawthorne's version of those intellectual histories variously entitled "Science and Religion in the Seventeenth Century."[11]

II

But if Hawthorne is only examining the problematic birth of the new science, his reference to Digby is still puzzling. It is, after all, Newton, not Digby, who is the inevitable hero of the other science-and-religion studies. To see why Digby is chosen as representative figure, we must return to Aylmer's library and examine the remaining volumes, ones much darker than the innocently jubilant *Transactions.* The presence there of works by "Albertus Magnus, Cornelius Agrippa, Paracelsus, and the famous friar who created the prophetic Brazen Head" (p. 48) suggests that the story covers a wider range than expected, that, though Digby is surely the *point d'appui,* **"The Birthmark"** goes beyond chronicling the foibles of the Royal Society to attack a whole tradition of problematic magico-science.

That at the most elementary level the works of Cornelius Agrippa belong in Digby's library is clear. Digby's meeting in the "Loose Fantasies" with the Brachman who shows him an image of Stelliana's suffering condition is merely an incident lifted from the famous legend of Agrippa's similar revelations in the reflections of his magic mirror.[12] Yet more importantly, the mention of this most notorious Renaissance magus alters the terms used to characterize Aylmer's experiments, as a tradition of magic is associated with the more innocent combination of science and religion. The significance of this addition is seen in examining the role Agrippa plays in the history of Renaissance science. Compiler of the clearest and most useful survey of Renaissance magic, Agrippa overturns Marsilio Ficino's delicate attempt to reconcile Hermetic and Neoplatonic religious traditions with orthodox Christianity, and, by identifying Ficino's "influences" as planetary demons which can be compelled to perform services, systematizes as a powerfully magical cosmology what is in the earlier man only a

very vague psychological process.[13] The meaning of a uniquely Christian experience is threatened, as religious rites, pagan and Christian, simply become more magic incantations, attempts to appeal to the same powers which he, as magician, approaches as demonic familiars. In his syncretism, a conflict begins to develop between three frames of reference that cannot exist simultaneously. Any two of the three might perhaps work out a compromise model for coexistence; but when the world is seen to be at once magical, scientific, and religious, competition is bound to result in the death of one of these world views.

The mention of the alchemist Theophrastus Paracelsus reinforces the suspicion that the sources of Aylmer's failure lie at least in part in the challenge magic offers to traditional Christian principles. Paracelsus too, even more than Agrippa, hastens the process by which Ficino's natural, "spiritual" magic is revealed to be actually of an irreligious "demonic" variety. Totally discounting, as Agrippa did not, the possibility of the purely psychological influence of a cosmic presence on the human soul, Paracelsus pictured magic instead as closely related to medicine, a wholly practical science operating not on any nebulously defined "spirit" but directly on the intellect. "And as poison or a remedy with all its effects can be introduced into man by man, so the Astrologer—Magus—can imbue man with firmamental power."[14] This alliance of science and magic, which allows that the firmamental power of demonic spirits can be dispensed as easily as aspirin, affords little room for a defense of spirituality as something distinct from a world mechanism. Hawthorne worries over the substitution when, in the "history of the long dynasty of the Alchemists" that Aylmer gives Georgiana, the Golden Rule of the New Testament is replaced by the "Golden Principle" as a means of eliciting the pure from the vile and base (p. 46).

Yet even more telling than the reductively mechanical aspect of his demonic magic is the problematic concept of Prime Matter which lies at the heart of the Paracelsian cosmology. In a traditional Aristotelian definition of the hylomorphic composition of material substance, matter is imagined as the passive state of pure potentiality, with the quasi-platonic form as the universal principle which places the body in its specific class and determines its essence. Paracelsus, however, operating in a tradition descended from the Stoics and more directly from Avicebron, tries to invert this definition, placing matter immediately below God in the cosmic hierarchy, and claiming, contra Aristotle, that it is form and not matter that is the principle of individuation.[15] Prime Matter thus becomes equivalent to the Platonic Idea, static and eternal, an element not of sensual perception but of contemplation.

Although Paracelsus argues that his spiritualization of matter involves no threat of materialism, others may not be willing so easily to agree. The monistic vision of a unified cosmos whose creation is a separation, the fall of an undifferentiated spiritual Prime Matter into specificity and physical presence, tends to represent spirit as merely the kernel of the visible body, the state of finest corporeality. Since all man can truly know is discovered in and through the fallen matter of the real world, the characteristics of that matter inevitably color his conception of spirit, however much he may try to "purify" out the baseness. Paracelsus himself demonstrates the problem as he uses "prime matter" in the second, less metaphysical sense to mean simply something raw and unprepared, such as the wheat which will become first bread and finally the flesh of the organism. Such a definition of spiritual matter as the wheat of the flesh may ultimately destroy any sense of a spirit truly different in kind from the stuff of the world.[16]

It is this tradition of magic as crypto-materialism that lies behind Hawthorne's historical allusions in the tale. The misdefinition of spirit as etherealized matter clearly unites the alchemical works on Aylmer's shelf. Agrippa's magic, by imagining between the World Spirit and the human one an intermediary realm of demons whom man can control by physical means, tends finally to debase the upper realm, pulling it down to man's earthly level. Indeed the very idea of a systematic magic, where physiological changes can be regularly effected by an established sequence of incantations and talismans, prevents the pseudo-spiritualism from ever becoming wholly free of the taint of mechanism. Similarly it is this confusion which links Digby's science, however more exact than that of the alchemists, with the earlier magic. His belief, inherited from Paracelsus, that physical birthmarks are the result of the "astral" impressions of the imagination, unites matter and spirit in a way ultimately fatal to the latter. Finally even the Royal Society aligns itself with these earlier materialists, though Hawthorne need not call Newton "the last of the Magi" to establish the bond. The mistake lies not in their credulity, but with their confidence that the guidebook to the miraculous is not essentially different from a notebook of one of their meetings, that in Sprat's words "by long studying of the *Spirits,* of the *Bloud,* of the *Nourishment,* of the parts of the *Diseases,* of the *Advantages,* of the accidents which belong to *humane bodies* . . . there, without question be very near ghesses made, even at the more *exalted,* and *immediate* Actions of the Soul" (p. 83).

And what of Albertus and the Brazen Head? Modern scholarship has identified the issue of the Egyptian talking statues as central to the differentiation of spiritual from demonic magic. Focusing on a passage in the Hermetic *Asclepius* which describes the Egyptian practise of calling down spirits to act as temporary souls for magic religious idols, critics see in the Renaissance debate over the spiritual or demonic nature of the influences thus summoned an epitome of the whole problem of the dangerous potential of magic.[17] From our point of view, the inability of the apologists of magic to convince their contemporaries that the animation was the result of general spiritual influence rather than of planetary demons embodies with comic clarity the persistent failure of the magicians to imagine a spirit that is anything more than a gauzy matter. For Hawthorne then to link Albertus, inventor of the first automaton,[18] and Roger Bacon, builder of a talking brazen head, with the rest of our spiritualizing materialists shows a remarkable ability to grasp intuitively philosophical connections which scholars are only today beginning to delineate. The mistake is the same again and again; Bacon constructing his head, Agrippa drawing his pentagrams, Digby injecting his geranium with "spiritual" salts, Harvey dissecting a witch's toad: all foolishly search in the material for the source of spiritual ills. With such historical insights Hawthorne prepares the reader to respond to the claim that Aylmer "handled physical details, as if there were nothing beyond them; yet spiritualized them all, and redeemed himself from materialism, by his strong and eager aspiration towards the infinite" (p. 49) not with Georgiana's wide-eyed admiration, but with horror.

III

Having seen that the books in Aylmer's library outline a whole tradition of confused "alchemical" attempts to spiritualize the material, a history to which Aylmer's own experiment is the natural conclusion, the reader can proceed to read correctly the troublesome tone of the story, to sort out the multiple ironies and uncover the moral center in Hawthorne's criticism of Aylmer's mistaking a wholly physical fact for a mark of spiritual inadequacy. The association of the scientist not only with the virtuosi, but with the far less reputable Digby, Agrippa, and Paracelsus, lays to rest any lingering doubts that his experiment, though misconceived, is yet basically noble. Aylmer, no less than his teachers, is led by a faulty definition of spirit to act foolishly and finally destructively. Moreover, the skill evident in Hawthorne's subtle delineation of the tradition answers those who find the story and its science clumsy and sophomoric; the stiff language and cardboard apparatus are not inventions, but part of the historical original, the tone of which Hawthorne has duplicated with extreme care and great facility. But most important, the intricacy of the relation between Aylmer and his scientific precursors, the enormous attention to detail in this recreation of a specific historical situation, suggests that the focus is quite precisely on science's problematic concept of spirit, rather than on some "larger" question of art, sex, or possession.[19]

But the difficulty remains of the contemporaneity of the tale, of why Hawthorne chooses to explore this particular confusion in 1843. Perhaps the best approach to the question is through the related problem of the story's own temporal setting. Although our magic tradition stretches from the Middle Ages through the seventeenth century, Hawthorne in fact locates his tale later, "in the latter part of the last century" (p. 36). What then is the place of this period in our history? The French Enlightenment, of course, suggests a characteristically reductive variation on the mechanical men of Friar Bacon and Albertus in its model of man the machine. The anti-spiritual, anti-church bias of the *philosophes* leads them to bring Locke's empiricism even closer to a thorough-going materialism. In his attack on the Englishman's postulation of the mind's capacity for "reflection," Condillac tries to prove that a proper theory of sensation can sufficiently account for all the faculties of the mind. To demonstrate how, he imagines a statue which has at first only the sense of smell. With this single sense, the statue, he argues, would yet possess many faculties, such as memory, comparison, judgment, and imagination. By the gradual super-addition of the other senses, he claims, all human faculties can finally be duplicated by a statue with the capacity for sensation. Although Condillac himself does not mean to propose a purely materialist philosophy and does in fact affirm the existence of a spiritual soul, yet the tendency of his comparison is clear. If man's abilities can be wholly explained as the sum of his sensations, if the statue is indeed an adequate model for man, the postulation of a spiritual element becomes unnecessary.[20]

Yet it is unlikely that Hawthorne felt such a simple-minded materialism, the transmutation of the mechanical man into man the machine, to be his most serious problem. His early **"Virtuoso's Collection"** exists to suggest the ease with which the threat of the virtuosi-materialist sons of Bayle may be dismissed. More dangerous, in that it seems to speak a more earnestly spiritual language, is the philosophy of Emanuel Swedenborg. Unlike the systems of the *philosophes,* who only toy with magical categories, Swedenborg's cosmology is a direct descendant of the magico-scientific program, one of his early works using a vocabulary borrowed not only from the seventeenth-century Cambridge Platonists, but, more interestingly, from Paracelsus himself. There are, in addition, some suggestions that the tale may allude directly to the Swedish mystic. The story's setting in the second half of the eighteenth century, of course, falls closer to the years of Swedenborg's mystic career (1745-72) than to the period of any of the other figures mentioned. Moreover Aylmer's exploration "of the profoundest mines" (p. 42) early in his studies may recall the Swede's fame as a mining engineer. Most important, however, is that Aylmer's tendency to read Georgiana's blemish as "the symbol of his wife's liability to sin, sorrow, decay, and death" (p. 39) derives from the Swedenborgian notion of correspondences. All of the figures studied support, of course, some vaguely Neoplatonic theory of the hier-

archical structure of the universe, of an analogous microcosm and macrocosm. Only Swedenborg, however, literalized this rather poetic analogical principle into a series of exact mystical equations, making of nature a divine cryptogram the meaning of which can be read off with the appropriate bilingual dictionary. Thus while Paracelsus and Digby can tell Aylmer that Georgiana's birthmark is of spiritual origin, only the lexicographer Swede can tell him that it means precisely "falsity or evil."[21]

Despite the rampant mysticism of Swedenborg's later career, his program, like those of his alchemical ancestors, was fundamentally a scientific one. Indeed Swedenborg's position as the greatest proponent of Cartesian science in the eighteenth century is exactly equivalent to that of Digby in the seventeenth. The basically scientific paradigms he would use "to prove the immortality of the soul to the senses themselves" are especially prominent in his early anatomies of the animal kingdom. Everything starts as mechanics; he assures us "that this body of ours is mechanical, that its organs are mechanical, that its senses are mechanical, the intellect, the reason, and the soul itself" and that "if we had the microscopes, we might be able to see the entire structure of both the soul and the spirit." His faith that such physiological visions are nevertheless underwritten by divinity assumes the same continuity of matter and spirit that allows the alchemists to insist that their distillations are governed primarily by the spiritual condition of the adept. The mystic conversion of 1743 alters nothing. The change from the study of nerve cells as the center of spiritual influx to the examination of the celestial realm as *Maximus Homo* represents merely an inversion of the same materialistic assumptions; and the nature of spirit mystically revealed in cosmic flights shows itself no less mechanistic than when scientifically discovered in microscopic probings.[22] Swedenborg is not, then, a freak, but merely the culmination of the whole tradition here outlined, the man who, taking Sprat's faith in method as miracle a little more seriously than anyone else yet had, sees through his microscope the layout of the celestial city.

Once we have established Swedenborg at the end of our line of spiritualizing materialists, we are home free; the transition from the *Heavenly Arcana* to the American Renaissance is instantaneous and inevitable. Not only does Swedenborgianism as a creed have its greatest success in mid-century America, but more simply, as Emerson tells us, "this age is Swedenborg's"; the Swedish mystic stands as the symbolic father of the whole period of spiritual ferment, in which a subjective philosophy teaches "that the soul makes its own world." Well, almost so. Although the 1830's and '40's present a veritable chowder of misguided idealisms, in fact not all subjectivists are closet materialists. Indeed Emerson himself, retracting an earlier statement that lumped to-

gether Swedenborg and Christ, mesmerism and eloquence and prayer, seems to get the drop on all materialist physicians whose "spirit is matter reduced to an
extreme thinness."[23] Still, the reduction is fair enough.
In Rochester two sisters convince willing spiritualists,
including joyful Swedenborgian ministers, that the
sound of their snapping kneecaps brings communications from the other world. In Salem are published advertisements for a seed which, with the aid of an "elec-
tric machine," will, like Digby's injected plants, grow
to maturity in a few minutes. And in New York, the one
poet who of all American writers seemed the most
purely aesthetic, the champion of the Beautiful in art, is
yet preparing a lecture on the universe which will diagram the course of history as a pseudo-Newtonian machine wherein gravity mechanically forces dispersed
matter back to an annihilating reunion in the "spiritual"
matter of the unparticled particle.[24]

Alchemy was alive and well in mid-century America.
And Hawthorne worried, as the threat of death by viper
wine pressed uncomfortably near. When his fiancée
found her headaches relieved by a mesmerist's influence, fear, not contempt, was the only sensible response.
"And what delusion," Hawthorne writes Sophia, "can
be more lamentable and mischievous than to mistake
the physical and material for the spiritual? What so
miserable as to lose the soul's true, though hidden,
knowledge and consciousness of heaven, in the mist of
an earth-born vision?" Later in his novel *The Blithedale
Romance,* he made it clear that his fear was not simply
that these materializing spiritualists were wrong, but
that their anti-spiritual campaign, though wrong, might
yet succeed.

> If these phenomena have not humbug at the bottom, so
> much the worse for us. What can they indicate, in a
> spiritual way, except that the soul of man is descending
> to a lower point than it has ever before reached while
> incarnate? We are pursuing a downward course in the
> eternal march, and thus bringing ourselves into the
> same range with beings whom death, in requital of
> their gross and evil lives, has degraded below human-
> ity. To hold intercourse with spirits of this order, we
> must stoop and grovel in some element more vile than
> earthly dust.
>
> . . . The less we have to say to them the better, lest we
> share their fate.[25]

To take up pen in 1843, then, and turn to an alchemical
tradition of spiritualized matter, of transfigured lead, is
not to create effete allegories but to cry out against the
follies of yesterday and tomorrow. If Coleridge will
persist in announcing that today's subjective revolution
finds in the mere "creaturely" state only the resurgent
ashes of the alchemists' phoenix or of Digby's reviving
flowers, then to expose the dangers of these past "reviv-
als" becomes not antiquarianism, but the first order of
business.[26]

Notes

1. Hawthorne's career may be divided roughly into
four periods of high productivity. The misnamed
"solitary years" (1825-37) are years of apprenticeship, of reading and writing, culminating in a series of tales dealing with seventeenth- and
eighteenth-century problems, especially those relating to Puritanism. During the next five years,
Hawthorne, occupied with the Boston Custom
House, Brook Farm, and his new fiancée, produces only a collection of children's stories and
an edition of Horatio Bridge's *Journal of an African Cruiser.* A second period of high activity
(1842-45) coincides with his stay at the Old
Manse. The stories of this period treat contemporary issues and thus form a history of his own
times to parallel the earlier history of the Puritans.
After the years at the Salem Custom House comes
the "major phase," during which are published
Hawthorne's three major novels (1850-52). A final
late period (1859-64) produces *The Marble Faun*
and the four uncompleted romances.

2. Alfred S. Reid, "Hawthorne's Humanism: 'The
Birthmark' and Sir Kenelm Digby," *American Literature,* 38 (1966), 337-351.

3. Criticism has thus far tended to play the two periods of stories off against each other to the benefit
of neither period. The general feeling that the earlier Puritan tales are superior to the later allegories leads some to assume that history, though not
itself the center of Hawthorne's art, was at least a
clear stimulus to his moral imagination. Yet while
the later tales are considered less successful than
the earlier, their presumed unhistorical character is
still read back into the first period as proof that
history is only a medium for meaning, and not the
meaning itself. To argue, then, that a later story
has an interesting historical reading is to suggest
two things at once: first that the Transcendental
tales, though difficult, are not exactly less successful than the Puritan ones; and second that the history in the later works implies the centrality of the
historical imagination throughout his career. "The
Birthmark" is a particularly convenient test case
for this theory, for while critics usually agree it
has a kind of power, the tale in general receives
less attention than, say, "Rappaccini's Daughter"
or "The Artist of the Beautiful." In the numerous
book-length studies of Hawthorne, the story receives extended treatment only once, in Richard
Harter Fogle's *Hawthorne's Fiction: The Light
and the Dark* (Norman: Univ. of Oklahoma, 1964).
If a contextual reading can render a means to define the hitherto elusive excellence of the tale, this
reclamation of one more underrated work should
of itself convince readers of the pragmatic value,

at least, of historical analysis. For a discussion of history and the two periods, see Randall Stewart, *Nathaniel Hawthorne* (New Haven: Yale Univ. Press, 1948), pp. 69-71; and Frederick Crews, *The Sins of the Fathers* (London: Oxford Univ. Press, 1966), pp. 27-43.

4. Digby's salt solution and his mention of Drebel's vial are both from "A Discourse concerning the Vegetation of Plants," appended to *Of Bodies and of Man's Soul* (London, 1669), pp. 222-224. Reid's similar discussion of Digby's plants is on p. 340, his version of Digby's moles, p. 345. See Reid, *passim,* for speculation on how Hawthorne could have learned Digby's history. Although it is uncertain where Hawthorne first learned of Digby, my own guess is that it was in the scientist's "Observations upon *Religio Medici,*"; appended to most editions of Browne's essay. The critique contains most of what Hawthorne would need to know about Digby's science, including a heated discussion of the famous ash-plant; Venetia, however, is not mentioned. The corresponding experiments by Aylmer appear on pp. 53, 47, and 41 respectively of *The Centenary Edition of the Works of Nathaniel Hawthorne* (Columbus: Ohio State Univ. Press, 1974), X. All future references to the tale will cite the page number of this edition in the text.

5. The manuscript "Loose Fantasies" were published as Digby's *Private Memoirs* in 1827. The unsigned introduction to this edition (London: Saunders and Otley) gives all the necessary facts about Venetia, including the brothel comment, quoted from John Aubrey on p. xxx. The biographer is E. W. Bligh in *Sir Kenelm Digby and His Venetia* (London: Sampson Low, Marston & Co., 1932), p. 13.

6. Quoted by Reid, p. 338.

7. For an analysis of Ann Hutchinson in *The Scarlet Letter,* see Michael J. Colacurcio, "Footsteps of Ann Hutchinson," *ELH,* 39 (1972), 439-494. For analyses of Endicott in "Endicott and the Red Cross," see Sacvan Bercovitch, "Endicott's Breast-plate," *Studies in Short Fiction,* 4 (1967), 289-299; and his "Diabolus in Salem," *English Language Notes,* 6 (1969), 280-285. Behind all such attempts to read Hawthorne as seriously interested in history lies Roy Harvey Pearce's pioneering study of "My Kinsman, Major Molineux," "Hawthorne and the Sense of the Past," *ELH,* 21 (1954), 327-349.

8. Stubbe's attack is mentioned in Joseph Glanvill, *A Praefatory Answer to Mr. Henry Stubbe . . . in his Animadversions* (London, 1671), p. 162, and in all subsequent biographies of Digby. The obituary is in Thomas Birch, *A History of the Royal Society . . . from its Rise* (London, 1756-57), II, 82. *The Philosophical Transactions . . . abridged* (London, 1809), I, 10, 20; 6, 16, 120 *et passim.* The unicorn experiment is in Birch, I, 35; and the powder requests, I, 25, 26, 29, *et passim.*

9. Digby is mentioned as an acquaintance of Chillingworth in Ch. 9, "The Leech," *Centenary Ed., I,* 121.

10. Thomas Sprat, *History of the Royal Society* (London, 1667), p. 29.

11. R. B. Heilman, "Hawthorne's 'The Birthmark': Science as Religion," *South Atlantic Quarterly,* 48 (1949), 575-583. Some of the science-and-religion studies are: Paul H. Kocher, *Science and Religion in Elizabethan England* (San Marino: Huntington Library, 1953); Richard S. Westfall, *Science and Religion in Seventeenth-Century England* (Ann Arbor: Univ. of Michigan, 1973); Edwin Arthur Burtt, *The Metaphysical Origins of Modern Science* (Garden City: Doubleday, 1934); Alexandre Koyré, *From the Closed World to the Infinite Universe* (New York: Harper, 1958). See Westfall's bibliographical essay for a more complete list.

12. *Memoirs,* pp. 119-153. Hawthorne mentions the mirror in "The Virtuoso's Collection" (*Centenary Ed.,* X, 482). The story of the vision of the distant lover was most readily available to Hawthorne in Sir Walter Scott's *Lay of the Last Minstrel,* Canto VI, xvi.

13. For a study of the transition effected by Agrippa, see D. P. Walker, *Spiritual and Demonic Magic from Ficino to Campanella* (London: Warburg Institute, 1958), esp. pp. 90-96.

14. Quoted in Walter Pagel, *Paracelsus, an Introduction to Philosophical Medicine in the Era of the Renaissance* (Basel: S. Karger, 1958), p. 62. See also Walker, pp. 96-106; and, for a general introduction to Hawthorne and alchemy, Raymona E. Hull, "Hawthorne and the Magic Elixir of Life," *ESQ,* 67 (1972), 97-107.

15. Pagel, pp. 227-236. See also his article, "The Prime Matter of Paracelsus," *Ambix,* 9 (1961), 117-135.

16. *Labyrinthus Medicorum Errantium,* V, in *The Hermetic and Alchemical Writings of Paracelsus,* ed. Arthur Edward Waite (1894; rpt. Berkeley: Shambhala, 1976), II, 167.

17. See Walker, pp. 40-44; and Frances A. Yates, *Giordano Bruno and the Hermetic Tradition* (New York: Random House, 1969), pp. 36-38, 66-68.

18. Hawthorne mentions this fabled aspect of Albertus' career in "The Artist of the Beautiful," *Centenary Ed.,* X, 465. The coupling of Albertus' man

of brass and Bacon's brazen head with Owen's own automaton may, in fact, measure the degree to which Warland is himself infected by the materialism which so misleads Aylmer.

19. The major statements of the positions alluded to are Cleanth Brooks, Jr., and Robert Penn Warren, *Understanding Fiction* (New York: Appleton-Century-Crofts, 1943), pp. 103-106; Kenneth Payson Kempton, *The Short Story* (Cambridge: Harvard, 1947), pp. 74-78, 82-83; Millicent Bell, *Hawthorne's View of the Artist* (New York: SUNY, 1962), pp. 182-185; and Crews, pp. 125-126. While I do not imagine my historical reading provides a final response to these other positions, it does, at least, suggest a standard against which to measure ironies which Fogle fears to be "almost unfathomable" (p. 131).

20. On Condillac's model, see Frederick Copleston, S. J., *A History of Philosophy* (Garden City: Doubleday, 1964), VI, i, 44-49.

21. *Arcana Coelestia* (New York: Swedenborg Foundation, 1954), IX, 596. For a general introduction to the idea of correspondence, see Inge Jonsson, *Emanuel Swedenborg* (New York: Twayne, 1971), pp. 104-118.

22. Swedenborg's program, stated several times during his early career, is quoted by Jonsson, p. 48. The mechanism quotations are cited in Signe Toksvig, *Emanuel Swedenborg, Scientist and Mystic* (New Haven: Yale Univ. Press, 1948), pp. 88, 87. For the argument on the continuity of the career, see Jonsson, *passim.*

23. Emerson makes this statement early in "Experience" (1844), thereby retracting a more materialistic definition of spirit made near the end of *Nature* (1836). The comment on Swedenborg is made in the journal for 1854. H. Bruce Franklin in *Future Perfect* (London: Oxford, 1966), makes the transition from the eighteenth to the nineteenth century in a different way, suggesting convincingly that Aylmer's scientific "miracles" are really recent nineteenth-century inventions (p. 14). I would, however, want to distinguish between his picture of the story as science fiction and my own sense that it is a somewhat more critical historical fiction about the problematic origins of science.

24. The story of the Fox sisters is told by Alice Felt Tyler, *Freedom's Ferment* (New York: Harper, 1961), pp. 82-83. The advertisement appeared in the *Salem Observer* for July 9, 1836. A similar magic salad was announced on the following October 29. The poet-aesthete is, of course, Edgar Allan Poe, and his lecture, an early form of *Eureka*. For discussion of these and other examples,

see Elizabeth Ruth Hosmer, "Science and Pseudoscience in the Writings of Nathaniel Hawthorne," Diss. Univ. of Illinois, 1948.

25. Letter of October 18, 1841, *Love Letters of Nathaniel Hawthorne* (1907; rpt. Washington: NCR Microcards, 1972), p. 64. *The Blithedale Romance,* Ch. 23, "The Village Hall," *Centenary Ed.,* III, 199.

26. Coleridge, *The Friend* (Princeton: Princeton, 1969), i, p. 516n. The coupling of the alchemists and Digby in this footnote may lie directly behind Hawthorne's rather more negative delineation of the tradition.

John Gatta, Jr. (essay date summer 1978)

SOURCE: Gatta, John, Jr. "Aylmer's Alchemy in 'The Birthmark.'" *Philological Quarterly* 57, no. 3 (summer 1978): 399-413.

[*In the following essay, Gatta holds that "The Birthmark" represents Hawthorne's best use of "alchemical philosophy" as a metaphor for Romantic, Platonist, and Transcendentalist ideas and traditions.*]

In retrospect, it becomes all too apparent that Aylmer's scheme to "perfect" his wife Georgianna is tragically misguided. Ordinary human nature or singular character defects in Aylmer may be partly to blame. But the fatal error that Aylmer commits in **"The Birthmark"** also has discernible intellectual roots; it may be associated, in fact, with more than one historically-conditioned ideology. This pregnant ambiguity in the historical application of Hawthorne's parable is reflected in the curiously mixed identity of Aylmer himself. He is, perhaps most obviously, a scientist, and one useful reading of the story has centered upon its symbolic critique of the modern propensity to deify science.[1] Yet the "natural philosophy" professed by Aylmer seems in many respects more closely allied to the atmosphere of medieval occult wisdom than it does to the temper of modern rational science, as the "dark old tomes" in his professional library will attest. Critics have pointed out that Aylmer is not only a scientist, but fills as well the assorted roles of Romantic artist, Platonist, and Transcendentalist.[2]

In the medieval and Renaissance tradition of esoteric alchemy, Hawthorne discovered a metaphorical system capable of sustaining these several diverse associations within a single dramatic fable. The disparity between man's drive to achieve self-transcendence and his stubbornly fallible nature, the subtle intermingling of noble aspirations with ignoble ambition and self-deception in the questing human heart—all of this, too, for Hawthorne came to a natural artistic focus in the figure of the alchemist. Alchemical motifs, particularly allusions to the Great Elixir of Life, appear throughout Hawthorne's writing. They serve important functions in tales like **"Dr. Heiddeger's Experiment," "The Great Carbuncle," "Rappaccini's Daughter,"** and in the last unfinished romances. Further mention of alchemical themes occurs in the *American Notebooks* and in sketches like **"Sir William Pepperell"** and **"A Virtuoso's Collection."**[3] But Hawthorne was rarely able to exploit the symbolic resonances of alchemical philosophy as successfully as he did in composing **"The Birthmark."**

The general theme of the alchemist's quest for the Philosopher's Stone and the Elixir of Life, its liquid and medicinal counterpart, would have been available to Hawthorne through his reading in Gothic romance. Yet Hawthorne's acquaintance with the imagery, procedures, and spiritual theory of alchemy seems to have been more detailed than anything he could have gleaned solely from his reading in romancers like Scott and Godwin. In 1842, for example, he wrote himself a note about the idea of curing "Imaginary diseases . . . by impossible remedies—as, a dose of the Grand Elixir, in the yolk of a Phoenix's egg" (VIII, 229). Both the egg and the phoenix symbolize particular aspects of the transformation process in standard hermetic descriptions of the Great Work.[4] Hawthorne's writing also contains recurring references to key figures in the alchemical tradition—to Paracelsus (1493-1541), Roger Bacon (1214-94), Albertus Magnus (1193-1280), Cornelius Agrippa of Nettesheim (1486-1535)—and one mention of the Book of Hermes.[5] And he was sufficiently aware of alchemical color symbolism to recognize that the final stage in the Great Work was the *rubedo,* the moment when a red-colored tincture, powder, elixir, or miraculous Stone appeared in the laboratory vessel. In the *Dolliver Romance* Hawthorne observes how one drop of the doctor's elixir turns a goblet of water "to a rosy hue of great brilliancy."[6] His color-filled description of the flower species that is supposed to be a critical ingredient in Septimius Felton's elixir of immortality is even more fraught with Hermetic significance: "The flower was of the richest crimson, with a gleam of gold in its centre, which yet was partly hidden."[7]

Where Hawthorne obtained his knowledge of alchemy, beyond the Gothic trappings abundant in popular romances, is less certain. Some classic literary works, including Ben Jonson's *The Alchemist,* Goethe's *Faust,* and Chaucer's *Canon's Yeoman's Tale,* could have supplied him with the necessary details.[8] Yet probably Hawthorne would have been able to school himself most thoroughly and naturally in alchemical philosophy through his enthusiastic absorption in contemporary encyclopedias, biographical dictionaries, and journals, all of which contained discussions of the topic. Such sources not only related the history and exoteric procedures of the art, but often expressed a surprisingly tolerant recognition of the "spiritual" or "mystical" goals of serious alchemy.[9]

In **"The Birthmark,"** the most immediate indication of Aylmer's participation in the occult tradition is his own earnest discourse to Georgianna on "the resources of his art":

> He gave a history of the long dynasty of the Alchemists, who spent so many ages in quest of the universal solvent, by which the Golden Principle might be elicited from all things vile and base. Aylmer appeared to believe, that, by the plainest scientific logic, it was altogether within the limits of possibility to discover this long-sought medium; but, he added, a philosopher who should go deep enough to acquire the power, would attain too lofty a wisdom to stoop to the exercise of it. Not less singular were his opinions in regard to the Elixir Vitae. He more than intimated, that it was his option to concoct a liquid that should prolong life for years—perhaps interminably—but that it would produce a discord in nature, which all the world, and chiefly the quaffer of the immortal nostrum, would find cause to curse.

(X, 46)

The reservations Aylmer expresses about harnessing the vast powers of occult science help to establish the relative purity of his original character and aims. But only on the most literal plane is it true that he has disavowed any intention of seeking the Golden Principle. For in a larger symbolic sense, the critical action of the tale is nothing less than an attempt on Aylmer's part to transmute the *prima materia* of Georgianna's human nature to a "golden" state of perfection, purging it of those normal earthly impurities that come to appear comparatively "vile and base" to the eye of the impassioned seeker. The same point applies to his stated rejection of any plan to pursue the Elixir Vitae. For the draught he finally concocts for the removal of Georgianna's blemish, not to mention the "gold-colored liquid" he shows her earlier, is a recognizable type of the alchemist's Great Elixir: "He bore a crystal goblet, containing a liquid colorless as water, but bright enough to be the draught of immortality" (52-53). If its main object here is not the endless prolongation of life and restoration of youth, neither were these necessarily the main purposes assigned to the Elixir by traditional alchemy. The extraordinary curative, medicinal powers of the Elixir or Stone were often emphasized instead; thus Paracelsus insisted that it "purges the whole body of man, and cleanses it from all impurities"—including, one might imagine, a disfiguring birthmark.[10] Moreover, Aylmer's declaration to Georgianna that "You are fit for heaven without tasting death!" (53) indicates that he has some expectation of absolving her from the usual curse of mortality in the course of bringing about her bodily perfection. Even the disastrous effects finally produced by

Aylmer's mysterious draught, and associated earlier with his gold-colored "Elixir of Immortality," are quite consistent with traditional accounts of the Great Elixir, the use of which was normally conceded to be a perilous business.

In any case, what Aylmer hopes to achieve in eliminating Georgianna's sole physical defect is evidently more than a unique success in plastic surgery. His physical project is at once an outgrowth of the psychological obsession that begins to take hold in him from the first days of his marriage and an expression of his peculiar philosophical vision. Like alchemy itself, that vision combines various strands of idealism—including the Neoplatonic notion of a gradually ascending scale of spiritual reality and a principle of correspondences shared with the Swedenborgians: "The higher intellect, the imagination, the spirit, and even the heart, might all find their congenial aliment in pursuits which . . . would ascend from one step of powerful intelligence to another, until the philosopher should lay his hand on the secret of creative force, and perhaps make new worlds for himself" (36). The passage recalls Georgianna's later reflection on the way in which her husband's spirit "was ever on the march—ever ascending" (52) as well as the classic alchemical preoccupation with "steps or scales in the ladder of transmutation."[11] There is also a distinctly Hermetic flavor to Hawthorne's mention of a "secret of creative force," which the alchemists considered knowable through empirical investigation but which presumably afforded access to—or, by a less orthodox interpretation, mastery over—the invisible spiritual order. Thus Georgianna is said to be so impressed by Aylmer's optical marvels that she is almost ready to believe he "possessed sway over the spiritual world" (45). An alchemist's confidence in the correspondential relation between nature and spirit, and a concern with both the exoteric and esoteric aspects of alchemy, likewise emerges from the pages of Aylmer's scientific journal as Georgianna pores over them while awaiting her treatment: "He handled physical details, as if there were nothing beyond them; yet spiritualized them all, and redeemed himself from materialism, by his strong and eager aspiration towards the infinite. In his grasp, the veriest clod of earth assumed a soul" (49).

This last description of Aylmer's approach to the problem of spirit and experimental science parallels almost exactly the summary immediately preceding it of views held by the most renowned alchemical figures of the Middle Ages: "All these antique naturalists stood in advance of their centuries, yet were imbued with some of their credulity, and therefore were believed, and perhaps imagined themselves, to have acquired from the investigation of nature a power above nature, and from physics a sway over the spiritual world" (48). To speak of acquiring "from the investigation of nature a power above nature" is to echo, in turn, a cardinal principle of speculative alchemy attributed to Hermes himself: that "Whatever is below is like that which is above."[12] It is no coincidence that Aylmer's own journal of experimental research stands in the immediate company of other "sorcerer's books," works by Albertus Magnus, Cornelius Agrippa, Paracelsus, and Roger Bacon. Conversely, books by Francis Bacon or Newton seem to have no place in this library even though Hawthorne situates his tale sometime in the latter part of the eighteenth century. The period itself naturally tended to place the alchemist in an awkward position. Challenged on the one hand by the rationalistic outlook of the New Science, he was nevertheless encouraged on the other by a renewed Romantic interest in occult phenomena. And Hawthorne recognized clearly enough the residual presence of an older occult mentality even in new enterprises that purported to be strictly "scientific." Thus the discovery of electricity "seemed to open paths into the region of Miracle" (36), and the early volumes of the Transactions of the Royal Society in Aylmer's library are quite accurately represented as full of reports about recent magical occurrences.[13]

In this transitional intellectual atmosphere, which probably engaged Hawthorne's attention because it underscored the moral connection between competing ideologies, Aylmer's alchemical ambitions become only partially anachronistic. What he has instinctually done is to absorb certain speculative issues and technical resources of the New Science into the temper and philosophy of the old alchemy, with its incipient empiricism. But in nearly every case his most intensely pursued scientific projects turn out to be subtly modern adaptations of ancient Hermetic dreams. In addition to seeking the miraculous Stone and Elixir, for example, nearly all of the famous alchemists mentioned by Hawthorne reputedly involved themselves in efforts to create a homunculus, or artificial man.[14] Although Aylmer makes no overt attempt to construct a homunculus, Robert Arner has noticed that he tried in effect to "recreate" Georgianna by means of his experimental science, a theme Hawthorne enforces in his narrative through strategically placed allusions to the Pygmalion legend.[15] And despite the impressive legacy of chemical discoveries left to modern science by the medieval alchemist, the distinctive mark of his career was failure, since he inevitably failed to realize the one supreme object of all his experimentation. Similarly, Georgianna finds in reading her husband's scientific folio that he has accomplished many impressive scientific feats, but that "his most splendid successes were almost invariably failures, if compared to the ideal at which he aimed" (49).

Hawthorne elaborates the point using mineralogical imagery that suggests further alchemical associations with the great Stone: "His brightest diamonds were the merest pebbles, and felt to be so by himself, in comparison with the inestimable gems which lay hidden beyond his reach" (49). It is worth noting, too, that Aylmer's past research has taken the form of a methodical search into the secrets behind each of the four classic elements in the Hermetic cosmology. Having investigated "the highest cloud region," the "profoundest mines," "the fires of the volcano," and "the mystery of fountains" (42), he can at last feel prepared to lay open the ultimate Secret of spirit and perfection, the quintessence, through his transmutative experiment upon Georgianna.

Many more occult resemblances come to light as one moves from considerations of a general philosophical nature to a study of the palpable setting and substance of the tale. One notices first that the physical image Hawthorne presents of Aylmer corresponds almost stereotypically to the traditional pose of the alchemist: he is a "pale" and melancholic figure, who is later seen watching anxiously over the fires of his furnace, the presumed repository of the "philosophical fire." Completing a familiar tableau that could be drawn from any number of illustrations in actual alchemical tracts is the image of Aminidab, Aylmer's grimy and ill-clad assistant, in the background. The interpretation Hawthorne places upon the contrasting appearances of Aminidab—a figure of "man's physical nature"—and Aylmer—"a type of the spiritual element"—points up an ominous imbalance in the latter's character. Aylmer's later refusal to consider his assistant's advice to leave the birthmark alone contributes further to the impression that this "pale philosopher" has a fatal inclination to dwell amid abstractions. And the special thrust of his idealism, added to the antique sound of his name, suggests yet another cultural link—this one between Aylmer and Hawthorne's Puritan forebears. Like many Puritans, Aylmer is profoundly suspicious of the natural order and unappreciative of those elemental sources of happiness defined by Melville in *Moby Dick* as within the scope of "attainable felicity." From a disparaging point of view, one could say that Aylmer, in his zealous pride, rejects even the beautiful Georgianna, "the best that earth has to offer" (55), because her human loveliness comes to appear intolerably "vile and base" (44) set against the alchemist's all-possessing dream of the quintessence. At the same time, however, critics have rightly stressed the complex division of sympathies implied in the Alymer-Aminidab contrast, pointing out that the cruel laughter and unattractive presence of Aminidab are a measure of Hawthorne's willingness to affirm even the compulsive idealism and aspiring folly of Aylmer over the leaden complacency of his assistant.[16]

Aylmer proceeds to carry out his plan in two fairly distinct stages. First he leads Georgianna into the outer apartments of his laboratory, a setting of luxurious "enchantment" where he attempts to calm her fears by performing a series of preliminary experiments. This outer chamber where Georgianna is secluded recalls the rounded vessel, so shaped to represent the macrocosm,

that the alchemist used in preparing and totally isolating his primary materials for the Great Work. Hawthorne specifically mentions the way in which the chamber's richly hung curtains conceal "all angles and straight lines" and seem "to shut in the scene from infinite space" (44).[17] The impression that Aylmer wants to enclose Georgianna as *prima materia* within the rounded glass of his Hermetic vessel is strengthened still more with the mention of his confidence "that he could draw a magic circle round her, within which no evil might intrude" (44). The circle itself is also a familiar sign for gold, the sun, and perfection; like the magical feats performed to distract Georgianna during her confinement, it foreshadows the ultimate feat of transmutation that Aylmer hopes to work within her. One of Aylmer's distracting tricks of magic, his ability to make a flower burgeon spontaneously, may be readily identified as a version of palingenesis, a common alchemical image for the startling generation of the philosopher's stone. But obviously the instant withering of the plant is prophetic, too, and signifies the eventual failure of Aylmer's great experiment. Far from being emblematic of the culminating stage of transmutation, the flower as reduced to a "coal-black" color indicates a fatal regression of the process to its most primitive stages. The visual wonders that Aylmer conjures up to entertain his wife recall the legendary powers of Cornelius Agrippa's "magic glass," which Hawthorne describes elsewhere, at the same time that they may have reminded the author of more recent nineteenth-century inventions.[18] And though the idea of having Georgianna sing to Aylmer sprang most directly from a passage Hawthorne read in Combe's *Physiology,* it would be fascinating to suppose he was also aware that some alchemists considered music to be an important influence upon their operations.[19]

Once Georgianna finally enters the laboratory proper, the inner chamber where Aylmer has been arduously at work on his chemical draught, she is immediately struck by the "intense glow" of a furnace so surrounded by soot it "seemed to have been burning for ages" (50). The alchemist's oven or *athanor,* flanked by a distilling device and other chemical apparatus, marks the final stage of Georgianna's journey into the "heart" of Aylmer's laboratory.[20] The *athanor* has at times been regarded as a symbolic equivalent of the human body, and of the heart in particular; here it at least stands as the active center of Aylmer's Great Work and signals the impending climax of Hawthorne's tale.

As Aylmer completes his preparations for Georgianna's alchemical renewal, he finds his gaze returning often to the mysterious birthmark on her cheek. At this point it is well to ask just what this mark, the symbolic focal point of the story, is supposed to mean. For Aylmer the answer is simple enough: it is "the visible mark of earthly imperfection" (37), the "fatal flaw" (38) stamped upon her by nature, and an expression of the "ineludible gripe" (39) in which mortality clutches humanity. But like Melville's white whale or Hawthorne's own scarlet letter, the Crimson Hand is a complex symbol offering different meanings to different observers. Thus for Georgianna, it becomes a "horrible stigma" (52), a thing mysteriously able to summon up antipathy in her husband and rob her of his love. Yet the Hand does not have entirely negative connotations: many of Georgianna's former lovers had seen it as a magical "charm," with obvious overtones of captivating sexual force. Indeed it would be a serious mistake to assume that Aylmer's interpretation of the birthmark is identically Hawthorne's, even though one often finds it difficult to separate Aylmer's subjective analysis from the author's narrative voice. Hawthorne indicates clearly enough, however, that Aylmer has somewhat wilfully and arbitrarily *selected* the birthmark "as the symbol of his wife's liability to sin, sorrow, decay, and death" and has done so under the influence of a "sombre imagination" (39).

That is not to deny Hawthorne's acceptance of the reality of Original Sin or even his willingness to see in Georgianna's birthmark one sort of provisional analogy for the mortal imperfection of man. But the error of excess in Aylmer's interpretation comes when he restricts his moral vision to the point where his wife's bodily presence becomes *nothing but* an example of debasement and imperfection. By reducing Georgianna's humanity to the level of a mere symbol and allowing his self-serving fancy to turn her isolated blemish into an image of universal blight, Aylmer manages to avoid in some measure a frank confrontation with the mortal limits and moral imperfections of his own nature. He also ends up ignoring those subtler appearances of physical vibrancy and fleshy vitality in the birthmark that Hawthorne develops in such colorful descriptive language: the intensity of its rosy, sanguinary glow against the surrounding whiteness of Georgianna's cheek; and the awful poignancy of its departure, which the narrator compares to the mysterious waning of a rainbow in the sky.

Worst of all, Aylmer fails to recognize that the Hand of imperfection is likewise a token of "the bond by which an angelic spirit kept itself in union with a mortal frame" (55). Within the mortal sphere, at least, the surpassing beauty of Georgianna is inseparably wedded to a fallible human personality, just as the mark itself is "deeply interwoven . . . with the texture and substance of her face" (37). Indeed the powerful and intimate grip of the Crimson Hand should have signified even more to Aylmer than the principle of organic union between spirit and flesh that defines Georgianna's earthly identity. He has, after all, only recently entered into an intimate "union" (37) of his own with a most desirable woman, a wedding one might have expected to humanize his scientific zeal and bring his love of science into

yet another "union" with his love of humanity. But Aylmer in his lesser wisdom simply cannot see the redemptive possibility that Hawthorne, still euphoric in the season of composition over his recent wedding to Sophia, must have deemed implicit in the scientist's marriage and figuratively incarnate in the very shape of the blemish on his wife's cheek. Only once, and then "by a strange and unaccountable impulse" (54) does Aylmer reveal a subconscious sensitivity to this positive lesson as he presses the birthmark to his lips. But an ironic and ambiguous twist in the closing paragraph underscores the point that it is Aylmer's "fatal Hand," more than the Crimson Hand or any cosmic Hand of mortality, which tears asunder at one stroke the union constitutive of Georgianna's person and the sacred union between husband and wife.

The entire story, in fact, is built upon an ironic structure reinforced by what appears to be a well-orchestrated set of allusions to the background and symbolic language of alchemy. The title itself alludes to a familiar object of speculation in occult science, particularly in the seventeenth century when much was written about the prophetic import of moles—i.e., birthmarks.[21] But the two most significant points of possible contact between Hawthorne and the occult tradition have to do with the color symbolism of alchemy and the previously mentioned theme of marriage. In alchemical terms, the crimson shade of Georgianna's birthmark corresponds to the appearance of the philosopher's stone in its final, perfected stage of generation. Thus Thomas Norton, fifteenth-century author of the *Ordinall of Alchemy,* declared that "Red is last in work of *Alkimy*"; and this reddish tincture of the stone or elixir was often compared to the sight of blood—the *sanguis agni*—or to the color of a precious ruby.[22] Even these minor points of descriptive nuance are closely paralleled in Hawthorne's story, as when the Hand's prominent appearance is likened to "a bas-relief of ruby on the whitest marble" (39). The "snow" or "whitest marble" of Georgianna's cheek likewise corresponds to the intermediate or *albedo* stage of the alchemical process, where the material produced is typically of a "clear snow-white color."[23] The final substance of perfection is already present as an immediate potential in this intermediate stage of the Great Work.

In the author's judgment, all alchemists may have lacked the "profounder wisdom" needed to appreciate these distinctions; but Aylmer's actions mark him as a tragic failure even by the standards of his own occult profession. He has developed all of the alchemist's technical expertise and questing energy, but not enough of the prayerful humility and purity of heart that were also called for in the traditional manuals. Consequently he remains ignorant of the deeper implications of his own transmutative work, misreads the crucial signs of color, and destroys the very quintessence he is seeking to discover. The fatal results of his miscomprehension reveal in retrospect yet one more negative meaning of the birthmark, beyond its representation of depravity, since in popular culture the red hand is a common symbol of warning.[24]

It is possible to shed further light on the ironic design of Hawthorne's tale through a consideration of the marital and death symbolism that plays such a prominent role in traditional alchemical descriptions. Esoteric alchemists often discussed the way in which opposing qualities of Sol and Luna, sulphur and quicksilver, red and white, the masculine and feminine principle, had to "marry" each other in order to generate the stone of perfection during the stage known as "conjunction." Alternatively, the stripping and corruption of metals in preparation for the New Birth of gold could be described as a death and regeneration process on the model of that defined by Christian doctrine. Or it was sometimes said that the married King and Queen must die and be buried before the final transformation could occur.

Hawthorne seems to have invoked both of these alchemical images to ironic effect in **"The Birthmark."** Georgianna must die, for example, before she can become "the now perfect woman" (56), but in the context of the story this final turn of events is hardly apt to strike the reader as a joyous New Birth. And instead of moving toward the dramatic completion of a marital union, the story starts out informing us of a recently formed matrimony whose undoing will take up the remainder of its pages. Instead of seeking as close a natural conjunction as possible with Georgianna, and thereby reaching some fleeting contact with "the immortal essence" (56), Aylmer applies all of his efforts toward disjunction, toward "unclasping the firm gripe" of the Crimson Hand. This radically dissevering instinct expresses itself in particularly violent imagery when Aylmer dreams of trying to cut away the Crimson Hand with a knife.

Still, the author could afford to temper his irony, sympathizing to some degree with Aylmer's desire to transcend nature, because in one sense the philosophical disagreement between him and his main character was a fairly subtle one, however momentous its consequences. Hawthorne would not be inclined to dispute Aylmer's belief in the existence of something called "spirit," or scorn his desire to see the human self finally purged of its moral impurities and alchemized into the quintessential creature that is presently prefigured by an "immortal essence." Nor does Hawthorne's narrative voice project any less hope than Aylmer himself when it is able to censure him for failing "to look beyond the shadowy scope of Time, and living once for all in Eternity, to find the perfect Future in the present" (56). But as Heilman observes, Aylmer's philosophy diverges

most critically from Hawthorne's in its estimate of the precise relation between matter and spirit. Aylmer understands "spirit" to be nothing more than an infinite improvement and extension of matter, a kind of substance obtainable through physical means and defined by the simple absence of material impurity. For Hawthorne, however, Spirit would remain an utterly transcendent quality, distinct from matter as the "mortal" was distinct from the "celestial" yet co-existent with it, and joined to it in the earthly dispensation as integrally and inevitably as the conjunction of the sexes in marriage.

Hawthorne might therefore have been willing to endorse the Hermetic dictum that "Whatever is below is like that which is above," but only in a carefully restricted sense. For he was far from accepting the alchemical assumption that operations upon physical matter could influence the disposition of spiritual reality and likewise refused the suggestion that this reality could be rendered accesible by any amount of human ingenuity or exertion. So far the example of alchemy not only served Hawthorne as a neutral metaphor that could help support the ironic structure of **"The Birthmark,"** but also functioned as a symbol of the dangerous appeal that could be produced by any mode of false transcendence based on material suppositions. Elsewhere in Hawthorne mesmerism performs a similar function, as the contemporary equivalent of the alchemist's search for access to spiritual reality through material means. In a letter written October 18, 1841, from Brook Farm, Hawthorne urged Sophia not to seek relief from her persistent headaches in the "magnetic miracles" of the mesmerist, and the terms in which he couched his skepticism are equally revealing of the grounds upon which he questioned the spiritual claims of alchemy:

> I am unwilling that a power should be exercised on thee, of which we know neither the origin nor the consequence. . . . Supposing that this power arises from the transfusion of one spirit into another, it seems to me that the sacredness of an individual is violated by it; there would be an intrusion into thy holy of holies— and the intruder would not be thy husband! . . . I have no faith whatever that people are raised to the seventh heaven, or to any heaven at all, or that they gain any insight into the mysteries of life beyond death, by means of this strange science. Without distrusting that the phenomena which thou tellest me of . . . have really occurred, I think that they are to be accounted for as the result of a physical and material, not of a spiritual, influence.

Yet the same blend of sympathy and irony that informs Hawthorne's treatment of Aylmer reflects itself also in his portrayal of alchemy. It is telling that the letter to Sophia does not stop on a note of negative warning, but goes on to express in positive terms the author's own vision of a future transmutation of self and his belief in "mysteries" not unlike those which once absorbed the fascination of the Hermetic philosophers:

> And what delusion can be more lamentable and mischievous, than to mistake the physical and material for the spiritual? What so miserable as to lose the soul's true, though hidden, knowledge and consciousness of heaven, in the mist of an earth-born vision. Thou shalt not do this. If thou wouldst know what heaven is, before thou comest thither hand in hand with thy husband, then retire into the depths of thine own spirit, and thou wilt find it there . . . [but] do not let an earthly effluence from Mrs. Park's corporeal system . . . contaminate something spiritual and sacred. . . . And thou wilt know that the view which I take of this matter is caused by no want of faith in mysteries, but from a deep reverence of the soul, and of the mysteries which it knows within itself, but never transmits to the earthly eye or ear. Keep thy imagination sane—that is one of the truest conditions of communion with Heaven.[25]

Clearly, then, Hawthorne had his doubts about the efficacy and final authenticity of enterprises like alchemy and animal magnetism. But as one who thought he had himself experienced something of a radical interior transmutation—been alchemized, as it were—as a result of meeting Sophia, he was perhaps in no position to take a wholly scornful view of the alchemist's search for a marvelously transforming quintessence.

Notes

1. Robert B. Heilman, "Hawthorne's 'The Birthmark': Science as Religion," *South Atlantic Quarterly,* 48 (1949), 575-83.

2. See, for example, Richard H. Fogle, *Hawthorne's Fiction: The Light and the Dark* (U. of Oklahoma Press, 1964), pp. 126-28.

3. It is also worth remembering from *The Scarlet Letter* that Chillingworth has studied alchemy. In "Main Street," moreover, Hawthorne points out "the abode of an unsuccessful alchemist" in his native Salem and in the *American Notebooks* observes that "There have been other alchemists of old in this town,—one who kept his fire burning seven weeks, and then lost the elixir by letting it go out." See the *Centenary Edition of the Works* (Ohio State U. Press, 1972), VIII, 181; cf. 285 and 626n. on Michael Scott. Wherever possible, quotations from Hawthorne's writing are taken from this edition and identified by volume and page number in the text. For a general survey of alchemical themes in Hawthorne, with an emphasis on the unfinished works and some consideration of possible sources, see Raymona E. Hull, "Hawthorne and the Magic Elixir of Life: The Failure of a Gothic Theme," *Emerson Society Quarterly,* 18 (1972), 97-107. Two other pertinent articles appeared after I had completed this essay:

Mark Hennellly, "Hawthorne's *Opus Alchymicum*: 'Ethan Brand'," *Emerson Society Quarterly,* 22 (1976), 96-106; and David M. Van Leer, "Aylmer's Library: Transcendental Alchemy in Hawthorne's 'The Birthmark,'" *Emerson Society Quarterly,* 22 (1976), 211-20. Van Leer offers a detailed and perceptive analysis of Hawthorne's contemporary context and historical sources while my main intention here is to develop a close textual reading, but our conclusions are largely harmonious.

4. For detailed information on the points of alchemy discussed in this paper, the reader will find the following particularly useful: Titus Burckhardt, *Alchemy: Science of the Cosmos, Science of the Soul,* trans. W. Stoddart (London: Stuart & Watkins, 1967); F. Sherwood Taylor, *The Alchemists: Founders of Modern Chemistry* (New York: Henry Schuman, 1949); and Reinhard Federmann, *The Royal Art of Alchemy,* trans. R. Weber (Philadelphia: Chilton Book, 1964).

5. Outside of "The Birthmark," these figures are mentioned in "A Virtuoso's Collection" (X, 482 and 490-91) and "The Artist of the Beautiful" (X, 465). Since the life and writings of Sir Kenelm Digby (1603-65) have been discussed as a particular source of possible inspiration for the story (Alfred S. Reid, "Hawthorne's Humanism: 'The Birthmark' and Sir Kenelm Digby," *American Literature,* 38 [1966], 337-51), it is pertinent to recall that Digby, too, was very much involved in alchemical pursuits.

6. *The Works of Nathaniel Hawthorne,* ed. George Parsons Lathrop (Boston: Houghton Mifflin, 1883), XI, 49-50.

7. *Works* (1883), XI, 344.

8. See Hull, pp. 97-8 and William B. Stein, *Hawthorne's Faust: A Study of the Devil Archetype* (U. of Florida Press, 1953). One cannot be certain, however, about how much influence any one of these works may have had on Hawthorne prior to 1843, the date when "The Birthmark" first appeared. Not until 1855, for example, does he mention explicitly in the *English Notebooks* that he had read *The Alchemist* and found it "a great play." But J. Lasley Dameron, in "Hawthorne and *Blackwood's* Review of Goethe's *Faust*," *Emerson Society Quarterly,* 19 (1960), 25, has helped to establish the likelihood that Hawthorne was exposed to some version of Goethe's *Faust* and perhaps as early as 1827. The famous passage describing the occult experiments of Faust's father (in the scene "Before the Gate") is particularly rich in alchemical imagery.

9. See Marion L. Kesselring, "Hawthorne's Reading 1828-1850," *Bulletin of the New York Public Library,* 53 (1949), 55-71, 121-38, 173-94. The

record of Hawthorne's withdrawals from the Salem Athenaeum for the years prior to publication of "The Birthmark" includes many pertinent items, such as the entry under "Alchemy" in Vol. I of Abraham Rees' *Cyclopaedia: or Universal Dictionary of Arts, Sciences, and Literature* (Philadelphia, 1810-42); that in Vol. I of Francis Lieber's *Encyclopedia Americana* (Philadelphia: Carey & Lea, 1829), 140-42; the account of Paracelsus given in Vol. I of James Thatcher's *American Medical Biography* (1828; rpt. New York: Da Capo Press, 1967), 11-12; and the extensive commentary on the reputations and writings of every major alchemical figure presented by Pierre Bayle in his *Dictionary Historical and Critical* (London: Knapton, 1734), esp. I, 181-84 and 145-56. Significantly, Bayle describes a letter supposedly written by Cornelius Agrippa in which the latter argues that "whatever is to be found in Books concerning the Virtue of Magic, Astrology, and Alchimy, is false and deceitful when literally understood; that a Mystical Sense is to be looked for in them" (155). Hawthorne might also have seen the full-length article on "Alchymy" that appeared in the *Retrospective Review,* 14 (1826), 98-135, though this particular volume does not appear on the Kesselring list.

10. *The Fifth Book of the Archidoxies* in *The Hermetic and Alchemical Writings of Paracelsus.* trans. A. E. Waite (1894; rpt. New Hyde Park, N.Y.: University Books, 1967), II, 39.

11. "Alchymy," *Retrospective Review,* 130. Also C. A. Burland in *The Arts of the Alchemists* (New York: Macmillan, 1967), p. 43, points out that the term "the Rosary of Philosophers" was probably first applied to alchemy by Arnold of Villanova (1235-1311) to describe the ascending progress of the alchemist's work through a calculated series of experiments interspersed with periods of meditation and prayer.

12. Burckhardt, p. 76.

13. See Lynn Thorndike, *A History of Magic and Experimental Science* (Columbia U. Press, 1958), VIII, 234, 251-61. Sir Walter Scott, in his *Letters on Demonology and Witchcraft* (1830; rpt. East Ardsley: SR Pub., 1968), noted that at this time "the discovery of the philosopher's stone was daily hoped for; and electricity, magnetism, and other remarkable and misconceived phenomena were appealed to as proof of the reasonableness of their expectations" (159); while David Brewster, in his *Letters on Natural Magic Addressed to Sir Walter* (New York: J. & J. Harper, 1832), stated that "The science of chymistry has from its infancy been

pre-eminently the science of wonders" (268). Both books may be found on the Kesselring list of Hawthorne borrowings.

14. In "The Artist of the Beautiful," Hawthorne refers specifically to "the Man of Brass, constructed by Albertus Magnus, and the Brazen Head of Friar Bacon" (X, 465). Needless to say, much that was written about the medieval masters of alchemy and that came to Hawthorne as common knowledge consisted more of legend than of fact. The attitudes toward alchemy held by the "masters" themselves were often ambivalent at best, though such problems of strict historicity need not particularly concern us here.

15. "The Legend of Pygmalion in 'The Birthmark'," *American Transcendental Quarterly,* 14 (1972), 168-71.

16. See, for example, the analysis by Cleanth Brooks and Robert Penn Warren in *Understanding Fiction* (New York: F. S. Crofts, 1943), 103-06. A relatively sympathetic view of Aylmer is also implied by three much-cited entries in the *American Notebooks* (VII, 165, 184).

17. For this idea, for the point made earlier about Aylmer's relation to the four elements of the Hermetic cosmology, and for the reference supplied in note 21, I am gratefully indebted to Professor Leo Lensing of the Department of German, Wesleyan University.

18. See "A Virtuoso's Collection," X, 482; and H. Bruce Franklin, "Hawthorne and Science Fiction," *The Centennial Review,* 10 (1966), 117-23.

19. See John Read, *The Alchemist in Life, Literature and Art* (New York: T. Nelson, 1947), pp. 11 and 60.

20. For a fuller exploration of the heart metaphor, see Lewis B. Horne, "The Heart, the Hand and 'The Birthmark'," *American Transcendental Quarterly,* 1 (1969), 38-41.

21. Thorndike, VII, esp. pp. 237, 457-58.

22. Norton is cited in Read, p. 12. The image of the ruby as philosopher's stone appears in Jonson's *The Alchemist*; it may also be found in the seventeenth-century *Alchemical Writings of Edward Kelly,* ed. A. E. Waite (1893; rpt. Bath, England: Stuart & Watkins, 1970), p. 142.

23. This last description comes from the *Alchemical Writings of Edward Kelly,* p. 142.

24. Ad deVries, *Dictionary of Symbols and Imagery* (Amsterdam: North-Holland Pub., 1974), p. 236.

25. *Love Letters of Nathaniel Hawthorne* (Chicago: Society of the Dofobs, 1907), II, 62-65.

Judith Fetterley (essay date 1978)

SOURCE: Fetterley, Judith. "Women Beware Science: 'The Birthmark.'" In *Critical Essays on Hawthorne's Short Stories,* edited by Albert J. von Frank, pp. 164-72. Boston, Mass.: G. K. Hall & Co., 1991.

[*In the following essay, first published in* The Resisting Reader *in 1978, Fetterley notes the feminist perspective in "The Birthmark," and contends that "[i]n exploring the sources of men's compulsion to idealize women Hawthorne is writing a story about the sickness of men, not a story about the flawed and imperfect nature of women."*]

The scientist Aylmer in Nathaniel Hawthorne's **"The Birthmark"** . . . is squarely confronted with the realities of marriage, sex, and women. There are compensations, however, for as an adult he has access to a complex set of mechanisms for accomplishing the great American dream of eliminating women. It is testimony at once to Hawthorne's ambivalence, his seeking to cover with one hand what he uncovers with the other, and to the pervasive sexism of our culture that most readers would describe **"The Birthmark"** as a story of failure rather than as the success story it really is—the demonstration of how to murder your wife and get away with it. It is, of course, possible to read **"The Birthmark"** as a story of misguided idealism, a tale of the unhappy consequences of man's nevertheless worthy passion for perfecting and transcending nature; and this is the reading usually given it.[1] This reading, however, ignores the significance of the form idealism takes in the story. It is not irrelevant that **"The Birthmark"** is about a man's desire to perfect his wife, nor is it accidental that the consequence of this idealism is the wife's death. In fact, **"The Birthmark"** provides a brilliant analysis of the sexual politics of idealization and a brilliant exposure of the mechanisms whereby hatred can be disguised as love, neurosis can be disguised as science, murder can be disguised as idealization, and success can be disguised as failure. Thus, Hawthorne's insistence in his story on the metaphor of disguise serves as both warning and clue to a feminist reading.

Even a brief outline is suggestive. A man, dedicated to the pursuit of science, puts aside his passion in order to marry a beautiful woman. Shortly after the marriage he discovers that he is deeply troubled by a tiny birthmark on her left cheek. Of negligible importance to him before marriage, the birthmark now assumes the proportions of an obsession. He reads it as a sign of the inevitable imperfection of all things in nature and sees in it a challenge to man's ability to transcend nature. So nearly perfect as she is, he would have her be completely perfect. In pursuit of this lofty aim, he secludes her in chambers that he has converted for the purpose, subjects her to a series of influences, and finally presents her with a potion which, as she drinks it, removes at last the hated birthmark but kills her in the process. At the end of the story Georgiana is both perfect and dead.

One cannot imagine this story in reverse—that is, a woman's discovering an obsessive need to perfect her husband and deciding to perform experiments on him—nor can one imagine the story being about a man's conceiving such an obsession for another man. It is woman, and specifically woman as wife, who elicits the obsession with imperfection and the compulsion to achieve perfection, just as it is man, and specifically man as husband, who is thus obsessed and compelled. In addition, it is clear from the summary that the imagined perfection is purely physical. Aylmer is not concerned with the quality of Georgiana's character or with the state of her soul, for he considers her "fit for heaven without tasting death." Rather, he is absorbed in her physical appearance, and perfection for him is equivalent to physical beauty. Georgiana is an exemplum of woman as beautiful object, reduced to and defined by her body. And finally, the conjunction of perfection and nonexistence . . . develops [the point] that the only good woman is a dead one and that the motive underlying the desire to perfect is the need to eliminate. **"The Birthmark"** demonstrates the fact that the idealization of women has its source in a profound hostility toward women and that it is at once a disguise for this hostility and the fullest expression of it.

The emotion that generates the drama of **"The Birthmark"** is revulsion. Aylmer is moved not by the vision of Georgiana's potential perfection but by his horror at her present condition. His revulsion for the birthmark is insistent: he can't bear to see it or touch it; he has nightmares about it; he has to get it out. Until she is "fixed," he can hardly bear the sight of her and must hide her away in secluded chambers which he visits only intermittently, so great is his fear of contamination. Aylmer's compulsion to perfect Georgiana is a result of his horrified perception of what she actually is, and all his lofty talk about wanting her to be perfect so that just this once the potential of Nature will be fulfilled is but a cover for his central emotion of revulsion. But Aylmer is a creature of disguise and illusion. In order to persuade this beautiful woman to become his wife, he "left his laboratory to the care of an assistant, cleared his fine countenance from the furnace smoke, washed the stains of acid from his fingers." Best not to let her know who he really is or what he really feels, lest she might say before the marriage instead of after, "You cannot love what shocks you!" In the chambers where Aylmer secludes Georgiana, "airy figures, absolutely bodiless ideas, and forms of unsubstantial beauty" come disguised as substance in an illusion so nearly perfect as to "warrant the belief that her husband possessed sway over the spiritual world." While Aylmer does not really possess sway over the spiritual world, he certainly controls Georgiana and he does so in great part because of his mastery of the art of illusion.

If the motive force for Aylmer's action in the story is repulsion, it is the birthmark that is the symbolic location of all that repels him. And it is important that the birthmark is just that: a birth *mark,* that is, something physical; and a *birth* mark, that is, something not acquired but inherent, one of Georgiana's givens, in fact equivalent to her.[2] The close connection between Georgiana and her birthmark is continually emphasized. As her emotions change, so does the birthmark, fading or deepening in response to her feelings and providing a precise clue to her state of mind. Similarly, when her senses are aroused, stroked by the influences that pervade her chamber, the birthmark throbs sympathetically. In his efforts to get rid of the birthmark Aylmer has "administered agents powerful enough to do aught except change your entire physical system," and these have failed. The object of Aylmer's obsessive revulsion, then, is Georgiana's "physical system," and what defines this particular system is the fact that it is female. It is Georgiana's female physiology, which is to say her sexuality, that is the object of Aylmer's relentless attack. The link between Georgiana's birthmark and her sexuality is implicit in the birthmark's role as her emotional barometer, but one specific characteristic of the birthmark makes the connection explicit: the hand which shaped Georgiana's birth has left its mark on her in *blood.* The birthmark is redolent with references to the particular nature of female sexuality; we hardly need Aylmer's insistence on seclusion, with its reminiscences of the treatment of women when they are "unclean," to point us in this direction. What repels Aylmer is Georgiana's sexuality; what is imperfect in her is the fact that she is female; and what perfection means is elimination.

In Hawthorne's analysis the idealization of women stems from a vision of them as hideous and unnatural; it is a form of compensation, an attempt to bring them up to the level of nature. To symbolize female physiology as a blemish, a deformity, a birthmark suggests that women are in need of some such redemption. Indeed, **"The Birthmark"** is a parable of woman's relation to the cult of female beauty, a cult whose political function is to remind women that they are, in their natural state, unacceptable, imperfect, monstrous. Una Stannard in "The Mask of Beauty" has done a brilliant job of analyzing the implications of this cult:

> Every day, in every way, the billion-dollar beauty business tells women they are monsters in disguise. Every ad for bras tells a woman that her breasts need lifting, every ad for padded bras that what she's got isn't big enough, every ad for girdles that her belly sags and her hips are too wide, every ad for high heels that her legs need propping, every ad for cosmetics that her skin is too dry, too oily, too pale, or too ruddy, or her lips are not bright enough, or her lashes not long enough, every ad for deodorants and perfumes that her natural odors all need disguising, every ad for hair dye, curlers, and permanents that the hair she was born with is the wrong color or too straight or too curly, and lately ads for wigs tell her that she would be better off covering up nature's mistake completely. In this culture women are told they are the fair sex, but at the same time that their "beauty" needs lifting, shaping, dyeing, painting, curling, padding. Women are really being told that "the beauty" is a beast.[3]

The dynamics of idealization are beautifully contained in an analogy which Hawthorne, in typical fashion, remarks on casually: "But it would be as reasonable to say that one of those small blue stains which sometimes occur in the purest statuary marble would convert the Eve of Powers to a monster." This comparison, despite its apparent protest against just such a conclusion, implies that where women are concerned it doesn't take much to convert purity into monstrosity; Eve herself is a classic example of the ease with which such a transition can occur. And the transition is easy because the presentation of woman's image in marble is essentially an attempt to disguise and cover a monstrous reality. Thus, the slightest flaw will have an immense effect, for it serves as a reminder of the reality that produces the continual need to cast Eve in the form of purest marble and women in the molds of idealization.

In exploring the sources of men's compulsion to idealize women Hawthorne is writing a story about the sickness of men, not a story about the flawed and imperfect nature of women. There is a hint of the nature of Aylmer's ailment in the description of his relation to "mother" Nature, a suggestion that his revulsion for Georgiana has its root in part in a jealousy of the power which her sexuality represents and a frustration in the face of its inpenetrable mystery. Aylmer's scientific aspirations have as their ultimate goal the desire to create human life, but "the latter pursuit, however, Aylmer had long laid aside in unwilling recognition of the truth— against which all seekers sooner or later stumble—that our great creative Mother, while she amuses us with apparently working in the broadest sunshine, is yet severely careful to keep her own secrets, and, in spite of her pretended openness, shows us nothing but results. She permits us, indeed, to mar, but seldom to mend, and, like a jealous patentee, on no account to make." This passage is striking for its undercurrent of jealousy, hostility, and frustration toward a specifically female force. In the vision of Nature as playing with man, deluding him into thinking he can acquire her power, and then at the last minute closing him off and allowing him only the role of one who mars, Hawthorne provides another version of woman as enemy, the force that interposes between man and the accomplishment of his deepest desires. Yet Hawthorne locates the source of this attitude in man's jealousy of woman's having something he does not and his rage at being excluded from participating in it.

Out of Aylmer's jealousy at feeling less than Nature and thus less than woman—for if Nature is woman, woman is also Nature and has, by virtue of her biology, a power he does not—comes his obsessional program for perfecting Georgiana. Believing he is less, he has to convince himself he is more: "and then, most beloved, what will be my triumph when I shall have corrected what Nature left imperfect in her fairest work! Even Pygmalion, when his sculptured woman assumed life, felt not greater ecstasy than mine will be." What a triumph indeed to upstage and outdo Nature and make himself superior to her. The function of the fantasy that underlies the myth of Pygmalion, as it underlies the myth of Genesis (making Adam, in the words of Mary Daly, "the first among history's unmarried pregnant males"[4]), is obvious from the reality which it seeks to invert. Such myths are powerful image builders, salving man's injured ego by convincing him that he is not only equal to but better than woman, for he creates in spite of, against, and finally better than nature. Yet Aylmer's failure here is as certain as the failure of his other "experiments," for the sickness which he carries within him makes him able only to destroy, not to create.

If Georgiana is envied and hated because she represents what is different from Aylmer and reminds him of what he is not and cannot be, she is feared for her similarity to him and for the fact that she represents aspects of himself that he finds intolerable. Georgiana is as much a reminder to Aylmer of what he is as of what he is not. This apparently contradictory pattern of double-duty is understandable in the light of feminist analyses of female characters in literature, who frequently function this way. Mirrors for men, they serve to indicate the involutions of the male psyche with which literature is primarily concerned, and their characters and identities shift accordingly. They are projections, not people; and thus coherence of characterization is a concept that often makes sense only when applied to the male characters of a particular work. Hawthorne's tale is a classic example of the woman as mirror, for, despite Aylmer's belief that his response to Georgiana is an objective concern for the intellectual and spiritual problem she presents, it is obvious that his reaction to her is intensely subjective. "Shocks you, my husband?" queries Georgiana, thus neatly exposing his mask, for one is not shocked by objective perceptions. Indeed, Aylmer views Georgiana's existence as a personal insult and threat to him, which, of course, it is, because what he sees in her is that part of himself he cannot tolerate. By the desire she elicits in him to marry her and possess her birthmark, she forces him to confront his own earthiness and "imperfection."

But it is precisely to avoid such a confrontation that Aylmer has fled to the kingdom of science, where he can project himself as a "type of the spiritual element." Unlike Georgiana, in whom the physical and the spiritual are completely intertwined, Aylmer is hopelessly alienated from himself. Through the figure of Aminadab, the shaggy creature of clay, Hawthorne presents sharply the image of Aylmer's alienation. Aminadab symbolizes that earthly, physical, erotic self that has been split off from Aylmer, that he refuses to recognize as part of himself, and that has become monstrous and grotesque as a result: "With his vast strength, his shaggy hair, his smoky aspect, and the indescribable earthiness that incrusted him, he seemed to represent man's physical nature; while Aylmer's slender figure, and pale, intellectual face, were no less apt a type of the spiritual element." Aminadab's allegorical function is obvious and so is his connection to Aylmer, for while Aylmer may project himself as objective, intellectual, and scientific and while he may pretend to be totally unrelated to the creature whom he keeps locked up in his dark room to do his dirty work, he cannot function without him. It is Aminadab, after all, who fires the furnace for Aylmer's experiments; physicality provides the energy for Aylmer's "science" just as revulsion generates his investment in idealization. Aylmer is, despite his pretenses to the contrary, a highly emotional man: his scientific interests tend suspiciously toward fires and volcanoes; he is given to intense emotional outbursts; and his obsession with his wife's birthmark is a feeling so profound as to disrupt his entire life. Unable to accept himself for what he is, Aylmer constructs a mythology of science and adopts the character of a scientist to disguise his true nature and to hide his real motives, from himself as well as others. As a consequence, he acquires a way of acting out these motives without in fact having to be aware of them. One might describe **"The Birthmark"** as an exposé of science because it demonstrates the ease with which science can be invoked to conceal highly subjective motives. **"The Birthmark"** is an exposure of the realities that underlie the scientist's posture of objectivity and rationality and the claims of science to operate in an amoral and value-free world. Pale Aylmer, the intellectual scientist, is a mask for the brutish, earthy, soot-smeared Aminadab, just as the mythology of scientific research and objectivity finally masks murder, disguising Georgiana's death as just one more experiment that failed.

Hawthorne has not omitted from his treatment of men an image of the consequences of their ailments for the women who are involved with them. The result of Aylmer's massive self-deception is to live in an unreal world, a world filled with illusions, semblances, and appearances, one which admits of no sunlight and makes no contact with anything outside itself and at whose center is a laboratory, the physical correlative of his utter solipsism. Nevertheless, Hawthorne makes it clear that Aylmer has got someone locked up in that laboratory with him. While **"The Birthmark"** is by no means explicitly feminist, since Hawthorne seems as eager to be misread and to conceal as he is to be read and to reveal, still it is impossible to read his story without being aware that Georgiana is completely in Aylmer's power. For the subject is finally power. Aylmer is able to project himself onto Georgiana and to work out his obsession through her because as woman and as wife she is his possession and in his power; and because as man he has access to the language and structures of that science which provides the mechanisms for such a process and legitimizes it. In addition, since the power of definition and the authority to make those definitions stick is vested in men, Aylmer can endow his illusions with the weight of spiritual aspiration and universal truth.

The implicit feminism in **"The Birthmark"** is considerable. On one level the story is a study of sexual politics, of the powerlessness of women and of the psychology which results from that powerlessness. Hawthorne dramatizes the fact that woman's identity is a product of men's responses to her: "It must not be concealed, however, that the impression wrought by this fairy sign manual varied exceedingly, according to the difference of temperament in the beholders." To those who love Georgiana, her birthmark is evidence of her beauty; to those who envy or hate her, it is an object of disgust. It is Aylmer's repugnance for the birthmark that makes Georgiana blanch, thus causing the mark to emerge as a sharply-defined blemish against the whiteness of her cheek. Clearly, the birthmark takes on its character from the eye of the beholder. And just as clearly Georgiana's attitude toward her birthmark varies in response to different observers and definers. Her self-image derives from internalizing the attitudes toward her of the man or men around her. Since what surrounds Georgiana is an obsessional attraction expressed as a total revulsion, the result is not surprising: continual self-consciousness that leads to a pervasive sense of shame and a self-hatred that terminates in an utter readiness to be killed. **"The Birthmark"** demonstrates the consequences to women of being trapped in the laboratory of man's mind, the object of unrelenting scrutiny, examination, and experimentation.

In addition, **"The Birthmark"** reveals an implicit understanding of the consequences for women of a linguistic system in which the word "man" refers to both male people and all people. Because of the conventions of this system, Aylmer is able to equate his peculiarly male needs with the needs of all human beings, men and women. And since Aylmer can present his compulsion to idealize and perfect Georgiana as a human aspiration, Georgiana is forced to identify with it. Yet to identify with his aspiration is in fact to identify with his hatred of her and his need to eliminate her. Georgiana's situation is a fictional version of the experience that women undergo when they read a story like "Rip Van Winkle." Under the influence of Aylmer's mind, in the laboratory where she is subjected to his subliminal messages, Georgiana is co-opted into a view of herself as flawed and comes to hate herself as an impediment to Aylmer's aspiration; eventually she wishes to be dead rather than to remain alive as an irritant to him and as a reminder of his failure. And as she identifies with him in her attitude toward herself, so she comes to worship him for his hatred of her and for his refusal to tolerate her existence. The process of projection is neatly reversed: he locates in her everything he cannot accept in himself, and she attributes to him all that is good and then worships in him the image of her own humanity.

Through the system of sexual politics that is Aylmer's compensation for growing up, Hawthorne shows how men gain power over women, the power to create and kill, to "mar," "mend," and "make," without ever having to relinquish their image as "nice guys." Under such a system there need be very few power struggles, because women are programmed to deny the validity of their own perceptions and responses and to accept male illusions as truth. Georgiana does faint when she first enters Aylmer's laboratory and sees it for one second with her own eyes; she is also aware that Aylmer is filling her chamber with appearances, not realities; and she is finally aware that his scientific record is in his own terms one of continual failure. Yet so perfect is the program that she comes to respect him even more for these failures and to aspire to be yet another of them.

Hawthorne's unrelenting emphasis on "seems" and his complex use of the metaphors and structures of disguise imply that women are being deceived and destroyed by man's system. And perhaps the most vicious part of this system is its definition of what constitutes nobility in women: "Drink, then, thou lofty creature," exclaims Aylmer with "fervid admiration" as he hands Georgiana the cup that will kill her. Loftiness in women is directly equivalent to the willingness with which they die at the hands of their husbands, and since such loftiness is the only thing about Georgiana which does elicit admiration from Aylmer, it is no wonder she is willing. Georgiana plays well the one role allowed her, yet one might be justified in suggesting that Hawthorne grants her at the end a slight touch of the satisfaction of revenge: "'My poor Aylmer,' she repeated, with a more than human tenderness, 'you have aimed loftily; you have done nobly. Do not repent that with so high and pure a feeling, you have rejected the best the earth could offer.'" Since dying is the only option, best to make the most of it.

Notes

[This essay appeared in] *The Resisting Reader: A Feminist Approach to American Fiction* (Bloomington; Indiana University Press, 1978), 22-33.

1. See, for example, Brooks and Warren, *Understanding Fiction* (New York: Appleton-Century-Croft, 1943), pp. 103-106: "We are not, of course, to conceive of Aylmer as a monster, a man who would experiment on his own wife for his own greater glory. Hawthorne does not mean to suggest that Aylmer is depraved and heartless. . . . Aylmer has not realized that perfection is something never achieved on earth and in terms of mortality"; Richard Harter Fogle, *Hawthorne's Fiction: The Light and The Dark*, rev. ed. (Norman, Okla.: University of Oklahoma Press, 1964), pp. 117-31; Robert Heilman, "Hawthorne's 'The Birthmark': Science as Religion," *South Atlantic Quarterly* 48 (1949), 575-83: "Alymer, the overweening scientist, resembles less the villain than the tragic hero: in his catastrophic attempt to improve on human actuality there is not only pride and a deficient sense of reality but also disinterested aspiration"; F. O. Matthiessen, *American Renaissance* (New York: Oxford University Press, 1941), pp. 253-55; Arlin Turner, *Nathaniel Hawthorne* (New York: Holt, Rinehart, and Winston, 1961), pp. 88, 98, 132: "In 'The Birthmark' he applauded Aylmer's noble pursuit of perfection, in contrast to Aminadab's ready acceptance of earthiness, but Aylmer's achievement was tragic failure because he had not realized that perfection is not of this world." The major variation in these readings occurs as a result of the degree to which individual critics see Hawthorne as critical of Aylmer. Still, those who see Hawthorne as critical locate the source of his criticism in Aylmer's idealistic pursuit of perfection—e.g., Millicent Bell, *Hawthorne's View of the Artist* (New York: State University of New York, 1962), pp. 182-85: "Hawthorne, with his powerful Christian sense of the inextricable mixture of evil in the human compound, regards Aylmer as a dangerous perfectibilitarian"; William Bysshe Stein, *Hawthorne's Faust* (Gainesville: University of Florida Press, 1953), pp. 91-92: "Thus the first of Hawthorne's Fausts, in a purely symbolic line of action sacrifices his soul to conquer nature, the universal force of which man is but a tool." Even Simon Lesser, *Fiction and the Unconscious* (1957: rpt. New York: Vintage-Random, 1962), pp. 87-90 and pp. 94-98, who is clearly aware of the sexual implications of the story, subsumes his analysis under the reading of misguided idealism and in so doing provides a fine instance of phallic criticism in action: "The ultimate purpose of Hawthorne's attempt to present Aylmer in balanced perspective is to quiet our fears so that the wishes which motivate his experiment, which are also urgent, can be given their opportunity. Aylmer's sincerity and idealism give us a sense of kinship with him. We see that the plan takes shape gradually in his mind, almost against his conscious intention. We are reassured by the fact that he loves Georgiana and feels confident that his attempt to remove the birthmark will succeed. Thus at the same time that we recoil we can identify with Aylmer and through him act out some of our secret desires. . . . The story not only gives expression to impulses which are ordinarily repressed; it gives them a sympathetic hearing—an opportunity to show whether they can be gratified without causing trouble or pain. There are obvious gains in being able to conduct tests of this kind with no more danger and no greater expenditure of effort than is involved in reading a story." The one significant dissenting view is offered by Frederick Crews, *The Sins of the Fathers* (New York: Oxford University Press, 1966), whose scattered comments on the story focus on the specific form of Aylmer's idealism and its implications for his secret motives.

2. In the conventional reading of the story Georgiana's birthmark is seen as the symbol of original sin—see, for example, Heilman, p. 579; Bell, p. 185. But what this reading ignores are, of course, the implications of the fact that the symbol of original sin is female and that the story only "works" because men have the power to project that definition onto women.

3. Gornick and Moran, *Woman in Sexist Society,* p. 192.

4. Mary Daly, *Beyond God the Father,* p. 195.

Charles L. Proudfit (essay date 1980)

SOURCE: Proudfit, Charles L. "Eroticization of Intellectual Functions as an Oedipal Defence: A Psychoanalytic View of Nathaniel Hawthorne's 'The Birthmark.'" *International Review of Psycho-Analysis* 7, part 3 (1980): 375-83.

[*In the following essay, Proudfit declares that in "The Birthmark," Hawthorne "has given us a masterful description of the eroticization of intellectual functions as a major defence," anticipating Anna Freud's twentieth-century study,* The Ego and the Mechanisms of Defence.]

Although Nathaniel Hawthorne's short story, **'The Birthmark'** (1843), has engaged the critical attention of numerous literary scholars, only two critics, Simon

O. Lesser (1957), and Frederick Crews (1966), have written at some length of this tale from a psychoanalytic perspective. Both critics offer some interesting insights into the unconscious levels of meaning in this complex psychological story, though Lesser's emphasis is upon preconscious and unconscious reader response and Crews is primarily concerned with what the tale reveals about the author's unconscious wishes and fantasies, fears of adult sexuality, and overwhelming the sense of oedipal guilt.

Repeated teaching of this tale in the college classroom has convinced me, however, that Hawthorne has revealed far more about the unconscious workings of the human mind than has hitherto been recognized. Specifically, it is my conviction that through the art of fiction Hawthorne has given us a masterful description of the eroticization of intellectual functions as a major defence—a literary and psychological *tour de force* that antedates Anna Freud's classic study, *The Ego and the Mechanisms of Defence* (1936), by ninety-three years. Since many readers may not be familiar with Hawthorne's story, a brief synopsis follows.

Aylmer, a brilliant young scientist whose 'discoveries in the elemental powers of nature . . . had roused the admiration of all the learned societies in [late eighteenth century] Europe' (Hawthorne, p. 42), decided one day to leave his laboratory and find a wife. Although his first passion was science, his love for the beautiful Georgiana was stronger, though 'only . . . by intertwining itself with his love of science, and uniting the strength of the latter to its own' (p. 37). Shortly after their marriage, Aylmer became preoccupied with a birthmark in the centre of his bride's left cheek—a mark that resembled a tiny human hand. Some members of Georgiana's sex found that this 'Bloody Hand . . . quite destroyed the effect of . . . [her] beauty, and rendered her countenance even hideous' (p. 38). Many of her male lovers would have risked their lives to kiss it while others 'contented themselves with wishing it away, that the world might possess one living specimen of ideal loveliness, without the semblance of a flaw' (p. 38). Aylmer belonged to the latter.

When Georgiana realized that this imperfection troubled her husband, she became distraught. Aylmer's preoccupation quickly developed into an obsession, and one night he cried out in his sleep: '"It is in her heart now—we must have it out!"' (p. 40). At Georgiana's insistence, Aylmer related the following dream:

> He had fancied himself, with his servant Aminadab, attempting an operation for the removal of the birthmark. But the deeper went the knife, the deeper sank the Hand, until at length its tiny grasp appeared to have caught hold of Georgiana's heart; whence, however, her husband was inexorably resolved to cut or wrench it away.
>
> (p. 40)

When Aylmer finished telling his dream, Georgiana asked her scientist-husband to attempt the removal of the mark that made her '"the object of . . . [his] horror and disgust"' (p. 41) no matter what the cost.

Aylmer, overjoyed, converted part of his laboratory 'into a series of beautiful apartments, not unfit to be the secluded abode of a lovely woman' (p. 44), and, with Aminadab's help, submitted the unsuspecting Georgiana to several experiments that proved to be ineffective. Finally Aylmer developed a liquid that, when poured near the roots of a diseased geranium, rid the plant of the 'yellow blotches, which had overspread all its leaves' (p. 53). When Georgiana witnessed this, she drank the liquid, fell into a deep sleep, and Aylmer, sitting by her side, recorded every noticeable change in a volume containing the results of all his scientific endeavours. At one point during his vigil, the young scientist felt compelled to kiss the mark he so abhorred, though 'his spirit recoiled . . . in the very act' (p. 54). When the birthmark faded to the point where it was almost invisible, the apparently successful experiment brought forth a chuckle from Aminadab and laughter and exclamations from Aylmer. These sounds awakened Georgiana who first praised her husband for his lofty aims and then charged him not to repent that he had '"rejected the best that earth could offer"' (p. 55). At the moment the mark faded from her cheek, Georgiana died, and 'a hoarse, chuckling laugh was heard again!' (p. 56).

According to Hawthorne's third-person omniscient narrator, Georgiana's birthmark symbolizes 'the fatal flaw of humanity, which Nature, in one shape or another, stamps ineffaceably on all her productions, either to imply that they are temporary and finite, or that their perfection must be wrought by toil and pain' (pp. 38-9). Thus, Aylmer came to view the mark as 'the symbol of his wife's liability to sin, sorrow, decay, and death' (p. 39). Although the narrator is sympathetic with Aylmer's desire to perfect one of Nature's productions, he recognizes that 'had Aylmer reached a profounder wisdom, he need not thus have flung away the happiness, which would have woven his mortal life of the self-same texture with the celestial' (p. 56).

Lesser (1957) is the first psychoanalytic critic to observe that on an unconscious level **'The Birthmark'** has to do with Aylmer's ambivalent attitude toward his wife's sexuality. For Lesser, the birthmark symbolizes Georgiana's sexuality in general and perhaps female sexuality viewed as a castration threat in particular. He relates Aylmer to that class of men described by Freud (1912) who make a sharp distinction between tender and sensuous love, heavenly and earthly love. He also observes that Hawthorne's tale revolves around two unconscious oedipal wishes and unconscious defences against those wishes: first, that the mother be virginal;

and second, that the mother be sexless and therefore not a castration threat. He concludes his reading by explaining how this unconscious level of meaning satisfies simultaneously both the pleasure and reality principles in the unconscious mind of the reader.

Several of Lesser's insights are incorporated by Crews (1966) in his reading of Hawthorne's story. Crews notes that many of the heroes in Hawthorne's fiction are egotists whose sexual fears and anxieties either drive them to obsession or turn them into misanthropes. Furthermore, many of them are facing some kind of matrimonial challenge. Aylmer, for instance, is an example of one type of hero whom Crews designates as the 'strangely uneasy newlywed' (p. 111). He finds Aylmer to be a severely disturbed adolescent with unresolved oedipal problems. Thus, the young scientist's obsession with his wife's birthmark, his thinly disguised dream which contains the wish to destroy that which both attracts and frightens him, the act of kissing the very mark he abhors, and his scientific murder of Georgiana under the guise of perfecting her beauty, are all seen by Crews to be elaborations in fiction of Hawthorne's own deeply buried oedipal fears and wishes.

Although both Lesser and Crews have revealed levels of unconscious meaning in **'The Birthmark'** that reverberate subtly between reader and text and author and text, neither has offered a sustained psychoanalytic reading that both attests to the unconscious unity of the tale and demonstrates Hawthorne's insight into the psyche's use of intellectualization as a major defensive system. It is my intention in the remainder of this article to provide such a reading. Specifically, I propose to show how Aylmer's choice of a profession, of a wife, and of an obsession are unconsciously determined by the character's past; that is, that the wishes, fears, anxieties, guilt feelings, and preverbal traumas of Aylmer's childhood live on in the present, though buried in the unconscious, and influence the character's conscious actions accordingly.[1]

One might well hesitate to undertake such a psychoanalytic reading were it not for Hawthorne's third-person omniscient narrator who continually offers the reader glimpses of unconscious mental activity on the part of both husband and wife. The most obvious and perhaps well-known example of such a 'glimpse' in all of Hawthorne's fiction is the narrator's comments preceding and following the account of Aylmer's dream: 'The mind is in a sad note, when Sleep, the all-involving, cannot confine her spectres within the dim region of her sway, but suffers them to break forth, affrighting this actual life with secrets that perchance belong to a deeper one' (p. 40). And then: 'Truth often finds its way to the mind close-muffled in robes of sleep, and then speaks with uncompromising directness of matters in regard to which we practise an unconscious self-deception, dur-

ing our waking moments' (p. 40). Although the narrator understands Aylmer's dream to mean that he had not realized how obsessed he had become with his wife's birthmark, we know that the latent content of such a dream has hardly been exhausted by such an interpretation. An alert reader will gain further insight into Aylmer's unconscious mind by noting *how* the dream is first denied and then acknowledged by the dreamer, and then *what* is recalled of the manifest dream (and what may be left out) and *how* the dreamer *feels* as he tells the dream. Aylmer's *excessive denial* that he had even dreamed when confronted by Georgiana, then his affecting 'a dry, cold tone' in order to conceal 'the real depth of his emotion' (p. 40) when he acknowledges that he had dreamed, and then his *guilty feeling* in her presence after he has told what he consciously remembers of his dream, all suggest that the manifest dream has levels of latent meanings that are not apparent either to the dreamer or to the narrator. We shall return to this most important dream and its relationship to our understanding of this love affair that ends in tragedy after we have noted further glimpses into the unconscious minds of both characters.

Aylmer's obsession with his wife's birthmark during the early days of their honeymoon is certainly the result of overdetermination, and indicates unconscious mental conflict:

> At all the seasons which should have been their happiest, he invariably, and without intending it—nay, in spite of a purpose to the contrary—reverted to this one disastrous topic. Trifling as it at first appeared, it so connected itself with innumerable trains of thought, and modes of feeling, that it became the central point of all. With the morning twilight, Aylmer opened his eyes upon his wife's face, and recognized the symbol of imperfection; and when they sat together at the evening hearth, his eyes wandered stealthily to her cheek, and beheld, flickering with the blaze of the wood fire, the spectral hand that wrote mortality, where he fain would have worshipped.
>
> (p. 39)

Descriptions of the young scientist's responses to the birthmark, such as 'Aylmer sat gazing at his wife, with a trouble in his countenance that grew stronger, until he spoke' (p. 37) and 'Aylmer's sombre imagination was not long in rendering the birth-mark a frightful object, causing him more trouble and horror than ever Georgiana's beauty, whether of soul or sense, had given him delight' (p. 39) also attest to an emotional involvement that exceeds the actual state of affairs; namely, that his wife has a small imperfection on her left cheek. Finally, Aylmer's hasty interruption of Georgiana's remarks concerning her desire for the removal of the birthmark suggest unconscious guilt that is related to more primitive desires for the removal of the mark. This is confirmed by Aylmer's impulsive kissing of the mark and immediate aversion to the act while Georgiana slept during Aylmer's final attempt to remove what is now hateful to them both.

Although Georgiana's psychological portrait is not drawn as deeply as Aylmer's, she, too, is seen to have an unconscious life within the tale. Her readiness to take over her husband's obsessive and negative view of her birthmark, for example, contrasts strongly with her earlier view that "'it . . . [had] been so often called a charm, that I was simple enough to imagine it might be so'" (p. 37) and suggests an unconscious willingness that might well satisfy deeply buried masochistic and/or destructive wishes. Placing herself at her husband's disposal for experiments which could result in the loss of her life as well as the removal of the detested birthmark also suggests an unconscious wish for suffering and/or death at the hands of her lover. Such a masochistic response on Georgiana's part might well be explained by her own unconscious unresolved oedipal problems, specifically the little girl's rage at father's rejection and her feelings of impotence in being unable to keep him for herself and be given a child. Viewed from this perspective, Georgiana's turning her rage and revenge upon herself enables her to achieve 'victory in defeat'; that is, her death effectively thwarts Aylmer's most ambitious scientific experiment, thereby symbolically castrating his phallicized intellectual effort.

Although the narrator provides other glimpses into the unconscious workings of the characters' minds, the above examples will suffice for the purpose of this paper. Hawthorne has indeed created two characters who are driven by unconscious conflicts that destroy that which ought to result from the marriage of two such people; that is, a relatively happy, healthy, and non-conflicted marital union. Furthermore, as I now intend to demonstrate, the ultimate cause of the tragic ending of **'The Birthmark'** is to be found in the psycho-sexual problems experienced by Aylmer in early childhood and adolescence. Once again the narrator comes to our aid, for he not only provides us with insights into current unconscious conflicts but he also details Aylmer's early psychological development with an accuracy heretofore unnoticed. We must, therefore, begin at the beginning.

We are informed in the first paragraph of the tale that in Aylmer's day 'it was not unusual for the love of science to rival the love of woman, in its depth and absorbing energy' (p. 36). Aylmer, however, who 'had devoted himself . . . too unreservedly to scientific studies, ever to be *weaned* [my italics] from them by any second passion' (p. 36), seems to have solved any problem of precedence by combining the two in one. According to my reading of the story, however, Aylmer's uniting his love for science with his love for woman is illusory, for in his unconscious mind Georgiana, science, Nature, and mother—the latter the son's first love object—are

one. Hawthorne's use of a profound pun helps to substantiate this interpretation, for 'science' = *scientia* = knowledge; and, in the author's day as well as in our own, to *know* a woman is a euphemism for carnal knowledge. Aylmer's desire to *know* in this sense, therefore, represents an unconscious incestuous wish. Furthermore, Aylmer's early experiments, his choice of a profession, and his choice of a wife are, from a psychoanalytic point of view, repetitious at different developmental stages of unconscious conflicts that become acute during the oedipal years, then are reactivated with great intensity in adolescence, and, if not surmounted at this time, break out again in later life. Our story begins, therefore, shortly after Aylmer has suffered such an outbreak of the return of the repressed. In an attempt once again to resolve his unconscious conflicts, Aylmer takes a wife who must of psychological necessity be sacrificed by her husband in an attempt to slay the intolerable guilt and anxiety that afflict him. Although both the narrator and Georgiana view Aylmer's experiment as a noble attempt to perfect "'the best that earth could offer'" (p. 55), we perceive the young scientist's 'failure' as a symbolic and multiply determined act. The unconscious and conscious determinants of this act are to be found in Aylmer's childhood as vividly described by the narrator.

It is of crucial importance that Aylmer's entire scientific career has taken place in the apartments of his laboratory in which he attempts his final experiment. We are told that *prior* to 'his toilsome youth, [when] he had made discoveries in the elemental powers of nature, that had roused the admiration of all the learned societies in Europe' (p. 42), Aylmer 'had studied the wonders of the human frame, and attempted to fathom the very process by which Nature assimilates all her precious influences from earth and air, and from the spiritual world, to create and foster Man, her masterpiece' (p. 42). He had had to relinquish his scientific investigations, however, for 'our great creative Mother, while she amuses us with apparently working in the broadest sunshine, is yet severely careful to keep her own secrets, and, in spite of her pretended openness, shows us nothing but results. She permits us indeed, to mar, but seldom to mend, and, like a jealous patentee, on no account to make' (p. 42). This period of scientific curiosity relates to the pre-oedipal and oedipal child's curiosity about sexual matters ranging from anatomical differences to coitus and pregnancy, and it ends abruptly for the male child when he is forced to realize that not only can he not have mother but that he could do nothing with her even if he had exclusive possession of her. Hawthorne's choice of the term 'patentee' in the preceding quotation enhances the ironic dilemma inherent in a small boy's oedipal victory; for a 'patentee' is one who is licensed to use certain lands.[2] Such a narcissistic wound is never forgotten, and when Aylmer enters adolescence and has grandiose fantasies about his sexual powers, the hurt and humiliation from these early years are never far away:

> Seated calmly in this laboratory, the pale philosopher had investigated the secrets of the highest cloud-region, and of the profoundest mines; he had satisfied himself of the causes that kindled and kept alive the fires of the volcano; and had explained the mystery of fountains, and how it is that they gush forth, some so bright and pure, and others with such rich medicinal virtues, from the dark bosom of the earth.

(p. 42)

Whether our narrator is offering us in the above-quoted passage an exaggerated account of Aylmer's scientific achievements or whether he is providing a description of adolescent omnipotent fantasies, or both, the sexual symbolism is obvious. 'The secrets of the highest cloud-region, and of the profoundest mines' have to do with the activities that occur behind the closed doors of the parental bedroom. When Georgiana enters that part of Aylmer's laboratory that was formerly 'smoky, dingy, sombre rooms, where he had spent his brightest years in recondite pursuits' (p. 44), and that now has been converted 'into a series of beautiful apartments, not unfit to be the secluded abode of a lovely woman' (p. 44), Georgiana (surrogate mother) finds herself in the primal scene room. 'The walls were hung with gorgeous curtains . . . [that] fell from the ceiling to the floor' (p. 44), and, according to our narrator, 'for aught Georgiana knew, it might be a pavilion among the clouds' (p. 44). This is, indeed, the home of the gods (parents), and it was in such a room (parental bedroom) that father's caresses 'kindled and kept alive the fires of the volcano [vagina]' and where the 'fountains [phallus] . . . gush[ed] forth . . . from the dark bosom of the earth' (p. 42). One is indeed impressed with Hawthorne's description of eroticized intellectual functions used defensively by the young adolescent who is at the mercy of his reactivated unconscious oediapal conflicts that are now even more frightening since the little boy who could not act is now a man who can.

When Aylmer enters young adulthood, his sexual curiosity and unconscious feelings of guilt and rage are sublimated through scientific activity that has brought him fame. Yet the repetition compulsion extracts its pound of flesh, and Aylmer is driven to marry and confront his deepest longings and ambivalent feelings for the mother of the early years in Georgiana, her surrogate. Although our narrator tells us that Aylmer 'thought little or nothing' (p. 38) about Georgiana's birthmark before their marriage, he leaves the door open for our surmise that the mark both attracted and repulsed Aylmer during their courtship. And when Georgiana informs her husband that the mark had '"been so often called a charm, that I was simple enough to imagine it

might be so"' (p. 37) we wonder how she could have failed to observe Aylmer's response that had drawn such diverse and strong reactions from members of both sexes. The subsequent events that occur during their brief and tragic honeymoon, particularly Aylmer's growing obsession and Georgiana's acquiescence in his desire for the mark's removal, strongly suggest that these lovers were doomed from the moment that their unconscious minds recognized that their deeply buried sadistic and masochistic fantasies and wishes could be fulfilled by each other.

It is at this point that we must take up Aylmer's dream once again. As with all dreams, no one interpretation will ever suffice; for when one thinks that he has finally unravelled all the threads of the pattern, he discovers often to his chagrin that untouched patterns have been revealed in the process. Aylmer's dream is no exception, and though we may not exhaust all its possible meanings, we can offer several interpretations that further our understanding of the unconscious levels of meaning in this tale. The first thing to note about Aylmer's dream is its pivotal nature; that is, it points both ways: forward, to the tragic conclusion, and backward, into the past. Second, this dream—like the unconscious itself—is, in a sense, timeless; that is, there is no past, no present, no future, only the immediacy of the dream itself. And third, Aylmer's recollection of the dream at his wife's insistence is in all probability not the whole of the dream that was dreamed, even though the narrator asserts that 'Aylmer sat in his wife's presence with a guilty feeling . . . [after] the dream had shaped itself perfectly in his memory' (p. 40). Although it is fruitless to speculate about the untold part of the dream in the absence of associations, Aylmer's affect, a sense of guilt, suggests levels of meaning beyond the one given us by the narrator.

The most obvious interpretation of Aylmer's dream is, of course, the narrator's; that is, the young scientist's concern with the removal of the birthmark has become such as obsession that it troubles his sleep as well as his waking hours. Crews (1966) offers the first analytic interpretation when he observes that Aylmer's 'plunging his knife into the birthmark until it reaches Georgiana's heart reveals a fantasy of sadistic revenge and a scarcely less obvious fantasy of sexual consummation' (p. 126). Although Crews does not go on to say that Aylmer's dream also contains parricidal and incestuous wishes, he does comment upon these unconscious desires as they appear in other works by Hawthorne. An awareness of the sadistic, incestuous, and parricidal fantasies that lie behind the manifest content of the dream certainly helps the reader understand Aylmer's complex reaction to his wife's questioning about his dream, especially his feelings of guilt. Yet more can be learned about Aylmer's unconscious life by submitting his dream to further analysis.

Aylmer's dream can also be seen as an attempt to ward off castration anxiety while, at the same time, symbolically obtaining the incestuous object of one's desire. Thus, Aylmer, the son, in the presence of Aminadab, the father, performs a surgical operation on Georgiana, the mother, ostensibly to make her 'perfect', thus 'proving' to the father that the son's intentions are honourable. This symbolic operation is open-ended, however, for Aylmer also obtains with his knife (phallus) what he unconsciously desires—sexual union with the mother. It also allows for the expression of sadistic impulses felt toward the mother.

Although sons fear castration at the hands of their fathers, they, in time, must come to fear the phallic power of their own sons. Given this universal psychic phenomenon, one wonders if perhaps Aylmer's dream does not also contain a deeply buried wish to destroy Georgiana's potential to produce a son, a potential threat that is symbolized by a birthmark that is variously described as a 'little Hand', a 'Bloody Hand', a 'Crimson Hand', and a 'fatal Hand'. If the young scientist's dream is interpreted in this manner, then Aylmer's 'strange and unaccountable impulse' to kiss 'the fatal Hand' while Georgiana sleeps and his revulsion as 'he press[es] it with his lips' is seen not to be 'strange and unaccountable' (p. 54); for Aylmer, an Oedipus who is also a potential Laius, both acknowledges and is repelled by his own parricidal wishes symbolized by the tiny, bloody Hand. One is reminded of Macbeth's bloody hands, and that his parricidical slaying of Duncan is soon followed by his fear of Fleance as his successor.

On another level, Aylmer's dream can be viewed as an attempt to master primal scene anxiety and guilt. According to Freud (1896), primal scene fantasies or actual experiences prior to four years are preverbal and hence untranslatable into words. If such experiences, either fantasied or observed, continue beyond the age of four, then the child's experiences are translated into words, and obsessive symptoms are generated. There can be no doubt that Aylmer is an obsessive compulsive individual whose major defence is intellectualization. In this dream, Aylmer is performing a surgical operation with his assistant's help; that is, the son, whose primal scene memories are sadistically tinged, helps the father master the seductive mother. On one level, he defends against his own incestuous wishes toward the mother by trying to remove her sexuality; on another level, he assumes the father's role and phallus and fulfills sadistically his childish fantasies of intercourse with the mother, thereby generating primal scene guilt. Little wonder that Aylmer cried out in his sleep: '"It is in her heart now—*we* [my italics] must have it out!"' (p. 40).

Viewed from another perspective, Aylmer's dream contains a deeply buried murderous wish to be avenged upon the mother in particular and Mother Nature in

general for their ability to create and sustain life. At the beginning of the story, the narrator tells us that in Aylmer's day some 'ardent votaries' of natural philosophy [science] believed that with continued effort 'the philosopher should [be able to] *lay his hand* [my italics] on the secret of creative force, and perhaps make new worlds for himself' (p. 36). Although the narrator is uncertain as to whether or not 'Aylmer possessed this degree of faith in man's ultimate control over nature' (p. 36), we are told that Aylmer's first attempt to understand female creativity had to be abandoned, for 'our great creative Mother . . . permits us, indeed, to mar, but seldom to mend, and, like a jealous patentee, *on no account to make* [my italics]' (p. 42). Later, after Georgiana has requested Aylmer to attempt the removal of the birthmark, the young scientist goes into raptures:

> "Noblest—dearest—tenderest wife! . . . Doubt not my power. I have already given this matter the deepest thought—thought which might almost have enlightened me to create a being less perfect than yourself. Georgiana, you have led me deeper than ever into the heart of science. I feel myself fully competent to render this dear cheek as faultless as its fellow; and then, most beloved, what will be my triumph, when I shall have corrected what Nature left imperfect, in her fairest work! Even Pygmalion, when his sculptured woman assumed life, felt not greater ecstasy than mine will be."
>
> (p. 41)

Although Aylmer's surgical dream demonstrates his narcissistic desire to go one step beyond Mother Nature by perfecting her creation, we also perceive the young scientist's murderous wish to revenge himself upon that which can create life.

When Aylmer's dream is interpreted from this perspective, Hawthorne's irony takes on added depth. Although Mother Nature 'amuses us with apparently working in the broadest sunshine . . . yet [is] severely careful to keep her own secrets' (p. 42), Aylmer closes out the sunshine 'which would have interfered with his chemical processes' (p. 44) and lights his converted laboratory 'with perfumed lamps . . . [that] emit[ted] flames of various hue . . . uniting [all] in a soft, empurpled radiance' (p. 44). It is only when he thinks that his experiment has been successful that he draws 'aside the window-curtain, and suffer[s] the light of natural day to fall into the room, and rest upon her cheek' (p. 55). Mother Nature is not to be outwitted, however, and in taking Georgiana to herself in broad daylight, ironically thwarts Aylmer's scientific curiosity for the last time. She, too, effectively castrates the son.

The feasibility of this psychoanalytic interpretive rendering is finally confirmed, I believe, by the narrator's comments upon Aylmer's folio volume, that handwritten book 'in which he had recorded every experiment of his scientific career, with its original aim, the methods adopted for its development, and its final success or failure, with the circumstances to which either event was attributable' (pp. 48-9). It serves, as our narrator suggests, as 'both the history and emblem of his ardent, ambitious, imaginative, yet practical and laborious, life' (p. 49). It is also the tragic record of an idealist whose 'most splendid successes were almost invariably failures, if compared with the ideal at which he aimed' (p. 49). And when we are told that as Aylmer records Georgiana's every symptom while she sleeps during the final disastrous experiment, that 'the thoughts of years were all concentrated upon the last [page]' (p. 54), we could not give our assent more readily. It is most appropriate that Aylmer should believe that 'his brightest diamonds were the merest pebbles, and *felt to be so by himself,* [my italics] in comparison with the inestimable gems which lay hidden beyond his reach' (p. 49)[3] for the unconscious defence mechanisms employed by the beleaguered ego (primarily intellectualization in Aylmer's case), *defend against but do not relieve* the unconscious conflict that has periodically plagued Aylmer throughout most of his life. When our young hero's commitment to scientific discovery and truth is seen to have the unconscious determinants detailed above, then the first sentence in **'The Birthmark'** must take its place as one of the most devastating ironic lines in all of Hawthorne's fiction: 'In the latter part of the last century, there lived a man of science—an eminent proficient in every branch of natural philosophy—who, not long before our story opens, had made experience of a spiritual affinity, more attractive than any chemical one' (p. 36).

Notes

1. The development of this reading was enhanced by discussions with Drs Joan Fleming, David Metcalf, and Professor James Folsom, and by the interest of Professor John Graham.

2. Hawthorne himself won such an oedipal victory since his sea-faring father died in a faraway port when Nathaniel was four.

3. Cf. Milton, *Paradise Regained,* iv, 321-30.

References

Crews, F. (1966). *The Sins of the Fathers: Hawthorne's Psychological Themes.* New York: Oxford Univ. Press.

Freud, A. (1936). *The Ego and the Mechanisms of Defence.* New York: Int. Univ. Press, 1966.

Freud, S. (1896). Draft K. The neuroses of defence. *S. E.* [*The Standard Edition of the Complete Psychological Works of Sigmund Freud,* 24 volumes, translated under the general editorship of James Strachey in collaboration with Anna Freud, assisted by Alix Strachey and Alan Tyson (London: Hogarth Press, 1953-1974)] 1.

Freud, S. (1912). On the universal tendency to debasement in the sphere of love. *S. E.* 11.

Hawthorne, N. (1843). 'The Birthmark.' In W. Charvat, R. H. Pearce, C. M. Simpson *et al.* (eds.), *Mosses From an Old Manse,* vol. 10. The Centenary Edition of the Works of Nathaniel Hawthorne. Columbus: Ohio State Univ. Press, 1974.

Lesser, S. (1957). *Fiction and the Unconscious.* Boston: Beacon Press.

James Quinn and Ross Baldessarini (essay date 1981)

SOURCE: Quinn, James, and Ross Baldessarini. "'The Birth-Mark': A Deathmark." *Hartford Studies in Literature* 13, no. 2 (1981): 91-8.

[*In the following essay, Quinn and Baldessarini delineate how Hawthorne utilizes the narrative device of offering various characters' responses to a particular symbol in "The Birthmark."*]

Hawthorne's art in the creation of character in many ways anticipates modern psychoanalytic psychology. As a literary psychologist, he excels at revealing unconscious sources of obsessed behavior. In **"The Birth-Mark,"** Aylmer, a scientist whose ambition may be to control nature, provides an exceptionally good example of an obsessive character. He is obsessed with imperfection in human nature and is unable to achieve a mature human relationship.

In this tale, although we are presented with Aylmer's intense reactions to an apparently solitary imperfection in his bride, Hawthorne does not explicitly analyze them. Indeed, the reader is conditioned to accept ambiguity and multiplicity as inevitable features of human nature. Hawthorne evidently values a balanced view of a complex world and his appreciation of complexity is no more forcefully demonstrated than in his psychological analysis of character. As we noted earlier in our analysis of **"The Minister's Black Veil,"**[1] a crucial technique Hawthorne employs to achieve his psychological revelations is the literary device of multiple reactions of observers to a central symbol. Here the central symbol is a red nevus on the face of Georgiana, her birth-mark.[2] Its power to evoke strong responses stems partly from the details which Hawthorne offers about its appearance. It is in the form of a hand appearing on her left (sinister and heart side) cheek. Hawthorne makes the red more vibrant by setting it off against Georgiana's changing complexion.

This method of the central symbol provides Hawthorne with a way to intrigue us by his revelations of the thoughts, feelings, and moods of leading characters as well as lesser observers. A short passage from **"The Birth-Mark"** illustrates his method:

Some fastidious persons—but they were exclusively of her own sex—affirmed that the Bloody Hand, as they chose to call it, quite destroyed the effect of Georgiana's beauty, and rendered her countenance even hideous. But it would be as reasonable to say, that one of those small blue stains which sometimes occur in purest statuary marble, would convert the Eve of Powers to a monster. Masculine observers, if the birth-mark did not heighten their admiration, contented themselves with wishing it away, that the world might possess one living specimen of ideal loveliness, without the semblance of a flaw.[3]

We also know that "many a desperate swain would have risked life for the privilege of pressing his lips to the mysterious hand" (p. 38) and, toward the end of the tale, Aylmer himself, while attempting to eradicate the mark, "by a strange and unaccountable impulse . . . pressed it with his lips" (p. 54). Reactions to Georgiana's birth-mark vary from the attraction of Aminadab and other men, to the ambivalence of Georgiana, to the negative reactions of Aylmer. In short, the chief narrative foci are the *perceptions* of the characters themselves. Hawthorne tells us that reactions to the hand-like blemish on Georgiana's cheek vary "according to the difference of temperament in the beholders" (p. 38).[4] That is to say, the "meaning" of this symbol is complex and colored by the personality of the observer. This is one of the clearest revelations by Hawthorne of his method and psychology.[5] Hawthorne shows that an object becomes what each viewer's personalized perceptions would have it become.

Hawthorne skillfully establishes the governing centrality of the birth-mark by describing its effect mainly from the standpoint of Aylmer's "sombre imagination." Specifically, Hawthorne gives overpowering sway to Aylmer's attitude toward the birth-mark and at the same time contrasts his view with Georgiana's initially more innocent perspective. We are told, for example, that before his marriage Aylmer had thought "little or nothing of the matter" (p. 38), while Georgiana had always imagined that the mark on her cheek was a kind of "charm" which, if anything, enhanced rather than detracted from her beauty. Soon after marrying, however, Aylmer discovers that he can think of little else but the birth-mark, "in spite of a purpose to the contrary" (p. 39), and that it has become a "frightful object, causing him more trouble and horror than ever Georgiana's beauty, whether of soul or sense, had given him delight" (p. 39). What has happened to make Aylmer feel this way? What indeed ails him? The question is a natural one, but useless. Hawthorne does not supply an answer and by this omission seems to suggest that insights into human behavior are likely to be subjective, imperfect, unsatisfying. What is important is not the cause of obsessive thought or compulsive behavior but the effects.

The dramatic situation here is that Aylmer, by marrying Georgiana, is forced to deal with a conflict between his earlier, somewhat distant view of her as an intellectualized feminine ideal and her present tangible reality. Clearly one meaning of the red hand is a mark of her accessibility to touch, that is, of her sexuality. It also includes conflict between personal idealization and reality—a classical and ubiquitous obsessional neurotic conflict. While Aylmer's struggle is virtually universal, his fixation on Georgiana's blemish approaches a symptom that is considered characteristic of obsessive-compulsive neurosis in modern-day psycho-pathological terms.[6] The function of such neurotic symptoms in the psychic economy is to inhibit intolerable anxiety by focusing on an isolated and somewhat concrete representation so as to avoid a larger emotional conflict.

The psychoanalytic theorist Fenichel has written, "Many compulsive neurotics have to worry very much about small and apparently insignificant things. In analysis, these small things turn out to be substitutes for important ones."[7] And further: "Compulsive neurotics try to use external objects for the solution or relief of their inner conflicts."[8] As "the compulsive neurotic tends . . . to extend the range of his symptoms . . ."[9] so Aylmer's reaction to the birth-mark grew "more and more intolerable with every moment of their lives" (p. 38), presumably as a result of Georgiana's unavoidable presence. What at first seemed a trifling matter "so connected itself with innumerable trains of thoughts and modes of feeling, that it became the *central point of all*"; (p. 39) [Stress added]. Like Parson Hooper, Aylmer is another Hawthornian victim of morbid forces, largely internal, beyond his control. Surely Aylmer's aversion owes its intensity and its obsessive character precisely to the fact that it is not accessible to conscious examination.[10]

In his morbid striving toward perfection for himself, Aylmer erects a monstrous structure to avoid engaging his bride directly and intimately. It is not clear that Aylmer has ever had a mature human relationship with Georgiana. Rather, his wife appears to be a wonderful possession meant to contribute to his own self-esteem. Having captured this object of desire, he then proceeds to isolate her in a setting of stagelike opulence.

> Aylmer had converted those smoky, dingy, sombre rooms, where he had spent his brightest years in recondite pursuits, into a series of beautiful apartments, not unfit to be the secluded abode of a lovely woman. The walls were hung with gorgeous curtains, which imparted the combination of grandeur and grace, that no other species of adornment can achieve; and as they fell from the ceiling to the floor, their rich and ponderous folds, concealing all angles and straight lines, appeared to shut in the scene from infinite space.
>
> (p. 44)

The description seems to reinforce the distance at which he wants to keep Georgiana. Again he is master and controller and isolates Georgiana from the real world in rooms unearthly and enchanted. Intimate and sexual desires he feels for Georgiana are presumably transferred to his efforts to create the perfect chamber for the perfect woman he desires. Yet Aylmer's attempt to "shut in the scene" hints at something concealed, secretive and perhaps guilty about his quest. This impression of Aylmer's aloofness is supported by his detached and icy approach toward life generally: "He had left his laboratory to the care of an assistant, cleared his fine countenance from the furnace-smoke, washed the stains of acids from his fingers, and persuaded a beautiful woman to become his wife" (p. 36).

Given the aloof nature of their relationship as well as Aylmer's obsession, it is perhaps not surprising that Georgiana is victimized by her husband's ill-disguised "horror and disgust." From Hawthorne's description of the birth-mark it is clear that it would not even be visible if Aylmer could accept Georgiana's humanity, her passion and sexuality:

> In the usual state of her complexion—a healthy, though delicate bloom—the mark wore a tint of deeper crimson, which imperfectly defined its shape amid the surrounding rosiness. When she blushed, it gradually became more indistinct, and finally vanished amid the triumphant rush of blood, that bathed the whole cheek with its brilliant glow. But, if any shifting emotion caused her to turn pale, there was the mark again, a crimson stain upon the snow, in what Aylmer sometimes deemed an almost fearful distinctness.
>
> (pp. 37-38)

But rather than keeping her happy, he ironically unleashes a vicious circle: his discomfort infects her with anxiety; her pallor makes the birth-mark more obvious; and his heightened anxiety completes the vicious circle. His coldness makes the problem worse: "It needed but a glance, with the peculiar expression that his face often wore, to change the roses of her cheek into a death-like paleness, amid which the Crimson Hand was brought strongly out, like a bas-relief of ruby on the whitest marble" (p. 39). Then Aylmer "so startled with the intense glow of the birth-mark upon the whiteness of her cheek . . . could not restrain a strong convulsive shudder" (p. 43). This reaction clearly typifies a neurotic vicious circle: Aylmer's anxiety leading to neurotic compromise, leading to more anxiety.

Eventually Aylmer corrupts Georgiana into accepting his deluded quest for omnipotence and perfection. She never feels the birth-mark is evil as Aylmer does, but she suddenly realizes "you cannot love what shocks you" (p. 37). Rather than drawing the reasonable conclusion that Aylmer's feelings toward her are grotesque, she misleads herself into believing how much more "precious" was Aylmer's sentiment "than that meaner kind which would have borne imperfection for her sake . . ." (p. 52). This feat of illogic closely resembles a shared delusion and paves the way for Georgiana's ultimate destruction.

The mocking laugh of Aminadab, an ordinary if somewhat peculiar man, suggests he realizes the irony of the situation and mocks his master, Aylmer, for trying to reach too high to attain perfection and reject humanity.[11] He senses that escape from the human condition is hubris and death; that the attempt to scale the heights leads to descent into hell; that the more man struggles to be god-like, the more he makes misery for himself and others. In fact, the odd earthman Aminadab, an embodiment of humanity's long past, in contrast to Aylmer, has a rational and pragmatic attitude: "If she were my wife, I'd never part with that birth-mark" (p. 43).

Aylmer, unlike Aminadab, alternates between blacks and whites rather than accepting the grays of life. He draws distinct lines between good and bad as does Young Goodman Brown, who must see Faith, indeed all women, as Madonna or whore and who therefore remains immature and uncommitted. Aylmer, too, is like an adolescent, unable to find a point of equilibrium between two poles of thought, not realizing that "to be is to be imperfect, that the price of human existence is imperfection."[12]

An ironic aspect of such obsessed and morbid behavior so often seen in Hawthorne's works, is that the more one struggles to attain perfection or to retain an unreasonable fixed idea, the more one is caught up in dealing with its opposite—imperfection and destruction. Obsessional behavior characteristically presents such ironies: those who seek perfect cleanliness are preoccupied with dirt. Elsewhere in Hawthorne, Endicott and the Puritans in **"The Maypole of Merry Mount,"** in their attempt to deny sensual pleasure, are constantly preoccupied with it and deal with it sadistically. While Aylmer aspires to perfection, his daily world is a secret, hellish, smokey, fume-filled place of labor cloaked with heavy curtains and giving him a strong identification with the powers of darkness, a devilish and fiendish quality. As Georgiana found:

> The first thing that struck her eyes was the furnace, that *hot* and *feverish* worker, with the intense glow of its fire, which by the quantities of *soot* clustered above it, seemed to have been *burning* for *ages* . . . The atmosphere felt *oppressively* close, and was *tainted* with gaseous odors, which had been *tormented* forth by the processes of science.
>
> (p. 50) [Stress added]

The culmination of this diabolical side of Aylmer is Georgiana's destruction and death in the attempt to offer her the "elixir of immortality."

There are numerous foreshadowings of the ultimate outcome of Aylmer's crazed drive. There is Georgiana's discovery of her husband's past failures, of his inability to carry past experiments to fruition. The symbol itself is characterized by Hawthorne as a mark of Original

Sin or the imperfection born with man as a race, as "the fatal flaw of humanity, which Nature, in one shape or another, stamps ineffaceably on all her productions . . . to imply that they are temporary and finite . . ." (pp. 38-39). Most significant is Aylmer's dream that explicitly suggests the intense, violent and remarkably sexual reaction the birth-mark evokes in Aylmer:

> He had fancied himself, with his servant Aminadab, attempting an operation for the removal of the birth-mark. But the deeper went the knife, the deeper sank the Hand, until at length its tiny grasp appeared to have caught hold of Georgiana's heart; whence, however, her husband was inexorably resolved to cut or wrench it away.
>
> (p. 40)

This dream seems to arise from a waking fantasy ["for before I fell asleep, it had taken a pretty firm hold of my fancy" (p. 40)] of the vivid and often destructive and violent kind so typical in obsessional neurosis.[13] Hawthorne makes an extremely perceptive statement for one living in the pre-Freudian world of 1843:

> When the dream had shaped itself perfectly in his memory, Aylmer sat in his wife's presence with a guilty feeling. Truth often finds its way to the mind close-muffled in robes of sleep, and then speaks with uncompromising directness of matters in regard to which we practise an *unconscious self-deception,* during our waking moments.
>
> (p. 40) [Stress added][14]

Again typical of obsessional neurotics, Aylmer goes on to act upon his omnipotent fantasies in a most compulsive and repetitive way by drawing Georgiana into a series of experiments with "drugs, elixers and concoctions" that eventually prove fatally toxic.

Up to this point we have been concerned with Hawthorne's presentation of Aylmer as one more neurotic and troubled obsessional soul. More important, however, is Aylmer's dramatically exaggerated representation of a more general struggle to adjust the ideal and the real. Likewise the birth-mark can be viewed on more than one level. It is a mark of Georgiana's accessibility to touch, of her sexuality. It is suggestive of the scarlet letter—another public sign of secret and lustful sin, of "putting hands upon" in a sexual sense, of being touched, tainted, having sexuality and womanly characteristics. And, within the Judeo-Christian tradition, as noted above, it seems to Hawthorne to symbolize the fallen and sinful nature of man. In an even wider application, it symbolizes the mortality of all mankind.

We miss the point, however, if we connect the birth-mark solely with neurotic conflicts of atypical individuals or even with the hold death has on everyone, for the mark is also connected with sexuality and new life, indeed with aspiration to beauty and achievement and with the joy and energy for living. The importance of Hawthorne's psychological symbol is not the susceptibility of man to sin and death, but the special manner in which the marked woman suffers her fate: it is Aylmer who kills her. When the inward life concentrates narcissistically on self, demonic violence flares up in the lust to control and possess another person. Yet the first to be destroyed is Aylmer himself, who steps out of the procession of life, suffering from an incapacity to accept and integrate human emotions. The price of perfection is spiritual atrophy or death, a withdrawal from what Hawthorne called "the magnetic chain of humanity."[15]

Notes

1. See James Quinn and Ross Baldessarini, "Literary Technique and Psychological Effect in Hawthorne's 'The Minister's Black Veil,'" *Literature and Psychology,* XXIV (November, 1974), 115-23.

2. The spelling of the word "birth-mark" in this article will be consistent with Hawthorne's spelling of the world.

3. *The Centenary Edition of the Works of Nathaniel Hawthorne,* eds. William Charvat, Roy Harvey Pearce, and Claude Simpson (Columbus, Ohio, 1974), X, 38. All future references from Volume X will appear in the body of the text of this article.

4. The influence of "temperament upon perception" is often alluded to by Hawthorne. For example, in *The House of the Seven Gables,* writing of the effect the Pyncheon mansion made upon people, Hawthorne noted that the ". . . person of imaginative temperament . . . would be conscious of something deeper than he saw" (*The Centenary Edition,* VII, 285).

5. It is strikingly similar to Milton Stern's description of Melville's procedure in *Moby-Dick* (from the chapter entitled "The Doubloon"): "the filtering of a constant through diverse intelligences." Melville needed a method to reveal the nature of the hearts of the crew and utilized Ahab's coin as his "constant." By having the men advance, each in his turn, to the mainmast and soliloquize about the meaning of the doubloon, Melville created a situation from which could arise a variety of different attitudes. See Herman Melville, *Moby-Dick,* eds. Harrison Hayford and Hershel Parker (Norton Critical Editions, New York: W. W. Norton and Company, 1967), p. 362.

6. Most of the characteristics of the illness can be found in the official definition of obsessive-compulsive disorder stated in the third edition of the American Psychiatric Association's (1980) *Di-

agnostic and Statistical Manual of Mental Disorders (DSM-III):

> The essential features are recurrent obsessions and/or compulsions. Obsessions are defined as recurrent, persistent ideas, thoughts, images or impulses which are ego-alien; that is, they are not experienced as voluntarily produced, but rather as ideas that invade the field of consciousness. Attempts are made to ignore or suppress them. Compulsions are behaviors which are not experienced as the outcome of the individual's own volition, but are accompanied by both a sense of subjective compulsion and a desire to resist (at least initially).

(p. 234)

7. Otto Fenichel, *The Psychoanalytic Theory of Neurosis* (New York, 1945), p. 290.

8. Fenichel, p. 293

9. Fenichel, p. 294.

10. In Freudian theory, certain ideas heavily charged or invested with affect or emotion constantly press toward conscious recognition or awareness, and certain impulses toward overt satisfaction or fulfillment. What we note in this tale is something close to "isolation of affect" or suppression and limitation or restriction of a highly charged emotion. The feeling and its source seem to be a form of anxiety, fear of being harmed through intimacy—metaphorically a problem in the category of castration anxiety or fear of being found wanting (already castrated). The idea that the birthmark is a castration symbol has already been suggested by Simon Lesser, *Fiction and the Unconscious*, p. 88.

11. W. R. Thompson suggests that the significance of the name Aminadab derives from the fact it is a variant of "Amminadab," a Levite high priest mentioned ten times in the Old Testament and who represents an old and traditional order and prescientific humanism. See "Aminadab in Hawthorne's 'The Birth-mark,'" *Modern Language Notes*, LXX (June, 1955), 413-15. One may also take the name in reverse, as a pun: Aylmer's "bad anima."

12. Terence Martin, *Nathaniel Hawthorne* (New Haven, 1965), p. 70.

13. Modern psychoanalysis suggests, "One of the striking features of patients with obsessive-compulsive disorder is the degree to which they are preoccupied with aggression or dirt, either overtly in the content of their symptoms or in the associations that lie behind them [*Comprehensive Textbook of Psychiatry/III*, eds. Harold I. Kaplan, Alfred M. Freedman, Benjamin J. Sadock (Baltimore/London, 1980), II, 1508.

14. That dreams might provide some clues to personality problems Hawthorne seemed to hold as a hope. In *The House of the Seven Gables* he expressed such an expectation. Writing of ". . . the topsy-turvy commonwealth of sleep," he said: "Modern psychology, it may be, will endeavor to reduce these alleged necromancies within a system, instead of rejecting them as altogether fabulous" (*The Centenary Edition*, II, 26).

15. *The Centenary Edition*, XI, 99.

Steven Youra (essay date June 1986)

SOURCE: Youra, Steven. "'The Fatal Hand': A Sign of Confusion in Hawthorne's 'The Birth-Mark.'" *American Transcendental Quarterly*, no. 60 (June 1986): 43-51.

[*In the following essay, Youra considers the interpretive significance of the apparent confusion between the birthmark and the hand at the conclusion of "The Birth-mark."*]

One thing is clear: Hawthorne's **"The Birth-Mark"** depends upon confusion. Aylmer's conflation of matter and spirit is but one of many confusions which the protagonist formulates for himself and others. As a result, surface is mistaken for depth, secrecy for openness, hypocrisy for idealisim, selfishness for selflessness, science for nature, head for heart, life for immortality. Emphasis on Aylmer's entanglement in one or another of these pairings has produced a variety of readings which examine what have become familiar Hawthorne themes.[1] However, the most remarkable confusion in **"The Birth-Mark"** is the final one—neither Aylmer's nor his wife's, but a *narrative* confusion so obvious, it has thus far evaded critical attention. When the story pronounces its closing moral, we are told that "The fatal Hand had grappled with the mystery of life, and was the bond by which an angelic spirit kept itself in union with a mortal frame" (55). This is not exactly right. Consciously or unconsciously, two hands are here confused; the "bond" refers to the birthmark, but the "fatal Hand" in this case is Aylmer's own, the one which has brought about the fatality by grappling with secrets of existence. Whether unconscious authorial slip or sly narrative strategy, this closing mixup indicates the extent to which the birthmark is Aylmer's projection—in a very real sense the product of his own hand. It also underlines distinctions between narrator and author which previous commentators have blurred. By calling attention to the narrative situation, the doubling of hands thematizes the act of reading. While it demonstrates how "marks" are projected and interpreted with excessive zeal and peculiar blindness, **"The Birth-Mark"** emphasizes the necessity and danger of reading the world metaphorically.

The equation of both hands culminates a series of instances which confirm that Aylmer himself creates the mark he vows to eradicate. As with other central symbols around which Hawthorne builds narratives (black veils, scarlet letters, etc.), the exact significance of the birthmark is left open to individual interpretation—an act which reveals much about the interpreter. "[T]he impression wrought . . . varied exceedingly, according to the difference of temperament in the beholders." Georgiana's male admirers declare that the mark is evidence of a "fairy" hand, indicating the "magic endowments that were to give her such sway over all hearts." Less admiring men wish away this singular "flaw" which mars her potential perfection. By contrast, women apparently jealous of her beauty declare that the mark renders her face "hideous" (38). Like a Rorschach image, the birthmark acts as a medium upon which observers project their individual psychology. Georgiana herself thinks it a "charm"—until her husband suggests otherwise.

At first, Aylmer thinks "little or nothing of the matter," and finds the small mark "trifling." But immediately after the marriage, he becomes intolerant of this "defect." Yet the radical transformation from innocuous trifling to distressing defect is a matter of interpretive choice. To Aylmer, the mark suddenly signifes that humans are directly connected to the lowest life forms; that we are mortal; that we bear (or more precisely, that woman has cast man into) original sin. "*[S]electing* it as the symbol of his wife's liability to sin, sorrow, decay and death, Aylmer's sombre imagination was not long in *rendering* the birth-mark a frightful object" (39; emphasis mine). Aylmer (perhaps unconsciously) chooses his aversion and then invests it with transcendental significance.

Not only is Aylmer's obsession self-created, it is also self-generating. Usually, the tiny hand is only slightly redder than Georgiana's rosy complexion. But when startled or frightened, she pales, and the tiny hand is suddenly highlighted against her whitened cheek, "a crimson stain upon the snow" (38). By his insistent gaze, Aylmer actually causes it to stand out in "fearful distinctness." The fear, of course, is his own—the cause, and not the result of the distinctness. "It needed but a glance, with the peculiar expression that his face often wore, to change the roses of her cheek into a deathlike paleness, amid which the Crimson Hand was brought strongly out, like a bas-relief of ruby on the whitest marble" (39). Another sequence reiterates and emphasizes Aylmer's part in generating and perpetuating his own obsession. Toward the end of the story, when Georgiana wanders into the laboratory, Aylmer is so angered by her intrusion that he grabs her arm with such force that his fingers leave an imprint. In this violent gesture, he reproduces on her arm an emblem of the birthmark, unwittingly confirming his complicity in creating the fingerprints on her cheek as well. Such episodes suggest

that **"The Birth-Mark"** relates the case history of an obsessive personality—a man who suffers from the self-created "tyrannizing influence acquired by one idea over his mind" and for whom a trifling matter soon becomes "the central point of all" (40, 39).[2]

Ironically, Aylmer has turned away from life in order to study it, withdrawing from the human contact which the dreaded hand connotes. Isolated in a "smoky, dingy, sombre" laboratory, he has "spent his brightest years in recondite persuits" (44). He has chosen as his mentors alchemists—protoscientists who manipulate elements in order to purify matter and thereby release its spiritual aspect. Aylmer apparently sees the stuff of the world as charged with transcendental meaning. To him, a clump of earth has a soul. Yet, although he commits his life to the investigation of physical processes, he seems to be "redeemed" from base materialism "by his strong and eager aspiration towards the infinite" (49). Such lofty vision appears to be admirable, but in fact, he uses the spiritual as a refuge from contact with the daily world and as a substitute for fellow-feeling. Immersion in the smoky, enclosed lab is a precise image for his situation. As he observes and notes down with self-congratulation his wife's last moments, his love reveals itself for what it is—an absolute intolerance for (what he perceives as) his wife's "imperfection." Aylmer "reject[s] the best that earth could offer" and cultivates instead an infatuation with his own fantasy of perfection (55); couched in idealism, his love is "so pure and lofty that it would accept nothing less than perfection, nor miserably make itself contented with an earthlier nature than he had dreamed of" (52). Although he assures Georgiana that he doesn't love her for her body, Aylmer can't get his mind off his wife's physical appearance.

The closing scene, which highlights his obsession, would be highly amusing if it weren't tragic. At her husband's prompting, Georgiana has just taken the "draught of immortality" to eradicate the mark on her cheek (53). She knows that she is dying, and we do too. Yet, as Anthony Trollope observed of *The Scarlet Letter*, "through all this intensity of suffering, through this blackness of narrative, there is ever running a vein of drollery" (quoted in Fogle 118). In this case, the potential humor comes from the fact that Aylmer is oblivious to his wife's passing, not because he isn't there to witness it, but precisely because he is! Aylmer gazes with intense, detached scrutiny, the "philosophic investigation, characteristic of the man of science." Noting down every detail in his experimental log ("A heightened flush of the cheek—a slight irregularity of breath—a quiver of the eyelid—a hardly perceptible tremor through the frame" [54]), he ignores the significance of these observations, even as he describes them into his huge book of failures. Though Aylmer is the abstracted, nearsighted professor, he certainly is not innocuous. While intently focused on the fading hand, apparent sign of his success, he—in effect—documents his slow murder of his wife. Even (or especially) the feeling Aminadab, "thing of senses," understands this fact. While the scientist is ecstatically proclaiming his apparent success ("'My peerless bride, it is successful! You are perfect!'" [55]), Georgiana herself breaks in to proclaim the obvious truth; with her last breath she announces "'Aylmer—dearest Aylmer—I am dying!'" At this point, we might well wonder who, indeed, is the earthy "clod."

Like the anecdote about the obtuse surgeon who addresses the anxious faces in the waiting room with the good and bad news ("The operation was a complete success . . . but the patient died"), **"The Birth-Mark"** derides that form of "philosophic investigation" which dispassionately measures, probes and analyzes, gauging success solely by quantifiable criteria—an attitude we sometimes call "scientific detachment" (although, as other Hawthorne tales demonstrate, it is hardly limited to scientists). Hardly a laughing matter, however, **"The Birth-Mark"** suggests that even cosmetic surgery can be lethal when idealization masks selfish manipulation.

The protagonist of **"The Birth-Mark"** is but one of many Hawthorne scientist-types who violate the sanctity of the human heart. Aylmer resembles both Chillingworth (a fellow alchemist) and Rappaccini, who also strives for omnipotence by gradually poisoning a beautiful woman he loves. **"The Birth-Mark"** depends on the fact that "the most precious poison," dispensed with homeopathic care, is potentially the "Elixir of Life" (47). When the "perfect and lovely flower" (45) he creates for Georgiana withers at her touch (prefiguring her own end, when all senses close over her spirit "like the leaves round the heart of a rose, at sunset" [54]), Aylmer realizes, with unknowingly ironic understatement, "'There was too powerful a stimulus'" (45).[3]

In their single-minded devotion to questionable creative projects, in their blindness to omens of failure, in their insensitivity to or violation of others under the guise of idealism, Hawthorne's artists and scientists resemble each other. The isolated painter in **"The Prophetic Pictures,"** for example, probes on canvas the hidden traits of his sitters with a heartless lack of concern for them, even when the picture forecasts the subject's destruction. He is coldly indifferent to anything but his art. Scientist and artist merge in Owen Warland, **"Artist of the Beautiful,"** (published just one year after **"The Birth-Mark,"** and also collected in *Mosses From An Old Manse*) who crafts a "spiritual mechanism"—an exquisite, delicate mechanical butterfly. Yet this attempt to transmute physical substance into the spiritual (an alchemy) can't survive harsh reality, the strong grasp of a human child.

Aylmer, too, is a figure for the artist as well as scientist. He is a writer whose experiment on his wife provides literary material for his logbook. A visual artist as well, he tries to calm and distract Georgiana with a succession of lifelike illusions, airy figures for entertainment. Then he produces a kind of TV screen: "The scenery and the figures of actual life were perfectly represented, but with that bewitching, yet indescribable difference, which always makes a picture, an image, or a shadow, so much more attractive than the original" (45). When she becomes bored, he instantly produces a flower which withers at Georgiana's touch. Then, when he makes her portrait with a photographic process of his own invention, he apparently fails again. But, in fact, he has actually produced a true picture of how he sees her—a blurred image whose only distinct feature is the minute hand imprinted on her cheek. Anticipating an ecstatic climax, Aylmer compares himself to the artist Pygmalion. In transforming a blushing woman into perfect pale sculpture, Aylmer exactly inverts his predecessor's activity, ironically improving on the attractive "original" by turning life into art. Aylmer, too, has retreated from sexuality, only to fall in love with his *fantasy* of female perfection. Like the ancient sculptor, the scientist marks his beloved's body with the imprint of his hand.[4]

Since the narrative is overloaded from the start with such foreboding omens, the ending of the story comes as no surprise. The signs are excessively clear to us, however oblivious the man of science may be. For example, Alymer's knife-plunging dream prefigures the end, as does Georgiana's "deathlike faintness" when she enters the boudoir (43-44). Through her, we discover Aylmer's documented history of repeated failure, and rightly anticipate that he is headed toward yet another. We fear the powerful "stimulus" which blights the "lovely flower" and understand the terrible implications of Georgiana's declaration that she will imbibe the concoction on "the same principle that would induce me to take a dose of poison, if offered by your hand" (45, 51). When his wife asks about this "Elixir of Life," Aylmer is quick to correct her; "Elixir of Immortality" is the more precise term for the tincture which will indeed immortalize her. Finally, although any birthmark, sign of generation, is invariably "fatal," the recurrent tag accrues resonance with each iteration—until the ultimate confusion of fatal hands. Unlike the birthmark, these signs are straightforward.

The voice which narrates these matters assumes an objective authority, a mastery over the story it tells, introducing it as history. "In the latter part of the last century, there lived . . ." (36). Enamored of its own story from the start, it excitedly announces that "truly remarkable" events will lead to a "deeply impressive" moral (37)—a moral which embodies the narrative's own interpretation of the events it has shaped to fit the conclusion. But the narrative voice reveals its ultimate subjectivity when, tripped up in its zeal to pronounce its sentential conclusion, it confounds two hands.

Although it purports to be "history," the story is a fairy tale, or the Gothic inversion of a fairy tale, in which the idealistic prince is a sham, his squire a shaggy hulk, his wakeful princess permanently put to sleep by the climactic kiss. Not only does the eager voice confound the two hands, it also doesn't seem to hear its own story, since it duplicates in its zeal Aylmer's impatient leap to conclusions. Apparently self-satisfied, the narrative announces at the end that "had Aylmer reached a profounder wisdom, he need not thus have flung away the happiness, which would have woven his mortal life of the self-same texture with the celestial" (56). This conclusion is not wrong, just a bit flabby; it fits the tale with too much room to spare, hardly doing justice to the story's complexities. The pronouncement is utterly flat and predictable, fully implied by the very first paragraph, and overly reinforced throughout. From the start, we know that "He had devoted himself . . . too unreservedly to scientific studies, ever to be weaned from them by any second passion" (36). Only by "Intertwining" (37) his two loves (like the fingers of two joined hands?) could Aylmer force his affection for Georgiana to exceed his devotion to science.

In the midst of an overdetermined moral conclusion, the narrator stumbles into a handy confusion. Although the conflation of hands might be symbolically appropriate, it also suggests a more insidious aspect of Hawthorne's narrative. For Aylmer suffers from a serious case of overreading, indiscriminately ascribing referential significance to all details. ("In his grasp, the veriest clod of earth assumed a soul" [49].) By creating a metaphorical link between the birthmark and the hand which eradicates it, the narrator unwittingly indicates the extent to which he is taken in by his own story, misguided by Aylmer—emulating him, even while apparently aware of the scientist's shortcomings.

Aylmer's ailment is transmitted by language, and the narrator's words suggest that he, too, is infected. When Aylmer first recoils from the birthmark, he explains to Georgiana that she "'came so nearly perfect from the *hand of Nature,* that this slightest possible defect . . . shocks me'" (37). He soon determines that the "superficial" mark "'has *clutched its grasp'*" (51) into her very being. Swept up in his obsession, Georgiana picks up Aylmer's language and pledges her life to "'unclasping *the firm gripe* of this little Hand'" (41; emphases mine). Similarly, when the narrator refers to the "fairy sign-manual" (38), he is taking a cue from his characters. With metaphorical versatility, the narrator proliferates such images. "The Crimson Hand expressed the ineludible *gripe,* in which mortality *clutches* the highest and purest of earthly mould" (39; emphasis mine). We are told that Aylmer cannot take his eyes off "the spectral Hand that *wrote* mortality" (39; emphasis mine). Later, the narrator observes that in Aylmer's dream, the knife plunges ever deeper, "until at length its tiny *grasp* appeared to have *caught hold* of Georgiana's heart" (40; emphases mine). Thus, by the end, when this figurative pattern has been firmly established, a reader is quick to associate that hand "which grappled with the mystery of life" with the birthmark, and not with Aylmer—especially since the metaphorical pattern has been firmly cast by the characters and reinforced by the narrator. In fact, the final confusion hints at a further proliferation of hands which mark life. While the narrator perceives the birthmark as a spectral hand writing mortality, *Aylmer's* hand can also be seen as a spectre which eventually inscribes Georgiana's mortality in word (his book) and deed. Furthermore, by its frequent ominous suggestions, the narrator's is a spectral hand which writes of mortality. Behind that hand lurks the author's.

As a detached scientific observer, an artist who worked in isolation writing tales of protagonists who explored the deep recesses of other's hearts, perhaps Hawthorne wondered about the extent to which he himself was immune from Aylmer's ailment. The biographical speculation is tempting: when he met and fell in love with Sophia Peabody in 1838, she was an invalid, tormented by chronic headaches. She had suffered at the hands of physicians since she was fifteen, barely enduring large doses of "curative" poisons. Although she was in love with Hawthorne, she refused to inflict herself on him, and declined his marriage proposal.

Sophia became a firm believer in the medicinal powers of infinitesimal homeopathic dosages, as did her father, Dr. Nathaniel Peabody, one of the first American practitioners of homeopathy (Stoehr 41-49; 107-108). Hawthorne, however, was skeptical, if not contemptuous of mesmerists, spiritualists, pseudo-scientists and fanatical purists of all stripes. When his fiancee's debilitating headaches were apparently cured by a mesmerist, Hawthorne was horrified by these "magnetic miracles" and begged her to "take no part in them," asking rhetorically, ". . . what delusion can be more lamentable and mischievous, than to mistake the physical and material for the spiritual? What so miserable as to lose the soul's true, though hidden, knowledge and consciousness of heaven, in the mist of an earth-born vision?" ("To Sophia Peabody," 18 Oct. 1841, letter 216 of *Letters*). In 1842, when they finally married, her symptoms ceased. After the marriage, Hawthorne quipped to his sister that "We are as happy as people can be, without making themselves ridiculous, and might be even happier; but, as a matter of taste, we choose to stop short at this point" ("To Louisa Hawthorne," 10 July 1842, letter 246 of *Letters*). But a letter to his New York magazine editors reveals that Hawthorne had anticipated that the marriage and new lack of isolation would prevent him from further writing ("To Cornelius Matthews and Evert A. Duyckinck," 22 December 1841, letter 222 of *Letters*). Fortunately, he was wrong. Perhaps presenting the author with an opportunity to intertwine two passions, **"The Birth-Mark"** was the first story he wrote following the wedding.

At about the same time he composed **"The Birth-Mark,"** Hawthorne was playfully experimenting in his journals with amusing conflations of literal and metaphorical meanings. "Flesh and Blood—a firm of butchers" and "Miss Polly Syllable—a schoolmistress." He mused about the entertaining possibilities of such wordplay:

> To make literal pictures of figurative expressions;—for instance, he burst into tears—a man suddenly turned into a shower of briny drops. An explosion of laughter—a man blowing up, and his fragments flying about on all sides. He cast his eyes upon the ground—a man standing eyeless, with his eyes on the ground, staring up at him in wonderment & c & c & c.
>
> (*Notebooks* 254)[5]

By spiritualizing all physical details and by seeing in his wife's face only the symbol of earthly imperfection, Aylmer plays the author's game by inverting it, making a figurative expression of a literal picture. But the result of *his* experiment is deadly serious.

Aylmer's dilemma and Hawthorne's amusement are, finally, ours too—precisely to the extent that we find ourselves tempted into speculating about the "significance" of (for example) spectral hands. However, the trap is not metaphorical thinking, *per se*. For, in a world in which nature chooses to show only results, we are left to intuit processes, to puzzle out implications, to interpret meanings—or remain illiterate. But **"The Birth-Mark"** emphasizes that in making sense, we must be certain not to do away with lively, pulsing possibilities.

Notes

1. Aylmer's confusions are not "mere" intellectual folly; they lead to bad science and philosophy, delusion, blasphemy or the subjugation and murder of women. See, for example, Shannon Burns, "Alchemy and 'The Birth-Mark,'" *American Transcendental Quarterly*, 48 (1979): 147-158; David Van Leer, "Aylmer's Library: Transcendental Alchemy in Hawthorne's 'The Birth-Mark,'" *ESQ*, 22 (1976): 211-219; Robert Heilman, "Hawthorne's 'The Birth-Mark': Science as Religion," *South Atlantic Quarterly*, 48 (1949): 575-583; Thomas F. Scheer, "Aylmer's Divine Roles in 'The Birth-Mark,'" *American Transcendental Quarterly*, 22 (Spring, 1974): 108; Judith Fetterley, "Women Beware Science: 'The Birth-Mark," *The Resisting Reader: A Feminist Approach to American Fiction* (Bloomington: Indiana University Press, 1978): 22-23.

2. Quinn and Baldessarini fruitfully examine the obsessive pattern, although in their rigid categorizing and failure to explore the fullest symbolic resonances of the throbbing red hand, they are both excessively and inadequately psychoanalytic in their approach. Furthermore, like most of those who have discussed the tale, they fail to distingush between author and narrator.

3. See Stoehr (103-104) on homeopathy.

4. Fondling his ivory statue, Pygmalion
   > Holds her, believes his fingers almost leave
   > An imprint on her limbs, and fears to bruise her.

   > (Ovid X)

   The Pygmalion motif is emphasized by the recurrent comparison of Georgiana's complexion to statuary marble (38; 39; 54). "The Birth-Mark" deflects the eroticsm of Pygmalion's story into a grotesque honeymoon parody, in which Aylmer carries his new bride across the "threshold" of the sumptuous laboratory/"boudoir" (43). In this sensuous place of enclosure, Aylmer finally unites his two passions by what amounts to an attack on his wife's blood-engorged sign of generation "glimmerng to-and-fro with every pulse of emotion that throbbed within her heart" (38). See Arner for further speculation about "Pygmalion." Fetterley offers insightful analysis of the "sexual politics of idealization."

5. These remarks appear on p. 61 of the original *Notebooks*. Immediately above them, on the same page, Hawthorne describes another scientst who sensualizes his scientific investigations—with disasterous results:

   > The case is quoted in Combe's *Physiology,* from Pinel, of a young man of great talents and profound knowledge of chemistry, who had in view some new discovery of importance. In order to put his mind into the highest possible activity, he shut himself up, for several successive days, and used various methods of excitement; he had a singing girl with him; he drank spirits; smelled penetrating odors, sprinkled cologne-water round the room & c & c. Eight days thus passed, when he was seized with a fit of frenzy, which terminated in mania.
   >
   > (*Notebooks* 235-236)

   These notebook entries are dated June 1, 1842. "The Birth-Mark" first appeared in March, 1843.

Works Cited

Arner, Robert D. "The Legend of Pygmalion in 'The Birth-Mark.'" *American Transcendental Quarterly*, 14 (1972): 168.

Fogle, Richard Harter. *Hawthorne's Fiction: The Light & The Dark.* Norman: Universty of Oklahoma Press, 1964.

Hawthorne, Nathaniel. "The Birth-Mark." *The Centenary Edition of the Works of Nathaniel Hawthorne.* Ed. William Charvat. XVI vols. to date. Columbus: Ohio State University Press, 1974. Vol. X: 36-56.

———. *The Letters, 1813-1843. The Centenary Edition of the Works of Nathaniel Hawthorne.* Ed. Thomas Woodson et al. XVI vols. to date. Columbus: Ohio State Unversity Press, 1984. Vol. XV: 588-589; 600; 639.

———. *The American Notebooks. The Centenary Edition of the Works of Nathaniel Hawthorne.* Ed. Claude M. Simpson. XVI vols. to date. Columbus: Ohio State University Press, 1972. Vol. VIII.

Ovid [Naso, Publius Ovidius]. "The Story of Pygmalion." *Metamorphoses.* Trans. Rolphe Humphries. Bloomington: Indiana Universty Press, 1955.

Quinn, James and Ross Baldessarini. "'The Birth-Mark': A Deathmark." *Hartford Studies In Literature,* 13 (1982): 91-98.

Stoehr, Taylor. *Hawthorne's Mad Scientists.* Hamden, Connecticut: The Shoe String Press, 1978.

Thomas Pribek (essay date 1987)

SOURCE: Pribek, Thomas. "Hawthorne's Aminadab: Sources and Significance." In *Studies in the American Renaissance,* edited by Joel Myerson, pp. 177-86. Charlottesville: The University Press of Virginia, 1987.

[*In the following essay, Pribek studies several possible Biblical and literary sources for the character of Aminadab in "The Birthmark."*]

Nathaniel Hawthorne's choice of the name "Aminadab" in **"The Birth-Mark"** has attracted much critical attention, with the tendency toward suggesting a single source or an ingenious meaning for "Aminadab." The name is certainly exotic; and although Hawthorne very often used conceptual names, historical characters who have emblematic meaning, and common New England Christian and surnames which point to a particular character type, he rarely chose anything as foreign-sounding and apparently cryptic as "Aminadab." Consequently, critics have read much into the name, as though Hawthorne's choice was a singularly important part of the plot. For instance, there is discussion of the possibility that Aminadab has a biblical source,[1] or that the word is an anagram.[2] All of these discussions assume "Aminadab" is a careful and deliberately significant choice of an unusual name.

The fact is, however, Aminadab can be found in English literature from the Renaissance to the Victorian period. There are some relatively contemporary literary sources and analogues of Aminadab beyond what critics already know. One, for instance, a novel by William Makepeace Thackeray, was published just a year before Hawthorne's tale was written. This story, or some popular stage comedies, may have provided Hawthorne with an appropriate name for Aylmer's assistant. "Aminadab" is an exotic name fitted to a kind of grubby person in a series of texts available to Hawthorne, directly and indirectly, and his own use of the character is similar to these works. Therefore, to begin evaluating the significance of Aminadab in the tale, critics should recognize that the choice of name may be only a casual literary borrowing and that the name itself should not be used as some sort of lever to push forward an interpretation. Although there are Aminadabs in three centuries of English literature, it may be too much to say that there is a popular literary tradition on which Hawthorne drew; nonetheless, in this context Aminadab has connotations without need of elaborate critical conjecture. The evidence suggests that Hawthorne was working with a wider range of sources and allusions than critics have yet pointed out and indicates that he had no need to resort to abstruse anagrammatic coding or refer to obscure biblical characters to make his own character meaningful in the plot of **"The Birth-Mark."**

"Aminadab" appears as a foolish servant or common laborer in the literary works Hawthorne might have drawn from. In the only lengthy description of him in **"The Birth-Mark,"** Hawthorne calls his Aminadab an emblem of "man's physical nature," then later "a brute" and, through Aylmer, a "man of clay" (pp. 43, 46, 51)—all descriptions that point to an allegorical reading of the character.[3] More often—and even before actually giving him any emblematical meaning—Hawthorne just refers to him briefly, and then he simply calls him the "servant Aminadab," an "underworker," "human machine," and "assistant" (pp. 40, 43, 51, 55). Of course, as the servant of a scientist in **"The Birth-Mark,"** Aminadab is more than only a necessary minor character who does the dirty work, so to speak, to carry the plot along. For example, if one allegorizes the story from Hawthorne's reference to Aminadab's merely "physical nature" and Aylmer's comment on this "thing of the senses" (p. 55), in an appropriate Lockean scheme, Aylmer then represents knowledge of the head (Georgiana of the heart) and Aminadab the mere body or sensual being. The assistant thus lives at a lower level of being than his master, morally and epistemologically, for he lacks deliberateness and consciousness. Although, this contrast can be read two ways: his lack of reflection makes him either a savage animal or, perhaps, a wise fool of essentially good or uncorrupted instincts. In the context of the tale, however, Aminadab, the true servant, always does his master's bidding. He has vocation, but not volition.

Such character is consistent with the roles Aminadab, the servant and foil, often plays in comedy. He is a fool who needs his master's more thoughtful guidance, or, less likely, he is an ironic contrast to the more sophisticated and misguided protagonist. In **"The Birth-Mark,"** Hawthorne's Aminadab is a more significant character than he is in other literature, but he is so probably as an adaptation of an existing literary type, and probably not a direct reference to a biblical personage or a figurative creation whose name itself holds the hidden clue to his meaning—a meaning which exists solely in the context of Hawthorne's tale.

The source studies about the biblical Aminadab are generally reasonable, though somewhat arbitrary. However, neither are they exclusive, nor are they convincing in arguing that the scriptural personage is vital to interpreting Hawthorne's use of his own character. For one, Alfred Reid says the name supports the view that Aminadab is inferior to his master. While the scientist is an idealist, his assistant is "limited, confined, and earthbound," and his name suggests the "narrow legalism of religious orthodoxy." However, Hugo McPherson, W. R. Thompson, and Thomas Scheer say the opposite; Aminadab is an Old Testament priest, perhaps more intuitively in touch with human nature and wiser than his master, so that his name implies a contrast to the modern scientist who has no reverence for the human soul. Aminadab is the unwitting henchman in a blasphemous experiment by a man who would be God; finally, he is more humane than Aylmer.

These views generally outline the critical debate over how to read the contrast of the two characters, master and man; nonetheless, these discussions have not been the last word on "Aminadab" because of an inherent weakness in trying to use the biblical references. In scripture, he is such a nondescript figure that his character and meaning are principally the critic's own choice. There is just one Aminadab in the Old Testament, and he is mentioned ten times, but only in genealogical listings, and the King James translation consistently spells his name "Amminadab." He is noted only insofar as he "begat" some person or family line, and he never figures in any narrative. Therefore, he has a character only by placing him within a tribe (the Levites) and generalizing about its historical relevance, or simply by guessing what significance he could have to Hawthorne. All this cannot be anything better than speculation, though it may be fitting that as a Levite, Aminadab belonged to a tribe of priests who guarded the ark of God. Still, there is no scriptural evidence that he was a high priest or had any recognizable historical importance. In the case of Thompson's argument, for example, one must simply assume that Hawthorne's use of Aminadab is ironic. Thompson says that "Aminadab is a symbol of an early authority which is now discredited; the priestcraft for which he stands is no longer significant." But even by this evidence, instead of concluding as Thompson does that Aminadab stands for an outmoded "compassion," one might see Aminadab more probably as a primitive character who stands for superstition. After all, he is among those men sensitive to the magic "charm" of the birthmark.[4]

Edward Van Winkle correctly notes the flaw in the biblical reading, the lack of any precise character for Aminadab. However, his alternative explanation—and others that assume "Aminadab" is a cipher—is even more speculative and dubious. He reads the name as an anagram: "Aminadab" means *bad anima* (soul or spirit). Aylmer has created, as it were, a false man, or bad soul, by his manipulation of Aminadab for an inhuman end. The *bad anima* is ultimately his own, though he can use his assistant as an extension of himself—it is merely one instance of his perverting human character and his dehumanizing work. Reid also suggests taking Aminadab as an anagram for *bad in man,* "a succinct play on the creed of human depravity." Thus, because of the human imperfection emphasized in the presence of Aminadab, Aylmer's efforts to transform his wife into the perfect woman must inevitably fail.

The applications of these readings too are consistent with common critical views of Hawthorne's tale and Aminadab's function as a contrast to Aylmer. Nonetheless, this use of "Aminadab" still seems extravagant and a bit overstrained. Reid, for example, even theorizes that the contrast in sound between "Aylmer" and "Aminadab" is significant; the former soft-sounding and ethereal, and the latter harsh—assuming a New England pronunciation would not make any difference. "Aylmer" may also be a pun, he says, "ail more."

There are no other characters in Hawthorne's tales and romances who suggest this kind of immoderate word play (at least, none that critics have found). There is no habit of Poe-like anagrammatic puzzle-making or hinting at hidden significance in names. So, if "Aminadab" is an anagram, it is a notable exception to Hawthorne's customary use of names. As noted above, when Hawthorne intends a name to be meaningful, that meaning is usually immediately accessible: *Chill*ingworth or *Dimm*esdale, for example. Historical characters like Thomas Morton and John Endicott are fairly easy to type, and often explicitly so: "Jollity and gloom were contending for an empire." Even foreign names like Rappaccini and Baglioni often suggest little more than Hawthorne's use of the gothic conventions of unfamiliar character and setting, so as to have unnatural occurrences become more credible.[5]

A possible point to consider in connection with the author's possible use of anagrams is his relationship to Delia Bacon. She held that clues to the real authorship of Shakespeare's plays (Francis Bacon, Walter Raleigh, and others) and a great new philosophical system were concealed in ciphers in the plays. Hawthorne wrote a preface to her book on the subject, and his good offices helped her to find a publisher. However, Hawthorne's remarks in *Our Old Home* and the *English Notebooks* show that he never regarded her thesis as anything more than a manifestation of insanity, even though he gave her credit for eloquently arguing the depth of meaning in Shakespeare's work. He scoffed at such research that looks for surreptitious clues in literature, and it is thus unlikely that he would employ such indirection and subtlety himself.

Even so, the name "Aylmer" has likewise been subjected to elaborate analysis by means of etymology and anagram-translation, but this name too may only be a casual borrowing from contemporary literature. For instance, there is an "Aylmer" in Walter Scott's *Woodstock* (1826) and *Ivanhoe* (1819; here spelled "Aymer"). This borrowing might very well be accounted for by Hawthorne's awareness of its meaning, "noble" and "famous" (Old English), perhaps by way of its modern equivalent, Elmer. It is less likely that Hawthorne knew what "Aminadab" signifies: "trustworthy," "loyal," or "faithful" (Hebrew and Arabic). However, the meaning of the name, and the scriptural evidence that Aminadab could only have been a lesser priest, an assistant of sorts, suggests the conventional literary use of the name for a retainer, instrument, or subordinate—a use reflected in the Thackeray novel, some eighteenth-century satires, and some Elizabethan comedies which were still in print in the early nineteenth century.

There is reason to believe, then, that whatever his final intent, Hawthorne first chose the name essentially for its connotations of villain (low type) and servant, and nothing more specific than this. Furthermore, there is no spelling discrepancy for any of the Aminadab-characters in literary sources (a single "m" in each instance), indicating that Hawthorne's recognition of Aminadab was primarily literary. **"The Birth-Mark"** was probably written in early 1843 and published later that year.[6] Thackeray's *The Great Hoggarty Diamond,* which contains a minor character called Aminadab, was serialized in *Fraser's Magazine* in 1841 (September-December). Here, Aminadab is a Jewish bondsman, a minor officer in the Court of Chancery: he is a crude, money-grubbing, filthy fellow—self-centered and rather dull. Except for his coarseness and narrow-mindedness, he has little similarity to Hawthorne's character. However, if Hawthorne did know the story, this may be all the likeness he had in mind. Thackeray used the same type again in two later works: *Men's Wives* and "Codlingsby" in *Novels by Eminent Hands,* the latter a series of parodies. In the former he is a cigar-seller; in the latter Aminadab is an "obsequious clerk." These works come after **"The Birth-Mark"**; nonetheless, they further suggest that "Aminadab" is a conventional, comic, literary type.

The first American publication of *The Great Hoggarty Diamond* in book form was 1848. However, the text is substantially the same as in the 1841 volumes of *Fraser's Magazine*; the characters are the same. Marion Kesselring, in *Hawthorne's Reading,* has no listing of Hawthorne's having borrowed any of Thackeray's novels or issues of *Fraser's Magazine.* Of course, this does not preclude the possibility of his having read the novel, especially since, as Kesselring observes, Hawthorne read magazines regularly and kept up with recent literature. Hawthorne's own letters and reports from acquaintances also testify to his reading in contemporary literature, even during his occasional Custom House employment. His publisher, James T. Fields, goes so far as to say that he read "every book in the [Salem] Athenæum." References in both the *English Notebooks* and *American Notebooks* indicate Hawthorne did read Thackeray, in particular. Furthermore, an acquaintance in Italy records his having called Thackeray the "greatest living novelist." Moreover, Hawthorne's *Letters* contain several comments on Thackeray, including the observation that "I enjoy Thackeray's books above all things" but that Hawthorne's own technique is essentially different from this writer of magazine serials. He once declined a request to compose a serial himself by contrasting himself to Thackeray. It is significant, to understanding Hawthorne's familiarity with Thackeray, that he considered Thackeray a pre-eminent model of the serial writer, rather than a writer of long romances.[7]

There are, in addition, less proximate examples of Aminadab than in Thackeray, which extend through the previous two centuries of English literature as well. The closest is found in Oliver Goldsmith's *She Stoops to Conquer* (1773). Here, Aminadab is included among a "low, paltry set of fellows" at the ale house, the one "that grinds the music box." Hawthorne never recorded any specific reference to this play, though it would be odd if he was unfamiliar with Goldsmith's most popular work. Washington Irving's Goldsmith-imitations in *The Sketch Book* (1819-20) and elsewhere and his biography of the author (1840) kept him quite in vogue, so much so that Herman Melville complained particularly about his pernicious influence on American writers in "Hawthorne and His Mosses." In this play, the alehouse musician is "Little Aminadab," his low stature suggesting his coarse character. Hawthorne's own laboratory assistant is likewise of "low stature."[8]

A lesser-known play containing an Aminadab is Christopher Bullock's *The Adventures of Half an Hour* (1716). Aminadab here is the apprentice of Tagg, a haberdasher, who is anxious about the faithfulness of a young wife. Tagg does not appreciate his lively wife and is justifiably cuckolded. Incompetently, then, he tries to kill her and her lover, with Aminadab a complaining but willing accomplice. The apprentice offers him a continuous stream of bad advice for dealing with his wife's supposed infidelity—at the same time, he belittles his master's foolish impulsiveness. Aminadab is rather more earthy, since he accepts the woman's human frailty and worries more about saving his own skin and getting his next meal or drink than any abstract conception of female virtue or male honor. Tagg thinks he is enacting tragedy; Aminadab helps make it domestic comedy.

The author, Bullock, was better known to his contemporaries as an actor than a playwright, and his own plays were mostly derivative of other popular works. For example, he borrowed from John Marston and Thomas Middleton, among others, both of whom have plays with Aminadabs (discussed below). Bullock borrowed more than once from Marston's *The Dutch Courtesan* and its ever-popular cuckold plot. The latest of five editions of *The Adventures of Half an Hour* was printed in 1767; there was no collected works of Bullock. He was a popular, if ephemeral, playwright and performer, but his reputation did not endure into the nineteenth century. Probably, Hawthorne would not have much chance of coming across any of his work, though this particular play is still significant in illustrating a characterization of the servant Aminadab which remained fairly conventional even among authors Hawthorne could read.

Moreover, in eighteenth-century literature, "Aminadab" is a name used often to designate a Quaker and usually a term of contempt for this low-church character, portrayed as a self-righteous hypocrite, a provincial fool, or a fanatic.[9] For example, Edward Ward, who enjoyed a considerable vogue in his lifetime as an author of plays, doggerel verse, and coarse humorous prose, has an Aminadab in *The London Terraefilius* (1703), a prose satire in the vein of his better-known *The London Spy* (1698), and again in the play *The Tory Quaker, or Aminadab's New Vision* (1717). A topical satirist, Ward was prolific and popular but briefly, and although he was still read somewhat in England during the next century, only *The London Spy* received much attention in the United States. His only collection, the *Miscellaneous Writings* (1717-24), was not reprinted in any nineteenth-century edition. Nonetheless, the presence of Aminadab in such literary works of the previous century further helps establish the existence of a literary continuity from the Renaissance to Thackeray.

The Elizabethan plays were, in fact, more immediately available to Hawthorne and his contemporaries, and the servant Aminadab who is occasionally present seems like a more immediate character model, for Hawthorne,

at least, than the coarse satirical targets of Ned Ward, which Thackeray might have drawn upon for his urban, low-life characters. For example, the servant Aminadab is a character in Middleton's *The Mayor of Quinborough* (1627), included in Robert Dodsley's *A Select Collection of Old English Plays* (1744). In this play, Aminadab is a minor character; a clerk or personal secretary, a trusty servant who runs his master's errands. The third edition of Dodsley's text, a standard collection in libraries and universities for more than a century after its original publication, was printed in 1825-27. Melville, for instance, was given an edition of Dodsley by Evert Duyckinck after asking him for some Elizabethan drama excluding well-read authors like Shakespeare and Marlowe.[10]

Another available Elizabethan play, by Thomas Heywood (as "Joshua Cooke"), *How to Chuse a Good Wife from a Bad* (1602), has an Aminadab who figures prominently in a young husband's plot to poison his wife. At one point in this comedy, the poor tutor Aminadab and the noble Arthur compete for the attention of the same courtesan. Arthur is not reconciled to his social marriage and hesitates in choosing between a practically ideal wife and a whore. Since Aminadab realizes he cannot have the courtesan himself, he decides to die by poison, but he is given only a sleeping potion by a sympathetic observer of his intention. However, Arthur takes it from him and uses it to kill his wife—so he thinks. He is reconciled finally to domestic life with a woman who is, by all other characters' reports, the closest thing to earthly perfection in a wife. The play was republished separately in 1824 and was then important enough to nineteenth-century readers for W. Carew Hazlitt to include it in the fourth edition of Dodsley's collection (1874-76).

A lesser-known work in the early nineteenth century, Marston's *The Dutch Courtesan* (1605), possibly based on the Heywood play, also has an Aminadab, one Sir Aminadab Ruth. Here, he is just someone noted in dialogue, one of Mrs. Mulligrub's many lovers; his nobility is only ironic, of course, and his attentions on her are no compliment to her character. However, the Marston play was not available in any recent printing, so it is doubtful Hawthorne knew of it. Still, it reinforces the supposition that "Aminadab" was a literary type—only a passing reference to Sir Aminadab supplies his low character.

Even though *The Mayor of Quinborough* and *How to Chuse a Good Wife from a Bad* were still in print, apparently neither was performed in the United States.[11] In addition, Kesselring does not record that Hawthorne checked out copies of Dodsley's collection of plays, which was readily available in the United States, although he did see Dodsley's collection of poetry, another standard text. Of course, familiarity with any of the stage comedies would be unnecessary if the Thackeray novel were Hawthorne's immediate source of a servant called "Aminadab."

In the texts available to Hawthorne, Aminadab is generally a comic type whose importance is only as a foil for a major character. *How to Chuse a Good Wife from a Bad* does have some plot parallels to **"The Birth-Mark"** which invite comparison and speculation about a particular source for the Aminadab in Hawthorne's tale: simple choice between woman as Madonna or whore which is, in Hawthorne's tale, a kind of childish morality and psychology; a competition between master and man for the same woman; poisoning a wife with Aminadab an unwitting accomplice; and an ironic ending. It is possible that this play or several of these sources were known to Hawthorne from his extensive reading after his graduation from Bowdoin, in preparation for and during his career as a writer.

Still, the best critics can say is that Hawthorne might have read the Heywood play, for instance; even then, it may be no more important than any other literary source, including the Bible. However much, or little, of these works Hawthorne knew we cannot be certain; and multiplying the sources of Aminadab just to stress Hawthorne's reading is not the most valuable application of this evidence. Though Hawthorne may have encountered an Aminadab in several literary works, his own tale is not significantly illuminated by any one source. In **"The Birth-Mark,"** Aminadab is too ambiguous a character to be just a comic foil, and the lack of a single source which might narrow his significance points to the ambiguity of the tale itself.

There is sufficient evidence for thinking that in Aminadab Hawthorne transformed a number of similar uses of a literary type of the faithful servant, which is ironic in **"The Birth-Mark,"** into a more complex literary symbol of man's baser nature. And the multiplicity of sources should caution critics against limiting the meaning of the character by pointing only to one possible source or some clever play on words. The evidence suggests that critics should avoid narrowing the meaning of Aminadab too much, and particularly avoid trying to use him merely as an indirect authorial spokesman and values-character.

Notes

1. Hugo McPherson, *Hawthorne as Myth-Maker: A Study in Imagination* (Toronto: University of Toronto Press, 1969), p. 222; Alfred S. Reid, "Hawthorne's Humanism: 'The Birthmark' and Sir Kenelm Digby," *American Literature,* 38 (November 1966): 337-51; Thomas F. Scheer, "Aylmer's Divine Roles in 'The Birthmark,'" *American Transcendental Quarterly,* no. 22 (Spring 1974): 108; and W. R. Thompson, "Aminadab in Hawthorne's 'The Birthmark,'" *Modern Language Notes,* 70 (June 1955): 413-15.

2. Edward S. Van Winkle, "Aminadab, the Unwitting 'Bad Anima,'" *American Notes & Queries,* 8 (May 1970): 131-33. In addition, John O. Rees, "Aminadab in 'The Birth-mark': The Name Again," *Names,* 28 (September 1980): 171-82, has reviewed the opinions represented in the above notes.

3. *The Centenary Edition of the Works of Nathaniel Hawthorne,* ed. William L. Charvat et al., 16 vols. to date (Columbus: Ohio State University Press, 1962-), vol. 10, *Mosses from an Old Manse* (1974); referred to subsequently in the text.

4. See David J. Baxter, "'The Birthmark' in Perspective," *Nathaniel Hawthorne Journal 1975,* ed. C. E. Frazer Clark, Jr. (Englewood, Col.: Microcard Editions, 1975), pp. 232-40, who argues that Aminadab represents the primitive man from whom humanity must mature.

5. See Jane Lundblad, *Nathaniel Hawthorne and the Tradition of Gothic Romance* (New York: Haskell House, 1964 [1946]), pp. 18-19. She specifically notes that "Aminadab" may be in this tale only for his antique and oriental (scriptural) connotations (p. 52).

6. Lea Bertani Vozar Newman, *A Reader's Guide to the Short Stories of Nathaniel Hawthorne* (Boston: G. K. Hall, 1979), p. 29; and *Mosses,* p. 501.

7. See Marion L. Kesselring, *Hawthorne's Reading: 1828-1850* (New York: New York Public Library, 1949), p. 8; James T. Fields, *Yesterdays with Authors* (Boston: Houghton, Osgood, 1900 [1879]), p. 47; Danny Robinson, "Hawthorne in the Boston Athenæum," *Hawthorne Society Newsletter,* 10 (Spring 1984): 1-2; Raymona E. Hull, *Nathaniel Hawthorne: The English Experience, 1853-64* (Pittsburgh: University of Pittsburgh Press, 1980), p. 147; and *The Centenary Edition of the Works of Nathaniel Hawthorne,* vol. 16, *The Letters: 1843-1853* (1985), pp. 488, 627.

8. In addition to pointing out an Aminadab in the Goldsmith play, Rees suggests similarity between Hawthorne's character and Caliban in *The Tempest,* though he can offer only a resemblance of the vowel sounds in the names to support such a specific allusion. Ultimately, Rees rather doubts any direct literary influences and prefers "plain" explanations for Hawthorne's choice of name: for instance, its "strangeness" and "strong hints of exoticism and the past," or its still-current use as a Christian name in New England. B. Bernard Cohen, who is working on a new study of Haw-

thorne's reading, has written to me that "it is safe to assume that during his college days he read widely in the [Bowdoin Athenæum Society] library," which owned an edition of Goldsmith's works, though there is no record for the contents of this edition nor what Hawthorne read in it.

9. See E. Cobham Brewer, *The Dictionary of Phrase and Fable,* rev. ed. (New York: Avenel Books, 1978 [1894]).

10. Merton M. Sealts, Jr., *Melville's Reading* (Madison: University of Wisconsin Press, 1966), p. 57.

11. See Don L. Hixon and Don A. Hennessee, *Nineteenth-Century American Drama: A Finding Guide* (Metuchen, N.J.: Scarecrow Press, 1977); and Robert L. Sherman, *Drama Cyclopedia: A Bibliography of Plays and Players* (Chicago: n. p., 1944).

Ellen E. Westbrook (essay date June 1989)

SOURCE: Westbrook, Ellen E. "Probable Improbabilities: Verisimilar Romance in Hawthorne's 'The Birth-Mark.'" *American Transcendental Quarterly* 3, no. 2 (June 1989): 203-17.

[*In the following essay, Westbrook illustrates that Hawthorne's "verisimilar fictional world" in "The Birth-mark," as well as in some of his other works, "enable[s] us to perceive what familiarity masks."*]

"Puff away, my pet! Puff away, pretty one!" Mother Rigby kept repeating, with her pleasantest smile. "It is the breath of life to ye; and that you may take my word for!"

Beyond all question, the pipe was bewitched. . . . The figure, after a few doubtful attempts, at length blew forth a volley of smoke. . . . The shrivelled yellow face, which heretofore had been no face at all, had already a thin, fantastic haze, as it were, of human likeness. . . . The whole figure, in like manner, assumed a show of life, such as we impart to ill-defined shapes among the clouds, and half-deceive ourselves with the pastime of our own fancy.

("Feathertop")

How does the language of fiction invoke a probable, or verisimilar, "show of life?" Often in our discussions of how, we focus either on narrative strategies that imitate our non-fictional world of lived experience or on strategies that violate the norms of our everyday world. In the passage I have just quoted from Hawthorne's last tale **"Feathertop"** (1852), for example, we perceive a fictional character as a woman because the narrator identifies her as a mother who speaks our language and who expresses emotion; we perceive the second figure whose identity is less clear as having a recognizable human countenance and manner. Our shared assumptions about what constitutes a universe shaped by nature and by human activity help us to understand and to accept as credible what this fiction presents to us. We take for granted that people are thinking, feeling, imagining, remembering, speaking creatures (Culler 140); we assume as part of everyday life cultural artifacts such as pipes and houses, causal relationships among events, and values and beliefs that shape our behavior and understanding of events.

But of course the probable worlds that authors create with literary language are not simply mirror images of our lived experience. In **"Feathertop,"** it is a witch who mothers a scarecrow son and who asks us to accept her word on the life-giving properties of her pipe; it is a puckered pumpkin that becomes an expressive face. Our shared assumptions about what can happen in fiction, then, here specifically in nineteenth-century American romance, also influence our understanding and acceptance of what fictions present to us; in the case of **"Feathertop,"** what would be improbable events in our lived experience become probable events. These shared assumptions about fictions constitute our notions of genre and the conventions that govern them. Hawthorne, for example, draws on conventions of nineteenth-century romance to affirm the credibility of his fictions. By invoking the individual or the particular of our taken-for-granted reality and general types or abstract patterns typical of romance, the possible and the marvelous, and the historical with the fictive (Stubbs 7, 8-48), he generates "an artistic distance from human experience" (Stubbs 5). From this perspective, Hawthorne's narratives reshape the tenets of what is probable to our everyday experience, by which we meaningfully order that reality. His narratives thereby transform our expectations for what might happen in fiction and transform our conception of everyday lived experience. Fiction reminds us that what can happen within its boundaries is not limited by what does happen in our everyday world; mimetic representation is only one possibility for verisimilar representation.

Hawthorne typically exploits an aesthetic latitude greater than mimesis allows as he develops credible realities in his short fiction. He explores this latitude in a variety of patterns that he shapes among kinds of verisimilitude. These patterns afford him flexibility and diversity in his form, and they typically invoke less extreme, and thereby less immediately visible contrasts than mischievous witches and engaging scarecrows dramatize. The standard method of his short fiction, one of four that I have identified in a longer study and the one which I will examine below, is to displace our everyday conception of reality with an other, seemingly unfamiliar world. Hawthorne later refers to his method as "establish[ing] a theatre, a little removed from the highway of ordinary travel" (III 1). When we oppose mimetic and comparatively non-mimetic styles, we emphasize how this canonical Hawthorne defines narrative boundaries different from those of everyday consensus reality. Yet Hawthorne's displacing fictions are not just separate from our everyday reality; they also are associated with it intimately. Not only do these narratives direct us to loosen our expectations for a probable world shaped primarily by the natural and cultural norms—the particular, the mimetic, the historical. They also engage us repeatedly with those conceptions of reality in order to perceive and to make sense of general types, the marvelous, and explicit fictionalizing. We become familiar with Hawthorne's unfamiliar worlds of romance and accept them as probable partly by means of the ongoing dialogue he generates among what in the twentieth century we designate as different styles of literary discourse. Indeed, Hawthorne generates probable worlds in this form of romance from an essential rhetorical engagement between what later theoreticians distinguish as novelistic and romance styles. Mimetic representation and allusion are not merely alternative possibilities for fictional representation in this form of Hawthorne's romance, but are an essential ingredient. Hawthorne "establish[es] a theatre, a *little* removed" (emphasis added).[1]

"THE BIRTH-MARK": A CASE STUDY

The theater of **"The Birth-Mark"** (1843) and the nature of our engagement with it illustrate how Hawthorne's method for distancing us into the perspective of romance originates from what is probable to our everyday world and what is not. The tale seems to progress from our everyday world toward a discrete framework of romance, from the domestic scene in which Aylmer first mentions the possibility of removing Georgiana's birthmark, to her death in the seemingly artificial environment of the boudoir of his laboratory. But our taken-for-granted assumptions about an everyday world are constantly engaged as we acquaint ourselves with this narrative's other reality in order to understand it. We are drawn into this fictional reality by the recognition and interpretation that Hawthorne's dialogue between his Actual and Imaginary demand of us.

Such movement between everyday norms and transformations of them is established as early as the title. The image of a birthmark initially grounds us in a natural world by focusing our attention on a mark of its fundamental generative process. Only insofar as we are familiar with Hawthorne's concern for the symbolic and therefore universal quality of his material, and with the conventions of romance that project abstract patterns, does the title expand into a less directly referential framework of romance.

Similarly, the way Hawthorne locates the tale within time both links us with our normative world and severs us from it: "In the latter part of the last century, there lived a man of science—an eminent proficient in every branch of natural philosophy" (X 36). This historical perspective, though here loosely defined, bridges the frame of reference with which we come to the tale and that of the narrative. But the distancing effect of this shared temporal dimension also loosens the narrative from our immediate present and thereby from our immediate practical concerns.

More striking in **"The Birth-Mark"** is the extent to which Hawthorne integrates different conceptions of reality by developing his representative characters in particular and normative terms. His portrayals of Aylmer and Georgiana emphasize selective characteristics. This emphasis creates a representative quality in their portrayals and is an aspect of what Northrop Frye identifies as the major characteristic of romance, "stylized figures which expand into psychological archetypes" (304). But because these portrayals are so particularized and exist within such a normative context, they are not primarily representative types, allegorical figures, or disembodied idealizations. Partly by means of such particularized characterization, the narrator not only avoids calling attention to the aesthetically distanced, unfamiliar world in which Aylmer and Georgiana live; he also consistently affirms that world as an everyday one.

The narrator develops this affirmation from the start by appealing to our assumptions about natural and culturally-shaped human behavior. Following natural impulse and social ritual, this eminent man of the last century falls in love with, courts, and eventually marries a beautiful woman. Aylmer is defined initially, then, by the two culturally-determined roles of husband and scientist, and these roles are not of equal value to him. If we gloss over such referential details in our readings, we camouflage the narrator's reliance on allusions to everyday experience as a means of defining and evaluating both characters' choices. Such camouflaging in turn masks the ethical implications of those choices, masks fiction's capacity to speak to lived experience, and masks how language generates aesthetic experience.

The narrator initiates such ethical choices by the terms that shape each character's introduction. Aylmer first appears in representative terms typical of romance, and the tale turns on the conflicts inherent to his characterization. The narrator signals the potential for Aylmer's specific conflict within a representative context when he continues to introduce the professional Aylmer in the context of attitudes toward science in his historical setting.

> The higher intellect, the imagination, the spirit, and even the heart, might all find their congenial aliment in pursuits which . . . would ascend from one step of powerful intelligence to another, until the philosopher

should lay his hand on the secret of creative force, and perhaps make new worlds for himself. We know not whether Aylmer possessed this degree of faith in man's ultimate control over nature.

(X 36)

The narrator's inflated and repeatedly qualifying diction draws our attention to a conventional conflict in romance between the efficacy of nature and the power of culture. As the tale develops, he poses the conflict in the more referential terms of how a particular character will resolve that conflict. By his identity as husband and scientist, Aylmer is grounded in cultural norms both in his private life and in his public role. The tale asks how Aylmer will respond to Georgiana's birthmark and what role will science play in that response.

But of course Aylmer also is in the tradition of the gothic villain, perceiving himself domestically and professionally as beyond the controlling, conserving influence of those norms. The setting of the tale initially reinforces Aylmer's perception, and our own, that he is loosed from ordinary constraints. Aylmer increasingly separates himself and his wife from conventional social settings, whether domestic or professional. But as Jules Zanger notes in his argument that the main settings of **"The Birth-Mark"** dramatize Aylmer's dominance over Georgiana, Aylmer's laboratory "looks remarkably like a nineteenth-century factory. . . . By placing Coketown and cloud pavilion literally under the same roof and next door to each other, Hawthorne has erased the physical and social distance that conventionally separates the genteel lady from the noxious factory and disguises their organic relationship and the dependence of one upon the other" (367). Such subtle housing points to a greater range of normative cultural values embedded in Hawthorne's portrayal of Aylmer's seemingly private enterprise. The narrative moves conceptually and imagistically in two directions: on the one hand, Aylmer and Georgiana live in a world increasingly separate from everyday lived experience; on the other, their world increasingly replicates normative reality; the narrative removes us into a world of romance only to confront us with what we think we have left.

The initial dramatic tension between Aylmer's two roles of husband and scientist introduces Hawthorne's familiar theme of obsession and thereby loosens the referential hold of the language of fiction. Aylmer's love for science, the narrator says, could never be subordinated to his love for his wife because "He had devoted himself . . . too unreservedly to scientific studies, ever to be weaned from them by any second passion" (X 36). As always in Hawthorne's work, obsessive choices necessarily violate other aspects of life that he values, especially "the truth of the human heart." The narrator hints at another resolution when he comments that Aylmer's "love for his young wife might prove the stron-

ger of the two; but it could only be by intertwining itself with his love of science, and uniting the strength of the latter to its own" (X 37). Implicitly, the tale asks how Aylmer and Georgiana will resolve the developing conflict between the cultural norms of husband/scientist and wife that they represent.

The developing, displacing perspective of romance suggests an answer, specifically through the agency of Georgiana. Like many of Hawthorne's female characters, she is potentially a mediating figure, here between Hawthorne's distinct yet sometimes complementary male worlds of intellectual activity and physical labor. Typically of romance, she is a representative wife insofar as she embodies the ideal domestic virtues of devotion and subservience to her husband.[2] Despite the couple's physical isolation from a larger social world, in terms of her social class Georgiana also is an idealization of social relationships; by definition the genteel lady affirms her husband's intellectual success and, like the isolated boudoir of Aylmer's laboratory, her deference and decorum camouflage the harsh realities that make this particular domestic situation possible (Zanger 366-367). She is idealized not only in her particular domestic role, one link to our everyday world, but also in the more fundamental terms of her gender—with fatal results. In Judith Fetterly's words, Aylmer attempts to idealize her as "an exemplum of woman as beautiful object, reduced to and defined by her body" (24). Aylmer, then, becomes an exemplar of culture by the values he expresses in his actions both as husband and scientist: his desire for a normal, domestic relationship of which a beautiful wife is emblematic, and his professional ambition. Georgiana develops in two, increasingly opposed directions: first, she becomes the tale's exemplar of the natural, as represented by her own birthmark; and, second, she too represents the cultural, as defined by her husband's increasingly suspicious project of embodying the natural in an idealized union of matter and spirit.

The preponderance of dramatic development in **"The Birth-Mark"** also accentuates the shaping influence of an everyday world upon this less referential world of romance. Much of the narrative before the scene in Aylmer's laboratory is comprised of dialogue set in two domestic scenes. In the first of these, Aylmer proposes removing his wife's blemish because it disgusts him. In the second scene, Georgiana essentially pleads with her husband to remove what also has become a curse for her. If her request enables Aylmer to "intertwin[e 'his love for his young wife'] with his love of science" (37), it also affirms his impulse to give his psychological obsession/expression in "lived" experience; he wants to give substance to his subjective reality in the form of practical applications of science. The narrative progressively manifests psychological archetypes typical of romance in referential terms.

These preparatory scenes ease us into this tale's particular perspective of romance not by removing us from an everyday world. Instead, they do so by blending its domestic and professional spheres with the psychological intensification, and the physical and psychic isolation, that we expect of romance. This intensification and isolation are figured in Aylmer's obsessive laboratory project. Even in this deep retreat from the conventional society of men and women, however, the brilliant Aylmer is governed by the constraints of nature and culture. When Georgiana faints at the sight of her husband's revulsion, Aylmer responds as a gothic villain but also as a husband; he "stamp[s] violently on the floor" but he also shouts for his assistant's help (X 43). Even before the domestic enters into this protected world. Aylmer depends on what he would supersede. Aminadab, the bestial servant to master science, represents the material world. His "great mechanical readiness, and the skill with which . . . he executed all the practical details of his master's experiments" make him "admirably fitted" to be Aylmer's assistant. But Aylmer fails to account for the dependence of his own intellectual activity on the material, or to consider that part of Aminadab's admirable fit may derive from the brutish but greater insight derived precisely from his sympathy with the material world. The events of the narrative confirm the implications of Aminadab's aside on Aylmer's experiment, and as an aside Aminadab's remarks point us to the confrontational relationship that Aylmer is shaping between the natural and the cultural: "'If she were my wife, I'd never part with that birthmark'" (X 43).

Similarly, Aylmer's developing experiment assumes shape and credibility from its mix of mimetic and explicitly fictional references. When Georgiana wakes after her collapse in the apartments of the lab, the "scene around her looked *like enchantment*"; Aylmer is "confident in his science, and felt that he could draw *a magic circle* round her, within which no evil might intrude" (44, emphasis added). Aylmer attempts to draw this magic circle within a concrete, specific setting of furnace, artificial lights and perfumes, and various laboratory paraphernalia, activities aided by and recorded in scientific volumes. For the most part, the narrator carefully presents Aylmer's work and even his proposal to remove Georgiana's birthmark as scientific experiment. But with Georgiana's awakening, he subtly subverts science as validation for Aylmer's project by referring to the experiment with a metaphor of magic; he reinforces this subversion by ascribing the language to Aylmer and thereby catching the scientist in a momentary confession of aspiring to powers inexplicable by natural laws or by any scientific manipulation of them. Georgiana's less authoritative but crucially complicit role is reflected in her less powerful figure of a simile, asserting only a flawed similarity between unlike things. Again the narrator displaces responsibility for this struc-

ture of thought from himself to the character; he thereby minimizes his apparent influence on shaping the character's perceptions, and he heightens the authority of the reported thought as representative of her.

We need to remember here that the "authority" and "power" of these rhetorical relationships are rooted in the opposition set up by Aylmer's project; Georgiana cannot supersede Aylmer. But Georgiana's rhetorical inability to weld her reality and Aylmer's hints at a yet more authoritative and credible point of view within the narrative which already has surfaced in Aminidab's aside. Indeed, Aylmer's self-exposure is foreshadowed by Georgiana's structure of thought, and both characters' comments foreshadow the empirical evidence that accumulates in the remainder of the narrative. Aylmer's credibility becomes so undermined that the authority for his confidence comes to rest upon the strength of his projected self-image and not on the strength of his skills—magic is what he will need. Only from our modern perspective, by which we minimize how mimetic representation and allusion function in less referential styles, does it seem paradoxical that "realism" here denies credibility to "romance" within its own territory.

Our assumptions about natural and cultural norms come into more specific play in the drama within the laboratory. Aylmer, Georgiana, and Aminadab think and speak; significantly, this play on our assumptions about what "people" do relies less on the narrator's summaries than on the more conventionally authoritative form of report. The characters also act, of course, and in ways that do not radically violate assumptions about normative reality. Aylmer induces fantasies in Georgiana "to release her mind from the burthen of actual things"; he intimates knowledge of how to concoct "the Elixir Vitae"; he releases a powerful perfumed substance; he tells his wife of a substance that is both a powerful poison and has the power to prolong life; and he demonstrates a cosmetic solution that removes spots from a plant (X 44-48). The narrator pointedly humanizes this man of science; as brilliant as he may be, Aylmer also is quite capable of failure: the plant he causes to grow and flower with astounding rapidity withers and dies; his attempt "to take [Georgiana's] portrait . . . [with] rays of light striking upon a polished plate of metal" produces the image she has assumed in his mind instead of her outward appearance, a portrait that blurs all of her features except the "minute figure of a hand . . . where the cheek should have been"; and his scientific work comes under unedited scrutiny as Georgiana reads of other failures in his notebooks recording earlier experiments (X 45, 48-49).

Similarly the characters' emotional responses emerge from our shared understanding of natural human behavior. Given the tale's cultural context, we are not entirely surprised either that Aylmer thinks his wife is physically imperfect or that Georgiana comes to identify with her husband's view. We are not surprised that Georgiana increasingly admires Aylmer when she sees his skills put to concrete use, nor that she has more loving faith in him and fear of the unknown when his efforts fail. And we are not surprised when Aylmer, projecting his own self-doubt onto his wife, thinks that Georgiana mistrusts his abilities. Aylmer's obsession-become-self-contradiction, which finally becomes prophecy, perhaps exemplifies the weakness of this magic and sums up his deluded ambition: he tells Georgiana that he would not concoct the Elixir Vitae because "it would produce a discord in nature, which all the world, and chiefly the quaffer of the immortal nostrum, would find cause to curse" (X 46). But of course he refuses or is unable to see the discord in nature implicit in his proposed removal of the birthmark. He fails to foresee that he himself would be the most likely to curse if he should fail.

Responding to Aminadab's laughter at the closing sight of Georgiana, Aylmer triumphantly comments on the method of his achievement before either knows that she soon will die: "'Ah, clod! Ah, earthly mass!' cried Aylmer, laughing in a sort of frenzy. 'You have served me well! Matter and Spirit—Earth and Heaven—have both done their part in this!'" (X 55). They have indeed. But of course this is not a story of successfully idealizing the natural by embodying pure spirit in matter. Even if unwittingly, Aylmer does not refer here to uniting the two. Instead, the chain of events and the intensifying symbolic import of Georgiana's birthmark expose how very committed Aylmer has been to the superseding powers of magic; Aylmer's project has been to eradicate that most fundamental matter, the natural.

We bring to this narrative an understanding of lived experience and of literary conventions for representing it that guide our judgment of Aylmer's and Hawthorne's projects. Not the least of our knowledge is Hawthorne's consistent judgment throughout his work against the solitary (usually male) figure who is obsessed with a single idea at the expense of natural sensibilities. **"The Birth-Mark"** exemplifies Hawthorne's attitude in its judgment against Aylmer by such devices as the narrator's commentary and by the dramatized fault-line between Aylmer's claims and his actual achievements. These judgments finally assert that a conserving, everyday world embodies values, even "truths" that Aylmer's distorted reality violates. That distortion becomes visible not only because the narrative subtly juxtaposes everyday world norms and explicitly fictional norms. More importantly, the less referential and seemingly distanced world of romance in **"The Birth-Mark"** is generated from some of our fundamental normative assumptions and is represented partially in normative terms.

But **"The Birth-Mark"** does not affirm norms of the everyday world that we breathing readers take for granted; it generates renewed values from the conflict among the three characters and from the interpretative guidance of the narrator. At issue, of course, are not the ethical implications of striving for one's notion of perfection in itself. Instead, the narrative exposes the potentially fatal implications of such an ambition when pursued at the expense of what the narrator identifies as a fundamental aspect of reality that too often is taken for granted: Georgiana's birthmark "was the fatal flaw of humanity, which Nature, in one shape or another, stamps ineffaceably on all her productions, either to imply that they are temporary and finite, or that their perfection must be wrought by toil and pain" (37-38).

In light of the tale's events, this explicit moral is a resounding understatement of what already has been demonstrated with much greater power by the tale's confluence of drama and symbol. This confluence occurs within Hawthorne's narrative play between the particular and the general pattern, the mimetic and the seemingly marvelous, the historical and the explicitly fictive, a play authorized as probable by standard conventions of romance. The understated moral does remind us when we listen closely that we are in a fictional world and under the guiding influence of a narrator's ordering consciousness. The crown of that ordering in this particular tale is the narrator's anti-climactic moral statement. Paradoxically, that statement lends credibility to the authority of the lived (fictional) experience over which the narrator's moral seems to assert judging authority by the very contrast invoked between statement and drama, cool observation and fatal event. The narrator's moral provides a neat and safe closure to the tale, then, but it is deceptively so. The almost empty resonance of this moral's generalization against the particular, referential events of the tale directs us back to those events to decipher what the specific conflict is all about.

Glancing backward, we recognize the narrator's fictional challenge to fundamental cultural values by the tension he creates between the symbolic value of a natural phenomenon and its cultural context. By means of Georgiana's death, the narrator affirms the value of nature within everyday lived experience. He does so over and against Georgiana's perspective and that of her husband. Both of these perspectives are shaped by shared assumptions of what is natural as well as by shared cultural values that proscribe a deferential role to women and an assertive, controlling role to men. But if Aylmer's and Georgiana's fictional drama is fatally problematic, the narrator's affirmation of nature in the shape of Georgiana's death is equally so. As Georgiana lives out her role under Aylmer's tutelage, she is forced in effect to comply with her own death. The narrator's affirmation of nature, then, does not supplant Aylmer's magical endeavors with an alternative that the character of Georgiana can effectively embody. Indeed, the narrator's affirmation of nature shears those endeavors of their very physical and culturally-grounded material. He thereby allots character and reader sheer loss. Hawthorne's dramatized perspective of romance implicitly asks us a fundamental question: how can we live humanely within inescapably acculturated lives?

Hawthorne brings these fundamental contradictions between nature and culture before us in part by generating his perspective of romance from what we expect within our natural and acculturated reality. His mingling of the Actual and Imaginary dislodges our point of view from our taken-for-granted everyday world and dislodges our corresponding expectations for normatively mimetic narrative. But his method only displaces us superficially from our familiar world; finally it enables Hawthorne to direct us back with a horrific glance at the potential implications of our choices as we shape cultural values at the expense of humane motives. Hawthorne's "theatre" is indeed "a little removed." But to describe his process of romance accurately, and to recognize the nature of his commitment to unseating our taken-for-granted frameworks of perception, we need to recognize his theater's proximity to everyday experience as well as its departure from it.

Our methods for such recognition have become both problematic and enriched by our debate about the relationship between fictional and non-fictional experience, by our "focus on referentiality as a problem rather than as something that reliably and unambiguously relates a reader to the 'real world' of history, of society, and of people acting within society on the stage of history" (Miller 283). Hawthorne's tales invited us into this problem long before we separated, by our theoretical debates, lived experience from aesthetic artifact, before we considered language our singularly rich and resisting access to reality, and before we contemplated the inscription of history within fiction as our means to clarify the miasma of fictional and critical discourse.

Our sometimes heated explorations of the relationship between theory, reading, and meaning help us to understand Hawthorne's particular style, his aesthetic concerns, and his place within our literary and larger social culture. They also enable us to interpret more subtly the problem Hawthorne shapes by the form of romance that he develops in his short fiction. With our discrete theoretical filters, however, we also continue to risk rarefying the problem. Symptomatic of our discretion is our critical separatingout of "the Actual" from "the Imaginary" in our analysis of Hawthorne's work, an interpretative strategy that assumes methodological authority in our historical, psychoanalytic, generic, and formalist discourse. We can comprehend the problems posed by Hawthorne's short fictions more clearly if our critical methods less insistently separate what Hawthorne's forms of narrative representation integrate. We can do so by confronting directly Hawthorne's use of what is

verisimilar to our natural and cultural reality in the context of his use of literary conventions.

By focusing on such standard methods of nineteenth-century American romance as idealizing, as marvelous events, and as explicit fictionalizing, we have emphasized what Hawthorne referred to as the "Imaginary" in order to explicate narrative techniques that imaginatively transform everyday experience. By focusing on the historical (Colacurcio), we have emphasized Hawthorne's "Actual" in order to explicate what we think romance transforms, usually the historical underpinnings of the fictional artistry. Rarely in our criticism of Hawthorne's work have we considered the role of everyday objects or usual circumstances (Brodhead; Schlegel; DeJong). Shannon Burns does discuss five kinds of verisimilitude used by Hawthorne in his tales: present and actual circumstances, history, character, straightforward description of the physical world, and the realism of domestic, homey detail, especially the household hearth. These categories help considerably to establish Hawthorne's use of verisimilitude. But Hawthorne's practice is considerably broader than Burns's isolated examples of what is naturally and culturally verisimilar suggest. We have considered even less the relationships among the various types of references (Michael; Kinkead-Weekes; Carton).

Further segrating the Actual and the Imaginary, we have categorized Hawthorne's longer prose fictions as romances in contrast to novels, based on loose notions of their degree of mimetic representation, and we apply similar criteria to his short fiction. The mimeticism of novelistic styles asserts a correspondence between fictions and our assumptions about nature and our acculturated lives; the less mimetic form of romance asserts its ready departure from those assumptions. We are engaged by illusion as reality in novelistic styles, and in the nineteenth-century American romance by illusion as illusion. Novelistic styles create the illusion of reality in part by heightening the impression that what literature portrays in its unnatural, artificial form is natural or at least conventional. In contrast to novelistic styles, romance makes our everyday world appear unfamiliar in order to acquaint us with a different conception of reality, yet somehow probable nevertheless. Often we conclude that romance poses against our normative perspective an other reality that claims for itself a more authoritative world view. The generic distinctions that underlie such conclusions contrast sharply with how flexible the terms "novel" and "romance" were in the nineteenth century (Baym). They also disguise that period's concern with the distinction between fiction and fact and not between kinds of fiction such as novels and romances (Bell 9).

Hawthorne's use of different kinds of verisimilitude in a tale such as **"The Birth-Mark"** demonstrates an artistic style and project that are much more complex than our dichotomy between novelistic and romance styles suggests. Hawthorne himself draws our attention to the complexity of his method. Glancing backward to his tales as well as forward to *The Scarlet Letter,* Hawthorne states in **"The Custom-House"** that under the influence of moonlight, "The floor of our familiar room has become a neutral territory, somewhere between the real world and fairy-land, where the Actual and Imaginary may meet, and each imbue itself with the nature of the other. . . ." But "the somewhat dim coal-fire has an essential influence in producing the effect which I would describe. . . . This warmer light mingles itself with the cold spirituality of the moonbeams, and communicates, as it were, a heart and sensibilities of human tenderness to the forms which fancy summons up" (I 36). Hawthorne's worlds of romance become credible not because we suspend our disbelief in the face of elderly women-become-witches, scientists/ministers-become-gothic-villains, or meteors-become-symbols radiating in the sky. Instead, Hawthorne generates the perspective of his other worlds of romance partly from the confluence of such apparent oppositions; for the imaginative activity of romance, Hawthorne's early method depends upon the transforming power of coal-fire as well as of moonlight.

Hawthorne's method in a tale such as **"The Birth-Mark"** suggests what is at stake in the frameworks of perception that characters enact in their fiction and that we choose as readers while we make sense of the theaters we enter. Georgiana embodies the values traditionally assigned to women and with which the narrator is most sympathetic; the narrator grants her the greatest potential to resolve the ethical conflicts raised by the tale. As a near-perfected representative of our imperfect sisters, she represents our potential to choose ethical lives within an everyday world. Conversely, Aylmer introduces a deviant reality that the narrator undermines in part by portraying him in less idealized, more referential terms. As a near-perfected representative of our less imperfect brothers, he too represents our potential choices within consensus reality but ones that we typically camouflage with our taken-for-granted modes of everyday perception—a world of judgment without compassion, of rational endeavor without humane purpose. **"The Birth-Mark"** does not promote the idealized reality of Georgiana. Nor of course does **"The Birth-Mark"** promote Aylmer's divergent reality that curiously reflects our own more than does Georgiana's. Instead, Hawthorne's narrative makes perceptible the subtle, here fatal violence of both characters' realities that we typically do not see, precisely because of their familiarity. He does so by drawing on a range of narrative conventions to shape a verisimilar fictional world. That world portrays our everyday lives in the unfamiliar, exaggerated form allowed by the license of romance. Because the techniques of this form of Hawthorne's romance reveal difference, the unfamiliar

perspectives they create enable us to perceive what familiarity masks. From these different vantage points, we are better able to renew our ethical stance within both lived and fictional experience.

Notes

1. Prefacing his own argument for how central the cultural context is to an understanding of *Blithedale,* James McIntosh makes a similar point about this preface. Although not concerned with verisimilitude per se, from a framework of intellectual history he cogently illustrates the thematic and structural function of what is culturally verisimilar within *Blithedale* and suggests its close relationship to what becomes credible by laws of genre: "When beliefs are unsettled and appear as fictions we are ready to entertain the notion of the fictionality of life itself. This notion . . . is presented without consolation or crafty reversals in *The Blithedale Romance* . . ." (99).

2. Judith Fetterly's concise feminist critique of "The Birthmark" as Hawthorne's critique of male idealization of women implicitly comments both on the romance structures within consensus reality and on consensus reality within this romance narrative:

> "The Birthmark" demonstrates the consequences to women of being trapped in the laboratory of man's [idealizing] mind, the object of unrelenting scrutiny, examination, and experimentation. In addition, [it] reveals an implicit understanding of the consequences for women of a linguistic system in which the word "man" refers to both male people and all people. . . . Since Aylmer can present his compulsion to idealize and perfect Georgiana as a human aspiration, Georgiana is forced to identify with it. Yet to identify with his aspiration is in fact to identify with his hatred of her and his need to eliminate her.

(32)

Works Cited

Brodhead, Richard. *Hawthorne, Melville, and the Novel.* Chicago: University of Chicago Press, 1976.

Burns, Shannon. "Hawthorne's Literary Theory." *The Nathaniel Hawthorne Journal* 1977: 261-277.

Baym, Nina. "Concepts of Romance in Hawthorne's America." *Nineteenth-Century Fiction* 38 (1984): 426-443.

Bell, Michael Davitt. *The Development of American Romance: The Sacrifice of Relation.* Chicago: University of Chicago Press, 1980.

Carton, Evan. "Hawthorne and the Province of Romance." *ELH* 47 (1980): 331-354.

Colacurcio, Michael J. *The Province of Piety: Moral History in Hawthorne's Early Tales.* Cambridge: Harvard University Press, 1984.

———. "Visible Sanctity and Specter Evidence: The Moral World of Hawthorne's 'Young Goodman Brown.'" *Essex Institute Historical Collection* 110 (1974): 259-299.

Culler, Jonathan. *Structuralist Poetics: Structuralism, Linguistics, and the Study of Literature.* Ithaca, New York: Cornell University Press, 1975.

De Jong, Mary Lou Gosselink. *The Rhetoric of the Romancer and the Realist: A Comparative Study of Nathaniel Hawthorne and George Eliot.* Diss. University of South Carolina, 1979, Ann Arbor, University of Michigan, 1979. 8002241.

Fetterly, Judith. *The Resisting Reader: A Feminist Approach to American Fiction.* Bloomington: Indiana University Press, 1978.

Frye, Northrop. *Anatomy of Criticism.* Princeton, New Jersey: Princeton University Press, 1957.

Hawthorne, Nathaniel. *The Centenary Edition of the Works of Nathaniel Hawthorne.* 18 vols. to date. Ed. William Charvet et al. Columbus: Ohio State University Press, 1962-.

Hume, Kathryn. *Fantasy and Mimesis: Responses to Reality in Western Literature.* New York: Methuen, 1984.

Kinkead-Weekes, Mark. "The Letter, the Picture, and the Mirror: Hawthorne's Framing of *The Scarlet Letter.*" In *Nathaniel Hawthorne: New Critical Essays.* Ed. A. Robert Lee. London and Totowa, New Jersey: Vision and Barnes and Noble, 1982. 68-87.

McIntosh, James. "The Instability of Belief in *The Blithedale Romance.*" *Prospects* 9 (1984): 71-114.

Michael, John. "History and Romance, Sympathy and Uncertainty: The Moral of the Stones in Hawthorne's *Marble Faun. PMLA* 103 (1988): 150-161.

Miller, J. Hillis. "Presidential Address 1986. The Triumph of Theory, the Resistance to Reading, and the Question of the Material Base." *PMLA* 102 (1987): 281-291.

Schlegel, Janice Miller. *Nathaniel Hawthorne's "The Blithedale Romance": A Study of Romance and Realism.* Diss. State University of New York at Albany, 1979. Ann Arbor: University of Michigan, 1979. 8004021.

Stubbs, John Caldwell. *The Pursuit of Form: A Study of Hawthorne and the Romance.* Urbana: University of Illinois Press, 1970.

Zanger, Jules. "Speaking of the Unspeakable: Hawthorne's 'The Birth-mark.'" *Modern Philology* 80 (1983): 364-371.

Barbara Eckstein (essay date fall 1989)

SOURCE: Eckstein, Barbara. "Hawthorne's 'The Birthmark': Science and Romance as Belief." *Studies in Short Fiction* 26, no. 4 (fall 1989): 511-19.

[*In the following essay, Eckstein discusses Hawthorne's treatment of science and romance as "ideologies" in "The Birthmark," and comments that "science and romance can both be particularly dangerous because they offer the highly coveted reward of immortality to their believers."*]

> They drew upon that science, however, in an apocalyptic, wildly romantic fashion.
>
> —Robert Jay Lifton, *The Nazi Doctors*

In 1949 Robert B. Heilman published the essay "Hawthorne's **'The Birthmark'**: Science as Religion."[1] The year of the Soviet Union's first successful test of an atomic bomb and four years after the United States' use of atomic weapons against the Japanese, 1949 was a year inclined to provoke concern about the practice of science as religion. Heilman's reading of Aylmer as a tragic overreacher who looks to science for "an ultimate account of reality" is a significant interpretation of the story's most salient text.[2] But when Heilman asserts that science "has become religion not only for Aylmer but also for Georgiana,"[3] he fails to credit the significant "absence" of the text: the plot and ideology of romance. Romance is Georgiana's religion. It contributes to the metaphysical excesses of science as science contributes to the metaphysical excesses of romance. Combined, these two ideologies define the distribution of work in the story, the work of man and woman and of master and servant. The destructive effects of overreaching science and romance are evident in the work of the scientist Aylmer, his wife Georgiana, and his "earthly" assistant Aminadab. If Hawthorne's narrator warns the reader about the excesses of science but not of romance, it may be because the domestic dangers of romance were too near the heart of the newlywed Hawthorne to be openly exposed when he wrote **"The Birthmark"** in 1843.

Two late twentieth-century texts illuminate the ideologies of science and romance and their definitions of labor by gender and class: Brian Easlea's *Fathering the Unthinkable: Masculinity, Scientists and the Nuclear Arms Race* and Rachel Brownstein's *Becoming a Heroine: Reading About Women in Novels.* I will consider Easlea's argument about science, gender, and labor and the relevance of his argument to Hawthorne's story before turning to the imperatives of the romance plot and the relevance of Brownstein's argument to **"The Birthmark."**

Easlea's thesis is that "modern science is basically a masculine endeavor" and that this male behavior . . . is a consequence of an unsatisfactory sexual division of labor between men and women in both the "domestic" and "public" domains, in particular in the domestic domain of childbirth, baby and infant care and in the public domain of control over nature.[4]

Tracing the history of the philosophy of science from prescientific magic and alchemy to Francis Bacon, Rene Descartes, Sir Ernest Rutherford, the Manhattan Project and beyond, Easlea argues that scientists are motivated to conquer nature, consistently described by feminine metaphors, and that this history and these metaphors reveal man's desire to create life (to transmute matter) without the help of women's childbearing capacity. Easlea further asserts that in his zeal to succeed at this task, the competitive scientist isolates himself from society in general and domestic life in particular and, in so doing, loses his sense of the correct moral place of his achievements in society. To help explain his thesis, Easlea draws upon Mary Shelley's *Frankenstein*; he might just as fruitfully have examined **"The Birthmark."** Both authors' imaginations were stirred by the transmutational possibility of the new discovery, electricity. Could it change matter into life, life into immortality? If so, what would the consequences be?

It is clear that Aylmer's obsession with his science makes him unfit for human companionship,[5] but what so motivates him to "correct . . . Nature"?[6] His past, his beliefs, which are consistent with the history of science, and the behavior he exhibits in relation primarily to his wife but also to his assistant provide some insight into his motivations. Most of what Hawthorne reveals of Aylmer's past Georgiana discovers in his folio, his record of failures to meet his own expectations. Between the discoveries of Aylmer's youth, which "roused the admiration of all the learned societies in Europe" (208), and his determination to conquer the birthmark lie these accumulated failures of his middle years.

At some point, amidst these failures, Aylmer decided to wash the acid from his fingers and leave the lab to court Georgiana. Donohue vehemently argues that Aylmer left his lab because he needed a new source of experiment in the process of creation. His failures may also have provoked in him a need for domestic reassurance. Whatever his motivation, while courting Georgiana, Aylmer did not express the disgust he later expresses at the sight of the birthmark, for his revulsion surprises his bride. Zanger explains this shift in Aylmer's behavior by reading the crimson hand as a symbol of menstrual blood, a courting secret but a marital reality.[7] This is a very credible explanation, but another, less emblematic one is also possible: that in society—in Georgiana's home with her mother and, it is implied, other suitors—Aylmer is not obsessed with correcting nature and creating perfection. Away from the isolation

of his lab, Aylmer sees and seduces Georgiana in a social context in which he refrains from analyzing "physical details" or "aspir[ing] toward the infinite" (214) at least to a degree sufficient to win her as his bride. Such is the story of Aylmer's past, preceding but contained in the plot of **"The Birthmark."**

The placement of Aylmer's type in the history of science is a more obvious feature of the plot. Easlea gives Francis Bacon a prominent place in this history as the initiator of modern science (and a practitioner of "scientific" gender metaphors). Bacon chastises pre-modern, Greek science as boyish, "too immature to breed."[8] He calls for mature men who will discover "still laid up in the womb of nature many secrets of excellent use."[9] Descartes adds to this cry for dominion the conviction that Nature is matter, mindless and lifeless, yet still metaphorically female.[10] The male mind is then the only measure of existence: he thinks; therefore, he is. And science is, as Bacon put it, a "chaste and lawful marriage between Mind and Nature," successfully consummated when it brings forth a "race of Heroes."[11]

Aylmer's goals and his metaphors are consistent with Bacon's. Hawthorne's narrator tells us on first introducing Aylmer that he loved this science which wished to "lay [its] hand on the secret of creative force," to have "ultimate control over Nature" (203). The narrator concludes this passage with the significant remark: "His love for his young wife might prove the stronger of the two; but it could only be by intertwining itself with his love of science and uniting the strength of the latter to his own" (203). Aylmer does precisely this when he feels "fully competent," indeed compelled, to "correct what Nature left imperfect" (207)—the birthmark—despite his own "unwilling recognition," recorded in his folio, that Mother Nature "keeps her own secrets" and permits us to "mar," perhaps to "mend," but "on no account to make" (208). Once isolated in his lab, Aylmer leaves this truth far behind: he brings to Georgiana a vial of fragrance "capable of impregnating all the breezes" (212) without the help of a female. And of this paradoxical, poisonous elixir of immortality, he assures his wife: "Its virtuous potency is yet greater than its harmful one" (212). (Pierre Curie, though more modestly, said much the same of radiation.)[12] Aylmer's past experiments, his dream,[13] every evidence tells him this experiment will be fatal for Georgiana, yet he proceeds. As she dies, he is recording details in his folio.

That she dies is nonetheless as much her own doing as his. Or, to be more precise, her death is the doing of her gender role as defined by romance. Before her marriage to Aylmer, Georgiana had a mother to protect her, lovers to court her, and other women—as the narrator tells it—to compete with. In this realm of romance, lovers made of Georgiana's birthmark a fairy mythology. Flattered, Georgiana did not know that some, or at least Aylmer, would wish the birthmark away. It is no wonder that "soon after their marriage," when Aylmer proposes removing the crimson hand, Georgiana is hurt and angered (204). Nothing in courtship has prepared her for this.

Georgiana is a heroine like those described by Brownstein in *Becoming A Heroine*. Her success is measured by her ability to attract suitors and, at the height of her beauty, to marry one. But at the point she succeeds, her story is over.[14] It is, according to this code, better for Georgiana to die for love and perfect beauty, the rewards of a heroine, than to live beyond the romance plot—in marriage where her flaws are acknowledged.

Romance prepared Georgiana only for submission, even martyrdom, in marriage. So after several "seasons" (205), aware that Aylmer's obsession has entered his dreams, Georgiana "voluntarily took up the subject" of removing the hand (206). She perceives her life to be a "burden" (207), "a sad possession" (217), "which [she] would fling down with joy" (207), a martyr's ecstasy. True to the code of romantic heroines, she worships Aylmer even more after reading of his ambitions and failures, and she projects her romantic exultation onto him, imagining, "trembling . . . at his honorable love—so pure and lofty" (217). Just as he loves her because she is a willing subject and admiring audience (not the woman who "love[s] life for life's sake" and thus whose interference Pierre Curie feared),[15] she loves him because he is obsessed with his singular power of creation, which she imagines includes her—in fact, *is* she. They both imagine she is his creation. Neither his overreaching code of science nor her overreaching code of romance addresses the physical creation possible through sex.

Georgiana is neither a mythic spiritual guide[16] nor a passive-aggressive manipulator;[17] like Aylmer, she is a victim who participates in her own destruction. They are people of their class and time (or Hawthorne's class and time). Domestic life no longer requires manual work of Georgiana's class and gender; it provides only the power and danger of childbearing, for which neither his science nor her romance prepares them. Given this situation, the crimson hand may well be the symbol of menstruation, the womb, the frightening source of life, which its color has suggested to Zanger, Young and others. If Aylmer could eliminate his wife's crimson mark of creation, then he would be the only one in the family with creative powers. He could then usurp Georgiana's crimson sexuality and childbearing potential. In the code of science, she is passive Nature on whom the Mind of the scientist works. But in the code of romance she is also the passive bride to whom her husband's destructive obsession seems pure and noble love.

Science and romance conspire to take from Georgiana her crimson mark, a red sign of her sex's power. But an equally serious transgression is the attempt to remove the mark which is a *hand*, a tool of useful work. In the rarified atmosphere of the boudoir, the home that is dependent upon the man's work,[18] Georgiana is a kept and useless creature. At first she reads—though only to learn about Aylmer—but then, restless and bored, she enters the lab. There, however, she is perceived as a curse. Returned to the boudoir, she nevertheless thinks only of her husband's great love. When he brings her the fatal vial, she drinks, eagerly, sleeps and dies. She fulfills the role of the perfect romantic heroine.

When Aylmer brings her the draught, she says to him:

> . . . I might wish to put off this birthmark of mortality by relinquishing mortality itself in preference to any other mode. Life is but a sad possession to those who have attained precisely the degree of moral advancement at which I stand. . . . Were I stronger, it might be endured hopefully. But, being what I find myself, methinks I am of all mortals the most fit to die.
>
> (217)

This sad statement is true within the code Georgiana lives by—except for her use of the word "moral." It is the degree of *social* advancement, gender confinement, which impedes her progress in life, as a woman and as a worker.

A worker permitted to use his hands, Aminadab, is nonetheless also confined. Ironically, his confinement in the public labor class is what has allowed Georgiana to be trapped in purposeless leisure. The industrial worker who carries out what the mind of management would have him do, Aminadab is also the "invisible" servant privy to marriage's intimacies, about which he has opinions that carry no weight. His past is unknown: some critics suggest he was made by Aylmer as Frankenstein made the monster.[19] Whether or not Aylmer literally made Aminadab, it seems clear he perceives Aminadab as a mindless machine, a worker who, like Georgiana, would have no purpose if Aylmer himself did not give him one.

When Aminadab first appears in the story by name, he is asked to enter the boudoir and "burn a pastille" (209). Though Georgiana lies unconscious in her quarters, Aylmer shows no self-consciousness about asking another man to enter the room. It is understandable that Aminadab would look at the supine and beautiful woman and "mutter to himself, 'If she were my wife, I'd never part with that birthmark'" (209). His opinion does not necessarily demonstrate Aminadab's moral superiority to Aylmer. Rather it seems an obvious sexual and wishful statement by a man to whom such ladies are not available. In addition, to a grimy, shaggy man accustomed to poor women equally shabby, Aylmer's obsession with a small birthmark may well seem a silly, upper-class affectation.

Nevertheless Aminadab goes along with the work, not only because it is the work he is given, but also because, even if he did protest, he could not save two willing victims. Indeed, he seems little inclined to save anyone. He acquiesces to the situation, deriving his only pleasure from Aylmer's failure. Apparently, he is the same assistant who had witnessed other experiments and failures; then, as now, he may well have laughed because the mighty had fallen. For the same hoarse chuckle that Aylmer perceives as delight at his success is heard again after Georgiana dies. The narrator interprets this final laugh as the "triumph" of what is "gross" and "earthly" (220), but there is very little triumph for one whose only success is in his employer's failure.

The extreme division of labor by gender and by class serves none of the characters. In fact, the ideologies and "advances" of science and romance, and their divisions of labor by gender and class, together defeat all of the characters. And yet at some point in the story, each character actually "succeeds" according to the code he or she lives by. Aylmer's scientific Mind controls Georgiana's passive Nature. Georgiana dies a martyr to romance. Even Aminadab has his moment, the last laugh. The narrator, however, does not acknowledge these separate ideologies as such. The narrator, who both appreciates and condemns the scientists' ambition, does not note how science intertwines with romance (thus dividing labor) and produces not tragedy—as Heilman describes the plot—but ironic failure.

"The Birthmark" has been described as an "indictment of modern science,"[20] but the text and modern life both acknowledge the extraordinary achievements of science. Science is not unequivocally evil; it is, however, dangerous in isolation from human society's other influences, including sexuality, work of all kinds, and familial relations. It is dangerous in the speed with which it progresses, an incredible pace far outrunning the cumbersome gait of social and moral change. And it is dangerous when the study of minute details becomes a system of belief, as it is for Aylmer. He says to Georgiana that her birthmark can be removed because it is a "trifle" compared to this or that achievement of "deep science," just as in this century we say that the removal of all pollution or the obsolescence of nuclear weapons is, if not a trifle, at least a possibility, because "we put a man on the moon." But as Aylmer *once* knew, creation, let alone resurrection, is not the business of isolated science. These tasks require considerable human cooperation.

Aylmer, however, does not want to cooperate by seeing his science as one study among many: his science must also be philosophy and religion. The narrator explains: "He handled physical details as if there were nothing beyond them; yet spiritualized them all and redeemed himself from materialism by his strong and eager aspiration towards the infinite" (214). Aylmer makes infinity of his empirical observations rather than accepting how far beyond his own mind knowledge and infinity extend. The irony of his eschewing the very physical details that his scientific work requires presents Aylmer as a hapless descendent of Franklin and Emerson or of the Puritans, those material survivors and spiritual autocrats. The inherited contradiction of materialism and spiritualism produces in Aylmer a belief in the oxymoron, science deity. In this century the result of mistaking the physical for the metaphysical may be seen in the belief that a nuclear holocaust would be the Armageddon that God had in mind.

But it is not science alone which can be dangerous; romance can also be a code of belief which turns against life, preferring perfection in annihilation to the birthmarks and shaggy characters of life. Georgiana, the romantic heroine, succeeds not only in dying perfect but in having the opportunity to say so: "You [Aylmer] have rejected the best the earth could offer" (219). In this position of romantic power, perverse though it be, she can pity him. "My poor Aylmer" (219). Her soul then takes a "heavenward flight" (220), and he is left with another failure to add to his folio. Thus, with help from a science pursuing the secret of transmutation, the romantic heroine escapes the imperfections and dangers of life. In our century, in which real transmutation *is* possible—matter into energy—science together with romance has given us the opportunity to imagine, to desire, a *more* perfect annihilation: extinction. This would remove all the world's flaws. Robert Lifton argues that modern humanity is fascinated in this way by the bomb, a product of science whose power approaches the infinite.[21]

As ideologies, science and romance can both be particularly dangerous because they offer the highly coveted reward of immortality to their believers. Through children, works of the imagination, the continuation of nature, or spiritual attainment,[22] every individual seeks if not the promise at least the hope of immortality. But that hope too easily becomes conviction. Science promises immortality in exchange for a unique discovery, sometimes regardless of the cost to life. Easlea, in fact, argues that one of the primary motivations of research scientists is the desire to announce a history-making breakthrough.[23] Just so, Aylmer pushes ahead despite the warnings of his past experience and troubled dreams. He records the details of his work—to be discovered if not in his generation, then in the next. Romance, on the other hand, promises immortality (and moral superiority) through transcendence of (one could say, *desertion* of) life. Just so, Georgiana rather quickly acquiesces to life-threatening experiments to prove her love (as well as her husband's love of her) and sacrifices her life to teach a lesson her lover may well not have learned. Separated from the physical labor and sexuality that Aminadab's earthly form embodies, Aylmer and Georgiana try to leap painlessly beyond the modest possibilities for immortality which are to be found in work or in the conception, birth, and rearing of children.

The narrator's final comment on eternity would suggest that he draws rather different conclusions. Judging Aylmer's ideology but not Georgiana's, he asserts, "The momentary circumstance was too strong for him; he failed to look beyond the shadowy scope of time, and, living once for all in eternity, to find the perfect future in the present" (220). But if I consider all of the overt and covert beliefs that rule the text, this moral is not very clear. In fact, Aylmer *was* living in history, recording his findings, knowing what discoveries came before him and imagining what would follow. Unfortunately, he could too well imagine his unforgettable place in that history. He could have lived in an "eternity," a "perfect future" which is "present," only if he had lived by Georgiana's romantic code. Only by arresting history, a function of romance, can a perfect future seem to be lived in the present. And yet to maintain such a present—which after all *is* subject to time and imperfection—the only thing one can do is die.

Marriage, beyond the romantic's plot, outside the scientist's lab is not a perfect future, though in 1843 Hawthorne, like most newlyweds, may have wished it so. It is a social institution subject to gender codes which sexually divide labor in order to propagate the myths of romance, science, and class division, and quite a few others that modest seeking will uncover.

Notes

1. Heilman's essay was first printed in *South Atlantic Quarterly* (October 1949), 575-83; I use the reprint in *Nathaniel Hawthorne's Tales,* ed. James McIntosh, Norton Critical Edition (New York: W. W. Norton, 1987), pp. 421-27.

2. Heilman, p. 422. Many others have since contributed to the critical discussion of the story. For example, Agnes McNeill Donohue [*Hawthorne: Calvin's Ironic Stepchild* (Kent, OH: Kent State Univ. Press, 1985)] perceives Aylmer as an Emersonian idealist, Georgiana as a passive aggressive manipulator. Rita K. Gollin [*Nathaniel Hawthorne and the Truth of Dreams* (Baton Rouge: Louisiana State Univ. Press, 1979)], argues Aylmer's dream is proof he knew the experiment would be fatal. Allan Gardner Lloyd Smith [*Eve Tempted: Writing and Sexuality in Hawthorne's Fiction* (London: Croom Helm, 1984)], Philip Young [*Hawthorne's Secret: An Un-Told Tale* (Boston: David R. Godine, 1984)], and Jules Zanger ["Speaking of the Unspeakable: Hawthorne's 'The Birthmark,'" *Modern Philology,* 80 (May 1983), 364-71] all

pursue the theme of sexuality deferred and the misused power which attends it. Taylor Stoehr [*Hawthorne's Mad Scientists: Pseudoscience and Social Science in Nineteenth-Century Life and Letters* (Hamden, CT: Archon Books, 1978] examines the effect of the pseudosciences on nineteenth-century America in general and Hawthorne in particular.

3. Heilman, p. 422.

4. Brian Easlea, *Fathering the Unthinkable: Masculinity, Scientists and the Nuclear Arms Race* (London: Pluto Press, 1983), p. 5.

5. Stoehr, *Hawthorne's Mad Scientists,* p. 2.

6. Nathaniel Hawthorne, "The Birthmark," in *The Celestial Railroad and Other Stories* (New York: Signet, 1963), p. 207. All subsequent references to the story, noted parenthetically in the text, are from this edition.

7. Zanger, "Speaking of the Unspeakable," p. 368.

8. Benjamin Farrington, *The Philosophy of Francis Bacon* (Liverpool: Liverpool Univ. Press, 1964), p. 129.

9. Cited in Easlea, note 11 on p. 20.

10. Easlea, pp. 22-23.

11. Cited in Farrington, p. 131.

12. In his Nobel Prize acceptance speech in 1903 (cited in Easlea, p. 46), Pierre Curie acknowledged that radiation could one day be used for mass destruction and wondered "whether it be to the advantage of humanity to know the secrets of nature, whether we be sufficiently mature to profit by them." Yet he believed "humanity will obtain more good than evil from future discoveries."

13. See Gollin, *Nathaniel Hawthorne and the Truth of Dreams,* p. 113.

14. Rachel M. Brownstein, *Becoming a Heroine: Reading About Women in Novels* (New York: Viking, 1982).

15. Easlea (p. 45) quotes Curie's diary from Marie Curie's biography *Pierre Curie* (1923; rpt. New York: Dover, 1963, p. 36).

16. William Bysshe Stein, *Hawthorne's Faust: A Study of the Devil Archetype* (Hamden, CT: Archon Books, 1968), p. 148.

17. Donohue, *Hawthorne: Calvin's Ironic Stepchild,* pp. 227-28.

18. Zanger, pp. 366-67.

19. For a balanced overview of opinions about Aminadab, his character and his name, see John O. Rees, "Aminadab in 'The Birthmark,'" *Names,* 28 (September 1980), 171-82.

20. Stein, p. 91.

21. Robert Jay Lifton with Richard Falk, *Indefensible Weapons: The Political and Psychological Case Against Nuclearism* (New York: Basic Books, 1982), p. 13.

22. Lifton, pp. 64-65.

23. Easlea, pp. 49-58.

Liz Rosenberg (essay date spring 1993)

SOURCE: Rosenberg, Liz. "'The Best That Earth Could Offer': 'The Birth-Mark,' A Newlywed's Story." *Studies in Short Fiction* 30, no. 2 (spring 1993): 145-51.

[*In the following essay, Rosenberg argues that "Hawthorne . . . suggests in 'The Birthmark' that human nature is its own proof of divinity and human love its highest expression."*]

"The Birth-Mark" is a love story, like most of Hawthorne's greatest fiction, concerned with the relation between men and women. The "love" in Hawthorne's fiction seldom takes any other form—his women are not mothers but wives, not angels but household saints: even in one notable exception, Hester's relation to her daughter Pearl comes to seem peripheral to her union (or disunion) with Reverend Dimmesdale.

This question of marriage—and the larger issue of union and separation—has a special piquancy in **"The Birth-Mark,"** perhaps largely for biographical reasons. Written in 1843, it was Hawthorne's first work of fiction following his own marriage to Sophia. It remains clearly a newlywed's story, fresh with the author's anxieties, hopes, and fears. This very freshness helps make the story as peculiar in Hawthorne's oeuvre as it is characteristic. In **"The Birth-Mark"** Hawthorne takes to task his own "etherealizing" protagonist; he reveals a deep suspicion of mind/body theories current in his time; and, strangest of all, he ends by praising the imperfect and mortal quality of human nature.

The story's problematic "hero," Aylmer, is a scientist, artist, aesthete—and newlywed. An idealist by nature and profession, he falls prey soon after his marriage to a haunting awareness of "his wife's liability to sin, sorrow, decay and death" (39), symbolized by the tiny birthmark on her cheek. This mark becomes to him "the spectral Hand that wrote mortality, where he would fain have worshipped" (39). Aylmer's personality resists this: his lifelong search, Hawthorne suggests, has been for "ultimate control over nature" (36).

"The Birth-Mark" examines Aylmer's dilemma chiefly by way of three systems of thought: alchemy, animism, and Emersonian Transcendentalism. All three systems address the issue of union versus separation—all three also bear upon "marriage," in its larger context of spirit and matter.

Alchemical references and imagery recur throughout **"The Birth-Mark,"** as has been amply documented by Shannon Burns, David Van Leer and others. Aylmer's scientific aims are at one with alchemy, to "ascend from one step of powerful intelligence to another, until the philosopher should lay his hand on the secret of creative force, and perhaps make new worlds for himself" (36). Aylmer relates to his wife "a history of the long dynasty of the Alchemists," and his library is filled with alchemical and other pseudo-scientific works.

The alchemists' fundamental project stems from an ambition to "peer beyond the experimental veil in their search for an all-embracing cosmical scheme" (Read 24) and further, to effect this transformation by human will. This kind of overweening pride renders Chillingworth—Hawthorne's most famous alchemist—"a demon," and Ethan Brand "a fiend," since it suggests not only a supplanting of God's powers but a violation of the "Mystery of life." For Aylmer, as for Chillingworth and Ethan Brand, this pride leads inevitably to the Unpardonable Sin: "an intellect that triumphed over the sense of brotherhood with man, and reverence for God, and sacrificed everything to its own mighty claims!" (**"Ethan Brand"** 90)

Aylmer is not only an alchemist, which is bad enough: he is a bad alchemist besides. As Burns points out, "The old alchemists searched for an integrated, unified personality; Aylmer wants a perfect and pure distillation" (Burns 154). According to Burns, the alchemical process "was carried out by a man and woman working together" (Burns 148) and several alchemical texts point to alchemy as a kind of marriage: "The Great Work . . . being equivalent to the marriage of the King and Queen" (Read 19) and "the conjunction of the masculine and feminine principles . . . sometimes indicated as a hermaphroditic figure or androgyne" (Read 17).

What Aylmer effects is not a marriage but his own wife's death, the ultimate divorce. Distillation leads to separation, separation to loss. Aylmer's failures arise from his confusion about spirit and matter. In 1841, Hawthorne had written to Sophia, at that time his fiancée, regarding mesmerism: ". . . what delusion can be more lamentable and mischievous, than to mistake the physical and material for the spiritual?" In Aylmer's "delusion," he mistakes Georgiana's physical imperfection for a spiritual one, and, in trying to cure her of her human nature, he kills her.

Animism—a word coined in the mid nineteenth century—is a system of thought that simultaneously conflates and divorces spirit and matter. The nineteenth-century animists believed that inanimate objects—stones, clods of earth—were imbued with spirit; they also believed in "the existence of soul or spirit apart from matter" ("Animism").

Aylmer's laboratory assistant or "under-worker" (43) is Aminadab, whose name is a reverse anagram for "bad anima." He embodies man's physical nature in its lowest form. Aylmer calls him "thou human machine . . . thou man of clay!" (51), and "Ah, clod! Ah, earthly mass!" (55) Aminadab is a "clod" imbued with spirit, a "bad anima" of the almost-purely physical. Aylmer represents an opposite "bad anima," etherealized man who creates "Airy figures, absolutely bodiless ideas, and forms of unsubstantial beauty . . ." (44). Only in his repeated failures as a scientist does Aylmer reveal "the short-comings of the composite man—the spirit burthened with clay and working in matter . . ." (49).

Aminadab and Aylmer are alter-egos, mirror images. Aylmer is introduced to us as "an eminent proficient in every branch of natural philosophy," while Aminadab enters as one "issued from an inner apartment, a man of low stature" (36, 43). Aylmer possesses "the higher nature," Aminadab "the grunt or growl of a brute" (49, 46). To make matters perfectly clear, Hawthorne tells us in an authorial aside that Aminadab "seemed to represent man's physical nature; while Aylmer's slender figure, and pale, intellectual face, were no less apt a type of the spiritual element" (43). What is "bad" in both is their lack of integration. Here, as elsewhere, Hawthorne reveals his distrust of polarizing extremes: "There is no surer method of arriving at the Hall of Fantasy, than to throw oneself into the current of a theory . . ." (**"The Hall of Fantasy"** 180). Fanaticism, Hawthorne suggests, kills the real.

Between Aylmer, the airy intellectual, and his "bad anima," the cloddish Aminadab, stands Aylmer's wife Georgiana—associated throughout the story with love, marriage, blood, and the heart. Her name, as Burns points out, is a feminized masculine, suggesting the "Two-thing" of the alchemical process, and perhaps also *geo,* "earth," poised between the "highest cloud-region" (42) of Aylmer and the underworld "furnace" of Aminadab. Georgiana's birthmark is controlled by her heart's blood, as is Georgiana herself: she feels the effects of Aylmer's remedy as a "tingling, half painfully, half pleasurably, at her heart" (48). In a story about the dangers of one-strandedness, Georgiana's failure of excessive heart—while to Hawthorne the most pardonable of sins—is ultimately deadly to her. As Barbara Eckstein has pointed out, "Romance is Georgiana's religion" (511) and she dies its martyr.

If the heart sees only the heart's truth, **"The Birth-Mark"** indicates that it is nonetheless closer to reality than either abstraction or cloddishness. Georgiana differs from Aylmer and Aminadab not only in the nature of her failure but in her clear-sightedness. Aylmer never truly *sees* his wife; even when she is dying, he misperceives the true import of her symptoms. Aminadab, on the other hand, feels only the physical: he says, "If she were my wife, I'd never part with that birth-mark" and expresses "delight" in a "gross, hoarse chuckle" while Georgiana lies dying (43, 55). But Georgiana observes her husband's failures clearly, even while she admires him for his passionate convictions. She sees herself and her situation no less accurately: "Life is but a sad possession to those who have attained precisely the degree of moral advancement at which I stand. Were I weaker and blinder, it might be happiness. Were I stronger, it might be endured hopefully" (53). It is Georgiana who proposes the operation, Georgiana who first observes its failure: "My poor Aylmer! . . . Do not repent, that, with so high and pure a feeling, you have rejected the best that earth could offer. Aylmer—dearest Aylmer—I am dying!" (55).

Aylmer—failed scientist, failed husband—is the very type and symbol of Emersonian Transcendentalism at its worst. He appears, indeed, almost a caricature of Emerson himself. In his journals, Hawthorne described Emerson as "a great searcher for facts; but they seem to melt away and become unsubstantial in his grasp" (Mellow 208). Of Aylmer he writes, "He handled physical details, as if there were nothing beyond them; yet spiritualized them all. . . . In his grasp, the veriest clod of earth assumed a soul" (49).

As E. Michael Jones points out in *The Angel and the Machine,* "The age of Emerson was preeminently the age of the opposition of mind and matter, the age of the great clash between the mechanist and idealist philosophies" (Jones 18). Emerson was, at least according to Hawthorne, the victim of both: "Mr. Emerson—the mystic, stretching his hand out of cloud-land, in vain search for something real; and the man of sturdy sense, all whose ideas seem to be dug out of his mind, hard and substantial, as he digs potatoes" (Mellow 208). Transcendentalists like Orestes A. Brownson addressed themselves directly to this "clash" and sought to "reconcile spirit and matter" (Miller 120):

> We cannot then go back either to exclusive Spiritualism, or to exclusive Materialism. Both these systems have received so full a development, have acquired so much strength, that neither can be subdued. Both have their foundation in our nature, and both will exist and exert their influence. Shall they exist as antagonist principles? Shall the spirit forever lust against the flesh, and the flesh against the spirit? Is the bosom of Humanity to be eternally torn by these two contending factions? No. It cannot be. The war must end. Peace must be made.
>
> This discloses our Mission. We are to reconcile spirit and matter; that is, we must realize the atonement.
>
> (Miller 120)

While Brownson proposes a reconciliation and an "atonement," Hawthorne proposes a marriage. Aylmer's failure to see, love, and accept Georgiana's imperfect, human nature is the failure to live "once for all in Eternity, to find the perfect Future in the present" (56). What Aylmer has rejected is "the happiness, which would have woven his mortal life of the self-same texture with the celestial" (56). The recommendation is so radical that Hawthorne—while often suggesting it again in his fiction's imagery or his sympathies with some of his "darker" characters—never again proposed it so directly. The ramifications of his own beliefs would—and did—appall him. There is no great leap from Georgiana's scarlet birthmark to Hester's scarlet letter. The difference is one of degree. Georgiana is not guilty, like Hawthorne's greatest heroines, of adultery or murder—she is guilty only of being human—liable to "sin, sorrow, decay and death." Yet if love between human beings, with all their innate imperfections and frailties, is "the best that earth could offer," then Hester's final question to Dimmesdale must be read in a new light—"Shall we not spend our immortal life together? Surely, surely, we have ransomed one another, with all this woe!" (*Scarlet Letter* 256)—as must the minister's response: "'Hush, Hester, hush!' said he, with tremulous solemnity. 'The law we broke!—the sin here so awfully revealed!—let these alone be in thy thoughts! I fear! I fear! . . .'" (256).

What is it that Dimmesdale and Hester are guilty of, if not expressing their human nature? Is a pro-forma marriage a stronger link in the "magnetic chain of humanity" than love? What can their adultery be if not the very thing that Aylmer has tossed away, "the happiness, which would have woven his mortal life of the self-same texture with the celestial" (56)? Miriam's speech to Kenyon goes still further:

> ". . . How wonderful is this! I tremble at my own thoughts, yet must needs probe them to their depths. Was the crime—in which he and I were wedded—was it a blessing in that strange disguise? . . . And may we follow the analogy yet farther? Was that very sin—into which Adam precipitated himself and all his race—was it the destined means by which, over a long pathway of toil and sorrow, we are to attain a higher, brighter, and profounder happiness, than our lost birthright gave?"
>
> (*Marble Faun* 434)

In *The Marble Faun*, Hawthorne's only answer is to "tremble" at the mystery, "the riddle of the Soul's growth, taking its first impulse amid remorse and pain, and struggling through the incrustations of the senses" (*Marble Faun* 381). But that is in 1860, after years of his own struggle, remorse and pain. In 1843, writing **"The Birth-Mark"** he was still the hopeful newlywed, critiquing not human nature but its critic, Aylmer.

"The Birth-Mark" proposes that human nature is a compound—a sacred mystery. The only way to effect a celebration of the body is not through distillation—separateness, voyeurism, science, etc.—but through uni-

fication, sympathy and love. **"The Birth-Mark"** is a hymn to earthly marriage, just as the story that immediately preceded it, **"The Hall of Fantasy,"** is a hymn to the earth itself.

> "Oh, you are ungrateful to our Mother Earth!" rejoined I. "Come what may, I never will forget her! Neither will it satisfy me to have her exist merely in idea. I want her great, round, solid self to endure interminably, and still to be peopled with the kindly race of man, whom I uphold to be much better than he thinks himself. . . ."
>
> (**"The Hall of Fantasy"** 184-85)

Aylmer's sin is in wanting "the ideal" (271) instead of what Hawthorne in **"The Artist of the Beautiful"** would call "the enjoyment of the Reality." In 1843, Hawthorne's love of reality was inseparable from his love for Sophia. He told her as much, in his letters: "Thou art my reality; and nothing is real for me, unless thou give it that golden quality by thy touch" (*Love Letters* 231). She was, to use the alchemist's terms, his Active Agent, her love and understanding his Philosopher's Stone. Had these been his active agents, the author of *The Scarlet Letter* preface suggests, he might have come to better love this world, the Custom House of Earth:

> It was a folly, with the materiality of this daily life pressing so intrusively upon me, to attempt to fling myself back into another age; or to insist on creating the semblance of a world out of airy matter. . . . The wiser effort would have been, to diffuse thought and imagination through the opaque substance of to-day, and thus to make it a bright transparency; to spiritualize the burden that began to weigh so heavily; to seek, resolutely, the true and indestructible value that lay hidden in the petty and wearisome incidents, and ordinary characters, with which I was now conversant. The fault was mine. The page of life that was spread out before me seemed dull and commonplace, only because I had not fathomed its deeper import. A better book than I shall ever write was there; leaf after leaf presenting itself to me, just as it was written out by the reality of the flitting hour, and vanishing as fast as written, only because my brain wanted the insight and my hand the cunning to transcribe it. At some future day, it may be, I shall remember a few scattered fragments and broken paragraphs, and write them down, and find the letters turned to gold upon the page.
>
> (*Scarlet Letter* 37)

Here is the true alchemy of connection, a marriage between spirit and matter, the love of "the best that earth could offer." It has been said that the Romantics found proof of God in nature, while the Victorians found proof of God in human doubt. Hawthorne, poised as he was between the two, suggests in **"The Birth-Mark"** that human nature is its own proof of divinity and human love its highest expression. It was a daring supposition, one he himself could bear neither to sustain nor to follow out to its logical conclusions. But in 1843, he set out clearly enough the questions that were to haunt him all the rest of his life.

Works Cited

"Animism." *Oxford English Dictionary.* 1971 ed.

Burns, Shannon. "Alchemy and 'The Birth-Mark.'" *American Transcendental Quarterly* 48 (1979): 147-58.

Charvat, William, et al., eds. *The Centenary Edition of the Works of Nathaniel Hawthorne.* 20 vols. Columbus: Ohio State UP, 1962-85.

Hawthorne, Nathaniel. "The Birth-mark." *Mosses* 36-56.

————. "Ethan Brand." *Snow-Image* 83-102.

————. "The Hall of Fantasy." *Mosses* 172-85.

————. *The Love Letters of Nathaniel Hawthorne: 1839-1863.* Washington. NCR Microcard Editions, 1972.

————. *The Marble Faun.* Columbus: Ohio State UP, 1968. Vol. 4 of Charvat et al.

————. *Mosses from an Old Manse.* Columbus: Ohio State UP, 1974. Vol. 10 of Charvat et al.

————. *The Scarlet Letter.* Columbus: Ohio State UP, 1962. Vol. 1 of Charvat et al.

————. *The Snow-Image and Uncollected Tales.* Columbus: Ohio State UP, 1974. Vol. 11 of Charvat et al.

Jones, E. Michael. *The Angel and the Machine.* Peru, IL: Sherwood Sugden, 1991.

Mellow, James. *Nathaniel Hawthorne in his Times.* Boston: Houghton, 1980.

Miller, Perry. *The Transcendentalists.* An Anthology. Cambridge: Harvard UP, 1950.

Read, John. *The Alchemist in Life, Literature and Art.* Edinburgh: Thomas Nelson, 1947.

Van Leer, David M. "Aylmer's Library: Transcendental Alchemy in Hawthorne's 'The Birth-Mark.'" *ESQ* 22 (1976): 211-20.

Lynn Shakinovsky (essay date December 1995)

SOURCE: Shakinovsky, Lynn. "The Return of the Repressed: Illiteracy and the Death of the Narrative in Hawthorne's 'The Birthmark.'" *American Transcendental Quarterly* 9, no. 4 (December 1995): 269-81.

[*In the following essay, Shakinovsky centers on the relationship between the symbol of the birthmark itself and the narrative structure of "The Birthmark."*]

Nathaniel Hawthorne's **"The Birthmark"** is the story of a marked body and a murder. Aylmer, a brilliant scientist, becomes obsessed with a mark on his wife's cheek, determines to eradicate it, and in doing so kills her. From the outset, the story, which revolves around the removal of a "bloody mark" in the shape of a hand from the woman's body, foregrounds not only the sexuality but also the textuality of the mark[1] and in so doing winds the ambiguities of reading and writing into the action of the story itself. Just as the mark's presence is the focal point which impels the narrative forward in the form of Aylmer's deathly desire, so the removal of the mark, signifying the satiation of that desire, results in the effacement of the narrative; Aylmer's act of destruction works not only on the body inside the story but becomes a destruction of the story itself, and the murder that is enacted inside the story is mirrored in the structure of the narrative.

In *Bodywork,* Peter Brooks explores the literary notion of the token, the identifying mark on the body: "The sign imprints the body," he says, "making it part of the signifying process. Signing or marking the body signifies its passage into writing, its becoming a literary body, and generally also a narrative body" (3). He continues:

> [I]n modern narrative literature, a protagonist often desires a body . . . and that body comes to represent for the protagonist an apparent ultimate good, since it appears to hold within itself—as itself—the key to satisfaction, power, and meaning. On the plane of reading, desire for knowledge of that body and its secrets becomes the desire to master the text's symbolic system, its key to knowledge, pleasure, and the very creation of significance. . . . Narrative seeks to make such a body semiotic, to mark or imprint it as a linguistic and narrative sign.
>
> (8)

The mark on Georgiana's body does act as her signature in precisely the way that Brooks describes—serving to enter her body into writing. From the outset, however, Brooks' comments reflect upon Hawthorne's tale in a peculiar way. In his work, Brooks focuses strongly on the narrative attempt to inscribe the body—to create, identify, or discover its particular mark or token as an aspect of a larger epistemophilic urge. In **"The Birthmark"** the notion of the marked body works in precisely the opposite way. The identifying mark is present at the beginning of the story, and the tale is about the protagonist's attempts to eradicate the mark; for him, it is the *removal* of the mark which holds the "key to satisfaction, power, and meaning." This inversion is crucial. The marking of the body is the process of entering it into writing, narrative, and desire; the removal of the mark implies the destruction of desire and narrative and hence the dissolution of the "text's symbolic system" (*BW* [*Bodywork*] 8). The unmarking of Georgiana's body becomes an undoing of the act of signification.

The mark, as the subject around which the entire narrative revolves, is quite obviously of central thematic and structural concern in the story, but, from the outset, what is regarded as most interesting about it is its signifying quality. Its capacity for different readings by different readers is presented to us as one of its first and major characteristics:

> It must not be concealed, however, that the impression wrought by this fairy sign manual varied exceedingly, according to the difference of the temperament in the beholders. Some fastidious persons—but they were exclusively of her own sex—affirmed that the bloody hand, as they chose to call it, quite destroyed the effect of Georgiana's beauty and rendered her countenance even hideous. But it would be as reasonable to say that one of those small blue stains which sometimes occur in the purest statuary marble would convert the Eve of Powers to a monster. Masculine observers, if the birthmark did not heighten their admiration, contented themselves with wishing it away, that the world might possess one living specimen of ideal loveliness without the semblance of a flaw. After his marriage—for he thought little or nothing of the matter before—Aylmer discovered that this was the case with himself.
>
> (38)

The narrator's focus on conflicting ways of reading the mark reveals various social and cultural responses to the mark. In comparing the mark to a "manual" which emphasizes its readability and openness to interpretation, his very language serves, from the outset, to foreground the notion of its textuality. He reveals both Aylmer's attitude to the mark—the one "flaw" in "ideal loveliness" and Georgiana's, which, up until this opening point in the story, has been to regard it as a "charm" (37). Most significantly, and seemingly inadvertently, the narrator, under the guise of offering us ordered, reasonable, normative comments, reveals his own attitudes to the mark. It is "reason," he argues, that should correct the vision of "some fastidious persons," but from the outset it is clear that the narrator is not as objective or reasonable as he considers himself to be. His response manifests ambiguities and biases of which he is completely unaware. It is noteworthy that he disagrees with the unreasonable assumptions of those of Georgiana's "own sex," but avoids deconstructing the assumptions of "masculine observers" in general, and of Aylmer in particular. His very imagery—"Eve of Powers," "statutory marble," "monster"—indicates that his vision is more contaminated than he knows. From the outset the ambiguities of reading are built into the narrative itself, functioning in Steven Youra's words, to "thematise the act of reading" (43).

Much critical attention has been focused on the mark; clearly the way in which the mark is "read" is funda-

mental to any interpretation of the story.[2] Of course, one of the most crucial readers of the mark is Aylmer himself; the story's plot revolves around the way in which he chooses to interpret the mark. But Aylmer cannot see his own response as an interpretation; it is precisely the mark's capacity to signify, its availability for symbolization, that Aylmer is incapable of apprehending. Trapped in an obsessional, fixed world view, he reduces the mark of many significations to a single signification or to no signification; his relationship to the mark is a commitment to its *literal* removal. Thus, although Aylmer may be said to *see* the mark, he really cannot read it at all.

But the ambiguities surrounding the mark's capacity for figuration extend beyond the limitations created by Aylmer's (murderous) illiteracy into not only the other main characters in the tale but also into the entire process of narration. Alymer's distortions are perfectly mirrored by Georgiana's—the two of them collude in her destruction—and the "deeply impressive moral" which the narrator promises at the beginning of the story and delivers at its conclusion is filled with enough bizarre ambiguities and incongruities to throw his capacity to read severely into question. In general, the narrative is so filled with its own contradictions regarding the mark and its significance that the process of narration tends to efface itself, mirroring the vanishing of the mark inside the story. If, as Peter Brooks argues, narrative "is life-giving in that it arouses and sustains desire" (*RP* [*Reading for the Plot*] 61), Alymer's murderousness, the consequence of a hideous illiteracy, results not only in the satiation of his desire and the death of his wife, but also in the death of the narrative itself.

All of this begs the question of why the mark should be so particularly illegible to Aylmer, to the narrator, and even to Georgiana herself. The answer lies not so much in the mark itself but in the body whose signature it is. If the mark signifies the passage of the body into writing, it is utterly significant that the body is a female one.[3] It is the female signed body that creates such havoc; its signification and very capacity to signify are so disruptive that not only are the two protagonists destroyed but so is the entire process of narration. The femaleness of the mark is one of its most emphasized characteristics:

> But if any shifting motion caused her to turn pale there was the mark again, a crimson stain upon the snow, in which Aylmer sometimes deemed an almost fearful distinctness. Its shape bore not a little similarity to the human hand, though of the smallest pygmy size.
>
> (37-38)

That the mark is in the shape of a hand is, in itself, very interesting. Brooks, commenting on the formulaic *croix de ma mere* of melodrama, says that the body is marked with a special sign which looks "suspiciously like a linguistic signifier" (*BW* 3). In this story, the shape of the mark invites a particular association with the world of writing, foregrounding its signifying quality. This, in conjunction with the notion that it is a "bloody hand," a "crimson stain" (429), announces it as a kind of women's writing. The particular conjunction of femininity and assertiveness that is embodied in the mark appears to be precisely what Aylmer cannot tolerate. It is the mark's utter determination to exist that offends him; the story describes repeatedly how the mark refuses to subject itself to Aylmer's vision. The autonomy of the mark emerges most clearly in the description of its relationship to its background:

> [I]n the centre of Georgiana's left cheek there was a singular mark, deeply interwoven, as it were, with the texture and substance of her face. In the usual state of her complexion—a healthy but delicate bloom—the mark wore the tint of deeper crimson, which imperfectly defined its shape amid the surrounding rosiness. When she blushed it gradually became more indistinct, and finally vanished amid the triumphant rush of blood that bathed the whole cheek with its brilliant glow. But if any shifting motion caused her to turn pale there was the mark again, a crimson stain upon the snow.
>
> (37-38)

Barbara Johnson, commenting upon the mark's relation to its background, sees it as the "mark of intersubjectivity; it is interpreted differently by different beholders, and it interprets *them* in response. . . . what Aylmer wishes to do in erasing the mark is to erase the difference—to erase sexual difference—by reducing woman to 'all,' to ground, to blankness" (259). Since Alymer cannot read (a female body entered into writing), he cannot see the mark is "one of Georgiana's givens, in fact equivalent to her" (Fetterley 25). It is a metaphor for her identity, her sexuality, her being. As he cannot read the mark in its metaphoric (metonymic) capacity as associated with (and representative of) the whole, Aylmer does not realize that in removing the mark, he removes all there is of her. The story reminds us repeatedly, and through each of its characters, of the unbreachable connection between Georgiana and her mark. The narrator tells us that the mark is "deeply interwoven . . . with the texture and substance of her face" (37). Aminadab comments that "if she were [his] wife, [he'd] never part with that birthmark" (43), and Georgiana, herslef, tells us that "the stain goes as deep as life itself" (41). The motif even surfaces in Aylmer's dream:

> . . . the deeper went the knife, the deeper sank the hand, until at length its tiny grasp appeared to have caught hold of Georgiana's heart.
>
> (40)

All of the characters in the story—Aylmer, Georgiana, Aminadab, and the narrator—know (and evade the fact) that the mark cannot be removed because it cannot be separated from Georgiana, or she from it. The mark is Aylmer's object, and since, as the sign of her subjectivity, it represents Georgiana, it becomes she who is his object. The corollary is also true; since Georgiana (together with her mark) is already an object, the object of his scientific and sexual attention and scrutiny, he is incapable of reading her subjectivity. Aylmer's illiteracy results in the death, not only of Georgiana's body, but the textual body that constitutes the narrative.

The notion of scrutiny, the act of looking, is crucial in this tale; Aylmer cannot take his eyes from Georgiana's mark. The gaze becomes the privilege of the male subject with the woman constituted as the object "of representation, of discourse, of desire" (Irigaray 133), and Aylmer's stare becomes an important aspect of the social, scientific, and sexual power he has over her. Indeed, Georgiana's physical beauty is stressed as a vital motivation for Aylmer's attraction towards her. In the second sentence of the story, we are told that Aylmer "persuaded a beautiful woman to become his wife" (36). The use of the indefinite article emphasizes her beauty as the crucial element in his choice. The motif of looking is reiterated again and again throughout the tale:

> One day, very soon after their marriage, Aylmer sat gazing at his wife with a trouble in his countenance.
>
> (37)

> . . . it became the central point of all. With the morning twilight Aylmer opened his eyes upon his wife's face . . . when they sat together at the evening hearth his eyes wandered stealthily to her cheek and beheld. . . .
>
> (39)

> While thus employed, he failed not to gaze often at the fatal hand, and not without a shudder.
>
> (54)

Aylmer's gaze exerts a powerful influence over Georgiana. She, as the focus of the gaze, colludes entirely with her own destruction; she absorbs his shameful view of her and echoes his shudder with her own:

> Georgiana soon learned to shudder at his gaze. It needed but a glance with the peculiar expression on his face.
>
> (39)

> . . . she placed a hand over her cheek to hide the terrible mark from her husband's eyes.
>
> (44)

What would happen, Luce Irigaray asks, "if the 'object' started to speak? Which also means beginning to 'see,' etc. What disaggregation of the subject would that entail?" (135). But Georgiana never speaks, never fractures Aylmer's vision of the world; indeed, eventually she matches Aylmer's hatred of the mark with her own. The progression of her deterioration is carefully plotted. Her response to his comments at the beginning of the story demonstrates an insight and power that vanishes as the tale develops. Thus at the beginning of the story, she is able to confront Aylmer with "momentary anger": "'Then why did you take me from my mother's side? You cannot love what shocks you!'" (430), she says. But by the end of the narrative, this insight has transformed into: "'life, while this hateful mark makes me the object of your horror and disgust—life is a burden which I would fling down with joy'" (430).

The significant symptom of her deterioration is that she also loses the capacity to read the mark. The sense of play present in her initial response to the mark where she regards it as a "charm" with all the overtones of attractiveness, luckiness, and delight gives way to a fixed sense of herself (as obsessional as Aylmer's) as an object of horror and disgust. After her first angry response at the beginning of the story, Georgiana never questions Aylmer's judgment again. If anything, once she begins to perceive the mark upon her cheek in his terms, it works to provoke her desire to make a total gift to him of her body and her self, to enslave herself absolutely to him. She increasingly wishes to become his object. Her newly learned, but extremely successful, illiteracy is beautifully demonstrated in the scene in which she reads the record of Aylmer's work. Although she notes that it is a record of failure, we are told that as she reads, she "reverenced Aylmer and loved him more profoundly than ever, but with a less entire dependence on his judgment than heretofore" (434). The confusion present in her response—the increase in reverence along with the loss of trust—is made manifest at the end of the story when, in spite of possessing a "less entire dependence" on Aylmer's judgement than previously, she drinks the draught that kills her. Since this text—the record of Aylmer's failures—is precisely the text in which her own story (his most devastating failure) will be written, it is her own story (her own mark) that becomes illegible and incomprehensible to her. This is inevitable since in giving up her own subjectivity, she gives up her own story. Significantly, the only time that she does see is when she sees herself seeing herself, that is, looking at herself in the mirror, seeing herself as the object of the gaze:

> Still, whenever she dared look into the mirror, there she beheld herself pale as a white rose and with the crimson birthmark stamped upon her cheek. Not even Aylmer now hated it as much as she.
>
> (48)

Beth Newman comments that perhaps the sight that makes the Medusa "threatening to the male spectator may be understood as the sight of someone else's look—the knowledge that the other sees and resists being reduced to an appropriate object":

> [T]he Medusa defies the male gaze as Western culture has constructed it . . . such defiance is surely unsettling, disturbing the pleasure the male subject takes in gazing and the hierarchical relations by which he asserts his dominance.
>
> (1031)

Luce Irigaray makes a similar observation:

> Once imagine that woman imagines and the object loses its fixed obsessional character. As a benchmark that is ultimately more crucial than the subject, for he can sustain himself only by bouncing off against some objectness, some objective. If there is no more 'earth' to press down/repress, to work to represent . . . then what pedestal remains for the ex-sistence of the 'subject'?
>
> (133)

Georgiana joins in creating herself as the object for Aylmer to "work." Not wishing to interrupt the fixedness of his gaze, she never reconstitutes herself as subject. It is therefore as much a product of Georgiana's vision as Alymer's that the removal of the mark results in her death. For Georgiana as well as for Aylmer, the mark is all there is.

But Aylmer's gazing at Georgiana is not just about the sexual and emotional power that it gives him over her. Since this story is centrally about the sight of the mark and the way that the protagonist interprets it, it also investigates the relationship between sight and narration, between seeing and telling. The story ties the "gaze inextricably to the signifier, the process of narration producing the signified, the theme and 'content'" (Newman 1033).

The narrator is also centrally concerned with the notion of the gaze; his tale is crucially involved with his own act of looking and begins with his own account of staring at the mark. Having described the different ways in which the mark might be viewed according to the temperament of the observer, he goes on to provide us with his own point of view, significantly explained in the language of looking:

> But it would be as reasonable to say that one of those small blue stains which sometimes occur in the purest statuary marble would convert the Eve of powers to a monster.
>
> (38)

This observation is crucial as it links the narrator firmly with Aylmer. He stares at Georgiana in a way that is extremely reminiscent of Aylmer, and his view of the mark is essentially not very different from either Aylmer's or Georgiana's.

For Aylmer, the mark supposedly represents Georgiana's connection to earthliness, her lack of heavenly perfection, and is therefore unacceptable. The narrator shifts this view only slightly. Like Aylmer, he regards the mark as a blemish; he simply sees it as a blemish which, precisely because it indicates Georgiana's earthliness, implies her true perfection. In all essentials, he is just like Aylmer and Georgiana; he cannot grasp the mark's symbolizing quality, its capacity for multiple significations or play. In this sense the narrative is as obsessive as the tale it recounts. Georgiana and Aylmer see their actions as the actions of idealism; the narrator shifts only in that he tells a story of misguided idealism. His own peculiar repressions are particularly evident in the inadequate moral that he draws at the end of the story: "Yet had Aylmer reached a profounder wisdom, he need not thus have flung away the happiness which would have woven his mortal life of the selfsame texture with the celestial. . . . he failed to look beyond the shadowy scope of Time, and living once for all in Eternity, to find the perfect Future in the present" (56). Like Georgiana and Aylmer he reads the story as a story of failure rather than, in Judith Fetterley's words, "the success story it really is—the demonstration of how to murder your wife and get away with it" (22). In this sense, the narrative is as repressed as the two protagonists whose tale forms its basic content. This repression is manifested through the similarities that emerge between Aylmer and the narrator, similarities that are expressed in terms of the motif of gazing and that link the destructiveness of Aylmer's look firmly to the narrative act. The point of view of the narrator (a concept expressed significantly in terms of the language of looking) is more contaminated than he knows.

A central aspect of the repression that is enacted in this story is the deceit that permeates the tale. It appears that in all cases what is being concealed is the violence of desire—desire to love, to murder, or a mixture of the two. This emerges clearly in Aylmer's dream, a dream which thinly disguises his wish to murder Georgiana. The narrator informs us that "[t]ruth often finds its way to the mind close-muffled in robes of sleep, and then speaks with uncompromising directness of matters in regard to which we practise an unconscious self-deception, during our waking moments" (40). Aylmer's capacity to conceal his true desires from himself manifests itself in his recollection of his dream. After his dream has shaped itself "perfectly in his memory," Aylmer sits in his wife's presence with a "guilty feeling." His private acknowledgement, on the one hand, of the "lengths which he might find it in his heart to go, for the sake of giving himself peace" bears no relation to his reassurance to his wife of the "perfect practicability" of his plan.

Since mutual deception practiced towards self and other is a hall-mark of this relationship, concealment is the most crucial feature of the second home that Aylmer creates for Georgiana in his laboratory:

The walls were hung with gorgeous curtains, which imparted the combination of grandeur and grace, that no other species of adornment can achieve; and as they fell from the ceiling to the floor, their rich and ponderous folds, concealing all angles and straight lines, appeared to shut in the scene from infinite space.

(44)

In this artificial and deceptive space he creates a magic show for her which is designed to distract her (and no doubt himself) from his murderous intentions. This second home that Aylmer creates for Georgiana replaces a first home which is hardly mentioned in the story. The lack of description of their first home functions, in itself, as a kind of repression or evasion, a repression which is repeated in the narrative by the fact that the only two references to their original home occur in terms of the light that it casts on the birthmark. The narrator states: ". . . when they sat together at the evening hearth his eyes wandered stealthily to her cheek, and beheld, flickering with the blaze of the wood-fire, the spectral hand that wrote mortality where he fain would have worshipped" (39). His second reference to their home also occurs in terms of the light that it casts on the mark, "[l]ate one night, when the lights were growing dim, so as hardly to betray the stain on the poor wife's cheek" (39). The lack of information about the first home is matched by the abundantly available detail about the second home. The narrative emphasis implies that this second place—the place of the artificial, the hidden, and the unreal—which is created by Aylmer as a place in which he can murder Georgiana is their true home. It is in this abode that he "[leads] her over the threshold" (43) in an action reminiscent of the traditional action of the groom when he takes his bride into their marital home. The peculiar absence of information about their first home (where the play of light illuminates the birthmark) and the narrative concentration on the second (the place of extreme concealment) highlight the sense that something very gross needs to be hidden; information is only available in the place of concealment. The violence which emerges in their second home has been a present but repressed aspect of their relationship in their first.

The notion of repressed violence and the perversion of desire are evident in the bizarre language of sexual ecstasy that pervades all their conversations about the mark. The first words of love and tenderness that we hear Aylmer utter towards Georgiana are when she asks him to remove the mark: "'Noblest—dearest—tenderest wife!' cried Aylmer rapturously" (41). This ecstasy pervades all their discussions about the removal of the mark: "Do not shrink from me! Believe me Georgiana, I even rejoice in this single imperfection, since it will be such rapture to remove it" (44). The sense for both of them of satisfaction obtained, of repleted desire, is clear in the drinking of the fatal potion: "'It allays a feverish thirst that had parched me for many days,'" Georgiana says (54), while for Aylmer the operation is accompanied by "almost irrepressible ecstasy" (55). The eroticism of Georgiana's death brings together the unacknowledged arousal, revulsion, and murderousness present in both of them.

The repressions that pervade this story are a hallmark not only of Georgiana and Aylmer's relationship, but also of the narrative itself. The bizarrely evasive moral offered by the narrator at the end of the tale replaces and represses the true end of the story. We never learn of Aylmer's response to Georgiana's final comment to him that she is dying—almost the only time since the very beginning of the story that she feels free to correct his perception. His silence, which mirrors here a textual silence or gap, is replaced by the narrator's "interpretation" of events, an interpretation which in fact appears thoroughly contradicted by the events of the story itself. In short, the ending of the story functions as evasion or concealment, a concealment that has pervaded the story and that is indicative of the monstrousness and fearfulness of the repressed desires with which this story concerns itself.[4]

The narrative concealments imitate Aylmer and Georgiana's, thereby announcing the coincidence of the mark with text and writing itself. That the mark signifies the body's passage into writing is indicated not only by its very nature as a mark, or its particular shape as a hand, but also by the way in which it is woven deep into the fabric of the text. Its presence "appears everywhere in the tale" (Smith 98):

> . . . until the Philosopher should lay his hand on the secret of creative force.
>
> (36)

> The Crimson hand expressed the ineludible gripe, in which mortality clutches the highest and purest of earthly mould.
>
> (39)

> . . . it had taken a pretty firm hold of my fancy.
>
> (40)

> By its aid, I could apportion the lifetime of any mortal at whom you might point your finger.
>
> (47)

> In his grasp, the veriest clod of earth assumed a soul.
>
> (49)

Finally, the removal of the mark is mirrored in the structure of the narrative itself in the scene where Georgiana misreads the book—a "large folio from her husband's own hand . . . yet as melancholy a record as ever mortal hand had penned" (48-49)—in which her own story will be inscribed. The hand here is identified overtly with the pen emphasizing its passage and the passage of

the body that it marks into the written text. The inclusion of the body into the texture of the narrative is most powerfully conveyed in the confusion exhibited by the narrator himself in his closing moral to the story. The narrator informs us that "The Fatal hand had grappled with the mystery of life, and was the bond by which an angelic spirit kept itself in union with a mortal frame" (55). He confuses here the "Fatal hand" of Aylmer with the mark ("the bond") itself and in so doing colludes with Aylmer and Georgiana's own projection of fatality onto the mark.[5]

Thus the female body marked and imprinted by desire is entered into the structure of the narrative. By destroying the impulse of desire, Aylmer's act of destruction perpetrated against the signed body also destroys the act of narrating. Aylmer's act is mirrored in the signifying process (which comprises the narrative act) in various ways. It occurs in the inability of all of the principal characters to read the mark, so that the complexities surrounding the act of reading, with which the tale concerns itself, become included in the narrative itself. It occurs in the way Aylmer's destructive gazing at Georgiana is imitated by the narrator who also takes on a poit of view very similar to Aylmer's own and, finally, in the way in which the narrator represses aspects of his own tale, an act of repression which mirrors the repression of violence and desire that occurs inside the story. Brooks says: "[t]hat desiring subject may be in the narrative and is always also the creator of the narrative, whose desire for the body is part of a semiotic project to make the body signify, to make it part of the narrative dynamic" (*BW* 25). Here, the desiring subject is the destroyer of the woman, desire, and the text itself. The effacement of the mark on Georgiana's body figures the inevitable termination of the narrative text which is the story of his desire.

Notes

1. A number of critics have commented on the connection between the mark and Georgiana's sexuality. See for example: Smith 97, 99; Quinn and Baldessarini 92; Millington 27; Fetterley 25; Zanger 368; Eckstein 515. Barbara Johnson suggests that the mark can be seen as a figure for women's writing: "Georgiana's 'bloody hand,' a kind of *ecriture feminine* that is both corporal and cheeky, throbs to its own rhythms in response to the world until she is taught to feel so ashamed of it that she is ready to die rather than to live with her horrible deformity" (263).

2. It is possible to divide the critical response into two camps. Critics who read the mark with the assumption that it is a "blemish" tend to see Aylmer, in one form or another, as an idealist, albeit failed, whose "fault" then lies in having longed for perfection on earth. Concomitantly, Georgiana's col-

lusion with him is a sign of her spiritual perfection. See, for example, Brooks and Warren: "What the story emphasises is not Aylmer's self conceit but rather his possession of the questing spirit which will not resign itself to the limitations and imperfections of nature" (104); Turner: "Two concluding sentences detract nothing from the loftiness of Aylmer's purpose or from his wife's understanding and heroism. . . . In 'The Birthmark' an obsession with a noble purpose produces tragic results" (163-4); Fogle: Aylmer's purposes are controlled by morality (129).

Critics who read the mark as a signifier for Georgiana's femininity and sexuality see Aylmer as sexually perverse, sadistic, and murderous. See Smith who discusses Aylmer's perversion (97-98), Crews who discusses his sadism (20). For other readings along these lines, see also Quinn and Baldessarini 92; Lesser 88; Zanger 368; Crews 126; Millington 27; Fetterley 25.2.

3. The genderised nature of Alymer's obsession is foregrounded by the identification of the mark with Georgiana's sexuality. Various critics comment on the fact that it is a female body that Aylmer wishes to destroy. Judith Fetterley, for example, emphasizes that "it is woman and specifically woman as wife, who elicits the obsession with imperfection and the compulsion to achieve perfection" (23). See also Crews 126; Johnson 259; Smith 97.

4. Fetterley attributes this desire for concealment to Hawthorne, stating that he seems as "eager to be misread and to conceal as he is to be read and to reveal" (31). It seems to me more useful to focus on the narrative ambiguities, noticeable throughout, but most particularly at the end of the tale. This is highlighted by Smith's comment about the ending: "[t]he story pretends to the conclusion: she is perfect, but, alas, she is dead! It secretly concludes: She is dead but [therefore] she is perfect!" (100).

5. For an extended discussion of the doubling of hands, see Youra 43-51.

Works Cited

Brooks, Cleanth and Austin Warren. *Understanding Fiction.* New York: F. S. Crofts & Company, 1944.

Brooks, Peter, *Bodywork: Objects of Desire in Modern Narrative.* Cambridge, Massachusetts: Harvard University Press, 1993.

———. *Reading for the Plot: Design and Intention in Narrative.* New York: Vintage, 1985.

Crews, Frederick. *The Sins of the Fathers: Hawthorne's Psychological Themes.* New York: Oxford University Press, 1966.

Eckstein, Barbara. "Hawthorne's 'The Birthmark': Science and Romance as Belief." *Studies in Short Fiction.* 26: 1989, 511-19.

Fetterley, Judith. *The Resisting Reader: A Feminist Approach to American Fiction.* Bloomington: Indiana, 1978.

Fogle, Richard Harter. *Hawthorne's Fiction: The Light and the Dark.* Norman: University of Oklahoma Press, 1964.

Hawthorne, Nathaniel. "The Birthmark." *The Centenary Edition of the Works of Nathaniel Hawthorne.* Ed. William Charvat. Columbus, Ohio: University State Press, 1974. Vol. X: 36-56.

Irigaray, Luce. *Speculum of the Other Woman.* Trans. by Gillian C. Gill. Ithaca, New York: Cornell University Press, 1974.

Johnson, Barbara. "Is Female to Male as Ground is to Figure?" *Feminism and Psychoanalysis.* Ed. Richard Feldstein and Judith Roof. Ithaca & London: Cornell University Press, 1989.

Lesser, Simon O. *Fiction and the Unconscious.* Chicago & London: University of Chicago Press, 1957.

Millington, Richard H. *Practising Romance: Narrative Form and Cultural Engagement in Hawthorne's Fiction.* Princeton: Princeton University Press, 1992.

Newman, Beth. "'The Situation of the Looker On': Gender, Narration, and Gaze in *Wuthering Heights.*" *PMLA.* October, 1990, 105:5, 1029-1041.

Quinn, James and Ross Baldessarini. "'The Birthmark': A Deathmark." *University of Hartford Studies in Literature: A Journal of Interdisciplinary-Criticism.* 1981, 13: 2, 91-98.

Smith, Allan Gardner Lloyd. *Eve Tempted: Writing and Sexuality in Hawthorne's Fiction.* Totowa, New Jersey: Barnes & Noble, 1983.

Turner, Arlin. *Nathaniel Hawthorne: A Biography.* New York: Oxford University Press, 1980.

Youra, Steven. "'The Fatal hand': A Sign of Confusion in Hawthorne's 'The Birth-Mark.'" *American Transcendental Quarterly.* June 1986, 60, 43-51.

Zanger, Jules. "Speaking of the Unspeakable: Hawthorne's 'The Birthmark.'" *Modern Philology.* May 1983, 80:4, 364-71.

Kary Meyers Skredsvig (essay date July-December 2000)

SOURCE: Skredsvig, Kary Meyers. "Eve's Daughter, Mary's Child: Women's Representation in Hawthorne's

'The Birthmark.'" *Revista de Filología y Lingüística de la Universidad de Costa Rica* 26, no. 2 (July-December 2000): 95-105.

[*In the following essay, Skredsvig asserts that issues of "gendered identities" serve as a means of developing characters, plot, and themes in "The Birthmark."*]

Anaïs Nin once made the following characteristically astute statement about human nature: "We don't see things as they are, we see them as we are." Although this affirmation might initially appear to render testimony to humans' capacity for self-deception, or perhaps a penchant for denial, closer examination suggests an even more significant aspect of human nature, which is no less real for being intangible: the fact that we are inevitably and inextricably bound to our perceptions, which in turn evolve from and depend upon our sense of self. In other words, "reality" is a construction, not a given; subjective, not objective; dynamic, not fixed. Whatever its conception, it is very closely aligned with human subjectivity at both personal and collective levels. In Nathaniel Hawthorne's short story **"The Birthmark,"** which was originally published in 1843, the ways in which human perceptions of reality are both pre-ordained by the cultural context and tempered by the inidividual appears to be peripheral to the larger, obvious conflict between humanism and science; however, they are really at the very heart of it.

The issues surrounding the concept of human subjectivity are as complex and diverse as those who contemplate them, but for the purposes of this discussion, human subjectivity will be understood as essentially refering to our sense of identity. This identity is in itself fundamentally a perception; our sense of self is a combination of the personal—our private apprehension of who and how we are, the social—our understanding and assimilation of others' views, and the cultural—the inculcation of a variety of collective components which constitute our identity as a member of a larger group. These categories obviously include a series of constitutive elements which interact continuously and significantly, such as age, ethnicity, gender, language, education, and experience, which exponentially enhance individual possibilities. The focus of this discussion is the gender factor and its crucial significance in identity issues: how is one's sense of self constituted; to what extent is biology (nature) a factor in determining one's mentality, temperament, and behavior; to what extent is cultural conditioning a determinant in the aforementioned areas; what are the repercussions of gendered identities. In **"The Birthmark,"** these concerns are not only the basis for character development of all three characters, but also the prime component of plot and the harbingers of theme; at issue are gendered politics and the juxtaposition of gendered identities.

Traditionally, patriarchal discussions of the human condition have followed the pattern of assuming that male concerns, perceptions, and assumptions are somehow universal, as clearly seen, for example, in the choice of "Man" as a synonym for humankind. As suggested above, traditional criticism of Hawthorne's story has centered on a perceived polarization of humanism and science, which responds to traditional patriarchal concerns with "man's place" in the universal scheme of things. Quite literally, this place has been occupied by males only, with women being significant only to the extent that they affect the men around them. Recognition of this fact and commitment to changing this patriarchal reality has been a cornerstone of the feminist movement since its onset—considered by some to be more of an onslaught—in the 1960s. Even before then, of course, many women (and a few men) were aware of and unhappy about the "sexual politics," to borrow Kate Millett's phrase, which ordained that men were by nature superior and a woman's place was necessarily subordinate to them. In 1970 Millett asserted "What goes largely unexamined, often even unacknowledged . . . in our social order, is the birthright priority whereby males rule females . . . [despite the fact that] sexual dominion [is] the most pervasive ideology of our culture and provides its most fundamental concept of power" (25). Sherry Ortner enlarges the discussion by identifying three basic dimensions of gender hegemonies: prestige and social status, male domination vs. female subordination, and female power (140), which although differentiated are closely intertwined. Ortner suggests that these are related to issues of cultural and personal space, nature/culture debates, agency/subjectivity, and, of course, sociopolitical structures and functions.

Writing decades earlier, Simone de Beauvoir shares many of their concerns and questions, as well as conclusions. In *The Second Sex,* Beauvoir argues that men have appropriated the "center," with women's collusion: "She is defined and differentiated with reference to man and not he with reference to her . . . He is the Subject, he is the Absolute—she is the Other" (xxii). Of great importance here is not only the hegemony, but also the establishment of identities. Beauvoir suggests that differentiation with an "other" is one means of self-definition, and she provides a wealth of illustrations and examples to explain women's significance as "Other" to men. She begins by differentiating two types of alterity, one in which a reciprocity exists which confers a degree of equality as subjects, and another in which there is no direct, autonomous relationship and therefore no true duality. In the case of male/female relationships, Beauvoir asserts that women have always been regarded as "the absolute Other," as the inessential, and therefore have been subordinated as inferior, a situation which is "validated" historically in patriarchal arguments in which "the dominant class bases its argument on a state of affairs that it has itself created" (xxx) and then tauto-logically presents as evidence of "absolute truth." Beau-voir provides many different patriarchal definitions of female "otherness," from "flesh" to "nature" to "media-trix" to "mystery," concluding that each patriarchal so-ciety and each male individual establishes its/his own self-image first, then assigns a correlative meaning to the female "other." Most significantly, in every case women's identity and significance are decided by an-other, never self-defined.

Female "otherness" thus takes on a variety of character-istics and roles to serve patriarchal needs and purposes, and they are generally perceived in terms of masculine/feminine polarities which are omnipresent in patriarchal patterns and norms to the present. Following the lead of Aristotle, who defined the male role in reproduction as that of providing the form or essence, while women merely supply the material, patriarchal dichotomies have tended to associate men with everything intellec-tual and abstract—ideas, ideals, truth, law—while women have been ascribed the emotional and physi-cal—feelings, nurturing, caretaking, the practical. As Mary Ellmann has examined so effectively in *Thinking About Women,* male/female differences have come to be polarized as not only the abstract vs. materiality, but also art vs. artifice. Men are perceived as those capable of all that is lofty, imaginative, creative, and original, while women are relegated to "lower" (this valuation is in itself a construct, of course) realms of reproduction, imitation, supplementation, and maintenance.

A very significant outgrowth of this type of Manichean polarization is the dichotomous association of men with culture and women with nature. As Sherry Ortner de-scribes it, culture is "broadly equated[d] with the notion of human consciousness, or with the products of human consciousness (i.e., systems of thought and technology) by means of which humanity attempts to assert control over nature" while nature is used as a label for "that which is non-human" and that which is most disturb-ingly human, that is, the inevitability of the life cycle (25-6). Ortner asserts that nature is universally devalued as a "lower order of existence" than culture and that all culture is "engaged in the process of generating and sustaining systems of meaningful forms by means of which humanity transcends the givens of natural exist-ence, bends them to its purposes, controls them in its interest" (25). Moreover, "[s]ince it is always culture's project to subsume and transcend nature, . . . then cul-ture would find it 'natural' to subordinate, not to say oppress, [women]" (27). As Beauvoir sees it, this not only explains the cultural mythology which serves as the foundation of all patriarchal societies, but also pro-vokes a fundamental ambivalence in men's attitudes and behavior towards women: "man desires to possess . . . that which he *is not,* he seeks union with what ap-pears to be Other than himself," at the same time that

he rejects and frees himself from nature when he "es-capes her hold" (74-75).

According to Beauvoir, it is this curiously paradoxical relationship of men with women/nature, one in which men are both inescapably bound to nature but wish to transcend it, that explains "why woman incarnates no stable concept": "through her is made unceasingly the passage from hope to frustration, from hate to love, from good to evil, from evil to good" (144). Millett also sees this ambivalence as closely related to men's "fear of otherness" (46) and rationalization of women's "inferiority." In literature, as has been amply analyzed and documented by at least two generations of feminist critics and theorists, this ambivalence has been trans-lated into two traditional, contradictory, female repre-sentations, commonly identified as the angel, or ideal-ized woman, and the demon, or villified woman. Drawing upon the Christian heritage of western societ-ies, these categories are often seen as derivatives of the Bible's most famous females: Eve, Adam's companion, and Mary, the mother of Jesus.

Both women are defined in terms of the men in their lives, thus identifying them as essentially "other": Eve is described as quite literally having been formed from Adam's rib as an afterthought, a means for providing companionship, while Mary is little more than a willing vessel through which the Holy Spirit can incarnate God's will. Eve, a descendent of the Pandora of classi-cal mythology, is canonized as the very spirit of disobe-dience and credited with no less than the fall from grace of all humanity; because she succumbed to temptation, and worse yet, persuded Adam to follow her terrible ex-ample, all humans are punished with lives of hardship. Mary, on the other hand, is presented as the pinnacle of virtue: unquestioning, submissive, obedient, gentle, pure (so pure that no sexuality taints her motherhood). De-scendants of Eve include all those women who manifest characteristics of seduction, temptation, disobedience, rebelliousness, autonomy, and carnality (all of which are frequently associated with beauty), while Mary's metophorical daughters are those who maintain their in-nocence, virtue, purity, gentility, nurturing, subservi-ence, docility, and silence. It is important to emphasize that the above traits are perceived as being inherited ex-clusively by their female "children," perhaps again fol-lowing Aristotle's lead in ascribing all that is most nega-tive to women and all that is most positive to men. Mary's "attributes" are perceived as positive from a pa-triarchal perspective only as desirable qualities in women, never in men, and Eve's intellectual curiosity, proclivity for action, and initiative are lauded only in men, never in women.

Whether as saints or sinners, traditional literary repre-sentations of women have been remarkably consistent; Hawthorne's innovation in **"The Birthmark"** consists of combining them into a single character, Georgiana. According to David Reynolds' analysis of Hawthorne's place within the cultural and literary contexts of his time, this is characteristic of Hawthorne's female protagonists during the time period in which **"The Birthmark"** was published. Although Reynolds does not discuss this particular short story, he asserts that the heroines of Hawthorne's early stories (1828-1837) are characterized by their heterogeneity and those of the middle period by "fusions" of different qualities, while in his later works there is a "fairly straightforward division between a 'light' . . . and a 'dark' heroine" (375).

Reynolds elaborates rather extensively on the ways in which these female characters are representative not only of literary trends of the nineteenth century U.S., but also of cultural patterns and norms of the time. Reynolds' version of the "saint," the "moral exemplar" tended to be represented as one of two types: the "angelic" or "gentle" variety was rarely gender-specific and basically "replaced" the formerly sacrosanct male moral-authority figures (especially clergy) as a "benign version of God's relation with humanity," while the "practical woman" embodied a "tougher alternative to America's powerful orthodox religious tradition" by the way in which she "flew in the face of Calvinistic gloom, and her persevering good works put the lie to Calvinistic predestination" (342-3). Reynolds' sinner, the "female rogue" also has a variety of guises, from the "female criminal" to the "fallen woman" to the "sensual woman," not to be confused with the "adventure feminist" of the frontier novels or the "female victim" of social reform texts. According to Reynolds, the woman-as-moral-model responds to "conventional" sentimental-domestic fiction which attempted to "avoid or defeat [social] ambiguities," while the other evolved from "subversive" sensational and/or "radical/democrat" writing which allowed these ambiguities to erupt (9). It goes without saying that Reynolds, while careful not to slight the literary genesis and repercussions of "major" authors of the American Renaissance, finds it necessary to examine their works from a cultural perspective in which Hawthorne emerges as himself "representative" of the multiple social realities of the time.

"The Birthmark" clearly revolves around a major concern of mid-nineteenth century U.S. society, the role of science in humans' lives, but in so doing it manifests crucial issues of gender identity and roles at personal and social levels. There is even a significant question in terms of which character should be considered the protagonist. From a patriarchal perspective, Aylmer is the protagonist, and the conflict is between science and humanism, or to put it another way, between mind and matter. From a feminist perspective, Georgiana is the protagonist, and the conflict is between autonomy and submission. The ways in which Aylmer, Aminadab, and Georgiana are represented reveal an overlapping of gender, moral, and philosophical issues in this story.

Aylmer is not only introduced in the loftiest of terms, but is consistently associated throughout the story with the highest of intentions, standards, and worth. The narrator initiates this deification by identifying Aylmer foremost, in the very first sentence, as "a man of science—an eminent proficient in every branch of natural philosophy" (2147). It is not insignificant that "natural philosophy" is used as a synonym for "science," given the traditional status accorded to philosophy. In this context, "natural" does not suggest anything innate or instinctual, of course, but rather is used as an adjective for what today would be called physical sciences. The word "science" itself was (and is) a term associated with critical thinking, analysis, abstraction (even if "applied"), and objectivity. According to the narrator, the incredible potential of science was just beginning to be perceived: "In those days, when the comparatively recent discovery of electricity, and other kindred mysteries of nature, seemed to open paths into the region of miracle . . ." (2147). So powerful was this realm of science that it appeared to have no limit: "The higher intellect, the imagination, the spirit, and even the heart, might all find their congenial aliment in pursuits which . . . would ascend from one steep of powerful intelligence to another, until the philosopher should lay his hand on the secret of creative force, and perhaps make new worlds for himself" (2147).

Perhaps because science as a field of inquiry was perceived as still so new, it was mixed with feelings and desires, for the narrator affirms that Aylmer's love for his new wife could only become strong by "intertwining itself with his love of science, and uniting the strength of the latter to its own." More importantly, the narrator speculates whether or not Aylmer "possessed this degree of faith in man's ultimate control over nature." The choice of the word "faith" is an interesting concession to possible limitations or inadequacies, but there is no such hesitancy in stating the ultimate goal or agency. "Man" is the only being capable of such achieving such aspirations, which more than aspirations, are presented as a necessity; clearly, it is man's "higher intellect" which permits him to vanquish, an intelligence beyond the realm of possibility for women, once again dating back philosophically to Aristotle's conviction that only men (and in particular, masters) had the capacity for and access to truth, while women were unable to surpass "opinion." Georgiana herself describes her own level of comprehension as "simple," and the narrator concurs by describing her understanding of the marvelous optical phenomena with which her husband amused her as merely "some indistinct idea."

Aylmer's professional, psychological, and physical features are all construed as manifestations of his superior nature. In classic physiognymic fashion, his insubstantial physical features are seen to represent illusive "higher" qualities of the human condition: "Aylmer's slender figure, and pale, intellectual face, were . . . apt[ly] a type of the spiritual element" (2151). He was not only confident, but arrogant about his professional abilities: he was "confident in his science" to the point where he felt sure "he could draw a magic circle round [Georgiana], within which no evil might intrude" (2151). He declares, "I feel myself fully competent to render this dear cheek as faultless as its fellow; and then . . . what will be my triumph, when I shall have corrected what Nature left imperfect, in her fairest work!" (2150). His fame is as extensive as his ambition: his scientific successes began while he was "yet in his youth," when "he had made discoveries in the elemental powers of nature, that had roused the admiration of all the learned societies in Europe" (2150). In short, Aylmer had had an "ardent, ambitious, imaginative, yet practical and laborious, life" during which he had "redeemed himself from materialism, by his strong and eager aspiration towards the infinite" (2154). His ambition has no limits; he even aspires to producing the very Elixir of Immortality and Elixir Vitae—goals which he believed possible "by the plainest scientific logic," even though he believes that "a philosopher who should go deep enough to acquire the power, would attain too lofty a wisdom to stoop to the exercise of it" (2152). Once again, materiality is subordinated to intellect, and Aylmer is the exclusive representative of "mind and spirit" in this story.

Georgiana's attitudes and feelings toward Aylmer's scientific abilities essentially reinforce his self-image and public image, although, like the narrator's, they are not unequivocal. On the basis of his reputation, she beseeches him to remove her birthmark: "You have deep science! All the world bears witness of it. You have achieved great wonders" (2149). However, when she reads his folio of scientific experiments, she is forced to modify her perception of him somewhat: "Georgiana, as she read, reverenced Aylmer, and loved him more profoundly than ever, but with a less entire dependence on his judgment than heretofore. Much as he had accomplished, she could not but observe that his most splendid successes were almost invariably failures, if compared with the ideal at which he aimed" (2154). The male intellectual circle emphasizes what is written, the theory, while Georgiana is concerned about practical results. Nevertheless, she claims that her reading has made her "worship [Aylmer] more than ever," an attitude of which he entirely approves: "Ah! wait for this one success, . . . then worship me if you will. I shall deem myself hardly unworthy of it" (2154).

So great is her respect for and awe of Aylmer, however, that Georgiana affirms—even as she is dying—that he has "aimed loftily" and "done nobly" and "should not repent" of "so high and pure a feeling" (2157). This is either amazingly delusional or unbelievably masochistic, considering that Georgiana "well knew" that even should the experiment be successful, she could "satisfy his highest and deepest conception" only momentarily because "his spirit was ever on the march—ever ascending—and each instant required soething that was beyond the scope of the instant before" (2156). Georgiana not only recognizes but also supports Aylmer's desire to surpass human limits; she "joyfully stake[s] all upon [his] word", as she herself acknowledges, "on the same principle that would induce me to take a dose of poison, if offered by [Aylmer's] hand" (2155). Perhaps Georgiana's unwillingness to diminish Aylmer's reputation and her eagerness to maintain his monumental ego are somehow related to comments by the narrator to the effect that, no matter how godlike his scientific knowledge and talents might be, Aylmer is merely mortal, after all. Georgiana pragmatically accepts human limitations, while Aylmer either denies or fights against them.

Georgiana and the narrator seem to concur that Aylmer's volume of experiments, "rich with achievements that had won renown for its author, was yet as melancholy a record as ever mortal hand had penned": "It was the sad confession, and continual exemplification, of the short-comings of the composite man—the spirit burthened with clay and working in matter—and of the despair that assails the higher nature, at finding itself so miserably thwarted by the earthly part" (2154). In other words, Aylmer, as a living human being, cannot escape the limitations of his physical nature, no matter how longingly he aspires to "the completeness of a higher state" (2157). The narrator is quite sympathetic in blaming human nature rather than individuals, observing that the tomes of the philosophers of the middle ages (all men, naturally) "stood in advance of their centuries, yet were imbued with some of their credulity, and therefore were believed, and perhaps imagined themselves, to have acquired from the investigation of nature a power above, nature, and from physics a sway over the spiritual world" (2153-4). The choice of the verbs "believe" and "imagine" suggests that these masculine aspirations are doomed to failure, more a figment of wishful thinking than a portent of future success.

This is reinforced in the character of Aylmer when he literally dreams of eliminating Georgiana's birthmark, fully unaware how accurate his subconscious drama would prove to be. Ironically, his dream is more "realistic" than his science. The visual illusions he creates for her are "almost perfect enough to warrant the belief, that her husband possessed sway over the spiritual world"; conversely, this dream, which appears to be mere imagination, proves to be an unheeded forewarning of imminent failure. The narrator also subtly undercuts Aylmer's pretensions by commenting that the early volumes of the Transactions of the Royal Society, "in which the members, knowing little of the limits of natural possibility, were continually recording wonders, or proposing methods whereby wonders might be wrought" in ways which were "hardly less curious and imaginative" than those of earlier tomes. The fact that the discussion of Aylmer's personal folio follows these observations tends to reveal it as merely the latest in a long, historical progression of failed attempts to surpass human limits.

Aminadab serves as a sort of alterego for Aylmer, embodying that "gross Fatality of Earth" (2157) which is the counterpart to Aylmer's intellectual and spiritual nature. Aminadab is described as "a man of low stature, but bulky frame, with shaggy hair hanging about his visage," a creature of "vast strength . . . and indescribably earthiness" who "seemed to represent man's physical nature" (2150-1). His "harsh, uncouth, misshapen tones" were "more like the grunt or growl of a brute than human speech" (2152). He had been Aylmer's assistant for his entire professional life, and "was admirably fitted for that office by his great mechanical readiness." Unlike Aylmer, however, this earthly version was "incapable of comprehending a single principle," although he "executed all the practical details of his master's experiments" (2151); as a representative of mere matter, he can acquire manual skills but not intellectual ones. Like the traditional representation of women as nature, he can reproduce, but not create on his own; he is totally dependent upon Aylmer's higher nature to provide the ideas, the essence, while his contribution is purely physical. The ways in which Aylmer addresses Aminadab clearly reinforce their opposition and the fact that Aminadab is only body: "thou human machine", "thou man of clay", "clod", "earthly mass", "thing of senses." Moreover, in a rare moment of appreciation, he affirms that Aminadab has "served him well! Matter and Spirit—Earth and Heaven—have both done their part in this!" (2157), acknowledging the participation of that specimen of lower nature, if not granting it equality.

Aminadab's setting is also appropriate to his nature and to his function. As a representative of physicality, it is "natural" that he should be found in the basement chambers, in the grimy bowels of the laboratory, illuminated by the primal fires of the furnace. If the physical dimension of human nature is considered "inferior", "lower", "gross", "fatal", it makes sense to banish it to the netherlands of the cavelike part of the laboratory. For the same reasons, it makes sense to establish Georgiana's quarters there as well. But although these two people both represent human physicality, there is one important difference: Aminadab, as a male—no matter how "primitive"—has privileges that Georgiana will never have. He is allowed to participate actively in Aylmer's science, while Georgiana's participation can only be passive. Georgiana's quarters are decorated with

beautiful curtains, scents, and other amenities, which both the narrator and Aylmer present as an attempt to make her sojourn there as pleasant as possible; however, the real objective is to strictly limit her personal space within the laboratory. For all practical purposes, Georgiana is a prisoner in her quarters, which is why her first entrance into the laboratory is described as an "intrusion" and her husband's initial reaction is to accuse her of risking the success of his scientific ventures by "throw[ing] a blight . . . over [his] labors" (2155). Quite clearly, each person has his/her "proper" place, and it is Aylmer who decides what that is.

Feminist critics, notably Sandra Gilbert and Susan Gubar, have frequently noted a literary penchant for female confinement which parallels the restrictions on women's real lives. In *The Madwoman in the Attic,* Gilbert and Gubar demonstrate how, for example, in Victorian fiction, a favorite strategy was literally to lock "mad" (rebellious?) women in the attic, a very graphic symbol of enclosure. Metaphors of enclosure and confinement abound in relation to literary women: houses and rooms are commonly used as symbolic spaces. Gilbert and Gubar (ironically) agree with Freud that a cave is "a female place, a womb-shaped enclosure, a house of earth, secret and often sacred." Perhaps the primary metaphor for "containment," however, is patriarchal insistence on restricting women to their own bodies, a clearly defined, "appropriately" limited space. In *Gender/Body/Knowledge,* Susan Bordo, among others, reminds us that "the body is not only a *text* of culture [but] also a *practical,* direct locus of social control" (13). Bordo differentiates between the "useful" body, a register of the cultural body following Foucault's ideas, and the "intelligible" body, our cultural conceptions of the body, which may be complementary or contradictory. As a female, Georgiana is a potential threat who is best incapacitated by "enclosing" her in a "safe" place. A significant step towards dominating nature is to attempt to bind it, to limit its realm.

The symbol of Georgiana's physicality is, of course, her birthmark. It is "a singular mark, deeply interwoven . . . with the texture and substance of her face", and its shape "bore not a little similarity to the human hand" (2147-8). Its hue varies from the "deeper crimson" in the "healthy, though delicate bloom" of her usual complexion, to becoming nearly imperceptible in the midst of blush, to "a crimson stain upon the snow" when she turned pale. Reactions to it varied, also: some women called it the "Bloody Hand" and saw it as a hideous detraction to her beauty, while male admirers speculated that it was the handprint of a fairy at the hour of birth, "in token of the magic endowments that were to give her such sway over all hearts" (2148). This male association of the birthmark with magic is in keeping with patriarchal tradition associating women with all that is mysterious, changeable, unintelligible, intangible, intuitive, or inexplicable. Other male observers simply wished it were not there to keep Georgiana from "ideal loveliness." It is not insignificant that her birthmark is compared to "one of those small blue stains, which sometimes occur in the purest statuary marble" and which could debatably "convert the Eve of Powers to a monster." At its most negative, this birthmark is what transforms Georgiana from the embodiment of an ideal into the personification of "the fatal flaw of humanity": "The Crimson Hand expressed the ineludible gripe [sic], in which mortality clutches the highest and purest of earthly mould, degrading them into kindred with the lowest, and even with the very brutes" (2148). In other words, Georgiana's birthmark is visible confirmation not only of human mortality but of human inferiority, which is represented as female.

Aylmer perceives Georgiana's birthmark as "the symbol of his wife's liability to sin, sorrow, decay, and death" (2148), and thus understandably becomes obsessed with removing it. Interestingly, the birthmark did not seem to bother him until Georgiana became his wife; it is only when she "belongs" to him that he sees her physicality as a reflection on himself, and quickly finds the mark unbearable. One day "very soon after their marriage," Aylmer expresses his concern: "you came so nearly perfect from the hand of Nature, that this slightest possible defect . . . shocks me, as being the visible mark of earthly imperfection" (2147). Aylmer despises this reminder of his own mortality, at the same time that he aspires to having "the perfect wife," as befits his status as eminent scientist. Georgiana apparently qualifies well for that position in terms of temperament; she is liked and admired by all who know her (even Aminadab). She also embodies those traits considered desirable in a wife: she is demure, proper, delicate, supportive, refined, and, above all, submissive. Although her initial reaction to Aylmer's statement about her birthmark is anger, her anger is immediately subsumed in tears and very shortly transformed into solidarity with her husband's attitudes and feelings: "life—while this hateful mark makes me the object of your horror and disgust— life is a burthen [sic] which I would fling down with joy. Either remove this dreadful Hand, or take my wretched life!" (2149). Georgiana willingly revises her original estimation of the mark as a "charm" and accepts her husband's judgment unquestioningly.

Because the birthmark is so intimately connected to Georgiana, to the point where it serves as a sort of visible barometer of her feelings, it is transformed into something approximating essence. Both Aylmer and Georgiana suspect that "the stain goes as deep as life itself," which is consistent with its having been "laid upon [her] before [she] came into the world" (2149). In other words, this "defect" is both innate and inherited, and its significance becomes one of the very nature of Georgiana. The mark is a manifestation of human im-

perfection, yes, and because of it Georgiana believes she is "of all mortals the most fit to die" (2156). As much as Aylmer would like to idealize her into a symbol for perfection, the little hand prevents him from doing so successfully. When Georgiana professes her complete faith in his ability and knowledge, he responds by declaring "there is no taint of imperfection on thy spirit" (2156); clearly, spiritual perfection in a woman consists of accepting the superiority of her husband. And as hard as Georgiana tries to be the perfect wife, perfection is simply beyond the realm of the possible because of this physical flaw. The fact that she is even willing to risk death in order to please her husband must surely be recognized as the ultimate sacrifice. However, Aylmer is ironically not the least bit concerned about Georgiana or possible consequences for her; he sees this situation in terms of himself only. The operation is an opportunity for him to correct nature's mistake and to achieve personal glory; tellingly, it is also the only way to "give himself peace." Aylmer's self-absorption is as monumental as his arrogance in believing himself capable of improving over nature and as his capacity for denial in so quickly forgetting his "mortifying failures".

Georgiana sees her birthmark as a symbol for her self, also, and it is a flawed self which she perceives. She bemoans her inability to achieve not only physical, but also moral perfection: "Life is but a sad possession to those who have attained precisely the degree of moral advancement at which I stand. Were I weaker and blinder, it might be happiness. Were I stronger, it might be endured hopefully" (2156). What is most important in her perception of weakness and imperfection, however, is the way in which she assimilates Aylmer's attitudes of blame: she assumes personal guilt for the flaws of human nature. Aylmer projects the blame for human imperfection upon his wife, and Georgiana willingly accepts the guilt. Essentially she is negating her own intuition and her own capacity for knowing by concurring that Aylmer's knowledge and wisdom are superior to her own. In *Women's Ways of Knowing*, Mary Belenky and associates examine women's answers to questions concerning what is truth, what is authority, to whom do we listen, and especially how do we know what we know. They affirm that "our basic assumptions about the nature of truth and reality and the origins of knowledge shape the way we see the world and ourselves as participants in it" (3). Georgiana's perspective fits into the epistemological position of "received knowledge", that is, of women who "conceive of themselves as capable of receiving . . . knowledge from the all-knowing external authorities but not capable of creating knowledge on their own" (15). Aylmer, as a man and especially as a scientist, is ascribed the authority of knowledge, while Georgiana sees herself only as a receptacle for his wisdom. In spite of clear indications that she is able to reason, and more importantly, understand and question her husband's work, her acceptance of Aylmer's perception and judgment of her as inferior determines her behavior accordingly. Because she has been ascribed the place and status of a lesser "other", Georgiana also perceives herself as such, which explains (but does not justify) her almost casual attitude towards her own survival.

When human knowledge is understood as a construction, the knower is part of the known (Goldberger 5). Knowledge and selfhood are inseparable in the sense that our perceptions of who we are and what we are constitute our vision and version of reality. Eve's daughter, Mary's child. In a patriarchal society, men project their desire to transcend human limitations and neutralize their fear of the other by constructing an idealized version of women, females who inherit Mary's angelic qualities. She is the representation of otherness in its most perfect form: a complementation which enhances and aggrandizes men's self-image with no threatening overtones. But just as otherness is essential for self-definition, so it can never be fully understood and assimilated, at the risk of its disappearing entirely. In a patriarchy, the indomitable aspects of womanhood are projected onto the figure of Eve, who embodies everything which is problematic and negative about otherness. In analyzing **"The Birthmark"**, the thoughtful reader must question why Georgiana is chosen to represent flawed humanity, even though her nature would appear to be "higher" than Aminadab's and her husband is unequivocally revealed to be less than perfect himself. The explanation is quite simple: she is perceived and projected as inferior because she is not a man. It is ironic that while there is little of the personal in this valuation, Georgiana assumes responsibility not only for her own guilt, but also quite literally for all of "mankind." Even more ironically, in so doing she transforms herself from a demonic Eve into a self-sacrificing Mary, thus perpetuating those most sacred of patriarchal myths: women as both the active cause of fallen humanity and the passive vehicle for human redemption.

Bibliography

Auerbach, Nina. 1982. *Woman and the Demon: The Life of a Victorian Myth.* Cambridge: Harvard UP.

Beauvoir, Simone de. 1952. *The Second Sex.* Trans. H. M. Parshley. NY: Vintage.

Bordo, Susan. 1989. "The Body and the Reproduction of Femininity: A Feminist Appropriation of Foucault." *Gender/Body/Knowledge.* Eds. Alison M. Jaggar and Susan R. Bordo. New Brunswick: Rutgers. 13-33.

Ellmann, Mary. 1968. *Thinking About Women.* NY: Harcourt Brace Jovanovich.

Fetterley, Judith. 1978. *The Resisting Reader: A Feminist Approach to American Fiction.* Bloomington: Indiana UP.

Gilbert, Sandra M. and Susan Gubar. 1979. *The Madwoman in the Attic: The Woman Writer and the Nineteenth-Century Literary Imagination.* New Haven: Yale UP.

Goldberger, Nancy et al (eds.). 1996. *Knowledge, Difference, and Power.* NY: Basic/Harper Collins.

Hawthorne, Nathaniel. 1843. "The Birthmark." *The Heath Anthology of American Literature.* Vol. I. 2nd ed. Eds. Paul Lauter et al. 1994. 2147-2158.

Millett, Kate. 1970. *Sexual Politics.* NY: Doubleday.

Mitchell, W. J. T. 1995. "Representation." *Critical Terms for Literary Study.* 2nd ed. Eds. Frank Lentricchia and Thomas McLaughlin. Chicago: U Chicago P. 11-22.

Ortner, Sherry. 1996. *Making Gender: The Politics and Erotics of Culture.* Boston: Beacon.

Reynolds, David S. 1989. *Beneath the American Renaissance: The Subversive Imagination in the Age of Emerson and Melville.* Cambridge: Harvard UP.

Price McMurray (essay date 2001)

SOURCE: McMurray, Price. "'Love Is as Much Its Demand, as Perception': Hawthorne's 'Birth-Mark' and Emerson's 'Humanity of Science.'" *ESQ: A Journal of the American Renaissance* 47, no. 1 (2001): 1-31.

[*In the following essay, McMurray interprets "The Birthmark" as a careful consideration of Ralph Waldo Emerson's early writings on the nature of love.*]

"The Birth-Mark," written shortly after Hawthorne's relocation to the Old Manse and first published in the *Pioneer* in the spring of 1843, has a rich critical history.[1] Although some contemporary readers doubtless shared the sentiments of a reviewer who declared in the October 1860 *National Review* that the "tale has no imaginative beauty and . . . is only remarkable for the diseased mixture of emotions which it depicts,"[2] since the 1950s Hawthorne's story of a scientist's ill-fated marriage has provoked readings from interpreters of a wide range of methodological persuasions and has assumed canonical status. Scholars interested in traditional cultural history, for instance, have been quick to identify Aylmer as a frustrated Pygmalion and the tale as a rejoinder to romantic idealism.[3] At the same time, critics working in the vein of Simon O. Lesser have translated the story's vaguely theological gloom into the language of psychoanalysis with such success that it is now difficult to take the hand in which Aylmer sees "his wife's liability to sin sorrow, decay, and death" as anything other than the marker of a threatening female sexuality.[4] Contextual support for these readings is not far to seek: the opening tale in a collection whose genesis Hawthorne pointedly places in the study where Emerson wrote *Nature*, **"The Birth-Mark"** is almost of necessity an exploration of transcendental premises, while its subject matter—a man's obsession with something "he thought little or nothing of" before marriage (*TS*, 766)—suggests an obvious biographical element. The story is further illuminated by the larger context of the emerging industrial order of antebellum America, and a series of historically minded critics have situated **"The Birth-Mark"** in relation to class and gender construction, the "production of personal life," and the dynamics of a marketplace guided by the invisible hand of Adam Smith's *Wealth of Nations*.[5]

Without gainsaying the massed commentary on Hawthorne's tale or the real interpretive gains of recent criticism, I would like to consider **"The Birth-Mark"** as a meditation on Emerson. My aim is not so much to question the "old" historicist consensus—which has it that the story registers Hawthorne's ambivalent engagement with transcendental idealism—as it is to suggest that he was a more assiduous and critical reader of his neighbor's work than we generally recognize.[6] Specifically, I trace the tale's apparently implausible donnée to "Love," where Emerson oscillates between the gloomy conviction that we must "study the sentiment as it appear[s] in hope and not in history" and his vision of marriage as a project of Platonic purification.[7] Pursuing the notion that in "the particular society of his mate" the lover "attains a clearer sight of any spot, any taint, which her beauty has contracted from this world" to a tragic conclusion ("Love," 150), **"The Birth-Mark"** is clearly polemical—evidence of both Hawthorne's disagreement with the relative optimism of "Love" and his conviction that he, and not Emerson, is the authority in matters of the heart. Should we also suspect that, in its initial conception at least, Georgiana's fate was an object lesson designed to dampen Sophia's enthusiasm for transcendentalism, such an observation in no way diminishes Hawthorne's accomplishment. **"The Birth-Mark"** remains our best commentary on "Love" and a searching evaluation of the "humanity of science"—the projected union of poetic and empirical knowledge that underlies Emerson's early lectures and the triumphant "Prospects" section of *Nature*.

In saying as much, though, I do not want to give short shrift to the unresolved tensions of the story, for the notion that **"The Birth-Mark"** translates biographical dilemma into coherent cultural criticism is not without its difficulties. A case in point is the tale's "moral," where the narrator concludes of Aylmer, "The momentary circumstance was too strong for him; he failed to look beyond the shadowy scope of Time, and living once for all in Eternity, to find the perfect Future in the present" (*TS* [*Tales and Sketches*], 780). Tepid as this theology may be, it is consistent with Hawthorne's beliefs and

strikingly reminiscent of his correspondence to Sophia.[8] Christianity is not without something to say about marriage, of course, and even the sentimental idiom in which the Hawthornes and other antebellum couples constructed their relationships did not completely avoid the realities of human love. Still, readers who see Georgiana's birthmark as an emblem of female sexuality and the tale as an intimation of Freudian reality are likely to find the narrator's vocabulary at the close—"bond," "token of human imperfection," "gross Fatality of Earth," "momentary circumstance" (780)—evasive to the point of unwitting self-parody. Similarly, the earlier account of Aylmer's graphic surgical dream teases and disappoints, for the narrator observes pertinently that "[t]ruth often finds its way to the mind close-muffled in robes of sleep, and then speaks with uncompromising directness of matters in regard to which we practise an unconscious self-deception, during our waking moments," only to add the obvious and seemingly vague explanation that "[u]ntil now, [Aylmer] had not been aware of the tyrannizing influence acquired by one idea over his mind" (767). Thus, rather than expecting too much from psychoanalysis *avant la lettre,* we might argue that the tale's insistence on irrational compulsion, its silence about the reason for and specific nature of Aylmer's obsession, is attributable less to the requirements of decorum than to intellectual indecisiveness.

Hawthorne's awareness of the competing impulses propelling his tale is suggested by the misdirection of the story's preamble. If the narrator's explanation that the late eighteenth century was a time when "it was not unusual for the love of science to rival the love of woman" implies that a largely historical representation will follow, his observation that Aylmer's love for his wife could survive only "by intertwining itself with his love of science, and uniting the strength of the latter to its own," puts the matter in doubt, hinting that *this* scientist may well prove more eccentric case study than representative man (*TS,* 764). Lest we miss the point, the narrator underscores the novelty and the exemplarity of his story as he draws the curtain to reveal Aylmer gazing at Georgiana's cheek:

> Such a union accordingly took place, and was attended with truly remarkable consequences, and a deeply impressive moral. One day, very soon after their marriage, Aylmer sat gazing at his wife, with a trouble in his countenance that grew stronger, until he spoke.
>
> "Georgiana," said he, "has it never occurred to you that the mark upon your cheek might be removed?"
>
> "No, indeed," said she, smiling; but perceiving the seriousness of his manner, she blushed deeply. "To tell you the truth, it has been so often called a charm, that I was simple enough to imagine it might be so."
>
> "Ah, upon another face, perhaps it might," replied her husband. "But never on yours! No, dearest Georgiana, you came so nearly perfect from the hand of Nature,

that this slightest possible defect—which we hesitate to term a defect or a beauty—shocks me, as being the visible mark of earthly imperfection."

"Shocks you, my husband!" cried Georgiana, deeply hurt; at first reddening with momentary anger, but then bursting into tears. "Then why did you take me from my mother's side? You cannot love what shocks you!"

To explain this conversation. . . .

(*TS*, 764-65)

Accustomed as we are to Hawthorne's interest in outré psychological states and the "inveterate love of allegory" to which he confesses in the preface to **"Rappaccini's Daughter"** (*TS*, 975), we may not feel that this conversation needs much explanation. Yet the story's implausible premise does bear dwelling on, not simply because all commentary that would dissolve the symbolic hand into some discursive significance necessarily tropes Aylmer's experiment but, more fundamentally, because it matters a great deal to the narrator. Even if we grant that Aylmer's obsession is sexual in origin—finding the phrase "[o]ne day, very soon after their marriage," sufficiently direct by Victorian standards—to rationalize the text in this fashion dilutes its propositionality. Since the narrator could manage his material differently (and does immediately backtrack to review the history of the hand's reception), it is of some moment that he shuffles the chronological deck to make Aylmer's troubled gaze the terminus a quo for the "truly remarkable consequences" the tale records.

If we must wait a while to see how Aylmer's obsession with his wife's birthmark could have probative value in a cautionary tale about scientific idealism, suffice it for now to note that the story's unusual mise en scène not only has a certain rightness—what romantic episode does not begin with a gaze?—but also seems to be a daring allusion to "Love."[9] I think specifically of the middle of the essay, where Emerson envisions marriage as a mutual project of Platonic self-fashioning:

[I]f . . . the soul passes through the body, and falls to admire strokes of character, and the lovers contemplate one another in their discourses and their actions, then, they pass to the true palace of Beauty, more and more inflame their love of it, and by this love extinguishing the base affection, as the sun puts out the fire by shining on the hearth, they become pure and hallowed. By conversation with that which is in itself excellent, magnanimous, lowly and just, the lover comes to a warmer love of these nobilities, and a quicker apprehension of them. . . . In the particular society of his mate, he attains a clearer sight of any spot, any taint, which her beauty has contracted from this world, and is able to point it out, and this with mutual joy that they are now able without offence to indicate blemishes and hindrances in each other, and give to each all help and comfort in curing the same. And, beholding in many

souls the traits of the divine beauty, and separating in each soul that which is divine from the taint which they have contracted in the world, the lover ascends ever to the highest beauty, to the love and knowledge of the Divinity, by steps on this ladder of created souls.

("Love," 149-50)

For the reader of Hawthorne's tale, Emerson's account of marital intimacy cannot but occasion something like a shock of recognition. Indeed, the narrator's claims for the singularity of his material notwithstanding, one begins to suspect that **"The Birth-Mark"** is an example of that most Hawthornesque of genres, the twice-told tale. Hinting (probably rightly) that the "clearer sight" described in "Love" might not be as cheerful a thing as Emerson would have us believe, Hawthorne transforms Platonic asceticism into a Frankensteinian experiment.[10]

Yet **"The Birth-Mark"** is not simply a sexualized rejoinder to "Love" that—should we compare Emerson's promise of "mutual joy" with the ways in which Georgiana is "aroused" and Aylmer reaches "ecstasy" (*TS*, 777, 779)—reduces spiritual discipline to gothic kinkiness. Were the story only this, it would seem unjustifiably contentious, for Hawthorne himself is less than frank about sexual matters, while Emerson makes little attempt to hide his ambivalence about marriage and erotic love.[11] Even if we assume that the story is autobiographical in some significant way, or suspect Hawthorne of sublimating his various anxieties—about sexuality, about Sophia's fascination with Emerson, about artistic creation—into intellectual conflict, I would insist that he is not an Aylmerish reader who, given to projection and fixation, mistakes a sentence for an essay and so warps his neighbor's Platonism to a dark ending. Hawthorne was hardly the first to recognize the affinity between Platonism and alchemy (both disdain the taint of the world of matter). Moreover, his revision of Emerson arguably does nothing more than call attention to Emerson's own revisionism. Specifically, while the notion of readable blemishes reflects Emerson's adoption of Swedenborg's doctrine of correspondence, the passage quoted above is fundamentally anti-Swedenborgian.[12] The image of "the sun put[ting] out the fire by shining on the hearth," for instance, is subtly polemical and consistent with what we find in "Swedenborg," where Emerson describes *Conjugal Love* as "a fine Platonic development of the science of marriage" but adds that it "exaggerates the circumstance of marriage" and is "an attempt to eternize the fireside and nuptial chamber" (*LA*, 679, 680). More generally, as Hawthorne clearly saw, "Love" is inhabited by a remarkable undercurrent of doubt, much as if the Emerson who chose to conclude *Nature* by envisioning a "correspondent revolution" (94) were disinclined to entertain such bold prospects where matters of the heart were concerned.

Our first hint that the burden of the essay may be to forget (rather than transcend) the darkness investing the contingent comes early on, when Emerson lays down some unusual ground rules for writing well about love:

> [T]he first condition is, that we must leave a too close and lingering adherence to the actual, to facts, and study the sentiment as it appeared in hope and not in history. For, each man sees his own life defaced and disfigured, as the life of man is not, to his imagination. Each man sees over his own experience a certain slime of error, whilst that of other men looks fair and ideal. . . . Alas! I know not why, but infinite compunctions embitter in mature life all the remembrances of budding sentiment, and cover every beloved name. Every thing is beautiful seen from the point of the intellect, or as truth. But all is sour, if seen as experience. Details are always melancholy; the plan is seemly and noble. It is strange how painful is the actual world,— the painful kingdom of time and place. There dwells care and canker and fear. With thought, with the ideal, is immortal hilarity, the rose of joy. Round it all the muses sing. But with names and persons and the partial interests of to-day and yesterday, is grief.

> ("Love," 141)

Emerson never wavers in his conviction that the imagination leads us to see life "as the life of man is not," but he can do little more to alleviate the sourness of experience than recommend that we "leave a too close and lingering adherence to the actual." His acknowledgment of the inevitability and enigma of erotic grief invites comparison with Hawthorne's tale, for the declaration that each man "sees over his own experience a certain slime of error" (later softened to "stain of error") seems simply a franker version of the obsessive and inexplicable gloom with which Aylmer views his wife. Similarly, Emerson's conviction that there is an irreconcilable split between experience and the ideal finds a decent analogue in Aylmer's journal, "the sad confession, and continual exemplification, of the shortcomings of the composite man," in which "every man of genius, in whatever sphere, might recognize the image of his own experience" (*TS,* 775).

In the immediate context, Emerson's caveat serves to qualify the essay's later arguments before the fact. The point is not so much that his account of experience seems more sincerely felt than the self-consciously platitudinous treatment of romance which opens "Love" as it is that the cloud of the "actual" shadows both the essay's dramatic Platonism and the surprising endorsement of realism we encounter at the end. While Emerson warns us of the sad alchemy of memory and the "infinite compunctions [that] embitter in mature life all the remembrances of budding sentiment," his metaphors—"defaced and disfigured," "a certain slime of error"—are such that this passage seems to anticipate his depiction later in "Love" of the lover's "clearer sight of

any spot, any taint." So, too, the close of the essay reveals an Aylmerish perspicacity:

> Not always can flowers, pearls, poetry, protestations, nor even home in another heart, content the awful soul that dwells in clay. . . . The soul which is in the soul of each, craving for a perfect beatitude, detects incongruities, defects, and disproportion in the behavior of the other. Hence arises surprise, expostulation, and pain. Yet that which drew them to each other was signs of loveliness, signs of virtue: and these virtues are there, however eclipsed. They appear and reappear, and continue to attract; but the regard changes, quits the sign, and attaches to the substance. This repairs the wounded affection. Meantime, as life wears on, it proves a game of permutation and combination. . . . All that is in the world which is or ought to be known, is cunningly wrought into the texture of man, of woman. . . .

> . . . Their once flaming regard is sobered by time in either breast, and losing in violence what it gains in extent, it becomes a thorough good understanding. They resign each other, without complaint, to the good offices which man and woman are severally appointed to discharge in time, and exchange the passion which once could not lose sight of its object, for a cheerful, disengaged furtherance, whether present or absent, of each other's designs.

> ("Love," 153-54)

Moving from romance to realism, this passage effectively reprises the argument of "Love." The crucial difference is the foreshortening of the perfectionist prospect that is the emotional and ideological heart of the essay. Emerson's observation that the soul detects "incongruities, defects, and disproportion" recalls the "clearer sight" passage, but the Platonic promise of "mutual joy" has vanished, replaced by the sobering assurance that "the wounded affection" will be "repair[ed]" when "the regard changes, quits the sign, and attaches to the substance." In similar fashion, Emerson celebrates the idea of the spouse-as-microcosm, explaining that "[a]ll that is in the world . . . is cunningly wrought into the texture of man, of woman," and adding that "the purification of the intellect and the heart, from year to year, is the real marriage." But his punning vision of "a cheerful, disengaged furtherance" makes it clear that the honeymoon—and any hope of erotic transcendence—must end (154).

In effect, "Love" is an essay of several voices. The first evokes memorably the "care and canker and fear" of love under the sign of the actual; a second envisions lovers who scale the Platonic ladder to become "pure and hallowed"; and yet another focuses on a couple whose faded passion is proof positive that love is a child of time. Without insisting that Emerson abandons his promise of "mutual joy," or that his endorsement of a "thorough good understanding" is out of character, we might find that the essay's primary signifier is its ambivalence. If the gist of Emerson's self-revision lies in his assertion that the "regard changes, quits the sign," such a formulation indicates that the matter is both experiential and linguistic—as is implied by the repetition of "sign" and its cognates, which runs the gamut from the evanescent "signs of virtue," to the wisdom that elects "to quit the sign," to the lovers' decision to "resign each other" and assist in the furtherance of each other's "designs." In part a textualization of the notion that the other is not a static, transparent emblem of virtue but a symbol that can and must be inscribed in the varied narrative of a life of good (and perhaps not so good) offices and designs, or Emerson's way of "resigning" his text to the fact that "the angels that inhabit this temple of the body appear at the windows, and all the gnomes and vices also" ("Love," 153-54), this proliferation of "signs" qualifies the passage's explicit assertion. Never quite able to "quit the sign," Emerson asserts a prudential acceptance of human and linguistic limitation, all the while revealing his nostalgia for the Swedenborgian fantasy of perfect signification upon which the essay's Platonic prospect depends.

Emerson's essay is clearly suggestive for a reading of **"The Birth-Mark."** We need not determine the extent to which (or even if) Hawthorne identifies with Aylmer to see that the tale throws the tensions in "Love" into bold relief, recalling both its Swedenborgian semiotic drama and the experiential enigma that haunts Emerson's uneasy dialectic. Moreover, the possibility that **"The Birth-Mark"** shadows Emerson's essay may help explain one of the more puzzling features of the story, namely, the willingness of the principals to build the gloomiest of allegories on the slightest of blemishes. While we can understand the fact that "Aylmer's sombre imagination was not long in rendering the birthmark a frightful object" in psychological terms, and see Georgiana, who quickly abandons her coquettish notion that the birthmark is a "'charm'" and decides she would rather die than leave it unremoved, as an all-too-willing victim of gender construction (*TS*, 766, 764), the tale's action strains credibility.[13] This allegorical discontinuity—if we can so characterize the disastrous turn of events set in motion by Aylmer's sight of Georgiana's birthmark—does make sense as a deft conflation of the competing impulses in "Love," however, for the Swedenborgian intimacy in which Emerson's lovers note and expunge eminently readable blemishes is never far from the darkness of the actual, of facts.

Hawthorne's aggression bears lingering over. Although we might conclude that the tale makes the logical point that Emerson's decision to avert his gaze from experience necessarily vitiates his account of marriage, or take the narrator's somewhat Delphic moral as evidence that **"The Birth-Mark"** aims to recall Platonic ideal-

ism to the confines of Christian humanism, neither reading is entirely satisfactory. The difficulty is not that the former interpretation presents us with an overly corrosive irony, as if the story existed merely to suggest that Emerson's description of love "as it appear[s] in hope and not in history" is wishful thinking, or that the latter is inconsistent with Hawthorne's belief, for he appears to have been invested in similar sentiments. The problem is that **"The Birth-Mark"** tropes the willful blindness of Emerson's essay. Not only does the sexual content of the tale remain obscured until the end, but the narrator's vaguely Christianized conclusion also fails to capture the theological ironies of a story that it seems especially appropriate to attribute to Melville's neo-Calvinist Hawthorne. In another writer it might be an accident that the narrator is familiar with every term for human frailty except original sin, or that the characters of the tale enact an unwitting parody of the Puritan morphology of conversion, but not with the author of a tale like **"Young Goodman Brown."**[14] Thus, **"The Birth-Mark"** seems oddly irresolute or self-serving; it underscores the anxiety beneath Emerson's "clearer sight" but averts its own gaze from a "true sight of sin," as if Hawthorne feared the recoil of his most trenchant criticism.

Still, whether we decide that Hawthorne takes Emerson on his own (somewhat conflicted) terms, or simply conclude that all is fair in love and war, **"The Birth-Mark"** is a cogent piece of criticism, and this becomes evident when we consider the vehicle of the tale—science. Although "Love" is not particularly concerned with what was once called natural philosophy, Emerson's few remarks on the subject are suggestive of why Hawthorne chooses the vocation he does for his unhappy protagonist:

> But this dream of love, though beautiful, is only one scene in our play. In the procession of the soul from within outward, it enlarges its circles ever, like the pebble thrown into the pond, or the light proceeding from an orb. The rays of the soul alight first on things nearest, on every utensil and toy, on nurses and domestics, on the house and yard and passengers, on the circle of household acquaintance, on politics, and geography, and history. But by the necessity of our constitution, things are ever grouping themselves according to higher or more interior laws. Neighborhood, size, numbers, habits, persons, lose by degrees their power over us. Cause and effect, real affinities, the longing for harmony between the soul and the circumstance, the high progressive idealizing instinct, these predominate later, and ever the step backward from the higher to the lower relations is impossible. Thus even love, which is the deification of persons, must become more impersonal every day. Of this at first it gives no hint.

("Love," 151)

This passage does not describe science in any modern or empirical sense, but it is a characteristically Emersonian attempt to yoke the classificatory schemes of natural philosophy and Platonic ontology. What is most remarkable is Emerson's faith—apparently genuine—in the human capacity for self-correction. The "dream of love" inhabited by the young misapprehends both the world and the nature of love, but there is no cause for alarm; the human psyche is hard-wired for scientific method, and a "necessity of our constitution" predisposes us to the work of classification and an increasingly abstract view of the world. Albeit belatedly, we will come to know "real affinities" and arrive at a truth from which "the step backward . . . is impossible." Yet one might wonder how this transformation is to take place, for if the shifting rhetorical registers of the essay are any indicator, romance and science are very different things. Moreover, desire is inherently paradoxical: for both scientist and lover it is at once the agent of and greatest threat to the "procession of the soul." Emerson's brief sketch of the soul reprises the "Discipline" section of *Nature,* to be sure, but his appeal to ultimate realities and the ideal of impersonal "deification"—directed, a bit surprisingly, as much against the allures of "every utensil" as against the inevitable particularity of human attachments—leaves unanswered the question of how one might distinguish a "real affinity" from that love which has "no hint" of its final object. Far from reconciling love and science, Emerson's essentially Goethean argument reduces love to an intellectual error, a mistake of method. At the same time, he reveals that the scientist may share the lover's fatal attraction for the contingent—that, as he puts it elsewhere, empirical science may "bereave the student of the manly contemplation of the whole" (*Nature*, 82). Thus, it is not surprising that "Love" says little about science, choosing instead to trust to time's alchemy. Nor should it come as a surprise that Aylmer's excursion into the world of romance—an episode the narrator wryly describes as the "experience of a spiritual affinity, more attractive than any chemical one" (*TS*, 764)—only serves to make his scientific libido return with a vengeance.

What should doubtless be added is that the implied incompatibility of love and science is an anomaly in Emerson's work. Much more characteristic of his way of thinking is the conclusion of "Art," where he attributes "the selfish and even cruel aspect which belongs to our great mechanical works" to "the effect of the mercenary impulses which these works obey" and promises that, "[w]hen science is learned in love, and its powers are wielded by love, they will appear the supplements and continuations of the material creation" (*LA*, 440). While the call for a perceptual revolution was common currency among the romantics, who almost inevitably grappled with the task of how to reconcile the competing demands of poetry and science, few of Emerson's European peers or precursors promised as boldly or extravagantly as the Sage of Concord, and the vision of

"science . . . learned in love"—which is both an exuberant synonym for poetic science and something a bit more—is crucial to the argument of both *Nature* and *Essays: First Series*.[15] Indeed, the principal irony of "Love"—apparently not lost on Hawthorne—is that for all Emerson's gloom about erotic experience he could be quite enthusiastic about "marriage" in the context of science.

Scholarship has established the crucial role of natural philosophy in Emerson's development, and Stephen E. Whicher and Robert E. Spiller explain that Emerson's "closest study" of science was "coincident with the intellectual crisis which led to his resignation as pastor of the Second Church (1832) and culminated in the publication of *Nature* (1836)." At bottom, this vocational crisis was an epistemological crisis: it was Emerson's reaction to a world dominated by Locke and historical Christianity. Because he was unwilling, as his "Address" at Harvard Divinity School would later make clear, to accept a condition of spiritual belatedness and unable to abandon a desire for moral certainties, Emerson turned to the world of contemporary science. Deductive and a priori, the discipline of Georges Cuvier and the naturalists offered a new and immediate ground for the apprehension of moral truth and became "the principal agent in [Emerson's] shift from a theological to a secular base for his moral philosophy."[16]

The dramatic turning point came at the tail end of Emerson's 1832 European tour. After visiting the Cabinet of Natural History in the Jardin des Plantes, the one-time cleric confided: "It is a beautiful collection & makes the visiter as calm & genial as a bridegroom. . . . The Universe is a more amazing puzzle than ever as you glance along this bewildering series of animated forms,—the hazy butterflies, the carved shells, the birds, beasts, fishes, insects, snakes,—& the upheaving principle of life everywhere incipient in the very rock aping organized forms." There is "[n]ot a form so grotesque, so savage, nor so beautiful," he added, "but is an expression of some property inherent in man the observer,—an occult relation between the very scorpions and man. I feel the centipede in me—cayman, carp, eagle, & fox. I am moved by strange sympathies, I say continually, 'I will be a naturalist'" (*JMN*, 4:199-200).[17] If Emerson's intuition of "strange sympathies" is unsettling even today, and all the more provocative on account of its psychosexual baggage, it was nonetheless a decisive discovery of vocation. Upon his return to the United States, he devoted his first series of lectures to science: "The Uses of Natural History," "On the Relation of Man to the Globe," "Water," and "The Naturalist." This specifically scientific phase of Emerson's career was relatively short-lived—he never published the 1834 lectures, and his 1836 lecture series included only one talk devoted to science—but it did prepare for things to come. "The Uses of Natural History," for instance, lays out a hierarchy of the uses of nature that looks forward to *Nature,* while "Water," which is as metaphorical as it is scientific, seems an early instance of transcendental symbol making. Perhaps most importantly, it was in this brief period that Emerson formulated his own particular brand of natural philosophy: a moral, intuitive, and poetic wisdom that his polemical 1836 lecture calls "The Humanity of Science."[18]

The notion that science might be humanized (or poetry and science married), like Emerson's interest in the analogical possibilities of the classificatory schemes of the naturalists, is essential to the program of *Nature,* a text Whicher describes magisterially as "an audacious attempt to rescue nature from the natural scientists and to sketch instead a human or poetic science."[19] Where Emerson takes up the matter most directly is in the final chapter, "Prospects." Making the familiar argument that "the problems to be solved are precisely those which the physiologist and the naturalist omit to state," Emerson prefaces his famous exhortation to "[b]uild, therefore, your own world" with a methodological manifesto:

> He cannot be a naturalist, until he satisfies all the demands of the spirit. Love is as much its demand, as perception. Indeed, neither can be perfect without the other. In the uttermost meaning of the words, thought is devout, and devotion is thought. Deep calls unto deep. But in actual life, the marriage is not celebrated. There are innocent men who worship God after the tradition of their fathers, but their sense of duty has not yet extended to the use of all their faculties. And there are patient naturalists, but they freeze their subject under the wintry light of the understanding. . . . But when a faithful thinker, resolute to detach every object from personal relations, and see it in the light of thought, shall, at the same time, kindle science with the fire of the holiest affections, then will God go forth anew into the creation.
>
> (*Nature,* 83, 94, 91-92)[20]

While readers of this call to action and the subsequent account of a "correspondent revolution" are likely to come away with the impression that the author of *Nature* anticipates a world magically transformed until "evil is no more seen," Emerson is careful to defer the "kingdom of man over nature" to an indefinite future. Similarly, his promise that "Nature is not fixed, but fluid" in no way changes the fact that this apocalypse will be an apocalypse of the mind (95, 93). Lest we begin to suspect *Nature* of solipsism, however, as if the close of the treatise imagined nothing more than a private triumph of vision, we should keep in mind that Emerson was an involved observer of his times and that his book is a polemic about science.[21] Just what point

this polemic makes is suggested when we turn to Emerson's journal and a memorable portrait of Alcott—the most likely local source for the mode (if not the specific content) of the orphic sayings in "Prospects":

> This man entertained in his spirit all vast & magnificent problems. None came to him so much recommended as the most universal. He delighted in the fable of Prometheus; in all the dim gigantic pictures of the most ancient mythology; in the Indian & Egyptian traditions; in the history of magic, of palmistry, of temperaments, of astrology, of whatever showed any impatience of custom & limits, any impulse to dare the solution of the total problem of man's nature, finding in every such experiment an implied pledge & prophecy of worlds of Science & Power yet unknown to us. He seemed often to realize the pictures of the old Alchemists; for he stood brooding on the edge of discovery of the Absolute from month to month, ever & anon affirming that it was within his reach, & nowise discomfited by uniform short comings.
>
> (*JMN,* 8:214)

As this account of the reformer's fascination with "worlds of . . . Power yet unknown to us" makes clear, the idealist project was a direct descendant of the magical prehistory of science. For the intellectual impatient with the alienating effects of empiricism, magic and astrology were not pseudosciences but, as "History" has it, "efforts of the mind in a right direction" (*LA,* 253); similarly, the "old Alchemists" were not credulous children but models to emulate.

Understood thus, *Nature* is a fit thesis or pre-text for Hawthorne's antithetical tale. Not only is the protagonist of **"The Birth-Mark"** an alchemist who persists in the face of failure, but his fate is essentially propositional as well—a grim counter to Emerson's optimism.[22] Lest Hawthorne's story seem too literal a dramatization of what is nothing more than an epistemological stance in Emerson's work, I would reiterate that the argument of *Nature* is not as abstract as it appears. Emerson's review of the "occasional examples of the action of man upon nature with his entire force" (*Nature,* 90), perhaps the most overtly topical moment in "Prospects," not only positions the treatise as a solution to the problem of historical Christianity but also dignifies the contemporary reform impulse in startling fashion. Celebrating "Reason's momentary grasp of the sceptre," Emerson urges his audience to consider the "examples" of

> the traditions of miracles in the earliest antiquity of all nations; the history of Jesus Christ; the achievements of a principle, as in religious and political revolutions, and in the abolition of the Slave-trade; the miracles of enthusiasm, as those reported of Swedenborg, Hohenlohe, and the Shakers; many obscure and yet contested facts, now arranged under the name of Animal Magnetism; prayer; eloquence; self-healing; and the wisdom of children.
>
> (*Nature,* 90)[23]

What makes this sweeping roll call especially remarkable is Emerson's apparent willingness to press "obscure and yet contested facts" into the service of his argument. The author of *Nature* was not an unequivocal supporter of the pseudosciences, but for a baffled reader wandering through the short treatise, this catalog might have been a valuable heuristic device, serving, in effect, to explain what transcendentalism was.[24] Nor would it have taken the conservatism of an Andrews Norton to wonder if a willingness to lump Christ's miracles together with Alcott's educational experiments and animal magnetism did not suggest something problematic about the spirit of the times.

It is likely that Hawthorne would have been inclined to look critically at his neighbor's expansive claims, for his wife's illnesses brought him firsthand experience with the "obscure and yet contested facts" Emerson adduces as evidence of Reason's power. Plagued throughout her adult life by debilitating headaches, Sophia was offered a series of "treatments" for her ailment, ranging from Jones Very's program of self-sacrifice to homeopathic doses of poison.[25] Her experimentation with mesmerism in the spring of 1841 led Hawthorne to write from Brook Farm later that year: "I am unwilling that a power should be exercised on thee, of which we know neither the origin nor the consequence. . . . Supposing that this power arises from the transfusion of one spirit into another," he explained, "it seems to me that the sacredness of an individual is violated by it. . . . I have no faith whatever that people are raised to the seventh heaven, or to any heaven at all, or that they gain any insight into the mysteries of life beyond death, by means of this strange science." If Hawthorne's religiosity seems a bit like special pleading, especially when it takes the form of a concern lest Sophia allow an intruder other than her future husband "into [her] holy of holies," his doubt that mesmerism is anything more than a "physical and material" influence appears genuine, as does his admonition to keep the imagination "sane."[26] Needless to say, Hawthorne's reaction to his future wife's interest in pseudoscience suggests not only that he might have been attentive to the contemporary referents in Emerson's account of Reason, finding his neighbor's conflation of mesmerism and Christian miracle hardly an abstract proposition, but also that he might have noted the vehicle for Emerson's argument, namely, the "marriage" of poetic and empirical forms of knowledge.[27]

Hawthorne's response to *Nature* takes the form of a tale that R. B. Heilman long ago described as a parable of the "marriage of science and humanity" and that I would characterize—more specifically and tendentiously—as a skeptical allegory of the humanity of science.[28] The narrator's description of Aylmer's library, for instance, with its "tomes . . . full of romance and poetry" by those "antique naturalists" who "perhaps imagined themselves, to have acquired from the investigation of nature a power above nature, and from physics a sway over the spiritual world" (*TS*, 774), maps a genealogy of science consistent with Emerson's account of Alcott and the cryptic sayings of the orphic bard. More generally, Aylmer's scientific undertakings are divided between the magical effects wrought in Georgiana's boudoir and the grimy empiricism of his laboratory. Doubtless in part an expedient to secure Georgiana's cooperation, Aylmer's refashioning of his "dingy, sombre rooms" is also consistent with a conversion to the poetic science envisioned in *Nature*. Something like the Emerson who looks forward to a time when "evil is no more seen," Aylmer is "confident" that his "science" can "draw a magic circle . . . within which no evil might intrude," failing all the while to realize that he has entered a vicious circle in which his love for Georgiana fuels the *libido sciendi* that will precipitate her destruction (770). As the narrator observes after one of Aylmer's unsuccessful experiments: "Soon, however, he forgot these mortifying failures. In the intervals of study and chemical experiment, he came to her, flushed and exhausted, but seemed invigorated by her presence, and spoke in glowing language of the resources of his art" (772). While the modern reader is likely to conclude that Aylmer feels renewed vigor because his sexual libido is recharging his scientific libido, as is more transparently the case when he later seeks out Georgiana and departs from her boudoir "with a boyish exuberance of gaiety," we should not lose sight of the fact that the itinerary of this self-styled heir to the "long dynasty of the Alchemists" is essentially that of Emerson's dialectic (775, 772).

Aylmer finally removes the birthmark from Georgiana's cheek, but his success comes at a terrible cost. The story's final tableau, in which the scientist stands uncomprehendingly over his wife's corpse as "the gross Fatality of Earth exult[s] in its invariable triumph over the immortal essence" (*TS*, 780), provides a stark contrast to Emerson's conviction that "when a faithful thinker . . . shall . . . kindle science with the fire of the holiest affections, then will God go forth anew into the creation." A cautionary tale about the tragic consequences of erotic and intellectual enthusiasms, **"The Birthmark"** uses Emerson's preferred figure for his methodological revolution—marriage—to weigh the potential humanity of science. Hawthorne's syncretism, his gesture of folding Emerson's conflicted account of the "clearer sight of any spot" into the visionary Platonism of *Nature* (or vice versa), is not arbitrary: the "correspondent revolution" envisioned at the end of the treatise is a Swedenborgian business, and "Prospects," especially in its alchemical overtones, is an epithalamium of sorts. Hawthorne may not have found, as was apparently the case when he read the New England annalists' accounts of Merry Mount, that the pages before him "wrought themselves, almost spontaneously, into a sort of allegory" (*TS,* 360), but Emerson's catalog of the moral and physical evils destined to vanish before the "advancing spirit"—"disagreeable appearances, swine, spiders, snakes, pests, mad-houses, prisons" (*Nature,* 95, 94)—could hardly exclude the defects or blemishes he speaks of in "Love."[29]

Perhaps the best evidence of Hawthorne's syncretism (and its appropriateness) is the tale's central symbol itself. While we could read Georgiana's birthmark as an obsessive projection on Hawthorne's part—as if the indefinite blemish in "Love" were a sort of Rorschach test—the symbol's specificity arguably clarifies the thematic issues governing the aggressive intertextuality of **"The Birth-Mark."** Suggestive in light of such a hypothesis is an entry Hawthorne made in his notebook in August of 1842, when he paused to reflect on an encounter with his august new neighbor and Edmund Hosmer, a farmer and rustic philosopher who attended "conversations" at Emerson's house:

> It would be amusing to draw a parallel between him and his admirer, Mr. Emerson—the mystic, stretching his hand out of cloud-land, in vain search for something real; and the man of sturdy sense, all whose ideas seem to be dug out of his mind, hard and substantial, as he digs potatoes, beets, carrots, and turnips, out of the earth. Mr. Emerson is a great searcher for facts; but they seem to melt away and become unsubstantial in his grasp.[30]

Largely a satire of intellectual otherworldliness, Hawthorne's portrait makes a pertinent point, for the dilemmas of idealist epistemology and the "transfer of the world into the consciousness" (*LA,* 195) are central to *Nature* and Emerson's early essays.[31] Indeed, the passage intimates that Hawthorne had begun to sense in his neighbor the moods that would culminate in Emerson's punning declaration, in "Experience," that "this evanescence and lubricity of all objects, which lets them slip through our fingers then when we clutch hardest, [is] the most unhandsome part of our condition" (*LA,* 473).

A direct consideration of the alienating effects of post-Kantian subjectivity would not come until 1844 and the writing of **"The Christmas Banquet,"** but Hawthorne's characterization of Emerson is relevant to **"The Birth-Mark."** Such a notion may seem counterintuitive at first blush, in spite of the obvious suggestiveness of Hawthorne's synecdoche or the similarity between his journal entry and the narrator's observation that, in Aylmer's "grasp, the veriest clod of earth assumed a soul" (*TS,* 774), for the simple reason that the birthmark is an irreducible reality and not a shadow. Yet it is possible to trace a minor strain in Emerson's writing in which the hand figures both the intellect's grasp and a distinct

perceptual limit. In *Nature,* for instance, Emerson bemoans the "tedious training, day after day, year after year, never ending, . . . and all to form the Hand of the mind" (47). This passing complaint about common sense or what Emerson generally calls the Understanding is of a piece with the polemics in his lapidary sketch of a dreamy schoolboy in "The American Scholar":

> Thus to him, to this school-boy under the bending dome of day, is suggested, that he and it proceed from one root; one is leaf and one is flower; relation, sympathy, stirring in every vein. And what is that Root? Is not that the soul of his soul?—A thought too bold,—a dream too wild. Yet when this spiritual light shall have revealed the law of more earthly natures,—when he has learned to worship the soul, and to see that the natural philosophy that now is, is only the first gropings of its gigantic hand, he shall look forward to an ever expanding knowledge as to a becoming creator.
>
> (*LA,* 55-56)

This account of "sympathy" is reminiscent of Emerson's epiphany in the Jardin des Plantes, much as his anticipation that the scholar will surpass "the natural philosophy that now is" to acquire the "ever expanding knowledge" of a "becoming creator" seems an unmistakable reprise of "Prospects." What makes the passage noteworthy for my purposes, of course, is the Aylmerish vision of a giant hand. If Emerson's pejorative "groping" underscores the limitations of contemporary natural philosophy, his verbal pyrotechnics—the insistently verbal "Root," for instance, which confounds sublime gazing with subterranean grasping—make it clear that scientific reform will consist of the pursuit of analogies that are poetic, intuitive, and above all, visionary.

Our suspicion that the hand is a figure for Emerson's construction of contemporary science becomes stronger when we factor evil into the equation. Because evil does not exist for Emerson—without denying the reality of human suffering, he would nonetheless argue that evil has no ontological basis—this common metaphor can take unusual turns, as is the case in "The Uses of Natural History," where he considers the problem of ugliness. "A lobster," Emerson explains, "is monstrous to the eye the first time it is seen, but when we have been shown the use of the case, the color, the tentacula, and the proportion of the claws, and have seen that he has not a scale nor a bristle, nor any part, but fits exactly to some habit and condition of the creature; he then seems as perfect and suitable to his seahouse, as a glove to a hand. A *man* in the rocks under the sea," Emerson concedes, "would indeed be a monster; but a lobster is a most handy and happy fellow there." For all his puckishness, Emerson is in earnest, and he generalizes boldly, writing, "[T]here is not an object in nature so mean or loathsome, not a weed, not a toad, not an earwig, but a knowledge of its habits would lessen our disgust, and convert it into an object of some worth; perhaps of admiration."[32] A tempered version of the earlier discovery of an "occult relation between the very scorpions and man," Emerson's lecture anticipates the millennial turns of *Nature* and his prophecy that "[a]s fast as you conform your life to the pure idea in your mind . . . [s]o fast will disagreeable appearances . . . vanish" (*Nature*, 94).

We do not want to make too much of a lobster, but there can be no doubt that the hand is at the center of a constellation of value in Emerson's thought, figuring both the intellect's act of grasping and a perceptual limit associated with evil and scientific empiricism.[33] Nowhere is this imaginative economy more evident than in "Blight," a poem that laments the imaginative cost of scientific knowledge and provides a decent précis of Emerson's vision of the humanity of science:

> Give me truths;
> For I am weary of the surfaces,
> And die of inanition. If I knew
> Only the herbs and simples of the wood, . . .
> And rare and virtuous roots, which in these woods
> Draw untold juices from the common earth,
> Untold, unknown, and I could surely spell
> Their fragrance, and their chemistry apply
> By sweet affinities to human flesh,
> Driving the foe and stablishing the friend,—
> O, that were much, and I could be a part
> Of the round day, related to the sun
> And planted world, and full executor
> Of their imperfect functions.

Voicing a weariness of "the surfaces" that anticipates the moody ennui of "Experience," Emerson nostalgically imagines an immediate relationship with nature and contrasts the "young scholars" who "devastate" nature "unreligiously" and whose "botany is Latin names" with the "old men" who "studied magic in the flowers," "human fortunes in astronomy," and "an omnipotence in chemistry." Although the vanished ideal is never explicitly equated with alchemy, that it is pre-empirical and the product of a monistic metaphysics ("these were men, / Were unitarians of the united world") tends to imply as much, just as Emerson's desire to "be a part / Of the round day, related to the sun / And planted world" so that he might be the "full executor / Of their imperfect functions" recalls the orphic poet in *Nature*.[34]

Separating the current generation of naturalists from their predecessors is what we might call the original sin of scientific method. The speaker's yearning for a knowledge of herbs in order that he might "their chemistry apply / By sweet affinities to human flesh" is arguably a Goethean commonplace, but his lament that "the divine consents / Of man and earth, of world beloved and lover, / The nectar and ambrosia, are withheld"

verges on erotic melancholy. Most explicit, however, is the account of how the "divine consents" have been lost:

> But these young scholars, who invade our hills,
> Bold as the engineer who fells the wood,
> And travelling often in the cut he makes,
> Love not the flower they pluck, and know it not,
> And all their botany is Latin names.

If the image of the "[b]old" engineer "travelling often in the cut he makes" is clearly meant to evoke the rape of nature by the Understanding, the double entendres that follow—"pluck" and "know"—provide a more subtle but equally insistent sexualization of natural philosophy. The argument is a familiar one, and Emerson's paradoxical assertion that the young scholars "know it not" denounces as partial the knowledge of scholars who bypass intuitive, poetic insights for empiricism and Latin names.

The image of humanity's fallen condition, which Emerson understands as an alienated and delusional subjectivity, is the hand. Presumably the agent plucking the flower, the hand also appears as Emerson describes our estrangement from nature, the condition when the "injured elements / . . . yield to us / Only what to our griping toil is due":

> And in the midst of spoils and slaves, we thieves
> And pirates of the universe, shut out
> Daily to a more thin and outward rind,
> Turn pale and starve. Therefore, to our sick eyes,
> The stunted trees look sick, the summer short,
> Clouds shade the sun, which will not tan our hay,
> And nothing thrives to reach its natural term. . . .

Albeit something of a surprise, the political polemic of "spoils and slaves" is consistent with the main idea of the passage: our alienation is something of our own making, and it is our rapaciousness that impoverishes us. Because we look wrongly, the argument runs, "our sick eyes" can see only a blighted landscape—regardless of what may really be there—and life itself comes to a premature end:

> And life, shorn of its venerable length . . .
> With most unhandsome calculation taught,
> Even in the hot pursuit of the best aims
> And prizes of ambition, checks its hand,
> Like Alpine cataracts frozen as they leaped,
> Chilled with a miserly comparison
> Of the toy's purchase with the length of life.

The poem's conclusion is at once sublime and cognitively difficult. We need to remind ourselves, for instance, that the frozen Alpine cataract (an image of pristine natural beauty if ever there was one) is here an emblem for both misguided human striving and the effects of that striving on the natural world. In effect, the "unhandsome" state of a blighted nature, which is a result of the fall into utilitarianism and, Emerson generally insists, a product of human perception, marks an insurmountable limit in the quest for a humane science.

Since "Blight" did not appear in Emerson's notebooks until several months after Hawthorne's story was published in the *Pioneer,* it would be absurd to take the poem as a source for **"The Birth-Mark."** By the same token, the two men were clearly covering similar intellectual territory at about the same time.[35] The alchemical and erotic emphases in Emerson's construction of the humanity of science are reminiscent of Hawthorne's story, as is the poem's decidedly unprospective gloom. So, too, the synecdochical logic of "Blight," whereby the "hand" figures a wasted landscape, is consonant with what we find in **"The Birth-Mark,"** where Georgiana's blemish takes on a disastrously general significance as the symbol of her "liability to sin, sorrow, decay, and death." A brilliant intuition of Emerson's argument, Hawthorne's tale also seems, somewhat uncannily, to echo Emerson's poem before the fact. The wordplay in the line "Love not the flower they pluck, and know it not," for instance, calls to mind a scene in **"The Birth-Mark"** when Aylmer presents Georgiana with a "flower" and urges her to "'pluck it,'" only to see that she "no sooner touche[s] the flower than the whole plant suffer[s] a *blight,* its leaves turning coalblack" (**TS,** 771; emphasis mine).[36] Even if we are not in the realm of traceable textual influence, one has to wonder whether Hawthorne did not get wind of the sentiments that appear in "Blight" during one of his walks with Emerson.

Perhaps most importantly, Emerson's poem illuminates the dual nature of the central symbol in Hawthorne's tale. While most critics take the blemish on Georgiana's cheek as a marker of female sexuality, such a reading is really an allegorical reduction, for hands accumulate throughout the tale, especially in reference to Aylmer's acts of doing or perceiving. Of course, these various hands occupy different rhetorical registers: the mark on Georgiana's cheek is a symbol while Aylmer's "grasp" remains a metaphor that, since it passes unremarked by the narrator, seems more discursive than figurative. Yet inasmuch as **"The Birth-Mark"** is a story about the tragic consequences of symbolic overdetermination, perhaps it is wise to be both more and less Aylmerish than Aylmer. If the multiplication of hands throughout the tale is explicable in Foucauldian terms—repression does not so much conceal sexuality as cause it to proliferate into all areas of life and discourse—it also points to a repressed dialectic between Georgiana's sexuality and the scientist's obsessive investigation of that sexuality (however dimly perceived). Of particular importance in this respect is the end of the tale, where the

narrator confuses Georgiana's blemish with the hand that would remove it: "The fatal Hand had grappled with the mystery of life, and was the bond by which an angelic spirit kept itself in union with a mortal frame" (**TS,** 780). Albeit dramatically satisfying, this conflation of hands hints that the tale's central symbol—ostensibly a given that brings the unhappy Aylmer to ruin—is also a product of perception.[37]

The narrator stumbles onto the dialectical interplay between subject and object only late in the story, but his slip of the tongue is prepared for in a fashion that makes it difficult to believe Hawthorne did not intend to explore just this problem (or Emerson's vision of natural philosophy). In the middle of the tale, for instance, after Aylmer sequesters Georgiana in preparation for the final experiment, she reviews the contents of her husband's library and turns to his journal:

> But, to Georgiana, the most engrossing volume was a large folio from her husband's own hand, in which he had recorded every experiment of his scientific career. . . . He handled physical details, as if there were nothing beyond them; yet spiritualized them all, and redeemed himself from materialism, by his strong and eager aspiration towards the infinite. In his grasp, the veriest clod of earth assumed a soul. . . . The volume, rich with achievements that had won renown for its author, was yet as melancholy a record as ever mortal hand had penned.
>
> (**TS,** 774-75)

Were the accumulation of "hands" in this passage not sufficient evidence that the blemish on Georgiana's cheek is, at least in part, a product of Aylmer's scientific method, what happens when she trespasses into his laboratory is decisive:

> Aylmer raised his eyes hastily, and at first reddened, then grew paler than ever, on beholding Georgiana. He rushed towards her, and seized her arm with a gripe that left the print of his fingers upon it.
>
> "Why do you come hither? Have you no trust in your husband?" cried he impetuously. "Would you throw the blight of that fatal birth-mark over my labors?"
>
> (**TS,** 776)

The principal irony here is that Aylmer's attempt to protect his "labors" from the "blight of that fatal birthmark" only serves to make the blemish reappear in another form. The scientist, we might now conclude, inhabits a vicious circle in two senses: his love for his wife fuels a destructive *libido sciendi,* and his method predisposes him to see the very mark that he would eradicate.

Should the contrast between the calm melancholy of Aylmer's journal and his subsequent rage in the laboratory make us doubt the compatibility of the romantic prospective mode and the charged watchfulness of empiricism, this is much to the point, for the passage is decidedly Emersonian in its marking of categories. Leaving aside the fact that Hawthorne's tale is again couched in the idiom of his neighbor's poem ("gripe," "blight"), what makes this moment most suggestive vis-à-vis Emerson's vision of a humane science is that the hand is duplicated in the liminal space between Georgiana's boudoir and Aylmer's laboratory. While Emerson presumably would have it that the hand—and the naturalist's awareness of the "tyrannizing unity in his constitution" (*Nature,* 83)—vanishes when poetic intuition and empiricism are married, Hawthorne's tale of a naturalist and the "tyrannizing influence acquired by one idea over his mind" (*TS,* 767) implies that the crossing between poetry and science is where the hand must appear.[38] If *Nature* concludes with a call for a "correspondent revolution," promising that a world which "lies broken and in heaps" will be restored to its "original and eternal beauty" when science is sufficient to the needs of the spirit and recognizes that "[l]ove is as much its demand, as perception" (*Nature,* 91), Hawthorne's eccentric tale depicts the tragic consequences of such a visionary naturalism.

Notes

1. Published criticism on "The Birth-mark" is extensive. For a good, brief overview of the tale's critical history up to the early 1970s, see David J. Baxter, "'The Birthmark' in Perspective," *Nathaniel Hawthorne Journal* (1975): 232-40.

2. Richard Holt Hutton, review of Hawthorne in *National Review* 11 (October 1860); quoted in Baxter, "'The Birthmark' in Perspective," 232. For contemporary reviews, see J. Donald Crowley, ed., *Hawthorne: The Critical Heritage* (New York: Barnes and Noble, 1970).

3. Arguably a foundational treatment of the tale, especially for the New Critics, is R. B. Heilman, "Hawthorne's 'The Birthmark': Science as Religion," *South Atlantic Quarterly* 48 (1949): 575-83. Other studies in this vein include Richard Harter Fogle, *Hawthorne's Fiction: The Light and the Dark* (Norman: Univ. of Oklahoma Press, 1964), 117-31; Alfred S. Reid, "Hawthorne's Humanism: 'The Birthmark' and Sir Kenelm Digby," *American Literature* 38 (1966): 337-51; David M. Van Leer, "Aylmer's Library: Transcendental Alchemy in Hawthorne's 'The Birthmark,'" *ESQ: A Journal of the American Renaissance* 22 (1976): 211-20; John Gatta Jr., "Aylmer's Alchemy in 'The Birthmark,'" *Philological Quarterly* 57 (1978): 399-413; Mary E. Rucker, "Science and Art in Hawthorne's 'The Birth-mark,'" *Nineteenth-Century Literature* 41 (1987): 445-61; and Bar-

bara Eckstein, "Hawthorne's 'The Birthmark': Science and Romance as Belief," *Studies in Short Fiction* 26 (1989): 511-19.

4. See Nathaniel Hawthorne, *Tales and Sketches* (New York: Library of America, 1982), 766. All subsequent references to Hawthorne's fiction will be to this edition, cited parenthetically as *TS.* The most influential application of psychoanalytic theory to Hawthorne remains Frederick Crews, *The Sins of the Fathers: Hawthorne's Psychological Themes* (1966; Berkeley and Los Angeles: Univ. of California Press, 1989). Detailed psychological treatments of "The Birth-mark" include Simon O. Lesser, *Fiction and the Unconscious* (Boston: Beacon Hill, 1945), 87-98; James Quinn and Ross Baldessarini, "'The Birth-Mark': A Deathmark," *University of Hartford Studies in Literature* 13 (1981): 91-98; and Benjamin Franklin V, "Aylmer's Lovely Plant and Colorless Liquor; or the 'Birth-Mark' Reconsidered," *Journal of Evolutionary Psychology* 2 (1981): 125-36. More theorized psychological readings include the following: Barbara Johnson, "Is Female to Male as Ground Is to Figure?" in *Feminism and Psychoanalysis,* ed. Richard Feldstein and Judith Roof (Ithaca: Cornell Univ. Press, 1989), 255-68; and Lynn Shakinovsky, "The Return of the Repressed: Illiteracy and the Death of the Narrative in Hawthorne's 'The Birthmark,'" *ATQ,* n.s., 9 (1995): 269-81. Jules Zanger, in "Speaking of the Unspeakable: Hawthorne's 'The Birthmark,'" *Modern Philology* 80 (1983): 364-71, gives the psychological reading a historical twist by locating "The Birth-Mark" in the context of nineteenth-century taboos about menstruation.

5. See Nicholas K. Bromell, "'The Bloody Hand' of Labor: Work, Class, and Gender in Three Stories by Hawthorne," *American Quarterly* 42 (1990): 542-64; Joel Pfister, *The Production of Personal Life: Class, Gender, and the Psychological in Hawthorne's Fiction* (Stanford: Stanford Univ. Press, 1991), 29-48; and Cindy Weinstein, "The Invisible Hand Made Visible: 'The Birth-mark,'" *Nineteenth-Century Literature* 48 (1993): 44-73.

6. A selective list of studies that consider the problem of Hawthorne's transcendentalism includes Darrel Abel, "Hawthorne's Skepticism about Social Reform: With Especial Reference to *The Blithedale Romance,*" *University of Kansas City Review* 19 (1953): 181-93, revised and incorporated in Abel's book *The Moral Picturesque: Studies in Hawthorne's Fiction* (West Lafayette: Purdue Univ. Press, 1988), 270-97; B. R. McElderry Jr., "The Transcendental Hawthorne," *Midwest Quarterly* 2 (1961): 307-23; Joseph T. Gordon,

"Nathaniel Hawthorne and Brook Farm," *Emerson Society Quarterly* 33 (1963): 51-61; James M. Cox, "Emerson and Hawthorne: Trust and Doubt," *Virginia Quarterly Review* 45 (1969): 88-107; Gustaaf Van Cromphout, "Emerson, Hawthorne, and *The Blithedale Romance*," *Georgia Review* 25 (1971): 471-80; Nancy L. Bunge, "Beyond Transcendentalism: Hawthorne on Perspective and Reality," *North Dakota Quarterly* 45 (1977): 43-49; Patricia Ann Carlson, *Hawthorne's Functional Settings: A Study of Artistic Method* (Amsterdam: Rodopi, 1977), 30-61; Taylor Stoehr, "Art vs. Utopia: The Case of Nathaniel Hawthorne and Brook Farm," *Antioch Review* 36 (1978): 89-102; and Gay Wilson Allen, "Emerson and Hawthorne, Neighbors," *Essex Institute Historical Collections* 118 (1982): 20-30.

The following studies are devoted specifically to Hawthorne's Old Manse fiction and, in some cases, its Emersonianism: John C. Willoughby, "'The Old Manse' Revisited: Some Analogues for Art," *New England Quarterly* 46 (1973): 45-61; Stephen Adams, "Unifying Structures in *Mosses from an Old Manse*," *Studies in American Fiction* 8 (1980): 147-63; Teresa Toulouse, "Spatial Relations in 'The Old Manse,'" *ESQ: A Journal of the American Renaissance* 28 (1982): 154-66; James Walters, "'The Old Manse': The Pastoral Precinct of Hawthorne's Fiction," *American Transcendental Quarterly* 51 (1981): 195-209; John S. Martin, "The Other Side of Concord: A Critique of Emerson in Hawthorne's 'The Old Manse,'" *New England Quarterly* 58 (1985): 453-58; Larry J. Reynolds, "Hawthorne and Emerson in 'The Old Manse,'" *Studies in the Novel* 23 (1991): 60-81; Leland S. Person Jr., "Hawthorne's Bliss of Paternity: Sophia's Absence from 'The Old Manse,'" *Studies in the Novel* 23 (1991): 46-59; Joel Porte, *In Respect to Egotism: Studies in American Romantic Writing* (Cambridge: Cambridge Univ. Press, 1991), 125-33; and Jonathan A. Cook, "New Heavens, Poor Old Earth: Satirical Apocalypse in Hawthorne's *Mosses from an Old Manse*," *ESQ: A Journal of the American Renaissance* 39 (1993): 209-51.

Deserving separate mention is the work of John J. McDonald: "The Old Manse Period Canon," *Nathaniel Hawthorne Journal* (1972): 13-39; "'The Old Manse' and Its Mosses: The Inception and Development of *Mosses from an Old Manse*," *Texas Studies in Literature and Language* 16 (1974): 77-108; "A Sophia Hawthorne Journal, 1843-1844," *Nathaniel Hawthorne Journal* (1974):

1-30; and "A Guide to Primary Source Materials for the Study of Hawthorne's Old Manse Period," *Studies in the American Renaissance* (1977): 261-312.

7. Ralph Waldo Emerson, "Love," in *Essays* (Boston: James Munroe, 1841), 141; hereafter cited parenthetically. Inasmuch as I draw on several editions of Emerson's work, a word of explanation is in order. Because Emerson often revised his essays and lectures for republication (this is especially true of "Love" and *Nature*, the two texts that are central to my argument), and because I am concerned with Hawthorne's reaction to Emerson, it has seemed essential to use the earliest printings on occasion. Thus, all subsequent references to "Love" are to the first printing in *Essays*, and all references to *Nature* are to the first edition (Boston: James Munroe, 1836), also cited parenthetically. In the case of the journals and lesser-known early lectures, I have used the standard scholarly editions. Elsewhere it has seemed acceptable to be guided by convenience, and I quote from the Library of America edition of Emerson's *Essays and Lectures*, ed. Joel Porte (New York, 1983); hereafter cited parenthetically as *LA*.

8. See F. O. Matthiessen, *American Renaissance: Art and Expression in the Age of Emerson and Whitman* (New York: Oxford Univ. Press, 1941), 254. A recent essay in a traditional vein is Liz Rosenberg, "'The Best That Earth Could Offer': 'The Birth-mark,' A Newlywed's Story," *Studies in Short Fiction* 30 (1993): 145-51. For a provocative account of the ideological texturing of the Hawthorne marriage, see T. Walter Herbert, *Dearest Beloved: The Hawthornes and the Making of the Middle-Class Family* (Berkeley and Los Angeles: Univ. of California Press, 1993).

9. An excellent essay on Emerson and the topic of love is Eric Murphy Selinger's "'Too Pathetic, Too Pitiable': Emerson's Lessons in Love's Philosophy," *ESQ: A Journal of the American Renaissance* 40 (1994): 139-82. Also of interest is Carl F. Strauch, "Hatred's Swift Repulsions: Emerson, Margaret Fuller, and Others," *Studies in Romanticism* 7 (1967): 65-103. For a close reading of "Love," see Carol Clancey Harter, "Emerson's Rhetorical Failure in 'Love,'" *ESQ: A Journal of the American Renaissance* 18 (1972): 227-33.

10. Lest the suggestion that "Love" is a source for "The Birth-mark" seem an Aylmerish bit of source hunting, I would point out that at least two other critics have made a similar observation. Porte suggests in passing that "Hawthorne's tale may actu-

ally have been intended as a devastating gloss on a frigidly high-minded passage in Emerson's 'Love'" (*In Respect to Egotism,* 146), while Selinger remarks that "a counter" to Emerson's apparent belief in an "unbelievable process of mutual improvement" "seems to underlie the plot of 'The Birth-mark'" ("'Too Pathetic, Too Pitiable,'" 162).

11. Emerson confesses to reservations about his essay in a journal passage: "I finish this morning transcribing my old Essay on Love, but I see well its inadequateness." Imagining a future that we might, after Plato, describe as free love, Emerson continues: "In silence we must wrap much of our life, because it is too fine for speech. . . . We do not live as angels eager to introduce each other to new perfections in our brothers & sisters . . . but that which passes for love in the world gets official, & instead of embracing, hates all the divine traits that dare to appear in other persons. A better & holier society will mend this selfish cowardice and we shall have brave ties of affection not petrified by law . . . to last for one year, for five years, or for life; but drawing their date like all friendship from itself only; brave as I said because innocent & religiously abstinent from the connubial endearments, being a higher league on a purely spiritual basis" (*The Journals and Miscellaneous Notebooks of Ralph Waldo Emerson,* ed. William H. Gilman and Ralph H. Orth et al. [Cambridge: Harvard Univ. Press, Belknap Press, 1960-82], 7:368); hereafter cited parenthetically as *JMN.*

12. For Emerson's interest in Swedenborg and the idea of correspondence, as put forth in Sampson Reed's *Growth of the Mind,* see Stephen E. Whicher, *Freedom and Fate: An Inner Life of Ralph Waldo Emerson* (Philadelphia: Univ. of Pennsylvania Press, 1953), 87-88. On Clarence Hotson's extensive work on Emerson and Swedenborg, see Joel Myerson, ed., *The Transcendentalists: A Review of Research and Criticism* (New York: Modern Language Association, 1984), 148-49, 159, 374.

13. For the idea that Georgiana acts out the conventions of the romance heroine, see Eckstein, "Hawthorne's 'The Birthmark': Science and Romance as Belief"; and Ellen E. Westbrook, "Probable Improbabilities: Verisimilar Romance in Hawthorne's 'The Birth-mark,'" *ATQ,* n.s., 3 (1989): 203-17.

14. Thomas F. Scheer ("Aylmer's Divine Roles in 'The Birthmark,'" *American Transcendental Quarterly* 22 [1974]: 108) provides a short but insightful account of the tale's "Puritan" ironies, while Agnes McNeill Donohue observes flatly that the

narrator's account of Georgiana's "'liability to sin, sorrow, decay, and death'" is "a perfect Calvinist description of Original Sin" (*Hawthorne: Calvin's Ironic Stepchild* [Kent, OH: Kent State Univ. Press, 1985], 188).

15. A useful recent collection of essays on the topic is Andrew Cunningham and Nicholas Jardine, eds., *Romanticism and the Sciences* (Cambridge: Cambridge Univ. Press, 1990); see esp. David Van Leer, who offers a different estimate of Emerson's interest in science ("Nature's Book: The Language of Science in the American Renaissance," 307-21).

16. See Stephen E. Whicher and Robert E. Spiller, eds., *The Early Lectures of Ralph Waldo Emerson* (Cambridge: Harvard Univ. Press, Belknap Press, 1966), 1:1. On Emerson and science, see Harry Hayden Clark, "Emerson and Science," *Philological Quarterly* 10 (1931): 225-60; Jonathan Bishop, *Emerson on the Soul* (Cambridge: Harvard Univ. Press, 1964), 53-57; Gay Wilson Allen, "A New Look at Emerson and Science," in *Literature and Ideas in America: Essays in Memory of Harry Hayden Clark,* ed. Robert Falk (Athens: Ohio Univ. Press, 1975), 58-78, reprinted in *Critical Essays on Ralph Waldo Emerson,* ed. Robert E. Burkholder and Joel Myerson (Boston: G. K. Hall, 1983), 434-48; David Robinson, "Emerson's Natural Theology and the Paris Naturalists: Toward a Theory of Animated Nature," *Journal of the History of Ideas* 41 (1980): 69-88, reprinted in Burkholder and Myerson, *Critical Essays,* 501-20; and Eric Wilson, *Emerson's Sublime Science* (New York: St. Martin's Press, 1999).

17. For a detailed discussion of the impact of the visit to Paris, see Lee Rust Brown, *The Emerson Museum: Practical Romanticism and the Pursuit of the Whole* (Cambridge: Harvard Univ. Press, 1997), 59-168, who argues that the "association of natural history with the marriage ceremony persisted in Emerson's reflections on nature" (60).

18. Good overviews of the "humanity of science" can be found in Whicher, *Freedom and Fate,* 89-91; and Sherman Paul, *Emerson's Angle of Vision: Man and Nature in American Experience* (Cambridge: Harvard Univ. Press, 1952), 208-20. Robinson points out links between Emerson's early scientific lectures and his later work ("Emerson's Natural Theology and the Paris Naturalists").

19. Stephen E. Whicher, "Ralph Waldo Emerson," in *Eight American Writers: An Anthology of American Literature,* ed. Norman Foerster and Robert P. Falk (New York: Norton, 1963), 188 n. 1.

20. This passage is essentially a more poetic version of the "Humanity of Science" passage: "Hence arises a corollary which every page of modern history repeats; that is, that science should be humanly studied. It will publish all its plan to a spirit akin to that which framed it. When science shall be studied with piety; when in a soul alive with moral sentiments, the antecedence of spirits is presupposed; then humanity advances, step by step with the opening of the intellect and its command over nature. Shall the problems never be assayed in a feeling of their beauty? Is not the poetic side of science entitled to be felt and presented by its investigators? Is it quite impossible to unite severe science with a poetic vision? Nature's laws are as charming to Taste and as pregnant with moral meaning as they are geometrically exact. Why then must the student freeze his sensibilities and cease to be a man that he may be a chemist and physiologist?" (*Early Lectures,* 2:36). (N. B. In the 1836 edition of *Nature,* page 94 is misnumbered as 92.)

21. Discussions of *Nature* are legion. An illuminating account of the development of the treatise and the visionary ambiguities of its close is B[arbara] L. Packer, *Emerson's Fall: A New Interpretation of the Major Essays* (New York: Continuum, 1982), 22-84.

22. That Aylmer is an alchemist is well established. In addition to the studies by Van Leer ("Aylmer's Library") and John Gatta Jr. ("Aylmer's Alchemy in 'The Birthmark'"), see Shannon Burns, "Alchemy and 'The Birth-Mark,'" *American Transcendental Quarterly* 42 (1979): 147-58. On alchemy more generally, see Randall A. Clack, *The Marriage of Heaven and Earth: Alchemical Regeneration in the Works of Taylor, Poe, Hawthorne, and Fuller* (Westport, CT: Greenwood Press, 2000).

23. Just how little Emerson thought of human understanding is suggested by his observation that "[a]t present . . . [man's] relation to nature, his power over it, is through the understanding; as by manure; the economic use of fire, wind, water, and the mariner's needle; steam, coal, chemical agriculture; the repairs of the human body by the dentist and the surgeon" (*Nature,* 89-90). Notwithstanding Emerson's tonelessness, his giving manure pride of place here is likely a bit of polemical humor.

24. Less enthusiastic is "Nominalist and Realist," where Emerson writes: "Homœopathy is insignificant as an art of healing, but of great value as criticism on the hygeia or medical practice of the time. So with Mesmerism, Swedenborgism, Fourierism, and the Millennial Church; they are poor pretensions enough, but good criticism on the science, philosophy, and preaching of the day" (*LA,* 580).

25. For Sophia's illnesses and various treatments, see, for example, James R. Mellow, *Nathaniel Hawthorne in His Times* (Boston: Houghton Mifflin, 1980), 114-16, 131-35.

26. Nathaniel to Sophia Hawthorne, Brook Farm, 18 [16] October [1841], *The Letters, 1813-1843,* ed. Thomas Woodson, L. Neal Smith, and Norman Holmes Pearson, vol. 15 of *The Centenary Edition of the Works of Nathaniel Hawthorne* (Columbus: Ohio State Univ. Press, 1984), 588-90.

27. The most thorough treatment of Hawthorne and pseudoscience is Taylor Stoehr, *Hawthorne's Mad Scientists: Pseudoscience and Social Science in Nineteenth-Century Life* (Hamden, CT: Archon, 1978). Both Gatta ("Aylmer's Alchemy in 'The Birthmark'") and Steven Youra ("'The Fatal Hand': A Sign of Confusion in Hawthorne's 'The Birth-Mark,'" *American Transcendental Quarterly* 60 [1986]: 43-51) read the tale in the context of Hawthorne's experience with mesmerism.

28. Heilman, "Science as Religion," 582. One of the oddities of the tale's critical history is that commentators seem reluctant to acknowledge the possible local referents for Hawthorne's allegory. Heilman never mentions Emerson, and even interpreters who locate "The Birth-mark" in the context of transcendentalism do so in a way that seems to obscure the specificity of its critical energies. Baxter, for instance, reads the tale as a response to transcendentalism and even concludes his essay by recalling (via an introduction to Walt Whitman) Emerson's observation that empirical science is "'apt to cloud the sight,'" yet he never seems to see the matter as anything other than one of competing perspectives in the history of ideas ("'The Birthmark' in Perspective," 239).

29. "The American Scholar" hints that Emerson saw in Swedenborg an answer to the problem of (sexual) evil: "Especially did his shade-loving muse hover over and interpret the lower parts of nature; he showed the mysterious bond that allies moral evil to the foul material forms, and has given in epical parables a theory of insanity, of beasts, of unclean and fearful things" (*LA,* 69-70).

30. Nathaniel Hawthorne, *The American Notebooks,* ed. Claude M. Simpson, vol. 8 of *The Centenary Edition of the Works of Nathaniel Hawthorne* (Columbus: Ohio State Univ. Press, 1972), 336.

Emerson recounts Hosmer's practical wisdom in "Agriculture of Massachusetts," an essay that appeared in the *Dial* in July 1842 (123-27). "The Hall of Fantasy," written within a few months of Hawthorne's journal entry, describes Emerson in similar fashion: "Mr. Emerson was likewise there, leaning against one of the pillars, and surrounded by an admiring crowd of writers and readers of the Dial, and all manner of Transcendentalists and disciples of the Newness, most of whom betrayed the power of his intellect by its modifying influence upon their own. He had come into the hall, in search, I suppose, either of a fact or a real man; both of which he was as likely to find there as elsewhere. No more earnest seeker after truth than he, and few more successful finders of it; although, sometimes, the truth assumes a mystic unreality and shadowyness in his grasp" (*TS,* 1491 n. 740.34).

31. As we might deduce from Whicher's expedient of introducing *Freedom and Fate* with chronologies of Emerson's outer and inner lives (xiii-xvi), philosophical idealism is less a component of Emerson's thought than an attitude or perspective from which all else follows. The most searching treatment of Emerson's Kantianism is David M. Van Leer's brilliant, closely grained *Emerson's Epistemology: The Argument of the Essays* (Cambridge: Cambridge Univ. Press, 1986).

32. Emerson, *Early Lectures,* 1:17.

33. It is also worth recalling that Emerson read and quoted from Sir Charles Bell's work *The Hand: Its Mechanism and Vital Endowments as Evincing Design* (London: William Pickering, 1833). One of the Bridgewater treatises in natural theology, Bell's book might have made the hand a fit metaphor for marking the compatibility of science and religion. Hawthorne may have been familiar with the book as well. It is not mentioned in Marion L. Kesselring (*Hawthorne's Reading, 1828-1850: A Transcription and Identification of Titles Recorded in the Charge-Books of the Salem Athenaem* [New York: New York Public Library, 1949]), but John L. Idol Jr. ("A Show of Hands in 'The Artist of the Beautiful,'" *Studies in Short Fiction* 22 [1985]) alleges that Hawthorne owned a copy of the treatise, on the strength of a letter from B. Bernard Cohen (458 n. 6).

34. Ralph Waldo Emerson, "Blight," in *Collected Poems and Translations,* ed. Harold Bloom and Paul Kane (New York: Library of America, 1994), 111-12. Further passages from the poem are quoted from these pages.

35. A draft of the poem, which seems to have come as a reaction to a visit to Fruitlands with Ellery Channing, shows up in Emerson's notebooks in July 1843; see *JMN,* 8:433-38. Part of the poem was published in the *Dial* in January 1844 (405-6).

36. For the sexual overtones of this moment in Hawthorne's tale, see Franklin, "Aylmer's Lovely Plant."

37. While Youra tends to oversimplify the tale, I agree that "[t]he equation of hands culminates a series of instances which confirm that Aylmer himself creates the mark he vows to eradicate" ("'The Fatal Hand,'" 43).

38. A similar phrase crops up in "The American Scholar," where Emerson describes the "young mind . . . tyrannized over by its own unifying instinct" and prophesies that, when the schoolboy "has learned to worship the soul, and to see that the natural philosophy that now is, is only the first gropings of its gigantic hand, he shall look forward to an ever expanding knowledge as to a becoming creator" (*LA,* 55-56).

FURTHER READING

Criticism

Bromell, Nicholas K. "'The Bloody Hand' of Labor: Work, Class, and Gender in Three Stories by Hawthorne." *American Quarterly* 42, no. 4 (December 1990): 542-64.
> Compares "The Birthmark" to Hawthorne's "The Artist of the Beautiful" and "Drowne's Wooden Image" in terms of Hawthorne's exploration of the nature of art and artistic activity.

Brooks, Cleanth, and Robert Penn Warren. "Interpretation: 'The Birthmark.'" In *Literary Theories in Praxis,* edited by Shirley F. Staton, pp. 32-5. Philadelphia: The University of Pennsylvania Press, 1987.
> Expands on the characterization of the story as a simple parable.

Chambers, Jane. "Two Legends of Temperance: Spenser's and Hawthorne's." *ESQ: A Journal of the American Renaissance* 20, no. 4 (1974): 275-79.
> Discusses the influence of Spenser's *The Faerie Queene* on "The Birthmark."

Heilman, Robert Bechtold. "Hawthorne's 'The Birthmark': Science as Religion." In *Literary Theories in Praxis,* edited by Shirley F. Staton, pp. 35-42. Philadelphia: The University of Pennsylvania Press, 1987.

Asserts that the complex theme of the story informs and enhances the narrative strength of "The Birthmark."

Rucker, Mary E. "Science and Art in Hawthorne's 'The Birth-Mark.'" *Nineteenth-Century Literature* 41, no. 4 (March 1987): 445-61.

Examines the theme of "The Birthmark" within the context of Hawthorne's oeuvre.

Thompson, W. R. "Aminadab in Hawthorne's 'The Birthmark.'" *Modern Language Notes* 70, no. 6 (June 1955): 413-15.

Argues that the character Aminadab is based on a Biblical character and is used by Hawthorne to symbolize "religion subverted to the ends of science."

Weinstein, Cindy. "The Invisible Hand Made Visible: 'The Birth-Mark.'" *Nineteenth-Century Literature* 48, no. 1 (June 1993): 44-73.

Analyzes "the complex relations between allegory, the market, and the body" to illuminate Hawthorne's use of allegory in "The Birthmark."

Zanger, Jules. "Speaking of the Unspeakable: Hawthorne's 'The Birthmark.'" *Modern Philology* 80, no. 4 (May 1983): 364-71.

Discusses "[t]he particularly tabooed nature of menstruation in nineteenth-century American genteel society" and how this may be embedded in the depiction of action, symbols, and themes in "The Birthmark."

Additional coverage of Hawthorne's life and career is contained in the following sources published by Thomson Gale: *American Writers; American Writers: The Classics,* **Vol. 1;** *American Writers Retrospective Supplement,* **Vol. 1;** *Authors and Artists for Young Adults,* **Vol. 18;** *Beacham's Encyclopedia of Popular Fiction: Biography and Resources,* **Vol. 2;** *Beacham's Guide to Literature for Young Adults,* **Vol. 3;** *Children's Literature Review,* **Vol. 103;** *Concise Dictionary of American Literary Biography, 1640-1865; Dictionary of Literary Biography,* **Vols. 1, 74, 183, 223, 269;** *DISCovering Authors; DISCovering Authors: British; DISCovering Authors: Canadian; DISCovering Authors Modules: Most-Studied Authors* **and** *Novelists; DISCovering Authors 3.0; Exploring Novels; Exploring Short Stories; Gothic Literature: A Gale Critical Companion; Literature and Its Times,* **Vol. 1;** *Literature Resource Center; Nineteenth-Century Literature Criticism,* **Vols. 2, 10, 17, 23, 39, 79, 95, 158;** *Novels for Students,* **Vols. 1, 20;** *Reference Guide to American Literature,* **Ed. 4;** *Reference Guide to Short Fiction,* **Ed. 2;** *St. James Guide to Horror, Ghost, and Gothic Writers; Short Stories for Students,* **Vols. 1, 7, 11, 15;** *Short Story Criticism,* **Vols. 3, 29, 39;** *Supernatural Fiction Writers,* **Vol. 1;** *Twayne's United States Authors; World Literature Criticism; Writers for Children;* **and** *Yesterday's Authors of Books for Children,* **Vol. 2.**

Horacio Quiroga
1878-1937

(Full name Horacio Sylvestre Quiroga; also wrote under the pseudonym Guillermo Eynhardt) Uruguayan short story and novella writer, essayist, poet, playwright, and journalist.

The following entry provides an overview of Quiroga's life and works of short fiction.

INTRODUCTION

Considered one of Latin America's greatest short story writers, Quiroga is best known for stories portraying conflict between an individual and the natural hazards of the South American jungle. Reflecting the influence of the works of Edgar Allan Poe, Quiroga's stories reflect the author's preoccupation with madness, terror, and death, and, like Poe's, are often narrowly focused in order to evoke a single mood or stunning effect.

BIOGRAPHICAL INFORMATION

Quiroga was born December 31, 1878 in Salto, Uruguay, to an Argentine vice-consul and the daughter of a highly respected Salto family. Within three months of Quiroga's birth his father was accidentally shot and killed, and in 1895 his stepfather committed suicide. These deaths were the first in a series of bizarre tragedies that continued to plague Quiroga throughout his life and to which critics attribute his obsession with violence and the macabre. During his school years Quiroga preferred travel literature and periodicals to his formal studies and distinguished himself at the University of Montevideo through his skill in photography, bicycling, and carpentry rather than scholarship. His first essays were published in Salto newspapers in 1897 under the pseudonym Guillermo Eynhardt, the hero of a nineteenth-century French novel. Two years later he founded *Revista del Salto,* a short-lived literary magazine that featured works influenced by Poe and by *modernismo,* a literary movement that dominated Spanish American literature from approximately 1890 to 1910. Through their innovative use of language, meter, and rhyme, the *modernistas* revitalized Spanish literature, which had seen little change since the seventeenth century, and created a uniquely Latin American form. Influenced by literary Romanticism and French Symbolism, the *modernistas* characteristically rejected

Naturalism and materialism in an attempt to create timeless works that avoided historical or topical issues. An artistic pilgrimage to Paris in 1900 afforded Quiroga an opportunity to attend *modernista* gatherings and to meet the leader of the movement, the Nicaraguan poet Rubén Darío, but Quiroga quickly became disillusioned with the Parisian literary community and a few months later returned to South America. Upon his return, Quiroga founded the first *modernista* group in Uruguay, "El Consistorio de Gay Saber," and in 1901 he published his first book, *Los arrecifes de coral,* a collection of Decadent poetry and short stories that was critically unsuccessful.

In 1902 Quiroga accidentally shot and killed Federico Ferrando, a member of "El Consistorio" and one of Quiroga's best friends. Quiroga left Montevideo for Buenos Aires, where he was soon appointed by the Argentine government to a commission formed to study the ruins of ancient Jesuit settlements in Misiones, a jungle province in northern Argentina. The commission's research expedition had a dramatic effect on his life and career: captivated by pioneer life in the tropical virgin forest, Quiroga later made the area his home and the setting for many of his most famous stories. After an unsuccessful attempt to grow cotton in the Chaco region of northern Argentina, Quiroga returned to Buenos Aires to write and teach secondary school. In 1910 he made a second journey to Misiones, accompanied by his young wife, and the couple remained there for five years while Quiroga farmed and experimented with making charcoal and distilling orange liqueur. Marital discord, particularly arguments about childrearing, is believed to be the reason that Quiroga's wife committed suicide in 1915. After her death Quiroga returned to Buenos Aires and entered into the most prolific period of his literary career: between 1916 and 1926 he published six of his most popular story collections, numerous articles and essays, two series of weekly film reviews, and the drama *Las sacrificadas* (1920). Quiroga's literary output declined significantly after 1926. Failing health led to a constant preoccupation with death, reflected in the morbidity of his final story collection, *Más allá* (1935). In 1937, after learning that he had cancer, Quiroga committed suicide.

MAJOR WORKS OF SHORT FICTION

While his early writings in *Los arrecifes de coral* reflected the aestheticism of *modernismo*, Quiroga gradually turned to the realistic technique for which he later became known. His second collection, *El crimen del otro* (1904), depicts the abnormal and horrific, relying on careful attention to detail to evoke disturbed states of mind and achieve extremely vivid effects. The influence of Poe dominates the collection: the title story concerns two characters obsessed with the theme of madness in Poe's story "The Cask of Amontillado." As in the Poe story, one character inters the other alive. Quiroga's short story "Los perseguidos" ("The Pursued"; also collected in *El crimen del otro*) and the novella *Historia de un amor turbio* (1908) are among the earliest examples of his transformation of autobiographical episodes into fiction. Quiroga acknowledged that he was the model for the protagonist in *Historia de un amor turbio,* one of several pieces in which he portrayed a passionate affair between a young woman and an older man. These works also signify Quiroga's final renunciation of *modernismo* in favor of realism and psychological analysis influenced by the works of Fyodor Dostoevsky and Guy de Maupassant.

With the publication of the short story collection *Cuentos de amor, de locura y de muerte* (1917), his first book to include stories set in the jungle of Misiones, Quiroga achieved widespread popularity and critical acclaim. These stories and those in the collections that followed are distinguished by their simple, direct depiction of the brutality of jungle life. Many portray a lone individual struggling for survival, often in conflict with nature, which is seen as an omnipotent and merciless force. Typical of these is "La insolación" ("Sunstroke"), in which the protagonist, who underestimates the power of the afternoon sun and overestimates his own strength, is felled by sunstroke while attempting to clear his cotton plantation. Death, particularly the experience of dying, is a recurring motif in Quiroga's works, including "El hombre muerto" ("The Dead Man"), in which a man who has received a fatal machete wound struggles to accept his imminent death. Animals are featured as protagonists in many of the Misiones stories, particularly in his collection of children's fables, *Cuentos de la selva* (1918; *South American Jungle Tales*). In stories such as "Anaconda," Quiroga contrasts animal instinct with human reason, which he considers inferior to instinct and insufficient for survival in the wilderness. *Los desterrados* (1926) comprises portraits of the "exiles" peculiar to the Argentine jungle: pioneers, drunkards, derelicts, day laborers, and eccentrics fleeing civilization. Stories in this collection, such as "Los mensú" ("The Contract Workers") and "Una bofetada" ("A Slap in the Face"), also provide social commentary on the exploitation of the South American contract worker.

CRITICAL RECEPTION

Critics have praised Quiroga's treatment of physical suffering and death as objective and unsentimental, and have maintained that his terse prose style heightens the effect of his stories by eliminating all extraneous details. Quiroga's *South American Jungle Tales* have been favorably compared to Rudyard Kipling's animal stories, and some critics have noted that the objectivity with which Quiroga portrays his characters in the Misiones stories evokes sympathy for their plight. Commentators have disagreed about Quiroga's technical skill as a short story writer. Many have praised his masterful utilization of the tenets set out in his "Decálogo del perfecto cuentista" ("Decalogue of the Perfect Short Story Writer"; collected in *Obras inéditas y desconocidas*), while others maintain that his stories are undisciplined and uneven in style. Most critics, however, laud Quiroga's genius in evoking the atmosphere of Misiones in powerful, vivid narratives.

PRINCIPAL WORKS

Short Fiction

Los arrecifes de coral 1901
El crimen del otro 1904
Historia de un amor turbio 1908

Cuentos de amor, de locura y de muerte 1917
Cuentos de la selva [*South American Jungle Tales*] 1918
El salvaje 1920
Anaconda 1921
El desierto 1924
Los desterrados 1926
Pasado amor 1929
Más allá 1935
Cuentos. 13 vols. 1937-45
Obras inéditas y desconocidas. 8 vols. [edited by Ángel
    Rama] 1969-73
Our First Smoke 1972
The Decapitated Chicken, and Other Stories [translated
    by Margaret Sayers Peden] 1976
The Exiles and Other Stories [translated by J. David
    Danielson] 1987

Other Major Works

Las sacrificadas [first publication] (play) 1920
El mundo ideal de Horacio Quiroga (letters) 1975

CRITICISM

Jefferson Rea Spell (essay date 1944)

SOURCE: Spell, Jefferson Rea. "Renowned Short-Story
Writer, Horacio Quiroga." In *Contemporary Spanish-
American Fiction*, 1944. Reprint edition, pp. 153-78.
New York: Biblo and Tannen, 1968.

[*In the following essay, first published in 1944, Spell offers a detailed overview of Quiroga's life and works.*]

Among the forms of fiction for which writers of Spanish America have shown a decided preference, particularly during the present century, is the brief prose narrative, or *cuento*. Nearly all of the outstanding novelists
of this period—Gallegos, Güiraldes, Gálvez, Azuela,
and Barrios—in addition to their longer works, have
written *cuentos*. The word *cuento,* however, on account
of its various connotations, is a nondescript and consequently unsatisfactory term. It is used, as an examination of any complete collection of *cuentos* will testify,
to designate anecdotes and fables; legendary accounts,
such as the *tradiciones* of Ricardo Palma; essays of
manners and customs, in the manner of *Pago Chico, a*
collection of *cuentos* by the Argentine writer Roberto J.
Payró; prose poems, such as the *cuentos* by Amado
Nervo, Díaz Rodríguez, and others, with emphasis on
style rather than on other fictional elements; and short
stories in the modern sense of the word—unfortunately

rare both in Spain and Spanish America—such as "La
Galleguita" ("The Galician Girl") by Hernández Catá,
"El Milagro" ("The Miracle") by Mateo Booz, "El Al-
filer" ("The Pin") by V. García Calderón, and "María
del Carmen" by Francisco Espinola—all of which are
in technique lineal descendants of the short story as created by Poe and Maupassant.

Their brevity, as in the case of poetry, has facilitated the
publication, within the last two decades, of collections
of *cuentos*. The first of these, *Los mejores Cuentos
Americanos* (*The Best American Tales*), 1920, contains
the cream of Spanish-American short stories—in the
judgment of the compiler, Ventura García Calderón, an
excellent critic. The only other collection of a general
nature, exclusive of school texts, is the *Antología del
Cuento hispano-americano* (*Anthology of Spanish-
American Tales*), 1939, compiled by Antonio R. Man-
zor. Collections of the best *cuentos* of a single country
or region—Mexico, Venezuela, Colombia, Chile, and
the River Plate[1]—and of individual writers—Viana,
Lillo, Blanco Fombona, Quiroga, López Albújar, and
José de la Cuadra[2]—have also been compiled. As compared with the best of modern short stories, the *cuentos*
of these six writers are technically deficient; nevertheless the *criollismo* or vital concern of each for his native land and people has given them distinction. The
degeneracy of the *gaucho* of Viana's Uruguay; the piti-
less treatment of the unorganized workers in the coal
mines of Lillo's Chile; the most intimate vices of the
montuvios, a people of Indian, Negro, and white blood
who live on the coast of José de la Cuadra's Ecuador;
the ignorance and superstition of the people, the lack of
sincerity on the part of revolutionary leaders, and the
futility of democracy in Blanco Fombona's Venezuela;
and not only the injustice of the whites towards the Indians, but also their own cruelty and viciousness in López Albújar's Peru are all brought out in these *cuentos*.
Aside from their deep concern with these problems,
Blanco Fombona and López Albújar sought beauty in
style, both having been strongly influenced by the
"modernista" movement. Although subordinate to the
human element, the background—whether it be the
plains of Uruguay, the coal mines of Chile, the forests
of Venezuela, the Andean plateaus of Peru, or the
jungles of the Ecuadorian lowlands—is an important
factor with all these writers. In contrast, Horacio
Quiroga, acknowledged peer of Spanish-American
short-story writers, is less interested in people; instead,
in the stories on which his high reputation depends, it is
the background itself, the tropical Misiones of northern
Argentina, on which emphasis is laid.

Into a full appreciation of the work of Horacio Quiroga,
knowledge of his own life must enter. For it is his own
life, rich in experience, which furnishes him the material for most of his stories; he himself is his own chief
character; and in his work he reveals, to an extent true

of few writers, his own character and temperament. He was born, December 31, 1878, in Salto, Uruguay, where his father was the Argentine consul. After the accidental death of her husband, Horacio's mother took him, still very young, and her older children to reside in Córdoba (Argentina). Some five years later she returned to Salto, where Horacio attended the Hiram school, which was maintained by the Masonic order, and later completed the work of the Polytechnique Institute. Although he gave evidence of creative imagination and superior intelligence, he was an undependable, fractious, willful, and petulant schoolboy who shunned the society of others and found his pleasure in reading, especially books of travel and periodical literature. While enrolled in the University of Montevideo, he was a pronounced individualist who pursued only the subjects that interested him—history, chemistry, and philosophy—and sought the company only of those of similar interests. Outside of the university he distinguished himself for his hobbies—bicycling, photography, and the manual arts, especially carpentry and ironwork. Narcotics, too, fascinated him; not only did he take chloroform to allay suffering from asthma, but he experimented on himself with hashish. Besides being interested in the theater and in music, he was passionately fond of nineteenth-century French literature, particularly the works of the Parnassians. Pronouncedly influenced by these writers are his own first articles, which appeared under the pseudonym of Guillermo Eynhardt in two literary periodicals, *La Revista,* in 1897, and *Gil Blas,* the following year.

Experiences around the turn of the century, when he reached his majority, deeply influenced Quiroga's later life. With some of his youthful companions in literary interests, he visited Leopoldo Lugones in Buenos Aires, in 1898, and became an ardent admirer both of the man and of his verse. That same year, in keeping with his visionary and unrestrained nature, Quiroga fell desperately in love with a girl he met in Salto, María Esther; but he was doomed to bitter disappointment, for the girl's mother objected to him as a suitor. In September of that year he established a literary periodical, which lasted but five months; in this his work, influenced to a marked degree by Poe and Lugones, is decidedly modernistic. The following year brought the realization of the great dream of his life—to see Paris; but lack of funds while there entailed great hardships and shortened his visit to a few months. Back in Montevideo in 1900, he was for the next two years the moving spirit in one of the most important literary groups of the city, the "Consistorio del Gay Saber." His own writings for this period are to be found in the records of this society; in his first book, *Los Arrecifes de Coral* (*Coral Reefs*), 1901; in the daily newspapers; and in two literary periodicals, *Rojo y Blanco* and *La Alborada.* In 1902 he accidentally shot and killed one of his best friends, Fernando Ferrando, who had been closely associated with him. Shaken by the tragedy, Quiroga left Montevideo for Buenos Aires.

Through friends Quiroga soon found means of earning a living there, and early in 1903 he secured a position as teacher of Spanish in the Colegio Nacional. When he resigned shortly to join a historical commission that was leaving for Misiones in northern Argentina, he took a step that led directly to his fame as a *cuentista.* The commission, of which Lugones was in charge, had been appointed to study the ruins of the Jesuit settlements, which had given the name to the region. One of the most important of these was at San Ignacio on the banks of the Paraná River, in the midst of dense forests which covered an area remarkable for its fertile soil, heavy rainfall, and many streams subject to frequent and rapid rises. In this hot, sultry region the Jesuits for almost a century and a half maintained missions, but the native Indians wandered away after the expulsion of their spiritual leaders. Only the ruins of the cathedral, the college, and living quarters remained—mute witnesses in stone of Catholic attempts to Christianize and civilize the people of the region.

With all that he saw in Misiones—the broad expanse of the Paraná River, the tropical forests, the strange animals, and the deadly serpents—Quiroga was enthralled. He had known of them from childhood, but only through the eyes of others. On his return to Buenos Aires early in 1904 he published a volume of stories, *El Crimen del Otro* (*Another's Crime*); but the urge to return to the tropical jungle was strong within him. It was easy, consequently, for a friend to persuade him to join in the purchase of a tract of land in the Chaco, some seventy miles from Resistencia, for the purpose of growing cotton. The undertaking failed, and early in 1905 Quiroga returned to Buenos Aires. That same year he published a short story, **"Los Perseguidos" ("The Haunted Ones")**, and became closely connected with the leading literati of the city—Lugones, Roberto Payró, and the dramatist Florencio Sánchez. His contributions to various literary periodicals—*Caras y Caretas, El Hogar, El Atlántida*—also began that year. In 1906 he was appointed to a professorship of the Spanish language and literature in the Escuela Normal. Teaching, however, was not his forte, and the fact that he purchased at this time 185 hectares of land near San Ignacio in Misiones is evidence of his intention ultimately to return there. During his vacations he made the 800-mile journey up the Paraná River to improve his property. His dream of a small, lovely cottage in the midst of this vast virgin forest had never left him, and now he sought to make that dream a reality. By the end of 1908, which saw the publication of his novelette *Historia de un Amor turbio* (*An Ill-Fated Love*), he had built with his own hands a rough cottage in this untracked wilderness. He had feverishly hurried its completion, for he was deeply in love with Ana María Cires, one of his pupils in the Escuela Normal; and his dreams included marrying her and taking her to Misiones to live. Although Ana María's parents objected to Quiroga as an erratic individual, they finally gave their consent to the marriage, which took place on December 30, 1909.

Shortly afterward Quiroga and his bride set off up the Paraná for the wilds of Misiones. At once he began improving the house, which leaked copiously—for the unseasoned lumber had shrunk. The outdoor life and the opportunity of making his living with his hands delighted him; and in 1911 he broke with civilization by resigning from the Escuela Normal. He was not without a remunerative position, however, for the governor of the territory of Misiones, in appreciation of his literary work, had appointed him justice of the peace and also official recorder for the district of San Ignacio; but, intensely occupied with his own undertakings, he was very remiss in the execution of his public duties. While he enthusiastically embarked during the next few years on various enterprises—a stock company for the growing of *yerba mate,* the distillation of alcohol from oranges, the utilization of a particular wood for the making of charcoal, and the manufacturing of pottery—all proved, aside from furnishing him material for some of his best stories, unprofitable. He spent much time hunting, fishing, sailing his boat on the Paraná, and listening to stories and tales about the district.

Two children were born to him and Ana María: Eglé, in January of 1911, and Darío, in Buenos Aires, the following year. Eglé was born in Misiones without the aid of a physician, for Quiroga held that childbirth should be entrusted to Nature alone, and Ana María almost died. For the birth of her second child, she returned to Buenos Aires. Although Quiroga and Ana María loved each other, their lives came to be a long succession of quarrels and reconciliations. She was very excitable and easily provoked; he was irascible and headstrong. His ideas on rearing the children—for he wanted to bring them up like young animals, in what he regarded as Nature's way—particularly irritated her. In one of her fits of anger she took poison to end her life and, after much suffering, died in December, 1915. Quiroga then had to occupy himself with the duties of his household, for he was unable to keep a servant on account of his irritability; but at the end of a year he abandoned Misiones and returned with his children to Buenos Aires.

The next nine years seem to have been one of the most active and productive periods of his life. In 1917 he made the collection of stories *Cuentos de Amor, de Locura, y de Muerte*; he was given a position in the Uruguayan consulate; and he and three friends, in a boat he had made with his own hands, sailed the long way up the Paraná to pass their vacation on Quiroga's place in Misiones. Back in Buenos Aires he took a house in Agüeros Street, where he lived for more than seven years. His most distinctive work, *El Salvaje* (*The Savage*), 1920, was followed by *Cuentos de la Selva para Niños* (*Tales of the Jungle*), 1921, *Anaconda* and *Las Sacrificadas* (*The Sacrificed*), 1923, and *El Desierto* (*The Wilderness*), 1924. During this time his contributions to various periodicals and dailies—*La Nación, La Prensa, Caras y Caretas, Fray Mocho, Atlántida,* and *El Hogar*—were also numerous. Those were pleasant years, too, it seems. He spent hours in his shop working with his beloved tools; his house, although by no means pretentious, was visited by the literati of the city; and, devoted as he was to his children, he spent much time on their education, although in sudden fits of anger he would sometimes punish them severely. Through prominent friends in the federal government in Montevideo, he received promotions in the consular service and in 1922 was appointed secretary of the Uruguayan delegation that was sent to Rio de Janeiro to the centenary celebration of Brazil's independence. But Quiroga, subject as he was to whims and caprices, could not remain in any one groove. Obtaining a leave from the consulate in 1925, he left Buenos Aires suddenly and returned to Misiones, where he resumed his old life, working his farm and visiting his neighbors at odd times. Although the house and furniture brought back memories of his dead wife, they did not prevent him, now in his forty-seventh year, from falling desperately in love with a young girl in the neighborhood, again Ana María by name, whom he had known some eight years previously as a mere child. The girl responded to his prince-charming love, but her parents put an end to the affair by sending her away. He, too, left Misiones.

Back in Buenos Aires early in 1926, with his children, his menagerie of wild and tame animals, his souvenirs of Misiones, particularly the skins of the snakes and animals he had killed, he moved to Vicente López Street. Again a city dweller, he renewed acquaintance with his literary friends; he indulged himself in his favorite diversion, the "movies," of which he was a confirmed habitué; and in addition to publishing a series of sketches of types in Misiones—*Los Desterrados* (*Exiles*), 1926, and a novelette on his own recent ill-fated love affair, he wrote extensively for periodicals—articles, animal stories for children, and reviews of moving pictures. There was time too, unfortunately, for another love affair, with María Elena, a girl of twenty, whom he married in July, 1927. Differences early arose between the two. He was jealous; and she, it seems, had not married him for love but was interested in him only as a successful writer. The birth of a child did not help matters. Again weary of the life he was leading in Buenos Aires, Quiroga decided to seek contentment once more in Misiones. He succeeded in being transferred as consul to San Ignacio, for which he embarked, with his family and all his belongings, early in 1932. He himself was delighted with returning to his old way of living; but his wife, in spite of his efforts to content her, grew so weary of life in the tropics that he finally let her return to Buenos Aires. It was in those dark days of domestic friction that his last book, with its foreboding title, *Más Allá* (*The Great Beyond*), 1934, was published. Other difficulties also beset him. The closing of the Uruguayan consulate in San Ignacio left him without a position. In 1935, through the influence of friends, he was appointed honorary consul, but more than a year passed before he received any salary. Then ill health, caused by cancer, set in. When medical aid became imperative, he sailed down the Paraná, for the last time, in September, 1936, and entered a hospital in Buenos Aires, more or less as a charity patient. In the following February he ended his life by taking a deadly poison. The body was interred, at the expense of friends, in his native Salto.

Quiroga was, to say the least, a strange individual. Ill health was probably one of the causes of his fractiousness, for various diseases beset him at different periods in his life—asthma in his childhood, dyspepsia in his early manhood, and later prostate trouble. Inherently, too, he was capricious, morbid, and introspective. In school he was undependable, and as an official very remiss in his duties; yet he was capable of great energy and endurance in the prosecution of some plan or scheme that struck his fancy, whether it was building a house or a boat, clearing land, working his farm, or engaging in some agricultural or chemical experiment.

Between Quiroga the man and Quiroga the writer there is an inseparable bond. In many of his stories, he himself, faithfully delineated, is the principal character, and events from his own life—his disappointments in love, his experiences in the wilds of the Chaco and Misiones, his scientific experiments—provide him with the narratives. Highly imaginative by nature, he reveals, like the true romantic that he was, his obsession for the supernatural, particularly the thought of an existence after death, on which hinges a goodly number of his stories. Although he was indifferent toward religion, his observations in certain essays and allegories on human conduct bespeak a truly high and noble soul. His writings during his youth and his last years reveal that his mind was often occupied with thoughts on insanity, suicide, and murder.

His fondness for such morbid subjects appeared at the outset of his literary career. That he was very deeply impressed by d'Annunzio's *Il Trionfo della Morte* is evident in **"El Guardabosque comediante"** (**"The Actor Forest-Guard"**) and **"Sin Razón, pero cansado"** (**"Without Reason but Tired"**), two stories in his first book, *Los Arrecifes de Coral,* 1901. This novel of d'Annunzio traces the progress of insanity in the protagonist, Giorgio Aurispa, who, bored with existence, murders his mistress and takes his own life. Under the spell of this book, the central figure in **"El Guarda-**

bosque comediante" lets himself be devoured by a pack of wolves. There is no reference to d'Annunzio's novel in **"Sin Razón, pero cansado"**; its influence, however, is evident, particularly in Luciano, a bored individual, who, like his prototype, Giorgio, murders his mistress when he tires of her.

Quiroga admits also, in his early writings, an absorbing passion for Poe, who, as Englekirk observes in his *Edgar Allan Poe in Hispanic Lands,* had a very definite influence on him. **"El Crimen del Otro,"** the title story of one of his collections, is admittedly inspired by "The Cask of Amontillado." The two characters in the story are insane; infatuated with Poe's tales, each reveals their effect on him; and, finally, one of them, following Poe's story, buries the other alive. Insanity is the theme of **"La justa Proporción de las Cosas"** (**"Things in Exact Proportion"**)—another story in the collection—and also of **"Los Perseguidos."** The latter is unique in that it is a sort of case history, purportedly written by one suffering from a persecution complex, of another victim of the same malady. Two other stories in the collection seem to derive their inspiration from Poe: **"El triple robo de Bellamore"** (**"A Triple Robbery by Bellamore"**), a very lame attempt at a detective story, and **"Historia de Estilicón"** (**"The Story of Estilicón"**), in which the destiny of a man, a woman, and a gorilla are fatally interwoven—a queer story surpassing Poe in certain abnormalities.

D'Annunzio and Poe were not the only writers that influenced Quiroga. In his youth in Montevideo he was one of the leaders of a group of admirers of modernism. Particularly in the sketches in *El Crimen del Otro,* such as **"La Princesa bizantina"** (**"The Byzantine Princess"**), Quiroga was endeavoring to write in the modernist manner and striving for effect through rhythmic and figurative language. In his third work, *Historia de un Amor turbio,* he is not concerned with refinements of style but with psychological analysis. The influence of Dostoevski in this novelette Quiroga acknowledged some years later, and he added that the Russian was one of very few writers in whom he still retained an interest.

In all this early work, in which Quiroga was endeavoring to find himself, individuality was lacking; but nevertheless the direction his later work was to take, in technique and subject matter, is clearly indicated. Like his more mature productions, they are, first of all, impressionistic; for Quiroga aims primarily at creating in the mind of the reader a mood, to which the action of the story is entirely subservient. The prevailing tone is one of gloom, although, as in **"La Muerte del Canario"** (**"The Death of the Canary"**), there are occasional touches of humor. In the subject matter utilized to produce the desired effect, he shows a decided preference for mental abnormalities. Nor in his study of abnormal beings does he overlook himself, a by-no-means well-balanced person. This highly personal element that definitely characterizes Quiroga's writing appears very early. In **"Hashish,"** a sketch in *El Crimen del Otro,* he recounts an experiment upon himself with that narcotic; in **"Los Perseguidos,"** he himself appears by name as one of the abnormal characters, his recent journey to Misiones is mentioned, and his friend Lugones plays a minor rôle. Much of *Historia de un Amor Turbio* is probably based on his own experience. The central figure—the dyspeptic, romantically minded Rohán—is Quiroga himself. Like Quiroga, Rohán had been to Paris, and he had abandoned the city to work on a country place, just as Quiroga was himself contemplating doing when he wrote the story. It will also be recalled that Quiroga's daughter, born a few years after this novelette was published, was named Eglé—the name of the character that as a child, and later as a young woman, became so passionately enamoured of Rohán. Another story, **"Historia de Estilicón,"** suggests not only the prominent rôle animals were to occupy in Quiroga's later stories, but his passion for the tropics, the background of his Misiones tales.

The stories he wrote in Misiones between 1910 and 1916 brought him a very enviable reputation as a *cuentista*; and it was fifteen of the most representative that he republished in *Cuentos de Amor, de Locura y de Muerte.* According to content they fall roughly into three groups. **"Nuestro primer Cigarro"** (**"Our First Cigar"**), **"El Meningitis y su Sombra"** (**"Meningitis and its Delusion"**), **"Una Estación de Amor"** (**"A Season of Love"**), and **"La Muerte de Isolda"** (**"The Death of Isolde"**), have an intimate tone that connects them at once with Quiroga himself. The first of these is a humorous account of a boyish trick. The second reveals the wildly imaginative and romantic side of Quiroga's mind; it concerns a young girl who during a severe illness fell deeply in love with the narrator of the tale, but—and here the fanciful element enters—was conscious of her infatuation only when delirious. **"Una Estación de Amor,"** of which *Las Sacrificadas,* 1923, is a dialogued version, is based without a doubt on his first disappointment in love—a very bitter experience which he seems to have nursed all his life. A youthful couple who are romantically in love are separated by the young man's father; when the two meet years later the man is married and the young woman has been forced by poverty to degrade herself. Urged by the girl's mother, a drug addict, the man takes her as his mistress; but the relationship proves unsatisfactory, for both feel they have been false to their former love. The theme of this story, the futility of attempting to recapture love, is somewhat similar to that of the last story of this group, **"La Muerte de Isolda,"** which is motivated by unavailing remorse for having spurned a sincere love.

Four stories of a very morbid nature, in which critics have detected the influence of Poe, constitute the second group in the collection. Technically, these stories vary considerably. Two relate mere incidents: the suicide craze of a crew that had manned an abandoned ship, **"Buques suicidantes"** (**"Barks that Lure to Death"**); and the pining away of a young bride caused, as was discovered after her death, by a loathsome parasitic animal in her pillow, **"El Almohadón de Pluma"** (**"The Feather Pillow"**). The remaining two stories of this group, however, **"El Solitario"** (**"The Solitaire"**) and **"La Gallina degollada"** (**"The Beheaded Hen"**), come as near meeting the requirements of an artistic short story as anything that Quiroga wrote. Both are told in a very direct and straightforward manner; each creates a very definite mood; the plots, though simple, are well constructed, each having a very definite climax; and the characters—each facing an impending catastrophe—are well delineated. Particularly effective is the contrast, in **"El Solitario,"** between the poor, plodding, and patient jeweler, Kassim, and his vain, frivolous wife. He, sick and weak, worked long hours at his trade to gratify her whims; she, ungrateful and dissatisfied, continually rebuked him for their poverty. In time, too, she was possessed by an inordinate desire for gems which her husband's trade gave her an opportunity to see; on one occasion she became so envious of a beautiful diamond that Kassim was mounting on a scarf-pin as to fly into an ungovernable fit of anger, in which she unwittingly revealed her unfaithfulness. When calmer, she retracted what she had said; but Kassim, as if unmoved by it all, continued his work on the scarf-pin. When he finished it late in the night, he took it to her; then, as she lay asleep, he thrust it into her heart and quietly left the house. The most tragic story that Quiroga wrote, however, is doubtless **"La Gallina degollada,"** in which some idiot sons, imitating the cook whom they had seen behead a chicken, kill their sister, a beautiful child and the only normal one of the children. Both these stories have an urban background and derive dramatic effect from the startling ending and from the dialogue in which the characters reveal themselves; but in neither, as is true of all Quiroga's stories so far discussed, is the setting a vital factor.

On the other hand, the most important element of the seven stories which constitute the third group from this collection is setting or background. With these, twenty-two others—five in *El Salvaje,* seven in *Anaconda,* two in *El Desierto,* and three in *Los Desterrados*—must be considered, for all are concerned in one way or another with the Misiones territory that borders the Paraná River. The source of the passion that was aroused in Quiroga when he visited the region for the first time, and that swayed him for the rest of his life, lies in the contrast that the tropical forest region presented to the level, open, and less picturesque country around Montevideo and Buenos Aires. Not only did the spirit of the tropics enthrall him, as frequently befalls those that enter that realm, but he was converted at once from an urban resident apparently indifferent to Nature into her worshipful student. His passion for the region—its climate, its topography, its animal life, the human derelicts that had taken refuge there—found expression in this group of stories, which constitute his greatest achievement and give him his main claim to distinction as a writer.

In reading these stories, one senses first Quiroga's own imaginative personality and next his very close personal contact with Misiones. Particularly real and vivid are the details in these stories in regard to climate, topography, and animal life; the extremes of heat—**"La Insolación"** (**"Sunstroke"**) and of cold; the droughts and torrential rains—**"El Simún"** (**"The Simoom"**); the Paraná River, both at flood stage and in a normal state, with its dangerous rapids and high banks of black stone; and the broken terrain covered by forests in which lurked deadly snakes and other animal life hostile to man, such as army ants—**"La Miel silvestre"** (**"Wild Honey"**). True to life, also, are many of the events in those tales in which Quiroga himself is the chief actor—such as **"Los Fabricantes de Carbón"** (**"Charcoal Burners"**) and **"Los Destiladores de Naranja"** (**"The Distillers of Oranges"**), which bring to light certain of his unfortunate business ventures and which emphasize his love for scientific experiments; **"El Desierto,"** which is autobiographic in a number of details, particularly those in which the principal character is left in Misiones with two children after the death of his wife; **"El Techo de Incienso"** (**"The Roof of Incense Wood"**), which is reminiscent of Quiroga's life as a public official in that territory; and **"Polea loca"** (**"Off Balance"**), which centers about a person, like Quiroga, averse to answering, or even opening, official correspondence.

So real as to be unforgettable are the people of the region, in some thirteen stories of this group. Some of these are types found along the Paraná River in the Misiones section. **"Los Mensú"** (**"Hired Hands"**), which is undoubtedly one of Quiroga's best stories, recounts the experience of two laborers who, after contracting to work in a lumber camp where they faced enslavement and death from malignant fever, succeeded in escaping and, after untold hardships on a raft on the Paraná at flood stage, reached the town of Posadas. The story is remarkable, too, for its unexpected ending. For the laborers, after spending their first night of freedom in a state of drunkenness, signed up the next morning for the very sort of work from which they had just escaped. Other tales intimately connected with the Paraná and those that dwell along it are **"Los Pescadores de vigas"** (**"River Thieves"**), which presents those who steal the valuable logs being floated down the river; **"El Yaciyateré"** (**"The Sinister Call"**), which tells of the

riverfolk and their superstitions; and **"En la Noche"** (**"In the Night"**), which recounts a horrible experience of a European and his wife on the Paraná. In other sketches and narratives of this group, types peculiar to the region appear, with all of whom Quiroga had doubtlessly come into direct contact: day laborers, particularly one that had probably worked on Quiroga's own farm (**"El Peón"**); an overbearing landlord who paid dearly for an act of arrogance—**"Una Bofetada"** (**"A Slap"**); European immigrants who had come to take up land in Misiones—**"Inmigrantes"** (**"Immigrants"**) and **"La Voluntad"** (**"Will Power"**); a promoter who, after repeated failures, is finally successful—**"El Monte negro"** (**"Black Mountain"**); an ailing and drunken justice of the peace, of whose corpse the widow had a photograph made, probably by Quiroga himself—**"La Cámara oscura"** (**"The Dark Room"**); and other human flotsam and jetsam that had found a haven in the region (**"Los Desterrados,"** **"Van Houten,"** and **"Tacuara-Mansión"**).

While there is abundant evidence of a keen power of observation in the remaining stories with a Misiones background, realism is somewhat held in check and a freer rein given to romance and imagination. These stories are **"El Salvaje,"** **"Anaconda,"** **"El Regreso de Anaconda"** (**"The Return of Anaconda"**), and possibly two short sketches, **"A la Deriva"** (**"Down Stream"**) and **"El Hombre muerto"** (**"The Dead Man"**), which are identical in theme and technique, and in having a dying man as a single character. In **"A la Deriva,"** he had been bitten by a venomous snake, and the effects of the deadly poison, which Quiroga had no doubt observed, are described in detail. By sheer will power the afflicted man got into his boat to go down the Paraná to seek medical aid. The great pain he was suffering finally ceased, and his mind became clear. Then, by virtue of Quiroga's imagination, the reader is enabled to know the thoughts that passed through the mind of the doomed man. He recalled various friends in the town to which he was going, friends he had not seen for years, and he anticipated the joy he would have in seeing them again. But suddenly a convulsion seized him; his mind again became cloudy; and, there in his boat on the Paraná, he died. In **"El Hombre muerto"** is a man mortally wounded by falling on his machete as he was crawling through a fence. Again, in this sketch, the interest is in the train of thoughts that passed through the man's mind as he lay dying, out of reach of help.

The play of imagination is far greater in **"El Salvaje,"** which, despite the lack of unity between its first and second part, is to be numbered among Quiroga's most original tales. The background is the upper Paraná, above Iguazú Falls, a region of dense forests and heavy rainfall. Tired of civilization, an educated man—no other than Quiroga himself—had taken refuge there, set up a meteorological observatory, and begun sending in reports to Buenos Aires. According to those that he sent in one season, the rainfall was so excessive that an inspector was sent from the central office in Buenos Aires to verify his figures. Shortly after his arrival the rain began to fall as the man had never seen rain fall before, and he had to spend the night with the amateur meteorologist—a tall, thin, pale man with a long black beard and a strange look in his eyes that suggested an unbalanced mind. Rather uncommunicative at first, the meteorologist suddenly asked the inspector if he had ever seen a dinosaur, and when the newcomer acknowledged he had not, the refugee told a long, impossible story of his experiences with one there on the Paraná River. The next morning when the inspector was going down the river he was overcome by the humidity of the air and the stench of the forest after the deluge. This convinced him that the storyteller had experienced in a dream the reality of that past age as fully as if he had actually lived in it.

"La Realidad" (**"Reality"**), as the second part of **"El Salvaje"** is entitled, is a unit in itself and, despite the fact that it deals with the Tertiary period, one of the most dramatic stories that Quiroga wrote. The principal character is a tree-dweller; his habitat is a humid, forest-covered, tropical region such as that of the upper Paraná; and what happens to him—his progress from a herbivorous to a carnivorous animal, from a tree-dweller to a cave-dweller, and from insecurity to security after he accidentally pushed a huge stone against the entrance of the cave—is the story of several stages in the slow upward progress of man.

If one of Quiroga's best stories deals with primitive man, it is not at all strange that he also writes about animals. Two stories of the Misiones group, **"El Alambre de Pua"** (**"Barbed Wire"**) and **"Yaguai,"** show an intimate understanding of domestic animals. Of the animal kingdom, however, snakes fascinate Quiroga most. In many of his stories they appear, very realistically, as actual snakes. But in **"Los Cazadores de Ratas"** (**"Rat Hunters"**), **"Anaconda,"** and its sequel **"El regreso de Anaconda,"** they are endowed with the power of speech and certain other human characteristics. **"Anaconda,"** his masterpiece, pictures the consternation that ensued when the snakes in a certain district in Misiones learned that their natural enemy, man, had invaded their kingdom. A group of scientists, the serpents discovered, had come to catch venomous snakes, which abounded in that region, in order to extract their poison and make with it a serum that would render their one dangerous weapon ineffective. Preferring to die rather than to submit to such degradation, the snakes convened to discuss means of combating the intruder. In the convention there were two factions, the poisonous and non-poisonous snakes, whose leaders—a large cobra and Anaconda, a huge boa—moved as much by the natural

enmity between them as by the differences in viewpoint, almost came to the point of attacking each other. The cobra's plan, that the snakes in a body should attack the men, was finally adopted; and Anaconda, putting aside personal prejudice, yielded to the general will. The result was disastrous, for the snakes were routed and many were killed. Then followed a terrific battle between the two leaders who had survived; and although Anaconda killed the cobra, she herself at the end of the struggle lay senseless from his deadly poison. The men saved her, however, as they saw in her an ally against the poisonous snakes; and she lingered among them for a year, "nosing about and observing everything," before she returned to her natural habitat further north.

She was in that region, along the upper Paraná, when Quiroga writes of her again—this time in **"El Regreso de Anaconda."** "A young serpent she was then, some ten meters in length, in the fullness of her strength; and in all her vast hunting range, there was not a deer or a tiger capable of withstanding with a breath of life in his body one of her embraces." It was at this time, during a great drought, that she conceived a plan of damming the river itself in order to shut out man, who had already begun to invade the district. Aided by the other animals whom she would win over to her venture, it could easily be done, she thought, when the rains came, with all the debris that the flood would wash down. Finally the great hoped-for deluge came; and down the river with it there descended a vast army of birds, insects, snakes, alligators, tigers, and other dwellers of the forest. Anaconda herself was on a huge cedar tree that had been uprooted. Later, she crawled upon a floating island, on which she found a house and in it a dying man. Whether he excited pity in her or whether she saw in him a place to lay her eggs, as she did do, she did not destroy him but protected him from the poisonous snakes that swarmed about. But Anaconda's plan failed; no dam was formed, and she herself met death, through a bullet of a high-powered rifle that one of the crew of a steamboat on the river sent through her head.

In these two stories, **"Anaconda"** and **"El Regreso de Anaconda,"** Quiroga appears at his very best. In nothing else that he has written can there be found such a large number of excellent qualities. Here, imagination and observation have joined hands to make them the little masterpieces that they are. The background, particularly the Paraná River at flood stage, is intensely individual. The stories themselves are told with dramatic effect. The characters, whose psychology and bodily movements have been recorded with masterly precision, are interesting for themselves, that is as snakes, not solely, as in nearly all animal stories, for the human characteristics that have been attributed to them. If there is a supreme quality of excellence in these two stories, however, it is the feeling of admiration and of compassion that Quiroga arouses for the great boa herself. The style is very effective, being simple, unadorned by figures of speech but rhythmical.

The only remaining stories with the Misiones background are eight fables (*Cuentos de la Selva para Niños*) that deal with certain animals of that region. One of these, which tells of the alligators who erected a dam in order to keep man out of the Paraná River, recalls **"El Regreso de Anaconda."** The story of the lazy bee is the only one that has a definite moral: in general Quiroga's aim in these fables is primarily to amuse. In nearly all of them, nevertheless, certain moral values are presented more or less indirectly—for instance, the consequences of disobedience on the part of young animals of the forest, and the gratitude that some animals show man in return for kindness. Certain qualities of these stories—their easy-flowing, chatty style, and the free hand that fantasy takes—recall *Alice's Adventures in Wonderland.*

On the other hand, six apologues—five in *El Desierto* and one in *Más Allá*—differ from the fables in that their purpose is not so much to amuse as to exemplify some philosophic truth. In **"Los tres Besos"** (**"The Three Kisses"**), the only one of the stories in which animals do not figure, he shows that a desire which is long deferred on account of some other consideration finally ceases to be a desire. Liberty, even with hunger—and no one could have said this any more sincerely than Quiroga himself—is preferable to luxury that brings with it a false and circumscribed life—**"El Potro salvaje"** (**"The Wild Colt"**). **"La Patria"** (**"The Homeland"**) decries, through a story of discord that arose among the animals of a forest, the establishment of political boundaries between countries. The tenor of the three remaining stories—**"Juan Darién,"** which has points of similarity with Kipling's "Tiger! Tiger!," **"El León"** (**"The Lion"**), and **"La señorita Leona"** (**"The Young Lioness"**)—is that animals are in many respects superior to man. In each story a wild animal, after coming under the influence of human civilization, abandons it for the animal kingdom.

Motifs of an ethical nature are to be found also in the **"Cuadrivio laico"** (**"The Lay Cuadrivium"**), which is the general title of four stories in *El Salvaje.* One of these, **"Reyes"** (**"Kings"**), may be dismissed at once, as it is only a short prose poem in the "modernista" manner. The remaining three, which are genuine narratives, are significant in that they contain the only references in all of Quiroga's works to any phase of the Christian religion. Slightly ironical, **"La Navidad"** (**"Christmas"**) and **"La Pasión"** (**"The Passion of Jesus"**) recall the style of certain stories of Anatole France; both claim to be incidents in connection with Jesus Christ. When Herod sought Jesus, says the first story, and threatened to slay all the infants of a certain age unless the place where He was born were revealed, Salome, a Jewish girl, disclosed that information to her Roman soldier-lover. Later, to the dismay of Saint Peter, Salome was admitted to Heaven on the ground that she had shown a great tenderness of heart in preferring the betrayal of her God to the death of so many innocent infants. According to **"La Pasión,"** reunions were held from time to time in Heaven at which Jesus showed His absolute goodness by pardoning all that had taken any part in His crucifixion. Finally a man appeared whom Jesus refused to pardon, and thereafter no hymn to His absolute goodness could be sung. The man was Ahasvero, the wandering Jew, who, in this version, refused Christ water when He begged for it on the cross. In the last story of the group, **"Corpus"** (**"Corpus Christi"**)—which tells of the persecution and burning, in Geneva at the time of Calvin, of a young German for having made an image of Christ—there is a ring of true feeling. For Quiroga, although unaffected by religion, hated intolerance in any form.

The material in the collections that has not been discussed up to this point is of a heterogeneous nature. Especially is this true in the case of *El Salvaje,* which contains an account of a man that was stung to death by his bees—**"La Reina italiana"** (**"The Italian Queen"**); an essay picturing a scene in Belgium during the World War—**"Los Cementerios belgas"** (**"Belgian Cemeteries"**), one of the few instances in Quiroga's writings of references to contemporary events; five brief narratives—**"Estefanía," "La Llama"** (**"The Flame"**), **"Fanny," "Lucila Strinberg,"** and **"Un Idilio"** (**"An Idyl"**)—all rather plotless, thin in substance, and, if not downright wildly imaginary, at least inconsequential; a humorous skit on the tactics of the Buenos Aires "masher"—**"Tres Cartas y un Pie"** (**"Three Letters and a Foot"**); and a tragi-comic account of a squabble between a man and his wife, probably based on an actual event in Quiroga's life, when their baby waked them at night by its crying—**"Cuento Para Novios"** (**"A Story for the Betrothed"**). Of the remaining items in *Anaconda,* there are two articles dealing with climatic phenomena of tropical Africa—**"El Simún"** and **"Gloria tropical"** (**"Tropical Glory"**); a ludicrous tale of the sad experiences of a young man who married the daughter of an expert in dietetics—**"Dieta de Amor"** (**"The Diet of Love"**); and **"Miss Dorothy Phillips, mi Esposa"** (**"Miss Dorothy Phillips, My Wife"**), which, aside from being a rambling, highly fanciful story of a young Argentine who went from Buenos Aires to Hollywood and married his favorite "movie" star, contains much light satire on Hollywood actors and actresses. Another story of "movie" actors, also highly improbable, is **"El Espectro"** (**"The Spectre"**) (*El Desierto*), in which a deceased husband fascinates, through a picture in which he had had a part, his widow and her lover and prevents them from marrying. The same collection contains also a droll account of a woman's scheme to get an author to read a novel her husband had written—**"Una Conquista"** (**"A Conquest"**); a story of two souls that met in an outer world and became enamoured of each other—**"El Síncope blanco"** (**"In Another World"**), whose supernatural quality predominates in Quiroga's last book, *Más Allá*; and, lastly, **"Silvina y Montt,"** which foreshadows, in that it tells of a love affair between a middle-aged man and a young girl, a later event in Quiroga's own life.

Of that ill-fated love affair in Misiones in 1925 with Ana María, he has left a record in his novelette *Pasado Amor* (*Bygone Love*), which is mainly of interest as his most personal and definite confessional. Many of the incidents in the life of the chief character, Morán, have been clearly established as autobiographical—his return to Misiones, where everything reminded him of his dead wife; his falling madly in love with Magdalena, whom he had known as a child; and the opposition of her family, who succeeded in thwarting him. Another character, perhaps fictitious, is Alicia Hontou, who took her own life because she was deeply in love with Morán but unable to attract him.

The characterization of Morán is nothing more than a delineation of Quiroga himself; intensity of feeling is the quality that distinguishes him. It reveals itself in that inner force that drove him to work hard physically at the things that interested him: the clearing and cultivation of his fields, boat making, rowing up and down the Paraná River with its dangerous rapids. High-strung, over-wrought, verging on madness, in his love affair with Magdalena he acted more like an adolescent than a middle-aged man. So immoderate is his sentimentality as to arouse disgust in readers.

In this work Quiroga pays more attention than usual to the setting. Here, it is the country itself, the "mate" fields and the Paraná River, and the people of the region, rather than the animals and snakes, with which he concerns himself. An insight is afforded into the lives of three families of different social levels and points of view. There are comments, too, on the public dances, on that inevitable social institution, the bar, and on labor unions—organizations which had come into existence since Quiroga's earlier residence there. Interesting in themselves, these details of manners and customs fail, however, to contribute to the artistry of the novel; rather than being fused with the story, they seem entirely extraneous.

To the troubles that marred the last years of his life—domestic dissensions, financial difficulties, and ill health—are traceable in a measure the somber themes that characterize in general his last collection of stories, *Más Allá*. In at least seven of its eleven stories the preoccupation of the author with death, suicide, insanity, and an existence beyond the tomb seems not only to in-

dicate an unhealthy state of mind but to presage his own tragic end. **"Más Allá,"** the title story, tells how the souls of two lovers who had committed suicide were united on this earth for three months but then had to separate without knowing what awaited them in the great beyond. Two stories, probably the most absurd that Quiroga wrote, hark back to his interest in the "movies": **"El Vampiro"** (**"The Vampire"**), which tells how a devotee of occult science created from a screen picture of a deceased movie star a real, living vampire, which finally destroyed him; and **"El Puritano"** (**"The Puritan"**), which portrays a straight-laced married man who went night after night to see a picture featuring a woman he had loved but spurned until he, too, took his own life, in order to join her in ghostland.

Quiroga returns to the theme of insanity, the predilection of his early stories, in **"El Conductor del Rápido"** (**"The Conductor on the Flyer"**), which describes the symptoms of incipient madness in a locomotive engineer, pictures his distress when he began to suspect that he was losing his mind, and narrates graphically, when the crisis did come and the engineer became a raving maniac, how he brought his train safely to the end of his run; and in **"El Llamado"** (**"Voices"**) a woman in an insane asylum reveals that the tragic death of an only child, of which she had been warned by voices of the dead, had brought about her own mental derangement.

Two short sketches, **"Las Moscas"** (**"Flies"**) and **"El Hijo"** (**"The Son"**), present very vividly states of mind: the former, that of a man, who, having fallen and broken his back, knows by the large green flies that begin to swarm about him that death is nigh; and the latter, the mental anxiety of a father shaken by a premonition of the death of his young son. Both of these sketches are very similar in technique to **"A la Deriva"** and **"El Hombre muerto."**

A tone of levity, rather than of gloom, characterizes the three remaining stories in *Más Allá*. Based on a lapse of memory, one of these, **"La Ausencia"** (**"A Case of Amnesia"**), has the best plot in the collection. Roldán Berger, an engineer, finds himself one day with no knowledge of the last six years of his life but engaged to a very beautiful and intellectual woman who had been attracted to him by a renowned philosophical work attributed to him. The matter-of-fact engineer would have broken the engagement at once, but his physician counseled otherwise. Terribly bored, after his marriage, by the intellectuals who pursued him, he confessed to his wife that he had not written the book. As he had succeeded in making himself loved for his own sake, she did not forsake him; instead, before an open fireplace, they tore the leaves from the book and cast them into the flames. The theme, that love does not depend on literary accomplishments, appears also in the far less interesting **"La Bella y la Bestia"** (**"Beauty and the Beast"**), in which a young woman of literary interests sets out to find a husband of similar tastes but finally decides in favor of an ordinary business man. **"El Ocaso"** (**"Sunset"**), the last story in the volume, relates an incident in the life of an old *roué* and of a young girl none too chaste. Somewhat risqué in nature, it is entirely out of keeping with the general tone of the author's other works.

Quiroga's entire literary output is not extensive—one narrative in dialogue, two novelettes, and some ninety-six short stories, sketches, and articles. The total impact, too, of his work is slight. Thin in substance in general, it is on the whole not much better than the usual type of journalistic material that fills the pages of the literary supplement of Sunday editions of newspapers or of weekly periodicals such as *Caras y Caretas* and *El Hogar,* in which much of it appeared. The influence of Poe on Quiroga in regard to themes and motifs is indisputable, but not in regard to his short-story technique, for only a few of his stories—**"El Solitario,"** **"La Gallina degollada,"** and **"Los Mensú"**—can be cited as examples of fair narration. His forte, however, does not lie in narration or in the analysis of human character. It is his ability to transfer to his pages the atmosphere of Misiones, the scene of so many of his joys and sorrows, that catches the attention of his readers and gives him distinction as a writer. Of the many stories that have Misiones as their background, those that are outstanding are very limited in number. For only in three—**"El Salvaje,"** **"Anaconda,"** and **"El Regreso de Anaconda"**—does his genius find its highest expression. But they are enough to entitle him to international fame as a short-story writer.

Notes

1. Among the most outstanding are *Antología de Cuentos mexicanos* (*Anthology of Mexican Tales*), 1926, by Ortiz de Montellano; *Los mejores Cuentos Venezolanos* (*The Best Venezuelan Tales*), 1923, by Valentín de Pedro and a recent two-volume work, *Antología del Cuento venezolano* (*Anthology of Venezuelan Tales*), 1940, by A. Uslar Pietri and Julián Padrón; various volumes in the collection *Biblioteca Aldeana de Colombia* (*The Aldine Collection of Colombian Literature*), 1936, compiled by D. Samper Ortega; *Los Cuentistas chilenos* (*Story-Tellers of Chile*), n. d., by R. Silva Castro and *Antología de Cuentistas chilenos* (*Anthology of Chilean Tales*), 1938, by Manuel Latorre, one of Chile's best *cuentistas*; and *Los mejores Cuentos* (*The Best of Tales*), 1919, by Manuel Gálvez and *Antología de Cuentistas rioplatenses* (*Anthology of the River Plate Region*), both of which include *cuentos* of the River Plate region.

2. Only a few such writers can be mentioned here: Javier Viana, whose *Campo* (*In the Country*), in 1898, was followed by more than a dozen collections of stories; Baldomero Lillo's *Sub Terra,* 1904, and *Sub Sole,* 1907; Blanco Fombona's *Cuentos Americanos* (*American Stories*), 1904-13, 1920; Horacio Quiroga's stories concerning Misiones in *Cuentos de Amor, de Locura y de Muerte* (*Stories of Love, Madness, and Death*), 1917; López Albújar's *Cuentos Andinos* (*Andean Tales*), 1920, and *Nuevos Cuentos andinos* (*New Andean Tales*), 1937; and José de la Cuadra's *El Amor que dormía* (*The Love that Slept*), 1930, *Repisas* (*Brackets*), 1931, *La Vuelta de Locura* (*The Recurrence of Madness*), 1932, *Horno* (*The Furnace*), 1932, and *Los Sangurimas* (*The Sangurimas Family*), 1934.

George D. Schade (essay date 1976)

SOURCE: Schade, George D. Introduction to *The Decapitated Chicken and Other Stories by Horacio Quiroga,* selected and translated by Margaret Sayers Peden, pp. ix-xvii. Austin: University of Texas Press, 1976.

[*In the following essay, an introduction to a volume of English translations of Quiroga's short stories, Schade offers biographical details on Quiroga's life that are apparent in his narratives, and surveys several of the works contained in the collection* The Decapitated Chicken.]

A new edition of Horacio Quiroga stories—in this case, the first selective translation into English ranging over his complete work—reminds us of a superb writer and offers a pretext for talking about him. Of course, the round dozen stories which make up this volume can speak for themselves, and many translations appear unescorted by an introduction; nonetheless, readers who are not acquainted with Quiroga may wish to learn something further about this author, generally regarded by the critics as a classic and one of the finest short-story writers Latin America has produced. Surveying his work afresh, we find that this favorable verdict still holds true and that his achievement continues to be admirable. Quiroga stands apart from the bulk of his contemporaries in Spanish American literature and head and shoulders above most of them.

Certain thematic designs run through Quiroga's life and also through his stories. He was born the last day of the year 1878 in El Salto, Uruguay, and died by his own hand in February, 1937, in Buenos Aires, Argentina. The fifty-eight-year span of his lifetime was crammed with adventure, hazardous enterprise, and recurrent tragedy and violence, particularly suicide. When he was a babe in arms, his father was accidentally killed when a shotgun went off on a family outing. Later his stepfather, desperately ill and of whom Horacio was fond, shot himself, and the young Quiroga, seventeen at the time, was the first to come upon the grisly scene. In 1902 Quiroga accidentally shot and killed, with a pistol, one of his best friends and literary companions. In 1915 his first wife, unable to endure the hardships of life in the jungle of Misiones where Quiroga insisted on living, committed suicide by taking a fatal dose of poison, leaving the widower with two small children to raise. Finally, Quiroga himself took cyanide to end his own life when he realized he was suffering from an incurable cancer.

His love affairs and marriages were also turbulent. He married twice, both times very young women; his second wife, a friend of his daughter, was nearly thirty years his junior. The first marriage ended with his wife's suicide; the second, in separation. This singular amount of violence marring the writer's personal life cannot be overly stressed, for it explains a great deal about his obsession with death, which is so marked in his work.

Quiroga's zest for adventure and the magnetic attraction the jungle hinterland of northern Argentina held for him are also biographical details that have great impact on his work. His first trip to the province of Misiones occurred in 1903, when he accompanied his friend and fellow writer Leopoldo Lugones as photographer on an expedition to study the Jesuit ruins there. Next came a trip to the Chaco to plant cotton, where he built his own hut and had his first pioneering experience. In 1906 he bought some land in San Ignacio, Misiones, and from that date on divided his time between the hinterland and Buenos Aires. He tried various experiments in Misiones, such as the making of charcoal and the distillation of an orange liqueur. These endeavors ended in failure but provided him with good material for his stories, as did his myriad other activities there, like constructing his bungalow, furniture, and boats and hunting and studying the wildlife of the region.

In his teens Quiroga began writing under the aegis of the Modernist movement, which dominated the Spanish American literary scene at the turn of the century. Soon, however, he reacted against the decadent and highly artificial mode of his first book, *Los arrecifes de coral* (*Coral reefs,* published 1901), which contained Modernist poems, prose pieces, and stories, and turned to writing tales firmly rooted in reality, though they often emphasized the bizarre or the monstrous.

Commentators have tended to discount the significance or merit of some of Quiroga's early works, such as the longish story **"The Pursued."** Recently this tale has received more favorable critical attention. Our translator,

who has made an excellent selection of Quiroga's stories that few would quarrel with, maintains that **"The Pursued"** is the most modern piece he wrote because of what it anticipates. It is undeniably one of Quiroga's more ambiguous and inscrutable stories, lending itself to various interpretations as it elaborates on the theme of madness.

Another early story, **"The Feather Pillow,"** first published in 1907, is a magnificent example of his successful handling of the Gothic tale, reminiscent of Poe, whom he revered as master. The effects of horror, something mysterious and perverse pervading the atmosphere, are all there from the beginning of the story, and Quiroga skillfully, gradually readies the terrain, so that we are somewhat prepared for, though we do not anticipate, the sensational revelation at the end. But this story takes on much more meaning and subtlety when we realize that the anecdote can be interpreted on a symbolical level: the ailing Alicia suffers from hallucinations brought on by her husband's hostility and coldness, for he is the real monster.

For three decades Quiroga continued writing and publishing stories in great quantity—his total output runs over two hundred—many of them also of impressive quality. Certain collections should be singled out as high points: *Los desterrados* (*The exiled,* published 1926) and *Cuentos de amor, de locura, y de muerte* (*Stories of love, madness, and death,* published 1917). The splendid title of *Cuentos* sets forth his major themes and could properly be the heading for his entire work. Quiroga also achieved great popularity with his *Cuentos de la selva* (published 1918), translated into English as *Jungle Tales,* a volume for children of all ages, permeated with tenderness and humor and filled with whimsy. These delightful stories are peopled by talking animals and are cast in a fable mold, usually with an underlying moral.

"Anaconda," which describes a world of snakes and vipers and how they battle men and also one another, is one of Quiroga's most celebrated stories. It moves at a more leisurely pace than the typical Quiroga tale, with spun-out plot, lingering over realistic details. The characters in this ophidian world are more compelling than believable, and the animal characterization is not perhaps as striking as that of some shorter narratives like **"Sunstroke."** But Quiroga, the fluent inventor at work, can almost always make something interesting happen. **"Anaconda"** lies on the ill-defined frontier between the long story and the novella and will gainsay those who think Quiroga sacrifices everything to rapid narrative. Consequently, it loses something of the dramatic intensity of other stories, despite its original title of "A Drama in the Jungle: The Vipers' Empire." The tightknit, tense structure we can perceive in **"Drifting," "The Dead Man,"** and many other Quiroga stories is considerably slackened here. On the other hand, Quiroga compensates for this by offering us a story of exuberant imagination, rich in irony, with abundant satirical implications about man and his behavior. Like the *Jungle Tales,* "Anaconda" will have a special appeal for children, but, unlike the former, it is essentially directed to a mature audience.

If we examine Quiroga's stories attentively, we will find moments full of vision concerning mankind, often illuminating a whole character or situation in a flash. Quiroga has an astute awareness of the problems besetting man on every side, not only the pitfalls of savage Nature but also those pertaining to human relationships. Man is moved by greed and overweening ambition, hampered by fate, and often bound by circumstances beyond his control. Quiroga penetrates the frontiers of profound dissatisfaction and despair felt by man. His vision is clear and ruthless, and his comments on human illusions can be withering. Yet it is man's diversity that emerges in these stories, his abjectness and his heroism. Though Quiroga never palliates man's faults and weaknesses, the heroic virtues of courage, generosity, and compassion stand out in many of his stories.

All this rich and multifarious human material is shaped and patterned into story form by a master craftsman. Quiroga was very conscious of the problems involved in the technique and art of the short story, and, like Edgar Allan Poe and other masters of the genre, he wrote about them. His most famous document on technique is what he dubbed a "Manual of the Perfect Short Story Writer," a succinct decalogue filled with cogent and compelling advice. The usual warnings stressing economy of expression are here: for instance, "Don't use unnecessary adjectives"; and also those concerned with careful advance planning: "Don't start to write without knowing from the first word where you are going. In a story that comes off well, the first three lines are as important as the last three." It is easy to find apt examples of the latter dictum in Quiroga's work: **"Drifting," "The Dead Man," "The Decapitated Chicken," "The Feather Pillow,"** and so on, to cite only from the stories translated in this collection.

The last commandment in Quiroga's decalogue to the person desiring to write perfect short stories is probably the most suggestive: "Don't think about your friends when you write or the impression your story will make. Tell the tale as if the story's only interest lay in the small surroundings of your characters, of which you might have been one. In no other way is *life* achieved in the short story." Quite rightly Quiroga emphasizes the word *life,* for it is this elusive and vital quality which lies at the core of his stories. The idea that the author or his narrator might be one of the characters is also significant, for he often was one of the characters, at least in some aspect, or felt that he was one of them.

Certainly in his best stories Quiroga practiced the economy he talks about in his manual and which is characteristic of good short-story writers. Almost every page will bear testimony to this laconic quality. It is a brevity which excludes everything redundant but nothing which is really significant. Wonderful feats of condensation are common, as in **"The Dead Man,"** where he shows his powers in dramatic focus on a single scene, or in **"Drifting,"** a stark story in which everything seems reduced to the essential, the indispensable. The brief opening scene of **"Drifting,"** where a man is bitten by a venomous snake, contains the germs of all that comes afterward. The language is terse and pointed, the situation of tremendous intensity, the action straightforward and lineal. Everything moves in an unbroken line from beginning to end, like an arrow to its target, to use Quiroga's phrase referring to technique in the short story. The title, too, is particularly appropriate: while the dying protagonist literally drifts in his canoe downriver seeking aid, we see him helplessly adrift on the river of life, unable to control his fatal destiny from the moment the snake sinks its fangs into his foot.

In **"Drifting," "The Son," "The Dead Man,"** and other stories, Quiroga plays on a life/death vibration, juxtaposing the two. While the throes of death slowly diminish the protagonist of **"The Dead Man,"** Nature and the landscape surrounding him pulsate with life—the ordinary domestic quality of daily life he is so accustomed to—so that he cannot accept the fact of his dying. Our curiosity is kept unfalteringly alive by Quiroga's dramatic technique. At his finest moments Quiroga reaches and maintains a high degree of emotional intensity, as in the three stories cited above, which have in common their magnificent treatment of death. Quiroga flinches from none of the difficulties perhaps implicit in this theme. In his dealing with death he is natural and matter-of-fact; we find no mawkish romantic sentimentality, no glossing over of realistic attributes, and no gloating over ugly clinical details characteristic of naturalistic writers.

There is also much suggestion and implication, rather than outright telling, in Quiroga's best work. **"The Dead Man"** is probably the most skillful instance of this technique, but interesting examples abound throughout Quiroga's narratives. A case in point is the heartfelt story **"The Son,"** where the protagonist father, suffering from hallucinations, imagines that his young son, who went hunting in the forest, has had a fatal accident. The father stumbles along in a frenzy, cutting his way through the thick and treacherous jungle, seeking a sign of the boy. Suddenly he stifles a cry, for he has seen something in the sky. The suggestion, confirmed later by the boy's death at the end of the story, is that the father saw a buzzard.

Dialogue does not play a heavy role in Quiroga's work. Occasionally we listen to scraps of talk, but, in the main, his stories do not move by dialogue; they are thrust along by overt action. Exceptions to this rule are **"Anaconda"** and some other animal tales. A stunning example of Quiroga's handling of dialogue occurs in **"A Slap in the Face"** toward the end of the story where the peon wreaks his terrible revenge on Korner, beating the boss into a bloody, inert pulp with his riding whip. Here Quiroga contrasts most effectively Korner's silence, symbolical of his beaten condition, with the peon's crackling commands *Levántate* ("Get up") and *Caminá* ("Get going"), the only words uttered in the latter part of this violent, sadistic scene. The word *caminá*, repeated four times at slight intervals, suggests an onomatopoeic fusion with the sound of the cracking whip, another instance of Quiroga's technical genius—language functioning to blend auditory effects with content.

Narrative interest seems to prevail over other elements which often dominate in the short story, such as the poetical, symbolical, or philosophical. And Quiroga does not have a social ax to grind. But some of the most trenchant social commentary in Spanish American fiction can be perceived in his stories, particularly those concerned with the exploitation of Misiones lumberjacks, like **"Los mensú" ("The Monthly Wage Earners")** and **"A Slap in the Face."** In these tales no preaching is involved. Quiroga is clearly on the side of the oppressed but does not express their point of view exclusively. Consequently, the reader draws his own conclusions, and the social impact is more deeply felt.

Setting, as well as narrative technique, is vitally important to Quiroga, because it is inseparable from the real, the ordinary, domestic, day-to-day experience of human existence. Quiroga's feelings are bound up in place, in his adopted corner of Argentina, Misiones province, rather than the urban centers of Buenos Aires or Montevideo, where he also lived. He is vastly attracted to the rugged jungle landscape, where the majority of his best stories take place (nine of the twelve translated here). And he makes us feel the significance of his setting, too—the symbolic strength of the rivers, especially the Paraná, and the power and hypnotic force of its snake-infested jungles. So does this dot on the map that is Misiones come throbbingly alive for us. It is not just a framework in which to set his stories but an integral part of them, of Quiroga himself, brimming over with drama and life.

In the best stories, many of which appear in this collection, action is perfectly illustrative: the stories have not only movement but also depth. The apparent spareness allows for a greater complexity and suggestion. A fine short story should have implications which will continue to play in the reader's mind when the story is done and over, as we can attest in **"The Feather Pillow," "The Dead Man,"** and almost all the stories included here. We are struck at the end of **"A Slap in the Face"** by the dual function of the river, which provides the final solution. The peon thrusts the almost lifeless, despicable Korner onto a raft where he will drift inevitably to his death, while the peon takes off in a boat in the opposite direction toward haven on the Brazilian shore. Thus the river assumes the role of justice, meting out death to the guilty and life to the accused. **"Juan Darién"** is probably one of the most subtle and interesting stories Quiroga ever penned. Rich in suggestions, it opens up to us a world of fantastic reality in which the protagonist is a tiger/boy. At one point in the story Quiroga has the inspector say that truth can be much stranger than fiction. Interpretations of this story will vary, but the most rewarding one may well be that of Juan Darién as a Christ-like figure.

Swift recognition for his mastery of the short story came to Quiroga fairly early in his career, and he continued to enjoy fame throughout his lifetime. In the Spanish-speaking world he is still popular today and almost universally admired, though the type of story he excelled at, in which man is pitted against Nature and rarely if ever wins out, is no longer so commonly composed in Latin America. The contemporary Argentine Julio Cortázar, a writer very unlike Quiroga but also topflight in the short-story genre, has pointed out perspicaciously Quiroga's best and most lasting qualities: he knew his trade in and out; he was universal in dimension; he subjected his themes to dramatic form, transmitting to his readers all their virtues, all their ferment, all their projection in depth; he wrote tautly and described with intensity so that the story would make its mark on the reader, nailing itself in his memory.

Quiroga's is an art that speaks to us clearly and passionately, charged with the emotion of his jungle setting. The action is usually of heroic simplicity. Quiroga does not transcribe life; he dramatizes it. His vision is fresh, intense, dramatic. He seems caught up in it, and so are we.

Translator's Note

The Quiroga stories in this book are available in several Spanish editions. In translating these stories I used the Biblioteca Rodó Series (Horacio Quiroga, *Cuentos,* Biblioteca Rodó Series, Montevideo, 1937-1945), in which the stories are located as follows:

"Sunstroke" ("La insolación," vol. 2)

"The Pursued" ("Los perseguidos," vol. 7)

"The Decapitated Chicken" ("La gallina degollada," vol. 1)

"Drifting" ("A la deriva," vol. 1)

"A Slap in the Face" ("Una bofetada," vol. 1)

"In the Middle of the Night" ("En la noche," vol. 3)

"Juan Darién" ("Juan Darién," vol. 4)

"The Dead Man" ("El hombre muerto," vol. 2)

"Anaconda" ("Anaconda," vol. 3)

"The Incense Tree Roof" ("El techo de incienso," vol. 5)

"The Son" ("El hijo," vol. 1)

I took "The Feather Pillow" ("El almohadón de pluma") from Quiroga's *Sus mejores cuentos,* with introduction and notes by John A. Crow (Mexico City: Editorial Cultura, 1943).

John S. Brushwood (essay date 1983)

SOURCE: Brushwood, John S. "The Spanish American Short Story from Quiroga to Borges." In *The Latin American Short Story: A Critical History,* edited by Margaret Sayers Peden, pp. 71-96. Boston, Mass.: Twayne Publishers, 1983.

[*In the following excerpt, Brushwood discusses Quiroga's "statement of principles" regarding short story writing, examines the manifestation of these principles in Quiroga's works, and studies them in relation to two stories by other Latin American writers.*]

QUIROGA AND THE BASIS OF THE TWENTIETH-CENTURY SHORT STORY

If asked for the name of an outstanding Spanish American *cuentisa* ("short-story writer"), a specialist in the literature would very likely think of Horacio Quiroga (Uruguay, 1878-1937) or Jorge Luis Borges (Argentina, 1899-). A second probability is corollary—that two decades ago, the answer would have been Quiroga; more recently, Borges would come to mind first. The latter's substantial influence goes back farther than two decades to the mid-1940s, however, some years passed before his name became virtually a household word internationally. This [essay] does not undertake an analysis of the complete Borges phenomenon, but considers some of his early stories. From Quiroga's first important collection, *Cuentos de amor, de locura y de muerte* (*Stories of Love, Madness and Death*) in 1917 to Borges's *Ficciones* in 1944, the trajectory of short fiction shows a gradual but clear change in subject matter and in narrative technique.

Quiroga was the first Spanish American writer to pay close attention to how a story is made, and at the same time, dedicate himself almost exclusively to writing short fiction. In a statement of principles for the *cuentista,* he sets forth several ideas that are especially inter-esting because of his importance as *magister.*[1] Although Quiroga did not consistently assume such a role for himself and was quite aware that some younger writers were not entirely sympathetic to his work, his decalogue for the perfect *cuentista* states his case in no uncertain terms. He first exhorts the writer to have limitless faith in his literary master, and specifically mentions Poe, Maupassant, Kipling, and Chekov. The first two are quite clearly present in Quiroga's work; Kipling is apparent in the stories about anthropomorphized jungle beasts; Chekov's presence is not as easy to specify, but there is certainly no reason to doubt its existence. Beyond this oath of allegiance, Quiroga says that the writer should know before beginning the narration how the story is going to develop. It seems unlikely that he would have much patience with the writer whose characters take charge of the work. He warns against excessive use of adjectives, claiming that if the writer controls language well enough to choose the best substantive, modifiers need be used only sparingly. Writing under the impulse of emotion should be avoided, Quiroga says; once the emotion has cooled, however, the writer does well to re-create it in the experience of his work. Interesting an audience should not be a concern; rather, the *cuentista* should feel certain that what he writes is of interest to the characters about whom he is writing.

In general, these principles suggest a rather comfortable fit into the realist-naturalist tradition. That is indeed where Quiroga is based in literary history, but with modifications caused by the Spanish American literary milieu. He began writing in the early years of the twentieth century, toward the end of *modernismo* and at a time when realism and naturalism were generally recognized, but not always understood. One of his early stories, **"Cuento sin razó, pero cansado"** (1901; **"Story Without Cause, But Weary"**), may be safely thought of as *modernista* because one of its qualities is the sense of ennui associated with the French decadents. There is also in it some of naturalism's inevitability, and this characteristic becomes dominant in many stories, including the well-known **"La gallina degollada"** (1909; **"The Decapitated Chicken"**).[2]

In this story, four idiot brothers commit an act of violence that is suggested to them by their having witnessed an ordinary act that seems analogous—to them—and quite acceptable. Quiroga introduces the brothers in an initial scene, then provides some background followed by emphasis on the parents' marital problems. The conflict that is developed in much of the story is based on the attitude of the parents toward their offspring. When this conflict reaches a climax, it points the reader in a direction different from that actually taken by the story. The narrator—always completely in control of the characters and recounting their actions without detailed characterization—removes the brothers from their regular routine, relates how they witnessed the stimulus action, and returns them to the place in which he first described them. Their subsequent action, wordless and in common accord, is an inevitable result of their mental condition.

The action of **"La gallina degollada"** takes place in the environs of Buenos Aires, but the story is in no way regionalistic. Quiroga often placed his stories in settings that were familiar to him, but his themes are universal. In **"Juan Darién"** (1920), the jungle is a factor, but not in terms of the man-against-nature theme found in many works located in unsettled areas. Rather, **"Juan Darién"** is a story of human injustice in the most general sense, not in terms of an attack on a specific or localized social problem. An animal is transformed into a human being and when his identity is discovered, he suffers the fate of those who threaten society because they are different.

The general structure of **"Juan Darién"** is what one would expect in a realist story: introduction, exposition of conflict, development, climax, and denouement. It is not a realistic story; it is a fantasy, and Quiroga never leaves any room for doubt about what kind of tale we are reading. At the beginning, the narrator states the fact of the animal's marvelous transformation. There is no time to wonder whether or not there may be some natural explanation for this phenomenon. We are dealing with a kind of fairy tale, and the language so indicates when the narrator uses expressions that are similar to English. "Once there was . . ." or "Well, of course . . . ," as introductions to paragraphs. The conflict in **"Juan Darién"** is between animal violence and human violence. Humans are always unjust; their only redeeming trait appears to be in the maternal role—the mother alone knows "the sacred rights of life."

Violence is frequent in Quiroga's work, but its significance varies in important ways. In **"La gallina degollada,"** it creates horror; in **"Juan Darién,"** it is related to justice and injustice. In **"El hombre muerto"** (1920; **"The Dead Man"**), the protagonist comes to a violent end by accident, and one thinks less about the violence itself than about the man's awareness, or lack of awareness, of his condition. The general ambience of "el hombre muerto" tends to make the story appear more regionalistic than is actually the case. The setting is tropical and rural. The man falls on his machete in the course of his work and dies in a period of thirty minutes that are accounted for in the narration. There is no surprise ending, nothing that need be withheld in a discussion of how it works out. It is impossible to summarize the story without duplicating it, however, because the experience of this narrative is the man's growing awareness of his condition. The basic conflict is quite simply between life and death; its development is what the man thinks of his total situation (his immediate con-

dition and its implications). Quiroga uses repetition with good effect as his protagonist becomes increasingly aware of what is happening to him and what it means in terms of the world in which he has lived. The narrator speaks mainly in free, indirect style, so we see what the man sees even though we are being informed by the third-person voice; an occasional comment from this point of view does not alter the basic narration in any significant way. Probably the outstanding device used by Quiroga in this story is a shift of focus in the last paragraph so that we are no longer seeing as the man sees but as he is seen. This change justifies the title; before this conclusion, the man is dying, but has not reached the end. The fact that **"El hombre muerto"** cannot be synopsized satisfactorily characterizes it as a more modern story than the other two by Quiroga. It would be difficult, and pointless, to say that one manner is more typical of the author than the other.

The perspective in which we see Quiroga in the early twentieth century as a kind of pillar of the Spanish American short story may be illuminated by reference to two stories by authors of the same generation. One of these, "En provincia" (1914; "In the Provinces") is by Augusto D'Halmar [Augusto Geomine Thompson] (Chile, 1882-1950), who is considered a naturalist writer; the other is "El hombre que parecía un caballo" (1915; "The Man Who Resembled a Horse"), by Rafael Arévalo Martínez (Guatemala, 1884-), who may be called either modernist or postmodernist. Neither of these stories is *typical* of either naturalism or modernism; each, however, has sufficient characteristics of the heritage that was Quiroga's, that their publication, so contemporaneous to Quiroga's own stories, emphasizes the sense of change that one experiences in reading the latter's work.

The small-town atmosphere of D'Halmar's story is faithful to the title, but identification with a specific geographical area is extremely difficult. The protagonist, an unimportant employee of a commercial firm, is a confirmed bachelor whose only social contact is made through playing a musical instrument. The humdrum quality of his life and, indeed, the generally slow pace of the town are readily appreciable; however, the effect of the story is not to elicit sympathy for a lonely person—he is quite content with his life. The conflict is triggered by a woman who involves him in an adulterous affair, using him for her own benefit. "En provincia" will not do as a textbook example of naturalism, because the case of adultery is so extreme as to seem used as satire and because the situation is not treated as though it were a clinical study. It is narrative procedure that gives the story its special personality.

The protagonist is the first-person narrator. He introduces himself, describes his situation and the way he lives, and gives a few words about his background.

Then he comments on his ambivalence concerning whether or not to tell his story, and concludes that although he will write it, no one will ever see it. Now the reader enters into a fascinating relationship with the narrator—the secret is out, or is going to be. It is worth noting that D'Halmar does not use the familiar device of the "found" manuscript. Of course, if we are to believe the narrator, someone must have found what he wrote, and he did not intend to have it discovered. The important effect is that the narrator's attitude toward the telling is really a part of the story we read, and the first conflict we are aware of has to do with that attitude. Then the protagonist moves into an account of the most important event in his life. This second conflict develops on the basis of his natural rights as an individual against the exigencies of social organization. Repeated episodes of sustained emotional intensity bring this conflict to a climax. The man's acceptance of his role, at this point, completes his characterization of himself and brings the reader to the starting point of the story of the adultery.

Arévalo Martínez's "El hombre que parecía un caballo" is more character sketch than traditionally plotted story. The narrative does move in time, enough to indicate change taking place in a friendship, but even this process of change is essentially a means of characterizing Aretal, the principal figure. A metaphor is established in terms of the equine analogy, which begins with reference to physical appearance and then becomes relevant to the more subtle manifestations of Aretal's personality. Arévalo Martínez also uses many metaphors that are very *modernista,* such as references to jewels, and the word azure to indicate the soul or the finer side of human personality. The story has its amusing side, created especially by Aretal's exterior similarity to a horse. He holds his head to one side, trots around the salon, sidles up to ladies, and whinnies. The revelation of his character is far more profound than these examples might indicate, however, and since we see him entirely from the narrator's point of view, the story is actually an evaluation of Aretal's personality.

Arévalo Martínez's affinity for *modernismo* is apparent enough in "El hombre que parecía un caballo," but he avoids the lush estheticism that characterized some *modernista* work and provoked a movement by some writers toward portrayal of the commonplace, the familiar. This is the phenomenon frequently called *criollismo.*[3] In the early years of the century, there was a complex of "isms" that were different from each other in some respects but not in others, and were also concurrent to a degree. One of the functions of *modernismo* was as a reaction against the ugliness of realism and naturalism, and criollismo was a reaction against the hyperestheticism of the *modernistas,* but these movements and countermovements did not cancel the characteristics of any of the forces involved. No movement comes to a

standstill when a reaction makes itself felt. That is why "En provincia" and "El hombre que parecía un caballo" show characteristics of two different movements without being perfect examples. Change is taking place; at the same time, some stories continue to hew close to the line of one "ism" or another.

Alfonso Hernández Catá's (Cuba, 1885-1940) "Noventa días" ("Ninety Days") is a naturalist story about a deteriorating infatuation told as if it were a case history. Its development follows a very orthodox pattern in which the narrator establishes the setting, introduces the principal character, and then initiates the action, which in turn follows a standard pattern. Spring, an important factor in the atmosphere, becomes even more important in the action as the narrator personifies the season and shows how it inspires an infatuation that is doomed never to blossom into real love. The conflict is represented in the personalities of the two principals, who are entirely different from each other and little inclined to make concessions once the magic of spring is lost; it is developed through a series of similar incidents until the story ends in tragedy. Hernández Catá's story, on the trajectory of literary history, could fit comfortably before or after *modernismo.*

These early stories use a wide variety of anecdotal material, the nature of which says a great deal about what the authors were doing in ways that went beyond classification by literary movement. Of the three Quiroga stories, **"La gallina degollada"** may seem at first to be terrifyingly real. It is certainly terrifying, but on second thought it seems less a representation of reality than **"El hombre muerto,"** because in the first story Quiroga's material is a psychological principle rather than a normally observed happening. **"Juan Darién"** is a fantasy that may have been born of observed reality, but its incident comes no closer to experienced reality than allegory does. On the basis of **"La gallina degollada"** and **"Juan Darién,"** one would hardly call Quiroga a *criollista,* since these stories are not reproductions of everyday, familiar Spanish American reality. **"El hombre muerto"** is a different matter. Its theme is universal, but the actual happening takes place in the tropics where a man has a banana grove and works with a machete. These facts provide some of the quality of our-own-Spanish-American-reality sought by the *criollistas.*

In fact, the themes of all the stories mentioned so far are universal, although some of the material may be slightly less so. **"El hombre muerto"** uses the most clearly regionalistic material. The setting of "En provincia" is provincial, but not identified with a region in that the action itself is not influenced by regional characteristics; "Noventa días" belongs anyplace where spring suggests romance. In both stories, the authors are relating ordinary human situations, but it is doubtful that there is a sense of closeness, of personal relationship, between them and the material. Interestingly, the story that may seem most fanciful, "El hombre que parecía un caballo," is probably closest to real life, a fantasized account of something that really happened.

Narrative technique has a great deal to do with how the reader understands the story. Arévalo Martínez might have told of his friendship with Señor Aretal in countless different ways. His decision to use the horse analogy in combination with words suggesting great refinement creates a contrast that is both amusing and perceptive. If he had narrated a typically realist story, the actions of the two people with respect to each other would be the same, but the effect would be different. The story could be more psychological, for example, but the suggestive contrast would not be emphasized. In the case of **"La gallina degollada,"** Quiroga decided to characterize the parents more than the idiot sons. This creates a more complex understanding of the parents while presenting the four boys with clinical objectivity; as their role becomes preeminent, attention focuses on the psychological principle. The same story told any other way might change emphasis, but not the relationship of persons to actions. Quiroga might even have chosen to stress the ambience of a particular area, in which case the story would have seemed more *criollista,* as does **"Juan Darién."**

Notes

1. Horacio Quiroga, *Cuentos,* ed. R. Lazo (Mexico City: Porrúa, 1968, p. xxxiv. The decalogue appears in English in William Peden's "Some Notes on Quiroga's Stories," *Review* (Winter 1976): 41-43.

2. The dates of the Quiroga stories refer to the year of journal publication to emphasize the chronologic span of his work and the dates of different kinds of stories.

3. See Luis Leal, *Historia del cuento hispanoamericano,* (Mexico City, 1966) p. 69.

Lon Pearson (essay date 1986)

SOURCE: Pearson, Lon. "Horacio Quiroga's Obsessions with Abnormal Psychology and Medicine as Reflected in 'La gallina degollada.'" *Literature and Psychology* 32, no. 2 (1986): 32-46.

[*In the following essay, Pearson studies the sources of Quiroga's interest in medicine and abnormal psychology and illustrates how the author expresses these interests in the short story "La gallina degollada" ("The Decapitated Chicken").*]

Horacio Quiroga is one of the most famous and colorful short story writers to come out of Spanish America during the early part of this century. His biography is nearly

as intriguing as his stories, for his life was filled with as many tragedies as is the fiction of most authors:[1] his father accidentally set off a borrowed shotgun while stepping out of a boat after hunting, killing himself in the process;[2] a brother suffered a similar fate and a sister died before Quiroga was twenty two;[3] Quiroga's stepfather and first wife both committed suicide in a horrible fashion; and Quiroga accidentally shot and killed his poet friend, Federico Ferrando, as he was checking Ferrando's new pistol for him.[4] This propensity toward violence climaxes in Quiroga's suicide with cyanide in 1937 when he learned he had cancer of the prostate. An epilogue to this violent way to end life is the suicide of Quiroga's daughter Eglé in 1939 and of his son Darío in 1951.

Almost as if they were continuing this tragic course which his life epitomizes, several of Quiroga's stories emphasize a violent death.[5] Anderson Imbert calls these tales, "sus cuentos crueles, en . . . que se describe la enfermedad, la muerte, el fracaso, la alucinación, el miedo a lo sobrenatural, el alcoholismo."[6] Along with his writing about characters who fall victim to this same vein of erratic and abnormal behavior, Quiroga also became fascinated with medical, scientific and psychological problems that were stirred up during the first decade of the twentieth century.[7]

In this study my focus is on Quiroga's first writing period: his writings between about 1900 and 1910, a period in which his use of gruesome detail[8] and themes of abnormal psychology prevail.[9] I will not be examining Quiroga's psychological development of his characters; rather, this paper demonstrates how Quiroga's fascination with psychology and medicine led him to develop the short story **"La gallina degollada,"** where he experimented with his ideas about abnormal psychology. In essence, it will be necessary to examine portions of Quiroga's biography to find the links between his feelings about abnormal medical and psychological problems and thus discover how he developed such situations in his writings of that period.[10]

Quiroga was fascinated by science[11] (once he blew up a room in the family home and nearly burned down the entire house with a chemistry experiment).[12] He was extremely interested in spiritualism[13] and in psychology,[14] and he was very well-versed in both subjects.[15] To be able to disseminate his newly-found concepts of psychology, Quiroga founded in September of 1899 the *Revista de Salto,* which had as a subtitle (*Semanario de literatura y ciencias sociales*).[16] During its brief five-month existence, Quiroga published (besides some Poe-like tales he had written) his essays on topics as disperse as *Modernismo* and "Sadismo-masoquismo."[17] Also, writers in his group were fascinated by drugs, such as opium, chloroform,[18] morphine,[19] and hashish.[20] Quiroga was the most daring of his literary friends,[21] and he led the way for his group to examine the psychological effects that these drugs had on humans.[22] The young men often wrote on such topics and discussed the effects of hallucinogens in their literary sessions or "tertulias."[23] Quiroga's fascination with medicine and popular psychology led him to insert several of these topics as themes in his short stories. An Uruguayan compatriot of his, Alberto Zum Felde, relates to us this seldom-examined side of Quiroga's creative process:

> Sábese que era Quiroga un apasionado lector de libros y revistas científicas, sobre todo de ciencias psíquicas, aunque también naturales; que se nutría de ello más que de la literatura, que de ellos extraía inducciones y sugerencias. Puede suponerse lógicamente que lo que él buscaba en ese material científico era precisamente aquello que en la ciencia misma hay de misterioso, lo que está más allá de ella misma, pero se ve por sus ventanas.[24]

What one of these "windows of science" displayed to Quiroga was the rare and innovative subject matter which was to become the gruesome theme of **"La gallina degollada."** In this shocking story four unfortunate sons born to loving parents are suddenly afflicted with a strange congenital mental degeneracy. These four animal-like sons are harshly contrasted to the beautifully perfect daughter who was born after the four "monsters" causing their parents to ignore and neglect them because of their horrible condition.

"La gallina degollada" was published for the first time on July 10, 1909[25] (Quiroga's life changed drastically when he married his first wife on December 30, 1909). At this time he had gained enough of a reputation to be able to write for the popular magazine *Caras y caretas* (*Faces and masks*), where he had to learn to limit the length of his short stories to one or two pages each.[26] Later he reworked and polished these stories from *Caras y caretas* for his books. **"La gallina degollada"** appeared in his most widely known book of stories, ***Cuentos de amor, de locura y de muerte,*** which was published in 1917 by the Argentine novelist, Manuel Gálvez. Since that time, **"La gallina degollada"** has been known as one of the most morbid and macabre stories to ever have been published in South America. Because it was only recently translated to English as **"The Decapitated Chicken,"**[27] it has not had a wide dissemination in English-speaking circles.

The beginning of the story, though it focuses briefly on morbidity, does not allow one to suspect the tragedy that will come later:

> Todo el día, sentados en el patio, en un banco estaban los cuatro hijos idiotas del matrimonio Mazzini-Ferraz. Tenían la lengua entre los labios, los ojos estúpidos, y volvían la cabeza con toda la boca abierta.[28]

The mental image that Quiroga creates for the reader through the description of these four "slobbering idiots" appears at first to be one of "cretinism" or "mongol-

ism." Today, society prefers to say that such children appear to suffer from Down's Syndrome instead of calling them Mongolian idiots, a term that is now passé. But if the reader sees these boys as "idiots," then something is wrong with his approach to the story, because Down's Syndrome develops before birth, and these four children were all healthy at birth, continuing so until they were nearly two years old:

> La criatura creció bella y radiante hasta que tuvo año y medio. Pero en el vigésimo mes sacudiéronlo una noche convulsiones terribles y a la mañana siguiente no conocía más a sus padres. . . .
>
> Después de algunos días los miembros paralizados de la criatura recobraron el movimiento, pero la inteligencia, el alma, aun el instinto, se habían ido del todo. Había quedado profundamente idiota, baboso, colgante, muerto para siempre sobre las rodillas de su madre.

(p. 47)

It should be noted that Quiroga never uses the terms "cretino" nor "mongoloide" in this story, yet critics might be tempted to fall back on such terms referring to the four boys whose brains were virtually destroyed by high fevers and convulsions.[29]

Quiroga loves to play at being doctor during the narration.[30] He proposes different hypotheses for the illnesses, most of them based on genetic inheritance (which reminds one of Emile Zola's theses concerning Naturalism). Quiroga also mentions tuberculosis and menengitis as possible debilitating microbes which could have led to the boys' pathetic mental state. This confusion of idiocy and mental retardation with another mental disease called *autism* has been very common.

Autism was chosen as the name for this unusual children's disease because it means "extreme loneliness." Infantile autism denotes the withdrawal of a child from any group, as well as a loss of speech, and an obsessive desire for sameness and repetition.[31] It occurs in about one birth per every 2,500[32] (there are approximately 100,000 autistic children in the United States). Not all symptoms are found in every child, who run the gamut from deaf mutes to *idiots savants.*[33]

Because Infantile Autism was officially discovered only forty years ago, Quiroga appears to be among the first to have detailed many of the symptoms of the malady in literature. One of my objectives here is to define autism and show how it develops in **"La gallina degollada."** By approaching Quiroga's work in this way, I hope to make his story more acceptable to the skeptical reader, and I would like to demonstrate another aspect of his broad humanistic approach to literature.

Autism was discovered in 1943 by Leo Kanner, who worked with eleven autistic children at John Hopkins University. For this reason it is also known as Kanner's

Syndrome. The disease has no etiology—that is to say, no discernible cause—nor has any cure yet been discovered. Autism can also be brought on by or aggravated by birth injuries, cerebral palsy, viruses (such as meningitis), tuberose sclerosis, epilepsy, congenital rubella, infantile spasms, and the like:[34]

> Autism is a disorder beginning in the first two and a half years of life; characterised by a defect in the development of social relationships, a global language impairment and rigid or ritualistic patterns of behaviour; not primarily caused by psychogenic influences; and probably due to some variety of cognitive, perceptual or language deficit.[35]

In Quiroga's story, each of the four healthy boys suffer convulsions before they turn two, and, because of this unforseen attack on their normal brain functions, they forget all they had learned, becoming animal-like in their behavior. After the first child becomes an "idiot," a second child is born who suffers an identical trauma:

> Como es natural, el matrimonio puso todo su amor en la esperanza de otro hijo. Nació éste, y su salud y limpidez de risa reencendieron el porvenir extinguido. Pero a los dieciocho meses las convulsiones del primogénito se repetían, y al día signiente el segundo hijo amanecía idiota.
>
> (48)

After this second disastrous infancy, twins are born with the same congenital disorder. Finally Mazzini-Ferraz has a daughter who does not succumb to the same debilitating illness. The little girl turns four without suffering the convulsions that afflicted her brothers; however, the tragic conclusion of the story come about because the four boys imitate the maid who earlier that day had beheaded a chicken, bleeding it slowly to prepare it for the meal. The young boys' shocking imitative action comes about at a moment when the parents have gone for a walk. Something clicks in the boys' minds; they grab their little sister and cut off her head.

The many times I previously reached this shocking ending to the story and read Quiroga's careful detailing of the similarity and coincidence of the four brothers' illnesses, I had difficulty accepting the plausibility of the story. It did not seem likely that a daughter who was completely normal could be born into such a family. I wondered if Quiroga had not stretched his narrative credibility a bit too far, and the idea that four idiots could slaughter their little sister was adding insult to my badly injured reader's ego. Did Quiroga believe that all readers were naïve?

Then one day I was introduced to autism through an article in a local newspaper which outlined the similarities and differences between Down's syndrome and autism. Suddenly the four mentally retarded Mazzini-Ferraz boys came to life in my mind. The reality of their illness was as plausible to me now as if it had been an electrical shock that had awakened me to the possibility that it was so. I learned through subsequent research that, like Quiroga's fictive couple, many parents of autistic children insist that their infants were normal until they reached their eighteenth to twenty-fourth month. At that time, many parents state they underwent a personality and behavior change (similar to the Mazzini-Ferraz boys).[36] For example, when a child is autistic, it often rejects cuddling or holding, and the parent realizes that something serious has happened to the infant, especially if it was previously cuddly and alert. Before his crisis or trauma that brought on autism, the child may have talked, yet, immediately after, it could no longer speak. As many as half of all autistic children remain mute the rest of their lives.[37] A large middle group of autistic children (especially those who are trained early enough) may speak a few words, but they are mostly echolalic in their communication skills and cannot create with language. They merely repeat back what their interlocutor has said to them.[38] Some autistic children are flappers, twiddlers, twirlers, or rockers—seeking some form of self-stimulation—because they do not receive brain messages in the same way that normal humans do.[39] Some autistic children that I have personally observed slobber, and they can become self-destructive—banging their heads against objects—or they can cause danger to others because they have no concept of cause and effect.

In reference to autism in **"La gallina degollada,"** we find that Mazzini and his wife, Berta, do not give up hope of having normal children, something they have longed for, especially after their first two boys were born diseased:

> Del nuevo desastre brotaron nuevas llamaradas de dolorido amor, un loco anhelo de redimir de una vez para siempre la santidad de su ternura. Sobrevinieron mellizos, y punto por punto repitióse el proceso de los dos mayores.
>
> (p. 48)

That the third and fourth boys—twins—should also suffer from an inherited or congenital deficiency is important in establishing autism as the disease that plagues the Mazzini-Ferraz children. Autism occurs much more frequently in boys than in girls, at a ratio of nearly four or five to one. It also appears most often in first-born children, but it can and does affect siblings, as in this story. Of great interest to researchers has been the high incidence of autism in twins; it is such a strange illness that when autism attacks one twin, it generally will attack the other soon after.[40] This gene-related phenomenon makes the study of the disease of great interest to geneticists who are anxious to examine the hereditary factors of the disease in hopes of discovering a cause or cure.

Research on autism was held back more than twenty years, because several of the leading psychiatrists in the field believed that it was a form of self-willed schizophrenia,[41] caused or aggravated by parents who could not relate to their children.[42] Many mothers of autistic children who were brought to clinics for help were well-educated, middle-class women with careers—factors which blinded would-be objective researchers. More recently that particular idea concerning lack of attention has been rejected, but psychologists have also discovered that when children lack love or understanding, because parents fail to pay attention to the child's needs, then that child suffers a severe inability to progress within the limitations of the three groupings in which autistic children seem to fall.[43]

Even though the parents may not be to blame, most feel a great frustration in being totally unable to do anything constructive with their children.[44] Occasionally only professionals can handle autistics, especially the most severely handicapped, and in any case it is frustrating to parents and upsetting to a marriage to have an autistic child.[45]

Through Mazzini's comments, Quiroga portrays Berta's ambivalence toward her demented children together with her inability to love them, for she sees them as monsters:

> —Me parece—díjola una noche Mazzini, que acababa de entrar y se lavaba las manos—que podrías tener más limpios a los muchachos.
>
> Berta continuó leyendo como si no hubiera oído.
>
> (p. 49)

The couple then begins a heated discussion where the two each avoid the responsibility for their sons' births. Berta says, "tus hijos", but Mazzini corrects her, "nuestros hijos." Berta also contrasts the lack of affection she has for the boys with the great love she can freely express for her perfect daughter, Bertita:

> Si aun en los últimos tiempos Berta cuidaba siempre de sus hijos, al nacer Bertita olvidóse casi del todo de los ostros. Su solo recuerdo la horrorizaba como algo atroz que la hubieran obligado a cometer. A Mazzini, bien que en menor grado, pasábale lo mismo.
>
> (p. 50)

The more that Berta's love grows for her husband and four-year-old Bertita, "the greater her loathing for the monsters." Her husband is duly concerned about her attitude, and it becomes a point of contention between them:

> Con estos sentimientos, no hubo ya para los cuatro hijos mayores afecto posible. La sirvienta los vestía, les daba de comer, los acostaba, con visible brutalidad. No los lavaban casi nunca. Pasaban casi todo el día sentados frente al cerco, abandonados de toda remota caricia.
>
> (p. 51)

Berta's personal frustrations with the boys' pitiful condition eventually make things worse for the children, with the result that the boys are treated little better than animals because Berta prefers to ignore them.

By the time little Bertita turns four, the twins are seven, the second son is about nine, and the oldest boy is approximately twelve years old. Such are the ages of the children when the tragical murder takes place at the end of the story.

Mazzini and Berta both feel that their children's disorders have been passed on to them through their genes (and recent research into autism seems to substantiate this hypothesis). Mostly it is Mazzini's father who is blamed as the weak link in the genetic chain:

> —Pero dígame [doctor]: ¿Usted cree que es herencia, que . . . ?
>
> —En cuanto a la herencia paterna, ya le dije lo que creía cuando vi a su hijo. Respecto a la madre, hay allí un pulmón que so sopla bien. No veo nada más, pero hay un soplo un poco rudo. Hágala examinar detenidamente.
>
> (p. 47)

This problem of blame for their children's defects is also a constant sore point between Mazzini and Berta, who fight until they realize that their daughter Bertita has become ill. Berta retorts:

> —¡Pero yo he tenido padres sanos!, ¿oyes? ¡sanos! ¡Mi padre no ha muerto del delirio! ¡Yo hubiera tenido hijos como los de todo el mundo! ¡Esos son hijos tuyos, los cuatro tuyos!
>
> Mazzini explotó a su vez.
>
> —¡Víbora tísica! ¡Eso es lo que te dije, lo que te quiero decir! ¡Pregúntale, pregúntale al médico quién tiene la mayor culpa de la meningitis de tus hijos; mi padre o tu pulmón picado, víbora!
>
> Continuaron cada vez con mayor violencia, hasta que un gemido de Bertita selló instantáneamente sus bocas.
>
> (pp. 51-52)

Quiroga has given the mother's possible tuberculosis as one potential cause of the boys' disorders; Mazzini's father's alcoholism is another; and Quiroga's diagnosis of the disease through Mazzini's dialogue is meningitis, though it is not totally accurate.

Recent research at UCLA has led to the discovery that autistic children suffer from limited signals sent to their brains from the ears, eyes, and other sensory receptors (a disorder of sensorimotor integration).[46] Quiroga demonstrates this characteristic of autism in the boys in several passages, explaining that the boys were aware only of bright colors, like reds, and things like food or loud thunder:

No sabían deglutir, cambiar de sitio, ni aun sentarse. Aprendieron al fin caminar, pero chocaban contra tudo, por no darse cuenta de los obstáculos. Cuando los lavaban mugían hasta inyectarse de sangre el rostro. Animábanse sólo al comer o cuando veían colores brillantes u oían truenos. Se reían entonces, echando afuera lengua y ríos de baba, radiantes de frenesí bestial. Tenían, en cambio, cierta facultad imitativa; pero no se pudo obtener nada más.

(pp. 48-49)

These boys had no awareness of objects or obstacles; they ran into things.[47] An autistic child runs into objects in the same way and would readily walk into a busy street, unaware of the dangers there of being hit by a car. The autistic child has a nonfunctional use of objects and cannot see his hand connected to his body. He observes it with curiosity as if it were detached from him. Given a toy car, he would likely turn it over and spin the wheels, unaware that it had functionability.

For the Mazzini boys, food becomes a major reward, just as it does in training schools today (especially M&Ms candy, which is commonly used with autistics as a positive reinforcement by way of reward for proper responses and actions).[48] Food as a reward in this story is a major motif, for it leads to the final outcome of the plot.

The last point in the quotation before—the boys' "certain imitative facility"—reads as if Quiroga took it from a psychology text on autism. Often autistic children are limited to little more than imitation: they mirror actions and they mimic speech. Those who parrot language commonly repeat the second-person pronoun (you—a pathognomonic response) instead of transferring it to a first-person reply, or they will call themselves by their own name and repeat what others say (echolalia). Occasionally there are autistic children who can repeat an entire television advertisement or one side of a telephone conversation without comprehending what was said. Young autistic children love to do routines where they imitate the hand actions of others.[49] Moreover, this element of autistic-like imitation is essential for the culmination of the story:

Entre tanto los idiotas no se habían movido en todo el día de su banco . . . y ellos continuaban mirando los ladrillos, más inertes que nunca.

De pronto algo se interpuso entre su mirada y el cerco. Su hermana, cansada de cinco horas paternales, quería observar por su cuenta. Detenida al pie del cerco, miraba pensativa la cresta. Quería trepar, eso no ofrecía duda. . . .

Los cuatro idiotas, la mirada indiferente, vieron cómo su hermana lograba pacientemente dominar el equilibrio y cómo en puntas de pie apoyaba la garanta sobre la cresta del cerro, entre sus manos tirantes. Viéronla mirar a todos lados y buscar apoyo con el pie para alzarse más.

Pero la mirada de los idiotas se había animado; una misma luz insistente estaba fija en sus pupilas. No apartaban los ojos de su hermana mientras creciente sensacíon de gula bestial iba cambiando cada línea de sus rostros.

(p. 53)

As the little girl unwittingly imitated the chicken by putting her head on a block of sorts, thus awakening the boys' awareness of her as an object and stimulating their hunger, the boys imitated the maid, María, by decapitating and bleeding the girl with the same deliberate slowness the maid had been taught to show.

In the title of his book *Cuentos de amor, de locura y de muerte,* the volume where **"La gallina degollada"** was published, Quiroga establishes an evolution that his story will also follow: "love" can lead to "insanity," which in turn can end in "death."[50] Mazzini and his wife were madly in love, so much so that the only goal they had was to produce perfect fruits of their intense love. The "insanity" of the story is to be found in the demented state of the boys, and it was a condition that put to test and nearly destroyed the love the couple had so intensely insisted that they shared. The "death" in the story is a product of both conditions, love and insanity, but it causes a shocking conclusion, because it comes about through a sacrifice of the youngest and most cherished child.

Another important point for a proper interpretation of the story is to reiterate that either death or suicide was a favorite ending for Quiroga's fiction. Moreover, toward the end of his life Quiroga even began to promulgate his obsession with suicide.[51] In respect to this matter it should be pointed out that both the words "idiot" and "suicide" have similar Latin etymologies connoting "without oneself."[52]

If the reader still has any doubt that an autistic child might be able to accomplish such a hideous murder as the little boys in Quiroga's story carried out through imitation, let me give one more example of an autistic act. An autistic child has no ability to connect objects logically. One child, as an example of horrible imitation, was riding with his mother in a car. When he saw his mother light a cigarette with a lighter in the dashboard, he seized this lighter and burnt his mouth without seeming to feel anything.[53] He could imitate but not realize the consequences of his actions.

Now that we understand the genetic problems involved in autism we can accept the likelihood that a normal girl could be born in such a family. Also we should realize that it is impossible to define and categorize autism completely. Horacio Quiroga apparently came across a primitive but interesting case study published about autistic children in a family with several boys. He then modified it to fit his need for the interesting plot of **"La gallina degollada."** It is likely that what Quiroga read was a very early clinical study from Europe or the United States, where medical research was more advanced. The likelihood that it was a case study is supported by the inclusion of twins in the story, just as there often are in modern studies of autism. Should such a clinical study ever be discovered among the publications that reached Buenos Aires at the first of the century, the researcher who comes across it will have made quite a find.

Some elements that are found in the story, such as the slobbering-idiot look may have been added for effect by Quiroga, because most autistic children look very normal (though some do not). Down's syndrome children, however, do commonly tend to show such weaknesses as slobbering, yet, as has been shown, they do not have the other characteristics of the boys in the story.

Structuring his story on a scientific base of a psychological case study, Quiroga may then have mixed in elements that he had observed in real-life cases of demented individuals. The most important element is the weaving of the story, which Quiroga handled masterfully, and to drive home his experiment in portraying boys with an abnormal psychological makeup, he added a grotesque ending to shock readers, which causes them to remember the story.

In Quiroga's theory of literature, man is an animal—at times barely above the level of the beasts[54]—and these boys reflect well his thesis for they live on the margin of human and animal. The boys succumb to human (and animal) frailties such as hunger and imitation, and, because of these weaknesses, they rise up against their parents at an unexpected moment venting nature's vengeance on them. The parents, who had not counted on nature reacting against them in such a way, were the greatest losers because they had never solidified their love in the first place.

In **"La gallina degollada"** the parents had placed excessive importance on the perfection of their daughter; then, when she was taken from them, they did not know how to react. The shocking conclusion which is handled most dramatically by Quiroga makes one realize that without love, even the most abject and demented being can rise in a moment of power and wreak havoc on the unsuspecting, the helpless, on those who were too selfish to share with them just a small portion of love and understanding.

Notes

1. Quiroga's many financial reverses tended to make him reserved and humble, but the accidental deaths and suicides that came down around his head during his early years produced in him a feeling of "innocent blame" ("culpabilidad inocente"), which was a psychological handicap to him throughout his life. For example, his mother in his youth blamed him for his father's death, even though he was merely an infant in her arms suffering from whooping cough.

2. José M. Delgado and Alberto J. Brignole, *Vida y obra de Horacio Quiroga* (Montevideo: Claudio García y Cía., 1939), 22-23. Quiroga's friend, Elias Castelnuovo, in "La tragedia de Horacio Quiroga," *Claridad* (Buenos Aires), March, 1937, adds doubts to the accidental nature of the father's death when he says that they brought Quiroga's mother the father's body with three shotgun wounds in it. Cited in John A. Crow, "La locura de Horacio Quiroga," *Revista Iberoamericana,* 1:1 (May, 1939), 33-45.

3. Pedro G. Orgambide, *Horacio Quiroga: El hombre y su obra* (Buenos Aires: Editorial Stilcograf, 1954), 65. Cf. Delgado and Brignole, 140.

4. Compare the versions of the incident given in Delgado and Brignole, 138, and Orgambide, 65. The most accurate and the clearest information about the case seems to have been achieved through the research of Emir Rodríguez Monegal, *Genio y figura de Horacio Quiroga* (Montevideo: Editorial Universitaria de Buenos Aires, 1967), 32-34.

5. Leonardo Garet, *Obra de Horacio Quiroga* (Montevideo: Ministerio de Educación y Cultura, 1978), 13, interprets this violent depiction of death as Quiroga in a self-confrontation with death each time he narrates such a scene. See also Crow, note 2, above.

6. Enrique Anderson Imbert, *Historia de la literatura hispanoamericana,* (Mexico: Fondo de Cultura Económica, 1967), 1, 412. Cf. also, Emir Rodríguez Monegal, *Las raíces de Horacio Quiroga: Ensayos* (Montevideo: Ediciones Asir, 1961), 153:

   Es claro que hay relatos de esplendorosa crueldad. Hay relatos de horror. Quizá el más típico sea "La gallina degollada."

7. This was the decade that saw the establishment of pediatrics and children's hospitals. Psychology and psychiatry were also becoming popular even though they were still new fields in their formative years between the careers of their respective founders, William James and Sigmund Freud.

8. María E Rodés de Clérico and Ramón Bordoli Dolci, *Horacio Quiroga: Antología, estudio crítico y notas* (Montevideo: Arca, 1977), 25:

En los cuentos anteriores a esta época y principalmente en los iniciales, Quiroga hace uso y abuso de la descripción macabra . . . para suscitar el horror.

9. Juan Carlos Ghiano, "Temática y recursos expresivos: Los temas," *Aproximaciones a Horacio Quiroga,* ed. Angel Flores (Caracas: Monte Avila Editores, 1976), 83-85:

> A Quiroga lo tentaban las referencias patológicas, de dudosa procedencia cienfífica.
>
> (85)

10. Hanne Gabriele Reck, *Horacio Quiroga: Biografía y crítica* (Mexico: Ediciones De Andrea, 1966), 5:

> Durante toda la vida de Quiroga hay una estrecha relación entre sus experiencias y sus obras. . . .

> Rodríguez Monegal, *Raíces,* 157:

> La obra de Quiroga está enraizada en su vida.

11. He loved photography and did well in that field. (Delgado and Brignole, 58). He also came up with numerous scientific schemes during his lifetime to make himself wealthy, among them a charcoal plant (that burned down during its first operation), and an orange liquor operation. See also, Delgado and Brignole, 248, 299, 302, 351-52.

12. Delgado and Brignole, 57-58, 70.

13. Delgado and Brignole, 62-63.

14. Quiroga's best friend of that period and first biographer, the physician Alberto J. Brignole, says of Quiroga, "Buen psicólogo como era." Delgado and Brignole, 77.

15. Examples of Quiroga's caricaturization of psychology are found in Rodríguez Monegal, *Las raíces de Horadio Quiroga,* 44:

> Dos o tres definiciones:
>
> Genio—Neurosis intensa
>
> Amor—Crisis histérica
>
> Inspiración—Un trago más de agua ó un bocado más
>
> Amargura—Pobrez de glóbulos rojos
>
> Inteligencia—Más o menos fósforo
>
> Goce—Crispación de la médula espinal (Bartrina)
>
> Soñar—Rozamiento del cuerpo contra las sábanas

16. Delgado and Brignole, 93-95.

17. Rodríguez Monegal, *Raíces,* 48-50, and Angel Flores, "Cronología," *Aproximaciones a Horacio Quiroga,* 278.

18. See Quiroga's autobiographical story, "El haschich," *El crimen del otro* (1904), *Cuentos completos,* I (Montevideo: Ediciones de la Plaza, 1967), 95-98; and Delgado and Brignole, 74-75. Quiroga would take chloroform to alleviate his asthma, and once it nearly killed him when he fell asleep with it spilled all over his pillow. See note 20, below.

19. Rodés de Clérico and Bordoli Dolci, 13.

20. Quiroga, "El haschich," 95-98.

21. Rodríguez Monegal, *Genio y figura,* 22.

22. Delgado and Brignole, 114-15, 272-73, 309. See also 86: The young poet's first love, María Esther, whom Quiroga attempted to elope with because her family felt he was too poor, eventually became a drug addict.

23. The group—the earliest "modernista" gathering in Uruguay—was known as the "Consistorio del Gay Saber." Brignole, a leader in the group says of it, "Fue sólo una especie de cantina psíquica . . ." Delgado and Brignole, 111.

24. Alberto Zum Felde, *La narrativa en Hispanoamérica* (Madrid: Aguilar, 1964), 298. Cf. Reck, 84:

> Los casos psicológicos parencen haber ejercido una extraña fascinación sobre Quiroga. Su fértil y viva imaginación, inspirada por algunos casos reales que conoció personalmente o a través de informes médicos o reportajes de diarios, lo llevó a componer algunos relatos sumamente sugestivos.

25. *Caras y caretas,* 562, Vol. 12:5.

26. Jaime Alazraki, "Variaciones del tema de la muerte," *Aproximaciones a Horacio Quiroga,* ed. Angel Flores (Caracas: Monte Avila Editores, 1976), 160.

27. Horacio Quiroga, *The Decapitated Chicken and Other Stories,* trans. Margaret Sayers Peden (Austin: University of Texas, 1976), 56-67.

28. Horacio Quiroga, *Cuentos de amor, de locura y de muerte,* (Buenos Aires: Losada, 1954), 43-50. Subsequent references to this edition will be listed in parentheses in the body of the text.

29. Note the error in Leonardo Garet, 44:

> La gallina degollada' explicita el afán de conmover: desgracia hereditaria, derrumbe del matrimonio y esperanza febril, animalización y trato despersonalizado los *mongoloides,* detalles de la muerte y reacción de los padres.
>
> (Italics are mine)

30. Quiroga's closest friend, Alberto J. Brignole, was a medical student when they were in Montevideo around the turn of the century. After Brignole obtained his medical degree in Paris, Quiroga lived

with him in Buenos Aires much of the time between 1905 and 1907. When Brignole married in 1907 and Quiroga returned from the Chaco, Quiroga had to move to another house, but he still kept his tools and books at Brignole's house and ate supper most evenings there. Delgado and Brignole, 167-173.

31. Brian Roberts, "Description of the Condition of Autism and Theories of Causation," *Autistic Children: Teaching, Community and Research Approaches,* ed. Barbara Furneaux and Brian Roberts (London and Boston: Routledge and Kegan Paul, 1977), 21-42; cf., especially 39-41 concerning "The Kanner Criteria." Michael Rutter, "Diagnosis and Definition," *Autism: A Reappraisal of Concepts and Treatment,* ed. Michael Rutter and Eric Schopler (New York and London: Plenum press, 1978), 1-25.

32. Bruce Balow, "Research on Autism and Childhood Schizophrenia," *Autism: Diagnosis, Instruction, Management and Research,* ed. James E. Gilliam (Springfield, Illinois: Charles A. Thomas, Publisher, 1981), 241.

33. Joseph P. Blank, "The Miracle of May Lemke's Love," *Reader's Digest* Vol. 121, No. 726 (October, 1982), 86:

    For nearly two centuries authorities have puzzled over the phenomenon of the autistic savant (often called idiot savant)—a person, who, though mentally retarded by brain damage, is capable of an extraordinary specific talent.

    Cf. also, Bernard Rimland, "Inside the Autistic Savant," *Psychology Today,* 12 (August, 1978), 68-80.

34. W[ayne] S[age], "Making Sense of Autism," *The UCLA Monthly,* 10:6 (July-August, 1980), 3. Susan Folstein and Michael Rutter, "A Twin Study of Individuals with Infantile Autism," *Autism: A Reappraisal of Concepts and Treatment,* ed. Michael Rutter and Eric Schopler (New York and London: Plenum press, 1978), 219-242.

35. Michael Rutter, *Infantile Autism: Concepts, Characteristics, and Treatment. Study Group No. 1* (Edinburgh and London: Churchill Livingston, 1971, vii.

36. Several articles referred to here state this phenomenon, as also does the film cited on the next page in footnote 49.

37. Michael Rutter, "Language Disorder and Infantile Autism," *Autism: A Reappraisal of Concepts and Treatment,* ed. Michael Rutter and Eric Schopler (New York and London: Plenum press, 1978), 85-86, 90.

38. Harriett Slife Kaberline, "A Process for Assessing the Functional Hearing of the Autistic Child," *Autism,* ed. Gilliam (note 31 above), p. 84:

    Many autistic children demonstrate an echolalic quality in their language. They fail to generate any of their own language and instead respond with various degrees of imitation to questions and answers. If a child is echolalic, he is able to hear well enough to develop language. If a child appears mute, a language sample can sometimes be obtained by putting a tape recorder in the child's room at night. Some autistic children verbalize when not in the presence of adults.

39. This "faulty modulation of sensory input" has been researched at UCLA by Edward M. Ornitz, "Childhood Autism: A Disorder of Sensorimotor Integration," *Infantile Autism: Concepts, Characteristics, and Treatment. Study Group No. 1,* ed. Michael Rutter (Edinburgh and London: Churchill Livingston, 1971), 50-68. See especially the section on "Nystagmus," 62-66.

40. Leo Kanner had pairs of twins in his original group of autistic and schizophrenic children, and several groups studied have had autistic twins. This concern with genetic factors led to the study by Susan Folstein and Michael Rutter, "A Twin Study of Individuals with Infantile Autism," *Autism: A Reappraisal of Concepts and Treatment,* ed. Michael Rutter and Eric Schopler (New York and London: Plenum press, 1978), 219-242. This article was extracted by the authors from their more extensive study, "Infantile Autism: A Genetic Study of 211 Twin Paris," *Journal of Child Psychology and Psychiatry,* 18 (1977), 297-321. This study of twins was followed up by Edward M. Ornitz, "Biological Homogeneity or Heterogeneity?" *Autism: A Reappraisal of Concepts and Treatment,* ed. Michael Rutter and Eric Schopler (New York and London: Plenum press, 1978), 243-250.

41. Michael Rutter, Lawrence Bartak, and Steven Newman, "Autism—A Central Disorder of Cognition and Language?" *Infantile Autism: Concepts, Characteristics, and Treatment, Study Group No. 1,* ed. Michael Rutter (Edinburgh and London: Churchill Livingston, 1971, 150.

42. Alan J. Ward, *Childhood Autism and Structural Therapy: Selected Papers on Early Childhood Autism* (Chicago: Nelson-Hall, 1976), 61-72. C. B. Ferster, "The Autistic Child," *Readings in Psychology Today,* 2nd ed. (Del Mar, California: Communications Research Machines Books, 1972), 187-91. Much of Bruno Bettelheim's *The Empty Fortress; Infantile Autism and the Birth of the Self* (New York: The Free press, 1967), attempts to fortify this stand. Cf. also Mary Harrington Hall,

"A Conversation with Bruno Bettelheim: The Pychology of Involvement," *Readings in Psychology Today,* 2nd ed. (Del Mar, California: Communications Research Machines Books, 1972), 513-14 (originally published in *Psychology Today* 2 (12 (1969):21. Much of Ward's and Rimland's writings attempt to refute Bettelheim's "psychogenesis hypothesis." Cf., for example, Bernard Rimland, *Infantile Autism: The Syndrome and Its Implications for a Neural Theory of Behavior* (New York: Appleton-Century-Crofts, 1964), 61.

43. The lowest group is mute and virtually untrainable; the second is the one who has been diagnosed as autistic at an early age and has some language, though with little functionalability; the upper group apparently never received as severe brain damage as the others and can function in society, although occasionally as *idiots savants.*

44. An excellent book that develops the anguish of the parents (to the point of placing a great strain on their marital relationship) but discovers that a child previously diagnosed as autistic was not is Virginia M. Axline, *Dibs in Search of Self* (New York: Ballantine Books, 1967). Dibs's father was a famous scientist and his mother a physician.

45. Josh Greenfield (co-author of *Harry and Tonto*) as a frustrated father of a mute autistic boy has written two books about his pathetic personal situation: *A Child Called Noah: A Family Journey* (New York: Holt, Rinehart and Winston, 1972), a less pessimistic book written when Noah was still young, and *A Place for Noah* (New York: Holt, Rinehart and Winston, 1978). The passage that touched me was the statement that "other parents walk their dogs; I have to walk my son!"

46. Maria J. Paluszny, *Autism: A Practical Guide for Parents and Professionals* (Syracuse: Syracuse University press, 1979), 59-61. Edward M. Ornitz, "Neurophysiologic Studies," *Autism: A Reappraisal of Concepts and Treatment,* ed. Michael Rutter and Eric Schopler (New York and London: Plenum press, 1978), 117-139.

47. Ward, p. 147. Autistic children seem to be blind to obstacles; they run into obvious things that other people see. They would have no fear of an automobile coming down the street.

48. Because some autistics do not like food this produces problems with reinforcement. Barbara Furneaux, "Working With The Youngest Children," *Autistic Children: Teaching, Community and Research Approaches,* ed. Barbara Furneaux and Brian Roberts (London and Boston: Routledge and Kegan Paul, 1977), 94.

49. This aspect of imitation and ritualistic behavior is shown in the film, "Straight Talk," with Phyllis Haynes, interviewing Stella Chess (NYU Professor of Child Psychiatry), Tape No. 1537, aired 9 Aug 1975 on National Public Television.

50. Hiber Conteris, "El amor, la locura, la muerte," *Aproximaciones a Horacio Quiroga,* ed. Angel Flores (Caracas: Monte Avila Editores, 1976), 151-56.

51. Rodríguez Monegal, *Raíces,* 124-25.

52. *Webster's Third New International Dictionary of the English Language* (Unabridged) (Springfield, Massachusetts: G. & C. Merriam Company, 1968), 1124: "Idiot": . . . fr. Gk *idiōtēs* person in a private station . . . fr. *idios* one's own, private, peculiar; akin to L *sed, se* without, *sui* of oneself—more at SUICIDE, and p. 2286: "Suicide": [L *sui* (gen), *sibi* (dat., *se* (accus. & abl.) oneself + E-cide; akin to OE *sin* his . . . L *suus* one's own, Gk *he* (accus.) oneself. . . .

53. Cyrille Koupernik, "A Pathogenic Approach to Infantile Autism," *Infantile Autism: Concepts, Characteristics, and Treatment. Study Group No. 1,* ed. Michael Rutter (Edinburgh and London: Churchill Livingston, 1971, 38, who is citing M. S. Mahler, "On Child Psychosis in Schizophrenia: Autistic and Symbiotic Infantile Psychoses," *Psychoanalitical Study of the Child,* 12 (1952), 286.

54. Jean Franco, ed. *Horacio Quiroga: Cuentos escogidos* (London: Pergamon press, 1968), 7.

J. David Danielson (essay date 1987)

SOURCE: Danielson, J. David. Introduction to *The Exiles and Other Stories,* by Horacio Quiroga, selected and translated by J. David Danielson with the assistance of Elsa K. Gambarini, pp. vii-xii. Austin: University of Texas Press, 1987.

[*In the following essay, an introduction to his collection of English translations of some of Quiroga's short stories, Danielson highlights common themes, settings, and narrative devices in Quiroga's short fiction.*]

At the turn of the century the subtropical territory of Misiones, in northeastern Argentina, was a frontier region, not only by virtue of its location between Brazil to the east and north and Paraguay to the west, but also, and especially, because it was a land of pioneers, somewhat like Alaska and the Yukon at the same moment in the history of North America. It was populated by aboriginal natives, mestizos, blacks, and whites; by Argentines, Brazilians, Paraguayans, and foreigners from abroad; by speakers of Guaraní, of Spanish and Portuguese, and of a number of later immigrant languages from Europe. The zone was—and remains—important for its forest products, and above all its *yerbales* or plantations of *yerba mate,* the green tea especially favored in Uruguay, Argentina, Paraguay, and southern Brazil. Such plantations were first established by the Jesuits in the early seventeenth century, as a major economic venture of their *reducciones* (collective settlements) of Guaraní natives, which flourished till the company was expelled from the Spanish dominions in 1767. It is of course the missions they founded which gave Misiones its name.

This is the setting of almost all of the most celebrated stories of Horacio Quiroga, including those selected for the present volume—excepting the lead story, **"Beasts in Collusion,"** which is set in the Brazilian Mato Grosso to the north. They are tales of risk and danger, suffering, disease, horror, and death; but also of courage and dignity, hard work, and human endurance in the face of hostile nature and the frequent brutality of men. In most of the stories translated here (all but two appearing in English for the first time) there are piquant touches of humor and bemused irony as well.

Our title, *The Exiles and Other Stories,* echoes that of one of Quiroga's own volumes, *Los desterrados* (1926), often said to be his best book. Included here are five stories from that collection, seven written earlier (1908-1923), and one subsequently (1929). This latest tale, **"The Forerunners,"** picks up a theme introduced in the title story, **"The Exiles,"** and is one of five that present characters who appear in more than one story. All thirteen are similar in inspiration, and may be said to constitute a kind of loosely structured, episodic novel—along with some of those published in *The Decapitated Chicken and Other Stories* (Austin: University of Texas Press, 1976), especially **"Drifting," "A Slap in the Face," "In the Middle of the Night," "The Dead Man,"** and **"The Son."** These stories are held together by common themes, situations, and conflicts—and of course their common setting in Misiones—but most of all by their vision of man (of men and women) in that setting, including Quiroga himself, who appears in various guises, and according to A. H. Rodríguez "made of himself the best character in his work" (*El mundo ideal de Horacio Quiroga,* 3ª ed. [Posadas: Montoya, 1985], p. 47).

Quiroga has been compared to our own Jack London, his contemporary and fellow-practitioner of a characteristically New World type of fiction. But he was far less ideological and political than London, more bourgeois in origin, better educated, and more literary as a youth, having published before he was twenty and edited the *Revista de Salto* before his trip to Paris at twenty-one (1900). His formative years coincided with the apogee of the estheticist *modernista* movement in Spanish American literature (Rubén Darío arrived in Buenos

Aires in 1893, and stayed till 1898), and his first two books (1901, 1904) betray its influence, as well as that of Charles Baudelaire's exemplar, Mr. Edgar Allan Poe. At this time his interest in the dark side of life was still largely literary, though he had already suffered the death of his father, his stepfather, and a close friend. . . .

When he discovered Misiones, Quiroga apparently found a world free of the constraints of urban life, where he could forge an existence in accordance with his own designs. He was of course not a primitive, but a sophisticated modern who brought culture and technology to the wilderness. He had books, all sorts of tools, and even a Model T, the latter a decided rarity in the Misiones of that day. From 1903 on he would spend about half his time in the north (including the Chaco, Corrientes, and Paraguay as well as Misiones) and half in Buenos Aires, where he would continually long for the home he had built with his own hands, overlooking the Paraná near San Ignacio. . . . He had become a successful writer in the city, and did not need to struggle in Misiones, but that was where he wanted to be, where he felt he belonged. No doubt it was his destiny to confront life in its most basic forms, and to exploit the openness of the frontier, both directly, in his manual labor, and literarily, in his fiction. Though the urban Quiroga will always be remembered for such gripping tales as **"The Decapitated Chicken,"** it is in Misiones that he finds his truest and most authentic voice. And his intense feeling for the land and its people is unmistakable. Even a quasi-mystical communion with nature is detectable at times.

Quiroga's characters are a varied lot. In this book we find parents and children, servant girls, prostitutes, laborers, foremen and overseers, craftsmen, shopkeepers, landowners and lumber barons, river sailors, scientists, derelicts and drunks, and even union organizers. Some characters are mestizos, or creoles of European stock. Many others are immigrants: from Sweden, Holland, Belgium, and England; France, Spain, and Italy; Germany, Poland, Hungary, and Turkey. Like the United States, the River Plate region was a land of opportunity in those days, and the influx of immigrants was very large, especially as compared to the number of native-born. (In 1914 there were about a million Italians—to say nothing of other immigrants—living in Uruguay and Argentina, out of a total population of about nine million.) Though a few of Quiroga's foreigners ultimately break under the strains of life in their harsh new environment, almost all are hard workers, like most of the creoles and *indígenas* who live beside them.

Work, indeed, is a central concern in these stories. There are contract laborers (*mensualeros* or *mensús*) who slave for months under cruel supervision, only to splurge their advances on a week's orgy in Posadas and return to the hazards of tropical fever, brutality, and death in the lumber camps. There are *peones* and household servants who work for short-term wages and are likely to walk off and disappear as quickly and unexpectedly as they first came on the scene. A number of workers are fierce independents who will commit themselves to just one task at a time in order to maintain their freedom from bosses. Others are small entrepreneurs who pluck logs from the river, try to grow crops, or establish cottage industries like cooking charcoal or the distillation of liquor from oranges. And finally, in **"The Forerunners,"** we have the tragicomic story of the field hands on the *yerba* plantations and the first frustrated efforts to build their labor union.

Quiroga is no socialist, but his stories clearly reveal his sympathy for the victimized *mensús* and plantation workers and other *peones* subjected to the barbarities of cruel bosses. He does not lecture, but simply describes conditions as he finds them. He shows little interest in the class struggle but, as befits a writer of fiction, a great deal of interest in individuals. Their skills impress him, and he admires their strength and persistence in the face of adversity. (Many of his characters are closely modeled on persons he actually knew in Misiones.) His ethic of work may be viewed as a kind of metaphor for human dignity.

Our author's material is regional and local, and in this sense he is a *criollista* or nativist. But he is seldom merely picturesque. While his characters and their circumstances are authentic, and he sometimes presents their activities in considerable detail, he is much less concerned with documentation than with basic human problems: survival, taming nature, confronting injustice, raising and protecting children, mastering difficult tasks, rising to creativity—and showing compassion for those who fail and suffer, through weaknesses of their own or the villainy of others. The focus is characteristically Hispanic in that the psychological is far less important than the existential. In some of his urban stories Quiroga displays an interest—inherited at least in part from Poe—in abnormal mental states, but here, in Misiones, his concern is man among men, especially man in conflict—and sometimes in harmony—with nature. (A marginal exception is that of alcoholism, particularly in the case of Dr. Else in **"The Orange-Distillers."**)

Quiroga is probably the most important precursor of the so-called "Boom" in Latin American fiction, which coincided, roughly, with the third quarter of the twentieth century. In recent years the names of Borges, Carpentier, Cortázar, Sábato, Bioy Casares, Onetti, Donoso, Fuentes, Rulfo, Vargas Llosa, Cabrera Infante, Nobel prizewinners Miguel Angel Asturias and Gabriel García Márquez, and a number of others, have become internationally familiar, and justifiably so. But they did not emerge from the void; the ground had been prepared, by Quiroga and some of his contemporaries, who were

able to shed much of the artificiality, inflated rhetoric, and polemical tendentiousness, as well as many of the normative conventions (largely derived from European literature) of early twentieth-century fiction in Latin America. Their work became less shallow, less programmatic, less extraliterary in purpose. Quiroga in particular began to treat the more deep-seated, more central aspects of human experience—and to do so concretely, in strictly American terms. That he succeeded is shown most obviously by the fact that he is still widely read and appreciated, not only within but also beyond the Spanish-speaking world—indeed that his reputation has grown, his work now receiving increased attention from critics and literary historians.

But as a transitional figure he could hardly have risen to the formal mastery of a Borges, a Cortázar, or a García Márquez. He is not a great prose stylist, though his means, by and large, seem adequate to his purposes. Some of his weaknesses are evident in the melodramatic and somewhat heavy-handed (but nevertheless powerful) **"Beasts in Collusion,"** which he did not include in any of his books. A number of his stories lack a clear center, sharing two or more prominent themes, such as **"The Charcoal-Makers"** and **"The Exiles."** Others wander from one incident to the next, like **"A Workingman."** There are occasional small inconsistencies of detail, imprecisions of syntax, and more often lapses in semantic rigor. But there are just as many stylistic felicities—such as the control of substandard dialect in **"The Forerunners"**—and the whole is vivid, convincing, and oddly profound. Furthermore, the stories of Misiones present a coherent world-view, a kind of creole tragic sense of life, ranging from pure horror to the anthropological irony of **"The Contract Laborers," "The Log-Fishermen," "A Workingman," "The Exiles," "The Forerunners,"** and others. Quiroga remains unique, apparently inimitable.

He wrote about two hundred short stories, and at least a third of them remain memorable. He thoroughly understood the genre, and exploited almost all of its possibilities, including the fantastic, a mode generally restricted to his urban stories, and only tangentially represented here (most clearly in **"The Yaciyateré"**). For rather complicated reasons, including the decline of Hispanic prestige in Europe after 1588, he is less well known than some of his peers (and freely acknowledged masters), such as Poe, Maupassant, and Chekhov. But he is in the same class as they, even in his unevenness, and his best work belongs not only to Latin America, but the world.

We have mentioned his attachment to Misiones. But perhaps only a visit to that land can convince one of its immense attractiveness: its rich red earth, its forests and *yerbales,* its magnificent falls on the Iguazú, its remote towns and villages, the resplendent *jacarandás* along the streets of its lovely capital, Posadas—and above all the majestic river, Olivera's "devil of a Paraná" (**"A Workingman"**), which defines its long border with Paraguay. These stories, whatever their incidents and conflicts, whoever their characters, are preeminently tales of Misiones, their narratives compenetrated with Misiones, its trees and waters, its climate, it agriculture, its people. San Ignacio's Jesuit ruins and Quiroga's house outside town have been cleaned up now, for the tourists, but readers of his tales can still picture them as they were more than sixty years ago, when Dr. Else mistook his daughter for an enormous rat. Because sense of place is so important in Quiroga, and because most readers in our distant climes will never see Misiones, I have thought it important to provide a map, and a list of place names, which follow the text. (But if you can, take a plane to Rio, and continue on to Foz-do-Iguaçu. Cross the new bridge to Argentina, and take a long bus ride south, down through Misiones to Quiroga country.)

In these translations I have not attempted to improve upon Quiroga, nor to drag him out of his context and into Anglophone literature. I have tried to stay close to his Spanish, to avoid dipping too far below the surface in search of his underlying meaning. In the process I have no doubt stretched the capacities of English a bit, but intentionally, in the conviction that a translation should not conceal its origin, not read as though written directly in the receptor language, but rather exploit the rich possibilities of the bilingual encounter, while respecting the norms of that second language. In so doing I hope I have conveyed something of the special flavor of Quiroga's prose, which like Quiroga himself is *sui generis.*

Jennifer L. French (essay date January-June 2002)

SOURCE: French, Jennifer L. "A Geographical Inquiry into Historical Experience: The Misiones Stories of Horacio Quiroga." *Latin American Literary Review* 30, no. 59 (January-June 2002): 79-99.

[*In the following essay, French asserts that Quiroga's "nativist poetics" in his* relatos de ambiente, *a group of stories set in Misiones, grew "out of Quiroga's dialogue with other colonial writers of the time, the writers he considered his literary peers."*]

> *Creo que [el entendimiento] puede acaecer siempre que los dos amigos sigan la misma derrota—no espiritual, que sería lo de menos—, sino material. Por ejemplo si Vd. sintiera nacer en Vd. el amor a la tierra, al plantar, a hacer su casa, hacerla prosperar trabajando manualmente en ello, estoy seguro de que no se levantaría una nube sobre nuestras personas amigas.*
>
> —Quiroga to Ezequiel Martínez Estrada[1]

I. A Colonial Quiroga

In his famous study, *La nueva novela latinoamericana,* Carlos Fuentes identifies Uruguayan Horacio Quiroga (1887-1937) as a pivotal figure in "el tránsito de la antigua literatura naturalista y documental a la nueva novela diversificada, crítica y ambigua."[2] Julio Cortázar had already come to a similar conclusion, naming Quiroga along with Ricardo Güiraldes and Benito Lynch as the three Río de la Plata writers who had most helped his own generation define their narrative praxis.[3] Today Quiroga is commonly recognized as one of the founders of Latin America's nativist, anti-hegemonic narrative discourse, but as Carlos Alonso has recently written, "A number of Quiroga's reviews and other writings on literature make it clear that he never meant for his work to be read as part of the movement for an autochthonous literature at the beginning of the century."[4] Alonso's remarks raise an important question: how did the mature Quiroga, the author of *Cuentos de amor de locura y de muerte* and *Los desterrados,* identify himself as a writer? The answer is somewhat surprising, because I believe that Quiroga located himself among the authors of colonial literature, the international group of writers for whom the essential reality of modern life was the struggle for survival on the frontier of capitalist expansion. Certainly Quiroga himself experienced the frontier during the years he spent as a pioneer in northeastern Argentina. After the failure of his cotton plantation in El Chaco in 1905, Quiroga undertook the more modest experiment that would dominate his life and literature until his death in 1937: growing *yerba mate* in the mountainous, semi-tropical jungles of Misiones, a region that took its name from the Jesuit missions established there centuries earlier.[5] His observations of frontier life occupy the work for which he is best known, the group of roughly one hundred stories known as the *relatos de ambiente,* and I will argue that the nativist poetics for which he is rightfully admired developed out of Quiroga's dialogue with other colonial writers of the time, the writers he considered his literary peers.[6]

The "reviews and other writings" to which Alonso alludes include a series of articles Quiroga published in Argentinean magazines and journals in the 1920s and '30s. The most famous is "Ante el tribunal," a bitter piece that attests to Quiroga's sense of alienation from the Buenos Aires literary scene led by Jorge Luis Borges and the other *Martinfierristas* as it attempts to defend his work against the defamations of literary history.[7] Other articles Quiroga published around the same time show him shaping an alternative orientation for his work, outside the Argentinean *milieu* and within an international tradition of colonial adventure narrative. These texts convey an implicit sense of fellowship, particularly as Quiroga sets the knowledge drawn from experience of frontier society and direct contact with nature against the hollow urbanity of the literary establishment. In 1922, for example, he published "Kipling en la pantalla," a review of the film version of Kipling's "The Unmade Nest," in which he defends the Anglo-Indian writer from the clumsy adaptation of two Parisian cinematographers who are "absolutely ignorant" of "the aspects of nature and the life of a country" represented in the fiction.[8] A few months later he criticized a translator of Hudson's *The Ombu,* a "stranger to the country" who failed to understand and thus to interpret the reality of the pampa and the language of its inhabitants. August 1928 saw Quiroga's celebration of the adventure-fiction genre in an homage to Jules Verne, and two months later readers of *El Mundo Argentino* encountered a short, ironic report of news Quiroga claims to have heard via telegram from London: the ghost of Joseph Conrad had communicated with Arthur Conan Doyle (in fact a known spiritualist), pleading for assistance in completing a final, literally posthumous novel.[9] Quiroga includes just two Latin Americans, Argentinean Benito Lynch and Colombian José Eustasio Rivera, along with North American Bret Harte, in his fellowship of pioneering writers.[10]

It should be clear from the outset that my project is not to trace the "influence" that any of these writers may have had on Quiroga. Over the years a good deal of ink has been spent debating—and largely discrediting—Quiroga's assertions that Kipling was one of his literary "masters," a claim that has become all but inextricable from the untenable notion of the "cultural dependency" of the post-colonial world.[11] The question of affiliation first became an issue when Borges ungenerously commented that Quiroga "wrote the stories that Kipling had already written better." Subsequent writers have come to Quiroga's defense, but in asserting the value and originality of Quiroga's work they have effectively negated its concern with imperialism. One of the most recent, Abelardo Castillo, suggests that Borges' remark "today would be equivalent to thinking that Quiroga only wrote those stories [*Cuentos de la selva*] or forgetting that they were stories for children."[12] His own comment seems to imply that a talent for fable-writing is all that Quiroga and Kipling shared. By describing scholarship which points to the relationship between them as "a frivolity," Castillo, unintentionally perhaps, cordons off a crucial aspect of the historical and material context of Quiroga's writing: the reality of colonialism and informal imperialism in Argentina.

One purpose of this essay is to consider Quiroga's writing as a rare example of literature that addresses what I call the "Invisible Empire," the economic, social and political structures that developed during Britain's undeclared hegemony in Latin America between the mid-nineteenth century and the 1920s. The issue of Britain's informal imperialism rarely arises in literary and cultural studies because it is all but unmentioned in the literature and even the political discourse of the era. Nevertheless, historians frequently note that the Latin American republics served the same economic functions as Britain's official colonies elsewhere, providing markets for British manufactures and an abundant supply of cheap raw materials, without the expense and complication of formal annexation. Though few Latin Americans recognized it for what it was, perhaps because the interests of the local elites coincided with those of foreign capitalists, the results of informal imperialism also resembled those of formal colonialism. In addition to mounting national debts and dependence on imported technologies, the policy of "export-led development" stimulated an increase in agricultural production that led to the rapid, often violent incorporation of new lands and peoples into the capitalist economic system.[13] On these new economic frontiers—and particularly in Quiroga's Misiones region, where settlers from the Río de la Plata were joined by thousands of European pioneers as well as the agents of large-scale logging and *yerba mate* companies—the process resembled both the Hispanic conquest of America centuries earlier and northwestern Europe's colonization of Asia and Africa.[14]

My second intention is to examine the narrative practice that Quiroga develops in response to informal imperialism, by which I mean his observations and experiences in Misiones as well as the dialogue he engages in with other colonial writers. In this regard Quiroga's Misiones stories provide an opportunity to compare the rhetorical structures produced in response to informal imperialism to the more frequently studied discourse of formal colonialism, making Quiroga extremely relevant to the ongoing debate about Latin America's position in the field of postcolonial studies. At times Quiroga rehearses the narratives of Latin America's colonial past: "Piense en sus antepasados los conquistadores," he jocosely writes his friend Ezequiel Martínez Estrada, urging him to try the rustic life of Misiones for himself.[15] But a contradictory discourse emerges in Quiroga's work in the solidarity that develops between the colonist and the local worker, exposing the abuses of informal imperialism and countering the capitalistic assumptions about land and labor on which it is based. Quiroga's work, then, is both colonial and anti-hegemonic, vehemently critical of capitalist exploitation and dedicated to the personal and communal rejuvenation he finds in the settler's work.

That paradoxical positioning itself suggests a critique of imperialism that escapes the rigid Manichean oppositions that as Abdul R. JanMohamed and others have noted conventionally structure colonial (and very often postcolonial) discourse.[16] Quiroga's disinterest in colonial binaries, particularly in his later work, opens discursive space for a fluid aesthetic and the emergence of a powerful third term, nature or the land. He represents informal imperialism as a process of capitalist expansion which profoundly reorganizes the relationship between humans and nature within a given environment, empowering some while stripping others of their traditional livelihood, exposing them to exploitation, poverty, and disease. In Quiroga's work the typical colonial dyad becomes a triad formed by land, labor, and capital, and eventually disperses into the shape of a (bio)sphere: what becomes clear in the dialogue between Quiroga and the British writers is a sense that for him colonialism was something other than an encounter or confrontation between racially and culturally opposed peoples. It was a new or different relationship between a heterogeneous human population and its physical environment.

In *Culture and Imperialism* Edward Said explains that "land" is always the fundamental issue of colonialism, and that "At some very basic level, imperialism means thinking about, settling on, controlling land you do not possess, that is distant, that is lived on and owned by others."[17] In Quiroga's texts land takes on the primacy that Said ascribes to it: land itself becomes the basis of the action and interaction of his characters in the colonial jungle. His *relatos de ambiente* may be roughly divided among three categories: those representing isolated colonists' struggle to survive amid the perils of the jungle, those depicting local workers' exploitation by the timber and *yerba mate* companies, and others representing animals' response to development of the jungle. The importance of nature as the primary reality of the characters' lives is more visible in all three categories of Quiroga's stories than in the more conventional colonial literature Said discusses, which tends to focus on political or cultural conflict played out on the ground that is itself contested. In order to recuperate this suppressed materiality Said advocates a critical practice he calls a "geographical inquiry into historical experience"—but the same phrase might just as well describe Quiroga's authorial attention to the changing configurations of economic power, human freedom, and the use of land and natural resources.

Emir Rodríguez Monegal, Quiroga's biographer and the interviewer to whom Borges' comment was originally addressed, came closer than most to the kind of approach to the relationship between Quiroga and colonial literature that interests me when he described the difference between Quiroga and Kipling with the phrase, "Kipling never ceased to be a sahib." But in order to consider the affinities between Quiroga and the European writers it will be necessary to keep in mind, as few of Quiroga's critics have, that Kipling and Conrad were themselves deeply ambivalent on the subject of imperialism and its benefits for both the metropolitan agent and his native subjects. Around the turn of the twentieth century British adventure fiction began to show signs of what Martin Green has described as an

"anxiety of possession," a questioning among British intellectuals of the ideological assumptions that had supported the imperialist project of the Victorian era.[18] Their moral discomfort was reinforced by setbacks that demonstrated the unsteady progress of colonization, checking the hubris of the colonists and their supporters at home: indigenous resistance to demands for their land and labor, low or unpredictable agricultural yields, seemingly uncombatable tropical diseases, declining forests, soils and other natural resources. It was a time in which colonists around the world began to sense the limits of colonization, and to direct that sensibility back towards the metropolis.

The 1908 story **"La insolación"** offers an early example of Quiroga's engagement with the colonial adventure tradition. Rodríguez Monegal locates a possible source for the protagonist in Robert Hilton Scott, an Englishman whom Quiroga had encountered in Paraguay in 1907. "Perhaps," he writes, "the image of the drunken Englishman who disintegrates in the tropical jungle is too generic (it is magnificently developed in Hudson, in Conrad, and in Kipling, whom Quiroga was already avidly reading) to attempt a definitive identification."[19] **"La insolación"** relates the final hours of an English colonist who dies of sunstroke in the Argentinean jungle; the event, witnessed by his team of fox terriers, is so typical of British attitudes toward the tropics that it could have prompted playwright Noel Coward's famous quip that only "mad dogs and Englishmen go out in the mid-day sun."[20] But the story radically alters the norms of colonial discourse because it is narrated almost entirely from the limited perspective of the fox terriers, who are able to foresee Mr. Jones' death in the personified form of *la Muerte,* and must explain to the youngest among them what the loss of the master will mean in their lives. Thus Quiroga introduces an alternative narrative position: "Luego la Muerte," he writes, "y con ella el cambio de dueño, las miserias, las patadas, estaba sobre ellos! Pasaron el resto de la tarde al lado de su patrón, sombríos y alertas," (139). Jones dies of heatstroke the following day, and the final paragraph communicates the effect of his death on the human and animal community of the ranch:

> Los peones, que lo vieron caer, lo llevaron a prisa al rancho, pero fue inútil todo el agua; murió sin volver en sí. Mister Moore, su hermano materno, fue de Buenos Aires, estuvo una hora en la chacra y en cuatro días liquidó todo, volviéndose enseguida al sur. Los indios se repartieron los perros que vivieron en adelante flacos y sarnosos, e iban todas las noches con hambriento sigilo a robar espigas de maíz en las chacras ajenas.

(143)

The business-like, efficient brother who travels north from Buenos Aires does not understand Jones' values and rapidly converts the land into cash. In his ironic portrayal of Mr. Moore, Quiroga initiates a theme that often reappears in his stories, the distinction between the rugged and independent colonists and the "lesser" men who prefer the comforts of the city. Then, with an extraordinary degree of compassion and insight, Quiroga describes the cruel fate that reduces the fox terriers to miserable foragers after their master's death, evincing what at the time must have been an usually strong sense of the interconnectedness of human and non-human species. In his attention to the dogs' biological needs Quiroga introduces an ecological perspective that also draws out the native peoples' changing relationship to the land: the sudden appearance of *indios* in the final sentences encapsulates the redistribution of natural resources that occurs after Jones' death and by implication also occurred upon his arrival in Misiones. There is no prior mention of indigenous persons in the text, and in these last sentences they emerge, phantom-like, as if from the margins of the social space, to inhabit the land once again as the wage-laboring *peones* depart. The structure that appears in these final sentences is not a bipolar opposition between Jones and the dogs, on the one hand, and the hostile climate on the other; it is a more complex figure of the relationships among Jones, the environment, and the local people.

Quiroga's **"Una bofetada"** (1916) also resembles (anti)colonial literature of the period in its representation of the brutal conflict of interests between the agents of a large timber company and the local people they exploit.[21] The story exposes the company's tactics of trapping local people in debt-peonage and the beatings and dangerous working conditions to which they are subjected by following a series of encounters between an anonymous *mensualario* or *mensú* (so called because they were typically contracted on a month-to-month basis) and an overseer named Korner. Korner's troubles begin when rum, which is prohibited among the workers because it fortifies them to rebel against the strict order of the camps, enters the *obraje*. "En los obrajes," Quiroga writes, "hay resentimientos y amarguras que no conviene traer a la memoria de los mensú. Cien gramos de alcohol por cabeza, concluirían con el obraje más militarizado." One *mensú* in particular is singled out and beaten by Korner after a brief uprising of the workers; for subsequent "insolence" Korner banishes him from company territory. When the *mensú* reappears, the furious Korner fires a shot at him. The shot misses; the *mensú* overpowers and disarms Korner, then forces him on a trek through the jungle, unremittingly beating the overseer to death with his own whip. Quiroga accumulates detail to describe the humiliation and abuse that have driven the worker to violence, describing the anarchic brutality that destabilizes the appearance of order imposed by the logging company. The death-march on which the *mensú* leads Korner is an inverse and parodic imitation of the overseer's own grotesque idea of disciplining labor.

Stories like **"Una bofetada"** and others are crucial to establishing the new language with which Latin American writers would describe the experience of the jungle, stripping away the utopian, romantic tropology of earlier eras and replacing it with an unsparing representation of the frontier as the contested site of Latin America's ongoing insertion into the international capitalist economy. As such they are indispensable precursors of Latin America's postcolonial literature, but they are certainly related as well to the literature of colonialism in their close and particular accounts of the failures and abuses of capitalist enterprise on the frontier and their representation of local resistance to colonization. **"La insolación," "Una bofetada"** and the texts discussed in the pages to follow—**"Los pescadores de vigas," "Los desterrados,"** and **"El regreso de Anaconda"**—mark a momentary convergence between Spanish-American and British narrative, a moment when a disintegrating imperialism and an emergent postcoloniality briefly share discursive space, using the forms of colonial adventure fiction to contest the progress of colonization.

II. "Los pescadores de vigas": The Ecological Response

These stories vividly convey the intense relationships among land, labor, and capital in the colonial jungle, where the power exerted by metropolitan capital extracts surplus value by deforming beyond all reason the "natural" interaction between local people and their environment. In **"Una bofetada"** Quiroga emphasizes the dangerous and inhumane working conditions of the *mensú*, who labor "bajo un sol de fuego, tumbando vigas desde lo alto de la barranca al río, a punto de palanca, en esfuerzos congestivos que tendían como alambres los tendones del cuello a los siete mensú enfilados" (177-8). Later they stand shoulder-high in the Paraná River, tying together bundles of logs to be sent downstream. That job is so hazardous that the company supplies alcohol—otherwise strictly forbidden—to numb the workers to the danger and discomfort. In this emphasis on the role of nature within changing relations of production, and even as the instrument of exploitation, Quiroga's stories coincide with one of the most recent developments in Marxist critique, the move by scholars including Fernando Coronil, David Harvey, and Fernando Mires to integrate the "third term," land, more completely into the analysis of neo-colonial economic structures in the "developing" or postcolonial world.[22]

Marxists have traditionally neglected this crucial aspect of Marx's thought, expressed in the third volume of *Capital*:

> Just as the savage must wrestle with nature, in order to satisfy his wants, in order to maintain his life and reproduce it, so civilized man has to do it, and he must do it in all forms of society and under all possible

modes of production. With his development the realm of natural necessity expands, because his wants increase; but at the same time the forces of production increase, by which these wants are satisfied. The freedom in this field cannot consist of anything else but of the fact that socialized man, the associated producers, regulate their interchange with nature rationally, bring it under their common control, instead of being ruled by it as by some blind power; that they accomplish their task with the least expenditure of energy and under conditions most adequate to their human nature and most worthy of it.[23]

Marx's dialectical, punning style subtly articulates the staggering effect that the process of capitalist expansion can have on laborers' changing interaction with nature in the economic periphery. With the development of the metropolitan economy, the apparently unbridgeable distance between "civilized man" and "the savage" shrinks as the "realm of natural necessity" grows—both the scope of foods, raw materials and consumer goods needed to support the worker and the geographical space in which they are produced. They meet, of course, in the colonial periphery, where the metropolitan settler goes about adapting the native to the system of disciplined labor that capitalism requires.

"**Los pescadores de vigas**" (1913) represents the abuse of land and laborers in Misiones' timber industry. Here the worker is the mestizo Candiyú; the boss an English accountant referred to as Mister Hall. Hall hires Candiyú one evening to procure three logs in exchange for a gramophone and twenty records. Hall knows that Candiyú will illegally "fish" the logs out of the Paraná River when the logging company upstream sends them floating down to Buenos Aires; moreover he wants rosewood logs which, as Candiyú explains, are only "sent down" in times of severe flooding. A prolepsis is inserted immediately after this first scene. An indefinite time has passed; we are told only that Candiyú has lived beside the Paraná for thirty years and that he is dying of liver failure brought on by successive bouts of fever. Only his hands, "lívidas zarpas veteadas de verde," continue their monotonous motion, "con temblor de loro implume" (116).

This brief story is uncommonly sharp in delineating, as Jorge Lafforgue and Napoleón Baccino Ponce de León write, "the subject of modernity, and the first effects of modernity's arrival at the marginal world."[24] Elsewhere "**Los pescadores de vigas**" has been described as an allegorical representation of Latin America's production of primary goods and dependency on imported manufactures; but what scholars have interpreted as Quiroga's anticipation of the dependency theory of the 1960s may in fact be an implied analogy between the power Britishers wielded in the Río de la Plata and Britain's activities in its official Empire.[25] It is this comparison to the degenerate colonists of Kipling or Conrad's fiction

that makes Hall stereotypically English, and transforms the individual character into an archetype of the abusive colonist: ". . . como un inglés a la caída de la noche, en mangas de camisa por el calor y con una botella de whisky al lado, es cien veces más circunspecto que cualquier mestizo, Míster Hall no levantó la vista del disco. Con lo que vencido y conquistado, Candiyú concluyó por arrimar su caballo a la puerta . . ." (114). Although the phrasing is different in subsequent versions, when "**Los pescadores de vigas**" was originally published the word "inglés" was almost immediately repeated: Hall takes a good look at the worker before him and becomes a recognizable national type: "La mirada turbia, inexpresiva e insistente de míster Hall se aclaró. El contador inglés surgía" (114).[26]

If his representation of the simple, heroic Candiyú betrays an indelible class bias, the power of the text as critical realism lies in Quiroga's attention to the physical details of the worker's experience. The perspective and positionality of the narrator show a flexibility and fluidity that surpass the expectations of colonial discourse, because Quiroga positions the narrator between the foreigner who commands local labor and the worker himself. As Noé Jitrik, who remains one of Quiroga's most astute interpreters, explains, the shared experience of laboring in and against the physical environment creates a sense of empathy and solidarity by heightening Quiroga's understanding of the workers' material conditions: "He approached the common man and understood him, he saw the reason and the consistency of his struggle against nature and understood the universality of his destiny" (78). To represent this physical struggle against nature in "**Los pescadores de vigas**" Quiroga adopts a kind of ground-level perspective from which to narrate Candiyú's efforts in the surging river:

> Ahora bien, en una creciente del Alto Paraná se encuentran muchas cosas antes de llegar a la viga elegida. Arboles enteros, desde leugo, arrancados de cuajo y con las raíces negras al aire, como pulpos. Vacas y mulas muertas, en compañía de buen lote de animales salvajes ahogados, fusilados o con una flecha plantada aún en el vientre. Altos conos de hormigas amontonadas sobre un raigón. Algún tigre, tal vez; camalotes y espuma a discreción—sin contar, claro está, las víboras.
>
> (119)

In striking contrast to the elevated, panoramic view, the "sweeping visual mastery of a scene" that typifies colonial landscape description,[27] Quiroga's narrator is located near the surface of the water, practically encountering with Candiyú the dead and decaying matter borne by the current. The monstrous mixing of death and life is narrated from a position close to the man struggling to negotiate the river and not be pulled from his canoe into the sickening, disease-ridden water: details are described down to the horde of ants. The narrator, spatially aligned with Candiyú, is distanced from the "circumspect" Hall, who stays on the porch minding his own business. Hall looks on and directs the scene, while the narrator, Candiyú, and eventually the reader share this intimate knowledge of the hazards of the swollen river.

It should be said that this "ground-level" perspective is repeated in many of Quiroga's *relatos de ambiente* and becomes for this reader one of the most distinctive features of his narrative practice. In **"El hombre muerto,"** for example, a man walking alone across his settlement suddenly falls to the ground, mortally impaling himself on the machete he carries; lying there prostrate and helpless, the man contemplates his imminent death. The fascinating effect of the story is largely due to the fact that the narrative perspective follows the man's gaze wandering over the landscape he has labored to order according to his own will, projected from a position that is already aligned with the lowliest creatures and the earth itself: "Por entre los bananos, allá arriba, el hombre ve desde el duro suelo el techo rojo de su casa. A la izquierda, entrevé el monte y la capuera de canelas" (654). Quiroga's ability to sustain this ground-level view is also essential to his animal stories, including texts like **"La vitalidad de las víboras"** and **"El pique"** and longer works like the Anaconda stories to which we will soon turn.

In **"Los pescadores de vigas,"** Hall's exploitation of the native worker is explicitly represented as a perversion or distortion of his "interchange with nature". Far from the rational "common control" advocated by Marx, Candiyú is needlessly, senselessly exposed to the river at its most gruesome and fatal moment. An ecological perspective complementary to Quiroga's critique of labor abuse emerges in the depiction of the logging outfit Castelhum and Company juxtaposed with Candiyú's story. The legal employment of the company's workers is nearly as perilous as Candiyú's log-fishing; they too (hence the plural of the title) are exposed to hazardous working conditions, in "los esfuerzos malgastados en el barro líquido, la zafadura de las palancas, las costaladas bajo la lluvia torrencial. Y la fiebre" (118). The company, furthermore, grossly wastes timber resources in a region where, as Robert Eidt's *Frontier Settlement in Northeast Argentina* explains, the effects of deforestation on soil quality and erosion had been noted decades earlier.[28] In preparation for the flood they send one thousand logs downstream, a quantity so vast that the river becomes clogged and the majority are lost before reaching Buenos Aires.

Scholars have with some consistency recognized Quiroga's importance as a writer of socially-critical realism; but this environmental or ecological discourse that his *relatos de ambiente* also formulate has less often been considered. In fact, critics almost unanimously point to a fundamental conflict between human beings and the natural environment in Quiroga's fiction. For example, in his detailed and very convincing study of "underdevelopment, ideology, and worldview" in Quiroga's Misiones stories, Juan José Beauchamp writes: "In all of them . . . in one way or another, and sometimes indirectly, we perceive what Quiroga called his characters' struggles against poverty, or the struggle to conquer or at least survive against the hostile forces of nature" (97). It may be said, on the contrary, that Quiroga's work deconstructs the strict opposition between humans and their physical environment that underlies both Beauchamp's remark and the conventional Marxist framework of his study. In much of Quiroga's fiction the natural environment is not represented as inherently "hostile" to human survival and happiness: the problem, on the contrary, is that capitalist industry brings radical changes to the Misiones ecosystem, destroying the balance of the bioregional community. If the protagonists of **"A la deriva," "En la noche,"** and **"El desierto"** appear to be the hapless victims of a jungle infested with snakes and other deadly creatures, the conventionally anthropocentric focus of these stories is balanced by a different discourse, pluralistic and ecological, which explores from a range of perspectives the ways in which the settlers' efforts to extract surplus value from natural resources affect the human and non-human inhabitants of the frontier region.

In this regard Quiroga's aesthetic may be said to resemble the political ecology David Harvey outlines in *Justice, Nature and the Geography of Difference*. As Harvey explains, the contemporary fusion of Marxism and environmental concerns involves a critique of the instrumental view of nature that conventionally shapes Marxist ideas of emancipation from "social want" around the possibility of subjugating nature to human will. The necessary revision, he explains, incorporates a more dialectical understanding of the interdependence of human beings and the rest of the natural world in order to express both the environment's vulnerability to human destruction and (here drawing directly on Horkheimer and Adorno's critique of instrumental reason in *The Dialectic of Enlightenment*) "the connection between the domination of nature and the domination of others" (137). In many of Quiroga's stories, the problem is not the inherent malignity of the jungle, but the way that capitalist exploitation transforms local workers' reasonable relationship with the land into an irrational and mutually-destructive situation.

III. Environmental Figures

In *Los desterrados,* the 1926 collection on which my final remarks will focus, a sense of ecological equality animates the texts. Taken as a whole they represent Misiones as a "bioregional community," exploring the interrelated experiences of several human and non-human actors from their individual perspectives. **"Tacuará-Mansión"** and **"Los destiladores de naranjas"** consider the European expatriates who degenerate in Misiones, frustrated and disillusioned by the failure of their scientific and agricultural experiments. **"El hombre muerto"** considers humans' ultimate inability to separate themselves from the natural environment as a dying settler slowly watches the land he has worked to subdue slip from his control. **"El regreso de Anaconda"** looks at the effects of capitalist industry on the plants and animals of the upper Paraná, and **"Los desterrados"** presents two local workers who are fundamentally alienated from the land by the arrival of large-scale agriculture.

When *Los desterrados* was originally published in 1926, its full title was *Los desterrados: tipos de ambiente.* Idiomatically translated as "Exiles: frontier types," a more literal equivalent would read: "The unlanded: environmental figures." Although Quiroga was interested in presenting his readers with what he calls the "tipos pintorescos" of the frontier region—especially in stories like **"Los destiladores de naranjas"** and **"Tacuará-Mansión"**—the second, oxymoronic meaning is equally indicative of Quiroga's project in this, his most cohesive and critically successful collection, in which he represents the dispossession or alienation of persons who remain, essentially and inextricably, part of their environment. These stories demonstrate the sense of balance in Quiroga's ecologism, which oscillates between careful attention to the natural environment and the crucial fact that the control of nature is ultimately always a question of social, political, and economic power: the control of other people. The story of Joao Pedro and Tirafogo, two Brazilian laborers who die on the border between Argentina and Brazil, unable to return to their homeland, was originally published as **"Los proscriptos"** (literally, "the forbidden," or "the banished"), but in editing the collection Quiroga changed the title to **"Los desterrados."** As Lafforgue and Baccino Ponce de León write, the alteration tightens the text's political implications by suggesting that the men's alienation is less a question of geographic location than economic and environmental change (626). In fact what we learn is that these two men have been alienated from their customary relationship to the land by the arrival of large-scale *yerba-mate,* ranching, and logging industries in Misiones. "Ahora el país era distinto, nuevo, extraño y difícil. Y ellos, Tirafogo y Joao Pedro, estaban muy viejos para reconocerse en él" (294).

Neither of them fits stereotypes of "native" innocence—Joao Pedro has killed at least three men, and Tirafogo prides himself on his lack of legal identity—but they miss the old days in Misiones, when "no se conocía entonces la moneda, ni el Código Rural, ni las tranqueras con candado, ni los breeches" (294). (As Leonor Flem-

ing points out, the metonymic breeches indicate the arrival of the exploitative Britishers who wore riding pants on their plantations.[29]) The present differs from the past, "como la realidad de un sueño," and the men are nostalgic for the time "cuando no había límite para la extensión de los rozados, y éstos se efectuaban entre todos y para todos, por el sistema cooperativo" (294). Their nostalgia is antithetical to the positive value given to the standards of "progress" in one of the best-known Spanish-American regional novels, Rómulo Gallegos' *Doña Bárbara* (Venezuela, 1929). For Gallegos' heroic protagonist, Santos Luzardo, legitimizing and securing private property by fencing in individual land-holdings is the only way to incorporate Venezuela's plains or *llanos* into the modern state.

A "modern" and seemingly rational response to the exploitation of the workers takes place in Misiones simultaneous to Joao Pedro and Tirafogo's attempted departure, in the form of an organized labor movement. However the movement, which historically spread from Buenos Aires to the frontier in 1919, seems too foreign—and perhaps too urban—to have much success in Misiones. Quiroga ironically writes, "Viéronse huelgas de peones que esperaban a Boycott, como a un personaje de Posadas," and when the demonstration turned violent, "hasta se vio la muerte de un sahib" (295-296). The conspicuous choice of the term "sahib" for a foreign administrator killed during the protests indicates again Quiroga's desire to locate Misiones' history in the context of British imperialism, a hegemony that is being contested as much in the violence of the workers as in the narrator's own project. But the labor movement, misexplained and misunderstood by those it is intended to liberate, is uneasily juxtaposed with the nostalgic tone of the main narrative, as if to suggest that this is an "inorganic" and therefore unfeasible response to the problem of the dispossessed or displaced workers.

In **"El regreso de Anaconda"** as in **"Anaconda,"** published two years earlier, and **"La guerra de los yacarés,"** resistance to settlement and capitalist expansion is figured as the revolt of the natural world. In **"Anaconda"** the snakes of the Upper Paraná band together to drive out the men who have come to develop the Serotherapy Institute, capturing poisonous snakes and keeping them in cages in order to extract periodically their venom for use in serum. Anaconda survives the general slaughter of the final pages to reappear in **"El regreso de Anaconda"** (1925), in which she leads a failed attempt to keep steamships out of the upper Paraná by blockading the river. In representing her efforts Quiroga constructs what Said calls a "geographical inquiry into historical experience," a dialectical representation of the historically-dynamic relationships among the human, animal and plant species that inhabit a given environment and the water, soil, air and other resources they share. The story unfolds as a minute and particular examination of an ecosystem and the changes it undergoes when capitalist development enters the region. It begins during a severe drought, a time of privation and also (as in Kipling's *Jungle Book*) a time when the animals cooperate to ensure the survival of the species. Anaconda convinces them to work together against man, their common enemy, rallying them in language that Quiroga rather playfully borrows from the contemporary labor movement: "¡Hermanos! . . . Todos somos iguales, pero juntos. Cada uno de nosotros, de por sí, no vale gran cosa. Aliados, somos toda la zona tropical. ¡Lancémonos contra el hombre, hermanos!"[30]

When the deluge begins, she urges the animals to travel downstream with her to construct a blockade from the debris she knows will collect in the estuary. As the creatures of the jungle float along, Anaconda acquires a shelter, a lean-to that is carried by the current. Inside a *mensú* lies dying; without knowing why Anaconda defends him from the other creatures. When they arrive at the estuary her plan is defeated: the *camalotes,* immense water-plants she hoped to mass together with the logs and other matter, drift off to the banks in order to bloom: "Embriagados por el vaivén y la dulzura del ambiente, los camalotes cedían dóciles a las contra corrientes de la costa, remontaban suavemente el Paraná en dos grandes curvas, y paralizábanse por fin a lo largo de la playa a florecer," (283-284). Defeated, Anaconda lays her eggs near the man's corpse, and dies nearby when she is shot by one of the men on a steamboat.

By adopting the perspective of the boa, Quiroga explores a relationship with the environment outside the assumptions underpinning capitalism's exploitation of natural resources. In doing so, he addresses the Judeo-Christian "doctrine of dominion" expressed in the Genesis account of the Garden of Eden, in which the snake becomes the basest of creatures: "Then God said, 'Let us make man in our image, after our likeness; and let them have dominion over the fish of the sea and over the birds of the air, and over the cattle, and over all the earth, and over every creeping thing that creeps upon the earth'" (Genesis 26:1). In literature of the colonial jungle, the danger of poisonous snakes often elevates an ecological peril to a mythological, moral confrontation between good and evil, as is the case in Kipling's *Jungle Book.* "Rikki-Tikki-Tavi," for example, has a native mongoose protecting an English family from the cobras that would rule the garden of their bungalow. In fact, scholars have described Kipling's rewriting of the story of humankind's expulsion from paradise as an idealized negotiation with India's indigenous society, from which Kipling himself had been expelled in early childhood.[31] If Kipling longingly stages a kind of prelapsarian reintegration into (Indian) Nature, Quiroga's depiction of the serpent as the wisest of creatures suggests a cosmology which transcends both the distinctions of good and evil in the Western tradition and the Manichean allegory of colonialist discourse.

According to Anaconda's world-view, it is the settlers' desire to radically transform the Misiones environment—the God-given right of "dominion" of the Judeo-Christian tradition—that inherently alienates them from the rest of nature. She recalls the arrival of the colonists: "Un hombre, primero, con su miserable ansia de ver, tocar y cortar, había emergido tras del cabo de arena con su larga piragua. Luego otros hombres, con otros más, cada vez más frecuentes. Y todos ellos sucios de olor, sucios de machetes y quemazones incesantes" (610). For Anaconda, the process the settlers consider colonization is purely destructive. Quiroga's incorporation of the dying *mensú* into the narrative signals an important distinction between the local peoples' use of natural resources and the newcomers': the *mensú,* found in a poor shack, organically constructed and so lightweight that it is pulled along by the current upon a raft of *camalotes,* seems to have integrated his own activities into the natural biological order, rather than pursuing the kind of large-scale deforestation the newcomers intend.

Despite Quiroga's jocular, ironic deployment of the egalitarian language of labor unions in the speech of the somewhat bullying Anaconda, he develops a system of representation that disperses the set of hierarchies, boundaries, and binary oppositions that commonly structure colonialist discourse, including Kipling's. The floodwaters that threaten to wipe out human endeavor are here a liberating force that lifts up the different species and takes them sailing downstream: "Había llegado la hora. Ante los ojos de Anaconda, la zona al asalto desfiló. Victorias nacidas ayer, y viejos cocodrilos rojizos; hormigas y tigres; camalotes y víboras; espumas, tortugas y fibres, y el mismo clima diluviano que descargaba otra vez—la selva pasó, aclamando al boa, hacia el abismo de las grandes crecidas" (275). The joyful intermingling of species as they float downstream corresponds to the river's liberation from its banks and the great, unrestrained wash of water over the land. In their journey the narrative traces a complex and richly detailed geography of Misiones, all described as if through the gaze of the snake. The result is an awareness of place that is free of the topographical markers of Western rationalism: the precise, mathematical calculations of distances and demarcations of borders and property-lines that legitimate and regulate the commodification of the land. The narrating voice is once again strategically located at ground-level: "Toda serpiente de agua," Quiroga writes, "sabe más de hidrografía que hombre alguno" (620).

Anaconda's sympathy for the dying *mensú* places him within the bioregional community from which the new arrivals are excluded. She finds him with his throat slashed, and pities him because he is "un desgraciado mensú . . . Un pobre individuo, como todos los otros" (619). When the shelter on which he and Anaconda have been floating arrives in the estuary and draws near a steamship, one of the men standing on its bow shoots her, claiming as he does so that it is to avenge the death of the man inside. In this final scene, the jocular, sportsmanlike attitude of the newcomers, combined with their location on the steamship, reiterates their alienation from the bioregional community formed by Anaconda and the laborer on his floating hut. Meanwhile Anaconda and the *camalotes* relinquish their own construction project. Rather than building a barrier across the Paraná, each gives in to the cycles of birth and death that seem to pull them away from their common purpose. The otherwise unaccountable sexual connotations of the language describing the *camalotes'* withdrawal from the estuary, for example, suggest an incipient maternal instinct: "la pasión de la flora había quemado el brío de la gran crecida" (623). Anaconda, drawn by her sympathy for the dead mensú and strangely attracted to the warmth of his decaying body, draws near and deposits her eggs beside him so that his death will be "más que la resolución final y estéril del ser que ella había velado" (284). Her own death, when she is shot by the new arrivals, is a triumph of ultimate integration and creativity.

"El regreso de Anaconda" may present as clear a demonstration of Quiroga's politics as any of his stories, despite and perhaps even because the characters are nearly all animals. Not a fable, a representation of human qualities and relationships in animal forms, the narrative is a verbalization of the real relationships among Misiones' different species. As such, it stages the effects of capitalist development on Misiones' most disempowered inhabitants and demonstrates the kind of radical, epistemological change the ideal of political ecology entails. Quiroga's ground-level perspective is an important beginning, because it allows him to transcend the abstractions and valuations that characterize Western discourse on nature and to look at the environment instead as a dynamic system of minutely-interrelated parts. He is able to conceptualize nature in such a way that humans are not excluded from or set against the environment but symbiotically located within it.

Frequently cited as one of Latin America's first fully anti-hegemonic writers, Quiroga is also, as I have argued, a colonial writer whose literary production is profoundly shaped by informal imperialism and the modern experience of capitalist expansion. At the same time, his understanding of imperialism and colonialism is not structured by the stark opposition of cultures, races or political regimes that typifies both colonialist and postcolonial discourses on imperialism. It is relatively free of what Said calls the "metaphysical weight" of the project of imperialism, the nationalistic, Eurocentric civilizing imperative that bore upon Kipling and Conrad, but also upon the positivistic discourse that flourished in the Río de la Plata, most fully embodied in Domingo F. Sarmiento's *Facundo: Civilización o barbárie.* Instead, Quiroga's narratives are structured by more pluralistic configurations of power, which allow the geographical "subtext" of colonial literature to rise to the surface, becoming not only the site and subject of violent confrontation but the source of a new sense of communal identity and resistance to the alienating effects of capitalist development. Quiroga's solidarity with local workers therefore grows as what begins as an essentially colonial project of adaptation to new environmental conditions incorporates the region's indigenous human and non-human inhabitants: in the process, the capitalist's conception of territory as a commodity to be possessed and exploited becomes a vision of the land as a source of shared identity and ground for collective transformation.

Notes

1. Horacio Quiroga, letter to Ezequiel Martínez Estrada of April 11, 1936. *Cartas inéditas de Horacio Quiroga,* ed. Arturo Sergio Visca (Montevideo: Ministerio de Instrucción Pública y Previsión Social, 1959) 94-95.

2. Carlos Fuentes, *La nueva novela latinoamericana* (Mexico City: Cuadernos Joaquín Mortiz, 1969) 24.

3. Julio Cortázar, "Algunos aspectos del cuento," *Julio Cortázar: Obra crítica,* vol. II, ed. Jaime Alazraki (Madrid: Alfaguara, 1994) 367-385.

4. Carlos J. Alonso, *The Burden of Modernity: The Rhetoric of Cultural Discourse in Spanish America* (New York and Oxford: Oxford University Press, 1998) 201. Alonso considers Quiroga in the context of post-independence intellectuals' problematic relationship with the concept of the Modern, a (European) discursive construct to which the writers are ostensibly committed, but which they repeatedly subvert when the unavoidably un-modern social reality of Spanish America threatens to negate the authority of their writing. The present study sees Quiroga less concerned with the Modern as a discursive construct than with the socio-economic alterations that modernity—specifically defined as capitalist expansion—brought to Argentina's northern frontier.

5. Leonor Fleming provides a useful summary of Quiroga's life in El Chaco and Misiones in her introduction to *Horacio Quiroga: Cuentos* (Madrid: Cátedra, 1995) 78-83. The most extensive account is offered by Emir Rodríguez Monegal in *El desterrado: Vida y obra de Horacio Quiroga* (Buenos

Aires: Losada, 1968). As Jorge Marcone has written, Quiroga went to El Chaco and later Misiones in search of three things: economic independence, an alternative to alienated labor, and his own writerly identity. Marcone discusses Quiroga's project as a critique of both capitalist exploitation and the romantic myth of the return to nature in "'Nuevos descubrimientos del gran río de las Amazonas': La 'novela de la selva' y la crítica al imaginario de la Amazonía," *Estudios: Revista de investigaciones literarias y culturales* 16 (2000) 129-40; and "The Politics of Cultural Criticism and Sustainable Development in Amazonia: A Reading from the Spanish American Romance of the Jungle," *Hispanic Journal* 19, 2 (1998) 281-284.

6. Quiroga's first published works include poetry in the *modernista* style influenced by the Argentinean poet Leopoldo Lugones; he later turned to writing stories inspired by Edgar Allan Poe and Guy de Maupassant. See Noé Jitrik, *Horacio Quiroga: Una obra de experiencia y riesgo* (Buenos Aires: Ediciones Argentinas, 1959) 71-74, 104-105. As Jitrik concludes, Quiroga's mature work has more in common with that of contemporaries like Ernest Hemingway and Franz Kafka than with that of his early influences.

7. "Ante el tribunal," *Obras inéditas y desconocidas,* vol. VII, ed. Roberto Ibáñez and Jorge Ruffinello (Montevideo: ARCA, 1967) 135.

8. "Kipling en la pantalla," *Todos los cuentos,* ed. Napoleón Baccino Ponce de León and Jorge Lafforgue (Madrid: Colección Archivos, 1993) 1219.

9. In *Horacio Quiroga: Obras inéditas y desconocidas,* vol. VII: "Sobre *El ombú* de Hudson," 122-126; "La novela trunca de un espíritu," 108-110.

10. See, in *Horacio Quiroga: Obras inéditas y desconocidas,* vol. VII, "Carta abierta al señor Benito Lynch," 36-38; "Un poeta de la selva: José Eustasio Rivera," 118-122; "El cuento norteamericano," 126-128; and "El impudor literario nacional," 43-46.

11. The first rule of Quiroga's "Decálogo del perfecto cuentista," for example, is "Cree en un maestro—Poe, Maupassant, Kipling, Chejov—como en Dios mismo." *Textos inéditos y desconocidos,* VII, 86.

12. Abelardo Castillo, "Liminar: Horacio Quiroga," *Horacio Quiroga: Todos los cuentos,* xxviii.

13. A partial bibliography of economic and historical materials on the relationship between Britain and Latin America in the nineteenth and early twentieth centuries would include: Tulio Halperín Donghi, *The Contemporary History of Latin America,* trans. John Charles Chasteen (Durham and London: Duke University Press, 1993); John Gallagher and Ronald Robinson, "The Imperialism of Free Trade," *Economic History Review,* IV:1 (1953) 1-15; D. C. M. Platt, ed., *Business Imperialism: An Inquiry into the British Experience in Latin America, 1850-1914* (Oxford: Clarendon Press, 1977); Leslie Bethell, ed., *Latin America: Economy and Society, 1870-1914* (Cambridge and New York: Cambridge University Press, 1989) 1-57; Rory Miller, *Britain and Latin America in the Nineteenth and Twentieth Centuries* (London and New York: Longman, 1993); Richard Graham, "Robinson and Gallagher in Latin America: The Meaning of Informal Imperialism," *Imperialism: The Robinson and Gallagher Controversy,* ed. William Roger Louis (New York and London: New Viewpoints, 1976) 217-220; P. J. Cain and A. G. Hopkins, "Gentlemanly Capitalism and British Expansion Overseas II: New Imperialism, 1850-1945," *Economic History Review,* XL, I (1987) 1-26. Eric Hobsbawm's *The Age of Capital: 1848-1875* [1975] (New York: Random House, 1996) explains the expansion of capitalism in Latin America as part of a global trend.

14. Historian Oliver Marshall tells the fascinating story of the British in Misiones in "Planters or Peasants? British Pioneers on Argentina's Tropical Frontier," *The Land That England Lost,* 143-158. According to Marshall, the last of the British colonists did not abandon Misiones until the 1980s.

15. *Cartas inéditas de Horacio Quiroga,* ed. Arturo Sergio Visca (Montevideo: Ministerio de Instrucción Pública y Previsión Social, 1959) 100.

16. See Abdul R. JanMohamed, "The Economy of Manichean Allegory: The Function of Racial Difference in Colonialist Literature," *"Race," Writing and Difference,* ed. Henry Louis Gates, Jr. (Chicago: University of Chicago Press, 1985) 78-106. More recently, Michael Hardt and Antonio Negri address the same subject in "The Liberation of Hybridities, or Beyond Colonial Binaries," *Empire* (Cambridge: Harvard University Press, 2000) 143-145.

17. Edward Said, *Culture and Imperialism* (New York: Vintage, 1994) 7.

18. Martin Green, *Dreams of Adventure, Deeds of Empire* (New York: Basic Books, 1979) 228.

19. Rodríguez Monegal, 117.

20. Dane Kennedy describes late-Victorian paranoia towards tropical climates and the fetishization of protective garb in, "The Perils of the Midday Sun: Climatic Anxieties in the Colonial Tropics," *Imperialism and the Natural World,* ed. John M. MacKenzie (Manchester and New York: Manchester University Press, 1990) 118-140.

QUIROGA

SHORT STORY CRITICISM, Vol. 89

21. "Una bofetada" might be compared, for example, to the account of the death of the Danish colonialist Fresleven in Joseph Conrad's *Heart of Darkness*: Fresleven is speared by a young African while relentlessly "hammer[ing] the chief of the village with a stick" over a minor dispute. In the account of Fresleven's death, as in Korner's, the colonial agent's irrational use of violence provokes the native to an act which is implicitly justified by the circumstances; in both texts the jungle is represented as a place of lurking danger, but the conventional pattern of representing the native as an anarchic and unpredictable threat to the more stable, rational European is revised. Joseph Conrad, *Heart of Darkness* and *The Secret Sharer*, intro. Albert Guerard (New York: Penguin, 1983) 72.

22. See David Harvey, *Justice, Nature and the Geography of Difference* (Malden, MA: Blackwell, 1996); Fernando Coronil, *The Magical State: Nature, Money and Modernity in Venezuela* (Chicago and London: University of Chicago Press, 1997); Fernando Mires, *El discurso de la naturaleza: ecología y política en América Latina* (San José, Costa Rica: DEI, 1990).

23. Karl Marx, *Capital: A Critique of Political Economy,* vol. III, trans. Ernest Untermann (Chicago, Charles H. Kerr and Company, 1909) 954.

24. Jorge Lafforgue and Napoleón Baccino Ponce de León, endnote, "Los pescadores de vigas," *Horacio Quiroga: Todos los cuentos,* 121.

25. See, for example, Juan José Beauchamp, "Subdesarrollo, ideología y visión del mundo en los relatos de ambiente de Horacio Quiroga," *Revista de Estudios Hispánicos* 6:85-120 (1979) 97.

26. Quiroga later struck "English accountant" for "commercial accountant."

27. David Spurr, *The Rhetoric of Empire: Colonial Discourse in Journalism, Travel Writing, and Imperial Administration* (Durham and London: Duke University Press, 1993) 17.

28. Robert C. Eidt, *Frontier Settlement in Northeast Argentina* (Madison, Milwaukee and London: University of Wisconsin Press, 1971) 174.

29. Leonor Fleming, ed. *Horacio Quiroga: Cuentos* (Madrid: Cátedra, 1995) 295.

30. Fleming, 273.

31. John A. McClure, *Kipling and Conrad: The Colonial Fiction* (Cambridge, MA: Harvard University Press, 1981); James Harrison, "Kipling's Jungle Eden," *Critical Essays on Rudyard Kipling,* ed. Harold Orel (Boston: G. K. Hall, 1989) 77-92.

Works Cited

Alonso, Carlos J. *The Burden of Modernity: The Rhetoric of Cultural Discourse in Spanish America.* Oxford: Oxford University Press, 1998.

Beauchamp, Juan José. "Subdesarrollo, ideología y visión del mundo en los relatos de ambiente de Horacio Quiroga." *Revista de Estudios Hispánicos* 6 (1979) 85-120.

Cortázar, Julio. "Algunos aspectos del cuento." *Julio Cortázar: Obra crítica.* vol. 2. Ed. Jaime Alazraki. Madrid: Alfaguara, 1994.

Eidt, Robert C. *Frontier Settlement in Northeast Argentina.* Madison: University of Wisconsin P, 1971.

Fleming, Leonor. "Introduction." *Cuentos.* By Horacio Quiroga. Madrid: Cátedra, 1995.

Fuentes, Carlos. *La nueva novela latinoamericana.* Mexico City: Cuadernos Joaquín Mortiz, 1969.

Green, Martin. *Dreams of Adventure, Deeds of Empire.* New York: Basic Books, 1979.

JanMohamed, Abdul R. "The Economy of Manichean Allegory: The Function of Racial Difference in Colonialist Literature," *"Race," Writing and Difference,* ed. Henry Louis Gates, Jr. Chicago: Chicago, University Press, 1985. 78-106.

Kipling, Rudyard. *Rudyard Kipling.* Ed. and intro. by Daniel Karlin. Oxford: Oxford University Press, 1999.

———. *The Portable Kipling.* Ed. Irving Howe. New York and London: Penguin, 1982.

Marx, Karl. *Capital: A Critique of Political Economy.* 3 vol. Trans. Ernest Untermann. Ed. Frederick Engels. Chicago: Charles H. Kerr, 1909.

Quiroga, Horacio. *Cartas inéditas.* Ed. Arturo Sergio Visca. Montevideo: Ministerio de Instrucción Pública y Previsión Social, 1959.

———. *Obras inéditas y escondidas.* Dir. Angel Rama. 7 vols. Montevideo: ARCA, 1967.

———. *Todos los cuentos.* Ed. Jorge Lafforgue and Napoleón Baccino Ponce de Leon. Barcelona: Fondo de Cultura, 1993.

Said, Edward. *Culture and Imperialism.* New York: Vintage, 1994.

Spurr, David. *The Rhetoric of Empire: Colonial Discourse in Journalism, Travel Writing, and Imperial Administration.* Durham: Duke University Press, 1993.

FURTHER READING

Criticism

Holland, Norman S. "'Doctoring' in Quiroga." *Confluencia* 9, no. 2 (spring 1994): 64-72.

Notes that Quiroga, in his stories, was "debunking naturalism" and thus placing himself firmly within the tradition of modernism.

Montenegro, Ernesto. "A Literary Kin of Kipling and Jack London." *Review* 19 (winter 1976): 31-4.
Compares Quiroga's technique of writing from his own life experiences to the autobiographical techniques of Jack London and Rudyard Kipling.

Param, Charles. "Horacio Quiroga and His Exceptional Protagonists." *Hispania* 55, no. 3 (September 1972): 428-35.
Discusses what he asserts is the autobiographical nature of the theme of personal courage in eight of Quiroga's stories.

Rosser, Harry L. "Quiroga and Cortazar's Dream Crossings." *Revista/Review Interamericana* 13, nos. 1-4 (spring-winter 1983): 120-25.
Notes how Quiroga's themes relating to knowledge in both dream states and conscious life inform the works of Julio Cortazar.

Scroggins, Daniel C. "Vengeance with a Stickpin: Barreto, Quiroga, and García Calderón." *Romance Notes* 15, no. 1 (autumn 1973): 47-51.
Traces the source for a Quiroga story and a García Calderón story to a story by José Barreto, and notes that Quiroga's story is "clearly superior."

Additional coverage of Quiroga's life and career is contained in the following sources published by Thomson Gale: *Contemporary Authors,* **Vols. 117, 131;** *DISCovering Authors Modules: Multicultural Authors;* *Encyclopedia of World Literature in the 20th Century,* **Ed. 3;** *Hispanic Literature Criticism,* **Ed. 2;** *Hispanic Writers,* **Ed. 1;** *Latin American Writers; Literature Resource Center; Major 20th-Century Writers,* **Ed. 1;** *Reference Guide to Short Fiction,* **Ed. 2;** *Twentieth-Century Literary Criticism,* **Vol. 20; and** *World Literature and Its Times,* **Vol. 1.**

Yevgeny Zamyatin
1884-1937

(Full name Yevgeny Ivanovich Zamyatin; first name also transliterated as Evgeny, Evgenii, Yevgenii, Yevgeni, and Eugene; surname also transliterated as Zamiatin, Zamjatin, and Zamayatin) Russian novella and short story writer, novelist, playwright, essayist, critic, and autobiographer.

The following entry provides an overview of Zamyatin's life and works of short fiction.

INTRODUCTION

Zamyatin is considered one of the most influential Russian writers in the decade following the Russian Revolution. While Zamyatin's early writings satirize the philistinism of provincial life, his works written after the Revolution denounce obedience to dogmatic authority. Throughout his career Zamyatin experimented with form and language, renouncing the straightforward representation of life advocated by the nineteenth-century Russian realists. His work is praised for its arresting language, grotesque imagery, and ironic viewpoint.

BIOGRAPHICAL INFORMATION

The son of an orthodox priest, Zamyatin was born in the central Russian town of Lebedyan. As a child, he had few friends and occupied himself reading the works of such classic Russian authors as Fyodor Dostoevsky, Ivan Turgenev, and Nikolai Gogol. Zamyatin entered the Polytechnical Institute of St. Petersburg in 1902 to study naval engineering. His studies were interrupted when he was arrested and temporarily exiled for revolutionary activities in 1905, a sentence that was reenacted in 1911. Zamyatin graduated in 1908, remaining with the Institute as a lecturer in the Department of Naval Architecture. During this time, he began writing short fiction, and a few of his efforts were published in local journals. Zamyatin worked in England during World War I, designing and supervising the construction of Russian ships. After the 1917 Revolution, Zamyatin became disenchanted with the Soviet government's insistence on artistic conformity to standards of realism and political didacticism. It was during this post-revolutionary era that he wrote what many consider his most important work, the novel *My* (1927; *We*). Though not explicitly a reaction against Soviet communism,

Zamyatin's attack on the communists' vision of a regimented civilization is apparent. Zamyatin continued to write and lecture on literary subjects during the 1920s, having a particular influence on the Serapion Brothers, a group of young Russian writers that included formalist critic Viktor Shklovsky and short story writer Mikhail Zoshchenko. Although diverse in their aesthetic tenets, the Serapions shared an emphasis on the autonomy of art from political commitment and on experimentation with literary technique. In 1929 the Soviet government forbade publication of Zamyatin's works after an unauthorized portion of *We* appeared in the Soviet Union through a Russian *émigré* journal based in Prague. Zamyatin subsequently wrote to Soviet leader Joseph Stalin asserting his independence and requesting emigration. Through the appeals of socialist-realist author Maxim Gorky, Zamyatin was permitted to leave the country in 1931 and lived in Paris until his death in 1937.

MAJOR WORKS OF SHORT FICTION

With the publication of the novella *Uezdnoe* (1916; *A Provincial Tale*), a satire on Russian provincial life, Zamyatin was acknowledged as an important literary figure in his country. His satiric portrayal of military life, *Na kulichkakh* (1923; *At the World's End*), offended czarist authorities who accused Zamyatin of anti-militarism and subversion. Commentators generally divide Zamyatin's literary career into four periods. The first, which includes such works as *A Provincial Tale* and *At the World's End,* is characterized by stories and novellas with provincial settings and themes. In these works Zamyatin satirized the philistinism of rural society by focusing on characters whose coarse, prosaic lives are devoid of any cultural or moral qualities. Employing the *skaz* manner of narration, which incorporates local dialects and colloquialisms, these works feature grotesque images and metonymies, often attributed to the influence of Gogol. The second period of Zamyatin's career begins with the publication of the novella *Ostrovityane* (1922; *The Islanders*), which was collected with several short stories, and ends with the completion of *We* in 1920. The works of this phase are characterized by urban settings and depart from the *skaz* form of narration. Zamyatin's fiction of this period is noted for stylistic and formal innovations, including the use of a central, integrating metaphor, such as that of the iron stove in his short story "Peščera" ("The

Cave"). Zamyatin shifted his concerns from provincial backwardness to the automatization of human life and the alienation of humanity from nature. The transitional third stage of Zamyatin's literary career, from 1922 to 1927, reflects his search for new literary forms. "Rasskaz o samom glavnom" ("A Story about the Most Important Thing") presents actions on multiple planes of existence and is often interpreted as stressing the relative nature of all systems of meaning. The story is considered characteristic of Zamyatin's efforts to base a literary structure on the aesthetic theories presented in his essays, which emphasize continual revolution and dialectical conflict, rather than an adherence to any ultimate ideology. In the final phase of his career, which spans from 1928 until his death, Zamyatin returned to fiction based on stylistic simplicity, objective narration, and surprise endings. Critics regard works of this period as powerful expressions of the author's tragic conception of life.

CRITICAL RECEPTION

For the most part Zamyatin's essays advocate rebellion against all forms of tradition and authority and have contributed to his status as an uncompromising artist. Despite his relative obscurity in the Soviet Union after his death, he is recognized as a major influence on Russian writers who have appeared since the 1920s. Although commentators fault Zamyatin's fiction for excessive verbal effects and for focusing on central metaphors at the expense of character development, he has been lauded as a master technician and his writing is esteemed for its original language, effective imagery, and powerful satire. *We* remains prominent as a quintessential anti-utopian novel, and Zamyatin's work as a whole is viewed as central to the transitional period that established modernism in Russian literature.

PRINCIPAL WORKS

Short Fiction

*Uezdnoe [A Provincial Tale] 1916
Bolshim detyam skazki 1922
†Ostrovityane [The Islanders] 1922
Na kulichkakh [At the World's End] 1923; also translated as *A Godforsaken Hole*, 1988
‡Nechestivye rasskazy 1927
Navodnenie [The Flood] 1930
#Bich Bozhy 1939
‖Povesti i rasskazy 1963

§The Dragon [translated and edited by Mirra Ginsburg] 1966

Other Major Works

Ogni svyatogo Dominika [The Fires of St. Dominic; first publication] (play) 1922
Blokha [The Flea] (play) 1925
Obshchestvo pochetnykh zvonarey [The Society of Honorary Bell-Ringers] (play) 1926
**My [We] (novel) 1927; published partially in the journal *Volya Russy*
Sobranie sochiney. 4 vols. (autobiography, play, fables, novellas, and short stories) 1929
††Atilla [first publication] (play) 1950; published in the journal *Novy zhurnal*
Litsa (essays) 1955
A Soviet Heretic: Essays by Yevgeny Zamyatin [translated and edited by Ginsburg] (autobiography, essays, and letters) 1970

*Uezdnoe was first published as a novella in the journal *Zavety* in 1913.

†This collection includes the short story "Peščera" ("The Cave"), which was first published in the journal *Zapiski mečtatelej* in 1922.

‡This collection includes the short story "Rasskaz o samom glavnom" ("A Story about the Most Important Thing"), which was first published in the journal *Russkij sovremennik* in 1924.

#This volume contains the title work—an unfinished novel—and the short stories "Vstrecha," "Chasy," "Lev," and "Desyatiminutnaya Drama."

‖In addition to novellas and short stories, this collection includes Zamyatin's autobiography.

§In addition to novellas and short stories, this collection includes Zamyatin's letters.

**This work was written in 1920 and not published in its entirety until 1952.

††This work was written from 1925 to 1927.

CRITICISM

D. J. Richards (essay date 1962)

SOURCE: Richards, D. J. "Psychological Tales." In *Zamyatin: A Soviet Heretic*, pp. 73-83. London: Bowes & Bowes, 1962.

[*In the following essay, Richards discusses Zamyatin's treatment of the psychology of personal relationships in four of his short stories.*]

The unifying theme of what might be called Zamyatin's "main-stream" works is that of the clash between the forces of Entropy and Revolution in various guises. In his earliest works this clash takes place in provincial Russia; after the Revolution the stage is the whole of

Russia—or a comparable setting in the past (*Ogni Svyatova Dominika*) or in the future (*My*); towards the end of his life Zamyatin produced a play (*Atilla*) and the first part of a novel (*Bich Bozhii*), where the eternal struggle was manifested in the historical clash between the Western Roman Empire and the Eastern barbarians. This theme of warring Entropy and Revolution finds expression in short stories, novels and dramatic works. The mood is often satirical.

At the same time Zamyatin produced outside this "mainstream" several works in which attention is focused not on the cosmic struggle but primarily on personal relationships. To call these works "psychological" is perhaps a little misleading without a word of explanation. All Zamyatin's works are psychological, in the sense that he is interested above all in his heroes' states of mind, but his "main-stream" works, as is so often the case in Russian literature, are at least equally sociological—the individual's personal problems and attitudes of mind are closely linked with wider problems of social organisation, with the relationship between the individual and society in general. The four works to be examined in this [essay] are psychological in the narrower, personal sense: the heroes are shown in their relations not with society in general and its values and patterns of behaviour, but with one or two individual fellow men. The larger community to which these individuals belong recedes far into the background. In these tales Zamyatin also endeavours, rather like Chekhov, to create an atmosphere or to evoke a mood in the reader.

(1)

"Aprel" (**"April"**), published in 1915, occupies a place apart in Zamyatin's early work. It is concerned exclusively with youthful romantic love and is entirely free from preoccupations with animal lusts and provincial stagnation. **"Aprel"** is an idyllic tale of one day in the love of a young boy and girl, Kolya and Nastya, from their first kiss early in the morning through a day of frustration and unsympathetic clashes with the adult world to a final reconciliation in the evening. The tale is told largely from Nastya's point of view and it is her changing state of mind, her thoughts and plans, which form its main substance. Zamyatin's touch is so sure that in the many scenes such as the final one, where Kolya is kneeling outside Nastya's open window while she stretches out her hands towards him, there is never one trivial or false note despite the often naïve simplicity of the plot.

In these psychological tales, as in many of his other works, Zamyatin employs parallel planes of action to mirror his heroes' states of mind and to help evoke the mood or atmosphere of the situation. In **"Aprel"** the changing state of Nastya's mind is neatly reflected in the changing weather: a brilliant morning is followed by rain and later by descending darkness and finally by a calm and peaceful evening, while the showery month of April mirrors the capricious springtime of Nastya's life and love.

Although Zamyatin in his articles was fond of pointing out that children shared with artists and heretics that spontaneous response to life which modern civilised man had lost, **"Aprel"** is, strangely, Zamyatin's only story in which interest is centred directly on the thoughts of children and their attitude to the adult world.

* * *

In an article on Zamyatin, written in 1921, a Russian critic said of **"Zemlemer"** (**"The Land-Surveyor"**):

> The tender lyricism of this charming tale and the healthy approach to a sharp and somewhat *risqué* subject inspired thoughts of some turning point in Zamyatin's literary career, of a "return" to Chekhov.

But that Zamyatin was capable of a light, delicate touch had already been revealed in **"Aprel,"** and connoisseurs of that story doubtless found **"Zemlemer"** less surprising. Like Chekhov in so many of his works, Zamyatin is here concerned with evoking a mood—and indeed a truly Chekovian mood of regret and missed opportunity. The whole tale is a masterpiece of subtle suggestion. The love which the land-surveyor and Lizaveta Petrovna feel for each other is never once mentioned, while Lizaveta Petrovna's appearance is described only once—and then very briefly and impressionistically, seen through the eyes of the land-surveyor, who recalls no more than the golden mist of her hair and the light blue veins on her temples.

The land-surveyor (his name is never given) has spent two months measuring Lizaveta Petrovna's estate. During his stay there he has fallen in love with his employer but cannot find the courage to declare himself to her. It is the last evening of his stay; the next day he must return to his lonely room in Moscow.

At the very beginning of the tale the reader's sympathy is aroused for the land-surveyor by his sensitivity and by his awkward and helpless personality. He stutters slightly and is a little effeminate; he is very out of place in the country and the peasants find him amusing. The land-surveyor's pathetic attachment to Lizaveta Petrovna are suggested early, while the recurring words "the last time" help to create an atmosphere of sadness and urgency, tinged with a sense of inevitability. The land-surveyor is overcome by the farewells of the peasants; unexpectedly he finds himself asking after Lizaveta Petrovna; he imagines he hears her soft tread in the sitting-room, but there is no one there; as he packs his trunk we are given a snatch of his thoughts: "Ah, well then, back to Moscow, to my empty, tobacco-stained room, and perhaps never again in my life . . ." After dinner he sits with Lizaveta Petrovna on the balcony. She hugs her little dog closely. Neither of them can find anything to say.

On the following day some workmen play a cruel trick on the dog and it dies. The land-surveyor tries to comfort the distraught Lizaveta Petrovna and he momentarily forgets himself so far as to stroke her hair. By this time it is too late to catch his train that day and he has to stay.

That same day the land-surveyor and Lizaveta Petrovna are advised to leave the house—the action is set at the time of the Revolution—and they go together to a monastery, where they are mistaken for husband and wife and put in the same room. Their confusion gradually turns to amusement and then to tender feelings towards each other but, just as the land-surveyor is about to kiss Lizaveta Petrovna, the latter's old nurse enters, makes herself comfortable in an armchair and announces that there is still time for the land-surveyor to reach the station. He meekly leaves and, returning home, he sees from the train Lizaveta Petrovna's house burning in the distance.

The land-surveyor's relations with Lizaveta Petrovna have been from start to finish a series of missed opportunities, for his shyness has repeatedly prevented him from declaring his love. The tale is full of goodbyes: the land-surveyor bids farewell to the peasants; the dog dies; Lizaveta Petrovna has to leave her old house and servants; and finally the land-surveyor leaves Lizaveta Petrovna.

Moreover the poignancy of the inner drama, enacted between the land-surveyor and Lizaveta Petrovna, is heightened by the setting of the action at the end of the summer and at the beginning of the Russian Revolution, so that the frustration of the hero's love is paralleled on the natural plane by the end of the fine weather and on the historical by the passing of the old Russia.

* * *

A third psychological tale, **"Detskaya" ("The Nursery")**, though written a decade later and first published in 1923, is obviously a product of Zamyatin's naval life and probably reflects memories from one of those cruises which he enjoyed during his student years at the St. Petersburg Polytechnic. The content of the tale is negligible; its effectiveness stems from the tense, claustrophobic atmosphere and the personality of the leading characters which Zamyatin graphically evokes.

The scene is set in a crowded, smoke-filled, hard-drinking, erotic and unsavoury Merchant Navy officers' club with its Chinese waiter and its heavily made-up hostesses. Most of the action takes place in the "nursery"—a name given to a room set aside for gambling. The tough, heartless Captain Krug, because of an old jealousy, seizes the chance to break down the feeble Semyon Semyonych and reduces him to a pathetic, sobbing wreck, while pretending all the time that it is a joke. Krug, with his eternal cigar, his fierce eyebrows and his hard, copper-coloured face, involves Semyon Semyonych in a gambling game and, by a combination of cheating and skill, wins huge sums from him. He gradually brings Semyon Semyonych to such a state that the latter, who is a little tipsy, is finally persuaded as a last desperate measure to wager his wife. He loses and breaks down completely, seeing nothing but mocking faces everywhere. The whole experience becomes nightmarish to him and he loses all touch with reality. His last despairing words are: "Who am I? I do not exist. Nothing exists."

The claustrophobic atmosphere and Semyon Semyonych's pathetic state are both effectively mirrored in the fate of a fly trapped in a damp patch left by a glass of beer. It is interesting to follow the development of this fly image in the story, as a good example of Zamyatin's use of a parallel plane of action. First of all we read that Semyon Semyonych, when he starts to lose, always "begins to wash his face, as it were, as a fly does with its leg". Then Krug, commenting on this habit, tells how he once tore a fly's head off. Thirdly, when Semyon Semyonych is about to sign a vast I.O.U., we read: "On the edge of the table there is a sweet sticky ring, left by a glass; in the ring is a fly and a hand with a cigar is pushing a piece of white paper towards the fly." Semyon Semyonych and the fly have fused into one. Finally the last words of the tale are: "On the table-top in front of him, in the sweet sticky ring, the fly is still buzzing and trying in vain to tear itself away and take off." Semyon Semyonych and the fly are again separate, but Semyon Semyonych now sees his own predicament in that of the fly.

* * *

A similarly claustrophobic atmosphere is created in *Navodnenie (The Flood)*, published in 1930 in Leningrad by Izdatelstvo Pisatelei. This was the last of his works to be issued in the U.S.S.R., and in his letter to Stalin, Zamyatin paid tribute to the publishing house for standing by him when he had been abandoned by so many former friends and acquaintances after the 1929 campaign against him. Apart from publishing *Navodnenie* Izdatelstvo Pisatelei also employed Zamyatin on its board, and it was not until the spring of 1931 that R.A.p. p. succeeded in having him removed.

Navodnenie is a story of love, jealousy and murder. Sophia, married to Trofim, is approaching middle age but still childless. She finds herself jealously admiring the neighbour's daughter, Ganka, who is chased by the boys. When Ganka's father dies, Sophia, "unexpectedly even to herself", takes the girl into her home. She is motivated, we assume, by a mixture of love and hate, by a longing to recapture, as it were, her own lost youth and by the desire to have the rival within her power; for on the universal level Sophia might be said to represent middle-aged woman, while Ganka is young woman, the sexual rival.

Trofim takes a greater pride in his appearance now and gradually transfers his affection to the newcomer until he is regularly sleeping with her, while Sophia sobs alone. Eventually Sophia is driven to kill Ganka. Her husband comes back to her; she conceives and gives birth to a daughter, but still feels burdened until she confesses her crime, after which for the first time in many months she sleeps "evenly, peacefully, blissfully".

The human emotional storm is paralleled throughout the tale by the rising of the Neva and consequent flooding in Leningrad. This flooding adds to the claustrophobic atmosphere physically, in as much as Sophia, Trofim and Ganka are forced closer together when they have to evacuate their ground floor.

Three closely interwoven themes run through *Navodnenie.* Firstly, there is the life/death theme. After the girl's arrival Sophia endures a living death until Ganka's death seems to bring her back to life and child-bearing. Like Anfimya, the heroine of **"Chrevo,"** Sophia is forced to kill before she can give birth herself. Life feeds on life; without death, rebirth is impossible: "Sophia's stomach was round and full, like the Earth. In the Earth, deep down, visible to none, lay Ganka; and in the Earth, visible to none, the roots of the old corn were stirring." The birth of Sophia's daughter is almost a direct result of Ganka's death, but then Sophia herself will have to die because of her guilt.

Secondly, closely connected with the first theme, is the blood theme: the bloody murder of Ganka (Sophia kills her with an axe) somehow restores Sophia's flagging functions long enough for her to conceive a child.

Thirdly, the fly theme: as in **"Detskaya,"** and also earlier in *Uezdnoe,* the image of a trapped fly (in *Navodnenie* it is caught under an upturned jar) is used to parallel a human situation. Just after her husband has started to sleep regularly with Ganka, Sophia is disturbed by a fly. When she has killed the girl a fly alights on the corpse and then drops persistently on to Sophia's hand. During the hot summer nights the buzzing flies keep Sophia awake. Finally, as Sophia is feeding her baby daughter, it is the appearance of a fly on the white hospital wall which strikes sudden fear into her and drives her to confess her guilt.

In *Navodnenie,* Zamyatin adopts his usual impressionistic approach towards character description. Ganka is likened throughout to a cat and Sophia, her victim, to a bird, while the husband's coarse nature is suggested by the *leitmotif* of his teeth, white like the keys of an accordion.

With its tense plot, its keen insight into Sophia's mind, its mysterious, almost religious undertones and its brilliantly constructed patterns of themes and images *Navodnenie* is one of the best of all Zamyatin's stories.

(2)

Somewhere between these psychological tales and Zamyatin's satires on post-revolutionary Russian life stand the tales **"Desyatiminutnaya Drama"** (**"A Ten-Minute Drama"**), **"Lev"** (**"The Lion"**), and **"Vstrecha"** (**"The Meeting"**), all written during the 'thirties after Zamyatin had left Russia. Human relationships are the central theme—in **"Desyatiminutnaya Drama"** friction between a young dandy and an elderly workman is built up during a short bus ride across Leningrad; in **"Lev"** a young man tries to impress his beloved by playing the very minor part of a lion in a ballet; in **"Vstrecha"** a former police colonel, turned actor and finding himself playing the part of a police chief, is terrified to find one of his former victims playing the accused—but the tales are little more than humorous acecdotes, which rely for their effect on their bizarre settings (in two of them) and on the unexpected twist of fortune which is the central feature of each. In **"Desyatiminutnaya Drama"** and **"Vstrecha"** the impending catastrophe is in one sentence dissolved into farce, while in **"Lev"** the farcical situation is almost as swiftly turned into tragedy.

* * *

In his *Panorama de la Littérature Russe* Vl. Pozner remarked: "All Zamyatin's work lacks feeling . . . the pleasure experienced in reading his books is entirely intellectual: one admires without being moved." True though this may be of much of Zamyatin's work, where many of the negative characters are deliberately presented as caricatures and as unthinking, unfeeling automata, and the positive heroes themselves are often representatives (of Revolution or enlightenment) rather than individuals and are significant for their intellectual stand rather than for the emotional problems which they might share with common humanity, it is not true of the best of these psychological tales, where common human emotional experiences, such as first love, timidity and frustration, helplessness in the face of hostile strength and cruelty, desperate jealousy, etc., are presented sympathetically and movingly.

Select Bibliography

A. Works in Russian

(i) The fullest edition of Zamyatin's works up to the mid-'twenties (but not including *My*) is the four-volumed *Sobranie Sochinenii*, Federatsia, Moscow, 1929.

(ii) The only Russian edition of *My* is that of Chekhov Publishing House, New York, 1952.

(iii) *Navodnenie*: Krug, Moscow, 1927; and in *Grani* (Frankfurt), No. 32, 1956.

(iv) *Atilla*: published only in *Novy Zhurnal* (New York), No. 24, 1950.

(v) The posthumous volume *Bich Bozhii*, Dom Knigi, Paris, 1938, contains *Bich Bozhii* and the four later tales, "Vstrecha," "Chasy," "Lev," "Desyatiminutnaya Drama."

(vi) *Litsa*, Chekhov Publishing House, New York, 1955, contains many of Zamyatin's critical articles and also the text of his letter to Stalin.

B. English Translations

Unfortunately very few of Zamyatin's works are available in English.

(i) *We* (*My*): there is a translation by B. Guerney in his *Anthology of Soviet Stories*, Random House, New York, 1959, and also a Dutton *Everyman Paperback* translation by G. Zilboorg, New York, 1959.

(ii) "The Cave" ("Peschera") has been translated several times, most recently by A. Yarmolinsky in his *Soviet Short Stories*, New York, 1960.

(iii) "Mamai" ("Mamai") appeared in *Soviet Literature—An Anthology*, London, 1933.

C. French Translations

Much more is available in French than in English. Some of the more important works not obtainable in English are:

(i) *Le Chasseur d'Hommes* (*Lovets Chelovekov*) translated by Vl. Pozner in *Anthologie de la Presse Russe*, Paris, 1929.

(ii) *L'Inondation* (*Navodnenie*) in *La Revue de France*, 1932/2.

(iii) *Les Insulaires* (*Ostrovityane*) in *Europe*, 1939/6.

(iv) *L'Aventure du Diacre Indikopleff* (*Iks*) in *Monde*, 1932/6.

Alex M. Shane (essay date 1968)

SOURCE: Shane, Alex M. "Early Period, 1908-1917." In *The Life and Works of Evgenij Zamjatin*, pp. 97-130. Berkeley and Los Angeles: University of California Press, 1968.

[*In the following essay, Shane surveys Zamyatin's works written between 1908 and 1917.*]

During these years [1908-1910], amidst the blueprints and figures were several stories. I did not submit them for publication: in each still I felt something that was not quite "it." "It" turned up in 1911.

Zamjatin, *Autobiography*[1]

Using such criteria as the date of writing, theme, structure, and style, Zamjatin's creative work can be divided into four periods. The first period (1908-1917), beginning with his maiden story **"Odin"** and terminating with the story **"Pravda istinnaja,"** comprises his early works. The setting for most of these is provincial Russia—the small town, the village, or the distant garrison. Local dialects and colloquialisms are abundant, and the *skaz* manner of narration is employed extensively. The second period (1917-1921) begins with the tale *Ostrovitjane* and culminates with Zamjatin's only complete novel, *My*. The works of this period depart from the folksy *skaz* and are characterized by the elaboration of a concise, elliptical style in which the role of imagery is highly intensified; several are set in great urban communities. The third period (1922-1927) shows a decided drop in the production of prose fiction (only seven stories were written in those years); these pieces are distinguished by much experimentation with form and a comic treatment of post-Revolutionary life, accompanied by new forms of *skaz* narrative. The major works of the final period (1928-1935) are simpler, have less elaborate imagery, lack *skaz,* and reflect the influence of the modern European novella in their plot dynamism and their use of surprise endings and false resolutions. These generalizations suggest considerable variety in Zamjatin's literary technique. Indeed, in Zamjatin's work the elaboration of one technique was followed by a search for a new and different technique—a search that reflected his philosophy of never-ending revolution in all spheres of life.

Zamjatin's belief that life is essentially tragic is expressed in all his early works. In **"Odin"** the imprisoned student-revolutionary commits suicide because his love is frustrated. In **"Devuška"** the heroine's needs for love remain unfulfilled. In *Uezdnoe* the rise of the ignorant, bestial Anfim Baryba to a powerful administrative position is in itself a tragic reflection of provincial life. The hero of **"Neputevyj"** dies uselessly on the Moscow barricades, and the heroine of **"Črevo,"** thwarted in her irrepressible desire to have a child, murders her drunken husband whose beatings have caused her to miscarry. *Nakuličkax* depicts the spiritual bankruptcy of a distant army garrison and the destruction of a genuine love between Captain Šmit and his wife Marusja. In **"Alatyr'"** the dreams and aspirations of the central characters are thwarted, and in **"Krjaži"** the love between two strong personalities remains unrealized at the death of one. Konyč's inability to comprehend a situation (**"Staršina"**) provides one more tragic example of provincial ignorance. Dar'ja (**"Pis'menno"**), overjoyed by the imprisonment of her hated husband, discovers a year later that she loves him. Fedor Volkov ("**Afrika**") abandons his shrewish wife in search of happiness, only to die. In "**Pravda istinnaja**" the letter of a country girl working as a servant in the city unintentionally betrays her unhappiness with her life there. The sole bright spot in Zamjatin's early stories is blossoming puppy love between two teen-agers in "**Aprel'**," but even there a tragic note is sounded when the uncomprehending adult world momentarily turns the emotion into a source of shame for the girl.

Despite the characteristically pessimistic endings of his early works, Zamjatin believed that life's tragedies could be surmounted either by religion or by irony. In contrast to the Symbolists, who had turned to religious mysticism, Zamjatin chose irony. It is ironic that Marusja (*Na kuličkax*), who loves Šmit so deeply, is not present at his funeral, while General Azančeev, the man who destroys Šmit and his love for Marusja, delivers an impassioned eulogy. It is ironic that Konyč, who in his ignorant zeal to serve the government has transgressed the law, is incapable of recognizing his error even after the trial. It is ironic that the meek and submissive Kostja Edytkin ("**Alatyr'**"), upon perceiving the hopelessness of pitiful Alatyr' life, is led off to prison surrounded by a clamoring mob that considers him a dangerous killer. Permeating all of the early works, irony underscores life's incongruities and illuminates the contradiction between truth and what people think to be true. Since the ironic rejection of the lives depicted is accompanied neither by solutions, nor by comments from the author, nor by an explicit ideology, the reader must make his own deductions which, hopefully, will stimulate him to seek a better life.

The apparent pessimism of the early stories is only a literary device; the critic Gizetti astutely observed that the indignation aroused by the denouement of *Uezdnoe,* for example, was proof that beneath Zamjatin's artistic devices resided a firm faith in man's potential goodness.[2] Although Zamjatin once quipped that the Neorealists believed neither in God nor in man,[3] his critical essays left no doubt about his own deep-rooted belief in man's capacity for self-improvement on earth. His faith in the verbal whip of satire as the sole means of preventing man's reversion to lower, inhuman behavior underlay his early, essentially satiric works. On the other hand, Gizetti went too far in seeing "excellent opportunities for regeneration" in some of Zamjatin's early stories,[4] for within most of the stories themselves such hope is rare. The opportunity exists only for the reader.

Man's inhumanity, love, and revolution—set invariably in provincial Russia—are the central themes of Zamjatin's early period. The theme of man's inhumanity, which is basic to all three of Zamjatin's tales and the majority of his stories, is the keynote of the early pe-

riod. It is first introduced in *Uezdnoe,* Zamjatin's first extensive work in which he found "it" and which brought him widespread recognition. [In [470], 48, Mark Slonim wrote that Zamjatin's *Uezdnoe* had received 300 reviews within two months, a claim that was reiterated in 1962 by D. J. Richards [454], 31.] Beginning with Anfim Baryba's expulsion from school and home for laziness and stupidity, Zamjatin traces his activities over two years of theft, gluttony, sadism, rape, and professional perjury, until Baryba finally attains the position of town constable where, presumably, he can indulge his sadistic bullying unhindered. Although the adventures of Baryba are the organizing principle of the work, contemporary critics were correct in construing the author's aim to be the satiric depiction of the extremely negative aspects of provincial Russian life. As V. Polonskij put it:

> And when you have read to the end of the tale, it turns out that Anfim Baryba is of no importance, Anfim Baryba is simply an excuse, and the tale is not at all about Anfimka. One after another the little chapters flow together into one large chapter, they dissolve, drown in one general, unified picture, and the name of that picture is Russia, limited, dark, provincial Russia.[5]

Although Polonskij's conclusion is sound, one cannot agree that Baryba is simply a literary device, of no importance in himself. He is, after all, a product of his philistine environment and is neither better nor worse than the other characters of the tale. His crude, angular, and heavy features, especially his iron jaws, reflect the essence of his personality; and Zamjatin's frequent use of the epithet "stone" not only reinforces the basic picture of his heavy awkwardness but reveals the central problem of the tale: the petrification of human feelings within man.[6] Whatever human feelings Baryba may begin with (he yearns for human companionship while living among the dogs, and he is genuinely touched—if only momentarily—by Aprosja's care during his illness) are completely petrified by the tale's end, when he can neither bear the sound of human laughter nor recognize a momentary twinge of conscience. The final comparison—"as if it were not a man walking, but an old resurrected heathen idol, an absurd Russian stone idol"—endows the figure of Baryba with symbolic significance. It shows him as the embodiment of a cruel, stagnant, provincial Russia devoid of human compassion.

Resembling Baryba in their bestial, ignorant, and senseless existence, the other characters of *Uezdnoe* present variant expressions of inhumanity. Foremost among them is the well-to-do merchant's widow who owns the town bathhouse and leather factory, the incomparable Čebotarixa. A veritable mound of quivering, doughy flesh, she cannot resist the sight of young Baryba's tensed, firm, animal-like body, and, instead of punishing him for stealing her chickens, she takes him into her arms and her bed to feed her insatiable appetite. Timoša, the town tailor and philosopher who is aware of Baryba's lack of soul, nonetheless befriends him. A chronic alcoholic with consumption, Timoša forces his three children to eat from his plate in order to tempt God, in the tradition of the Dostoevskian rebels: Will He allow the suffering of innocent children? In a few instances Timoša serves as the author's ironic mouth-piece:

> It's nothing unusual [Baryba's being the 'companion' of a certain respected widow]. It's a matter of trade. Everything now, in accord with the times, is a matter of trade, that's how we make a living. The merchant sells herring, the gal sells her belly. Each has his own trade. And in what way is the belly any worse than herring, or the herring any worse than conscience? Everything is a commodity.
>
> (*S. S.* I, 86)
>
> [*Sobranie sočinenij*, I, [30], 86. Hereafter quotations from this four-volume edition of Zamjatin's collected works [30]-[33] will be identified in the text by the initials *S. S.* plus volume and page numbers in roman and arabic numerals, respectively.]

Timoša's words forecast all that follows: Baryba does indeed sell his conscience and even sends his friend Timoša to the gallows by perjuring himself for a hundred and fifty rubles and an appointment as town constable. The irony of Timoša's execution is purposely intensified: his intercession on behalf of one of the apprehended thieves, a slight lad who is being severely beaten by the tavern-keeper Čurilov, leads to his false conviction as an accessory to the crime: "Do you want to kill the kid because of a hundred rubles [the amount stolen]? Maybe you've already killed him? Look, he's not breathing. Devils, animals, isn't a man even worth a hundred rubles?" (*S. S.* I, 96.) The answer is an ironic negative, for this sole prominent humane impulse is rewarded by ostracism and death. This bleak picture is supplemented by a host of other grotesque characters: the fly-watching priest Father Evsej, the sensual and deceitful lawyer Morgunov, the presiding colonel at the military court whose upset stomach interests him more than justice, the prosecutor who wants a victim more than he wants the actual robber, and the district police officer who prefers pleasing his superiors to saving an innocent man.

Zamjatin's satire is not limited to any one group. In *Uezdnoe* he attacks small town inhabitants (Baryba, Čebotarixa, Aprosja, Timoša), the clergy (Evsej, Innokentij, d'jakonok, Savka), and the courts (the colonel, the prosecutor, the district police official, Morgunov). In *Na kuličkax,* which further develops the main theme of *Uezdnoe,* he shifts his attention to the military personnel of a remote Siberian garrison, but in this tale he endows some characters (Šmit, Marusja, Polovec, Tixmen') with human qualities which raise them above their environment. The tragedy is therefore all the more poignant when the three basic lines of action lead to the destruction of these four people. Polovec, ostensibly the central figure of the tale and a man of some capabilities and aspirations, cannot carry anything through to completion. Seeking love and fame, he decides to begin life anew out in the sticks, far away from his native Tambov. A dreamer and idealist, he resembles Lieutenant Romašov, the ill-fated hero of Aleksandr Kuprin's "Poedinok" ("The Duel"), to which *Na kuličkax* has frequently been compared. Both works give extremely negative pictures of garrison life, and they have similar plots: both heroes fall in love with married women, which forces them into duels; in both instances—for different reasons—the women request the heroes to play passive roles in order to ensure the husband's safety. The two women, however, differ greatly: Marusja has integrity and loves her husband, not the hero; Šuročka ("Poedinok") is a schemer who does not love her husband, but will sacrifice the hero Romašov's life for her own advancement. The outcome of the two works is quite different: Romašov is shot in cold blood, a victim of Šuročka's seduction, but Polovec, in despair at Marusja's enmity after her husband Šmit's suicide, is later drawn into the drunken, bestial revelry of the other officers: "Suddenly Andrej Ivanovič was swept up, whirled away by a drunken, hopeless revelry, by that very last revelry in which revels Russia, chased out into the sticks" (*S. S.* II, 129).

As in *Uezdnoe,* the finale takes on symbolic proportions. The frenzied, hopeless revelry of the garrison out in the sticks engulfs not only Polovec, but all of Russia. This apocalyptic vision of impending catastrophe, which anticipated World War I, the Revolution, and the Civil War, stresses the need of a spiritual regeneration within Russia.

The love between Šmit and his wife Marusja represents the second line of action. Their two-year marriage is based on an unusually personal, human, faithful relationship which, envied and despised by the others, stands in sharp contrast to "normal" garrison life. [Moločko and Katjuška speak enviously of it (*S. S.* II, 18) and Azančeev in a fit of rage lashes out at this relationship knowing it to be Šmit's only sensitive point (*S. S.* II, 35-36).] The tragic destruction of this unique love is effected by General Azančeev. In order to punish Šmit for mentioning his theft of government funds, Azančeev forces Marusja to submit to him. Unable to accept a profaned idol despite his continuing love, Šmit cruelly torments both Marusja and himself in a truly Dostoevskian love-hate relationship that culminates in his suicide.

The successful interweaving of three plot lines contributes a structural complexity to *Na kuličkax* which reflects Zamjatin's increasing literary maturity. Joined by a traditional love triangle (Polovec-Marusja-Šmit), the two major plot lines are resolved by the dissolution of the triangle (Šmit's suicide and Marusja's departure). And the tale's structural integration is strengthened by an undeniable spiritual harmony between Marusja and Polovec. Established at their first meeting, this rapport is symbolized by a light golden web floating through the blue air (*S. S.* II, 21, 25). The central figure in the third plot line is Lieutenant Tixmen', who (like the tailor Timoša) is afflicted with a penchant for thought; he seeks to discover whether he is the father of Katjuška's ninth child. The subordinate plot is allied to the major triangle by a relationship both prognostic and contrastive: The suicide of Tixmen' in the face of an insoluble problem foreshadows that of Šmit, but Katjuška's behavior sets a garrison norm from which Marusja's is sharply differentiated. All lines of action are ultimately united by the central theme of man's inhumanity, expressed in the ignorance, spiritual bankruptcy, and utter boredom of Zamjatin's extensive gallery of negative characters: General Azančeev, the froglike culinary artist, the Raphael of potatoes, who thrives on gluttony, embezzlement, and sex; the garrison cuckold Captain Nečesa whose favorite pastime is to skewer cockroaches with a needle; his round little wanton wife Katjuška; the garrison gossip and busybody, Lieutenant Moločko, who sleeps with the general's half-witted wife, with Katjuška and with anyone else who is available; the stupid, fish-eyed orderly Neprotošnov; the orderly Gusljakin whose predilection for keyholes furnishes the garrison with the details of each other's personal lives; the officers as a whole, flotsam of humanity who delight in howling endless songs at nightly drinking bouts and in shooting down passing coolies.

Although both tales depict the negative aspects of provincial life, there is a difference in their emphasis. In *Uezdnoe* Zamjatin focuses on the successful rise to power of an animal-like provincial amidst others like himself, while in *Na kuličkax* he shows the destruction of sensitive people amidst the animal-like inhabitants of a provincial garrison. The central tragedy of both works, however, is the same—man's inhuman behavior.

Love, the second major theme in Zamjatin's tales, is depicted in two aspects, the physical and the spiritual. For the negative characters of *Uezdnoe* there can be no question of a spiritual love. Baryba, for example, has liaisons with three women—Čebotarixa, her cook Pol'ka, and his landlady Aprosja. And in all three cases Baryba is merely satisfying a natural urge, without thought and without passion. The striking feature is Baryba's sexual indifference. Desire is aroused in him simply by the proximity of the woman, and, once gratified, it becomes an automatic daily function. The attitudes of the women vary. The sight of Baryba's body immediately arouses Čebotarixa, and, in showing him how to make the sign of the cross, she envelopes him in her doughy flesh. Baryba's reaction is instinctive: he turns, sinking his

hands into her flesh, and later falls asleep contented. Čebotarixa's desire proves to be too demanding even for such a fine animal as Baryba, and one day, as he watches the cook Pol'ka tearfully run to the cellar to escape his sadistic bullying, the idea of possessing her occurs to him. In her master's hands Pol'ka becomes a rag doll, submitting fearfully and tearfully, which gratifies Baryba's sadistic nature. Pol'ka is not a source of sexual gratification to Baryba, but represents a chance to bully someone, to avenge himself for Čebotarixa's demands. This primitive trait of vengeance is the mainspring of Baryba's personality, and as the story ends he is bullying others because his father has again repudiated him. His third affair begins like the first, but unlike the others it is satisfactory to both parties. Every night, after completing her chores, the tired Aprosja, yawning, takes off her clothes, carries Baryba's freshly shined boots to him, and half an hour later, still yawning, returns to her own room, says her prayers, and falls fast asleep. Love has been reduced to a passionless, everyday, physical function that does nothing to dispel the boredom of provincial life.

The treatment of love is considerably more varied in *Na kuličkax*. The automatic, instinctive, Baryba-like behavior is exemplified by Katjuška, who sleeps with any man. General Azančeev, like Katjuška, is interested only in physical love, and, like the lawyer Morgunov in *Uezdnoe,* he has a jaded desire for a variety of mates. By contrast, Polovec's love for Marusja is that of an idealistic dreamer, spiritual in nature. And the relationship between Marusja and Šmit, portrayed only fragmentarily in Gusljakin's gossip, appears to be a healthy combination of the spiritual and physical aspects, which sets them apart from the rest of the garrison. Nevertheless, for the majority in *Na kuličkax* and in *Uezdnoe* love is a physical function which becomes an automatic part of their humdrum daily routine.

In Zamjatin's third tale, **"Alatyr',"** the love theme assumes central importance. The women of the provincial town of Alatyr', once famed for its fertility, have come upon barren times, with a dearth of eligible bachelors. In particular, Glafira, the daughter of the district police chief, is like succulent rye, ripe for harvest. Her dreams of a lover-general on a white stallion manifest her physiological need for fulfillment; and her ideal of ultimate happiness is exemplified by the police chief's cat Milka, who is contentedly suckling her four new kittens. The presentation of physical love in a positive, even lyrical, manner contrasts strongly with the negative treatment in *Uezdnoe* and *Na kuličkax*. However, the archpriest's daughter Varavara, who is driven by the same physiological need and who is Glafira's chief rival for the affections of the new postmaster Prince Vadbol'skij, has a malicious character and is frequently likened to a dog, as her nickname Sobačeja (a derivation of the Russian word for dog) would indicate.

The masculine protagonists, both lacking this strong physiological urge, belong to the dreamer-thinker category and view Glafira as a godly embodiment of an ideal. In the third tale, however, the dreamer is not isolated amidst a mass of unthinking beings, since most inhabitants of Alatyr' are striving toward some particular dream or goal. It is true that their striving seems ridiculous and that, without exception, their aspirations are completely frustrated. Kostja Edytkin, a self-made peasant poet who is tutored by Glafira in preparation for civil-service examinations, seeks literary fame and aspires to Glafira's hand. Shy and timid, his romantic idolization of Glafira resembles Polovec's love for Marusja. His major work, *Vnutrennij ženskij dogmat božestva* (*The Inner Feminine Tenet of Godliness*), provokes the laughter of his whole audience, including Glafira, and his love is never reciprocated. Prince Vadbol'skij believes that all the problems of the world would be solved if everyone would speak one language. But his attempts to teach Esperanto to the townspeople fail miserably. Instead of establishing universal brotherhood and world peace, his efforts precipitate a pitched battle for his affection between his two best pupils, Glafira and Varvara. The police chief is always seeking to invent something beneficial to mankind, but all his attempts, including bread baked with bird droppings instead of yeast, are failures. Glafira's dreams of a general on a white stallion likewise remain unrealized. All of these dreams are needed to dispel the terrible tedium of the provinces, which is established in the first chapter: "All day in the police chief's home tedium loudly cuckoos like a cuckoo" (*S. S.* I, 116). And later, when Prince Vadbol'skij looks at the darkening sky, which appears "so terribly empty, so silent forever," there is a catch in his throat and he feels like howling (*S. S.* I, 145). In this environment all dreams are frustrated, and at the tale's end, in a moment of truth, Edytkin and the reader see how pitiful the people of Alatyr' are. There is prophecy in Edytkin's final cry of anguish, "We are doomed! Doomed, doomed . . . ," (*S. S.* I, 171) which recalls the symbolic finale of Zamjatin's other two tales.

Of the three tales, **"Alatyr'"** is the briefest and the most tightly structured. Centering on Glafira's need for a mate, the action develops quickly, with each of the eight chapters contributing to the forward movement of the plot. In integrating the motifs of frustration with the central love intrigue, Zamjatin displays great skill in attaining a remarkable unity of action. The police chief's frustrating experiment in bread baking introduces Edytkin into the narrative, thus altering the initial situation (suitorless Glafira). Edytkin's literary debacle not only foreshadows his failure in love, but makes him ridiculous in the eyes of his beloved, thus stimulating his envy and despair. The prince's Esperanto classes provide a field of rivalry for the two heroines and provoke the anonymous love notes which ultimately lead to the resolution of the love intrigue and the destruction of the

prince's hopes for world peace through Esperanto. In comparison, the three plot lines of *Na kuličkax* provide less actional unity. Of the two central thrusts of action, Polovec's love is treated directly and fully, while the Marusja-Šmit relationship is seen primarily through secondary sources and consequently is somewhat blurred. The third line of action (Tixmen') is primarily used to retard the others, and the major unifying element is theme, rather than action. The purely episodic structure of *Uezdnoe* deemphasizes action, thereby stressing descriptive elements and bringing the theme into prominence as the central unity. Although divided into twenty-six very short chapters, the tale contains not twenty-six individual "vignettes" or "watercolors," as claimed by some critics,[7] but seven episodes in the life of Baryba: his failure in final examinations (Chapter 1), life with the dogs (Chapters 2-3), Čebotarixa (Chapters 4-9), the theft of Father Evsej's money (Chapters 10-12), life at Aprosja's (Chapters 13-16), professional perjury for Morgunov (Chapters 17-19), and his appointment with the police (Chapters 20-26). The unity of action resides solely in the person of Baryba, who, like Gogol's Čičikov, serves as a structural device which enables the author to depict many scenes and characters. In their structure Zamjatin's early tales show a definite progress toward greater actional unity, from an episodic to an internally cohesive plot structure. Greater actional unity tended to deemphasize the unifying role of theme and descriptive elements, which was one of the main factors contributing to the diminishing force with which the theme of ignorant, inhuman, provincial Russia struck the reader in *Uezdnoe, Na kuličkax,* and **"Alatyr'."**

In sheer volume, the three tales comprise more than half of Zamjatin's output of imaginative prose for the years 1908 to 1917, and they are typical examples of the stylistic maturity he achieved prior to the Revolution. [The figure is closer to two-thirds if **"Odin"** and **"Devuska,"** his first two stories which he never allowed to be reprinted, are excluded. Zamjatin's prose of the early period covers 500 pages of the 1929 collected works (including projected equivalents for those two stories). Since each page holds about 165 words, Zamjatin's pre-Revolutionary output was only about 83,000 words.] Significant structural features distinguish the tales from Zamjatin's stories, which exhibit much greater thematic and stylistic variety. This variety is more pronounced in the stories, especially the earliest ones, because the short form is better suited for experimentation. The size of the tales, which average ninety pages each, considerably exceeds that of his stories— six of the eleven stories number fewer than twenty pages each, and only three exceed thirty pages. The importance of brevity in the perfection of Zamjatin's literary technique, is clearly indicated by a significant decrease in the length of the later stories. In contrast to his first six stories (written from 1908 to 1913) which average thirty pages, the next five (written from 1914 to 1917) average only ten pages each. Although some of the stories ("**Odin**," "**Neputevyj**," "**Črevo**," "**Krjaži**," "**Afrika**") contain numbered chapters, only in his tales does Zamjatin consistently use chapter titles which stress the central theme or event. Partly because of the greater length, each tale has eight to ten significant characters, while most of the stories, except "**Neputevyj**," have only one or two. The stories are comparatively static, often depicting only one or two events rather than a whole series, although "**Neputevyj**," "**Črevo**," and "**Afrika**" are exceptions to this. These distinguishing features testify to Zamjatin's acceptance of the established Russian genre differentiation between story and tale during the first decade of his literary career.

Although the love theme is central in Zamjatin's first four stories, which in many respects anticipate his tales, the treatment differs in that love is never reduced to the level of an automatic, daily physical function as in *Uezdnoe* and *Nakuličkax*. Apparently the negative depiction was dictated by the choice of man's inhumanity as the major theme. The student Belov (in "**Odin**"), who is in solitary confinement because of his revolutionary activities, disdainfully rejects love on the basis of rationalistic argumentation, yet his solitude and his illicit correspondence with his friend Lel'ka combine to produce dreams of happiness and, ultimately, of love. Despite occasional lapses into sensual thoughts, Belov's love for Lel'ka is a spiritual feeling that alters his outlook on life by being a source of hope and joy for him. Learning of her marriage, he dies spiritually, cursing his sacred love; his subsequent suicide is merely the physical counterpart of his spiritual death. Belov's idealization of his beloved is echoed in Polovec's love for Marusja and in Edytkin's and the prince's love for Glafira. The motif of a destroyed idol recurs in *Na kuličkax,* where Marusja's degradation results in Šmit's spiritual bankruptcy and ultimately in his suicide. In Zamjatin's second story, "**Devuška**," the heroine Vera experiences a strong desire for love, the product of daydreams stimulated by a strong physiological urge. In this respect Vera is the precursor of both Glafira and Varvara, and her behavior with the librarian on the park bench is remarkably similar to Varvara's behavior with the prince at the archpriest's home. The presentation of the love theme in "**Aprel'**," Zamjatin's third story, remains unique in his work. Told in a light and fresh tone from the point of view of Nastja, a teen-age girl, the story describes her first kiss and the growth of her first love. Threatened by the action of adults (Nastja's kiss was observed and reported to her mother) and by her boyfriend's feigned indifference, her budding love is reasserted with renewed vigor at the story's end. Unlike the love of Vera or Glafira, hers has no overwhelming physiological desires, but only a wonderful innocence and purity. The fourth story, "**Neputevyj**," is an ex-

tended character sketch of a lovable, good-for-nothing Moscow student, Senja Babuškin, whose character is endowed with the softness of a warm summer day in the Kostroma Province and an irreconcilable duality: he reveres old Russian things, especially those connected with the Orthodox church, yet as a radical student he denies the existence of God. He expounds cynical theories about love, reducing it to physiological function, and at the same time he mawkishly cherishes sentimental ideas about it. Senja's vacillation on love echoes Belov's. However, unlike Belov who spends much time in self-examination and rationalization, Senja simply falls in love without thinking—and, in his typically ingenuous manner, with two girls at the same time. Unable to reconcile his two loves, Senja directs his energies to the revolutionary movement and, discontented with his lot, chooses a useless death on the barricades to a life without love. Senja, whose love, despite his theories, is spiritual rather than physical, represents an interesting variation of the frustrated dreamer; and his death on the barricades, so reminiscent of the death of Turgenev's Rudin, is a form of suicide like Belov's and Šmit's.

All of the remaining six stories of the early period were written after Zamjatin had established a stylistic and thematic norm. They differ from the tales, however, in that the protagonists are peasants rather than merchants, officials, priests, intelligentsia, or nobility. Vanjatka Konyč Tjurin (in "**Staršina**"), a huge bull-like peasant noted for his stupidity, is by chance elevated to being a village elder and is awarded a gold medal for his service to the tsar. Inspired by rumors, he takes it upon himself to appropriate the land of the local nobility in the name of the tsar and distributes it among the peasants of Lenivka (Lazyplace). He is tried and acquitted, for it is evident that his misdemeanor stemmed from ignorance rather than malicious intent. Konyč, however, never understands his error and glows with righteous self-satisfaction: "Well, there you are: acquitted, I'm going home. I know. I acted by decree, in the proper manner. You can't fool me!" (*S. S.* II, 280). Konyč, with his extreme ignorance and bullying abuse of power, is a peasant version of Baryba, and the story is just an appendix to *Uezdnoe.* In describing Konyč's stupidity as a recruit, Zamjatin points out the incompatibility of the peasant with military order, a theme which he elaborates more directly in the peasant soldier Aržanoj in *Na kuličkax.*

The treatments of love, dreams, and aspirations in "**Črevo**," "**Krjaži**," and "**Afrika**" represent variations on motifs in "**Alatyr'**." The heroine of "**Črevo**," like Glafira, has a strong physiological urge which dominates the entire work, motivating all action: she must bear a child. Married to the old widower Petra against her wishes (the motif of forced marriage to a repulsive mate recurs in "**Pis'menno**"), Afim'ja fails to become pregnant after more than a year of marriage and takes a lover, Van'ka Selifontov. After conception all her attention centers on her womb and the developing fetus, but one night after a merciless beating by Petra, she suffers a miscarriage. The loss of her child fills Afim'ja with a deep, primeval hatred for her husband, so one night, mechanically, she kills him with an axe. With Van'ka Selifontov's aid, she buries him. The murder of vengeance brings no relief, and during a late summer hot spell she begins imagining that the stench of Petra's decomposing body fills the air, permeating her hut. She retrieves the body and, mechanically again, cuts it into pieces, salts it, and stores it in her cellar. But she gains no inner peace until she at last confesses and is taken into custody. This powerful story, one of the most extreme examples of Zamjatin's primitivism, ends with an expression of the Russian peasant's typical compassion for criminals: "Farewell, Afim'juška. God will forgive you" (*S. S.* II, 193).

On the other hand, **"Afrika,"** the first of three stories set in the distant north on the shores of the Arctic Ocean, shows a dreamer much in the fashion of **"Alatyr'."** Fedor Volkov, an Arctic boatman who ferries passengers from ships to shore, hears some gentry, including a lovely girl, speak a language that is not Russian. When he asks where they come from, they laughingly reply, "from Africa." Africa, the lovely girl, and Fedor's conception of ideal happiness merge into one illusory dream, quite different from his surrounding reality. The next spring Volkov attempts to realize his dream by earning passage to Africa as a harpoonist, but after missing the whale which would have brought his passage money, he falls dead. The author ironically comments: "There is an Africa. Fedor Volkov has reached it" (*S. S.* IV, 86). Unlike the dreamers of Alatyr', Volkov does not live to see his dreams and illusions frustrated. The author's message here seems to be that men should die striving for their goals, rather than live to discover them to be false illusions. This idea was to be stated explicitly two years later in the article "Skify-li?" A similar message can be extracted from the brief story **"Pis'menno,"** where Dar'ja is forced by her mother to marry Eremej, a repulsive, heavy-handed widower. She wishes for his death and is overjoyed at her freedom when he is sent to Siberia for killing a man. She takes a lover, Savos'ka, and lives happily for a year, until she receives a humble letter from her husband begging forgiveness and describing his dire circumstances. After much thought, Dar'ja forsakes her lover and sets out to Siberia to help her husband. The narrator's comment, "What fools women are, oh what fools!," leaves the reader in a quandary which lends the tale its charm. Was the author, in contrast to the narrator, in favor of the humaneness of her sacrifice, or did he agree with the narrator in lamenting Dar'ja's denial of her happiness with Savos'ka?

The story **"Krjaži"** expresses Zamjatin's opinion that neither pride nor convention should stand in the way of the realization of love. Through stubborn pride, the strong physical attraction between Ivan and Mar'ja remains unrealized. The need to prove his worth results in Ivan's death, which is Mar'ja's loss, for, although she loves him, she has been too proud to encourage him. Zamjatin's final story of the early period, **"Pravda istinnaja,"** is in the form of a peasant girl's letter to her mother. It reveals Dašutka's unhappiness as a domestic in town, despite her lip service to the happiness and the supposed benefits of town life. The letter, like many of Zamjatin's early works, discloses the negative aspects of provincial town life. Since the piece was written in England, one may speculate that it was inspired by a similar feeling on Zamjatin's part about his life in England.

It is rather surprising that the Revolution of 1905 to 1906 did not find a greater place in the works of Zamjatin, a onetime Bolshevik, exile, and student revolutionary. Discounting **"Tri dnja,"** an impressionistic, first-person, eye-witness account of the "Potemkin" mutiny, this revolution only appears as a minor theme in **"Odin"** and **"Neputevyj."** In **"Odin"** Belov, like Zamjatin, has been imprisoned for revolutionary activity, and we find a brief two-page narrative by his imprisoned fellow revolutionary Tifleev, telling how a government agent has been murdered. The sensational element in Tifleev's account and its psychological effect on Belov are of much greater importance in the story, however, than the theme of the Revolution itself. The same is true in **"Neputevyj,"** where Senja joins the movement of 1905 to fill an inner emptiness after losing Tanja and Vasilisa, and not because of political conviction: "I wouldn't set eyes on all those programs of theirs. Thank God, for the first time in ages we have overflowed the banks, and they want to put us back in them. I think that if it's flood time, then let it really flood, like the Volga. Right or not?" (*S. S.* II, 163). The revolutionary movement provides Senja with an opportunity to live, and the proximity of death makes life seem all the more valuable to him: "You queer fellow, it's gay, you understand, it's gay in the streets: life. I think that the people who are most alive are there now. A-ah, you say that they are close to death; that's why they are close to death, because they are most alive . . ." (*S. S.* II, 163). Never having been able to carry anything through to completion, Senja remains on the barricade after his comrades have wisely retreated. This does not indicate extraordinary bravery or extreme dedication to the Revolution; it is instead a tragic solution to his failures in life. For once, he finishes something.

The theme of revolution deserves fuller consideration here. It has been mentioned earlier that, under the influence of Robert Mayer, Zamjatin in 1920 and 1921 systematized his philosophic views, setting forth the thesis that energy (revolution) and entropy (stagnation) were the two cosmic forces governing the universe, man, and man's thought. The Communist critic Voronskij asserted that "all of the works published by Zamjatin . . . symbolize the struggle between these two principles,"[8] but this generalization, valid for Zamjatin's major works of the second period (1917-1921), does not hold true for his early efforts. In works like the tale **"Ostrovitjane"** and the novel *My,* revolution represents a conscious rebellion against the accepted norm, and love is treated as a primitive physical passion that disrupts the regulatory mechanisms created by an automated society. This is not true, with minor exceptions, in Zamjatin's early works. In *Uezdnoe* love itself has been degraded to a tedious physical process. The strong physiological urge of Glafira and Varvara is indeed a primitive feeling, but it does not represent a rebellion against the status quo and the surrounding environment, for these women seek gratification and fulfillment within the existing social framework. Essentially the same is true of Anfim'ja's desire to have a child. Although her love might be considered a manifestation of energy in revolt against the forces of entropy (represented by her husband), D. J. Richards has embarked on rather risky speculation in attributing political significance to the story ("the conspiracy of Anfimya and her young lover against the old man represents the rebellion of young, politically revolutionary Russia against the decaying old order").[9]

It is true that elements of revolution can be detected in Zamjatin's dreamers insomuch as their dreams represent rejection of the existing order, but the aspirations of these dreamers are presented in a comic light and never are coupled with a primitive revolt of the passions symbolic of man's irrational impulses. In depicting a growing primitivism, the entropy of human thought and feeling, Zamjatin's early works fail to portray the disruptive force of energy (revolution). And the retroactive application of the entropy-energy dichotomy to these works is not really justifiable. At most, it can be said that the tedium shown in Zamjatin's early works "is but an unconscious demand for freedom, for struggle, for the conversion of 'entropy,' of rest, into 'energy,' revolution."[10] As such, it is the seed from which Zamjatin's later theories developed.

In 1915 Zamjatin started writing his fables. Of the twenty he published, only four appeared before the Revolution, although two others evidently had been written by then.[11] A *skaz* narrative in which the narrator speaks a colloquial Russian studded with regional and substandard lexical items prevails in these fables, whose protagonists are often animals. Frequently oblique in meaning, the fables center on themes of human frailty and ignorance. In **"Bog"** (**"God"**) the carousing and bullying cockroach Sen'ka who does not believe in God is struck speechless with reverence for the poverty-stricken postman Mizjumin, a kind and omniscient di-

ety who rescues him after a disastrous fall. The fable is probably aimed at ridiculing stupid people who ignorantly glorify or diefy the ordinary and commonplace.

A similar moral can be drawn from **"D'jaček"** (**"The Deacon"**) and **"Pet'ka."** A stupid boy Pet'ka, "too bright for his age," is given a beautiful talking doll with moving eyes. Curious to discover what makes it move and speak, he takes it apart with a knife, only to find uninteresting bearings, sawdust, a diaphragm, and a horn. His angry parents repair the toy, but it is no longer the same, so they punish the boy. Probably the doll represents the unquestionable "truths" and beliefs that ignorant men blindly accept. To question these false "truths," is to destroy or alter them; therefore ignorant men punish those who are either intelligent or naïve enough to question them, just as parents punish questioning children. Latent in this fable is Zamjatin's conception of philistinism and heresy. The third fable **"D'jaček,"** tells of a deacon who, having won a 5,000 ruble lottery, decides to experience the vision of Moses, to look into the blue vault of the heavens from the top of Mt. Sinai. After forty days of fasting and climbing, he gains the mountaintop, only to discover that beautiful clouds are nothing but a damp, dark, autumnal, foggy drizzle. The moral is essentially that of **"Pet'ka,"** and in this formulation we can discern the beginnings of Zamjatin's idea (expressed two years later in "Skify li?") that the attainment of an ideal philistinizes it. Zamjatin again returned to this image (beautiful distant clouds becoming damp, dismal fog at close quarters) in describing the Symbolists' disillusionment with their search for the beautiful ideal on earth.[12] The basic message in these fables would seem to be that man should not only be intelligent and curious enough to examine his own and others' conceptions and ideals, but he also should have the strength to recognize, accept, and apply any newly found truth in his life, without despair and disillusionment. The fables **"Petr Petrovič"** and **"Angel Dormidon"** ridicule ignorance more openly by showing that haste coupled with uncomprehending stupidity leads to disastrous results.

No survey of Zamjatin's works would be complete without a discussion of style, perhaps the most distinctive aspect of his imaginative prose. A leading exponent of the Neorealist movement in Russian literature, Zamjatin was preoccupied with style and literary techniques as a direct consequence of his philosophy. As a firm believer in the Hegelian dialectic, Zamjatin considered Neorealism to be a synthesis of nineteenth-century Realism (thesis) and Symbolism (antithesis): "The symbolists did their part in the development of literature, and to replace them in the second decade of the twentieth century came the Neorealists, inheriting features of former Realists as well as features of the Symbolists."[13] The Realists were excellent mirrors—their stories attempted to depict a segment of life. The Symbolists sought to describe man's complex feelings and to depict the essence of man's spiritual being; in doing so, they rejected the "real" world. The Neorealists, like the Realists, depicted the real world, but they found their truth by focusing on a few, carefully chosen features, enlarging them to grotesque proportions. Zamjatin firmly believed that "apparent improbability—nightmarishness—reveals the true essence of a thing—its reality—more than probability does."

Quoting Dostoevskij's statement that "the real truth is always improbable," Zamjatin repeatedly utilized effective analogy to drive home his point.[14] Where the Realist saw only smooth skin covered with downy hair, the Neorealist with his cruel, ironic microscope saw gullies and mounds, thick stems of unknown plants (hair), and huge masses of earth and meteorites (dust particles).[15] In accordance with his aim, Zamjatin frequently used the grotesque in his early works. His depiction of life and people was exaggerated, deformed, and fantastic, which led some critics to protest Zamjatin's "excessively thickened paints" and moved some to contend that instead of depicting life, he caricatured it.[16] Others were more perceptive; in his review of Zamjatin's first collection of stories, A. Gvozdev made an excellent analysis of his technique:

> the author does not attempt to delineate the *byt* in detail, but is constantly drawn to a synthetic image, frequently resorting to the aid of comic grotesque. His art consists in the ability of imbuing exaggeratedly massive figures with a touch of some sort of bright truth of life. Isolating, in the characterization of his heroes, some one of their characteristics, E. Zamjatin imparts his character sketch with the extraordinary, sketches comic contours that border on the absurd, and widely utilizes exaggerated parody as a means of artistic embodiment. But angular contours, paradoxical situations, and the extraordinary harshness of the author's satirical inspiration do not keep the reader from the truth.[17]
>
> [*Byt*: a peculiarly Russian term which indicates the general tenor of life, from customs and habits to social and economic conditions (usually of a particular social group).]

In the characterization of Čebotarixa, for example, the primary, exaggerated feature was her excessive obesity, indicative of her unbridled gastronomic and sexual appetites. The reader's first glimpse of Čebotarixa comes through Baryba's eyes and immediately establishes her gluttony: "They finished eating, and Čebotarixa herself crawls out into the yard: red, settling, unable to walk because of overeating" (*S. S.* I, 29). When Čebotarixa is presented directly to the reader, the motif of not being able to walk recurs and is developed into an explicit presentation of the central characteristic:

> After the evening vespers or liturgy the priest of Pokrov Church would catch up with Čebotarixa, shake his head and say: "It's unseemly, mother. You must walk, take a promenade. Or before you know it, the flesh will completely conquer."

But Čebotarixa would spread out like dough on her wagon and, knitting her lips, would say: "It's impossible, father, kintinual heart murmur." And Čebotarixa rolls onward through the dust, stuck to her wagon, inseparable from it, corpulent, flowing, springy. So no one had ever seen Čebotarixa in the street on her own feet without wheels.

(*S. S.* I, 30)

The impression of doughy obesity was maintained by the recurrent use of key words or new words which were associated with the original presentation: "The smell of her sweaty, *sticky* flesh" (*S. S.* I, 38). "Nonetheless, she *flowed* off, . . ." (*S. S.* I, 52). "Čebotarixa turned white and began shaking like *leavened dough* that had swollen to the very edges of the mixing bowl" (*S. S.* I, 52). "'What's up, have you gone nuts?' said he, disentangling himself from her *flesh*. But she *stuck* to him like a spider" (*S. S.* I, 55). The last of these four examples is doubly effective in that it recalls another image associated with Čebotarixa's gluttony: "Her greedy mouth—a red wet hole" (*S. S.* I, 38). This mouth image is repeated with a variation ("a greedy, gaping, sucking mouth") some six lines before the spider comparison, which, because of its proximity and the easy association with a spider sucking its prey, recalls the "greedy mouth" sequence and reinforces the idea of Čebotarixa's unbridled appetite.

Zamjatin's use of grotesque to underline a single basic characteristic was motivated by his own central subjective impression of a character, in which he trusted firmly and completely. Frequently originating as an explicit comparison or simile, his impression is usually continued in a recurrent implicit comparison—a metaphor: "Kipa, all in bows, frills, gathers, with a comb on her forehead—a Brahmaputra hen. As soon as Senja saw the Brahmaputra, he stuck at her side . . ." (*S. S.* II, 148). And later: "Petr Petrovič . . . looked at Senja and the Brahmaputra hen. They were alone in the room, Senja and Kipa-Brahmaputra, in a corner behind the plam tree" (*S. S.* II, 149).

External description and character depiction are kept to a minimum in Zamjatin's early work and usually consist of a basic impression which undergoes varying degrees of development depending upon the story, the importance of the character, and the felicity of the chosen impression. The impression is usually conveyed in one of three ways: The character can be compared to some animal, as above, in which case he assumes both the external features and the character traits of that animal. The girl Kipa (**"Neputevyj"**) not only looks like a hen, but she is also a featherbrain. Pimen (**"Afrika"**), small and skinny and persistent, is compared to a mosquito: "Pimen . . . began to follow Fedor, hovering about him like a mosquito and biting him continually" (*S. S.* IV, 76). "Pimen hovered and hovered" (*S. S.* IV, 76). "Pimen sang, a caressing mosquito, and bit into Fedor Volkov's very ear" (*S. S.* IV, 77). "Pimen stretched forth his mosquito mug" (IV, 77). "Oh-ho! A mosquito soul?" (*S. S.* IV, 77). The same technique is used in characterizing General Azančeev as a frog (*Na kuličkax*); the tailor Timoša as a sparrow and the coachman Urvanka as a devil (*Uezdnoe*); Kostja Edytkin as a chicken, Varvara as a dog, Rodivon Rodivonovič as a rooster, the archpriest as a small, hairy sprite, and the county police chief's wife as an elephant ("Alatyr'"). In each case the physical and character similarities are equally important, and the numerous comparisons with animals are a major factor contributing to the central theme of animal-like provincial life.

A second technique for conveying the central impression consists in focusing attention on some physical characteristic associated with a basic character trait. The arctic fisherman Fedor Volkov is first described ("Afrika") as having huge shoulders, small ingenuous eyes, and a "crock-like head cropped like a kid's" (*S. S.* IV, 70). The crock-like head and ingenuous, inoffensive eyes are mentioned throughout the story in connection with his dreams of Africa; they symbolize his naïve simplicity:

He shook his cropped crock: "And what if it ain't—Africa—that is?"

(*S. S.* IV, 72)

. . . himself unseen, just a head, a cropped crock, rocking above the light sea. "What are you looking for, Fedor? Are you waiting for some guests from beyond the sea?" Fedor would glance with his ingenuous, inoffensive eyes and shake his crock-head. But whether he shook yes or no could not be fathomed.

(*S. S.* IV, 75-76)

Fedor Volkov was silent: only his inoffensive eyes dumbly spoke to Jausta, but what they said could not be fathomed.

(*S. S.* IV, 76)

And he tripped over something, began to cry woefully, put his cropped crock on the table. "I'll leave . . . I'll le-e-ave you all . . . Leave."

(*S. S.* IV, 78)

He kept standing at the rail, hanging his cropped crock over the water, and kept smiling to himself.

(*S. S.* IV, 80)

"Ugh!" Fedor only shook his crock, cropped like a kid's; only his small inoffensive eyes glimmered as a candle to God; and, really, what words could be found here?

(*S. S.* IV, 84)

The reader learns nothing more of Volkov's external appearance, nor does the author directly reveal any of Volkov's thoughts. There are no inner monologues, the narrator is not omniscient. The reader must deduce everything for himself from Volkov's actions and from the reported dialogues. The recurrent motifs of "cropped crock" and "ingenuous, inoffensive eyes" stress his most essential characteristic: a childlike simplicity which enables him to idolize distant Africa as the embodiment of all his dreams. The same technique is used with numerous other characters. Polovcc's broad forchcad, which contrasts sharply with the rest of his nondescript features, is symbolic of his intellectual and spiritual aspirations which are incapable of being realized. Marusja Šmit is characterized by a "hint of unchildish lines near her lips" which become marked and old-womanish after her relationship with Šmit has been destroyed by Azančeev. Prince Vadbol'skij's crafty nature ("Alatyr'") is indicated by his receding chin. Indrik's sad, unsmiling eyes ("Afrika") hint that he is aware of things forbidden to mortals, and they serve as a disquieting foreboding of the denouement, which imparts a genuinely tragic element to the story. Lieutenant Tixmen' (*Na kuličkax*) is endowed with a long nose that not only indicates his predilection for serious thought but also causes his shyness with women. The orderly Neprotošnov's stupidity is reflected in his inhuman, "hopelessly fishy eyes," yet the one time he experiences a human feeling, his eyes become human and pour forth tears (*S. S.* II, 127).

The association of one or several attributives with a given personage is Zamjatin's third method of conveying his impression. The effect of the attributives is produced, as in the other two methods, by their frequent recurrence. But in this method the same attributive refers to all aspects of the person—sometimes to a physical feature, sometimes to an action, and sometimes directly to his character. Roundness, for example, is the basic attribute of the captain's wife Katjuška Nečesa; and, associated with her yearly pregnancies, it recurs in different environments:

The captain's wife lay in bed, small and all round: a little round face, round quick eyes, round curls on her forehead, all of the captain's wife's charms were round.

(*S. S.* II, 17)

She laughed roundly . . .

(*S. S.* II, 18)

. . . she shook the round curls on her forehead.

(*S. S.* II, 51)

Tixmen' kissed her round little hand.

(*S. S.* II, 53)

The captain's wife's eyes, round as they were, became even rounder . . .

(*S. S.* II, 54)

She laughed so roundly, so clearly.

(*S. S.* II, 57)

The same is true of Baryba's squareness and of Captain Šmit's hardness, although in these cases, because both characters are of central importance, a combination of all three methods is used.

The basic impression associated with a personage is often reinforced by the choice of an appropriate name, for Zamjatin claimed that: "Surnames, names, become attached to personages just as firmly as to living people. And that is understandable: if the name is felt, chosen correctly, then it indispensibly contains a phonic characterization of the personage."[18] In some instances the choices and significance are obvious. In *Uezdnoe* a lawyer's slyness is indicated by his blinking eyes, by his blinking gait, and by his name Morgunov (derived from the Russian verb *morgat',* "to blink"). In other cases the choice is more subtle and depends on phonic features that evoke associations between the name and some physical feature or character trait. The surname Edytkin, used to designate a tall, lanky person with a pitiably thin neck, brings to mind—by means of the infrequent phonic combination *dytk*—the word for Adam's apple (*kadyk*), which reinforces the image of a thin neck. The ignorance of Polovec's orderly is exemplified by his recurrent mispronunciation of the phrase "exactly so, your excellency." And the mispronunciation *tak tošno, vaše-brodie,* which makes a significant play on the words "exactly" (*točno*) and "nauseating" (*tošno*), is echoed in the orderly's name Neprotošnov. Most frequently, however, the name of a personage is simply appropriate to his social position and psychological makeup. Čebotarixa is a typical, merchant-class name, and the suffix -*ixa* has an appropriate pejorative significance which the more usual suffix -*eva* lacks. The German name Šmit suits an unbending, honest military man whose severity borders on cruelty. In addition to using indicative and appropriate names, Zamjatin frequently employs such obvious nicknames as Sobačeja (a derivation of *sobaka,* "dog") for Varvara (**"Alatyr'"**), who is endowed with the characteristics and behavior of a dog.

The predominance of "a very strong, 90 proof *byt* that had been concentrated by centuries of aging"[19] was highly conducive to Zamjatin's grotesque imagery and would indicate that Zamjatin had utilized provincial Russia mainly as a stylistic device. The center of gravity in his treatment of bestial, ignorant, provincial life resided not in provincial life itself, but in bestiality and ignorance, which is in line with the humanism so basic to Zamjatin's world view and so dear to his lifelong heresy.

Furthermore, the provinces provided him with numerous colloquial and regional expressions to use in renovating the literary language. In all of his tales and in all but four of his earliest stories (**"Odin," "Devuška," "Aprel',"** and **"Tri dnja"**) Zamjatin used *skaz,* a special mode of narrative prose in which a narrator manipulated by the author, but usually differing from the author in language, social position, and outlook, is introduced explicitly or implicitly as a stylistic device. Zamjatin's narrator speaks a Russian which grammatically is basically correct, but which contains numerous regional words and colloquial expressions that normally would not be considered appropriate to standard literary Russian. The peculiarities of the narrator's language are not only lexical; his speech also displays a highly stylized syntactical structure characterized by numerous inversions. The following sample, from *Uezdnoe,* illustrates several typical features:

> Vstanet Baryba na utro smuryj i ves' den' kolobrodit. Zal'etsja do noči v monastyrskij les. Učilišče? A, da propadaj ono propadom!

> ["In the morning Baryba'd get up glumpy and fool around all day. He'd take off to the monastery woods till night. School? Aw, the hell with it!"]

> (*S. S.* I, 24)

The word *kolobrodit,* the expression *propadaj propadom,* and the use of *zal'etsja* with the meaning of "he set off" are all examples of colloquial speech; and the word *smuryj* is a substandard dialectal distortion of *xmuryj.* The inversion in the first sentences which places the verb in the initial position, the rhetorical question *Učilišče?,* and the use of the interjection *a* in the initial position followed by the emphatic particle *da* all contribute to the stylistically oral orientation of the narrative, so fundamental to *skaz.* In reported speech a few of Zamjatin's characters, unlike the narrator, use substandard phonetic and grammatical forms:

> "Gospodi, da pošli ž ty, štob učilišša sgorela i mne ba tuda ne itit' . . ."

> ["Lord, make the school burn down so I won't hab to goes there . . ."]

> (Konyč: *S. S.* II, 273)

> "Tak tošno, vaše-brodie . . ."

> ["Eksickly so, your beardship . . ."]

> (Neprotošnov: *S. S.* II, 9)

> "Vaše prevosxoditel'stvo, už dozvol'te pojtit' vzjat'. Ved' naše takoe, znyčt', delo krest'janskoe, den'gi-to vot kak nadobny, podatja opjat' že . . ."

> ["Your excellency, let me go git it. You knows, it's us peasants' business, we needs the money, taxes again . . ."]

> (Aržanoj: *S. S.* II, 69)

Such grammatically substandard speech, however, is not widespread in Zamjatin's writing, where it is restricted to peasants. On the other hand, substandard literary speech in the form of regional words, colloquial expressions, and casual syntax is extremely frequent and typical of most of his characters, including the implicit narrator. When Zamjatin's first collection of stories appeared in 1916, most critics censured his style severely. A. Derman wrote that "all of the author's remarks, all descriptions are expressed . . . by this repulsive, half-dead, vulgar language, depressive in its monotony and hopeless grayness."[20] Another critic was appalled by the "depressive . . . characterless deterioration of the language."[21] Critics notwithstanding, the *skaz* narrative became a hallmark of Russian literature of the twenties and was immortalized in the stories of Mixail Zoščenko, a student of Zamjatin.

Another characteristic of Zamjatin's early prose was a concise, compressed style that he said was dictated by life itself, which had become more complex, more rapid, feverish, and Americanized—especially in the cities that were the cultural centers for which he intended his works.[22] The Neorealists learned to say in ten lines what would have taken a page before and to condense material suitable for a novel into a tale or a story. This may explain why none of Zamjatin's works, except the novel *My*, ever exceeded one hundred and twenty-five small pages. In this respect the main teacher of the Neorealists was Anton Čexov, "who had provided amazing examples of brevity in the art of writing."[23] Čexov's legacy was not limited to brevity, for he was the first Russian to employ "impressionism." [Zamjatin, "Čexov," [38], 48. One example Zamjatin cited of Čexov's impressionism was: "the district elder and district clerk had become imbued with falsehood to such a degree, that the very skin on their faces was knavish."]

Directly related to his impressionistic imagery and his noted brevity was Zamjatin's tendency to demonstrate, rather than narrate. This was first pointed out by Ivanov-Razumnik early in 1914. In discussing L. Dobronravov's tale "Novaja bursa" ("The New Seminary"), he stated that "the young author knows how to observe and *to narrate* his observations. A. Terek and Evg. Zamjatin know how *to demonstrate*—that is the difference between them."[24] Seeking a greater economy of words and a more lively impression of life's activities, Zamjatin avoided static passages describing the hero and the setting. The external description and the character of a personage are indicated by a brief phrase or two, usually a recurrent motif, and any further information is demonstrated by the character's actions rather than being narrated by the author. Zamjatin himself cited his description of Morgunov's (Blinkman's) character as an example of demonstrating:

"Semen Semenovič blinked continually: blink, blink, as if he were ashamed of his own eyes. And why speak of eyes: all of him blinked. When he would go along the street and begin to limp on his left leg, actually all of him, his entire being, would blink." Here there is no

word of slyness, which comprised the essence of Morgunov's character; here action is given, and in the action, immediately, concisely, all of Morgunov, as if alive.[25]

Despite the importance of the Čexovian origins of Zamjatin's stylistic development, the latter's intense interest in verbal mastery was the result of much more immediate influences, namely the works of Aleksej Remizov and the Symbolists. In reviewing Zamjatin's first tale, Ivanov-Razumnik had written that: "The young author has not yet found himself; consciously or unconsciously there is much of Remizov in him, but already there is much of his own. If examples of how 'realism' can utilize the many technical achievements of 'modernism' are needed, then here is one of those examples, Evg. Zamjatin's tale."[26] Without a doubt, Zamjatin's great attention and interest in the style and form of his literary work was a legacy from the Symbolists, which Zamjatin himself freely admitted: "In the cultivation of the form of the work, in the perfection of the mastery of precisely the technique of writing, lies the greatest and fundamental service of the Symbolists."[27] Zamjatin did not, however, blindly ape Symbolist innovations; he adapted only those techniques that were congenial to his conception of art. Of specific importance to him were Sologub's *Melkij bes* (*The Petty Demon*), the novels and tales of Remizov, and to a lesser extent the prose works of Belyj. *Melkij bes* may justifiably be considered the forerunner of Russian Neorealism, for it was characterized by ironic laughter, by the depiction of provincial ignorance, by the grotesque, and by recurrent impressionistic imagery. Similar features frequently appeared in the early works of Remizov, who also developed a refined stylization of the *skaz* manner and showed a decided tendency toward colloquial and regional expressions. In respect to language, Remizov was the single most important influence on Zamjatin.

Considerably less discernible was the influence of Belyj, whose Neorealistic tendencies were most clearly expressed in his novel *Peterburg*, which first appeared in 1913 to 1914, well after Zamjatin had established his style.[28]

Traces of Zamjatin's interest in the rhythmic and musical qualities of prose were already manifest as early as 1914:

Zabeleli utrenniki, zazjabla zemlja, ležala neujutnaja, žalas': snežku by. I na Mixajlov den'—sneg povalil. Kak xlynuli belye xlop'ja—tak i utixlo vse. Tixim kolobkom belym laj sobačij plyvet. Molča moljatsja za ljudej staricy-sosny v klobukax belyx.

[The frosts whitened, the earth froze, lying uncozily, shriveling: oh for some snow. And on Mixajlov Day snow fell. As white flakes flowed, all became quiet. In a silent white ball dogs' barking floats. In their silent white cowls the monk-pines pray for people.]

(*S. S.* II, 267)

Zamjatin attempted here to create the impression of falling, circling snowflakes by the repetition of the clusters *xl* and *kl*,[29] but this only begins to suggest the rich rhythmic and phonic qualities of this passage. Each sentence is endowed with a syntactic rhythm that is reinforced by stress distribution, word order, and alliteration. In the first sentence, three di-stress phrases were followed by two mono-stresses, a rhythm which is further emphasized by the alliteration and assonance of *za, zazja, z, ža, ža,* and by the verb-noun contrast in the initial position. The next three sentences are each rythmically divided into equal halves emphasized twice by the dash (the stress distribution is two-two, three-three, three-three) and leads up to the final sentence, which has a three-two-two distribution reinforced by alliteration: *molča mol*jatsja; *s*taricy-*s*osny; *kl*obuka*x bel*y*x*. The continuity between sentences stems not only from the central motif of falling snow and the use of *xl* and *kl*, but also from the frequent repetition of the liquid *l*; the recurrence of the key words *sneg, snežku, belyj* (three instances of the latter, twice in inverted order); *utixlo, tixim* (connected semantically with *molča*); and by the phonetic similarity of *kolobkom* and *klobukax*. Such rhythmical and musical organization reflects conscious manipulation by the author and goes far beyond the scope of normal *skaz* narrative. Despite his use of such instrumental features as alliteration and assonance in his prose, however, Zamjatin rejected the use of metrical feet in prose, which was so typical of Belyj at that time.[30]

The preceding discussion of stylistic features has been accompanied by examples from Zamjatin's early works. However, although all of the stylistic features enumerated are present in varying degrees in all three of Zamjatin's tales, they exist only in some of his stories. His first stories (**"Odin," "Devuška,"** and **"Aprel'"**) seek neither to achieve a symbolic synthesis by means of grotesque, impressionistic, and recurrent images, nor do they utilize regional expressions and the *skaz* narrative. This is true also of the sketch **"Tri dnja,"** although Zamjatin did attempt there to recreate the spirit and feelings of the time by means of an impressionistic pastiche of events. Lacking the later compressed brevity and differing in thematic treatment, the earliest stories aim at narrating, not demonstrating. Close scrutiny reveals an interesting stylistic evolution, which was essentially complete by the time Zamjatin had written **"Alatyr'."** A comparison of the following two texts will graphically illustrate this evolution:

[Text A is from **"Devuška"** (*Novyj žurnal dlja vsex,* No. 25, Nov. 1910, 63-64), and Text B is from **"Alatyr',"** (*Russkaja mysl',* No. 9, Sept. 1915, 25-26).]

Text A

Beside them, nearby, the flowers smell pungently and sweetly. Vera inhales them and says: "Do you smell them? That's the flowers caressing each other and dying, and that's the scent of their caresses."

Vera feels his glance. Her heart pounds so that she wants to grab it with her hands and restrain it.

"How shameful, how shameful," Vera tells herself. "He's looking!"

And with terror she understands: she wants to grab and tear the lace on her breast and her dress, and give everything to him: look, here I am, for you alone . . . kiss me.

But he is silent. He has lowered his heavy head onto his arm.

Something was on the point of dying out and falling. She must grab it, hold it. She must quickly, quickly tell him something.

Vera's teeth rattle and she says: "Well, why do you sit like that? Amuse me."

And then she turns cold. Did she, did she say that? And it seems that she is on the verge of plunging into a hole, and, to keep from falling, she must grab the air with her hands.

Vera waves her arms and laughs loudly and strangely. He looks at her intently and says: "There you are laughing, Vera. But it seems to me that you are not at all gay. You have some sort of woe."

Vera again waves her hands and laughingly says: "Why, no. What sort of woe? You are such an interesting escort, I am gay with you."

Impatiently he stirs, and his voice is so strange: "I can't understand you. You are so . . . such a . . . It's difficult to talk to you."

He leans back, rustles in the grass behind the bench, looks for his cap. It's better to leave quickly, while this has passed. Why, even the musicians are leaving.

Vera screams to herself. I don't want to, I don't want to, and wrings her hands. Then she adjusts her hat and says: "Today the night is cold, you can catch a cold. It's time to go."

The distant lanterns die out. The flowers smell more furiously—they have but a minute to live. And it seems that the moon will move just once more and they will exhale the sickenly sweet breath of a corpse.

Vera inhales and speaks in a soundless voice, hidden by darkness: "Give me your hand."

She takes his hand and feels in it a scarcely perceptible caress. And suddenly, not knowing why, she slowly raises that hand to her lips. And at the end of the dark pathway stands the earlier Vera, waves her arms in mad terror and shouts at her: "What are you doing, what are you doing?"

She raises his hand to her lips and kisses it suddenly—quickly and greedily.

Then her whole body slips down from the bench onto the sand, she embraces his knees, presses to him with her breast and whispers, gasping: "I have never kissed, never kissed."

No, what is one to do with her? Bewildered, he grasps her head in his shaking hands. "Vera, I don't understand. Vera—forgive me. I'll go now. For God's sake."

He tears free his legs from her tenacious hands, the toe of his boot grazes something soft. Hurriedly he leaves, stumbling over tree roots crawling below. . . .

Text B

"Father is visiting the parish," Varvara greeted the prince. She fingered the lamp in her hands, but for some reason did not light it.

Only then did the prince notice: why, it's rather late. Beyond the window the moon rose, waning, dull, narrow. And the sky appeared so terribly empty, so silent forever, that his throat gagged, and he felt like howling.

To remain silent was terrible. The prince forced himself to smile: "You know, I was coming to your place in a cab. And a pig gave a gru-u-unt at the horse. Your pigs are so fleet-footed!"

Varvara was silent, gazed out the window at the moon.

"And you've got all sorts of fences, empty lots, empty lots, the dogs howl . . ."

Varvara covered her face with her hands and strangely slipped from the chair to the floor. The prince got up startled.

"Don't leave . . . No! No!," cried Varvara convulsively.

Her eyes had such an expression, such pity began to ache in the prince, that he lacked the strength to leave. He sat down again on the chair.

"Well, I hope that soon . . . We will begin our work for the general good . . . ," muttered the prince turning away; he was embarrassed to look at Varvara, she had such eyes . . .

It seemed that something was rubbing at his feet—the archpriest's dog. How did it get in from . . . He looked, but at his feet on the floor crept Sobačeja-Varvara. Caressingly she barred her canine teeth, pleaded with her eyes, pleaded: "Well, if you don't want to, then at least hit me, at least hit me," she rubbed against his legs . . .

The prince exclaimed, pushed away, jumped out onto the square without his hat. He broke into a run.

The situations in the two passages are essentially the same: a girl prompted by strong physiological drives throws herself at a man who does not reciprocate. But the styles differ. Zamjatin's progress toward a condensed style is reflected in the lengths of the passages: Text A is twice as long as Text B. Although Text B is not the best example of demonstrating, in comparison with the extensive description of the protagonist's thoughts in Text A, it definitely does indicate a tendency away from narrating. The extended use of an impressionistic image, absent in Text A, assumes central importance (Varvara—a dog) in Text B. In general, Text

A contains several literary clichés left over from the decadents: the furious caresses of dying flowers, the smell of corpses, rattling teeth, pounding heart. The mature Zamjatin was careful to purge his style of the trite and banal. In Text B the waning moon, the sole item of external description, is well integrated into the action (both the prince and Varvara look at it and presumably experience the same feeling); and the moon has symbolic significance in evoking the major mood of the tale—silent, empty, provincial Russia.

Zamjatin's early works, then, represent the evolution of an original literary style which is equally distant from the unhurried narrative of the Realists and the abstractions of the Symbolists. Irony and satire were the tools Zamjatin chose for surmounting the essential tragedy he saw in life; and his early works, with their seemingly pessimistic denouements, rejected the life they depicted, in the hope if inspiring the reader to strive for a better one.

The underlying philosophy of these writings is humanistic, and their primary subjects are bestiality and ignorance, not provincial Russia as it might at first appear. Mankind's lack of human values is shown especially in Zamjatin's portrayal of love either as a physical necessity (negatively as an automatic function and positively as a lyric expression of physiological drives) or as a spiritual need that is frustrated by the inhuman environment of provincial Russia. The theme of revolution, aside from a few references to the Revolution of 1905, is not explicit in Zamjatin's works.

These works do not stem from abstract generalizations, as those of the Symbolists did, but are firmly rooted in *byt*. One obvious sign of this is the quantity of colloquial and regional expressions which permeate both dialogue and *skaz* narrative. Unlike the Realists, Zamjatin sought neither to depict the minutiae of this *byt* nor to analyze the spiritual tribulations of his heroes; he attempted to convey both to the reader by a seemingly fantastic grotesque which would underline the significant features and thereby create a synthesis which was symbolic not only of the individual character but of the universal human condition as well. In character depiction Zamjatin developed one central impression, relying heavily on animal imagery and the recurrence of select attributes and physical features having symbolic significance. Related to this technique, also, was his growth toward brevity and demonstration.

Inspired by a genuine humanism, Zamjatin's early works in many respects did represent a synthesis between the two divergent schools of Realism and Symbolism, and, as such, they played a significant role in the manifestation of Russian Neo-realism during the second decade of the twentieth century.

Notes

1. Epigraph: [179a], 16.

2. [575], 309.

3. [164], 95.

4. [777n], 246.

5. [442], 260.

6. The idea of the gradual petrification of human feelings within Baryba was first discussed by Ju. Ajxenval'd in [777a].

7. [454], 30, and [442], 264.

8. [496], 310.

9. [454], 33.

10. [335], 229.

11. The date of writing for both "Petr Petrovič" (date of first publication not known) and "Angel Dormidon" (published in *Novaja žizn'*, No. 83 [May 4, 1918], 1) was given as 1916 in [33], 263, 270. See [93]-[112] for publication data on the other fables.

12. [164], 92, 94.

13. [164], 93.

14. [164], 95.

15. [164], 95, and "O sintetizme," [38], 234-235.

16. [577], 690.

17. [777p], 137.

18. "Zakulisy," [38], 267.

19. [164], 97.

20. [777l].

21. [777h], 304.

22. [164], 98.

23. [164], 98.

24. [595], 96.

25. [164], 98.

26. [595], 95.

27. [164], 93.

28. In 1914 Zamjatin had written an extremely negative review of *Peterburg,* comparing Belyj to an unfortunate contortionist [171]. (Although Zamjatin's authorship of this review is a surmise, the style of the review, the initialed signature "Evg. Z.," and his association with the journal at the time support the conjecture strongly.) But four years later in 1918, Zamjatin cited *Peterburg* sev-

eral times as an example of certain Neorealistic features, refraining from negative pronouncements about the novel itself ([164], 93, 95-96, 97, 99). Sixteen years later in his obituary of Belyj, Zamjatin spoke of *Peterburg* in glowing terms: "In this book, the best of everything written by Belyj, Petersburg has found its true artist for the first time since Gogol' and Dostoevskij" ("Andrej Belyj," [38], 78). Although the rather different evaluations in part reflect the very nature of the articles, they also indicate a gradual but definite change in Zamjatin's opinion, which may have been influenced by personal friendship.

29. [164], 99.

30. [169], 97.

A Bibliography of Zamjatiana

No adequate bibliography of Zamjatin's works and relevant secondary literature has previously been published. The few items included in K. D. Muratova's *Istorija russkoj literatury konca XIX-načala XX veka; bibliografičeskij ukazatel'* (Moskva-Leningrad, 1963) are woefully inadequate, and the exclusion of a section on Zamjatin from the current six-volume *Russkie sovetskie pisateli prozaiki; bibliografičeskij ukazatel'* (Leningrad, 1959-) indicates that no bibliography from Soviet sources will be forthcoming soon. Although the four-volume *Sobranie sočinenij* (Moskva, 1929) contains much of Zamjatin's prose fiction, it is far from complete. The critical investigator must search out materials on his own by referring to a myriad of literary histories and general bibliographies, many of which are outdated or highly selective. The following is an attempt to remedy this situation and, while making no claim to completeness except in Section I, is the single most extensive bibliography of Zamjatiana published to date.

Section I, which comprises all of Zamjatin's published works, as well as his unpublished plays and some letters, has been subdivided into archives, monographs, prose fiction, fables, plays, essays, reviews, autobiographies, letters, and edited works. The month of publication has been determined by consulting *Knižnaja letopis',* review literature, and advertisements. Although the resultant chronological order is admittedly approximate, the reader can reasonably assume that the works were already in circulation by the date indicated.

Section II, which comprises published translations of Zamjatin's works, is intended as a guide for persons who do not read Russian, future translators, and comparativists interested in Zamjatin's reception and influence abroad.

The secondary materials listed in Section III include works on Zamjatin, general works which mention him, reviews, and a list of other works cited in my discussion of the campaign against the VSp. Although articles on Zamjatin in Western encyclopedias have been plagued by factual inaccuracies, they may prove of use to comparativists' reception studies and therefore are included in Section III. Introductions to all Russian-language editions of Zamjatin's works are listed, but brief translators' introductions are not, unless they are of special interest. Even the most cursory mentions of Zamjatin in Soviet sources are included because of their value in determining Zamjatin's position in Russian letters and the critical attitudes toward him, but most cursory mentions in Western sources are excluded. Some one hundred anonymous announcements and factual references in literary chronicles have been omitted, but they are listed in the bibliography of my dissertation [460]. Among the general works in Section III, page references are provided for the Russian books, which usually lack indexes, but they are not given for indexed Western scholarly studies. Titles of review articles are cited only when they differ from the work reviewed (many reviews of essays and stories bear the titles of the journals in which Zamjatin's works originally appeared). The code ZA is explained in [1]. Items which I have been unable to examine are marked with asterisks, as in [2]*.

I. THE WORKS OF EVGENIJ IVANOVIC ZAMJATIN

ARCHIVAL MATERIALS

[1] Archive of Russian and East European History and Culture, Columbia University, New York City. Zamjatin Collection (1923-1936). References in the footnotes and bibliography are to materials on microfilm and are identified by the code ZA, followed by the folio number and then the frame number (folio title page has been counted as zero).

[2]* Central'nyj gosudarstvennyj arxiv literatury i iskusstva SSSR (CGALI), Moskva, fond 1776, 10 edinic xranenija (1920-1927).

MONOGRAPHS LISTED CHRONOLOGICALLY BY DATE OF PUBLICATION

[30] *Uezdnoe; povesti, teatr.* (*Sobranie sočinenij,* Tom I.) Moskva: Federacija, 1929. 256 pp. [Pub. Jan.] Contents: Avtobiografija [1929], Uezdnoe, Alatyr', [novoe] Predislovie [k Bloxe], Bloxa, Priloženie k "Bloxe."

[31] *Na kuličkax; povesti, rasskazy.* (*Sobranie sočinenij,* Tom II.) Moskva: Federacija, 1929. 286 pp. [Pub. Feb.] Contents: Na kuličkax, Neputevyj, Črevo, Znamenie, Aprel', Spodručnica grešnyx, Pis'menno, Krjaži, Staršina, Pravda istinnaja.

[32] *Ostrovitjane; povesti, rasskazy, teatr.* (*Sobranie sočinenij,* Tom III.) Moskva: Federacija, 1929. 324 pp. [Pub. Mar.] Contents: Ostrovitjane, Lovec čelovekov, Zemlemer, Detskaja, Mamaj, Peščera, Glaza, Rasskaz o samom glavnom, Ogni svjatogo Dominika.

[33] *Sever; povesti, rasskazy, skazki.* (*Sobranie sočinenij,* Tom IV.) Moskva: Federacija, 1929. 287 pp. [Pub. Apr.] Contents: Sever; Afrika; Ela; Rus'; Iks; Slovo predostavljaetsja tovariščču Čuryginu; Tri dnja; O tom, kak iscelen byl inok Erazm; O čude, proisšedšem v Pepel'nuju Sredu; Bog; Petr Petrovič; D'jaček; Angel Dormidon; Èlektričestvo; Kartinki; Drjan'-mal'čiška; Xeruvimy; Bibliografija.

[38] *Lica.* N'ju-Jork; Izdatel'stvo imeni Čexova, 1955. 285 pp. Contents: Ot izdatel'stva, Aleksandr Blok, Fedor Sologub, Čexov, L. Andreev, Vstreči s B. M. Kustodievym, Andrej Belyj, M. Gor'kij, Anatol' France (Nekrolog), Gerbert Uèlls, Genealogičeskoe derevo Uèllsa, O'Genri, Ričard Brinsli Šeridan, Zavtra, Cel', Ja bojus', Novaja russkaja proza, O segodnjašnem i o sovremennom, O sintetizme, O literature, revoljucii i èntropii, Dlja sbornika o knige, Zakulisy, Pis'mo Stalinu.

[40A] *Lica.* N'ju-Jork: Meždunarodnoe literaturnoe sodružestvo, 1967. 311 pp. Contents: same as [38] with the omission of "Ot izdatel'stva" and the addition of essays by M. Korjakov, "Lica i xari," and V. Bondarenko, "Evgenij Zamjatin i sovetskij period russkoj literatury."

FABLES (SKAZKI), LISTED ALPHABETICALLY WITH DATE OF WRITING AND OF FIRST PUBLICATION, IF KNOWN.

All twenty fables were published in the book *Bol'šim detjam skazki* (Berlin-Petrograd-Moskva: Z. I. Gržebin, 1922), which was in Gržebin's hands in manuscript form by 1920.

[93] "Angel Dormidon." *Novaja žizn'.* No. 83 (May 4, 1918), 1. [Written 1916.] Reprinted in [33].

[94] "Arapy." *Peterburgskij sbornik; poèty i belletristy.* Peterburg: Letopis' Doma literatorov, 1922, 43. [Pub. Apr.]

[95] "Bjaka i Kaka."

[96] "Bog." *Letopis'.* No. 4 (April 1916), 46-47. [Written 1915.] Reprinted in [29], [33].

[97] "Cerkov' Božija." *Peterburgskij sbornik; poèty i belletristy.* Peterburg: Letopis' Doma literatorov, 1922, 41-42. [Pub. Apr.]

[98] "Četverg." *Gazeta-Protest Sojuza russkix pisatelej* [odnodnevnaja petrogradskaja gazeta]. November 26, 1917, 2.

[99] "D'jaček." *Letopis'.* No. 4 (April 1916), 48-49. [Written 1915.] Reprinted in [29], [33].

[100] "Drjan'-mal'čiška." Originally published as "Pet'ka." *Letopis'.* No. 4 (April 1916), 50. [Written 1915.] Reprinted in [33].

[101] "Èlektričestvo." *Delo naroda.** 1918. [Written 1917.] Reprinted in [33].

[102] "Ivany."

[103] "Kartinki." *Prjanik osirotevšim detjam.* Petrograd: A. D. Baranovskaja, 1916, 72. [Written 1916.] Reprinted in [33].

[104] "Ognennoe A." *Novaja žizn'.* No. 106 (June 2, 1918), 2.

[105] "Pervaja skazka pro Fitu." Originally published as "Fita." *Delo naroda.* No. 198 (November 3, 1917), 2.

[106] "Petr Petrovič." [Written 1916.] Reprinted in [33].

[107] "Poslednjaja skazka pro Fitu."

[108] "Tret'ja skazka pro Fitu." Originally published as "Malen'-kijfel'eton; Fity." *Delo naroda.* No. 218 (November 24, 1917), 2-3.

[109] "Vtoraja skazka pro Fitu." Originally published as "Dejanija Fity." *Delo naroda.* No. 206 (November 11, 1917), 1.

[110] "Xaldej."

[111] "Xeruvimy." *Delo naroda.* No. 232 (December 14, 1917), 1. [Written 1917; much shortened in later versions.] Reprinted in [33].

[112] "Xrjapalo."

Essays (stat'i, predislovija), listed chronologically by date of first publication, with date of writing, if known.

The posthumous collection *Lica* [38] included twenty-one of these essays, five of which apparently were being published for the first time. The pagination of Zamjatin's articles in the new edition of *Lica* [40A], published after this biography was compiled, is identical to that in [38].

[164] "Sovremennaja russkaja literatura." *Grani.* No. 32 (October-December 1956), 90-101. A public lecture at the *Lebedjanskij narodnyj universitet* on September 8, 1918.

[169] "O jazyke." [Written 1919-1920.] *Novyj žurnal.* No. 77 (September 1964), 97-113.

Reviews (recenzii), listed chronologically.

[171] "Sirin. Sbornik pervyj vtoroj" (signed: Evg. Z.). *Ežemesjačnyj žurnal.* No. 4 (April 1914), 157-158.

Autobiographies, listed by date of publication, with subsequent reprintings.

[179] "Avtobiografija [1929]."

a. *Uezdnoe* [30], 1929, 5-19.

III. Secondary Sources

Works on Zamjatin, including articles, separate sections in books, and introductions to his works, arranged alphabetically by author.

[335] Braun, Ja. "Vzyskujuščij čeloveka; tvorčestvo Evgenija Zamjatina." *Sibirskie ogni.* No. 5/6 (September-December 1923), 225-240.

[442] Polonskij, V. "Zametki o molodyx; Čapygin, Nikandrov, Zamjatin." *Letopis'.* No. 3 (March 1916), 253-265.

[454] Richards, D. J. *Zamyatin; A Soviet Heretic.* London, 1962. 112 pp. Reviewed by E. J. Brown, *Slavic Review,* Vol. 23, No. 2 (June 1964), 389-390, and C. Collins, *Slavic and East European Journal,* Vol. 7, No. 1 (Spring 1963), 68-69.

[470] Slonim, Mark. *Portrety sovetskix pisatelej.* Pariž, 1933, 48-61. First published as "Portreti savremenix ruskix pisaca; 1. Evgenije Zamjatin." *Ruski arxiv.* No. 3 (1929); 99-112; and reprinted in *M. Slonim, *Portreti savremenix ruskix pisaca.* Beograd, 1933.

[496] Voronskij, A. "Literaturnye siluèty: III. Evg. Zamjatin." *Krasnaja nov'.* No. 6 (November-December 1922), 304-322. Reprinted in Aleksandr Voronskij, *Na styke; sbornik statej.* Moskva-Petrograd, 1923, 47-75; *Literaturnye tipy.* Moskva, 1927, 15-38; *Literaturnye portrety v dvux tomax.* Vol. I. Moskva, 1928, 76-110; *Literaturno-kritičeskie stat'i.* Moskva, 1963, 85-111.

[575] Gizetti, A. "Vozroždenie ili vyroždenie? (O žurnale *Letopis'*)." *Ežemesjačnyj žurnal.* No. 4 (April 1916), 299-318.

[577] Golikov, V. "Bessleznye glaza." *Vestnik znanija.* No. 7 (July 1913), 683-691.

[595] Ivanov-Razumnik, R. "Literatura i obščestvennost'; russkaja literatura v 1913 godu." *Zavety.* No. 1 (January 1914), 87-99. Reprinted in Ivanov-Razumnik, *Zavetnoe o kul'turnoj tradicii; stat'i 1912-1913 gg.* Peterburg, 1922, 35-56.

Reviews, listed alphabetically by author under the title of the work reviewed (reviews of translations are listed after reviews of the Russian originals).

[777] "Uezdnoe" and *Uezdnoe*

a. Ajxenval'd, Ju. *Reč'.* No. 54 (February 25, 1916), 2.

h. Anon. *Russkie zapiski.* No. 4 (April 1916), 303-305.

l. Derman, A. *Russkie vedomosti.* No. 155 (July 6, 1916), 5.

n. Gizetti, A. *Ežemesjačnyj žurnal.* No. 6 (June 1916), 245-246.

p. Gvozdev, A. *Severnye zapiski.* No. 6 (June 1916), 137-139.

Susan Layton (essay date fall 1976)

SOURCE: Layton, Susan. "The Symbolic Dimension of 'The Cave' by Zamjatin." *Studies in Short Fiction* 13, no. 4 (fall 1976): 455-63.

[In the following essay, Layton offers a close examination of "Peščera" ("The Cave").]

Evgenij Zamjatin is best known for the fantastical, anti-utopian novel *We,* which was a forerunner of *Brave New World* and *1984.* Of equal interest, however, are short stories such as **"The Cave," "Mamaj"** and **"The Dragon"** in which he dealt with the Bolshevik revolution in a nonrealistic manner. As does *We,* the stories oppose the optimism of the Marxist view of man and doctrine of historical progress, and they helped to establish Zamjatin's reputation in the Soviet Union as an anti-Bolshevik writer. However, it is inadequate to describe them narrowly as political works written in opposition to communism. Zamjatin had a revolutionary fervor which had led to a brief involvement with the impulse for radical political and social change in Russia. While he was a student in the early 1900's he joined the Bolshevik Party; arrested for his revolutionary activities, he was imprisoned for several months in 1905-1906, but by 1908 he had left the Party.[1] As an artist Zamjatin continued to uphold an anarchistic, bohemian concept of revolution, and he opposed the encroachment upon freedom of expression in the Soviet Union as one of the signs of a dogmatization of Bolshevism. In several essays and articles in the 1920's he protested against demands that the artist serve the state and provide a chronicle of the progressive development of socialism in the U.S.S.R. Attacking journalistic writing that followed the current Party line, he stated that genuine literature must have a symbolic dimension; it must be "artistically realized philosophy."[2] Repeatedly Zamjatin defended this notion that the artist must rise above the chaotic day-by-day progression of events and deal with the realities of being. Comparing the function of genuine art to a sailor on the watchtower of a ship, he wrote that

> In stormy weather you need a man aloft. And right now the weather is stormy. S.O.S. signals are coming in from all directions. . . . Right now we can look and think only as men do in the face of death: we shall die—and what then? How have we lived? If we are to live all over again in some new way, then by what shall we live and for what? Right now we need in literature the vast philosophical horizon, the vast sweep from the masthead, from the sky above; we need the most ultimate, the most fearsome "Whys?" and "What nexts?"[3]

"The Cave" is one of the most richly symbolic works in which Zamjatin placed the contemporary within a framework of universal experience. Concerned with the difficulty of maintaining traditional values and civilized behavior under harsh conditions in Russia after the revolution, **"The Cave"** depicts a grim regression of life. Focusing upon Martin Martinych and his wife Masha, the story covers approximately twenty-four hours during the winter of 1919-1920. Martin Martinych is desperate to get some firewood—especially because his wife, who is ill and weak, hopes to burn the stove throughout her nameday. When his request to borrow some logs from a neighbor is denied, Martin Martinych steals the wood; and his suffering over the meaning of that act is the essential material of **"The Cave."** Certainly there are realistic details in the story that point to the new political system. In the years of War Communism, supplies of food and fuel were minimal, and people literally lived in the dark much of the time because the government had to regulate strictly the use of electricity. Most directly to the point, the central occurrence of the story was drawn from Zamjatin's own experience in Soviet Petersburg. In the essay "Behind the Scenes" he relates: "One winter night in 1919 I was on watch duty in our yard. My partner—a frozen, half-starved professor—complained about the lack of firewood: 'Sometimes I am even tempted to steal some wood! But the trouble is that I cannot do it, I'd rather die than steal.' On the following day I sat down to write 'The Cave.'"[4] While Zamjatin clearly was dealing with the material of experience in contemporary society in this story, as in *We* and other works of this period of his career in **"The Cave"** he has transformed the particulars of life in Soviet Russia in order to make current history speak of the human condition.

The title, **"The Cave,"** poses the central metaphor which extends throughout the story[5]—and transforms contemporary Petersburg into a nightmarish world of fear and suspicion: life in a cave is a framing device that refers to natural history and renders the society of 1919 as alien and distant. With no direct reference to a city or to men, the first lines describe a snow-swept wasteland with a starkness that is heightened by the compressed, often elliptical sentences: "Glaciers, mammoths, wastes. Black nocturnal cliffs, somehow resembling houses; in the cliffs, caves. And no one knows who trumpets at night on the stony path between the cliffs, who blows up white snow-dust, sniffing out the path. Perhaps it is a gray-trunked mammoth, perhaps the wind. Or is the wind itself the icy roar of the king of mammoths?" (p. 138)[6] This god-forsaken wasteland in which winter seems eternal is preeminently a realm of necessity: "And you must clench your teeth as tightly as possible to keep them from chattering; and you must split wood with a stone axe; and you must carry your fire every night from cave to cave, deeper and deeper; and you must wrap yourself into shaggy animal hides, more and more of them" (ibid). As for their prehistoric ancestors, for the people inhabiting the fearfully transformed Petersburg, existence is essentially a struggle to survive.

Zamjatin presents Martin Martinych and Masha as the inhabitants of one of the caves. Unable to keep their entire apartment heated, they have retreated to the bedroom and light a fire in the stove for a few hours each day. In this situation the hero emerges as a life-like individual whose behavior has a complex psychological and philosophical basis—even though Zamjatin does not analyze his motivations. However, in exploring the predicament of that freezing professor whom he had encountered, Zamjatin represents Martin Martinych in a symbolic manner. There is no complete physical description of Martin Martinych, and he is not identified by full name or profession. Appearing as a figure of everyman, he undergoes a struggle which is referred back beyond the trials of the contemporary social upheaval. Existing now as cave men means being devoted to a fight for the material necessities; but in opposition to this terrifying realm, the story evokes another mode of being and suggests that the soul is the universally distinctive feature of humanity. Standing in **"The Cave"** as a remembered ideal, this world of spirit is summoned by references to love, art and Christian legend.

The hero in **"The Cave"** is a man who attributes primary value to the spiritual dimension of existence.[7] Considered within this broad tendency, his name suggests an association with Henride St. Martin, the man whose books exerted a major influence in the mid-eighteenth century upon the first Russian Masons. Zamjatin's hero can be regarded as a son of these original "Martinists"—the name which Catherine the Great applied to Novikov and his followers, only in the most general sense, of course. Martin Martinych professes no specific doctrines, but he, like the Masons, believes that authentic reality is the world of the spirit. As the only reference in the story to his physical appearance emphasizes, he is acutely aware that the soul is being lost in the realm of the cave: "his face is crumpled, claylike: many people had clay faces now—back to Adam" (p. 139). Compounding the image of the cave man, this biblical reference suggests that man attains fully human being only when animated by a divine inner spirit.

The cave of this person who has spiritual longings is a chaotic world that contains all manner of things and centers around a deity invented by man:

> In the Petersburg bedroom-cave things were much as they had been in Noah's ark not long ago: a confusion of beasts, clean and unclean, thrown together by the flood. A mahogany desk; books; stone-age pancakes that seemed to have been made of potter's clay; Scriabin, Opus 74; a flat-iron; five potatoes, scrubbed lovingly to gleaming whiteness; nickel bedsteads; an axe; a chiffonier; firewood. And in the center of this universe—it's god, the shortlegged, rusty-red, squat, greedy cave god: the cast-iron stove.
>
> (p. 138)

The jumbled, disordered quality of Martin Martinych's existence is not described essentially in terms of social upheaval—but is conveyed through the allusion to immemorial chaos—the Flood. The fact that the hero has retained a place in his life for things which are not necessary for physical survival underlines that he, like Noah, is notable as a man with a soul. Zamjatin juxta-

poses the objects which belong to the realm of the cast-iron god with products of civilization, indicating a discrepancy between Martin Martinych's spiritual aspirations and the possibilities of realizing them in his present existence.

The participation of Martin Martinych and Masha in the world of the soul is conveyed mainly through their personal recollections of the past. In opposition to the wintry realm of necessity, the world in which the spirit can thrive is summoned in the hero's thoughts by symbolic reference to the other seasons of the year. In the bedroom-cave the fire as a source of warmth is associated with spring, as the glow of the flames seems to regenerate Martin Martinych: "For a single hour it was spring in the cave; for one hour the animal hides, claws, fangs were discarded, and green shoots—thoughts— struggled up through the ice-crusted cortex of the brain" (pp. 138-139). References to autumn and summer elaborate upon this allusion to a specifically human world of mind, emphasizing not the intellectual but the spiritual, irrational faculty. Masha breaks into her husband's contemplation, accusing him of forgetting that tomorrow is her saint's day. Not answering immediately, he continues to dream, now recalling summer as a lost ideal and autumn as the falling away: "In October, when the leaves have yellowed, withered, drooped, there are sometimes blue-eyed days; you throw back your head on such a day, so as not to see the earth, and you almost believe that joy, that summer are still here. And so with Masha now: if you close your eyes and only listen to her voice, you can still believe she is the same, the old Masha" (p. 139). As evoked further in Masha's recollections on her nameday, the ideal world of spring and summer is a creation of love. Speaking in her "voice of old," she recalls a distant evening when their warm, beautiful "universe had been created:"

> Do you remember, Mart: my blue room, and the piano with the covered top, and the little wooden horse, the ashtray, on the piano? I played, and you came up to me from behind. . . .
>
> Do you remember, Mart—the open window, the green sky and below, out of another world, the hurdy-gurdy man? . . .
>
> And on the quay—remember? The branches still bare, the rosy water and a last ice floe, like a coffin floating by. And the coffin only made us laugh, for we would never die. Remember?
>
> (p. 142; ellipses in original)

In contrast to the grim world that is ruled by cold and hunger, this recollected universe stands in **"The Cave"** as an eternal ideal; experiencing love, Zamjatin's characters express a sense of immortality.

In contrast to Martin Martinych and Masha, other creatures are at home in the kingdom of the cast-iron god. Obertyshev is the cave man most in harmony with the environment in which only the fittest survive. When Martin Martinych goes to him to beg for firewood, Obertyshev opens the door—his face appearing as a "wasteland overgrown with rusty, dusty weeds" (p. 140). For Obertyshev to smile is like the scurrying of a lizard: "Through a tangle of weeds—yellow, stony teeth, and between the stones, a flick of a lizard's tail" (ibid.). Recurrently, the prominence of his teeth is noted, and this motif stresses his kinship with the mammoths of the frozen wasteland that is summoned in the opening paragraphs. As this episode procedes, the underlying metaphor of Obertyshev as a sub-human, animal-like person is "realized" so that he appears essentially as a monster trying to impersonate a man. As Martin Martinych anticipates his refusal to give him any firewood, "all of Obertyshev was sprouting teeth, and they grew longer and longer" (p. 141); later, after he has stolen some wood, the hero imagines the fury of Obertyshev, "all of him overgrown with teeth" (p. 142). Appearing increasingly grotesque, Obertyshev presents the most horrible aspect in **"The Cave"** of a man who is not human. Similarly, while the house chairman Selikhov does display some sympathy for Martin Martinych, Zamjatin also characterizes him by motifs of dehumanization that connect him with the mammoths and with the cast-iron stove and shows his ready adaptation to the laws of the harsh realm of Soviet cave men.

Unlike Obertyshev and Selikhov, Martin Martinych and his wife are conscious of their reduction in the realm of the cave. Throughout the story Masha appears "flat, cut-out of paper" (p. 143) and is never fully described. The suggestion that she is less than a vital, three-dimensional person is realized in her own words. At the end of **"The Cave"** she begs her husband to give her the single dose of poison that he has, as though to commit suicide would be to acknowledge her virtual death: "'There is nothing left of me anyway. This is no longer I . . .'" (p. 146). Reduced to a helpless, irritable creature, Masha is now unrecognizable as the fully human woman who is preserved in memory. During the critical twenty-four-hour period that is portrayed in **"The Cave,"** the old Martin Martinych also ceases to exist. As conveyed by motifs that externalize his mental state, he is falling to pieces and eventually seems annihilated spiritually. Unknown to Masha on the eve of her saint's day, their wood supply has been totally exhausted. Martin Martinych's anxiety about this is shattering: he hears the sound of Obertyshev's chopping logs and the "stone axe was splitting Martin Martinych into pieces" (p. 139). One part of him smiles at his wife while "another piece—like a bird that has flown into a room out of the open—dashed itself blindly, stupidly against the ceiling, the windows, the walls: 'Where can I get some wood—some wood—some wood?'" (p. 140). Flying to pieces, Martin Martinych desperately asks Obertyshev for some logs: "The strayed bird could be heard fluttering up, rustling, darting left, right—and suddenly, desperately,

it dashed its breast against the wall" (pp. 140-141). The metaphor of a shattered personality is realized when the hero stands alone before the big wood pile after Obertyshev has refused to give him any logs: ". . . two Martin Martinychs locked in mortal combat: the old one, who had loved Scriabin and who knew he must not, and the new one, the cave dweller, who knew—he must" (p. 141). The cave man throttles the old self, and Martin Martinych with the logs "bounded upstairs with great, animal leaps" (ibid.). By stealing, he believes that he has destroyed his former self and degenerated into a subhuman creature.

Virtually annihilated as a man from his own point of view, Martin Martinych appears increasingly like a clay figure. Even before the theft, the motif of the clay figure suggests not a human who still can respond to the external world but inanimate material that can be molded. When he first enters Obertyshev's apartment, the "clay Martin Martinych painfully struck his side against the wood—a deep dent formed in the clay" (p. 140). After the theft of the logs, the image of the clay figure is central in conveying what it means for the hero to have lost his soul. "Cold, blind, made of clay, Martin Martinych stumbled against the things piled in confusion, out of the flood" (p. 144). Similarly, he is described as "mechanical, faraway," but "still going through some motions" (p. 145). Lost in despair martin Martinych is transformed finally into an android figure.

Throughout the story Masha appears oblivious to her husband's suffering, and her anger at him brings the blackest moment for him. Stumbling about numbly, Martin Martinych knocks the tea kettle and pan from the stove, arousing his wife's irritation: "'Get out! Get out at once. I don't need anybody, I don't need anything—I want nothing, nothing!'" (ibid). As if the cry "nothing, nothing" overwhelms him, he now takes the vial of poison from the desk. At first he intends to drink it himself, but his wife catches sight of the vial. When she then asks for the poison, Martin Martinych hesitates in his own misery but does give it to her—perhaps thinking that to abandon Masha would be more dishonorable than the theft of firewood. For the pitiful Masha death is associated with a journey away from the wintry realm to a land of the sun. Almost joyfully she prepares to drink and appears "rosy, immortal—like the river at sunset long ago" (p. 146). In the name of the woman and of the entire joyful existence which are etched in memory, Martin Martinych allows his wife to escape from the cave. His own anguish is unrelieved, however. At his wife's request he goes outside, leaving her to die. The icy wasteland described in the opening paragraph of **"The Cave"** is represented once again, and the hero is left alone in a hostile universe of blizzards, ice and monster mammoths.

While surely the most sombre of any of Zamjatin's works, **"The Cave"** nevertheless does attest to the greatness of the human soul. Precisely because of his despair about falling from the ideal of the truly human, Martin Martinych transcends the realm of the cave men. Unlike Obertyshev and Selikhov, who exist as animals, experiencing no spiritual torment, he has lived with a sense of good and evil. By reducing him to the state in which his best choice is to mercifully kill his wife, Zamjatin very starkly underlines his hero's struggle to retain a residual humanity. As do many of Zamjatin's works, this story also represents passionate love as a peak of human experience.

When **"The Cave"** first appeared in the Soviet Union in 1920, Marxists interpreted it strictly in ideological terms; and, since Zamjatin did not celebrate the Bolshevik revolution, he was berated. He was attacked for compassionately depicting those "disappearing people who are unfit for life."[8] Zamjatin was well aware that works such as **"The Cave"** would provide grounds for this kind of charge from Communists. But instead of avoiding forbidden themes, he insisted that literature must arouse readers by exploring fundamental questions about life. Believing that the artist must consider all aspects of the revolution, he did draw upon the reality of contemporary Russia to depict the tragedy of an individual overwhelmed by history. Writing the story of a man who steals firewood in October 1919 in Petersburg, Zamjatin subsumed the realistic elements in philosophical speculation about what it means to be human.

Notes

1. Alex M. Shane, *The Life and Works of Evgenij Zamjatin* (Berkeley: University of California Press, 1968), pp. 9-12.

2. E. Zamjatin, "Serapionovy brat'ja," ("The Serapion Brothers"), *Literaturnye zapiski (Literary Notes)*, No. I (May 15, 1922), 8.

3. Zamjatin, "O literature, revoljucii i entropii," ("On Literature, Revolution and Entropy"), *Lica (Faces)* (New York: Cerov Press 1955), p. 252; see also "O sinteizm," ("On Synthesism"), p. 240; "Novaja russkaja proza," ("New Russian Prose"), p. 203; and "O segodnjassnem i o sovremennom," ("On the Topical and the Contemporary"), pp. 213-214, 229-230. All of these essays appear in *Lica*.

4. Zamjatin, "Zakulisy," ("Behind the Scenes"), p. 264.

5. Cf. Zamjatin on the system of imagery in "The Cave" in ibid., p. 270.

6. All page numbers refer to Zamjatin's *Povesti i rasskazy (Novellas and Stories)*, (Letchworth: Bradda Books 1969).

7. On the "Martinists," see James Billington, *The Icon and the Axe. An Interpretative History of*

Russian Culture (New York: Random House 1968), pp. 255-256.

8. Quoted by Shane, p. 147.

Andrew Barratt (essay date 1983)

SOURCE: Barratt, Andrew. "Adam and the Ark of Ice: Man and Revolution in Zamyatin's 'The Cave.'" *Irish Slavonic Studies*, no. 4 (1983): 20-37.

[*In the following essay, Barratt focuses on Zamyatin's neo-realism, his treatment of the October Revolution, and his views on revolution in general, as expressed in "Peščera" ("The Cave").*]

"The Cave" (**"Peshchera"**) is one of Zamyatin's most famous short stories, and arguably one of his finest achievements in any genre. Yet, like the rest of the author's shorter fiction, this story has tended to languish in the shadow of the anti-Utopian novel *We (My)*, which continues to attract the lion's share of critical attention.[1] In the case of **"The Cave,"** this relative neglect is doubly regrettable. In the first place, it is a story which makes for a perfect case-study in Zamyatin's so-called Neo-Realist technique. And, secondly, it sheds important light on the writer's understanding of the October Revolution. Quite different in scope and focus from *We*, it also provides a counterweight to some of the ideas put forward in Zamyatin's articles of the early Soviet period, highlighting the complexity (perhaps even the ambiguity) of his thinking on the all-important question of revolution. It is towards these issues that the present discussion of **"The Cave"** is directed.

The development of 'Neo-Realism' represented a new direction. It was conceived as a literary style fully consonant with the new themes which appeared in his post-revolutionary fiction, and its principal features have been neatly summarized by Alex Shane: the chatty, village *skaz* type of discourse, which had characterized most of the early fiction, is replaced by a narrative which is more condensed and self-consciously literary; imagery plays a far more prominent role and is developed into systems; and the rhythmic and musical properties of language are consciously exploited.[2] There is, however, one aspect of Neo-Realism which has escaped detailed scrutiny. This is the notion of *synthesis,* from which 'Synthetism' (Zamyatin's own alternative name for Neo-Realism) derives, and which is of paramount importance for an understanding of **"The Cave."**

As the word itself suggests, 'Synthetism' has its origin in dialectical thinking. The term was first introduced in the article 'On Synthetism' ('O sintetizme'), which begins with an attempt by Zamyatin to apply the dialectical method to an analysis of literary developments in early twentieth-century Russia. The result is a typically daring simplification: the notorious complexities of this period are reduced to the clash of two opposite principles—Realism and Symbolism. In Zamyatin's own words:

> Realism saw the world with the naked eye: Symbolism caught a glimpse of the skeleton through the surface of the world, and Symbolism turned away from the world. Here we have the thesis and antithesis: the synthesis has approached the world with a complex array of lenses, and grotesque, strange multitudes of worlds are being opened up to it.[3]

We should note that the writer is really saying two things here. Firstly, he is stating the case for the historical legitimacy of his own 'Synthetism' as the natural progression beyond Realism and Symbolism in the endless dialectic of literary development. Secondly, and more importantly in view of our present purpose, Zamyatin is defining 'Synthetism' as a literary method in which Realism and Symbolism (in his own idiosyncratic sense of these words) are combined to create an exciting new way of viewing the world.

In order to understand more precisely what is implied by 'Synthetism' in this latter, technical sense, we would perhaps do better to avoid the term 'Synthetism' itself and to use instead the more descriptive phrase 'dislocation of planes' ('smeshcheniye planov'), which crops up several times in the article and is evidently synonymous with the idea of 'Synthetic' technique. Yet even this phrase is not without its difficulties. From the discussion, both here and elsewhere in Zamyatin's critical writings, it would appear that it may be taken to refer to at least three quite distinct technical features, of which two are unmistakably present in **"The Cave."** The first is the combination, within the single 'plane' of the artistic work, of seemingly random, disconnected details drawn from disparate planes of experience. As an example Zamyatin cites a portrait of Gorky by Yuriy Annenkov, in which a street 'bristling with bayonets', a cupola, and a 'dreaming Buddha' appear alongside the writer's face.[4] This, of course, is the principle of collage, which has its literary analogue in Zamyatin's syncretic use of imagery and mythic allusions. **"The Cave"** itself will provide ample evidence of this technique, which challenges the reader to discover the logic governing the mixture of materials drawn from apparently incompatible sources.

The second meaning of 'dislocation of planes' may be comprehended if we look again at the passage from 'On Synthetism' quoted above. Prominent here, as in other of Zamyatin's articles, is the image of the lens. The extract cited is, in fact, preceded by one of the writer's most celebrated arguments, in which he compares the description of a piece of skin as viewed by the naked eye and as seen under a microscope, and concludes by

asking the reader to decide which is the more 'real'. Naturally, the question defies an answer; this is merely Zamyatin's way of insisting that 'reality' is a relative concept, and that what is perceived depends entirely upon the position of the observer and the mode of observation employed. It should be added that Zamyatin's example automatically implies that these different modes of observation are mutually exclusive; they belong, that is, to separate planes of experience and render quite dissimilar pictures of reality. 'Dislocation' of this type is a matter of *vision,* therefore, in both the literal and metaphorical sense of the word. In **"The Cave,"** as we shall see, the story of Martin Martinych and Masha is told on two different 'planes'. On the plane of 'Realism' (to borrow Zamyatin's own terminology), we have a moving personal story of an acute moral dilemma, which is rendered with compelling lyrical intensity. Simultaneously, on the plane of 'Symbolism', the same story is viewed from a perspective which grants us the ability to see the 'skeleton' beneath the surface. In this way, Zamyatin insists that we view the experiences of the characters on a different scale, as part of an ineluctable evolutionary process.[5]

With these ideas in mind, let us turn to the beginning of **"The Cave"**:

> Glaciers, mammoths, wastes. Black, nocturnal cliffs, somewhat similar to buildings; caves in the cliffs. And it is not known who trumpets at night on the stony path between the cliffs, sniffing the path and raising white, snowy dust. Perhaps it is a grey-trunked mammoth; perhaps it is the wind. Or perhaps the wind itself is the icy roar of a most mammoth mammoth?[6]

It is a bold start, quintessential Zamyatin. Yet readers of Dickens may well detect an echo in this passage of the opening of *Bleak House,* with its memorable comparison of the muddy city of London to the immediate post-diluvian world. Zamyatin was an admirer of Dickens, and his extended metaphor certainly suggests the working of a similar kind of literary imagination. Indeed, the comparison might even be extended down to minor points of detail. Zamyatin's mammoth has a counterpart in Dickens' Megalosaurus; and Dickens' reference to the Flood is picked up in the third paragraph of Zamyatin's story, where Martin Martinych's apartment is compared to Noah's Ark (p. 186).

Despite these affinities, there is, however, an important difference between the openings of the two works, a difference which lies principally in the authors' choice of tropes. Where Dickens employs a simile, Zamyatin opts for a metaphor, and the effects that they achieve provide a neat illustration of the opposite potential residing in the two figures. The simile, by definition, works on the principle of explicit comparison. Thus Dickens begins by introducing his reader to a stable, recognizable world (London, the Chancery), which then provides a firm point of reference for the subsequent flight of fancy involving diluvian muds and pre-historic monsters. The metaphor, on the other hand, suppresses the subject of comparison, a feature which ensures that it has an inbuilt capacity for generating instability. And what, in fact, could be more unstable, than Zamyatin's opening paragraph? When first we pick up the story, there is every likelihood that we might imagine that this is an actual Ice-Age landscape that is being described. It is only when we learn, in the second paragraph, that this is the place 'where, centuries ago, stood Petersburg', that we are able, retrospectively, to decipher the metaphor with confidence and realise that the 'cliffs, somewhat similar to buildings' *are* buildings, that the 'caves' are apartments, and that the 'icy roar of a most mammoth mammoth' is the cold, October wind.

The disturbing mood of uncertainty and ambiguity established in the opening paragraph is only partially alleviated in the narrative which follows. Indeed, in the very same sentence where the initial metaphor is exposed, Zamyatin introduces a difficulty of a different order: 'Among the cliffs, where *centuries ago* stood Petersburg, the grey-trunked mammoth roamed by night' (p. 185). The extended metaphor is now easy to penetrate and, with the subsequent mention of the modern 'cave men', Martin Martinych and Masha, it becomes fully transparent. But what are we to make of the phrase 'centuries ago'? An immediate reaction might well be to dismiss this as an hyperbole as unremarkable as its English equivalent 'ages ago', by means of which Zamyatin expresses the idea (equally unremarkable) of the immense gulf separating the St Petersburg era from the new age of post-revolutionary Petrograd. But this is only to sweep the problem under the carpet, for it recurs, although in reverse form, at the beginning of the third paragraph, where we are told that in Martin Martinych's 'Petersburg bedroom-cave, it was as it had been *not long ago* in Noah's Ark' (p. 186).[7] This expression, to be sure, cannot be discounted as a mere cliché; it is an arresting detail, which, like the previous phrase (although with greater insistence), strikes at the heart of conventional historical consciousness. The idea of time as sequence is supplanted by an analogical view of events which proclaims that contemporary Petrograd is 'close' to the distant time of the Flood, and 'distant' from the recent era of St Petersburg.

The reference to the Flood draws attention to a further dimension of the problem of time in the opening section of the story. The initial metaphor with its glaciers and mammoths, seems at first to invite a fairly simple interpretation: contemporary Petrograd is like an ancient Ice Age. But, by the end of the third paragraph it is apparent that the metaphor does not translate quite so readily into a convenient simile. As we have seen, revolutionary Petrograd is equated not only with the Ice Age, but also with the Deluge. And this is not all. The

description of the contents of Martin Martinych's apartment includes '*Stone-Age* pancakes' (p. 186; it is the Stone Age also, it should be added, which is most readily associated with cave dwelling). And the final item in the list ('the squat, greedy cave-god: the cast-iron stove'), besides evoking the spectre of a new paganism, hints at the other great era of prehistory, the Iron Age. In short, the metaphor has been transformed before our very eyes into a complex syncretic image, which, like the peculiar references to time, betrays the operation of a non-linear conception of history. The image, which might first have appeared only to convey (albeit most graphically) the grim inhospitability of Petrograd in 1919, carries a far greater burden of meaning. By means of this perplexing stratagem, the contemporary Russian experience is situated on the largest historical scale so that its epochal significance is revealed.

The opening three paragraphs, therefore, introduce the larger theme of **"The Cave"**: the problem of man and history. But, at the same time, they also function as a prologue to the story of Martin Martinych and the smaller theme of his ethical dilemma. In the second paragraph, Zamyatin quickly sketches in the relevant details of his hero's predicament: the perpetual and growing threat of cold and starvation, the gradual retreat into the single heated room, and so on. The discrepancy between the smallness of this world (Zamyatin surely has his tongue in his cheek when he calls it a 'universe', p. 186) and the vast icy wastes outside could hardly be more evident. Martin Martinych's vulnerability is almost palpable. But there is more to this than the mere question of size; also involved here is the fundamental matter of vision. The shift of narrative focus entails a radical change of perspective. As Zamyatin's camera 'zooms in' on the apartment of Martin Martinych, 'Symbolism' gives way to 'Realism', or, to state the matter in more conventional literary terms, the epic voice (distinguished above all by the initial syncretic metaphor) is replaced by free indirect discourse, in which the lyric voice of Martin Martinych himself is a dominant presence.[8] The two voices compete briefly for the reader's attention, but the epic voice, which sounds clearly at the beginning of paragraph 4 ('In the dark cave: a fiery miracle. People—Martin Martinych and Masha—silently, thankfully, stretched out their hands towards it') is soon drowned out by the free indirect style, which, at the end of paragraph 6, is indistinguishable from Martin Martinych's speech ('but if you were to close your eyes and only listen to her, you could still believe she was the same', p. 186).

The narrative sections of **"The Cave"** which follow are rendered almost entirely in the form of free indirect discourse. What is more, within this mode the lyric voice of Martin Martinych becomes increasingly prominent as the plot rushes towards its dénouement. But the epic voice is not completely excluded; it recurs briefly in two parenthetic remarks:

> And in the light it can clearly be seen: his face is crumpled, clay, (many have clay faces nowadays: back to Adam).
>
> (p. 187)

> Martin Martinych put on his coat, belted tight with a leather belt on top (the cave men have a myth that it is warmer like this).
>
> (p. 188)

Nothing more is needed to maintain the tension between the two narrative voices. Even as we become absorbed in the human drama of Martin Martinych, these tiny interpretations serve to remind us that we are to be anthropologists as well. At the very end of the story, as we shall see, the epic voice resurfaces, intersecting with the lyric voice of Martin Martinych to reinforce and expand our understanding of the larger theme. But, for the time being, this larger theme is left, as it were, in suspension; the reader is released at least temporarily, from the need to ponder the full implications of the epic voice, and is thereby allowed to become immersed in the inner world of Zamyatin's hero.

Martin Martinych's story is one of classic simplicity, fully meeting the rigorous standard of economy that Zamyatin was now demanding both of himself and of other writers.[9] Martin Martinych (his surname is never given), an intellectual, wishes to enable his wife, Masha, to celebrate her name-day properly by heating their apartment. As their own stock of firewood has been exhausted, he goes to his downstairs neighbour, Obertyshev, in the hope that the latter will offer him some. When Obertyshev refuses to help, Martin Martinych steals the logs he needs, returns with them to his own apartment, and the celebration goes ahead. But Obertyshev, having discovered the theft, has already reported it to Selikhov, the head of the housing committee. Selikhov has an interview with Martin Martinych, whom he instructs to return the firewood to its rightful owner. Martin Martinych is now conscience-stricken. He cannot return the firewood, as it has already been burnt, nor can he live with the thought that he has offended against his personal code of morality, first by the very theft itself, and then by lying to Selikhov. Contemplating suicide, he returns to his wife, who begs him to let her have the contents of a blue phial (presumably a narcotic of some sort) so that she can put an end to her own life.[10] Acceding to her wish, Martin Martinych goes out into the cold Petrograd night.

The bare summary, although it fails to do justice to the complexity of Zamyatin's narrative, brings out its most striking surface feature—the nobility of Martin Martinych's sacrifice. This nobility is displayed in the initial motive for the theft, which he undertakes, unselfishly, for the sake of his wife. It is displayed also in his subsequent intense and unfeigned anguish, which derives not from the fear of external retribution, but from the acknowledgement that he has transgressed against his own absolute moral standard. And, finally, it is displayed in the altruistic gesture of denying himself an easy suicide, again for the sake of his wife. However we read the story's open ending (will Martin Martinych return to the apartment, or will he simply perish from deliberately exposing himself to the elements?) this nobility remains, to the last, uncompromised.

Martin Martinych engages our sympathies not only because of his own qualities, but also due to the fact that the other characters in the story are manifestly less attractive than he is. Let us take his wife, Masha, for example. Where Martin Martinych's decision to commit suicide is the result of a moral dilemma which raises him truly to the level of tragedy, Masha's desire for death fails to transcend mere pathos. Weak and sickly though she is, her selfishness and her blindness to her husband's crisis tend even to make her slightly more repellent than appealing. As for the others, there can be no question of sympathy at all. Obertyshev clearly represents man reduced to the level of the animal. One of Zamyatin's most uncharitable portraits, he can trace his pedigree back to some of the writer's earlier characters—to Anton Baryba in *A Provincial Tale* (*Uyezdnoye*) and to Captain Nechesa in *At the Back of Beyond* (*Na kulichkakh*). Just as the latter's progeny are described not as children, but 'Nechesa cubs' (*nechesyata*), so Obertyshev's family comprises an 'Obertyshev female and three Obertyshev cubs' (p. 189).[11] Theirs is a life dedicated only to the problem of physical survival, a daily battle which Obertyshev seems likely to win. Unencumbered by moral principles (where, one wonders, did *his* stock of firewood come from?) or by any susceptibility to compassion, Obertyshev is perfectly equipped to ensure the safety of his brood, an ability which immediately distinguishes him from Martin Martinych, who is quite incapable of coping with the lesser demand of looking after himself and an ailing, neurotic wife.

Obertyshev is a genius of physical adaptation, the apple of a Lamarckian eye, and it is this feature which is constantly stressed in the imagery used to describe him. His unshaven face is a 'wasteland overgrown with a sort of red, dusty tumbleweed', his teeth are of 'yellow stone', and the flick of his tongue is compared to the movement of the tail of a lizard, a creature, appropriately enough, quite perfectly adapted to the rigours of desert life and cave dwelling (p. 188).

Selikhov, by contrast, is no mere beast, yet he is, no less than Obertyshev, one in whom the instinct for self-preservation is developed in the highest degree. On the face of it, Selikhov is more attractive than Obertyshev. During his interview with Martin Martinych, he reveals himself to be a man not insensitive to the plight of others and he seems sincerely to regret having to defend the interests of Obertyshev and his ilk. Yet, beneath this veneer of concern there is a cynicism in Selikhov which is perhaps even more repugnant than Obertyshev's brute self-interest. For all his professed sympathy with Martin Martinych, he does no more to help him than Obertyshev, and his repeated refrain—'What a laugh!' *(Potekha!)*—severely undermines his claim to humanity. For him the revolution is ultimately little more than a source of amusing anecdotes. If Selikhov *does* have any principles, he is never the less quite willing to jettison them when it is expedient to do so; his path to survival lies along the line of least resistance. What is more, Selikhov's behaviour places him, willy nilly, in a symbiotic relationship with Obertyshev; each relies on the other to ensure the continuance of their species.

At this point, it may also be noted that the very names of the characters seem to have been selected deliberately to harmonize with their roles in the story. Obertyshev is the most interesting in this respect. His surname derives from the verb *obyortyvat'/obernut'*, which has the primary meaning 'to wrap up'. In the harsh world of the new Ice Age, wrapping up is an activity of the most crucial importance; it is the first essential for survival and one which is, moreover, specifically mentioned in both the first and the second paragraphs of the story: 'more and more hairy animal skins have to be *wound about* oneself'; 'the cave men, *swathed* in skins, in overcoats, in rags' (p. 185). The Russian verbs in both these extracts *(navyortyvat', zavyornutyye)* are from the same root as *obyortyvat'*, making the connection both semantic and etymological. It seems quite fitting, therefore, that when we first encounter Obertyshev, he is kitted out, as the complete cave man surely should be, in a 'coat tied tightly with a string' (p. 188). Apart from this literal meaning the same Russian verb is also commonly encountered in the phrase 'obernut' v svoyu pol'zu' ('to turn something to one's own advantage'), an ability that Obertyshev, it hardly needs saying, possesses in the highest degree. Finally, his name is related to *oboroten'* ('werewolf'), an association which again seems uncannily appropriate to one whose humanity is so severely compromised.

Selikhov's name is less complex. It has its root in the verb *selit'* ('to settle'), and is hence eminently suitable for one who has become chairman of a housing committee. The names Martin Martinych and Masha, on the other hand, are less obviously meaningful. That we never learn their surname at all might be taken as a sign that the characters themselves have somehow lost their 'meaning', that they have no designated place in the new world. It has been pointed out to me that the name Martin Martinych is not, however, altogether devoid of

connotations:[12] Martyn is a character who figures in a number of Russian proverbs, in which he is distinguished by his impracticality.[13] Martin Martinych, of course, shares this failing. What is more, his impracticality is constantly linked in the story with the Obertyshev motif of 'wrapping up'. Martin Martinych's prime objective, we should remember, is not simply to heat his apartment, but to heat it to such a degree that he and Masha will be able to throw off their 'animal skins' (p. 186). Natural though this urge might seem, it would have been an almost criminal extravagance in the conditions of the time. The notion of 'wrapping up' is also called forth in the repeated refrain '*tuzhe uzel, yeshchyo tuzhe*' ('tighten the knot, tighter still'), which occurs at those moments in the story when Martin Martinych attempts to defy his own nature and act in accordance with the cave-man ethos.

From the discussion so far, it would seem that **"The Cave"** amply justifies the charge laid against it by A. K. Voronsky, who complained that the story would afford 'undoubted satisfaction to the most violent enemies of October'.[14] The Bolshevik Revolution, in Zamyatin's version, has unleashed an implacable evolutionary process, in which survival, true to the Darwinian principle, is guaranteed to the fittest. Quite obviously, this is a process which offers little hope for humanity, as positive qualities reside only in the one character most certainly doomed to extinction. This is the argument developed, almost in realization of Voronsky's fears, by Susan Layton, in whose eyes Martin Martinych is the embodiment specifically of the intellectual values which are inevitably forfeit under the selective pressures unleashed by revolution.[15]

To interpret **"The Cave"** in this way, however, is to read it on one 'plane' only, reducing it to a rather crude propaganda piece, and hence ignoring the profound ambivalence in Zamyatin's treatment of his central hero. It is also to impute to Zamyatin a reverence for the pre-revolutionary intelligentsia and its culture that he, as a self-professed 'Scythian', certainly did not entertain.[16] His concern for the plight of the contemporary Russian intellectual was, in fact, tempered with a strong element of criticism. In his memoir of Blok, for example (whose death was somehow emblematic of the fate of the pre-revolutionary intelligentsia), he wrote with wry humour: 'We had all become used to surrogates; we ate pancakes made from potato peelings and drank water instead of wine. But Blok tried persistently to turn the water into wine'.[17] The intelligentsia, in Zamyatin's eyes, had fallen victim not simply to the times, but also to its own unwillingness, or inability, to cast off an attachment to habits of mind and behaviour which had no place in the post-revolutionary world. This idea finds cruel, satirical expression in **"The Land Surveyor"** (**"Zemlemer"**) and **"Mamay."** The latter story is especially pertinent here, as it deals with the central problem of the relationship between the intellectual and the cultural heritage. The grotesque account of Mamay's lust for a rare second-hand book (it is described specifically in terms of sublimated sexuality) is perhaps the most graphic illustration of Zamyatin's Scythian scorn for the 'man of culture', who is exposed here as nothing more than a bourgeois fetishist.

"Mamay" is an extreme case; there is obviously a world of difference between the crude caricature in that story and the infinitely more subtle and sensitive characterization of Martin Martinych in "The Cave." Yet Martin Martinych is not entirely without taint: when scratched, it is with the blood of Mamay that he bleeds. Consider, for example, the description of the apartment:

> In the Petersburg bedroom-cave it was as it had been not long ago in Noah's Ark: a diluvian disorder of beasts clean and unclean. A desk of mahogany; books; Stone-Age pancakes that looked like pottery; Skryabin, Opus 74; a flat-iron; five potatoes scrubbed lovingly to shining whiteness; nickel-plated bedstead frames; an axe; a chiffonier; firewood.
>
> (p. 186)

This is a perfect example of Zamyatin's extreme economy of means; it is 'high-voltage' prose in action.[18] Each detail is carefully chosen not only to characterize the lifestyle of the apartment's occupants, but also to highlight their present crisis. The objects divide equally into those which conjure up the spirit of past grandeur (the desk, the books, the piano music, the bedsteads, and the chiffonier), and those which manifest the threat of present exigencies (the pancakes, the iron, the potatoes, the axe, and the firewood). The objects from the past, it should be emphasized, identify Martin Martinych from the outset not so much as the guardian of cultural values, but rather as one who has enjoyed bourgeois luxury. As is so often the case in literature, the listing device functions here as a grand leveller; cultural items and luxury items are lumped together indiscriminately so that they become virtually indistinguishable. So it is with Martin Martinych's entire endeavour: his refusal to sacrifice the life of the spirit to the demands of the flesh is, at the same time (and quite paradoxically), a refusal to be parted from what can now only be a symbolic reminder of the life of luxury and ease that he had previously enjoyed. In the disturbing logic of the story, the one seems to be inextricably bound up with the other. A concern for cultural values, Zamyatin implies, is essentially a bourgeois concern, and here he places his finger on one of the most troublesome issues of the early Soviet period.[19]

Apart from their immediate relevance, several of the objects listed in the initial description of the apartment prove to be of direct importance in the story which follows. The firewood, of course, is the axis around which

the whole plot revolves. The books and the furniture are also mentioned again later, featuring prominently in the all-important conversation between Obertyshev and Martin Martinych:

> 'Well then, how's the wife? How's the wife? How's the wife?'
>
> 'Just the same, Aleksey Ivanych, just the same. Bad. And tomorrow her name-day too, and I've nothing for the fire'.
>
> 'You should use the chairs, Martin Martinych, and the cupboards . . . The books too: books make an excellent fire, excellent, excellent . . .'
>
> 'But you know yourself that none of the furniture is ours, except for the piano . . .'
>
> 'Of course. Yes, of course . . . A terrible shame, a terrible shame'.
>
> (p. 189)

Fully evident in this extract is Zamyatin's fine ear for dialogue. Tone and expression are captured perfectly: Martin Martinych's woefully inadequate disingenuousness, Obertyshev's patent insincerity and odious familiarity (in the untranslatable diminutives *stul'chiki, shkafchiki*) are all rendered with a ruthless and impressive authenticity. But this is no mere black-and-white confrontation between civilized humanity and the new 'cave man'. Although our sympathies will tend naturally to lie with Martin Martinych, we cannot ignore the deeper implications of this conversation. Obertyshev, despite the fact that he would no more consider offering firewood to his neighbour than he would contemplate depriving himself of a limb, is not all callous disregard. His suggestions are typically and eminently practicable. The use of books and furniture as fuel was, of course, commonplace at the time. Moreover, Martin Martinych's explanation of why he is unable to follow this advice is hollow in the extreme. Whilst we might accept his unwillingness to burn furniture that isn't his own (would Obertyshev have been troubled by such scruples, however?), he offers no reason at all why the books, or the piano, which *are* his property, cannot be put to the purpose. Obertyshev doesn't push the matter; Martin Martinych' welfare is, after all, his own affair, and Obertyshev probably knows from experience that his practical suggestions will fall on deaf ears.

The conversation with Obertyshev casts a different light upon Martin Martinych's behaviour. Whilst there is still no doubt about his essential humanity, he can no longer be viewed simply as the innocent plaything of fate. Ultimately, at least in part, the problem is of his own making; if Martin Martinych feels that he is obliged to steal, it is because the combination of his impracticality and his unrealistic objectives has made it necessary.

These considerations lead inevitably to a re-examination of Martin Martinych's motives and of his entire endeavour. What, precisely, is he trying to do? Ostensibly, as we have seen, his objective is to ensure that his wife is able to celebrate her name-day in comfort. But that will not explain why the books or the piano cannot be burnt. The real explanation lies elsewhere. Martin Martinych, albeit unconsciously, is being less than honest with himself when he imagines he is acting purely in his wife's interests. Masha's name-day is, in fact, a convenient accident which allows him to realise, and, more importantly, to legitimate, his own desire to escape from a threatening present into the safety of a Golden Age of the past. This imperative is detectable from the very outset, even as we learn that it is Masha's name-day:

> But if you were to close your eyes and only listen to her, you could still believe that she's the same, and that any moment now she will laugh, get out of bed and embrace you. And that knife against glass an hour ago wasn't her voice, not her at all . . .
>
> (p. 186)

Martin Martinych wants to recreate a past which exists in his and Masha's fantasy. For the illusion to succeed, not a single book nor a stick of furniture must be destroyed: hence his intransigence on that point.

Martin Martinych's efforts are rewarded; when the 'celebration' begins, Masha plays her own part in conjuring up the comforting myth:

> 'Do you remember, Marty: my blue room, and the piano with its cover, and the little wooden horse, the ashtray, on the piano? And you came up from behind . . .'
>
> Yes, that evening the universe had been created, and there was the amazing, wise muzzle of the moon, and the nightingale trill of the bells in the corridor.
>
> 'Do you remember, Marty: the open window, the green sky—and, down below, from another world, the organ-grinder?'
>
> Organ-grinder, miraculous organ-grinder, where are you?
>
> 'And on the quay . . . Remember? The branches still bare, the water rosy, and a last blue ice-floe, like a coffin, floating by. And the coffin was only funny because we would never die. Remember?'
>
> (p. 192)

This is a moment of lyrical intensity; once more, the narrative voice briefly becomes one with Martin Martinych's own. But the idyllic fantasy is obviously fragile. Martin Martinych himself is conscious all the while that the illusion cannot be sustained for very long. Even as he listens to Masha, he is aware of Obertyshev, downstairs, discovering the theft of the logs and setting the process of nemesis in motion. And the very lyricism of the passage is equally fragile, as it is consistently exposed to the pressure of irony, which is generated by the fact that the images by which Martin Martinych's

and Masha's idyll is conveyed (the ice-floe and the rosy waters of the river) distinctly recall two prominent details from the story's 'epic' opening: the metaphorical glaciers and the allusion to the Flood. The images of ice and water are, however, put to quite opposite uses. On the epic scale they are symbols of danger and catastrophe; here, on the other hand, they are transformed into harmless and comforting emblems of security.

Just as the lyric voice is undercut by the reminders of the epic vision, so the private world of myth is unable to hold out against the tide of historical reality. The 'universe' created by Martin Martinych and Masha (again Zamyatin's ironic tone is unmistakeable in the use of this word), like their faith in their immortality, is a grotesque conceit. And it is this conceit which is finally exposed as the story reaches its climax.

The turning point comes during Martin Martinych's fateful interview with Selikhov. The conversation between the two men is rendered dramatically, but it is interspersed with brief passages which go far beyond the function of simple commentary:

> . . . Martin Martinych laughed louder and louder, so as to throw more firewood into Selikhov, so that he wouldn't stop . . .
>
> . . . . .
>
> In boots and fur coat—mammoth-like—(Selikhov) straightened up and recovered his breath.
>
> . . . . .
>
> The study floor is an ice-floe; barely audibly, the ice-floe cracked, broke away from the shore, and swept away, whirling Martin Martinych round, and from the distant shore of the divan over there Selikhov can hardly be heard.
>
> . . . . .
>
> The ice-floe went faster and faster. Tiny, flattened, barely visible—a mere wood-chip—Martin Martinych answered . . .
>
> . . . . .
>
> In the cave it was still dark. Martin Martinych—cold, clay, blind—stumbled dully into the diluvian disorder of objects in the cave.
>
> (pp. 194-5)

What is involved here is something incomparably more serious than the threat of being made to answer for a minor misdemeanour: this is the moment when the theme of man and history, which had been held in abeyance since the opening paragraphs, is finally resolved.

Before considering this passage in detail, two general comments are in order. The first relates to the curious status of the narrative voice in the extracts cited. What are we dealing with here, the epic or the lyric voice? Ultimately, it is impossible to say, because the 'epic' and the 'lyric' have now fused in such a way as to have become indistinguishable. This is the sign of a new awareness in Martin Martinych, whose consciousness has been expanded to accommodate a far broader scale of understanding. We are witnessing a moment of tragic *anagnorisis*. Secondly, it should be stressed that the narrative at this point is of extreme density. These brief extracts constitute a complex web of metaphorical and mythic associations which reverberate throughout the entire story. But, as is commonly the case with Zamyatin's writing of this period, it is at the point of the greatest density that the key to the system of imagery is provided. The system is obviously not a static one (although much of the critical literature on Zamyatin's style tends to give this impression); on the contrary, it is highly dynamic. And it must also be realised that the reader is given to penetrate the system at the precise moment in the story when Martin Martinych too arrives at a new level of awareness. In this way, Zamyatin forges a disturbing bond of identification between the reader and his hero.

Let us now return to the passage under discussion. I shall take the details individually and in order. The first two (Selikhov as stove/cave-god; Selikhov as mammoth) serve simply to signal the return of the epic voice, permitting us to see beyond the surface of events (housing-committee chairman upbraiding erring resident) to the deeper meaning that lies beyond. The image of the ice-floe similarly requires little in the way of commentary. It is a cruel, yet undeniable, law that demands that Martin Martinych should experience nemesis in terms of the very images of ice and water which had symbolized the security and serenity of the private world of fantasy. The fantasy, of course, is rudely disrupted by Martin Martinych's present experience. He is no longer a placid observer looking out on the river from the safety of a room; he is a desperate victim, cast adrift on the icy flood waters of history. The ironic reversal is neatly recapitulated in the subsequent oxymoron: 'the immortal organ-grinder is dead' (p. 196).

The image of the swirling waters of the river naturally recalls the earlier allusion to the Deluge. Indeed, the earlier passage is specifically called to mind by the repetition of the exact phrase, 'diluvian disorder', which had accompanied the initial comparison of Martin Martinych's apartment to Noah's Ark. The effect again is clearly ironic, as the mythic subtext is now turned on its head. In the biblical story, Noah and his family, chosen by God as the only people worthy of salvation in a world overrun by decadence, are *survivors,* and their survival itself constitutes a pledge of the underlying justice of the divine process. Martin Martinych only too obviously fails to emulate the example of his biblical counterpart. His 'ark' is as unsubstantial as the other products of his fantasy world.

Instead of enabling him to survive, it is transformed into the treacherous ice-floe which will sweep him away to inevitable destruction. Just as the biblical myth is inverted, so is its meaning: Zamyatin's 'Noah' occupies a world which is governed not by the will of a wise, just God, but by a blind, natural process in which justice has no place.

Survival, in this world, goes not to the best, but to the fittest. Selikhov, even though he has not been unaffected by the rigours of life in the cave (his massive bulk has been halved in weight), will never the less be untouched by the flood waters; he remains safely on the shore as Martin Martinych's ice-floe drifts away. Obertyshev too, is perfectly equipped to deal with this adversity. The significance of an earlier image now becomes apparent. The first mention of Obertyshev had come when Martin Martinych had heard him chopping his firewood: 'downstairs, at the Obertyshevs', the stone axe chips the snag from the barge, the stone axe chops Martin Martinych to pieces' (pp. 187-8—this image is echoed in the metaphor of Martin Martinych as a 'wood-chip'). Obertyshev's 'barge' is the very antithesis of Martin Martinych's 'ark'. The biblical vessel, as it turns out, is the perfect (though ironic) symbol for Martin Martinych's endeavour, being richly suggestive both of his unwarrented faith in his own destiny and of his adherence to a system of values which Zamyatin would certainly have considered completely outmoded. To an equal extent, the barge is a most appropriate metaphor for the totally utilitarian voyage on which Obertyshev has embarked. Whilst Martin Martinych's ark proves completely unseaworthy, Obertyshev's barge, we feel sure, will safely negotiate the flood waters of history, its progress having been guaranteed by its master's careful preparatory work in clearing it of the snag represented by such antediluvian types as Martin Martinych.

Two other important images recur in the above extracts. When Martin Martinych stumbles blindly onto the objects in his apartment, we are reminded of an earlier passage in which he was compared to a 'bird which had flown into a room from the open air, dashing itself senselessly, blindly against the ceiling' (p. 188). The notions of captivity and inescapability conveyed by this simile are reinforced, on the same page, by the comparison of his clanking bucket to the rattle of convicts' fetters. Retrospectively, these images are imbued with a significance which is both prophetic and symbolic. The room into which Martin Martinych has flown may be understood both literally and metaphorically: it is both the last heated room of the apartment and the 'room' of private fantasy into which admission is gained by closing the eyes, an act of self-imposed, albeit temporary, 'blindness'. Either way, the refuge is illusory; both rooms are prison cells from which there is no possibility of escape or release.

There remains one final detail: the epithet 'clay'. Taken in isolation, this repeated metaphor would seem transparent enough, suggesting the softness and vulnerability of Martin Martinych's character and contrasting with the 'stone' features of Obertyshev (hence, Martin Martinych 'dents' his clay flesh when he knocks against the pile of logs in Obertyshev's apartment, p. 189). The epithet acquires a peculiar opacity, however, because of its association with the mythic figure of Adam, an association which is established in the first of the 'epic' asides: '(many have clay faces nowadays: back to Adam)' (p. 187). The purpose of this biblical allusion is most difficult to ascertain, all the more so as it is bound to cause confusion due to its close proximity to the reference to Noah's Ark. Is Zamyatin proposing Martin Martinych both as a new Noah, *and* as a new Adam, we might wonder on an initial reading? Even when the ironic purpose of the Noah allusion is finally understood, the full significance of the association with Adam is still, however, far from clear. Whilst it may safely be assumed that this mythic reference is intended to raise the story of Martin Martinych to the level of existential tragedy, this assumption in itself leads us no closer to comprehension. A literal reading of the myth would lead to an interpretation of **"The Cave"** as a re-enactment of the fall of man, with Masha as a sort of Eve figure leading Martin Martinych into error. There may well be something to this line of reasoning: certainly, it should not be forgotten that Zamyatin *does* use the Fall as the central sub-text in *We*.[20] But there are, I suspect, few readers who would wish to insist too strongly on such a standard 'biblical' interpretation of **"The Cave."** Indeed, it is possible that the real clue to the Adam reference resides not in the bible itself, but in Zamyatin's own article 'On Synthetism', where the author refers to Adam in the context of his argument about Realism and Symbolism. In the Realist vision, Zamyatin explains (in terms which make the connection with **"The Cave"** quite unmistakable), 'Adam is only clay, the world is only clay'.[21] The Symbolist vision, on the other hand, has created an Adam deprived of flesh and blood; he is a creature of pure spirit located in a realm far removed from the brute world of clay. It is the task of Neo-Realism, the author concludes, to provide for a synthesis of the two competing visions.

The relevance of this discussion to **"The Cave"** will become apparent if we substitute sociological categories for the terms Realism and Symbolism. Martin Martinych is an intellectual who has come to live a rarefied existence, in which the exigencies of the flesh and the world of mere clay have been conveniently forgotten. His experience of the Revolution, therefore, has served primarily to alert him to this fundamental conceit and to remind him, alas painfully, that he is a man like any other, even such a brutish individual as Obertyshev. In this interpretation, of course, the reference to Adam has been stripped of its mythic meaning (this is true of 'On Synthetism' as well); Zamyatin has invoked the name of our mythic forbear simply as a novel way of stating

the age-old Russian problem of the gulf between the intelligentsia and the people. Like the Eloi and the Morlocks in H. G. Wells' *The Time Machine,* Martin Martinych and Obertyshev are the extreme representatives of two social classes which have grown so far apart as to be considered different biological species. The problem, as Zamyatin was only too obviously aware, was how to achieve the synthesis which would re-unite spirit and flesh and provide the basis for new progress.

The fate of Martin Martinych may be read, therefore, as Zamyatin's obituary both on Symbolism (hence his hero's predilection for Skryabin, the Symbolist composer *par excellence*) and, more broadly, on the 'entropic' state of pre-revolutionary Russian culture.[22]

Mention of entropy returns us inevitably to the point with which we began—the place of **"The Cave"** amongst Zamyatin's other statements, fictional and non-fictional, on the subject of revolution. **"The Cave"** is, without doubt, one of the writer's most pessimistic works, fully justifying Voronsky's misgiving about it. In the first place, it is a story in which Zamyatin expresses the fear, common enough amongst the intellectuals of his day, that the Revolution had unleashed an indiscriminate brute force which was sweeping away the good along with the bad. For Zamyatin, however, this also signified a retreat from the Scythian joy in the destruction of the old world which had informed **"The Land Surveyor"** and **"Mamay."** **"The Cave"** explores precisely the possibilities that the Scythian formula had ignored: that animal vigour not only promises to renew life but also threatens to reduce it to the level of primitive bestiality; and that bourgeois society, although decadent, has never the less fostered positive human attributes. What would probably have been far worse in the eyes of those like Voronsky, however, was the fact that **"The Cave"** implicitly challenged the belief in social progress which is the basic tenet of the Marxist view of history. Zamyatin's story offers a far less attractive vision of the historical process; here we witness the operation of a blind evolutionary force which guarantees no improvement for mankind, but only the endless repetition of a seemingly inescapable tragedy.

These remarks suggest that there is a profound ambivalence in Zamyatin's thoughts on revolution, a tension between his idealistic hopes for what revolution might achieve and his more sober reflections on its actual results. One need look no further for confirmation of this supposition than the article 'Tomorrow' ('Zavtra'), which dates from the same period as **"The Cave"** and provides an important gloss on it. 'Tomorrow' begins with a bold assertion of Zamyatin's faith in progress, which, as usual, is expressed in dialectical terms: 'Every today is simultaneously a cradle and a shroud: a shroud for yesterday, a cradle for tomorrow . . . Yesterday, the thesis; today, the antithesis; tomorrow, the synthesis'.[23] Zamyatin proceeds to illustrate this optimistic principle by referring to the example of the Revolution itself: 'Yesterday there was a tsar and there were slaves; today there is no tsar, but the slaves remain; tomorrow there will be only tsars'.[24] But it was, inevitably, from the position of 'today' that Zamyatin was writing, and the main thrust of his article is to expose the present dangers which threaten the realization of the future synthesis. In one of his most memorable statements, he laments: 'Man is dying. Proud *homo erectus* is going down on all fours, growing fangs and fur; the beast is gaining ascendency over man'.[25]

The connections between **"The Cave"** and 'Tomorrow' are obvious. Obertyshev, the new cave man, is the embodiment of Zamyatin's worst fears for humanity. He is the man of 'today'. Martin Martinych, on the other hand, is identified as the man of 'yesterday', and the failure of his endeavour is described specifically in the language of the article:

> The 29th of October was dead, and the immortal organ-grinder was dead too, as were the ice-floes on the rosy sunset waters and Masha herself. And that was good. There must be no fantastic tomorrow, no Obertyshev or Selikhov, no Masha and no Martin Martinych: everything must die.
>
> (p. 196)

The same terms had cropped up earlier in the formulation of the 'law' of cave life: '"tomorrow" is incomprehensible in the cave; only in centuries' time would people come to know "tomorrow", "the day after tomorrow"' (p. 191)

If 'Tomorrow' helps to bring Zamyatin's concerns in **"The Cave"** into sharper focus, the story itself, in its own turn, points up the major weakness of the dialectic expounded in the article. How, we may ask, is the qualitative jump to the future synthesis to be achieved? **"The Cave"** supplies no answer; indeed, the very logic of the story points towards the *impossibility* of any higher state. The world of **"The Cave"** is populated only by 'slaves'—slaves of 'yesterday', and slaves of 'today'. Martin Martinych and Masha, as slaves of yesterday, can, by definition, have no place in the world of tomorrow. But Selikhov and Obertyshev are also barred from entry. They are the slaves of today; their very survival has depended on their singular ability *not* to think of tomorrow. If they are to be the only survivors, what hope can there possibly be for a future when 'there will be only tsars'?

As a statement of faith in revolutionary progress, 'Tomorrow', although undoubtedly sincere, is patently unconvincing. And by comparing the article with **"The Cave,"** we can easily see why this should be so. The dialectical model employed in 'Tomorrow' offers a false

resolution to the binary opposition which finds literary expression in **"The Cave."** Like Zamyatin's other major works of this period, *The Islanders* and *We,* **"The Cave"** demands that it be understood in terms of the clash of 'energy' and 'entropy'. In *The Islanders* and *We,* however, this basic opposition is developed rather differently than in **"The Cave."** Both works tell the story of a battle between heretics (Didi Lloyd; I-330) and representatives of the *status quo* (Vicar Dewly; the One State) for the soul of an individual who vacillates between the two extremes (Campbell, D-503). The outcome, in both cases, is a victory for the forces of entropy, this being the tragic law of life. The forces of energy in these works, we should note, are bold and life-affirming, whilst the forces of entropy (particularly the odious Vicar Dewly) inspire our moral disgust. In **"The Cave,"** as we have seen, our moral sympathies are aligned quite differently. Here it is the forces of energy that are repugnant. Obertyshev and Selikhov are no heretics; their instinct for survival can provoke neither respect nor admiration. Martin Martinych, on the other hand, is far more attractive. He is no militant defender of the *status quo* and no hypocrite; what is more, he brings about the ruin of no one but himself. But, whichever way the conflict is stated, the result is equally tragic for humanity, for it is man's nobler instincts—be it the urge for freedom or an innate moral integrity—which are destroyed.

The tragic vision of **"The Cave,"** like that of *The Islanders* and *We,* is obviously born of an intense idealism, the 'morbus rossica', as Zamyatin called it, a 'love demanding all or nothing'.[26] The cruel nihilism of **"The Cave"** might perhaps be compared to Dostoyevsky's famous 'furnace of doubt': it embodies a spirit of negation against which Zamyatin was constantly struggling. Time and again we find him striving towards a more optimistic statement, both in his articles, like 'Tomorrow', and in such fictional works as **"The Story of the Most Important Thing."** Even in *We,* Zamyatin leaves a 'loophole' by having the pregnant 0-90 escape to the other side of the Green Wall. Yet it might be argued that the dialectic of hope is never quite convincing. In **"The Story of the Most Important Thing"** it is simply too contrived; in *We* the potential promise offered by what is happening on the other side of the Green Wall remains vague and insubstantial, in marked contrast to the stark immediacy of the events we actually witness on *this* side of it.

In **"The Cave,"** as in Zamyatin's work as a whole, it is the tragic vision which prevails. It has been suggested that the pessimism of Zamyatin's fiction is more apparent than real, that it should be understood as 'a literary device to spur the reader to thought and action'.[27] Zamyatin himself would certainly have liked to think so. Most revealing in this respect is the following comment from his article on Sologub, whose satirical genius he describes as a 'whip':

> The whip is still undervalued as an instrument for human progress. I know of nothing more effective than the whip for raising man from all fours, for stopping man from falling on his knees before anyone and anything. I am, of course, not speaking of whips woven from things; I am speaking of whips woven from words . . .[28]

Such faith in the power of literature to transform humanity seems typically and unmistakably Russian. Yet it is difficult to read **"The Cave"** as a call to action. It is more likely, in our own cynical age at least, that it will be seen as the ghost which refused to be exorcised and as the expression of Zamyatin's deep-seated acknowledgement that revolution is an impossible dream.

Notes

I would like to express my gratitude to my colleague at Otago University, Peter Stupples, and to my former teacher and colleague, Svetlana le Fleming, both of whom read an earlier version of this article and made generous and valuable suggestions for its improvement.

1. See, however, Susan Layton, 'The Symbolic Dimension of *The Cave* by Zamjatin', (*Studies in Short Fiction*, XIII, 1976, pp. 455-61); J. J. van Baak, 'Zamjatin's Cave: on Troglodyte versus Urban Culture, Myth, and the Semiotics of Literary Space' (*Russian Literature*, X, 1981, pp. 381-422). Van Baak reads *The Cave* as a clash of cultural codes, depicted through 'recurrent features of binarity'.

2. Alex M. Shane, *The Life and Works of Evgenij Zamjatin*, Berkeley and Los Angeles, 1968, pp. 165-6.

3. Ye. Zamyatin, *Litsa*, New York, 1967, p. 237.

4. Ibid., p. 238.

5. For the third meaning of 'dislocation of planes', see 'The New Russian Prose' ('Novaya Russkaya Proza'), ibid., p. 200, where it occurs in a discussion of Pil'nyak's writing and refers to the technique of combining separate stories within the one narrative framework.

6. Ye. Zamyatin, *Sobraniye sochineniy,* Vol. III, Moscow, 1929, p. 185. All further references to *The Cave* will be incorporated in the text, noting the page number. Other references to this edition will be abbreviated in the footnotes, using the notation SS, followed by the volume and page numbers. All translations and italics are my own.

7. Cf. the opening of *A Fisher of Men (Lovets chelovekov),* where wartime London is described as follows: 'The light columns of druid temples, which only yesterday were factory chimneys' (SS, III, p. 95).

8. For a brief but lucid account of this style, see: Roy Pascal, *The Dual Voice. Free Indirect Speech and its Functioning in the Nineteenth-Century European Novel,* Manchester and New Jersey, 1977.

9. See 'On Story and Plot' ('O syuzhete i fabule'), translated as 'Theme and Plot' in *A Soviet Heretic. Essays by Yevgeniy Zamyatin,* edited and translated by Mirra Ginsburg, Chicago, 1970, pp. 165-74.

10. In an earlier story, *April (Aprel'),* a similar blue phial had contained medicine used to cure migraine.

11. SS, II, p. 86.

12. I am indebted to Svetlana le Fleming for this piece of information.

13. The change of the name from the Russian Martyn to the Europeanized Martin would support the view of Martin Martinych as an effete intellectual, cut off from his national roots. See below.

14. A. Voronsky, *Stat'i,* Ann Arbor, 1980, p. 76.

15. Layton, op. cit.

16. See, in particular, 'Scythians,' ('Skify li?'), *A Soviet Heretic,* pp. 21-33.

17. *Litsa,* p. 20.

18. The term is Zamyatin's own, see: *Litsa,* p. 255.

19. For a short, but wide-ranging, discussion of this subject, see Boris Thomson, *Lot's Wife and the Venus of Milo: Conflicting Attitudes to the Cultural Heritage in Modern Russia,* Cambridge, 1978.

20. See, R. Gregg, 'Two Adams and Eve in the Crystal Palace', in *Major Soviet Writers,* edited by E. J. Brown, New York, 1973, pp. 202-8.

21. *Litsa,* pp. 233-4.

22. It is typical of Zamyatin's quirky humour that he should have chosen the music of Skryabin to adorn Martin Martinych's piano. The author himself had the highest regard for Skryabin's work. In a letter to Annenkov, he placed the Russian composer's name alongside those of Shakespeare and Dostoyevsky as an example of the artistic heretic (Yu. Annenkov, *Dnevnik moikh vstrech. Tsikl tragedii,* I, New York, 1966, p. 258). Readers of *We* will, of course, remember that it is Skryabin's music that D-503 hears performed by I-330.

23. *Litsa,* p. 173.

24. Loc. cit.

25. Ibid., p. 174.

26. Ibid., p. 37.

27. Shane, p. 132.

28. *Litsa*, p. 35.

Philip Cavendish (essay date 2000)

SOURCE: Cavendish, Philip. "Playing Devil's Advocate: Paradox and Parody in Zamiatin's 'The Miracle of Ash Wednesday'." In *Russian Literature and Its Demons*, edited by Pamela Davidson, pp. 441-72. New York: Berghahn Books, 2000.

[*In the following essay, Cavendish delineates how Zamyatin "adopts 'devil's advocacy' as a form of post-symbolist literary conceit" in his story "O chude, prois-shed shem v Pepel' nuiu Sredu" ("The Miracle of Ash Wednesday").*]

To discuss demonism in the work of Evgenii Zamiatin might at first glance appear misguided. Despite an Orthodox background—his father was a priest and his mother the daughter of a priest—Zamiatin was either an agnostic or an atheist for whom the sacred truths of Christian belief were essentially fictions. For much of his career, both in terms of his fiction and his journalistic writing, he preached the values of heresy and intellectual rebellion, quoting approvingly in 1924 Anatole France's paradoxical statement that "it requires extraordinary strength of spirit to be a non-believer."[1] Like France, Zamiatin adhered in his fiction to the values of relativism, irony, and scepticism, preferring to believe in the virtue of revolt for its own sake, irrespective of the prevailing ideological system. As is well known, his persistent challenge to Bolshevik "orthodoxies" in the field of literature and the arts after the October Revolution led to his gradual exclusion from cultural life and subsequent exile abroad in 1931.

Unlike the symbolists, for whom the relationship between religion and art was a central element in their philosophical and aesthetic inquiry, Zamiatin would doubtless have denied the ontological status of the Devil. This did not mean, however, that he denied the Devil symbolic status, or status as a cultural, social, or psychological metaphor. Zamiatin's Romantic identification with Lucifer as the "spirit of doubt and eternal rebellion" is present both in his art and in his journalism.[2] Furthermore, he was perfectly capable of donning a Satanic mask when his narrative conceit required it, a prime example being the three "miracle tales" or *chudesa*: **"The Saintly Sin of the Precious Virgin. A Eulogy"** (**"O sviatom grekhe Zenitsy-devy. Slovo pokhval'noe,"** 1917), **"The Healing of the Novice Erasmus"** (**"O tom, kak istselen byl otrok Erazm,"** 1922), and **"The Miracle of Ash Wednesday"** (**"O chude, proisshedshem v Pepel'nuiu Sredu,"** 1926).[3] If, citing Erasmus, the work of the Devil consists of "anything that deters us from Christ and his teaching," then these tales are clearly demonically inspired.[4] Not only are they blasphemous attacks on the values promoted in the legends of the saints, but as parodies which assume the guises of sacred texts only to subvert their edificatory function, they can be read as literary forgeries whose *jouissance,* to borrow briefly from Barthes, consists of gradually stripping away the impression of authenticity to reveal the underlying burlesque and carnivalesque intent.[5] Indeed, in their use of the obscene, the bawdy, and the grotesque, and in their general formalistic playfulness, they have their roots in the sphere which Bakhtin has defined as carnival, laughter, or "anti-world" culture, a sphere in which official values, rituals, and modes of expression are mocked and subverted.[6] Thus the demon which haunts these narratives is not so much the defiant and gloomy rebel of Romantic poetry, but rather the scandal-mongering joker of the folk-religious imagination. He is the demon of vaudevillean laughter and street theatre, the mask-wearing charlatan, manipulator, and intriguer, the crude vulgarian who seeks to provoke, corrupt, and play tricks on the naive and gullible.[7]

In **"The Miracle of Ash Wednesday"** Zamiatin adopts "devil's advocacy" as a form of post-symbolist literary conceit. The fatal paradox, according to which art is viewed as a collaborative continuation with God of Creation, but a collaboration inevitably tainted with the Satanic because it rivals that Creation, is here radically transformed, even parodied, in a display of ludic provocation. The artist-demiurge of symbolist poetics is replaced by the artist-buffoon or *skomorokh,* the strolling minstrel whose bawdy laughter and song was associated in the medieval imagination with the work of the Devil.[8] The antics of the modern artist-*skomorokh*, insofar as they applied to literature and art, envisaged a wide range of transgressive behaviour: commitment to "low genres," such as *skaz*-style narration; interest in the apocryphal, marginal, and censored; subversion of religious and secular institutions; celebration of the erotic, the obscene, and the sexually taboo; promotion of the verbal prank and whimsical joke as legitimate literary subjects; and a penchant for the fanciful, absurd, and bizarre. In spirit, Zamiatin's hagiographical parodies are influenced greatly by the carnivalesque experiments of Gogol, in particular his vision of the Devil as the embodiment of the absurd and the deceptive.[9] **"The Miracle of Ash Wednesday"** features the Devil as a fictional character in his own right; furthermore, as an authorial alter ego, this Devil is a subversive and corrupting presence who threatens the coherence and logicality of the text. This text constitutes a surreal riddle which challenges not only the desired norms of serious and ideologically correct Soviet literature in the 1920s, but also the expectation of sense on the part of the reader. It is the challenge of unravelling this riddle, and drawing out the demonic strategy inherent in Zamiatin's tale, which provides the central focus of this essay.

In order to appreciate **"The Miracle of Ash Wednesday"** as an example of demonic mask-play, consideration needs to be given to a broad range of literary and aesthetic influences. The first part of this essay examines Zamiatin's interest in hagiography, an interest shared by many writers in the second half of the nineteenth century and after. The adaptations of *vitae* undertaken by Leo Tolstoi and Anatole France, for example, in Zamiatin's view the great religious heretics of his time, are important in this regard. I will be drawing attention to the stylized, parodic features of Zamiatin's earlier *chudesa*, their use of bawdy and obscene images, and the ways in which they constitute a transgression of ecclesiastical norms.

In this context, it is important to appreciate the influence of Aleksei Remizov, a writer with whom Zamiatin enjoyed a close personal and professional relationship at this time. The conceit of the modern artist as *skomorokh,* for example, derives primarily from Remizov, and I will be examining his pornographic aetiological tale "What Tobacco Is" ("Chto est' tabak," 1908) as a prototypical example of carnivalesque playfulness. It is instructive that Zamiatin was coopted into Remizov's Great and Free Order of Apes (Obezvelvolpal), a mock-literary society devoted to anarchic and subversive laughter, in the immediate aftermath of the October Revolution.[10] The fate of the artists associated with this society is symptomatic of the continuation of various forms of censorship into the post-Revolutionary era and the appearance under a secular authority of new forms of political, social, and cultural taboo. While it was appropriate now to mock and ridicule the Orthodox Church as an institution (a fact which gave rise to numerous anti-ecclesiastical subjects), the Bolsheviks were puritan and conservative as far as sexual mores were concerned; indeed, they despised and sought to suppress all forms of carnivalesque activity, including the very carnival itself.[11] Literature devoted to parody, satire, and the subversion of secular norms was quickly relegated to the margins of cultural activity and officially disparaged, if not banned altogether.

As pseudo-hagiography, Zamiatin's *chudesa* belong to the wave of interest in hagiographic materials characteristic of a number of Russian writers, including such literary giants as Dostoevsky, Tolstoi, Leskov, and Merezhkovsky.[12] In the main these writers were concerned with the moral values promoted in the *Lives* and their relevance for modern-day humanity. It was common to borrow standard themes (*topoi*) from well-known *vitae,* to model fictional characters on celebrated saintly types, to adapt a particular *vita* for a modern, secular audience, and to rework entire narratives for po-

lemical, sometimes anti-ecclesiastical purposes. If parody and stylization were not a primary concern of these writers, their approaches ranged from the reverent to the extremely irreverent (it was not uncommon, for example, to use the legends as a literary "Trojan horse" with which to disarm the Tsarist censors).[13] The attitudes of these writers towards the hagiographic sources themselves varied. Tolstoi, for example, considered the miracles in the legends of the saints to be "fairy tales" for the uninitiated; while Leskov considered the various tales in the Russian *Synaxary* (*Prolog*) to be "rubbish," but argued that they provided unusual and interesting raw material on which the artist could profitably draw.[14] In many cases, the adaptations of these writers constituted arguments about revealed religion, the value of certain forms of ritual and worship (kenotic versus ascetic), and the practices of the Russian Orthodox Church, in particular the clergy. If Tolstoi was excommunicated, for example, this was not because he rejected belief in a Supreme Being as such, but because he rejected certain important aspects of Orthodox doctrine and was vehemently critical of the hierarchy.[15]

For Zamiatin, Tolstoi was one of the great religious heretics of his time. Along with Anatole France, a writer well known for his scepticism, he was an important champion of free thinking in the modern era, the proof of his heresy reflected in the banning of his fiction by the Russian Orthodox Church. We may presume that the iconoclastic views of both writers were influential in shaping Zamiatin's attitude towards religion; moreover, it is interesting to note that both men adapted *vitae* as a means by which to polemicize with their opponents. Zamiatin, however, was careful to draw a distinction between the philosophical and moral outlooks of the two men.[16] France's adaptions of hagiographic legends were tainted by a neo-paganist eroticism which would have been unacceptable to the puritan Tolstoi.[17] Indeed, his penchant for libertinage and gauloiserie, an aspect of his writing which derives primarily from the Enlightenment works of Voltaire and Diderot, in many respects prefigures Zamiatin's own amoral tendencies in his reworkings of similar types of material. Another influence was undoubtedly the fascination for the obscene and sexually perverse in the first decades of the twentieth century on the part of certain symbolist and decadent writers in Russia.[18] While it is true that this interest was explored within a specifically religious and mystical context, this made it no less acceptable to the Orthodox Church or to the Tsarist autocracy—hence the continuing problem with the censors during this period with regard to supposed depravity and the corruption of public morals.[19]

One of the figures from this milieu to whom Zamiatin owed a great debt was Remizov, a writer whose interest in the transgressional was well established by the time Zamiatin made his acquaintance in 1913 in the editorial offices of *Zavety,* the Socialist Revolutionaries' cultural almanac. In 1908 Remizov founded the society Obezvelvolpal, adopting as his pseudonym the name of the Vogul Prince who had allegedly murdered the Bishop of Perm in the fifteenth century.[20] His anti-ecclesiastical prejudices were particularly strident at this time, as can be witnessed by the pornographic tale "What Tobacco Is," which he published in the very same year. Printed privately in twenty-five copies, and allegedly the product of meetings between himself, Rozanov, Kuzmin, Bakst, Somov, and Nuvel in 1906 to explore the nature of the erotic, this is a scurrilous, bawdy, and seedy tale with few rivals in terms of its frivolous, anarchic, and nihilistic spirit.[21] Generically speaking, "What Tobacco Is" is a demonic aetiological tale with strong roots in Russia's folk tradition.[22] It is ostensibly written at Christmas, a time of licensed festivity on the part of the Church, and a key stylistic device involves the attribution of authorship to a fictitious narrator. This was a device typical of the purveyors of obscene material in Russia—see, for example, the false bibliographical details given in the first emigré edition of Afanas'ev's celebrated *Secret Tales of Russia* (*Russkie zavetnye skazki*), which was actually published in Geneva in 1872.[23] Remizov introduces his tale as the account of Gonosius, an ancient sage concerned to correct various popular but misconceived notions about the origins of the evil weed (his story might be read as a malicious riposte to Tolstoi's public renunciation of tobacco in his article "Why Do Men Stupefy Themselves?").[24] Gonosius's account opens with a brief review of the more intriguing popular fables regarding the origins of tobacco; he then proceeds to expound his own version, according to which the tobacco plant is spawned from the gigantic loins of a monk calling himself Savrasius. The story takes place in a pious fraternity called the "Monastery of Miracles" ("Chudov Monastyr'"). The antics of Savrasius, who arrives mysteriously at the monastery and is suspected by many to be a *iurodivyi* (holy fool) possessed by the Devil, are obscene and loathsome; suffice to say, the climax of the tale involves a violent and bizarre confrontation between Savrasius and a monk called Niukh, the outcome of which leads to their mutual destruction and dissolution into a lake of tar, in the middle of which floats a large penis. The burial of their remains gives rise next spring to a flower, the aroma of which is so seductive that the monks use the leaves to make cigars and export them for recreational use. Hence the origin of the tobacco plant which, after a brief period of official approval, is then angrily condemned as the work of the Devil.

It has been argued that Remizov's entire career consists of a buffoon-like transgression of the official.[25] His position vis-à-vis ecclesiastical culture, however, is more ambiguous than such a statement would allow. If "What Tobacco Is" is the epitome of *skomorokh*-style obscenity, and plays mischievously with the ambiguous status of the *iurodivyi* in Russian culture, it is a rather extreme example of Remizov's "black art" and is not characteristic of his work as a whole. His attitude towards the spiritual and cultural heritage of Orthodox Christianity was celebratory, rather than subversive, as can be witnessed by the tales of *Leimonarium* (*Limonar'*, 1907), *Paraleipomenon* (*Paralipomenon*, 1912), and *The Golden Chain* (*Tsep' zlataia*, 1913), the last of which Zamiatin himself reviewed in 1914.[26] The apparent paradox which underlines Remizov's position is vividly illustrated in Zamiatin's own depiction of him in his short story **"Alatyr"** (**"Alatyr',"** 1914) as the character of the archpriest Father Peter, a man renowned locally for his interest in marsh-demons (bolotnye cherti) and for his learned treatise "On the Lives and Subsistence of Devils" ("O zhitii i propitanii diavolov"), but unmistakably a man of religion.[27] On the other hand, Remizov's private correspondence with such friends as Rozanov (chief "phallus-bearer" in the society Obezvelvolpal), and his interest in linguistic transgression (swear words) and newspaper stories about exotic sexual-religious practices (the Flagellants), stands somewhat at odds with his respectful attitude towards Orthodox religious culture in general. While moving in a milieu which was critical of the institutions of Orthodoxy, but sought nevertheless to renew contact with religion and mysticism through the exploration of Eros, there can be little doubt that Remizov's position was essentially ambiguous. However provocative and obscene, "What Tobacco Is" is not ultimately an erotic piece of work, or even a celebration of the carnival in the free-wheeling style of Rabelais, but rather a dark, sinister tale with disturbing imagery and a distaste for the physically sexual. Like a church gargoyle, it is a crude and vulgar grotesque which provokes revulsion on the part of the reader, as well as laughter at its more outrageous, fanciful episodes.[28]

Remizov's stylizations of folk-ecclesiastical genres, while not parodies, are important precursors for Zamiatin. He was certainly acquainted with "What Tobacco Is," although it is not clear how early in his career. In his mock epistle "The Turkish Drum" ("Tulumbas," 1920), an open response to Remizov's Obezvelvolpal manifesto, he manages to include a reference to the evil habit of smoking and "Savrasius's gigantic, loathsome member" ("Savrasieva merzkogo udishcha").[29] On the whole, Zamiatin possesses a far less ambiguous attitude towards the sacred traditions of the Orthodox Church. At the same time, the main difference between his ecclesiastical parodies and Remizov's aetiological tale lies not in the aesthetic impulse, but rather in the sphere of literary strategy. While anti-ecclesiastical in spirit, "What Tobacco Is" does not pretend to formal respectability. By contrast, Zamiatin seeks to give the illusion of an official or semi-official document, while at the same time undermining its piety through thematic subversion and the incorporation of bawdy, grotesque details. Remizov's tale is diabolical because it boasts a demonic subject (the Devil as the originator of tobacco) and an "author" who does not purport to belong to the Church (Gonosius's status as "sage" suggests a pagan magus). Zamiatin's parodies are demonic because the author adopts a saintly mask behind which he conceals his diabolical intentions. Disguise, of course, is part of the Devil's armoury of weapons; thus Zamiatin's fictions might be said to constitute the fictional equivalents of the devils in hagiographic literature who assume disguises in order to corrupt the pure and innocent.

Although first published in 1917, we now know, thanks to the release of archival materials, that **"The Precious Virgin"** was written in 1915 and entrusted to Remizov for publication while Zamiatin was working in Great Britain on a ship-building mission.[30] In his own words, the tale was an attempt to give the "illusion" of an early medieval narrative.[31] The title in Russian refers to a type of hagiographic sub-genre—the encomiastic sermon—with stylistic origins in the sermons of the early Christian period.[32] As a stylization, the work purports to be that of a medieval chronicler: draft versions reveal that Zamiatin conceived the author of the tale either as an anonymous monk, or a monk calling himself Gleb, who had witnessed the events of the narrative—in other words, the text was intended to be read as a "found document," and thus essentially as apocryphal in origin.[33] The narrative incorporates several themes from the virginmartyr *passiones* and subverts several *topoi* from the legends of female and male saints. These include the expelling of serpents from the womb;[34] the healing of mutilated breasts after torture;[35] and the preservation of the body from mortal decay.[36] A similar exploitation of hagiographic themes occurs in Zamiatin's second tale, **"The Healing of the Novice Erasmus,"** which tells the story of a gifted and talented icon-painter whose erotic visions prove dangerous to the religious community in which he serves. The plot of this tale incorporates the menological account of the *Life of Saint Mary of Egypt,* the harlot whose conversion and many years of penitence spent in solitude in the Egyptian desert inspired such writers as Dostoevsky, Boris Almazov, and Elizaveta Shakhova, and was twice celebrated by Remizov in 1907 and 1915.[37] Like **"The Precious Virgin," "The Healing of the Novice Erasmus"** purports to be the work of a hagiographer, this time a scribe called Innokentii who has compiled his account for the "edification" and "instruction" of the elders in his monastery. The conceit of ecclesiastical authenticity extended even to the design of the original booklet in which the story was first published in Berlin; it carried a series of grotesque chimeras by Kustodiev very much in the style of medieval hagiographic collections.[38]

Gor'ky's complaint that **"The Healing of the Novice Erasmus"** was little more than a "vulgar joke" ("grubaia shutka"), and a failed reworking of the stories of Remizov and France, rather missed the point.[39] It is very much an element of the carnival text that the joke is a permitted literary form. This is not to ignore the polemical strategy which informs Zamiatin's writing in this vein. On the one hand, his parodies are allegorical vehicles with which to satirize contemporary events (I argue elsewhere that **"The Precious Virgin"** alludes to the rumours of a royally-negotiated "separate peace" circulating in Petersburg towards the end of 1915).[40] On the other hand, they also constitute an attempt to polemicize with certain doctrines of the Orthodox Church—in particular, the celebration of virginity as a spiritual ideal. In their reversal of the usual edificatory themes of hagiographic literature, and the incorporation of bawdy details into the fabric of what purports to be a pious text, the author's blasphemous strategy becomes transparent. The miracles of the saints, a feature of their *Lives* which served as important proof of their divine powers in the posthumous bid for canonization, are ironized; the laudatory function of the genre itself is subverted, if not reversed; and the Orthodox teaching on the insoluble link between bodily and spiritual purity is openly challenged. Common to both stories is the acceptance, rather than rejection of sexual sin as an act of virtue; furthermore, in both texts demons are figuratively present. In **"The Precious Virgin,"** it is the barbarian warlord Erman, described as a "proud king and architect of evil" (3:65): he is the person to whom the Precious Virgin gives herself, thus sacrificing her vows of celibacy, but saving her compatriots from further invasion and brutal repression. In **"The Healing of the Novice Erasmus,"** it is the laughing devils (besy) which besiege Erasmus's cell in true medieval style (in his drawings Kustodiev used the conventional images of ugly beasts with horns and tails) and are representative of the sexual licentiousness to which the entire monastery falls victim. The demonic is synonymous in this story with the forces of erotic liberation. As a result of the "divine" instruction given to Pamva, Erasmus's guardian—"Release the arrow, and the bowstring will lose its tension, and the bow will no longer be deathly" ("Spusti strelu, i oslabnet tetiva, i uzhe ne budet bolee smertonosen luk," 1:474)—Erasmus is permitted knowledge of the forbidden secrets of the flesh in order fully and accurately to depict the penitent whore as she stands naked in the desert.

Although the miracle tales are not as vulgar as Remizov's "What Tobacco Is," there can be little doubting their fundamental obscenity. The description of Erman licking the severed breasts of the Precious Virgin as they are brought to him on a plate after her torture (3:67); the mention of Erasmus's erection as Saint Mary reveals her naked body to him (1:469); the droplets of sperm which rain down on the assembled monks during his reading of Solomon's "Song of Songs" (1:466); and the curious aroma of the virginal Mary's "fourth secret"

(1:468) all belong to the realm of the "lower bodily world," and therefore to the carnivalesque in the Bakhtinian understanding. Hand in hand with such transgression goes Zamiatin's authorial pact with the Devil of lust and carnal desire. It is symptomatic that in a later article on Kustodiev he mentioned the *topos* of temptation in the menological collections, and wondered whether he himself, like the demons who visited the saints of old in the wilderness, had not tempted Kustodiev into impious transgression.[41] Unlike Remizov, Zamiatin took great pleasure in the employment of sexually explicit material. One thinks of his description of Nelson's column in terms of a phallus in **"Fisher of Men"** (**"Lovets chelovekov,"** 1921), a story which would not be published in Britain for several decades because of its barely-concealed eroticism.[42] In **"A Reliable Place"** (**"Nadezhnoe mesto,"** 1924), we read the story of a pious woman on a pilgrimage to Zadonsk who has her life's savings stolen after succumbing to the devilish charms of a male travelling companion: he has the red hair of a Russian folk devil (ryzhii chert), and the "reliable place" in question turns out to be inside her knickers![43] These works are striking illustrations of Zamiatin's Boccaccio-like treatment of nominally religious subjects. Indeed, as I hope to show, the bawdy Western humour of *The Decameron,* as well as the Russian folk bawdy tradition itself, is a shaping influence in **"The Miracle of Ash Wednesday,"** and constitutes a key element in Zamiatin's carnival-style humour.

Although first published in 1926 in the journal *Novaia Rossiia,* Zamiatin's **"The Miracle of Ash Wednesday"** was actually written in the summer of 1923 at the same time as his article "About Literature, Revolution and Entropy" ("O literature, revoliutsii i entropii," 1924).[44] In a letter to Lev Lunts, his erstwhile student at the House of Arts, Zamiatin characterized his tale as tiny and "indecorous" ("neprilichen"), and compared it to **"The Healing of the Novice Erasmus,"** explaining that it was conceived during a heatwave, "when, as you know, the demon of carnal desire is powerful."[45] The view that these two stories should be read as companion pieces is supported by the fact that they were both parodied in a humorous account of the conception and staging of *The Flea* (*Blokha,* 1924) which Zamiatin himself composed in December 1926 for a special evening of parody at FIGA (Fizeo-geotsentricheskaia assotsiatsiia).[46] Furthermore, they were reprinted alongside each other in **Impious Tales** (**Nechestivye rasskazy,** 1927), a collection which included several examples of Zamiatin's anti-ecclesiastical whimsy.[47]

The uncanny quality of this text lies partly in the incongruity between the event described and the setting in which it takes place. Approaching **"The Miracle of Ash Wednesday"** from the parodies ostensibly set in Russia, the reader is initially unsettled by the unfamiliar surroundings. The location purports to be that of a Benedictine monastery somewhere in Central or Eastern Europe, and the story opens with a young canon and a doctor discussing a supposed miracle which neither is able to explain scientifically. The nature of this miracle is only gradually revealed during the course of the narrative. We learn that during mass to celebrate the Festival of the Apostle Peter-in-Chains (1 August), the young Simplicius begins to feel faint at the moment when he lifts the bread at Eucharist. After a few months of nervous fretting, during which his stomach has increased in size, he is examined by a friend, Dr Voichek, and allegedly found to be pregnant. The doctor decides to operate immediately. On Ash Wednesday, Simplicius is wheeled into surgery and made to wait briefly alongside a woman about to give birth for the third time; he is then given a general anaesthetic. After regaining consciousness the next morning, he is appalled to discover that he has apparently given birth to a baby boy; at the same time he learns that the woman awaiting surgery in the room alongside him has died. Dr Voichek advises Simplicius to pretend that the boy belonged to the dead woman, and that he has adopted him out of a sense of charity. This is the act of generosity, presumably, for which the young canon becomes venerated in later years, and which, according to the mock-hagiographical conceit of the narrative, provides the impulse for the account of the "miracle." On his deathbed, however, Simplicius admits to being his son's mother; more bizarrely, he claims that the father of the child is Archbishop Benedict, the head of the monastery who, we have been told, returned from a visit to Rome and entertained Simplicius with wine and crayfish only seven days before the mass took place. The story concludes with the image of Dr Voichek laughing through tears as his former patient drifts quietly off into eternal sleep.

Unsurprisingly, perhaps, contemporary readers were bewildered by this narrative, and slightly scornful. A correspondent for the Berlin emigré newspaper *Dni,* after attending a reading of the story in May 1924 along with Akhmatova, Chukovsky, Efros, and Pil'niak, dismissed the story as "rubbish" ("vzdor") and "utter nonsense" ("chep ukha narochitaia").[48] Clearly there is a sense in which Zamiatin is trivializing the purpose and function of literature in an epic, revolutionary age. Chudakova observes that as literature in the 1920s became ever more serious, grandiose, and ideologically pretentious, so the conceit of the artist-*skomorokh* inspired Zamiatin to ever greater acts of "buffoonery" ("shutovstvo").[49] Certainly, this is one method of approaching the story's undeniable surrealism. It can fruitfully be argued, for example, that the absurdity and frivolity of the story challenges epic expectation and seriousness of purpose in much the same way as Gogol's surreal fantasy "The Nose" ("Nos," 1836) cocked a snook at the reactionary demand for morally edifying literature in the 1830s.[50] The meaning of the tale may thus be seen to lie in the deliberate discomfiting and unsettling of reader expectations as to what constitutes acceptable forms of literature. A microcosm of this problem is introduced into the very text itself in the form of Dr Voichek's remark to Simplicius regarding the postponement of deadlines: he suggests that travelling continuously westwards, and winding one's watch backwards as one does so, is a way of gaining crucial time (1:476). This is a riddle, rather than a scientific explanation of time-differences around the world; nevertheless, it torments Simplicius by means of its mathematical legerdemain in much the same way as the reader is baffled by the biological sleight of hand at the heart of the story's narrative.[51] This is literature as enigma or opaque joke, with the reader forced into the position of trying to restore logic to the text and make sense of the author's purpose. Not for nothing, perhaps, was Zamiatin's pseudonym in Obezvelvolpal "Zamutius, Bishop of the Apes," his name deriving from the Russian verb meaning "to muddy" or "to make obscure."[52]

The modern reader may well share the bafflement expressed by the early "victims" of **"The Miracle of Ash Wednesday."** Nevertheless, it is important to recognize that this is a conscious literary strategy, and that the confusion which arises is the product of Zamiatin's authorial pact with the Devil. This pact exists on various different levels. Another way of approaching this story, for example, would be as a carnivalized text which deliberately subverts Orthodox norms. While obviously not a counterfeit product in the anachronistic style of the two earlier *chudesa*, **"The Miracle of Ash Wednesday"** is nevertheless a parody of an ecclesiastical mode of writing. The title alludes specifically to the *chudo*, a short text of hagiographic provenance which forms a part of the individual *vita* or can sometimes appear as a self-contained fragment on its own. Examining the story in this light, we see that several of the defining features of hagiographic literature are present. The main protagonist is a saintly type, and the narrative, although set in modern times, and employing a transparently modern idiom, is also clearly intended as an "instructive" and "edificatory" account of the act of virtue with which his life is associated. Like the two earlier *chudesa*, Zamiatin's strategy lies in the subversion of these stock elements. The very idea of saintliness is ridiculed; moreover, in its deliberate playing with notions of credibility and credulity, **"The Miracle of Ash Wednesday"** questions the value of didactic literature generally and mocks the gullibility of those who are prepared to accept the fantastic nature of the miracles attributed to the saints. The central joke or absurdity in this tale is that the miracle in question defies medical science and the known facts of human biology. Indeed, as distinct from the medieval hagiographer, who warns readers in ad-

vance of the fantastic events to be described, but attributes them to the powers of divine intervention, Zamiatin's author is unable to explain the miracle at the heart of the narrative and seems not even to wish to do so.[53] Not only does he willingly repudiate authorial omnipotence, he seems to suggest that if there are divine mechanisms in operation in this world, they operate in a mystifying and bizarre fashion. As we will see, his subversion of fantastic *topoi* relate not only to the legends of the saints, but also to the *topos* of the miraculous birth in the Old and New Testaments.

A related approach to **"The Miracle of Ash Wednesday"** would be to view it as a post-symbolist demonological tale—in other words, as a tale which plays with the conceit of the artist-*skomorokh*. Alex Shane, for instance, considers Zamiatin's story "in all probability a parody of some ribald medieval Czech tale about the evil powers of the Devil."[54] Although this proposition is unconvincing as far as the literary origin of the parody is concerned, it is interesting to observe that he places Dr Voichek at the centre of the tale's labyrinth as a palpably demonic presence. Voichek, in fact, "corrupts" the text in two ways: firstly, as a fictional character, he may be responsible for playing some kind of joke on Simplicius, just as the joker of the bawdy tradition plays tricks on the gullible clergyman;[55] secondly, as the only person to have witnessed the events in question, he enjoys a status equal to the author. His laughter through tears at the end of the story suggests privileged information; and if readers are tempted to solve the riddle of the text and restore logic by trying to guess the content of his knowledge, then this is very much part of the tantalizing game which Zamiatin is playing. This view of the Devil combines various traditions into one composite: the Devil as evil-doer who seeks to tempt the innocent from the path of virtue (the expression "the Devil has led me astray" [chert menia poputal] is common in Russian);[56] as magician who seeks to pull the wool over the eyes of the public and overturn scientific logic; and as Satanic, post-symbolist *skomorokh* or clown who seeks to disrupt the normal procedures of literature in favour of surrealism. This Devil is a master of parody; but he is also one who "tempts" the reader into fitting all the pieces into a coherent whole. It is precisely this aspect of Zamiatin's tale which is most intriguing, and what follows is an attempt to establish a rationale for the events which take place.

One explanation which restores logic to the text, but which still relies on a degree of implausibility, is that Zamiatin's humble protagonist is not a young man at all, but a young woman—in other words, like the main character in Johann Jacob Grimmelshausen's celebrated seventeenth-century novel, with whom he shares a first name, Simplicius might well be so perfectly ignorant of life generally that he is unaware even of his own gender.[57] Although this stretches the bounds of credibility, it is subtly implied at several intervals in the course of the narrative. At no point is objective proof of the young canon's masculinity furnished by the author; indeed, a number of remarks are made in relation to Simplicius which stress his fresh-faced youthfulness and effeminate qualities. He is wide-eyed and innocent, we are told, his eyes described as "two little babes with thumbs in their mouths" (1:476); he has fetching dimples, which make him endearing to those around him (1:476); and he has a plumpish body, which is compared to a chair in a woman's bedroom, "upholstered in pink satin, full of warm creases and folds, and alive—almost ready to replace the mistresses who normally occupy them" (1:477). From this, more logical point of view, only Dr Voichek and Archbishop Benedict need be aware of Simplicius's true gender; moreover, an early indication that the doctor might in fact be colluding in the young canon's ignorance is given when he first asks Simplicius to undress for a physical examination. This is followed by a smile and the characteristic twisting of his curly "horns" (1:477), an indication either of his surprise in relation to the size of Simplicius's swollen stomach (he is at least seven months pregnant), or a hint perhaps that something more fundamental is amiss. Could it be knowledge of Simplicius's bizarre secret that causes the doctor's mirth at the end of the story?

The plausibility of this interpretation is certainly strengthened by the fact that concealed sexual identity and illegitimate birth are *topoi* in a number of female saints' *Lives*. These are young women, many of them virgins converted to Christianity, who are forced to marry pagans against their will by their parents. Invariably, they escape from home disguised in male clothing and later serve with model humility in monasteries until revealed to be female on their deathbeds; quite frequently, they find themselves accused of seducing women from secular society or nuns from neighbouring convents. Saint Margaret (feast day, 8 October), for example, enters a monastery disguised as a man, is rewarded for her uncommon devotion by being placed in charge of a neighbouring convent, and is later accused of seducing a nun under her care.[58] A similar circumstance, although differing in certain details (the heroine is happily married, but betrays her husband and joins a monastery so that he will not be able to find her), arises in the *Life* of Saint Theodora (feast day, 11 September), a text reworked by the radical thinker and writer Aleksandr Herzen in 1836.[59] A stock theme in this kind of narrative involves the (female) monk being amorously pursued by a woman from outside the monastery who labours under a comic and almost grotesque misapprehension with regard to her love object's true identity. In the case of Theodora, it is the daughter of a local hotel owner in Alexandria who solicits her attentions and, her attempted seduction rebuffed, later accuses her of fa-

thering her baby. Theodora's protestations of innocence are not believed by the authorities; she is banished beyond the monastery walls as punishment and forced to bring up the illegitimate child on her own; and it is only after her death, when burial preparations reveal that she is a woman after all, that she receives proper vindication. Another variation on the disguise theme occurs in the *Life* of Saint Euphrosine, which Anatole France adapted in 1891, although in her case the *topos* of the failed seduction and accusation of fatherhood is absent.[60]

It is not suggested here that Simplicius is synonymous with these errant female "monks"—these virgins were obviously aware of their own gender, but sought to conceal it from outsiders—merely that there is an established tradition in certain *vitae* of male impersonation and falsely attributed pregnancy which Zamiatin sought consciously to parody. There are certain important similarities, for example, between his treatment of this subject and Herzen's secular adaptation of Theodora's legend. Like Zamiatin, Herzen exploits ignorance of Theodora's gender as a device with which to increase dramatic tension; by entitling his tale simply "The Legend," and giving his heroine the name Theodor, Herzen endeavoured to disguise his literary source and thus hopefully to prevent his readers from guessing the curious denouement. Indeed, in terms very similar to the description of Simplicius in Zamiatin, the true nature of her secret is implied discreetly early on in the tale (Herzen focuses on the youthful innocence and "girl-like" locks of the young boy's hair).[61] Ultimately, however, the two authors have a different strategic purpose. Herzen was interested in the legend as a proto-feminist document, as a refutation of the widespread prejudice among certain religious circles that women were incapable of serious feats of ascetic discipline—thus by disguising the gender of his protoganist, he causes the reader to consider carefully, or reconsider, his or her pre-conceived ideas of male and female behaviour (a key *topos*, for example, is the scene in which the misogynistic abbot or Father Superior, without realizing the virgin's true identity, warns her on entering the monastery about the evil, fickle, and corrupting nature of women). Zamiatin's project is imbued with a more anarchic and nihilistic spirit. The revelation at the end of **"The Miracle of Ash Wednesday"** is essentially a mock revelation. If true, it confirms only that Simplicius, admittedly innocent and gullible, is far from the pure or virtuous model of the legends, a fact which somewhat compromises his "saintly" act of adoption. Zamiatin's narrative thus takes its place among a number of tales in the Eastern and Western bawdy tradition which tell of sexual malpractice at the very heart of religious worship. An interesting precedent, since it demonstrates that the *topoi* of sexual indeterminacy and monastic effeminacy may have crossed from hagiography into oral literature, is the bawdy Russian folktale entitled "The Monk and the Mother Superior" ("Monakh i igumen'ia"), which Afanas'ev recorded in the nineteenth century.[62] There is no evidence that Zamiatin actually knew this tale directly. It is intriguing, nonetheless, that the denouement involves the mysterious impregnation of a young nun by a male monk dressed in female garb, and that the story culminates with a joke about sexually indeterminate babies.[63]

If we accept this suspicion about Simplicius's true gender, but approach the text from a different angle, an obviously blasphemous, rather than merely anti-clerical dimension emerges. There are several hints in **"The Miracle of Ash Wednesday"** that Simplicius's inexplicable pregnancy may have a precedent in the story of the Virgin Birth.[64] On two occasions, both of them significant junctures in the text, Simplicius raises an exclamation in the name of the Blessed Virgin. The first occurs when Dr Voichek examines his belly for the first time and announces that he will operate: "But why? What do I have? In the name of the Holy Mary?" (1:478); while the second takes place as he is presented in hospital with the child to which he has ostensibly given birth: "But I . . . Holy Virgin! But I'm, after all, a man!" ("No ved' ia zhe . . . Presviataia Deva!—ved' ia zhe vse-taki muzhchina!," 1:480). The syntactical ambiguity here, lost in English translation, does more than hint at Simplicius's sexual androgyny. Moreover, the day on which we are led to believe that the conception of his child takes place—the Archbishop's party is given seven days prior to 1 August on 25 July—happens to coincide with the feast of Saint Anne, the mother of the Virgin Mary. Simplicius is thus linked with two women celebrated by the Church for miraculous births which take place thanks to divine intervention. In the case of Anne, of course, the surrealism is somewhat spectacular, since she is barren for much of her life and conceives after lengthy supplication only at the age of seventy (!); whereas for Mary, the birth of Jesus occurs after the annunciation by the Archangel Gabriel through the power of the Holy Spirit. The joke at the heart of **"The Miracle of Ash Wednesday"** derives from the fact that no one would possibly believe such miraculous conceptions if they were to occur in modern, scientific times.[65] Indeed, much humour is derived from the comic reversal, according to which the young canon, a religious believer brought up strictly on the articles of the Catholic faith, and one who readily accepts the resurrection of the dead, nevertheless finds the miracle of Felix's conception incredible, while his friend, a doctor and a man of science, has no such rational qualms: "Nevertheless . . . You understand, I am a doctor, it's much more difficult for me to believe in a miracle than it is for you—a priest. And yet, it can't be helped! I must believe" (1:480).

The irony is doubly felicitous here. It is absurd that a young canon should forget the celebrated legend of the Virgin Birth as a historical precedent for his own pregnancy. Further humour is derived retrospectively from the inquiry to his friend regarding the historical precedents for such an event at the very beginning of the tale: "But still . . . still, have you found nothing, nothing at all in your books, perhaps another case—perhaps in antiquity?" (1:475). Simplicius is referring to medical books here, but the reader will undoubtedly be reminded of that most ancient of texts—the New Testament. When the reader learns that Archbishop Benedict is the father, along with various hints that something sinful happened on the night when he returned from Rome, the biblical myth is ridiculed and the supposedly inexplicable and fantastic miracle revealed to have a normal biological explanation after all.

This approach to Zamiatin's tale depends on Simplicius's ignorance of his own gender and the assumption that he was named by his parents without his gender being taken into consideration. Such a reading is thus undeniably absurd. Nevertheless, the committing of sin and the acceptance of guilt are clearly two of the story's themes. This holds true even if we construct a reading of the text on the basis that Simplicius is a young man, albeit a rather effeminate one. According to this reading, the birth of Felix, his son, is a miraculous event indeed, so miraculous that no logical or biological explanation can be offered at all, and the tale acquires the hallmarks of a grotesque parody of the Virgin Birth, one in which the sex of the Mother of God has been obscenely reversed. It remains for the reader to speculate on the possibility that Simplicius has been in some way punished for an illicit homosexual encounter, the true nature of which remains something of a mystery to him. The title of the story hints that the punishment of sins and the acceptance of guilt is a central theme. According to the calendar, Ash Wednesday is the first day of the Lenten Fast, an occasion on which Christians celebrate the start of Jesus' forty days in the wilderness by marking their foreheads with a cross made of ash in symbolic recognition of their sins. Dr Voichek himself speculates on the possibility that the child has been conceived as a punishment and should best be viewed as a "test" ("ispytanie," 1:480) of the canon's faith. This seems to be recognized even by Simplicius himself. It is with a sense of guilt—likened to the admission of sins at confession (na ispovedi, 1:476)—that Simplicius first tells Dr Voichek of the events preceding his sudden illness; indeed later, after the birth of Felix, we are informed that Simplicius bears his burden humbly precisely because he understands why God might have chosen him for such punishment: "The canon submitted to it and bore it as meekly as the

Apostle Peter bore his iron chains. It even seemed to him that he knew why heaven had so punished and rewarded him" (1:480).

The literary precedents for Simplicius's "sin" in anti-clerical literature are extensive. For Boccaccio, the practice of sodomy on the part of monks and friars was traditional, and several of his stories in *The Decameron* employ deliberate homosexual innuendo;[66] moreover, as Adam Olearius records, the depiction of "vile sodomies" by street entertainers was apparently an integral part of Russian folk culture in the seventeenth century.[67] In this context, it is interesting to note the images of phallic penetration which punctuate Zamiatin's story, often in the vicinity of anus-like orifices. A particularly important sequence occurs at the very beginning of the tale. When Dr Voichek inquires after the health of the Archbishop, for example, he is smoking a cigarette (1:475). Simplicius's embarrassment in relation to this question is described in terms of being roasted alive like a woodcock on a spit (1:475). A few sentences later, the young canon's eyes are compared to two babies sucking their thumbs (1:476), an image of fellatio and/or anal penetration made even more suggestive perhaps by the mention immediately afterwards of the "dimples" (literally, "little trenches" [iamochki]) on his "cheeks" (1:476). These images hint at a counter-narrative of homoerotic impropriety. Naturally, for a successful reading of this kind, it must be assumed that the canon's confession to Felix at the end of the story reflects not so much the truth of his feminine gender, but rather his confused conviction that since he gave birth to a baby, he must therefore, technically, be his "mother." Even the admission of motherhood does not de facto rule out masculinity, since it could simply be recognition of his nurturing role.

The precedents for bizarre pregnancies of this kind, especially where it is a man who is thought to be giving birth, are well established in the folk tradition. The subject draws on the medical and cultural phenomenon of couvade, and is essentially Western and medieval in origin, although it is clear that certain versions migrated into Russian folk culture at some point later. In Boccaccio's *The Decameron*, for instance, the painter Calandrino is persuaded by his friends and a doctor called Master Simone that he is pregnant.[68] It turns out that the painter is the naive victim of a ruse to extract money from him by means of a miraculous cure which results a few days later in a "miscarriage"; hilariously, he has earlier concluded that the pregnancy must have been the result of unconventional sexual practices with this wife (she prefers to straddle him during love-making, rather than assume the missionary position). A similarly absurd situation arises in the bawdy Russian folktale about the priest who gives birth mysteriously to a calf, one version of which can be found in the emigré edi-

tions of Afanas'ev's *Secret Tales of Russia,* and another of which was published legally by Onchukov in his 1908 collection of Northern Russian folktales.[69] Initially, according to the latter version, there is evidence that the priest has something medically wrong with him: his stomach is said to have increased in size over several months "until it has grown quite large."[70] Worried by this development, he sends a sample of urine in an earthenware pot to the local doctor for diagnosis via one of his servant-girls. Unfortunately, the young girl trips over en route, spills the contents of the pot all over the road, but instead substitutes a sample taken from a cow in a nearby field which later turns out to be pregnant. The doctor informs the priest that he is due to give birth to a bullock, the priest spends the night in a local cowshed to avoid the embarrassment of giving birth in front of his wife, and this turns out to be the very same shed in which the pregnant cow is about to give birth herself. The priest wakes up the next morning to find that the diagnosis has proved accurate. He gives his thanks to the Lord for having avoided the humiliation of a home birth, and rushes home to tell his wife the good news.

If these tales are based on unlikely coincidences, and involve a certain degree of stupidity on the part of their victims, they do at least conform to the known facts of biology. Boccaccio makes no attempt to disguise the fact that Calandrino is not really pregnant; indeed, none of the physical symptoms usually associated with the condition are betrayed. Likewise, although the priest in the Russian folktale might initially exhibit similar symptoms (we never discover the true cause of his swollen belly), it is quite clear that he is not pregnant either. If these bizarre stories have a rationale, therefore, it would appear to lie in the mocking of ignorance and gullibility. Like Simplicius, whose name derives from the Latin for "simplicity" ("simplicitas"), Calandrino is renowned for his naivety, so much so that his name has become coterminous in the Italian language with a simpleton.[71] By the same token, priests in the Russian bawdy tradition are frequently mocked and ridiculed for their naivety or wilful blindness in sexual matters, so regularly are they cuckolded by labourers, jokers (shuty), and other representatives of secular society. One *topos* of the bawdy tale involves a member of the clergy as the victim of a prank or joke, the result of which is the sexual abuse of his kith and kin (usually his wife or daughter).[72] One might speculate that the pregnancy *topos* derives from the popular analogy in anti-clerical literature between the fat-bellied priest (puzatyi pop) and the pregnant woman. Avvakum, for instance, denounced the representatives of the Nikonian hierarchy in precisely such terms.[73] He also mocked the effeminacy of the clergy and their penchant for luxurious, silk-lined clothing.[74] Zamiatin might well have been aware of this kind of popular analogy. He uses the expression "fat-bellied priest" in his discussion of religious entropy in "Scythians?" ("Skify li?"), an essay written in 1918.[75] Moreover, it is intriguing that he employs a vulgar turn of phrase ("to sit on your backside"), attributed to Avvakum, in the very same letter to Lunts in which he describes the writing of **"The Miracle of Ash Wednesday."**[76] The fact that Simplicius is also described in terms of a silky obesity might lead us to speculate that he is not pregnant at all, merely overweight; this possibility is surely strengthened when he remarks that his friends think he has "put on weight" (1:477). The time-symbolism of the story—Ash Wednesday follows Shrovetide (Maslenitsa), and thus marks the launch of the Lenten Fast after a period of dietary self-indulgence—is also suggestive in this regard.[77]

Since the joke at the expense of the innocent victim is a commonplace in the bawdy tradition, we should perhaps also consider the possibility that Simplicius is the victim of a sleight of hand, this time at the hands of his friend, the sinister Dr Voichek; indeed, the latter might be considered akin to the joker or *shut* in the bawdy tradition who plays a carnivalesque trick on the hapless and gullible representative of the church.

We need not doubt the doctor's essentially devilish provenance, even if Zamiatin has taken care to disguise him thinly in the form of a doctor. His goat-like eyes and russet-red "horns," and the description of him as a "demon" (1:479) in the scene immediately after the operation is testament to the Devil's power to assume any disguise in order to further his aims.[78] Without a doubt, the doctor is an unnerving and paradoxical presence in the story. It is ironic that he should represent the medical profession, one dedicated to restoring the health of its patients, rather than inflicting harm. This is reflected in his symbolic association with the colour white—the colour of clinical efficiency, health, and purity—rather than the traditional black, as witnessed in the description of his "other-worldly" surgery.[79] The doctor's love of dominoes, however, should make us wary of this façade. The domino, as well as being a black piece of ivory on which numbers of white dots appear, also functions in Italian as a word for the black cloak and half-mask worn at masquerades; in other words, it is a garment used to conceal one's true identity.[80] The fact that Dr Voichek is fond of games—in the Russian folk-religious imagination, devils have a passion for cards, dice, and chess (like Dr Voichek, they are also associated with the smoking of cigarettes)[81]—should also alert us to the possibility that his friendship with Simplicius is not disinterested. As I have already pointed out, one "game" he plays with Simplicius, a game which parallels his interest in dominoes, and thus in numbers generally (the Devil's association with numbers—three sixes being the "number of the beast" in the Book of Revelation [13:18]—is traditional), involves the idea

that by travelling continuously in a westward direction one can halt time and postpone the future (on two occasions, intriguingly, this deadline is couched explicitly in terms of the Last Judgement).[82] This is unscientific, of course, and hints at Dr Voichek's disruptive potential and his power to torment his victims by means of mental trickery. Like Goethe's Mephistopheles, who appears before Faust in the guise of a travelling scholar, the doctor is also said to possess an "extraordinary mind" (1:476).

Voichek's diabolic role in **"The Miracle of Ash Wednesday"** operates on two levels. As a symbolic presence in the narrative, his association with temptation provides an ironic commentary on the events connected with the Archbishop's party: the image of the goat—an image associated in the folk imagination with the carnival and the cuckold—links neatly with the idea that Simplicius's downfall has been caused by over-indulgence in food and drink, both of them symbolic of the carnival.[83] Simultaneously, Voichek's propensity for jokes and pranks—the traditional role of demons in the folk-religious imagination—provides a second explanation for the curious events which occur. It is not inconceivable, for example, that Simplicius is not really pregnant at all, and that his alleged sinning is the product of slanderous insinuation on the part of the doctor. There is no evidence of the pregnancy as such. We are treated only to the testimony of others that he has put on weight; to the information that he feels dizzy during the celebration of Mass; and to the sensation of heaviness in his stomach, all of which may have an ordinary explanation.[84] Secondly, the doctor's diagnosis that a Caesarian section should be undertaken immediately seems premature from the medical point of view; indeed, the subsequent assertion that the baby belongs to Simplicius need not be taken at face value (in the Russian folk-religious imagination, for example, the Devil's penchant for abducting small babies is well known).[85] Since the operation takes place while Simplicius is unconscious—the second occasion when a crucial event takes place while the canon is under the influence of a drug (the first, we are led to suspect, being the alcohol consumed at the Archbishop's party)—we cannot exclude the possibility that the doctor has taken the baby from the dead peasant woman and passed it off as belonging to Simplicius. While it is obvious that the boy is sired by the Archbishop—the twofold mention of his huge forehead (1:480, 481) is explicit—the identity of the mother is open to question if we suspect that the doctor's word cannot be trusted (the Devil, after all, is the father of all lies).[86] It is interesting to note that the woman's boots are the same colour as the doctor's hair (1:479), a sinister detail which establishes a partial, if essentially unfathomable connection between the two. It is insinuated, furthermore, that she is the very same woman who is taken ill at the same time as Simplicius during the Festival of Apostle Peter-in-Chains—thus she is a person with a connection to the same religious institution, and thus, potentially, to Archbishop Benedict. The possibility of Voichek's direct involvement in the train of events, like the reading of Simplicius as a woman, also reduces the miraculous to the level of the banal, although it establishes a clear kinship between fictional character and ostensible author, both of whom are indulging in deceptions.

"The Miracle of Ash Wednesday" is a story which plays subtly with the idea of confusion and clarity. If, as Simon Franklin maintains in his contribution to this volume, hagiographers employed dramatic irony in their works so that the participants remained ignorant or temporarily deceived, while the implied author and reader saw with knowledge and clarity, then Zamiatin has pushed the device beyond the realms of the plausible. Not only does the participant remain ignorant of the edificatory message which the narrative contains, but the reader is denied access to crucial facts which make comprehension of this message possible. The text is full of innuendo and insinuation, rather than unambiguous information; furthermore, it unfolds in an atmosphere of the uncanny which encourages the reader to view the events described as the product of dream or nightmare. The final line, which expresses the canon's vision of the laughing Dr Voichek in terms of a dream (kak skvoz' son, 1:481), is suggestive. We are reminded of Gogol's warning not to trust the streetlamps on Nevsky Prospect because they have been lit by the "demon himself" ("sam demon") and present things "in an unreal light" ("ne v nastoiashchem vide");[87] we should recall also Dostoevsky's warning in *The Brothers Karamazov* (*Brat'ia Karamazovy,* 1880) that Ivan Karamazov's encounter with the devil (chert) may be the product of a feverish hallucination.[88] The disorientating power of Zamiatin's tale owes much to the fact that crucial events occur "off-stage" while the leading protagonist is unconscious or semi-conscious. It is significant that his death is described in terms of falling asleep.[89] We might add to this sensation the indeterminate location of the narrative (Poland, Germany, the Ukraine, or Czechoslovakia are all possibilities) and the strange tricks played with time. I am referring here to the repeated use of the word *mladenets* in relation to Simplicius both at the beginning and end of the story; the fact that he gives birth and dies in February; and the fact that Dr Voichek discovers about the pregnancy after seven months, yet we are told that Simplicius sought his advice when it "first started" ("kak s kanonikom eto nachalos'," 1:476). This suggests that time has not elapsed according to the normal laws of nature. Further uncanny details emerge as a result of Zamiatin's use of colour imagery. The dying peasant woman's boots, as we have already noted, are the same colour as the doctor's hair; the crayfish eaten at the Archbishop's party

are as "rosy as a new-born baby" (1:476); Simplicius's flesh is compared to "rosy silk" (1:477); and Felix, the new-born baby, is described as a "red baby" (1:479). This establishes the doctor at the centre of a sinister nexus based around the colour red, although it is not clear whether these links should be considered significant or not.

As a dream or nonsense text, **"The Miracle of Ash Wednesday"** clearly owes much to Gogol, in particular his vision of the "demon of disorder and stupidity" ("demon putanitsy i gluposti") which Shevyrev observed stalking the pages of *Dead Souls* (*Mertvye dushi,* 1842).[90] It is a world, to paraphrase Gogol himself, which has been crumbled into idiotic fragments by some demon and presented in an unreal light, a world of absurdity and illogicality, of incredible events which border on the nonsensical. Shevyrev pinpoints this world as the fixed axis of Gogol's comic genius. However, we must draw a distinction between the early and late works of Gogol's fiction, and the fact that while Zamiatin clearly sought to embrace this absurd world, it was, for Gogol, the embodiment of moral bankruptcy and dehumanized existence. He drew a sharp distinction between the humour of his later works and the kind of humour encountered at the vaudeville or carnival. In one statement, for example, he juxtaposed the "elevated, triumphant" laughter of *Dead Souls* with the tomfoolery (krivlian'e) of the fairground *skomorokh*.[91] In his view, the laughter which functioned purely as festive entertainment was light-hearted, licentious, and spiritually empty, whereas his own brand of humour grew out of a love of humanity and exhibited a serious moral concern.[92] He also drew a distinction between his early works of fiction, which were full of "pure, unalloyed humour," and the later works, for example after *The Inspector General* (*Revizor,* 1836), which sought to communicate sad truths beyond their surface gaiety.[93] If **"The Miracle of Ash Wednesday"** bears a Gogolian imprint, therefore, it does so without the later moral and philosophical concerns, owing more to the freewheeling, carnivalesque tradition of the Dikanka stories and the bawdy innuendo of "The Nose." It is significant that the Ukraine is one of the locations in which Zamiatin's tale could take place, since this is a key space in Gogol's folk-religious fantasy world.

In "I Am Afraid" ("Ia boius'," 1921), an essay on the dangers of the new culture of conformity, Zamiatin declared that true literature existed only where it was produced by "madmen, hermits, visionaries, rebels and sceptics."[94] He should, perhaps, have included buffoons and clowns on his list. **"The Miracle of Ash Wednesday"** shows his penchant for the absurd, the bizarre, and the farcical, and his fascination for the anecdotal, whimsical, and vaudevillean. More importantly, it illustrates his interest in art as pure play. This aspect of his artistic temperament is also revealed in *The Flea*, the adaptation for stage of Leskov's "A Tale About the Cross-Eyed Left-Hander of Tula and the Steel Flea" ("Skaz o tul'skom kosom Levshe i o stal'noi blokhe," 1881) which drew its stylistic inspiration from the carnival tradition of Russian street theatre and the Italian *commedia dell'arte*. The central conceit of this play is the buffonade (skomorosh'ia igra), with the buffoons in question—the Chaldeans (Khaldei)—modelled on the participants of the medieval Russian Furnace Play (Peshchnoe deistvo). This was a sacred ritual which took place in churches in the days between Christmas and Epiphany. The Chaldeans themselves, however, were demonic figures who belonged to the sphere of carnival culture. Like the devils who took part in the medieval French *diablerie,* and roamed the streets in special costumes prior to their performance in the mystery plays of the time, these entertainers were given licence to play fun and games in the days before Epiphany as a concession to the festive spirit of Yuletide.[95] Zamiatin's identification with them as author was later made explicit in his essay "Popular Theatre" ("Narodnyi teatr," 1927): just as the Chaldeans were reported to have run amok gaily setting fire to the beards of peasant onlookers, so his modern mummers would aim, through their merry escapades, to "inflame" ("podzhigat'") their audience.[96] It is symptomatic that in an earlier letter to the producer Aleksei Diky, written during the preparations for the play's production in Moscow, he signed himself "Your Buffoon" ("Vash khaldei").[97]

"The Miracle of Ash Wednesday" demonstrates how demonism could make the transition from the mystical inquiries of the symbolists into the age of secular art. This is the age in which the demons of the medieval imagination have been banished through the study of medicine and psychology, the age in which, as illustrated by Sigmund Freud's 1923 study of seventeenth-century demonization in Germany, the Devil is now understood as a neurotic symptom, a symbol of all that men and women sexually desire in secret, but cannot admit openly for fear of social and moral retribution.[98] Freud's analysis neatly anticipates the hysteria of modern ideological politics, according to which secular authority taps into deep-seated anxieties and neuroses in order to blacken the reputation of political opponents. Zamiatin found himself at the receiving end of such a campaign of political persecution in 1929, and it is interesting to note that in his letter to Stalin he borrows the language of medieval demonization in order to describe it: "Just as the Christians created the devil (chert) as a convenient personification of all evil, so the critics have transformed me into the devil of Soviet literature. Spitting at the devil is regarded as a good deed, and ev-

eryone spat to the best of his ability. In each of my published works, these critics have inevitably discovered some diabolical intent."[99]

"Diabolical," here, means "anti-Soviet" and "criminal," not "anti-Christian," and is an indication of the degree to which the word "devil" was a free-floating signifier in Zamiatin's lexicon, one which could take on a variety of meanings, depending on the context. The devilish mask of his fiction, and the diabolical provocation of some of his public antics—most famously, his adoption of aristocratic English dress-codes and pipe-smoking at a time of spartan commissarial, military fashion—were self-conscious reflections of this fact. Indeed, it might be argued, paraphrasing Voltaire, that if the Devil did not exist, Zamiatin would have had to invent him.

Notes

1. See "Anatol' Frans (Nekrolog)" (1924), in Evgenii Zamiatin, *Sochineniia,* 4 vols. (Munich: Neimanis, 1970-88), 4:196. Henceforth, unless otherwise stated, all citations of Zamiatin will be from this edition and will be given in the text and notes by volume and page number. Unless otherwise indicated, all translations are my own.

2. As an example, see his allusion to the myth of Lucifer as rebel angel in the essay "Rai" (1921), 4:524-31. The theme of Satanic rebellion has also been identified in the dystopian novel *We* (*My,* 1927). See Richard A. Gregg, "Two Adams and Eve in the Crystal Palace: Dostoevsky, the Bible, and 'We,'" *Slavic Review* 24 (1965):680-87.

3. The dates given refer to the date of publication, rather than to the time of writing. "O sviatom grekhe Zenitsy-devy. Slovo pokhval'noe" (3:64-67) first appeared in the SR newspaper *Delo naroda* on 15 October (Old Style) 1917. "O tom, kak istselen byl otrok Erazm" (1:463-74) was first published as a booklet with illustrations by the artist Boris Kustodiev—see *O blazhennom startse Pamve Nereste, o narochitoi premudrosti ego, o mnogikh proisshedshikh chudesnykh znameniiakh i o tom, kak istselen byl inok Erazm* (Berlin: Petropolis, 1922). "O chude, proisshedshem v Pepel'nuiu Sredu" (1:475-81) was first published in the journal *Novaia Rossiia*, 1926, no. 1:57-62. Translations of "O tom, kak byl istselen otrok Erazm" and "O chude, proisshedshem v Pepel'nuiu Sredu" are taken from Yevgeny Zamyatin, *The Dragon and Other Stories,* trans. and ed. Mirra Ginsburg (London: Penguin, 1975), 150-63 and 208-15, respectively. Henceforth, for the sake of simplicity, the first miracle tale will be called "The Precious Virgin."

4. Cited in Peter Stanford, *The Devil. A Biography* (London: Heinemann, 1996), 181.

5. "Text of sexual enjoyment (texte de jouissance): one that brings about a state of loss, one that causes discomfort (even a certain annoyance), shakes the historical, cultural, psychological bases of the reader, the consistency of his tastes, his values, his memories, causes a crisis in his relationship with language." See Roland Barthes, *Le Plaisir du texte* (Paris: Les Editions du Seuil, 1973), 26. For a detailed examination of Zamiatin's miracle stories as hagiographic parodies, see the fifth chapter of my doctoral dissertation, "Evgenii Zamiatin and the Literary Stylization of Rus'" (Ph.D. diss., School of Slavonic and East European Studies, University of London, 1997), 257-350.

6. Bakhtin discusses hagiographic parodies as carnivalized texts in Mikhail Bakhtin, *Rabelais and His World,* trans. Hélène Iswolsky (Bloomington: Indiana University Press, 1984), 1-58, esp. 13-15. For a discussion of Bakhtin's conception of carnival laughter as it relates to medieval Russian culture, see D. S. Likhachev, A. M. Panchenko, and N. V. Ponyrko, eds., *Smekh v drevnei rusi* (Leningrad: Nauka, 1984), 3-25.

7. For the folk-religious view of the devil in terms of a clown (shut), one whose evil machinations include various types of prank (koznia), intrigue (prokaza), and joke (shutka), see Sergei Maksimov, *Nechistaia, nevedomaia i krestnaia sila* [1903], 2 vols. (reprint, Moscow: Kniga, 1989), 1:6-22.

8. The Orthodox Church condemned all forms of laughter and secular music and entertainment as the work of the Devil. See Ju. M. Lotman and B. A. Uspenskij, "New Aspects in the Study of Early Russian Culture," in their *The Semiotics of Russian Culture,* ed. Ann Shukman, Michigan Slavic Contributions, no. 11 (Ann Arbor: Department of Slavic Languages and Literatures, University of Michigan, 1984), 36-52. For a history of the *skomorokhi* and their formal proscription by the Church, see Russell Zguta, *Russian Minstrels. A History of the "Skomorokhi"* (Oxford: Clarendon Press, 1978).

9. For an examination of this tendency in Gogol's work, see "Komicheskii alogizm," in Aleksandr L. Slonimskii, *Tekhnika komicheskogo u Gogolia* [1923] (reprint, Providence, R.I.: Brown University Press, 1963), 33-65.

10. Remizov's Great and Free Order of Apes (Obez'ian'ia Velikaia i Vol'naia Palata [Obezvelvolpal]) was founded in 1908, but proclaimed officially only in 1917, after the February Revolution—for details regarding the Order's es-

tablishment, membership, and activities during this period, see S. S. Grechishkin, "Arkhiv Remizova," in *Ezhegodnik rukopisnogo otdela Pushkinskogo Doma na 1975 god,* ed. M. p. Alekseev and others (Leningrad: Nauka, 1977), 20-44. It is not known when exactly Zamiatin was coopted into the Order. Remizov first mentions his pseudonym (Bishop Zamutius) in connection with the series of arrests made by the Cheka in February 1919 of artistic figures believed to be sympathetic to the Left Socialist Revolutionaries—see the relevant sections of the diary he was keeping at the time, reprinted in A. Remizov, *Vzvikhrennaia Rus'* (Moscow: Sovetskii pisatel', 1991), 377. These arrests gave rise to Remizov's "Manifest," issued in the name of his pseudonym, Asyka the First, in which the anarchic principles of the Order were enunciated. The text of this document, his *skomorokh* manifesto ("Tulumbas"), and other texts relating to the establishment of the Order were first published together in *AKHRU. Povest' Peterburgskaia* (Berlin and St. Petersburg, Moscow: Izdatel'stvo Z. I. Grzhebina, 1922), 47-51.

11. For a discussion of official attitudes towards street culture in the immediate aftermath of the Revolution, see Catriona Kelly, *Petrushka. The Russian Carnival Puppet Theatre* (Cambridge: Cambridge University Press, 1990), 179-211.

12. For a detailed discussion of this literary phenomenon, see Margaret Ziolkowski, *Hagiography and Modern Russian Literature* (Princeton: Princeton University Press, 1988), 3-33.

13. Ibid., 83.

14. Ibid.

15. For a discussion of Tolstoi's attitude towards religion and the doctrines of the Russian Orthodox Church, see Ernest J. Simmons, *Introduction to Tolstoy's Writings* (Chicago and London: University of Chicago Press, 1968), 94-117.

16. "From Tolstoi—the absolute, pathos, faith (although this is compromised by virtue of his faith in reason). From France—relativism, irony, scepticism (. . .): both are great heretics; and many of their works belong to that most prestigious category for writers: the banned book." See "Anatol' Frans (Nekrolog)," 4:195.

17. See, for example, "Scholastica" (1889), *Légende de Thaïs, comédienne* (1889), "Sainte Euphrosine" (1891), "La Légende des saintes Oliverie et Liberette" (1891), and "Le Miracle du grand saint Nicolas" (1909). For a more detailed discussion of this subject in France's work, see the chapter entitled "Eroticism and *Gauloiserie,*" in Dushan Bresky,

The Art of Anatole France (The Hague and Paris: Mouton, 1969), 159-78.

18. For a more detailed discussion of Tsarist censorship as it related to taboo subjects, see N. Bogomolov, "'My—dva grozoi zazhzhennye stvola'," in *Anti-mir russkoi kul'tury. Iazyk. Fol'klor. Literatura,* ed. N. Bogomolov (Moscow: Ladomir, 1996), 297-327.

19. Ibid.

20. For the origins of this sobriquet, and its connection with hagiographic sources, see the footnote in Grechishkin, "Arkhiv Remizova," 32.

21. Slobin reports that after the abolition of censorship in 1905 these artists were allegedly collaborating on an encyclopaedia of erotica, to be entitled "On Love" ("O liubvi"), which would comprise folk notions and advice on sex. See Greta N. Slobin, *Remizov's Fictions. 1900-1921* (DeKalb: Northern Illinois University Press, 1991), 66.

22. In the folk-religious imagination, the production of both spirits and tobacco is attributed to the devil: "In stories about the origins of tobacco there is even more difference of opinion: either it sprouted from the grave of a brother and sister who had been involved in an incestuous relationship, or from the head of a Biblical whore (Viatka province), or from the body of a nun who had strayed from the path of piety and been struck down by lightning (Penza province), or, finally, from the grave of some unknown person (Simbirsk province)." See Maksimov, *Nechistaia, nevedomaia i krestnaia sila,* 1:10.

23. Bizarrely, in view of the contents, the editors of Afanas'ev's *Secret Tales of Russia* tried to conceal the true identity of the author-collector by pretending that the book had been published by the Valaam Monastery, universally recognized as one of the most pious in Russia. Presumably, this was to protect Afanas'ev from potential legal action. See *Secret Tales of Russia,* with an introduction by G. Legman (New York: Brussel and Brussel, 1966), v.

24. The name of Remitzov's sage, rather amusingly in light of his account, derives from the Greek word *gnosos,* meaning someone who possesses a special knowledge of spiritual mysteries. The name also alludes to the Gnostics, a heretical Christian sect in the first to the third centuries, the members of which claimed to possess such knowledge.

25. "In medieval life, Remizov would have been one of the *skomorokhi* (merry folk), the entertainers forbidden by the Orthodox church. In his own

versions of the established literary tradition, he rejected all authority, whether religious or secular." See Slobin, *Remizov's Fictions,* 34-35.

26. See "Sirin. Sbornik pervyi i vtoroi" (1914), 4:497-99.

27. Zamiatin revealed Remizov as the model for this character in "Zakulisy" (1930), 4:304. It is worth noting that the information given in "Alatyr'" (1:158) about marsh-demons, including the use of the word *khokhlik* to indicate their hirsute qualities, echoes extremely closely the discussion of this phenomenon in Maksimov, *Nechistaia, nevedomaia i krestnaia sila,* 1:8.

28. An important part of Remizov's grotesque strategy involves the use of chimeras—for example, the demonic Sea-Monster (Chudo morskoe) which makes an appearance early in the tale. This is presumably based on a *lubok* picture described in the celebrated collection of Dmitrii Rovinsky. See the version of this picture reprinted in T. A. Novichkova, *Russkii demonologicheskii slovar'* (St. Petersburg: Peterburgskii pisatel', 1995), 97.

29. "Tulumbas," 3:72-73. The archaic term employed here to mean "private part" (ud, udishche) was used earlier in Remizov's tale and, interestingly, can also be found with the same meaning in "The Precious Virgin": "udy zhe nezhnyia ikh opaliaemy byli povsiudu lampadami ognennymi," 3:65.

30. In a letter written to Remizov while in Great Britain, Zamiatin inquired after the progress of his short story "Africa" ("Afrika," 1916) and "The Precious Virgin," which suggests that they were both written prior to his departure in March 1916. See Zamiatin's letter to Remizov dated 22 April (Old Style) 1916, in "Pis'ma E. I. Zamiatina A. M. Remizovu," ed. V. V. Buznik, *Russkaia literatura* 1 (1992):177-78.

31. "'The Precious Virgin'—a difficult, but successful experiment in the stylization of language: a work which is not written in medieval Russian, but one which gives the illusion of having been so." See "O iazyke," the title of Zamiatin's lecture given at the Petrograd House of Arts in 1920-21, and published for the first time in "Evg. Zamiatin. Tekhnika khudozhestvennoi prozy," ed. A. Strizhev, *Literaturnaia ucheba* 6 (1988):81.

32. For further discussion of this genre in the early Christian and medieval periods, see Julia Alissandratos, *Medieval Slavic and Patristic Eulogies* (Florence: Sansoni, 1982).

33. See Zamiatin's archive in the Institute of World Literature of the Academy of Sciences in Moscow (IMLI), fond 47, opis' 1, ed. khr. 58-61.

34. The healing of a woman who has swallowed a snake while drinking a cup of water occurs, for example, in the *Life* of Simeon the Stylite. See the modern Russian version, "Zhizn' i deianiia blazhennogo Simeona Stolpnika," in *Vizantiiskie legendy,* ed. S. V. Poliakova (Moscow: Ladomir, 1994), 29.

35. Breast mutilation as a *topos* in the legends of the virgin-martyrs is discussed in Thomas J. Heffernan, *Sacred Biography. Saints and Their Biographers in the Middle Ages* (New York and Oxford: Oxford University Press, 1988), 282-83.

36. For the stock theme of the fragrant body, see Al'bert Opulskii, *Zhitiia sviatykh v tvorchestve russkikh pisatelei XIX veka* (East Lansing, Mich.: Russian Language Journal, 1986), 21.

37. For further discussion of Saint Mary's popularity in nineteenth-century Russia, see Ziolkowski, *Hagiography and Modern Russian Literature,* 73-78.

38. See n. 6. Interestingly, Bakhtin draws attention to the paradox that hagiographic texts in the Middle Ages were often accompanied by illustrations of a grotesque nature. See Bakhtin, *Rabelais and His World,* 96.

39. See Gor'ky's letter to Nikolai Tikhonov dated 23 October 1924, cited in N. Primochkina, "M. Gor'kii i E. Zamiatin (K istorii literaturnykh vzaimootnoshenii)," *Russkaia literatura* 4 (1987): 151.

40. See Cavendish, "Evgenii Zamiatin and the Literary Stylisation of Rus'," 279-85.

41. See "Vstrechi s B. M. Kustodievym" (1927), 4:169.

42. See 1:347.

43. See 4:48-50.

44. See Zamiatin's letter to Lunts dated 13 November 1923, in "L. Lunts i Serapionovy brat'ia," *Novyi zhurnal* 82 (1966):185.

45. Ibid.

46. See "Shutochnaia miniatiura 'Zhitie Blokhi'" (1929), 2:507-18.

47. See Zamiatin, *Nechestivye rasskazy* (Moscow: Artel' pisatelei "Krug," 1927), 129-52, 153-66.

48. Cited in M. Chudakova, "Eretik, ili matros na machte," in *Evgenii Zamiatin, Sochineniia* (Moscow: Kniga, 1988), 504. It is interesting to note that these words echo Gogol's narrator in "Nos." At one point he exclaims: "All sorts of nonsense (chepukha) takes place in the world."

Later, he dismisses one possible interpretation of the story (offered by himself!) as "rubbish" ("vzdor"). See "Nos," in N. V. Gogol', *Sobranie sochinenii,* 6 vols. (Moscow: Khudozhestvennaia literatura, 1976-79), 3:61, 63.

49. See Chudakova, "Eretik, ili matros na machte," 504.

50. See Ann Shukman, "Gogol's *The Nose* or the Devil in the Works," in *Nikolay Gogol. Text and Context,* ed. Jane Grayson and Faith Wigzell (Basingstoke and London: Macmillan, 1989), 64-82.

51. "Every evening, at departure, Doctor Voichek left some such thorny point stuck in the canon's head. Afterwards the canon twisted and tossed in bed, thinking and thinking, turning the matter this way and that" (1:476).

52. The verb *zamutit'* in modern Russian means simply "to make cloudy or turgid." However, its archaic sense means "to create disorder" and "to sow discord" ("privesti v bespokoistvo, smiatenie"). See *Slovar' russkogo iazyka,* 4 vols. (Moscow: Izdatel'stvo "Russkii iazyk," 1981-84), 1:547.

53. Bishop Sophronius, by comparison, introduces the extraordinary events in his *Life of Saint Mary of Egypt* as follows: "No one should have any doubts about believing me, for I am writing about what I have heard, and no one should think in astonishment over the magnitude of the miracles that I am inventing fables. God deliver me from inventing and falsifying an account in which his name comes . . . If, however, such readers of this narrative are found, who are so overcome by the miraculous nature of this account that they will not want to believe it, may the Lord be merciful to them! For they consider the infirmity of human nature and think that miracles related about people are impossible." See Sophronius, *Life of Saint Mary of Egypt,* in *Harlots of the Desert,* trans. and ed. Benedicta Ward (London and Oxford: Mowbray, 1987), 36.

54. See Shane, *The Life and Works of Evgenij Zamjatin,* 178.

55. This *topos* in the bawdy tale will be examined in detail below.

56. See Maksimov, *Nechistaia, nevedomaia i krestnaia sila,* 1:6-22.

57. "But as to knowledge of things divine, none shall ever persuade me that any lad of my age in all Christendom could there beat me, for I knew nought of god or man, of heaven or hell, of angel

or devil, nor could discern between good and evil. So may it be easily understood that I, with such knowledge of theology, lived like our first parents in Paradise, which in their innocence knew nought of sickness or death or dying, and still less of the Resurrection . . . Yes, I was so perfected in ignorance that I knew not that I knew nothing." See Johann Jacob Grimmelshausen, *Simplicissimus,* trans. S. Goodrich (Sawtry, Cambridgeshire: Dedalus/ Hippocrene, 1989), 3.

58. See the abridged version of Saint Margaret's legend in *The Golden Legend of Jacobus de Voragine,* trans. from the Latin by William Granger Ryan and Helmut Ripperger (New York, London and Toronto: Longmans, Green & Co., 1948), 613-14.

59. See "Legenda," in A. I. Gertsen, *Sobranie sochinenii,* 30 vols. (Moscow: Izdatel'stvo Akademii nauk SSSR, 1954-66), 1:81-106.

60. See "Saint Euphrosine," in Anatole France, *Oeuvres,* 4 vols. (Paris: Gallimard, 1964-91), 1:903-13.

61. "His white face was extraordinarily tender, and every time he flicked away the curly locks which fell across his eyes with his hand, he might have been mistaken for a young girl." See Gertsen, "Legenda," 84-85.

62. See *Narodnye russkie skazki A. N. Afanas'eva,* 3 vols. (Moscow: Nauka, 1986), 3:318.

63. "Time passed—and the nun gave birth. I was at the christening, only I couldn't make out the sex of the child: a boy or a girl?" Ibid., 3:319.

64. It is worth noting, perhaps, that this was the subject of Pushkin's *Gavriiliada* (1821), which had been published legally for the first time in Russia only in 1918. See M. p. Alekseev, "Zametki o Gavriiliade," in his *Pushkin: Sravnitel'no-istoricheskie issledovaniia* (Leningrad: Nauka, 1962), 281-325, esp. 283-84.

65. This is reflected in the author's opening address to the reader: "If you take a miracle that happened long ago, to someone else—that's somehow easier to accept. I could believe in it, and so could you. But just imagine—if it should happen now, if it happened yesterday, to you—yes, precisely, to you!" (1:475).

66. See, for example, the homosexual innuendo in Fr. Cipolla's sermon (tenth story of the sixth day), in Giovanni Boccaccio, *The Decameron,* trans. with an introduction and notes by G. H. McWilliam, 2d ed. (Harmondsworth: Penguin, 1995), 469-77.

67. "But as [the Muscovites] are given up to all licentiousness, even to sins against Nature, not only

with Men, but also with Beasts, he who can tell most stories of that kind, and set them out in most gestures, is accompted the bravest Man." Cited in Kelly, *Petrushka. The Russian Carnival Puppet Theatre,* 50.

68. See Boccaccio, *The Decameron* (third story of the ninth day), 658-63.

69. The Afanas'ev version, "Skazka o tom, kak pop rodil telenka" [1872], is reprinted in *Russkie zavetnye skazki* (St. Petersburg: Biblioteca Erotica, 1994), 136-39. The Onchukov version, "Pop telenka rodil," is reprinted in *Zavetnye skazki iz sobranii N. E. Onchukova* (Moscow: Ladomir, 1996), 226-27.

70. Ibid., 226.

71. See Boccaccio, *The Decameron,* cxl.

72. See, in particular, the following tales from Onchukov's collection: "Shut," "Pop ispovednik," "Pop i rabotnik," "Na glazakh u popa," "Pro popa," "Popad'ia ponemetski zagovorila," "Ispoved'," "Smekh i slezy," "Chudov monastyr'," and "Popovna i monakhi."

73. "You, you pregnant woman, careful not to damage the baby in your stomach by placing a belt around your breasts!" ("Ty, chto chrevataia zhenka, ne izvredit' by v briukhe robenka, podpoiasyvaesse po titkam!"). Cited in V. p. Adrianova-Peretts, *Russkaia demokraticheskaia satira XVII veka* (Moscow and Leningrad: Izdatel'stvo Akademii nauk SSSR, 1954), 158.

74. Ibid., 157.

75. "And worse—Christ victorious in practice is the fat-bellied priest (puzatyi pop) in a silk-lined, purple cassock giving his blessing with his right hand and collecting alms with his left." See "Skify li?," 4:504.

76. "The censors, to coin a phrase from Archpriest Avvakum, have 'sat their back side' on my novel" ("Na roman moi zdes' tsenzura 'gubkom sela'— protopopoavvakumovski govoria")—see Zamiatin's letter to Lunts, 185. Unfortunately, the misprint in *Novyi zhurnal* distorts Zamiatin's allusion. *Gubkom,* the meaning of which is unclear, should read *guznom,* a vulgar expression for the backside—see *Slovar' russkogo iazyka,* 1:356. This can be seen from a letter written by Zamiatin a month earlier, this time to Maksimilian Voloshin, in which exactly the same expression is used: "I arrived—and was greeted straightaway with the news that the Katkovs have, to coin a phrase from Avvakum, 'sat their backside' on my novel" ("Priekhal—pervoe, s chem pozdravili: Katkovy

na moi roman 'guznom seli'—po avvakumovski govoria"). See "'Pishu vam iz Rossii . . .' (Pis'ma E. I. Zamiatina M. A. Voloshinu)," ed. V. Kupchenko, *Pod''em* 5 (1988):121.

77. It is also mentioned in the story itself: "And it was on Wednesday, Ash Wednesday, the first day of Lent (postom na pervoi nedele) that it all happened" (1:478).

78. See Maksimov, *Nechistaia, nevedomaia i krestnaia sila,* 1:10.

79. "The room was quiet, with eerily white walls, doors, and benches, as if it were no longer here, on earth, where everything is varicoloured, noisy, where black and white are always intermingled" (1:478).

80. See *Entsiklopedicheskii slovar' Brokgauza i Efrona,* 42 vols. and 4 suppl. vols. (St. Petersburg: Tipografiia I. A. Efrona, 1890-1907), 10a:959.

81. See Maksimov, *Nechistaia, nevedomaia i krestnaia sila,* 1:9.

82. "My dear friend, if you are troubled by the thought of the next world, of retribution and all that—which is understandable—I can put your mind at ease" (1:476).

83. The idea that food, wine, "the genital force" and the organs of the body are the driving forces of the carnival experience is mentioned in Bakhtin, *Rabelais and his World,* 62.

84. Couvade is a custom in some cultures whereby a man takes to his bed and enacts certain rituals when his wife bears a child. It is now used more as a medical term which refers to men who experience phantom pregnancies or illnesses akin to those of their wives during pregnancy. It is discussed as a source for the story of Calandrino's pregnancy in A.C. Lee, *The Decameron. Its Sources and Analogues* (London: David Nutt, 1909), 277-81.

85. Maksimov, *Nechistaia, nevedomaia i krestnaia sila,* 1:17.

86. See John 8:44.

87. "Nevskii prospekt" (1835), in Gogol', *Sobranie sochinenii,* 3:39.

88. See F. M. Dostoevskii, *Polnoe sobranie sochinenii v tridtsati tomakh,* ed. V. G. Bazanov and others, 30 vols. (Leningrad: Nauka, 1972-90), 15:69-70.

89. "However, all this came to him mistily, from far away, as in a dream: the babe was already going off to sleep" (1:481).

90. Cited in Slonimskii, *Tekhnika komicheskogo u Gogolia,* 33.

91. Ibid., 9.

92. Ibid., 10.

93. Ibid.

94. See 4:255.

95. For a discussion of carnival rituals in medieval Russia, in particular the Furnace Play and its relation to the French *diablerie,* see Likhachev, Panchenko, and Ponyrko, eds., *Smekh v drevnei rusi,* 158-75.

96. See "Narodnyi teatr" (1927), 4:429.

97. See Zamiatin's letter to Diky dated 12 November 1924, in "Perepiska s E. I. Zamiatinym i B. M. Kustodievym po povodu spektaklia 'Blokha'," in *A. Dikii. Stat'i. Perepiska. Vospominaniia* (Moscow: Iskusstvo, 1967), 302.

98. See Freud, "A Seventeenth-Century Demonological Neurosis" (Eine Teufelsneurose im siebzehnten Jahrhundert, 1923), in *Sigmund Freud. Standard Edition,* trans. and under the General Editorship of James Strachey, 24 vols (London: The Hogarth Press, 1953-74), 19:72-105.

99. "Pis'mo Stalinu" (1931), 4:310-11.

FURTHER READING

Biographies

Alexandrova, Vera. "Yevgeny Zamyatin (1884-1937)." In *A History of Soviet Literature,* translated by Mirra Ginsburg, pp. 84-96. Garden City, N.Y.: Doubleday & Company, 1963.

A general biographical sketch of Zamyatin's life.

Richards, D. J. *Zamyatin: A Soviet Heretic.* London: Bowes & Bowes, 1962, 112 p.

Detailed biographical overview of Zamyatin's life and career.

Criticism

Collins, Christopher. "Islanders." In *Major Soviet Writers: Essays in Criticism,* edited by Edward J. Brown, pp. 209-20. London and New York: Oxford University Press, 1973.

Discusses the portrayal of alienation in modern society in *Ostrovityane (Islanders).*

Connolly, Julian W. "A Modernist's Palette: Color in the Fiction of Evgenij Zamjatin." *Russian Language Journal* 33, no. 115 (spring 1979): 82-98.

   Studies the development of color imagery in *Uezdnoe,* "Sever," and *Navodnenie.*

Ginsburg, Mirra. "Translator's Introduction." In *The Dragon: Fifteen Stories,* translated and edited by Mirra Ginsburg, n.p. New York: Random House, 1966.

   Discusses Zamyatin's literary career and aesthetic tenets.

Mihajlov, Mihajlo. "Evgeny Zamyatin: The Chagall of Russian Literature." In *Russian Themes,* translated by Marija Mihajlov, pp. 288-97. New York: Farrar, Straus and Giroux, 1968.

Examines Zamyatin's themes and modernist influence.

Slonim, Marc. "Evgeny Zamyatin: The Ironic Dissident." In *Soviet Russian Literature: Writers and Problems,* pp. 80-9. New York: Oxford University Press, 1964.

   Assesses Zamyatin's distinct writing style and his impact on Russian literature during the 1920s.

Van Baak, J. J. "Zamjatin's Cave—On Troglodyte versus Urban Culture, Myth, and the Semiotics of Literary Space." *Russian Literature* 10, no. 4 (15 November 1981): 381-422.

   Views culture conflict in the story "Peščera" ("The Cave") to illustrate "how certain semiotic properties of cultures find expression in a narrative text."

How to Use This Index

The main references

> **Calvino, Italo**
> 1923-1985 .... **CLC 5, 8, 11, 22, 33, 39,**
> **73; SSC 3, 48**

list all author entries in the following Gale Literary Criticism series:

AAL = Asian American Literature
BG = The Beat Generation: A Gale Critical Companion
BLC = Black Literature Criticism
BLCS = Black Literature Criticism Supplement
CLC = Contemporary Literary Criticism
CLR = Children's Literature Review
CMLC = Classical and Medieval Literature Criticism
DC = Drama Criticism
HLC = Hispanic Literature Criticism
HLCS = Hispanic Literature Criticism Supplement
HR = Harlem Renaissance: A Gale Critical Companion
LC = Literature Criticism from 1400 to 1800
NCLC = Nineteenth-Century Literature Criticism
NNAL = Native North American Literature
PC = Poetry Criticism
SSC = Short Story Criticism
TCLC = Twentieth-Century Literary Criticism
WLC = World Literature Criticism, 1500 to the Present
WLCS = World Literature Criticism Supplement

The cross-references

> See also CA 85-88, 116; CANR 23, 61;
> DAM NOV; DLB 196; EW 13; MTCW 1, 2;
> RGSF 2; RGWL 2; SFW 4; SSFS 12

list all author entries in the following Gale biographical and literary sources:

AAYA = Authors & Artists for Young Adults
AFAW = African American Writers
AFW = African Writers
AITN = Authors in the News
AMW = American Writers
AMWR = American Writers Retrospective Supplement
AMWS = American Writers Supplement
ANW = American Nature Writers
AW = Ancient Writers
BEST = Bestsellers
BPFB = Beacham's Encyclopedia of Popular Fiction: Biography and Resources
BRW = British Writers
BRWS = British Writers Supplement
BW = Black Writers
BYA = Beacham's Guide to Literature for Young Adults
CA = Contemporary Authors
CAAS = Contemporary Authors Autobiography Series
CABS = Contemporary Authors Bibliographical Series
CAD = Contemporary American Dramatists
CANR = Contemporary Authors New Revision Series
CAP = Contemporary Authors Permanent Series
CBD = Contemporary British Dramatists
CCA = Contemporary Canadian Authors
CD = Contemporary Dramatists
CDALB = Concise Dictionary of American Literary Biography
CDALBS = Concise Dictionary of American Literary Biography Supplement
CDBLB = Concise Dictionary of British Literary Biography

CMW = *St. James Guide to Crime & Mystery Writers*
CN = *Contemporary Novelists*
CP = *Contemporary Poets*
CPW = *Contemporary Popular Writers*
CSW = *Contemporary Southern Writers*
CWD = *Contemporary Women Dramatists*
CWP = *Contemporary Women Poets*
CWRI = *St. James Guide to Children's Writers*
CWW = *Contemporary World Writers*
DA = *DISCovering Authors*
DA3 = *DISCovering Authors 3.0*
DAB = *DISCovering Authors: British Edition*
DAC = *DISCovering Authors: Canadian Edition*
DAM = *DISCovering Authors: Modules*
   DRAM: Dramatists Module; MST: Most-studied Authors Module;
   MULT: Multicultural Authors Module; NOV: Novelists Module;
   POET: Poets Module; POP: Popular Fiction and Genre Authors Module
DFS = *Drama for Students*
DLB = *Dictionary of Literary Biography*
DLBD = *Dictionary of Literary Biography Documentary Series*
DLBY = *Dictionary of Literary Biography Yearbook*
DNFS = *Literature of Developing Nations for Students*
EFS = *Epics for Students*
EXPN = *Exploring Novels*
EXPP = *Exploring Poetry*
EXPS = *Exploring Short Stories*
EW = *European Writers*
FANT = *St. James Guide to Fantasy Writers*
FW = *Feminist Writers*
GFL = *Guide to French Literature,* Beginnings to 1789, 1798 to the Present
GLL = *Gay and Lesbian Literature*
HGG = *St. James Guide to Horror, Ghost & Gothic Writers*
HW = *Hispanic Writers*
IDFW = *International Dictionary of Films and Filmmakers: Writers and Production Artists*
IDTP = *International Dictionary of Theatre: Playwrights*
LAIT = *Literature and Its Times*
LAW = *Latin American Writers*
JRDA = *Junior DISCovering Authors*
MAICYA = *Major Authors and Illustrators for Children and Young Adults*
MAICYAS = *Major Authors and Illustrators for Children and Young Adults Supplement*
MAWW = *Modern American Women Writers*
MJW = *Modern Japanese Writers*
MTCW = *Major 20th-Century Writers*
NCFS = *Nonfiction Classics for Students*
NFS = *Novels for Students*
PAB = *Poets: American and British*
PFS = *Poetry for Students*
RGAL = *Reference Guide to American Literature*
RGEL = *Reference Guide to English Literature*
RGSF = *Reference Guide to Short Fiction*
RGWL = *Reference Guide to World Literature*
RHW = *Twentieth-Century Romance and Historical Writers*
SAAS = *Something about the Author Autobiography Series*
SATA = *Something about the Author*
SFW = *St. James Guide to Science Fiction Writers*
SSFS = *Short Stories for Students*
TCWW = *Twentieth-Century Western Writers*
WLIT = *World Literature and Its Times*
WP = *World Poets*
YABC = *Yesterday's Authors of Books for Children*
YAW = *St. James Guide to Young Adult Writers*

Literary Criticism Series
Cumulative Author Index

Arden, John 1930- .... **CLC 6, 13, 15**
  See also BRWS 2; CA 13-16R; CAAS 4;
  CANR 31, 65, 67, 124; CBD; CD 5, 6;
  DAM DRAM; DFS 9; DLB 13, 245;
  EWL 3; MTCW 1

Arenas, Reinaldo 1943-1990 .. **CLC 41; HLC 1**
  See also CA 124; 128; 133; CANR 73, 106;
  DAM MULT; DLB 145; EWL 3; GLL 2;
  HW 1; LAW; LAWS 1; MTCW 2; MTFW
  2005; RGSF 2; RGWL 3; WLIT 1

Arendt, Hannah 1906-1975 .... **CLC 66, 98**
  See also CA 17-20R; 61-64; CANR 26, 60;
  DLB 242; MTCW 1, 2

Aretino, Pietro 1492-1556 .... **LC 12**
  See also RGWL 2, 3

Arghezi, Tudor .... **CLC 80**
  See Theodorescu, Ion N.
  See also CA 167; CDWLB 4; DLB 220;
  EWL 3

Arguedas, Jose Maria 1911-1969 .... **CLC 10, 18; HLCS 1; TCLC 147**
  See also CA 89-92; CANR 73; DLB 113;
  EWL 3; HW 1; LAW; RGWL 2, 3; WLIT 1

Argueta, Manlio 1936- .... **CLC 31**
  See also CA 131; CANR 73; CWW 2; DLB
  145; EWL 3; HW 1; RGWL 3

Arias, Ron(ald Francis) 1941- .... **HLC 1**
  See also CA 131; CANR 81, 136; DAM
  MULT; DLB 82; HW 1, 2; MTCW 2;
  MTFW 2005

Ariosto, Lodovico
  See Ariosto, Ludovico
  See also WLIT 7

Ariosto, Ludovico 1474-1533 ... **LC 6, 87; PC 42**
  See Ariosto, Lodovico
  See also EW 2; RGWL 2, 3

Aristides
  See Epstein, Joseph

Aristophanes 450B.C.-385B.C. .... **CMLC 4, 51; DC 2; WLCS**
  See also AW 1; CDWLB 1; DA; DA3;
  DAB; DAC; DAM DRAM, MST; DFS
  10; DLB 176; LMFS 1; RGWL 2, 3; TWA

Aristotle 384B.C.-322B.C. .... **CMLC 31; WLCS**
  See also AW 1; CDWLB 1; DA; DA3;
  DAB; DAC; DAM MST; DLB 176;
  RGWL 2, 3; TWA

Arlt, Roberto (Godofredo Christophersen) 1900-1942 .... **HLC 1; TCLC 29**
  See also CA 123; 131; CANR 67; DAM
  MULT; DLB 305; EWL 3; HW 1, 2;
  IDTP; LAW

Armah, Ayi Kwei 1939- . **BLC 1; CLC 5, 33, 136**
  See also AFW; BRWS 10; BW 1; CA 61-
  64; CANR 21, 64; CDWLB 3; CN 1, 2,
  3, 4, 5, 6, 7; DAM MULT, POET; DLB
  117; EWL 3; MTCW 1; WLIT 2

Armatrading, Joan 1950- .... **CLC 17**
  See also CA 114; 186

Armitage, Frank
  See Carpenter, John (Howard)

Armstrong, Jeannette (C.) 1948- .... **NNAL**
  See also CA 149; CCA 1; CN 6, 7; DAC;
  SATA 102

Arnette, Robert
  See Silverberg, Robert

Arnim, Achim von (Ludwig Joachim von Arnim) 1781-1831 .. **NCLC 5, 159; SSC 29**
  See also DLB 90

Arnim, Bettina von 1785-1859 ...... **NCLC 38, 123**
  See also DLB 90; RGWL 2, 3

Arnold, Matthew 1822-1888 ..... **NCLC 6, 29, 89, 126; PC 5; WLC**
  See also BRW 5; CDBLB 1832-1890; DA;
  DAB; DAC; DAM MST, POET; DLB 32,
  57; EXPP; PAB; PFS 2; TEA; WP

Arnold, Thomas 1795-1842 .... **NCLC 18**
  See also DLB 55

Arnow, Harriette (Louisa) Simpson 1908-1986 .... **CLC 2, 7, 18**
  See also BPFB 1; CA 9-12R; 118; CANR
  14; CN 2, 3, 4; DLB 6; FW; MTCW 1, 2;
  RHW; SATA 42; SATA-Obit 47

Arouet, Francois-Marie
  See Voltaire

Arp, Hans
  See Arp, Jean

Arp, Jean 1887-1966 .... **CLC 5; TCLC 115**
  See also CA 81-84; 25-28R; CANR 42, 77;
  EW 10

Arrabal
  See Arrabal, Fernando

Arrabal (Teran), Fernando
  See Arrabal, Fernando
  See also CWW 2

Arrabal, Fernando 1932- ... **CLC 2, 9, 18, 58**
  See Arrabal (Teran), Fernando
  See also CA 9-12R; CANR 15; DLB 321;
  EWL 3; LMFS 2

Arreola, Juan Jose 1918-2001 .... **CLC 147; HLC 1; SSC 38**
  See also CA 113; 131; 200; CANR 81;
  CWW 2; DAM MULT; DLB 113; DNFS
  2; EWL 3; HW 1, 2; LAW; RGSF 2

Arrian c. 89(?)-c. 155(?) .... **CMLC 43**
  See also DLB 176

Arrick, Fran .... **CLC 30**
  See Gaberman, Judie Angell
  See also BYA 6

Arrley, Richmond
  See Delany, Samuel R(ay), Jr.

Artaud, Antonin (Marie Joseph) 1896-1948 .... **DC 14; TCLC 3, 36**
  See also CA 104; 149; DA3; DAM DRAM;
  DFS 22; DLB 258, 321; EW 11; EWL 3;
  GFL 1789 to the Present; MTCW 2;
  MTFW 2005; RGWL 2, 3

Arthur, Ruth M(abel) 1905-1979 ..... **CLC 12**
  See also CA 9-12R; 85-88; CANR 4; CWRI
  5; SATA 7, 26

Artsybashev, Mikhail (Petrovich) 1878-1927 .... **TCLC 31**
  See also CA 170; DLB 295

Arundel, Honor (Morfydd) 1919-1973 .... **CLC 17**
  See also CA 21-22; 41-44R; CAP 2; CLR
  35; CWRI 5; SATA 4; SATA-Obit 24

Arzner, Dorothy 1900-1979 .... **CLC 98**

Asch, Sholem 1880-1957 .... **TCLC 3**
  See also CA 105; EWL 3; GLL 2

Ascham, Roger 1516(?)-1568 .... **LC 101**
  See also DLB 236

Ash, Shalom
  See Asch, Sholem

Ashbery, John (Lawrence) 1927- .. **CLC 2, 3, 4, 6, 9, 13, 15, 25, 41, 77, 125; PC 26**
  See Berry, Jonas
  See also AMWS 3; CA 5-8R; CANR 9, 37,
  66, 102, 132; CP 1, 2, 3, 4, 5, 6, 7; DA3;
  DAM POET; DLB 5, 165; DLBY 1981;
  EWL 3; INT CANR-9; MAL 5; MTCW
  1, 2; MTFW 2005; PAB; PFS 11; RGAL
  4; TCLE 1:1; WP

Ashdown, Clifford
  See Freeman, R(ichard) Austin

Ashe, Gordon
  See Creasey, John

Ashton-Warner, Sylvia (Constance) 1908-1984 .... **CLC 19**
  See also CA 69-72; 112; CANR 29; CN 1,
  2, 3; MTCW 1, 2

Asimov, Isaac 1920-1992 ..... **CLC 1, 3, 9, 19, 26, 76, 92**
  See also AAYA 13; BEST 90:2; BPFB 1;
  BYA 4, 6, 7, 9; CA 1-4R; 137; CANR 2,
  19, 36, 60, 125; CLR 12, 79; CMW 4;
  CN 1, 2, 3, 4, 5; CPW; DA3; DAM POP;
  DLB 8; DLBY 1992; INT CANR-19;
  JRDA; LAIT 5; MAICYA 1; MAL 5;
  MTCW 1, 2; MTFW 2005; NFS 5; SFW
  RGAL 4; SATA 1, 26, 74; SCFW 1, 2;
  SFW 4; SSFS 17; TUS; YAW

Askew, Anne 1521(?)-1546 .... **LC 81**
  See also DLB 136

Assis, Joaquim Maria Machado de
  See Machado de Assis, Joaquim Maria

Astell, Mary 1666-1731 .... **LC 68**
  See also DLB 252; FW

Astley, Thea (Beatrice May) 1925-2004 .... **CLC 41**
  See also CA 65-68; 229; CANR 11, 43, 78;
  CN 1, 2, 3, 4, 5, 6, 7; DLB 289; EWL 3

Astley, William 1855-1911
  See Warung, Price

Aston, James
  See White, T(erence) H(anbury)

Asturias, Miguel Angel 1899-1974 .... **CLC 3, 8, 13; HLC 1**
  See also CA 25-28; 49-52; CANR 32; CAP
  2; CDWLB 3; DA3; DAM MULT, NOV;
  DLB 113, 290; EWL 3; HW 1; LAW;
  LMFS 2; MTCW 1, 2; RGWL 2, 3; WLIT 1

Atares, Carlos Saura
  See Saura (Atares), Carlos

Athanasius c. 295-c. 373 .... **CMLC 48**

Atheling, William
  See Pound, Ezra (Weston Loomis)

Atheling, William, Jr.
  See Blish, James (Benjamin)

Atherton, Gertrude (Franklin Horn) 1857-1948 .... **TCLC 2**
  See also CA 104; 155; DLB 9, 78, 186;
  HGG; RGAL 4; SUFW 1; TCWW 1, 2

Atherton, Lucius
  See Masters, Edgar Lee

Atkins, Jack
  See Harris, Mark

Atkinson, Kate 1951- .... **CLC 99**
  See also CA 166; CANR 101; DLB 267

Attaway, William (Alexander) 1911-1986 .... **BLC 1; CLC 92**
  See also BW 2, 3; CA 143; CANR 82;
  DAM MULT; DLB 76; MAL 5

Atticus
  See Fleming, Ian (Lancaster); Wilson,
  (Thomas) Woodrow

Atwood, Margaret (Eleanor) 1939- ... **CLC 2, 3, 4, 8, 13, 15, 25, 44, 84, 135; PC 8; SSC 2, 46; WLC**
  See also AAYA 12, 47; AMWS 13; BEST
  89:2; BPFB 1; CA 49-52; CANR 3, 24,
  33, 59, 95, 133; CN 2, 3, 4, 5, 6, 7; CP 1,
  2, 3, 4, 5, 6, 7; CPW; CWP; DA; DA3;
  DAB; DAC; DAM MST, NOV, POET;
  DLB 53, 251; EWL 3; EXPN; FL 1:5;
  FW; GL 2; INT CANR-24; LAIT 5;
  MTCW 1, 2; MTFW 2005; NFS 4, 12,
  13, 14, 19; PFS 7; RGSF 2; SATA 50;
  SSFS 3, 13; TCLE 1:1; TWA; WWE 1;
  YAW

Aubigny, Pierre d'
  See Mencken, H(enry) L(ouis)

Aubin, Penelope 1685-1731(?) .... **LC 9**
  See also DLB 39

EXPS; LAIT 5; MAL 5; MTCW 1, 2; MTFW 2005; NCFS 4; NFS 4; RGAL 4; RGSF 2; SATA 9; SATA-Obit 54; SSFS 2, 18; TUS

Baldwin, William c. 1515-1563 .... **LC 113**
See also DLB 132

Bale, John 1495-1563 .... **LC 62**
See also DLB 132; RGEL 2; TEA

Ball, Hugo 1886-1927 .... **TCLC 104**

Ballard, J(ames) G(raham) 1930- . **CLC 3, 6, 14, 36, 137; SSC 1, 53**
See also AAYA 3, 52; BRWS 5; CA 5-8R; CANR 15, 39, 65, 107, 133; CN 1, 2, 3, 4, 5, 6, 7; DA3; DAM NOV, POP; DLB 14, 207, 261, 319; EWL 3; HGG; MTCW 1, 2; MTFW 2005; NFS 8; RGEL 2; RGSF 2; SATA 93; SCFW 1, 2; SFW 4

Balmont, Konstantin (Dmitriyevich) 1867-1943 .... **TCLC 11**
See also CA 109; 155; DLB 295; EWL 3

Baltausis, Vincas 1847-1910
See Mikszath, Kalman

Balzac, Honore de 1799-1850 ... **NCLC 5, 35, 53, 153; SSC 5, 59; WLC**
See also DA; DA3; DAB; DAC; DAM MST, NOV; DLB 119; EW 5; GFL 1789 to the Present; LMFS 1; RGSF 2; RGWL 2, 3; SSFS 10; SUFW; TWA

Bambara, Toni Cade 1939-1995 .... **BLC 1; CLC 19, 88; SSC 35; TCLC 116; WLCS**
See also AAYA 5, 49; AFAW 2; AMWS 11; BW 2, 3; BYA 12, 14; CA 29-32R; 150; CANR 24, 49, 81; CDALBS; DA; DA3; DAC; DAM MST, MULT; DLB 38, 218; EXPS; MAL 5; MTCW 1, 2; MTFW 2005; RGAL 4; RGSF 2; SATA 112; SSFS 4, 7, 12, 21

Bamdad, A.
See Shamlu, Ahmad

Bamdad, Alef
See Shamlu, Ahmad

Banat, D. R.
See Bradbury, Ray (Douglas)

Bancroft, Laura
See Baum, L(yman) Frank

Banim, John 1798-1842 .... **NCLC 13**
See also DLB 116, 158, 159; RGEL 2

Banim, Michael 1796-1874 .... **NCLC 13**
See also DLB 158, 159

Banjo, The
See Paterson, A(ndrew) B(arton)

Banks, Iain
See Banks, Iain M(enzies)
See also BRWS 11

Banks, Iain M(enzies) 1954- .... **CLC 34**
See Banks, Iain
See also CA 123; 128; CANR 61, 106; DLB 194, 261; EWL 3; HGG; INT CA-128; MTFW 2005; SFW 4

Banks, Lynne Reid .... **CLC 23**
See Reid Banks, Lynne
See also AAYA 6; BYA 7; CLR 86; CN 4, 5, 6

Banks, Russell (Earl) 1940- .... **CLC 37, 72, 187; SSC 42**
See also AAYA 45; AMWS 5; CA 65-68; CAAS 15; CANR 19, 52, 73, 118; CN 4, 5, 6, 7; DLB 130, 278; EWL 3; MAL 5; MTCW 2; MTFW 2005; NFS 13

Banville, John 1945- .... **CLC 46, 118**
See also CA 117; 128; CANR 104; CN 4, 5, 6, 7; DLB 14, 271; INT CA-128

Banville, Theodore (Faullain) de 1832-1891 .... **NCLC 9**
See also DLB 217; GFL 1789 to the Present

Baraka, Amiri 1934- .... **BLC 1; CLC 1, 2, 3, 5, 10, 14, 33, 115, 213; DC 6; PC 4; WLCS**
See Jones, LeRoi
See also AAYA 63; AFAW 1, 2; AMWS 2; BW 2, 3; CA 21-24R; CABS 3; CAD; CANR 27, 38, 61, 133; CD 3, 5, 6; CDALB 1941-1968; CP 4, 5, 6, 7; CPW; DA; DA3; DAC; DAM MST, MULT, POET, POP; DFS 3, 11, 16; DLB 5, 7, 16, 38; DLBD 8; EWL 3; MAL 5; MTCW 1, 2; MTFW 2005; PFS 9; RGAL 4; TCLE 1:1; TUS; WP

Baratynsky, Evgenii Abramovich 1800-1844 .... **NCLC 103**
See also DLB 205

Barbauld, Anna Laetitia 1743-1825 .... **NCLC 50**
See also DLB 107, 109, 142, 158; RGEL 2

Barbellion, W. N. P. .... **TCLC 24**
See Cummings, Bruce F(rederick)

Barber, Benjamin R. 1939- .... **CLC 141**
See also CA 29-32R; CANR 12, 32, 64, 119

Barbera, Jack (Vincent) 1945- .... **CLC 44**
See also CA 110; CANR 45

Barbey d'Aurevilly, Jules-Amedee 1808-1889 .... **NCLC 1; SSC 17**
See also DLB 119; GFL 1789 to the Present

Barbour, John c. 1316-1395 .... **CMLC 33**
See also DLB 146

Barbusse, Henri 1873-1935 .... **TCLC 5**
See also CA 105; 154; DLB 65; EWL 3; RGWL 2, 3

Barclay, Alexander c. 1475-1552 .... **LC 109**
See also DLB 132

Barclay, Bill
See Moorcock, Michael (John)

Barclay, William Ewert
See Moorcock, Michael (John)

Barea, Arturo 1897-1957 .... **TCLC 14**
See also CA 111; 201

Barfoot, Joan 1946- .... **CLC 18**
See also CA 105; CANR 141

Barham, Richard Harris 1788-1845 .... **NCLC 77**
See also DLB 159

Baring, Maurice 1874-1945 .... **TCLC 8**
See also CA 105; 168; DLB 34; HGG

Baring-Gould, Sabine 1834-1924 ... **TCLC 88**
See also DLB 156, 190

Barker, Clive 1952- .... **CLC 52, 205; SSC 53**
See also AAYA 10, 54; BEST 90:3; BPFB 1; CA 121; 129; CANR 71, 111, 133; CPW; DA3; DAM POP; DLB 261; HGG; INT CA-129; MTCW 1, 2; MTFW 2005; SUFW 2

Barker, George Granville 1913-1991 .... **CLC 8, 48**
See also CA 9-12R; 135; CANR 7, 38; CP 1, 2, 3, 4; DAM POET; DLB 20; EWL 3; MTCW 1

Barker, Harley Granville
See Granville-Barker, Harley
See also DLB 10

Barker, Howard 1946- .... **CLC 37**
See also CA 102; CBD; CD 5, 6; DLB 13, 233

Barker, Jane 1652-1732 .... **LC 42, 82**
See also DLB 39, 131

Barker, Pat(ricia) 1943- ...... **CLC 32, 94, 146**
See also BRWS 4; CA 117; 122; CANR 50, 101; CN 6, 7; DLB 271; INT CA-122

Barlach, Ernst (Heinrich) 1870-1938 .... **TCLC 84**
See also CA 178; DLB 56, 118; EWL 3

Barlow, Joel 1754-1812 .... **NCLC 23**
See also AMWS 2; DLB 37; RGAL 4

Barnard, Mary (Ethel) 1909- .... **CLC 48**
See also CA 21-22; CAP 2; CP 1

Barnes, Djuna 1892-1982 .... **CLC 3, 4, 8, 11, 29, 127; SSC 3**
See Steptoe, Lydia
See also AMWS 3; CA 9-12R; 107; CAD; CANR 16, 55; CN 1, 2, 3; CWD; DLB 4, 9, 45; EWL 3; GLL 1; MAL 5; MTCW 1, 2; MTFW 2005; RGAL 4; TCLE 1:1; TUS

Barnes, Jim 1933- .... **NNAL**
See also CA 108, 175; CAAE 175; CAAS 28; DLB 175

Barnes, Julian (Patrick) 1946- . **CLC 42, 141**
See also BRWS 4; CA 102; CANR 19, 54, 115, 137; CN 4, 5, 6, 7; DAB; DLB 194; DLBY 1993; EWL 3; MTCW 2; MTFW 2005

Barnes, Peter 1931-2004 .... **CLC 5, 56**
See also CA 65-68; 230; CAAS 12; CANR 33, 34, 64, 113; CBD; CD 5, 6; DFS 6; DLB 13, 233; MTCW 1

Barnes, William 1801-1886 .... **NCLC 75**
See also DLB 32

Baroja (y Nessi), Pio 1872-1956 .... **HLC 1; TCLC 8**
See also CA 104; EW 9

Baron, David
See Pinter, Harold

Baron Corvo
See Rolfe, Frederick (William Serafino Austin Lewis Mary)

Barondess, Sue K(aufman) 1926-1977 .... **CLC 8**
See Kaufman, Sue
See also CA 1-4R; 69-72; CANR 1

Baron de Teive
See Pessoa, Fernando (Antonio Nogueira)

Baroness Von S.
See Zangwill, Israel

Barres, (Auguste-)Maurice 1862-1923 .... **TCLC 47**
See also CA 164; DLB 123; GFL 1789 to the Present

Barreto, Afonso Henrique de Lima
See Lima Barreto, Afonso Henrique de

Barrett, Andrea 1954- .... **CLC 150**
See also CA 156; CANR 92; CN 7

Barrett, Michele .... **CLC 65**

Barrett, (Roger) Syd 1946- .... **CLC 35**

Barrett, William (Christopher) 1913-1992 .... **CLC 27**
See also CA 13-16R; 139; CANR 11, 67; INT CANR-11

Barrett Browning, Elizabeth 1806-1861 ... **NCLC 1, 16, 61, 66; PC 6, 62; WLC**
See also AAYA 63; BRW 4; CDBLB 1832-1890; DA; DA3; DAB; DAC; DAM MST, POET; DLB 32, 199; EXPP; FL 1:2; PAB; PFS 2, 16, 23; TEA; WLIT 4; WP

Barrie, J(ames) M(atthew) 1860-1937 .... **TCLC 2, 164**
See also BRWS 3; BYA 4, 5; CA 104; 136; CANR 77; CDBLB 1890-1914; CLR 16; CWRI 5; DA3; DAB; DAM DRAM; DFS 7; DLB 10, 141, 156; EWL 3; FANT; MAICYA 1, 2; MTCW 2; MTFW 2005; SATA 100; SUFW; WCH; WLIT 4; YABC 1

Barrington, Michael
See Moorcock, Michael (John)

Barrol, Grady
See Bograd, Larry

Barry, Mike
See Malzberg, Barry N(athaniel)

Barry, Philip 1896-1949 .... **TCLC 11**
See also CA 109; 199; DFS 9; DLB 7, 228; MAL 5; RGAL 4

Bart, Andre Schwarz
See Schwarz-Bart, Andre

Barth, John (Simmons) 1930- ... **CLC 1, 2, 3, 5, 7, 9, 10, 14, 27, 51, 89, 214; SSC 10, 89**
See also AITN 1, 2; AMW; BPFB 1; CA 1-4R; CABS 1; CANR 5, 23, 49, 64, 113; CN 1, 2, 3, 4, 5, 6, 7; DAM NOV; DLB 2, 227; EWL 3; FANT; MAL 5; MTCW 1; RGAL 4; RGSF 2; RHW; SSFS 6; TUS

Barthelme, Donald 1931-1989 ... **CLC 1, 2, 3, 5, 6, 8, 13, 23, 46, 59, 115; SSC 2, 55**
See also AMWS 4; BPFB 1; CA 21-24R; 129; CANR 20, 58; CN 1, 2, 3, 4; DA3; DAM NOV; DLB 2, 234; DLBY 1980, 1989; EWL 3; FANT; LMFS 2; MAL 5; MTCW 1, 2; MTFW 2005; RGAL 4; RGSF 2; SATA 7; SATA-Obit 62; SSFS 17

Barthelme, Frederick 1943- ...... **CLC 36, 117**
See also AMWS 11; CA 114; 122; CANR 77; CN 4, 5, 6, 7; CSW; DLB 244; DLBY 1985; EWL 3; INT CA-122

Barthes, Roland (Gerard) 1915-1980 .... **CLC 24, 83; TCLC 135**
See also CA 130; 97-100; CANR 66; DLB 296; EW 13; EWL 3; GFL 1789 to the Present; MTCW 1, 2; TWA

Bartram, William 1739-1823 .... **NCLC 145**
See also ANW; DLB 37

Barzun, Jacques (Martin) 1907- ..... **CLC 51, 145**
See also CA 61-64; CANR 22, 95

Bashevis, Isaac
See Singer, Isaac Bashevis

Bashkirtseff, Marie 1859-1884 .... **NCLC 27**

Basho, Matsuo
See Matsuo Basho
See also RGWL 2, 3; WP

Basil of Caesaria c. 330-379 .... **CMLC 35**

Basket, Raney
See Edgerton, Clyde (Carlyle)

Bass, Kingsley B., Jr.
See Bullins, Ed

Bass, Rick 1958- .... **CLC 79, 143; SSC 60**
See also ANW; CA 126; CANR 53, 93, 145; CSW; DLB 212, 275

Bassani, Giorgio 1916-2000 .... **CLC 9**
See also CA 65-68; 190; CANR 33; CWW 2; DLB 128, 177, 299; EWL 3; MTCW 1; RGWL 2, 3

Bastian, Ann .... **CLC 70**

Bastos, Augusto (Antonio) Roa
See Roa Bastos, Augusto (Jose Antonio)

Bataille, Georges 1897-1962 .... **CLC 29; TCLC 155**
See also CA 101; 89-92; EWL 3

Bates, H(erbert) E(rnest) 1905-1974 .... **CLC 46; SSC 10**
See also CA 93-96; 45-48; CANR 34; CN 1; DA3; DAB; DAM POP; DLB 162, 191; EWL 3; EXPS; MTCW 1, 2; RGSF 2; SSFS 7

Bauchart
See Camus, Albert

Baudelaire, Charles 1821-1867 . **NCLC 6, 29, 55, 155; PC 1; SSC 18**
See also DA; DA3; DAB; DAC; DAM MST, POET; DLB 217; EW 7; GFL 1789 to the Present; LMFS 2; PFS 21; RGWL 2, 3; TWA

Baudouin, Marcel
See Peguy, Charles (Pierre)

Baudouin, Pierre
See Peguy, Charles (Pierre)

Baudrillard, Jean 1929- .... **CLC 60**
See also DLB 296

Baum, L(yman) Frank 1856-1919 .. **TCLC 7, 132**
See also AAYA 46; BYA 16; CA 108; 133; CLR 15; CWRI 5; DLB 22; FANT; JRDA; MAICYA 1, 2; MTCW 1, 2; NFS 13; RGAL 4; SATA 18, 100; WCH

Baum, Louis F.
See Baum, L(yman) Frank

Baumbach, Jonathan 1933- .... **CLC 6, 23**
See also CA 13-16R; CAAS 5; CANR 12, 66, 140; CN 3, 4, 5, 6, 7; DLBY 1980; INT CANR-12; MTCW 1

Bausch, Richard (Carl) 1945- .... **CLC 51**
See also AMWS 7; CA 101; CAAS 14; CANR 43, 61, 87; CN 7; CSW; DLB 130; MAL 5

Baxter, Charles (Morley) 1947- . **CLC 45, 78**
See also CA 57-60; CANR 40, 64, 104, 133; CPW; DAM POP; DLB 130; MAL 5; MTCW 2; MTFW 2005; TCLE 1:1

Baxter, George Owen
See Faust, Frederick (Schiller)

Baxter, James K(eir) 1926-1972 .... **CLC 14**
See also CA 77-80; CP 1; EWL 3

Baxter, John
See Hunt, E(verette) Howard, (Jr.)

Bayer, Sylvia
See Glassco, John

Baynton, Barbara 1857-1929 .... **TCLC 57**
See also DLB 230; RGSF 2

Beagle, Peter S(oyer) 1939- .... **CLC 7, 104**
See also AAYA 47; BPFB 1; BYA 9, 10, 16; CA 9-12R; CANR 4, 51, 73, 110; DA3; DLBY 1980; FANT; INT CANR-4; MTCW 2; MTFW 2005; SATA 60, 130; SUFW 1, 2; YAW

Bean, Normal
See Burroughs, Edgar Rice

Beard, Charles A(ustin) 1874-1948 .... **TCLC 15**
See also CA 115; 189; DLB 17; SATA 18

Beardsley, Aubrey 1872-1898 .... **NCLC 6**

Beattie, Ann 1947- ..... **CLC 8, 13, 18, 40, 63, 146; SSC 11**
See also AMWS 5; BEST 90:2; BPFB 1; CA 81-84; CANR 53, 73, 128; CN 4, 5, 6, 7; CPW; DA3; DAM NOV, POP; DLB 218, 278; DLBY 1982; EWL 3; MAL 5; MTCW 1, 2; MTFW 2005; RGAL 4; RGSF 2; SSFS 9; TUS

Beattie, James 1735-1803 .... **NCLC 25**
See also DLB 109

Beauchamp, Kathleen Mansfield 1888-1923
See Mansfield, Katherine
See also CA 104; 134; DA; DA3; DAC; DAM MST; MTCW 2; TEA

Beaumarchais, Pierre-Augustin Caron de 1732-1799 .... **DC 4; LC 61**
See also DAM DRAM; DFS 14, 16; DLB 313; EW 4; GFL Beginnings to 1789; RGWL 2, 3

Beaumont, Francis 1584(?)-1616 .. **DC 6; LC 33**
See also BRW 2; CDBLB Before 1660; DLB 58; TEA

Beauvoir, Simone (Lucie Ernestine Marie Bertrand) de 1908-1986 .... **CLC 1, 2, 4, 8, 14, 31, 44, 50, 71, 124; SSC 35; WLC**
See also BPFB 1; CA 9-12R; 118; CANR 28, 61; DA; DA3; DAB; DAC; DAM MST, NOV; DLB 72; DLBY 1986; EW 12; EWL 3; FL 1:5; FW; GFL 1789 to the Present; LMFS 2; MTCW 1, 2; MTFW 2005; RGSF 2; RGWL 2, 3; TWA

Becker, Carl (Lotus) 1873-1945 ..... **TCLC 63**
See also CA 157; DLB 17

Becker, Jurek 1937-1997 .... **CLC 7, 19**
See also CA 85-88; 157; CANR 60, 117; CWW 2; DLB 75, 299; EWL 3

Becker, Walter 1950- .... **CLC 26**

Beckett, Samuel (Barclay) 1906-1989 .. **CLC 1, 2, 3, 4, 6, 9, 10, 11, 14, 18, 29, 57, 59, 83; DC 22; SSC 16, 74; TCLC 145; WLC**
See also BRWC 2; BRWR 1; BRWS 1; CA 5-8R; 130; CANR 33, 61; CBD; CDBLB 1945-1960; CN 1, 2, 3, 4; CP 1, 2, 3, 4; DA; DA3; DAB; DAC; DAM DRAM, MST, NOV; DFS 2, 7, 18; DLB 13, 15, 233, 319, 321; DLBY 1990; EWL 3; GFL 1789 to the Present; LATS 1:2; LMFS 2; MTCW 1, 2; MTFW 2005; RGSF 2; RGWL 2, 3; SSFS 15; TEA; WLIT 4

Beckford, William 1760-1844 .... **NCLC 16**
See also BRW 3; DLB 39, 213; GL 2; HGG; LMFS 1; SUFW

Beckham, Barry (Earl) 1944- .... **BLC 1**
See also BW 1; CA 29-32R; CANR 26, 62; CN 1, 2, 3, 4, 5, 6; DAM MULT; DLB 33

Beckman, Gunnel 1910- .... **CLC 26**
See also CA 33-36R; CANR 15, 114; CLR 25; MAICYA 1, 2; SAAS 9; SATA 6

Becque, Henri 1837-1899 .... **DC 21; NCLC 3**
See also DLB 192; GFL 1789 to the Present

Becquer, Gustavo Adolfo 1836-1870 .... **HLCS 1; NCLC 106**
See also DAM MULT

Beddoes, Thomas Lovell 1803-1849 .. **DC 15; NCLC 3, 154**
See also BRWS 11; DLB 96

Bede c. 673-735 .... **CMLC 20**
See also DLB 146; TEA

Bedford, Denton R. 1907-(?) .... **NNAL**

Bedford, Donald F.
See Fearing, Kenneth (Flexner)

Beecher, Catharine Esther 1800-1878 .... **NCLC 30**
See also DLB 1, 243

Beecher, John 1904-1980 .... **CLC 6**
See also AITN 1; CA 5-8R; 105; CANR 8; CP 1, 2, 3

Beer, Johann 1655-1700 .... **LC 5**
See also DLB 168

Beer, Patricia 1924- .... **CLC 58**
See also CA 61-64; 183; CANR 13, 46; CP 1, 2, 3, 4; CWP; DLB 40; FW

Beerbohm, Max
See Beerbohm, (Henry) Max(imilian)

Beerbohm, (Henry) Max(imilian) 1872-1956 .... **TCLC 1, 24**
See also BRWS 2; CA 104; 154; CANR 79; DLB 34, 100; FANT; MTCW 2

Beer-Hofmann, Richard 1866-1945 .... **TCLC 60**
See also CA 160; DLB 81

Beg, Shemus
See Stephens, James

Begiebing, Robert J(ohn) 1946- .... **CLC 70**
See also CA 122; CANR 40, 88

Begley, Louis 1933- .... **CLC 197**
See also CA 140; CANR 98; DLB 299; TCLE 1:1

Behan, Brendan (Francis) 1923-1964 .... **CLC 1, 8, 11, 15, 79**
See also BRWS 2; CA 73-76; CANR 33, 121; CBD; CDBLB 1945-1960; DAM DRAM; DFS 7; DLB 13, 233; EWL 3; MTCW 1, 2

Behn, Aphra 1640(?)-1689 .. **DC 4; LC 1, 30, 42; PC 13; WLC**
See also BRWS 3; DA; DA3; DAB; DAC; DAM DRAM, MST, NOV, POET; DFS 16; DLB 39, 80, 131; FW; TEA; WLIT 3

Bishop, John Peale 1892-1944 ..... **TCLC 103**
See also CA 107; 155; DLB 4, 9, 45; MAL
5; RGAL 4

Bissett, Bill 1939- .... **CLC 18; PC 14**
See also CA 69-72; CAAS 19; CANR 15;
CCA 1; CP 1, 2, 3, 4, 5, 6, 7; DLB 53;
MTCW 1

Bissoondath, Neil (Devindra)
1955- .... **CLC 120**
See also CA 136; CANR 123; CN 6, 7;
DAC

Bitov, Andrei (Georgievich) 1937- ... **CLC 57**
See also CA 142; DLB 302

Biyidi, Alexandre 1932-
See Beti, Mongo
See also BW 1, 3; CA 114; 124; CANR 81;
DA3; MTCW 1, 2

Bjarme, Brynjolf
See Ibsen, Henrik (Johan)

Bjoernson, Bjoernstjerne (Martinius)
1832-1910 .... **TCLC 7, 37**
See also CA 104

Black, Robert
See Holdstock, Robert P.

Blackburn, Paul 1926-1971 .... **CLC 9, 43**
See also BG 1:2; CA 81-84; 33-36R; CANR
34; CP 1; DLB 16; DLBY 1981

Black Elk 1863-1950 .... **NNAL; TCLC 33**
See also CA 144; DAM MULT; MTCW 2;
MTFW 2005; WP

Black Hawk 1767-1838 .... **NNAL**

Black Hobart
See Sanders, (James) Ed(ward)

Blacklin, Malcolm
See Chambers, Aidan

Blackmore, R(ichard) D(oddridge)
1825-1900 .... **TCLC 27**
See also CA 120; DLB 18; RGEL 2

Blackmur, R(ichard) P(almer)
1904-1965 .... **CLC 2, 24**
See also AMWS 2; CA 11-12; 25-28R;
CANR 71; CAP 1; DLB 63; EWL 3;
MAL 5

Black Tarantula
See Acker, Kathy

Blackwood, Algernon (Henry)
1869-1951 .... **TCLC 5**
See also CA 105; 150; DLB 153, 156, 178;
HGG; SUFW 1

Blackwood, Caroline (Maureen)
1931-1996 .... **CLC 6, 9, 100**
See also BRWS 9; CA 85-88; 151; CANR
32, 61, 65; CN 3, 4, 5, 6; DLB 14, 207;
HGG; MTCW 1

Blade, Alexander
See Hamilton, Edmond; Silverberg, Robert

Blaga, Lucian 1895-1961 .... **CLC 75**
See also CA 157; DLB 220; EWL 3

Blair, Eric (Arthur) 1903-1950 .... **TCLC 123**
See Orwell, George
See also CA 104; 132; DA; DA3; DAB;
DAC; DAM MST, NOV; MTCW 1, 2;
MTFW 2005; SATA 29

Blair, Hugh 1718-1800 .... **NCLC 75**

Blais, Marie-Claire 1939- .... **CLC 2, 4, 6, 13,
22**
See also CA 21-24R; CAAS 4; CANR 38,
75, 93; CWW 2; DAC; DAM MST; DLB
53; EWL 3; FW; MTCW 1, 2; MTFW
2005; TWA

Blaise, Clark 1940- .... **CLC 29**
See also AITN 2; CA 53-56, 231; CAAE
231; CAAS 3; CANR 5, 66, 106; CN 4,
5, 6, 7; DLB 53; RGSF 2

Blake, Fairley
See De Voto, Bernard (Augustine)

Blake, Nicholas
See Day Lewis, C(ecil)
See also DLB 77; MSW

Blake, Sterling
See Benford, Gregory (Albert)

Blake, William 1757-1827 . **NCLC 13, 37, 57,
127; PC 12, 63; WLC**
See also AAYA 47; BRW 3; BRWR 1; CD-
BLB 1789-1832; CLR 52; DA; DA3;
DAB; DAC; DAM MST, POET; DLB 93,
163; EXPP; LATS 1:1; LMFS 1; MAI-
CYA 1, 2; PAB; PFS 2, 12; SATA 30;
TEA; WCH; WLIT 3; WP

Blanchot, Maurice 1907-2003 .... **CLC 135**
See also CA 117; 144; 213; CANR 138;
DLB 72, 296; EWL 3

Blasco Ibanez, Vicente 1867-1928 . **TCLC 12**
See Ibanez, Vicente Blasco
See also BPFB 1; CA 110; 131; CANR 81;
DA3; DAM NOV; EW 8; EWL 3; HW 1,
2; MTCW 1

Blatty, William Peter 1928- .... **CLC 2**
See also CA 5-8R; CANR 9, 124; DAM
POP; HGG

Bleeck, Oliver
See Thomas, Ross (Elmore)

Blessing, Lee (Knowlton) 1949- .... **CLC 54**
See also CA 236; CAD; CD 5, 6

Blight, Rose
See Greer, Germaine

Blish, James (Benjamin) 1921-1975 . **CLC 14**
See also BPFB 1; CA 1-4R; 57-60; CANR
3; CN 2; DLB 8; MTCW 1; SATA 66;
SCFW 1, 2; SFW 4

Bliss, Frederick
See Card, Orson Scott

Bliss, Reginald
See Wells, H(erbert) G(eorge)

Blixen, Karen (Christentze Dinesen)
1885-1962
See Dinesen, Isak
See also CA 25-28; CANR 22, 50; CAP 2;
DA3; DLB 214; LMFS 1; MTCW 1, 2;
SATA 44; SSFS 20

Bloch, Robert (Albert) 1917-1994 .... **CLC 33**
See also AAYA 29; CA 5-8R; 179; 146;
CAAE 179; CAAS 20; CANR 5, 78;
DA3; DLB 44; HGG; INT CANR-5;
MTCW 2; SATA 12; SATA-Obit 82; SFW
4; SUFW 1, 2

Blok, Alexander (Alexandrovich)
1880-1921 .... **PC 21; TCLC 5**
See also CA 104; 183; DLB 295; EW 9;
EWL 3; LMFS 2; RGWL 2, 3

Blom, Jan
See Breytenbach, Breyten

Bloom, Harold 1930- .... **CLC 24, 103**
See also CA 13-16R; CANR 39, 75, 92,
133; DLB 67; EWL 3; MTCW 2; MTFW
2005; RGAL 4

Bloomfield, Aurelius
See Bourne, Randolph S(illiman)

Bloomfield, Robert 1766-1823 ..... **NCLC 145**
See also DLB 93

Blount, Roy (Alton), Jr. 1941- .... **CLC 38**
See also CA 53-56; CANR 10, 28, 61, 125;
CSW; INT CANR-28; MTCW 1, 2;
MTFW 2005

Blowsnake, Sam 1875-(?) .... **NNAL**

Bloy, Leon 1846-1917 .... **TCLC 22**
See also CA 121; 183; DLB 123; GFL 1789
to the Present

Blue Cloud, Peter (Aroniawenrate)
1933- .... **NNAL**
See also CA 117; CANR 40; DAM MULT

Bluggage, Oranthy
See Alcott, Louisa May

Blume, Judy (Sussman) 1938- .... **CLC 12, 30**
See also AAYA 3, 26; BYA 1, 8, 12; CA 29-
32R; CANR 13, 37, 66, 124; CLR 2, 15,
69; CPW; DA3; DAM NOV, POP; DLB
52; JRDA; MAICYA 1, 2; MAICYAS 1;
MTCW 1, 2; MTFW 2005; SATA 2, 31,
79, 142; WYA; YAW

Blunden, Edmund (Charles)
1896-1974 .... **CLC 2, 56; PC 66**
See also BRW 6; BRWS 11; CA 17-18; 45-
48; CANR 54; CAP 2; CP 1, 2; DLB 20,
100, 155; MTCW 1; PAB

Bly, Robert (Elwood) 1926- .... **CLC 1, 2, 5,
10, 15, 38, 128; PC 39**
See also AMWS 4; CA 5-8R; CANR 41,
73, 125; CP 1, 2, 3, 4, 5, 6, 7; DA3; DAM
POET; DLB 5; EWL 3; MAL 5; MTCW
1, 2; MTFW 2005; PFS 6, 17; RGAL 4

Boas, Franz 1858-1942 .... **TCLC 56**
See also CA 115; 181

Bobette
See Simenon, Georges (Jacques Christian)

Boccaccio, Giovanni 1313-1375 ... **CMLC 13,
57; SSC 10, 87**
See also EW 2; RGSF 2; RGWL 2, 3; TWA;
WLIT 7

Bochco, Steven 1943- .... **CLC 35**
See also AAYA 11; CA 124; 138

Bode, Sigmund
See O'Doherty, Brian

Bodel, Jean 1167(?)-1210 .... **CMLC 28**

Bodenheim, Maxwell 1892-1954 .... **TCLC 44**
See also CA 110; 187; DLB 9, 45; MAL 5;
RGAL 4

Bodenheimer, Maxwell
See Bodenheim, Maxwell

Bodker, Cecil 1927-
See Bodker, Cecil

Bodker, Cecil 1927- .... **CLC 21**
See also CA 73-76; CANR 13, 44, 111;
CLR 23; MAICYA 1, 2; SATA 14, 133

Boell, Heinrich (Theodor)
1917-1985 ..... **CLC 2, 3, 6, 9, 11, 15, 27,
32, 72; SSC 23; WLC**
See Boll, Heinrich (Theodor)
See also CA 21-24R; 116; CANR 24; DA;
DA3; DAB; DAC; DAM MST, NOV;
DLB 69; DLBY 1985; MTCW 1, 2;
MTFW 2005; SSFS 20; TWA

Boerne, Alfred
See Doeblin, Alfred

Boethius c. 480-c. 524 .... **CMLC 15**
See also DLB 115; RGWL 2, 3

Boff, Leonardo (Genezio Darci)
1938- .... **CLC 70; HLC 1**
See also CA 150; DAM MULT; HW 2

Bogan, Louise 1897-1970 .... **CLC 4, 39, 46,
93; PC 12**
See also AMWS 3; CA 73-76; 25-28R;
CANR 33, 82; CP 1; DAM POET; DLB
45, 169; EWL 3; MAL 5; MAWW;
MTCW 1, 2; PFS 21; RGAL 4

Bogarde, Dirk
See Van Den Bogarde, Derek Jules Gaspard
Ulric Niven
See also DLB 14

Bogosian, Eric 1953- .... **CLC 45, 141**
See also CA 138; CAD; CANR 102; CD 5,
6

Bograd, Larry 1953- .... **CLC 35**
See also CA 93-96; CANR 57; SAAS 21;
SATA 33, 89; WYA

Boiardo, Matteo Maria 1441-1494 .... **LC 6**

Boileau-Despreaux, Nicolas 1636-1711 . **LC 3**
See also DLB 268; EW 3; GFL Beginnings
to 1789; RGWL 2, 3

Boissard, Maurice
See Leautaud, Paul

Bojer, Johan 1872-1959 .... **TCLC 64**
See also CA 189; EWL 3

Bok, Edward W(illiam)
1863-1930 .... **TCLC 101**
See also CA 217; DLB 91; DLBD 16

Boker, George Henry 1823-1890 . **NCLC 125**
See also RGAL 4

Boland, Eavan (Aisling) 1944- .. **CLC 40, 67, 113; PC 58**
See also BRWS 5; CA 143, 207; CAAE 207; CANR 61; CP 1, 7; CWP; DAM POET; DLB 40; FW; MTCW 2; MTFW 2005; PFS 12, 22

Boll, Heinrich (Theodor)
See Boell, Heinrich (Theodor)
See also BPFB 1; CDWLB 2; EW 13; EWL 3; RGSF 2; RGWL 2, 3

Bolt, Lee
See Faust, Frederick (Schiller)

Bolt, Robert (Oxton) 1924-1995 ...... **CLC 14; TCLC 175**
See also CA 17-20R; 147; CANR 35, 67; CBD; DAM DRAM; DFS 2; DLB 13, 233; EWL 3; LAIT 1; MTCW 1

Bombal, Maria Luisa 1910-1980 .... **HLCS 1; SSC 37**
See also CA 127; CANR 72; EWL 3; HW 1; LAW; RGSF 2

Bombet, Louis-Alexandre-Cesar
See Stendhal

Bomkauf
See Kaufman, Bob (Garnell)

Bonaventura .... **NCLC 35**
See also DLB 90

Bonaventure 1217(?)-1274 .... **CMLC 79**
See also DLB 115; LMFS 1

Bond, Edward 1934- .... **CLC 4, 6, 13, 23**
See also AAYA 50; BRWS 1; CA 25-28R; CANR 38, 67, 106; CBD; CD 5, 6; DAM DRAM; DFS 3, 8; DLB 13, 310; EWL 3; MTCW 1

Bonham, Frank 1914-1989 .... **CLC 12**
See also AAYA 1; BYA 1, 3; CA 9-12R; CANR 4, 36; JRDA; MAICYA 1, 2; SAAS 3; SATA 1, 49; SATA-Obit 62; TCWW 1, 2; YAW

Bonnefoy, Yves 1923- . **CLC 9, 15, 58; PC 58**
See also CA 85-88; CANR 33, 75, 97, 136; CWW 2; DAM MST, POET; DLB 258; EWL 3; GFL 1789 to the Present; MTCW 1, 2; MTFW 2005

Bonner, Marita .... **HR 1:2**
See Occomy, Marita (Odette) Bonner

Bonnin, Gertrude 1876-1938 .... **NNAL**
See Zitkala-Sa
See also CA 150; DAM MULT

Bontemps, Arna(ud Wendell)
1902-1973 .. **BLC 1; CLC 1, 18; HR 1:2**
See also BW 1; CA 1-4R; 41-44R; CANR 4, 35; CLR 6; CP 1; CWRI 5; DA3; DAM MULT, NOV, POET; DLB 48, 51; JRDA; MAICYA 1, 2; MAL 5; MTCW 1, 2; SATA 2, 44; SATA-Obit 24; WCH; WP

Boot, William
See Stoppard, Tom

Booth, Martin 1944-2004 .... **CLC 13**
See also CA 93-96; 188; 223; CAAE 188; CAAS 2; CANR 92; CP 1, 2, 3, 4

Booth, Philip 1925- .... **CLC 23**
See also CA 5-8R; CANR 5, 88; CP 1, 2, 3, 4, 5, 6, 7; DLBY 1982

Booth, Wayne C(layson) 1921-2005 . **CLC 24**
See also CA 1-4R; CAAS 5; CANR 3, 43, 117; DLB 67

Borchert, Wolfgang 1921-1947 .... **TCLC 5**
See also CA 104; 188; DLB 69, 124; EWL 3

Borel, Petrus 1809-1859 .... **NCLC 41**
See also DLB 119; GFL 1789 to the Present

Borges, Jorge Luis 1899-1986 ... **CLC 1, 2, 3, 4, 6, 8, 9, 10, 13, 19, 44, 48, 83; HLC 1; PC 22, 32; SSC 4, 41; TCLC 109; WLC**
See also AAYA 26; BPFB 1; CA 21-24R; CANR 19, 33, 75, 105, 133; CDWLB 3; DA; DA3; DAB; DAC; DAM MST,

MULT; DLB 113, 283; DLBY 1986; DNFS 1, 2; EWL 3; HW 1, 2; LAW; LMFS 2; MSW; MTCW 1, 2; MTFW 2005; RGSF 2; RGWL 2, 3; SFW 4; SSFS 17; TWA; WLIT 1

Borowski, Tadeusz 1922-1951 .... **SSC 48; TCLC 9**
See also CA 106; 154; CDWLB 4; DLB 215; EWL 3; RGSF 2; RGWL 3; SSFS 13

Borrow, George (Henry)
1803-1881 .... **NCLC 9**
See also DLB 21, 55, 166

Bosch (Gavino), Juan 1909-2001 ..... **HLCS 1**
See also CA 151; 204; DAM MST, MULT; DLB 145; HW 1, 2

Bosman, Herman Charles
1905-1951 .... **TCLC 49**
See Malan, Herman
See also CA 160; DLB 225; RGSF 2

Bosschere, Jean de 1878(?)-1953 ... **TCLC 19**
See also CA 115; 186

Boswell, James 1740-1795 ... **LC 4, 50; WLC**
See also BRW 3; CDBLB 1660-1789; DA; DAB; DAC; DAM MST; DLB 104, 142; TEA; WLIT 3

Bottomley, Gordon 1874-1948 ..... **TCLC 107**
See also CA 120; 192; DLB 10

Bottoms, David 1949- .... **CLC 53**
See also CA 105; CANR 22; CSW; DLB 120; DLBY 1983

Boucicault, Dion 1820-1890 .... **NCLC 41**

Boucolon, Maryse
See Conde, Maryse

Bourdieu, Pierre 1930-2002 .... **CLC 198**
See also CA 130; 204

Bourget, Paul (Charles Joseph)
1852-1935 .... **TCLC 12**
See also CA 107; 196; DLB 123; GFL 1789 to the Present

Bourjaily, Vance (Nye) 1922- .... **CLC 8, 62**
See also CA 1-4R; CAAS 1; CANR 2, 72; CN 1, 2, 3, 4, 5, 6, 7; DLB 2, 143; MAL 5

Bourne, Randolph S(illiman)
1886-1918 .... **TCLC 16**
See also AMW; CA 117; 155; DLB 63; MAL 5

Bova, Ben(jamin William) 1932- ...... **CLC 45**
See also AAYA 16; CA 5-8R; CAAS 18; CANR 11, 56, 94, 111; CLR 3, 96; DLBY 1981; INT CANR-11; MAICYA 1, 2; MTCW 1; SATA 6, 68, 133; SFW 4

Bowen, Elizabeth (Dorothea Cole)
1899-1973 . **CLC 1, 3, 6, 11, 15, 22, 118; SSC 3, 28, 66; TCLC 148**
See also BRWS 2; CA 17-18; 41-44R; CANR 35, 105; CAP 2; CDBLB 1945-1960; CN 1; DA3; DAM NOV; DLB 15, 162; EWL 3; EXPS; FW; HGG; MTCW 1, 2; MTFW 2005; NFS 13; RGSF 2; SSFS 5; SUFW 1; TEA; WLIT 4

Bowering, George 1935- .... **CLC 15, 47**
See also CA 21-24R; CAAS 16; CANR 10; CN 7; CP 1, 2, 3, 4, 5, 6, 7; DLB 53

Bowering, Marilyn R(uthe) 1949- .... **CLC 32**
See also CA 101; CANR 49; CP 4, 5, 6, 7; CWP

Bowers, Edgar 1924-2000 .... **CLC 9**
See also CA 5-8R; 188; CANR 24; CP 1, 2, 3, 4, 5, 6, 7; CSW; DLB 5

Bowers, Mrs. J. Milton 1842-1914
See Bierce, Ambrose (Gwinett)

Bowie, David .... **CLC 17**
See Jones, David Robert

Bowles, Jane (Sydney) 1917-1973 ..... **CLC 3, 68**
See Bowles, Jane Auer
See also CA 19-20; 41-44R; CAP 2; CN 1; MAL 5

Bowles, Jane Auer
See Bowles, Jane (Sydney)
See also EWL 3

Bowles, Paul (Frederick) 1910-1999 . **CLC 1, 2, 19, 53; SSC 3**
See also AMWS 4; CA 1-4R; 186; CAAS 1; CANR 1, 19, 50, 75; CN 1, 2, 3, 4, 5, 6; DA3; DLB 5, 6, 218; EWL 3; MAL 5; MTCW 1, 2; MTFW 2005; RGAL 4; SSFS 17

Bowles, William Lisle 1762-1850 . **NCLC 103**
See also DLB 93

Box, Edgar
See Vidal, (Eugene Luther) Gore
See also GLL 1

Boyd, James 1888-1944 .... **TCLC 115**
See also CA 186; DLB 9; DLBD 16; RGAL 4; RHW

Boyd, Nancy
See Millay, Edna St. Vincent
See also GLL 1

Boyd, Thomas (Alexander)
1898-1935 .... **TCLC 111**
See also CA 111; 183; DLB 9; DLBD 16, 316

Boyd, William (Andrew Murray)
1952- .... **CLC 28, 53, 70**
See also CA 114; 120; CANR 51, 71, 131; CN 4, 5, 6, 7; DLB 231

Boyesen, Hjalmar Hjorth
1848-1895 .... **NCLC 135**
See also DLB 12, 71; DLBD 13; RGAL 4

Boyle, Kay 1902-1992 .... **CLC 1, 5, 19, 58, 121; SSC 5**
See also CA 13-16R; 140; CAAS 1; CANR 29, 61, 110; CN 1, 2, 3, 4, 5; CP 1, 2, 3, 4; DLB 4, 9, 48, 86; DLBY 1993; EWL 3; MAL 5; MTCW 1, 2; MTFW 2005; RGAL 4; RGSF 2; SSFS 10, 13, 14

Boyle, Mark
See Kienzle, William X(avier)

Boyle, Patrick 1905-1982 .... **CLC 19**
See also CA 127

Boyle, T. C.
See Boyle, T(homas) Coraghessan
See also AMWS 8

Boyle, T(homas) Coraghessan
1948- .... **CLC 36, 55, 90; SSC 16**
See Boyle, T. C.
See also AAYA 47; BEST 90:4; BPFB 1; CA 120; CANR 44, 76, 89, 132; CN 6, 7; CPW; DA3; DAM POP; DLB 218, 278; DLBY 1986; EWL 3; MAL 5; MTCW 2; MTFW 2005; SSFS 13, 19

Boz
See Dickens, Charles (John Huffam)

Brackenridge, Hugh Henry
1748-1816 .... **NCLC 7**
See also DLB 11, 37; RGAL 4

Bradbury, Edward P.
See Moorcock, Michael (John)
See also MTCW 2

Bradbury, Malcolm (Stanley)
1932-2000 .... **CLC 32, 61**
See also CA 1-4R; CANR 1, 33, 91, 98, 137; CN 1, 2, 3, 4, 5, 6, 7; CP 1; DA3; DAM NOV; DLB 14, 207; EWL 3; MTCW 1, 2; MTFW 2005

Bradbury, Ray (Douglas) 1920- .... **CLC 1, 3, 10, 15, 42, 98; SSC 29, 53; WLC**
See also AAYA 15; AITN 1, 2; AMWS 4; BPFB 1; BYA 4, 5, 11; CA 1-4R; CANR 2, 30, 75, 125; CDALB 1968-1988; CN 1, 2, 3, 4, 5, 6, 7; CPW; DA; DA3; DAB; DAC; DAM MST, NOV, POP; DLB 2, 8;

EXPN; EXPS; HGG; LAIT 3, 5; LATS 1:2; LMFS 2; MAL 5; MTCW 1, 2; MTFW 2005; NFS 1, 22; RGAL 4; RGSF 2; SATA 11, 64, 123; SCFW 1, 2; SFW 4; SSFS 1, 20; SUFW 1, 2; TUS; YAW

Braddon, Mary Elizabeth 1837-1915 .... **TCLC 111**
See also BRWS 8; CA 108; 179; CMW 4; DLB 18, 70, 156; HGG

Bradfield, Scott (Michael) 1955- ..... **SSC 65**
See also CA 147; CANR 90; HGG; SUFW 2

Bradford, Gamaliel 1863-1932 .... **TCLC 36**
See also CA 160; DLB 17

Bradford, William 1590-1657 .... **LC 64**
See also DLB 24, 30; RGAL 4

Bradley, David (Henry), Jr. 1950- .... **BLC 1; CLC 23, 118**
See also BW 1, 3; CA 104; CANR 26, 81; CN 4, 5, 6, 7; DAM MULT; DLB 33

Bradley, John Ed(mund, Jr.) 1958- . **CLC 55**
See also CA 139; CANR 99; CN 6, 7; CSW

Bradley, Marion Zimmer 1930-1999 .... **CLC 30**
See Chapman, Lee; Dexter, John; Gardner, Miriam; Ives, Morgan; Rivers, Elfrida
See also AAYA 40; BPFB 1; CA 57-60; 185; CAAS 10; CANR 7, 31, 51, 75, 107; CPW; DA3; DAM POP; DLB 8; FANT; FW; MTCW 1, 2; MTFW 2005; SATA 90, 139; SATA-Obit 116; SFW 4; SUFW 2; YAW

Bradshaw, John 1933- .... **CLC 70**
See also CA 138; CANR 61

Bradstreet, Anne 1612(?)-1672 ...... **LC 4, 30; PC 10**
See also AMWS 1; CDALB 1640-1865; DA; DA3; DAC; DAM MST, POET; DLB 24; EXPP; FW; PFS 6; RGAL 4; TUS; WP

Brady, Joan 1939- .... **CLC 86**
See also CA 141

Bragg, Melvyn 1939- .... **CLC 10**
See also BEST 89:3; CA 57-60; CANR 10, 48, 89; CN 1, 2, 3, 4, 5, 6, 7; DLB 14, 271; RHW

Brahe, Tycho 1546-1601 .... **LC 45**
See also DLB 300

Braine, John (Gerard) 1922-1986 . **CLC 1, 3, 41**
See also CA 1-4R; 120; CANR 1, 33; CDBLB 1945-1960; CN 1, 2, 3, 4; DLB 15; DLBY 1986; EWL 3; MTCW 1

Braithwaite, William Stanley (Beaumont) 1878-1962 .... **BLC 1; HR 1:2; PC 52**
See also BW 1; CA 125; DAM MULT; DLB 50, 54; MAL 5

Bramah, Ernest 1868-1942 .... **TCLC 72**
See also CA 156; CMW 4; DLB 70; FANT

Brammer, Billy Lee
See Brammer, William

Brammer, William 1929-1978 .... **CLC 31**
See also CA 235; 77-80

Brancati, Vitaliano 1907-1954 .... **TCLC 12**
See also CA 109; DLB 264; EWL 3

Brancato, Robin F(idler) 1936- ...... **CLC 35**
See also AAYA 9, 68; BYA 6; CA 69-72; CANR 11, 45; CLR 32; JRDA; MAICYA 2; MAICYAS 1; SAAS 9; SATA 97; WYA; YAW

Brand, Dionne 1953- .... **CLC 192**
See also BW 2; CA 143; CANR 143; CWP

Brand, Max
See Faust, Frederick (Schiller)
See also BPFB 1; TCWW 1, 2

Brand, Millen 1906-1980 .... **CLC 7**
See also CA 21-24R; 97-100; CANR 72

Branden, Barbara .... **CLC 44**
See also CA 148

Brandes, Georg (Morris Cohen) 1842-1927 .... **TCLC 10**
See also CA 105; 189; DLB 300

Brandys, Kazimierz 1916-2000 .... **CLC 62**
See also CA 239; EWL 3

Branley, Franklyn M(ansfield) 1915-2002 .... **CLC 21**
See also CA 33-36R; 207; CANR 14, 39; CLR 13; MAICYA 1, 2; SAAS 16; SATA 4, 68, 136

Brant, Beth (E.) 1941- .... **NNAL**
See also CA 144; FW

Brant, Sebastian 1457-1521 .... **LC 112**
See also DLB 179; RGWL 2, 3

Brathwaite, Edward Kamau 1930- .... **BLCS; CLC 11; PC 56**
See also BW 2, 3; CA 25-28R; CANR 11, 26, 47, 107; CDWLB 3; CP 1, 2, 3, 4, 5, 6, 7; DAM POET; DLB 125; EWL 3

Brathwaite, Kamau
See Brathwaite, Edward Kamau

Brautigan, Richard (Gary) 1935-1984 .... **CLC 1, 3, 5, 9, 12, 34, 42; TCLC 133**
See also BPFB 1; CA 53-56; 113; CANR 34; CN 1, 2, 3; CP 1, 2, 3, 4; DA3; DAM NOV; DLB 2, 5, 206; DLBY 1980, 1984; FANT; MAL 5; MTCW 1; RGAL 4; SATA 56

Brave Bird, Mary .... **NNAL**
See Crow Dog, Mary (Ellen)

Braverman, Kate 1950- .... **CLC 67**
See also CA 89-92; CANR 141

Brecht, (Eugen) Bertolt (Friedrich) 1898-1956 ..... **DC 3; TCLC 1, 6, 13, 35, 169; WLC**
See also CA 104; 133; CANR 62; CDWLB 2; DA; DA3; DAB; DAC; DAM DRAM, MST; DFS 4, 5, 9; DLB 56, 124; EW 11; EWL 3; IDTP; MTCW 1, 2; MTFW 2005; RGWL 2, 3; TWA

Brecht, Eugen Berthold Friedrich
See Brecht, (Eugen) Bertolt (Friedrich)

Bremer, Fredrika 1801-1865 .... **NCLC 11**
See also DLB 254

Brennan, Christopher John 1870-1932 .... **TCLC 17**
See also CA 117; 188; DLB 230; EWL 3

Brennan, Maeve 1917-1993 ... **CLC 5; TCLC 124**
See also CA 81-84; CANR 72, 100

Brenner, Jozef 1887-1919
See Csath, Geza
See also CA 240

Brent, Linda
See Jacobs, Harriet A(nn)

Brentano, Clemens (Maria) 1778-1842 .... **NCLC 1**
See also DLB 90; RGWL 2, 3

Brent of Bin Bin
See Franklin, (Stella Maria Sarah) Miles (Lampe)

Brenton, Howard 1942- .... **CLC 31**
See also CA 69-72; CANR 33, 67; CBD; CD 5, 6; DLB 13; MTCW 1

Breslin, James 1930-
See Breslin, Jimmy
See also CA 73-76; CANR 31, 75, 139; DAM NOV; MTCW 1, 2; MTFW 2005

Breslin, Jimmy .... **CLC 4, 43**
See Breslin, James
See also AITN 1; DLB 185; MTCW 2

Bresson, Robert 1901(?)-1999 .... **CLC 16**
See also CA 110; 187; CANR 49

Breton, Andre 1896-1966 .. **CLC 2, 9, 15, 54; PC 15**
See also CA 19-20; 25-28R; CANR 40, 60; CAP 2; DLB 65, 258; EW 11; EWL 3; GFL 1789 to the Present; LMFS 2; MTCW 1, 2; MTFW 2005; RGWL 2, 3; TWA; WP

Breytenbach, Breyten 1939(?)- .. **CLC 23, 37, 126**
See also CA 113; 129; CANR 61, 122; CWW 2; DAM POET; DLB 225; EWL 3

Bridgers, Sue Ellen 1942- .... **CLC 26**
See also AAYA 8, 49; BYA 7, 8; CA 65-68; CANR 11, 36; CLR 18; DLB 52; JRDA; MAICYA 1, 2; SAAS 1; SATA 22, 90; SATA-Essay 109; WYA; YAW

Bridges, Robert (Seymour) 1844-1930 .... **PC 28; TCLC 1**
See also BRW 6; CA 104; 152; CDBLB 1890-1914; DAM POET; DLB 19, 98

Bridie, James .... **TCLC 3**
See Mavor, Osborne Henry
See also DLB 10; EWL 3

Brin, David 1950- .... **CLC 34**
See also AAYA 21; CA 102; CANR 24, 70, 125, 127; INT CANR-24; SATA 65; SCFW 2; SFW 4

Brink, Andre (Philippus) 1935- . **CLC 18, 36, 106**
See also AFW; BRWS 6; CA 104; CANR 39, 62, 109, 133; CN 4, 5, 6, 7; DLB 225; EWL 3; INT CA-103; LATS 1:2; MTCW 1, 2; MTFW 2005; WLIT 2

Brinsmead, H. F(ay)
See Brinsmead, H(esba) F(ay)

Brinsmead, H. F.
See Brinsmead, H(esba) F(ay)

Brinsmead, H(esba) F(ay) 1922- ...... **CLC 21**
See also CA 21-24R; CANR 10; CLR 47; CWRI 5; MAICYA 1, 2; SAAS 5; SATA 18, 78

Brittain, Vera (Mary) 1893(?)-1970 . **CLC 23**
See also BRWS 10; CA 13-16; 25-28R; CANR 58; CAP 1; DLB 191; FW; MTCW 1, 2

Broch, Hermann 1886-1951 .... **TCLC 20**
See also CA 117; 211; CDWLB 2; DLB 85, 124; EW 10; EWL 3; RGWL 2, 3

Brock, Rose
See Hansen, Joseph
See also GLL 1

Brod, Max 1884-1968 .... **TCLC 115**
See also CA 5-8R; 25-28R; CANR 7; DLB 81; EWL 3

Brodkey, Harold (Roy) 1930-1996 .. **CLC 56; TCLC 123**
See also CA 111; 151; CANR 71; CN 4, 5, 6; DLB 130

Brodsky, Iosif Alexandrovich 1940-1996
See Brodsky, Joseph
See also AITN 1; CA 41-44R; 151; CANR 37, 106; DA3; DAM POET; MTCW 1, 2; MTFW 2005; RGWL 2, 3

Brodsky, Joseph . **CLC 4, 6, 13, 36, 100; PC 9**
See Brodsky, Iosif Alexandrovich
See also AMWS 8; CWW 2; DLB 285; EWL 3; MTCW 1

Brodsky, Michael (Mark) 1948- .... **CLC 19**
See also CA 102; CANR 18, 41, 58; DLB 244

Brodzki, Bella ed. .... **CLC 65**

Brome, Richard 1590(?)-1652 .... **LC 61**
See also BRWS 10; DLB 58

Bromell, Henry 1947- .... **CLC 5**
See also CA 53-56; CANR 9, 115, 116

Bromfield, Louis (Brucker)
1896-1956 .... **TCLC 11**
See also CA 107; 155; DLB 4, 9, 86; RGAL 4; RHW

Broner, E(sther) M(asserman)
1930- .... **CLC 19**
See also CA 17-20R; CANR 8, 25, 72; CN 4, 5, 6; DLB 28

Bronk, William (M.) 1918-1999 .... **CLC 10**
See also CA 89-92; 177; CANR 23; CP 3, 4, 5, 6, 7; DLB 165

Bronstein, Lev Davidovich
See Trotsky, Leon

Bronte, Anne 1820-1849 ..... **NCLC 4, 71, 102**
See also BRW 5; BRWR 1; DA3; DLB 21, 199; TEA

Bronte, (Patrick) Branwell
1817-1848 .... **NCLC 109**

Bronte, Charlotte 1816-1855 ...... **NCLC 3, 8, 33, 58, 105, 155; WLC**
See also AAYA 17; BRW 5; BRWC 2; BRWR 1; BYA 2; CDBLB 1832-1890; DA; DA3; DAB; DAC; DAM MST, NOV; DLB 21, 159, 199; EXPN; FL 1:2; GL 2; LAIT 2; NFS 4; TEA; WLIT 4

Bronte, Emily (Jane) 1818-1848 ... **NCLC 16, 35, 165; PC 8; WLC**
See also AAYA 17; BPFB 1; BRW 5; BRWC 1; BRWR 1; BYA 3; CDBLB 1832-1890; DA; DA3; DAB; DAC; DAM MST, NOV, POET; DLB 21, 32, 199; EXPN; FL 1:2; GL 2; LAIT 1; TEA; WLIT 3

Brontes
See Bronte, Anne; Bronte, Charlotte; Bronte, Emily (Jane)

Brooke, Frances 1724-1789 .... **LC 6, 48**
See also DLB 39, 99

Brooke, Henry 1703(?)-1783 .... **LC 1**
See also DLB 39

Brooke, Rupert (Chawner)
1887-1915 ..... **PC 24; TCLC 2, 7; WLC**
See also BRWS 3; CA 104; 132; CANR 61; CDBLB 1914-1945; DA; DAB; DAC; DAM MST, POET; DLB 19, 216; EXPP; GLL 2; MTCW 1, 2; MTFW 2005; PFS 7; TEA

Brooke-Haven, P.
See Wodehouse, P(elham) G(renville)

Brooke-Rose, Christine 1926(?)- ..... **CLC 40, 184**
See also BRWS 4; CA 13-16R; CANR 58, 118; CN 1, 2, 3, 4, 5, 6, 7; DLB 14, 231; EWL 3; SFW 4

Brookner, Anita 1928- .. **CLC 32, 34, 51, 136**
See also BRWS 4; CA 114; 120; CANR 37, 56, 87, 130; CN 4, 5, 6, 7; CPW; DA3; DAB; DAM POP; DLB 194; DLBY 1987; EWL 3; MTCW 1, 2; MTFW 2005; TEA

Brooks, Cleanth 1906-1994 . **CLC 24, 86, 110**
See also AMWS 1; CA 17-20R; 145; CANR 33, 35; CSW; DLB 63; DLBY 1994; EWL 3; INT CANR-35; MAL 5; MTCW 1, 2; MTFW 2005

Brooks, George
See Baum, L(yman) Frank

Brooks, Gwendolyn (Elizabeth)
1917-2000 ... **BLC 1; CLC 1, 2, 4, 5, 15, 49, 125; PC 7; WLC**
See also AAYA 20; AFAW 1, 2; AITN 1; AMWS 3; BW 2, 3; CA 1-4R; 190; CANR 1, 27, 52, 75, 132; CDALB 1941-1968; CLR 27; CP 1, 2, 3, 4, 5, 6, 7; CWP; DA; DA3; DAC; DAM MST, MULT, POET; DLB 5, 76, 165; EWL 3; EXPP; FL 1:5; MAL 5; MAWW; MTCW 1, 2; MTFW 2005; PFS 1, 2, 4, 6; RGAL 4; SATA 6; SATA-Obit 123; TUS; WP

Brooks, Mel .... **CLC 12, 217**
See Kaminsky, Melvin
See also AAYA 13, 48; DLB 26

Brooks, Peter (Preston) 1938- .... **CLC 34**
See also CA 45-48; CANR 1, 107

Brooks, Van Wyck 1886-1963 .... **CLC 29**
See also AMW; CA 1-4R; CANR 6; DLB 45, 63, 103; MAL 5; TUS

Brophy, Brigid (Antonia)
1929-1995 .... **CLC 6, 11, 29, 105**
See also CA 5-8R; 149; CAAS 4; CANR 25, 53; CBD; CN 1, 2, 3, 4, 5, 6; CWD; DA3; DLB 14, 271; EWL 3; MTCW 1, 2

Brosman, Catharine Savage 1934- ..... **CLC 9**
See also CA 61-64; CANR 21, 46

Brossard, Nicole 1943- .... **CLC 115, 169**
See also CA 122; CAAS 16; CANR 140; CCA 1; CWP; CWW 2; DLB 53; EWL 3; FW; GLL 2; RGWL 3

Brother Antoninus
See Everson, William (Oliver)

The Brothers Quay
See Quay, Stephen; Quay, Timothy

Broughton, T(homas) Alan 1936- ..... **CLC 19**
See also CA 45-48; CANR 2, 23, 48, 111

Broumas, Olga 1949- .... **CLC 10, 73**
See also CA 85-88; CANR 20, 69, 110; CP 7; CWP; GLL 2

Broun, Heywood 1888-1939 .... **TCLC 104**
See also DLB 29, 171

Brown, Alan 1950- .... **CLC 99**
See also CA 156

Brown, Charles Brockden
1771-1810 .... **NCLC 22, 74, 122**
See also AMWS 1; CDALB 1640-1865; DLB 37, 59, 73; FW; GL 2; HGG; LMFS 1; RGAL 4; TUS

Brown, Christy 1932-1981 .... **CLC 63**
See also BYA 13; CA 105; 104; CANR 72; DLB 14

Brown, Claude 1937-2002 ... **BLC 1; CLC 30**
See also AAYA 7; BW 1, 3; CA 73-76; 205; CANR 81; DAM MULT

Brown, Dan 1964- .... **CLC 209**
See also AAYA 55; CA 217; MTFW 2005

Brown, Dee (Alexander)
1908-2002 .... **CLC 18, 47**
See also AAYA 30; CA 13-16R; 212; CAAS 6; CANR 11, 45, 60; CPW; CSW; DA3; DAM POP; DLBY 1980; LAIT 2; MTCW 1, 2; MTFW 2005; NCFS 5; SATA 5, 110; SATA-Obit 141; TCWW 1, 2

Brown, George
See Wertmueller, Lina

Brown, George Douglas
1869-1902 .... **TCLC 28**
See Douglas, George
See also CA 162

Brown, George Mackay 1921-1996 ... **CLC 5, 48, 100**
See also BRWS 6; CA 21-24R; 151; CAAS 6; CANR 12, 37, 67; CN 1, 2, 3, 4, 5, 6; CP 1, 2, 3, 4; DLB 14, 27, 139, 271; MTCW 1; RGSF 2; SATA 35

Brown, (William) Larry 1951-2004 . **CLC 73**
See also CA 130; 134; 233; CANR 117, 145; CSW; DLB 234; INT CA-134

Brown, Moses
See Barrett, William (Christopher)

Brown, Rita Mae 1944- .... **CLC 18, 43, 79**
See also BPFB 1; CA 45-48; CANR 2, 11, 35, 62, 95, 138; CN 5, 6, 7; CPW; CSW; DA3; DAM NOV, POP; FW; INT CANR-11; MAL 5; MTCW 1, 2; MTFW 2005; NFS 9; RGAL 4; TUS

Brown, Roderick (Langmere) Haig-
See Haig-Brown, Roderick (Langmere)

Brown, Rosellen 1939- .... **CLC 32, 170**
See also CA 77-80; CAAS 10; CANR 14, 44, 98; CN 6, 7

Brown, Sterling Allen 1901-1989 ...... **BLC 1; CLC 1, 23, 59; HR 1:2; PC 55**
See also AFAW 1, 2; BW 1, 3; CA 85-88; 127; CANR 26; CP 3, 4; DA3; DAM MULT, POET; DLB 48, 51, 63; MAL 5; MTCW 1, 2; MTFW 2005; RGAL 4; WP

Brown, Will
See Ainsworth, William Harrison

Brown, William Hill 1765-1793 .... **LC 93**
See also DLB 37

Brown, William Wells 1815-1884 ...... **BLC 1; DC 1; NCLC 2, 89**
See also DAM MULT; DLB 3, 50, 183, 248; RGAL 4

Browne, (Clyde) Jackson 1948(?)- ... **CLC 21**
See also CA 120

Browne, Sir Thomas 1605-1682 .... **LC 111**
See also BRW 2; DLB 151

Browning, Robert 1812-1889 . **NCLC 19, 79; PC 2, 61; WLCS**
See also BRW 4; BRWC 2; BRWR 2; CD-BLB 1832-1890; CLR 97; DA; DA3; DAB; DAC; DAM MST, POET; DLB 32, 163; EXPP; LATS 1:1; PAB; PFS 1, 15; RGEL 2; TEA; WLIT 4; WP; YABC 1

Browning, Tod 1882-1962 .... **CLC 16**
See also CA 141; 117

Brownmiller, Susan 1935- .... **CLC 159**
See also CA 103; CANR 35, 75, 137; DAM NOV; FW; MTCW 1, 2; MTFW 2005

Brownson, Orestes Augustus
1803-1876 .... **NCLC 50**
See also DLB 1, 59, 73, 243

Bruccoli, Matthew J(oseph) 1931- ..... **CLC 34**
See also CA 9-12R; CANR 7, 87; DLB 103

Bruce, Lenny .... **CLC 21**
See Schneider, Leonard Alfred

Bruchac, Joseph III 1942- .... **NNAL**
See also AAYA 19; CA 33-36R; CANR 13, 47, 75, 94, 137; CLR 46; CWRI 5; DAM MULT; JRDA; MAICYA 2; MAICYAS 1; MTCW 2; MTFW 2005; SATA 42, 89, 131

Bruin, John
See Brutus, Dennis

Brulard, Henri
See Stendhal

Brulls, Christian
See Simenon, Georges (Jacques Christian)

Brunetto Latini c. 1220-1294 .... **CMLC 73**

Brunner, John (Kilian Houston)
1934-1995 .... **CLC 8, 10**
See also CA 1-4R; 149; CAAS 8; CANR 2, 37; CPW; DAM POP; DLB 261; MTCW 1, 2; SCFW 1, 2; SFW 4

Bruno, Giordano 1548-1600 .... **LC 27**
See also RGWL 2, 3

Brutus, Dennis 1924- ... **BLC 1; CLC 43; PC 24**
See also AFW; BW 2, 3; CA 49-52; CAAS 14; CANR 2, 27, 42, 81; CDWLB 3; CP 1, 2, 3, 4, 5, 6, 7; DAM MULT, POET; DLB 117, 225; EWL 3

Bryan, C(ourtlandt) D(ixon) B(arnes)
1936- .... **CLC 29**
See also CA 73-76; CANR 13, 68; DLB 185; INT CANR-13

Bryan, Michael
See Moore, Brian
See also CCA 1

Bryan, William Jennings
1860-1925 .... **TCLC 99**
See also DLB 303

Bryant, William Cullen 1794-1878 . **NCLC 6, 46; PC 20**
See also AMWS 1; CDALB 1640-1865; DA; DAB; DAC; DAM MST, POET; DLB 3, 43, 59, 189, 250; EXPP; PAB; RGAL 4; TUS

Bryusov, Valery Yakovlevich
1873-1924 .... **TCLC 10**
See also CA 107; 155; EWL 3; SFW 4

Buchan, John 1875-1940 .... **TCLC 41**
See also CA 108; 145; CMW 4; DAB; DAM POP; DLB 34, 70, 156; HGG; MSW; MTCW 2; RGEL 2; RHW; YABC 2

Buchanan, George 1506-1582 .... **LC 4**
See also DLB 132

Buchanan, Robert 1841-1901 .... **TCLC 107**
See also CA 179; DLB 18, 35

Buchheim, Lothar-Guenther 1918- .... **CLC 6**
See also CA 85-88

Buchner, (Karl) Georg
1813-1837 .... **NCLC 26, 146**
See also CDWLB 2; DLB 133; EW 6; RGSF 2; RGWL 2, 3; TWA

Buchwald, Art(hur) 1925- .... **CLC 33**
See also AITN 1; CA 5-8R; CANR 21, 67, 107; MTCW 1, 2; SATA 10

Buck, Pearl S(ydenstricker)
1892-1973 .... **CLC 7, 11, 18, 127**
See also AAYA 42; AITN 1; AMWS 2; BPFB 1; CA 1-4R; 41-44R; CANR 1, 34; CDALBS; CN 1; DA; DA3; DAB; DAC; DAM MST, NOV; DLB 9, 102; EWL 3; LAIT 3; MAL 5; MTCW 1, 2; MTFW 2005; RGAL 4; RHW; SATA 1, 25; TUS

Buckler, Ernest 1908-1984 .... **CLC 13**
See also CA 11-12; 114; CAP 1; CCA 1; CN 1, 2, 3; DAC; DAM MST; DLB 68; SATA 47

Buckley, Christopher (Taylor)
1952- .... **CLC 165**
See also CA 139; CANR 119

Buckley, Vincent (Thomas)
1925-1988 .... **CLC 57**
See also CA 101; CP 1, 2, 3, 4; DLB 289

Buckley, William F(rank), Jr. 1925- . **CLC 7, 18, 37**
See also AITN 1; BPFB 1; CA 1-4R; CANR 1, 24, 53, 93, 133; CMW 4; CPW; DA3; DAM POP; DLB 137; DLBY 1980; INT CANR-24; MTCW 1, 2; MTFW 2005; TUS

Buechner, (Carl) Frederick 1926- . **CLC 2, 4, 6, 9**
See also AMWS 12; BPFB 1; CA 13-16R; CANR 11, 39, 64, 114, 138; CN 1, 2, 3, 4, 5, 6, 7; DAM NOV; DLBY 1980; INT CANR-11; MAL 5; MTCW 1, 2; MTFW 2005; TCLE 1:1

Buell, John (Edward) 1927- .... **CLC 10**
See also CA 1-4R; CANR 71; DLB 53

Buero Vallejo, Antonio 1916-2000 ... **CLC 15, 46, 139; DC 18**
See also CA 106; 189; CANR 24, 49, 75; CWW 2; DFS 11; EWL 3; HW 1; MTCW 1, 2

Bufalino, Gesualdo 1920-1996 .... **CLC 74**
See also CA 209; CWW 2; DLB 196

Bugayev, Boris Nikolayevich
1880-1934 .... **PC 11; TCLC 7**
See Bely, Andrey; Belyi, Andrei
See also CA 104; 165; MTCW 2; MTFW 2005

Bukowski, Charles 1920-1994 ... **CLC 2, 5, 9, 41, 82, 108; PC 18; SSC 45**
See also CA 17-20R; 144; CANR 40, 62, 105; CN 4, 5; CP 1, 2, 3, 4; CPW; DA3; DAM NOV, POET; DLB 5, 130, 169; EWL 3; MAL 5; MTCW 1, 2; MTFW 2005

Bulgakov, Mikhail (Afanas'evich)
1891-1940 ..... **SSC 18; TCLC 2, 16, 159**
See also BPFB 1; CA 105; 152; DAM DRAM, NOV; DLB 272; EWL 3; MTCW 2; MTFW 2005; NFS 8; RGSF 2; RGWL 2, 3; SFW 4; TWA

Bulgya, Alexander Alexandrovich
1901-1956 .... **TCLC 53**
See Fadeev, Aleksandr Aleksandrovich; Fadeev, Alexandr Alexandrovich; Fadeyev, Alexander
See also CA 117; 181

Bullins, Ed 1935- ... **BLC 1; CLC 1, 5, 7; DC 6**
See also BW 2, 3; CA 49-52; CAAS 16; CAD; CANR 24, 46, 73, 134; CD 5, 6; DAM DRAM, MULT; DLB 7, 38, 249; EWL 3; MAL 5; MTCW 1, 2; MTFW 2005; RGAL 4

Bulosan, Carlos 1911-1956 .... **AAL**
See also CA 216; DLB 312; RGAL 4

Bulwer-Lytton, Edward (George Earle Lytton) 1803-1873 .... **NCLC 1, 45**
See also DLB 21; RGEL 2; SFW 4; SUFW 1; TEA

Bunin, Ivan Alexeyevich 1870-1953 ... **SSC 5; TCLC 6**
See also CA 104; DLB 317; EWL 3; RGSF 2; RGWL 2, 3; TWA

Bunting, Basil 1900-1985 ...... **CLC 10, 39, 47**
See also BRWS 7; CA 53-56; 115; CANR 7; CP 1, 2, 3, 4; DAM POET; DLB 20; EWL 3; RGEL 2

Bunuel, Luis 1900-1983 ... **CLC 16, 80; HLC 1**
See also CA 101; 110; CANR 32, 77; DAM MULT; HW 1

Bunyan, John 1628-1688 ..... **LC 4, 69; WLC**
See also BRW 2; BYA 5; CDBLB 1660-1789; DA; DAB; DAC; DAM MST; DLB 39; RGEL 2; TEA; WCH; WLIT 3

Buravsky, Alexandr .... **CLC 59**

Burckhardt, Jacob (Christoph)
1818-1897 .... **NCLC 49**
See also EW 6

Burford, Eleanor
See Hibbert, Eleanor Alice Burford

Burgess, Anthony . **CLC 1, 2, 4, 5, 8, 10, 13, 15, 22, 40, 62, 81, 94**
See Wilson, John (Anthony) Burgess
See also AAYA 25; AITN 1; BRWS 1; CDBLB 1960 to Present; CN 1, 2, 3, 4, 5; DAB; DLB 14, 194, 261; DLBY 1998; EWL 3; RGEL 2; RHW; SFW 4; YAW

Burke, Edmund 1729(?)-1797 .... **LC 7, 36; WLC**
See also BRW 3; DA; DA3; DAB; DAC; DAM MST; DLB 104, 252; RGEL 2; TEA

Burke, Kenneth (Duva) 1897-1993 ... **CLC 2, 24**
See also AMW; CA 5-8R; 143; CANR 39, 74, 136; CN 1, 2; CP 1, 2, 3, 4; DLB 45, 63; EWL 3; MAL 5; MTCW 1, 2; MTFW 2005; RGAL 4

Burke, Leda
See Garnett, David

Burke, Ralph
See Silverberg, Robert

Burke, Thomas 1886-1945 .... **TCLC 63**
See also CA 113; 155; CMW 4; DLB 197

Burney, Fanny 1752-1840 .... **NCLC 12, 54, 107**
See also BRWS 3; DLB 39; FL 1:2; NFS 16; RGEL 2; TEA

Burney, Frances
See Burney, Fanny

Burns, Robert 1759-1796 ... **LC 3, 29, 40; PC 6; WLC**
See also AAYA 51; BRW 3; CDBLB 1789-1832; DA; DA3; DAB; DAC; DAM MST, POET; DLB 109; EXPP; PAB; RGEL 2; TEA; WP

Burns, Tex
See L'Amour, Louis (Dearborn)

Burnshaw, Stanley 1906- .... **CLC 3, 13, 44**
See also CA 9-12R; CP 1, 2, 3, 4, 5, 6, 7; DLB 48; DLBY 1997

Burr, Anne 1937- .... **CLC 6**
See also CA 25-28R

Burroughs, Edgar Rice 1875-1950 . **TCLC 2, 32**
See also AAYA 11; BPFB 1; BYA 4, 9; CA 104; 132; CANR 131; DA3; DAM NOV; DLB 8; FANT; MTCW 1, 2; MTFW 2005; RGAL 4; SATA 41; SCFW 1, 2; SFW 4; TCWW 1, 2; TUS; YAW

Burroughs, William S(eward)
1914-1997 .. **CLC 1, 2, 5, 15, 22, 42, 75, 109; TCLC 121; WLC**
See Lee, William; Lee, Willy
See also AAYA 60; AITN 2; AMWS 3; BG 1:2; BPFB 1; CA 9-12R; 160; CANR 20, 52, 104; CN 1, 2, 3, 4, 5, 6; CPW; DA; DA3; DAB; DAC; DAM MST, NOV, POP; DLB 2, 8, 16, 152, 237; DLBY 1981, 1997; EWL 3; HGG; LMFS 2; MAL 5; MTCW 1, 2; MTFW 2005; RGAL 4; SFW 4

Burton, Sir Richard F(rancis)
1821-1890 .... **NCLC 42**
See also DLB 55, 166, 184; SSFS 21

Burton, Robert 1577-1640 .... **LC 74**
See also DLB 151; RGEL 2

Buruma, Ian 1951- .... **CLC 163**
See also CA 128; CANR 65, 141

Busch, Frederick 1941- ... **CLC 7, 10, 18, 47, 166**
See also CA 33-36R; CAAS 1; CANR 45, 73, 92; CN 1, 2, 3, 4, 5, 6, 7; DLB 6, 218

Bush, Barney (Furman) 1946- .... **NNAL**
See also CA 145

Bush, Ronald 1946- .... **CLC 34**
See also CA 136

Bustos, F(rancisco)
See Borges, Jorge Luis

Bustos Domecq, H(onorio)
See Bioy Casares, Adolfo; Borges, Jorge Luis

Butler, Octavia E(stelle) 1947- .. **BLCS; CLC 38, 121**
See also AAYA 18, 48; AFAW 2; AMWS 13; BPFB 1; BW 2, 3; CA 73-76; CANR 12, 24, 38, 73, 145; CLR 65; CN 7; CPW; DA3; DAM MULT, POP; DLB 33; LATS 1:2; MTCW 1, 2; MTFW 2005; NFS 8, 21; SATA 84; SCFW 2; SFW 4; SSFS 6; TCLE 1:1; YAW

Butler, Robert Olen, (Jr.) 1945- ...... **CLC 81, 162**
See also AMWS 12; BPFB 1; CA 112; CANR 66, 138; CN 7; CSW; DAM POP; DLB 173; INT CA-112; MAL 5; MTCW 2; MTFW 2005; SSFS 11

Butler, Samuel 1612-1680 .... **LC 16, 43**
See also DLB 101, 126; RGEL 2

Butler, Samuel 1835-1902 .... **TCLC 1, 33; WLC**
See also BRWS 2; CA 143; CDBLB 1890-1914; DA; DA3; DAB; DAC; DAM MST, NOV; DLB 18, 57, 174; RGEL 2; SFW 4; TEA

Butler, Walter C.
See Faust, Frederick (Schiller)

Butor, Michel (Marie Francois)
1926- .... **CLC 1, 3, 8, 11, 15, 161**
See also CA 9-12R; CANR 33, 66; CWW
2; DLB 83; EW 13; EWL 3; GFL 1789 to
the Present; MTCW 1, 2; MTFW 2005
Butts, Mary 1890(?)-1937 .... **TCLC 77**
See also CA 148; DLB 240
Buxton, Ralph
See Silverstein, Alvin; Silverstein, Virginia
B(arbara Opshelor)
Buzo, Alex
See Buzo, Alexander (John)
See also DLB 289
Buzo, Alexander (John) 1944- .... **CLC 61**
See also CA 97-100; CANR 17, 39, 69; CD
5, 6
Buzzati, Dino 1906-1972 .... **CLC 36**
See also CA 160; 33-36R; DLB 177; RGWL
2, 3; SFW 4
Byars, Betsy (Cromer) 1928- .... **CLC 35**
See also AAYA 19; BYA 3; CA 33-36R,
183; CAAE 183; CANR 18, 36, 57, 102;
CLR 1, 16, 72; DLB 52; INT CANR-18;
JRDA; MAICYA 1, 2; MAICYAS 1;
MTCW 1; SAAS 1; SATA 4, 46, 80, 163;
SATA-Essay 108; WYA; YAW
Byatt, A(ntonia) S(usan Drabble)
1936- .... **CLC 19, 65, 136**
See also BPFB 1; BRWC 2; BRWS 4; CA
13-16R; CANR 13, 33, 50, 75, 96, 133;
CN 1, 2, 3, 4, 5, 6; DA3; DAM NOV,
POP; DLB 14, 194; EWL 3; MTCW 1, 2;
MTFW 2005; RGSF 2; RHW; TEA
Byrd, William II 1674-1744 .... **LC 112**
See also DLB 24, 140; RGAL 4
Byrne, David 1952- .... **CLC 26**
See also CA 127
Byrne, John Keyes 1926-
See Leonard, Hugh
See also CA 102; CANR 78, 140; INT CA-
102
Byron, George Gordon (Noel)
1788-1824 ..... **DC 24; NCLC 2, 12, 109,
149; PC 16; WLC**
See also AAYA 64; BRW 4; BRWC 2; CD-
BLB 1789-1832; DA; DA3; DAB; DAC;
DAM MST, POET; DLB 96, 110; EXPP;
LMFS 1; PAB; PFS 1, 14; RGEL 2; TEA;
WLIT 3; WP
Byron, Robert 1905-1941 .... **TCLC 67**
See also CA 160; DLB 195
C. 3. 3.
See Wilde, Oscar (Fingal O'Flahertie Wills)
Caballero, Fernan 1796-1877 .... **NCLC 10**
Cabell, Branch
See Cabell, James Branch
Cabell, James Branch 1879-1958 .... **TCLC 6**
See also CA 105; 152; DLB 9, 78; FANT;
MAL 5; MTCW 2; RGAL 4; SUFW 1
Cabeza de Vaca, Alvar Nunez
1490-1557(?) .... **LC 61**
Cable, George Washington
1844-1925 .... **SSC 4; TCLC 4**
See also CA 104; 155; DLB 12, 74; DLBD
13; RGAL 4; TUS
Cabral de Melo Neto, Joao
1920-1999 .... **CLC 76**
See Melo Neto, Joao Cabral de
See also CA 151; DAM MULT; DLB 307;
LAW; LAWS 1
Cabrera Infante, G(uillermo)
1929-2005 ..... **CLC 5, 25, 45, 120; HLC
1; SSC 39**
See also CA 85-88; 236; CANR 29, 65, 110;
CDWLB 3; CWW 2; DA3; DAM MULT;
DLB 113; EWL 3; HW 1, 2; LAW; LAWS
1; MTCW 1, 2; MTFW 2005; RGSF 2;
WLIT 1

Cade, Toni
See Bambara, Toni Cade
Cadmus and Harmonia
See Buchan, John
Caedmon fl. 658-680 .... **CMLC 7**
See also DLB 146
Caeiro, Alberto
See Pessoa, Fernando (Antonio Nogueira)
Caesar, Julius .... **CMLC 47**
See Julius Caesar
See also AW 1; RGWL 2, 3
Cage, John (Milton), (Jr.)
1912-1992 .... **CLC 41; PC 58**
See also CA 13-16R; 169; CANR 9, 78;
DLB 193; INT CANR-9; TCLE 1:1
Cahan, Abraham 1860-1951 .... **TCLC 71**
See also CA 108; 154; DLB 9, 25, 28; MAL
5; RGAL 4
Cain, G.
See Cabrera Infante, G(uillermo)
Cain, Guillermo
See Cabrera Infante, G(uillermo)
Cain, James M(allahan) 1892-1977 .. **CLC 3,
11, 28**
See also AITN 1; BPFB 1; CA 17-20R; 73-
76; CANR 8, 34, 61; CMW 4; CN 1, 2;
DLB 226; EWL 3; MAL 5; MSW; MTCW
1; RGAL 4
Caine, Hall 1853-1931 .... **TCLC 97**
See also RHW
Caine, Mark
See Raphael, Frederic (Michael)
Calasso, Roberto 1941- .... **CLC 81**
See also CA 143; CANR 89
Calderon de la Barca, Pedro
1600-1681 .... **DC 3; HLCS 1; LC 23**
See also EW 2; RGWL 2, 3; TWA
Caldwell, Erskine (Preston)
1903-1987 .... **CLC 1, 8, 14, 50, 60; SSC
19; TCLC 117**
See also AITN 1; AMW; BPFB 1; CA 1-4R;
121; CAAS 1; CANR 2, 33; CN 1, 2, 3,
4; DA3; DAM NOV; DLB 9, 86; EWL 3;
MAL 5; MTCW 1, 2; MTFW 2005;
RGAL 4; RGSF 2; TUS
Caldwell, (Janet Miriam) Taylor (Holland)
1900-1985 .... **CLC 2, 28, 39**
See also BPFB 1; CA 5-8R; 116; CANR 5;
DA3; DAM NOV, POP; DLBD 17;
MTCW 2; RHW
Calhoun, John Caldwell
1782-1850 .... **NCLC 15**
See also DLB 3, 248
Calisher, Hortense 1911- ..... **CLC 2, 4, 8, 38,
134; SSC 15**
See also CA 1-4R; CANR 1, 22, 117; CN
1, 2, 3, 4, 5, 6, 7; DA3; DAM NOV; DLB
2, 218; INT CANR-22; MAL 5; MTCW
1, 2; MTFW 2005; RGAL 4; RGSF 2
Callaghan, Morley Edward
1903-1990 ..... **CLC 3, 14, 41, 65; TCLC
145**
See also CA 9-12R; 132; CANR 33, 73;
CN 1, 2, 3, 4; DAC; DAM MST; DLB
68; EWL 3; MTCW 1, 2; MTFW 2005;
RGEL 2; RGSF 2; SSFS 19
Callimachus c. 305B.C.-c.
240B.C. .... **CMLC 18**
See also AW 1; DLB 176; RGWL 2, 3
Calvin, Jean
See Calvin, John
See also GFL Beginnings to 1789
Calvin, John 1509-1564 .... **LC 37**
See also Calvin, Jean
Calvino, Italo 1923-1985 .... **CLC 5, 8, 11, 22,
33, 39, 73; SSC 3, 48**
See also AAYA 58; CA 85-88; 116; CANR
23, 61, 132; DAM NOV; DLB 196; EW
13; EWL 3; MTCW 1, 2; MTFW 2005;
RGSF 2; RGWL 2, 3; SFW 4; SSFS 12;
WLIT 7

Camara Laye
See Laye, Camara
See also EWL 3
Camden, William 1551-1623 .... **LC 77**
See also DLB 172
Cameron, Carey 1952- .... **CLC 59**
See also CA 135
Cameron, Peter 1959- .... **CLC 44**
See also AMWS 12; CA 125; CANR 50,
117; DLB 234; GLL 2
Camoens, Luis Vaz de 1524(?)-1580
See Camoes, Luis de
See also EW 2
Camoes, Luis de 1524(?)-1580 . **HLCS 1; LC
62; PC 31**
See Camoens, Luis Vaz de
See also DLB 287; RGWL 2, 3
Campana, Dino 1885-1932 .... **TCLC 20**
See also CA 117; DLB 114; EWL 3
Campanella, Tommaso 1568-1639 .... **LC 32**
See also RGWL 2, 3
Campbell, John W(ood, Jr.)
1910-1971 .... **CLC 32**
See also CA 21-22; 29-32R; CANR 34;
CAP 2; DLB 8; MTCW 1; SCFW 1, 2;
SFW 4
Campbell, Joseph 1904-1987 .... **CLC 69;
TCLC 140**
See also AAYA 3, 66; BEST 89:2; CA 1-4R;
124; CANR 3, 28, 61, 107; DA3; MTCW
1, 2
Campbell, Maria 1940- .... **CLC 85; NNAL**
See also CA 102; CANR 54; CCA 1; DAC
Campbell, (John) Ramsey 1946- ..... **CLC 42;
SSC 19**
See also AAYA 51; CA 57-60; 228; CAAE
228; CANR 7, 102; DLB 261; HGG; INT
CANR-7; SUFW 1, 2
Campbell, (Ignatius) Roy (Dunnachie)
1901-1957 .... **TCLC 5**
See also AFW; CA 104; 155; DLB 20, 225;
EWL 3; MTCW 2; RGEL 2
Campbell, Thomas 1777-1844 .... **NCLC 19**
See also DLB 93, 144; RGEL 2
Campbell, Wilfred .... **TCLC 9**
See Campbell, William
Campbell, William 1858(?)-1918
See Campbell, Wilfred
See also CA 106; DLB 92
Campbell, William Edward March
1893-1954
See March, William
See also CA 108
Campion, Jane 1954- .... **CLC 95**
See also AAYA 33; CA 138; CANR 87
Campion, Thomas 1567-1620 .... **LC 78**
See also CDBLB Before 1660; DAM POET;
DLB 58, 172; RGEL 2
Camus, Albert 1913-1960 ...... **CLC 1, 2, 4, 9,
11, 14, 32, 63, 69, 124; DC 2; SSC 9,
76; WLC**
See also AAYA 36; AFW; BPFB 1; CA 89-
92; CANR 131; DA; DA3; DAB; DAC;
DAM DRAM, MST, NOV; DLB 72, 321;
EW 13; EWL 3; EXPN; EXPS; GFL 1789
to the Present; LATS 1:2; LMFS 2;
MTCW 1, 2; MTFW 2005; NFS 6, 16;
RGSF 2; RGWL 2, 3; SSFS 4; TWA
Canby, Vincent 1924-2000 .... **CLC 13**
See also CA 81-84; 191
Cancale
See Desnos, Robert
Canetti, Elias 1905-1994 .. **CLC 3, 14, 25, 75,
86; TCLC 157**
See also CA 21-24R; 146; CANR 23, 61,
79; CDWLB 2; CWW 2; DA3; DLB 85,
124; EW 12; EWL 3; MTCW 1, 2; MTFW
2005; RGWL 2, 3; TWA

Canfield, Dorothea F.
See Fisher, Dorothy (Frances) Canfield
Canfield, Dorothea Frances
See Fisher, Dorothy (Frances) Canfield
Canfield, Dorothy
See Fisher, Dorothy (Frances) Canfield
Canin, Ethan 1960- .... **CLC 55; SSC 70**
See also CA 131; 135; MAL 5
Cankar, Ivan 1876-1918 .... **TCLC 105**
See also CDWLB 4; DLB 147; EWL 3
Cannon, Curt
See Hunter, Evan
Cao, Lan 1961- .... **CLC 109**
See also CA 165
Cape, Judith
See Page, P(atricia) K(athleen)
See also CCA 1
Capek, Karel 1890-1938 .... **DC 1; SSC 36;**
TCLC 6, 37; WLC
See also CA 104; 140; CDWLB 4; DA;
DA3; DAB; DAC; DAM DRAM, MST,
NOV; DFS 7, 11; DLB 215; EW 10; EWL
3; MTCW 2; MTFW 2005; RGSF 2;
RGWL 2, 3; SCFW 1, 2; SFW 4
Capote, Truman 1924-1984 . **CLC 1, 3, 8, 13,**
19, 34, 38, 58; SSC 2, 47; TCLC 164;
WLC
See also AAYA 61; AMWS 3; BPFB 1; CA
5-8R; 113; CANR 18, 62; CDALB 1941-
1968; CN 1, 2, 3; CPW; DA; DA3; DAB;
DAC; DAM MST, NOV, POP; DLB 2,
185, 227; DLBY 1980, 1984; EWL 3;
EXPS; GLL 1; LAIT 3; MAL 5; MTCW
1, 2; MTFW 2005; NCFS 2; RGAL 4;
RGSF 2; SATA 91; SSFS 2; TUS
Capra, Frank 1897-1991 .... **CLC 16**
See also AAYA 52; CA 61-64; 135
Caputo, Philip 1941- .... **CLC 32**
See also AAYA 60; CA 73-76; CANR 40,
135; YAW
Caragiale, Ion Luca 1852-1912 ...... **TCLC 76**
See also CA 157
Card, Orson Scott 1951- .... **CLC 44, 47, 50**
See also AAYA 11, 42; BPFB 1; BYA 5, 8;
CA 102; CANR 27, 47, 73, 102, 106, 133;
CPW; DA3; DAM POP; FANT; INT
CANR-27; MTCW 1, 2; MTFW 2005;
NFS 5; SATA 83, 127; SCFW 2; SFW 4;
SUFW 2; YAW
Cardenal, Ernesto 1925- .... **CLC 31, 161;**
HLC 1; PC 22
See also CA 49-52; CANR 2, 32, 66, 138;
CWW 2; DAM MULT, POET; DLB 290;
EWL 3; HW 1, 2; LAWS 1; MTCW 1, 2;
MTFW 2005; RGWL 2, 3
Cardinal, Marie 1929-2001 .... **CLC 189**
See also CA 177; CWW 2; DLB 83; FW
Cardozo, Benjamin N(athan)
1870-1938 .... **TCLC 65**
See also CA 117; 164
Carducci, Giosue (Alessandro Giuseppe)
1835-1907 .... **PC 46; TCLC 32**
See also CA 163; EW 7; RGWL 2, 3
Carew, Thomas 1595(?)-1640 . **LC 13; PC 29**
See also BRW 2; DLB 126; PAB; RGEL 2
Carey, Ernestine Gilbreth 1908- ...... **CLC 17**
See also CA 5-8R; CANR 71; SATA 2
Carey, Peter 1943- .... **CLC 40, 55, 96, 183**
See also CA 123; 127; CANR 53, 76, 117;
CN 4, 5, 6, 7; DLB 289; EWL 3; INT CA-
127; MTCW 1, 2; MTFW 2005; RGSF 2;
SATA 94
Carleton, William 1794-1869 .... **NCLC 3**
See also DLB 159; RGEL 2; RGSF 2
Carlisle, Henry (Coffin) 1926- .... **CLC 33**
See also CA 13-16R; CANR 15, 85
Carlsen, Chris
See Holdstock, Robert P.

Carlson, Ron(ald F.) 1947- .... **CLC 54**
See also CA 105, 189; CAAE 189; CANR
27; DLB 244
Carlyle, Thomas 1795-1881 ..... **NCLC 22, 70**
See also BRW 4; CDBLB 1789-1832; DA;
DAB; DAC; DAM MST; DLB 55, 144,
254; RGEL 2; TEA
Carman, (William) Bliss 1861-1929 ... **PC 34;**
TCLC 7
See also CA 104; 152; DAC; DLB 92;
RGEL 2
Carnegie, Dale 1888-1955 .... **TCLC 53**
See also CA 218
Carossa, Hans 1878-1956 .... **TCLC 48**
See also CA 170; DLB 66; EWL 3
Carpenter, Don(ald Richard)
1931-1995 .... **CLC 41**
See also CA 45-48; 149; CANR 1, 71
Carpenter, Edward 1844-1929 .... **TCLC 88**
See also CA 163; GLL 1
Carpenter, John (Howard) 1948- ... **CLC 161**
See also AAYA 2; CA 134; SATA 58
Carpenter, Johnny
See Carpenter, John (Howard)
Carpentier (y Valmont), Alejo
1904-1980 . **CLC 8, 11, 38, 110; HLC 1;**
SSC 35
See also CA 65-68; 97-100; CANR 11, 70;
CDWLB 3; DAM MULT; DLB 113; EWL
3; HW 1, 2; LAW; LMFS 2; RGSF 2;
RGWL 2, 3; WLIT 1
Carr, Caleb 1955- .... **CLC 86**
See also CA 147; CANR 73, 134; DA3
Carr, Emily 1871-1945 .... **TCLC 32**
See also CA 159; DLB 68; FW; GLL 2
Carr, John Dickson 1906-1977 .... **CLC 3**
See Fairbairn, Roger
See also CA 49-52; 69-72; CANR 3, 33,
60; CMW 4; DLB 306; MSW; MTCW 1,
2
Carr, Philippa
See Hibbert, Eleanor Alice Burford
Carr, Virginia Spencer 1929- .... **CLC 34**
See also CA 61-64; DLB 111
Carrere, Emmanuel 1957- .... **CLC 89**
See also CA 200
Carrier, Roch 1937- .... **CLC 13, 78**
See also CA 130; CANR 61; CCA 1; DAC;
DAM MST; DLB 53; SATA 105
Carroll, James Dennis
See Carroll, Jim
Carroll, James P. 1943(?)- .... **CLC 38**
See also CA 81-84; CANR 73, 139; MTCW
2; MTFW 2005
Carroll, Jim 1951- .... **CLC 35, 143**
See also AAYA 17; CA 45-48; CANR 42,
115; NCFS 5
Carroll, Lewis ..... **NCLC 2, 53, 139; PC 18;**
WLC
See Dodgson, Charles L(utwidge)
See also AAYA 39; BRW 5; BYA 5, 13; CD-
BLB 1832-1890; CLR 2, 18; DLB 18,
163, 178; DLBY 1998; EXPN; EXPP;
FANT; JRDA; LAIT 1; NFS 7; PFS 11;
RGEL 2; SUFW 1; TEA; WCH
Carroll, Paul Vincent 1900-1968 ...... **CLC 10**
See also CA 9-12R; 25-28R; DLB 10; EWL
3; RGEL 2
Carruth, Hayden 1921- ..... **CLC 4, 7, 10, 18,**
84; PC 10
See also CA 9-12R; CANR 4, 38, 59, 110;
CP 1, 2, 3, 4, 5, 6, 7; DLB 5, 165; INT
CANR-4; MTCW 1, 2; MTFW 2005;
SATA 47
Carson, Anne 1950- .... **CLC 185; PC 64**
See also AMWS 12; CA 203; DLB 193;
PFS 18; TCLE 1:1
Carson, Ciaran 1948- .... **CLC 201**
See also CA 112; 153; CANR 113; CP 7

Carson, Rachel
See Carson, Rachel Louise
See also AAYA 49; DLB 275
Carson, Rachel Louise 1907-1964 .... **CLC 71**
See Carson, Rachel
See also AMWS 9; ANW; CA 77-80; CANR
35; DA3; DAM POP; FW; LAIT 4; MAL
5; MTCW 1, 2; MTFW 2005; NCFS 1;
SATA 23
Carter, Angela (Olive) 1940-1992 ...... **CLC 5,**
41, 76; SSC 13, 85; TCLC 139
See also BRWS 3; CA 53-56; 136; CANR
12, 36, 61, 106; CN 3, 4, 5; DA3; DLB
14, 207, 261, 319; EXPS; FANT; FW; GL
2; MTCW 1, 2; MTFW 2005; RGSF 2;
SATA 66; SATA-Obit 70; SFW 4; SSFS
4, 12; SUFW 2; WLIT 4
Carter, Nick
See Smith, Martin Cruz
Carver, Raymond 1938-1988 ..... **CLC 22, 36,**
53, 55, 126; PC 54; SSC 8, 51
See also AAYA 44; AMWS 3; BPFB 1; CA
33-36R; 126; CANR 17, 34, 61, 103; CN
4; CPW; DA3; DAM NOV; DLB 130;
DLBY 1984, 1988; EWL 3; MAL 5;
MTCW 1, 2; MTFW 2005; PFS 17;
RGAL 4; RGSF 2; SSFS 3, 6, 12, 13;
TCLE 1:1; TCWW 2; TUS
Cary, Elizabeth, Lady Falkland
1585-1639 .... **LC 30**
Cary, (Arthur) Joyce (Lunel)
1888-1957 .... **TCLC 1, 29**
See also BRW 7; CA 104; 164; CDBLB
1914-1945; DLB 15, 100; EWL 3; MTCW
2; RGEL 2; TEA
Casal, Julian del 1863-1893 .... **NCLC 131**
See also DLB 283; LAW
Casanova, Giacomo
See Casanova de Seingalt, Giovanni Jacopo
See also WLIT 7
Casanova de Seingalt, Giovanni Jacopo
1725-1798 .... **LC 13**
See Casanova, Giacomo
Casares, Adolfo Bioy
See Bioy Casares, Adolfo
See also RGSF 2
Casas, Bartolome de las 1474-1566
See Las Casas, Bartolome de
See also WLIT 1
Casely-Hayford, J(oseph) E(phraim)
1866-1930 .... **BLC 1; TCLC 24**
See also BW 2; CA 123; 152; DAM MULT
Casey, John (Dudley) 1939- .... **CLC 59**
See also BEST 90:2; CA 69-72; CANR 23,
100
Casey, Michael 1947- .... **CLC 2**
See also CA 65-68; CANR 109; CP 2, 3;
DLB 5
Casey, Patrick
See Thurman, Wallace (Henry)
Casey, Warren (Peter) 1935-1988 .... **CLC 12**
See also CA 101; 127; INT CA-101
Casona, Alejandro .... **CLC 49**
See Alvarez, Alejandro Rodriguez
See also EWL 3
Cassavetes, John 1929-1989 .... **CLC 20**
See also CA 85-88; 127; CANR 82
Cassian, Nina 1924- .... **PC 17**
See also CWP; CWW 2
Cassill, R(onald) V(erlin)
1919-2002 .... **CLC 4, 23**
See also CA 9-12R; 208; CAAS 1; CANR
7, 45; CN 1, 2, 3, 4, 5, 6, 7; DLB 6, 218;
DLBY 2002
Cassiodorus, Flavius Magnus c. 490(?)-c.
583(?) .... **CMLC 43**
Cassirer, Ernst 1874-1945 .... **TCLC 61**
See also CA 157

Chapman, John Jay 1862-1933 .... **TCLC 7**
See also AMWS 14; CA 104; 191
Chapman, Lee
See Bradley, Marion Zimmer
See also GLL 1
Chapman, Walker
See Silverberg, Robert
Chappell, Fred (Davis) 1936- .... **CLC 40, 78, 162**
See also CA 5-8R, 198; CAAE 198; CAAS 4; CANR 8, 33, 67, 110; CN 6; CP 7; CSW; DLB 6, 105; HGG
Char, Rene(-Emile) 1907-1988 .... **CLC 9, 11, 14, 55; PC 56**
See also CA 13-16R; 124; CANR 32; DAM POET; DLB 258; EWL 3; GFL 1789 to the Present; MTCW 1, 2; RGWL 2, 3
Charby, Jay
See Ellison, Harlan (Jay)
Chardin, Pierre Teilhard de
See Teilhard de Chardin, (Marie Joseph) Pierre
Chariton fl. 1st cent. (?)- .... **CMLC 49**
Charlemagne 742-814 .... **CMLC 37**
Charles I 1600-1649 .... **LC 13**
Charriere, Isabelle de 1740-1805 .. **NCLC 66**
See also DLB 313
Chartier, Alain c. 1392-1430 .... **LC 94**
See also DLB 208
Chartier, Emile-Auguste
See Alain
Charyn, Jerome 1937- .... **CLC 5, 8, 18**
See also CA 5-8R; CAAS 1; CANR 7, 61, 101; CMW 4; CN 1, 2, 3, 4, 5, 6, 7; DLBY 1983; MTCW 1
Chase, Adam
See Marlowe, Stephen
Chase, Mary (Coyle) 1907-1981 .... **DC 1**
See also CA 77-80; 105; CAD; CWD; DFS 11; DLB 228; SATA 17; SATA-Obit 29
Chase, Mary Ellen 1887-1973 .... **CLC 2; TCLC 124**
See also CA 13-16; 41-44R; CAP 1; SATA 10
Chase, Nicholas
See Hyde, Anthony
See also CCA 1
Chateaubriand, Francois Rene de 1768-1848 .... **NCLC 3, 134**
See also DLB 119; EW 5; GFL 1789 to the Present; RGWL 2, 3; TWA
Chatelet, Gabrielle-Emilie Du
See du Chatelet, Emilie
See also DLB 313
Chatterje, Sarat Chandra 1876-1936(?)
See Chatterji, Saratchandra
See also CA 109
Chatterji, Bankim Chandra 1838-1894 .... **NCLC 19**
Chatterji, Saratchandra .... **TCLC 13**
See Chatterje, Sarat Chandra
See also CA 186; EWL 3
Chatterton, Thomas 1752-1770 .... **LC 3, 54**
See also DAM POET; DLB 109; RGEL 2
Chatwin, (Charles) Bruce 1940-1989 .... **CLC 28, 57, 59**
See also AAYA 4; BEST 90:1; BRWS 4; CA 85-88; 127; CPW; DAM POP; DLB 194, 204; EWL 3; MTFW 2005
Chaucer, Daniel
See Ford, Ford Madox
See also RHW
Chaucer, Geoffrey 1340(?)-1400 .. **LC 17, 56; PC 19, 58; WLCS**
See also BRW 1; BRWC 1; BRWR 2; CD-BLB Before 1660; DA; DA3; DAB; DAC; DAM MST, POET; DLB 146; LAIT 1; PAB; PFS 14; RGEL 2; TEA; WLIT 3; WP

Chavez, Denise (Elia) 1948- .... **HLC 1**
See also CA 131; CANR 56, 81, 137; DAM MULT; DLB 122; FW; HW 1, 2; LLW; MAL 5; MTCW 2; MTFW 2005
Chaviaras, Strates 1935-
See Haviaras, Stratis
See also CA 105
Chayefsky, Paddy .... **CLC 23**
See Chayefsky, Sidney
See also CAD; DLB 7, 44; DLBY 1981; RGAL 4
Chayefsky, Sidney 1923-1981
See Chayefsky, Paddy
See also CA 9-12R; 104; CANR 18; DAM DRAM
Chedid, Andree 1920- .... **CLC 47**
See also CA 145; CANR 95; EWL 3
Cheever, John 1912-1982 ..... **CLC 3, 7, 8, 11, 15, 25, 64; SSC 1, 38, 57; WLC**
See also AAYA 65; AMWS 1; BPFB 1; CA 5-8R; 106; CABS 1; CANR 5, 27, 76; CDALB 1941-1968; CN 1, 2, 3; CPW; DA; DA3; DAB; DAC; DAM MST, NOV, POP; DLB 2, 102, 227; DLBY 1980, 1982; EWL 3; EXPS; INT CANR-5; MAL 5; MTCW 1, 2; MTFW 2005; RGAL 4; RGSF 2; SSFS 2, 14; TUS
Cheever, Susan 1943- .... **CLC 18, 48**
See also CA 103; CANR 27, 51, 92; DLBY 1982; INT CANR-27
Chekhonte, Antosha
See Chekhov, Anton (Pavlovich)
Chekhov, Anton (Pavlovich) 1860-1904 .... **DC 9; SSC 2, 28, 41, 51, 85; TCLC 3, 10, 31, 55, 96, 163; WLC**
See also AAYA 68; BYA 14; CA 104; 124; DA; DA3; DAB; DAC; DAM DRAM, MST; DFS 1, 5, 10, 12; DLB 277; EW 7; EWL 3; EXPS; LAIT 3; LATS 1:1; RGSF 2; RGWL 2, 3; SATA 90; SSFS 5, 13, 14; TWA
Cheney, Lynne V. 1941- .... **CLC 70**
See also CA 89-92; CANR 58, 117; SATA 152
Chernyshevsky, Nikolai Gavrilovich
See Chernyshevsky, Nikolay Gavrilovich
See also DLB 238
Chernyshevsky, Nikolay Gavrilovich 1828-1889 .... **NCLC 1**
See Chernyshevsky, Nikolai Gavrilovich
Cherry, Carolyn Janice 1942-
See Cherryh, C. J.
See also CA 65-68; CANR 10
Cherryh, C. J. .... **CLC 35**
See Cherry, Carolyn Janice
See also AAYA 24; BPFB 1; DLBY 1980; FANT; SATA 93; SCFW 2; SFW 4; YAW
Chesnutt, Charles W(addell) 1858-1932 .... **BLC 1; SSC 7, 54; TCLC 5, 39**
See also AFAW 1, 2; AMWS 14; BW 1, 3; CA 106; 125; CANR 76; DAM MULT; DLB 12, 50, 78; EWL 3; MAL 5; MTCW 1, 2; MTFW 2005; RGAL 4; RGSF 2; SSFS 11
Chester, Alfred 1929(?)-1971 .... **CLC 49**
See also CA 196; 33-36R; DLB 130; MAL 5
Chesterton, G(ilbert) K(eith) 1874-1936 . **PC 28; SSC 1, 46; TCLC 1, 6, 64**
See also AAYA 57; BRW 6; CA 104; 132; CANR 73, 131; CDBLB 1914-1945; CMW 4; DAM NOV, POET; DLB 10, 19, 34, 70, 98, 149, 178; EWL 3; FANT; MSW; MTCW 1, 2; MTFW 2005; RGEL 2; RGSF 2; SATA 27; SUFW 1
Chettle, Henry 1560-1607(?) .... **LC 112**
See also DLB 136; RGEL 2

Chiang, Pin-chin 1904-1986
See Ding Ling
See also CA 118
Chief Joseph 1840-1904 .... **NNAL**
See also CA 152; DA3; DAM MULT
Chief Seattle 1786(?)-1866 .... **NNAL**
See also DA3; DAM MULT
Ch'ien, Chung-shu 1910-1998 .... **CLC 22**
See Qian Zhongshu
See also CA 130; CANR 73; MTCW 1, 2
Chikamatsu Monzaemon 1653-1724 ... **LC 66**
See also RGWL 2, 3
Child, L. Maria
See Child, Lydia Maria
Child, Lydia Maria 1802-1880 .. **NCLC 6, 73**
See also DLB 1, 74, 243; RGAL 4; SATA 67
Child, Mrs.
See Child, Lydia Maria
Child, Philip 1898-1978 .... **CLC 19, 68**
See also CA 13-14; CAP 1; CP 1; DLB 68; RHW; SATA 47
Childers, (Robert) Erskine 1870-1922 .... **TCLC 65**
See also CA 113; 153; DLB 70
Childress, Alice 1920-1994 . **BLC 1; CLC 12, 15, 86, 96; DC 4; TCLC 116**
See also AAYA 8; BW 2, 3; BYA 2; CA 45-48; 146; CAD; CANR 3, 27, 50, 74; CLR 14; CWD; DA3; DAM DRAM, MULT, NOV; DFS 2, 8, 14; DLB 7, 38, 249; JRDA; LAIT 5; MAICYA 1, 2; MAICYAS 1; MAL 5; MTCW 1, 2; MTFW 2005; RGAL 4; SATA 7, 48, 81; TUS; WYA; YAW
Chin, Frank (Chew, Jr.) 1940- .... **AAL; CLC 135; DC 7**
See also CA 33-36R; CAD; CANR 71; CD 5, 6; DAM MULT; DLB 206, 312; LAIT 5; RGAL 4
Chin, Marilyn (Mei Ling) 1955- .... **PC 40**
See also CA 129; CANR 70, 113; CWP; DLB 312
Chislett, (Margaret) Anne 1943- ...... **CLC 34**
See also CA 151
Chitty, Thomas Willes 1926- .... **CLC 11**
See Hinde, Thomas
See also CA 5-8R; CN 7
Chivers, Thomas Holley 1809-1858 .... **NCLC 49**
See also DLB 3, 248; RGAL 4
Choi, Susan 1969- .... **CLC 119**
See also CA 223
Chomette, Rene Lucien 1898-1981
See Clair, Rene
See also CA 103
Chomsky, (Avram) Noam 1928- ..... **CLC 132**
See also CA 17-20R; CANR 28, 62, 110, 132; DA3; DLB 246; MTCW 1, 2; MTFW 2005
Chona, Maria 1845(?)-1936 .... **NNAL**
See also CA 144
Chopin, Kate .... **SSC 8, 68; TCLC 127; WLCS**
See Chopin, Katherine
See also AAYA 33; AMWR 2; AMWS 1; BYA 11, 15; CDALB 1865-1917; DA; DAB; DLB 12, 78; EXPN; EXPS; FL 1:3; FW; LAIT 3; MAL 5; MAWW; NFS 3; RGAL 4; RGSF 2; SSFS 2, 13, 17; TUS
Chopin, Katherine 1851-1904
See Chopin, Kate
See also CA 104; 122; DA3; DAC; DAM MST, NOV
Chretien de Troyes c. 12th cent. - . **CMLC 10**
See also DLB 208; EW 1; RGWL 2, 3; TWA
Christie
See Ichikawa, Kon

Clutha, Janet Paterson Frame 1924-2004
See Frame, Janet
See also CA 1-4R; 224; CANR 2, 36, 76, 135; MTCW 1, 2; SATA 119

Clyne, Terence
See Blatty, William Peter

Cobalt, Martin
See Mayne, William (James Carter)

Cobb, Irvin S(hrewsbury)
1876-1944 .... **TCLC 77**
See also CA 175; DLB 11, 25, 86

Cobbett, William 1763-1835 .... **NCLC 49**
See also DLB 43, 107, 158; RGEL 2

Coburn, D(onald) L(ee) 1938- .... **CLC 10**
See also CA 89-92

Cocteau, Jean (Maurice Eugene Clement)
1889-1963 ...... **CLC 1, 8, 15, 16, 43; DC 17; TCLC 119; WLC**
See also CA 25-28; CANR 40; CAP 2; DA; DA3; DAB; DAC; DAM DRAM, MST, NOV; DLB 65, 258, 321; EW 10; EWL 3; GFL 1789 to the Present; MTCW 1, 2; RGWL 2, 3; TWA

Codrescu, Andrei 1946- .... **CLC 46, 121**
See also CA 33-36R; CAAS 19; CANR 13, 34, 53, 76, 125; CN 7; DA3; DAM POET; MAL 5; MTCW 2; MTFW 2005

Coe, Max
See Bourne, Randolph S(illiman)

Coe, Tucker
See Westlake, Donald E(dwin)

Coen, Ethan 1958- .... **CLC 108**
See also AAYA 54; CA 126; CANR 85

Coen, Joel 1955- .... **CLC 108**
See also AAYA 54; CA 126; CANR 119

The Coen Brothers
See Coen, Ethan; Coen, Joel

Coetzee, J(ohn) M(axwell) 1940- ..... **CLC 23, 33, 66, 117, 161, 162**
See also AAYA 37; AFW; BRWS 6; CA 77-80; CANR 41, 54, 74, 114, 133; CN 4, 5, 6, 7; DA3; DAM NOV; DLB 225; EWL 3; LMFS 2; MTCW 1, 2; MTFW 2005; NFS 21; WLIT 2; WWE 1

Coffey, Brian
See Koontz, Dean R.

Coffin, Robert P(eter) Tristram
1892-1955 .... **TCLC 95**
See also CA 123; 169; DLB 45

Cohan, George M(ichael)
1878-1942 .... **TCLC 60**
See also CA 157; DLB 249; RGAL 4

Cohen, Arthur A(llen) 1928-1986 ...... **CLC 7, 31**
See also CA 1-4R; 120; CANR 1, 17, 42; DLB 28

Cohen, Leonard (Norman) 1934- ...... **CLC 3, 38**
See also CA 21-24R; CANR 14, 69; CN 1, 2, 3, 4, 5, 6; CP 1, 2, 3, 4, 5, 6, 7; DAC; DAM MST; DLB 53; EWL 3; MTCW 1

Cohen, Matt(hew) 1942-1999 .... **CLC 19**
See also CA 61-64; 187; CAAS 18; CANR 40; CN 1, 2, 3, 4, 5, 6; DAC; DLB 53

Cohen-Solal, Annie 1948- .... **CLC 50**
See also CA 239

Colegate, Isabel 1931- .... **CLC 36**
See also CA 17-20R; CANR 8, 22, 74; CN 4, 5, 6, 7; DLB 14, 231; INT CANR-22; MTCW 1

Coleman, Emmett
See Reed, Ishmael (Scott)

Coleridge, Hartley 1796-1849 .... **NCLC 90**
See also DLB 96

Coleridge, M. E.
See Coleridge, Mary E(lizabeth)

Coleridge, Mary E(lizabeth)
1861-1907 .... **TCLC 73**
See also CA 116; 166; DLB 19, 98

Coleridge, Samuel Taylor
1772-1834 ...... **NCLC 9, 54, 99, 111; PC 11, 39, 67; WLC**
See also AAYA 66; BRW 4; BRWR 2; BYA 4; CDBLB 1789-1832; DA; DA3; DAB; DAC; DAM MST, POET; DLB 93, 107; EXPP; LATS 1:1; LMFS 1; PAB; PFS 4, 5; RGEL 2; TEA; WLIT 3; WP

Coleridge, Sara 1802-1852 .... **NCLC 31**
See also DLB 199

Coles, Don 1928- .... **CLC 46**
See also CA 115; CANR 38; CP 7

Coles, Robert (Martin) 1929- .... **CLC 108**
See also CA 45-48; CANR 3, 32, 66, 70, 135; INT CANR-32; SATA 23

Colette, (Sidonie-Gabrielle)
1873-1954 .... **SSC 10; TCLC 1, 5, 16**
See Willy, Colette
See also CA 104; 131; DA3; DAM NOV; DLB 65; EW 9; EWL 3; GFL 1789 to the Present; MTCW 1, 2; MTFW 2005; RGWL 2, 3; TWA

Collett, (Jacobine) Camilla (Wergeland)
1813-1895 .... **NCLC 22**

Collier, Christopher 1930- .... **CLC 30**
See also AAYA 13; BYA 2; CA 33-36R; CANR 13, 33, 102; JRDA; MAICYA 1, 2; SATA 16, 70; WYA; YAW 1

Collier, James Lincoln 1928- .... **CLC 30**
See also AAYA 13; BYA 2; CA 9-12R; CANR 4, 33, 60, 102; CLR 3; DAM POP; JRDA; MAICYA 1, 2; SAAS 21; SATA 8, 70; WYA; YAW 1

Collier, Jeremy 1650-1726 .... **LC 6**

Collier, John 1901-1980 . **SSC 19; TCLC 127**
See also CA 65-68; 97-100; CANR 10; CN 1, 2; DLB 77, 255; FANT; SUFW 1

Collier, Mary 1690-1762 .... **LC 86**
See also DLB 95

Collingwood, R(obin) G(eorge)
1889(?)-1943 .... **TCLC 67**
See also CA 117; 155; DLB 262

Collins, Billy 1941- .... **PC 68**
See also AAYA 64; CA 151; CANR 92; MTFW 2005; PFS 18

Collins, Hunt
See Hunter, Evan

Collins, Linda 1931- .... **CLC 44**
See also CA 125

Collins, Tom
See Furphy, Joseph
See also RGEL 2

Collins, (William) Wilkie
1824-1889 .... **NCLC 1, 18, 93**
See also BRWS 6; CDBLB 1832-1890; CMW 4; DLB 18, 70, 159; GL 2; MSW; RGEL 2; RGSF 2; SUFW 1; WLIT 4

Collins, William 1721-1759 .... **LC 4, 40**
See also BRW 3; DAM POET; DLB 109; RGEL 2

Collodi, Carlo .... **NCLC 54**
See Lorenzini, Carlo
See also CLR 5; WCH; WLIT 7

Colman, George
See Glassco, John

Colman, George, the Elder
1732-1794 .... **LC 98**
See also RGEL 2

Colonna, Vittoria 1492-1547 .... **LC 71**
See also RGWL 2, 3

Colt, Winchester Remington
See Hubbard, L(afayette) Ron(ald)

Colter, Cyrus J. 1910-2002 .... **CLC 58**
See also BW 1; CA 65-68; 205; CANR 10, 66; CN 2, 3, 4, 5, 6; DLB 33

Colton, James
See Hansen, Joseph
See also GLL 1

Colum, Padraic 1881-1972 .... **CLC 28**
See also BYA 4; CA 73-76; 33-36R; CANR 35; CLR 36; CP 1; CWRI 5; DLB 19; MAICYA 1, 2; MTCW 1; RGEL 2; SATA 15; WCH

Colvin, James
See Moorcock, Michael (John)

Colwin, Laurie (E.) 1944-1992 .... **CLC 5, 13, 23, 84**
See also CA 89-92; 139; CANR 20, 46; DLB 218; DLBY 1980; MTCW 1

Comfort, Alex(ander) 1920-2000 .... **CLC 7**
See also CA 1-4R; 190; CANR 1, 45; CN 1, 2, 3, 4; CP 1, 2, 3, 4, 5, 6, 7; DAM POP; MTCW 2

Comfort, Montgomery
See Campbell, (John) Ramsey

Compton-Burnett, I(vy)
1892(?)-1969 .... **CLC 1, 3, 10, 15, 34**
See also BRW 7; CA 1-4R; 25-28R; CANR 4; DAM NOV; DLB 36; EWL 3; MTCW 1, 2; RGEL 2

Comstock, Anthony 1844-1915 ...... **TCLC 13**
See also CA 110; 169

Comte, Auguste 1798-1857 .... **NCLC 54**

Conan Doyle, Arthur
See Doyle, Sir Arthur Conan
See also BPFB 1; BYA 4, 5, 11

Conde (Abellan), Carmen
1901-1996 .... **HLCS 1**
See also CA 177; CWW 2; DLB 108; EWL 3; HW 2

Conde, Maryse 1937- ..... **BLCS; CLC 52, 92**
See also BW 2, 3; CA 110, 190; CAAE 190; CANR 30, 53, 76; CWW 2; DAM MULT; EWL 3; MTCW 2; MTFW 2005

Condillac, Etienne Bonnot de
1714-1780 .... **LC 26**
See also DLB 313

Condon, Richard (Thomas)
1915-1996 .... **CLC 4, 6, 8, 10, 45, 100**
See also BEST 90:3; BPFB 1; CA 1-4R; 151; CAAS 1; CANR 2, 23; CMW 4; CN 1, 2, 3, 4, 5, 6; DAM NOV; INT CANR-23; MAL 5; MTCW 1, 2

Condorcet .... **LC 104**
See Condorcet, marquis de Marie-Jean-Antoine-Nicolas Caritat
See also GFL Beginnings to 1789

Condorcet, marquis de
Marie-Jean-Antoine-Nicolas Caritat
1743-1794
See Condorcet
See also DLB 313

Confucius 551B.C.-479B.C. .... **CMLC 19, 65; WLCS**
See also DA; DA3; DAB; DAC; DAM MST

Congreve, William 1670-1729 ... **DC 2; LC 5, 21; WLC**
See also BRW 2; CDBLB 1660-1789; DA; DAB; DAC; DAM DRAM, MST, POET; DFS 15; DLB 39, 84; RGEL 2; WLIT 3

Conley, Robert J(ackson) 1940- .... **NNAL**
See also CA 41-44R; CANR 15, 34, 45, 96; DAM MULT; TCWW 2

Connell, Evan S(helby), Jr. 1924- . **CLC 4, 6, 45**
See also AAYA 7; AMWS 14; CA 1-4R; CAAS 2; CANR 2, 39, 76, 97, 140; CN 1, 2, 3, 4, 5, 6; DAM NOV; DLB 2; DLBY 1981; MAL 5; MTCW 1, 2; MTFW 2005

Connelly, Marc(us Cook) 1890-1980 . **CLC 7**
See also CA 85-88; 102; CAD; CANR 30; DFS 12; DLB 7; DLBY 1980; MAL 5; RGAL 4; SATA-Obit 25

Connor, Ralph .... **TCLC 31**
See Gordon, Charles William
See also DLB 92; TCWW 1, 2

Dimont, Penelope
   See Mortimer, Penelope (Ruth)
Dinesen, Isak ..... **CLC 10, 29, 95; SSC 7, 75**
   See Blixen, Karen (Christentze Dinesen)
   See also EW 10; EWL 3; EXPS; FW; GL
   2; HGG; LAIT 3; MTCW 1; NCFS 2;
   NFS 9; RGSF 2; RGWL 2, 3; SSFS 3, 6,
   13; WLIT 2
Ding Ling .... **CLC 68**
   See Chiang, Pin-chin
   See also RGWL 3
Diphusa, Patty
   See Almodovar, Pedro
Disch, Thomas M(ichael) 1940- ... **CLC 7, 36**
   See Disch, Tom
   See also AAYA 17; BPFB 1; CA 21-24R;
   CAAS 4; CANR 17, 36, 54, 89; CLR 18;
   CP 7; DA3; DLB 8; HGG; MAICYA 1, 2;
   MTCW 1, 2; MTFW 2005; SAAS 15;
   SATA 92; SCFW 1, 2; SFW 4; SUFW 2
Disch, Tom
   See Disch, Thomas M(ichael)
   See also DLB 282
d'Isly, Georges
   See Simenon, Georges (Jacques Christian)
Disraeli, Benjamin 1804-1881 ... **NCLC 2, 39,
   79**
   See also BRW 4; DLB 21, 55; RGEL 2
Ditcum, Steve
   See Crumb, R(obert)
Dixon, Paige
   See Corcoran, Barbara (Asenath)
Dixon, Stephen 1936- .... **CLC 52; SSC 16**
   See also AMWS 12; CA 89-92; CANR 17,
   40, 54, 91; CN 4, 5, 6, 7; DLB 130; MAL
   5
Dixon, Thomas, Jr. 1864-1946 ..... **TCLC 163**
   See also RHW
Djebar, Assia 1936- .... **CLC 182**
   See also CA 188; EWL 3; RGWL 3; WLIT
   2
Doak, Annie
   See Dillard, Annie
Dobell, Sydney Thompson
   1824-1874 .... **NCLC 43**
   See also DLB 32; RGEL 2
Doblin, Alfred .... **TCLC 13**
   See Doeblin, Alfred
   See also CDWLB 2; EWL 3; RGWL 2, 3
Dobroliubov, Nikolai Aleksandrovich
   See Dobrolyubov, Nikolai Alexandrovich
   See also DLB 277
Dobrolyubov, Nikolai Alexandrovich
   1836-1861 .... **NCLC 5**
   See Dobroliubov, Nikolai Aleksandrovich
Dobson, Austin 1840-1921 .... **TCLC 79**
   See also DLB 35, 144
Dobyns, Stephen 1941- .... **CLC 37**
   See also AMWS 13; CA 45-48; CANR 2,
   18, 99; CMW 4; CP 4, 5, 6, 7; PFS 23
Doctorow, E(dgar) L(aurence)
   1931- .... **CLC 6, 11, 15, 18, 37, 44, 65,
   113, 214**
   See also AAYA 22; AITN 2; AMWS 4;
   BEST 89:3; BPFB 1; CA 45-48; CANR
   2, 33, 51, 76, 97, 133; CDALB 1968-
   1988; CN 3, 4, 5, 6, 7; CPW; DA3; DAM
   NOV, POP; DLB 2, 28, 173; DLBY 1980;
   EWL 3; LAIT 3; MAL 5; MTCW 1, 2;
   MTFW 2005; NFS 6; RGAL 4; RHW;
   TCLE 1:1; TCWW 1, 2; TUS
Dodgson, Charles L(utwidge) 1832-1898
   See Carroll, Lewis
   See also CLR 2; DA; DA3; DAB; DAC;
   DAM MST, NOV, POET; MAICYA 1, 2;
   SATA 100; YABC 2
Dodsley, Robert 1703-1764 .... **LC 97**
   See also DLB 95; RGEL 2

Dodson, Owen (Vincent) 1914-1983 .. **BLC 1;
   CLC 79**
   See also BW 1; CA 65-68; 110; CANR 24;
   DAM MULT; DLB 76
Doeblin, Alfred 1878-1957 .... **TCLC 13**
   See Doblin, Alfred
   See also CA 110; 141; DLB 66
Doerr, Harriet 1910-2002 .... **CLC 34**
   See also CA 117; 122; 213; CANR 47; INT
   CA-122; LATS 1:2
Domecq, H(onorio Bustos)
   See Bioy Casares, Adolfo
Domecq, H(onorio) Bustos
   See Bioy Casares, Adolfo; Borges, Jorge
   Luis
Domini, Rey
   See Lorde, Audre (Geraldine)
   See also GLL 1
Dominique
   See Proust, (Valentin-Louis-George-Eugene)
   Marcel
Don, A
   See Stephen, Sir Leslie
Donaldson, Stephen R(eeder)
   1947- .... **CLC 46, 138**
   See also AAYA 36; BPFB 1; CA 89-92;
   CANR 13, 55, 99; CPW; DAM POP;
   FANT; INT CANR-13; SATA 121; SFW
   4; SUFW 1, 2
Donleavy, J(ames) P(atrick) 1926- .... **CLC 1,
   4, 6, 10, 45**
   See also AITN 2; BPFB 1; CA 9-12R;
   CANR 24, 49, 62, 80, 124; CBD; CD 5,
   6; CN 1, 2, 3, 4, 5, 6, 7; DLB 6, 173; INT
   CANR-24; MAL 5; MTCW 1, 2; MTFW
   2005; RGAL 4
Donnadieu, Marguerite
   See Duras, Marguerite
Donne, John 1572-1631 ... **LC 10, 24, 91; PC
   1, 43; WLC**
   See also AAYA 67; BRW 1; BRWC 1;
   BRWR 2; CDBLB Before 1660; DA;
   DAB; DAC; DAM MST, POET; DLB
   121, 151; EXPP; PAB; PFS 2, 11; RGEL
   3; TEA; WLIT 3; WP
Donnell, David 1939(?)- .... **CLC 34**
   See also CA 197
Donoghue, Denis 1928- .... **CLC 209**
   See also CA 17-20R; CANR 16, 102
Donoghue, P. S.
   See Hunt, E(verette) Howard, (Jr.)
Donoso (Yanez), Jose 1924-1996 ... **CLC 4, 8,
   11, 32, 99; HLC 1; SSC 34; TCLC 133**
   See also CA 81-84; 155; CANR 32, 73; CD-
   WLB 3; CWW 2; DAM MULT; DLB 113;
   EWL 3; HW 1, 2; LAW; LAWS 1; MTCW
   1, 2; MTFW 2005; RGSF 2; WLIT 1
Donovan, John 1928-1992 .... **CLC 35**
   See also AAYA 20; CA 97-100; 137; CLR
   3; MAICYA 1, 2; SATA 72; SATA-Brief
   29; YAW
Don Roberto
   See Cunninghame Graham, Robert
   (Gallnigad) Bontine
Doolittle, Hilda 1886-1961 . **CLC 3, 8, 14, 31,
   34, 73; PC 5; WLC**
   See H. D.
   See also AAYA 66; AMWS 1; CA 97-100;
   CANR 35, 131; DA; DAC; DAM MST,
   POET; DLB 4, 45; EWL 3; FW; GLL 1;
   LMFS 2; MAL 5; MAWW; MTCW 1, 2;
   MTFW 2005; PFS 6; RGAL 4
Doppo, Kunikida .... **TCLC 99**
   See Kunikida Doppo
Dorfman, Ariel 1942- .... **CLC 48, 77, 189;
   HLC 1**
   See also CA 124; 130; CANR 67, 70, 135;
   CWW 2; DAM MULT; DFS 4; EWL 3;
   HW 1, 2; INT CA-130; WLIT 1

Dorn, Edward (Merton)
   1929-1999 .... **CLC 10, 18**
   See also CA 93-96; 187; CANR 42, 79; CP
   1, 2, 3, 4, 5, 6, 7; DLB 5; INT CA-93-96;
   WP
Dor-Ner, Zvi .... **CLC 70**
Dorris, Michael (Anthony)
   1945-1997 .... **CLC 109; NNAL**
   See also AAYA 20; BEST 90:1; BYA 12;
   CA 102; 157; CANR 19, 46, 75; CLR 58;
   DA3; DAM MULT, NOV; DLB 175;
   LAIT 5; MTCW 2; MTFW 2005; NFS 3;
   RGAL 4; SATA 75; SATA-Obit 94;
   TCWW 2; YAW
Dorris, Michael A.
   See Dorris, Michael (Anthony)
Dorsan, Luc
   See Simenon, Georges (Jacques Christian)
Dorsange, Jean
   See Simenon, Georges (Jacques Christian)
Dorset
   See Sackville, Thomas
Dos Passos, John (Roderigo)
   1896-1970 ... **CLC 1, 4, 8, 11, 15, 25, 34,
   82; WLC**
   See also AMW; BPFB 1; CA 1-4R; 29-32R;
   CANR 3; CDALB 1929-1941; DA; DA3;
   DAB; DAC; DAM MST, NOV; DLB 4,
   9, 274, 316; DLBD 1, 15; DLBY 1996;
   EWL 3; MAL 5; MTCW 1, 2; MTFW
   2005; NFS 14; RGAL 4; TUS
Dossage, Jean
   See Simenon, Georges (Jacques Christian)
Dostoevsky, Fedor Mikhailovich
   1821-1881 .. **NCLC 2, 7, 21, 33, 43, 119;
   SSC 2, 33, 44; WLC**
   See Dostoevsky, Fyodor
   See also AAYA 40; DA; DA3; DAB; DAC;
   DAM MST, NOV; EW 7; EXPN; NFS 3,
   8; RGSF 2; RGWL 2, 3; SSFS 8; TWA
Dostoevsky, Fyodor
   See Dostoevsky, Fedor Mikhailovich
   See also DLB 238; LATS 1:1; LMFS 1, 2
Doty, M. R.
   See Doty, Mark (Alan)
Doty, Mark
   See Doty, Mark (Alan)
Doty, Mark (Alan) 1953(?)- .... **CLC 176; PC
   53**
   See also AMWS 11; CA 161, 183; CAAE
   183; CANR 110
Doty, Mark A.
   See Doty, Mark (Alan)
Doughty, Charles M(ontagu)
   1843-1926 .... **TCLC 27**
   See also CA 115; 178; DLB 19, 57, 174
Douglas, Ellen .... **CLC 73**
   See Haxton, Josephine Ayres; Williamson,
   Ellen Douglas
   See also CN 5, 6, 7; CSW; DLB 292
Douglas, Gavin 1475(?)-1522 .... **LC 20**
   See also DLB 132; RGEL 2
Douglas, George
   See Brown, George Douglas
   See also RGEL 2
Douglas, Keith (Castellain)
   1920-1944 .... **TCLC 40**
   See also BRW 7; CA 160; DLB 27; EWL
   3; PAB; RGEL 2
Douglas, Leonard
   See Bradbury, Ray (Douglas)
Douglas, Michael
   See Crichton, (John) Michael
Douglas, (George) Norman
   1868-1952 .... **TCLC 68**
   See also BRW 6; CA 119; 157; DLB 34,
   195; RGEL 2
Douglas, William
   See Brown, George Douglas

Enchi, Fumiko (Ueda) 1905-1986 ..... **CLC 31**
  See Enchi Fumiko
  See also CA 129; 121; FW; MJW
Enchi Fumiko
  See Enchi, Fumiko (Ueda)
  See also DLB 182; EWL 3
Ende, Michael (Andreas Helmuth)
  1929-1995 .... **CLC 31**
  See also BYA 5; CA 118; 124; 149; CANR
  36, 110; CLR 14; DLB 75; MAICYA 1,
  2; MAICYAS 1; SATA 61, 130; SATA-
  Brief 42; SATA-Obit 86
Endo, Shusaku 1923-1996 ..... **CLC 7, 14, 19,**
  54, 99; SSC 48; TCLC 152
  See Endo Shusaku
  See also CA 29-32R; 153; CANR 21, 54,
  131; DA3; DAM NOV; MTCW 1, 2;
  MTFW 2005; RGSF 2; RGWL 2, 3
Endo Shusaku
  See Endo, Shusaku
  See also CWW 2; DLB 182; EWL 3
Engel, Marian 1933-1985 .... **CLC 36; TCLC**
  137
  See also CA 25-28R; CANR 12; CN 2, 3;
  DLB 53; FW; INT CANR-12
Engelhardt, Frederick
  See Hubbard, L(afayette) Ron(ald)
Engels, Friedrich 1820-1895 .. **NCLC 85, 114**
  See also DLB 129; LATS 1:1
Enright, D(ennis) J(oseph)
  1920-2002 .... **CLC 4, 8, 31**
  See also CA 1-4R; 211; CANR 1, 42, 83;
  CN 1, 2; CP 1, 2, 3, 4, 5, 6, 7; DLB 27;
  EWL 3; SATA 25; SATA-Obit 140
Ensler, Eve 1953- .... **CLC 212**
  See also CA 172; CANR 126
Enzensberger, Hans Magnus
  1929- .... **CLC 43; PC 28**
  See also CA 116; 119; CANR 103; CWW
  2; EWL 3
Ephron, Nora 1941- .... **CLC 17, 31**
  See also AAYA 35; AITN 2; CA 65-68;
  CANR 12, 39, 83; DFS 22
Epicurus 341B.C.-270B.C. .... **CMLC 21**
  See also DLB 176
Epsilon
  See Betjeman, John
Epstein, Daniel Mark 1948- .... **CLC 7**
  See also CA 49-52; CANR 2, 53, 90
Epstein, Jacob 1956- .... **CLC 19**
  See also CA 114
Epstein, Jean 1897-1953 .... **TCLC 92**
Epstein, Joseph 1937- .... **CLC 39, 204**
  See also AMWS 14; CA 112; 119; CANR
  50, 65, 117
Epstein, Leslie 1938- .... **CLC 27**
  See also AMWS 12; CA 73-76, 215; CAAE
  215; CAAS 12; CANR 23, 69; DLB 299
Equiano, Olaudah 1745(?)-1797 . **BLC 2; LC**
  16
  See also AFAW 1, 2; CDWLB 3; DAM
  MULT; DLB 37, 50; WLIT 2
Erasmus, Desiderius 1469(?)-1536 ..... **LC 16,**
  93
  See also DLB 136; EW 2; LMFS 1; RGWL
  2, 3; TWA
Erdman, Paul E(mil) 1932- .... **CLC 25**
  See also AITN 1; CA 61-64; CANR 13, 43,
  84
Erdrich, (Karen) Louise 1954- .. **CLC 39, 54,**
  120, 176; NNAL; PC 52
  See also AAYA 10, 47; AMWS 4; BEST
  89:1; BPFB 1; CA 114; CANR 41, 62,
  118, 138; CDALBS; CN 5, 6, 7; CP 7;
  CPW; CWP; DA3; DAM MULT, NOV,
  POP; DLB 152, 175, 206; EWL 3; EXPP;

  FL 1:5; LAIT 5; LATS 1:2; MAL 5;
  MTCW 1, 2; MTFW 2005; NFS 5; PFS
  14; RGAL 4; SATA 94, 141; SSFS 14;
  TCWW 2
Erenburg, Ilya (Grigoryevich)
  See Ehrenburg, Ilya (Grigoryevich)
Erickson, Stephen Michael 1950-
  See Erickson, Steve
  See also CA 129; SFW 4
Erickson, Steve .... **CLC 64**
  See Erickson, Stephen Michael
  See also CANR 60, 68, 136; MTFW 2005;
  SUFW 2
Erickson, Walter
  See Fast, Howard (Melvin)
Ericson, Walter
  See Fast, Howard (Melvin)
Eriksson, Buntel
  See Bergman, (Ernst) Ingmar
Eriugena, John Scottus c.
  810-877 .... **CMLC 65**
  See also DLB 115
Ernaux, Annie 1940- .... **CLC 88, 184**
  See also CA 147; CANR 93; MTFW 2005;
  NCFS 3, 5
Erskine, John 1879-1951 .... **TCLC 84**
  See also CA 112; 159; DLB 9, 102; FANT
Eschenbach, Wolfram von
  See Wolfram von Eschenbach
  See also RGWL 3
Eseki, Bruno
  See Mphahlele, Ezekiel
Esenin, Sergei (Alexandrovich)
  1895-1925 .... **TCLC 4**
  See Yesenin, Sergey
  See also CA 104; RGWL 2, 3
Eshleman, Clayton 1935- .... **CLC 7**
  See also CA 33-36R; 212; CAAE 212;
  CAAS 6; CANR 93; CP 1, 2, 3, 4, 5, 6,
  7; DLB 5
Espriella, Don Manuel Alvarez
  See Southey, Robert
Espriu, Salvador 1913-1985 .... **CLC 9**
  See also CA 154; 115; DLB 134; EWL 3
Espronceda, Jose de 1808-1842 ..... **NCLC 39**
Esquivel, Laura 1951(?)- ... **CLC 141; HLCS**
  1
  See also AAYA 29; CA 143; CANR 68, 113;
  DA3; DNFS 2; LAIT 3; LMFS 2; MTCW
  2; MTFW 2005; NFS 5; WLIT 1
Esse, James
  See Stephens, James
Esterbrook, Tom
  See Hubbard, L(afayette) Ron(ald)
Estleman, Loren D. 1952- .... **CLC 48**
  See also AAYA 27; CA 85-88; CANR 27,
  74, 139; CMW 4; CPW; DA3; DAM
  NOV, POP; DLB 226; INT CANR-27;
  MTCW 1, 2; MTFW 2005; TCWW 1, 2
Etherege, Sir George 1636-1692 . **DC 23; LC**
  78
  See also BRW 2; DAM DRAM; DLB 80;
  PAB; RGEL 2
Euclid 306B.C.-283B.C. .... **CMLC 25**
Eugenides, Jeffrey 1960(?)- .... **CLC 81, 212**
  See also AAYA 51; CA 144; CANR 120;
  MTFW 2005
Euripides c. 484B.C.-406B.C. .... **CMLC 23,**
  51; DC 4; WLCS
  See also AW 1; CDWLB 1; DA; DA3;
  DAB; DAC; DAM DRAM, MST; DFS 1,
  4, 6; DLB 176; LAIT 1; LMFS 1; RGWL
  2, 3
Evan, Evin
  See Faust, Frederick (Schiller)
Evans, Caradoc 1878-1945 ... **SSC 43; TCLC**
  85
  See also DLB 162

Evans, Evan
  See Faust, Frederick (Schiller)
Evans, Marian
  See Eliot, George
Evans, Mary Ann
  See Eliot, George
  See also NFS 20
Evarts, Esther
  See Benson, Sally
Everett, Percival
  See Everett, Percival L.
  See also CSW
Everett, Percival L. 1956- .... **CLC 57**
  See Everett, Percival
  See also BW 2; CA 129; CANR 94, 134;
  CN 7; MTFW 2005
Everson, R(onald) G(ilmour)
  1903-1992 .... **CLC 27**
  See also CA 17-20R; CP 1, 2, 3, 4; DLB 88
Everson, William (Oliver)
  1912-1994 .... **CLC 1, 5, 14**
  See Antoninus, Brother
  See also BG 1:2; CA 9-12R; 145; CANR
  20; CP 2, 3, 4; DLB 5, 16, 212; MTCW 1
Evtushenko, Evgenii Aleksandrovich
  See Yevtushenko, Yevgeny (Alexandrovich)
  See also CWW 2; RGWL 2, 3
Ewart, Gavin (Buchanan)
  1916-1995 .... **CLC 13, 46**
  See also BRWS 7; CA 89-92; 150; CANR
  17, 46; CP 1, 2, 3, 4; DLB 40; MTCW 1
Ewers, Hanns Heinz 1871-1943 ..... **TCLC 12**
  See also CA 109; 149
Ewing, Frederick R.
  See Sturgeon, Theodore (Hamilton)
Exley, Frederick (Earl) 1929-1992 .... **CLC 6,**
  11
  See also AITN 2; BPFB 1; CA 81-84; 138;
  CANR 117; DLB 143; DLBY 1981
Eynhardt, Guillermo
  See Quiroga, Horacio (Sylvestre)
Ezekiel, Nissim (Moses) 1924-2004 .. **CLC 61**
  See also CA 61-64; 223; CP 1, 2, 3, 4, 5, 6,
  7; EWL 3
Ezekiel, Tish O'Dowd 1943- .... **CLC 34**
  See also CA 129
Fadeev, Aleksandr Aleksandrovich
  See Bulgya, Alexander Alexandrovich
  See also DLB 272
Fadeev, Alexandr Alexandrovich
  See Bulgya, Alexander Alexandrovich
  See also EWL 3
Fadeyev, A.
  See Bulgya, Alexander Alexandrovich
Fadeyev, Alexander .... **TCLC 53**
  See Bulgya, Alexander Alexandrovich
Fagen, Donald 1948- .... **CLC 26**
Fainzilberg, Ilya Arnoldovich 1897-1937
  See Ilf, Ilya
  See also CA 120; 165
Fair, Ronald L. 1932- .... **CLC 18**
  See also BW 1; CA 69-72; CANR 25; DLB
  33
Fairbairn, Roger
  See Carr, John Dickson
Fairbairns, Zoe (Ann) 1948- .... **CLC 32**
  See also CA 103; CANR 21, 85; CN 4, 5,
  6, 7
Fairfield, Flora
  See Alcott, Louisa May
Fairman, Paul W. 1916-1977
  See Queen, Ellery
  See also CA 114; SFW 4
Falco, Gian
  See Papini, Giovanni
Falconer, James
  See Kirkup, James

Author Index

Field, Andrew 1938- .... **CLC 44**
   See also CA 97-100; CANR 25
Field, Eugene 1850-1895 .... **NCLC 3**
   See also DLB 23, 42, 140; DLBD 13; MAI-
   CYA 1, 2; RGAL 4; SATA 16
Field, Gans T.
   See Wellman, Manly Wade
Field, Michael 1915-1971 .... **TCLC 43**
   See also CA 29-32R
Fielding, Helen 1958- .... **CLC 146, 217**
   See also AAYA 65; CA 172; CANR 127;
   DLB 231; MTFW 2005
Fielding, Henry 1707-1754 .... **LC 1, 46, 85;**
   WLC
   See also BRW 3; BRWR 1; CDBLB 1660-
   1789; DA; DA3; DAB; DAC; DAM
   DRAM, MST, NOV; DLB 39, 84, 101;
   NFS 18; RGEL 2; TEA; WLIT 3
Fielding, Sarah 1710-1768 .... **LC 1, 44**
   See also DLB 39; RGEL 2; TEA
Fields, W. C. 1880-1946 .... **TCLC 80**
   See also DLB 44
Fierstein, Harvey (Forbes) 1954- ..... **CLC 33**
   See also CA 123; 129; CAD; CD 5, 6;
   CPW; DA3; DAM DRAM, POP; DFS 6;
   DLB 266; GLL; MAL 5
Figes, Eva 1932- .... **CLC 31**
   See also CA 53-56; CANR 4, 44, 83; CN 2,
   3, 4, 5, 6, 7; DLB 14, 271; FW
Filippo, Eduardo de
   See de Filippo, Eduardo
Finch, Anne 1661-1720 .... **LC 3; PC 21**
   See also BRWS 9; DLB 95
Finch, Robert (Duer Claydon)
   1900-1995 .... **CLC 18**
   See also CA 57-60; CANR 9, 24, 49; CP 1,
   2, 3, 4; DLB 88
Findley, Timothy (Irving Frederick)
   1930-2002 .... **CLC 27, 102**
   See also CA 25-28R; 206; CANR 12, 42,
   69, 109; CCA 1; CN 4, 5, 6, 7; DAC;
   DAM MST; DLB 53; FANT; RHW
Fink, William
   See Mencken, H(enry) L(ouis)
Firbank, Louis 1942-
   See Reed, Lou
   See also CA 117
Firbank, (Arthur Annesley) Ronald
   1886-1926 .... **TCLC 1**
   See also BRWS 2; CA 104; 177; DLB 36;
   EWL 3; RGEL 2
Firdawsi, Abu al-Qasim
   See Ferdowsi, Abu'l Qasem
   See also WLIT 6
Fish, Stanley
   See Fish, Stanley Eugene
Fish, Stanley E.
   See Fish, Stanley Eugene
Fish, Stanley Eugene 1938- .... **CLC 142**
   See also CA 112; 132; CANR 90; DLB 67
Fisher, Dorothy (Frances) Canfield
   1879-1958 .... **TCLC 87**
   See also CA 114; 136; CANR 80; CLR 71;
   CWRI 5; DLB 9, 102, 284; MAICYA 1,
   2; MAL 5; YABC 1
Fisher, M(ary) F(rances) K(ennedy)
   1908-1992 .... **CLC 76, 87**
   See also CA 77-80; 138; CANR 44; MTCW
   2
Fisher, Roy 1930- .... **CLC 25**
   See also CA 81-84; CAAS 10; CANR 16;
   CP 1, 2, 3, 4, 5, 6, 7; DLB 40
Fisher, Rudolph 1897-1934 . **BLC 2; HR 1:2;**
   SSC 25; TCLC 11
   See also BW 1, 3; CA 107; 124; CANR 80;
   DAM MULT; DLB 51, 102

Fisher, Vardis (Alvero) 1895-1968 .... **CLC 7;**
   TCLC 140
   See also CA 5-8R; 25-28R; CANR 68; DLB
   9, 206; MAL 5; RGAL 4; TCWW 1, 2
Fiske, Tarleton
   See Bloch, Robert (Albert)
Fitch, Clarke
   See Sinclair, Upton (Beall)
Fitch, John IV
   See Cormier, Robert (Edmund)
Fitzgerald, Captain Hugh
   See Baum, L(yman) Frank
FitzGerald, Edward 1809-1883 ...... **NCLC 9,**
   153
   See also BRW 4; DLB 32; RGEL 2
Fitzgerald, F(rancis) Scott (Key)
   1896-1940 .... **SSC 6, 31, 75; TCLC 1, 6,**
   14, 28, 55, 157; WLC
   See also AAYA 24; AITN 1; AMW; AMWC
   2; AMWR 1; BPFB 1; CA 110; 123;
   CDALB 1917-1929; DA; DA3; DAB;
   DAC; DAM MST, NOV; DLB 4, 9, 86,
   219, 273; DLBD 1, 15, 16; DLBY 1981,
   1996; EWL 3; EXPN; EXPS; LAIT 3;
   MAL 5; MTCW 1, 2; MTFW 2005; NFS
   2, 19, 20; RGAL 4; RGSF 2; SSFS 4, 15,
   21; TUS
Fitzgerald, Penelope 1916-2000 . **CLC 19, 51,**
   61, 143
   See also BRWS 5; CA 85-88; 190; CAAS
   10; CANR 56, 86, 131; CN 3, 4, 5, 6, 7;
   DLB 14, 194; EWL 3; MTCW 2; MTFW
   2005
Fitzgerald, Robert (Stuart)
   1910-1985 .... **CLC 39**
   See also CA 1-4R; 114; CANR 1; CP 1, 2,
   3, 4; DLBY 1980; MAL 5
FitzGerald, Robert D(avid)
   1902-1987 .... **CLC 19**
   See also CA 17-20R; CP 1, 2, 3, 4; DLB
   260; RGEL 2
Fitzgerald, Zelda (Sayre)
   1900-1948 .... **TCLC 52**
   See also AMWS 9; CA 117; 126; DLBY
   1984
Flanagan, Thomas (James Bonner)
   1923-2002 .... **CLC 25, 52**
   See also CA 108; 206; CANR 55; CN 3, 4,
   5, 6, 7; DLBY 1980; INT CA-108; MTCW
   1; RHW; TCLE 1:1
Flaubert, Gustave 1821-1880 .... **NCLC 2, 10,**
   19, 62, 66, 135; SSC 11, 60; WLC
   See also DA; DA3; DAB; DAC; DAM
   MST, NOV; DLB 119, 301; EW 7; EXPS;
   GFL 1789 to the Present; LAIT 2; LMFS
   1; NFS 14; RGSF 2; RGWL 2, 3; SSFS
   6; TWA
Flavius Josephus
   See Josephus, Flavius
Flecker, Herman Elroy
   See Flecker, (Herman) James Elroy
Flecker, (Herman) James Elroy
   1884-1915 .... **TCLC 43**
   See also CA 109; 150; DLB 10, 19; RGEL
   2
Fleming, Ian (Lancaster) 1908-1964 . **CLC 3,**
   30
   See also AAYA 26; BPFB 1; CA 5-8R;
   CANR 59; CDBLB 1945-1960; CMW 4;
   CPW; DA3; DAM POP; DLB 87, 201;
   MSW; MTCW 1, 2; MTFW 2005; RGEL
   2; SATA 9; TEA; YAW
Fleming, Thomas (James) 1927- ...... **CLC 37**
   See also CA 5-8R; CANR 10, 102; INT
   CANR-10; SATA 8
Fletcher, John 1579-1625 .... **DC 6; LC 33**
   See also BRW 2; CDBLB Before 1660;
   DLB 58; RGEL 2; TEA

Fletcher, John Gould 1886-1950 .... **TCLC 35**
   See also CA 107; 167; DLB 4, 45; LMFS
   2; MAL 5; RGAL 4
Fleur, Paul
   See Pohl, Frederik
Flieg, Helmut
   See Heym, Stefan
Flooglebuckle, Al
   See Spiegelman, Art
Flora, Fletcher 1914-1969
   See Queen, Ellery
   See also CA 1-4R; CANR 3, 85
Flying Officer X
   See Bates, H(erbert) E(rnest)
Fo, Dario 1926- .... **CLC 32, 109; DC 10**
   See also CA 116; 128; CANR 68, 114, 134;
   CWW 2; DA3; DAM DRAM; DLBY
   1997; EWL 3; MTCW 1, 2; MTFW 2005;
   WLIT 7
Fogarty, Jonathan Titulescu Esq.
   See Farrell, James T(homas)
Follett, Ken(neth Martin) 1949- .... **CLC 18**
   See also AAYA 6, 50; BEST 89:4; BPFB 1;
   CA 81-84; CANR 13, 33, 54, 102; CMW
   4; CPW; DA3; DAM NOV, POP; DLB
   87; DLBY 1981; INT CANR-33; MTCW
   1
Fondane, Benjamin 1898-1944 ..... **TCLC 159**
Fontane, Theodor 1819-1898 . **NCLC 26, 163**
   See also CDWLB 2; DLB 129; EW 6;
   RGWL 2, 3; TWA
Fonte, Moderata 1555-1592 .... **LC 118**
Fontenot, Chester .... **CLC 65**
Fonvizin, Denis Ivanovich
   1744(?)-1792 .... **LC 81**
   See also DLB 150; RGWL 2, 3
Foote, Horton 1916- .... **CLC 51, 91**
   See also CA 73-76; CAD; CANR 34, 51,
   110; CD 5, 6; CSW; DA3; DAM DRAM;
   DFS 20; DLB 26, 266; EWL 3; INT
   CANR-34; MTFW 2005
Foote, Mary Hallock 1847-1938 .. **TCLC 108**
   See also DLB 186, 188, 202, 221; TCWW
   2
Foote, Samuel 1721-1777 .... **LC 106**
   See also DLB 89; RGEL 2
Foote, Shelby 1916-2005 .... **CLC 75**
   See also AAYA 40; CA 5-8R; 240; CANR
   3, 45, 74, 131; CN 1, 2, 3, 4, 5, 6, 7;
   CPW; CSW; DA3; DAM NOV, POP;
   DLB 2, 17; MAL 5; MTCW 2; MTFW
   2005; RHW
Forbes, Cosmo
   See Lewton, Val
Forbes, Esther 1891-1967 .... **CLC 12**
   See also AAYA 17; BYA 2; CA 13-14; 25-
   28R; CAP 1; CLR 27; DLB 22; JRDA;
   MAICYA 1, 2; RHW; SATA 2, 100; YAW
Forche, Carolyn (Louise) 1950- .... **CLC 25,**
   83, 86; PC 10
   See also CA 109; 117; CANR 50, 74, 138;
   CP 4, 5, 6, 7; CWP; DA3; DAM POET;
   DLB 5, 193; INT CA-117; MAL 5;
   MTCW 2; MTFW 2005; PFS 18; RGAL
   4
Ford, Elbur
   See Hibbert, Eleanor Alice Burford
Ford, Ford Madox 1873-1939 ... **TCLC 1, 15,**
   39, 57, 172
   See Chaucer, Daniel
   See also BRW 6; CA 104; 132; CANR 74;
   CDBLB 1914-1945; DA3; DAM NOV;
   DLB 34, 98, 162; EWL 3; MTCW 1, 2;
   RGEL 2; TEA
Ford, Henry 1863-1947 .... **TCLC 73**
   See also CA 115; 148
Ford, Jack
   See Ford, John

French, Albert 1943- .... **CLC 86**
See also BW 3; CA 167

French, Antonia
See Kureishi, Hanif

French, Marilyn 1929- .. **CLC 10, 18, 60, 177**
See also BPFB 1; CA 69-72; CANR 3, 31, 134; CN 5, 6, 7; CPW; DAM DRAM, NOV, POP; FL 1:5; FW; INT CANR-31; MTCW 1, 2; MTFW 2005

French, Paul
See Asimov, Isaac

Freneau, Philip Morin 1752-1832 .. **NCLC 1, 111**
See also AMWS 2; DLB 37, 43; RGAL 4

Freud, Sigmund 1856-1939 .... **TCLC 52**
See also CA 115; 133; CANR 69; DLB 296; EW 8; EWL 3; LATS 1:1; MTCW 1, 2; MTFW 2005; NCFS 3; TWA

Freytag, Gustav 1816-1895 .... **NCLC 109**
See also DLB 129

Friedan, Betty (Naomi) 1921- .... **CLC 74**
See also CA 65-68; CANR 18, 45, 74; DLB 246; FW; MTCW 1, 2; MTFW 2005; NCFS 5

Friedlander, Saul 1932- .... **CLC 90**
See also CA 117; 130; CANR 72

Friedman, B(ernard) H(arper)
1926- .... **CLC 7**
See also CA 1-4R; CANR 3, 48

Friedman, Bruce Jay 1930- ...... **CLC 3, 5, 56**
See also CA 9-12R; CAD; CANR 25, 52, 101; CD 5, 6; CN 1, 2, 3, 4, 5, 6, 7; DLB 2, 28, 244; INT CANR-25; MAL 5; SSFS 18

Friel, Brian 1929- .... **CLC 5, 42, 59, 115; DC 8; SSC 76**
See also BRWS 5; CA 21-24R; CANR 33, 69, 131; CBD; CD 5, 6; DFS 11; DLB 13, 319; EWL 3; MTCW 1; RGEL 2; TEA

Friis-Baastad, Babbis Ellinor
1921-1970 .... **CLC 12**
See also CA 17-20R; 134; SATA 7

Frisch, Max (Rudolf) 1911-1991 ... **CLC 3, 9, 14, 18, 32, 44; TCLC 121**
See also CA 85-88; 134; CANR 32, 74; CD-WLB 2; DAM DRAM, NOV; DLB 69, 124; EW 13; EWL 3; MTCW 1, 2; MTFW 2005; RGWL 2, 3

Fromentin, Eugene (Samuel Auguste)
1820-1876 .... **NCLC 10, 125**
See also DLB 123; GFL 1789 to the Present

Frost, Frederick
See Faust, Frederick (Schiller)

Frost, Robert (Lee) 1874-1963 .. **CLC 1, 3, 4, 9, 10, 13, 15, 26, 34, 44; PC 1, 39; WLC**
See also AAYA 21; AMW; AMWR 1; CA 89-92; CANR 33; CDALB 1917-1929; CLR 67; DA; DA3; DAB; DAC; DAM MST, POET; DLB 54, 284; DLBD 7; EWL 3; EXPP; MAL 5; MTCW 1, 2; MTFW 2005; PAB; PFS 1, 2, 3, 4, 5, 6, 7, 10, 13; RGAL 4; SATA 14; TUS; WP; WYA

Froude, James Anthony
1818-1894 .... **NCLC 43**
See also DLB 18, 57, 144

Froy, Herald
See Waterhouse, Keith (Spencer)

Fry, Christopher 1907-2005 ... **CLC 2, 10, 14**
See also BRWS 3; CA 17-20R; 240; CAAS 23; CANR 9, 30, 74, 132; CBD; CD 5, 6; CP 1, 2, 3, 4, 5, 6, 7; DAM DRAM; DLB 13; EWL 3; MTCW 1, 2; MTFW 2005; RGEL 2; SATA 66; TEA

Frye, (Herman) Northrop
1912-1991 .... **CLC 24, 70; TCLC 165**
See also CA 5-8R; 133; CANR 8, 37; DLB 67, 68, 246; EWL 3; MTCW 1, 2; MTFW 2005; RGAL 4; TWA

Fuchs, Daniel 1909-1993 .... **CLC 8, 22**
See also CA 81-84; 142; CAAS 5; CANR 40; CN 1, 2, 3, 4, 5; DLB 9, 26, 28; DLBY 1993; MAL 5

Fuchs, Daniel 1934- .... **CLC 34**
See also CA 37-40R; CANR 14, 48

Fuentes, Carlos 1928- .. **CLC 3, 8, 10, 13, 22, 41, 60, 113; HLC 1; SSC 24; WLC**
See also AAYA 4, 45; AITN 2; BPFB 1; CA 69-72; CANR 10, 32, 68, 104, 138; CDWLB 3; CWW 2; DA; DA3; DAB; DAC; DAM MST, MULT, NOV; DLB 113; DNFS 2; EWL 3; HW 1, 2; LAIT 3; LATS 1:2; LAW; LAWS 1; LMFS 2; MTCW 1, 2; MTFW 2005; NFS 8; RGSF 2; RGWL 2, 3; TWA; WLIT 1

Fuentes, Gregorio Lopez y
See Lopez y Fuentes, Gregorio

Fuertes, Gloria 1918-1998 .... **PC 27**
See also CA 178, 180; DLB 108; HW 2; SATA 115

Fugard, (Harold) Athol 1932- . **CLC 5, 9, 14, 25, 40, 80, 211; DC 3**
See also AAYA 17; AFW; CA 85-88; CANR 32, 54, 118; CD 5, 6; DAM DRAM; DFS 3, 6, 10; DLB 225; DNFS 1, 2; EWL 3; LATS 1:2; MTCW 1; MTFW 2005; RGEL 2; WLIT 2

Fugard, Sheila 1932- .... **CLC 48**
See also CA 125

Fujiwara no Teika 1162-1241 .... **CMLC 73**
See also DLB 203

Fukuyama, Francis 1952- .... **CLC 131**
See also CA 140; CANR 72, 125

Fuller, Charles (H.), (Jr.) 1939- .... **BLC 2; CLC 25; DC 1**
See also BW 2; CA 108; 112; CAD; CANR 87; CD 5, 6; DAM DRAM, MULT; DFS 8; DLB 38, 266; EWL 3; INT CA-112; MAL 5; MTCW 1

Fuller, Henry Blake 1857-1929 .... **TCLC 103**
See also CA 108; 177; DLB 12; RGAL 4

Fuller, John (Leopold) 1937- .... **CLC 62**
See also CA 21-24R; CANR 9, 44; CP 1, 2, 3, 4, 5, 6, 7; DLB 40

Fuller, Margaret
See Ossoli, Sarah Margaret (Fuller)
See also AMWS 2; DLB 183, 223, 239; FL 1:3

Fuller, Roy (Broadbent) 1912-1991 ... **CLC 4, 28**
See also BRWS 7; CA 5-8R; 135; CAAS 10; CANR 53, 83; CN 1, 2, 3, 4, 5; CP 1, 2, 3, 4; CWRI 5; DLB 15, 20; EWL 3; RGEL 2; SATA 87

Fuller, Sarah Margaret
See Ossoli, Sarah Margaret (Fuller)

Fuller, Sarah Margaret
See Ossoli, Sarah Margaret (Fuller)
See also DLB 1, 59, 73

Fuller, Thomas 1608-1661 .... **LC 111**
See also DLB 151

Fulton, Alice 1952- .... **CLC 52**
See also CA 116; CANR 57, 88; CP 7; CWP; DLB 193

Furphy, Joseph 1843-1912 .... **TCLC 25**
See Collins, Tom
See also CA 163; DLB 230; EWL 3; RGEL 2

Fuson, Robert H(enderson) 1927- .... **CLC 70**
See also CA 89-92; CANR 103

Fussell, Paul 1924- .... **CLC 74**
See also BEST 90:1; CA 17-20R; CANR 8, 21, 35, 69, 135; INT CANR-21; MTCW 1, 2; MTFW 2005

Futabatei, Shimei 1864-1909 .... **TCLC 44**
See Futabatei Shimei
See also CA 162; MJW

Futabatei Shimei
See Futabatei, Shimei
See also DLB 180; EWL 3

Futrelle, Jacques 1875-1912 .... **TCLC 19**
See also CA 113; 155; CMW 4

Gaboriau, Emile 1835-1873 .... **NCLC 14**
See also CMW 4; MSW

Gadda, Carlo Emilio 1893-1973 ...... **CLC 11; TCLC 144**
See also CA 89-92; DLB 177; EWL 3; WLIT 7

Gaddis, William 1922-1998 ... **CLC 1, 3, 6, 8, 10, 19, 43, 86**
See also AMWS 4; BPFB 1; CA 17-20R; 172; CANR 21, 48; CN 1, 2, 3, 4, 5, 6; DLB 2, 278; EWL 3; MAL 5; MTCW 1, 2; MTFW 2005; RGAL 4

Gaelique, Moruen le
See Jacob, (Cyprien-)Max

Gage, Walter
See Inge, William (Motter)

Gaiman, Neil (Richard) 1960- .... **CLC 195**
See also AAYA 19, 42; CA 133; CANR 81, 129; DLB 261; HGG; MTFW 2005; SATA 85, 146; SFW 4; SUFW 2

Gaines, Ernest J(ames) 1933- .. **BLC 2; CLC 3, 11, 18, 86, 181; SSC 68**
See also AAYA 18; AFAW 1, 2; AITN 1; BPFB 2; BW 2, 3; BYA 6; CA 9-12R; CANR 6, 24, 42, 75, 126; CDALB 1968-1988; CLR 62; CN 1, 2, 3, 4, 5, 6, 7; CSW; DA3; DAM MULT; DLB 2, 33, 152; DLBY 1980; EWL 3; EXPN; LAIT 5; LATS 1:2; MAL 5; MTCW 1, 2; MTFW 2005; NFS 5, 7, 16; RGAL 4; RGSF 2; RHW; SATA 86; SSFS 5; YAW

Gaitskill, Mary (Lawrence) 1954- .... **CLC 69**
See also CA 128; CANR 61; DLB 244; TCLE 1:1

Gaius Suetonius Tranquillus
See Suetonius

Galdos, Benito Perez
See Perez Galdos, Benito
See also EW 7

Gale, Zona 1874-1938 .... **TCLC 7**
See also CA 105; 153; CANR 84; DAM DRAM; DFS 17; DLB 9, 78, 228; RGAL 4

Galeano, Eduardo (Hughes) 1940- . **CLC 72; HLCS 1**
See also CA 29-32R; CANR 13, 32, 100; HW 1

Galiano, Juan Valera y Alcala
See Valera y Alcala-Galiano, Juan

Galilei, Galileo 1564-1642 .... **LC 45**

Gallagher, Tess 1943- .... **CLC 18, 63; PC 9**
See also CA 106; CP 3, 4, 5, 6, 7; CWP; DAM POET; DLB 120, 212, 244; PFS 16

Gallant, Mavis 1922- ..... **CLC 7, 18, 38, 172; SSC 5, 78**
See also CA 69-72; CANR 29, 69, 117; CCA 1; CN 1, 2, 3, 4, 5, 6, 7; DAC; DAM MST; DLB 53; EWL 3; MTCW 1, 2; MTFW 2005; RGEL 2; RGSF 2

Gallant, Roy A(rthur) 1924- .... **CLC 17**
See also CA 5-8R; CANR 4, 29, 54, 117; CLR 30; MAICYA 1, 2; SATA 4, 68, 110

Gallico, Paul (William) 1897-1976 .... **CLC 2**
See also AITN 1; CA 5-8R; 69-72; CANR 23; CN 1, 2; DLB 9, 171; FANT; MAICYA 1, 2; SATA 13

Gallo, Max Louis 1932- .... **CLC 95**
See also CA 85-88

Gallois, Lucien
See Desnos, Robert

Gallup, Ralph
See Whitemore, Hugh (John)

Galsworthy, John 1867-1933 .... **SSC 22; TCLC 1, 45; WLC**
See also BRW 6; CA 104; 141; CANR 75; CDBLB 1890-1914; DA; DA3; DAB; DAC; DAM DRAM, MST, NOV; DLB 10, 34, 98, 162; DLBD 16; EWL 3; MTCW 2; RGEL 2; SSFS 3; TEA

Galt, John 1779-1839 .... **NCLC 1, 110**
See also DLB 99, 116, 159; RGEL 2; RGSF 2

Galvin, James 1951- .... **CLC 38**
See also CA 108; CANR 26

Gamboa, Federico 1864-1939 .... **TCLC 36**
See also CA 167; HW 2; LAW

Gandhi, M. K.
See Gandhi, Mohandas Karamchand

Gandhi, Mahatma
See Gandhi, Mohandas Karamchand

Gandhi, Mohandas Karamchand
1869-1948 .... **TCLC 59**
See also CA 121; 132; DA3; DAM MULT; MTCW 1, 2

Gann, Ernest Kellogg 1910-1991 ..... **CLC 23**
See also AITN 1; BPFB 2; CA 1-4R; 136; CANR 1, 83; RHW

Gao Xingjian 1940- .... **CLC 167**
See Xingjian, Gao
See also MTFW 2005

Garber, Eric 1943(?)-
See Holleran, Andrew
See also CANR 89

Garcia, Cristina 1958- .... **CLC 76**
See also AMWS 11; CA 141; CANR 73, 130; CN 7; DLB 292; DNFS 1; EWL 3; HW 2; LLW; MTFW 2005

Garcia Lorca, Federico 1898-1936 ...... **DC 2; HLC 2; PC 3; TCLC 1, 7, 49; WLC**
See Lorca, Federico Garcia
See also AAYA 46; CA 104; 131; CANR 81; DA; DA3; DAB; DAC; DAM DRAM, MST, MULT, POET; DFS 4, 10; DLB 108; EWL 3; HW 1, 2; LATS 1:2; MTCW 1, 2; MTFW 2005; TWA

Garcia Marquez, Gabriel (Jose)
1928- .... **CLC 2, 3, 8, 10, 15, 27, 47, 55, 68, 170; HLC 1; SSC 8, 83; WLC**
See also AAYA 3, 33; BEST 89:1, 90:4; BPFB 2; BYA 12, 16; CA 33-36R; CANR 10, 28, 50, 75, 82, 128; CDWLB 3; CPW; CWW 2; DA; DA3; DAB; DAC; DAM MST, MULT, NOV, POP; DLB 113; DNFS 1, 2; EWL 3; EXPN; EXPS; HW 1, 2; LAIT 2; LATS 1:2; LAW; LAWS 1; LMFS 2; MTCW 1, 2; MTFW 2005; NCFS 3; NFS 1, 5, 10; RGSF 2; RGWL 2, 3; SSFS 1, 6, 16, 21; TWA; WLIT 1

Garcilaso de la Vega, El Inca
1539-1616 .... **HLCS 1**
See also DLB 318; LAW

Gard, Janice
See Latham, Jean Lee

Gard, Roger Martin du
See Martin du Gard, Roger

Gardam, Jane (Mary) 1928- .... **CLC 43**
See also CA 49-52; CANR 2, 18, 33, 54, 106; CLR 12; DLB 14, 161, 231; MAICYA 1, 2; MTCW 1; SAAS 9; SATA 39, 76, 130; SATA-Brief 28; YAW

Gardner, Herb(ert George)
1934-2003 .... **CLC 44**
See also CA 149; 220; CAD; CANR 119; CD 5, 6; DFS 18, 20

Gardner, John (Champlin), Jr.
1933-1982 ...... **CLC 2, 3, 5, 7, 8, 10, 18, 28, 34; SSC 7**
See also AAYA 45; AITN 1; AMWS 6; BPFB 2; CA 65-68; 107; CANR 33, 73; CDALBS; CN 2, 3; CPW; DA3; DAM NOV, POP; DLB 2; DLBY 1982; EWL 3;

FANT; LATS 1:2; MAL 5; MTCW 1, 2; MTFW 2005; NFS 3; RGAL 4; RGSF 2; SATA 40; SATA-Obit 31; SSFS 8

Gardner, John (Edmund) 1926- .... **CLC 30**
See also CA 103; CANR 15, 69, 127; CMW 4; CPW; DAM POP; MTCW 1

Gardner, Miriam
See Bradley, Marion Zimmer
See also GLL 1

Gardner, Noel
See Kuttner, Henry

Gardons, S. S.
See Snodgrass, W(illiam) D(e Witt)

Garfield, Leon 1921-1996 .... **CLC 12**
See also AAYA 8; BYA 1, 3; CA 17-20R; 152; CANR 38, 41, 78; CLR 21; DLB 161; JRDA; MAICYA 1, 2; MAICYAS 1; SATA 1, 32, 76; SATA-Obit 90; TEA; WYA; YAW

Garland, (Hannibal) Hamlin
1860-1940 .... **SSC 18; TCLC 3**
See also CA 104; DLB 12, 71, 78, 186; MAL 5; RGAL 4; RGSF 2; TCWW 1, 2

Garneau, (Hector de) Saint-Denys
1912-1943 .... **TCLC 13**
See also CA 111; DLB 88

Garner, Alan 1934- .... **CLC 17**
See also AAYA 18; BYA 3, 5; CA 73-76; 178; CAAE 178; CANR 15, 64, 134; CLR 20; CPW; DAB; DAM POP; DLB 161, 261; FANT; MAICYA 1, 2; MTCW 1, 2; MTFW 2005; SATA 18, 69; SATA-Essay 108; SUFW 1, 2; YAW

Garner, Hugh 1913-1979 .... **CLC 13**
See Warwick, Jarvis
See also CA 69-72; CANR 31; CCA 1; CN 1, 2; DLB 68

Garnett, David 1892-1981 .... **CLC 3**
See also CA 5-8R; 103; CANR 17, 79; CN 1, 2; DLB 34; FANT; MTCW 2; RGEL 2; SFW 4; SUFW 1

Garnier, Robert c. 1545-1590 .... **LC 119**
See also GFL Beginnings to 1789

Garos, Stephanie
See Katz, Steve

Garrett, George (Palmer, Jr.) 1929- . **CLC 3, 11, 51; SSC 30**
See also AMWS 7; BPFB 2; CA 1-4R; 202; CAAE 202; CAAS 5; CANR 1, 42, 67, 109; CN 1, 2, 3, 4, 5, 6, 7; CP 1, 2, 3, 4, 5, 6, 7; CSW; DLB 2, 5, 130, 152; DLBY 1983

Garrick, David 1717-1779 .... **LC 15**
See also DAM DRAM; DLB 84, 213; RGEL 2

Garrigue, Jean 1914-1972 .... **CLC 2, 8**
See also CA 5-8R; 37-40R; CANR 20; CP 1; MAL 5

Garrison, Frederick
See Sinclair, Upton (Beall)

Garrison, William Lloyd
1805-1879 .... **NCLC 149**
See also CDALB 1640-1865; DLB 1, 43, 235

Garro, Elena 1920(?)-1998 .. **HLCS 1; TCLC 153**
See also CA 131; 169; CWW 2; DLB 145; EWL 3; HW 1; LAWS 1; WLIT 1

Garth, Will
See Hamilton, Edmond; Kuttner, Henry

Garvey, Marcus (Moziah, Jr.)
1887-1940 ... **BLC 2; HR 1:2; TCLC 41**
See also BW 1; CA 120; 124; CANR 79; DAM MULT

Gary, Romain .... **CLC 25**
See Kacew, Romain
See also DLB 83, 299

Gascar, Pierre .... **CLC 11**
See Fournier, Pierre
See also EWL 3

Gascoigne, George 1539-1577 .... **LC 108**
See also DLB 136; RGEL 2

Gascoyne, David (Emery)
1916-2001 .... **CLC 45**
See also CA 65-68; 200; CANR 10, 28, 54; CP 1, 2, 3, 4, 5, 6, 7; DLB 20; MTCW 1; RGEL 2

Gaskell, Elizabeth Cleghorn
1810-1865 .... **NCLC 5, 70, 97, 137; SSC 25**
See also BRW 5; CDBLB 1832-1890; DAB; DAM MST; DLB 21, 144, 159; RGEL 2; RGSF 2; TEA

Gass, William H(oward) 1924- . **CLC 1, 2, 8, 11, 15, 39, 132; SSC 12**
See also AMWS 6; CA 17-20R; CANR 30, 71, 100; CN 1, 2, 3, 4, 5, 6, 7; DLB 2, 227; EWL 3; MAL 5; MTCW 1, 2; MTFW 2005; RGAL 4

Gassendi, Pierre 1592-1655 .... **LC 54**
See also GFL Beginnings to 1789

Gasset, Jose Ortega y
See Ortega y Gasset, Jose

Gates, Henry Louis, Jr. 1950- ... **BLCS; CLC 65**
See also BW 2, 3; CA 109; CANR 25, 53, 75, 125; CSW; DA3; DAM MULT; DLB 67; EWL 3; MAL 5; MTCW 2; MTFW 2005; RGAL 4

Gautier, Theophile 1811-1872 .. **NCLC 1, 59; PC 18; SSC 20**
See also DAM POET; DLB 119; EW 6; GFL 1789 to the Present; RGWL 2, 3; SUFW; TWA

Gay, John 1685-1732 .... **LC 49**
See also BRW 3; DAM DRAM; DLB 84, 95; RGEL 2; WLIT 3

Gay, Oliver
See Gogarty, Oliver St. John

Gay, Peter (Jack) 1923- .... **CLC 158**
See also CA 13-16R; CANR 18, 41, 77; INT CANR-18

Gaye, Marvin (Pentz, Jr.)
1939-1984 .... **CLC 26**
See also CA 195; 112

Gebler, Carlo (Ernest) 1954- .... **CLC 39**
See also CA 119; 133; CANR 96; DLB 271

Gee, Maggie (Mary) 1948- .... **CLC 57**
See also CA 130; CANR 125; CN 4, 5, 6, 7; DLB 207; MTFW 2005

Gee, Maurice (Gough) 1931- .... **CLC 29**
See also AAYA 42; CA 97-100; CANR 67, 123; CLR 56; CN 2, 3, 4, 5, 6, 7; CWRI 5; EWL 3; MAICYA 2; RGSF 2; SATA 46, 101

Geiogamah, Hanay 1945- .... **NNAL**
See also CA 153; DAM MULT; DLB 175

Gelbart, Larry
See Gelbart, Larry (Simon)
See also CAD; CD 5, 6

Gelbart, Larry (Simon) 1928- .... **CLC 21, 61**
See Gelbart, Larry
See also CA 73-76; CANR 45, 94

Gelber, Jack 1932-2003 ...... **CLC 1, 6, 14, 79**
See also CA 1-4R; 216; CAD; CANR 2; DLB 7, 228; MAL 5

Gellhorn, Martha (Ellis)
1908-1998 .... **CLC 14, 60**
See also CA 77-80; 164; CANR 44; CN 1, 2, 3, 4, 5, 6 7; DLBY 1982, 1998

Genet, Jean 1910-1986 .. **CLC 1, 2, 5, 10, 14, 44, 46; DC 25; TCLC 128**
See also CA 13-16R; CANR 18; DA3; DAM DRAM; DFS 10; DLB 72, 321; DLBY 1986; EW 13; EWL 3; GFL 1789 to the Present; GLL 1; LMFS 2; MTCW 1, 2; MTFW 2005; RGWL 2, 3; TWA

Glanville, Brian (Lester) 1931- .... **CLC 6**
See also CA 5-8R; CAAS 9; CANR 3, 70; CN 1, 2, 3, 4, 5, 6, 7; DLB 15, 139; SATA 42

Glasgow, Ellen (Anderson Gholson) 1873-1945 .... **SSC 34; TCLC 2, 7**
See also AMW; CA 104; 164; DLB 9, 12; MAL 5; MAWW; MTCW 2; MTFW 2005; RGAL 4; RHW; SSFS 9; TUS

Glaspell, Susan 1882(?)-1948 ..... **DC 10; SSC 41; TCLC 55, 175**
See also AMWS 3; CA 110; 154; DFS 8, 18; DLB 7, 9, 78, 228; MAWW; RGAL 4; SSFS 3; TCWW 2; TUS; YABC 2

Glassco, John 1909-1981 .... **CLC 9**
See also CA 13-16R; 102; CANR 15; CN 1, 2; CP 1, 2, 3; DLB 68

Glasscock, Amnesia
See Steinbeck, John (Ernst)

Glasser, Ronald J. 1940(?)- .... **CLC 37**
See also CA 209

Glassman, Joyce
See Johnson, Joyce

Gleick, James (W.) 1954- .... **CLC 147**
See also CA 131; 137; CANR 97; INT CA-137

Glendinning, Victoria 1937- .... **CLC 50**
See also CA 120; 127; CANR 59, 89; DLB 155

Glissant, Edouard (Mathieu) 1928- .... **CLC 10, 68**
See also CA 153; CANR 111; CWW 2; DAM MULT; EWL 3; RGWL 3

Gloag, Julian 1930- .... **CLC 40**
See also AITN 1; CA 65-68; CANR 10, 70; CN 1, 2, 3, 4, 5, 6

Glowacki, Aleksander
See Prus, Boleslaw

Gluck, Louise (Elisabeth) 1943- .. **CLC 7, 22, 44, 81, 160; PC 16**
See also AMWS 5; CA 33-36R; CANR 40, 69, 108, 133; CP 1, 2, 3, 4, 5, 6, 7; CWP; DA3; DAM POET; DLB 5; MAL 5; MTCW 2; MTFW 2005; PFS 5, 15; RGAL 4; TCLE 1:1

Glyn, Elinor 1864-1943 .... **TCLC 72**
See also DLB 153; RHW

Gobineau, Joseph-Arthur 1816-1882 .... **NCLC 17**
See also DLB 123; GFL 1789 to the Present

Godard, Jean-Luc 1930- .... **CLC 20**
See also CA 93-96

Godden, (Margaret) Rumer 1907-1998 .... **CLC 53**
See also AAYA 6; BPFB 2; BYA 2, 5; CA 5-8R; 172; CANR 4, 27, 36, 55, 80; CLR 20; CN 1, 2, 3, 4, 5, 6; CWRI 5; DLB 161; MAICYA 1, 2; RHW; SAAS 12; SATA 3, 36; SATA-Obit 109; TEA

Godoy Alcayaga, Lucila 1899-1957 .. **HLC 2; PC 32; TCLC 2**
See Mistral, Gabriela
See also BW 2; CA 104; 131; CANR 81; DAM MULT; DNFS; HW 1, 2; MTCW 1, 2; MTFW 2005

Godwin, Gail 1937- ...... **CLC 5, 8, 22, 31, 69, 125**
See also BPFB 2; CA 29-32R; CANR 15, 43, 69, 132; CN 3, 4, 5, 6, 7; CPW; CSW; DA3; DAM POP; DLB 6, 234; INT CANR-15; MAL 5; MTCW 1, 2; MTFW 2005

Godwin, Gail Kathleen
See Godwin, Gail

Godwin, William 1756-1836 .. **NCLC 14, 130**
See also CDBLB 1789-1832; CMW 4; DLB 39, 104, 142, 158, 163, 262; GL 2; HGG; RGEL 2

Goebbels, Josef
See Goebbels, (Paul) Joseph

Goebbels, (Paul) Joseph 1897-1945 .... **TCLC 68**
See also CA 115; 148

Goebbels, Joseph Paul
See Goebbels, (Paul) Joseph

Goethe, Johann Wolfgang von 1749-1832 . **DC 20; NCLC 4, 22, 34, 90, 154; PC 5; SSC 38; WLC**
See also CDWLB 2; DA; DA3; DAB; DAC; DAM DRAM, MST, POET; DLB 94; EW 5; GL 2; LATS 1; LMFS 1:1; RGWL 2, 3; TWA

Gogarty, Oliver St. John 1878-1957 .... **TCLC 15**
See also CA 109; 150; DLB 15, 19; RGEL 2

Gogol, Nikolai (Vasilyevich) 1809-1852 .... **DC 1; NCLC 5, 15, 31, 162; SSC 4, 29, 52; WLC**
See also DA; DAB; DAC; DAM DRAM, MST; DFS 12; DLB 198; EW 6; EXPS; RGSF 2; RGWL 2, 3; SSFS 7; TWA

Goines, Donald 1937(?)-1974 ... **BLC 2; CLC 80**
See also AITN 1; BW 1, 3; CA 124; 114; CANR 82; CMW 4; DA3; DAM MULT, POP; DLB 33

Gold, Herbert 1924- ... **CLC 4, 7, 14, 42, 152**
See also CA 9-12R; CANR 17, 45, 125; CN 1, 2, 3, 4, 5, 6, 7; DLB 2; DLBY 1981; MAL 5

Goldbarth, Albert 1948- .... **CLC 5, 38**
See also AMWS 12; CA 53-56; CANR 6, 40; CP 3, 4, 5, 6, 7; DLB 120

Goldberg, Anatol 1910-1982 .... **CLC 34**
See also CA 131; 117

Goldemberg, Isaac 1945- .... **CLC 52**
See also CA 69-72; CAAS 12; CANR 11, 32; EWL 3; HW 1; WLIT 1

Golding, Arthur 1536-1606 .... **LC 101**
See also DLB 136

Golding, William (Gerald) 1911-1993 ..... **CLC 1, 2, 3, 8, 10, 17, 27, 58, 81; WLC**
See also AAYA 5, 44; BPFB 2; BRWR 1; BRWS 1; BYA 2; CA 5-8R; 141; CANR 13, 33, 54; CD 5; CDBLB 1945-1960; CLR 94; CN 1, 2, 3, 4; DA; DA3; DAB; DAC; DAM MST, NOV; DLB 15, 100, 255; EWL 3; EXPN; HGG; LAIT 4; MTCW 1, 2; MTFW 2005; NFS 2; RGEL 2; RHW; SFW 4; TEA; WLIT 4; YAW

Goldman, Emma 1869-1940 .... **TCLC 13**
See also CA 110; 150; DLB 221; FW; RGAL 4; TUS

Goldman, Francisco 1954- .... **CLC 76**
See also CA 162

Goldman, William (W.) 1931- ...... **CLC 1, 48**
See also BPFB 2; CA 9-12R; CANR 29, 69, 106; CN 1, 2, 3, 4, 5, 6, 7; DLB 44; FANT; IDFW 3, 4

Goldmann, Lucien 1913-1970 .... **CLC 24**
See also CA 25-28; CAP 2

Goldoni, Carlo 1707-1793 .... **LC 4**
See also DAM DRAM; EW 4; RGWL 2, 3; WLIT 7

Goldsberry, Steven 1949- .... **CLC 34**
See also CA 131

Goldsmith, Oliver 1730-1774 .... **DC 8; LC 2, 48, 122; WLC**
See also BRW 3; CDBLB 1660-1789; DA; DAB; DAC; DAM DRAM, MST, NOV, POET; DFS 1; DLB 39, 89, 104, 109, 142; IDTP; RGEL 2; SATA 26; TEA; WLIT 3

Goldsmith, Peter
See Priestley, J(ohn) B(oynton)

Gombrowicz, Witold 1904-1969 .... **CLC 4, 7, 11, 49**
See also CA 19-20; 25-28R; CANR 105; CAP 2; CDWLB 4; DAM DRAM; DLB 215; EW 12; EWL 3; RGWL 2, 3; TWA

Gomez de Avellaneda, Gertrudis 1814-1873 .... **NCLC 111**
See also LAW

Gomez de la Serna, Ramon 1888-1963 .... **CLC 9**
See also CA 153; 116; CANR 79; EWL 3; HW 1, 2

Goncharov, Ivan Alexandrovich 1812-1891 .... **NCLC 1, 63**
See also DLB 238; EW 6; RGWL 2, 3

Goncourt, Edmond (Louis Antoine Huot) de 1822-1896 .... **NCLC 7**
See also DLB 123; EW 7; GFL 1789 to the Present; RGWL 2, 3

Goncourt, Jules (Alfred Huot) de 1830-1870 .... **NCLC 7**
See also DLB 123; EW 7; GFL 1789 to the Present; RGWL 2, 3

Gongora (y Argote), Luis de 1561-1627 .... **LC 72**
See also RGWL 2, 3

Gontier, Fernande 19(?)- .... **CLC 50**

Gonzalez Martinez, Enrique
See Gonzalez Martinez, Enrique
See also DLB 290

Gonzalez Martinez, Enrique 1871-1952 .... **TCLC 72**
See Gonzalez Martinez, Enrique
See also CA 166; CANR 81; EWL 3; HW 1, 2

Goodison, Lorna 1947- .... **PC 36**
See also CA 142; CANR 88; CP 7; CWP; DLB 157; EWL 3

Goodman, Paul 1911-1972 ..... **CLC 1, 2, 4, 7**
See also CA 19-20; 37-40R; CAD; CANR 34; CAP 2; CN 1; DLB 130, 246; MAL 5; MTCW 1; RGAL 4

GoodWeather, Harley
See King, Thomas

Googe, Barnabe 1540-1594 .... **LC 94**
See also DLB 132; RGEL 2

Gordimer, Nadine 1923- ...... **CLC 3, 5, 7, 10, 18, 33, 51, 70, 123, 160, 161; SSC 17, 80; WLCS**
See also AAYA 39; AFW; BRWS 2; CA 5-8R; CANR 3, 28, 56, 88, 131; CN 1, 2, 3, 4, 5, 6, 7; DA; DA3; DAB; DAC; DAM MST, NOV; DLB 225; EWL 3; EXPS; INT CANR-28; LATS 1:2; MTCW 1, 2; MTFW 2005; NFS 4; RGEL 2; RGSF 2; SSFS 2, 14, 19; TWA; WLIT 2; YAW

Gordon, Adam Lindsay 1833-1870 .... **NCLC 21**
See also DLB 230

Gordon, Caroline 1895-1981 . **CLC 6, 13, 29, 83; SSC 15**
See also AMW; CA 11-12; 103; CANR 36; CAP 1; CN 1, 2; DLB 4, 9, 102; DLBD 17; DLBY 1981; EWL 3; MAL 5; MTCW 1, 2; MTFW 2005; RGAL 4; RGSF 2

Gordon, Charles William 1860-1937
See Connor, Ralph
See also CA 109

Gordon, Mary (Catherine) 1949- .... **CLC 13, 22, 128, 216; SSC 59**
See also AMWS 4; BPFB 2; CA 102; CANR 44, 92; CN 4, 5, 6, 7; DLB 6; DLBY 1981; FW; INT CA-102; MAL 5; MTCW 1

Gordon, N. J.
See Bosman, Herman Charles

Gordon, Sol 1923- .... **CLC 26**
See also CA 53-56; CANR 4; SATA 11

Gordone, Charles 1925-1995 .. **CLC 1, 4; DC 8**
See also BW 1, 3; CA 93-96, 180; 150; CAAE 180; CAD; CANR 55; DAM DRAM; DLB 7; INT CA-93-96; MTCW 1

Gore, Catherine 1800-1861 .... **NCLC 65**
See also DLB 116; RGEL 2

Gorenko, Anna Andreevna
See Akhmatova, Anna

Gorky, Maxim .... **SSC 28; TCLC 8; WLC**
See Peshkov, Alexei Maximovich
See also DAB; DFS 9; DLB 295; EW 8; EWL 3; TWA

Goryan, Sirak
See Saroyan, William

Gosse, Edmund (William)
1849-1928 .... **TCLC 28**
See also CA 117; DLB 57, 144, 184; RGEL 2

Gotlieb, Phyllis (Fay Bloom) 1926- .. **CLC 18**
See also CA 13-16R; CANR 7, 135; CN 7; CP 1, 2, 3, 4; DLB 88, 251; SFW 4

Gottesman, S. D.
See Kornbluth, C(yril) M.; Pohl, Frederik

Gottfried von Strassburg fl. c.
1170-1215 .... **CMLC 10**
See also CDWLB 2; DLB 138; EW 1; RGWL 2, 3

Gotthelf, Jeremias 1797-1854 .... **NCLC 117**
See also DLB 133; RGWL 2, 3

Gottschalk, Laura Riding
See Jackson, Laura (Riding)

Gould, Lois 1932(?)-2002 .... **CLC 4, 10**
See also CA 77-80; 208; CANR 29; MTCW 1

Gould, Stephen Jay 1941-2002 .... **CLC 163**
See also AAYA 26; BEST 90:2; CA 77-80; 205; CANR 10, 27, 56, 75, 125; CPW; INT CANR-27; MTCW 1, 2; MTFW 2005

Gourmont, Remy(-Marie-Charles) de
1858-1915 .... **TCLC 17**
See also CA 109; 150; GFL 1789 to the Present; MTCW 2

Gournay, Marie le Jars de
See de Gournay, Marie le Jars

Govier, Katherine 1948- .... **CLC 51**
See also CA 101; CANR 18, 40, 128; CCA 1

Gower, John c. 1330-1408 .... **LC 76; PC 59**
See also BRW 1; DLB 146; RGEL 2

Goyen, (Charles) William
1915-1983 .... **CLC 5, 8, 14, 40**
See also AITN 2; CA 5-8R; 110; CANR 6, 71; CN 1, 2, 3; DLB 2, 218; DLBY 1983; EWL 3; INT CANR-6; MAL 5

Goytisolo, Juan 1931- .... **CLC 5, 10, 23, 133; HLC 1**
See also CA 85-88; CANR 32, 61, 131; CWW 2; DAM MULT; DLB 322; EWL 3; GLL 2; HW 1, 2; MTCW 1, 2; MTFW 2005

Gozzano, Guido 1883-1916 .... **PC 10**
See also CA 154; DLB 114; EWL 3

Gozzi, (Conte) Carlo 1720-1806 .... **NCLC 23**

Grabbe, Christian Dietrich
1801-1836 .... **NCLC 2**
See also DLB 133; RGWL 2, 3

Grace, Patricia Frances 1937- .... **CLC 56**
See also CA 176; CANR 118; CN 4, 5, 6, 7; EWL 3; RGSF 2

Gracian y Morales, Baltasar
1601-1658 .... **LC 15**

Gracq, Julien .... **CLC 11, 48**
See Poirier, Louis
See also CWW 2; DLB 83; GFL 1789 to the Present

Grade, Chaim 1910-1982 .... **CLC 10**
See also CA 93-96; 107; EWL 3

Graduate of Oxford, A
See Ruskin, John

Grafton, Garth
See Duncan, Sara Jeannette

Grafton, Sue 1940- .... **CLC 163**
See also AAYA 11, 49; BEST 90:3; CA 108; CANR 31, 55, 111, 134; CMW 4; CPW; CSW; DA3; DAM POP; DLB 226; FW; MSW; MTFW 2005

Graham, John
See Phillips, David Graham

Graham, Jorie 1950- .... **CLC 48, 118; PC 59**
See also AAYA 67; CA 111; CANR 63, 118; CP 4, 5, 6, 7; CWP; DLB 120; EWL 3; MTFW 2005; PFS 10, 17; TCLE 1:1

Graham, R(obert) B(ontine) Cunninghame
See Cunninghame Graham, Robert (Gallnigad) Bontine
See also DLB 98, 135, 174; RGEL 2; RGSF 2

Graham, Robert
See Haldeman, Joe (William)

Graham, Tom
See Lewis, (Harry) Sinclair

Graham, W(illiam) S(idney)
1918-1986 .... **CLC 29**
See also BRWS 7; CA 73-76; 118; CP 1, 2, 3, 4; DLB 20; RGEL 2

Graham, Winston (Mawdsley)
1910-2003 .... **CLC 23**
See also CA 49-52; 218; CANR 2, 22, 45, 66; CMW 4; CN 1, 2, 3, 4, 5, 6, 7; DLB 77; RHW

Grahame, Kenneth 1859-1932 ...... **TCLC 64, 136**
See also BYA 5; CA 108; 136; CANR 80; CLR 5; CWRI 5; DA3; DAB; DLB 34, 141, 178; FANT; MAICYA 1, 2; MTCW 2; NFS 20; RGEL 2; SATA 100; TEA; WCH; YABC 1

Granger, Darius John
See Marlowe, Stephen

Granin, Daniil 1918- .... **CLC 59**
See also DLB 302

Granovsky, Timofei Nikolaevich
1813-1855 .... **NCLC 75**
See also DLB 198

Grant, Skeeter
See Spiegelman, Art

Granville-Barker, Harley
1877-1946 .... **TCLC 2**
See Barker, Harley Granville
See also CA 104; 204; DAM DRAM; RGEL 2

Granzotto, Gianni
See Granzotto, Giovanni Battista

Granzotto, Giovanni Battista
1914-1985 .... **CLC 70**
See also CA 166

Grass, Guenter (Wilhelm) 1927- ... **CLC 1, 2, 4, 6, 11, 15, 22, 32, 49, 88, 207; WLC**
See Grass, Gunter (Wilhelm)
See also BPFB 2; CA 13-16R; CANR 20, 75, 93, 133; CDWLB 2; DA; DA3; DAB; DAC; DAM MST, NOV; DLB 75, 124; EW 13; EWL 3; MTCW 1, 2; MTFW 2005; RGWL 2, 3; TWA

Grass, Gunter (Wilhelm)
See Grass, Guenter (Wilhelm)
See also CWW 2

Gratton, Thomas
See Hulme, T(homas) E(rnest)

Grau, Shirley Ann 1929- .... **CLC 4, 9, 146; SSC 15**
See also CA 89-92; CANR 22, 69; CN 1, 2, 3, 4, 5, 6, 7; CSW; DLB 2, 218; INT CA-89-92; CANR-22; MTCW 1

Gravel, Fern
See Hall, James Norman

Graver, Elizabeth 1964- .... **CLC 70**
See also CA 135; CANR 71, 129

Graves, Richard Perceval
1895-1985 .... **CLC 44**
See also CA 65-68; CANR 9, 26, 51

Graves, Robert (von Ranke)
1895-1985 .. **CLC 1, 2, 6, 11, 39, 44, 45; PC 6**
See also BPFB 2; BRW 7; BYA 4; CA 5-8R; 117; CANR 5, 36; CDBLB 1914-1945; CN 1, 2, 3; CP 1, 2, 3, 4; DA3; DAB; DAC; DAM MST, POET; DLB 20, 100, 191; DLBD 18; DLBY 1985; EWL 3; LATS 1:1; MTCW 1, 2; MTFW 2005; NCFS 2; NFS 21; RGEL 2; RHW; SATA 45; TEA

Graves, Valerie
See Bradley, Marion Zimmer

Gray, Alasdair (James) 1934- .... **CLC 41**
See also BRWS 9; CA 126; CANR 47, 69, 106, 140; CN 4, 5, 6, 7; DLB 194, 261, 319; HGG; INT CA-126; MTCW 1, 2; MTFW 2005; RGSF 2; SUFW 2

Gray, Amlin 1946- .... **CLC 29**
See also CA 138

Gray, Francine du Plessix 1930- ..... **CLC 22, 153**
See also BEST 90:3; CA 61-64; CAAS 2; CANR 11, 33, 75, 81; DAM NOV; INT CANR-11; MTCW 1, 2; MTFW 2005

Gray, John (Henry) 1866-1934 ...... **TCLC 19**
See also CA 119; 162; RGEL 2

Gray, John Lee
See Jakes, John (William)

Gray, Simon (James Holliday)
1936- .... **CLC 9, 14, 36**
See also AITN 1; CA 21-24R; CAAS 3; CANR 32, 69; CBD; CD 5, 6; CN 1, 2, 3; DLB 13; EWL 3; MTCW 1; RGEL 2

Gray, Spalding 1941-2004 .... **CLC 49, 112; DC 7**
See also AAYA 62; CA 128; 225; CAD; CANR 74, 138; CD 5, 6; CPW; DAM POP; MTCW 2; MTFW 2005

Gray, Thomas 1716-1771 .... **LC 4, 40; PC 2; WLC**
See also BRW 3; CDBLB 1660-1789; DA; DA3; DAB; DAC; DAM MST; DLB 109; EXPP; PAB; PFS 9; RGEL 2; TEA; WP

Grayson, David
See Baker, Ray Stannard

Grayson, Richard (A.) 1951- .... **CLC 38**
See also CA 85-88; 210; CAAE 210; CANR 14, 31, 57; DLB 234

Greeley, Andrew M(oran) 1928- ...... **CLC 28**
See also BPFB 2; CA 5-8R; CAAS 7; CANR 7, 43, 69, 104, 136; CMW 4; CPW; DA3; DAM POP; MTCW 1, 2; MTFW 2005

Green, Anna Katharine
1846-1935 .... **TCLC 63**
See also CA 112; 159; CMW 4; DLB 202, 221; MSW

Green, Brian
See Card, Orson Scott

Green, Hannah
See Greenberg, Joanne (Goldenberg)

Green, Hannah 1927(?)-1996 .... **CLC 3**
See also CA 73-76; CANR 59, 93; NFS 10

Green, Henry .... **CLC 2, 13, 97**
See Yorke, Henry Vincent
See also BRWS 2; CA 175; DLB 15; EWL 3; RGEL 2

Green, Julian .... **CLC 3, 11, 77**
See Green, Julien (Hartridge)
See also EWL 3; GFL 1789 to the Present; MTCW 2

Green, Julien (Hartridge) 1900-1998
See Green, Julian
See also CA 21-24R; 169; CANR 33, 87;
CWW 2; DLB 4, 72; MTCW 1, 2; MTFW
2005

Green, Paul (Eliot) 1894-1981 .... CLC 25
See also AITN 1; CA 5-8R; 103; CAD;
CANR 3; DAM DRAM; DLB 7, 9, 249;
DLBY 1981; MAL 5; RGAL 4

Greenaway, Peter 1942- .... CLC 159
See also CA 127

Greenberg, Ivan 1908-1973
See Rahv, Philip
See also CA 85-88

Greenberg, Joanne (Goldenberg)
1932- .... CLC 7, 30
See also AAYA 12, 67; CA 5-8R; CANR
14, 32, 69; CN 6, 7; SATA 25; YAW

Greenberg, Richard 1959(?)- .... CLC 57
See also CA 138; CAD; CD 5, 6

Greenblatt, Stephen J(ay) 1943- ...... CLC 70
See also CA 49-52; CANR 115

Greene, Bette 1934- .... CLC 30
See also AAYA 7; BYA 3; CA 53-56; CANR
4, 146; CLR 2; CWRI 5; JRDA; LAIT 4;
MAICYA 1, 2; NFS 10; SAAS 16; SATA
8, 102, 161; WYA; YAW

Greene, Gael .... CLC 8
See also CA 13-16R; CANR 10

Greene, Graham (Henry)
1904-1991 .... CLC 1, 3, 6, 9, 14, 18, 27,
37, 70, 72, 125; SSC 29; WLC
See also AAYA 61; AITN 2; BPFB 2;
BRWR 2; BRWS 1; BYA 3; CA 13-16R;
133; CANR 35, 61, 131; CBD; CDBLB
1945-1960; CMW 4; CN 1, 2, 3, 4; DA;
DA3; DAB; DAC; DAM MST, NOV;
DLB 13, 15, 77, 100, 162, 201, 204;
DLBY 1991; EWL 3; MSW; MTCW 1, 2;
MTFW 2005; NFS 16; RGEL 2; SATA
20; SSFS 14; TEA; WLIT 4

Greene, Robert 1558-1592 .... LC 41
See also BRWS 8; DLB 62, 167; IDTP;
RGEL 2; TEA

Greer, Germaine 1939- .... CLC 131
See also AITN 1; CA 81-84; CANR 33, 70,
115, 133; FW; MTCW 1, 2; MTFW 2005

Greer, Richard
See Silverberg, Robert

Gregor, Arthur 1923- .... CLC 9
See also CA 25-28R; CAAS 10; CANR 11;
CP 1, 2, 3, 4, 5, 6, 7; SATA 36

Gregor, Lee
See Pohl, Frederik

Gregory, Lady Isabella Augusta (Persse)
1852-1932 .... TCLC 1, 176
See also BRW 6; CA 104; 184; DLB 10;
IDTP; RGEL 2

Gregory, J. Dennis
See Williams, John A(lfred)

Grekova, I. .... CLC 59
See Ventsel, Elena Sergeevna
See also CWW 2

Grendon, Stephen
See Derleth, August (William)

Grenville, Kate 1950- .... CLC 61
See also CA 118; CANR 53, 93; CN 7

Grenville, Pelham
See Wodehouse, P(elham) G(renville)

Greve, Felix Paul (Berthold Friedrich)
1879-1948
See Grove, Frederick Philip
See also CA 104; 141, 175; CANR 79;
DAC; DAM MST

Greville, Fulke 1554-1628 .... LC 79
See also BRWS 11; DLB 62, 172; RGEL 2

Grey, Lady Jane 1537-1554 .... LC 93
See also DLB 132

Grey, Zane 1872-1939 .... TCLC 6
See also BPFB 2; CA 104; 132; DA3; DAM
POP; DLB 9, 212; MTCW 1, 2; MTFW
2005; RGAL 4; TCWW 1, 2; TUS

Griboedov, Aleksandr Sergeevich
1795(?)-1829 .... NCLC 129
See also DLB 205; RGWL 2, 3

Grieg, (Johan) Nordahl (Brun)
1902-1943 .... TCLC 10
See also CA 107; 189; EWL 3

Grieve, C(hristopher) M(urray)
1892-1978 .... CLC 11, 19
See MacDiarmid, Hugh; Pteleon
See also CA 5-8R; 85-88; CANR 33, 107;
DAM POET; MTCW 1; RGEL 2

Griffin, Gerald 1803-1840 .... NCLC 7
See also DLB 159; RGEL 2

Griffin, John Howard 1920-1980 ..... CLC 68
See also AITN 1; CA 1-4R; 101; CANR 2

Griffin, Peter 1942- .... CLC 39
See also CA 136

Griffith, D(avid Lewelyn) W(ark)
1875(?)-1948 .... TCLC 68
See also CA 119; 150; CANR 80

Griffith, Lawrence
See Griffith, D(avid Lewelyn) W(ark)

Griffiths, Trevor 1935- .... CLC 13, 52
See also CA 97-100; CANR 45; CBD; CD
5, 6; DLB 13, 245

Griggs, Sutton (Elbert)
1872-1930 .... TCLC 77
See also CA 123; 186; DLB 50

Grigson, Geoffrey (Edward Harvey)
1905-1985 .... CLC 7, 39
See also CA 25-28R; 118; CANR 20, 33;
CP 1, 2, 3, 4; DLB 27; MTCW 1, 2

Grile, Dod
See Bierce, Ambrose (Gwinett)

Grillparzer, Franz 1791-1872 .... DC 14;
NCLC 1, 102; SSC 37
See also CDWLB 2; DLB 133; EW 5;
RGWL 2, 3; TWA

Grimble, Reverend Charles James
See Eliot, T(homas) S(tearns)

Grimke, Angelina (Emily) Weld
1880-1958 .... HR 1:2
See Weld, Angelina (Emily) Grimke
See also BW 1; CA 124; DAM POET; DLB
50, 54

Grimke, Charlotte L(ottie) Forten
1837(?)-1914
See Forten, Charlotte L.
See also BW 1; CA 117; 124; DAM MULT,
POET

Grimm, Jacob Ludwig Karl
1785-1863 .... NCLC 3, 77; SSC 36, 88
See also DLB 90; MAICYA 1, 2; RGSF 2;
RGWL 2, 3; SATA 22; WCH

Grimm, Wilhelm Karl 1786-1859 .. NCLC 3,
77; SSC 36, 88
See also CDWLB 2; DLB 90; MAICYA 1,
2; RGSF 2; RGWL 2, 3; SATA 22; WCH

Grimmelshausen, Hans Jakob Christoffel
von
See Grimmelshausen, Johann Jakob Christoffel von
See also RGWL 2, 3

Grimmelshausen, Johann Jakob Christoffel
von 1621-1676 .... LC 6
See Grimmelshausen, Hans Jakob Christoffel von
See also CDWLB 2; DLB 168

Grindel, Eugene 1895-1952
See Eluard, Paul
See also CA 104; 193; LMFS 2

Grisham, John 1955- .... CLC 84
See also AAYA 14, 47; BPFB 2; CA 138;
CANR 47, 69, 114, 133; CMW 4; CN 6,
7; CPW; CSW; DA3; DAM POP; MSW;
MTCW 2; MTFW 2005

Grosseteste, Robert 1175(?)-1253 . CMLC 62
See also DLB 115

Grossman, David 1954- .... CLC 67
See also CA 138; CANR 114; CWW 2;
DLB 299; EWL 3; WLIT 6

Grossman, Vasilii Semenovich
See Grossman, Vasily (Semenovich)
See also DLB 272

Grossman, Vasily (Semenovich)
1905-1964 .... CLC 41
See Grossman, Vasilii Semenovich
See also CA 124; 130; MTCW 1

Grove, Frederick Philip .... TCLC 4
See Greve, Felix Paul (Berthold Friedrich)
See also DLB 92; RGEL 2; TCWW 1, 2

Grubb
See Crumb, R(obert)

Grumbach, Doris (Isaac) 1918- . CLC 13, 22,
64
See also CA 5-8R; CAAS 2; CANR 9, 42,
70, 127; CN 6, 7; INT CANR-9; MTCW
2; MTFW 2005

Grundtvig, Nikolai Frederik Severin
1783-1872 .... NCLC 1, 158
See also DLB 300

Grunge
See Crumb, R(obert)

Grunwald, Lisa 1959- .... CLC 44
See also CA 120

Gryphius, Andreas 1616-1664 .... LC 89
See also CDWLB 2; DLB 164; RGWL 2, 3

Guare, John 1938- .... CLC 8, 14, 29, 67; DC
20
See also CA 73-76; CAD; CANR 21, 69,
118; CD 5, 6; DAM DRAM; DFS 8, 13;
DLB 7, 249; EWL 3; MAL 5; MTCW 1,
2; RGAL 4

Guarini, Battista 1537-1612 .... LC 102

Gubar, Susan (David) 1944- .... CLC 145
See also CA 108; CANR 45, 70, 139; FW;
MTCW 1; RGAL 4

Gudjonsson, Halldor Kiljan 1902-1998
See Halldor Laxness
See also CA 103; 164

Guenter, Erich
See Eich, Gunter

Guest, Barbara 1920- .... CLC 34; PC 55
See also BG 1:2; CA 25-28R; CANR 11,
44, 84; CP 1, 2, 3, 4, 5, 6, 7; CWP; DLB
5, 193

Guest, Edgar A(lbert) 1881-1959 ... TCLC 95
See also CA 112; 168

Guest, Judith (Ann) 1936- .... CLC 8, 30
See also AAYA 7, 66; CA 77-80; CANR
15, 75, 138; DA3; DAM NOV, POP;
EXPN; INT CANR-15; LAIT 5; MTCW
1, 2; MTFW 2005; NFS 1

Guevara, Che .... CLC 87; HLC 1
See Guevara (Serna), Ernesto

Guevara (Serna), Ernesto
1928-1967 .... CLC 87; HLC 1
See Guevara, Che
See also CA 127; 111; CANR 56; DAM
MULT; HW 1

Guicciardini, Francesco 1483-1540 ..... LC 49

Guild, Nicholas M. 1944- .... CLC 33
See also CA 93-96

Guillemin, Jacques
See Sartre, Jean-Paul

Guillen, Jorge 1893-1984 . CLC 11; HLCS 1;
PC 35
See also CA 89-92; 112; DAM MULT,
POET; DLB 108; EWL 3; HW 1; RGWL
2, 3

Guillen, Nicolas (Cristobal)
1902-1989 .... **BLC 2; CLC 48, 79; HLC 1; PC 23**
See also BW 2; CA 116; 125; 129; CANR 84; DAM MST, MULT, POET; DLB 283; EWL 3; HW 1; LAW; RGWL 2, 3; WP

Guillen y Alvarez, Jorge
See Guillen, Jorge

Guillevic, (Eugene) 1907-1997 .... **CLC 33**
See also CA 93-96; CWW 2

Guillois
See Desnos, Robert

Guillois, Valentin
See Desnos, Robert

Guimaraes Rosa, Joao 1908-1967 .... **HLCS 2**
See Rosa, Joao Guimaraes
See also CA 175; LAW; RGSF 2; RGWL 2, 3

Guiney, Louise Imogen
1861-1920 .... **TCLC 41**
See also CA 160; DLB 54; RGAL 4

Guinizelli, Guido c. 1230-1276 ...... **CMLC 49**
See Guinizzelli, Guido

Guinizzelli, Guido
See Guinizelli, Guido
See also WLIT 7

Guiraldes, Ricardo (Guillermo)
1886-1927 .... **TCLC 39**
See also CA 131; EWL 3; HW 1; LAW; MTCW 1

Gumilev, Nikolai (Stepanovich)
1886-1921 .... **TCLC 60**
See Gumilyov, Nikolay Stepanovich
See also CA 165; DLB 295

Gumilyov, Nikolay Stepanovich
See Gumilev, Nikolai (Stepanovich)
See also EWL 3

Gump, P. Q.
See Card, Orson Scott

Gunesekera, Romesh 1954- .... **CLC 91**
See also BRWS 10; CA 159; CANR 140; CN 6, 7; DLB 267

Gunn, Bill .... **CLC 5**
See Gunn, William Harrison
See also DLB 38

Gunn, Thom(son William)
1929-2004 . **CLC 3, 6, 18, 32, 81; PC 26**
See also BRWS 4; CA 17-20R; 227; CANR 9, 33, 116; CDBLB 1960 to Present; CP 1, 2, 3, 4, 5, 6, 7; DAM POET; DLB 27; INT CANR-33; MTCW 1; PFS 9; RGEL 2

Gunn, William Harrison 1934(?)-1989
See Gunn, Bill
See also AITN 1; BW 1, 3; CA 13-16R; 128; CANR 12, 25, 76

Gunn Allen, Paula
See Allen, Paula Gunn

Gunnars, Kristjana 1948- .... **CLC 69**
See also CA 113; CCA 1; CP 7; CWP; DLB 60

Gunter, Erich
See Eich, Gunter

Gurdjieff, G(eorgei) I(vanovich)
1877(?)-1949 .... **TCLC 71**
See also CA 157

Gurganus, Allan 1947- .... **CLC 70**
See also BEST 90:1; CA 135; CANR 114; CN 6, 7; CPW; CSW; DAM POP; GLL 1

Gurney, A. R.
See Gurney, A(lbert) R(amsdell), Jr.
See also DLB 266

Gurney, A(lbert) R(amsdell), Jr.
1930- .... **CLC 32, 50, 54**
See Gurney, A. R.
See also AMWS 5; CA 77-80; CAD; CANR 32, 64, 121; CD 5, 6; DAM DRAM; EWL 3

Gurney, Ivor (Bertie) 1890-1937 ... **TCLC 33**
See also BRW 6; CA 167; DLBY 2002; PAB; RGEL 2

Gurney, Peter
See Gurney, A(lbert) R(amsdell), Jr.

Guro, Elena (Genrikhovna)
1877-1913 .... **TCLC 56**
See also DLB 295

Gustafson, James M(oody) 1925- ... **CLC 100**
See also CA 25-28R; CANR 37

Gustafson, Ralph (Barker)
1909-1995 .... **CLC 36**
See also CA 21-24R; CANR 8, 45, 84; CP 1, 2, 3, 4; DLB 88; RGEL 2

Gut, Gom
See Simenon, Georges (Jacques Christian)

Guterson, David 1956- .... **CLC 91**
See also CA 132; CANR 73, 126; CN 7; DLB 292; MTCW 2; MTFW 2005; NFS 13

Guthrie, A(lfred) B(ertram), Jr.
1901-1991 .... **CLC 23**
See also CA 57-60; 134; CANR 24; CN 1, 2, 3; DLB 6, 212; MAL 5; SATA 62; SATA-Obit 67; TCWW 1, 2

Guthrie, Isobel
See Grieve, C(hristopher) M(urray)

Guthrie, Woodrow Wilson 1912-1967
See Guthrie, Woody
See also CA 113; 93-96

Guthrie, Woody .... **CLC 35**
See Guthrie, Woodrow Wilson
See also DLB 303; LAIT 3

Gutierrez Najera, Manuel
1859-1895 .... **HLCS 2; NCLC 133**
See also DLB 290; LAW

Guy, Rosa (Cuthbert) 1925- .... **CLC 26**
See also AAYA 4, 37; BW 2; CA 17-20R; CANR 14, 34, 83; CLR 13; DLB 33; DNFS 1; JRDA; MAICYA 1, 2; SATA 14, 62, 122; YAW

Gwendolyn
See Bennett, (Enoch) Arnold

H. D. .... **CLC 3, 8, 14, 31, 34, 73; PC 5**
See Doolittle, Hilda
See also FL 1:5

H. de V.
See Buchan, John

Haavikko, Paavo Juhani 1931- .. **CLC 18, 34**
See also CA 106; CWW 2; EWL 3

Habbema, Koos
See Heijermans, Herman

Habermas, Juergen 1929- .... **CLC 104**
See also CA 109; CANR 85; DLB 242

Habermas, Jurgen
See Habermas, Juergen

Hacker, Marilyn 1942- ...... **CLC 5, 9, 23, 72, 91; PC 47**
See also CA 77-80; CANR 68, 129; CP 3, 4, 5, 6, 7; CWP; DAM POET; DLB 120, 282; FW; GLL 2; MAL 5; PFS 19

Hadewijch of Antwerp fl. 1250- ... **CMLC 61**
See also RGWL 3

Hadrian 76-138 .... **CMLC 52**

Haeckel, Ernst Heinrich (Philipp August)
1834-1919 .... **TCLC 83**
See also CA 157

Hafiz c. 1326-1389(?) .... **CMLC 34**
See also RGWL 2, 3; WLIT 6

Hagedorn, Jessica T(arahata)
1949- .... **CLC 185**
See also CA 139; CANR 69; CWP; DLB 312; RGAL 4

Haggard, H(enry) Rider
1856-1925 .... **TCLC 11**
See also BRWS 3; BYA 4, 5; CA 108; 148; CANR 112; DLB 70, 156, 174, 178; FANT; LMFS 1; MTCW 2; RGEL 2; RHW; SATA 16; SCFW 1, 2; SFW 4; SUFW 1; WLIT 4

Hagiosy, L.
See Larbaud, Valery (Nicolas)

Hagiwara, Sakutaro 1886-1942 .... **PC 18; TCLC 60**
See Hagiwara Sakutaro
See also CA 154; RGWL 3

Hagiwara Sakutaro
See Hagiwara, Sakutaro
See also EWL 3

Haig, Fenil
See Ford, Ford Madox

Haig-Brown, Roderick (Langmere)
1908-1976 .... **CLC 21**
See also CA 5-8R; 69-72; CANR 4, 38, 83; CLR 31; CWRI 5; DLB 88; MAICYA 1, 2; SATA 12; TCWW 2

Haight, Rip
See Carpenter, John (Howard)

Hailey, Arthur 1920-2004 .... **CLC 5**
See also AITN 2; BEST 90:3; BPFB 2; CA 1-4R; 233; CANR 2, 36, 75; CCA 1; CN 1, 2, 3, 4, 5, 6, 7; CPW; DAM NOV, POP; DLB 88; DLBY 1982; MTCW 1, 2; MTFW 2005

Hailey, Elizabeth Forsythe 1938- ..... **CLC 40**
See also CA 93-96, 188; CAAE 188; CAAS 1; CANR 15, 48; INT CANR-15

Haines, John (Meade) 1924- .... **CLC 58**
See also AMWS 12; CA 17-20R; CANR 13, 34; CP 1, 2, 3, 4; CSW; DLB 5, 212; TCLE 1:1

Hakluyt, Richard 1552-1616 .... **LC 31**
See also DLB 136; RGEL 2

Haldeman, Joe (William) 1943- .... **CLC 61**
See Graham, Robert
See also AAYA 38; CA 53-56, 179; CAAE 179; CAAS 25; CANR 6, 70, 72, 130; DLB 8; INT CANR-6; SCFW 2; SFW 4

Hale, Janet Campbell 1947- .... **NNAL**
See also CA 49-52; CANR 45, 75; DAM MULT; DLB 175; MTCW 2; MTFW 2005

Hale, Sarah Josepha (Buell)
1788-1879 .... **NCLC 75**
See also DLB 1, 42, 73, 243

Halevy, Elie 1870-1937 .... **TCLC 104**

Haley, Alex(ander Murray Palmer)
1921-1992 .... **BLC 2; CLC 8, 12, 76; TCLC 147**
See also AAYA 26; BPFB 2; BW 2, 3; CA 77-80; 136; CANR 61; CDALBS; CPW; CSW; DA; DA3; DAB; DAC; DAM MST, MULT, POP; DLB 38; LAIT 5; MTCW 1, 2; NFS 9

Haliburton, Thomas Chandler
1796-1865 .... **NCLC 15, 149**
See also DLB 11, 99; RGEL 2; RGSF 2

Hall, Donald (Andrew, Jr.) 1928- ...... **CLC 1, 13, 37, 59, 151**
See also AAYA 63; CA 5-8R; CAAS 7; CANR 2, 44, 64, 106, 133; CP 1, 2, 3, 4, 5, 6, 7; DAM POET; DLB 5; MAL 5; MTCW 2; MTFW 2005; RGAL 4; SATA 23, 97

Hall, Frederic Sauser
See Sauser-Hall, Frederic

Hall, James
See Kuttner, Henry

Hall, James Norman 1887-1951 ..... **TCLC 23**
See also CA 123; 173; LAIT 1; RHW 1; SATA 21

Hall, Joseph 1574-1656 .... **LC 91**
See also DLB 121, 151; RGEL 2

Harrison, Elizabeth (Allen) Cavanna
1909-2001
See Cavanna, Betty
See also CA 9-12R; 200; CANR 6, 27, 85, 104, 121; MAICYA 2; SATA 142; YAW

Harrison, Harry (Max) 1925- .... **CLC 42**
See also CA 1-4R; CANR 5, 21, 84; DLB 8; SATA 4; SCFW 2; SFW 4

Harrison, James (Thomas) 1937- ...... **CLC 6, 14, 33, 66, 143; SSC 19**
See Harrison, Jim
See also CA 13-16R; CANR 8, 51, 79, 142; DLBY 1982; INT CANR-8

Harrison, Jim
See Harrison, James (Thomas)
See also AMWS 8; CN 5, 6; CP 1, 2, 3, 4, 5, 6, 7; RGAL 4; TCWW 2; TUS

Harrison, Kathryn 1961- .... **CLC 70, 151**
See also CA 144; CANR 68, 122

Harrison, Tony 1937- .... **CLC 43, 129**
See also BRWS 5; CA 65-68; CANR 44, 98; CBD; CD 5, 6; CP 2, 3, 4, 5, 6, 7; DLB 40, 245; MTCW 1; RGEL 2

Harriss, Will(ard Irvin) 1922- .... **CLC 34**
See also CA 111

Hart, Ellis
See Ellison, Harlan (Jay)

Hart, Josephine 1942(?)- .... **CLC 70**
See also CA 138; CANR 70; CPW; DAM POP

Hart, Moss 1904-1961 .... **CLC 66**
See also CA 109; 89-92; CANR 84; DAM DRAM; DFS 1; DLB 7, 266; RGAL 4

Harte, (Francis) Bret(t)
1836(?)-1902 ... **SSC 8, 59; TCLC 1, 25; WLC**
See also AMWS 2; CA 104; 140; CANR 80; CDALB 1865-1917; DA; DA3; DAC; DAM MST; DLB 12, 64, 74, 79, 186; EXPS; LAIT 2; RGAL 4; RGSF 2; SATA 26; SSFS 3; TUS

Hartley, L(eslie) P(oles) 1895-1972 ... **CLC 2, 22**
See also BRWS 7; CA 45-48; 37-40R; CANR 33; CN 1; DLB 15, 139; EWL 3; HGG; MTCW 1, 2; MTFW 2005; RGEL 2; RGSF 2; SUFW 1

Hartman, Geoffrey H. 1929- .... **CLC 27**
See also CA 117; 125; CANR 79; DLB 67

Hartmann, Sadakichi 1869-1944 ... **TCLC 73**
See also CA 157; DLB 54

Hartmann von Aue c. 1170-c. 1210 .... **CMLC 15**
See also CDWLB 2; DLB 138; RGWL 2, 3

Hartog, Jan de
See de Hartog, Jan

Haruf, Kent 1943- .... **CLC 34**
See also AAYA 44; CA 149; CANR 91, 131

Harvey, Caroline
See Trollope, Joanna

Harvey, Gabriel 1550(?)-1631 .... **LC 88**
See also DLB 167, 213, 281

Harwood, Ronald 1934- .... **CLC 32**
See also CA 1-4R; CANR 4, 55; CBD; CD 5, 6; DAM DRAM, MST; DLB 13

Hasegawa Tatsunosuke
See Futabatei, Shimei

Hasek, Jaroslav (Matej Frantisek)
1883-1923 .... **SSC 69; TCLC 4**
See also CA 104; 129; CDWLB 4; DLB 215; EW 9; EWL 3; MTCW 1, 2; RGSF 2; RGWL 2, 3

Hass, Robert 1941- ... **CLC 18, 39, 99; PC 16**
See also AMWS 6; CA 111; CANR 30, 50, 71; CP 3, 4, 5, 6, 7; DLB 105, 206; EWL 3; MAL 5; MTFW 2005; RGAL 4; SATA 94; TCLE 1:1

Hastings, Hudson
See Kuttner, Henry

Hastings, Selina .... **CLC 44**

Hathorne, John 1641-1717 .... **LC 38**

Hatteras, Amelia
See Mencken, H(enry) L(ouis)

Hatteras, Owen .... **TCLC 18**
See Mencken, H(enry) L(ouis); Nathan, George Jean

Hauptmann, Gerhart (Johann Robert)
1862-1946 .... **SSC 37; TCLC 4**
See also CA 104; 153; CDWLB 2; DAM DRAM; DLB 66, 118; EW 8; EWL 3; RGSF 2; RGWL 2, 3; TWA

Havel, Vaclav 1936- ..... **CLC 25, 58, 65, 123; DC 6**
See also CA 104; CANR 36, 63, 124; CD-WLB 4; CWW 2; DA3; DAM DRAM; DFS 10; DLB 232; EWL 3; LMFS 2; MTCW 1, 2; MTFW 2005; RGWL 3

Haviaras, Stratis .... **CLC 33**
See Chaviaras, Strates

Hawes, Stephen 1475(?)-1529(?) .... **LC 17**
See also DLB 132; RGEL 2

Hawkes, John (Clendennin Burne, Jr.)
1925-1998 .. **CLC 1, 2, 3, 4, 7, 9, 14, 15, 27, 49**
See also BPFB 2; CA 1-4R; 167; CANR 2, 47, 64; CN 1, 2, 3, 4, 5, 6; DLB 2, 7, 227; DLBY 1980, 1998; EWL 3; MAL 5; MTCW 1, 2; MTFW 2005; RGAL 4

Hawking, S. W.
See Hawking, Stephen W(illiam)

Hawking, Stephen W(illiam) 1942- . **CLC 63, 105**
See also AAYA 13; BEST 89:1; CA 126; 129; CANR 48, 115; CPW; DA3; MTCW 2; MTFW 2005

Hawkins, Anthony Hope
See Hope, Anthony

Hawthorne, Julian 1846-1934 .... **TCLC 25**
See also CA 165; HGG

Hawthorne, Nathaniel 1804-1864 ... **NCLC 2, 10, 17, 23, 39, 79, 95, 158; SSC 3, 29, 39, 89; WLC**
See also AAYA 18; AMW; AMWC 1; AMWR 1; BPFB 2; BYA 3; CDALB 1640-1865; CLR 103; DA; DA3; DAB; DAC; DAM MST, NOV; DLB 1, 74, 183, 223, 269; EXPN; EXPS; GL 2; HGG; LAIT 1; NFS 1, 20; RGAL 4; RGSF 2; SSFS 1, 7, 11, 15; SUFW 1; TUS; WCH; YABC 2

Hawthorne, Sophia Peabody
1809-1871 .... **NCLC 150**
See also DLB 183, 239

Haxton, Josephine Ayres 1921-
See Douglas, Ellen
See also CA 115; CANR 41, 83

Hayaseca y Eizaguirre, Jorge
See Echegaray (y Eizaguirre), Jose (Maria Waldo)

Hayashi, Fumiko 1904-1951 .... **TCLC 27**
See Hayashi Fumiko
See also CA 161

Hayashi Fumiko
See Hayashi, Fumiko
See also DLB 180; EWL 3

Haycraft, Anna (Margaret) 1932-2005
See Ellis, Alice Thomas
See also CA 122; 237; CANR 90, 141; MTCW 2; MTFW 2005

Hayden, Robert E(arl) 1913-1980 ..... **BLC 2; CLC 5, 9, 14, 37; PC 6**
See also AFAW 1, 2; AMWS 2; BW 1, 3; CA 69-72; 97-100; CABS 2; CANR 24, 75, 82; CDALB 1941-1968; CP 1, 2, 3; DA; DAC; DAM MST, MULT, POET; DLB 5, 76; EWL 3; EXPP; MAL 5; MTCW 1, 2; PFS 1; RGAL 4; SATA 19; SATA-Obit 26; WP

Haydon, Benjamin Robert
1786-1846 .... **NCLC 146**
See also DLB 110

Hayek, F(riedrich) A(ugust von)
1899-1992 .... **TCLC 109**
See also CA 93-96; 137; CANR 20; MTCW 1, 2

Hayford, J(oseph) E(phraim) Casely
See Casely-Hayford, J(oseph) E(phraim)

Hayman, Ronald 1932- .... **CLC 44**
See also CA 25-28R; CANR 18, 50, 88; CD 5, 6; DLB 155

Hayne, Paul Hamilton 1830-1886 . **NCLC 94**
See also DLB 3, 64, 79, 248; RGAL 4

Hays, Mary 1760-1843 .... **NCLC 114**
See also DLB 142, 158; RGEL 2

Haywood, Eliza (Fowler)
1693(?)-1756 .... **LC 1, 44**
See also DLB 39; RGEL 2

Hazlitt, William 1778-1830 ...... **NCLC 29, 82**
See also BRW 4; DLB 110, 158; RGEL 2; TEA

Hazzard, Shirley 1931- .... **CLC 18, 218**
See also CA 9-12R; CANR 4, 70, 127; CN 1, 2, 3, 4, 5, 6, 7; DLB 289; DLBY 1982; MTCW 1

Head, Bessie 1937-1986 ...... **BLC 2; CLC 25, 67; SSC 52**
See also AFW; BW 2, 3; CA 29-32R; 119; CANR 25, 82; CDWLB 3; CN 1, 2, 3, 4; DA3; DAM MULT; DLB 117, 225; EWL 3; EXPS; FL 1:6; FW; MTCW 1, 2; MTFW 2005; RGSF 2; SSFS 5, 13; WLIT 2; WWE 1

Headon, (Nicky) Topper 1956(?)- ..... **CLC 30**

Heaney, Seamus (Justin) 1939- ..... **CLC 5, 7, 14, 25, 37, 74, 91, 171; PC 18; WLCS**
See also AAYA 61; BRWR 1; BRWS 2; CA 85-88; CANR 25, 48, 75, 91, 128; CD-BLB 1960 to Present; CP 1, 2, 3, 4, 5, 6, 7; DA3; DAB; DAM POET; DLB 40; DLBY 1995; EWL 3; EXPP; MTCW 1, 2; MTFW 2005; PAB; PFS 2, 5, 8, 17; RGEL 2; TEA; WLIT 4

Hearn, (Patricio) Lafcadio (Tessima Carlos)
1850-1904 .... **TCLC 9**
See also CA 105; 166; DLB 12, 78, 189; HGG; MAL 5; RGAL 4

Hearne, Samuel 1745-1792 .... **LC 95**
See also DLB 99

Hearne, Vicki 1946-2001 .... **CLC 56**
See also CA 139; 201

Hearon, Shelby 1931- .... **CLC 63**
See also AITN 2; AMWS 8; CA 25-28R; CANR 18, 48, 103, 146; CSW

Heat-Moon, William Least .... **CLC 29**
See Trogdon, William (Lewis)
See also AAYA 9

Hebbel, Friedrich 1813-1863 . **DC 21; NCLC 43**
See also CDWLB 2; DAM DRAM; DLB 129; EW 6; RGWL 2, 3

Hebert, Anne 1916-2000 .... **CLC 4, 13, 29**
See also CA 85-88; 187; CANR 69, 126; CCA 1; CWP; CWW 2; DA3; DAC; DAM MST, POET; DLB 68; EWL 3; GFL 1789 to the Present; MTCW 1, 2; MTFW 2005; PFS 20

Hecht, Anthony (Evan) 1923-2004 .... **CLC 8, 13, 19**
See also AMWS 10; CA 9-12R; 232; CANR 6, 108; CP 1, 2, 3, 4, 5, 6, 7; DAM POET; DLB 5, 169; PFS 6; WP

Hecht, Ben 1894-1964 ..... **CLC 8; TCLC 101**
See also CA 85-88; DFS 9; DLB 7, 9, 25, 26, 28, 86; FANT; IDFW 3, 4; RGAL 4

Hedayat, Sadeq 1903-1951 .... **TCLC 21**
See also CA 120; EWL 3; RGSF 2

Hewes, Cady
See De Voto, Bernard (Augustine)

Heyen, William 1940- .... **CLC 13, 18**
See also CA 33-36R; 220; CAAE 220;
CAAS 9; CANR 98; CP 3, 4, 5, 6, 7; DLB
5

Heyerdahl, Thor 1914-2002 .... **CLC 26**
See also CA 5-8R; 207; CANR 5, 22, 66,
73; LAIT 4; MTCW 1, 2; MTFW 2005;
SATA 2, 52

Heym, Georg (Theodor Franz Arthur)
1887-1912 .... **TCLC 9**
See also CA 106; 181

Heym, Stefan 1913-2001 .... **CLC 41**
See also CA 9-12R; 203; CANR 4; CWW
2; DLB 69; EWL 3

Heyse, Paul (Johann Ludwig von)
1830-1914 .... **TCLC 8**
See also CA 104; 209; DLB 129

Heyward, (Edwin) DuBose
1885-1940 .... **HR 1:2; TCLC 59**
See also CA 108; 157; DLB 7, 9, 45, 249;
MAL 5; SATA 21

Heywood, John 1497(?)-1580(?) .... **LC 65**
See also DLB 136; RGEL 2

Heywood, Thomas 1573(?)-1641 .... **LC 111**
See also DAM DRAM; DLB 62; LMFS 1;
RGEL 2; TEA

Hibbert, Eleanor Alice Burford
1906-1993 .... **CLC 7**
See Holt, Victoria
See also BEST 90:4; CA 17-20R; 140;
CANR 9, 28, 59; CMW 4; CPW; DAM
POP; MTCW 2; MTFW 2005; RHW;
SATA 2; SATA-Obit 74

Hichens, Robert (Smythe)
1864-1950 .... **TCLC 64**
See also CA 162; DLB 153; HGG; RHW;
SUFW

Higgins, Aidan 1927- .... **SSC 68**
See also CA 9-12R; CANR 70, 115; CN 1,
2, 3, 4, 5, 6, 7; DLB 14

Higgins, George V(incent)
1939-1999 .... **CLC 4, 7, 10, 18**
See also BPFB 2; CA 77-80; 186; CAAS 5;
CANR 17, 51, 89, 96; CMW 4; CN 2, 3,
4, 5, 6; DLB 2; DLBY 1981, 1998; INT
CANR-17; MSW; MTCW 1

Higginson, Thomas Wentworth
1823-1911 .... **TCLC 36**
See also CA 162; DLB 1, 64, 243

Higgonet, Margaret ed. .... **CLC 65**

Highet, Helen
See MacInnes, Helen (Clark)

Highsmith, (Mary) Patricia
1921-1995 .... **CLC 2, 4, 14, 42, 102**
See Morgan, Claire
See also AAYA 48; BRWS 5; CA 1-4R; 147;
CANR 1, 20, 48, 62, 108; CMW 4; CN 1,
2, 3, 4, 5; CPW; DA3; DAM NOV, POP;
DLB 306; MSW; MTCW 1, 2; MTFW
2005

Highwater, Jamake (Mamake)
1942(?)-2001 .... **CLC 12**
See also AAYA 7; BPFB 2; BYA 4; CA 65-
68; 199; CAAS 7; CANR 10, 34, 84; CLR
17; CWRI 5; DLB 52; DLBY 1985;
JRDA; MAICYA 1, 2; SATA 32, 69;
SATA-Brief 30

Highway, Tomson 1951- ...... **CLC 92; NNAL**
See also CA 151; CANR 75; CCA 1; CD 5,
6; CN 7; DAC; DAM MULT; DFS 2;
MTCW 2

Hijuelos, Oscar 1951- .... **CLC 65; HLC 1**
See also AAYA 25; AMWS 8; BEST 90:1;
CA 123; CANR 50, 75, 125; CPW; DA3;
DAM MULT, POP; DLB 145; HW 1, 2;
LLW; MAL 5; MTCW 2; MTFW 2005;
NFS 17; RGAL 4; WLIT 1

Hikmet, Nazim 1902-1963 .... **CLC 40**
See Nizami of Ganja
See also CA 141; 93-96; EWL 3; WLIT 6

Hildegard von Bingen 1098-1179 . **CMLC 20**
See also DLB 148

Hildesheimer, Wolfgang 1916-1991 .. **CLC 49**
See also CA 101; 135; DLB 69, 124; EWL
3

Hill, Geoffrey (William) 1932- ...... **CLC 5, 8,
18, 45**
See also BRWS 5; CA 81-84; CANR 21,
89; CDBLB 1960 to Present; CP 1, 2, 3,
4, 5, 6, 7; DAM POET; DLB 40; EWL 3;
MTCW 1; RGEL 2

Hill, George Roy 1921-2002 .... **CLC 26**
See also CA 110; 122; 213

Hill, John
See Koontz, Dean R.

Hill, Susan (Elizabeth) 1942- ...... **CLC 4, 113**
See also CA 33-36R; CANR 29, 69, 129;
CN 2, 3, 4, 5, 6, 7; DAB; DAM MST,
NOV; DLB 14, 139; HGG; MTCW 1;
RHW

Hillard, Asa G. III .... **CLC 70**

Hillerman, Tony 1925- .... **CLC 62, 170**
See also AAYA 40; BEST 89:1; BPFB 2;
CA 29-32R; CANR 21, 42, 65, 97, 134;
CMW 4; CPW; DA3; DAM POP; DLB
206, 306; MAL 5; MSW; MTCW 2;
MTFW 2005; RGAL 4; SATA 6; TCWW
2; YAW

Hillesum, Etty 1914-1943 .... **TCLC 49**
See also CA 137

Hilliard, Noel (Harvey) 1929-1996 ... **CLC 15**
See also CA 9-12R; CANR 7, 69; CN 1, 2,
3, 4, 5, 6

Hillis, Rick 1956- .... **CLC 66**
See also CA 134

Hilton, James 1900-1954 .... **TCLC 21**
See also CA 108; 169; DLB 34, 77; FANT;
SATA 34

Hilton, Walter (?)-1396 .... **CMLC 58**
See also DLB 146; RGEL 2

Himes, Chester (Bomar) 1909-1984 .. **BLC 2;
CLC 2, 4, 7, 18, 58, 108; TCLC 139**
See also AFAW 2; BPFB 2; BW 2; CA 25-
28R; 114; CANR 22, 89; CMW 4; CN 1,
2, 3; DAM MULT; DLB 2, 76, 143, 226;
EWL 3; MAL 5; MSW; MTCW 1, 2;
MTFW 2005; RGAL 4

Himmelfarb, Gertrude 1922- .... **CLC 202**
See also CA 49-52; CANR 28, 66, 102

Hinde, Thomas .... **CLC 6, 11**
See Chitty, Thomas Willes
See also CN 1, 2, 3, 4, 5, 6; EWL 3

Hine, (William) Daryl 1936- .... **CLC 15**
See also CA 1-4R; CAAS 15; CANR 1, 20;
CP 1, 2, 3, 4, 5, 6, 7; DLB 60

Hinkson, Katharine Tynan
See Tynan, Katharine

Hinojosa(-Smith), Rolando (R.)
1929- .... **HLC 1**
See Hinojosa-Smith, Rolando
See also CA 131; CAAS 16; CANR 62;
DAM MULT; DLB 82; HW 1, 2; LLW;
MTCW 2; MTFW 2005; RGAL 4

Hinton, S(usan) E(loise) 1950- .. **CLC 30, 111**
See also AAYA 2, 33; BPFB 2; BYA 2, 3;
CA 81-84; CANR 32, 62, 92, 133;
CDALBS; CLR 3, 23; CPW; DA; DA3;
DAB; DAC; DAM MST, NOV; JRDA;
LAIT 5; MAICYA 1, 2; MTCW 1, 2;
MTFW 2005 !**; NFS 5, 9, 15, 16; SATA
19, 58, 115, 160; WYA; YAW

Hippius, Zinaida (Nikolaevna) .... **TCLC 9**
See Gippius, Zinaida (Nikolaevna)
See also DLB 295; EWL 3

Hiraoka, Kimitake 1925-1970
See Mishima, Yukio
See also CA 97-100; 29-32R; DA3; DAM
DRAM; GLL 1; MTCW 1, 2

Hirsch, E(ric) D(onald), Jr. 1928- .... **CLC 79**
See also CA 25-28R; CANR 27, 51; DLB
67; INT CANR-27; MTCW 1

Hirsch, Edward 1950- .... **CLC 31, 50**
See also CA 104; CANR 20, 42, 102; CP 7;
DLB 120; PFS 22

Hitchcock, Alfred (Joseph)
1899-1980 .... **CLC 16**
See also AAYA 22; CA 159; 97-100; SATA
27; SATA-Obit 24

Hitchens, Christopher (Eric)
1949- .... **CLC 157**
See also CA 152; CANR 89

Hitler, Adolf 1889-1945 .... **TCLC 53**
See also CA 117; 147

Hoagland, Edward (Morley) 1932- .. **CLC 28**
See also ANW; CA 1-4R; CANR 2, 31, 57,
107; CN 1, 2, 3, 4, 5, 6, 7; DLB 6; SATA
51; TCWW 2

Hoban, Russell (Conwell) 1925- ... **CLC 7, 25**
See also BPFB 2; CA 5-8R; CANR 23, 37,
66, 114, 138; CLR 3, 69; CN 4, 5, 6, 7;
CWRI 5; DAM NOV; DLB 52; FANT;
MAICYA 1, 2; MTCW 1, 2; MTFW 2005;
SATA 1, 40, 78, 136; SFW 4; SUFW 2;
TCLE 1:1

Hobbes, Thomas 1588-1679 .... **LC 36**
See also DLB 151, 252, 281; RGEL 2

Hobbs, Perry
See Blackmur, R(ichard) P(almer)

Hobson, Laura Z(ametkin)
1900-1986 .... **CLC 7, 25**
See also BPFB 2; CA 17-20R; 118; CANR
55; CN 1, 2, 3, 4; DLB 28; SATA 52

Hoccleve, Thomas c. 1368-c. 1437 ...... **LC 75**
See also DLB 146; RGEL 2

Hoch, Edward D(entinger) 1930-
See Queen, Ellery
See also CA 29-32R; CANR 11, 27, 51, 97;
CMW 4; DLB 306; SFW 4

Hochhuth, Rolf 1931- .... **CLC 4, 11, 18**
See also CA 5-8R; CANR 33, 75, 136;
CWW 2; DAM DRAM; DLB 124; EWL
3; MTCW 1, 2; MTFW 2005

Hochman, Sandra 1936- .... **CLC 3, 8**
See also CA 5-8R; CP 1, 2, 3, 4; DLB 5

Hochwaelder, Fritz 1911-1986 .... **CLC 36**
See Hochwalder, Fritz
See also CA 29-32R; 120; CANR 42; DAM
DRAM; MTCW 1; RGWL 3

Hochwalder, Fritz
See Hochwaelder, Fritz
See also EWL 3; RGWL 2

Hocking, Mary (Eunice) 1921- .... **CLC 13**
See also CA 101; CANR 18, 40

Hodgins, Jack 1938- .... **CLC 23**
See also CA 93-96; CN 4, 5, 6, 7; DLB 60

Hodgson, William Hope
1877(?)-1918 .... **TCLC 13**
See also CA 111; 164; CMW 4; DLB 70,
153, 156, 178; HGG; MTCW 2; SFW 4;
SUFW 1

Hoeg, Peter 1957- .... **CLC 95, 156**
See also CA 151; CANR 75; CMW 4; DA3;
DLB 214; EWL 3; MTCW 2; MTFW
2005; NFS 17; RGWL 3; SSFS 18

Hoffman, Alice 1952- .... **CLC 51**
See also AAYA 37; AMWS 10; CA 77-80;
CANR 34, 66, 100, 138; CN 4, 5, 6, 7;
CPW; DAM NOV; DLB 292; MAL 5;
MTCW 1, 2; MTFW 2005; TCLE 1:1

Hoffman, Daniel (Gerard) 1923- . **CLC 6, 13,
23**
See also CA 1-4R; CANR 4, 142; CP 1, 2,
3, 4, 5, 6, 7; DLB 5; TCLE 1:1

Hunter, Robert (?)-1734 .... **LC 7**

Hurston, Zora Neale 1891-1960 .... **BLC 2;
CLC 7, 30, 61; DC 12; HR 1:2; SSC 4,
80; TCLC 121, 131; WLCS**
  See also AAYA 15; AFAW 1, 2; AMWS 6;
  BW 1, 3; BYA 12; CA 85-88; CANR 61;
  CDALBS; DA; DA3; DAC; DAM MST,
  MULT, NOV; DFS 6; DLB 51, 86; EWL
  3; EXPN; EXPS; FL 1:6; FW; LAIT 3;
  LATS 1:1; LMFS 2; MAL 5; MAWW;
  MTCW 1, 2; MTFW 2005; NFS 3; RGAL
  4; RGSF 2; SSFS 1, 6, 11, 19, 21; TUS;
  YAW

Husserl, E. G.
  See Husserl, Edmund (Gustav Albrecht)

Husserl, Edmund (Gustav Albrecht)
  1859-1938 .... **TCLC 100**
  See also CA 116; 133; DLB 296

Huston, John (Marcellus)
  1906-1987 .... **CLC 20**
  See also CA 73-76; 123; CANR 34; DLB
  26

Hustvedt, Siri 1955- .... **CLC 76**
  See also CA 137

Hutten, Ulrich von 1488-1523 .... **LC 16**
  See also DLB 179

Huxley, Aldous (Leonard)
  1894-1963 .... **CLC 1, 3, 4, 5, 8, 11, 18,
  35, 79; SSC 39; WLC**
  See also AAYA 11; BPFB 2; BRW 7; CA
  85-88; CANR 44, 99; CDBLB 1914-1945;
  DA; DA3; DAB; DAC; DAM MST, NOV;
  DLB 36, 100, 162, 195, 255; EWL 3;
  EXPN; LAIT 5; LMFS 2; MTCW 1, 2;
  MTFW 2005; NFS 6; RGEL 2; SATA 63;
  SCFW 1, 2; SFW 4; TEA; YAW

Huxley, T(homas) H(enry)
  1825-1895 .... **NCLC 67**
  See also DLB 57; TEA

Huygens, Constantijn 1596-1687 .... **LC 114**
  See also RGWL 2, 3

Huysmans, Joris-Karl 1848-1907 ... **TCLC 7,
  69**
  See also CA 104; 165; DLB 123; EW 7;
  GFL 1789 to the Present; LMFS 2; RGWL
  2, 3

Hwang, David Henry 1957- .... **CLC 55, 196;
  DC 4, 23**
  See also CA 127; 132; CAD; CANR 76,
  124; CD 5, 6; DA3; DAM DRAM; DFS
  11, 18; DLB 212, 228, 312; INT CA-132;
  MAL 5; MTCW 2; MTFW 2005; RGAL
  4

Hyde, Anthony 1946- .... **CLC 42**
  See Chase, Nicholas
  See also CA 136; CCA 1

Hyde, Margaret O(ldroyd) 1917- ..... **CLC 21**
  See also CA 1-4R; CANR 1, 36, 137; CLR
  23; JRDA; MAICYA 1, 2; SAAS 8; SATA
  1, 42, 76, 139

Hynes, James 1956(?)- .... **CLC 65**
  See also CA 164; CANR 105

Hypatia c. 370-415 .... **CMLC 35**

Ian, Janis 1951- .... **CLC 21**
  See also CA 105; 187

Ibanez, Vicente Blasco
  See Blasco Ibanez, Vicente
  See also DLB 322

Ibarbourou, Juana de
  1895(?)-1979 .... **HLCS 2**
  See also DLB 290; HW 1; LAW

Ibarguengoitia, Jorge 1928-1983 ..... **CLC 37;
  TCLC 148**
  See also CA 124; 113; EWL 3; HW 1

Ibn Battuta, Abu Abdalla
  1304-1368(?) .... **CMLC 57**
  See also WLIT 2

Ibn Hazm 994-1064 .... **CMLC 64**

Ibsen, Henrik (Johan) 1828-1906 .... **DC 2;
  TCLC 2, 8, 16, 37, 52; WLC**
  See also AAYA 46; CA 104; 141; DA; DA3;
  DAB; DAC; DAM DRAM, MST; DFS 1,
  6, 8, 10, 11, 15, 16; EW 7; LAIT 2; LATS
  1:1; MTFW 2005; RGWL 2, 3

Ibuse, Masuji 1898-1993 .... **CLC 22**
  See Ibuse Masuji
  See also CA 127; 141; MJW; RGWL 3

Ibuse Masuji
  See Ibuse, Masuji
  See also CWW 2; DLB 180; EWL 3

Ichikawa, Kon 1915- .... **CLC 20**
  See also CA 121

Ichiyo, Higuchi 1872-1896 .... **NCLC 49**
  See also MJW

Idle, Eric 1943- .... **CLC 21**
  See Monty Python
  See also CA 116; CANR 35, 91

Idris, Yusuf 1927-1991 .... **SSC 74**
  See also AFW; EWL 3; RGSF 2, 3; RGWL
  3; WLIT 2

Ignatow, David 1914-1997 .... **CLC 4, 7, 14,
  40; PC 34**
  See also CA 9-12R; 162; CAAS 3; CANR
  31, 57, 96; CP 1, 2, 3, 4, 5, 6; DLB 5;
  EWL 3; MAL 5

Ignotus
  See Strachey, (Giles) Lytton

Ihimaera, Witi (Tame) 1944- .... **CLC 46**
  See also CA 77-80; CANR 130; CN 2, 3, 4,
  5, 6, 7; RGSF 2; SATA 148

Ilf, Ilya .... **TCLC 21**
  See Fainzilberg, Ilya Arnoldovich
  See also EWL 3

Illyes, Gyula 1902-1983 .... **PC 16**
  See also CA 114; 109; CDWLB 4; DLB
  215; EWL 3; RGWL 2, 3

Imalayen, Fatima-Zohra
  See Djebar, Assia

Immermann, Karl (Lebrecht)
  1796-1840 .... **NCLC 4, 49**
  See also DLB 133

Ince, Thomas H. 1882-1924 .... **TCLC 89**
  See also IDFW 3, 4

Inchbald, Elizabeth 1753-1821 ...... **NCLC 62**
  See also DLB 39, 89; RGEL 2

Inclan, Ramon (Maria) del Valle
  See Valle-Inclan, Ramon (Maria) del

Infante, G(uillermo) Cabrera
  See Cabrera Infante, G(uillermo)

Ingalls, Rachel (Holmes) 1940- .... **CLC 42**
  See also CA 123; 127

Ingamells, Reginald Charles
  See Ingamells, Rex

Ingamells, Rex 1913-1955 .... **TCLC 35**
  See also CA 167; DLB 260

Inge, William (Motter) 1913-1973 ..... **CLC 1,
  8, 19**
  See also CA 9-12R; CAD; CDALB 1941-
  1968; DA3; DAM DRAM; DFS 1, 3, 5,
  8; DLB 7, 249; EWL 3; MAL 5; MTCW
  1, 2; MTFW 2005; RGAL 4; TUS

Ingelow, Jean 1820-1897 .... **NCLC 39, 107**
  See also DLB 35, 163; FANT; SATA 33

Ingram, Willis J.
  See Harris, Mark

Innaurato, Albert (F.) 1948(?)- ... **CLC 21, 60**
  See also CA 115; 122; CAD; CANR 78;
  CD 5, 6; INT CA-122

Innes, Michael
  See Stewart, J(ohn) I(nnes) M(ackintosh)
  See also DLB 276; MSW

Innis, Harold Adams 1894-1952 .... **TCLC 77**
  See also CA 181; DLB 88

Insluis, Alanus de
  See Alain de Lille

Iola
  See Wells-Barnett, Ida B(ell)

Ionesco, Eugene 1912-1994 ... **CLC 1, 4, 6, 9,
  11, 15, 41, 86; DC 12; WLC**
  See also CA 9-12R; 144; CANR 55, 132;
  CWW 2; DA; DA3; DAB; DAC; DAM
  DRAM, MST; DFS 4, 9; DLB 321; EW
  13; EWL 3; GFL 1789 to the Present;
  LMFS 2; MTCW 1, 2; MTFW 2005;
  RGWL 2, 3; SATA 7; SATA-Obit 79;
  TWA

Iqbal, Muhammad 1877-1938 .... **TCLC 28**
  See also CA 215; EWL 3

Ireland, Patrick
  See O'Doherty, Brian

Irenaeus St. 130- .... **CMLC 42**

Irigaray, Luce 1930- .... **CLC 164**
  See also CA 154; CANR 121; FW

Iron, Ralph
  See Schreiner, Olive (Emilie Albertina)

Irving, John (Winslow) 1942- ... **CLC 13, 23,
  38, 112, 175**
  See also AAYA 8, 62; AMWS 6; BEST
  89:3; BPFB 2; CA 25-28R; CANR 28, 73,
  112, 133; CN 3, 4, 5, 6, 7; CPW; DA3;
  DAM NOV, POP; DLB 6, 278; DLBY
  1982; EWL 3; MAL 5; MTCW 1, 2;
  MTFW 2005; NFS 12, 14; RGAL 4; TUS

Irving, Washington 1783-1859 . **NCLC 2, 19,
  95; SSC 2, 37; WLC**
  See also AAYA 56; AMW; CDALB 1640-
  1865; CLR 97; DA; DA3; DAB; DAC;
  DAM MST; DLB 3, 11, 30, 59, 73, 74,
  183, 186, 250, 254; EXPS; GL 2; LAIT
  1; RGAL 4; RGSF 2; SSFS 1, 8, 16;
  SUFW 1; TUS; WCH; YABC 2

Irwin, P. K.
  See Page, P(atricia) K(athleen)

Isaacs, Jorge Ricardo 1837-1895 ... **NCLC 70**
  See also LAW

Isaacs, Susan 1943- .... **CLC 32**
  See also BEST 89:1; BPFB 2; CA 89-92;
  CANR 20, 41, 65, 112, 134; CPW; DA3;
  DAM POP; INT CANR-20; MTCW 1, 2;
  MTFW 2005

Isherwood, Christopher (William Bradshaw)
  1904-1986 .... **CLC 1, 9, 11, 14, 44; SSC
  56**
  See also AMWS 14; BRW 7; CA 13-16R;
  117; CANR 35, 97, 133; CN 1, 2, 3; DA3;
  DAM DRAM, NOV; DLB 15, 195; DLBY
  1986; EWL 3; IDTP; MTCW 1, 2; MTFW
  2005; RGAL 4; RGEL 2; TUS; WLIT 4

Ishiguro, Kazuo 1954- . **CLC 27, 56, 59, 110,
  219**
  See also AAYA 58; BEST 90:2; BPFB 2;
  BRWS 4; CA 120; CANR 49, 95, 133;
  CN 5, 6, 7; DA3; DAM NOV; DLB 194;
  EWL 3; MTCW 1, 2; MTFW 2005; NFS
  13; WLIT 4; WWE 1

Ishikawa, Hakuhin
  See Ishikawa, Takuboku

Ishikawa, Takuboku 1886(?)-1912 ..... **PC 10;
  TCLC 15**
  See Ishikawa Takuboku
  See also CA 113; 153; DAM POET

Iskander, Fazil (Abdulovich) 1929- .. **CLC 47**
  See Iskander, Fazil' Abdulevich
  See also CA 102; EWL 3

Iskander, Fazil' Abdulevich
  See Iskander, Fazil (Abdulovich)
  See also DLB 302

Isler, Alan (David) 1934- .... **CLC 91**
  See also CA 156; CANR 105

Ivan IV 1530-1584 .... **LC 17**

Ivanov, Vyacheslav Ivanovich
  1866-1949 .... **TCLC 33**
  See also CA 122; EWL 3

Jordan, June (Meyer)
  1936-2002 .. **BLCS; CLC 5, 11, 23, 114; PC 38**
  See also AAYA 2, 66; AFAW 1, 2; BW 2, 3; CA 33-36R; 206; CANR 25, 70, 114; CLR 10; CP 3, 4, 5, 6, 7; CWP; DAM MULT, POET; DLB 38; GLL 2; LAIT 5; MAICYA 1, 2; MTCW 1; SATA 4, 136; YAW

Jordan, Neil (Patrick) 1950- .... **CLC 110**
  See also CA 124; 130; CANR 54; CN 4, 5, 6, 7; GLL 2; INT CA-130

Jordan, Pat(rick M.) 1941- .... **CLC 37**
  See also CA 33-36R; CANR 121

Jorgensen, Ivar
  See Ellison, Harlan (Jay)

Jorgenson, Ivar
  See Silverberg, Robert

Joseph, George Ghevarughese .... **CLC 70**

Josephson, Mary
  See O'Doherty, Brian

Josephus, Flavius c. 37-100 .... **CMLC 13**
  See also AW 2; DLB 176

Josiah Allen's Wife
  See Holley, Marietta

Josipovici, Gabriel (David) 1940- ...... **CLC 6, 43, 153**
  See also CA 37-40R, 224; CAAE 224; CAAS 8; CANR 47, 84; CN 3, 4, 5, 6, 7; DLB 14, 319

Joubert, Joseph 1754-1824 .... **NCLC 9**

Jouve, Pierre Jean 1887-1976 .... **CLC 47**
  See also CA 65-68; DLB 258; EWL 3

Jovine, Francesco 1902-1950 .... **TCLC 79**
  See also DLB 264; EWL 3

Joyce, James (Augustine Aloysius)
  1882-1941 .... **DC 16; PC 22; SSC 3, 26, 44, 64; TCLC 3, 8, 16, 35, 52, 159; WLC**
  See also AAYA 42; BRW 7; BRWC 1; BRWR 1; BYA 11, 13; CA 104; 126; CD-BLB 1914-1945; DA; DA3; DAB; DAC; DAM MST, NOV, POET; DLB 10, 19, 36, 162, 247; EWL 3; EXPN; EXPS; LAIT 3; LMFS 1, 2; MTCW 1, 2; MTFW 2005; NFS 7; RGSF 2; SSFS 1, 19; TEA; WLIT 4

Jozsef, Attila 1905-1937 .... **TCLC 22**
  See also CA 116; 230; CDWLB 4; DLB 215; EWL 3

Juana Ines de la Cruz, Sor
  1651(?)-1695 ...... **HLCS 1; LC 5; PC 24**
  See also DLB 305; FW; LAW; RGWL 2, 3; WLIT 1

Juana Inez de La Cruz, Sor
  See Juana Ines de la Cruz, Sor

Judd, Cyril
  See Kornbluth, C(yril) M.; Pohl, Frederik

Juenger, Ernst 1895-1998 .... **CLC 125**
  See Junger, Ernst
  See also CA 101; 167; CANR 21, 47, 106; DLB 56

Julian of Norwich 1342(?)-1416(?) . **LC 6, 52**
  See also DLB 146; LMFS 1

Julius Caesar 100B.C.-44B.C.
  See Caesar, Julius
  See also CDWLB 1; DLB 211

Junger, Ernst
  See Juenger, Ernst
  See also CDWLB 2; EWL 3; RGWL 2, 3

Junger, Sebastian 1962- .... **CLC 109**
  See also AAYA 28; CA 165; CANR 130; MTFW 2005

Juniper, Alex
  See Hospital, Janette Turner

Junius
  See Luxemburg, Rosa

Junzaburo, Nishiwaki
  See Nishiwaki, Junzaburo
  See also EWL 3

Just, Ward (Swift) 1935- .... **CLC 4, 27**
  See also CA 25-28R; CANR 32, 87; CN 6, 7; INT CANR-32

Justice, Donald (Rodney)
  1925-2004 .... **CLC 6, 19, 102; PC 64**
  See also AMWS 7; CA 5-8R; 230; CANR 26, 54, 74, 121, 122; CP 1, 2, 3, 4, 5, 6, 7; CSW; DAM POET; DLBY 1983; EWL 3; INT CANR-26; MAL 5; MTCW 2; PFS 14; TCLE 1:1

Juvenal c. 60-c. 130 .... **CMLC 8**
  See also AW 2; CDWLB 1; DLB 211; RGWL 2, 3

Juvenis
  See Bourne, Randolph S(illiman)

K., Alice
  See Knapp, Caroline

Kabakov, Sasha .... **CLC 59**

Kabir 1398(?)-1448(?) .... **LC 109; PC 56**
  See also RGWL 2, 3

Kacew, Romain 1914-1980
  See Gary, Romain
  See also CA 108; 102

Kadare, Ismail 1936- .... **CLC 52, 190**
  See also CA 161; EWL 3; RGWL 3

Kadohata, Cynthia (Lynn)
  1956(?)- .... **CLC 59, 122**
  See also CA 140; CANR 124; SATA 155

Kafka, Franz 1883-1924 ... **SSC 5, 29, 35, 60; TCLC 2, 6, 13, 29, 47, 53, 112; WLC**
  See also AAYA 31; BPFB 2; CA 105; 126; CDWLB 2; DA; DA3; DAB; DAC; DAM MST, NOV; DLB 81; EW 9; EWL 3; EXPS; LATS 1:1; LMFS 1; MTCW 1, 2; MTFW 2005; NFS 7; RGSF 2; RGWL 2, 3; SFW 4; SSFS 3, 7, 12; TWA

Kahanovitsch, Pinkhes
  See Der Nister

Kahn, Roger 1927- .... **CLC 30**
  See also CA 25-28R; CANR 44, 69; DLB 171; SATA 37

Kain, Saul
  See Sassoon, Siegfried (Lorraine)

Kaiser, Georg 1878-1945 .... **TCLC 9**
  See also CA 106; 190; CDWLB 2; DLB 124; EWL 3; LMFS 2; RGWL 2, 3

Kaledin, Sergei .... **CLC 59**

Kaletski, Alexander 1946- .... **CLC 39**
  See also CA 118; 143

Kalidasa fl. c. 400-455 .... **CMLC 9; PC 22**
  See also RGWL 2, 3

Kallman, Chester (Simon)
  1921-1975 .... **CLC 2**
  See also CA 45-48; 53-56; CANR 3; CP 1, 2

Kaminsky, Melvin 1926-
  See Brooks, Mel
  See also CA 65-68; CANR 16; DFS 21

Kaminsky, Stuart M(elvin) 1934- ..... **CLC 59**
  See also CA 73-76; CANR 29, 53, 89; CMW 4

Kamo no Chomei 1153(?)-1216 .... **CMLC 66**
  See also DLB 203

Kamo no Nagaakira
  See Kamo no Chomei

Kandinsky, Wassily 1866-1944 .... **TCLC 92**
  See also AAYA 64; CA 118; 155

Kane, Francis
  See Robbins, Harold

Kane, Henry 1918-
  See Queen, Ellery
  See also CA 156; CMW 4

Kane, Paul
  See Simon, Paul (Frederick)

Kanin, Garson 1912-1999 .... **CLC 22**
  See also AITN 1; CA 5-8R; 177; CAD; CANR 7, 78; DLB 7; IDFW 3, 4

Kaniuk, Yoram 1930- .... **CLC 19**
  See also CA 134; DLB 299

Kant, Immanuel 1724-1804 ..... **NCLC 27, 67**
  See also DLB 94

Kantor, MacKinlay 1904-1977 .... **CLC 7**
  See also CA 61-64; 73-76; CANR 60, 63; CN 1, 2; DLB 9, 102; MAL 5; MTCW 2; RHW; TCWW 1, 2

Kanze Motokiyo
  See Zeami

Kaplan, David Michael 1946- .... **CLC 50**
  See also CA 187

Kaplan, James 1951- .... **CLC 59**
  See also CA 135; CANR 121

Karadzic, Vuk Stefanovic
  1787-1864 .... **NCLC 115**
  See also CDWLB 4; DLB 147

Karageorge, Michael
  See Anderson, Poul (William)

Karamzin, Nikolai Mikhailovich
  1766-1826 .... **NCLC 3**
  See also DLB 150; RGSF 2

Karapanou, Margarita 1946- .... **CLC 13**
  See also CA 101

Karinthy, Frigyes 1887-1938 .... **TCLC 47**
  See also CA 170; DLB 215; EWL 3

Karl, Frederick R(obert)
  1927-2004 .... **CLC 34**
  See also CA 5-8R; 226; CANR 3, 44, 143

Karr, Mary 1955- .... **CLC 188**
  See also AMWS 11; CA 151; CANR 100; MTFW 2005; NCFS 5

Kastel, Warren
  See Silverberg, Robert

Kataev, Evgeny Petrovich 1903-1942
  See Petrov, Evgeny
  See also CA 120

Kataphusin
  See Ruskin, John

Katz, Steve 1935- .... **CLC 47**
  See also CA 25-28R; CAAS 14, 64; CANR 12; CN 4, 5, 6, 7; DLBY 1983

Kauffman, Janet 1945- .... **CLC 42**
  See also CA 117; CANR 43, 84; DLB 218; DLBY 1986

Kaufman, Bob (Garnell) 1925-1986 . **CLC 49**
  See also BG 1:3; BW 1; CA 41-44R; 118; CANR 22; CP 1; DLB 16, 41

Kaufman, George S. 1889-1961 ...... **CLC 38; DC 17**
  See also CA 108; 93-96; DAM DRAM; DFS 1, 10; DLB 7; INT CA-108; MTCW 2; MTFW 2005; RGAL 4; TUS

Kaufman, Moises 1964- .... **DC 26**
  See also CA 211; DFS 22; MTFW 2005

Kaufman, Sue .... **CLC 3, 8**
  See Barondess, Sue K(aufman)

Kavafis, Konstantinos Petrou 1863-1933
  See Cavafy, C(onstantine) P(eter)
  See also CA 104

Kavan, Anna 1901-1968 .... **CLC 5, 13, 82**
  See also BRWS 7; CA 5-8R; CANR 6, 57; DLB 255; MTCW 1; RGEL 2; SFW 4

Kavanagh, Dan
  See Barnes, Julian (Patrick)

Kavanagh, Julie 1952- .... **CLC 119**
  See also CA 163

Kavanagh, Patrick (Joseph)
  1904-1967 .... **CLC 22; PC 33**
  See also BRWS 7; CA 123; 25-28R; DLB 15, 20; EWL 3; MTCW 1; RGEL 2

Keynes, John Maynard
1883-1946 .... **TCLC 64**
See also CA 114; 162, 163; DLBD 10;
MTCW 2; MTFW 2005

Khanshendel, Chiron
See Rose, Wendy

Khayyam, Omar 1048-1131 ... **CMLC 11; PC 8**
See Omar Khayyam
See also DA3; DAM POET; WLIT 6

Kherdian, David 1931- .... **CLC 6, 9**
See also AAYA 42; CA 21-24R; 192; CAAE
192; CAAS 2; CANR 39, 78; CLR 24;
JRDA; LAIT 3; MAICYA 1, 2; SATA 16,
74; SATA-Essay 125

Khlebnikov, Velimir .... **TCLC 20**
See Khlebnikov, Viktor Vladimirovich
See also DLB 295; EW 10; EWL 3; RGWL
2, 3

Khlebnikov, Viktor Vladimirovich 1885-1922
See Khlebnikov, Velimir
See also CA 117; 217

Khodasevich, Vladislav (Felitsianovich)
1886-1939 .... **TCLC 15**
See also CA 115; DLB 317; EWL 3

Kielland, Alexander Lange
1849-1906 .... **TCLC 5**
See also CA 104

Kiely, Benedict 1919- ... **CLC 23, 43; SSC 58**
See also CA 1-4R; CANR 2, 84; CN 1, 2,
3, 4, 5, 6, 7; DLB 15, 319; TCLE 1:1

Kienzle, William X(avier)
1928-2001 .... **CLC 25**
See also CA 93-96; 203; CAAS 1; CANR
9, 31, 59, 111; CMW 4; DA3; DAM POP;
INT CANR-31; MSW; MTCW 1, 2;
MTFW 2005

Kierkegaard, Soren 1813-1855 ..... **NCLC 34, 78, 125**
See also DLB 300; EW 6; LMFS 2; RGWL
3; TWA

Kieslowski, Krzysztof 1941-1996 .... **CLC 120**
See also CA 147; 151

Killens, John Oliver 1916-1987 .... **CLC 10**
See also BW 2; CA 77-80; 123; CAAS 2;
CANR 26; CN 1, 2, 3, 4; DLB 33; EWL
3

Killigrew, Anne 1660-1685 .... **LC 4, 73**
See also DLB 131

Killigrew, Thomas 1612-1683 .... **LC 57**
See also DLB 58; RGEL 2

Kim
See Simenon, Georges (Jacques Christian)

Kincaid, Jamaica 1949- ...... **BLC 2; CLC 43, 68, 137; SSC 72**
See also AAYA 13, 56; AFAW 2; AMWS 7;
BRWS 7; BW 2, 3; CA 125; CANR 47,
59, 95, 133; CDALBS; CDWLB 3; CLR
63; CN 4, 5, 6, 7; DA3; DAM MULT,
NOV; DLB 157, 227; DNFS 1; EWL 3;
EXPS; FW; LATS 1:2; LMFS 2; MAL 5;
MTCW 2; MTFW 2005; NCFS 1; NFS 3;
SSFS 5, 7; TUS; WWE 1; YAW

King, Francis (Henry) 1923- .... **CLC 8, 53, 145**
See also CA 1-4R; CANR 1, 33, 86; CN 1,
2, 3, 4, 5, 6, 7; DAM NOV; DLB 15, 139;
MTCW 1

King, Kennedy
See Brown, George Douglas

King, Martin Luther, Jr. 1929-1968 . **BLC 2; CLC 83; WLCS**
See also BW 2, 3; CA 25-28; CANR 27,
44; CAP 2; DA; DA3; DAB; DAC; DAM
MST, MULT; LAIT 5; LATS 1:2; MTCW
1, 2; MTFW 2005; SATA 14

King, Stephen 1947- .... **CLC 12, 26, 37, 61, 113; SSC 17, 55**
See also AAYA 1, 17; AMWS 5; BEST
90:1; BPFB 2; CA 61-64; CANR 1, 30,
52, 76, 119, 134; CN 7; CPW; DA3; DAM
NOV, POP; DLB 143; DLBY 1980; HGG;
JRDA; LAIT 5; MTCW 1, 2; MTFW
2005; RGAL 4; SATA 9, 55, 161; SUFW
1, 2; WYAS 1; YAW

King, Stephen Edwin
See King, Stephen

King, Steve
See King, Stephen

King, Thomas 1943- .... **CLC 89, 171; NNAL**
See also CA 144; CANR 95; CCA 1; CN 6,
7; DAC; DAM MULT; DLB 175; SATA
96

Kingman, Lee .... **CLC 17**
See Natti, (Mary) Lee
See also CWRI 5; SAAS 3; SATA 1, 67

Kingsley, Charles 1819-1875 .... **NCLC 35**
See also CLR 77; DLB 21, 32, 163, 178,
190; FANT; MAICYA 2; MAICYAS 1;
RGEL 2; WCH; YABC 2

Kingsley, Henry 1830-1876 .... **NCLC 107**
See also DLB 21, 230; RGEL 2

Kingsley, Sidney 1906-1995 .... **CLC 44**
See also CA 85-88; 147; CAD; DFS 14, 19;
DLB 7; MAL 5; RGAL 4

Kingsolver, Barbara 1955- .... **CLC 55, 81, 130, 216**
See also AAYA 15; AMWS 7; CA 129; 134;
CANR 60, 96, 133; CDALBS; CN 7;
CPW; CSW; DA3; DAM POP; DLB 206;
INT CA-134; LAIT 5; MTCW 2; MTFW
2005; NFS 5, 10, 12; RGAL 4; TCLE 1:1

Kingston, Maxine (Ting Ting) Hong
1940- .... **AAL; CLC 12, 19, 58, 121; WLCS**
See also AAYA 8, 55; AMWS 5; BPFB 2;
CA 69-72; CANR 13, 38, 74, 87, 128;
CDALBS; CN 6, 7; DA3; DAM MULT,
NOV; DLB 173, 212, 312; DLBY 1980;
EWL 3; FL 1:6; FW; INT CANR-13;
LAIT 5; MAL 5; MAWW; MTCW 1, 2;
MTFW 2005; NFS 6; RGAL 4; SATA 53;
SSFS 3; TCWW 2

Kinnell, Galway 1927- ..... **CLC 1, 2, 3, 5, 13, 29, 129; PC 26**
See also AMWS 3; CA 9-12R; CANR 10,
34, 66, 116, 138; CP 1, 2, 3, 4, 5, 6, 7;
DLB 5; DLBY 1987; EWL 3; INT CANR-
34; MAL 5; MTCW 1, 2; MTFW 2005;
PAB; PFS 9; RGAL 4; TCLE 1:1; WP

Kinsella, Thomas 1928- .... **CLC 4, 19, 138; PC 69**
See also BRWS 5; CA 17-20R; CANR 15,
122; CP 1, 2, 3, 4, 5, 6, 7; DLB 27; EWL
3; MTCW 1, 2; MTFW 2005; RGEL 2;
TEA

Kinsella, W(illiam) P(atrick) 1935- . **CLC 27, 43, 166**
See also AAYA 7, 60; BPFB 2; CA 97-100,
222; CAAE 222; CAAS 7; CANR 21, 35,
66, 75, 129; CN 4, 5, 6, 7; CPW; DAC;
DAM NOV, POP; FANT; INT CANR-21;
LAIT 5; MTCW 1, 2; MTFW 2005; NFS
15; RGSF 2

Kinsey, Alfred C(harles)
1894-1956 .... **TCLC 91**
See also CA 115; 170; MTCW 2

Kipling, (Joseph) Rudyard 1865-1936 . **PC 3; SSC 5, 54; TCLC 8, 17, 167; WLC**
See also AAYA 32; BRW 6; BRWC 1, 2;
BYA 4; CA 105; 120; CANR 33; CDBLB
1890-1914; CLR 39, 65; CWRI 5; DA;
DA3; DAB; DAC; DAM MST, POET;
DLB 19, 34, 141, 156; EWL 3; EXPS;
FANT; LAIT 3; LMFS 1; MAICYA 1, 2;

MTCW 1, 2; MTFW 2005; NFS 21; PFS
22; RGEL 2; RGSF 2; SATA 100; SFW
4; SSFS 8, 21; SUFW 1; TEA; WCH;
WLIT 4; YABC 2

Kircher, Athanasius 1602-1680 .... **LC 121**
See also DLB 164

Kirk, Russell (Amos) 1918-1994 .. **TCLC 119**
See also AITN 1; CA 1-4R; 145; CAAS 9;
CANR 1, 20, 60; HGG; INT CANR-20;
MTCW 1, 2

Kirkham, Dinah
See Card, Orson Scott

Kirkland, Caroline M. 1801-1864 . **NCLC 85**
See also DLB 3, 73, 74, 250, 254; DLBD
13

Kirkup, James 1918- .... **CLC 1**
See also CA 1-4R; CAAS 4; CANR 2; CP
1, 2, 3, 4, 5, 6, 7; DLB 27; SATA 12

Kirkwood, James 1930(?)-1989 .... **CLC 9**
See also AITN 2; CA 1-4R; 128; CANR 6,
40; GLL 2

Kirsch, Sarah 1935- .... **CLC 176**
See also CA 178; CWW 2; DLB 75; EWL
3

Kirshner, Sidney
See Kingsley, Sidney

Kis, Danilo 1935-1989 .... **CLC 57**
See also CA 109; 118; 129; CANR 61; CD-
WLB 4; DLB 181; EWL 3; MTCW 1;
RGSF 2; RGWL 2, 3

Kissinger, Henry A(lfred) 1923- ..... **CLC 137**
See also CA 1-4R; CANR 2, 33, 66, 109;
MTCW 1

Kivi, Aleksis 1834-1872 .... **NCLC 30**

Kizer, Carolyn (Ashley) 1925- ... **CLC 15, 39, 80; PC 66**
See also CA 65-68; CAAS 5; CANR 24,
70, 134; CP 1, 2, 3, 4, 5, 6, 7; CWP; DAM
POET; DLB 5, 169; EWL 3; MAL 5;
MTCW 2; MTFW 2005; PFS 18; TCLE
1:1

Klabund 1890-1928 .... **TCLC 44**
See also CA 162; DLB 66

Klappert, Peter 1942- .... **CLC 57**
See also CA 33-36R; CSW; DLB 5

Klein, A(braham) M(oses)
1909-1972 .... **CLC 19**
See also CA 101; 37-40R; CP 1; DAB;
DAC; DAM MST; DLB 68; EWL 3;
RGEL 2

Klein, Joe
See Klein, Joseph

Klein, Joseph 1946- .... **CLC 154**
See also CA 85-88; CANR 55

Klein, Norma 1938-1989 .... **CLC 30**
See also AAYA 2, 35; BPFB 2; BYA 6, 7,
8; CA 41-44R; 128; CANR 15, 37; CLR
2, 19; INT CANR-15; JRDA; MAICYA
1, 2; SAAS 1; SATA 7, 57; WYA; YAW

Klein, T(heodore) E(ibon) D(onald)
1947- .... **CLC 34**
See also CA 119; CANR 44, 75; HGG

Kleist, Heinrich von 1777-1811 ...... **NCLC 2, 37; SSC 22**
See also CDWLB 2; DAM DRAM; DLB
90; EW 5; RGSF 2; RGWL 2, 3

Klima, Ivan 1931- .... **CLC 56, 172**
See also CA 25-28R; CANR 17, 50, 91;
CDWLB 4; CWW 2; DAM NOV; DLB
232; EWL 3; RGWL 3

Klimentev, Andrei Platonovich
See Klimentov, Andrei Platonovich

Klimentov, Andrei Platonovich
1899-1951 .... **SSC 42; TCLC 14**
See Platonov, Andrei Platonovich; Platonov,
Andrey Platonovich
See also CA 108; 232

Kubrick, Stanley 1928-1999 .... **CLC 16;**
   TCLC 112
   See also AAYA 30; CA 81-84; 177; CANR
   33; DLB 26
Kumin, Maxine (Winokur) 1925- ..... **CLC 5,**
   13, 28, 164; PC 15
   See also AITN 2; AMWS 4; ANW; CA
   1-4R; CAAS 8; CANR 1, 21, 69, 115,
   140; CP 2, 3, 4, 5, 6, 7; CWP; DA3; DAM
   POET; DLB 5; EWL 3; EXPP; MTCW 1,
   2; MTFW 2005; PAB; PFS 18; SATA 12
Kundera, Milan 1929- . **CLC 4, 9, 19, 32, 68,**
   115, 135; SSC 24
   See also AAYA 2, 62; BPFB 2; CA 85-88;
   CANR 19, 52, 74, 144; CDWLB 4; CWW
   2; DA3; DAM NOV; DLB 232; EW 13;
   EWL 3; MTCW 1, 2; MTFW 2005; NFS
   18; RGSF 2; RGWL 3; SSFS 10
Kunene, Mazisi (Raymond) 1930- ... **CLC 85**
   See also BW 1, 3; CA 125; CANR 81; CP
   1, 7; DLB 117
Kung, Hans .... **CLC 130**
   See Kung, Hans
Kung, Hans 1928-
   See Kung, Hans
   See also CA 53-56; CANR 66, 134; MTCW
   1, 2; MTFW 2005
Kunikida Doppo 1869(?)-1908
   See Doppo, Kunikida
   See also DLB 180; EWL 3
Kunitz, Stanley (Jasspon) 1905- .. **CLC 6, 11,**
   14, 148; PC 19
   See also AMWS 3; CA 41-44R; CANR 26,
   57, 98; CP 1, 2, 3, 4, 5, 6, 7; DA3; DLB
   48; INT CANR-26; MAL 5; MTCW 1, 2;
   MTFW 2005; PFS 11; RGAL 4
Kunze, Reiner 1933- .... **CLC 10**
   See also CA 93-96; CWW 2; DLB 75; EWL
   3
Kuprin, Aleksander Ivanovich
   1870-1938 .... **TCLC 5**
   See Kuprin, Aleksandr Ivanovich; Kuprin,
   Alexandr Ivanovich
   See also CA 104; 182
Kuprin, Aleksandr Ivanovich
   See Kuprin, Aleksander Ivanovich
   See also DLB 295
Kuprin, Alexandr Ivanovich
   See Kuprin, Aleksander Ivanovich
   See also EWL 3
Kureishi, Hanif 1954- .. **CLC 64, 135; DC 26**
   See also BRWS 11; CA 139; CANR 113;
   CBD; CD 5, 6; CN 6, 7; DLB 194, 245;
   GLL 2; IDFW 4; WLIT 4; WWE 1
Kurosawa, Akira 1910-1998 ..... **CLC 16, 119**
   See also AAYA 11, 64; CA 101; 170; CANR
   46; DAM MULT
Kushner, Tony 1956- .... **CLC 81, 203; DC 10**
   See also AAYA 61; AMWS 9; CA 144;
   CAD; CANR 74, 130; CD 5, 6; DA3;
   DAM DRAM; DFS 5; DLB 228; EWL 3;
   GLL 1; LAIT 5; MAL 5; MTCW 2;
   MTFW 2005; RGAL 4; SATA 160
Kuttner, Henry 1915-1958 .... **TCLC 10**
   See also CA 107; 157; DLB 8; FANT;
   SCFW 1, 2; SFW 4
Kutty, Madhavi
   See Das, Kamala
Kuzma, Greg 1944- .... **CLC 7**
   See also CA 33-36R; CANR 70
Kuzmin, Mikhail (Alekseevich)
   1872(?)-1936 .... **TCLC 40**
   See also CA 170; DLB 295; EWL 3
Kyd, Thomas 1558-1594 .... **DC 3; LC 22**
   See also BRW 1; DAM DRAM; DFS 21;
   DLB 62; IDTP; LMFS 1; RGEL 2; TEA;
   WLIT 3
Kyprianos, Iossif
   See Samarakis, Antonis

L. S.
   See Stephen, Sir Leslie
La3amon
   See Layamon
   See also DLB 146
Labe, Louise 1521-1566 .... **LC 120**
Labrunie, Gerard
   See Nerval, Gerard de
La Bruyere, Jean de 1645-1696 .... **LC 17**
   See also DLB 268; EW 3; GFL Beginnings
   to 1789
Lacan, Jacques (Marie Emile)
   1901-1981 .... **CLC 75**
   See also CA 121; 104; DLB 296; EWL 3;
   TWA
Laclos, Pierre-Ambroise Francois
   1741-1803 .... **NCLC 4, 87**
   See also DLB 313; EW 4; GFL Beginnings
   to 1789; RGWL 2, 3
Lacolere, Francois
   See Aragon, Louis
La Colere, Francois
   See Aragon, Louis
La Deshabilleuse
   See Simenon, Georges (Jacques Christian)
Lady Gregory
   See Gregory, Lady Isabella Augusta (Persse)
Lady of Quality, A
   See Bagnold, Enid
La Fayette, Marie-(Madelaine Pioche de la
   Vergne) 1634-1693 .... **LC 2**
   See Lafayette, Marie-Madeleine
   See also GFL Beginnings to 1789; RGWL
   2, 3
Lafayette, Marie-Madeleine
   See La Fayette, Marie-(Madelaine Pioche
   de la Vergne)
   See also DLB 268
Lafayette, Rene
   See Hubbard, L(afayette) Ron(ald)
La Flesche, Francis 1857(?)-1932 ...... **NNAL**
   See also CA 144; CANR 83; DLB 175
La Fontaine, Jean de 1621-1695 .... **LC 50**
   See also DLB 268; EW 3; GFL Beginnings
   to 1789; MAICYA 1, 2; RGWL 2, 3;
   SATA 18
Laforgue, Jules 1860-1887 . **NCLC 5, 53; PC**
   14; SSC 20
   See also DLB 217; EW 7; GFL 1789 to the
   Present; RGWL 2, 3
Lagerkvist, Paer (Fabian)
   1891-1974 ..... **CLC 7, 10, 13, 54; TCLC**
   144
   See Lagerkvist, Par
   See also CA 85-88; 49-52; DA3; DAM
   DRAM, NOV; MTCW 1, 2; MTFW 2005;
   TWA
Lagerkvist, Par .... **SSC 12**
   See Lagerkvist, Paer (Fabian)
   See also DLB 259; EW 10; EWL 3; RGSF
   2; RGWL 2, 3
Lagerloef, Selma (Ottiliana Lovisa)
   .... **TCLC 4, 36**
   See Lagerlof, Selma (Ottiliana Lovisa)
   See also CA 108; MTCW 2
Lagerlof, Selma (Ottiliana Lovisa)
   1858-1940
   See Lagerloef, Selma (Ottiliana Lovisa)
   See also CA 188; CLR 7; DLB 259; RGWL
   2, 3; SATA 15; SSFS 18
La Guma, (Justin) Alex(ander)
   1925-1985 . **BLCS; CLC 19; TCLC 140**
   See also AFW; BW 1, 3; CA 49-52; 118;
   CANR 25, 81; CDWLB 3; CN 1, 2, 3;
   CP 1; DAM NOV; DLB 117, 225; EWL
   3; MTCW 1, 2; MTFW 2005; WLIT 2;
   WWE 1
Laidlaw, A. K.
   See Grieve, C(hristopher) M(urray)

Lainez, Manuel Mujica
   See Mujica Lainez, Manuel
   See also HW 1
Laing, R(onald) D(avid) 1927-1989 . **CLC 95**
   See also CA 107; 129; CANR 34; MTCW 1
Laishley, Alex
   See Booth, Martin
Lamartine, Alphonse (Marie Louis Prat) de
   1790-1869 .... **NCLC 11; PC 16**
   See also DAM POET; DLB 217; GFL 1789
   to the Present; RGWL 2, 3
Lamb, Charles 1775-1834 ..... **NCLC 10, 113;**
   WLC
   See also BRW 4; CDBLB 1789-1832; DA;
   DAB; DAC; DAM MST; DLB 93, 107,
   163; RGEL 2; SATA 17; TEA
Lamb, Lady Caroline 1785-1828 ... **NCLC 38**
   See also DLB 116
Lamb, Mary Ann 1764-1847 .... **NCLC 125**
   See also DLB 163; SATA 17
Lame Deer 1903(?)-1976 .... **NNAL**
   See also CA 69-72
Lamming, George (William) 1927- ... **BLC 2;**
   CLC 2, 4, 66, 144
   See also BW 2, 3; CA 85-88; CANR 26,
   76; CDWLB 3; CN 1, 2, 3, 4, 5, 6, 7; CP
   1; DAM MULT; DLB 125; EWL 3;
   MTCW 1, 2; MTFW 2005; NFS 15;
   RGEL 2
L'Amour, Louis (Dearborn)
   1908-1988 .... **CLC 25, 55**
   See also AAYA 16; AITN 2; BEST 89:2;
   BPFB 2; CA 1-4R; 125; CANR 3, 25, 40;
   CPW; DA3; DAM NOV, POP; DLB 206;
   DLBY 1980; MTCW 1, 2; MTFW 2005;
   RGAL 4; TCWW 1, 2
Lampedusa, Giuseppe (Tomasi) di
   .... **TCLC 13**
   See Tomasi di Lampedusa, Giuseppe
   See also CA 164; EW 11; MTCW 2; MTFW
   2005; RGWL 2, 3
Lampman, Archibald 1861-1899 ... **NCLC 25**
   See also DLB 92; RGEL 2; TWA
Lancaster, Bruce 1896-1963 .... **CLC 36**
   See also CA 9-10; CANR 70; CAP 1; SATA
   9
Lanchester, John 1962- .... **CLC 99**
   See also CA 194; DLB 267
Landau, Mark Alexandrovich
   See Aldanov, Mark (Alexandrovich)
Landau-Aldanov, Mark Alexandrovich
   See Aldanov, Mark (Alexandrovich)
Landis, Jerry
   See Simon, Paul (Frederick)
Landis, John 1950- .... **CLC 26**
   See also CA 112; 122; CANR 128
Landolfi, Tommaso 1908-1979 .... **CLC 11, 49**
   See also CA 127; 117; DLB 177; EWL 3
Landon, Letitia Elizabeth
   1802-1838 .... **NCLC 15**
   See also DLB 96
Landor, Walter Savage
   1775-1864 .... **NCLC 14**
   See also BRW 4; DLB 93, 107; RGEL 2
Landwirth, Heinz 1927-
   See Lind, Jakov
   See also CA 9-12R; CANR 7
Lane, Patrick 1939- .... **CLC 25**
   See also CA 97-100; CANR 54; CP 3, 4, 5,
   6, 7; DAM POET; DLB 53; INT CA-97-
   100
Lang, Andrew 1844-1912 .... **TCLC 16**
   See also CA 114; 137; CANR 85; CLR 101;
   DLB 98, 141, 184; FANT; MAICYA 1, 2;
   RGEL 2; SATA 16; WCH
Lang, Fritz 1890-1976 .... **CLC 20, 103**
   See also AAYA 65; CA 77-80; 69-72;
   CANR 30

Leblanc, Maurice (Marie Emile)
1864-1941 .... **TCLC 49**
See also CA 110; CMW 4

Lebowitz, Fran(ces Ann) 1951(?)- ... **CLC 11, 36**
See also CA 81-84; CANR 14, 60, 70; INT CANR-14; MTCW 1

Lebrecht, Peter
See Tieck, (Johann) Ludwig

le Carre, John .... **CLC 3, 5, 9, 15, 28**
See Cornwell, David (John Moore)
See also AAYA 42; BEST 89:4; BPFB 2; BRWS 2; CDBLB 1960 to Present; CMW 4; CN 1, 2, 3, 4, 5, 6, 7; CPW; DLB 87; EWL 3; MSW; MTCW 2; RGEL 2; TEA

Le Clezio, J(ean) M(arie) G(ustave)
1940- .... **CLC 31, 155**
See also CA 116; 128; CWW 2; DLB 83; EWL 3; GFL 1789 to the Present; RGSF 2

Leconte de Lisle, Charles-Marie-Rene
1818-1894 .... **NCLC 29**
See also DLB 217; EW 6; GFL 1789 to the Present

Le Coq, Monsieur
See Simenon, Georges (Jacques Christian)

Leduc, Violette 1907-1972 .... **CLC 22**
See also CA 13-14; 33-36R; CANR 69; CAP 1; EWL 3; GFL 1789 to the Present; GLL 1

Ledwidge, Francis 1887(?)-1917 .... **TCLC 23**
See also CA 123; 203; DLB 20

Lee, Andrea 1953- .... **BLC 2; CLC 36**
See also BW 1, 3; CA 125; CANR 82; DAM MULT

Lee, Andrew
See Auchincloss, Louis (Stanton)

Lee, Chang-rae 1965- .... **CLC 91**
See also CA 148; CANR 89; CN 7; DLB 312; LATS 1:2

Lee, Don L. .... **CLC 2**
See Madhubuti, Haki R.
See also CP 2, 3, 4

Lee, George W(ashington)
1894-1976 .... **BLC 2; CLC 52**
See also BW 1; CA 125; CANR 83; DAM MULT; DLB 51

Lee, (Nelle) Harper 1926- . **CLC 12, 60, 194; WLC**
See also AAYA 13; AMWS 8; BPFB 2; BYA 3; CA 13-16R; CANR 51, 128; CDALB 1941-1968; CSW; DA; DA3; DAB; DAC; DAM MST, NOV; DLB 6; EXPN; LAIT 3; MAL 5; MTCW 1, 2; MTFW 2005; NFS 2; SATA 11; WYA; YAW

Lee, Helen Elaine 1959(?)- .... **CLC 86**
See also CA 148

Lee, John .... **CLC 70**

Lee, Julian
See Latham, Jean Lee

Lee, Larry
See Lee, Lawrence

Lee, Laurie 1914-1997 .... **CLC 90**
See also CA 77-80; 158; CANR 33, 73; CP 1, 2, 3, 4; CPW; DAB; DAM POP; DLB 27; MTCW 1; RGEL 2

Lee, Lawrence 1941-1990 .... **CLC 34**
See also CA 131; CANR 43

Lee, Li-Young 1957- .... **CLC 164; PC 24**
See also AMWS 15; CA 153; CANR 118; CP 7; DLB 165, 312; LMFS 2; PFS 11, 15, 17

Lee, Manfred B(ennington)
1905-1971 .... **CLC 11**
See Queen, Ellery
See also CA 1-4R; 29-32R; CANR 2; CMW 4; DLB 137

Lee, Nathaniel 1645(?)-1692 .... **LC 103**
See also DLB 80; RGEL 2

Lee, Shelton Jackson 1957(?)- .. **BLCS; CLC 105**
See Lee, Spike
See also BW 2, 3; CA 125; CANR 42; DAM MULT

Lee, Spike
See Lee, Shelton Jackson
See also AAYA 4, 29

Lee, Stan 1922- .... **CLC 17**
See also AAYA 5, 49; CA 108; 111; CANR 129; INT CA-111; MTFW 2005

Lee, Tanith 1947- .... **CLC 46**
See also AAYA 15; CA 37-40R; CANR 53, 102, 145; DLB 261; FANT; SATA 8, 88, 134; SFW 4; SUFW 1, 2; YAW

Lee, Vernon .... **SSC 33; TCLC 5**
See Paget, Violet
See also DLB 57, 153, 156, 174, 178; GLL 1; SUFW 1

Lee, William
See Burroughs, William S(eward)
See also GLL 1

Lee, Willy
See Burroughs, William S(eward)
See also GLL 1

Lee-Hamilton, Eugene (Jacob)
1845-1907 .... **TCLC 22**
See also CA 117; 234

Leet, Judith 1935- .... **CLC 11**
See also CA 187

Le Fanu, Joseph Sheridan
1814-1873 .... **NCLC 9, 58; SSC 14, 84**
See also CMW 4; DA3; DAM POP; DLB 21, 70, 159, 178; GL 3; HGG; RGEL 2; RGSF 2; SUFW 1

Leffland, Ella 1931- .... **CLC 19**
See also CA 29-32R; CANR 35, 78, 82; DLBY 1984; INT CANR-35; SATA 65

Leger, Alexis
See Leger, (Marie-Rene Auguste) Alexis Saint-Leger

Leger, (Marie-Rene Auguste) Alexis Saint-Leger 1887-1975 .. **CLC 4, 11, 46; PC 23**
See Perse, Saint-John; Saint-John Perse
See also CA 13-16R; 61-64; CANR 43; DAM POET; MTCW 1

Leger, Saintleger
See Leger, (Marie-Rene Auguste) Alexis Saint-Leger

Le Guin, Ursula K(roeber) 1929- ..... **CLC 8, 13, 22, 45, 71, 136; SSC 12, 69**
See also AAYA 9, 27; AITN 1; BPFB 2; BYA 5, 8, 11, 14; CA 21-24R; CANR 9, 32, 52, 74, 132; CDALB 1968-1988; CLR 3, 28, 91; CN 2, 3, 4, 5, 6, 7; CPW; DA3; DAB; DAC; DAM MST, POP; DLB 8, 52, 256, 275; EXPS; FANT; FW; INT CANR-32; JRDA; LAIT 5; MAICYA 1, 2; MAL 5; MTCW 1, 2; MTFW 2005; NFS 6, 9; SATA 4, 52, 99, 149; SCFW 1, 2; SFW 4; SSFS 2; SUFW 1, 2; WYA; YAW

Lehmann, Rosamond (Nina)
1901-1990 .... **CLC 5**
See also CA 77-80; 131; CANR 8, 73; CN 1, 2, 3, 4; DLB 15; MTCW 2; RGEL 2; RHW

Leiber, Fritz (Reuter, Jr.)
1910-1992 .... **CLC 25**
See also AAYA 65; BPFB 2; CA 45-48; 139; CANR 2, 40, 86; CN 2, 3, 4, 5; DLB 8; FANT; HGG; MTCW 1, 2; MTFW 2005; SATA 45; SATA-Obit 73; SCFW 1, 2; SFW 4; SUFW 1, 2

Leibniz, Gottfried Wilhelm von
1646-1716 .... **LC 35**
See also DLB 168

Leimbach, Martha 1963-
See Leimbach, Marti
See also CA 130

Leimbach, Marti .... **CLC 65**
See Leimbach, Martha

Leino, Eino .... **TCLC 24**
See Lonnbohm, Armas Eino Leopold
See also EWL 3

Leiris, Michel (Julien) 1901-1990 ..... **CLC 61**
See also CA 119; 128; 132; EWL 3; GFL 1789 to the Present

Leithauser, Brad 1953- .... **CLC 27**
See also CA 107; CANR 27, 81; CP 7; DLB 120, 282

le Jars de Gournay, Marie
See de Gournay, Marie le Jars

Lelchuk, Alan 1938- .... **CLC 5**
See also CA 45-48; CAAS 20; CANR 1, 70; CN 3, 4, 5, 6, 7

Lem, Stanislaw 1921- ...... **CLC 8, 15, 40, 149**
See also CA 105; CAAS 1; CANR 32; CWW 2; MTCW 1; SCFW 1, 2; SFW 4

Lemann, Nancy (Elise) 1956- .... **CLC 39**
See also CA 118; 136; CANR 121

Lemonnier, (Antoine Louis) Camille
1844-1913 .... **TCLC 22**
See also CA 121

Lenau, Nikolaus 1802-1850 .... **NCLC 16**

L'Engle, Madeleine (Camp Franklin)
1918- .... **CLC 12**
See also AAYA 28; AITN 2; BPFB 2; BYA 2, 4, 5, 7; CA 1-4R; CANR 3, 21, 39, 66, 107; CLR 1, 14, 57; CPW; CWRI 5; DA3; DAM POP; DLB 52; JRDA; MAICYA 1, 2; MTCW 1, 2; MTFW 2005; SAAS 15; SATA 1, 27, 75, 128; SFW 4; WYA; YAW

Lengyel, Jozsef 1896-1975 .... **CLC 7**
See also CA 85-88; 57-60; CANR 71; RGSF 2

Lenin 1870-1924
See Lenin, V. I.
See also CA 121; 168

Lenin, V. I. .... **TCLC 67**
See Lenin

Lennon, John (Ono) 1940-1980 .. **CLC 12, 35**
See also CA 102; SATA 114

Lennox, Charlotte Ramsay
1729(?)-1804 .... **NCLC 23, 134**
See also DLB 39; RGEL 2

Lentricchia, Frank, (Jr.) 1940- .... **CLC 34**
See also CA 25-28R; CANR 19, 106; DLB 246

Lenz, Gunter .... **CLC 65**

Lenz, Jakob Michael Reinhold
1751-1792 .... **LC 100**
See also DLB 94; RGWL 2, 3

Lenz, Siegfried 1926- .... **CLC 27; SSC 33**
See also CA 89-92; CANR 80; CWW 2; DLB 75; EWL 3; RGSF 2; RGWL 2, 3

Leon, David
See Jacob, (Cyprien-)Max

Leonard, Elmore (John, Jr.) 1925- . **CLC 28, 34, 71, 120**
See also AAYA 22, 59; AITN 1; BEST 89:1, 90:4; BPFB 2; CA 81-84; CANR 12, 28, 53, 76, 96, 133; CMW 4; CN 5, 6, 7; CPW; DA3; DAM POP; DLB 173, 226; INT CANR-28; MSW; MTCW 1, 2; MTFW 2005; RGAL 4; SATA 163; TCWW 1, 2

Leonard, Hugh .... **CLC 19**
See Byrne, John Keyes
See also CBD; CD 5, 6; DFS 13; DLB 13

Leonov, Leonid (Maximovich)
1899-1994 .... **CLC 92**
See Leonov, Leonid Maksimovich
See also CA 129; CANR 76; DAM NOV; EWL 3; MTCW 1, 2; MTFW 2005

Limonov, Edward 1944- .... CLC 67
See Limonov, Eduard
See also CA 137
Lin, Frank
See Atherton, Gertrude (Franklin Horn)
Lin, Yutang 1895-1976 .... TCLC 149
See also CA 45-48; 65-68; CANR 2; RGAL
4
Lincoln, Abraham 1809-1865 .... NCLC 18
See also LAIT 2
Lind, Jakov .... CLC 1, 2, 4, 27, 82
See Landwirth, Heinz
See also CAAS 4; DLB 299; EWL 3
Lindbergh, Anne (Spencer) Morrow
1906-2001 .... CLC 82
See also BPFB 2; CA 17-20R; 193; CANR
16, 73; DAM NOV; MTCW 1, 2; MTFW
2005; SATA 33; SATA-Obit 125; TUS
Lindsay, David 1878(?)-1945 .... TCLC 15
See also CA 113; 187; DLB 255; FANT;
SFW 4; SUFW 1
Lindsay, (Nicholas) Vachel
1879-1931 .... PC 23; TCLC 17; WLC
See also AMWS 1; CA 114; 135; CANR
79; CDALB 1865-1917; DA; DA3; DAC;
DAM MST, POET; DLB 54; EWL 3;
EXPP; MAL 5; RGAL 4; SATA 40; WP
Linke-Poot
See Doeblin, Alfred
Linney, Romulus 1930- .... CLC 51
See also CA 1-4R; CAD; CANR 40, 44,
79; CD 5, 6; CSW; RGAL 4
Linton, Eliza Lynn 1822-1898 .... NCLC 41
See also DLB 18
Li Po 701-763 .... CMLC 2; PC 29
See also PFS 20; WP
Lipsius, Justus 1547-1606 .... LC 16
Lipsyte, Robert (Michael) 1938- ...... CLC 21
See also AAYA 7, 45; CA 17-20R; CANR
8, 57; CLR 23, 76; DA; DAC; DAM
MST, NOV; JRDA; LAIT 5; MAICYA 1,
2; SATA 5, 68, 113, 161; WYA; YAW
Lish, Gordon (Jay) 1934- ... CLC 45; SSC 18
See also CA 113; 117; CANR 79; DLB 130;
INT CA-117
Lispector, Clarice 1925(?)-1977 .... CLC 43;
HLCS 2; SSC 34
See also CA 139; 116; CANR 71; CDWLB
3; DLB 113, 307; DNFS 1; EWL 3; FW;
HW 2; LAW; RGSF 2; RGWL 2, 3; WLIT
1
Littell, Robert 1935(?)- .... CLC 42
See also CA 109; 112; CANR 64, 115;
CMW 4
Little, Malcolm 1925-1965
See Malcolm X
See also BW 1, 3; CA 125; 111; CANR 82;
DA; DA3; DAB; DAC; DAM MST,
MULT; MTCW 1, 2; MTFW 2005
Littlewit, Humphrey Gent.
See Lovecraft, H(oward) P(hillips)
Litwos
See Sienkiewicz, Henryk (Adam Alexander
Pius)
Liu, E. 1857-1909 .... TCLC 15
See also CA 115; 190
Lively, Penelope 1933- .... CLC 32, 50
See also BPFB 2; CA 41-44R; CANR 29,
67, 79, 131; CLR 7; CN 5, 6, 7; CWRI 5;
DAM NOV; DLB 14, 161, 207; FANT;
JRDA; MAICYA 1, 2; MTCW 1, 2;
MTFW 2005; SATA 7, 60, 101, 164; TEA
Lively, Penelope Margaret
See Lively, Penelope

Livesay, Dorothy (Kathleen)
1909-1996 .... CLC 4, 15, 79
See also AITN 2; CA 25-28R; CAAS 8;
CANR 36, 67; CP 1, 2, 3, 4; DAC; DAM
MST, POET; DLB 68; FW; MTCW 1;
RGEL 2; TWA
Livy c. 59B.C.-c. 12 .... CMLC 11
See also AW 2; CDWLB 1; DLB 211;
RGWL 2, 3
Lizardi, Jose Joaquin Fernandez de
1776-1827 .... NCLC 30
See also LAW
Llewellyn, Richard
See Llewellyn Lloyd, Richard Dafydd Viv-
ian
See also DLB 15
Llewellyn Lloyd, Richard Dafydd Vivian
1906-1983 .... CLC 7, 80
See Llewellyn, Richard
See also CA 53-56; 111; CANR 7, 71;
SATA 11; SATA-Obit 37
Llosa, (Jorge) Mario (Pedro) Vargas
See Vargas Llosa, (Jorge) Mario (Pedro)
See also RGWL 3
Llosa, Mario Vargas
See Vargas Llosa, (Jorge) Mario (Pedro)
Lloyd, Manda
See Mander, (Mary) Jane
Lloyd Webber, Andrew 1948-
See Webber, Andrew Lloyd
See also AAYA 1, 38; CA 116; 149; DAM
DRAM; SATA 56
Llull, Ramon c. 1235-c. 1316 .... CMLC 12
Lobb, Ebenezer
See Upward, Allen
Locke, Alain (Le Roy)
1886-1954 .... BLCS; HR 1:3; TCLC 43
See also AMWS 14; BW 1, 3; CA 106; 124;
CANR 79; DLB 51; LMFS 2; MAL 5;
RGAL 4
Locke, John 1632-1704 .... LC 7, 35
See also DLB 31, 101, 213, 252; RGEL 2;
WLIT 3
Locke-Elliott, Sumner
See Elliott, Sumner Locke
Lockhart, John Gibson 1794-1854 .. NCLC 6
See also DLB 110, 116, 144
Lockridge, Ross (Franklin), Jr.
1914-1948 .... TCLC 111
See also CA 108; 145; CANR 79; DLB 143;
DLBY 1980; MAL 5; RGAL 4; RHW
Lockwood, Robert
See Johnson, Robert
Lodge, David (John) 1935- .... CLC 36, 141
See also BEST 90:1; BRWS 4; CA 17-20R;
CANR 19, 53, 92, 139; CN 1, 2, 3, 4, 5,
6, 7; CPW; DAM POP; DLB 14, 194;
EWL 3; INT CANR-19; MTCW 1, 2;
MTFW 2005
Lodge, Thomas 1558-1625 .... LC 41
See also DLB 172; RGEL 2
Loewinsohn, Ron(ald William)
1937- .... CLC 52
See also CA 25-28R; CANR 71; CP 1, 2, 3,
4
Logan, Jake
See Smith, Martin Cruz
Logan, John (Burton) 1923-1987 .... CLC 5
See also CA 77-80; 124; CANR 45; CP 1,
2, 3, 4; DLB 5
Lo Kuan-chung 1330(?)-1400(?) .... LC 12
Lombard, Nap
See Johnson, Pamela Hansford
Lombard, Peter 1100(?)-1160(?) ... CMLC 72
London, Jack 1876-1916 .. SSC 4, 49; TCLC
9, 15, 39; WLC
See London, John Griffith
See also AAYA 13; AITN 2; AMW; BPFB
2; BYA 4, 13; CDALB 1865-1917; DLB

8, 12, 78, 212; EWL 3; EXPS; LAIT 3;
MAL 5; NFS 8; RGAL 4; RGSF 2; SATA
18; SFW 4; SSFS 7; TCWW 1, 2; TUS;
WYA; YAW
London, John Griffith 1876-1916
See London, Jack
See also CA 110; 119; CANR 73; DA; DA3;
DAB; DAC; DAM MST, NOV; JRDA;
MAICYA 1, 2; MTCW 1, 2; MTFW 2005;
NFS 19
Long, Emmett
See Leonard, Elmore (John, Jr.)
Longbaugh, Harry
See Goldman, William (W.)
Longfellow, Henry Wadsworth
1807-1882 .... NCLC 2, 45, 101, 103; PC
30; WLCS
See also AMW; AMWR 2; CDALB 1640-
1865; CLR 99; DA; DA3; DAB; DAC;
DAM MST, POET; DLB 1, 59, 235;
EXPP; PAB; PFS 2, 7, 17; RGAL 4;
SATA 19; TUS; WP
Longinus c. 1st cent. - .... CMLC 27
See also AW 2; DLB 176
Longley, Michael 1939- .... CLC 29
See also BRWS 8; CA 102; CP 1, 2, 3, 4, 5,
6, 7; DLB 40
Longstreet, Augustus Baldwin
1790-1870 .... NCLC 159
See also DLB 3, 11, 74, 248; RGAL 4
Longus fl. c. 2nd cent. - .... CMLC 7
Longway, A. Hugh
See Lang, Andrew
Lonnbohm, Armas Eino Leopold 1878-1926
See Leino, Eino
See also CA 123
Lonnrot, Elias 1802-1884 .... NCLC 53
See also EFS 1
Lonsdale, Roger ed. .... CLC 65
Lopate, Phillip 1943- .... CLC 29
See also CA 97-100; CANR 88; DLBY
1980; INT CA-97-100
Lopez, Barry (Holstun) 1945- .... CLC 70
See also AAYA 9, 63; ANW; CA 65-68;
CANR 7, 23, 47, 68, 92; DLB 256, 275;
INT CANR-7, -23; MTCW 1; RGAL 4;
SATA 67
Lopez de Mendoza, Inigo
See Santillana, Inigo Lopez de Mendoza,
Marques de
Lopez Portillo (y Pacheco), Jose
1920-2004 .... CLC 46
See also CA 129; 224; HW 1
Lopez y Fuentes, Gregorio
1897(?)-1966 .... CLC 32
See also CA 131; EWL 3; HW 1
Lorca, Federico Garcia
See Garcia Lorca, Federico
See also DFS 4; EW 11; PFS 20; RGWL 2,
3; WP
Lord, Audre
See Lorde, Audre (Geraldine)
See also EWL 3
Lord, Bette Bao 1938- .... AAL; CLC 23
See also BEST 90:3; BPFB 2; CA 107;
CANR 41, 79; INT CA-107; SATA 58
Lord Auch
See Bataille, Georges
Lord Brooke
See Greville, Fulke
Lord Byron
See Byron, George Gordon (Noel)
Lorde, Audre (Geraldine)
1934-1992 .... BLC 2; CLC 18, 71; PC
12; TCLC 173
See Domini, Rey; Lord, Audre
See also AFAW 1, 2; BW 1, 3; CA 25-28R;
142; CANR 16, 26, 46, 82; CP 2, 3, 4;
DA3; DAM MULT, POET; DLB 41; FW;
MAL 5; MTCW 1, 2; MTFW 2005; PFS
16; RGAL 4

McGinley, Patrick (Anthony) 1937- . **CLC 41**
See also CA 120; 127; CANR 56; INT CA-127

McGinley, Phyllis 1905-1978 .... **CLC 14**
See also CA 9-12R; 77-80; CANR 19; CP 1, 2; CWRI 5; DLB 11, 48; MAL 5; PFS 9, 13; SATA 2, 44; SATA-Obit 24

McGinniss, Joe 1942- .... **CLC 32**
See also AITN 2; BEST 89:2; CA 25-28R; CANR 26, 70; CPW; DLB 185; INT CANR-26

McGivern, Maureen Daly
See Daly, Maureen

McGrath, Patrick 1950- .... **CLC 55**
See also CA 136; CANR 65; CN 5, 6, 7; DLB 231; HGG; SUFW 2

McGrath, Thomas (Matthew)
1916-1990 .... **CLC 28, 59**
See also AMWS 10; CA 9-12R; 132; CANR 6, 33, 95; CP 1, 2, 3, 4; DAM POET; MAL 5; MTCW 1; SATA 41; SATA-Obit 66

McGuane, Thomas (Francis III)
1939- .... **CLC 3, 7, 18, 45, 127**
See also AITN 2; BPFB 2; CA 49-52; CANR 5, 24, 49, 94; CN 2, 3, 4, 5, 6, 7; DLB 2, 212; DLBY 1980; EWL 3; INT CANR-24; MAL 5; MTCW 1; MTFW 2005; TCWW 1, 2

McGuckian, Medbh 1950- .... **CLC 48, 174; PC 27**
See also BRWS 5; CA 143; CP 4, 5, 6, 7; CWP; DAM POET; DLB 40

McHale, Tom 1942(?)-1982 .... **CLC 3, 5**
See also AITN 1; CA 77-80; 106; CN 1, 2, 3

McHugh, Heather 1948- .... **PC 61**
See also CA 69-72; CANR 11, 28, 55, 92; CP 4, 5, 6, 7; CWP

McIlvanney, William 1936- .... **CLC 42**
See also CA 25-28R; CANR 61; CMW 4; DLB 14, 207

McIlwraith, Maureen Mollie Hunter
See Hunter, Mollie
See also SATA 2

McInerney, Jay 1955- .... **CLC 34, 112**
See also AAYA 18; BPFB 2; CA 116; 123; CANR 45, 68, 116; CN 5, 6, 7; CPW; DA3; DAM POP; DLB 292; INT CA-123; MAL 5; MTCW 2; MTFW 2005

McIntyre, Vonda N(eel) 1948- .... **CLC 18**
See also CA 81-84; CANR 17, 34, 69; MTCW 1; SFW 4; YAW

McKay, Claude .... **BLC 3; HR 1:3; PC 2; TCLC 7, 41; WLC**
See McKay, Festus Claudius
See also AFAW 1, 2; AMWS 10; DAB; DLB 4, 45, 51, 117; EWL 3; EXPP; GLL 2; LAIT 3; LMFS 2; MAL 5; PAB; PFS 4; RGAL 4; WP

McKay, Festus Claudius 1889-1948
See McKay, Claude
See also BW 1, 3; CA 104; 124; CANR 73; DA; DAC; DAM MST, MULT, NOV, POET; MTCW 1, 2; MTFW 2005; TUS

McKuen, Rod 1933- .... **CLC 1, 3**
See also AITN 1; CA 41-44R; CANR 40; CP 1

McLoughlin, R. B.
See Mencken, H(enry) L(ouis)

McLuhan, (Herbert) Marshall
1911-1980 .... **CLC 37, 83**
See also CA 9-12R; 102; CANR 12, 34, 61; DLB 88; INT CANR-12; MTCW 1, 2; MTFW 2005

McManus, Declan Patrick Aloysius
See Costello, Elvis

McMillan, Terry (L.) 1951- . **BLCS; CLC 50, 61, 112**
See also AAYA 21; AMWS 13; BPFB 2; BW 2, 3; CA 140; CANR 60, 104, 131; CN 7; CPW; DA3; DAM MULT, NOV, POP; MAL 5; MTCW 2; MTFW 2005; RGAL 4; YAW

McMurtry, Larry 1936- .... **CLC 2, 3, 7, 11, 27, 44, 127**
See also AAYA 15; AITN 2; AMWS 5; BEST 89:2; BPFB 2; CA 5-8R; CANR 19, 43, 64, 103; CDALB 1968-1988; CN 2, 3, 4, 5, 6, 7; CPW; CSW; DA3; DAM NOV, POP; DLB 2, 143, 256; DLBY 1980, 1987; EWL 3; MAL 5; MTCW 1, 2; MTFW 2005; RGAL 4; TCWW 1, 2

McNally, T. M. 1961- .... **CLC 82**

McNally, Terrence 1939- ... **CLC 4, 7, 41, 91; DC 27**
See also AAYA 62; AMWS 13; CA 45-48; CAD; CANR 2, 56, 116; CD 5, 6; DA3; DAM DRAM; DFS 16, 19; DLB 7, 249; EWL 3; GLL 1; MTCW 2; MTFW 2005

McNamer, Deirdre 1950- .... **CLC 70**

McNeal, Tom .... **CLC 119**

McNeile, Herman Cyril 1888-1937
See Sapper
See also CA 184; CMW 4; DLB 77

McNickle, (William) D'Arcy
1904-1977 .... **CLC 89; NNAL**
See also CA 9-12R; 85-88; CANR 5, 45; DAM MULT; DLB 175, 212; RGAL 4; SATA-Obit 22; TCWW 1, 2

McPhee, John (Angus) 1931- .... **CLC 36**
See also AAYA 61; AMWS 3; ANW; BEST 90:1; CA 65-68; CANR 20, 46, 64, 69, 121; CPW; DLB 185, 275; MTCW 1, 2; MTFW 2005; TUS

McPherson, James Alan 1943- . **BLCS; CLC 19, 77**
See also BW 1, 3; CA 25-28R; CAAS 17; CANR 24, 74, 140; CN 3, 4, 5, 6; CSW; DLB 38, 244; EWL 3; MTCW 1, 2; MTFW 2005; RGAL 4; RGSF 2

McPherson, William (Alexander)
1933- .... **CLC 34**
See also CA 69-72; CANR 28; INT CANR-28

McTaggart, J. McT. Ellis
See McTaggart, John McTaggart Ellis

McTaggart, John McTaggart Ellis
1866-1925 .... **TCLC 105**
See also CA 120; DLB 262

Mead, George Herbert 1863-1931 . **TCLC 89**
See also CA 212; DLB 270

Mead, Margaret 1901-1978 .... **CLC 37**
See also AITN 1; CA 1-4R; 81-84; CANR 4; DA3; FW; MTCW 1, 2; SATA-Obit 20

Meaker, Marijane (Agnes) 1927-
See Kerr, M. E.
See also CA 107; CANR 37, 63, 145; INT CA-107; JRDA; MAICYA 1, 2; MAICYAS 1; MTCW 1; SATA 20, 61, 99, 160; SATA-Essay 111; YAW

Medoff, Mark (Howard) 1940- .... **CLC 6, 23**
See also AITN 1; CA 53-56; CAD; CANR 5; CD 5, 6; DAM DRAM; DFS 4; DLB 7; INT CANR-5

Medvedev, P. N.
See Bakhtin, Mikhail Mikhailovich

Meged, Aharon
See Megged, Aharon

Meged, Aron
See Megged, Aharon

Megged, Aharon 1920- .... **CLC 9**
See also CA 49-52; CAAS 13; CANR 1, 140; EWL 3

Mehta, Deepa 1950- .... **CLC 208**

Mehta, Gita 1943- .... **CLC 179**
See also CA 225; CN 7; DNFS 2

Mehta, Ved (Parkash) 1934- .... **CLC 37**
See also CA 1-4R, 212; CAAE 212; CANR 2, 23, 69; MTCW 1; MTFW 2005

Melanchthon, Philipp 1497-1560 .... **LC 90**
See also DLB 179

Melanter
See Blackmore, R(ichard) D(oddridge)

Meleager c. 140B.C.-c. 70B.C. ...... **CMLC 53**

Melies, Georges 1861-1938 .... **TCLC 81**

Melikow, Loris
See Hofmannsthal, Hugo von

Melmoth, Sebastian
See Wilde, Oscar (Fingal O'Flahertie Wills)

Melo Neto, Joao Cabral de
See Cabral de Melo Neto, Joao
See also CWW 2; EWL 3

Meltzer, Milton 1915- .... **CLC 26**
See also AAYA 8, 45; BYA 2, 6; CA 13-16R; CANR 38, 92, 107; CLR 13; DLB 61; JRDA; MAICYA 1, 2; SAAS 1; SATA 1, 50, 80, 128; SATA-Essay 124; WYA; YAW

Melville, Herman 1819-1891 ..... **NCLC 3, 12, 29, 45, 49, 91, 93, 123, 157; SSC 1, 17, 46; WLC**
See also AAYA 25; AMW; AMWR 1; CDALB 1640-1865; DA; DA3; DAB; DAC; DAM MST, NOV; DLB 3, 74, 250, 254; EXPN; EXPS; GL 3; LAIT 1, 2; NFS 7, 9; RGAL 4; RGSF 2; SATA 59; SSFS 3; TUS

Members, Mark
See Powell, Anthony (Dymoke)

Membreno, Alejandro .... **CLC 59**

Menand, Louis 1952- .... **CLC 208**
See also CA 200

Menander c. 342B.C.-c. 293B.C. .... **CMLC 9, 51; DC 3**
See also AW 1; CDWLB 1; DAM DRAM; DLB 176; LMFS 1; RGWL 2, 3

Menchu, Rigoberta 1959- .. **CLC 160; HLCS 2**
See also CA 175; CANR 135; DNFS 1; WLIT 1

Mencken, H(enry) L(ouis)
1880-1956 .... **TCLC 13**
See also AMW; CA 105; 125; CDALB 1917-1929; DLB 11, 29, 63, 137, 222; EWL 3; MAL 5; MTCW 1, 2; MTFW 2005; NCFS 4; RGAL 4; TUS

Mendelsohn, Jane 1965- .... **CLC 99**
See also CA 154; CANR 94

Mendoza, Inigo Lopez de
See Santillana, Inigo Lopez de Mendoza, Marques de

Menton, Francisco de
See Chin, Frank (Chew, Jr.)

Mercer, David 1928-1980 .... **CLC 5**
See also CA 9-12R; 102; CANR 23; CBD; DAM DRAM; DLB 13, 310; MTCW 1; RGEL 2

Merchant, Paul
See Ellison, Harlan (Jay)

Meredith, George 1828-1909 .. **PC 60; TCLC 17, 43**
See also CA 117; 153; CANR 80; CDBLB 1832-1890; DAM POET; DLB 18, 35, 57, 159; RGEL 2; TEA

Meredith, William (Morris) 1919- .... **CLC 4, 13, 22, 55; PC 28**
See also CA 9-12R; CAAS 14; CANR 6, 40, 129; CP 1, 2, 3, 4, 5, 6, 7; DAM POET; DLB 5; MAL 5

Merezhkovsky, Dmitrii Sergeevich
See Merezhkovsky, Dmitry Sergeyevich
See also DLB 295

Min, Anchee 1957- .... **CLC 86**
See also CA 146; CANR 94, 137; MTFW
2005

Minehaha, Cornelius
See Wedekind, (Benjamin) Frank(lin)

Miner, Valerie 1947- .... **CLC 40**
See also CA 97-100; CANR 59; FW; GLL
2

Minimo, Duca
See D'Annunzio, Gabriele

Minot, Susan (Anderson) 1956- ...... **CLC 44,
159**
See also AMWS 6; CA 134; CANR 118;
CN 6, 7

Minus, Ed 1938- .... **CLC 39**
See also CA 185

Mirabai 1498(?)-1550(?) .... **PC 48**

Miranda, Javier
See Bioy Casares, Adolfo
See also CWW 2

Mirbeau, Octave 1848-1917 .... **TCLC 55**
See also CA 216; DLB 123, 192; GFL 1789
to the Present

Mirikitani, Janice 1942- .... **AAL**
See also CA 211; DLB 312; RGAL 4

Mirk, John (?)-c. 1414 .... **LC 105**
See also DLB 146

Miro (Ferrer), Gabriel (Francisco Victor)
1879-1930 .... **TCLC 5**
See also CA 104; 185; DLB 322; EWL 3

Misharin, Alexandr .... **CLC 59**

Mishima, Yukio ... **CLC 2, 4, 6, 9, 27; DC 1;
SSC 4; TCLC 161**
See Hiraoka, Kimitake
See also AAYA 50; BPFB 2; GLL 1; MJW;
RGSF 2; RGWL 2, 3; SSFS 5, 12

Mistral, Frederic 1830-1914 .... **TCLC 51**
See also CA 122; 213; GFL 1789 to the
Present

Mistral, Gabriela
See Godoy Alcayaga, Lucila
See also DLB 283; DNFS 1; EWL 3; LAW;
RGWL 2, 3; WP

Mistry, Rohinton 1952- ... **CLC 71, 196; SSC
73**
See also BRWS 10; CA 141; CANR 86,
114; CCA 1; CN 6, 7; DAC; SSFS 6

Mitchell, Clyde
See Ellison, Harlan (Jay)

Mitchell, Emerson Blackhorse Barney
1945- .... **NNAL**
See also CA 45-48

Mitchell, James Leslie 1901-1935
See Gibbon, Lewis Grassic
See also CA 104; 188; DLB 15

Mitchell, Joni 1943- .... **CLC 12**
See also CA 112; CCA 1

Mitchell, Joseph (Quincy)
1908-1996 .... **CLC 98**
See also CA 77-80; 152; CANR 69; CN 1,
2, 3, 4, 5, 6; CSW; DLB 185; DLBY 1996

Mitchell, Margaret (Munnerlyn)
1900-1949 .... **TCLC 11, 170**
See also AAYA 23; BPFB 2; BYA 1; CA
109; 125; CANR 55, 94; CDALBS; DA3;
DAM NOV, POP; DLB 9; LAIT 2; MAL
5; MTCW 1, 2; MTFW 2005; NFS 9;
RGAL 4; RHW; TUS; WYAS 1; YAW

Mitchell, Peggy
See Mitchell, Margaret (Munnerlyn)

Mitchell, S(ilas) Weir 1829-1914 .... **TCLC 36**
See also CA 165; DLB 202; RGAL 4

Mitchell, W(illiam) O(rmond)
1914-1998 .... **CLC 25**
See also CA 77-80; 165; CANR 15, 43; CN
1, 2, 3, 4, 5, 6; DAC; DAM MST; DLB
88; TCLE 1:2

Mitchell, William (Lendrum)
1879-1936 .... **TCLC 81**
See also CA 213

Mitford, Mary Russell 1787-1855 ... **NCLC 4**
See also DLB 110, 116; RGEL 2

Mitford, Nancy 1904-1973 .... **CLC 44**
See also BRWS 10; CA 9-12R; CN 1; DLB
191; RGEL 2

Miyamoto, (Chujo) Yuriko
1899-1951 .... **TCLC 37**
See Miyamoto Yuriko
See also CA 170, 174

Miyamoto Yuriko
See Miyamoto, (Chujo) Yuriko
See also DLB 180

Miyazawa, Kenji 1896-1933 .... **TCLC 76**
See Miyazawa Kenji
See also CA 157; RGWL 3

Miyazawa Kenji
See Miyazawa, Kenji
See also EWL 3

Mizoguchi, Kenji 1898-1956 .... **TCLC 72**
See also CA 167

Mo, Timothy (Peter) 1950- .... **CLC 46, 134**
See also CA 117; CANR 128; CN 5, 6, 7;
DLB 194; MTCW 1; WLIT 4; WWE 1

Modarressi, Taghi (M.) 1931-1997 ... **CLC 44**
See also CA 121; 134; INT CA-134

Modiano, Patrick (Jean) 1945- .... **CLC 18,
218**
See also CA 85-88; CANR 17, 40, 115;
CWW 2; DLB 83, 299; EWL 3

Mofolo, Thomas (Mokopu)
1875(?)-1948 .... **BLC 3; TCLC 22**
See also AFW; CA 121; 153; CANR 83;
DAM MULT; DLB 225; EWL 3; MTCW
2; MTFW 2005; WLIT 2

Mohr, Nicholasa 1938- .... **CLC 12; HLC 2**
See also AAYA 8, 46; CA 49-52; CANR 1,
32, 64; CLR 22; DAM MULT; DLB 145;
HW 1, 2; JRDA; LAIT 5; LLW; MAICYA
2; MAICYAS 1; RGAL 4; SAAS 8; SATA
8, 97; SATA-Essay 113; WYA; YAW

Moi, Toril 1953- .... **CLC 172**
See also CA 154; CANR 102; FW

Mojtabai, A(nn) G(race) 1938- ..... **CLC 5, 9,
15, 29**
See also CA 85-88; CANR 88

Moliere 1622-1673 ..... **DC 13; LC 10, 28, 64;
WLC**
See also DA; DA3; DAB; DAC; DAM
DRAM, MST; DFS 13, 18, 20; DLB 268;
EW 3; GFL Beginnings to 1789; LATS
1:1; RGWL 2, 3; TWA

Molin, Charles
See Mayne, William (James Carter)

Molnar, Ferenc 1878-1952 .... **TCLC 20**
See also CA 109; 153; CANR 83; CDWLB
4; DAM DRAM; DLB 215; EWL 3;
RGWL 2, 3

Momaday, N(avarre) Scott 1934- ...... **CLC 2,
19, 85, 95, 160; NNAL; PC 25; WLCS**
See also AAYA 11, 64; AMWS 4; ANW;
BPFB 2; BYA 12; CA 25-28R; CANR 14,
34, 68, 134; CDALBS; CN 2, 3, 4, 5, 6,
7; CPW; DA; DA3; DAB; DAC; DAM
MST, MULT, NOV, POP; DLB 143, 175,
256; EWL 3; EXPP; INT CANR-14;
LAIT 4; LATS 1:2; MAL 5; MTCW 1, 2;
MTFW 2005; NFS 10; PFS 2, 11; RGAL
4; SATA 48; SATA-Brief 30; TCWW 1,
2; WP; YAW

Monette, Paul 1945-1995 .... **CLC 82**
See also AMWS 10; CA 139; 147; CN 6;
GLL 1

Monroe, Harriet 1860-1936 .... **TCLC 12**
See also CA 109; 204; DLB 54, 91

Monroe, Lyle
See Heinlein, Robert A(nson)

Montagu, Elizabeth 1720-1800 .... **NCLC 7,
117**
See also FW

Montagu, Mary (Pierrepont) Wortley
1689-1762 .... **LC 9, 57; PC 16**
See also DLB 95, 101; FL 1:1; RGEL 2

Montagu, W. H.
See Coleridge, Samuel Taylor

Montague, John (Patrick) 1929- ..... **CLC 13,
46**
See also CA 9-12R; CANR 9, 69, 121; CP
1, 2, 3, 4, 5, 6, 7; DLB 40; EWL 3;
MTCW 1; PFS 12; RGEL 2; TCLE 1:2

Montaigne, Michel (Eyquem) de
1533-1592 .... **LC 8, 105; WLC**
See also DA; DAB; DAC; DAM MST; EW
2; GFL Beginnings to 1789; LMFS 1;
RGWL 2, 3; TWA

Montale, Eugenio 1896-1981 ... **CLC 7, 9, 18;
PC 13**
See also CA 17-20R; 104; CANR 30; DLB
114; EW 11; EWL 3; MTCW 1; PFS 22;
RGWL 2, 3; TWA; WLIT 7

Montesquieu, Charles-Louis de Secondat
1689-1755 .... **LC 7, 69**
See also DLB 314; EW 3; GFL Beginnings
to 1789; TWA

Montessori, Maria 1870-1952 ...... **TCLC 103**
See also CA 115; 147

Montgomery, (Robert) Bruce 1921(?)-1978
See Crispin, Edmund
See also CA 179; 104; CMW 4

Montgomery, L(ucy) M(aud)
1874-1942 .... **TCLC 51, 140**
See also AAYA 12; BYA 1; CA 108; 137;
CLR 8, 91; DA3; DAC; DAM MST; DLB
92; DLBD 14; JRDA; MAICYA 1, 2;
MTCW 2; MTFW 2005; RGEL 2; SATA
100; TWA; WCH; WYA; YABC 1

Montgomery, Marion H., Jr. 1925- .... **CLC 7**
See also AITN 1; CA 1-4R; CANR 3, 48;
CSW; DLB 6

Montgomery, Max
See Davenport, Guy (Mattison, Jr.)

Montherlant, Henry (Milon) de
1896-1972 .... **CLC 8, 19**
See also CA 85-88; 37-40R; DAM DRAM;
DLB 72, 321; EW 11; EWL 3; GFL 1789
to the Present; MTCW 1

Monty Python
See Chapman, Graham; Cleese, John
(Marwood); Gilliam, Terry (Vance); Idle,
Eric; Jones, Terence Graham Parry; Palin,
Michael (Edward)
See also AAYA 7

Moodie, Susanna (Strickland)
1803-1885 .... **NCLC 14, 113**
See also DLB 99

Moody, Hiram (F. III) 1961-
See Moody, Rick
See also CA 138; CANR 64, 112; MTFW
2005

Moody, Minerva
See Alcott, Louisa May

Moody, Rick .... **CLC 147**
See Moody, Hiram (F. III)

Moody, William Vaughan
1869-1910 .... **TCLC 105**
See also CA 110; 178; DLB 7, 54; MAL 5;
RGAL 4

Mooney, Edward 1951-
See Mooney, Ted
See also CA 130

Mooney, Ted .... **CLC 25**
See Mooney, Edward

Mourning Dove 1885(?)-1936 .... **NNAL**
See also CA 144; CANR 90; DAM MULT; DLB 175, 221

Mowat, Farley (McGill) 1921- .... **CLC 26**
See also AAYA 1, 50; BYA 2; CA 1-4R; CANR 4, 24, 42, 68, 108; CLR 20; CPW; DAC; DAM MST; DLB 68; INT CANR-24; JRDA; MAICYA 1, 2; MTCW 1, 2; MTFW 2005; SATA 3, 55; YAW

Mowatt, Anna Cora 1819-1870 ..... **NCLC 74**
See also RGAL 4

Moyers, Bill 1934- .... **CLC 74**
See also AITN 2; CA 61-64; CANR 31, 52

Mphahlele, Es'kia
See Mphahlele, Ezekiel
See also AFW; CDWLB 3; CN 4, 5, 6; DLB 125, 225; RGSF 2; SSFS 11

Mphahlele, Ezekiel 1919- ... **BLC 3; CLC 25, 133**
See Mphahlele, Es'kia
See also BW 2, 3; CA 81-84; CANR 26, 76; CN 1, 2, 3; DA3; DAM MULT; EWL 3; MTCW 2; MTFW 2005; SATA 119

Mqhayi, S(amuel) E(dward) K(rune Loliwe) 1875-1945 .... **BLC 3; TCLC 25**
See also CA 153; CANR 87; DAM MULT

Mrozek, Slawomir 1930- .... **CLC 3, 13**
See also CA 13-16R; CAAS 10; CANR 29; CDWLB 4; CWW 2; DLB 232; EWL 3; MTCW 1

Mrs. Belloc-Lowndes
See Lowndes, Marie Adelaide (Belloc)

Mrs. Fairstar
See Horne, Richard Henry Hengist

M'Taggart, John M'Taggart Ellis
See McTaggart, John McTaggart Ellis

Mtwa, Percy (?)- .... **CLC 47**
See also CD 6

Mueller, Lisel 1924- .... **CLC 13, 51; PC 33**
See also CA 93-96; CP 7; DLB 105; PFS 9, 13

Muggeridge, Malcolm (Thomas) 1903-1990 .... **TCLC 120**
See also AITN 1; CA 101; CANR 33, 63; MTCW 1, 2

Muhammad 570-632 .... **WLCS**
See also DA; DAB; DAC; DAM MST; DLB 311

Muir, Edwin 1887-1959 . **PC 49; TCLC 2, 87**
See Moore, Edward
See also BRWS 6; CA 104; 193; DLB 20, 100, 191; EWL 3; RGEL 2

Muir, John 1838-1914 .... **TCLC 28**
See also AMWS 9; ANW; CA 165; DLB 186, 275

Mujica Lainez, Manuel 1910-1984 ... **CLC 31**
See Lainez, Manuel Mujica
See also CA 81-84; 112; CANR 32; EWL 3; HW 1

Mukherjee, Bharati 1940- ..... **AAL; CLC 53, 115; SSC 38**
See also AAYA 46; BEST 89:2; CA 107, 232; CAAE 232; CANR 45, 72, 128; CN 5, 6, 7; DAM NOV; DLB 60, 218; DNFS 1, 2; EWL 3; FW; MAL 5; MTCW 1, 2; MTFW 2005; RGAL 4; RGSF 2; SSFS 7; TUS; WWE 1

Muldoon, Paul 1951- .... **CLC 32, 72, 166**
See also BRWS 4; CA 113; 129; CANR 52, 91; CP 2, 3, 4, 5, 6, 7; DAM POET; DLB 40; INT CA-129; PFS 7, 22; TCLE 1:2

Mulisch, Harry (Kurt Victor) 1927- .... **CLC 42**
See also CA 9-12R; CANR 6, 26, 56, 110; CWW 2; DLB 299; EWL 3

Mull, Martin 1943- .... **CLC 17**
See also CA 105

Muller, Wilhelm .... **NCLC 73**

Mulock, Dinah Maria
See Craik, Dinah Maria (Mulock)
See also RGEL 2

Multatuli 1820-1887 .... **NCLC 165**
See also RGWL 2, 3

Munday, Anthony 1560-1633 .... **LC 87**
See also DLB 62, 172; RGEL 2

Munford, Robert 1737(?)-1783 .... **LC 5**
See also DLB 31

Mungo, Raymond 1946- .... **CLC 72**
See also CA 49-52; CANR 2

Munro, Alice (Anne) 1931- .... **CLC 6, 10, 19, 50, 95; SSC 3; WLCS**
See also AITN 2; BPFB 2; CA 33-36R; CANR 33, 53, 75, 114; CCA 1; CN 1, 2, 3, 4, 5, 6, 7; DA3; DAC; DAM MST, NOV; DLB 53; EWL 3; MTCW 1, 2; MTFW 2005; RGEL 2; RGSF 2; SATA 29; SSFS 5, 13, 19; TCLE 1:2; WWE 1

Munro, H(ector) H(ugh) 1870-1916 .... **WLC**
See Saki
See also AAYA 56; CA 104; 130; CANR 104; CDBLB 1890-1914; DA; DA3; DAB; DAC; DAM MST, NOV; DLB 34, 162; EXPS; MTCW 1, 2; MTFW 2005; RGEL 2; SSFS 15

Murakami, Haruki 1949- .... **CLC 150**
See Murakami Haruki
See also CA 165; CANR 102, 146; MJW; RGWL 3; SFW 4

Murakami Haruki
See Murakami, Haruki
See also CWW 2; DLB 182; EWL 3

Murasaki, Lady
See Murasaki Shikibu

Murasaki Shikibu 978(?)-1026(?) .. **CMLC 1, 79**
See also EFS 2; LATS 1:1; RGWL 2, 3

Murdoch, (Jean) Iris 1919-1999 ... **CLC 1, 2, 3, 4, 6, 8, 11, 15, 22, 31, 51; TCLC 171**
See also BRWS 1; CA 13-16R; 179; CANR 8, 43, 68, 103, 142; CBD; CDBLB 1960 to Present; CN 1, 2, 3, 4, 5, 6; CWD; DA3; DAB; DAC; DAM MST, NOV; DLB 14, 194, 233; EWL 3; INT CANR-8; MTCW 1, 2; MTFW 2005; NFS 18; RGEL 2; TCLE 1:2; TEA; WLIT 4

Murfree, Mary Noailles 1850-1922 .. **SSC 22; TCLC 135**
See also CA 122; 176; DLB 12, 74; RGAL 4

Murnau, Friedrich Wilhelm
See Plumpe, Friedrich Wilhelm

Murphy, Richard 1927- .... **CLC 41**
See also BRWS 5; CA 29-32R; CP 1, 2, 3, 4, 5, 6, 7; DLB 40; EWL 3

Murphy, Sylvia 1937- .... **CLC 34**
See also CA 121

Murphy, Thomas (Bernard) 1935- ... **CLC 51**
See Murphy, Tom
See also CA 101

Murphy, Tom
See Murphy, Thomas (Bernard)
See also DLB 310

Murray, Albert L. 1916- .... **CLC 73**
See also BW 2; CA 49-52; CANR 26, 52, 78; CN 7; CSW; DLB 38; MTFW 2005

Murray, James Augustus Henry 1837-1915 .... **TCLC 117**

Murray, Judith Sargent 1751-1820 .... **NCLC 63**
See also DLB 37, 200

Murray, Les(lie Allan) 1938- .... **CLC 40**
See also BRWS 7; CA 21-24R; CANR 11, 27, 56, 103; CP 1, 2, 3, 4, 5, 6, 7; DAM POET; DLB 289; DLBY 2001; EWL 3; RGEL 2

Murry, J. Middleton
See Murry, John Middleton

Murry, John Middleton 1889-1957 .... **TCLC 16**
See also CA 118; 217; DLB 149

Musgrave, Susan 1951- .... **CLC 13, 54**
See also CA 69-72; CANR 45, 84; CCA 1; CP 2, 3, 4, 5, 6, 7; CWP

Musil, Robert (Edler von) 1880-1942 .... **SSC 18; TCLC 12, 68**
See also CA 109; CANR 55, 84; CDWLB 2; DLB 81, 124; EW 9; EWL 3; MTCW 2; RGSF 2; RGWL 2, 3

Muske, Carol .... **CLC 90**
See Muske-Dukes, Carol (Anne)

Muske-Dukes, Carol (Anne) 1945-
See Muske, Carol
See also CA 65-68, 203; CAAE 203; CANR 32, 70; CWP

Musset, (Louis Charles) Alfred de 1810-1857 .... **DC 27; NCLC 7, 150**
See also DLB 192, 217; EW 6; GFL 1789 to the Present; RGWL 2, 3; TWA

Mussolini, Benito (Amilcare Andrea) 1883-1945 .... **TCLC 96**
See also CA 116

Mutanabbi, Al-
See al-Mutanabbi, Ahmad ibn al-Husayn Abu al-Tayyib al-Jufi al-Kindi
See also WLIT 6

My Brother's Brother
See Chekhov, Anton (Pavlovich)

Myers, L(eopold) H(amilton) 1881-1944 .... **TCLC 59**
See also CA 157; DLB 15; EWL 3; RGEL 2

Myers, Walter Dean 1937- ..... **BLC 3; CLC 35**
See also AAYA 4, 23; BW 2; BYA 6, 8, 11; CA 33-36R; CANR 20, 42, 67, 108; CLR 4, 16, 35; DAM MULT, NOV; DLB 33; INT CANR-20; JRDA; LAIT 5; MAICYA 1, 2; MAICYAS 1; MTCW 2; MTFW 2005; SAAS 2; SATA 41, 71, 109, 157; SATA-Brief 27; WYA; YAW

Myers, Walter M.
See Myers, Walter Dean

Myles, Symon
See Follett, Ken(neth Martin)

Nabokov, Vladimir (Vladimirovich) 1899-1977 .... **CLC 1, 2, 3, 6, 8, 11, 15, 23, 44, 46, 64; SSC 11, 86; TCLC 108; WLC**
See also AAYA 45; AMW; AMWC 1; AMWR 1; BPFB 2; CA 5-8R; 69-72; CANR 20, 102; CDALB 1941-1968; CN 1, 2; CP 2; DA; DA3; DAB; DAC; DAM MST, NOV; DLB 2, 244, 278, 317; DLBD 3; DLBY 1980, 1991; EWL 3; EXPS; LATS 1:2; MAL 5; MTCW 1, 2; MTFW 2005; NCFS 4; NFS 9; RGAL 4; RGSF 2; SSFS 6, 15; TUS

Naevius c. 265B.C.-201B.C. .... **CMLC 37**
See also DLB 211

Nagai, Kafu .... **TCLC 51**
See Nagai, Sokichi
See also DLB 180

Nagai, Sokichi 1879-1959
See Nagai, Kafu
See also CA 117

Nagy, Laszlo 1925-1978 .... **CLC 7**
See also CA 129; 112

Naidu, Sarojini 1879-1949 .... **TCLC 80**
See also EWL 3; RGEL 2

Naipaul, Shiva(dhar Srinivasa) 1945-1985 .... **CLC 32, 39; TCLC 153**
See also CA 110; 112; 116; CANR 33; CN 2, 3; DA3; DAM NOV; DLB 157; DLBY 1985; EWL 3; MTCW 1, 2; MTFW 2005

Niven, Larry .... **CLC 8**
See Niven, Laurence Van Cott
See also AAYA 27; BPFB 2; BYA 10; DLB 8; SCFW 1, 2

Niven, Laurence Van Cott 1938-
See Niven, Larry
See also CA 21-24R, 207; CAAE 207; CAAS 12; CANR 14, 44, 66, 113; CPW; DAM POP; MTCW 1, 2; SATA 95; SFW 4

Nixon, Agnes Eckhardt 1927- .... **CLC 21**
See also CA 110

Nizan, Paul 1905-1940 .... **TCLC 40**
See also CA 161; DLB 72; EWL 3; GFL 1789 to the Present

Nkosi, Lewis 1936- .... **BLC 3; CLC 45**
See also BW 1, 3; CA 65-68; CANR 27, 81; CBD; CD 5, 6; DAM MULT; DLB 157, 225; WWE 1

Nodier, (Jean) Charles (Emmanuel)
1780-1844 .... **NCLC 19**
See also DLB 119; GFL 1789 to the Present

Noguchi, Yone 1875-1947 .... **TCLC 80**

Nolan, Christopher 1965- .... **CLC 58**
See also CA 111; CANR 88

Noon, Jeff 1957- .... **CLC 91**
See also CA 148; CANR 83; DLB 267; SFW 4

Norden, Charles
See Durrell, Lawrence (George)

Nordhoff, Charles Bernard
1887-1947 .... **TCLC 23**
See also CA 108; 211; DLB 9; LAIT 1; RHW 1; SATA 23

Norfolk, Lawrence 1963- .... **CLC 76**
See also CA 144; CANR 85; CN 6, 7; DLB 267

Norman, Marsha (Williams) 1947- . **CLC 28, 186; DC 8**
See also CA 105; CABS 3; CAD; CANR 41, 131; CD 5, 6; CSW; CWD; DAM DRAM; DFS 2; DLB 266; DLBY 1984; FW; MAL 5

Normyx
See Douglas, (George) Norman

Norris, (Benjamin) Frank(lin, Jr.)
1870-1902 .... **SSC 28; TCLC 24, 155**
See also AAYA 57; AMW; AMWC 2; BPFB 2; CA 110; 160; CDALB 1865-1917; DLB 12, 71, 186; LMFS 2; NFS 12; RGAL 4; TCWW 1, 2; TUS

Norris, Leslie 1921- .... **CLC 14**
See also CA 11-12; CANR 14, 117; CAP 1; CP 1, 2, 3, 4, 5, 6, 7; DLB 27, 256

North, Andrew
See Norton, Andre

North, Anthony
See Koontz, Dean R.

North, Captain George
See Stevenson, Robert Louis (Balfour)

North, Captain George
See Stevenson, Robert Louis (Balfour)

North, Milou
See Erdrich, (Karen) Louise

Northrup, B. A.
See Hubbard, L(afayette) Ron(ald)

North Staffs
See Hulme, T(homas) E(rnest)

Northup, Solomon 1808-1863 ...... **NCLC 105**

Norton, Alice Mary
See Norton, Andre
See also MAICYA 1; SATA 1, 43

Norton, Andre 1912-2005 .... **CLC 12**
See Norton, Alice Mary
See also AAYA 14; BPFB 2; BYA 4, 10, 12; CA 1-4R; 237; CANR 68; CLR 50; DLB 8, 52; JRDA; MAICYA 2; MTCW 1; SATA 91; SUFW 1, 2; YAW

Norton, Caroline 1808-1877 .... **NCLC 47**
See also DLB 21, 159, 199

Norway, Nevil Shute 1899-1960
See Shute, Nevil
See also CA 102; 93-96; CANR 85; MTCW 2

Norwid, Cyprian Kamil
1821-1883 .... **NCLC 17**
See also RGWL 3

Nosille, Nabrah
See Ellison, Harlan (Jay)

Nossack, Hans Erich 1901-1978 .... **CLC 6**
See also CA 93-96; 85-88; DLB 69; EWL 3

Nostradamus 1503-1566 .... **LC 27**

Nosu, Chuji
See Ozu, Yasujiro

Notenburg, Eleanora (Genrikhovna) von
See Guro, Elena (Genrikhovna)

Nova, Craig 1945- .... **CLC 7, 31**
See also CA 45-48; CANR 2, 53, 127

Novak, Joseph
See Kosinski, Jerzy (Nikodem)

Novalis 1772-1801 .... **NCLC 13**
See also CDWLB 2; DLB 90; EW 5; RGWL 2, 3

Novick, Peter 1934- .... **CLC 164**
See also CA 188

Novis, Emile
See Weil, Simone (Adolphine)

Nowlan, Alden (Albert) 1933-1983 ... **CLC 15**
See also CA 9-12R; CANR 5; CP 1, 2, 3; DAC; DAM MST; DLB 53; PFS 12

Noyes, Alfred 1880-1958 ...... **PC 27; TCLC 7**
See also CA 104; 188; DLB 20; EXPP; FANT; PFS 4; RGEL 2

Nugent, Richard Bruce
1906(?)-1987 .... **HR 1:3**
See also BW 1; CA 125; DLB 51; GLL 2

Nunn, Kem .... **CLC 34**
See also CA 159

Nussbaum, Martha Craven 1947- .. **CLC 203**
See also CA 134; CANR 102

Nwapa, Flora (Nwanzuruaha)
1931-1993 .... **BLCS; CLC 133**
See also BW 2; CA 143; CANR 83; CD-WLB 3; CWRI 5; DLB 125; EWL 3; WLIT 2

Nye, Robert 1939- .... **CLC 13, 42**
See also BRWS 10; CA 33-36R; CANR 29, 67, 107; CN 1, 2, 3, 4, 5, 6, 7; CP 1, 2, 3, 4, 5, 6, 7; CWRI 5; DAM NOV; DLB 14, 271; FANT; HGG; MTCW 1; RHW; SATA 6

Nyro, Laura 1947-1997 .... **CLC 17**
See also CA 194

Oates, Joyce Carol 1938- .. **CLC 1, 2, 3, 6, 9, 11, 15, 19, 33, 52, 108, 134; SSC 6, 70; WLC**
See also AAYA 15, 52; AITN 1; AMWS 2; BEST 89:2; BPFB 2; BYA 11; CA 5-8R; CANR 25, 45, 74, 113, 129; CDALB 1968-1988; CN 1, 2, 3, 4, 5, 6, 7; CP 7; CPW; CWP; DA; DA3; DAB; DAC; DAM MST, NOV, POP; DLB 2, 5, 130; DLBY 1981; EWL 3; EXPS; FL 1:6; FW; GL 3; HGG; INT CANR-25; LAIT 4; MAL 5; MAWW; MTCW 1, 2; MTFW 2005; NFS 8; RGAL 4; RGSF 2; SATA 159; SSFS 1, 8, 17; SUFW 2; TUS

O'Brian, E. G.
See Clarke, Arthur C(harles)

O'Brian, Patrick 1914-2000 .... **CLC 152**
See also AAYA 55; CA 144; 187; CANR 74; CPW; MTCW 2; MTFW 2005; RHW

O'Brien, Darcy 1939-1998 .... **CLC 11**
See also CA 21-24R; 167; CANR 8, 59

O'Brien, Edna 1932- ..... **CLC 3, 5, 8, 13, 36, 65, 116; SSC 10, 77**
See also BRWS 5; CA 1-4R; CANR 6, 41, 65, 102; CDBLB 1960 to Present; CN 1, 2, 3, 4, 5, 6, 7; DA3; DAM NOV; DLB 14, 231, 319; EWL 3; FW; MTCW 1, 2; MTFW 2005; RGSF 2; WLIT 4

O'Brien, Fitz-James 1828-1862 .... **NCLC 21**
See also DLB 74; RGAL 4; SUFW

O'Brien, Flann .... **CLC 1, 4, 5, 7, 10, 47**
See O Nuallain, Brian
See also BRWS 2; DLB 231; EWL 3; RGEL 2

O'Brien, Richard 1942- .... **CLC 17**
See also CA 124

O'Brien, (William) Tim(othy) 1946- . **CLC 7, 19, 40, 103, 211; SSC 74**
See also AAYA 16; AMWS 5; CA 85-88; CANR 40, 58, 133; CDALBS; CN 5, 6, 7; CPW; DA3; DAM POP; DLB 152; DLBD 9; DLBY 1980; LATS 1:2; MAL 5; MTCW 2; MTFW 2005; RGAL 4; SSFS 5, 15; TCLE 1:2

Obstfelder, Sigbjoern 1866-1900 .... **TCLC 23**
See also CA 123

O'Casey, Sean 1880-1964 .... **CLC 1, 5, 9, 11, 15, 88; DC 12; WLCS**
See also BRW 7; CA 89-92; CANR 62; CBD; CDBLB 1914-1945; DA3; DAB; DAC; DAM DRAM, MST; DFS 19; DLB 10; EWL 3; MTCW 1, 2; MTFW 2005; RGEL 2; TEA; WLIT 4

O'Cathasaigh, Sean
See O'Casey, Sean

Occom, Samson 1723-1792 .... **LC 60; NNAL**
See also DLB 175

Ochs, Phil(ip David) 1940-1976 .... **CLC 17**
See also CA 185; 65-68

O'Connor, Edwin (Greene)
1918-1968 .... **CLC 14**
See also CA 93-96; 25-28R; MAL 5

O'Connor, (Mary) Flannery
1925-1964 .... **CLC 1, 2, 3, 6, 10, 13, 15, 21, 66, 104; SSC 1, 23, 61, 82; TCLC 132; WLC**
See also AAYA 7; AMW; AMWR 2; BPFB 3; BYA 16; CA 1-4R; CANR 3, 41; CDALB 1941-1968; DA; DA3; DAB; DAC; DAM MST, NOV; DLB 2, 152; DLBD 12; DLBY 1980; EWL 3; EXPS; LAIT 5; MAL 5; MAWW; MTCW 1, 2; MTFW 2005; NFS 3, 21; RGAL 4; RGSF 2; SSFS 2, 7, 10, 19; TUS

O'Connor, Frank .... **CLC 23; SSC 5**
See O'Donovan, Michael Francis
See also DLB 162; EWL 3; RGSF 2; SSFS 5

O'Dell, Scott 1898-1989 .... **CLC 30**
See also AAYA 3, 44; BPFB 3; BYA 1, 2, 3, 5; CA 61-64; 129; CANR 12, 30, 112; CLR 1, 16; DLB 52; JRDA; MAICYA 1, 2; SATA 12, 60, 134; WYA; YAW

Odets, Clifford 1906-1963 ..... **CLC 2, 28, 98; DC 6**
See also AMWS 2; CA 85-88; CAD; CANR 62; DAM DRAM; DFS 3, 17, 20; DLB 7, 26; EWL 3; MAL 5; MTCW 1, 2; MTFW 2005; RGAL 4; TUS

O'Doherty, Brian 1928- .... **CLC 76**
See also CA 105; CANR 108

O'Donnell, K. M.
See Malzberg, Barry N(athaniel)

O'Donnell, Lawrence
See Kuttner, Henry

O'Donovan, Michael Francis
1903-1966 .... **CLC 14**
See O'Connor, Frank
See also CA 93-96; CANR 84

Oskison, John Milton
1874-1947 .... **NNAL; TCLC 35**
See also CA 144; CANR 84; DAM MULT;
DLB 175
Ossian c. 3rd cent. - .... **CMLC 28**
See Macpherson, James
Ossoli, Sarah Margaret (Fuller)
1810-1850 .... **NCLC 5, 50**
See Fuller, Margaret; Fuller, Sarah Margaret
See also CDALB 1640-1865; FW; LMFS 1;
SATA 25
Ostriker, Alicia (Suskin) 1937- .... **CLC 132**
See also CA 25-28R; CAAS 24; CANR 10,
30, 62, 99; CWP; DLB 120; EXPP; PFS
19
Ostrovsky, Aleksandr Nikolaevich
See Ostrovsky, Alexander
See also DLB 277
Ostrovsky, Alexander 1823-1886 .. **NCLC 30,
57**
See Ostrovsky, Aleksandr Nikolaevich
Otero, Blas de 1916-1979 .... **CLC 11**
See also CA 89-92; DLB 134; EWL 3
O'Trigger, Sir Lucius
See Horne, Richard Henry Hengist
Otto, Rudolf 1869-1937 .... **TCLC 85**
Otto, Whitney 1955- .... **CLC 70**
See also CA 140; CANR 120
Otway, Thomas 1652-1685 ... **DC 24; LC 106**
See also DAM DRAM; DLB 80; RGEL 2
Ouida .... **TCLC 43**
See De la Ramee, Marie Louise (Ouida)
See also DLB 18, 156; RGEL 2
Ouologuem, Yambo 1940- .... **CLC 146**
See also CA 111; 176
Ousmane, Sembene 1923- ... **BLC 3; CLC 66**
See Sembene, Ousmane
See also BW 1, 3; CA 117; 125; CANR 81;
CWW 2; MTCW 1
Ovid 43B.C.-17 .... **CMLC 7; PC 2**
See also AW 2; CDWLB 1; DA3; DAM
POET; DLB 211; PFS 22; RGWL 2, 3;
WP
Owen, Hugh
See Faust, Frederick (Schiller)
Owen, Wilfred (Edward Salter)
1893-1918 ... **PC 19; TCLC 5, 27; WLC**
See also BRW 6; CA 104; 141; CDBLB
1914-1945; DA; DAB; DAC; DAM MST,
POET; DLB 20; EWL 3; EXPP; MTCW
2; MTFW 2005; PFS 10; RGEL 2; WLIT
4
Owens, Louis (Dean) 1948-2002 .... **NNAL**
See also CA 137, 179; 207; CAAE 179;
CAAS 24; CANR 71
Owens, Rochelle 1936- .... **CLC 8**
See also CA 17-20R; CAAS 2; CAD;
CANR 39; CD 5, 6; CP 1, 2, 3, 4, 5, 6, 7;
CWD; CWP
Oz, Amos 1939- ...... **CLC 5, 8, 11, 27, 33, 54;
SSC 66**
See also CA 53-56; CANR 27, 47, 65, 113,
138; CWW 2; DAM NOV; EWL 3;
MTCW 1, 2; MTFW 2005; RGSF 2;
RGWL 3; WLIT 6
Ozick, Cynthia 1928- .... **CLC 3, 7, 28, 62,
155; SSC 15, 60**
See also AMWS 5; BEST 90:1; CA 17-20R;
CANR 23, 58, 116; CN 3, 4, 5, 6, 7;
CPW; DA3; DAM NOV, POP; DLB 28,
152, 299; DLBY 1982; EWL 3; EXPS;
INT CANR-23; MAL 5; MTCW 1, 2;
MTFW 2005; RGAL 4; RGSF 2; SSFS 3,
12
Ozu, Yasujiro 1903-1963 .... **CLC 16**
See also CA 112
Pabst, G. W. 1885-1967 .... **TCLC 127**
Pacheco, C.
See Pessoa, Fernando (Antonio Nogueira)

Pacheco, Jose Emilio 1939- .... **HLC 2**
See also CA 111; 131; CANR 65; CWW 2;
DAM MULT; DLB 290; EWL 3; HW 1,
2; RGSF 2
Pa Chin .... **CLC 18**
See Li Fei-kan
See also EWL 3
Pack, Robert 1929- .... **CLC 13**
See also CA 1-4R; CANR 3, 44, 82; CP 1,
2, 3, 4, 5, 6, 7; DLB 5; SATA 118
Padgett, Lewis
See Kuttner, Henry
Padilla (Lorenzo), Heberto
1932-2000 .... **CLC 38**
See also AITN 1; CA 123; 131; 189; CWW
2; EWL 3; HW 1
Page, James Patrick 1944-
See Page, Jimmy
See also CA 204
Page, Jimmy 1944- .... **CLC 12**
See Page, James Patrick
Page, Louise 1955- .... **CLC 40**
See also CA 140; CANR 76; CBD; CD 5,
6; CWD; DLB 233
Page, P(atricia) K(athleen) 1916- ...... **CLC 7,
18; PC 12**
See Cape, Judith
See also CA 53-56; CANR 4, 22, 65; CP 1,
2, 3, 4, 5, 6, 7; DAC; DAM MST; DLB
68; MTCW 1; RGEL 2
Page, Stanton
See Fuller, Henry Blake
Page, Stanton
See Fuller, Henry Blake
Page, Thomas Nelson 1853-1922 .... **SSC 23**
See also CA 118; 177; DLB 12, 78; DLBD
13; RGAL 4
Pagels, Elaine Hiesey 1943- .... **CLC 104**
See also CA 45-48; CANR 2, 24, 51; FW;
NCFS 4
Paget, Violet 1856-1935
See Lee, Vernon
See also CA 104; 166; GLL 1; HGG
Paget-Lowe, Henry
See Lovecraft, H(oward) P(hillips)
Paglia, Camille (Anna) 1947- .... **CLC 68**
See also CA 140; CANR 72, 139; CPW;
FW; GLL 2; MTCW 2; MTFW 2005
Paige, Richard
See Koontz, Dean R.
Paine, Thomas 1737-1809 .... **NCLC 62**
See also AMWS 1; CDALB 1640-1865;
DLB 31, 43, 73, 158; LAIT 1; RGAL 4;
RGEL 2; TUS
Pakenham, Antonia
See Fraser, Antonia (Pakenham)
Palamas, Costis
See Palamas, Kostes
Palamas, Kostes 1859-1943 .... **TCLC 5**
See Palamas, Kostis
See also CA 105; 190; RGWL 2, 3
Palamas, Kostis
See Palamas, Kostes
See also EWL 3
Palazzeschi, Aldo 1885-1974 .... **CLC 11**
See also CA 89-92; 53-56; DLB 114, 264;
EWL 3
Pales Matos, Luis 1898-1959 .... **HLCS 2**
See Pales Matos, Luis
See also DLB 290; HW 1; LAW
Paley, Grace 1922- .. **CLC 4, 6, 37, 140; SSC
8**
See also AMWS 6; CA 25-28R; CANR 13,
46, 74, 118; CN 2, 3, 4, 5, 6, 7; CPW;
DA3; DAM POP; DLB 28, 218; EWL 3;
EXPS; FW; INT CANR-13; MAL 5;
MAWW; MTCW 1, 2; MTFW 2005;
RGAL 4; RGSF 2; SSFS 3, 20

Palin, Michael (Edward) 1943- .... **CLC 21**
See Monty Python
See also CA 107; CANR 35, 109; SATA 67
Palliser, Charles 1947- .... **CLC 65**
See also CA 136; CANR 76; CN 5, 6, 7
Palma, Ricardo 1833-1919 .... **TCLC 29**
See also CA 168; LAW
Pamuk, Orhan 1952- .... **CLC 185**
See also CA 142; CANR 75, 127; CWW 2;
WLIT 6
Pancake, Breece Dexter 1952-1979
See Pancake, Breece D'J
See also CA 123; 109
Pancake, Breece D'J .... **CLC 29; SSC 61**
See Pancake, Breece Dexter
See also DLB 130
Panchenko, Nikolai .... **CLC 59**
Pankhurst, Emmeline (Goulden)
1858-1928 .... **TCLC 100**
See also CA 116; FW
Panko, Rudy
See Gogol, Nikolai (Vasilyevich)
Papadiamantis, Alexandros
1851-1911 .... **TCLC 29**
See also CA 168; EWL 3
Papadiamantopoulos, Johannes 1856-1910
See Moreas, Jean
See also CA 117
Papini, Giovanni 1881-1956 .... **TCLC 22**
See also CA 121; 180; DLB 264
Paracelsus 1493-1541 .... **LC 14**
See also DLB 179
Parasol, Peter
See Stevens, Wallace
Pardo Bazan, Emilia 1851-1921 .... **SSC 30**
See also EWL 3; FW; RGSF 2; RGWL 2, 3
Pareto, Vilfredo 1848-1923 .... **TCLC 69**
See also CA 175
Paretsky, Sara 1947- .... **CLC 135**
See also AAYA 30; BEST 90:3; CA 125;
129; CANR 59, 95; CMW 4; CPW; DA3;
DAM POP; DLB 306; INT CA-129;
MSW; RGAL 4
Parfenie, Maria
See Codrescu, Andrei
Parini, Jay (Lee) 1948- .... **CLC 54, 133**
See also CA 97-100, 229; CAAE 229;
CAAS 16; CANR 32, 87
Park, Jordan
See Kornbluth, C(yril) M.; Pohl, Frederik
Park, Robert E(zra) 1864-1944 ..... **TCLC 73**
See also CA 122; 165
Parker, Bert
See Ellison, Harlan (Jay)
Parker, Dorothy (Rothschild)
1893-1967 . **CLC 15, 68; PC 28; SSC 2;
TCLC 143**
See also AMWS 9; CA 19-20; 25-28R; CAP
2; DA3; DAM POET; DLB 11, 45, 86;
EXPP; FW; MAL 5; MAWW; MTCW 1,
2; MTFW 2005; PFS 18; RGAL 4; RGSF
2; TUS
Parker, Robert B(rown) 1932- .... **CLC 27**
See also AAYA 28; BEST 89:4; BPFB 3;
CA 49-52; CANR 1, 26, 52, 89, 128;
CMW 4; CPW; DAM NOV, POP; DLB
306; INT CANR-26; MSW; MTCW 1;
MTFW 2005
Parkin, Frank 1940- .... **CLC 43**
See also CA 147
Parkman, Francis, Jr. 1823-1893 .. **NCLC 12**
See also AMWS 2; DLB 1, 30, 183, 186,
235; RGAL 4
Parks, Gordon (Alexander Buchanan)
1912- .... **BLC 3; CLC 1, 16**
See also AAYA 36; AITN 2; BW 2, 3; CA
41-44R; CANR 26, 66, 145; DA3; DAM
MULT; DLB 33; MTCW 2; MTFW 2005;
SATA 8, 108

Pepys, Samuel 1633-1703 ... **LC 11, 58; WLC**
See also BRW 2; CDBLB 1660-1789; DA; DA3; DAB; DAC; DAM MST; DLB 101, 213; NCFS 4; RGEL 2; TEA; WLIT 3

Percy, Thomas 1729-1811 .... **NCLC 95**
See also DLB 104

Percy, Walker 1916-1990 .... **CLC 2, 3, 6, 8, 14, 18, 47, 65**
See also AMWS 3; BPFB 3; CA 1-4R; 131; CANR 1, 23, 64; CN 1, 2, 3, 4; CPW; CSW; DA3; DAM NOV, POP; DLB 2; DLBY 1980, 1990; EWL 3; MAL 5; MTCW 1, 2; MTFW 2005; RGAL 4; TUS

Percy, William Alexander
1885-1942 .... **TCLC 84**
See also CA 163; MTCW 2

Perec, Georges 1936-1982 .... **CLC 56, 116**
See also CA 141; DLB 83, 299; EWL 3; GFL 1789 to the Present; RGWL 3

Pereda (y Sanchez de Porrua), Jose Maria de 1833-1906 .... **TCLC 16**
See also CA 117

Pereda y Porrua, Jose Maria de
See Pereda (y Sanchez de Porrua), Jose Maria de

Peregoy, George Weems
See Mencken, H(enry) L(ouis)

Perelman, S(idney) J(oseph)
1904-1979 .. **CLC 3, 5, 9, 15, 23, 44, 49; SSC 32**
See also AITN 1, 2; BPFB 3; CA 73-76; 89-92; CANR 18; DAM DRAM; DLB 11, 44; MTCW 1, 2; MTFW 2005; RGAL 4

Peret, Benjamin 1899-1959 .... **PC 33; TCLC 20**
See also CA 117; 186; GFL 1789 to the Present

Peretz, Isaac Leib
See Peretz, Isaac Loeb
See also CA 201

Peretz, Isaac Loeb 1851(?)-1915 ...... **SSC 26; TCLC 16**
See Peretz, Isaac Leib
See also CA 109

Peretz, Yitzkhok Leibush
See Peretz, Isaac Loeb

Perez Galdos, Benito 1843-1920 ..... **HLCS 2; TCLC 27**
See Galdos, Benito Perez
See also CA 125; 153; EWL 3; HW 1; RGWL 2, 3

Peri Rossi, Cristina 1941- .. **CLC 156; HLCS 2**
See also CA 131; CANR 59, 81; CWW 2; DLB 145, 290; EWL 3; HW 1, 2

Perlata
See Peret, Benjamin

Perloff, Marjorie G(abrielle)
1931- .... **CLC 137**
See also CA 57-60; CANR 7, 22, 49, 104

Perrault, Charles 1628-1703 .... **LC 2, 56**
See also BYA 4; CLR 79; DLB 268; GFL Beginnings to 1789; MAICYA 1, 2; RGWL 2, 3; SATA 25; WCH

Perry, Anne 1938- .... **CLC 126**
See also CA 101; CANR 22, 50, 84; CMW 4; CN 6, 7; CPW; DLB 276

Perry, Brighton
See Sherwood, Robert E(mmet)

Perse, St.-John
See Leger, (Marie-Rene Auguste) Alexis Saint-Leger

Perse, Saint-John
See Leger, (Marie-Rene Auguste) Alexis Saint-Leger
See also DLB 258; RGWL 3

Persius 34-62 .... **CMLC 74**
See also AW 2; DLB 211; RGWL 2, 3

Perutz, Leo(pold) 1882-1957 .... **TCLC 60**
See also CA 147; DLB 81

Peseenz, Tulio F.
See Lopez y Fuentes, Gregorio

Pesetsky, Bette 1932- .... **CLC 28**
See also CA 133; DLB 130

Peshkov, Alexei Maximovich 1868-1936
See Gorky, Maxim
See also CA 105; 141; CANR 83; DA; DAC; DAM DRAM, MST, NOV; MTCW 2; MTFW 2005

Pessoa, Fernando (Antonio Nogueira)
1888-1935 ..... **HLC 2; PC 20; TCLC 27**
See also CA 125; 183; DAM MULT; DLB 287; EW 10; EWL 3; RGWL 2, 3; WP

Peterkin, Julia Mood 1880-1961 ...... **CLC 31**
See also CA 102; DLB 9

Peters, Joan K(aren) 1945- .... **CLC 39**
See also CA 158; CANR 109

Peters, Robert L(ouis) 1924- .... **CLC 7**
See also CA 13-16R; CAAS 8; CP 1, 7; DLB 105

Petofi, Sandor 1823-1849 .... **NCLC 21**
See also RGWL 2, 3

Petrakis, Harry Mark 1923- .... **CLC 3**
See also CA 9-12R; CANR 4, 30, 85; CN 1, 2, 3, 4, 5, 6, 7

Petrarch 1304-1374 .... **CMLC 20; PC 8**
See also DA3; DAM POET; EW 2; LMFS 1; RGWL 2, 3; WLIT 7

Petronius c. 20-66 .... **CMLC 34**
See also AW 2; CDWLB 1; DLB 211; RGWL 2, 3

Petrov, Evgeny .... **TCLC 21**
See Kataev, Evgeny Petrovich

Petry, Ann (Lane) 1908-1997 .. **CLC 1, 7, 18; TCLC 112**
See also AFAW 1, 2; BPFB 3; BW 1, 3; BYA 2; CA 5-8R; 157; CAAS 6; CANR 4, 46; CLR 12; CN 1, 2, 3, 4, 5, 6; DLB 76; EWL 3; JRDA; LAIT 1; MAICYA 1, 2; MAICYAS 1; MTCW 1; RGAL 4; SATA 5; SATA-Obit 94; TUS

Petursson, Halligrimur 1614-1674 .... **LC 8**

Peychinovich
See Vazov, Ivan (Minchov)

Phaedrus c. 15B.C.-c. 50 .... **CMLC 25**
See also DLB 211

Phelps (Ward), Elizabeth Stuart
See Phelps, Elizabeth Stuart
See also FW

Phelps, Elizabeth Stuart
1844-1911 .... **TCLC 113**
See Phelps (Ward), Elizabeth Stuart
See also DLB 74

Philips, Katherine 1632-1664 . **LC 30; PC 40**
See also DLB 131; RGEL 2

Philipson, Morris H. 1926- .... **CLC 53**
See also CA 1-4R; CANR 4

Phillips, Caryl 1958- .... **BLCS; CLC 96**
See also BRWS 5; BW 2; CA 141; CANR 63, 104, 140; CBD; CD 5, 6; CN 5, 6, 7; DA3; DAM MULT; DLB 157; EWL 3; MTCW 2; MTFW 2005; WLIT 4; WWE 1

Phillips, David Graham
1867-1911 .... **TCLC 44**
See also CA 108; 176; DLB 9, 12, 303; RGAL 4

Phillips, Jack
See Sandburg, Carl (August)

Phillips, Jayne Anne 1952- .... **CLC 15, 33, 139; SSC 16**
See also AAYA 57; BPFB 3; CA 101; CANR 24, 50, 96; CN 4, 5, 6, 7; CSW; DLBY 1980; INT CANR-24; MTCW 1, 2; MTFW 2005; RGAL 4; RGSF 2; SSFS 4

Phillips, Richard
See Dick, Philip K(indred)

Phillips, Robert (Schaeffer) 1938- .... **CLC 28**
See also CA 17-20R; CAAS 13; CANR 8; DLB 105

Phillips, Ward
See Lovecraft, H(oward) P(hillips)

Philostratus, Flavius c. 179-c.
244 .... **CMLC 62**

Piccolo, Lucio 1901-1969 .... **CLC 13**
See also CA 97-100; DLB 114; EWL 3

Pickthall, Marjorie L(owry) C(hristie)
1883-1922 .... **TCLC 21**
See also CA 107; DLB 92

Pico della Mirandola, Giovanni
1463-1494 .... **LC 15**
See also LMFS 1

Piercy, Marge 1936- .... **CLC 3, 6, 14, 18, 27, 62, 128; PC 29**
See also BPFB 3; CA 21-24R; 187; CAAE 187; CAAS 1; CANR 13, 43, 66, 111; CN 3, 4, 5, 6, 7; CP 1, 2, 3, 4, 5, 6, 7; CWP; DLB 120, 227; EXPP; FW; MAL 5; MTCW 1, 2; MTFW 2005; PFS 9, 22; SFW 4

Piers, Robert
See Anthony, Piers

Pieyre de Mandiargues, Andre 1909-1991
See Mandiargues, Andre Pieyre de
See also CA 103; 136; CANR 22, 82; EWL 3; GFL 1789 to the Present

Pilnyak, Boris 1894-1938 . **SSC 48; TCLC 23**
See Vogau, Boris Andreyevich
See also EWL 3

Pinchback, Eugene
See Toomer, Jean

Pincherle, Alberto 1907-1990 ...... **CLC 11, 18**
See Moravia, Alberto
See also CA 25-28R; 132; CANR 33, 63, 142; DAM NOV; MTCW 1; MTFW 2005

Pinckney, Darryl 1953- .... **CLC 76**
See also BW 2, 3; CA 143; CANR 79

Pindar 518(?)B.C.-438(?)B.C. .... **CMLC 12; PC 19**
See also AW 1; CDWLB 1; DLB 176; RGWL 2

Pineda, Cecile 1942- .... **CLC 39**
See also CA 118; DLB 209

Pinero, Arthur Wing 1855-1934 .... **TCLC 32**
See also CA 110; 153; DAM DRAM; DLB 10; RGEL 2

Pinero, Miguel (Antonio Gomez)
1946-1988 .... **CLC 4, 55**
See also CA 61-64; 125; CAD; CANR 29, 90; DLB 266; HW 1; LLW

Pinget, Robert 1919-1997 .... **CLC 7, 13, 37**
See also CA 85-88; 160; CWW 2; DLB 83; EWL 3; GFL 1789 to the Present

Pink Floyd
See Barrett, (Roger) Syd; Gilmour, David; Mason, Nick; Waters, Roger; Wright, Rick

Pinkney, Edward 1802-1828 .... **NCLC 31**
See also DLB 248

Pinkwater, D. Manus
See Pinkwater, Daniel Manus

Pinkwater, Daniel
See Pinkwater, Daniel Manus

Pinkwater, Daniel M.
See Pinkwater, Daniel Manus

Pinkwater, Daniel Manus 1941- .... **CLC 35**
See also AAYA 1, 46; BYA 9; CA 29-32R; CANR 12, 38, 89, 143; CLR 4; CSW; FANT; JRDA; MAICYA 1, 2; SAAS 3; SATA 8, 46, 76, 114, 158; SFW 4; YAW

Pinkwater, Manus
See Pinkwater, Daniel Manus

MAL 5; MAWW; MTCW 1, 2; MTFW
2005; NFS 14; RGAL 4; RGSF 2; SATA
39; SATA-Obit 23; SSFS 1, 8, 11, 16;
TCWW 2; TUS

Porter, Peter (Neville Frederick)
    1929- .... **CLC 5, 13, 33**
    See also CA 85-88; CP 1, 2, 3, 4, 5, 6, 7;
    DLB 40, 289; WWE 1

Porter, William Sydney 1862-1910
    See Henry, O.
    See also CA 104; 131; CDALB 1865-1917;
    DA; DA3; DAB; DAC; DAM MST; DLB
    12, 78, 79; MAL 5; MTCW 1, 2; MTFW
    2005; TUS; YABC 2

Portillo (y Pacheco), Jose Lopez
    See Lopez Portillo (y Pacheco), Jose

Portillo Trambley, Estela 1927-1998 .. **HLC 2**
    See Trambley, Estela Portillo
    See also CANR 32; DAM MULT; DLB
    209; HW 1

Posey, Alexander (Lawrence)
    1873-1908 .... **NNAL**
    See also CA 144; CANR 80; DAM MULT;
    DLB 175

Posse, Abel .... **CLC 70**

Post, Melville Davisson
    1869-1930 .... **TCLC 39**
    See also CA 110; 202; CMW 4

Potok, Chaim 1929-2002 ... **CLC 2, 7, 14, 26,
    112**
    See also AAYA 15, 50; AITN 1, 2; BPFB 3;
    BYA 1; CA 17-20R; 208; CANR 19, 35,
    64, 98; CLR 92; CN 4, 5, 6; DA3; DAM
    NOV; DLB 28, 152; EXPN; INT CANR-
    19; LAIT 4; MTCW 1, 2; MTFW 2005;
    NFS 4; SATA 33, 106; SATA-Obit 134;
    TUS; YAW

Potok, Herbert Harold -2002
    See Potok, Chaim

Potok, Herman Harold
    See Potok, Chaim

Potter, Dennis (Christopher George)
    1935-1994 .... **CLC 58, 86, 123**
    See also BRWS 10; CA 107; 145; CANR
    33, 61; CBD; DLB 233; MTCW 1

Pound, Ezra (Weston Loomis)
    1885-1972 .. **CLC 1, 2, 3, 4, 5, 7, 10, 13,
    18, 34, 48, 50, 112; PC 4; WLC**
    See also AAYA 47; AMW; AMWR 1; CA
    5-8R; 37-40R; CANR 40; CDALB 1917-
    1929; CP 1; DA; DA3; DAB; DAC; DAM
    MST, POET; DLB 4, 45, 63; DLBD 15;
    EFS 2; EWL 3; EXPP; LMFS 2; MAL 5;
    MTCW 1, 2; MTFW 2005; PAB; PFS 2,
    8, 16; RGAL 4; TUS; WP

Povod, Reinaldo 1959-1994 .... **CLC 44**
    See also CA 136; 146; CANR 83

Powell, Adam Clayton, Jr.
    1908-1972 .... **BLC 3; CLC 89**
    See also BW 1, 3; CA 102; 33-36R; CANR
    86; DAM MULT

Powell, Anthony (Dymoke)
    1905-2000 .... **CLC 1, 3, 7, 9, 10, 31**
    See also BRW 7; CA 1-4R; 189; CANR 1,
    32, 62, 107; CDBLB 1945-1960; CN 1,
    2, 3, 4, 5, 6; DLB 15; EWL 3; MTCW 1, 2;
    MTFW 2005; RGEL 2; TEA

Powell, Dawn 1896(?)-1965 .... **CLC 66**
    See also CA 5-8R; CANR 121; DLBY 1997

Powell, Padgett 1952- .... **CLC 34**
    See also CA 126; CANR 63, 101; CSW;
    DLB 234; DLBY 01

Powell, (Oval) Talmage 1920-2000
    See Queen, Ellery
    See also CA 5-8R; CANR 2, 80

Power, Susan 1961- .... **CLC 91**
    See also BYA 14; CA 160; CANR 135; NFS
    11

Powers, J(ames) F(arl) 1917-1999 ..... **CLC 1,
    4, 8, 57; SSC 4**
    See also CA 1-4R; 181; CANR 2, 61; CN
    1, 2, 3, 4, 5, 6; DLB 130; MTCW 1;
    RGAL 4; RGSF 2

Powers, John J(ames) 1945-
    See Powers, John R.
    See also CA 69-72

Powers, John R. .... **CLC 66**
    See Powers, John J(ames)

Powers, Richard (S.) 1957- .... **CLC 93**
    See also AMWS 9; BPFB 3; CA 148;
    CANR 80; CN 6, 7; MTFW 2005; TCLE
    1:2

Pownall, David 1938- .... **CLC 10**
    See also CA 89-92, 180; CAAS 18; CANR
    49, 101; CBD; CD 5, 6; CN 4, 5, 6, 7;
    DLB 14

Powys, John Cowper 1872-1963 ... **CLC 7, 9,
    15, 46, 125**
    See also CA 85-88; CANR 106; DLB 15,
    255; EWL 3; FANT; MTCW 1, 2; MTFW
    2005; RGEL 2; SUFW

Powys, T(heodore) F(rancis)
    1875-1953 .... **TCLC 9**
    See also BRWS 8; CA 106; 189; DLB 36,
    162; EWL 3; FANT; RGEL 2; SUFW

Pozzo, Modesta
    See Fonte, Moderata

Prado (Calvo), Pedro 1886-1952 ... **TCLC 75**
    See also CA 131; DLB 283; HW 1; LAW

Prager, Emily 1952- .... **CLC 56**
    See also CA 204

Pratchett, Terry 1948- .... **CLC 197**
    See also AAYA 19, 54; BPFB 3; CA 143;
    CANR 87, 126; CLR 64; CN 6, 7; CPW;
    CWRI 5; FANT; MTFW 2005; SATA 82,
    139; SFW 4; SUFW 2

Pratolini, Vasco 1913-1991 .... **TCLC 124**
    See also CA 211; DLB 177; EWL 3; RGWL
    2, 3

Pratt, E(dwin) J(ohn) 1883(?)-1964 . **CLC 19**
    See also CA 141; 93-96; CANR 77; DAC;
    DAM POET; DLB 92; EWL 3; RGEL 2;
    TWA

Premchand .... **TCLC 21**
    See Srivastava, Dhanpat Rai
    See also EWL 3

Prescott, William Hickling
    1796-1859 .... **NCLC 163**
    See also DLB 1, 30, 59, 235

Preseren, France 1800-1849 .... **NCLC 127**
    See also CDWLB 4; DLB 147

Preussler, Otfried 1923- .... **CLC 17**
    See also CA 77-80; SATA 24

Prevert, Jacques (Henri Marie)
    1900-1977 .... **CLC 15**
    See also CA 77-80; 69-72; CANR 29, 61;
    DLB 258; EWL 3; GFL 1789 to the
    Present; IDFW 3, 4; MTCW 1; RGWL 2,
    3; SATA-Obit 30

Prevost, (Antoine Francois)
    1697-1763 .... **LC 1**
    See also DLB 314; EW 4; GFL Beginnings
    to 1789; RGWL 2, 3

Price, (Edward) Reynolds 1933- ... **CLC 3, 6,
    13, 43, 50, 63, 212; SSC 22**
    See also AMWS 6; CA 1-4R; CANR 1, 37,
    57, 87, 128; CN 1, 2, 3, 4, 5, 6, 7; CSW;
    DAM NOV; DLB 2, 218, 278; EWL 3;
    INT CANR-37; MAL 5; MTFW 2005;
    NFS 18

Price, Richard 1949- .... **CLC 6, 12**
    See also CA 49-52; CANR 3; CN 7; DLBY
    1981

Prichard, Katharine Susannah
    1883-1969 .... **CLC 46**
    See also CA 11-12; CANR 33; CAP 1; DLB
    260; MTCW 1; RGEL 2; RGSF 2; SATA
    66

Priestley, J(ohn) B(oynton)
    1894-1984 .... **CLC 2, 5, 9, 34**
    See also BRW 7; CA 9-12R; 113; CANR
    33; CDBLB 1914-1945; CN 1, 2, 3; DA3;
    DAM DRAM, NOV; DLB 10, 34, 77,
    100, 139; DLBY 1984; EWL 3; MTCW
    1, 2; MTFW 2005; RGEL 2; SFW 4

Prince 1958- .... **CLC 35**
    See also CA 213

Prince, F(rank) T(empleton)
    1912-2003 .... **CLC 22**
    See also CA 101; 219; CANR 43, 79; CP 1,
    2, 3, 4, 5, 6, 7; DLB 20

Prince Kropotkin
    See Kropotkin, Peter (Alekseevich)

Prior, Matthew 1664-1721 .... **LC 4**
    See also DLB 95; RGEL 2

Prishvin, Mikhail 1873-1954 .... **TCLC 75**
    See Prishvin, Mikhail Mikhailovich

Prishvin, Mikhail Mikhailovich
    See Prishvin, Mikhail
    See also DLB 272; EWL 3

Pritchard, William H(arrison)
    1932- .... **CLC 34**
    See also CA 65-68; CANR 23, 95; DLB
    111

Pritchett, V(ictor) S(awdon)
    1900-1997 ... **CLC 5, 13, 15, 41; SSC 14**
    See also BPFB 3; BRWS 3; CA 61-64; 157;
    CANR 31, 63; CN 1, 2, 3, 4, 5, 6; DA3;
    DAM NOV; DLB 15, 139; EWL 3;
    MTCW 1, 2; MTFW 2005; RGEL 2;
    RGSF 2; TEA

Private 19022
    See Manning, Frederic

Probst, Mark 1925- .... **CLC 59**
    See also CA 130

Procaccino, Michael
    See Cristofer, Michael

Proclus c. 412-485 .... **CMLC 81**

Prokosch, Frederic 1908-1989 ...... **CLC 4, 48**
    See also CA 73-76; 128; CANR 82; CN 1,
    2, 3, 4; CP 1, 2, 3, 4; DLB 48; MTCW 2

Propertius, Sextus c. 50B.C.-c.
    16B.C. .... **CMLC 32**
    See also AW 2; CDWLB 1; DLB 211;
    RGWL 2, 3

Prophet, The
    See Dreiser, Theodore (Herman Albert)

Prose, Francine 1947- .... **CLC 45**
    See also CA 109; 112; CANR 46, 95, 132;
    DLB 234; MTFW 2005; SATA 101, 149

Proudhon
    See Cunha, Euclides (Rodrigues Pimenta)
    da

Proulx, Annie
    See Proulx, E. Annie

Proulx, E. Annie 1935- .... **CLC 81, 158**
    See also AMWS 7; BPFB 3; CA 145;
    CANR 65, 110; CN 6, 7; CPW 1; DA3;
    DAM POP; MAL 5; MTCW 2; MTFW
    2005; SSFS 18

Proulx, Edna Annie
    See Proulx, E. Annie

**Proust, (Valentin-Louis-George-Eugene)
    Marcel** 1871-1922 ..... **SSC 75; TCLC 7,
    13, 33; WLC**
    See also AAYA 58; BPFB 3; CA 104; 120;
    CANR 110; DA; DA3; DAB; DAC; DAM
    MST, NOV; DLB 65; EW 8; EWL 3; GFL
    1789 to the Present; MTCW 1, 2; MTFW
    2005; RGWL 2, 3; TWA

Prowler, Harley
    See Masters, Edgar Lee

Reyes y Basoalto, Ricardo Eliecer Neftali
See Neruda, Pablo
Reymont, Wladyslaw (Stanislaw)
1868(?)-1925 .... **TCLC 5**
See also CA 104; EWL 3
Reynolds, John Hamilton
1794-1852 .... **NCLC 146**
See also DLB 96
Reynolds, Jonathan 1942- .... **CLC 6, 38**
See also CA 65-68; CANR 28
Reynolds, Joshua 1723-1792 .... **LC 15**
See also DLB 104
Reynolds, Michael S(hane)
1937-2000 .... **CLC 44**
See also CA 65-68; 189; CANR 9, 89, 97
Reznikoff, Charles 1894-1976 .... **CLC 9**
See also AMWS 14; CA 33-36; 61-64; CAP
2; CP 1, 2; DLB 28, 45; WP
Rezzori (d'Arezzo), Gregor von
1914-1998 .... **CLC 25**
See also CA 122; 136; 167
Rhine, Richard
See Silverstein, Alvin; Silverstein, Virginia
B(arbara Opshelor)
Rhodes, Eugene Manlove
1869-1934 .... **TCLC 53**
See also CA 198; DLB 256; TCWW 1, 2
R'hoone, Lord
See Balzac, Honore de
Rhys, Jean 1890-1979 .... **CLC 2, 4, 6, 14, 19,
51, 124; SSC 21, 76**
See also BRWS 2; CA 25-28R; 85-88;
CANR 35, 62; CDBLB 1945-1960; CD-
WLB 3; CN 1, 2; DA3; DAM NOV; DLB
36, 117, 162; DNFS 2; EWL 3; LATS 1:1;
MTCW 1, 2; MTFW 2005; NFS 19;
RGEL 2; RGSF 2; RHW; TEA; WWE 1
Ribeiro, Darcy 1922-1997 .... **CLC 34**
See also CA 33-36R; 156; EWL 3
Ribeiro, Joao Ubaldo (Osorio Pimentel)
1941- .... **CLC 10, 67**
See also CA 81-84; CWW 2; EWL 3
Ribman, Ronald (Burt) 1932- .... **CLC 7**
See also CA 21-24R; CAD; CANR 46, 80;
CD 5, 6
Ricci, Nino (Pio) 1959- .... **CLC 70**
See also CA 137; CANR 130; CCA 1
Rice, Anne 1941- .... **CLC 41, 128**
See Rampling, Anne
See also AAYA 9, 53; AMWS 7; BEST
89:2; BPFB 3; CA 65-68; CANR 12, 36,
53, 74, 100, 133; CN 6, 7; CPW; CSW;
DA3; DAM POP; DLB 292; GL 3; GLL
2; HGG; MTCW 2; MTFW 2005; SUFW
2; YAW
Rice, Elmer (Leopold) 1892-1967 ...... **CLC 7,
49**
See Reizenstein, Elmer Leopold
See also CA 21-22; 25-28R; CAP 2; DAM
DRAM; DFS 12; DLB 4, 7; IDTP; MAL
5; MTCW 1, 2; RGAL 4
Rice, Tim(othy Miles Bindon)
1944- .... **CLC 21**
See also CA 103; CANR 46; DFS 7
Rich, Adrienne (Cecile) 1929- ... **CLC 3, 6, 7,
11, 18, 36, 73, 76, 125; PC 5**
See also AMWR 2; AMWS 1; CA 9-12R;
CANR 20, 53, 74, 128; CDALBS; CP 1,
2, 3, 4, 5, 6, 7; CSW; CWP; DA3; DAM
POET; DLB 5, 67; EWL 3; EXPP; FL 1:6;
FW; MAL 5; MAWW; MTCW 1, 2;
MTFW 2005; PAB; PFS 15; RGAL 4; WP
Rich, Barbara
See Graves, Robert (von Ranke)
Rich, Robert
See Trumbo, Dalton
Richard, Keith .... **CLC 17**
See Richards, Keith

Richards, David Adams 1950- .... **CLC 59**
See also CA 93-96; CANR 60, 110; CN 7;
DAC; DLB 53; TCLE 1:2
Richards, I(vor) A(rmstrong)
1893-1979 .... **CLC 14, 24**
See also BRWS 2; CA 41-44R; 89-92;
CANR 34, 74; CP 1, 2; DLB 27; EWL 3;
MTCW 2; RGEL 2
Richards, Keith 1943-
See Richard, Keith
See also CA 107; CANR 77
Richardson, Anne
See Roiphe, Anne (Richardson)
Richardson, Dorothy Miller
1873-1957 .... **TCLC 3**
See also CA 104; 192; DLB 36; EWL 3;
FW; RGEL 2
**Richardson (Robertson), Ethel Florence
Lindesay** 1870-1946
See Richardson, Henry Handel
See also CA 105; 190; DLB 230; RHW
Richardson, Henry Handel .... **TCLC 4**
See Richardson (Robertson), Ethel Florence
Lindesay
See also DLB 197; EWL 3; RGEL 2; RGSF
2
Richardson, John 1796-1852 .... **NCLC 55**
See also CCA 1; DAC; DLB 99
Richardson, Samuel 1689-1761 ...... **LC 1, 44;
WLC**
See also BRW 3; CDBLB 1660-1789; DA;
DAB; DAC; DAM MST, NOV; DLB 39;
RGEL 2; TEA; WLIT 3
Richardson, Willis 1889-1977 .... **HR 1:3**
See also BW 1; CA 124; DLB 51; SATA 60
Richler, Mordecai 1931-2001 .... **CLC 3, 5, 9,
13, 18, 46, 70, 185**
See also AITN 1; CA 65-68; 201; CANR
31, 62, 111; CCA 1; CLR 17; CN 1, 2, 3,
4, 5, 7; CWRI 5; DAC; DAM MST, NOV;
DLB 53; EWL 3; MAICYA 1, 2; MTCW
1, 2; MTFW 2005; RGEL 2; SATA 44,
98; SATA-Brief 27; TWA
Richter, Conrad (Michael)
1890-1968 .... **CLC 30**
See also AAYA 21; BYA 2; CA 5-8R; 25-
28R; CANR 23; DLB 9, 212; LAIT 1;
MAL 5; MTCW 1, 2; MTFW 2005;
RGAL 4; SATA 3; TCWW 1, 2; TUS;
YAW
Ricostranza, Tom
See Ellis, Trey
Riddell, Charlotte 1832-1906 .... **TCLC 40**
See Riddell, Mrs. J. H.
See also CA 165; DLB 156
Riddell, Mrs. J. H.
See Riddell, Charlotte
See also HGG; SUFW
Ridge, John Rollin 1827-1867 ...... **NCLC 82;
NNAL**
See also CA 144; DAM MULT; DLB 175
Ridgeway, Jason
See Marlowe, Stephen
Ridgway, Keith 1965- .... **CLC 119**
See also CA 172; CANR 144
Riding, Laura .... **CLC 3, 7**
See Jackson, Laura (Riding)
See also CP 1, 2, 3, 4; RGAL 4
Riefenstahl, Berta Helene Amalia 1902-2003
See Riefenstahl, Leni
See also CA 108; 220
Riefenstahl, Leni .... **CLC 16, 190**
See Riefenstahl, Berta Helene Amalia
Riffe, Ernest
See Bergman, (Ernst) Ingmar
Riggs, (Rolla) Lynn
1899-1954 .... **NNAL; TCLC 56**
See also CA 144; DAM MULT; DLB 175

Riis, Jacob A(ugust) 1849-1914 ..... **TCLC 80**
See also CA 113; 168; DLB 23
Riley, James Whitcomb 1849-1916 .... **PC 48;
TCLC 51**
See also CA 118; 137; DAM POET; MAI-
CYA 1, 2; RGAL 4; SATA 17
Riley, Tex
See Creasey, John
Rilke, Rainer Maria 1875-1926 .... **PC 2;
TCLC 1, 6, 19**
See also CA 104; 132; CANR 62, 99; CD-
WLB 2; DA3; DAM POET; DLB 81; EW
9; EWL 3; MTCW 1, 2; MTFW 2005;
PFS 19; RGWL 2, 3; TWA; WP
Rimbaud, (Jean Nicolas) Arthur
1854-1891 ... **NCLC 4, 35, 82; PC 3, 57;
WLC**
See also DA; DA3; DAB; DAC; DAM
MST, POET; DLB 217; EW 7; GFL 1789
to the Present; LMFS 2; RGWL 2, 3;
TWA; WP
Rinehart, Mary Roberts
1876-1958 .... **TCLC 52**
See also BPFB 3; CA 108; 166; RGAL 4;
RHW
Ringmaster, The
See Mencken, H(enry) L(ouis)
Ringwood, Gwen(dolyn Margaret) Pharis
1910-1984 .... **CLC 48**
See also CA 148; 112; DLB 88
Rio, Michel 1945(?)- .... **CLC 43**
See also CA 201
Rios, Alberto (Alvaro) 1952- .... **PC 57**
See also AAYA 66; AMWS 4; CA 113;
CANR 34, 79, 137; CP 7; DLB 122; HW
2; MTFW 2005; PFS 11
Ritsos, Giannes
See Ritsos, Yannis
Ritsos, Yannis 1909-1990 .... **CLC 6, 13, 31**
See also CA 77-80; 133; CANR 39, 61; EW
12; EWL 3; MTCW 1; RGWL 2, 3
Ritter, Erika 1948(?)- .... **CLC 52**
See also CD 5, 6; CWD
Rivera, Jose Eustasio 1889-1928 ... **TCLC 35**
See also CA 162; EWL 3; HW 1, 2; LAW
Rivera, Tomas 1935-1984 .... **HLCS 2**
See also CA 49-52; CANR 32; DLB 82;
HW 1; LLW; RGAL 4; SSFS 15; TCWW
2; WLIT 1
Rivers, Conrad Kent 1933-1968 .... **CLC 1**
See also BW 1; CA 85-88; DLB 41
Rivers, Elfrida
See Bradley, Marion Zimmer
See also GLL 1
Riverside, John
See Heinlein, Robert A(nson)
Rizal, Jose 1861-1896 .... **NCLC 27**
Roa Bastos, Augusto (Jose Antonio)
1917-2005 .... **CLC 45; HLC 2**
See also CA 131; 238; CWW 2; DAM
MULT; DLB 113; EWL 3; HW 1; LAW;
RGSF 2; WLIT 1
Robbe-Grillet, Alain 1922- .... **CLC 1, 2, 4, 6,
8, 10, 14, 43, 128**
See also BPFB 3; CA 9-12R; CANR 33,
65, 115; CWW 2; DLB 83; EW 13; EWL
3; GFL 1789 to the Present; IDFW 3, 4;
MTCW 1, 2; MTFW 2005; RGWL 2, 3;
SSFS 15
Robbins, Harold 1916-1997 .... **CLC 5**
See also BPFB 3; CA 73-76; 162; CANR
26, 54, 112; DA3; DAM NOV; MTCW 1,
2
Robbins, Thomas Eugene 1936-
See Robbins, Tom
See also CA 81-84; CANR 29, 59, 95, 139;
CN 7; CPW; CSW; DA3; DAM NOV,
POP; MTCW 1, 2; MTFW 2005

Robbins, Tom .... **CLC 9, 32, 64**
    See Robbins, Thomas Eugene
    See also AAYA 32; AMWS 10; BEST 90:3;
    BPFB 3; CN 3, 4, 5, 6, 7; DLBY 1980
Robbins, Trina 1938- .... **CLC 21**
    See also AAYA 61; CA 128
Roberts, Charles G(eorge) D(ouglas)
    1860-1943 .... **TCLC 8**
    See also CA 105; 188; CLR 33; CWRI 5;
    DLB 92; RGEL 2; RGSF 2; SATA 88;
    SATA-Brief 29
Roberts, Elizabeth Madox
    1886-1941 .... **TCLC 68**
    See also CA 111; 166; CLR 100; CWRI 5;
    DLB 9, 54, 102; RGAL 4; RHW; SATA
    33; SATA-Brief 27; TCWW 2; WCH
Roberts, Kate 1891-1985 .... **CLC 15**
    See also CA 107; 116; DLB 319
Roberts, Keith (John Kingston)
    1935-2000 .... **CLC 14**
    See also BRWS 10; CA 25-28R; CANR 46;
    DLB 261; SFW 4
Roberts, Kenneth (Lewis)
    1885-1957 .... **TCLC 23**
    See also CA 109; 199; DLB 9; MAL 5;
    RGAL 4; RHW
Roberts, Michele (Brigitte) 1949- .... **CLC 48,
    178**
    See also CA 115; CANR 58, 120; CN 6, 7;
    DLB 231; FW
Robertson, Ellis
    See Ellison, Harlan (Jay); Silverberg, Rob-
    ert
Robertson, Thomas William
    1829-1871 .... **NCLC 35**
    See Robertson, Tom
    See also DAM DRAM
Robertson, Tom
    See Robertson, Thomas William
    See also RGEL 2
Robeson, Kenneth
    See Dent, Lester
Robinson, Edwin Arlington
    1869-1935 .... **PC 1, 35; TCLC 5, 101**
    See also AMW; CA 104; 133; CDALB
    1865-1917; DA; DAC; DAM MST,
    POET; DLB 54; EWL 3; EXPP; MAL 5;
    MTCW 1, 2; MTFW 2005; PAB; PFS 4;
    RGAL 4; WP
Robinson, Henry Crabb
    1775-1867 .... **NCLC 15**
    See also DLB 107
Robinson, Jill 1936- .... **CLC 10**
    See also CA 102; CANR 120; INT CA-102
Robinson, Kim Stanley 1952- .... **CLC 34**
    See also AAYA 26; CA 126; CANR 113,
    139; CN 6, 7; MTFW 2005; SATA 109;
    SCFW 2; SFW 4
Robinson, Lloyd
    See Silverberg, Robert
Robinson, Marilynne 1944- ...... **CLC 25, 180**
    See also CA 116; CANR 80, 140; CN 4, 5,
    6, 7; DLB 206; MTFW 2005
Robinson, Mary 1758-1800 .... **NCLC 142**
    See also DLB 158; FW
Robinson, Smokey .... **CLC 21**
    See Robinson, William, Jr.
Robinson, William, Jr. 1940-
    See Robinson, Smokey
    See also CA 116
Robison, Mary 1949- .... **CLC 42, 98**
    See also CA 113; 116; CANR 87; CN 4, 5,
    6, 7; DLB 130; INT CA-116; RGSF 2
Roches, Catherine des 1542-1587 ...... **LC 117**
Rochester
    See Wilmot, John
    See also RGEL 2

Rod, Edouard 1857-1910 .... **TCLC 52**
Roddenberry, Eugene Wesley 1921-1991
    See Roddenberry, Gene
    See also CA 110; 135; CANR 37; SATA 45;
    SATA-Obit 69
Roddenberry, Gene .... **CLC 17**
    See Roddenberry, Eugene Wesley
    See also AAYA 5; SATA-Obit 69
Rodgers, Mary 1931- .... **CLC 12**
    See also BYA 5; CA 49-52; CANR 8, 55,
    90; CLR 20; CWRI 5; INT CANR-8;
    JRDA; MAICYA 1, 2; SATA 8, 130
Rodgers, W(illiam) R(obert)
    1909-1969 .... **CLC 7**
    See also CA 85-88; DLB 20; RGEL 2
Rodman, Eric
    See Silverberg, Robert
Rodman, Howard 1920(?)-1985 .... **CLC 65**
    See also CA 118
Rodman, Maia
    See Wojciechowska, Maia (Teresa)
Rodo, Jose Enrique 1871(?)-1917 .... **HLCS 2**
    See also CA 178; EWL 3; HW 2; LAW
Rodolph, Utto
    See Ouologuem, Yambo
Rodriguez, Claudio 1934-1999 .... **CLC 10**
    See also CA 188; DLB 134
Rodriguez, Richard 1944- .... **CLC 155; HLC
    2**
    See also AMWS 14; CA 110; CANR 66,
    116; DAM MULT; DLB 82, 256; HW 1,
    2; LAIT 5; LLW; MTFW 2005; NCFS 3;
    WLIT 1
Roelvaag, O(le) E(dvart) 1876-1931
    See Rolvaag, O(le) E(dvart)
    See also CA 117; 171
Roethke, Theodore (Huebner)
    1908-1963 .... **CLC 1, 3, 8, 11, 19, 46,
    101; PC 15**
    See also AMW; CA 81-84; CABS 2;
    CDALB 1941-1968; DA3; DAM POET;
    DLB 5, 206; EWL 3; EXPP; MAL 5;
    MTCW 1, 2; PAB; PFS 3; RGAL 4; WP
Rogers, Carl R(ansom)
    1902-1987 .... **TCLC 125**
    See also CA 1-4R; 121; CANR 1, 18;
    MTCW 1
Rogers, Samuel 1763-1855 .... **NCLC 69**
    See also DLB 93; RGEL 2
Rogers, Thomas Hunton 1927- .... **CLC 57**
    See also CA 89-92; INT CA-89-92
Rogers, Will(iam Penn Adair)
    1879-1935 .... **NNAL; TCLC 8, 71**
    See also CA 105; 144; DA3; DAM MULT;
    DLB 11; MTCW 2
Rogin, Gilbert 1929- .... **CLC 18**
    See also CA 65-68; CANR 15
Rohan, Koda
    See Koda Shigeyuki
Rohlfs, Anna Katharine Green
    See Green, Anna Katharine
Rohmer, Eric .... **CLC 16**
    See Scherer, Jean-Marie Maurice
Rohmer, Sax .... **TCLC 28**
    See Ward, Arthur Henry Sarsfield
    See also DLB 70; MSW; SUFW
Roiphe, Anne (Richardson) 1935- .. **CLC 3, 9**
    See also CA 89-92; CANR 45, 73, 138;
    DLBY 1980; INT CA-89-92
Rojas, Fernando de 1475-1541 ... **HLCS 1, 2;
    LC 23**
    See also DLB 286; RGWL 2, 3
Rojas, Gonzalo 1917- .... **HLCS 2**
    See also CA 178; HW 2; LAWS 1
Roland (de la Platiere), Marie-Jeanne
    1754-1793 .... **LC 98**
    See also DLB 314

**Rolfe, Frederick (William Serafino Austin
    Lewis Mary)** 1860-1913 .... **TCLC 12**
    See Al Siddik
    See also CA 107; 210; DLB 34, 156; RGEL
    2
Rolland, Romain 1866-1944 .... **TCLC 23**
    See also CA 118; 197; DLB 65, 284; EWL
    3; GFL 1789 to the Present; RGWL 2, 3
Rolle, Richard c. 1300-c. 1349 ...... **CMLC 21**
    See also DLB 146; LMFS 1; RGEL 2
Rolvaag, O(le) E(dvart) .... **TCLC 17**
    See Roelvaag, O(le) E(dvart)
    See also DLB 9, 212; MAL 5; NFS 5;
    RGAL 4
Romain Arnaud, Saint
    See Aragon, Louis
Romains, Jules 1885-1972 .... **CLC 7**
    See also CA 85-88; CANR 34; DLB 65,
    321; EWL 3; GFL 1789 to the Present;
    MTCW 1
Romero, Jose Ruben 1890-1952 .... **TCLC 14**
    See also CA 114; 131; EWL 3; HW 1; LAW
Ronsard, Pierre de 1524-1585 . **LC 6, 54; PC
    11**
    See also EW 2; GFL Beginnings to 1789;
    RGWL 2, 3; TWA
Rooke, Leon 1934- .... **CLC 25, 34**
    See also CA 25-28R; CANR 23, 53; CCA
    1; CPW; DAM POP
Roosevelt, Franklin Delano
    1882-1945 .... **TCLC 93**
    See also CA 116; 173; LAIT 3
Roosevelt, Theodore 1858-1919 ..... **TCLC 69**
    See also CA 115; 170; DLB 47, 186, 275
Roper, William 1498-1578 .... **LC 10**
Roquelaure, A. N.
    See Rice, Anne
Rosa, Joao Guimaraes 1908-1967 ... **CLC 23;
    HLCS 1**
    See Guimaraes Rosa, Joao
    See also CA 89-92; DLB 113, 307; EWL 3;
    WLIT 1
Rose, Wendy 1948- . **CLC 85; NNAL; PC 13**
    See also CA 53-56; CANR 5, 51; CWP;
    DAM MULT; DLB 175; PFS 13; RGAL
    4; SATA 12
Rosen, R. D.
    See Rosen, Richard (Dean)
Rosen, Richard (Dean) 1949- .... **CLC 39**
    See also CA 77-80; CANR 62, 120; CMW
    4; INT CANR-30
Rosenberg, Isaac 1890-1918 .... **TCLC 12**
    See also BRW 6; CA 107; 188; DLB 20,
    216; EWL 3; PAB; RGEL 2
Rosenblatt, Joe .... **CLC 15**
    See Rosenblatt, Joseph
    See also CP 3, 4, 5, 6, 7
Rosenblatt, Joseph 1933-
    See Rosenblatt, Joe
    See also CA 89-92; CP 1, 2; INT CA-89-92
Rosenfeld, Samuel
    See Tzara, Tristan
Rosenstock, Sami
    See Tzara, Tristan
Rosenstock, Samuel
    See Tzara, Tristan
Rosenthal, M(acha) L(ouis)
    1917-1996 .... **CLC 28**
    See also CA 1-4R; 152; CAAS 6; CANR 4,
    51; CP 1, 2, 3, 4; DLB 5; SATA 59
Ross, Barnaby
    See Dannay, Frederic
Ross, Bernard L.
    See Follett, Ken(neth Martin)
Ross, J. H.
    See Lawrence, T(homas) E(dward)
Ross, John Hume
    See Lawrence, T(homas) E(dward)

Ross, Martin 1862-1915
See Martin, Violet Florence
See also DLB 135; GLL 2; RGEL 2; RGSF 2

Ross, (James) Sinclair 1908-1996 ... **CLC 13; SSC 24**
See also CA 73-76; CANR 81; CN 1, 2, 3, 4, 5, 6; DAC; DAM MST; DLB 88; RGEL 2; RGSF 2; TCWW 1, 2

Rossetti, Christina 1830-1894 ... **NCLC 2, 50, 66; PC 7; WLC**
See also AAYA 51; BRW 5; BYA 4; DA; DA3; DAB; DAC; DAM MST, POET; DLB 35, 163, 240; EXPP; FL 1:3; LATS 1:1; MAICYA 1, 2; PFS 10, 14; RGEL 2; SATA 20; TEA; WCH

Rossetti, Christina Georgina
See Rossetti, Christina

Rossetti, Dante Gabriel 1828-1882 . **NCLC 4, 77; PC 44; WLC**
See also AAYA 51; BRW 5; CDBLB 1832-1890; DA; DAB; DAC; DAM MST, POET; DLB 35; EXPP; RGEL 2; TEA

Rossi, Cristina Peri
See Peri Rossi, Cristina

Rossi, Jean-Baptiste 1931-2003
See Japrisot, Sebastien
See also CA 201; 215

Rossner, Judith (Perelman) 1935- . **CLC 6, 9, 29**
See also AITN 2; BEST 90:3; BPFB 3; CA 17-20R; CANR 18, 51, 73; CN 4, 5, 6, 7; DLB 6; INT CANR-18; MAL 5; MTCW 1, 2; MTFW 2005

Rostand, Edmond (Eugene Alexis)
1868-1918 .... **DC 10; TCLC 6, 37**
See also CA 104; 126; DA; DA3; DAB; DAC; DAM DRAM, MST; DFS 1; DLB 192; LAIT 1; MTCW 1; RGWL 2, 3; TWA

Roth, Henry 1906-1995 ..... **CLC 2, 6, 11, 104**
See also AMWS 9; CA 11-12; 149; CANR 38, 63; CAP 1; CN 1, 2, 3, 4, 5, 6; DA3; DLB 28; EWL 3; MAL 5; MTCW 1, 2; MTFW 2005; RGAL 4

Roth, (Moses) Joseph 1894-1939 ... **TCLC 33**
See also CA 160; DLB 85; EWL 3; RGWL 2, 3

Roth, Philip (Milton) 1933- ... **CLC 1, 2, 3, 4, 6, 9, 15, 22, 31, 47, 66, 86, 119, 201; SSC 26; WLC**
See also AAYA 67; AMWR 2; AMWS 3; BEST 90:3; BPFB 3; CA 1-4R; CANR 1, 22, 36, 55, 89, 132; CDALB 1968-1988; CN 3, 4, 5, 6, 7; CPW 1; DA; DA3; DAB; DAC; DAM MST, NOV, POP; DLB 2, 28, 173; DLBY 1982; EWL 3; MAL 5; MTCW 1, 2; MTFW 2005; RGAL 4; RGSF 2; SSFS 12, 18; TUS

Rothenberg, Jerome 1931- .... **CLC 6, 57**
See also CA 45-48; CANR 1, 106; CP 1, 2, 3, 4, 5, 6, 7; DLB 5, 193

Rotter, Pat ed. .... **CLC 65**

Roumain, Jacques (Jean Baptiste)
1907-1944 .... **BLC 3; TCLC 19**
See also BW 1; CA 117; 125; DAM MULT; EWL 3

Rourke, Constance Mayfield
1885-1941 .... **TCLC 12**
See also CA 107; 200; MAL 5; YABC 1

Rousseau, Jean-Baptiste 1671-1741 ...... **LC 9**

Rousseau, Jean-Jacques 1712-1778 .... **LC 14, 36, 122; WLC**
See also DA; DA3; DAB; DAC; DAM MST; DLB 314; EW 4; GFL Beginnings to 1789; LMFS 1; RGWL 2, 3; TWA

Roussel, Raymond 1877-1933 .... **TCLC 20**
See also CA 117; 201; EWL 3; GFL 1789 to the Present

Rovit, Earl (Herbert) 1927- .... **CLC 7**
See also CA 5-8R; CANR 12

Rowe, Elizabeth Singer 1674-1737 ..... **LC 44**
See also DLB 39, 95

Rowe, Nicholas 1674-1718 .... **LC 8**
See also DLB 84; RGEL 2

Rowlandson, Mary 1637(?)-1678 .... **LC 66**
See also DLB 24, 200; RGAL 4

Rowley, Ames Dorrance
See Lovecraft, H(oward) P(hillips)

Rowley, William 1585(?)-1626 ... **LC 100, 123**
See also DFS 22; DLB 58; RGEL 2

Rowling, J. K. 1966- .... **CLC 137, 217**
See also AAYA 34; BYA 11, 13, 14; CA 173; CANR 128; CLR 66, 80; MAICYA 2; MTFW 2005; SATA 109; SUFW 2

Rowling, Joanne Kathleen
See Rowling, J.K.

Rowson, Susanna Haswell
1762(?)-1824 .... **NCLC 5, 69**
See also AMWS 15; DLB 37, 200; RGAL 4

Roy, Arundhati 1960(?)- .... **CLC 109, 210**
See also CA 163; CANR 90, 126; CN 7; DLBY 1997; EWL 3; LATS 1:2; MTFW 2005; NFS 22; WWE 1

Roy, Gabrielle 1909-1983 .... **CLC 10, 14**
See also CA 53-56; 110; CANR 5, 61; CCA 1; DAB; DAC; DAM MST; DLB 68; EWL 3; MTCW 1; RGWL 2, 3; SATA 104; TCLE 1:2

Royko, Mike 1932-1997 .... **CLC 109**
See also CA 89-92; 157; CANR 26, 111; CPW

Rozanov, Vasilii Vasil'evich
See Rozanov, Vassili
See also DLB 295

Rozanov, Vasily Vasilyevich
See Rozanov, Vassili
See also EWL 3

Rozanov, Vassili 1856-1919 .... **TCLC 104**
See Rozanov, Vasilii Vasil'evich; Rozanov, Vasily Vasilyevich

Rozewicz, Tadeusz 1921- ...... **CLC 9, 23, 139**
See also CA 108; CANR 36, 66; CWW 2; DA3; DAM POET; DLB 232; EWL 3; MTCW 1, 2; MTFW 2005; RGWL 3

Ruark, Gibbons 1941- .... **CLC 3**
See also CA 33-36R; CAAS 23; CANR 14, 31, 57; DLB 120

Rubens, Bernice (Ruth) 1923-2004 . **CLC 19, 31**
See also CA 25-28R; 232; CANR 33, 65, 128; CN 1, 2, 3, 4, 5, 6, 7; DLB 14, 207; MTCW 1

Rubin, Harold
See Robbins, Harold

Rudkin, (James) David 1936- .... **CLC 14**
See also CA 89-92; CBD; CD 5, 6; DLB 13

Rudnik, Raphael 1933- .... **CLC 7**
See also CA 29-32R

Ruffian, M.
See Hasek, Jaroslav (Matej Frantisek)

Ruiz, Jose Martinez .... **CLC 11**
See Martinez Ruiz, Jose

Ruiz, Juan c. 1283-c. 1350 .... **CMLC 66**

Rukeyser, Muriel 1913-1980 . **CLC 6, 10, 15, 27; PC 12**
See also AMWS 6; CA 5-8R; 93-96; CANR 26, 60; CP 1, 2, 3; DA3; DAM POET; DLB 48; EWL 3; FW; GLL 2; MAL 5; MTCW 1, 2; PFS 10; RGAL 4; SATA-Obit 22

Rule, Jane (Vance) 1931- .... **CLC 27**
See also CA 25-28R; CAAS 18; CANR 12, 87; CN 4, 5, 6, 7; DLB 60; FW

Rulfo, Juan 1918-1986 .. **CLC 8, 80; HLC 2; SSC 25**
See also CA 85-88; 118; CANR 26; CD-WLB 3; DAM MULT; DLB 113; EWL 3; HW 1, 2; LAW; MTCW 1; RGSF 2; RGWL 2, 3; WLIT 1

Rumi, Jalal al-Din 1207-1273 ...... **CMLC 20; PC 45**
See also AAYA 64; RGWL 2, 3; WLIT 6; WP

Runeberg, Johan 1804-1877 .... **NCLC 41**

Runyon, (Alfred) Damon
1884(?)-1946 .... **TCLC 10**
See also CA 107; 165; DLB 11, 86, 171; MAL 5; MTCW 2; RGAL 4

Rush, Norman 1933- .... **CLC 44**
See also CA 121; 126; CANR 130; INT CA-126

Rushdie, (Ahmed) Salman 1947- .... **CLC 23, 31, 55, 100, 191; SSC 83; WLCS**
See also AAYA 65; BEST 89:3; BPFB 3; BRWS 4; CA 108; 111; CANR 33, 56, 108, 133; CN 4, 5, 6, 7; CPW 1; DA3; DAB; DAC; DAM MST, NOV, POP; DLB 194; EWL 3; FANT; INT CA-111; LATS 1:2; LMFS 2; MTCW 1, 2; MTFW 2005; NFS 22; RGEL 2; RGSF 2; TEA; WLIT 4

Rushforth, Peter (Scott) 1945- .... **CLC 19**
See also CA 101

Ruskin, John 1819-1900 .... **TCLC 63**
See also BRW 5; BYA 5; CA 114; 129; CD-BLB 1832-1890; DLB 55, 163, 190; RGEL 2; SATA 24; TEA; WCH

Russ, Joanna 1937- .... **CLC 15**
See also BPFB 3; CA 25-28; CANR 11, 31, 65; CN 4, 5, 6, 7; DLB 8; FW; GLL 1; MTCW 1; SCFW 1, 2; SFW 4

Russ, Richard Patrick
See O'Brian, Patrick

Russell, George William 1867-1935
See A.E.; Baker, Jean H.
See also BRWS 8; CA 104; 153; CDBLB 1890-1914; DAM POET; EWL 3; RGEL 2

Russell, Jeffrey Burton 1934- .... **CLC 70**
See also CA 25-28R; CANR 11, 28, 52

Russell, (Henry) Ken(neth Alfred)
1927- .... **CLC 16**
See also CA 105

Russell, William Martin 1947-
See Russell, Willy
See also CA 164; CANR 107

Russell, Willy .... **CLC 60**
See Russell, William Martin
See also CBD; CD 5, 6; DLB 233

Russo, Richard 1949- .... **CLC 181**
See also AMWS 12; CA 127; 133; CANR 87, 114

Rutherford, Mark .... **TCLC 25**
See White, William Hale
See also DLB 18; RGEL 2

Ruyslinck, Ward .... **CLC 14**
See Belser, Reimond Karel Maria de

Ryan, Cornelius (John) 1920-1974 ..... **CLC 7**
See also CA 69-72; 53-56; CANR 38

Ryan, Michael 1946- .... **CLC 65**
See also CA 49-52; CANR 109; DLBY 1982

Ryan, Tim
See Dent, Lester

Rybakov, Anatoli (Naumovich)
1911-1998 .... **CLC 23, 53**
See Rybakov, Anatolii (Naumovich)
See also CA 126; 135; 172; SATA 79; SATA-Obit 108

Rybakov, Anatolii (Naumovich)
See Rybakov, Anatoli (Naumovich)
See also DLB 302

Ryder, Jonathan
　　See Ludlum, Robert
Ryga, George 1932-1987 .... **CLC 14**
　　See also CA 101; 124; CANR 43, 90; CCA
　　1; DAC; DAM MST; DLB 60
S. H.
　　See Hartmann, Sadakichi
S. S.
　　See Sassoon, Siegfried (Lorraine)
Sa'adawi, al- Nawal
　　See El Saadawi, Nawal
　　See also AFW; EWL 3
Saadawi, Nawal El
　　See El Saadawi, Nawal
　　See also WLIT 2
Saba, Umberto 1883-1957 .... **TCLC 33**
　　See also CA 144; CANR 79; DLB 114;
　　EWL 3; RGWL 2, 3
Sabatini, Rafael 1875-1950 .... **TCLC 47**
　　See also BPFB 3; CA 162; RHW
Sabato, Ernesto (R.) 1911- .... **CLC 10, 23;**
　　HLC 2
　　See also CA 97-100; CANR 32, 65; CD-
　　WLB 3; CWW 2; DAM MULT; DLB 145;
　　EWL 3; HW 1, 2; LAW; MTCW 1, 2;
　　MTFW 2005
Sa-Carneiro, Mario de 1890-1916 . **TCLC 83**
　　See also DLB 287; EWL 3
Sacastru, Martin
　　See Bioy Casares, Adolfo
　　See also CWW 2
Sacher-Masoch, Leopold von
　　1836(?)-1895 .... **NCLC 31**
Sachs, Hans 1494-1576 .... **LC 95**
　　See also CDWLB 2; DLB 179; RGWL 2, 3
Sachs, Marilyn 1927- .... **CLC 35**
　　See also AAYA 2; BYA 6; CA 17-20R;
　　CANR 13, 47; CLR 2; JRDA; MAICYA
　　1, 2; SAAS 2; SATA 3, 68, 164; SATA-
　　Essay 110; WYA; YAW
Sachs, Marilyn Stickle
　　See Sachs, Marilyn
Sachs, Nelly 1891-1970 .... **CLC 14, 98**
　　See also CA 17-18; 25-28R; CANR 87;
　　CAP 2; EWL 3; MTCW 2; MTFW 2005;
　　PFS 20; RGWL 2, 3
Sackler, Howard (Oliver)
　　1929-1982 .... **CLC 14**
　　See also CA 61-64; 108; CAD; CANR 30;
　　DFS 15; DLB 7
Sacks, Oliver (Wolf) 1933- .... **CLC 67, 202**
　　See also CA 53-56; CANR 28, 50, 76;
　　CPW; DA3; INT CANR-28; MTCW 1, 2;
　　MTFW 2005
Sackville, Thomas 1536-1608 .... **LC 98**
　　See also DAM DRAM; DLB 62, 132;
　　RGEL 2
Sadakichi
　　See Hartmann, Sadakichi
Sa'dawi, Nawal al-
　　See El Saadawi, Nawal
　　See also CWW 2
Sade, Donatien Alphonse Francois
　　1740-1814 .... **NCLC 3, 47**
　　See also DLB 314; EW 4; GFL Beginnings
　　to 1789; RGWL 2, 3
Sade, Marquis de
　　See Sade, Donatien Alphonse Francois
Sadoff, Ira 1945- .... **CLC 9**
　　See also CA 53-56; CANR 5, 21, 109; DLB
　　120
Saetone
　　See Camus, Albert
Safire, William 1929- .... **CLC 10**
　　See also CA 17-20R; CANR 31, 54, 91

Sagan, Carl (Edward) 1934-1996 .... **CLC 30,**
　　112
　　See also AAYA 2, 62; CA 25-28R; 155;
　　CANR 11, 36, 74; CPW; DA3; MTCW 1,
　　2; MTFW 2005; SATA 58; SATA-Obit 94
Sagan, Francoise .... **CLC 3, 6, 9, 17, 36**
　　See Quoirez, Francoise
　　See also CWW 2; DLB 83; EWL 3; GFL
　　1789 to the Present; MTCW 2
Sahgal, Nayantara (Pandit) 1927- .... **CLC 41**
　　See also CA 9-12R; CANR 11, 88; CN 1,
　　2, 3, 4, 5, 6, 7
Said, Edward W. 1935-2003 .... **CLC 123**
　　See also CA 21-24R; 220; CANR 45, 74,
　　107, 131; DLB 67; MTCW 2; MTFW
　　2005
Saint, H(arry) F. 1941- .... **CLC 50**
　　See also CA 127
St. Aubin de Teran, Lisa 1953-
　　See Teran, Lisa St. Aubin de
　　See also CA 118; 126; CN 6, 7; INT CA-
　　126
Saint Birgitta of Sweden c.
　　1303-1373 .... **CMLC 24**
Sainte-Beuve, Charles Augustin
　　1804-1869 .... **NCLC 5**
　　See also DLB 217; EW 6; GFL 1789 to the
　　Present
Saint-Exupery, Antoine (Jean Baptiste
　　Marie Roger) de 1900-1944 .... **TCLC 2,**
　　56, 169; WLC
　　See also AAYA 63; BPFB 3; BYA 3; CA
　　108; 132; CLR 10; DA3; DAM NOV;
　　DLB 72; EW 12; EWL 3; GFL 1789 to
　　the Present; LAIT 3; MAICYA 1, 2;
　　MTCW 1, 2; MTFW 2005; RGWL 2, 3;
　　SATA 20; TWA
St. John, David
　　See Hunt, E(verette) Howard, (Jr.)
St. John, J. Hector
　　See Crevecoeur, Michel Guillaume Jean de
Saint-John Perse
　　See Leger, (Marie-Rene Auguste) Alexis
　　Saint-Leger
　　See also EW 10; EWL 3; GFL 1789 to the
　　Present; RGWL 2
Saintsbury, George (Edward Bateman)
　　1845-1933 .... **TCLC 31**
　　See also CA 160; DLB 57, 149
Sait Faik .... **TCLC 23**
　　See Abasiyanik, Sait Faik
Saki .... **SSC 12; TCLC 3**
　　See Munro, H(ector) H(ugh)
　　See also BRWS 6; BYA 11; LAIT 2; RGEL
　　2; SSFS 1; SUFW
Sala, George Augustus 1828-1895 . **NCLC 46**
Saladin 1138-1193 .... **CMLC 38**
Salama, Hannu 1936- .... **CLC 18**
　　See also EWL 3
Salamanca, J(ack) R(ichard) 1922- .. **CLC 4,**
　　15
　　See also CA 25-28R; 193; CAAE 193
Salas, Floyd Francis 1931- .... **HLC 2**
　　See also CA 119; CAAS 27; CANR 44, 75,
　　93; DAM MULT; DLB 82; HW 1, 2;
　　MTCW 2; MTFW 2005
Sale, J. Kirkpatrick
　　See Sale, Kirkpatrick
Sale, Kirkpatrick 1937- .... **CLC 68**
　　See also CA 13-16R; CANR 10
Salinas, Luis Omar 1937- ... **CLC 90; HLC 2**
　　See also AMWS 13; CA 131; CANR 81;
　　DAM MULT; DLB 82; HW 1, 2
Salinas (y Serrano), Pedro
　　1891(?)-1951 .... **TCLC 17**
　　See also CA 117; DLB 134; EWL 3

Salinger, J(erome) D(avid) 1919- .. **CLC 1, 3,**
　　8, 12, 55, 56, 138; SSC 2, 28, 65; WLC
　　See also AAYA 2, 36; AMW; AMWC 1;
　　BPFB 3; CA 5-8R; CANR 39, 129;
　　CDALB 1941-1968; CLR 18; CN 1, 2, 3,
　　4, 5, 6, 7; CPW 1; DA; DA3; DAB; DAC;
　　DAM MST, NOV, POP; DLB 2, 102, 173;
　　EWL 3; EXPN; LAIT 4; MAICYA 1, 2;
　　MAL 5; MTCW 1, 2; MTFW 2005; NFS
　　1; RGAL 4; RGSF 2; SATA 67; SSFS 17;
　　TUS; WYA; YAW
Salisbury, John
　　See Caute, (John) David
Sallust c. 86B.C.-35B.C. .... **CMLC 68**
　　See also AW 2; CDWLB 1; DLB 211;
　　RGWL 2, 3
Salter, James 1925- .. **CLC 7, 52, 59; SSC 58**
　　See also AMWS 9; CA 73-76; CANR 107;
　　DLB 130
Saltus, Edgar (Everton) 1855-1921 . **TCLC 8**
　　See also CA 105; DLB 202; RGAL 4
Saltykov, Mikhail Evgrafovich
　　1826-1889 .... **NCLC 16**
　　See also DLB 238:
Saltykov-Shchedrin, N.
　　See Saltykov, Mikhail Evgrafovich
Samarakis, Andonis
　　See Samarakis, Antonis
　　See also EWL 3
Samarakis, Antonis 1919-2003 .... **CLC 5**
　　See Samarakis, Andonis
　　See also CA 25-28R; 224; CAAS 16; CANR
　　36
Sanchez, Florencio 1875-1910 .... **TCLC 37**
　　See also CA 153; DLB 305; EWL 3; HW 1;
　　LAW
Sanchez, Luis Rafael 1936- .... **CLC 23**
　　See also CA 128; DLB 305; EWL 3; HW 1;
　　WLIT 1
Sanchez, Sonia 1934- .... **BLC 3; CLC 5, 116,**
　　215; PC 9
　　See also BW 2, 3; CA 33-36R; CANR 24,
　　49, 74, 115; CLR 18; CP 2, 3, 4, 5, 6, 7;
　　CSW; CWP; DA3; DAM MULT; DLB 41;
　　DLBD 8; EWL 3; MAICYA 1, 2; MAL 5;
　　MTCW 1, 2; MTFW 2005; SATA 22, 136;
　　WP
Sancho, Ignatius 1729-1780 .... **LC 84**
Sand, George 1804-1876 ..... **NCLC 2, 42, 57;**
　　WLC
　　See also DA; DA3; DAB; DAC; DAM
　　MST, NOV; DLB 119, 192; EW 6; FL 1:3;
　　FW; GFL 1789 to the Present; RGWL 2,
　　3; TWA
Sandburg, Carl (August) 1878-1967 . **CLC 1,**
　　4, 10, 15, 35; PC 2, 41; WLC
　　See also AAYA 24; AMW; BYA 1, 3; CA
　　5-8R; 25-28R; CANR 35; CDALB 1865-
　　1917; CLR 67; DA; DA3; DAB; DAC;
　　DAM MST, POET; DLB 17, 54, 284;
　　EWL 3; EXPP; LAIT 2; MAICYA 1, 2;
　　MAL 5; MTCW 1, 2; MTFW 2005; PAB;
　　PFS 3, 6, 12; RGAL 4; SATA 8; TUS;
　　WCH; WP; WYA
Sandburg, Charles
　　See Sandburg, Carl (August)
Sandburg, Charles A.
　　See Sandburg, Carl (August)
Sanders, (James) Ed(ward) 1939- .... **CLC 53**
　　See Sanders, Edward
　　See also BG 1:3; CA 13-16R; CAAS 21;
　　CANR 13, 44, 78; CP 1, 2, 3, 4, 5, 6, 7;
　　DAM POET; DLB 16, 244
Sanders, Edward
　　See Sanders, (James) Ed(ward)
　　See also DLB 244
Sanders, Lawrence 1920-1998 .... **CLC 41**
　　See also BEST 89:4; BPFB 3; CA 81-84;
　　165; CANR 33, 62; CMW 4; CPW; DA3;
　　DAM POP; MTCW 1

Stephen, Adeline Virginia
See Woolf, (Adeline) Virginia
Stephen, Sir Leslie 1832-1904 .... **TCLC 23**
See also BRW 5; CA 123; DLB 57, 144, 190
Stephen, Sir Leslie
See Stephen, Sir Leslie
Stephen, Virginia
See Woolf, (Adeline) Virginia
Stephens, James 1882(?)-1950 .... **SSC 50; TCLC 4**
See also CA 104; 192; DLB 19, 153, 162; EWL 3; FANT; RGEL 2; SUFW
Stephens, Reed
See Donaldson, Stephen R(eeder)
Steptoe, Lydia
See Barnes, Djuna
See also GLL 1
Sterchi, Beat 1949- .... **CLC 65**
See also CA 203
Sterling, Brett
See Bradbury, Ray (Douglas); Hamilton, Edmond
Sterling, Bruce 1954- .... **CLC 72**
See also CA 119; CANR 44, 135; CN 7; MTFW 2005; SCFW 2; SFW 4
Sterling, George 1869-1926 .... **TCLC 20**
See also CA 117; 165; DLB 54
Stern, Gerald 1925- .... **CLC 40, 100**
See also AMWS 9; CA 81-84; CANR 28, 94; CP 3, 4, 5, 6, 7; DLB 105; RGAL 4
Stern, Richard (Gustave) 1928- ... **CLC 4, 39**
See also CA 1-4R; CANR 1, 25, 52, 120; CN 1, 2, 3, 4, 5, 6, 7; DLB 218; DLBY 1987; INT CANR-25
Sternberg, Josef von 1894-1969 .... **CLC 20**
See also CA 81-84
Sterne, Laurence 1713-1768 .... **LC 2, 48; WLC**
See also BRW 3; BRWC 1; CDBLB 1660-1789; DA; DAB; DAC; DAM MST, NOV; DLB 39; RGEL 2; TEA
Sternheim, (William Adolf) Carl 1878-1942 .... **TCLC 8**
See also CA 105; 193; DLB 56, 118; EWL 3; IDTP; RGWL 2, 3
Stevens, Margaret Dean
See Aldrich, Bess Streeter
Stevens, Mark 1951- .... **CLC 34**
See also CA 122
Stevens, Wallace 1879-1955 . **PC 6; TCLC 3, 12, 45; WLC**
See also AMW; AMWR 1; CA 104; 124; CDALB 1929-1941; DA; DA3; DAB; DAC; DAM MST, POET; DLB 54; EWL 3; EXPP; MAL 5; MTCW 1, 2; PAB; PFS 13, 16; RGAL 4; TUS; WP
Stevenson, Anne (Katharine) 1933- .. **CLC 7, 33**
See also BRWS 6; CA 17-20R; CAAS 9; CANR 9, 33, 123; CP 3, 4, 5, 6, 7; CWP; DLB 40; MTCW 1; RHW
Stevenson, Robert Louis (Balfour) 1850-1894 ...... **NCLC 5, 14, 63; SSC 11, 51; WLC**
See also AAYA 24; BPFB 3; BRW 5; BRWC 1; BRWR 1; BYA 1, 2, 4, 13; CD-BLB 1890-1914; CLR 10, 11; DA; DA3; DAB; DAC; DAM MST, NOV; DLB 18, 57, 141, 156, 174; DLBD 13; GL 3; HGG; JRDA; LAIT 1, 3; MAICYA 1, 2; NFS 11, 20; RGEL 2; RGSF 2; SATA 100; SUFW; TEA; WCH; WLIT 4; WYA; YABC 2; YAW
Stewart, J(ohn) I(nnes) M(ackintosh) 1906-1994 .... **CLC 7, 14, 32**
See Innes, Michael
See also CA 85-88; 147; CAAS 3; CANR 47; CMW 4; CN 1, 2, 3, 4, 5; MTCW 1, 2

Stewart, Mary (Florence Elinor) 1916- .... **CLC 7, 35, 117**
See also AAYA 29; BPFB 3; CA 1-4R; CANR 1, 59, 130; CMW 4; CPW; DAB; FANT; RHW; SATA 12; YAW
Stewart, Mary Rainbow
See Stewart, Mary (Florence Elinor)
Stifle, June
See Campbell, Maria
Stifter, Adalbert 1805-1868 .. **NCLC 41; SSC 28**
See also CDWLB 2; DLB 133; RGSF 2; RGWL 2, 3
Still, James 1906-2001 .... **CLC 49**
See also CA 65-68; 195; CAAS 17; CANR 10, 26; CSW; DLB 9; DLBY 01; SATA 29; SATA-Obit 127
Sting 1951-
See Sumner, Gordon Matthew
See also CA 167
Stirling, Arthur
See Sinclair, Upton (Beall)
Stitt, Milan 1941- .... **CLC 29**
See also CA 69-72
Stockton, Francis Richard 1834-1902
See Stockton, Frank R.
See also AAYA 68; CA 108; 137; MAICYA 1, 2; SATA 44; SFW 4
Stockton, Frank R. .... **TCLC 47**
See Stockton, Francis Richard
See also BYA 4, 13; DLB 42, 74; DLBD 13; EXPS; SATA-Brief 32; SSFS 3; SUFW; WCH
Stoddard, Charles
See Kuttner, Henry
Stoker, Abraham 1847-1912
See Stoker, Bram
See also CA 105; 150; DA; DA3; DAC; DAM MST, NOV; HGG; MTFW 2005; SATA 29
Stoker, Bram . **SSC 62; TCLC 8, 144; WLC**
See Stoker, Abraham
See also AAYA 23; BPFB 3; BRWS 3; BYA 5; CDBLB 1890-1914; DAB; DLB 304; GL 3; LATS 1:1; NFS 18; RGEL 2; SUFW; TEA; WLIT 4
Stolz, Mary (Slattery) 1920- .... **CLC 12**
See also AAYA 8; AITN 1; CA 5-8R; CANR 13, 41, 112; JRDA; MAICYA 1, 2; SAAS 3; SATA 10, 71, 133; YAW
Stone, Irving 1903-1989 .... **CLC 7**
See also AITN 1; BPFB 3; CA 1-4R; 129; CAAS 3; CANR 1, 23; CN 1, 2, 3, 4; CPW; DA3; DAM POP; INT CANR-23; MTCW 1, 2; MTFW 2005; RHW; SATA 3; SATA-Obit 64
Stone, Oliver (William) 1946- .... **CLC 73**
See also AAYA 15, 64; CA 110; CANR 55, 125
Stone, Robert (Anthony) 1937- ... **CLC 5, 23, 42, 175**
See also AMWS 5; BPFB 3; CA 85-88; CANR 23, 66, 95; CN 4, 5, 6, 7; DLB 152; EWL 3; INT CANR-23; MAL 5; MTCW 1; MTFW 2005
Stone, Ruth 1915- .... **PC 53**
See also CA 45-48; CANR 2, 91; CP 7; CSW; DLB 105; PFS 19
Stone, Zachary
See Follett, Ken(neth Martin)
Stoppard, Tom 1937- ... **CLC 1, 3, 4, 5, 8, 15, 29, 34, 63, 91; DC 6; WLC**
See also AAYA 63; BRWC 1; BRWR 2; BRWS 1; CA 81-84; CANR 39, 67, 125; CBD; CD 5, 6; CDBLB 1960 to Present; DA; DA3; DAB; DAC; DAM DRAM, MST; DFS 2, 5, 8, 11, 13, 16; DLB 13, 233; DLBY 1985; EWL 3; LATS 1:2; MTCW 1, 2; MTFW 2005; RGEL 2; TEA; WLIT 4

Storey, David (Malcolm) 1933- . **CLC 2, 4, 5, 8**
See also BRWS 1; CA 81-84; CANR 36; CBD; CD 5, 6; CN 1, 2, 3, 4, 5, 6; DAM DRAM; DLB 13, 14, 207, 245; EWL 3; MTCW 1; RGEL 2
Storm, Hyemeyohsts 1935- ... **CLC 3; NNAL**
See also CA 81-84; CANR 45; DAM MULT
Storm, (Hans) Theodor (Woldsen) 1817-1888 .... **NCLC 1; SSC 27**
See also CDWLB 2; DLB 129; EW; RGSF 2; RGWL 2, 3
Storni, Alfonsina 1892-1938 . **HLC 2; PC 33; TCLC 5**
See also CA 104; 131; DAM MULT; DLB 283; HW 1; LAW
Stoughton, William 1631-1701 .... **LC 38**
See also DLB 24
Stout, Rex (Todhunter) 1886-1975 ..... **CLC 3**
See also AITN 2; BPFB 3; CA 61-64; CANR 71; CMW 4; CN 2; DLB 306; MSW; RGAL 4
Stow, (Julian) Randolph 1935- ... **CLC 23, 48**
See also CA 13-16R; CANR 33; CN 1, 2, 3, 4, 5, 6, 7; CP 1, 2, 3, 4; DLB 260; MTCW 1; RGEL 2
Stowe, Harriet (Elizabeth) Beecher 1811-1896 .... **NCLC 3, 50, 133; WLC**
See also AAYA 53; AMWS 1; CDALB 1865-1917; DA; DA3; DAB; DAC; DAM MST, NOV; DLB 1, 12, 42, 74, 189, 239, 243; EXPN; FL 1:3; JRDA; LAIT 2; MAICYA 1, 2; NFS 6; RGAL 4; TUS; YABC 1
Strabo c. 64B.C.-c. 25 .... **CMLC 37**
See also DLB 176
Strachey, (Giles) Lytton 1880-1932 .... **TCLC 12**
See also BRWS 2; CA 110; 178; DLB 149; DLBD 10; EWL 3; MTCW 2; NCFS 4
Stramm, August 1874-1915 .... **PC 50**
See also CA 195; EWL 3
Strand, Mark 1934- .. **CLC 6, 18, 41, 71; PC 63**
See also AMWS 4; CA 21-24R; CANR 40, 65, 100; CP 1, 2, 3, 4, 5, 6, 7; DAM POET; DLB 5; EWL 3; MAL 5; PAB; PFS 9, 18; RGAL 4; SATA 41; TCLE 1:2
Stratton-Porter, Gene(va Grace) 1863-1924
See Porter, Gene(va Grace) Stratton
See also ANW; CA 137; CLR 87; DLB 221; DLBD 14; MAICYA 1, 2; SATA 15
Straub, Peter (Francis) 1943- ... **CLC 28, 107**
See also BEST 89:1; BPFB 3; CA 85-88; CANR 28, 65, 109; CPW; DAM POP; DLBY 1984; HGG; MTCW 1, 2; MTFW 2005; SUFW 2
Strauss, Botho 1944- .... **CLC 22**
See also CA 157; CWW 2; DLB 124
Strauss, Leo 1899-1973 .... **TCLC 141**
See also CA 101; 45-48; CANR 122
Streatfeild, (Mary) Noel 1897(?)-1986 .... **CLC 21**
See also CA 81-84; 120; CANR 31; CLR 17, 83; CWRI 5; DLB 160; MAICYA 1, 2; SATA 20; SATA-Obit 48
Stribling, T(homas) S(igismund) 1881-1965 .... **CLC 23**
See also CA 189; 107; CMW 4; DLB 9; RGAL 4
Strindberg, (Johan) August 1849-1912 ... **DC 18; TCLC 1, 8, 21, 47; WLC**
See also CA 104; 135; DA; DA3; DAB; DAC; DAM DRAM, MST; DFS 4, 9; DLB 259; EW 7; EWL 3; IDTP; LMFS 2; MTCW 2; MTFW 2005; RGWL 2, 3; TWA
Stringer, Arthur 1874-1950 .... **TCLC 37**
See also CA 161; DLB 92

Thackeray, William Makepeace
1811-1863 .... **NCLC 5, 14, 22, 43; WLC**
See also BRW 5; BRWC 2; CDBLB 1832-1890; DA; DA3; DAB; DAC; DAM MST, NOV; DLB 21, 55, 159, 163; NFS 13; RGEL 2; SATA 23; TEA; WLIT 3

Thakura, Ravindranatha
See Tagore, Rabindranath

Thames, C. H.
See Marlowe, Stephen

Tharoor, Shashi 1956- .... **CLC 70**
See also CA 141; CANR 91; CN 6, 7

Thelwall, John 1764-1834 .... **NCLC 162**
See also DLB 93, 158

Thelwell, Michael Miles 1939- .... **CLC 22**
See also BW 2; CA 101

Theobald, Lewis, Jr.
See Lovecraft, H(oward) P(hillips)

Theocritus c. 310B.C.- .... **CMLC 45**
See also AW 1; DLB 176; RGWL 2, 3

Theodorescu, Ion N. 1880-1967
See Arghezi, Tudor
See also CA 116

Theriault, Yves 1915-1983 .... **CLC 79**
See also CA 102; CCA 1; DAC; DAM MST; DLB 88; EWL 3

Theroux, Alexander (Louis) 1939- .... **CLC 2, 25**
See also CA 85-88; CANR 20, 63; CN 4, 5, 6, 7

Theroux, Paul (Edward) 1941- ..... **CLC 5, 8, 11, 15, 28, 46**
See also AAYA 28; AMWS 8; BEST 89:4; BPFB 3; CA 33-36R; CANR 20, 45, 74, 133; CDALBS; CN 1, 2, 3, 4, 5, 6, 7; CP 1; CPW 1; DA3; DAM POP; DLB 2, 218; EWL 3; HGG; MAL 5; MTCW 1, 2; MTFW 2005; RGAL 4; SATA 44, 109; TUS

Thesen, Sharon 1946- .... **CLC 56**
See also CA 163; CANR 125; CP 7; CWP

Thespis fl. 6th cent. B.C.- .... **CMLC 51**
See also LMFS 1

Thevenin, Denis
See Duhamel, Georges

Thibault, Jacques Anatole Francois 1844-1924
See France, Anatole
See also CA 106; 127; DA3; DAM NOV; MTCW 1, 2; TWA

Thiele, Colin (Milton) 1920- .... **CLC 17**
See also CA 29-32R; CANR 12, 28, 53, 105; CLR 27; CP 1, 2; DLB 289; MAICYA 1, 2; SAAS 2; SATA 14, 72, 125; YAW

Thistlethwaite, Bel
See Wetherald, Agnes Ethelwyn

Thomas, Audrey (Callahan) 1935- .... **CLC 7, 13, 37, 107; SSC 20**
See also AITN 2; CA 21-24R; 237; CAAE 237; CAAS 19; CANR 36, 58; CN 2, 3, 4, 5, 6, 7; DLB 60; MTCW 1; RGSF 2

Thomas, Augustus 1857-1934 .... **TCLC 97**
See also MAL 5

Thomas, D(onald) M(ichael) 1935- . **CLC 13, 22, 31, 132**
See also BPFB 3; BRWS 4; CA 61-64; CAAS 11; CANR 17, 45, 75; CDBLB 1960 to Present; CN 4, 5, 6, 7; CP 1, 2, 3, 4, 5, 6, 7; DA3; DLB 40, 207, 299; HGG; INT CANR-17; MTCW 1, 2; MTFW 2005; SFW 4

Thomas, Dylan (Marlais) 1914-1953 .... **PC 2, 52; SSC 3, 44; TCLC 1, 8, 45, 105; WLC**
See also AAYA 45; BRWS 1; CA 104; 120; CANR 65; CDBLB 1945-1960; DA; DA3; DAB; DAC; DAM DRAM, MST, POET;
DLB 13, 20, 139; EWL 3; EXPP; LAIT 3; MTCW 1, 2; MTFW 2005; PAB; PFS 1, 3, 8; RGEL 2; RGSF 2; SATA 60; TEA; WLIT 4; WP

Thomas, (Philip) Edward 1878-1917 . **PC 53; TCLC 10**
See also BRW 6; BRWS 3; CA 106; 153; DAM POET; DLB 19, 98, 156, 216; EWL 3; PAB; RGEL 2

Thomas, Joyce Carol 1938- .... **CLC 35**
See also AAYA 12, 54; BW 2, 3; CA 113; 116; CANR 48, 114, 135; CLR 19; DLB 33; INT CA-116; JRDA; MAICYA 1, 2; MTCW 1, 2; MTFW 2005; SAAS 7; SATA 40, 78, 123, 137; SATA-Essay 137; WYA; YAW

Thomas, Lewis 1913-1993 .... **CLC 35**
See also ANW; CA 85-88; 143; CANR 38, 60; DLB 275; MTCW 1, 2

Thomas, M. Carey 1857-1935 .... **TCLC 89**
See also FW

Thomas, Paul
See Mann, (Paul) Thomas

Thomas, Piri 1928- .... **CLC 17; HLCS 2**
See also CA 73-76; HW 1; LLW

Thomas, R(onald) S(tuart) 1913-2000 .... **CLC 6, 13, 48**
See also CA 89-92; 189; CAAS 4; CANR 30; CDBLB 1960 to Present; CP 1, 2, 3, 4, 5, 6, 7; DAB; DAM POET; DLB 27; EWL 3; MTCW 1; RGEL 2

Thomas, Ross (Elmore) 1926-1995 .. **CLC 39**
See also CA 33-36R; 150; CANR 22, 63; CMW 4

Thompson, Francis (Joseph) 1859-1907 .... **TCLC 4**
See also BRW 5; CA 104; 189; CDBLB 1890-1914; DLB 19; RGEL 2; TEA

Thompson, Francis Clegg
See Mencken, H(enry) L(ouis)

Thompson, Hunter S(tockton) 1937(?)-2005 .... **CLC 9, 17, 40, 104**
See also AAYA 45; BEST 89:1; BPFB 3; CA 17-20R; 236; CANR 23, 46, 74, 77, 111, 133; CPW; CSW; DA3; DAM POP; DLB 185; MTCW 1, 2; MTFW 2005; TUS

Thompson, James Myers
See Thompson, Jim (Myers)

Thompson, Jim (Myers) 1906-1977(?) .... **CLC 69**
See also BPFB 3; CA 140; CMW 4; CPW; DLB 226; MSW

Thompson, Judith (Clare Francesca) 1954- .... **CLC 39**
See also CA 143; CD 5, 6; CWD; DFS 22

Thomson, James 1700-1748 .... **LC 16, 29, 40**
See also BRWS 3; DAM POET; DLB 95; RGEL 2

Thomson, James 1834-1882 .... **NCLC 18**
See also DAM POET; DLB 35; RGEL 2

Thoreau, Henry David 1817-1862 .. **NCLC 7, 21, 61, 138; PC 30; WLC**
See also AAYA 42; AMW; ANW; BYA 3; CDALB 1640-1865; DA; DA3; DAB; DAC; DAM MST; DLB 1, 183, 223, 270, 298; LAIT 2; LMFS 1; NCFS 3; RGAL 4; TUS

Thorndike, E. L.
See Thorndike, Edward L(ee)

Thorndike, Edward L(ee) 1874-1949 .... **TCLC 107**
See also CA 121

Thornton, Hall
See Silverberg, Robert

Thorpe, Adam 1956- .... **CLC 176**
See also CA 129; CANR 92; DLB 231

Thubron, Colin (Gerald Dryden) 1939- .... **CLC 163**
See also CA 25-28R; CANR 12, 29, 59, 95; CN 5, 6, 7; DLB 204, 231

Thucydides c. 455B.C.-c. 395B.C. . **CMLC 17**
See also AW 1; DLB 176; RGWL 2, 3

Thumboo, Edwin Nadason 1933- .... **PC 30**
See also CA 194; CP 1

Thurber, James (Grover) 1894-1961 .. **CLC 5, 11, 25, 125; SSC 1, 47**
See also AAYA 56; AMWS 1; BPFB 3; BYA 5; CA 73-76; CANR 17, 39; CDALB 1929-1941; CWRI 5; DA; DA3; DAB; DAC; DAM DRAM, MST, NOV; DLB 4, 11, 22, 102; EWL 3; EXPS; FANT; LAIT 3; MAICYA 1, 2; MAL 5; MTCW 1, 2; MTFW 2005; RGAL 4; RGSF 2; SATA 13; SSFS 1, 10, 19; SUFW; TUS

Thurman, Wallace (Henry) 1902-1934 ..... **BLC 3; HR 1:3; TCLC 6**
See also BW 1, 3; CA 104; 124; CANR 81; DAM MULT; DLB 51

Tibullus c. 54B.C.-c. 18B.C. .... **CMLC 36**
See also AW 2; DLB 211; RGWL 2, 3

Ticheburn, Cheviot
See Ainsworth, William Harrison

Tieck, (Johann) Ludwig 1773-1853 .... **NCLC 5, 46; SSC 31**
See also CDWLB 2; DLB 90; EW 5; IDTP; RGSF 2; RGWL 2, 3; SUFW

Tiger, Derry
See Ellison, Harlan (Jay)

Tilghman, Christopher 1946- .... **CLC 65**
See also CA 159; CANR 135; CSW; DLB 244

Tillich, Paul (Johannes) 1886-1965 .... **CLC 131**
See also CA 5-8R; 25-28R; CANR 33; MTCW 1, 2

Tillinghast, Richard (Williford) 1940- .... **CLC 29**
See also CA 29-32R; CAAS 23; CANR 26, 51, 96; CP 2, 3, 4, 5, 6, 7; CSW

Timrod, Henry 1828-1867 .... **NCLC 25**
See also DLB 3, 248; RGAL 4

Tindall, Gillian (Elizabeth) 1938- ...... **CLC 7**
See also CA 21-24R; CANR 11, 65, 107; CN 1, 2, 3, 4, 5, 6, 7

Tiptree, James, Jr. .... **CLC 48, 50**
See Sheldon, Alice Hastings Bradley
See also DLB 8; SCFW 1, 2; SFW 4

Tirone Smith, Mary-Ann 1944- .... **CLC 39**
See also CA 118; 136; CANR 113; SATA 143

Tirso de Molina 1580(?)-1648 .... **DC 13; HLCS 2; LC 73**
See also RGWL 2, 3

Titmarsh, Michael Angelo
See Thackeray, William Makepeace

Tocqueville, Alexis (Charles Henri Maurice Clerel Comte) de 1805-1859 .. **NCLC 7, 63**
See also EW 6; GFL 1789 to the Present; TWA

Toer, Pramoedya Ananta 1925- ...... **CLC 186**
See also CA 197; RGWL 3

Toffler, Alvin 1928- .... **CLC 168**
See also CA 13-16R; CANR 15, 46, 67; CPW; DAM POP; MTCW 1, 2

Toibin, Colm 1955- .... **CLC 162**
See also CA 142; CANR 81; CN 7; DLB 271

Tolkien, J(ohn) R(onald) R(euel) 1892-1973 .... **CLC 1, 2, 3, 8, 12, 38; TCLC 137; WLC**
See also AAYA 10; AITN 1; BPFB 3; BRWC 2; BRWS 2; CA 17-18; 45-48; CANR 36, 134; CAP 2; CDBLB 1914-

Ustinov, Peter (Alexander)
1921-2004 .... **CLC 1**
See also AITN 1; CA 13-16R; 225; CANR
25, 51; CBD; CD 5, 6; DLB 13; MTCW
2

U Tam'si, Gerald Felix Tchicaya
See Tchicaya, Gerald Felix

U Tam'si, Tchicaya
See Tchicaya, Gerald Felix

Vachss, Andrew (Henry) 1942- .... **CLC 106**
See also CA 118, 214; CAAE 214; CANR
44, 95; CMW 4

Vachss, Andrew H.
See Vachss, Andrew (Henry)

Vaculik, Ludvik 1926- .... **CLC 7**
See also CA 53-56; CANR 72; CWW 2;
DLB 232; EWL 3

Vaihinger, Hans 1852-1933 .... **TCLC 71**
See also CA 116; 166

Valdez, Luis (Miguel) 1940- ..... **CLC 84; DC
10; HLC 2**
See also CA 101; CAD; CANR 32, 81; CD
5, 6; DAM MULT; DFS 5; DLB 122;
EWL 3; HW 1; LAIT 4; LLW

Valenzuela, Luisa 1938- .... **CLC 31, 104;
HLCS 2; SSC 14, 82**
See also CA 101; CANR 32, 65, 123; CD-
WLB 3; CWW 2; DAM MULT; DLB 113;
EWL 3; FW; HW 1, 2; LAW; RGSF 2;
RGWL 3

Valera y Alcala-Galiano, Juan
1824-1905 .... **TCLC 10**
See also CA 106

Valerius Maximus fl. 20- .... **CMLC 64**
See also DLB 211

Valery, (Ambroise) Paul (Toussaint Jules)
1871-1945 .... **PC 9; TCLC 4, 15**
See also CA 104; 122; DA3; DAM POET;
DLB 258; EW 8; EWL 3; GFL 1789 to
the Present; MTCW 1, 2; MTFW 2005;
RGWL 2, 3; TWA

Valle-Inclan, Ramon (Maria) del
1866-1936 .... **HLC 2; TCLC 5**
See del Valle-Inclan, Ramon (Maria)
See also CA 106; 153; CANR 80; DAM
MULT; DLB 134; EW 8; EWL 3; HW 2;
RGSF 2; RGWL 2, 3

Vallejo, Antonio Buero
See Buero Vallejo, Antonio

Vallejo, Cesar (Abraham)
1892-1938 .... **HLC 2; TCLC 3, 56**
See also CA 105; 153; DAM MULT; DLB
290; EWL 3; HW 1; LAW; RGWL 2, 3

Valles, Jules 1832-1885 .... **NCLC 71**
See also DLB 123; GFL 1789 to the Present

Vallette, Marguerite Eymery
1860-1953 .... **TCLC 67**
See Rachilde
See also CA 182; DLB 123, 192

Valle Y Pena, Ramon del
See Valle-Inclan, Ramon (Maria) del

Van Ash, Cay 1918-1994 .... **CLC 34**
See also CA 220

Vanbrugh, Sir John 1664-1726 .... **LC 21**
See also BRW 2; DAM DRAM; DLB 80;
IDTP; RGEL 2

Van Campen, Karl
See Campbell, John W(ood, Jr.)

Vance, Gerald
See Silverberg, Robert

Vance, Jack .... **CLC 35**
See Vance, John Holbrook
See also DLB 8; FANT; SCFW 1, 2; SFW
4; SUFW 1, 2

Vance, John Holbrook 1916-
See Queen, Ellery; Vance, Jack
See also CA 29-32R; CANR 17, 65; CMW
4; MTCW 1

**Van Den Bogarde, Derek Jules Gaspard
Ulric Niven** 1921-1999 .... **CLC 14**
See Bogarde, Dirk
See also CA 77-80; 179

Vandenburgh, Jane .... **CLC 59**
See also CA 168

Vanderhaeghe, Guy 1951- .... **CLC 41**
See also BPFB 3; CA 113; CANR 72, 145;
CN 7

van der Post, Laurens (Jan)
1906-1996 .... **CLC 5**
See also AFW; CA 5-8R; 155; CANR 35;
CN 1, 2, 3, 4, 5, 6; DLB 204; RGEL 2

van de Wetering, Janwillem 1931- ... **CLC 47**
See also CA 49-52; CANR 4, 62, 90; CMW
4

Van Dine, S. S. .... **TCLC 23**
See Wright, Willard Huntington
See also DLB 306; MSW

Van Doren, Carl (Clinton)
1885-1950 .... **TCLC 18**
See also CA 111; 168

Van Doren, Mark 1894-1972 .... **CLC 6, 10**
See also CA 1-4R; 37-40R; CANR 3; CN
1; CP 1; DLB 45, 284; MAL 5; MTCW
1, 2; RGAL 4

Van Druten, John (William)
1901-1957 .... **TCLC 2**
See also CA 104; 161; DLB 10; MAL 5;
RGAL 4

Van Duyn, Mona (Jane) 1921-2004 .. **CLC 3,
7, 63, 116**
See also CA 9-12R; 234; CANR 7, 38, 60,
116; CP 1, 2, 3, 4, 5, 6, 7; CWP; DAM
POET; DLB 5; MAL 5; MTFW 2005;
PFS 20

Van Dyne, Edith
See Baum, L(yman) Frank

van Itallie, Jean-Claude 1936- .... **CLC 3**
See also CA 45-48; CAAS 2; CAD; CANR
1, 48; CD 5, 6; DLB 7

Van Loot, Cornelius Obenchain
See Roberts, Kenneth (Lewis)

van Ostaijen, Paul 1896-1928 .... **TCLC 33**
See also CA 163

Van Peebles, Melvin 1932- .... **CLC 2, 20**
See also BW 2, 3; CA 85-88; CANR 27,
67, 82; DAM MULT

van Schendel, Arthur(-Francois-Emile)
1874-1946 .... **TCLC 56**
See also EWL 3

Vansittart, Peter 1920- .... **CLC 42**
See also CA 1-4R; CANR 3, 49, 90; CN 4,
5, 6, 7; RHW

Van Vechten, Carl 1880-1964 ... **CLC 33; HR
1:3**
See also AMWS 2; CA 183; 89-92; DLB 4,
9, 51; RGAL 4

van Vogt, A(lfred) E(lton) 1912-2000 . **CLC 1**
See also BPFB 3; BYA 13, 14; CA 21-24R;
190; CANR 28; DLB 8, 251; SATA 14;
SATA-Obit 124; SCFW 1, 2; SFW 4

Vara, Madeleine
See Jackson, Laura (Riding)

Varda, Agnes 1928- .... **CLC 16**
See also CA 116; 122

Vargas Llosa, (Jorge) Mario (Pedro)
1936- .... **CLC 3, 6, 9, 10, 15, 31, 42, 85,
181; HLC 2**
See Llosa, (Jorge) Mario (Pedro) Vargas
See also BPFB 3; CA 73-76; CANR 18, 32,
42, 67, 116, 140; CDWLB 3; CWW 2;
DA; DA3; DAB; DAC; DAM MST,
MULT, NOV; DLB 145; DNFS 2; EWL
3; HW 1, 2; LAIT 5; LATS 1:2; LAW;
LAWS 1; MTCW 1, 2; MTFW 2005;
RGWL 2; SSFS 14; TWA; WLIT 1

Varnhagen von Ense, Rahel
1771-1833 .... **NCLC 130**
See also DLB 90

Vasari, Giorgio 1511-1574 .... **LC 114**

Vasiliu, George
See Bacovia, George

Vasiliu, Gheorghe
See Bacovia, George
See also CA 123; 189

Vassa, Gustavus
See Equiano, Olaudah

Vassilikos, Vassilis 1933- .... **CLC 4, 8**
See also CA 81-84; CANR 75; EWL 3

Vaughan, Henry 1621-1695 .... **LC 27**
See also BRW 2; DLB 131; PAB; RGEL 2

Vaughn, Stephanie .... **CLC 62**

Vazov, Ivan (Minchov) 1850-1921 . **TCLC 25**
See also CA 121; 167; CDWLB 4; DLB
147

Veblen, Thorstein B(unde)
1857-1929 .... **TCLC 31**
See also AMWS 1; CA 115; 165; DLB 246;
MAL 5

Vega, Lope de 1562-1635 ... **HLCS 2; LC 23,
119**
See also EW 2; RGWL 2, 3

Vendler, Helen (Hennessy) 1933- ... **CLC 138**
See also CA 41-44R; CANR 25, 72, 136;
MTCW 1, 2; MTFW 2005

Venison, Alfred
See Pound, Ezra (Weston Loomis)

Ventsel, Elena Sergeevna 1907-2002
See Grekova, I.
See also CA 154

Verdi, Marie de
See Mencken, H(enry) L(ouis)

Verdu, Matilde
See Cela, Camilo Jose

Verga, Giovanni (Carmelo)
1840-1922 .... **SSC 21, 87; TCLC 3**
See also CA 104; 123; CANR 101; EW 7;
EWL 3; RGSF 2; RGWL 2, 3; WLIT 7

Vergil 70B.C.-19B.C. ... **CMLC 9, 40; PC 12;
WLCS**
See Virgil
See also AW 2; DA; DA3; DAB; DAC;
DAM MST, POET; EFS 1; LMFS 1

Vergil, Polydore c. 1470-1555 .... **LC 108**
See also DLB 132

Verhaeren, Emile (Adolphe Gustave)
1855-1916 .... **TCLC 12**
See also CA 109; EWL 3; GFL 1789 to the
Present

Verlaine, Paul (Marie) 1844-1896 .. **NCLC 2,
51; PC 2, 32**
See also DAM POET; DLB 217; EW 7;
GFL 1789 to the Present; LMFS 2; RGWL
2, 3; TWA

Verne, Jules (Gabriel) 1828-1905 ... **TCLC 6,
52**
See also AAYA 16; BYA 4; CA 110; 131;
CLR 88; DA3; DLB 123; GFL 1789 to
the Present; JRDA; LAIT 2; LMFS 2;
MAICYA 1, 2; MTFW 2005; RGWL 2, 3;
SATA 21; SCFW 1, 2; SFW 4; TWA;
WCH

Verus, Marcus Annius
See Aurelius, Marcus

Very, Jones 1813-1880 .... **NCLC 9**
See also DLB 1, 243; RGAL 4

Vesaas, Tarjei 1897-1970 .... **CLC 48**
See also CA 190; 29-32R; DLB 297; EW
11; EWL 3; RGWL 3

Vialis, Gaston
See Simenon, Georges (Jacques Christian)

Vian, Boris 1920-1959(?) .... **TCLC 9**
See also CA 106; 164; CANR 111; DLB
72, 321; EWL 3; GFL 1789 to the Present;
MTCW 2; RGWL 2, 3

Wakefield, Herbert Russell
1888-1965 .... **TCLC 120**
See also CA 5-8R; CANR 77; HGG; SUFW

Wakoski, Diane 1937- ...... **CLC 2, 4, 7, 9, 11, 40; PC 15**
See also CA 13-16R, 216; CAAE 216; CAAS 1; CANR 9, 60, 106; CP 1, 2, 3, 4, 5, 6, 7; CWP; DAM POET; DLB 5; INT CANR-9; MAL 5; MTCW 2; MTFW 2005

Wakoski-Sherbell, Diane
See Wakoski, Diane

Walcott, Derek (Alton) 1930- ... **BLC 3; CLC 2, 4, 9, 14, 25, 42, 67, 76, 160; DC 7; PC 46**
See also BW 2; CA 89-92; CANR 26, 47, 75, 80, 130; CBD; CD 5, 6; CDWLB 3; CP 1, 2, 3, 4, 5, 6, 7; DA3; DAB; DAC; DAM MST, MULT, POET; DLB 117; DLBY 1981; DNFS 1; EFS 1; EWL 3; LMFS 2; MTCW 1, 2; MTFW 2005; PFS 6; RGEL 2; TWA; WWE 1

Waldman, Anne (Lesley) 1945- .... **CLC 7**
See also BG 1:3; CA 37-40R; CAAS 17; CANR 34, 69, 116; CP 1, 2, 3, 4, 5, 6, 7; CWP; DLB 16

Waldo, E. Hunter
See Sturgeon, Theodore (Hamilton)

Waldo, Edward Hamilton
See Sturgeon, Theodore (Hamilton)

Walker, Alice (Malsenior) 1944- .... **BLC 3; CLC 5, 6, 9, 19, 27, 46, 58, 103, 167; PC 30; SSC 5; WLCS**
See also AAYA 3, 33; AFAW 1, 2; AMWS 3; BEST 89:4; BPFB 3; BW 2, 3; CA 37-40R; CANR 9, 27, 49, 66, 82, 131; CDALB 1968-1988; CN 4, 5, 6, 7; CPW; CSW; DA; DA3; DAB; DAC; DAM MST, MULT, NOV, POET, POP; DLB 6, 33, 143; EWL 3; EXPN; EXPS; FL 1:6; FW; INT CANR-27; LAIT 3; MAL 5; MAWW; MTCW 1, 2; MTFW 2005; NFS 5; RGAL 4; RGSF 2; SATA 31; SSFS 2, 11; TUS; YAW

Walker, David Harry 1911-1992 ...... **CLC 14**
See also CA 1-4R; 137; CANR 1; CN 1, 2; CWRI 5; SATA 8; SATA-Obit 71

Walker, Edward Joseph 1934-2004
See Walker, Ted
See also CA 21-24R; 226; CANR 12, 28, 53

Walker, George F(rederick) 1947- .. **CLC 44, 61**
See also CA 103; CANR 21, 43, 59; CD 5, 6; DAB; DAC; DAM MST; DLB 60

Walker, Joseph A. 1935-2003 .... **CLC 19**
See also BW 1, 3; CA 89-92; CAD; CANR 26, 143; CD 5, 6; DAM DRAM, MST; DFS 12; DLB 38

Walker, Margaret (Abigail)
1915-1998 .... **BLC; CLC 1, 6; PC 20; TCLC 129**
See also AFAW 1, 2; BW 2, 3; CA 73-76; 172; CANR 26, 54, 76, 136; CN 1, 2, 3, 4, 5, 6; CP 1, 2, 3, 4; CSW; DAM MULT; DLB 76, 152; EXPP; FW; MAL 5; MTCW 1, 2; MTFW 2005; RGAL 4; RHW

Walker, Ted .... **CLC 13**
See Walker, Edward Joseph
See also CP 1, 2, 3, 4, 5, 6, 7; DLB 40

Wallace, David Foster 1962- ... **CLC 50, 114; SSC 68**
See also AAYA 50; AMWS 10; CA 132; CANR 59, 133; CN 7; DA3; MTCW 2; MTFW 2005

Wallace, Dexter
See Masters, Edgar Lee

Wallace, (Richard Horatio) Edgar
1875-1932 .... **TCLC 57**
See also CA 115; 218; CMW 4; DLB 70; MSW; RGEL 2

Wallace, Irving 1916-1990 .... **CLC 7, 13**
See also AITN 1; BPFB 3; CA 1-4R; 132; CAAS 1; CANR 1, 27; CPW; DAM NOV, POP; INT CANR-27; MTCW 1, 2

Wallant, Edward Lewis 1926-1962 ... **CLC 5, 10**
See also CA 1-4R; CANR 22; DLB 2, 28, 143, 299; EWL 3; MAL 5; MTCW 1, 2; RGAL 4

Wallas, Graham 1858-1932 .... **TCLC 91**

Waller, Edmund 1606-1687 .... **LC 86**
See also BRW 2; DAM POET; DLB 126; PAB; RGEL 2

Walley, Byron
See Card, Orson Scott

Walpole, Horace 1717-1797 .... **LC 2, 49**
See also BRW 3; DLB 39, 104, 213; GL 3; HGG; LMFS 1; RGEL 2; SUFW 1; TEA

Walpole, Hugh (Seymour)
1884-1941 .... **TCLC 5**
See also CA 104; 165; DLB 34; HGG; MTCW 2; RGEL 2; RHW

Walrond, Eric (Derwent) 1898-1966 . **HR 1:3**
See also BW 1; CA 125; DLB 51

Walser, Martin 1927- .... **CLC 27, 183**
See also CA 57-60; CANR 8, 46, 145; CWW 2; DLB 75, 124; EWL 3

Walser, Robert 1878-1956 ..... **SSC 20; TCLC 18**
See also CA 118; 165; CANR 100; DLB 66; EWL 3

Walsh, Gillian Paton
See Paton Walsh, Gillian

Walsh, Jill Paton .... **CLC 35**
See Paton Walsh, Gillian
See also CLR 2, 65; WYA

Walter, Villiam Christian
See Andersen, Hans Christian

Walters, Anna L(ee) 1946- .... **NNAL**
See also CA 73-76

Walther von der Vogelweide c.
1170-1228 .... **CMLC 56**

Walton, Izaak 1593-1683 .... **LC 72**
See also BRW 2; CDBLB Before 1660; DLB 151, 213; RGEL 2

Wambaugh, Joseph (Aloysius), Jr.
1937- .... **CLC 3, 18**
See also AITN 1; BEST 89:3; BPFB 3; CA 33-36R; CANR 42, 65, 115; CMW 4; CPW 1; DA3; DAM NOV, POP; DLB 6; DLBY 1983; MSW; MTCW 1, 2

Wang Wei 699(?)-761(?) .... **PC 18**
See also TWA

Warburton, William 1698-1779 .... **LC 97**
See also DLB 104

Ward, Arthur Henry Sarsfield 1883-1959
See Rohmer, Sax
See also CA 108; 173; CMW 4; HGG

Ward, Douglas Turner 1930- .... **CLC 19**
See also BW 1; CA 81-84; CAD; CANR 27; CD 5, 6; DLB 7, 38

Ward, E. D.
See Lucas, E(dward) V(errall)

Ward, Mrs. Humphry 1851-1920
See Ward, Mary Augusta
See also RGEL 2

Ward, Mary Augusta 1851-1920 ... **TCLC 55**
See Ward, Mrs. Humphry
See also DLB 18

Ward, Nathaniel 1578(?)-1652 .... **LC 114**
See also DLB 24

Ward, Peter
See Faust, Frederick (Schiller)

Warhol, Andy 1928(?)-1987 .... **CLC 20**
See also AAYA 12; BEST 89:4; CA 89-92; 121; CANR 34

Warner, Francis (Robert le Plastrier)
1937- .... **CLC 14**
See also CA 53-56; CANR 11; CP 1, 2, 3, 4

Warner, Marina 1946- .... **CLC 59**
See also CA 65-68; CANR 21, 55, 118; CN 5, 6, 7; DLB 194; MTFW 2005

Warner, Rex (Ernest) 1905-1986 ...... **CLC 45**
See also CA 89-92; 119; CN 1, 2, 3, 4; CP 1, 2, 3, 4; DLB 15; RGEL 2; RHW

Warner, Susan (Bogert)
1819-1885 .... **NCLC 31, 146**
See also DLB 3, 42, 239, 250, 254

Warner, Sylvia (Constance) Ashton
See Ashton-Warner, Sylvia (Constance)

Warner, Sylvia Townsend
1893-1978 .. **CLC 7, 19; SSC 23; TCLC 131**
See also BRWS 7; CA 61-64; 77-80; CANR 16, 60, 104; CN 1, 2; DLB 34, 139; EWL 3; FANT; FW; MTCW 1, 2; RGEL 2; RGSF 2; RHW

Warren, Mercy Otis 1728-1814 ..... **NCLC 13**
See also DLB 31, 200; RGAL 4; TUS

Warren, Robert Penn 1905-1989 .. **CLC 1, 4, 6, 8, 10, 13, 18, 39, 53, 59; PC 37; SSC 4, 58; WLC**
See also AITN 1; AMW; AMWC 2; BPFB 3; BYA 1; CA 13-16R; 129; CANR 10, 47; CDALB 1968-1988; CN 1, 2, 3, 4; CP 1, 2, 3, 4; DA; DA3; DAB; DAC; DAM MST, NOV, POET; DLB 2, 48, 152; 320; DLBY 1980, 1989; EWL 3; INT CANR-10; MAL 5; MTCW 1, 2; MTFW 2005; NFS 13; RGAL 4; RGSF 2; RHW; SATA 46; SATA-Obit 63; SSFS 8; TUS

Warrigal, Jack
See Furphy, Joseph

Warshofsky, Isaac
See Singer, Isaac Bashevis

Warton, Joseph 1722-1800 .... **NCLC 118**
See also DLB 104, 109; RGEL 2

Warton, Thomas 1728-1790 .... **LC 15, 82**
See also DAM POET; DLB 104, 109; RGEL 2

Waruk, Kona
See Harris, (Theodore) Wilson

Warung, Price .... **TCLC 45**
See Astley, William
See also DLB 230; RGEL 2

Warwick, Jarvis
See Garner, Hugh
See also CCA 1

Washington, Alex
See Harris, Mark

Washington, Booker T(aliaferro)
1856-1915 .... **BLC 3; TCLC 10**
See also BW 1; CA 114; 125; DA3; DAM MULT; LAIT 2; RGAL 4; SATA 28

Washington, George 1732-1799 .... **LC 25**
See also DLB 31

Wassermann, (Karl) Jakob
1873-1934 .... **TCLC 6**
See also CA 104; 163; DLB 66; EWL 3

Wasserstein, Wendy 1950-2006 . **CLC 32, 59, 90, 183; DC 4**
See also AMWS 15; CA 121; 129; CABS 3; CAD; CANR 53, 75, 128; CD 5, 6; CWD; DA3; DAM DRAM; DFS 5, 17; DLB 228; EWL 3; FW; INT CA-129; MAL 5; MTCW 2; MTFW 2005; SATA 94

Waterhouse, Keith (Spencer) 1929- . **CLC 47**
See also CA 5-8R; CANR 38, 67, 109; CBD; CD 6; CN 1, 2, 3, 4, 5, 6, 7; DLB 13, 15; MTCW 1, 2; MTFW 2005

West, Dorothy 1907-1998 ...... **HR 1:3; TCLC 108**
See also BW 2; CA 143; 169; DLB 76

West, (Mary) Jessamyn 1902-1984 ... **CLC 7, 17**
See also CA 9-12R; 112; CANR 27; CN 1, 2, 3; DLB 6; DLBY 1984; MTCW 1, 2; RGAL 4; RHW; SATA-Obit 37; TCWW 2; TUS; YAW

West, Morris L(anglo) 1916-1999 ..... **CLC 6, 33**
See also BPFB 3; CA 5-8R; 187; CANR 24, 49, 64; CN 1, 2, 3, 4, 5, 6; CPW; DLB 289; MTCW 1, 2; MTFW 2005

West, Nathanael 1903-1940 .. **SSC 16; TCLC 1, 14, 44**
See also AMW; AMWR 2; BPFB 3; CA 104; 125; CDALB 1929-1941; DA3; DLB 4, 9, 28; EWL 3; MAL 5; MTCW 1, 2; MTFW 2005; NFS 16; RGAL 4; TUS

West, Owen
See Koontz, Dean R.

West, Paul 1930- .... **CLC 7, 14, 96**
See also CA 13-16R; CAAS 7; CANR 22, 53, 76, 89, 136; CN 1, 2, 3, 4, 5, 6, 7; DLB 14; INT CANR-22; MTCW 2; MTFW 2005

West, Rebecca 1892-1983 ... **CLC 7, 9, 31, 50**
See also BPFB 3; BRWS 3; CA 5-8R; 109; CANR 19; CN 1, 2, 3; DLB 36; DLBY 1983; EWL 3; FW; MTCW 1, 2; MTFW 2005; NCFS 4; RGEL 2; TEA

Westall, Robert (Atkinson) 1929-1993 .... **CLC 17**
See also AAYA 12; BYA 2, 6, 7, 8, 9, 15; CA 69-72; 141; CANR 18, 68; CLR 13; FANT; JRDA; MAICYA 1, 2; MAICYAS 1; SAAS 2; SATA 23, 69; SATA-Obit 75; WYA; YAW

Westermarck, Edward 1862-1939 . **TCLC 87**

Westlake, Donald E(dwin) 1933- . **CLC 7, 33**
See also BPFB 3; CA 17-20R; CAAS 13; CANR 16, 44, 65, 94, 137; CMW 4; CPW; DAM POP; INT CANR-16; MSW; MTCW 2; MTFW 2005

Westmacott, Mary
See Christie, Agatha (Mary Clarissa)

Weston, Allen
See Norton, Andre

Wetcheek, J. L.
See Feuchtwanger, Lion

Wetering, Janwillem van de
See van de Wetering, Janwillem

Wetherald, Agnes Ethelwyn
1857-1940 .... **TCLC 81**
See also CA 202; DLB 99

Wetherell, Elizabeth
See Warner, Susan (Bogert)

Whale, James 1889-1957 .... **TCLC 63**

Whalen, Philip (Glenn) 1923-2002 .... **CLC 6, 29**
See also BG 1:3; CA 9-12R; 209; CANR 5, 39; CP 1, 2, 3, 4, 5, 6, 7; DLB 16; WP

Wharton, Edith (Newbold Jones)
1862-1937 ... **SSC 6, 84; TCLC 3, 9, 27, 53, 129, 149; WLC**
See also AAYA 25; AMW; AMWC 2; AMWR 1; BPFB 3; CA 104; 132; CDALB 1865-1917; DA; DA3; DAB; DAC; DAM MST, NOV; DLB 4, 9, 12, 78, 189; DLBD 13; EWL 3; EXPS; FL 1:6; GL 3; HGG; LAIT 2, 3; LATS 1:1; MAL 5; MAWW; MTCW 1, 2; MTFW 2005; NFS 5, 11, 15, 20; RGAL 4; RGSF 2; RHW; SSFS 6, 7; SUFW; TUS

Wharton, James
See Mencken, H(enry) L(ouis)

Wharton, William (a pseudonym)
1925- .... **CLC 18, 37**
See also CA 93-96; CN 4, 5, 6, 7; DLBY 1980; INT CA-93-96

Wheatley (Peters), Phillis
1753(?)-1784 ... **BLC 3; LC 3, 50; PC 3; WLC**
See also AFAW 1, 2; CDALB 1640-1865; DA; DA3; DAC; DAM MST, MULT, POET; DLB 31, 50; EXPP; FL 1:1; PFS 13; RGAL 4

Wheelock, John Hall 1886-1978 .... **CLC 14**
See also CA 13-16R; 77-80; CANR 14; CP 1, 2; DLB 45; MAL 5

Whim-Wham
See Curnow, (Thomas) Allen (Monro)

White, Babington
See Braddon, Mary Elizabeth

White, E(lwyn) B(rooks)
1899-1985 .... **CLC 10, 34, 39**
See also AAYA 62; AITN 2; AMWS 1; CA 13-16R; 116; CANR 16, 37; CDALBS; CLR 1, 21; CPW; DA3; DAM POP; DLB 11, 22; EWL 3; FANT; MAICYA 1, 2; MAL 5; MTCW 1, 2; MTFW 2005; NCFS 5; RGAL 4; SATA 2, 29, 100; SATA-Obit 44; TUS

White, Edmund (Valentine III)
1940- .... **CLC 27, 110**
See also AAYA 7; CA 45-48; CANR 3, 19, 36, 62, 107, 133; CN 5, 6, 7; DA3; DAM POP; DLB 227; MTCW 1, 2; MTFW 2005

White, Hayden V. 1928- .... **CLC 148**
See also CA 128; CANR 135; DLB 246

White, Patrick (Victor Martindale)
1912-1990 ...... **CLC 3, 4, 5, 7, 9, 18, 65, 69; SSC 39; TCLC 176**
See also BRWS 1; CA 81-84; 132; CANR 43; CN 1, 2, 3, 4; DLB 260; EWL 3; MTCW 1; RGEL 2; RGSF 2; RHW; TWA; WWE 1

White, Phyllis Dorothy James 1920-
See James, P. D.
See also CA 21-24R; CANR 17, 43, 65, 112; CMW 4; CN 7; CPW; DA3; DAM POP; MTCW 1, 2; MTFW 2005; TEA

White, T(erence) H(anbury)
1906-1964 .... **CLC 30**
See also AAYA 22; BPFB 3; BYA 4, 5; CA 73-76; CANR 37; DLB 160; FANT; JRDA; LAIT 1; MAICYA 1, 2; RGEL 2; SATA 12; SUFW 1; YAW

White, Terence de Vere 1912-1994 ... **CLC 49**
See also CA 49-52; 145; CANR 3

White, Walter
See White, Walter F(rancis)

White, Walter F(rancis) 1893-1955 ... **BLC 3; HR 1:3; TCLC 15**
See also BW 1; CA 115; 124; DAM MULT; DLB 51

White, William Hale 1831-1913
See Rutherford, Mark
See also CA 121; 189

Whitehead, Alfred North
1861-1947 .... **TCLC 97**
See also CA 117; 165; DLB 100, 262

Whitehead, E(dward) A(nthony)
1933- .... **CLC 5**
See Whitehead, Ted
See also CA 65-68; CANR 58, 118; CBD; CD 5; DLB 310

Whitehead, Ted
See Whitehead, E(dward) A(nthony)
See also CD 6

Whiteman, Roberta J. Hill 1947- ...... **NNAL**
See also CA 146

Whitemore, Hugh (John) 1936- .... **CLC 37**
See also CA 132; CANR 77; CBD; CD 5, 6; INT CA-132

Whitman, Sarah Helen (Power)
1803-1878 .... **NCLC 19**
See also DLB 1, 243

Whitman, Walt(er) 1819-1892 .. **NCLC 4, 31, 81; PC 3; WLC**
See also AAYA 42; AMW; AMWR 1; CDALB 1640-1865; DA; DA3; DAB; DAC; DAM MST, POET; DLB 3, 64, 224, 250; EXPP; LAIT 2; LMFS 1; PAB; PFS 2, 3, 13, 22; RGAL 4; SATA 20; TUS; WP; WYAS 1

Whitney, Phyllis A(yame) 1903- .... **CLC 42**
See also AAYA 36; AITN 2; BEST 90:3; CA 1-4R; CANR 3, 25, 38, 60; CLR 59; CMW 4; CPW; DA3; DAM POP; JRDA; MAICYA 1, 2; MTCW 2; RHW; SATA 1, 30; YAW

Whittemore, (Edward) Reed, Jr.
1919- .... **CLC 4**
See also CA 9-12R; 219; CAAE 219; CAAS 8; CANR 4, 119; CP 1, 2, 3, 4, 5, 6, 7; DLB 5; MAL 5

Whittier, John Greenleaf
1807-1892 .... **NCLC 8, 59**
See also AMWS 1; DLB 1, 243; RGAL 4

Whittlebot, Hernia
See Coward, Noel (Peirce)

Wicker, Thomas Grey 1926-
See Wicker, Tom
See also CA 65-68; CANR 21, 46, 141

Wicker, Tom .... **CLC 7**
See Wicker, Thomas Grey

Wideman, John Edgar 1941- ... **BLC 3; CLC 5, 34, 36, 67, 122; SSC 62**
See also AFAW 1, 2; AMWS 10; BPFB 4; BW 2, 3; CA 85-88; CANR 14, 42, 67, 109, 140; CN 4, 5, 6, 7; DAM MULT; DLB 33, 143; MAL 5; MTCW 2; MTFW 2005; RGAL 4; RGSF 2; SSFS 6, 12; TCLE 1:2

Wiebe, Rudy (Henry) 1934- .. **CLC 6, 11, 14, 138**
See also CA 37-40R; CANR 42, 67, 123; CN 1, 2, 3, 4, 5, 6, 7; DAC; DAM MST; DLB 60; RHW; SATA 156

Wieland, Christoph Martin
1733-1813 .... **NCLC 17**
See also DLB 97; EW 4; LMFS 1; RGWL 2, 3

Wiene, Robert 1881-1938 .... **TCLC 56**

Wieners, John 1934- .... **CLC 7**
See also BG 1:3; CA 13-16R; CP 1, 2, 3, 4, 5, 6, 7; DLB 16; WP

Wiesel, Elie(zer) 1928- .... **CLC 3, 5, 11, 37, 165; WLCS**
See also AAYA 7, 54; AITN 1; CA 5-8R; CAAS 4; CANR 8, 40, 65, 125; CDALBS; CWW 2; DA; DA3; DAB; DAC; DAM MST, NOV; DLB 83, 299; DLBY 1987; EWL 3; INT CANR-8; LAIT 4; MTCW 1, 2; MTFW 2005; NCFS 4; NFS 4; RGWL 3; SATA 56; YAW

Wiggins, Marianne 1947- .... **CLC 57**
See also BEST 89:3; CA 130; CANR 60, 139; CN 7

Wigglesworth, Michael 1631-1705 .... **LC 106**
See also DLB 24; RGAL 4

Wiggs, Susan .... **CLC 70**
See also CA 201

Wight, James Alfred 1916-1995
See Herriot, James
See also CA 77-80; SATA 55; SATA-Brief 44

Wilbur, Richard (Purdy) 1921- ..... **CLC 3, 6, 9, 14, 53, 110; PC 51**
See also AMWS 3; CA 1-4R; CABS 2; CANR 2, 29, 76, 93, 139; CDALBS; CP 1, 2, 3, 4, 5, 6, 7; DA; DAB; DAC; DAM MST, POET; DLB 5, 169; EWL 3; EXPP;

Literary Criticism Series
Cumulative Topic Index

This index lists all topic entries in Thompson Gale's *Children's Literature Review* (CLR), *Classical and Medieval Literature Criticism* (CMLC), *Contemporary Literary Criticism* (CLC), *Drama Criticism* (DC), *Literature Criticism from 1400 to 1800* (LC), *Nineteenth-Century Literature Criticism* (NCLC), *Short Story Criticism* (SSC), and *Twentieth-Century Literary Criticism* (TCLC). The index also lists topic entries in the Gale Critical Companion Collection, which includes the following publications: *The Beat Generation* (BG), and *Harlem Renaissance* (HR).

American Romanticism NCLC 44: 74-138
overviews and general studies, 74-84
sociopolitical influences, 84-104
Romanticism and the American frontier, 104-15
thematic concerns, 115-37

American Western Literature TCLC 46: 1-100
definition and development of American Western literature, 2-7
characteristics of the Western novel, 8-23
Westerns as history and fiction, 23-34
critical reception of American Western literature, 34-41
the Western hero, 41-73
women in Western fiction, 73-91
later Western fiction, 91-9

American Writers in Paris TCLC 98: 1-156
overviews and general studies, 2-155

Anarchism NCLC 84: 1-97
overviews and general studies, 2-23
the French anarchist tradition, 23-56
Anglo-American anarchism, 56-68
anarchism: incidents and issues, 68-97

Angry Young Men TCLC 166: 1-80
overviews, 2-18
major figures, 18-58
themes and style, 58-79

Animals in Literature TCLC 106: 1-120
overviews and general studies, 2-8
animals in American literature, 8-45
animals in Canadian literature, 45-57
animals in European literature, 57-100
animals in Latin American literature, 100-06
animals in women's literature, 106-20

Antebellum South, Literature of the NCLC 112:1-188
overviews, 4-55
culture of the Old South, 55-68
antebellum fiction: pastoral and heroic romance, 68-120
role of women: a subdued rebellion, 120-59
slavery and the slave narrative, 159-85

Anti-Americanism TCLC 158: 1-98
overviews and general studies, 3-18
literary and intellectual perspectives, 18-36
social and political reactions, 36-98

Anti-Apartheid TCLC 162: 1-121
overviews, 3-45
major authors, 45-74
anti-apartheid literature and the liberal tradition, 74-101
writing under apartheid: historical views, 101-20

The Apocalyptic Movement TCLC 106: 121-69

Aristotle CMLC 31:1-397
philosophy, 3-100
poetics, 101-219
rhetoric, 220-301
science, 302-397

Art and Literature TCLC 54: 176-248
overviews and general studies, 176-93
definitions, 193-219
influence of visual arts on literature, 219-31
spatial form in literature, 231-47

Arthurian Literature CMLC 10: 1-127
historical context and literary beginnings, 2-27
development of the legend through Malory, 27-64
development of the legend from Malory to the Victorian Age, 65-81
themes and motifs, 81-95
principal characters, 95-125

Arthurian Revival NCLC 36: 1-77
overviews and general studies, 2-12
Tennyson and his influence, 12-43
other leading figures, 43-73
the Arthurian legend in the visual arts, 73-6

The Audience and Nineteenth-Century Literature NCLC 160: 1-158
overviews, 3-35
race, class, gender, 35-89
America, 89-102
Britain and Europe, 102-30
genre and audience, 130-57

Australian Cultural Identity in Nineteenth-Century Literature NCLC 124: 1-164
overviews and general studies, 4-22
poetry, 22-67
fiction, 67-135
role of women writers, 135-64

Australian Literature TCLC 50: 1-94
origins and development, 2-21
characteristics of Australian literature, 21-33
historical and critical perspectives, 33-41
poetry, 41-58
fiction, 58-76
drama, 76-82
Aboriginal literature, 82-91

Aztec Myths and Literature LC 122: 1-182
Overviews and General Studies, 3-68
Cosmology, 68-136
Language and Literature, 136-81

The Beat Generation BG 1:1-562
the Beat Generation: an overview, 1-137
primary sources, 3-32
overviews and general studies, 32-47
Beat Generation as a social phenomenon, 47-65
drugs, inspiration, and the Beat Generation, 65-92
religion and the Beat Generation, 92-124
women of the Beat Generation, 124-36
Beat "scene": East and West, 139-259
primary sources, 141-77
Beat scene in the East, 177-218
Beat scene in the West, 218-59
Beat Generation publishing: periodicals, small presses, and censorship, 261-349
primary sources, 263-74
overview, 274-88
Beat periodicals: "little magazines," 288-311
Beat publishing: small presses, 311-24
Beat battles with censorship, 324-49
performing arts and the Beat Generation, 351-417
primary sources, 353-58
Beats and film, 358-81
Beats and music, 381-415
visual arts and the Beat Generation, 419-91
primary sources, 421-24
critical commentary, 424-90

Beat Generation, Literature of the TCLC 42: 50-102
overviews and general studies, 51-9
the Beat generation as a social phenomenon, 59-62
development, 62-5
Beat literature, 66-96
influence, 97-100

The Bell Curve Controversy CLC 91: 281-330

Bildungsroman in Nineteenth-Century Literature NCLC 20: 92-168
surveys, 93-113
in Germany, 113-40
in England, 140-56
female *Bildungsroman,* 156-67
NCLC 152: 1-129
overview, 3-16

definition and issues, 16-52
female *Bildungsromane* , 52-83
ideology and nationhood, 83-128

Black Humor, Contemporary CLC 196: 1-128
overviews and general studies, 2-18
black humor in American fiction, 18-28
development and history, 29-62
major authors, 62-115
technique and narrative, 115-127

Bloomsbury Group TCLC 34: 1-73
history and major figures, 2-13
definitions, 13-7
influences, 17-27
thought, 27-40
prose, 40-52
and literary criticism, 52-4
political ideals, 54-61
response to, 61-71

The Bloomsbury Group TCLC 138: 1-59
representative members of the Bloomsbury Group, 9-24
literary relevance of the Bloomsbury Group, 24-36
Bloomsbury's hallmark works, 36-48
other modernists studied with the Bloomsbury Group, 48-54

The Blues in Literature TCLC 82: 1-71

Bly, Robert, *Iron John: A Book about Men and Men's Work* CLC 70: 414-62

The Book of J CLC 65: 289-311

The Book of Common Prayer LC 118: 1-76
overviews, 2-43
translation and diffusion, 44-63
influence of the Prayer Book, 63-76

Brazilian Literature TCLC 134: 1-126
overviews and general studies, 3-33
Brazilian poetry, 33-48
contemporary Brazilian writing, 48-76
culture, politics, and race in Brazilian writing, 76-100
modernism and postmodernism in Brazil, 100-25

British Ephemeral Literature LC 59: 1-70
overviews and general studies, 1-9
broadside ballads, 10-40
chapbooks, jestbooks, pamphlets, and newspapers, 40-69

Buddhism and Literature TCLC 70: 59-164
eastern literature, 60-113
western literature, 113-63

The *Bulletin* and the Rise of Australian Literary Nationalism NCLC 116: 1-121
overviews, 3-32
legend of the nineties, 32-55
Bulletin style, 55-71
Australian literary nationalism, 71-98
myth of the bush, 98-120

Businessman in American Literature TCLC 26: 1-48
portrayal of the businessman, 1-32
themes and techniques in business fiction, 32-47

The Calendar LC 55: 1-92
overviews and general studies, 2-19
measuring time, 19-28
calendars and culture, 28-60
calendar reform, 60-92

Captivity Narratives LC 82: 71-172
overviews, 72-107
captivity narratives and Puritanism, 108-34
captivity narratives and Native Americans, 134-49
influence on American literature, 149-72

Caribbean Literature TCLC 138: 60-135
overviews and general studies, 61-9
ethnic and national identity, 69-107

SSC Cumulative Nationality Index

Oe, Kenzaburo **20**
Shiga, Naoya **23**
Tanizaki, Junichirō **21**

MEXICAN

Arreola, Juan José **38**
Castellanos, Rosario **39, 68**
Fuentes, Carlos **24**
Rulfo, Juan **25**

NEW ZEALANDER

Frame, Janet **29**
Mansfield, Katherine **9, 23, 38, 81**

POLISH

Agnon, S(hmuel) Y(osef Halevi) **30**
Borowski, Tadeusz **48**
Conrad, Joseph **9, 71**
Peretz, Isaac Loeb **26**
Schulz, Bruno **13**
Singer, Isaac Bashevis **3, 53, 80**

PUERTO RICAN

Ferré, Rosario **36**

RUSSIAN

Babel, Isaak (Emmanuilovich) **16, 78**
Bulgakov, Mikhail (Afanas'evich) **18**
Bunin, Ivan Alexeyevich **5**
Chekhov, Anton (Pavlovich) **2, 28, 41, 51, 85**
Dostoevsky, Fedor Mikhailovich **2, 33, 44**

Gogol, Nikolai (Vasilyevich) **4, 29, 52**
Gorky, Maxim **28**
Kazakov, Yuri Pavlovich **43**
Leskov, Nikolai (Semyonovich) **34**
Nabokov, Vladimir (Vladimirovich) **11, 86**
Olesha, Yuri **69**
Pasternak, Boris (Leonidovich) **31**
Pilnyak, Boris **48**
Platonov, Andrei (Klimentov, Andrei Platonovich) **42**
Pushkin, Alexander (Sergeyevich) **27, 55**
Solzhenitsyn, Aleksandr I(sayevich) **32**
Tolstoy, Leo (Nikolaevich) **9, 30, 45, 54**
Turgenev, Ivan (Sergeevich) **7, 57**
Zamyatin, Yevgeny **89**
Zoshchenko, Mikhail (Mikhailovich) **15**

SCOTTISH

Davie, Elspeth **52**
Doyle, Arthur Conan **12**
Oliphant, Margaret (Oliphant Wilson) **25**
Scott, Walter **32**
Spark, Muriel (Sarah) **10**
Stevenson, Robert Louis (Balfour) **11, 51**

SOUTH AFRICAN

Gordimer, Nadine **17, 80**
Head, Bessie **52**

SPANISH

Alarcón, Pedro Antonio de **64**
Cela, Camilo José **71**

Cervantes (Saavedra), Miguel de **12**
Pardo Bazán, Emilia **30**
Unamuno (y Jugo), Miguel de **11, 69**

SWEDISH

Lagervist, Par **12**

SWISS

Hesse, Hermann **9, 49**
Meyer, Conrad Ferdinand **30**
Keller, Gottfried **26**
Walser, Robert **20**

TRINIDADIAN

Naipaul, V(idiadhar) S(urajprasad) **38**

UKRAINIAN

Aleichem, Sholom **33**

URUGUAYAN

Onetti, Juan Carlos **23**
Quiroga, Horacio **89**

WELSH

Evans, Caradoc **43**
Lewis, Alun **40**
Machen, Arthur **20**
Thomas, Dylan (Marlais) **3, 44**

YUGOSLAVIAN

Andrić, Ivo **36**

Nationality Index

SSC-89 Title Index

Title Index

ISBN 0-7876-8886-X

9 780787 688868